Marketing
Communications

"Covering the main aspects of communication
both in B2C and B2B environments, raising the
ethical issues and providing relevant case studies,
this book is a useful tool for students, teachers as
well as for practitioners eager to know more
about Marketing Communications."

The Catholic University of Mons

Visit the *Marketing Communications: engagement, strategies and practice, fourth edition* Companion Website at **www.pearsoned.co.uk/fill** to find valuable **student** learning material including:

- Multiple choice questions to test your understanding
- Weblinks to relevant, specific Internet resources to facilitate in-depth independent research

Chris Fill

University of Portsmouth

Marketing Communications

engagements, strategies and practice

Fourth edition

FT Prentice Hall
FINANCIAL TIMES

An imprint of Pearson Education
Harlow, England • London • New York • Boston • San Francisco • Toronto
Sydney • Tokyo • Singapore • Hong Kong • Seoul • Taipei • New Delhi
Cape Town • Madrid • Mexico City • Amsterdam • Munich • Paris • Milan

Pearson Education Limited
Edinburgh Gate
Harlow
Essex CM20 2JE
England

and Associated Companies throughout the world

Visit us on the World Wide Web at:
www.pearsoned.co.uk

First published under the Prentice Hall Europe imprint 1995
Fourth edition published 2005

© Prentice Hall Europe 1994, 1999
© Pearson Education Limited 2002
© Pearson Education Limited 2006

ISBN: 978-0-273-68772-6

British Library Cataloguing-in-Publication Data
A catalogue record for this book is available from the British Library

Library of Congress Cataloging-in-Publication Data
Fill, Chris.
    Marketing communications : contexts, strategies, and applications / Chris Fill. – 4th ed.
        p.   cm.
    Includes bibliographical references and index.
    ISBN 0-273-68772-7 (alk. paper)
        1. Communication in marketing.   2. Marketing channels.   3. Sales promotion.   I. Title.

    HF5415.123.F55 2005
    658.8'02–dc22   2005048672

10 9 8 7 6 5 4
11 10 09 08 07

Typeset in 9.5/12.5pt Stone serif by 35
Printed and Bound by Rotolito Lomborda S.p.A., Milan, Italy

The publisher's policy is to use paper manufactured from sustainable forests.

For my soulmate - Karen.

Brief Contents

Contents

Part 2   Understanding how marketing communications works   115

5   Understanding how customers process information   117

6   Customer decision-making   149

7   How marketing communications might work   177

Part 3   Strategies and planning   293

11   Integrated marketing communications   295

12   Marketing communications: strategies and planning   324

13   Marketing communications: objectives and positioning   360

31   Business-to-business marketing communications   841

32   Internal marketing communications   869

Supporting resources

Visit **www.pearsoned.co.uk/fill** to find valuable online resources

Companion Website for students
- Multiple choice questions to test your understanding
- Weblinks to relevant, specific Internet resources to facilitate in-depth independent research

For instructors
- Customisable PowerPoint slides, including key figures and tables from the main text
- Instructor's Manual, including a range of teaching schemes, as well as sample answers for question material in the book
- A test bank of multiple choice questions

Also: The Companion Website provides the following features:
- Search tool to help locate specific items of content
- E-mail results and profile tools to send results of quizzes to instructors
- Online help and support to assist with website usage and troubleshooting

For more information please contact your local Pearson Education sales representative or visit **www.pearsoned.co.uk/fill**

OneKey: All you and your students need to succeed

OneKey is an exclusive new resource for instructors and students, giving you access to the best online teaching and learning tools 24 hours a day, 7 days a week.

OneKey is all you need

Convenience. Simplicity. Success.

OneKey means all your resources are in one place for maximum convenience, simplicity and success.

A OneKey product is available for *Marketing Communications: engagement, strategies and practice, fourth edition* for use with Blackboard™, WebCT and CourseCompass. It contains:

- An online study guide providing up to 30 hours of enrichment materials, including video clips, interactive quizzes, multiple choice questions, and more.

For more information about the OneKey product please contact your local Pearson Education sales representative or visit **www.pearsoned.co.uk/onekey**

Guided tour

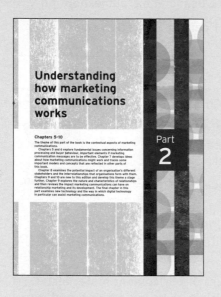

Part Openers summarise the Main themes in each chapter. ◄

Great **colour photography** from real, high profile marketing campaigns is used throughout the book. ►

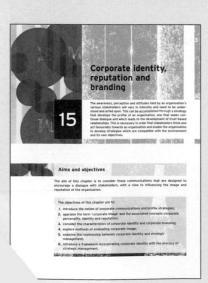

Aims and objectives enable you to focus on what you should have achieved by ◄ the end of the chapter.

Snappy **ViewPoints** boxes ► improve your understanding by providing examples of the application of theory in practice.

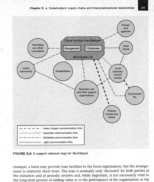

Margin notes help reinforce core concepts in the text body.

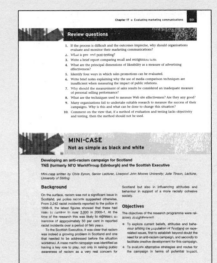

Figures and tables illustrate key points, concepts and processes visually to reinforce your learning.

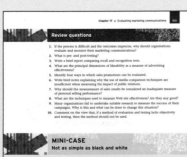

Summaries clinch the important concepts that have just been presented to reinforce the chapter.

Every chapter ends with **Review questions** that test your understanding and help you to track your progress.

Mini-Cases encourage stimulating debates and class discussion.

Each chapter is supported by a list of **References**, directing your independent study to both printed and electronic sources.

Guided tour of the website

Marketing
Communications
Website

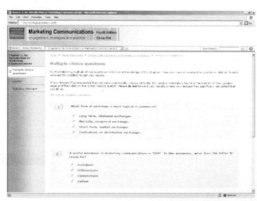

Multiple
Choice
Questions

Weblinks

Preface

Thank you for reading this book. This is the fourth edition of *Marketing Communications* and it is intended to help you engage with the increasingly complex world of marketing communications. This book has been written in the hope that you will enjoy the material, be stimulated to want to know more and wish to engage further with the world of marketing communications.

A world of marketing communications

All organisations, large and small, commercial, government, charities, educational and other not-for-profit organisations, need to communicate with a range of stakeholders. This may be in order to get materials and services to undertake their business activities or to collaborate and coordinate with others to secure suitable distribution of their goods and services. In addition, there are consumers, you and me, people who are free to choose among the many hundreds and thousands of product offerings. Marketing communications provides a core activity so that all interested parties can understand the intentions of others and appreciate the value of the goods and services offered.

Traditionally there are five main marketing communication disciplines or tools: advertising, sales promotion, personal selling, public relations and direct marketing. In addition, there are media in which time and space can be bought or used to deliver messages to target audiences. The appropriate mix of these tools and the choice of media have for a long time been largely predictable. Distinct mixes could be identified for business-to-consumer (b2c) and business-to-business (b2b) audiences. There were variations reflecting particular brand circumstances but essentially in the b2c market advertising was used to build brand values, sales promotions were used to encourage customer action and public relations sought to generate goodwill and interest about the company. Personal selling was regarded as the primary tool in b2b markets but also had a role to play in retail environments, for example selling consumer durables. In the 1990s direct marketing became a more prominent tool in the mix because technology had enabled a form of communication by appealing personally and directly to the target customer. This change introduced new media formats and the subsequent development of the Internet and related digital technologies has accelerated change in the marketing communications industry. There are now a myriad of opportunities to reach audiences, with the Internet representing a new, yet challenging, form of communication channel.

At the same time as the media world has splintered into many different parts so have the audiences with whom organisations need to communicate. Consumers now have a variety of different ways to spend their leisure time. Some of those that choose to incorporate the media as part of their relaxation now have not just 3 commercial television channels but nearly 200 channels, all have access to an increasing number of general and specific interest magazines, a multitude of new cinema complexes and, of course, the Internet with an explosion of Web sites offering a seemingly endless source of information, opportunities to buy online and a form of global entertainment. The world of marketing communications is bright, exciting, sometimes unpredictable, yet always challenging and evolving.

Managers are now not only required to find new ways to communicate but do so on reduced budgets and they must account for their communication spend. The development of long-term relationships with customers, whether this be in b2b or b2c markets, is now an essential aspect of marketing policy. Customer retention is crucial today and various devices, such as loyalty schemes, are used to shape long-term customer behaviour. Organisations now accept that the tools of the promotional mix are not the only way brands communicate. All parts of the marketing mix communicate: the behaviour of employees and the performance of products, the actions of competitors all serve to influence the way in which each customer perceives a brand. Corporate branding is now recognised as an integral part of the overall communication effort. Corporate reputation and the actions undertaken by organisations are perceived not only in terms of brand values and profits but also in terms of their ethics and the impact organisations have on the environment.

Marketing communication agencies are trying to adjust the way they can best serve the interests of their clients. One of the results is structural realignment (mergers and takeovers) which can lead to consolidation. Clients themselves are fighting to generate superior value for their customers and to find new ways of establishing competitive advantage. Globalisation and the development of partnerships, alliances and networks are all testimony to changing markets and expectations.

Where does this all lead? It leads to a new form and role for marketing communications and a vision that an organisation's entire marketing communications should be planned, coherent and consistent. This word consistency applies to internal policies and strategies, to messages to and from internal and external stakeholders, consistency with the values of their customers and with the relationships they forge with key suppliers and distributors.

This book introduces readers to this changing world of marketing communications and allows them to appreciate some of the conceptual underpinnings associated with marketing communications and associated aspects of integration. There are examples of the practical application of marketing communications and examples that demonstrate the application of theory in practice. This book does not just show how organisations use marketing communications, it also contains theoretical material to enable readers to understand why organisations use marketing communications in the ways they do.

Overview of the book

Despite the misuse and often laboured understanding of the term, this book presents marketing communications from a new strategic perspective. The interlinking of corporate, marketing and communication strategy, the blend of internal and external communications, the relational aspects of network communications, and the various objectives and strategies that flow from understanding the context within which marketing communications emanates, functions and forms a part of the fabric within which audiences frame and interpret marketing messages are presented to readers for consideration.

A key topic in this edition is engagement. Effective marketing communications enables audiences to engage with products, services, brands and organisations. Through engagement relationships can develop and this enables customers, stakeholders and organisations to achieve their various goals. The degree to which engagement occurs reflects audience perception, interpretation and meaning of the messages delivered. Through engagement brand value and equity can be developed or reduced. Engagement, therefore, encompasses a range of marketing communication activities and is referred to throughout the text.

This book has been written deliberately from an academic perspective and seeks to provide a suitably consistent appraisal of the ever-expanding world of marketing communications. This book seeks to stimulate thought and consideration about a wide range of interrelated issues, and to help achieve this aim a number of theories and models are advanced. Some of these theories reflect marketing practice, while others are offered as suggestions for moving the subject forward. Many of the theories are abstractions of actual practice, some are based on empirical research and others are pure conceptualisation. All seek to enrich the subject, but not all need carry the same weight of contribution. Readers should form their own opinions based upon their reading, experience and judgement.

There are a number of themes running through the text, but perhaps the two main ones concern relationship marketing and integrated communications. I am of the view that organisations will in the future perceive communications as a core strategic activity, central to strategic management and thought. Corporate and marketing communications will inevitably merge and integrate, the need to build and sustain relationships with a variety of stakeholders inside and outside the organisation will become paramount and communications will be a vital source in making it all work. Witness the branding developments at the grocery giants Procter & Gamble and Unilever to understand this point.

In this light, this text assumes relationship marketing to be essential and sees communication in the context of both transactional and relational exchanges. Corporate and marketing communications are considered as important components of the total process.

The structure of the book has been revised from the previous edition. It is now in five parts and several new chapters have been added:

Chapter 7   How marketing communications might work

Chapter 9   Marketing: relationships and communications

Chapter 10   The impact of technology on marketing communications.

Chapter 20, concerning traditional media, has been reintroduced and updated as a result of feedback and general demand. Several other chapters have been reworked and material moved around. In addition, all of the chapters have been revised, updated and refreshed. All chapters contain a mini-case study written by a variety of marketing tutors and practitioners and the vast majority are new to this edition.

Structure of the text

There are five main parts to the book:

Part 1 introduces readers to the subject from a general perspective and then seeks to establish some of the key factors that are necessary in order to provide an underpinning of the subject. This includes communication theory, the structure and dynamics of the marketing communications industry and the means by which the industry serves its audiences. In particular, this refers to the way in which organisations are controlled with respect to the messages delivered and the media used to carry them. Legislation and voluntary controls provide the context within which organisations behave with varying degrees of responsibility.

Part 2 considers the way in which marketing communications works and contains most of the new chapters in this edition. Based on the important aspects of buyer behaviour and customer decision-making, Chapter 7 considers some of the ways in which marketing communications is thought to work. This is followed by a review of relationship marketing concepts, the nature of new technology and the management of stakeholders associated with marketing communications. These elements provide a context in which marketing communications is used and managed.

Part 3 explores some of the managerial aspects associated with marketing communications. The core content concerns the various aspects of *strategy* and how organisations should develop their marketing communications in the light of their contextual positions. This part explores the concept of integrated marketing communications and follows on with an examination of strategy and planning concepts, product and corporate branding, financial and budgeting issues and the methods and issues associated with the evaluation and measurement of marketing communications.

Part 4 examines the individual disciplines of marketing communications and the ways in which they can be applied in order to communicate with target audiences.

Part 5 examines marketing communications in the context of some specific audiences. In particular, consideration is given to international dimensions, business-to-business communications and the hugely important internal or employee audiences.

Part 1: Introduction to marketing communications

This opening part serves to establish the scope of the book and provides a brief overview of the content and style adopted throughout the rest of the text. Chapter 1 provides an introductory perspective to marketing communications and sets out some key concepts. It also contains a brief overview of each of the disciplines (or tools) of the marketing communications mix. Chapter 2 addresses issues concerning communication theory and in particular moves on from the simple linear interpretation of how communication works to one that recognises the influence of people, behaviour and interactional elements on the communication process. Chapter 3 is concerned with the nature and characteristics of the UK marketing communications industry and specifically examines the strategic and operational issues of advertising agencies and their interaction with client organisations. The content of Chapter 4 follows on directly from the previous chapter and examines some of the ethical and social issues for which organisations have responsibility in terms of what they say and how they say it.

Part 2: Understanding how marketing communications works

This part considers not only how marketing communications works but also explores some of the key contextual issues that influence the nature and form of marketing communications.

The first two chapters consider the important aspects of buyer behaviour, upon which marketing communications should be developed. Only by understanding the market and the target audience can appropriate objectives, strategies, promotional methods, applications and resources be determined, allocated and implemented.

Chapter 7 considers various approaches to understanding how marketing communications works. Although some of these ideas are borrowed from the world of advertising the key notion is that effective marketing communications develops by establishing a level of engagement and delivering messages that provide significant value.

Chapter 8 seeks to develop an understanding of the interrelationships between the different organisations and stakeholders who impact on an organisation's marketing communications. The networks of stakeholders are considered primarily from a 'marketing channel' perspective, with particular emphasis upon the relationships that are of increasing importance. Chapter 9 is new and considers ideas of relationship marketing and associated factors concerning the fundamental basis upon which marketing and marketing communications is now considered by many to work. The final chapter in this part of the book considers issues about digital technology and the impact it has had on marketing communications.

Part 3: Strategies and planning

Part 3 of the book opens with Chapter 11. This chapter challenges ideas about the nature and validity of the 'integrated' view of marketing communications. This is a core chapter because it bridges the contextual elements and the application of the various disciplines. The notion that IMC is a valid and realistic concept is debated and readers are encouraged to consider the arguments for and against this approach. Chapter 12 is concerned with the nature of communication strategy and considers the interrelationship between strategy and planning. The second section of the chapter introduces the marketing communications planning framework and works through the model highlighting issues and linkages and ends with an operational approach to devising, formulating and implementing a strategic marketing communications plan.

Chapter 13 looks at the nature of objectives and positioning in marketing communications and is followed by a chapter on branding. This chapter is significant in that it focuses on the role marketing communications can play in the development and maintenance of brands. The branding and positioning connection is significant, which is why these strategically significant elements are located next to each other.

The next chapter develops the branding theme and considers corporate identity and branding issues. The focus is again on the role of marketing communications in the identity and branding process rather than pure identity work alone. These elements are of course interrelated but readers are helped to see how communications can be a pivotal aspect of brand development.

This part of the book concludes with a consideration of various budgeting approaches and the ways in which the performance of marketing communication activities can be evaluated. In effect this considers how much should be invested in the engagement process and how the engagement process should be measured.

Part 4: The marketing communications mix: disciplines and applications

This part looks at the individual marketing communication disciplines that are available to organisations to communicate with its external and internal audiences.

The first five chapters consider different aspects of advertising. The first, Chapter 18, considers different advertising strategies and is developed out of Chapter 7, which is about how marketing communications might work. The chapter traces the development of advertising strategies and ends by considering some contemporary approaches. The following chapter builds on this base material and considers the nature of advertising messages before Chapters 20 and 21 consider traditional and digital media respectively. The interactive media chapter should be read in conjunction with Chapter 10, which is about the impact of technology on marketing communications. In Chapter 21 much of the focus is on Web site characteristics and the role of the Web site within marketing communications. The final advertising chapter explores issues about media planning.

The rest of this part of the book deals with sales promotion, public relations, sponsorship, personal selling and direct marketing. The part closes with a view of exhibitions, product placement, packaging and field marketing.

Part 5: Marketing communications for special audiences

This part of the book considers issues associated with marketing communications and special audiences. The audiences are themselves not so much special but display characteristics that deserve special attention. The first of these is the international audience and the issues arising when using marketing communications across two or more countries. The following chapter examines business-to-business marketing communications. Reference to both business-to-consumer (b2c) and business-to-business (btb) are made throughout the book but here particular attention is given to the special contextual conditions that arise through interorganisational communications. The final chapter considers the role of marketing communications within organisations where the employees are the target audience. Increasingly recognised as a key part of a brand, the importance of engaging with employees and using them as a means of engaging with external audiences is actively considered.

Design features and presentation

In addition to the five-part structure of the book, there are a number of features that are intended to help readers navigate the material.

Chapter objectives

Each chapter opens with both the aims of what is to be covered and a list of (learning) objectives. This helps to signal the primary topics that are covered in the chapter and so guide the learning experience.

Navigation

Important key text is extracted and presented in the margin. This helps readers to locate relevant material quickly and highlight key issues. In addition, to assist readers through the various chapters, the left-hand page is used to identify the page number and in which part of the text it is located. To complement this, the right-hand page is used to flag the page number and the chapter title.

Visual supports

This book is produced in four colour and throughout the text there are numerous colour and black and white exhibits; figures (diagrams) and tables of information throughout the text serve to highlight, illustrate and bring life to the written word. The pictures used serve either to illustrate particular points by demonstrating theory in practice or they are used to complement individual examples. The examples are normally highlighted in the text as ViewPoints. These examples are easily distinguishable through the colour contrasts and serve to demonstrate how a particular aspect of marketing communications has been used by an organisation in a particular context. I hope you enjoy these ViewPoints of organisational practice.

Summaries and mini-cases

At the end of each chapter is a summary and a series of review and discussion questions. Readers are advised to test their own understanding of the content of each chapter by considering some or all of the discussion questions. In this sense the questions support self-study but tutors might wish to use some of these as part of a seminar or workshop programme. At the end of each chapter is a mini-case study. Most of these have been written by marketing academics from a variety of universities and colleges and some have been written by leading marketing practitioners. These short cases can be used in class for discussion purposes and to explore some of the salient issues raised in the chapter. Students working alone can use the mini-case to test their own understanding and they can use the questions that follow each mini-case to consolidate their understanding.

Support materials

Students and lecturers who adopt this text have a range of support materials and facilities to help them.

Readers are invited to visit the companion Web site for the book at www. booksites.net/fill. Here students have access to a range of mini-case studies, including a selection of recent Chartered Institute of Marketing examination cases for both the Integrated Marketing Communications and the new Marketing Communications modules.

There are various text files available for download, including answers to the case study in Chapter 12.

For lecturers and tutors not only is there an Instructor's Manual containing a range of teaching schemes, slides and exercises in downloadable format but there is also a password-protected section of the companion Web site for their use. From this site a much larger range of PowerPoint slides, teaching schemes and additional mini-cases can be downloaded.

A test bank of multiple-choice questions has also been developed for use by students and lecturers. In addition, there are hyperlinks to a range of related sites.

Acknowledgements

This book could not have been written without the support of a wide range of people. Contributions range from providing information and permissions, writing mini-case studies, to answering my questions and tolerating my persistent nagging, sending through photographs, answering phone calls and emails and simply liaising with others. Finally there are those who have read, reviewed drafts, made constructive comments and provided moral support and encouragement.

The list of individuals and organisations involved with this book is extensive. My thanks are offered to all of you. I have tried to list everyone but if anyone has been omitted then I offer my apologies.

Mini-case contributors

Ruth Ashford – Manchester Metropolitan University

Duncan Bennett – Yorkshire Water

Peter Betts – Manchester Metropolitan University

Selina Bichard – Specsavers Opticians

Lucy Bristowe – Channel 4

Jill Brown – University of Portsmouth

Anthony Byrne – Liverpool John Moores University

Yvonne Dixon – University of Sunderland

Alexander Dries – CRM Consultant

Chris Eynon – TNS System Three

Jill Finney – The British Library

Tony Garry – DeMontfort University

Angela Hall – Manchester Metropolitan University

Graham Hughes – Leeds Business School

Janet Hull – Institute of Practitioners in Advertising

Jeremy Miles – Consultant and Lecturer Manchester Metropolitan University

Mike Molesworth – Bournemouth University

Clive Nancarrow – Bristol Business School

Beth Rogers – University of Portsmouth

Stuart Roper – Manchester Business School

Andy Saxton – Galaxy Radio

Richard Scullion – Bournemouth University

Lynn Sudbury – Liverpool John Moores University

Julie Tinson – Stirling University

Gary Warnaby – Salford University

Kate Watts – Chime Communications

Gill Wood – The Write Marketing Consultancy

Other acknowledgements

Gary Akehurst – Aberystwyth University
Rozina Ali – Akzo Nobel
Vicky Allard – TBWA
Marion Baker – Procter & Gamble
Duncan Bruce – Pearson Education
Claire Burgess – Twinings
Vicky Charlesworth – Barclaycard
Richard Christy – University of Portsmouth
Paul Collier – Hewlett Packard
Lorien Coutts – B&Q
Anna Fenton – Leedex
Kate Goodfellow – Neville McCarthy Associates
Catherine Humphries – Webber-Shandwick
Judith Johnson – JCB
Jonathan Lace – London Institute
Justin Leyton – Citroën UK

Nigel Markwick – Wolff Olins
Gordon Oliver – Horndean
Ben Pearman – Bird's Eye Walls
Steve Pike – Photographer
Nick Pringle – D'arcy
Victoria Savill – Dyson
Catherine Sharp – TBWA
Richard Tansey – D'arcy
Pat Thomas – Reebok International
David Todman – Alfa Laval
Phil Toms – Meat and Livestock Commission
Vaia Valioti – Postgraduate Student of the University of Portsmouth
Debra Weatherley – Findphoto
Rachel West – American Express Europe
Neil Yoxall – Y&R

Above all perhaps are the various individuals at Pearson and their associates who have taken my manuscript, managed it and published it in this form. In particular I should like to thank Thomas Sigel for his constant support, professionalism and faith in my writing and Peter Hooper for his positive approach and for accommodating my preference to circumnavigate various Pearson procedures. In addition I should like to thank Tim Parker and his team for transforming the manuscript into the final product. Thank you all.

The biggest thank you is for my wife Karen. She has not only been insightful, made telling observations and significant contributions but she has also been supportive throughout the process, just as best friends are.

We would also like to thank the following for permission to reproduce copyright material:
Table 2.3 from *Interpersonal Processes: New Directions in Communication Research*, Sage Publications, Inc., (eds. Roloff, M.E. and Miller, G.R., 1987), Reprinted by Permission of Sage Publications, Inc.; Table 6.3 from *Organisational Buying Behaviour*, Prentice Hall Publishers (Webster, F.E. and Wind, Y. 1972); Table 9.1 reprinted from *Business Horizons*, Vol. 46, (Wagner, S. and Boutellier, R.) 'Capabilities for managing a portfolio of supplier relationships', pp. 78–9, 2002, with permission from Elsevier; Figure 9.3 from *Perceived Quality of Business Relationships*, Hanken Swedish School of Economics, (Holmund, M. 1997); Table 9.5 from 'The social function of trust and implications of e-commerce' in *International Journal of Advertising*, World Advertising Research Centre, (Morrison, D.E. and Firmstone, J. 2000); Table 11.3 from www.openplanning.org (Jenkinson, A. and Sain, B. 2004); Table 12.1 from *Formulation, Implementation and Control of Competitive Strategy*, The McGraw-Hill Companies Inc., (Pearce, J.A. and Robinson, R.B. Jr. 1997); Figure 14.1 and Table 14.1 from *The New Strategic Brand Management*, Kogan Page Publishers, (Kapferer, J-N. 2004); Figure 14.3 and Table 14.5 adapted from *Brand Management: A Theoretical and Practical Approach*, Pearson Education Ltd., (Riezebos, R. 2003); Figures 14.6 and 14.7 from 'Measurement and tracking of brand equity in the global marketplace – The PepsiCo Experience' in *International Marketing Review*, Vol. 18, 1, (Krish, P., Riskey, D.R. and Kerin, R. 2001), Republished with permission, Emerald Publishers Limited; Table 15.1 from 'Corporate brands: What are they? What of them?' in *European Journal of Marketing*, Vol. 37, 7/8,

MCP University Press Limited, (Balmer, J.M.T. and Gray, E.R. 2001) republished with permission, Emerald Group Publishing Limited; Figure 16.2 from 'Ad spending: Growing market share' *Harvard Business Review*, Jan/Feb edition, Harvard Business School Publishing Corporation, (Schroer, J. 1990); Figure 16.3 from 'Ad spending: Growing market share' *Harvard Business Review*, Jan/Feb edition, Harvard Business School Publishing Corporation, (Jones, J.P. 1990); Table 17.5 from The world wide web as an advertising medium: toward an understanding of conversion efficiency, *Journal of Advertising Research* (Berthon, P., Pitt, L. and Watson, R., 1996); Figure 18.3 from An all-embracing theory of how advertising works?, *Admap*, February, pp. 18–23 (Prue, T., 1988); Table 20.2 from *Advertising Statistics Year Book*, World Advertising Research Centre, 2003; Table 21.4 from 'Web site characteristics and business performance; some evidence from international business-to-business organisations' in *Marketing Intelligence and Planning*, Vol. 21, 2, © MCB University Press Limited (Karayanni, D.A. and Baltas, G.A. 2003) Republished with permission, Emerald Publishers Limited; Table 22.2 adapted from *Group Support Systems: New Perspectives*, Macmillan Publishers (Jessup, L.M. and Valacich, J.S.) used by permission of M.E. Sharpe, Inc.; Table 22.6 from Regency planning in *Admap*, February edition, World Advertising Research Centre, (Ephron, E. 1997) www.admapmagazine.com; Table 23.4 adapted from 'Loyalty trends for the 21st century' in *Journal of Targeting Measurement and Analysis for Marketing*, Vol. 12, 3, Henry Stewart Publications, (Capizzi, M., Ferguson, R. and Cuthbertson, R. 2004); Table 25.3 and Table 25.4 reprinted from *Public Relations Review*, Vol. 23, Benoit, W.L., 'Image repair discourse and crisis communication' pp. 309–329, 2001 with permission from Elsevier; Table 26.2 from 'Case study: The network approach to international sport sponsorship arrangement' in *The Journal of Business and Industrial Marketing*, © MCB University Press Limited, (Olkkonen, R. 2001) Republished with permission, Emerald Publishers Limited; Table 28.2 from *Strategic Marketing*, The McGraw-Hill Companies Inc., (Cravens, D.W. *et al.* 1987); Table 28.3 from 'Marketing business process and shareholder value: an organizationally embedded view of marketing activities and the discipline of marketing' in *Journal of Marketing*, Vol. 63, pp. 168–179, American Marketing Association, (Srivastava, R.K., Shervani, T.A. and Fahey, L. 1999); Table 28.4 from *Rethinking the Sales Force: Redefining Selling to Create and Capture Customer Value*, The McGraw-Hill Companies Inc., (Rackman, N. and DeVincentis, J.R. 1999); Figure 28.5 from K. Grant and D.W. Cravens (1999) Examining the antecedents of sales organization effectiveness: an Australian study, *European Journal of Marketing*, 33 (9/10), pp. 945–957, reprinted with permission from MCB University Press; Table 28.5 adapted from 'Infusing technology into personal selling' in *Journal of Personal Selling and Sales Management*, Vol. 22, 3, Summer, (Widmier, S.M., Jackson, Jnr, D.W. and McCabe, D.B. 2002) used by permission of M.E. Sharpe Inc.; Table 31.2 and Figure 31.3 reprinted from *Industrial Marketing Management*, vol. 26. Gilliland, D.I. and Johnston, W.J., Towards a model of business-to-business marketing communication effects, 15–29, copyright (1997), with permission from Elsevier Science; Figure 32.2 reprinted with permission from *Journal of Marketing*, published by the American Marketing association, Gilly, M.C. and Wolfinbarger, M. (1998, Vol. 62, pp. 69–88); Table 32.2 from *Research in Organisational Behavior*, The McGraw-Hill Companies Inc., (Albert, S. and Whetten, D.A., eds. Cummings, L.L. and Staw, B.M. 1985).

Exhibits

Exhibit 1.1 reproduced with the kind permission of the British Library; Exhibit 1.2 reproduced with the kind permission of Dyson; Exhibits 1.3 and 1.4 reproduced with the kind permission of Little Chef; Exhibits 1.5 and 1.6 reproduced with the kind permission of Michelin; Exhibit 2.1 Rainey Kelly Campbell Roalfe / Y & R. Art Director: Jerry Hollens, Copywriter: Mike Boles: Photographer: Nick Georghiou Client: Landrover; Exhibits 2.2 and 7.3 reproduced with the kind permission of Ronseal Ltd.; Exhibit 2.3 reproduced with the kind permission of Adidas; Exhibit 3.1 reproduced with the kind permission of Direct Line Insurance; Exhibits 5.1 and 5.2 reproduced with the kind permission of Fiat; Exhibits 5.3 and 29.7 reproduced with the kind permission of the Coca-Cola Company; Exhibit 5.4 reproduced with the kind permission of Subaru (UK) Ltd.; Exhibit 5.5 reproduced with the kind permission of Citroën UK. Exhibit 5.6 reproduced with the kind permission of the Kellog Company of Great Britain Ltd. All rights reserved.; Exhibit 6.1 reproduced with the kind permission of Ralph Lauren and Neville McCarthy Associates.; Exhibit 6.2 reproduced with the kind permission of Mitsubishi; Exhibits 7.1, 7.2, 13.6, 21.1 and 24.3 reproduced with the kind permission of the AA; Exhibit 7.4 reproduced with the kind permission of Twinings; Exhibit 7.5 reproduced with the kind permission of Cadbury Trebor Bassett; Exhibit 9.1 reproduced with the kind permission of Unilever UK foods; Exhibits 9.2 and 9.3 reproduced with the kind permission of International Musical Eisteddfod, Llangollen; Exhibit 10.1 reproduced with the kind permission of IBM; Exhibit 11.1 reproduced with the kind permission of Bird's Eye Walls; Exhibits 12.2 and 32.1 reproduced with the kind permission of B&Q; Exhibit 12.2 reproduced with the kind permission of Akzo Nobel; Exhibit 12.3 reproduced with the kind permission of Makita UK Ltd.; Exhibit 12.4 reproduced with the kind permission of the Meat and Livestock Commission; Exhibit 12.5 courtesy Alvey and Towers Picture Library; Exhibit 13.1 reproduced with the kind permission of Solvite on behalf of Henkel Consumer Adhesives and BDHTBWA; Exhibit 13.2 courtesy of Interbrew UK/Lowe. Director: Ivan Zacharias, Writers/AD's: Vince Squibb, Jason Lawes, Sam Cartmell Account, Director: Ben Sareen; Exhibits 13.3, 14.3 and 19.3 reproduced with the kind permission of Walkers Snack Foods; Exhibit 13.4 reproduced with the kind permission of Le Creuset; Exhibit 13.5 reproduced with the kind permission of Green & Blacks; Exhibit 14.1 reproduced with the kind permission of SCPhotos/Alamy (top) and Gianni Muratore/ Alamy (bottom); Exhibit 14.2 reproduced with the kind permission of Procter and Gamble UK; Exhibit 14.4 reproduced with the kind permission of Charnos and Lewis Moberly; Exhibit 14.5 reproduced with the kind permission of JCB; Exhibit 15.1 reproduced with the kind permission of BMW and WCRS; Exhibit 17.1 reproduced with the kind permission of the Scottish Executive; Exhibits 18.1 and 18.2 reproduced with the kind permission of Specsavers Opticians; Exhibit 18.3 reproduced with the kind permission of Amnesty International; Exhibits 18.4 and 19.7 reproduced with the kind permission of No More Nails on behalf of Henkel Consumer Adhesives and BDHTBWA; Exhibit 19.1 reproduced with the kind permission of Max Factor/Leo Burnett; Exhibit 19.2 picture kindly supplied by APA. Photograph by Steve Pike; Exhibit 19.4 reproduced with the kind permission of Toni & Guy Haircare; Exhibit 19.5 reproduced with the kind permission of Duracell; Exhibit 19.6 reproduced with the kind permission of Gieves and Hawkes; Exhibit 20.1 reproduced with the kind permission of Chris Brown/Action Plus; Exhibit 20.2 reproduced with the kind permission of Neil Tingle/Action Plus; Exhibit 20.3 reproduced with the kind permission of Plainpicture/Alamy; Exhibits 20.6, 20.7 and 20.8 reproduced with the kind permission of Galaxy Radio; Exhibit 21.2 reproduced with the kind permission of the NSPCC; Exhibit 23.1 reproduced with the kind permission of Centura Foods Ltd.; Exhibits 24.1 and 24.2 reproduced with the kind permission of Jeff Greenberg/Alamy; Exhibit 25.2 reproduced with the kind permission of Alton Towers; Exhibit 25.2 reproduced with the kind permission of Topfoto/National; Exhibit 25.3 reproduced with the kind permission of Hewlett Packard Ltd.; Exhibit 26.1 reproduced with the kind permission of Acero Miguelez/Action Plus; Exhibit 26.2 reproduced with the kind permission of Neil

Tingle/Action Plus; Exhibit 26.3 reproduced with the kind permission of Asia Pacific Breweries Ltd.; Exhibit 27.1 reproduced with the kind permission of Alton Towers; Exhibit 27.2 reproduced with the kind permission of Stan Gamester/Photofusion; Exhibit 27.3 the photographs of Felix cat food packaging are reproduced with the kind permission of Société des Produits Nestlé; Exhibit 27.4 reproduced with the kind permission of Dell; Exhibit 29.1 reproduced with the kind permission of the National Exhibition Centre, Birmingham; Exhibit 29.2 reproduced with the kind permission of Taisho Pharmaceutical (Europe) Ltd.; Exhibit 29.3 picture kindly supplied by Proctor and Gamble UK; Exhibit 29.4 reproduced with the kind permission of Elizabeth Arden; Exhibits 29.5 and 29.6 pictures kindly supplied by Recklitt Benckiser and LeverBros; Exhibit 31.1 reproduced with the kind permission of Barclaycard; Exhibit 31.2 reproduced with the kind permission of Reebok International Ltd.; Exhibit 32.2 reproduced with the kind permission of Vision Express and Webber Shandwick

Introduction to marketing communications

Chapters 1-4

Chapter 1 of this book is concerned with exploring the nature and diversity of marketing communications. It considers the role, nature and tasks of marketing communications and explores the increasing significance and importance of this aspect of marketing management. Chapter 2 is concerned with theories and methods associated with the way in which communication is thought to work.

Chapter 3 considers the structure, participants and issues facing the marketing communications industry, with particular emphasis on the UK, although the principles and many of the issues are transferable to many other parts of the world.

The final chapter in this introductory part explores the ways in which organisations manage their communications from an ethical and moral standpoint. Ethics, corporate social responsibility and overall industry controls, which serve to regulate and control marketing communications, are examined.

Part 1

MINI-CASE
Strategic marketing communication at the British Library

Mini-case written by Gary Warnaby, Senior Lecturer, School of Management, University of Salford;
Jill Finney, Director of Strategic Marketing and Communications, The British Library

The British Library

The British Library (BL) (see Exhibit 1.1) is the national library of the UK. It receives a copy of every publication produced in the UK and Ireland. Its collection comprises over 150 million items, with 3 million new items incorporated annually. The BL also houses manuscripts of major historical importance (ranging from Magna Carta and Leonardo da Vinci's notebooks to original Beatles' song lyrics), maps, newspapers, prints and drawings, music scores and over 49.5 million patents. The BL has an extensive science collection and is a vitally important information source for industrial and commercial organisations and researchers. In addition, over 8 million stamps and other philatelic items and a sound archive with recordings dating from the nineteenth century also form part of the collection. The BL also operates the world's largest document delivery service, providing 4 million items to customers annually.

The main collections (with reference, bibliographic and world-renowned research and conservation facilities and activities), are housed at St Pancras in London in a purpose-built site, which is the largest public building constructed in the UK in the twentieth century. Document supply and lending activities are based at Boston Spa in Yorkshire. The BL is not only a repository of the nation's knowledge. In line with UK central government's widening access and participation agendas, it also has a wider communication role – the BL's vision is 'to make the world's intellectual, scientific and cultural heritage accessible, and to bring the collections of the British Library to everyone – at work, school, college or home'. Clearly there is a significant potential role for marketing communications.

Until recently the BL had no coordinated marketing activity (other than a small Press/PR department). Commercial activities such as the document supply business were promoted through attendance at various UK and international trade exhibitions, but this activity was sales oriented, with little account

management structure or awareness of margins. Individual subject collections had their own separate communications activities that were organised by their curators. However, much of this activity could be regarded as product oriented, being aimed at subject specialists who already had a detailed knowledge of the area. Moreover, there was no uniformity of style. The only common communication theme was a logo (which itself was only used in the main BL building – the document supply business in Boston Spa had its own logo, and there was also a plethora of sub-brands). The perceived need for the organisation's identity and promotional activity to be improved and coordinated if the BL was to realise many aspects of its mission and objectives has led to a complete overhaul of its marketing and communications activity.

From product to marketing orientation

In 2001 five different market sectors for the BL were identified – business users, education (schools), researchers, the general public and the UK library network (both public and higher education libraries). A Head of Marketing for each sector was appointed, reporting to the Director of Strategic Marketing and Communication. In addition, a Marketing Support Services department was created. Management of exhibitions, BL bookshop, publications, development fund raising and developing a Web presence for the BL was also part of the remit. Indicative activities aimed at the five market sectors are shown in Table 1.1.

A new identity

At the end of 2001 it was decided that this adoption of a more marketing-oriented approach to the BL's activities would be facilitated by the development of a consistent, unifying new brand identity. The brand consultancy Interbrand was commissioned, and

EXHIBIT 1.1 The British Library – a structural and architectural success . . . now a challenge for marketing communications

implemented an extensive research programme on perceptions of the BL among both internal and external stakeholders. Resulting from this, the mission of the BL was articulated in terms of helping people *advance knowledge to enrich lives*. This mission incorporated three key values – *innovation*, *relevance* and *pride* – this last value building on the key strength of a committed and professional workforce, many of whom are world experts in their fields. Senior management engaged in an extensive internal

TABLE 1.1 Five market sectors for the British Library

Market sectors	Target audiences	Indicative activities
Business	High research- & development-oriented industries Professional services Creative industries Publishing industries SMEs	Research services Bespoke services Document supply Reprographics Business & Intellectual Property Centre Resource discovery
Education	Teachers Students (11–18 years old) School libraries	On-site visits School tours Workshops Web learning
Researchers	Postgraduate/undergraduate researchers Scholars Lifelong learners Commercial researchers	Reading rooms Bespoke services Reprographics Publishing Document supply Bibliographic services
Public	Visitors Lifelong learners	Exhibitions (physical & virtual) Events Tours (e.g. travelling exhibitions of collections) Publishing
Libraries (Acting as a channel to the public)	Librarians Public libraries Higher education libraries	Document supply Resource discovery Training Inter-library lending Bibliographic services

marketing campaign (including small group workshops and briefings) to communicate the new mission and values in order to get staff to 'buy in' to the process (and its results). Indeed, five 'core competences' of the BL were identified by which this mission was to be achieved:

● open, consultative management

● staff who feel valued and recognised

● an empowered, flexible and diverse workforce

● non-hierarchical, agile decision-making

● strong performance measurement.

Thus the strategy for the British Library moved to being 'demand driven', focusing on the targeted market sectors identified above, and with awareness of the BL improved by the adoption of a single coherent brand identity. The distinctive features of the BL – particularly its world-class collections, and the value-added services it could offer through the skills and expertise of its staff – would arguably guarantee customer satisfaction in these targeted sectors. Indeed, it was envisaged that the new strategy would be delivered through a renewed customer focus, whereby staff would interface more effectively and the potential of electronic communications would be embraced. Thus the BL Web site offers online catalogues, information and exhibitions, and changes to the Document Supply Service at Boston Spa have enabled digital delivery of research material on a far greater scale. In addition, partnerships with appropriate commercial partners are being developed in certain areas.

In order to develop consistency of approach, the theme of *advancing knowledge* became the focus for external communications. Marketing communications aimed at each of the targeted market sectors focus on case studies of how the BL has helped organisations and individuals advance their own knowledge in order to achieve their business and/or personal aims and objectives, through the resulting enhanced individual development and effectiveness or improved business performance. Thus the marketing communications activity explicitly highlights the contribution of the BL in the cycle of the production and dissemination of knowledge.

One key theme underlying all this communication is the role played by the BL in terms of *adding value* through the performance of the whole range of its activities. This applies not only to those individuals and organisations that comprise the various targeted market sectors, but also, as a consequence, to the nation as a whole, in line with its remit as a *national* library. Indeed, central government and other funding stakeholders are also an important target for marketing communications activity, and here the need to highlight the efficiency and cost effectiveness of the BL is paramount. This focus on *outcomes* and how the BL provides value-added, has been reinforced by an independent study of the economic impact of the organisation entitled *Measuring Our Value*. Using contingent valuation methodology, the study concludes that for the £83 million of public funding the BL receives annually, the total value produced totals £363 million – a benefit cost ratio of 4.4:1. Thus for every £1 of public funding the BL receives annually, £4.40 is generated for the UK

economy, again emphasising the value of its role in knowledge creation and dissemination, in addition to its cultural role.

Communicating the scope and effectiveness of its operations is, therefore, of critical importance to the British Library, particularly in a dynamic environment. The Internet has revolutionised the information storage and retrieval industry, and the BL, like all players in this industry, has to cope with the implications – grasping the huge opportunities arising, and also countering the threats to the traditional ways in which things have been done in the past. Another key marketing role in relation to the Internet is managing customer expectations – digitisation of the BL collection to make it available on the World Wide Web is a massive (and extremely costly) undertaking that cannot be accomplished overnight. Emphasising the role that the BL can play, in a targeted way to specific identified market sectors, as well as to potential funders, is a crucially important activity that is necessary to ensure its continued success.

Comment by Chris Fill

This brief overview of the changes at the British Library demonstrates some of the issues associated with marketing communications: the market conditions, the public's perceptions, positioning, branding, objectives, planning and strategy, relationships, technology, plus the utilisation of the tools of the promotional mix to deliver the marketing plan.

This book explores these ideas and considers some of the concepts and ideas underpinning these activities. It looks at communications in the business-to-business sector as well and considers a range of issues that impact on marketing communications. I hope you enjoy the indulgence.

Introduction to marketing communications

1

Marketing communications is a management process through which an organisation engages with its various audiences. Through understanding an audience's communications environment, organisations seek to develop and present messages for their identified stakeholder groups, before evaluating and acting upon the responses. By conveying messages that are of significant value, audiences are encouraged to offer attitudinal and behavioural responses.

Aims and objectives

The aims of this introductory chapter are to explore some of the concepts associated with marketing communications and to develop an appreciation of the key characteristics of the main tools of the communications mix.

The objectives of this chapter are to:

1. examine the concept of exchange in the marketing context;
2. assess the role of promotion in the context of the marketing mix;
3. consider the range and potential impact of marketing communications;
4. identify the key characteristics of each major tool in the communications mix;
5. examine the effectiveness of each communication tool;
6. establish a need for marketing communications;
7. compare marketing communications in the consumer and business markets.

Introduction

Organisations engage with a variety of audiences in order to pursue their marketing and business objectives. Engagement refers to the form of communication and whether the nature of the messages and media are essentially intellectual or emotional. Invariably organisations use a mixture of these two elements in order that they be heard, understood and engage their audiences in dialogue and mutually beneficial relationships.

> Organisations engage with a variety of audiences in order to pursue their marketing and business objectives.

MTV, Unilever, Virgin, Gucci, Oxfam, CNN, Singapore Airlines, easyJet, First-Pacific, Samsung and Disney operate across a number of sectors, markets and countries and use a variety of marketing communications tools to engage with their various audiences. These audiences consist not only of people who buy their products and services but also of people and organisations who might be able to influence them, who might help and support them by providing, for example, labour, finance, manufacturing facilities, distribution outlets and legal advice or who are interested because of their impact on parts of society or the business sector in particular.

The organisations mentioned earlier are all well-known brand names, but there are hundreds of thousands of smaller organisations that also need and use marketing communications to convey the essence of their products and services and to engage their audiences. Each of these organisations, large and small, is part of a network of companies, suppliers, retailers, wholesalers, value-added resellers, distributors and other retailers, which join together, often freely, so that each can achieve its own goals.

Effective communication is critically important to organisations, which is why they use a variety of promotional tools. Advertising, sales promotion, public relations, direct marketing, personal selling and added-value approaches such as sponsorship are the most used. To get their messages through they use traditional media such as print and broadcast, cinema and radio; but increasingly digital media, the Internet in particular, are used to 'talk' to and with their customers, potential customers, suppliers, financiers, distributors, communities and employees, among others.

> Increasingly digital media, the Internet in particular, are used to 'talk' to and with their customers, potential customers, suppliers, financiers, distributors, communities and employees, among others.

ViewPoint 1.1   Crisp marketing communications

Walkers, one of the best-known and market-leading brands in the UK, is synonymous with snack foods, and in particular, crisps. In order to communicate and develop its brand with customers and other stakeholders it uses a variety of communication methods. Some of the main ones are set out below.

Advertising   Web site   Point of purchase   Packaging
    Corporate identity   Direct marketing   Public relations
Personal selling   Exhibitions   Trade promotions   Sponsorship
    Product placement   Sales promotion   Field marketing
Merchandising   Vending machines   Customer contact centre
    Video conferencing   Discussion boards

The goal is to stimulate a dialogue that will, ideally, lead to a succession of purchases. Complete engagement.

Marketing communications provides the means by which brands and organisations are presented to their audiences. The goal is to stimulate a dialogue that will, ideally, lead to a succession of purchases. Complete engagement. This interaction represents an exchange between each organisation and each customer, and, according to the quality and satisfaction of the exchange process, will or will not be repeated. It follows, therefore, that communication is a very important and integral part of the exchange process, and it is the skill and judgement of management that determines, in most cases, success or failure.

Marketing communications is an audience-centred activity.

Marketing communications is an audience-centred activity.

The concept of marketing as an exchange

The concept of exchange, according to most marketing academics and practitioners, is central to our understanding of marketing. For an exchange to take place there must be two or more parties, each of whom can offer something of value to the other and who are prepared to enter freely into the exchange process, a transaction. It is possible to identify two main forms of exchange: market (or transactional) exchanges and relational (or collaborative) exchanges.

Market exchanges (Bagozzi, 1978; Houston and Gassenheimer, 1987) are transactions that occur independently of any previous or subsequent exchanges. They have a short-term orientation and are primarily motivated by self-interest. When a consumer buys a bag of Walkers Crisps, a brand they do not buy regularly, then a market exchange can be identified. In contrast to this, *relational exchanges* (Dwyer *et al.*, 1987) have a longer-term orientation and develop between parties who wish to build long-term supportive relationships. So, when a consumer buys Walkers Crisps on a regular basis, and even buys the same flavour, on a majority of purchase occasions, relational exchanges are considered to be taking place.

These two types of exchange represent the extremes in a spectrum of exchange transactions.

These two types of exchange represent the extremes in a spectrum of exchange transactions. In industrial societies market exchanges have tended to dominate commercial transactions although recently there has been a substantial movement towards relational exchanges. In other words there are a mixture of exchanges that occur and each organisation has a portfolio of differing types of exchange which it maintains with different customers, suppliers and other stakeholders. Communication is an essential element, similar to an oil, that lubricates these exchanges enabling them to function. However, to enable these different exchanges to function properly, different types of communication are necessary.

Relational exchanges form the basis of the ideas represented in relationship marketing. Many organisations use relationship marketing principles, manifest in the form of customer relationship marketing, or loyalty marketing programmes. This book is developed on relationship marketing principles and marketing communications is considered to be a means by which long-term relationships between organisations and between organisations and consumers are developed.

The role of communication in exchange transactions

Bowersox and Morash (1989) demonstrated how marketing flows, including the information flow, can be represented as a network that has as its sole purpose the satisfaction of customer needs and wants. Communication plays an important role in these exchange networks. At a basic level, communication can assume one of four main roles:

1. It can *inform* and make potential customers aware of an organisation's offering.

2. Communication may attempt to *persuade* current and potential customers of the desirability of entering into an exchange relationship.

3. Communications can also be used to *reinforce* experiences. This may take the form of *reminding* people of a need they might have or reminding them of the benefits of past transactions with a view to convincing them that they should enter into a similar exchange. In addition, it is possible to provide *reassurance* or comfort either immediately prior to an exchange or, more commonly, post-purchase. This is important as it helps to retain current customers and improve profitability. This approach to business is much more cost effective than constantly striving to lure new customers.

4. Finally, marketing communications can act as a *differentiator*, particularly in markets where there is little to separate competing products and brands. Mineral water products, such as Perrier and Highland Spring, are largely similar: it is the communications surrounding the products that have created various brand images, enabling consumers to make purchasing decisions. In these cases it is the images created by marketing communications that disassociates one brand from another and positions them so that consumers' purchasing confidence and positive attitudes are developed. Therefore, communication can inform, persuade, reinforce and build images to delineate a product or service (see Table 1.2).

> Marketing communications can act as a *differentiator*, particularly in markets where there is little to separate competing products and brands.

At a higher level, the communication process not only supports the transaction, by informing, persuading, reinforcing or differentiating, but also offers a means of

TABLE 1.2 DRIP elements of marketing communications

DRIP element	Examples
Differentiate	Burger King differentiates itself from market leader McDonald's by stating that its burgers are flame grilled for a better taste.
Reinforce	Specsavers Opticians work to bring people back into the eyecare market (see Mini case in Chapter 18).
Inform/make aware	The Environment Agency and Flood Action Week – to inform various organisations, such as the Met Office, local media and the general public of the new flood warning codes.
Persuade	So Good milk is better for us than ordinary milk.

ViewPoint 1.2   Dyson DRIP

Dyson manufactures a revolutionary type of cleaner and has 52 per cent of the UK market. Its communications have needed to:

differentiate it from conventional products – use of innovative technology;

remind/reassure customers that the cyclone system works better than any other and to resist the competition's attempts to gain top of mind awareness;

inform and educate the market about what is wrong with conventional appliances;

persuade potential customers to consider Dyson as the only option when next purchasing floor-cleaning appliances.

EXHIBIT 1.2 Dyson
The manufacturer of this revolutionary new domestic appliance uses marketing communications to differentiate, remind, inform and persuade audiences. Picture reproduced with the kind permission of Dyson.

exchange itself, for example communication for entertainment, for potential solutions and concepts for education and self-esteem. Communications involve intangible benefits, such as the psychological satisfactions associated with, for example, the entertainment value of television advertisements. Communications can also be seen as a means of perpetuating and transferring values and culture to different parts of society or networks. For example, it is argued that the way women are portrayed in the media and stereotypical images of very thin or anorexic women are dysfunctional in that they set up inappropriate role models. The form and characteristics of the communication process adopted by some organisations (both the deliberate and the unintentional use of signs and symbols used to convey meaning) help to provide stability and continuity.

> Communications involve intangible benefits, such as the psychological satisfactions associated with, for example, the entertainment value of television advertisements.

Other examples of intangible satisfactions can be seen in the social and psychological transactions involved increasingly with the work of the National Health Service (NHS), charities, educational institutions and other not-for-profit organisations, such as housing associations. Not only do these organisations increasingly recognise the need to communicate with various audiences, but also they perceive value in being seen to be 'of value' to their customers. There is also evidence that some brands are trying to meet the emerging needs of some consumers who want to know the track record of manufacturers with respect to their environmental policies and actions. For example, the growth in 'Fairtrade' products, designed to provide fairer and more balanced trading arrangements with producers and growers in emerging parts of the world, has influenced Kraft that they should engage with this form of commercial activity. Typhoo claims on its packaging, 'care for tea and our tea pickers'.

The notion of value can be addressed in a different way. All organisations have the opportunity to develop their communications to a point where the value of their messages represents a competitive advantage. This value can be seen in the consistency, timing, volume or expression of the message.

Communication can be used for additional reasons. The tasks of informing, persuading and reinforcing and differentiating are, primarily, activities targeted at consumers or end users. Organisations do not exist in isolation from each other as each one is a part of a wider system of corporate entities, where each enters into a series of exchanges to secure raw material inputs or resources and to discharge them as value-added outputs to other organisations in the network.

The exchanges that organisations enter into require the formation of relationships, however tenuous or strong. Andersson (1992) looks at the strength of the relationship between organisations in a network and refers to them as 'loose or tight couplings'. These couplings, or partnerships, are influenced by the communications that are transmitted and received. The role that organisations assume in a network and the manner in which they undertake and complete their tasks are, in part, shaped by the variety and complexity of the communications in transmission throughout the network. Issues of channel or even network control, leadership, subservience and conflict are implanted in the form and nature of the communications exchanged in any network.

> The exchanges that organisations enter into require the formation of relationships, however tenuous or strong.

Within market exchanges, communications are characterised by formality and planning. Relational exchanges are supported by more frequent communication activity. As Mohr and Nevin (1990) state, there is a bidirectional flow to communications and an informality to the nature and timing of the information flows. This notion of relational exchange has been popularised by the term 'relationship marketing' and is a central theme in this text.

ViewPoint 1.3 — Influencing and directing perception

The charity concerned with the welfare of homeless people, Crisis, ran a direct response television campaign in 2004 in an attempt to boost fundraising in the run-up to the crucial Christmas period. Marketing communications was used to raise awareness about homelessness and to confront people's perception of homelessness. This was achieved through the use of real stories about people, such as a nurse and a soldier, who had become homeless (Whitehead, 2004).

Marketing communications can be used to persuade target audiences in a variety of ways. For example, speaking on BBC Radio 4, Bob Waller (1996) claimed that publicity had been used effectively by the Peak District National Park. However, instead of using publicity to attract tourists, they had deliberately used their publicity opportunities to divert visitors away from particular areas in the Park, in order to repair, preserve and protect them for visitors in the future.

In 2001, with the foot and mouth crisis mounting, the government realised that its previous policy to restrict the public's access to the countryside was deterring tourism and threatening the economy. To correct this perception it used public relations to encourage access to particular areas that were uninfected with the disease.

Marketing communications and the process of exchange

The exchange process is developed and managed by researching consumer/stakeholder needs, identifying, selecting and targeting particular groups of consumers/stakeholders who share similar discriminatory characteristics, including needs and wants, and developing an offering that satisfies the identified needs at an acceptable price, which is available through particular sets of distribution channels. The next task is to make the target audience aware of the existence of the offering. Where competition or other impediments to positive consumer action exist, such as lack of motivation or conviction, a promotional programme is developed and used to communicate with the targeted group.

> Where competition or other impediments to positive consumer action exist, such as lack of motivation or conviction, a promotional programme is developed and used to communicate with the targeted group.

Collectively, these activities constitute the marketing mix (the 4Ps as McCarthy (1960) originally referred to them), and the basic task of marketing is to combine these 4Ps into a marketing programme to facilitate the exchange process. The use of these 4Ps approach has been criticised as limiting the scope of the marketing manager. The assumption by McCarthy was that the tools of the marketing mix allow adaptation to the uncontrollable external environment. It is now seen that the external environment can be influenced and managed strategically and the rise and influence of the service sector is not easily accommodated within the original 4Ps. To do this, additional Ps such as Processes, Political Power and People have been suggested. A marketing mix of 20Ps has even been proposed by some but the essence of the mix remains the same and this deterministic approach has raised concerns and doubts about its usefulness in a marketing environment that is so different to that when the 4Ps was conceived.

Promotion, therefore, is one of the elements of the marketing mix and is responsible for the communication of the marketing offer to the target market. While recognising that there is implicit and important communication through the other elements of the marketing mix (through a high price, for example, symbolic of high quality), it is the task of a planned and integrated set of communication activities to communicate effectively with each of an organisation's stakeholder groups. Marketing communications is sometimes perceived as only dealing with communications that are external to the organisation. It should be recognised that good communications with internal stakeholders, such as employees, are also vital if, in the long term, successful favourable images, perceptions and attitudes are to be established. This book considers the increasing importance of suitable internal communications (Chapter 32) and their vital role in helping to form a strong and consistent corporate identity (Chapter 15).

> It should be recognised that good communications with internal stakeholders, such as employees, are also vital.

ViewPoint 1.4   Social forces of obesity

The influence of social forces on marketing, and marketing communications in particular, can be immense. For example, in the past few years increasing media and public attention has been given to issues concerning healthy eating, obesity and the role food manufacturers and retailers play in helping us (or not) to be slimmer.

Little Chef, which owns several hundred roadside restaurants, has used the brand icon of a chef called Charlie, who has carried a discernible paunch (Exhibit 1.3) since he first appeared in the 1970s. As part of an overall marketing strategy to provide guests with a healthy range of menu items, using less salt and more fruit, it was decided to slim Charlie down (Exhibit 1.4). Part of Little Chef's research

EXHIBIT 1.3 Original Charlie with slight paunch

EXHIBIT 1.4 Proposed but rejected slimmed-down Charlie

EXHIBIT 1.5 Original Michelin Man

EXHIBIT 1.6 Revised, toned and accepted Michelin Man

programme included the use of focus groups and an online voting system for the public to decide which icon they preferred. The public decided, quite emphatically, that Charlie should *not* be slimmed down.

The Michelin Man (Exhibit 1.5) used to drink and smoke before social pressures forced out these habits. In 1998 he lost weight as well in an effort to avoid unattractive associations (Exhibit 1.6). These changes can also be interpreted by the public as a measure of an organisation's image and reputation.

Source: Adapted from Gray (2004).

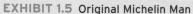

New forms of promotion have been developed in response to changing market and environmental conditions.

New forms of promotion have been developed in response to changing market and environmental conditions. For example, public relations is now seen by some to have a marketing and a corporate dimension (Chapters 15 and 25). Direct marketing is now recognised as an important way of developing closer relationships with buyers, both consumer and organisational (Chapters 12, 14, 15, 25 and 27), while new and innovative forms of communication through sponsorship (Chapter 26), floor advertising, video screens on supermarket trolleys and check-out coupon dispensers (Chapters 10 and 20) and the Internet and associated technologies (Chapters 10 and 21) mean that effective communication requires the selection and integration of an increasing variety of communication tools. The marketing communication mix depicted in Figure 1.1 attempts to reflect these developments and represents a new promotional configuration for organisations.

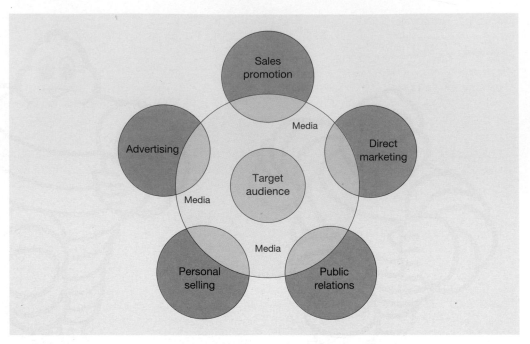

FIGURE 1.1 The tools and position of the marketing communications mix

Defining marketing communications

There is no universal definition of marketing communications and there are many interpretations of the subject. Table 1.3 depicts some of the main orientations through which marketing communications has evolved. The origin of many definitions rests with a promotional outlook where the purpose was to use communications to persuade people to buy products and services. The focus was on products, one-way communications, and there was a short-term perspective. The expression marketing communications emerged as a wider range of tools and media evolved and as the scope of the tasks these communications activities were expected to accomplish expanded. In addition to awareness and persuasion, new goals such as developing understanding and preference, reminding and reassuring customers were recognised as important aspects of the communications effort. Direct marketing activities heralded a new approach as one-to-one, two-way communications began to shift the focus from mass to personal communications efforts. Now a large number of definitions refer to an integrated perspective. This view has gathered momentum over the last 10 years and is even an integral part of the marketing communications vocabulary. This topic is discussed in greater depth in Chapter 11. However, this transition to an integrated perspective raises questions and debate about the purpose of marketing communications. For example, should the focus extend beyond products and services, should corporate communications be integrated in the organisation's marketing communications, should the range of stakeholders move beyond customers, and what does integration mean and is it achievable? With the integrative perspective a strong strategic and long-term orientation developed, although the basis for many marketing communication strategies appears still to rest with a promotional mix orientation.

Some of these interpretations fail to draw out the key issue that marketing communications provides added value, through enhanced product and organisational symbolism.

Some of these interpretations fail to draw out the key issue that marketing communications provides added

TABLE 1.3 The developing orientation of marketing communications

Orientation	Explanation
Information and promotion	Communications are used to persuade people into product purchase using mass media communications. Emphasis on rational, product-based information.
Process and imagery	Communications are used to influence the different stages of the purchase process that customers' experience. A range of tools is used. Emphasis on product imagery and emotional messages.
Integration	Communication resources are used in an efficient and effective way to enable customers to have a clear view of the brand proposition. Emphasis on strategy, media neutrality and a balance between rational and emotional communication.
Relational	Communication is used as an integral part of the different relationships that organisations share with customers. Emphasis on mutual value and meaning plus a recognition of the different communication needs and processing styles of different stakeholder groups.

value, through enhanced product and organisational symbolism. They also fail to recognise that it is the context within which marketing communications flows that impacts upon the meaning and interpretation given to such messages. Its ability to frame and associate offerings with different environments is powerful. Today, in an age where the word 'integration' is used to express a variety of marketing and communication-related activities, where corporate marketing is emerging as the next important development within the subject (Balmer and Gray, 2003) and where relationship marketing is the preferred paradigm (Gronroos, 2004) marketing communications now needs to embrace a wider remit, to move beyond the product information model and become an integral part of an organisation's overall communications and relationship management strategy. This perspective embraces communications as a one-way, two-way, interactive and dialogic approach necessary to meet the varying needs of different audiences. The integration stage focuses on the organisation, whereas the next development may have its focus on the relationships that an organisation has with its various audiences. Above all else, marketing communications should be an audience-centred activity.

> *Marketing communications is a management process through which an organisation engages with its various audiences. By understanding an audience's communications environment, organisations seek to develop and present messages for its identified stakeholder groups, before evaluating and acting upon the responses. By conveying messages that are of significant value, audiences are encouraged to offer attitudinal and behavioural responses.*

Marketing communications can be used to engage with a variety of audiences in such a way that one-way, two-way and dialogic communications are used.

This definition has three main themes. The first concerns the word *engages*. By recognising the different transactional and relationship needs of the target audience, marketing communications can be used to engage with a variety of audiences in such a way that one-way, two-way and dialogic communications are used (Chapters 2 and 9) that meet the needs of the audience. It is incorrect to think that all audiences always want a relationship with your organisation, and for some, one-way communication is just fine. However, messages should encourage individual members of target audiences to respond to the focus organisation (or product/brand). This response can be immediate through, for example, purchase behaviour or use of customer care lines, or it can be deferred as information is assimilated and considered for future use. Even if the information is discarded at a later date, the communication will have prompted attention and consideration of the message.

ViewPoint 1.5   Water communications

The growth in consumption of bottled water is well known, accounts for 10 per cent of the soft drinks market and is only surpassed by cola and fruit juice (ACNielsen). However, the market is evolving such that consumers do not want straight water just for hydration purposes, now they want bottled 'water-plus' products; for example with added minerals and vitamins, low carbonated for exercise (Lucozade Hydro Active) and functional, fortified and 'wellness' waters to support healthy lifestyles and to reduce or guard against obesity.

Marketing communications plays an active role in shaping our perception of these various bottled waters and helps construct brands. Vittel used 'reVittelise' to change perceptions of its brand beyond hydration. Malvern mineral water uses advertising to position itself as 'Not quite Middle England' and reinforces this with celebrities such as Ali G.

However, advertising spend on these bottled brands has fallen as more activity takes place below-the-line. For example, attention has been given to packaging in an attempt not only to achieve shelf stand-out but also to reflect changing social trends. Evian has introduced an 'easy-to-carry' Nomad bottle with a belt clip for 'active consumers'.

Source: Adapted from Sweney (2004).

The second theme concerns the *audiences* for marketing communications. Traditionally marketing communications has been used to convey product-related information to customer based audiences. Today, a range of stakeholders have connections and relationships of varying dimensions and marketing communications needs to incorporate this breadth and variety. Stakeholder audiences, including customers, are all interested in a range of corporate issues, sometimes product related and sometimes related to the policies, procedures and values of the organisation itself. Marketing communications should be an audience-centred activity and in that sense it is important that messages be based on a firm understanding of both the needs and environment of the audience. To be successful, marketing communications should be grounded in the behaviour and information-processing needs and style of the target audience. This is referred to as understanding the context in which the communications event is to occur (Chapters 5, 6 and 12). From this base it is easier to present and position brands in order that they are perceived to be different and of value to the target audience.

> Marketing communications should be grounded in the behaviour and information-processing needs and style of the target audience.

The third theme from the definition concerns the *cognitive response*. This refers to the outcomes of the communication process, and a measure of whether a communication event has been successful. The audience should be regarded as active problem solvers and they use marketing communications to help them in their lives, in purchasing products and services and in managing organisation-related activities. For example, brands are developed partly to help consumers and partly to assist the marketing effort of the host organisation. A brand can inform consumers quickly that, among other things, 'this brand means x quality', and through experience of similar brand purchases consumers are assured that their risk is minimised. If the problem facing a consumer is 'which new soup to select for dinner', by choosing one from a familiar family brand the consumer is able to solve it with minimal risk and great speed. As explained later (Chapter 5) individuals may or may not be aware of the cognitive processing they engage in, as it varies according to a variety of factors.

Marketing communications, therefore, can be considered from a number of perspectives. It is a complex activity and is used by organisations with varying degrees of sophistication and success.

The role of marketing communications

From the above it is possible to deduce that marketing communications is about the promotion of both the organisation and its offerings. Marketing communications recognises the increasing role the organisation plays in the marketing process and the impact that organisational factors can have on the minds of audiences. As the structure, composition and sheer number of offerings in some markets proliferate, so differences between products diminish, to the extent that differentiation between products has become much more difficult. This results in a decrease in the number of available and viable positioning opportunities. One way to resolve this problem is to use the parent organisation as an umbrella, to provide greater support and leadership in the promotion of any offerings. Hence the earlier reference to the emerging strength of corporate marketing.

> As the structure, composition and sheer number of offerings in some markets proliferate, so differences between products diminish.

A view which is becoming increasingly popular is that corporate strategy should be supported by the organisation's key stakeholders, if the strategy is to be successful. Strategy must be communicated in such a way that the messages are consistent through time and targeted accurately at appropriate stakeholder audiences. Each organisation must constantly guard against the transmission of confusing messages, whether this be through the way in which the telephone is answered, the navigability of a Web site, the impact of sales literature or the way salespersons approach prospective clients. These and other stakeholder issues are discussed at length in Chapter 8.

> Strategy must be communicated in such a way that the messages are consistent through time and targeted accurately at appropriate stakeholder audiences.

Many organisations recognise the usefulness and importance of good public relations. This is because of the high credibility attached to the messages received and the relatively low operational costs. As a result, the use of corporate advertising has grown.

Finally, marketing communications recognises the development of channel or trade marketing. Many organisations have moved away from the traditional control of a brand manager to a system that focuses upon the needs of distributors and intermediaries in the channel. The organisations in the channel work together to satisfy their individual and collective objectives. The degree of conflict and cooperation in the

Marketing communications must address the specific communication needs of members of the distribution network and those other stakeholders who impact on or who influence the performance of the network.

channel network depends upon a number of factors, but some of the most important factors are the form and quality of the communications between member organisations. This means that marketing communications must address the specific communication needs of members of the distribution network and those other stakeholders who impact on or who influence the performance of the network. Indeed, marketing communications recognises the need to contribute to the communications in the channel network, to support and sustain the web of relationships.

For example, many organisations in the airline industry have shifted their attention to the needs of the travel trade, customers and competitors. United Airlines, British Airways, KLM and Qantas and other airlines have changed their approach, attitude and investment priorities so that channel partnerships and alliances are of particular priority. Now there is a clear emphasis on working with their partners and their competitors (e.g. British Airways and KLM), and this entails agreement, collaboration and joint promotional activity in order that all participants achieve their objectives.

The marketing communications mix

The marketing communications mix consists of a set of tools (disciplines) that can be used in various combinations and different degrees of intensity in order to communicate with a target audience. In addition to these tools or methods of communication, there is the media, or the means by which marketing communications messages are conveyed. Tools and media should not be confused as they have different characteristics and seek to achieve different goals.

There are five principal marketing communications tools: these are advertising, sales promotion, public relations, direct marketing and personal selling. However, there

There are five principal marketing communications tools.

have been some major changes in the environment and in the way organisations communicate with their target audiences. New technology has given rise to a raft of different media while people have developed a variety of ways to spend their leisure time. This is referred to as media and audience fragmentation and organisations have developed fresh combinations of the promotional mix in order to reach their audiences effectively. For example, there has been a dramatic rise in the use of direct-response media as direct marketing becomes adopted as part of the marketing plan for many products. The Internet and digital technologies have enabled new interactive forms of communication, where the receiver has greater responsibility for their part in the communication process. An increasing number of organisations are using public relations to communicate messages about the organisation (corporate public relations) and also messages about their brands (marketing public relations).

What has happened therefore is that the promotional mix has developed such that the original emphasis on heavyweight mass communication (above-the-line) campaigns has given way to more direct and highly targeted promotional activities using direct marketing and the other tools of the mix. Using the jargon, through-the-line and below-the-line communications are used much more these days. Figure 1.2 brings these elements together.

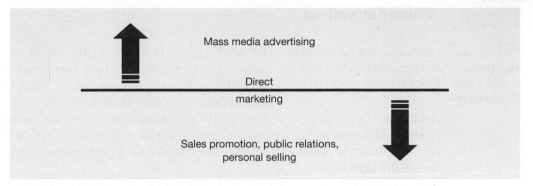

FIGURE 1.2 Above- and below-the-line communications

The shift is from an *intervention*-based approach to marketing communications (one based on seeking the attention of a customer who might not necessarily be interested), towards *permission*-based communications (where the focus is upon communications with members of an audience who have already expressed an interest in a particular offering). In other words with permission communications the seedlings for a relationship are established by the audience, not the brand owner. This has a particular impact on direct marketing, online communications and to some extent personal selling.

Advertising

Advertising is a non-personal form of mass communication that offers a high degree of control for those responsible for the design and delivery of advertising messages. However, the ability of advertising to persuade the target audience to think or behave in a particular way is suspect. Furthermore, the effect on sales is extremely hard to measure. Advertising also suffers from low credibility in that audiences are less likely to believe messages delivered through advertising than they are messages received through some other tools.

The flexibility of this tool is good because it can be used to communicate with a national audience or a particular specialised segment. Although the costs can be extremely large, a vast number of people can be reached with a message, so the cost per contact can be the lowest of all the tools in the mix. Advertising and related media are considered at some depth in Chapters 18 to 22.

Sales promotion

Sales promotion comprises various marketing techniques, which are often used tactically to provide added value to an offering, with the aim of accelerating sales and gathering marketing information. Like advertising, sales promotion is a non-personal form of communication but has a greater capability to be targeted at smaller audiences. It is controllable and, although it has to be paid for, the associated costs can be much lower than those of advertising. As a generalisation, credibility is not very high, as the sponsor is, or should be, easily identifiable. However, the ability to add value and to bring forward future sales is strong and complements a macroeconomic need, which focuses upon short-term financial performance. Sales promotion techniques and approaches are the subject of Chapters 23 and 24.

Personal selling

Personal selling is traditionally perceived as an interpersonal communication tool that involves face-to-face activities undertaken by individuals.

Personal selling is traditionally perceived as an interpersonal communication tool that involves face-to-face activities undertaken by individuals, often representing an organisation, in order to inform, persuade or remind an individual or group to take appropriate action, as required by the sponsor's representative. A salesperson engages in communication on a one-to-one basis where instantaneous feedback is possible. The costs associated with interpersonal communication are normally very large.

This tool, the focus of Chapter 28, differs from the previous two in that, while still lacking in relative credibility and control, the degree of control is potentially lower. This is because the salesperson is free at the point of contact to deliver a message other than that intended (Lloyd, 1997). Indeed, many different messages can be delivered by a single salesperson. Some of these messages may enhance the prospect of the salesperson's objectives being reached (making the sale), or they may retard the process and so incur more time and hence costs. Whichever way it is viewed, control is lower than with advertising.

Public relations

Public relations is 'the art and social science of analysing trends, predicting their consequences, counselling organisations' leadership, and implementing planned programmes of action which will serve both the organisation's and the public interest' (Mexican Statement, 1978). This definition suggests that public relations should be a part of the wider perspective of corporate strategy, and this is discussed at length in Chapter 25. The increasing use of public relations, and in particular publicity, is a reflection of the high credibility attached to this form of communication. Publicity involves the dissemination of messages through third-party media, such as magazines, newspapers or news programmes. There is no charge for the media space or time but there are costs incurred in the production of the material. (There is no such thing as a free lunch or free promotion.) There is a wide range of other tools used by public relations, such as event management, sponsorship and lobbying. It is difficult to control a message once it is placed in the channels, but the endorsement offered by a third party can be very influential and have a far greater impact on the target audience than any of the other tools in the promotional mix.

The increasing use of public relations, and in particular publicity, is a reflection of the high credibility attached to this form of communication.

ViewPoint 1.6	Audi football placement

German car manufacturer Audi, a part of the Volkswagen group, has agreements with both Manchester United and Real Madrid to be their 'car partner' for several seasons, usually three. Not only does this provide Audi opportunities for its cars to be seen associated with some of the leading footballers (celebrities) but it gives Audi opportunities to be seen worldwide as well as inside Old Trafford and the Bernabéu stadiums.

When David Beckham was negotiating his contract to move to Real Madrid the media was intense. He was provided with three Audis during his 36-hour stay, during which he undertook icals, a contract signing event and an official reception. The cars were constantly on prime time news programmes and in newspaper photographs around the globe, to the extent that the equivalent advertising media costs would have been impossible to pay and would not have had the credibility that the product placement event provided.

This non-personal form of communication offers organisations a different way to communicate, not only with consumers but also with many other stakeholders.

The four elements of the promotional mix discussed so far have a number of strengths and weaknesses. As a response to some of the weaknesses that revolve around costs and effectiveness, direct marketing emerged in the 1990s as a new and effective way of building relationships with customers over the long term.

Direct marketing

The growing utilisation of direct marketing by organisations over recent years has been significant. It signals a shift in focus from mass to personalised communications.

> The growing utilisation of direct marketing by organisations over recent years has been significant.

In particular, the use of direct mail, telemarketing and the fast developing area of interactive communications represents through-the-line communications. By removing the face-to-face aspect of personal selling and replacing it with an email communication, a telephone conversation or a direct mail letter, many facets of the traditional salespersons' tasks can be removed, freeing them to concentrate on their key skill areas.

Direct marketing seeks to target individual customers with the intention of delivering personalised messages and building a relationship with them based upon their responses to the direct communications. In contrast to conventional approaches, direct marketing attempts to build a one-to-one relationship, a partnership with each customer, by communicating with the customers on a direct and personal basis. If an organisation chooses to use direct marketing then it has to incorporate the approach within a marketing plan. This is because distribution is different and changes in the competitive environment may mean that prices need to change. For example, charges for packing and delivery need to be incorporated. The product may also need to be altered or adapted to the market. For example, some electrical products are marketed through different countries on home shopping channels and Web sites. The electrical requirements of each country or region need to be incorporated within the product specification of each country's offering. In addition to these changes, the promotion component is also different, simply because communication is required directly with each targeted individual. To do this, direct-response media must be used.

In many cases direct-response media are a derivative of advertising, such as direct mail, magazine inserts, and television and print advertisements that use telephone numbers to encourage a direct response. However, direct response can also be incorporated within personal selling through telemarketing and sales promotions with competitions to build market knowledge and develop the database, which is the key to the direct marketing approach.

This text regards direct marketing as the management process associated with building mutually satisfying customer relationships through a personal and intermediary-free

...ect-response media are the primary communication tools when direct ... an integral part of the marketing plan. Further discussion of direct mar-... direct-response communications can be found in Chapters 21 and 27.

The Internet is a distribution channel and communication medium that enables consumers and organisations to communicate in radically different ways. It allows for interactivity and is possibly the best medium to enable dialogue. Communication is two-way and interactive, is ... ist, allowing businesses and individuals to find information and enter exchange tra... ctions in such a way that some traditional communication practices and shopping patterns are being reconfigured.

The communication mix is changing: no longer can the traditional grouping of promotional tools be assumed to be the most effective forms of communication. This brief outline of the elements of the promotions mix signals some key characteristics. These are the extent to which each element is controllable, whether it is paid for by the sponsor and whether communication is by mass medium or undertaken personally. One additional characteristic concerns the receiver's perception of the credibility of the source of the message. If the credibility factor is high then there is a greater likelihood that messages from that source will be accepted by the receivers.

The 4Cs Framework (Table 1.4) represents the key characteristics and shows the relative effectiveness of the tools of promotion across a number of different characteristics. The three primary groupings are the ability of each to communicate, the costs involved and the control that each tool can maintain.

TABLE 1.4 The 4Cs Framework – a summary of the key characteristics of the tools of marketing communications

	Advertising	Sales promotion	Public relations	Personal selling	Direct marketing
Communications					
Ability to deliver a personal message	Low	Low	Low	High	High
Ability to reach a large audience	High	Medium	Medium	Low	Medium
Level of interaction	Low	Low	Low	High	High
Credibility					
Given by the target audience	Low	Medium	High	Medium	Medium
Costs					
Absolute costs	High	Medium	Low	High	Medium
Cost per contact	Low	Medium	Low	High	High
Wastage	High	Medium	High	Low	Low
Size of investment	High	Medium	Low	High	Medium
Control					
Ability to target particular audiences	Medium	High	Low	Medium	High
Management's ability to adjust the deployment of the tool as circumstances change	Medium	High	Low	Medium	High

Effectiveness of the promotional tools

Each element of the promotions mix has different capacities to communicate and to achieve different objectives. The effectiveness of each tool can be tracked against the purchase decision process. Here consumers can be assumed to move from a state of unawareness through product comprehension to purchase. Advertising is better for creating awareness, and personal selling is more effective at promoting action and purchase behaviour.

> **Advertising is better for creating awareness, and personal selling is more effective at promoting action and purchase behaviour.**

Readers are encouraged to see the elements of the mix as a set of complementary ingredients, each drawing on the potential of the others. The tools are, to a limited extent, partially interchangeable and in different circumstances different tools are used to meet different objectives. For example, network marketing organisations, such as Avon Cosmetics, use personal selling to complete the majority of activities in the purchase decision sequence. The high cost of this approach is counterbalanced by the effectiveness of the communications. However, this aspect of interchangeability only serves to complicate matters. If management's task was simply to identify problems and then select the correct precision tool to solve the problem, then the issue of the selection of the 'best' promotions mix would evaporate (Figure 1.3).

These five elements of the promotional mix are supplemented by one of the most effective forms of marketing communication, *word-of-mouth* recommendation. As we shall see later, word-of-mouth recommendation is one of the most powerful marketing communication tools and, if an organisation can develop a programme to harness and accelerate the use of personal recommendation effectively, the more likely it will be that the marketing programme will be successful.

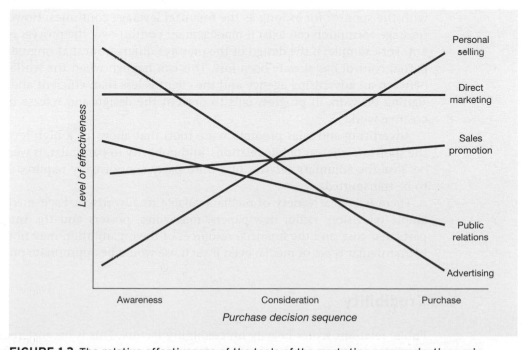

FIGURE 1.3 The relative effectiveness of the tools of the marketing communications mix

Selection criteria

The key criteria governing an organisation's selection and use of each tool are as follows:

1. the degree of control required over the delivery of the message;
2. the financial resources available to pay a third party to transmit messages;
3. the level of credibility that each tool bestows on the organisation;
4. the size and geographic dispersion of the target audiences.

Control

Control over the message is necessary to ensure that the intended message is trans-mitted to and received by the target audience. Furthermore, this message must be capable of being understood in order that the receiver can act appropriately. Message control is complicated by interference or negative 'noise' that can corrupt and distort messages. For example, an airline's advertising may be discredited by a major news story about safety checks or even an accident.

> Control over the message is necessary to ensure that the intended message is transmitted to and received by the target audience.

Advertising and sales promotion allow for a high level of control over the message, from design to transmission. Interestingly, they afford only partial control or influence over the feedback associated with the original message.

Financial resources

Control is also a function of financial power. In other words, if an organisation is pre-pared to pay a third party to transmit the message, then long-term control will rest with the sponsor for as long as the financial leverage continues. However, short-term message corruption can exist if management control over the process is less than vigil-ant. For example, if the design of the message differs from that originally agreed, then partial control has already been lost. This can happen when the working relationship between an advertising agency and the client is less than efficient and the process for signing off work in progress fails to prevent the design and release of inappropriate creative work.

Advertising and sales promotion are tools that allow for a high level of control by the sponsor, whereas public relations, and publicity in particular, is weak in this aspect because the voluntary services of a third party are normally required for the message to be transmitted.

There is a great variety of media available to advertisers. Each media type (for example television, radio, newspapers, magazines, posters and the Internet) carries a particular cost, and the financial resources of the organisation may not be available to use particular types of media, even if such use would be appropriate on other grounds.

Credibility

Public relations scores heavily on credibility factors. This is because receivers perceive the third party as unbiased and to be endorsing the offering. They view the third party's comments as objective and trustworthy in the context of the media in which the comments appear.

At a broad level, advertising, sales promotion and, to a slightly lesser extent, personal selling are tools that can lack credibility, as perceived by the target audience. Because of this, organisations often use celebrities and 'experts' to endorse their offerings. The credibility of the spokesperson is intended to distract the receiver from the sponsor's prime objective, which is to sell the offering. Credibility, as we see shall later, is an important aspect of the communication process and of marketing communications.

> The credibility of the spokesperson is intended to distract the receiver from the sponsor's prime objective, which is to sell the offering.

Size and geographic dispersion

The final characteristic concerns the size and geographic dispersion of the target audience. A consumer audience, often national, can only be reached effectively if tools of mass communication are used, such as advertising and sales promotion. Similarly, various specialist businesses require personal attention to explain, design, demonstrate, install and service complex equipment. In these circumstances personal selling, one-to-one contact, is of greater significance. The tools of marketing communications can enable an organisation to speak to vast national and international audiences through advertising and satellite technology, or to single persons or small groups through personal selling and the assistance of word-of-mouth recommendation.

Management of the promotional tools

Traditionally, each of the promotional tools has been regarded as the domain of particular groups within organisations:

1. Personal selling is the domain of the sales director, and traditionally uses an internally based and controlled sales force.
2. Public relations is the domain of the chairperson and is often administered by a specialist PR agency.
3. Advertising and sales promotion are the domain of the marketing director or brand manager. Responsibility for the design and transmission of messages for mass communications is often devolved to an external advertising agency.

Many organisations have evolved without marketing being recognised as a key function, let alone as a core philosophy. There are a number of reasons why this might be so. First, the organisation may have developed with a public relations orientation in an environment without competition, where the main purpose of the organisation was to disperse resources according to the needs of their clients. The most obvious examples are to be drawn from the public sector, local authorities and the NHS in particular. A second reason would be because a selling perspective ('our job is to sell it') dominated. There would invariably be no marketing director on the board, just a sales director representing the needs of the market.

It is not surprising that these various organisational approaches have led to the transmission of a large number of different messages. Each function operates with good intent, but stakeholders receive a range of diverse and often conflicting messages.

Context and marketing communications

Organisations can be seen as open social systems (Katz and Kahn, 1978) in which all of the components of the unit or system are interactive and interdependent (Goldhaber, 1986). Modify one part of a system and adjustments are made by all the other components to accommodate the change. This effect can be seen at the micro and macro levels. At the macro level the interdependence of organisations has been noted by a number of researchers. Stern and El-Ansary (1995) depict distribution channels as 'a network of systems', and so recognise organisations as interdependent units. At the micro level, the individual parts of an organisation accommodate each other as the organisation adjusts to its changing environment. By assembling the decisions associated with the development and delivery of a marketing communications strategy (Figure 1.4), it becomes possible to see the complexity and sensitivity of each of the decision components.

Organisations can be seen as open social systems.

The marketing communications undertaken by organisations within these systems can be regarded as a series of communication episodes. These episodes can often be construed as a dialogue and can be seen to be continuous. The amount of time between episodes may vary from the very small, such as those associated with many major FMCG (fast-moving consumer goods) brand campaigns, which run and run, or very

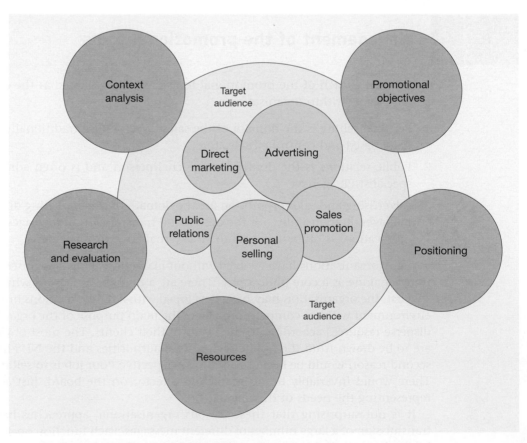

FIGURE 1.4 The system of marketing communications

large, such as those associated with some business-to-business campaigns or one-off events associated with a single task, such as government drink-driving campaigns held annually each Christmas period.

These episodes occur within situations where specific factors can be identified and where the circumstances are characteristically individual. Indeed, it is unlikely that any two episodes will occur with exactly the same circumstances. The use of market-ing communications as a means of influencing others is therefore determined by the specific circumstances or the context in which the episode is to occur. Marketing com-munications become part of the context and influences and are influenced by the particular circumstances.

> The use of marketing communications as a means of influencing others is therefore determined by the specific circumstances or the context in which the episode is to occur.

It is important therefore, when considering the elements and factors that contribute to marketing communications, to account for the context in which the communica-tions will contribute. For example, falling sales often provoke a response by manage-ment to increase or change the advertising. The perception of the brand by the target audience might be inaccurate or not what was intended, or a new product might be launched into a competitive market where particular positions have been adopted by competitors. These contexts contain a set of specific circumstances in which a market-ing communication episode might (will) occur. It should be borne in mind that the list of possible contexts is endless and that the task facing marketing communications managers is to identify the key aspects of any situation and deliver promotional messages that complement the context. This enables audiences to interpret messages correctly and maintain a dialogue.

The main tasks facing the management team responsible for marketing commun-ications are to decide the following:

1. who should receive the messages;
2. what the messages should say;
3. what image of the organisation/brand receivers are to form and retain;
4. how much is to be spent establishing this new image;
5. how the messages are to be delivered;
6. what actions the receivers should take;
7. how to control the whole process once implemented;
8. determining what was achieved.

These tasks are undertaken within a context within which there may be many episodes or only a few. Note that more than one message is often transmitted and that there is more than one target audience. This is important, as recognition of the need to com-municate with multiple audiences and their different information requirements, often simultaneously, lies at the heart of marketing communications. The aim is to generate and transmit messages that present the organisation and its offerings to their various target audiences, encouraging them to enter into a dialogue and relationship. These messages must be presented consistently and they must address the points stated above. It is the skill and responsibility of the marketing communications manager to blend the communication tools and create a mix that satisfies these elements.

Consequently, contexts are not independent or isolated sets of easily identifiable circumstances, but are inter-related and overlapping circumstances in which it is rare for any one organisation to have total knowledge of any single context. Management makes judgements based upon its experience, marketing research and limited knowledge of any one identifiable

> Consequently, contexts are not independent or isolated sets of easily identifiable circumstances, but are interrelated and overlapping circumstances.

part context, and it might be said that each time a marketing communications programme is rolled out management takes an educated leap into the unknown.

Communication differences

Having identified the need to communicate with a number of different audiences, it seems appropriate to conclude this opening chapter by examining the differences between communications used by and targeted at two very different and specific audiences. These are organisations (commonly referred to as business-to-business) and those aimed at consumer markets. Some writers (Brougaletta, 1985; Gilliland and Johnston, 1997) have documented a variety of differences between consumer and business-to-business markets. The following is intended to set out some of the more salient differences (see also Table 1.5):

1. *Message reception*

   The contextual conditions in which messages are received and ascribed meanings are very different. In the organisational setting the context is much more formal, and as the funding for the purchase is to be derived from company sources (as opposed to personal sources for consumer market purchases) there may be a lower orientation to the price as a significant variable in the purchase decision. The purchase is intended to be used by others for company usage, whereas products bought in a consumer context are normally intended for personal consumption.

2. *Number of decision-makers*

   In consumer markets a single person very often makes the decision. In organisational markets decisions are made by many people within the buying centre. This means that the interactions of the individuals needs to be considered. In addition, a variety of different individuals need to be reached and influenced and this may involve the use of different media and message strategies.

3. *The balance of the communications mix*

   The role of advertising and sales promotions in business-to-business communications is primarily to support the personal selling effort. This contrasts with the mix that predominates in consumer markets. Personal selling has a relatively minor role and is only significant at the point of purchase in some product categories where involvement is high (cars, white goods and financial services), reflecting high levels of perceived risk. However, the increasing use of direct marketing in consumer markets suggests that personal communications are becoming more prevalent and in some ways increasingly similar to the overall direction of business-to-business communications.

4. *The constituents of the marketing communications mix*

   Business-to-business markets have traditionally been quite specific in terms of the promotional tools and media used to target audiences. While the use of advertising literature is very important, there has been a tendency to use a greater proportion of below-the-line activities. This compares with consumer markets, where a greater proportion of funds have been allocated to above-the-line activities. It is interesting that the communications in the consumer market are moving towards a more integrated format, more similar in form to the business-to-business model than was previously considered appropriate.

TABLE 1.5 Differences between consumer and business-to-business marketing communications

	Consumer-oriented markets	Business-to-business markets
Message reception	Informal	Formal
Number of decision-makers	Single or few	Many
Balance of the promotional mix	Advertising and sales promotions dominate	Personal selling dominates
Specificity and integration	Broad use of promotional mix with a move towards integrated mixes	Specific use of below-the-line tools but with a high level of integration
Message content	Greater use of emotions and imagery	Greater use of rational, logic- and information-based messages although there is evidence of a move towards the use of imagery
Length of decision time	Normally short	Longer and more involved
Negative communications	Limited to people close to the purchaser/user	Potentially an array of people in the organisation and beyond
Target marketing and research	Great use of sophisticated targeting and communication approaches	Limited but increasing use of targeting and segmentation approaches
Budget allocation	Majority of budget allocated to brand management	Majority of budget allocated to sales management
Evaluation and measurement	Great variety of techniques and approaches used	Limited number of techniques and approaches used

5. *Message content*

   Generally, there is high involvement in many business-to-business purchase decisions, so communications tend to be much more rational and information based than in consumer markets. However, there are signs that businesses are making increased use of imagery and emotions in the messages (see Chapter 19).

6. *Length of purchase decision time*

   The length of time taken to reach a decision is much greater in the organisation market. This means that the intensity of any media plan can be dissipated more easily in the organisational market.

7. *Negative communications*

   The number of people affected by a dissatisfied consumer, and hence negative marketing communication messages, is limited. The implications of a poor purchase decision in an organisational environment may be far reaching, including those associated with the use of the product, the career of participants close to the locus of the decision and, depending upon the size and spread, perhaps the whole organisation.

8. *Target marketing and research*

   The use of target marketing processes in the consumer market has been more advanced and sophisticated than in the organisational market. This impacts on the quality of the marketing communications used to reach the target audience. However, there is much evidence that the business-to-business markets organisations are becoming more aware and sophisticated in their approach to segmentation techniques and processes.

9. *Budget allocation*

The sales department receives the bulk of the marketing budget in the organisation market and little is spent on research in comparison with the consumer market.

10. *Measurement and evaluation*

The consumer market employs a variety of techniques to evaluate the effectiveness of communications. In the organisation market, sales volume, value, number of enquiries and market share are the predominant measures of effectiveness.

There can be no doubt that there are a number of major differences between consumer and organisational communications. These reflect the nature of the environments, the tasks involved and the overall need of the recipients for particular types of information. Information need, therefore, can be seen as a primary reason for the differences in the way promotional mixes are configured. Advertising in organisational markets has to provide a greater level of information and is geared to generating leads that can be followed up with personal selling, which is traditionally the primary tool in the promotional mix. In consumer markets, advertising plays the primary role with support from the other tools of the promotional mix. Interestingly, new media appears to be reconfiguring the marketing communications mix and perhaps reducing the gulf and distinction between the mix used in business-to-business and consumer markets. Throughout this book, reference will be made to the characteristics, concepts and processes associated with marketing communications and each of these two main sectors.

> Advertising in organisational markets has to provide a greater level of information and is geared to generating leads.

Summary

The concept of exchange transactions is seen by many commentators as underpinning the marketing concept. Of the different types of exchange, market and relational are the two that can be observed most often in industrial societies.

Marketing communications has a number of roles to play in the context of both these types of exchange but, as will be seen later in this book, there is a strong movement away from the reliance on market exchanges to the longer-term perspective that relational exchanges enjoy and to the development of partnerships. This approach is referred to as 'relationship marketing', and it is here that changes in the use and deployment of marketing communications can be best observed.

Marketing communications is an audience-centred activity and uses five traditional elements of the promotional mix: advertising, sales promotion, public relations, direct marketing and personal selling. Each has strengths and weaknesses, and these tools are now beginning to be used in different ways to develop relationships with customers, whether they be consumers or organisational buyers. An example of these changes is the use of the Internet, a communication medium, which has grown rapidly since the mid-1990s and is threatening to reconfigure the way marketing as well as marketing communications is practised.

Marketing communications has an important role to play in communicating and promoting the products and services not only to consumers but also to the business-to-business sector and other organisations that represent other stakeholders. The development of partnerships between brands and consumers and between organisations within distribution channels or networks is an important perspective of marketing communications. Communications in this context will be an important part of this text.

Finally, marketing communications can be seen as a series of episodes that occur within a particular set of circumstances or contexts. Marketing managers need to be able to identify principal characteristics of the context they are faced with and contribute to the context with a suitable promotional programme.

Review questions

1. Briefly compare and contrast the different types of exchange transaction.

2. How does communication assist the exchange process?

3. Name the five main elements of the marketing communications mix.

4. Write a brief description of each element of the marketing communications mix.

5. How do each of the elements compare across the following criteria: control, communication effectiveness and cost?

6. How does direct marketing differ from the other elements of the mix?

7. Identify five different advertisements that you think are using direct-response media. How effective do you think they might be?

8. Explain contexts and episodes. Describe the main tasks facing the management team responsible for marketing communications.

9. What is systems theory and how might it apply to marketing communications?

10. Explain how marketing communications supports the marketing and business strategies of the organisation.

References

Andersson, P. (1992) Analysing distribution channel dynamics. *European Journal of Marketing*, **26**(2), pp. 47–68.

Bagozzi, R. (1978) Marketing as exchange: a theory of transactions in the market place. *American Behavioral Science*, **21**(4), pp. 257–61.

Balmer, J.M.T. and Gray, E.R. (2003) Corporate brands: what are they? What of them?, *European Journal of Marketing*, **37**(7/8), pp. 972–97.

Bowersox, D. and Morash, E. (1989) The integration of marketing flows in channels of distribution. *European Journal of Marketing*, **23**, p. 2.

Brougaletta, Y. (1985) What business-to-business advertisers can learn from consumer advertisers. *Journal of Advertising Research*, **25**(3), pp. 8–9.

Dwyer, R., Schurr, P. and Oh, S. (1987) Developing buyer–seller relationships. *Journal of Marketing*, **51** (April), pp. 11–27.

Gilliland, D.I. and Johnston, W.J. (1997) Toward a model of business-to-business marketing communications effects. *Industrial Marketing Management*, **26**, pp. 15–29.

Goldhaber, G.M. (1986) *Organisational Communication*. Dubuque, IA: W.C. Brown.

Gray, R. (2004) Why the fatboys slimmed, *Marketing*, 25 August, p. 14.

Gronroos, C. (2004) The relationship marketing process: communication, interaction, dialogue, value. *Journal of Business and Industrial Marketing*, **19**(2), pp. 99–113.

Houston, F. and Gassenheimer, J. (1987) Marketing and exchange. *Journal of Marketing*, **51** (October), pp. 3–18.

Katz, D. and Kahn, R.L. (1978) *The Social Psychology of Organisations*, 2nd edn. New York: Wiley.

Lloyd, J. (1997) Cut your rep free. *Pharmaceutical Marketing* (September), pp. 30–2.

McCarthy, E.J. (1960) *Basic Marketing: A Managerial Approach*. Homewood, IL: Irwin.

Mexican Statement (1978) *The Place of Public Relations in Management Education*. Public Relations Education Trust, June.

Mohr, J. and Nevin, J. (1990) Communication strategies in marketing channels. *Journal of Marketing* (October), pp. 36–51.

Stern, L. and El-Ansary, A. (1995) *Marketing Channels*. 5th edn. Englewood Cliffs, NJ: Prentice-Hall.

Sweney, M. (2004) Sector insight: bottled water – beyond the functional. *Marketing*. Retrieved 18 August 2004 from Brand Republic at http://www.brandrepublic.co.uk/news/newsArticle.

Waller, R. (1996) BBC Radio 4 *Today* programme, 29 July.

Whitehead, J. (2004) Crisis uses real-life stories as inspiration for ad campaign. Retrieved 19 November 2004 from Brand Republic at http://www.brandrepublic.com/.

Communication theory

2

Only by sharing meaning with members of the target audience and reducing levels of ambiguity can it be hoped to create a dialogue through which marketing goals can be accomplished. To share meaning successfully may require the support of significant others: those who may be expert, knowledgeable or have access to appropriate media channels.

Aims and objectives

The aims of this chapter are to introduce communication theory and to set it in the context of marketing communications.

The objectives of this chapter are to:

1. understand the basic model of the communication process;
2. appreciate how the components of the model contribute to successful communications;
3. provide an analysis of the linkages between components;
4. examine the impact of the media on the communication process;
5. examine the impact of personal influences on the communication process;
6. introduce more recent explanations of communication theory, including networks;
7. explain how communication theory underpins our understanding of marketing communications.

An introduction to the communication process

It was established in the previous chapter that marketing communications is partly an attempt by an organisation/brand to create and sustain a dialogue with its various constituencies. Communication itself is the process by which individuals share meaning. Therefore, for dialogue to occur, each participant needs to be able to interpret the meaning embedded in the others messages and be able to respond. For this overall process to work, information needs to be transmitted by all participants. It is important, therefore, that those involved with marketing communications understand the complexity of the transmission process. Through knowledge and understanding of the communications process they are more likely to achieve their objective of sharing meaning with each member of their target audiences and so have an opportunity to enter into a dialogue.

Communication itself is the process by which individuals share meaning.

In the previous chapter the point was established that there are a variety of reasons why organisations need to communicate with various groups. Of these, one of the more prominent is the need to influence or persuade.

As an initial observation, persuasive communications can be seen in three different contexts. These are set out in Table 2.1.

These three perspectives focus upon the use of persuasion, but there is a strong need for organisations also to inform and remind. Furthermore, these approaches are too specific for general marketing purposes and fail to provide assistance to those who wish to plan and manage particular communications.

TABLE 2.1 Forms of persuasion

Form of persuasion	Explanation
Negotiation	Individuals use a variety of overt and subtle rewards and punishments to persuade the other of the superiority of their point of view.
Propaganda	Organisations seek to influence their target audiences through the use of symbols, training and cultural indoctrination.
Use of speakers	When a speaker addresses a large group influence is achieved through the structure of the material presented, the manner in which the presentation is delivered and the form of evidence used to influence the group.

Linear model of communication

Wilbur Schramm (1955) developed what is now accepted as the basic model of mass communications (Figure 2.1). The components of the linear model of communication are:

1. Source: the individual or organisation sending the message.
2. Encoding: transferring the intended message into a symbolic style that can be transmitted.
3. Signal: the transmission of the message using particular media.

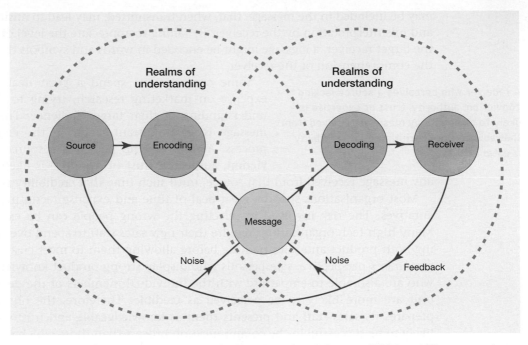

FIGURE 2.1 A linear model of communication (Based on Schramm (1955) and Shannon and Weaver (1962).)

4. Decoding: understanding the symbolic style of the message in order to understand the message.

5. Receiver: the individual or organisation receiving the message.

6. Feedback: the receiver's communication back to the source on receipt of the message.

7. Noise: distortion of the communication process, making it difficult for the receiver to interpret the message as intended by the source.

This is a linear model that emphasises the 'transmission of information, ideas, attitudes, or emotion from one person or group to another (or others), primarily through symbols' (Theodorson and Theodorson, 1969). The model and its components are straightforward, but it is the quality of the linkages between the various elements in the process that determine whether the communication will be successful.

> This is a linear model that emphasises the 'transmission of information, ideas, attitudes, or emotion from one person or group to another (or others), primarily through symbols'.

Source/encoding

> The source, an individual or organisation, identifies a need to transmit a message and then selects a combination of appropriate words, pictures, symbols and music to represent the message to be transmitted.

The source, an individual or organisation, identifies a need to transmit a message and then selects a combination of appropriate words, pictures, symbols and music to represent the message to be transmitted. This is called encoding. The purpose is to create a message that is capable of being understood by the receiver.

There are a number of reasons why the source/encoding link might break down; for example, the source may fail to diagnose a particular situation accurately. By not fully understanding a stakeholder's problem or level of knowledge, inappropriate information may be included in the message, that, when transmitted, may lead to misunderstanding and misinterpretation by the receiver. By failing to appreciate the level of education of the target receiver, a message might be encoded in words and symbols that are beyond the comprehension of the receiver.

A receiver who perceives a source lacking conviction, authority, trust or expertise is likely to discount any message received from that source, until such time that credibility is established.

Some organisations spend a great deal of time and expense on marketing research, trying to develop their understanding of their target audience. The source of a message is an important factor in the communication process. A receiver who perceives a source lacking conviction, authority, trust or expertise is likely to discount any message received from that source, until such time that credibility is established.

Most organisations spend a great deal of time and expense recruiting sales representatives. The risk involved in selecting the wrong people can be extremely large. Many high-tech organisations require their new sales staff to spend over a year receiving both product and sales training before allowing them to meet customers. From a customer's perspective, salespersons who display strong product knowledge skills and who are also able to empathise with the individual members of the decision-making unit are more likely to be perceived as credible. Therefore, the organisation that prepares its sales staff and presents them as knowledgeable and trustworthy is more likely to be successful in the communication process than those which do not take the same level of care.

The source is a part of the communication process, not just the generator of detached messages. Patzer (1983) determined that the physical attractiveness of the communicator, particularly if it is the source, contributes significantly to the effectiveness of persuasive communications.

This observation can be related to the use, by organisations, of spokespersons and celebrities to endorse products. Spokespersons can be better facilitators of the communication process if they are able to convey conviction, if they are easily associated with the object of the message, if they have credible expertise and if they are attractive to the receiver, in the wider sense of the word.

Spokespersons can be better facilitators of the communication process if they are able to convey conviction.

This legitimate authority is developed in many television advertisements by the use of the 'white coat', or product-specific clothing, as a symbol of expertise. By dressing the spokesperson in a white coat, he or she is perceived immediately as a credible source of information ('they know what they are talking about'), and so is much more likely to be believed.

Signal

Once encoded, the message must be put into a form that is capable of transmission. It may be oral or written, verbal or non-verbal, in a symbolic form or in a sign. Whatever the format chosen, the source must be sure that what is being put into the message is what is wanted to be decoded by the receiver. The importance of this aspect of the communication process will be developed later when different message strategies are examined in Chapter 19.

The channel is the means by which the message is transmitted from the source to the receiver. These channels may be personal or non-personal. The former involves face-to-face contact and word-of-mouth communications, which can be extremely influential. Non-personal channels are characterised by mass media advertising, which can reach large audiences.

Information received directly from personal influence channels is generally more persuasive than information received through mass media.

Information received directly from personal influence channels is generally more persuasive than information received through mass media. This may be a statement of the obvious, but the reasons for this need to be understood. First, the individual approach permits greater flexibility in the delivery of the message. The timing and power with which a message is delivered can be adjusted to suit the immediate 'selling' environment. Secondly, a message can be adapted to meet the needs of the customer as the sales call progresses. This flexibility is not possible with mass media messages, as these have to be designed and produced well in advance of transmission and often without direct customer input.

ViewPoint 2.1   Encoding/decoding problems

When developing names or taglines for global brands it is important to choose a name that translates appropriately into all the languages. The encoding process, the name of the car, cleaner, biscuit or fashion accessory should be well researched and capable of being decoded by the target audience in such a way that there is meaning, sense and value. The following are examples where the encoding process had not be properly considered:

● When the European hardware store chain 'Götzen' opened in Istanbul it had to change the name as 'Göt' means 'ass' in Turkish.

● Traficante is an Italian brand of mineral water. In Spanish, it means drug dealer.

● Clairol's 'Mist Stick' curling iron had problems when launched in Germany because 'mist' is slang for manure.

A mainstream UK bank informed audiences in a recent advertising campaign that to show the soles of your feet in Thailand is a very rude gesture, and to give the thumbs up sign in Turkey has quite the opposite meaning to its symbolism of cool acceptance here in the UK.

Finally, workers in an African port saw a consignment with the international symbol for 'fragile' (a wine glass with snapped stem) on the side. They assumed it meant that they had been sent a cargo of broken glass and immediately pitched all the cases overboard into the harbour.

Source: Adapted from: www.i18nguy.com/translations and http://www.sourceuk.net/indexf.html?03590; used with permission.

Decoding/receiver

Decoding is the process of transforming and interpreting a message into thought. This process is influenced by the receiver's realm of understanding, which encompasses the experiences, perceptions, attitudes and values of both the source and the receiver. The more the receiver understands about the source and the greater his or her experience in decoding the source's messages, the more able the receiver will be to decode the message successfully.

EXHIBIT 2.1 Freelander print ad. The decoding of this message requires understanding the picture of the Maasai tribe in terms of being 'freelanders' and in terms of their visual and symbolic representation of the vehicle.

Feedback/response

The set of reactions a receiver has after seeing, hearing or reading the message is known as the response. These reactions may vary from the extreme of dialing an enquiry telephone number, returning a coupon or even buying the product, to storing information in long-term memory for future use. Feedback is that part of the response that is sent back to the sender, and it is essential for successful communication. The need to understand not just whether the message has been received but also which message has been received is vital. For example, the receiver may have decoded the message incorrectly and a completely different set of responses may have been elicited. If a suitable feedback system is not in place then the source will be unaware that the communication has been unsuccessful and is liable to continue wasting resources. This represents inefficient and ineffective marketing communications.

The evaluation of feedback is, of course, vital if sound communications are to be developed. Only through evaluation can the success of any communication be judged.

> Only through evaluation can the success of any communication be judged.

Feedback through personal selling can be instantaneous, through overt means such as questioning, raising objections or signing an order form. Other means, such as the use of gestures and body language, are less overt, and the decoding of the feedback needs to be accurate if an appropriate response is to be given. For the advertiser, the process is much more vague and prone to misinterpretation and error.

Feedback through mass media channels is generally much more difficult to obtain, mainly because of the inherent time delay involved in the feedback process. There are some exceptions, namely the overnight ratings provided by the Broadcasters' Audience Research Board to television contractors, but as a rule feedback is normally delayed and not as fast. Some commentators argue that the only meaningful indicator of communication success is sales. However, there are many other influences that affect the level of sales, such as price, the effect of previous communications, the recommendations of opinion leaders or friends, poor competitor actions or any number of government or regulatory developments. Except in circumstances such as direct marketing, where immediate and direct feedback can be determined, organisations should use other methods to gauge the success of their communications activities, for example the level and quality of customer inquiries, the number and frequency of store visits, the degree of attitude change and the ability to recognise or recall an advertisement. All of these represent feedback but, as a rough distinction, the evaluation of feedback for mass communications is much more difficult to judge than is the case for interpersonal communications.

Noise

A complicating factor that may influence the quality of the reception and the feedback is noise. Noise, according to Mallen (1977), is 'the omission and distortion of information', and there will always be some noise present in all communications. Management's role is to ensure that levels of noise are kept to a minimum, wherever it is able to exert influence.

> Noise occurs when a receiver is prevented from receiving the message.

Noise occurs when a receiver is prevented from receiving the message. This may be because of either cognitive or physical factors. For example, a cognitive factor may be that the encoding of the message was inappropriate, so making it difficult for the receiver to decode the message. In this circumstance it is said that the realms of understanding of the source and the receiver were not matched. Another reason why noise may enter the system is that the receiver may have been physically prevented from decoding the message accurately because the receiver was distracted. Examples of distraction are that the telephone rang, or someone in the room asked a question or coughed. A further reason could be that competing messages screened out the targeted message.

Some sales promotion practitioners use the word 'noise' to refer to the ambience and publicity surrounding a particular sales promotion event. In other words, the word is being used as a positive, advantageous element in the communication process. This approach is not adopted in this text.

Realms of understanding

The concept of the 'realm of understanding' was introduced earlier. It is an important element in the communication process because it recognises that successful communications are more likely to be achieved if the source and the receiver understand each other. This understanding concerns attitudes, perceptions, behaviour and experience: the values of both parties to the communication process. Therefore, effective communication is more likely when there is some common ground, a realm of understanding between the source and receiver.

Some organisations, especially those in the private sector, spend a huge amount of money researching their target markets and testing their advertisements to ensure that their messages can be decoded and understood by the target audience. The more organisations understand their receivers, the more confident they become in constructing and transmitting messages to them. Repetition and learning, as we shall see later, are important elements in marketing communications. Learning is a function of knowledge and, the more we know, the more likely we are to understand.

Influences of the communication process

The linear, sequential interpretation of the communication process fails to accurately represent all forms of communication. Indeed it is probable that there is not a single model or framework which is entirely satisfactory and capable of covering all forms of communication. However there are two particular influences on the communication process that need to be considered. First the media used to convey information and, secondly, the influence of people on the communication process. These are considered in turn.

The influence of media within the communication process

The dialogue that marketing communications seeks to generate with audiences is partially constrained by an inherent time delay based upon the speed at which responses are generated by the participants in the communication process. Technological advances now allow participants to conduct marketing communication-based 'conversations' at electronic speeds. The essence of this speed attribute is that it allows for interactively based communications, where enquiries are responded to more or less instantly (see Chapter 10).

> Technological advances now allow participants to conduct marketing communication-based 'conversations' at electronic speeds.

New technology, and the Internet in particular, provide an opportunity for real dialogue with customers. With traditional media the tendency is for monologue or at best delayed and inferred dialogue. One of the first points to be made about these new media-based communications is that the context within which marketing communications occurs is redefined. Traditionally, dialogue occurs in a context that is familiar

Providers implant their messages into the various environments of their targets.

(relatively) and which is driven by providers who deliberately present their messages via a variety of communication devices into the environments that they expect their audiences may well pass through or recognise. Providers implant their messages into the various environments of their targets. Yuan *et al.* (1998) refer to advertising messages being 'unbundled', such as direct marketing, which has no other content, or 'bundled' and embedded with other news content such as television, radio and Web pages with banner ads. Perhaps more pertinently, they refer to direct and indirect online advertising. Direct advertising is concerned with advertising messages delivered to the customers (email) while indirect advertising is concerned with messages that are made available for customers to access at their leisure (Web sites).

New media-based communications tend to make providers become relatively passive. Their messages are presented in an environment that requires targets to use specific equipment to actively search them out. The roles are reversed, so that the drivers in the new context are active information seekers, represented by the target audience (members of the public and other information providers such as organisations), not just the information-providing organisations.

The drivers in the new context are active information seekers.

A further development resulting from the use of new media in marketing communications is the target of the communication activity. Interactivity, as stated above, has increased in speed, but interactivity can occur not only between people as a result of a message conveyed through a particular medium but also with machines or cyberspace. As Hoffman and Novak (1996) state, people interactivity is now supplemented by machine interactivity. This means that the dialogue that previously occurred through machines now occurs with the equipment facilitating the communication exchanges (see Figure 2.2).

The dialogue that previously occurred through machines now occurs with the equipment facilitating the communication exchanges.

These authors refer to the work of Steuer (1992), who suggests that the principal relationship is with what is referred to as a *mediated environment* and not between sender and receiver. This is important, as it is the potential of all participants in the communication activity to mediate or influence the environment (especially the message content) in which the dialogue occurs that makes interactive marketing communications so dynamic and such a radically revolutionary new promotional medium.

The linear model assumes information content to be essentially one-dimensional.

The linear model assumes information content to be essentially one-dimensional, that is, just the spoken word (as in a presentation), just the written word (as in a product leaflet) or just in a visual format (as in a print or television advertisement). New media and the development of multimedia facilities have enabled the simultaneous delivery of messages through a variety of formats. Media Richness theory (MRT), developed before the influence of the Internet and related digital technologies, suggests that there is a range or depth of message content embedded within different media and is concerned with the capacity of media types to process ambiguous communication in organisations. According to Daft and Lengel (1986, p. 560) richness refers to the 'ability of information to change understanding within a time interval'. The criteria used are the availability of instant feedback, the capacity to transmit multiple cues, expressions such as tone of voice, body language and eye contact, the use of natural language and finally the personal focus of the medium. Face-to-face communication is the richest medium because it helps establish a personal connection. At the other end of the scale, numeric and formal written communication is slow, often visually limited and impersonal. Such media is said to be leaner. The scale starts with face-to-face and is followed by the telephone, email, letter, note, memo, special report, fliers and bulletins. It is argued that rich media have a greater capacity to reduce ambiguity and allow for

Richness refers to the 'ability of information to change understanding within a time interval'.

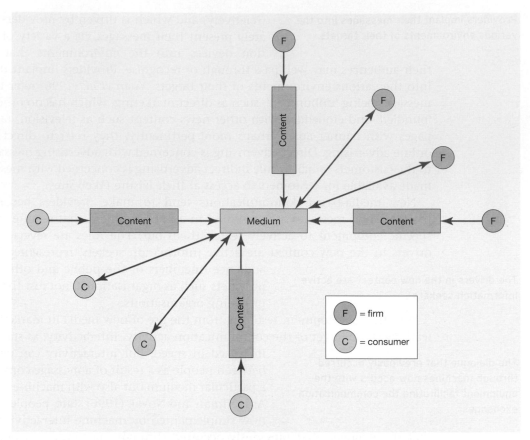

FIGURE 2.2 A model of marketing communications in a hypermedia computer-mediated environment. From Hoffman and Novak (1996); reprinted with permission from the *Journal of Marketing*, published by the American Marketing Association

more complex and difficult communications. Lean media is more cost effective for simple or routine communications. By fitting the right media to the right type of task, it is argued that managerial performance can be improved or optimized. Media Richness theory provides a scale or ranking of different media concerning the richness of information each medium is capable of communicating. With the advent of digital technologies it might be expected that new media would be relatively rich and hence impact positively on task performance. However, although intuitively appealing, there is little empirical evidence to support MRT. Dennis and Kinney (1998) found that new media did allow for quicker decision-making but they argue that MRT is an old theory and not necessarily relevant in the digital age. Other, subsequent theories have evolved and these will be considered in greater depth in Chapter 25.

The influence of people on the communication process

The traditional view of communication holds that the process consists essentially of one step. Information is directed and shot at prospective audiences, rather like a bullet is propelled from a gun. The decision of each member of the audience to act on the message or not is the result of a passive role or participation in the process (Figure 2.3).

Organisations can communicate with different target audiences simply by varying the message and the type and frequency of channels used. The one-step model has been criticised for its oversimplification, and it certainly ignores the effect of personal influences on the communication process and potential for information deviance.

The one-step model has been criticised for its oversimplification.

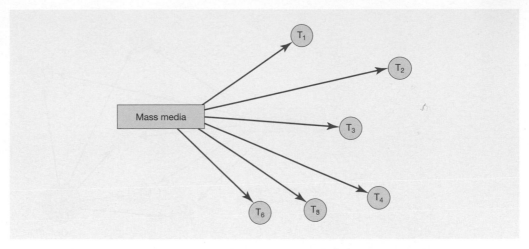

FIGURE 2.3 One-step model of communication. T = member of the target audience

EXHIBIT 2.2 Brushing Wax print ad. This uses the principles of opinion leadership (a representative of the target audience) to convey product benefits

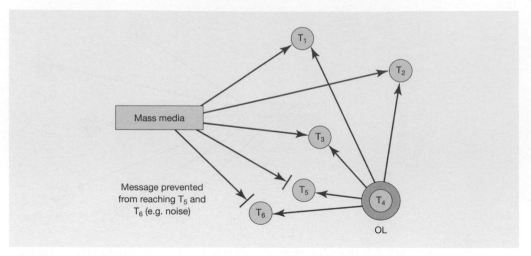

FIGURE 2.4 Two-step model of communication. OL = opinion leader

Two-step flow of communication

This model depicts information flowing via media channels to particular types of people (opinion leaders and opinion formers; see later) to whom other members of the audience refer for information and guidance. Through interpersonal networks, opinion leaders not only reach members of the target audience who may not have been exposed to the message, but may reinforce the impact of the message for those members that did receive it (Figure 2.4). For example, editors of travel sections in the Sunday press and television presenters of travel programmes fulfil the role of opinion former and can influence the decision of prospective travellers. It can be seen that targets 5 and 6 were not exposed to the original message, so the opinion leader (OL; T_4) acts as an original information source for them and as a reinforcer for targets 1, 2 and 3.

The implication of the two-step model is that the mass media do not have a direct and all-powerful effect over their audiences. If the primary function of the mass media is to provide information, then personal influences are necessary to be persuasive and to exert direct influence on members of the target audience.

Multi-step flow of communications

This model proposes that the process involves interaction among all parties to the communication process; see Figure 2.5. This interpretation closely resembles the network of participants that are often involved in the communication process.

Word-of-mouth communications

The multi-step model suggests that opinion leaders/formers and members of the target audience all influence each other. Indeed, successful communication is characterised by interaction and word-of-mouth (WoM) communications can assist and enrich this communication process.

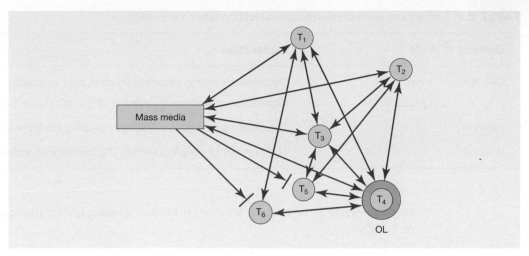

FIGURE 2.5 Multi-step model of communication

Personal influence upon the communication process is important if communication is to be successful.

Therefore, personal influence upon the communication process is important if communication is to be successful. Customers use word-of-mouth recommendations to provide information and to support and reinforce their purchasing decisions. At the heart of this approach is the source credibility that is assigned to people whose opinions are sought after and used in the purchase decision process. In comparison to advertising messages, word of mouth communications are more robust (Berkman and Gilson, 1986).

Stokes and Lomax (2002) define word-of-mouth communication as 'interpersonal communication regarding products or services where the receiver regards the communicator as impartial'. This definition was developed from some of the more established interpretations that did not accommodate such communication through new media and restrictions concerning perceived independence of the communicator. Organisations now use WoM techniques commercially in order to generate a point of differentiation.

People like to talk about their product (service) experiences, for a variety of reasons that are explored in the next section. However, by talking with a neighbour or colleague about the good experiences associated with a new car, for example, the first-hand 'this has actually happened to someone I know' effect will be instrumental in the same views being passed on to other colleagues, irrespective of their validity or overall representation of similar cars. eViral marketing (see Chapter 21) is an electronic version of the spoken endorsement of a product or service where messages, screen savers and other information are targeted at key individuals who then voluntarily pass the message to friends and colleagues and in doing so bestow, endorse and provide the message with much valued credibility.

But why do people want to discuss products or advertising messages? Bone (1995) cited by Stokes and Lomax (2002) refers to three elements of WoM. See Table 2.2.

Dichter (1966) determined that there were four main categories of output WoM.

Dichter (1966) determined that there were four main categories of output WoM:

1. *Product involvement*
   People, he found, have a high propensity to discuss matters that are either distinctly pleasurable or unpleasurable. Such discussion serves to provide an opportunity for

TABLE 2.2 Elements of word-of-mouth communication (after Bone 1995)

Element of WoM		Explanation
Direction	Input WoM	Customers seeking recommendation prior to purchase
	Output WoM	Expression of feelings as a result of the purchase experience
Valence		The positive or negative feelings resulting from the experience
Volume		The number of people to which the message is conveyed

the experience to be relived, whether it be the 'looking for' or the 'use' experience, or both.

2. *Self-involvement*

Discussion offers a means for ownership to be established and signals aspects of prestige and levels of status to the receiver. More importantly, perhaps, dissonance can be reduced as the purchaser seeks reassurance about the decision.

3. *Other involvement*

Products can assist motivations to help others and to express feelings of love, friendship and caring. These feelings can be released through a sense of sharing the variety of benefits that products can bestow.

4. *Message involvement*

The final motivation to discuss products is derived, according to Dichter, from the messages that surround the product itself, in particular the advertising messages and, in the business-to-business market, seminars, exhibitions and the trade press, which provide the means to provoke conversation and so stimulate word-of-mouth recommendation.

It is interesting to note that Dichter's various forms of involvement, in particular the 'self' and 'other' categories, bear a strong similarity to the market exchanges and reciprocal exchanges explored in Chapter 1. However, word-of-mouth communications are often undertaken by those who identify very closely with a brand, to the extent that they might be termed brand advocates. Advocacy can be demonstrated not only through word-of-mouth communications but also through behaviour, for example by wearing branded clothing or using tools and equipment. Watts (2000) reports the claim made by the group marketing director of Dyson that 70 per cent of sales are generated through recommendation by family and friends, to the extent that some people would ring up others and offer to lend out their machine. The issue of advocacy is explored further in Chapter 9 in the section on loyalty and retention schemes.

> Advocacy can be demonstrated not only through word-of-mouth communications but also through behaviour.

These motivations to discuss products and their associative experiences vary between individuals and with the intensity of the motivation at any one particular moment. There are two main persons involved in this process of word-of-mouth communications: a sender and receiver. Research indicates that the receiver's evaluation of a message is far from stable over time and accuracy of recall decays (expectedly) through time. What this means for marketing communications is that those people who have a positive product experience, especially in the service sector, should be encouraged to talk as soon as possible after the event (Christiansen and Tax, 2000).

> Those people who have a positive product experience, especially in the service sector, should be encouraged to talk as soon as possible after the event.

ViewPoint 2.2	WoM to attract hotel guests

A hotel manager noticed that input WoM for his hotel given by travel agents was much stronger than the output WoM, even though the overseas guests reported very favourable satisfaction levels. In order 'to align the input WoM needs of potential customers with activities designed to encourage appropriate output WoM', a range of activities was introduced to prompt WoM opportunities.

One of these required guests to tell the agents of their experience, and the manager also communicated with the agents by sending them copies of the guest comment cards. He also provided complimentary rooms for the agents so that they could experience the hotel at first hand and then sent them teddy bears (a reminder of England) when they made a certain number of bookings. Later he sent them jars of honey. Guests were also given teddy bears on departure.

One other notable activity included restoring one of the hotel rooms to how it would have been when the hotel opened in 1860. People perceived this as novel, interesting, and it gave rise to extensive positive output WoM. This activity also gave rise to a number of public relations activities.

Source: Stokes and Lomax (2002). Used with kind permission.

According to Reichheld (2003) cited by Mazur (2004) organisations should measure word-of-mouth communication because those who speak up about a brand are risking their own reputation when they recommend a brand. Looking at the financial services sector, Reichheld argues that measures based on customer satisfaction or retention rates can mask real growth potential because they are measures of defection and switching barriers may induce inertia. He found three particular groups based on their type of word-of-mouth endorsement: Promoters, Passively Satisfied and Detractors. In particular he identified a strong correlation between an organisation's growth rate and the percentage of customers who are active Promoters.

For organisations it is important to target messages at those individuals who are predisposed to such discussion, as this may well propel word-of-mouth recommendations and the success of the communications campaign. The target, therefore, is not necessarily the target market, but those in the target market who are most likely to volunteer their positive opinions about the offering or those who, potentially, have some influence over members. There are three types of such volunteers: opinion leaders, formers and followers.

Opinion leaders

Katz and Lazerfeld (1955) first identified individuals who were predisposed to receiving information and then reprocessing it to influence others. Their studies of American voting and purchase behaviour led to their conclusion that those individuals who could exert such influence were more persuasive than information received directly from the mass media. These opinion leaders, according to Rogers (1962), tend 'to be of the same social class as non-leaders, but may enjoy a higher social status within the group'. Williams (1990) uses the work of Reynolds and Darden (1971) to suggest that they are more gregarious and more self-confident than non-leaders. In addition, they have a greater exposure to relevant mass media (print) and as a result have more

> Those individuals who could exert such influence were more persuasive than information received directly from the mass media.

knowledge/familiarity and involvement with the product class, are more innovative and more confident of their role as influencer (leader) and appear to be less dogmatic than non-leaders (Chan and Misra, 1990).

Opinion leadership can be simulated in advertising by the use of product testimonials. Using ordinary people to express positive comments about a product to each other is a very well-used advertising technique.

ViewPoint 2.3   French fashion clothing

Vernette (2004) reports that a typical profile of an opinion leader in the French women's fashion market is aged 15 to 35 years, is female and is either employed or is a student. Their dominant values are that they are open-minded, full of wanderlust and they attach a high level of importance to their friends. They favour advertising more than non-leaders (or followers) and they prefer to talk about advertising more than non-leaders do. Vernette confirmed that (these) leaders read more women's magazines than non-leaders but also found that it is possible to rank these magazines according to the penetration among leaders. This suggests that media planning can be developed around those media vehicles that reach a disproportionately high number of opinion leaders.

Source: Adapted from Vernette (2004).

The importance of opinion leaders in the design and implementation of communication plans should not be underestimated.

The importance of opinion leaders in the design and implementation of communication plans should not be underestimated. Midgley and Dowling (1993) refer to *innovator communicators*: those who are receptive to new ideas and who make innovation-based purchase decisions without reference to or from other people. However, while the importance of these individuals is not doubted, a major difficulty exists in trying to identify just who these opinion leaders and innovator communicators are. While they sometimes display some distinctive characteristics, such as reading specialist media vehicles, often being first to return coupons, enjoying attending exhibitions or just involving themselves with new, innovative techniques or products, they are by their very nature invisible outside their work, family and social groups.

Opinion formers

Opinion formers are individuals who are able to exert personal influence because of their authority, education or status associated with the object of the communication process.

Opinion formers are individuals who are able to exert personal influence because of their authority, education or status associated with the object of the communication process. Like opinion leaders, they are looked to by others to provide information and advice, but this is because of the formal expertise that opinion formers are adjudged to have. For example, community pharmacists are often consulted about symptoms and medicines, and film critics carry such conviction in their reviews that they can make or break a new production.

ViewPoint 2.4	Delia followers

Many celebrities develop a band of followers, who are keen to support the opinion former or spokesperson. Sainsbury's was said to be able to predict the volume of ingredients and food it would sell the day following the broadcast of a Jamie Oliver advertisement. Delia Smith has a similar fan base to the extent that the day after she used fresh cranberries in a TV recipe, sales of cranberries rose 200 per cent. When she fried and boiled eggs on *How to Cook* average egg sales rose by 54 million.

Source: Adapted from Keating (2004).

The BBC radio programme *The Archers*, an everyday story of country folk, has been used to deliver messages about farming issues. The actors in the programme are opinion formers and they direct messages to farmers about farming techniques and methods. The educational use was very important after the Second World War.

Popular television programmes, such as *EastEnders*, *Emmerdale* and *Coronation Street*, all of which attract huge audiences, have been used as vehicles to bring to attention and open up debates about many controversial social issues, such as contraception, abortion, drug use and abuse, and serious illness and mental health concerns.

The influence of opinion formers can be great. For example, the editor of a journal or newspaper may be a recognised source of expertise, and any offering referred to by the editor in the media vehicle is endowed with great credibility. In this sense the editor acts as a gatekeeper, and it is the task of the marketing communicator to ensure that all relevant opinion formers are identified and sent appropriate messages.

The credibility of opinion formers is vital for communication effectiveness.

However, the credibility of opinion formers is vital for communication effectiveness. If there is a suspicion or doubt about the impartiality of the opinion former, then the objectivity of their views and comments is likely to be perceived as tainted and not believed so that damage may be caused to the reputation of the brand and those involved.

ViewPoint 2.5	Wine buffs

The views of an independent third party can be very beneficial, as witnessed by Chittenden (2000) who reported that when a Liubimetz merlot was mentioned on the BBC's *Food and Drink* programme, sales of the wine soared by 888 per cent.

So it was not surprising when an allegation by a member of the Circle of Wine Tasters that some members were not sufficiently independent to give unbiased views of wines caused much resentment. It was suggested that some members were tied into supermarket contracts or television programmes such that there was a conflict of interest and that the advice and recommendations they gave consumers were inevitably biased.

Source: Chittenden (2000).

Many organisations constantly lobby key members of parliament in an effort to persuade them to pursue 'favourable' policies. Opinion formers are relatively easy to identify, as they need to be seen shaping the opinion of others, usually opinion followers.

Opinion followers

Some people actively seek information from those they believe are well informed, while others prefer to use the mass media for information and guidance.

The vast majority of consumers can be said to be opinion followers. The messages they receive via the mass media are tempered by the opinions of the two groups of personal influencers just discussed. Some people actively seek information from those they believe are well informed, while others prefer to use the mass media for information and guidance (Robinson, 1976). However, this should not detract from the point that, although followers, they still process information independently and use a variety of inputs when sifting information and responding to marketing stimuli.

Ethical drug manufacturers normally launch new drugs by enlisting the support of particular doctors who have specialised in the therapy area and who are recognised by other doctors as experts. These opinion formers are invited to lead symposia and associated events to build credibility and activity around the new product. At the same time, public relations agencies prepare press releases with the aim that the information will be used by the mass media (opinion formers) for editorial purposes and create exposure for the product across the target audience, which, depending upon the product and/or the media vehicle, may be GPs, hospital doctors, patients or the general public. All these people, whether they be opinion leaders or formers, are active influencers or talkers (Kingdom, 1970).

Process of adoption

An interesting extension to the concept of opinion followers and the discussion on word-of-mouth communications is the process by which individuals become committed to the use of a new product. Rogers (1983) has identified this as the process of adoption and the stages of his innovation decision process are represented in Figure 2.6. These stages in the adoption process are sequential and are characterised by the different factors that are involved at each stage (e.g. the media used by each individual).

1. *Knowledge*
   The innovation becomes known to consumers, but they have little information and no well-founded attitudes. Information must be provided through mass media to institutions and people that active seekers of information are likely to contact. Information for passive seekers should be supplied through the media and channels that this group habitually uses to look for other kinds of information (Windahl *et al.*, 1992).

   Jack cleans his teeth regularly, but he is beginning to notice a sensitivity to both hot and cold drinks. He becomes aware of an advertisement for Special Paste on television.

2. *Persuasion*
   The consumer becomes aware that the innovation may be of use in solving known and potential problems. Information from those who have experience of the product becomes very important.

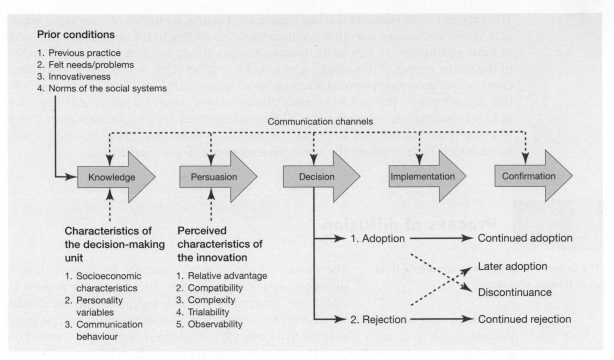

Prior conditions

1. Previous practice
2. Felt needs/problems
3. Innovativeness
4. Norms of the social systems

Communication channels

Knowledge → Persuasion → Decision → Implementation → Confirmation

Characteristics of the decision-making unit

1. Socioeconomic characteristics
2. Personality variables
3. Communication behaviour

Perceived characteristics of the innovation

1. Relative advantage
2. Compatibility
3. Complexity
4. Trialability
5. Observability

1. Adoption → Continued adoption
→ Later adoption
→ Discontinuance
2. Rejection → Continued rejection

FIGURE 2.6 Stages in the innovation decision process of adoption. Reprinted from Rogers (1983) with the permission of the Free Press. Copyright 1962, 1971, 1983 by the Free Press

> *Jack notices that the makers of Special Paste claim that their brand reduces the amount of sensitive reaction to hot and cold drinks. Special Paste has also been recommended to him by someone he overheard in the pub last week. Modelling behaviour predominates.*

3. *Decision*

   An attitude may develop and may be either favourable or unfavourable, but as a result a decision is reached whether to trial the offering or not. Communications need to assist this part of the process by continual prompting.

   > *Jack is prepared to believe (or not to believe) the messages and the claims made on behalf of Special Paste. He thinks that Special Paste is potentially a very good brand (or not). He intends trying Special Paste because he was given a free sample (or because it was on a special price deal).*

4. *Implementation*

   For the adoption to proceed in the absence of a sales promotion, buyers must know where to get it and how to use it. The product is then tested in a limited way. Communications must provide this information in order that the trial experience be developed.

   > *Jack buys Special Paste and tests it.*

5. *Confirmation*

   The innovation is accepted or rejected on the basis of the experience during trial. Planned communications play an important role in maintaining the new behaviour by dispelling negative thoughts and positively reaffirming the original 'correct' decision. McGuire, as reported in Windahl *et al.* (1992), refers to this as post-behavioural consolidation.

   > *It works; Jack's teeth are not as sensitive to hot and cold drinks as they were before he started using 'Special Paste'. He reads an article which reports that large numbers of people are using these types of products satisfactorily. Jack resolves to buy Special Paste next time.*

This process can be terminated at any stage and, of course, a number of competing brands may vie for consumers' attention simultaneously, so adding to the complexity and levels of noise in the process. Generally, mass communications are seen to be more effective in the earlier phases of the adoption process for products that buyers are actively interested in, and more interpersonal forms are more appropriate at the later stages, especially trial and adoption. This model assumes that the stages occur in a predictable sequence, but this clearly does not happen in all purchase activity, as some information that is to be used later in the trial stage may be omitted, which often happens when loyalty to a brand is high or where the buyer has experience in the marketplace.

Process of diffusion

The process of adoption in aggregate form, over time, is diffusion.

The process of adoption in aggregate form, over time, is diffusion. According to Rogers, diffusion is the process by which an innovation is communicated through certain channels over a period of time among the members of a social system. This is a group process and Rogers again identified five categories of adopters. Figure 2.7 shows how diffusion may be fast or slow and that there is no set speed at which the process occurs. The five categories are as follows:

1. *Innovators*: these groups like new ideas and have a large disposable income. This means they are more likely to take risks associated with new products.

2. *Early adopters*: research has established that this group contains a large proportion of opinion leaders and they are therefore important in speeding the diffusion process. Early adopters tend to be younger than any other group and above average in education. Other than innovators, this group takes more publications and consults more salespeople than all others. This group is important to the

Early adopters tend to be younger than any other group and above average in education.

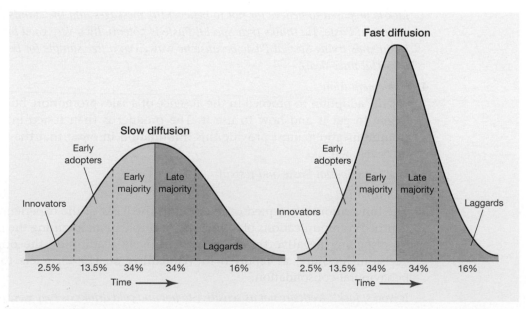

FIGURE 2.7 Fast and slow diffusion of an innovation (From Hawkins *et al.* (1989); used with kind permission.)

marketing communications process because they can determine the speed at which diffusion occurs.

3. *Early majority*: usually, opinion followers are a little above average in age, education, social status and income. They rely on informal sources of information and take fewer publications than the previous two groups.

4. *Late majority*: this group of people is sceptical of new ideas and only adopts new products because of social or economic factors. They take few publications and are below average in education, social status and income.

5. *Laggards*: a group of people who are suspicious of all new ideas and set in their opinions. Lowest of all the groups in terms of income, social status and education, this group takes a long time to adopt an innovation.

This framework suggests that, at the innovation stage, messages should be targeted at relatively young people in the target group, with a high level of income, education and social status. This will speed word-of-mouth recommendation and the diffusion process. Mahajan *et al.* (1990) observe that the personal influence of word-of-mouth communications does not work in isolation from the other communication tools. Early adopters are more likely to adopt an innovation in response to 'external influences' and only through time will the effect of 'internal influences' become significant. In other words, mass media communications need time to work before word-of-mouth communications can begin to build effectiveness.

A major difficulty associated with the use of this framework, however, is the inability to define which stage of the diffusion process is operating at any time. Furthermore, Gatignon and Robertson (1985) suggest that there are three elements to the diffusion process which need to be taken into account, particularly for the fast-moving consumer goods sector:

1. the rate of diffusion or speed at which sales occur;

2. the pattern of diffusion or shape of the curve;

3. the potential penetration level or size of the market.

Care should be taken to ensure that all three of these elements are considered when attempting to understand the diffusion process. It can be concluded that if a promotional campaign is targeted at innovators and the early majority and is geared to stimulating word-of-mouth communications, then the diffusion process is more likely to be successful than if these elements are ignored.

Interactional approaches to communications

The models and frameworks of the communication process discussed to date can be interpreted as an abstraction. The one-step model is linear and unidirectional, and it suggests that the receiver plays a passive role in the process. The two-step and multi-step models attempt to account for the interactive nature of communication and they proffer a mutually participative role for all parties to the communication process. These models emphasise individual behaviour and exclude the social behaviour implicit in the process. Goffman (1969) advocates an 'interactional' approach that focuses on the roles adopted by the players in the communication process. Through mutual understanding of each other's behaviour the rules of

The two-step and multi-step models attempt to account for the interactive nature of communication.

the communication process are established. McEwan (1992) suggests that this permits formal and informal communication procedures to be established, and that mutual understanding (Rogers and Kincaid, 1981) and increased levels of trust can be developed by the participants.

This is an interesting perspective, as strands of the importance of source credibility can be identified in this approach. Evidence of Goffman's approach can be seen in personal selling. Sellers and buyers, meeting for the first time, often enter negotiations at a formal level, each adopting a justifiable, self-protective position. As negotiations proceed, so the two parties adjust their roles, and, as the likelihood of a mutual exchange increases, so the formal roles give way to more informal ones.

Relational or contextual approaches to communications

The previous model accounts for social behaviour but does not account for the context within which the behaviour occurs. Communication events always occur within a context (Littlejohn, 1992) or particular set of circumstances, which not only influence the form of the communication but also the nature and the way the communication is received, interpreted and acted upon. There are a huge number of variables that can influence the context, including the disposition of the people involved, the physical environment, the nature of the issue, the history and associated culture, the goals of the participants and the expected repercussions of the dialogue itself.

Littlejohn identifies four main contextual levels. These are interpersonal, group, organisational and mass communication. These levels form part of a hierarchy whereby higher levels incorporate the lower levels but 'add something new of their own'.

The relational approach means that communication events are linked together in an organised manner.

The relational approach means that communication events are linked together in an organised manner, one where the events are 'punctuated' by interventions from one or more of the participants. These interventions occur whenever the participants attempt cooperation or if conflict arises.

Soldow and Thomas (1984), referring to a sales negotiation, state that a relationship develops through the form of negotiations rather than the content. An agreement is necessary about who is to control the relationship or whether there will be equality. Rothschild (1987) reports that 'sparring will continue' until agreement is reached or the negotiations are terminated. In other words, without mutual agreement over the roles of the participants, the true purpose of the interaction, to achieve an exchange, cannot be resolved.

An interesting aspect of relational communication theory is social penetration (Taylor and Altman, 1987). Through the disclosure of increasing amounts of information about themselves, partners in a relationship (personal or organisational) develop levels of intimacy that serve to build interpersonal (interorganisational?) relationships. The relationship moves forward as partners reveal successive layers of information about each other and, as a greater amount or breadth of information is shared, confidence grows. These levels can be seen to consist of orientation, exploratory affective exchange, affective exchange and stable exchange; see Table 2.3. These layers are not uncovered in a logical, orderly sequence. It is likely that partners will return to previous levels, test the outcomes and rewards and reconsider their positions as the relationships unfold through time. This suggests that social penetration theory may lie at the foundation of the development of trust, commitment and relational exchanges between organisations.

TABLE 2.3 Layers of social penetration

Orientation	The disclosure of public information only.
Exploratory affective exchange	Expansion and development of public information.
Affective exchange	Disclosure, based upon anticipated relationship rewards, of deeper feelings, values and beliefs.
Stable exchange	High level of intimacy where partners are able to predict each other's reactions with a good level of accuracy.

Source: Adapted from Taylor and Altman (1987).

> Participants engage in communication based upon their perception of the environment in which the communication occurs and the way in which each participant relates to each other.

Relationships need not be just dyadic, as the interactional approach suggests, but could be triadic or even encompass a much wider network or array of participants. Through this perspective a 'communication network' can be observed, through which information can flow. Participants engage in communication based upon their perception of the environment in which the communication occurs and the way in which each participant relates to each other.

Rogers (1986) identifies a communication network as 'consisting of interconnected individuals who are linked by patterned communication flows'. This is important, as it views communication as transcending organisational boundaries. In other words, it is not only individuals within an organisation that develop patterned communication flows but also individuals across different organisations. These individuals participate with one another (possibly through exchanges) and use communication networks to achieve their agenda items.

The extent to which individuals are linked to the network is referred to as connectedness. The more a network is connected, the greater the likelihood that a message will be disseminated, as there are few isolated individuals. Similarly, the level of integration in a network refers to the degree to which members of the network are linked to one another. The greater the integration, the more potential channels there are for a message to be routed through.

Systems theory, as discussed in the previous chapter, recognises that organisations are made of interacting units. The relational approach to communications is similar to systems theory. The various 'criss-crossing' flows of information between reciprocating units allow individuals and groups to modify the actions of others in the 'net', and this permits the establishment of a pattern of communication (Tichy, 1979).

Network approaches to communications

The regular use of these patterned flows leads to the development of communication networks, which have been categorised as prescribed and emergent (Weick, 1987).

> The regular use of these patterned flows leads to the development of communication networks.

Prescribed networks are formalised patterns of communication, very often established by senior management within an organisation or by organisational representatives when interorganisational communications are considered.

It follows that emergent networks are informal and emerge as a response to the social and task-oriented needs of the participants.

Undoubtedly some of these more recent approaches have made significant contributions to our understanding of communication. They need to be developed further, and for a fuller account of these approaches to communication readers are referred to McEwan (1992). These later approaches, like their predecessors, have been developed as a result of our understanding of individual behaviour, often within an organisational context.

Summary

An appreciation of the way in which communication works is important to understanding and developing planned communications. The classic approach to communication views the process as linear, similar to the actions of a hypodermic syringe injecting its audience with information. Here the sender, message, channel, receiver approach is prevalent. Subsequent models have attempted to reflect the two-way perspective and to account for the interpersonal components of communications, which in themselves stress mutuality and shared perceptions (Windahl *et al.*, 1992).

The linear approach is not rejected, as there are circumstances where a one-way transmission of information is required, such as a flood warning by the National Rivers Authority or the announcement that a product specification has been altered to meet new legislative requirements. However, in the context of developing relational exchanges (Chapter 1), the network approach to communications is both justified and compatible. Individuals are seen to engage in patterned flows of communication that partly reflect the diversity of their interests.

This text recognises the importance of the linear and interactional approaches to communication, but uses the concept of communication networks, a contextual perspective, to explore marketing communications.

Review questions

1. Name the elements of the linear model of communication and briefly describe the role of each element.
2. Make brief notes explaining why the linear interpretation of the communication process is not entirely valid.
3. Discuss the nature and characteristics of Media Richness theory.
4. Discuss the differences between one-step, two-step and multi-step communications.
5. How do opinion leaders differ from opinion formers and opinion followers?
6. Why is word-of-mouth communication so important to marketing communications?
7. What are the three elements of word-of-mouth communication identified by Bone?
8. Sketch an outline diagram to show the difference between fast and slow diffusion.
9. What is the relational approach to communications? How might social penetration theory assist our understanding of this interpretation of how communication works?
10. Identify two forms of communication networks.

MINI-CASE
Adidas Originals training shoes

Mini-case written by Lynn Sudbury, Senior Lecturer, Liverpool John Moores University; Anthony Byrne, Senior Lecturer, Liverpool John Moores University

I currently own around 140 pairs of old school training shoes, 100 of which are adidas. I tend to buy these from eBay or from outlets like size? and Aspecto. I don't just collect the shoes, I also collect adidas memorabilia, information, magazines, anything really historical to do with adidas. Yes, I do get asked about training shoes quite a bit! (Graham K. – opinion leader)

'Old school' or 'classic' are terms commonly used to describe sports training shoes originally produced and retailed during 1960–80. Adidas, Nike, Reebok and Puma have all reproduced models from this era that are now positioned as leisurewear, and are available on most major high streets. While the market for old school training shoes is small in comparison to the training shoes market overall, there are several benefits of producing back catalogue products. These include a reduction in resources and expenditure into research and development because the designs, patents and manufacturing capabilities are already owned. Additionally, a back catalogue of shoes that are considered 'classics' adds to brand equity and builds or maintains consumer franchise.

Adidas has maintained a high profile in sport over the last five decades resulting in its becoming a global household brand. The adidas Originals line is identifiable by the adidas trefoil logo, and is an addition to the adidas portfolio that, in a market where brand differentiation is paramount, aims to reinforce brand values and steer consumers away from price considerations through leveraging the heritage and history of the brand. Sometimes this reaches areas outside sport; for example, the adidas Superstar shoe was the footwear of choice during the formative era of hip-hop culture. Leading American hip-hop artists Run DMC even performed a song, entitled 'My adidas' in the brand's honour. This was reciprocated by adidas, which produced a model named in honour of deceased Run DMC member Jam Master Jay.

The overall creative strategy of the marketing communications for Originals is the authenticity and history of the brand. There has been relatively little advertising of the range, with the small amount that has been employed using the theme 'Every adidas has a story'. These ads draw on the history of the product by using people who may be of interest to the Originals target audience reminiscing about their first experience with the product at the time of its launch.

Contemporary magazines, positioned at the leading edge of fashion, art and culture, have also played a part in the communications mix through publicity. The adidas Originals range has received sizeable coverage in magazines such as *The Face*, *Wallpaper* and *I-D*. For example, *The Face* dedicated a full page to espousing the virtues of the denim adidas Italia shoe, as well as coverage to Jay Kay of the band Jamiroquai, who was endorsing the Oregon shoe. Adidas Originals products have also been given to Liam Gallagher, Robbie Williams and Madonna. Celebrities also played a large part in the launch of the Originals 83-C tracksuit top, which was not initially advertised. Rather, celebrities were given the garment and then 'captured' wearing it by the style press. Demand for the limited product resulted in it being offered only through selected retailers, which skimmed the market with a price tag in excess of £300.

In another creative move, adidas Originals leveraged the authenticity of the brand through the opening of a store in Central London. The store, named SET, was open for two weeks only, and did not sell anything. Rather, it contained an exhibition of adidas tennis shoes dating back to the 1920s. In addition to generating considerable publicity, it also created a buzz with adidas enthusiasts, fuelling word-of-mouth communications via interpersonal sources and the Web. Indeed, for an increasing number of people the traditional social circle of friends and family is growing to include people with similar interests from around the world via specialist groups and e-forums. An example of a Web site where word-of-mouth marketing is prevalent is Terrace Retro, an e-forum dedicated to football terrace culture and fashions of

EXHIBIT 2.3 Adidas Originals
Adidas, the Trefoil logo and the 3-stripe trade mark are registered trade marks of the adidas-Salomon group, used with permission.

the 1980s and early 1990s. Here, among other topics, visitors swap information about classic training shoes, including where certain models can be purchased, and delve into the history of the shoe with regard to terrace culture.

Questions

1 Identify the different opinion leaders and opinion formers in the case study.

2 Explain the different ways in which adidas Originals use opinion leaders and opinion formers to generate word-of-mouth communications.

3 Why is word-of-mouth communication so important to adidas Originals?

4 Suggest ways in which adidas can further encourage word-of-mouth communications about the Originals brand.

5 In what ways could adidas monitor word-of-mouth communications?

References

Berkman, H. and Gilson, C. (1986) *Consumer Behaviour: Concepts and Strategies.* Boston, MA: Vent.

Bone P.F. (1995) Word of mouth effects on short-term and long-term product judgements. *Journal of Business Research*, **21**(3), pp. 213–23.

Chan, K.K. and Misra, S. (1990) Characteristics of the opinion leader: a new dimension. *Journal of Advertising*, **19**(3), pp. 53–60.

Chittenden, M. (2000) Store links 'taint' wine critics taste. *Sunday Times*, 26 November, p. 3.

Christiansen, T. and Tax, S.S. (2000) Measuring word of mouth: the questions of who and when. *Journal of Marketing Communications*, **6**, pp. 185–99.

Daft, R.L. and Lengel, R.H. (1986) Organizational information requirements, media richness and structural design. *Managerial Science*, no. 32.

Dennis, A.R. and Kinney, S.T. (1998) Testing media richness theory in the new media. *Information Systems Research*, **9**(3), pp. 256–74.

Dichter, E. (1966) How word-of-mouth advertising works. *Harvard Business Review*, **44** (November/December), pp. 147–66.

Gatignon, H. and Robertson, T. (1985) A propositional inventory for new diffusion research. *Journal of Consumer Research*, **11**, pp. 849–67.

Goffman, E. (1969) *Strategic Interaction.* New York: Doubleday.

Hawkins, D.I., Best, R.J. and Coney, K.A. (1989) *Consumer Behavior: Implications for Marketing Strategy.* Homewood, IL: Irwin.

Hoffman, D.L. and Novak, P.T. (1996) Marketing in hyper computer-mediated environments: conceptual foundations. *Journal of Marketing*, **60** (July), pp. 50–68.

Katz, E. and Lazarfeld, P.F. (1955) *Personal Influence.* Glencoe, IL: Free Press.

Keating, S. (2004) Food heroes: Delia Smith. *The Magazine*, 27 November, p. 122.

Kingdom, J.W. (1970) Opinion leaders in the electorate. *Public Opinion Quarterly*, **34**, pp. 256–61.

Littlejohn, S.W. (1992) *Theories of Human Communication*, 4th edn. Belmont, CA: Wadsworth.

McEwan, T. (1992) Communication in organisations. In *Hospitality Management* (ed. L. Mullins). London: Pitman.

Mahajan, V., Muller, E. and Bass, F.M. (1990) New product diffusion models in marketing. *Journal of Marketing*, **54** (January), pp. 1 26.

Mallen, B. (1977) *Principles of Marketing Channel Management.* Lexington, MA: Lexington Books.

Mazur, L. (2004) Keep it simple. *Marketing Business*, March, p. 17.

Midgley, D. and Dowling, G. (1993) Longitudinal study of product form innovation: the interaction between predispositions and social messages. *Journal of Consumer Research*, **19** (March), pp. 611–25.

Patzer, G.L. (1983) Source credibility as a function of communicator physical attractiveness. *Journal of Business Research*, **11**, pp. 229–41.

Reynolds, F.D. and Darden, W.R. (1971) Mutually adaptive effects of interpersonal communication. *Journal of Marketing Research*, **8** (November), pp. 449–54.

Reichheld, F.F. (2003) The one number you need to grow. *Harvard Business Review* (December) pp. 47–54

Robinson, J.P. (1976) Interpersonal influence in election campaigns: two step flow hypothesis. *Public Opinion Quarterly*, **40**, pp. 304–19.

Rogers, E.M. (1962) *Diffusion of Innovations*, 1st edn. New York: Free Press.

Rogers, E.M. (1983) *Diffusion of Innovations*, 3rd edn. New York: Free Press.

Rogers, E.M. (1986) *Communication Technology: The New Media in Society.* New York: Free Press.

Rogers, E.M. and Kincaid, D.L. (1981) *Communication Networks: Toward a Paradigm for Research*. New York: Free Press.

Rothschild, M. (1987) *Marketing Communications*. Lexington, MA: D.C. Heath.

Schramm, W. (1955) How communication works. In *The Process and Effects of Mass Communications* (ed. W. Schramm). Urbana, IL: University of Illinois Press, pp. 3–26.

Shannon, C. and Weaver, W. (1962) *The Mathematical Theory of Communication*. Urbana, IL: University of Illinois Press.

Soldow, G. and Thomas, G. (1984) Relational communication: form versus content in the sale interaction. *Journal of Marketing*, **48** (Winter), pp. 84–93.

Steuer, J. (1992) Defining virtual reality: dimensions determining telepresence. *Journal of Communication*, **42**(4), pp. 73–93.

Stokes, D. and Lomax, W. (2002) Taking control of word of mouth marketing: the case of an entrepreneurial hotelier. *Journal of Small Business and Enterprise Development*, **9**(4), pp. 349–57.

Taylor, D. and Altman, I. (1987) Communication in interpersonal relationships: social penetration theory. In *Interpersonal Processes: New Directions in Communication Research* (eds M.E. Roloff and G.R. Miller). Newbury Park, CA: Sage, pp. 257–77.

Theodorson, S.A. and Theodorson, G.R. (1969) *A Modern Dictionary of Sociology*. New York: Cromwell.

Tichy, N. (1979) Social network analysis for organisations. *Academy of Management Review*, **4**, pp. 507–19.

Vernette, E. (2004) Targeting women's clothing fashion opinion leaders in media planning: an application for magazines. *Journal of Advertising Research*, March, pp. 90–107.

Watts, J. (2000) Dyson abandons strategy of in-house advertising. *Campaign*, 11 August, p. 22.

Weick, K. (1987) Prescribed and emergent networks. In *Handbook of Organisational Communication* (ed. F. Jablin). London: Sage.

Williams, K. (1990) *Behavioural Aspects of Marketing*. Oxford: Heinemann.

Windahl, S., Signitzer, B. and Olson, J.T. (1992) *Using Communication Theory*. London: Sage.

Yuan, Y., Caulkins, J.P. and Roehrig, S. (1998) The relationship between advertising and content provision on the Internet. *European Journal of Marketing*, **32**(7/8), pp. 667–87.

The marketing communications industry

3

The marketing communications industry is evolving rapidly as new technology and increasing competition induces audience and media fragmentation. Clients, media and agencies continually adapt themselves to the changing environment as they attempt to understand the complexity and opportunities that are constantly arising around them.

Aims and objectives

The aims of this chapter are to introduce the communications industry, the various organisations involved and some of the issues affecting the operation of the industry.

The objectives of this chapter are to:

1. provide an introduction to the communications industry;
2. consider the nature and role of the main types of organisations involved;
3. explore relationships and methods of remuneration used within the industry;
4. introduce some of the wider European and global issues facing the industry;
5. anticipate some of the future trends that might affect the industry.

Introduction

The marketing communications industry consists of four principal actors. These are the media, the clients, the agencies (the most notable of which are advertising agencies) and finally the thousands of support organisations, such as production companies and fulfilment houses, that enable the whole process to function. It is the operations and relationships between these organisations that not only drive the industry but also form an important context within which marketing communications needs to be understood. Figure 3.1 sets out the main actor organisations in the industry.

The number of relationships that can be developed in this industry, as with others, is enormous. To further complicate matters, the slow yet enduring move towards integrated marketing communications (Chapter 11) requires participants to form new relationships and acquire new skills. The argument that marketing communications activities should be kept in-house is now weak, as manufacturing and service industry providers continue to increase their level of outsourcing activities and de-layer and hollow out their organisations even more finely. There is little or no room to maintain people with skills and expertise who are only drawn upon infrequently and where the notion of critical mass is important for media buying. Most observers would argue that it could only be accomplished by agencies and others that are dealing with a large number of clients and which are, by definition, in constant touch with developments in the industry. In the field of media buying, for example, many would argue that it is unlikely that the necessary expertise could be developed in-house. The increased emphasis on accountability and efficiency means that it is necessary to outsource such activities in order to use expertise, specialised resources and take advantage of collective discounts from media houses. Marketing practitioners, therefore, need to use some of the other organisations in the communications industry. A level of interdependence exists that requires cooperative and collaborative behaviour if the system is to function efficiently.

> The argument that marketing communications activities should be kept in-house is now weak, as manufacturing and service industry providers continue to increase their level of outsourcing activities.

> A level of interdependence exists which requires cooperative and collaborative behaviour if the system is to function efficiently.

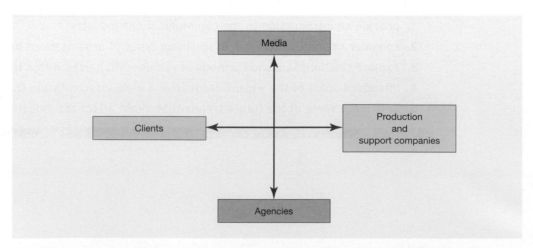

FIGURE 3.1 The principal organisations in the marketing communications industry

Dimensions of the UK marketing communications industry

It is useful to consider the size and value of the industry by considering the sums of money spent by clients on marketing communications. Some of these figures are acknowledged to be estimates, and there is some evidence of 'double counting' (one or more sectors claiming part of the overall spend for itself), so any figures produced cannot be seen as being totally accurate. That said, however, the total spend for advertising, as can be seen from Table 3.1, was £17.2 billion in 2003.

TABLE 3.1 Total UK advertising expenditure (including direct mail) £ million

	2003 (£m)	2000 (£m)	1996 (£m)
Press	8,382	8,604	6,413
Television	4,374	4,646	3,379
Direct mail	2,431	2,049	1,404
Outdoor and transit	901	810	466
Radio	582	595	344
Cinema	180	128	73
Internet	376	155	NA
Total	**17,227**	**16,988**	**12,080**

Source: *Advertising Statistics Yearbook*. Used with kind permission.

ViewPoint 3.1   Industry issues

In a recent article the Director-General of the Incorporated Society of British Advertisers, Malcolm Earnshaw, referred to three main issues facing the marketing industry in the coming year.

The first of these was the need for advertisers to defend their rights to advertise responsibly and not to be constrained by increasing legislation and government regulations. In particular, he referred to a recent government White Paper regarding food advertising and public health (obesity).

The second issue concerned the continuing consolidation in the media and the possible negative impact on clients in the advertising market.

The third issue referred to clients using the services of procurement specialists in order to drive down advertising costs with the consequent impact on agency margins and overall profitability. His argument is based on the need for agencies to offer better value to clients rather than to win pitches based on price alone.

Source: Earnshaw (2005).

The Institute of Sales Promotion claims that the growth of sales promotion has been 'explosive', but measuring the growth is difficult because there are no rate cards (price lists) and the breadth of activities that are attributable to sales promotion are many and varied. However, the Institute estimates that expenditure on sales promotion has

Expenditure on sales promotion has grown from £9 billion in 1996 to perhaps £15 billion in 2003.

grown from £9 billion in 1996 to perhaps £15 billion in 2003. Although not yet formally exceeding the spend on advertising, this area of activity is fast catching up and, despite published figures, it is widely believed inside the industry that sales promotion has already overtaken advertising in terms of the proportion of client spend.

Estimates vary, mainly because of problems of definition, but of the other areas in the industry sponsorship has grown significantly to £793 million in 2003. Direct marketing spend has increased steadily as confidence has grown in the industry. However, a downturn in the economy brought this increase to an abrupt halt with two years of little or no growth. Goften (2004) reports that there are some tentative signs of recovery with expenditure on direct mail, the dominant aspect of the industry, rising 2.2 per cent in 2003 to £2.43 billion (Direct Mail Information Service (DMIS)).

Other areas of the industry include public relations, which has experienced steady development and was worth approximately £2 billion in 2003, and exhibitions, of which there were 858 in 2003, each over 2,000 sq ft and in total worth approximately £1,800 million.

Expenditure patterns do change, albeit at different rates, and, given the domination of advertising and sales promotion, the overall balance is unlikely to change dramatically in the short term. However, it is clearly important for those responsible for the future and current planning of marketing communications activities to monitor trends, particularly those in the fastest growing sectors of the industry, in order to identify and target creative opportunities.

Structure and development of the UK marketing communications industry

As with any industry, growth and development spawn new types and structures.

As with any industry, growth and development spawn new types and structures. Adaptation to the environment is important for survival. The same applies to the marketing communications industry, where, to take the advertising industry as an example, many different organisational configurations have evolved. Before considering some of the structural issues it is useful to establish the main types of organisation that populate the industry. These are set out at Figure 3.1.

Clients can decide to undertake the communications functions in-house. However, this is both costly and inefficient, and most outsource their requirements. Of the four main groups the production and media houses require that the clients and agencies agree and specify campaigns in order that they are able to contribute. So, to some extent, agencies and clients are the lead players in this industry.

To some extent, agencies and clients are the lead players in this industry.

Agency types and structures

The marketing communications industry consists of a number of different types of organisations whose purpose is to enable clients to communicate effectively and efficiently with their target audiences. Originally these organisations acted as agents on behalf of media owners who wanted to sell media time and space. This was basically a production and selling role but one that has changed drastically. These agents learned to work more closely with their clients and in doing so became more customer oriented. As will be seen later agents undertook two main roles: creative message design and media planning and buying. The media component has subsequently been spun off to specialist agencies and might be regarded as a direct function of the media owners yet again. However, the interest and drive towards integrated communications, including media neutrality, means that agents will probably assume new, more independent roles in the shape of the communications industry in the future. The result of this development is that a number of different types of agency have emerged, none of which is right or wrong.

> Agents undertook two main roles: creative message design and media planning and buying.

Full-service agencies

The first and most common type of agency (advertising) is the full-service agency. This type of organisation offers the full range of services that a client requires in order to advertise its products and services. Agencies such as J. Walter Thompson and Leo Burnett offer a full service consisting of strategic planning, research, creative development, production and media planning. Some of these activities may be subcontracted, but overall responsibility rests with the full-service agency. Further discussion of some of the issues concerning full-service agencies follows later.

Creative shops

A derivative of this type of agency is the creative shop, which often forms when creative personnel (teams) leave full-service agencies to set up their own business. These 'HotShops' provide specialist services for clients who wish to use particular styles and approaches for their creative work.

> The creative shop often forms when creative personnel (teams) leave full-service agencies to set up their own business.

ViewPoint 3.2   It's not advertising, it's communication

Many aspects of the marketing communications industry have changed and are continuing to change. Some of these changes concern the nature and size of agencies. Many large dominant groups are emerging, such as the four major organisations that recently pitched for Samsung's worldwide branding account. These four – Interpublic (using its FCB operation), Omnicom (using BBDO agency), WPP (using J. Walter Thompson and Red Cell) and Publicis Groupe (using Leo Burnett and Saatchi & Saatchi). The fact that WPP won the account is not the point.

These organisations evolved as advertising agencies but have now transformed themselves into 'communication partners'. This reflects the increasing attention given to relationship marketing, the development of integrated marketing communications and the relative decline in the dominance of advertising within the communications mix. Organisations now seek to communicate different messages and this involves using a variety of (neutral) media. The term 'communication agencies', or partners, suggests variety and flexibility and reflects a change in core business.

Media independents

Similarly, media independents provide specialist media services for planning, buying and monitoring the purchase of a client's media schedule. There are two main forms:

Media dependents, where the organisation is a subsidiary of a creative or full-service organisation.

media independents, where the organisation is owned and run free of the direction and policy requirements of a full-service agency, and media dependents, where the organisation is a subsidiary of a creative or full-service organisation. The largest dependent in the UK is ZenithOptimedia, owned originally by Saatchi & Saatchi, and the largest independent is Carat.

A la carte

Partly in response to the changing needs of clients and consumers, many organisations require greater flexibility in the way their advertising is managed. Consequently these clients prefer to use the services of a range of organisations. So, the planning skills of a full-service agency, the creative talent of a particular HotShop and the critical mass of a media-buying independent provide an *à la carte* approach. This process needs to be managed by the client, because when the services of other marketing communications providers are included flexibility is increased while coordination and control become more complex and problematic.

New media

New media agencies have developed as a result of the growth of the new media industry, which has seen huge growth in recent years. The growth has come from two main areas. The first concerns the surge of online brands that hit the market full of expectation of transforming the way business is conducted and the second concerns established offline brands seeking to reach customers by adding to their marketing channels.

The provision of Internet facilities has been the main area of work, mainly communication and business operations activities. This has been followed by WAP technology activity and interactive television (see Chapters 10 and 21). The market appears to have formed into three main parts of a spectrum of activities. At one end are those agencies that are marketing oriented and at the other are technology-based organisations.

Growth is likely to develop in the middle, with organisations referred to as 'interactive architects'.

Murphy (2000) feels that the real growth is likely to develop in the middle, with organisations referred to as 'interactive architects' that can offer a blend of skills and consultancy services. Merger and acquisition activity has been intense, mainly a reaction to rapid industry growth that was not capable of being sustained. The move towards what is referred to as 'integrated marketing communications' (see Chapter 11) has been accelerated by the greater efficiency and harmonisation that digital technology brings.

Industry structure

The structure of the industry has changed through time. Some may argue that it has not changed enough but the shape and size of the industry has developed. Over the last 20 years the size of the industry has increased in response to the growth in the number of marketing communications activities and with it the real value of advertising, sales promotion, public relations and direct marketing. The growth distribution

The growth distribution among these tools has been variable with only direct marketing showing consistent levels of real growth.

The configuration of the agency services industry partly reflects the moves made by the larger agencies to consolidate their positions. They have attempted to buy either smaller, often medium-sized competitors, in an attempt to protect their market share or provide an improved range of services for their clients. (See the section later on one-stop shopping.) This has led to an industry characterised by a large number of very big agencies and an even larger number of very small agencies. These smaller agencies have formed as the result of people formerly employed in large agencies becoming frustrated with having to work within tight margins and increased administration leaving and setting up their own fledgling businesses. This is currently evident in the direct marketing part of the industry, according to Billings (2004). She argues that there are now two distinct structural models emerging: those direct marketing agencies that are attached to advertising agencies (for example *Elvis* and *Hall Moore CHI*) and those which are entirely independent (for example *Barraclough Edwards Chamberlain* and *Keevill Lee Kershaw*). This pattern was also observed in the 1990s when media planning houses developed. Some were entirely independent and others, such as Zenith, were dependent upon a parent organisation.

> Two distinct structural models are emerging: those direct marketing agencies that are attached to advertising agencies and those which are entirely independent.

Although ownership has been an important factor driving industry development the current preference for loose, independent networks has given some large organisations the ability to offer clients an improved range of services (integrated marketing communications – IMC) and the small agencies a chance to work with some of the bigger accounts.

Miln (2004) speculates that structural changes to the way in which clients and agencies work together may give rise to what he refers to as 'new agencies' that will provide a limited range of specific communication services, most commonly involved with the thinking around the creative or media elements, but will outsource or delegate the implementation to a third-party organisation. These organisations possess the core skills associated with project management and are better placed to fulfil this specialist role. The agency will remain responsible to the client for the implementation but is in a better position to continue advising about the overall communication strategy and media imperatives.

> 'New agencies' will provide a limited range of specific communication services, most commonly involved with the thinking around the creative or media elements, but will outsource or delegate the implementation.

One-stop shopping

As with most industries, the structure of the communications industry has evolved in response to changes in the environment. However, if there is a 'holy grail' of communications it is an organisation's ability to offer clients a single point from which all of their integrated communication needs can be met. In search of this goal, WPP and Saatchi & Saatchi set about building the largest marketing communications empires in the world. According to Green (1991), Saatchi & Saatchi attempted to become the largest marketing services company in the world. The strategy adopted in the early 1980s was to acquire companies outside its current area of core competence, media advertising. Organisations in direct marketing, market research, sales promotion and public relations were brought under the Saatchi banner.

By offering a range of services under a single roof, rather like a 'supermarket', the one-stop shopping approach made intrinsic sense. Clients could put a package together, rather like eating from a buffet table, and solve a number of their marketing requirements – without the expense and effort of searching through each sector to find a company with which to work.

Green also refers to the WPP experience in the late 1980s. J. Walter Thompson and Ogilvy & Mather were grouped together under the umbrella of WPP and it was felt that synergies were to be achieved by bringing together their various services. Six areas were identified: strategic marketing services, media advertising, public relations, market research, non-media advertising and specialist communications. A one-stop shopping approach was advocated once again.

The recession of the early 1990s brought problems to both of these organisations, as well as others. The growth had been built on acquisition, which was partly funded from debt. This required considerable interest payments, but the recession brought a sharp decline in the revenues of the operating companies, and cash flow problems forced WPP and Saatchi & Saatchi to restructure their debt and their respective organisations. As Phillips (1991) points out, the financial strain and the complex task of managing operations on such a scale began to tell.

However, underpinning the strategy was the mistaken idea that clients actually wanted a one-stop shopping facility. It was unlikely that the best value for money was going to be achieved through this, so it came as no surprise when clients began to question the quality of the services for which they were paying. There was no guarantee that they could obtain from one large organisation the best creative, production, media and marketing solutions to their problems. Many began to shop around and engage specialists in different organisations (*à la carte*) in an attempt to receive not only the best quality of service but also the best value for money. Evidence for this might be seen in the resurgence of the media specialists whose very existence depends on their success in media planning and buying. By 1990 it was estimated that in the UK 30 per cent of market share in media buying was handled by media specialist companies.

It is no wonder, then, that clients, and indeed many media people working in agencies who felt constrained decided to leave and set up on their own account, and felt that full-service agencies were asking too much of their staff, not only in terms of providing a wide range of integrated marketing services generally, but also in giving full attention and bringing sufficient expertise to bear in each of the specific services it has to offer (account management, creative, production, media research, etc.).

The debate about whether or not to use a full-service agency becomes even more crucial, perhaps, for those in specialist areas. For example, a large number of business-to-business communication agencies have been set up by people leaving full-service agencies. They spotted opportunities to provide specialist services in a market area that at the time was under resourced, often marginalised or even ignored. In many ways it comes back to the quality of relationships. Arguments for the specialist agency were based upon the point that, while there may be some convergence of approaches between consumer goods marketing and business-to-business advertising, it can be easier for a business-to-business advertising agency to do consumer advertising than it is to do the reverse.

As a general view, business-to-business shops survive on their ability to execute some very fundamental techniques for clients, such as direct mail or sales promotion.

In contrast, the large, consumer goods-oriented shops, whose traditional skills are market research, planning and media advertising, often lack the core skills, initiative or expertise to deliver business-to-business marketing services.

The same has been said of direct marketing where there appears to be the same sort of disenchantment with the full-service agency. Criticisms include the exclusion of direct marketing experts from presentations to clients, a lack of education among mainstream agency types as to what direct marketing actually does or the complaint that clients don't want to be force-fed a direct marketing subsidiary that may be incompetent or inappropriate. The experience of those involved in direct marketing has been further destabilised by the growth in the Internet. Direct mail has gained rather than lost because many online brands have used direct mail as offline promotion to drive Web site traffic. Telemarketing has flourished because call centres have repositioned themselves as multimedia contact centres and have extended their range of services.

> Direct mail has gained rather than lost because many online brands have used direct mail as offline promotion to drive Web site traffic.

There is a spectrum of approaches for clients. They can find an agency that can provide all of the required marketing communication services under one roof, or find a different agency for each of the services, or mix and match. Clearly the first solution can be used only if the budget holder is convinced that the best level of service is being provided in *all* areas, and the second only if there are sufficient gains in efficiency (and savings in expenditure) to warrant the amount of additional time he or she would need to devote to the task of managing marketing communications.

> Industry concentration and the development of global networks have shifted the structure and composition of the industry.

One area that has experienced significant change has been media. Industry concentration and the development of global networks have shifted the structure and composition of the industry. Clients have responded by centralising their business into a single media network agency in search of higher discounts and improved efficiency. As a general rule, the stronger the competitive forces, the lower the profitability in the market. An organisation needs to determine a competitive approach that will allow it to influence the industry's competitive rules, protect it from competitive forces as much as possible and give it a strong position from which to compete. The media networks have yet to find a competitive form of differentiation, although some are offering additional services as a way of trying to enhance brand identities (Griffiths, 2000). It appears that the power of the media agencies, the low switching costs of buyers and the large threat of substitute products make this a relatively unattractive industry in its current form. Finer segmentation to determine markets that permit higher margins and a move to provide greater differentiation among agencies, together with a policy to reduce the threats from substitute products, perhaps through more visible alliances and partnerships, would enable the industry to recover its position and provide greater stability. It is interesting to note that many leading agencies have moved into strategic consultancy, away from the reliance on mass media, where a substantially higher margin can be generated. Many direct marketing companies have evolved out of sales promotion agencies. According to Goften (2000), both have tried to reposition themselves with the sales promotion houses adopting a wide variety of promotional activities and direct marketing agencies moving their focus of business activity to one that is either oriented towards ecommerce or customer relationship management.

Selecting an agency

In the areas that have traditionally dominated marketing communications, advertising and sales promotion, there has never been a shortage of advice on how to select an agency. Articles informing readers how to select an agency (Young and Steilen, 1996; Woolgar, 1998; Finch, 2000; McKee, 2004) appear regularly, and there are a large number of publications and organisations to assist in the process.

ViewPoint 3.3   Direct Line agency selection

In August 2004 Direct Line, a major insurance company, was thought to have called for a review of its £40 million advertising account. It shortlisted four agencies for the pitch and did not invite its current agency to bid for the work, with whom it has worked for eight years.

Recent work by the incumbent agency had not been received well by everyone and was thought to have contributed to the decision to change agency. Direct Line was seeking to launch a major brand campaign, increasing its adspend by 15 per cent.

EXHIBIT 3.1 Direct Line telephone
The red telephone identifies Direct Line, one of the first to establish direct marketing as its principal form of marketing communications. Picture reproduced with the kind permission of Direct Line Insurance.

Source: Adapted from Whitehead (2004).

The process of selecting an agency that is set out below appears to be rational and relatively straightforward. Readers should be aware that the reality is that the process is infused with political and personal issues, some of which can be contradictory. Logically the process commences with a *search,* undertaken to develop a list of potential candidates. This is accomplished by referring to publications such as *Campaign Portfolio* and the *Advertising Agency Roster*, together with personal recommendations. The latter is perhaps the most potent and influential of

> The process is infused with political and personal issues, some of which can be contradictory.

ViewPoint 3.4   Making agency selection easier

In 2003 discussion began among advertising industry groups (1,500 agencies and 500 clients in the UK) to develop a single database to provide a central online source of information designed to improve the process of finding an ad agency.

Some of the industry's leading Web sites including AdForum, ISBA, the Marketing Society, IPA, Media Guardian and Brand Republic will provide access to the database. Users will be able to view a range of agency credentials and information, plus creative work including TV commercials, print ads, radio, mail packs, discipline-specialist campaigns and interactive work. Creative showreels are also planned with sites carrying text, video and still images, with some ads played live.

Agency profiles can be uploaded and managed online by clicking a button on any of the participating sites to access a data input tool. Agencies need only update their details once to ensure that they reach all UK clients.

This facility should allow client organisations to benchmark their own work on a regular basis and agency credentials can be considered online as part of the selection process.

these sources. As many as 10 agencies could be included at this stage although 6 or 7 are to be expected.

Next, the client will visit each of the short-listed candidates in what is referred to as a *credentials presentation*. This is a crucial stage in the process, as it is now that the agency is evaluated for its degree of fit with the client's expectations and requirements. Agencies could develop their Web sites to fulfil this role, which would save time and costs. The agency's track record, resources, areas of expertise and experience can all be made available on the Internet, from which it should be possible to short-list three or possibly four agencies for the next stage in the process: the pitch.

In the PR industry agencies are selected to pitch on the basis of the quality and experience of the agency people, its image and reputation and relationships with existing clients.

In the PR industry agencies are selected to pitch on the basis of the quality and experience of the agency people, its image and reputation and relationships with existing clients. In addition, Pawinska (2000) reports that the track record of the agency and the extent of its geographical coverage are also regarded as important.

To be able to make a suitable bid the agencies are given a brief and then required to make a formal presentation (the *pitch*) to the client some 6–8 weeks later. This presentation is about how the agency would approach the strategic and creative issues and the account is awarded to whichever produces the most suitable proposal. Suitability is a relative term, and a range of factors needs to be considered when selecting an organisation to be responsible for a large part of a brand's visibility. A strategic alliance is being formed and therefore a strong understanding of the strategic objectives of both parties is necessary, as is an appreciation of the structure and culture of the two organisations. The selection process is a bringing together of two organisations whose expectations may be different but whose cooperative behaviour is essential for these expectations to have any chance of materialising. For example, agencies must have access to comprehensive and often commercially confidential data about products and markets if they are to operate efficiently. Otherwise, they cannot provide the service that is expected. However, it

The selection process is a bringing together of two organisations whose expectations may be different but whose cooperative behaviour is essential for these expectations to have any chance of materialising.

should be noted that pitches are not mandatory, and as Jones (2004) reports, nearly a third of clients move their accounts without involving pitches. One of the reasons for this is the increasing cost involved in running the whole process, as much as £50,000 according to Jones.

The immediate selection process is finalised when terms and conditions are agreed and the winner is announced to the contestants and made public, often through trade journals such as *Campaign*, *Marketing* and *Marketing Week*.

This formalised process is now being questioned as to its suitability. The arrival of new media companies and their need to find communication solutions in one rather than eight weeks has meant that new methods have had to be found. In addition, agencies felt that they were having to invest a great deal in a pitch with little or no reward if the pitch failed. Their response has been to ask for payment to pitch, which has not been received well by many clients. The tension that arises is that each agency is required to generate creative ideas over which they have little control once a pitch has been lost. The pitching process also fails to give much insight into the probable working relationships and is very often led by senior managers who will not be involved in the day-to-day operations. One solution adopted by Iceland and Dyson (Jardine, 2000) has been to invite agencies to discuss mini-briefs. These are essentially discussion topics about related issues rather than the traditional challenge about how to improve a brand's performance. By issuing the mini-brief on the day it eliminates weeks of preparation and associated staff costs, and enables the client to see agency teams working together.

> **Mini-briefs are essentially discussion topics about related issues rather than the traditional challenge about how to improve a brand's performance.**

Agency operations

Most communications agencies are generally organised on a functional basis. There have been moves to develop matrix structures utilising a customer orientation, but this is very inefficient and the low margins prohibit such luxuries. There are departments for planning, creative and media functions coordinated on behalf of the client by an account handler or executive.

> **The account handler fulfils a very important role in that these people are responsible for the flow of communications between the client and the agency.**

The account handler fulfils a very important role in that these people are responsible for the flow of communications between the client and the agency. The quality of the communications between the two main parties can be critical to the success of the overall campaign and to the length of the relationship between the two organisations. Acting at the boundary of the agency's operations, the account handler needs to perform several roles, from internal coordinator and negotiator to presenter (of the agency's work), conflict manager and information gatherer. Very often account handlers will experience tension as they seek to achieve their clients' needs while trying to balance the needs of their employer and colleagues. These tensions are similar to those experienced by salespersons and need to be managed in a sensitive manner by management.

Once an account has been signed a client brief is prepared that provides information about the client organisation (Figure 3.2). It sets out the nature of the industry it operates in together with data about trends, market share, customers, competitors and the problem that the agency is required to address. This is used to inform agency personnel. In particular, the account planner will undertake research to determine market,

Project management – Provide basic project details, e.g. timescales, contacts and people, project numbers
Where are we now? – Describe current brand details, e.g. background, position, competitors, key issues
Where do we want to be? – What needs to be achieved in terms of goals, e.g. sales, market share, ROI, shareholder value, awareness, perception, etc.
What are we doing to get there? – What is the context in terms of the marketing strategy, overall communication strategy and campaign strategy?
Who do we need to talk to? – What is understood about the audiences the communications are intended to influence?
How will we know if we have arrived? – What will be measured, by whom, how and when to determine whether the activity has been successful?
Practicalities – Budgets, timings and schedules, creative and media imperatives
Approvals – Who has the authority to sign off the brief and the agency work?

FIGURE 3.2 A new briefing structure

ViewPoint 3.5   Agency operations

New technology has been used to assist different aspects of campaign management. A large majority have been supplier driven but more recent contributions have attempted to enable both clients and agencies to participate more equally in the campaign development process. For example, Kickfire have developed Marketing Resource Management (MRM), a software system designed specifically to enable organisations to manage the development processes associated with campaigns.

The software application provides for a large degree of ubiquity and freedom as suppliers and clients can work on marketing projects regardless of location. Using a specific password protected Web site, parties can share data and documents, develop schedules, allocate individuals to particular tasks, check project progress and produce relevant and timely reports.

The system uses digital asset management functionality to store logos, images and copy that can be utilised by all participants. Public relations activities are also assisted as there are templates for writing press releases. This helps develop coordinated marketing communications through the promotion of image consistency and usage.

Source: Adapted from Murphy (2002).

---

media and audience characteristics and make proposals to the rest of the account team as to how the client problem is to be resolved.

Briefing is a process that is common across all client agency relationships in the communication industry. Regardless of whether working in direct marketing, sales promotion, advertising, public relations, media planning and buying or other specialist areas, the brief has a special importance in making the

> Briefing is a process that is common across all client agency relationships in the communication industry.

process work and the outcomes significant. However, the importance of preparing a brief of suitable quality has for some been underestimated. With agencies having to brief themselves and some briefs insufficiently detailed, a recent joint industry initiative sought to establish common working practices. The outcome of the process was a briefing template intended to be used by all across the communications agencies in the industry. Eight key headings emerged from the report and these can be seen at Figure 3.2.

In addition to the account handler, whose role might be regarded as one of traffic management, is the role undertaken by account planners (or creative planners). The role of the account planner has been the subject of a recent flurry of debate (Grant *et al.*, 2003; Collin, 2003; Zambarino and Goodfellow, 2003). The general conclusion of these papers is that the role of account planner, which has evolved since the beginning of the 1960s, has changed as the communications industry has fragmented and that a new role is emerging in response to integrated marketing communication and media neutral planning initiatives (see Chapter 11 for details about these concepts).

The traditional role of the account planner, which began in full-service agencies, was to understand the client's target consumers and develop strategies for the creative and media departments. As media broke away from full-service agencies so the role of the account planner shifted to the creative aspect of agency work. Media planners assumed the same type of work in media companies although their work focused on planning the right media mix to reach the target audience. With the development of integrated perspectives and the move towards a broader view of a client's communication needs there is an expectation that the planning role will evolve into a strategic role. The role will be to work with a broad range of marketing disciplines (tools) and media but not to brief creatives or media planners directly (Collin, 2003).

> As media broke away from full-service agencies so the role of the account planner shifted to the creative aspect of agency work.

Creative teams work as a pair, a copy writer and an art director, supported by a service team. This team is responsible for translating the proposal into an advertisement. In a full-service agency, a media brief will also be generated, informing the media planning and buying department of the media required and the type of media vehicles required. However, the vast majority of media planning work is now undertaken by specialist media agencies, media independents, and these will be briefed by the client, with some support from those responsible for the creative.

In recent years, partly as a response to the growth of new media, a raft of small entrepreneurial agencies have emerged, to exploit the new opportunities arising from the digital revolution. Although these agencies are often founded by people who have started their careers in larger and highly structured agencies, many of them run their own organisations in a more organic manner. While dedicated teams might theoretically be the best way to manage a client's project, reality in many cases is the use of project teams comprising expert individuals working on a number of projects simultaneously. This is not, of course, a new phenomenon, but as a result many people are multitasking and they assume many roles with new titles. For example, the title head of content has arisen to reflect the significance of content issues in the new media market. Project managers assume responsibility for the implementation phase and the coordination of all aspects of a client's technological facilities. In addition, there are positions such as head of marketing, mobile (increasing focus on WAP technology), production and technology. The result is no hierarchies, flat structures and flexible working practices and similar expectations.

> A raft of small entrepreneurial agencies have emerged, to exploit the new opportunities arising from the digital revolution.

Relationships

The nature of the relationships that exist in the industry shapes and influences the strategies and operations. There are a vast number of relationships that form between various clients and agencies, disciplines, and within individual organisations.

Client/agency relationships

If the briefing process provides the mechanism for the agency operations, it is the relationship between the agency and the client that very often determines the length of the contract and the strength of the solutions advanced for the client.

There are a number of agency/client relationships that have flourished over a very long period of time, and some for several decades. There are a huge number of other accounts which have excellent relationships that have lasted a long time. However, these appear to be in the minority, as many relationships appear to founder as clients abandon agencies and search for better, fresher solutions, because a contract expires, the client needs change or because of takeovers and mergers between agencies, which require that they forfeit accounts that cause a conflict of interest.

From a contextual perspective these buyer/seller relationships can be seen to follow a pattern of formation, maintenance and severance, or pre-contract, contracting process and post-contract stages (Davidson and Kapelianis, 1996). Clients and agencies enter into a series of interactions (West and Paliwoda, 1996) or exchanges through which trust and commitment are developed. Hakansson (1982) identified different contexts or atmospheres within which a relationship develops. These contexts had several dimensions: closeness/distance, cooperation/conflict, power/dependence, trustworthiness and expectations. Therefore, the client/agency relationship should be seen in the context of the network of organisations and the exchanges or interactions that occur in that network. It is through these interactions that the tasks that need to be accomplished are agreed, resources made available, strategies determined and goals achieved. The quality of the agency/client relationship is a function of trust, which is developed through the exchanges and that fosters confidence. Commitment is derived from a belief that the relationship is worth continuing and that maximum effort is warranted at maintaining the relationship (Morgan and Hunt, 1994). The development of new forms of remuneration (see below), based around payment by results, also signifies a new client focus and a willingness to engage with clients and to be paid according to the success and contribution the agency can provide (Lace and Brocklehurst, 2000).

Poor relationships between agencies and clients are likely to result from a lack of trust and falling commitment. As it appears that communication is a primary element in the formation and substance of relational exchanges, clients might be advised to consider the agencies in their roster as an extended department of the core organisation and use internal marketing communication procedures to assist the development of identity and belonging.

One last point to be made is the increasing age gap between those in the industry, both agency and client, and their audiences. Those who produce marketing communications tend to be under 35 and the average age of those targeted to receive the communications is rising. According to Starkey (1999), this may increase the chance of misunderstanding of older consumers and this misunderstanding becomes a self-fulfilling prophecy.

ViewPoint 3.6   Agency relationships

Timex is a well-known brand but its overall share in the UK is relatively small compared to the 30 per cent market share it holds in the US. There it sells more watches than the next 18 best-selling brands combined.

In 2002 Timex USA decided to end its 16-year relationship with its lead agency Fallon Worldwide. According to Timex spokesman Jim Katz: 'After 16 years, we feel we want to see what else is out there.' The account is thought to be worth around £6 million.

Marketing and public relations

A further example of the potential problems that can arise in the industry concerns the role and structural position within organisations of public relations, relative to the marketing function. The issue concerns where in an organisation public relations should be located and, more importantly, to whom they should report.

The role that public relations should assume and its structural position within an organisation have become increasingly complex and a source of much debate. Traditionally, public relations has been regarded as a function of public affairs or corporate communication that reports directly to the CEO. Control over the activities of public relations is direct and the purpose is to convey appropriate information about the corporate entity and to create goodwill and understanding with other stakeholders. To that end, public relations was seen as separate to and distinct from marketing. A publication by the Public Relations Educational Trust (1991) declared that 'PR is NOT Marketing'. The substantiation for this is based on an interpretation of marketing, one that is strictly profit oriented. This does not reflect reality, as self-help groups and organisations such as the NHS and charities would not be able to practise marketing if such a narrow perspective was supported.

Kotler and Mindak (1978) set out five ways in which organisations can manage the marketing and public relations functions. These are depicted in Figure 3.3. It can be seen that the structural relationship of marketing and public relations can range from the traditional view, where they are separate and totally unconnected, fulfilling different roles, through various other forms where one subsumes the other, to model E. Here, both share an equal and mutually supportive relationship. In this form, both recognise the need to segment markets and to provide different satisfactions. Each function needs the support of the other and both have similar needs in terms of understanding the attitudes, perceptions and awareness held by each market or stakeholder. Internal conflict is effectively reduced, and this in turn facilitates the transmission of consistent, positive and coordinated messages to all stakeholders.

Kotler and Mindak highlight these key relationships well, but the models can also be used to depict the development of public relations and marketing in organisations.

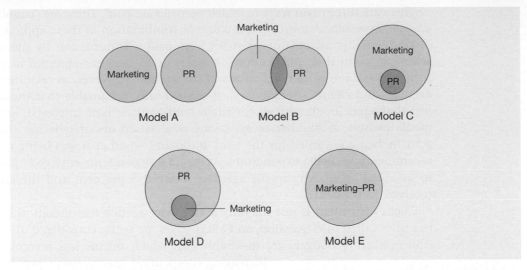

FIGURE 3.3 Relationships between marketing and public relations (From Kotler and Mindak (1978); used with kind permission.)

For example, local authorities have for a long time had a public relations department, but only recently have they begun to appoint marketing managers in response to their changing responsibilities, environments and new competitive orientation. Hospitals are having to focus on market needs rather than the needs of internal experts. Many are increasing the level of public relations activities and are also introducing marketing as a distinct function, partly to assist the necessary change in culture.

Many private sector organisations are making a transition from model C to model D or E, depending upon their experiences and organisational culture, market environments and the perspective of the CEO and senior management team towards the roles of public relations and marketing.

The level of interest and strength of voice given to integrated marketing communications has been a force for bringing these two disciplines together. Increasingly campaigns are being used in a coordinated way and public relations is used in conjunction with the other marketing communication instruments. Clients are not normally structured internally so that they have an integrated communications department and until the benefits of this type of approach are recognised it is likely that the gulf between these two functions will continue.

> The level of interest and strength of voice given to integrated marketing communications has been a force for bringing these two disciplines together.

Agency remuneration

One factor that has a significant impact on the quality of the relationship between the parties is the remuneration or reward for the effort (added value) the agency makes in attempting to meet and satisfy the needs of its client. One major cause for concern and complaint among marketing managers is the uncertainty over how much their marketing communications programmes will finally cost and the complexity surrounding the remuneration system itself.

There are three main ways in which agencies are paid. These are *commission, fees* and *payment by results*. A fourth is a mixture or combination of these approaches.

Traditionally, advertising agencies were paid a commission by media owners for selling space in their publications. A figure of 15 per cent emerged as the norm and seemed a fair reward for the efforts of the agency. However, as relationships between agencies and clients strengthened, it seemed only reasonable that the clients should feel that agencies should act for them (and in their best interests), and not for the media owners. A number of questions were raised about whether the agency was actually being rewarded for the work it did and whether it was being objective when recommending media expenditure. As media independents emerged, questions started to be asked about why media agencies received 3 per cent and the creative agency received 12 per cent.

Client discontent is not the only reason why agency remuneration by commission has been called into question, and alternatives are being considered. In times of recession marketing budgets are inevitably cut, which means less revenue for agencies.

> Client discontent is not the only reason why agency remuneration by commission has been called into question.

Increasing competition means lower profit margins if an agency is to retain the business, and if costs are increasing at the same time the very survival of the agency is in question. As Snowden stated as long ago as 1993, 'Clients are demanding more for less'. She goes on to say, 'It is clear to me that the agency business needs to address a number of issues; most important amongst them, how agencies get paid. It is the key to the industry's survival.'

During the early 1990s there was a great deal of discussion and energy directed towards non-commission payment systems. This was a direct result of the recession, in which clients cut budgets and there was a consequent reduction in the quantity of media purchased and hence less revenue for the agencies. Fees became more popular, and some experimented with payment by results. Interestingly, as the recession died and the economy lifted, more revenue resulted in larger commission possibilities, and the death throes of the commission system were quickly replaced by its resuscitation and revival.

> It is likely that there will continue to be a move away from a reliance on the payment of commission as the only form of remuneration to the agency.

It is likely that there will continue to be a move away from a reliance on the payment of commission as the only form of remuneration to the agency. Fees have been around for a long time, either in the form of retainers or on a project-by-project basis. Indeed, many agencies charge a fee for services over and above any commission earned from media owners. The big question is about the basis for calculation of fees (and this extends to all areas of marketing communications, not just advertising), and protracted, complicated negotiations can damage client/agency relationships.

For many, payment by results (PBR) seems a good solution. There are some problems, however, in that the agency does not have total control over its performance and the final decisions about how much is spent and which creative ideas should be used

> For many, payment by results seems a good solution.

are the client's. The agency has no control over the other marketing activities of the client, which might determine the degree of success of the campaign. Indeed, this raises the very thorny question of what 'success' is and how it might be measured. Despite these considerations, it appears that PBR is starting to become an established form of remuneration, with over 30 per cent of agency–client contracts containing an element of PBR. Lace (2000) explains that this is due to the inadequacies of both commission- and fee-based systems in the 'new age of cost cutting and accountability'.

A different way of looking at this is to consider what the client thinks the agency does and from this evaluate the outcomes from the relationship. Jensen (1995) proposes that advertising agencies can be seen as an *ideas business* which seeks to build brands for clients. An alternative view is that agencies are *advertising factories*, where the majority of the work is associated with administration, communication, coordination and general running around to ensure that the advertisement appears on the page or screen as desired.

If the 'ideas business' view is accepted then the ideas generated add value for the client, so the use the client makes of the idea should be rewarded by way of a royalty type payment. If the 'factory concept' is adopted, then it is the resources involved in the process that need to be considered and a fee-based system is more appropriate. Both parties will actively seek to reduce costs that do not contribute to the desired outcomes. These are different approaches to remuneration and avoid the volume of media purchased as a critical and controversial area.

> The use the client makes of the idea should be rewarded by way of a royalty type payment.

Agency structures and IMC

The development of integrated marketing communications has been mentioned earlier, and although the concept is subject to considerable debate and uncertainty the underlying good sense inherent in the concept has started to resonate with clients and agencies. As a result the influence of IMC on agencies and clients should not be underestimated.

In order for messages to be developed and conveyed through an integrated approach, the underlying structure supporting this strategy needs to be reconsidered. Just as the structure of the industry had a major impact on the way in which messages were developed and communicated as the industry developed, so the structural underpinning needs to adapt to the new and preferred approaches of clients.

The use of outside agencies that possess skills, expertise and purchasing advantages which are valued by clients is not new and is unlikely to change. However, the way in which these outsourced skills are used and how they are structured has been changing. Aspects of client–agency relationships are important and are considered in Chapter 9. What is important for this part of the text is a consideration of the way in which those organisations that provide outsourcing facilities and contribute to a client's IMC can be configured to provide optimal servicing and support. Gronstedt and Thorsen (1996) suggest five ways in which agencies could be configured to provide integrated marketing communications. The research is centred upon US-based advertising agencies so, while not immediately transferable to the European, Asian or other regional markets, their proposals provide a base from which other agencies might evolve in other geographic markets.

The models are presented in Figure 3.4, and although the authors acknowledge that a mix of forms could be identified, one particular form tended to dominate each agency. The forms denote a continuum, at one end of which is a highly centralised organisation that can provide a high level of integration for a variety of communication disciplines. Staffed by generalists with no particular media bias, these organisations are structured according to client needs, not functional specialisms. Total integration is offered at the expense of in-depth and leading-edge knowledge in new and developing areas. Clients who seek to use a marketing communications campaign

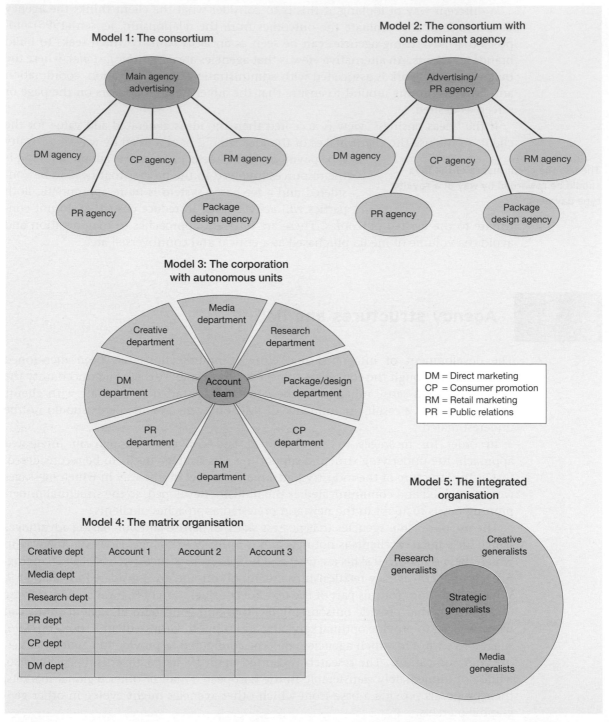

FIGURE 3.4 An overview of the five agency structures (From Gronstedt and Thorson (1996); used with kind permission.)

which draws on more than one marketing communications discipline, have a basic choice of four main options. These are set out in Table 3.2.

Neither of these four approaches can provide a perfect solution and the variety of integrated possibilities reflects different client structures and cultures and hence different needs and relationships which need to be satisfied (Murphy, 2004). The Mini-Group option is a relatively recent development and can include the use of product

TABLE 3.2 Integrated agency options

Type of agency	Explanation
Integrated agency	A single agency which provides the full range of communication disciplines.
Complementary agencies	The client selects a range of different agencies, each from a different discipline and self manages or appoints a lead agency.
Networked agencies	A single group agency is appointed (eg WPP or Interpublic) who then appoints agencies within their own profit-oriented network.
Mini-group agencies	Clusters of small independent specialist agencies who work on a non-competitive basis for a client.

development, research, design and interactive services. This means that this approach serves a broad range of needs, typical of smaller client organisations whose budgets do not match those of mainstream firms.

At the other end of the continuum are those providers who group themselves in the form of a network. Often led by a main advertising agency that has divested itself of expensive overheads, the independent yet interdependent network players each provide specialist skills under the leadership of the main contractor agency. One of the two main weaknesses associated with this model concerns the deficiency associated with communications across the players in the network. This horizontal aspect means that individual members of the network tend to identify with their own area of expertise and advance their specialism, possibly at the expense of the client's overriding requirements. The other main weakness concerns the transitory or temporary nature of a member organisation's involvement within such networks. Therefore, the level of potential integration is possibly weakest in this model, although the level of expertise available to clients is highest at this end of the continuum.

One of the essential points emerging from this research is that there seems to be a trade-off between levels of integration and the expertise provided by different agencies. Clients who want to retain control over their brands and to find an integrated agency where all the required services are of the exact level and quality demanded may be expecting too much. The inevitability of this position is that clients may choose to select marketing communication expertise from a variety of sources, and the integrated agency may well lose out.

> There seems to be a trade-off between levels of integration and the expertise provided by different agencies.

Furthermore, environmental factors should not be ignored, and it may be that clients in the future will state their preferred structural requirements at the pitching or client briefing stage of the agency–client relationship. Increasingly, agencies may well be required to mix and match their structures and provide structural flexibility to meet the varying needs of their clients.

A further point concerns global branding and the standardisation/adaptation debate when considered in the light of IMC. One argument is that standardisation is the only way in which IMC can be achieved. However, as it is generally accepted that there are few examples of truly standardised global brands, does that suggest that IMC is not possible for global brands? A strong counter-view is that glocalisation encourages integration where it matters, at the point of implementation. Furthermore, to have adaptation, there must be strong internal integration between

> A strong counter-view is that glocalisation encourages integration where it matters, at the point of implementation.

head office (and business/marketing strategies) and those responsible for local adaptation and implementation. For example, Fielding (2000) shows that many Japanese and Korean advertising messages emphasise product-related information, whereas many Western brands require an emphasis on the development of brand personality and character. For IMC to succeed, a consistent core message and local or regional flavour need to be delivered if such a difference is to be overcome.

Summary

This chapter has attempted to demonstrate the complex nature of the marketing communications industry by considering the size, trends, players, operations and competitive aspects. It should be noted, however, that in the space available this analysis has not attempted to be, and cannot be regarded as, a comprehensive treatment.

The structure that advertising agencies have adopted and the operational aspects may be a little outdated, and the industry might be advised to find new ways of presenting itself to its buyers. Of the many issues facing the industry one of the key ones concerns the relationships between agencies and their clients. The context that the industry presents and which influences the relationships of the main participants, the media, clients and agencies, must not be ignored.

The industry will continue to evolve and further integration between agencies and those that own and manage many of the new marketing communication tools is likely to accelerate.

Review questions

1. Find the most up-to-date figures for the amount spent on each of the promotional disciplines in your country.
2. Which are the principal types of organisation in the marketing communication industry?
3. Write notes for a presentation explaining the different types of agency available to clients.
4. Outline the arguments for and against using an agency.
5. What factors should be taken into consideration and what procedure might be followed when selecting an agency?
6. What problems might be encountered in agency/client relationships?
7. What are the basic dimensions for the development of good agency/client relationships?
8. Write brief notes about the briefing system.
9. Explain the commission payment system, and outline alternative approaches.
10. How can an organisation best acquaint itself with the relevant controls in a chosen area of marketing communications?

MINI-CASE
Revealed: how food firms target children

Mini-case written by Tony Garry, Senior Lecturer, DeMontfort University

The way children are influenced by what they see and hear has been the subject of debate for some time. However, criticisms are not just restricted to TV sex and violence anymore. Parents, consumer associations and the EU are increasingly concerned about the impact that marketing may have on children. To quote Rowan Williams, the Archbishop of Canterbury: 'What can we say about a marketing culture that so openly feeds and colludes with obsession?'

The pre-school market alone is estimated to be worth around £4.3 billion a year, and if you add those areas where children influence their parents' purchases (clothing, food, leisure activities, holidays, etc.), the estimate goes up to £30 billion a year.

Principal among these markets is the lucrative after-school snacking market, where a recent Mintel report suggests there are an estimated 9 million children aged between 7 and 16 who buy food on their way home from school. Recently there has been much controversy surrounding the way food manufacturers have targeted this market given increasing concerns about obesity in general and child obesity in particular. Some estimates suggest child obesity has tripled in the UK in the last 20 years.

As a result the food and advertising industries have been put on notice to change their pricing and promotion policies to help tackle the epidemic. As one newspaper states: 'Methods used by the food industry to target children include bypassing parents and deploying "viral marketing" and "underground communication"'. It reveals how manufacturers are using text messages to target children's mobile phones with advertisements for sweets and snacks. More than 50 per cent of children aged between 7 and 15 own mobile phones according to a recent NOP survey. Children are encouraged to text a number or a word to see if they have won a prize under campaigns that have been run by companies such as Masterfoods, Walkers Snacks, Coca-Cola and McDonald's. The companies can then retain the senders' numbers and send them back promotional information.

Matt Jones, Business Development manager for 12snap, a specialist mobile phone marketing company, said texting was becoming an increasingly effective way of contacting potential customers. 'Brands build up a relationship with the person texting in, get close to them. It's the easiest and most convincing way to talk to a teenage audience.' He went on to say, 'I understand concerns about marketing snack foods but if companies can get in the minds of a teenage audience like this then maybe their healthy competitors should look at using the same medium.'

Particular criticism has been aimed at a recent campaign for Kellogg's Real Fruit Winders, which was awarded the 'Tooth Rot' award by the parents' jury of the Food Commission. Using 'mutant fruit characters' the firm's advertising agency, Leo Burnett, has revealed in a submission to the Institute of Practitioners in Advertising for its effectiveness awards how it spread the word about the brand virally (by word of mouth) following an 'initial underground communication campaign'. It was able to 'seed' the characters through a secret language used at concerts, magazines and cinemas. It also used clothing to place the characters with children's celebrities, gaining exposure on TV shows and music channels popular with children.

'We have a clear indication that it infiltrated the kid's conversations' the ad agency states. It quotes typical responses from children including 'it's cool – it's more secret than text messaging – my mum wouldn't know what was going on'. The campaign also encouraged children to interact with its Web sites while retrieving emails. New micro sites were created on sites popular with children. All this activity was unbranded. The advertising agency claims it managed to reach nearly 60 per cent of children with only PR and Web activity. It was only after this that it started TV advertising to reach mothers, who are seen as the main purchasers.

Healthy eating campaigners are enraged by this latest use of technology and attempts are being made to regulate the advertising of food based on its nutritional quality. One such campaigner is Debra Shipley, Labour MP for Stourbridge, who states: 'If the government fails to act, it is clear it is working hand in glove with the vested interests of the food industry rather than the best interests of the children'; and she adds 'I'm shocked to hear of this cynical targeting of young people. It's outrageous.' John Reid, the (then) Health Secretary, is looking at moves that could ban junk food manufacturers from advertising during children's television programmes. Reid's aides said he considered the 'nuclear option' of banning such advertising altogether during children's programmes.

There is also mounting criticism of the way fast food companies are being allowed to sponsor and subsidise sports to the tune of £40 million a year. For example, the Cadbury's Get Active promotion encouraged pupils to swap chocolate wrappers for school sports equipment; however it was dropped when critics pointed out that it would require 5,440 wrappers to secure one football net.

The Food Standards Agency recently published evidence that there was a clear link between the types of food promoted to children and what they ate. The food industry refuses to admit there is a direct link but continues to invest heavily in advertising. Privately, however, Department of Health officials admit that there is a paralysis over how to proceed. Ministers are wary of accusations of nannying the public. 'We know people don't want to be told how to run their lives, but we don't really have a mechanism for finding out what sort of measures they would put up with,' said one official.

Sources

Croft, M. (2003) Seen and not heard. *Marketing Week*, 30 January, pp. 33–5.

Food Standards Agency Consumer Committee (2003) The promotion of foods to children. For discussion. ConsComm D023/03, FSA, September.

Lawrence, F. (2004) Revealed: how food firms target children, *Guardian*, 27 May.

Mintel (2003) Snacks. Mintel International Group Ltd, April.

NOP (2004) Teen and tween influentials. *NOP World*, September.

Rogers, L. and Carr-Brown, J. (2004) Food firms text sweet ads to children, *Guardian*, 30 May.

Questions

1 'Cynical targeting of young people' or 'Getting in the minds of a teenage audience'. Are the food manufacturers being unethical in their communication techniques?

2 Should food manufacturers take greater responsibility for the promotion of their products or should there be legislation to regulate the way products are promoted?

3 How should the food manufacturers respond in the light of the threatened legislative action?

References

Billings, C. (2004) DM's new wave. *Campaign*, 7 September. Retrieved from http://www.brandrepublic.com/news/newsArticle.cfm.

Collin, W. (2003) The interface between account planning and media planning – a practitioner perspective. *Marketing Intelligence and Planning*, **21**(7), pp. 440–5.

Curtis, J. (1999) Why grey is golden. *Marketing*, 15 July, pp. 25–6.

Davidson, S. and Kapelianis, D. (1996) Towards an organisational theory of advertising: agency–client relationships in South Africa. *International Journal of Advertising*, **15**, pp. 48–60.

Earnshaw, M. (2005) New year, new challenges. *Marketing*, 5 January, p. 10.

Fielding, S. (2000) Developing global brands in Asia. *Admap* (June), pp. 26–9.

Finch, M. (2000) How to choose the right marketing agency, *Admap* (October), pp. 46–7.

Goften, K. (2000) Mergers shake up DM and SP groups. *Agency 2001 Marketing Report 13*, 30 November, pp. 15–16.

Grant, I., Gilmore, C. and Crosier, K. (2003) Account planning: whose role is it anyway? *Marketing Intelligence and Planning*, **21**(7), pp. 462–72.

Green, A. (1991) Death of the full-service ad agency? *Admap* (January), pp. 21–4.

Griffiths, A. (2000) More than a media network. *Campaign Report*, 20 October, pp. 3–4.

Gronstedt, A. and Thorsen, E. (1996) Five approaches to organise an integrated marketing communications agency. *Journal of Advertising Research* (March/April), pp. 48–58.

Hakansson, H. (1982) *International Marketing and Purchasing of Industrial Goods: An Interaction Approach*. Chichester: Wiley.

Jardine, A. (2000) Will workshops replace the pitch? *Marketing*, 13 April, p. 16.

Jensen, B. (1995) Using agency remuneration as a strategic tool. *Admap* (January), pp. 20–2.

Jones, M. (2004) 10 things agencies need to know about clients. *Admap*, **39**(5) (May), pp. 21–3.

Kotler, P. and Mindak, W. (1978) Marketing and public relations. *Journal of Marketing*, **42** (October), pp. 13–20.

Lace, J.M. (2000) Payment-by-results. Is there a pot of gold at the end of the rainbow? *International Journal of Advertising*, **19**, pp. 167–83.

Lace, J.M. and Brocklehurst, D. (2000) You both win when you play the same game. *Admap* (October), pp. 40–2.

McKee, S. (2004) Pick an agency . . . any agency. *Admap*, **39**(5) (May), pp. 24–5.

Miln, D. (2004) New marketing, new agency? *Admap*, **39**(7) (July/August), pp. 47–8.

Morgan, R.M. and Hunt, S.D. (1994) The commitment–trust theory of relationship marketing. *Journal of Marketing*, **58** (July), pp. 20–38.

Murphy, C. (2004) Small but perfectly formed? *Marketing*, 15 December, p. 12.

Murphy, D. (2000) New media's year of good fortunes. *Agency 2001 Marketing Report 13*, 30 November, p. 33.

Murphy, D. (2002) Automation assists business efficiency. *Marketing*, 30 May, p. 23.

Pawińska, M. (2000) The passive pitch. *PR Week*, 12 May, pp. 14–15.

Phillips, W. (1991) From bubble to rubble. *Admap* (April), pp. 14–19.

Public Relations Educational Trust (1991) *The Place of Public Relations in Management Education*. London: Institute of Public Relations.

Snowden, S. (1993) The remuneration squeeze. *Admap* (January), pp. 26–8.

Starkey, R. (1999) cited in Curtis (1999).

West, D.C. and Paliwoda, S.J. (1996) Advertising client–agency relationships. *European Journal of Marketing*, **30**(8), pp. 22–39.

Whitehead, J. (2004) MWO out of running for £40m Direct Line ad account. *Brand Republic* 17 August. Retrieved from http://www.brandrepublic.com/news/newsArticle.

Woolgar, T. (1998) Choosing an agency. *Campaign Report*, 9 October, pp. 6–7.

Young, M. and Steilen, C. (1996) Strategy based advertising agency selection: an alternative to 'spec' presentation. *Business Horizons*, **39** (November/December), pp. 77–80.

Zambarino, A. and Goodfellow, J. (2003) Account planning in the new marketing and communications environment (has the Stephen King challenge been met?) *Marketing Intelligence and Planning*, **21**(7), pp. 424–34.

Ethics in marketing communications

Richard Christy

4

Ethical considerations – questions of right and wrong – are an inseparable part of real-life marketing communications. Any part of an organisation's marketing communications can send messages about its ethical stance, either intentionally or otherwise. Organisations need to cultivate an active awareness of the ethical consequences of their marketing communications.

Aims and objectives

The aim of this chapter is to introduce ideas of business ethics and to review how they are relevant to marketing communications.

The objectives of this chapter are to:

1. review briefly the main ideas in ethics and the way they are applied to business in general;
2. discuss the differing viewpoints of the ethics of marketing communications as a whole;
3. understand how ethical considerations affect specific issues in marketing communications, such as truth-telling, respect for personal privacy, the treatment of vulnerable groups and questions of taste and decency;
4. introduce frameworks and models that can help managers to think through these issues in planning their marketing communications.

Introduction

In this book, the word 'good' is probably used dozens of times, often in the sense of 'likely to contribute to effective marketing communications', or something similar. 'Good', however, can also have a moral, or ethical (the two words are used interchangeably here), connotation, which may be quite distinct: something that is functionally effective may or may not be ethically acceptable. This chapter looks at how ethical questions of good and bad or right and wrong might be applied to marketing communications.

Something that is functionally effective may or may not be ethically acceptable.

Familiar concerns

How do these questions make themselves felt in real life? Everyone will have their own list, but common concerns include:

- misleading or false advertising;
- shocking, tasteless or indecent material in marketing communications;
- high-pressure sales techniques, particularly when applied to vulnerable groups;
- telesales calls that seem to intrude on personal privacy;
- PR communications that seem to distract and obfuscate, rather than inform;
- the payment of bribes to win business.

Why is it worth paying attention to these matters? For many, the main reason for wanting to understand how ethics may bear upon marketing communications will be a natural desire to know how good things can be promoted and bad things avoided. For others, interest in these questions will result from a realisation that if a company conducts its marketing communications (or any other aspect of its business) in a way that others find unethical, then it may have negative consequences which can outweigh any functional benefits. Finally, many may believe that there is no necessary contradiction between being effective in business and behaving ethically, and perhaps even that true long-term effectiveness in business is more likely to be achieved by companies which set and stick to high ethical standards.

Importance of judgement and experience

There has been a growing emphasis on business ethics in recent years, partly as a consequence of an increased public interest in how businesses behave (i.e. not just in the products and services they produce) and a more sceptical and less respectful attitude to the place of business and business people in society. This growing awareness has also been fuelled by a far wider availability of information about corporate actions: it is much more difficult to keep things permanently secret in the Internet age. Business ethics as a subject addresses itself to the complete range of activities of an organisation, part of which is to do with the ethical implications of the way an organisation approaches its marketing communications. As we shall see, many of the issues that arise are not simple 'black-and-white' questions, but more complex situations in which judgement and experience have to be applied to arrive at an ethically acceptable solution.

Complex situations in which judgement and experience have to be applied to arrive at an ethically acceptable solution.

For example, most people would presumably object to a sales presentation whose content was designed to mislead consumers about a product or make deliberately false claims about its benefits, but few would go as far as to require every marketing communication to provide full 'warts and all' detail about the advantages and possible disadvantages of buying and using the product. Finding the balance between these two extremes is not wholly an ethical question – practical and legal issues, for example, are also likely to intrude – but one in which an understanding of ethics as applied to the conduct of business can be very valuable.

This chapter provides a brief introduction to some of the main ideas in ethics and to the way in which ethical thinking can be applied to business. For all that common sense plays a major role in the resolution of many real-life ethical questions, these issues can be highly complex, with solutions sometimes depending strongly on the approach adopted to analysis. Understanding moral concepts may help a decision-maker to analyse the ethical ramifications of a situation in order to make a better ethical choice. Sometimes, in real-life business situations, resolving to do the right thing can be easier than determining what the right thing actually *is*.

> Resolving to do the right thing can be easier than determining what the right thing actually *is*.

Ideas in business ethics

> Ethics is the study of morality: those practices and activities that are importantly right and wrong.

Ethics is the study of morality: those practices and activities that are importantly right and wrong (De George, 1999); business ethics considers the application of ethical principles to the conduct of business. This distinction may seem obvious, but it makes an important point: just as medical ethics considers the application of ethics to medicine, business ethics is about the way general ethical principles should be applied to business. In particular, business is not 'exempt' from the moral considerations that apply to human affairs in general, nor should a separate set of moral standards be developed for the set of human activities that fall under the heading of business (or marketing communications in particular).

Questions of right and wrong have occupied thinkers and writers over many millennia, and it is impossible to provide anything but a superficial overview in the space available here. Those who wish to follow up in more detail some of the theoretical ideas mentioned here should consult a specialist business ethics text: De George's (1999) book, for example, is one of many in the field that provide a clear and accessible account of the application of ethical principles to business.

Duties and consequences

Two major schools of thought can be distinguished in ethics, which broadly lie on either side of the means/ends debate:

● The first is concerned with *duties*, and argues that some actions are always bad and others always good.

● The second approach focuses on *consequences*, holding that whether an act is good or bad depends on what happens as a result of taking that action, no matter what the action is. Utilitarianism is a well-known form of this approach, seeking to identify actions that (very broadly) can be expected to result in the greatest good of the greatest number.

Problems of the main approaches

To make this distinction is to oversimplify a very complex and long-running debate and also to overlook the many sophisticated variants and hybrid theories that have been developed. In the course of this debate, the problems inherent in either approach have been well rehearsed – an approach to ethics based on duty alone is likely to be inflexible and difficult to put into practice in a complex real world. By contrast, the alternative approach of considering only outcomes seems unsatisfactory to many. Crude utilitarianism, for example, is (by definition) 'unprincipled' and insufficiently concerned with the idea of justice. Also, in practical terms, it can also be very difficult to arrive at a satisfactory assessment of 'the greatest good', however that is defined.

Neither approach on its own seems to offer a practical and foolproof guide to ethical business decision-making. As has been suggested above, a simple and apparently unarguable duty-based rule such as 'Always tell the truth in marketing communications' may cause problems as soon as we start to plan an advertising campaign. Is it our duty to provide a detailed and reasoned discussion of all of the reasons for and against buying the product, whatever the medium we are using? Must we refrain from using ironic statements that are plainly designed to entertain, rather than inform?

Basing the ethical evaluation of our actions only on the expected consequences brings a separate set of problems. If, for example, a company designs an advertising campaign that most people will find mildly amusing but which a small religious minority will find highly offensive, then the publication of research data showing a weighted average calculation of approval for the adverts will be unlikely to reassure most people's intuitive concerns about the campaign. In practical terms, it can also be extraordinarily difficult to forecast all of the consequences of a proposed action, however concerned one may be to achieve a balanced assessment.

Other approaches to business ethics

These practical difficulties in applying simple rules or methods to complex real-life situations have caused many writers in business ethics to leave the theoretical ends/ means argument to one side and to propose alternative bases for judging the ethical implications of proposed business actions. Jackson (1996), for example, explains how a focus on moral virtues in business life can provide a much more practical basis for assessing good conduct in business. The concept of virtues seeks to express those qualities and dispositions in a person that will help to ensure a good life, often seeking a 'mean' between two undesirable poles. Finding the 'mean', however, is far from straightforward. Murphy (1999) argues that a virtues approach is appropriate and useful in analysing the ethics of organisations as well as individuals, and discusses five virtues which are particularly relevant to the ethical conduct of international marketing: integrity, fairness, trust, respect and empathy.

A different alternative is proposed by Sternberg (2000), in which the assessment of business ethics is based upon a definition of the *purpose* of the company (for this reason, her approach to business ethics is described as teleological):

> *To be an ethical business, an organisation must be a business and must conduct its activities ethically. An organisation is a business if its objective is maximising long-term owner value; a business acts ethically, if its actions are compatible with that aim and with distributive justice and ordinary decency.*

(p. 93)

'Distributive justice' refers to the principle by which rewards are allocated in proportion to the contribution made to organisational ends.

In this definition, 'distributive justice' refers to the principle by which rewards are allocated in proportion to the contribution made to organisational ends, while the constraint of 'ordinary decency' obliges a firm to refrain from coercion, lying, cheating and so on, whether or not they appear at the time to further the business purpose. These two restrictions acknowledge the vital importance of confidence and trust in the business world.

In adopting this approach, a manager would be mainly concerned with the consequences of a proposed action, but would concentrate on those consequences that are directly or indirectly relevant to the firm's long-term interests, rather than seeking to judge what is in the general interest. On first reading, this may seem to some to be nothing more than a formal statement of the 'Greed is good' values that are sometimes associated with the aggressive 'Anglo-Saxon' model of capitalism of the 1980s. The teleological approach, however, is importantly different from the excesses of that era:

● The concept of 'long-term owner value' is not the same thing as that of short-term rewards: the pursuit of long-term value may require very different actions from a policy designed to maximise, say, the next dividend payment.

● The requirement to behave with 'common decency' firmly excludes actions on the part of the firm such as lying, cheating, stealing and coercion, no matter how expedient or financially attractive they may seem in the short term: these things are always unethical.

● An intelligently self-interested firm will generally not wish to pursue activities that give it a bad reputation among customers, suppliers, potential recruits and so on, because to do so would be to fail to maximise long-term owner value. This is not to say that individual employees may have no other reasons for this restraint, but rather to suggest that the teleological principle will often provide sufficient reason to behave ethically in business.

An intelligently self-interested firm will generally not wish to pursue activities that give it a bad reputation.

This teleological principle, and the primacy it accords to the interests of the shareholders, has been criticised as incomplete by some (see, for example, Sorrell, 1994) and many argue for a much more extensive view of corporate social responsibility. However, thinking broadly and clearly about the long-term interests of a business can in many cases help to identify the ethical way forward, as will be argued in this chapter.

Stakeholder theories

Although it is framed in terms that may seem to be disconcertingly stark – even provocative – this teleological principle may help to illuminate the difference between the ideas of 'stakeholder' theory and the seemingly narrower concerns of what De George (1999) refers to as the organisational view of business. One example of this view is provided by Milton Friedman's (1970) suggestion that the social responsibility of business is to use its resources to engage in activities designed to increase its profits, within the 'rules' of free competition and without deception or fraud. This type of approach views directors and managers as agents of the owners, with a prime duty to maximise their wealth. By contrast, some forms of stakeholder theory define a far wider set of external interests, to which the firm is in some way 'accountable' (see Chapter 8 for a fuller discussion of the implications of stakeholder theory).

Whatever view is taken of a firm's relationship with and duties towards its various stakeholders, the mere acknowledgement of complexity and plurality does not of itself help managers to know what to *do* about this plurality in practice. Managers seeking to 'balance' stakeholder interests will quickly encounter the very practical problem of how that 'balance' should be defined. Consider, for example, opportunities for a firm to contribute to or become involved with charitable causes. The available range of local, national and global causes will in total outweigh any conceivable budget. What is needed is both an ethical basis for deciding whether to lend support at all and, if so, which causes to support. Asking the question 'Which actions best support the long-term goals of this firm?' in an intelligent and enlightened way may well help to illuminate the complex ethical issues facing firms today. The word 'enlightened' is used here to describe an outlook that deliberately considers the long term as well as the short term, which thinks more broadly than the immediate transactions carried out by the firm and is active and searching, rather than passive.

The teleological principle requires that stakeholder interests be acknowledged and taken into account.

The teleological principle requires that stakeholder interests be acknowledged and taken into account, because not to do so would be a violation of the principle. Importantly, it also provides guidance on *how* those interests are to be taken into account (i.e. by assessing their impact on the long-term interests of the owners of the firm).

The scope of ethical issues in marketing communications

Before looking at the application of these ideas to marketing communications, one or two things need to be clarified. The first of these is the importance of distinguishing between:

● those critiques of marketing communications that are based upon a belief that the activity as a whole is undesirable;

● criticisms of some aspects of marketing communications in practice which are based on an acceptance that the activity is in principle justifiable.

The next section provides a brief review of some of the first type of critique, not least because these arguments are frequently encountered in public debate; in effect, they are part of the world in which marketing takes place. The rest of the chapter, however, concerns itself with the second category of criticisms – ethical issues which are raised by the practice of marketing communications, with a clear implication that advertising, selling, PR and so on are things that can be done ethically or unethically, depending upon the choices that are made.

It is also important to clarify that the discussion here concentrates on marketing communications in particular, rather than marketing in general, meaning that many issues relating to marketing as a whole have been excluded. It is certainly unethical to advertise a product that is known to be so badly designed or manufactured as to be dangerous, for example, but the ethical issue in this case has more to do with the practice of product management than advertising. Those interested in ethical issues affecting marketing in general should consult a specialised text such as Schlegelmilch (1998), or the review of the literature presented in Tsalikis and Fritzsche (1989).

The final clarification is to point out that the main ethical questions in marketing communications are considered one by one in this chapter, rather than looking at the individual elements of the promotional mix in turn. Questions of truth-telling, decency, privacy and so on have some bearing on every part of the promotional mix, although the context of each medium may affect the way in which ethical considerations have to be applied.

Marketing communications: a diabolical liberty?

In the 1968 comedy film *Bedazzled* Peter Cook plays a jaded, weary devil, who complains that since introducing the seven deadly sins he has done very little except invent advertising. The line is just a joke, of course, but does rely upon one familiar view of advertising: that it is inherently bad, manipulative or corrupting. Nor is this disapproval confined to advertising: the image of the smooth, fast-talking 'snake oil' salesman is an enduring one, with many modern counterparts. Similarly, the public relations industry has suffered from some extremely *poor* PR in recent years: the term 'PR' sometimes seems to be used in a way that is almost synonymous with half-truths, insincerity and manipulation. In contemporary politics, the term 'spin' is generally pejorative, suggesting a growing impatience with slick presentation at the expense of candour and truth.

If these views – in effect, that marketing communications is inherently undesirable and unworthy – are taken seriously, then the ethical response must presumably be to indulge in these activities as little as possible, if at all. Happily, however, this is not the only view that can be taken: an alternative view regards marketing communications as playing a key role in the market economy, assisting the process through which consumer needs are identified and satisfied. From this perspective, the ethics of advertising, PR and so on depend upon how they are carried out: in themselves, these activities are ethically neutral. Most of this chapter takes the latter perspective, but it is certainly worth briefly highlighting the more fundamental critiques of advertising.

Advertising as mass manipulation?

Vance Packard's famous book about mass communications, *The Hidden Persuaders* (1960), had a major impact. His concern was what he saw as the manipulative, widespread use of psychological techniques in advertising, PR, politics and so on:

> *many of us are being influenced and manipulated – far more than we realise – in the patterns of our everyday lives. Large-scale efforts are being made, often with impressive success, to channel our unthinking habits, our purchasing decisions, and our thought processes by the use of insights gained from psychiatry and the social sciences. Typically these efforts take place beneath our level of awareness, so that the appeals which move us are often, in a sense, 'hidden'.*

(p. 11)

Today's hard-pressed advertisers, trying to engage the attention of a sophisticated, knowing and demanding public, might be forgiven for wryly wishing that anything like that level of influence could be achieved. However, Packard's book provided a powerful expression of a point of view that is often found in press and academic commentaries on advertising, sometimes linked to more fundamental political critiques of the capitalistic society in which advertising takes place. Forty years later, a similar concern is evident in Klein's (2000) account of the anti-capitalist protests that have taken place in several cities internationally. One of the strands of this diverse movement has been concern about the dominance of global brands in everyday life.

Pollay's (1986) review of social science commentaries on advertising drew together a wide range of material into a general framework. This synthesis suggested that advertising was seen – by social scientists – as a powerful and intrusive means of communication and persuasion, whose (unintended) effects could be to reinforce materialism, cynicism, irrationality, selfishness and a number of other undesirable outcomes. Holbrook's (1987) reply to this paper challenged some of its implicit assumptions (e.g. that advertising is monolithic, somehow acting in concert; that it appeals to a mass audience; that it manipulates social values; that it relies mainly upon emotional impact) and suggested that the 'conventional wisdom or prevailing opinion' represented in the Pollay model was unfairly destructive of a much more diverse reality.

Space does not permit anything like an adequate discussion of these serious and important arguments. The important point to be taken forward is that this discussion of ethics in marketing communications takes for granted a number of much broader issues to do with the ethical acceptability of marketing as an activity and of the capitalist system which engendered it. As Robin and Reidenbach (1993) point out:

> *The degree to which the basic marketing functions are seen to be ethical or unethical must . . . be measured within our understanding of their history, the times in which they are applied, the context in which they are applied, the expectations of society, the requirements of capitalism and our best understanding of human behaviour.*

(p. 104)

Truth-telling

The general ethical requirement to tell the truth is one that bears upon every type of marketing communication.

The general ethical requirement to tell the truth is one that bears upon every type of marketing communication. Reflecting the widespread public distaste for lying and deceit, there are plenty of legal and other regulatory deterrents to this type of unethical conduct in advertising, selling, public relations and so on. Clearly, no responsible business will wish to be found on the wrong side of these requirements, but there remains plenty of scope for judgement in respect of which aspects of the truth are to be presented in marketing communications and how they are to be put across.

As discussed at the beginning of this chapter, we expect a salesperson not to lie to us, but few would require from a salesperson a full and balanced account of the advantages and disadvantages of our entering into the proposed transaction. There are perhaps two reasons why: mainly, it is unreasonable to expect the salesperson or advertiser to have enough information about us to be able to carry this out; also, however, there is a general acceptance that the principle of *caveat emptor* (let the buyer beware) should play some sort of moderating role.

As Sternberg (2000) observes, the aim of a salesperson is to sell the company's products, not to provide consumer guidance. Both buyer and seller have their own interests and it is normally up to either party to look after these interests during the purchase process. Thus there is no ethical requirement that customers should ensure that the transaction is profitable for the seller, nor – in every case – that the seller must go to great lengths to ensure that the buyer is making a wise and prudent purchase (although many sellers will choose to provide some advice of this nature, in order to appeal more effectively to customers). Much depends on the context of the sales dialogue: the nature of the product or service, the awareness and expectations of the customer and so on (see also Smith's (1995) 'Consumer sovereignty' test discussed below). It is also usually important for the seller to make it plain in some way that selling is actually taking place: the Market Research Society, for example, defines the unacceptable practice of 'sugging' – selling under guise (of conducting research). The distinction between selling and giving independent advice is also embodied in the regulations relating to the marketing of financial services in the UK.

Misrepresentation and 'puffery'

Some way short of the extreme of deceit or lying, but nonetheless the wrong side (for most people) of the ethical divide, is the problem of deliberate or reckless misrepresentation in selling. Chonko (1995) defines misrepresentation as occurring when salespeople make incorrect statements or false promises about a product or service. The dividing line is not always absolutely clear: a salesperson can be generally expected to show enthusiasm for the product, which may result in some degree of exaggeration. Up to a point, of course, a sales negotiation can be seen as a performance in which both buyer and seller may make some claims that do not represent their actual or final position. Most, however, would accept this as perfectly normal, perhaps even seeing it as an effective way of identifying and delineating the area within which both buyer and seller are prepared to participate.

Misrepresentation in advertising is likely to be condemned by codes of practice, if not by actual statute.

Misrepresentation in advertising is likely to be condemned by codes of practice, if not by actual statute. The American Marketing Association's code of ethics, for example, is clear that it is the responsibility of members to avoid false and misleading advertising and sales promotions that use deception or manipulation (American Marketing Association, n.d.). Much advertising, however, contains some degree of what might be called 'embellishment' or 'puffery' – the enthusiastic use of language and images to convey the most optimistic view of the product or service being portrayed. Those who find embellishment to be a natural, obvious and harmless aspect of advertising language will have some difficulty in providing a firm dividing line between harmless embellishment and deception. Chonko (1995) points out that the American Federal Trade Commission regards puffery as acceptable because such statements are not likely to be relied upon by consumers in making their choice. However, this approach seems itself to place great reliance upon being able to identify those parts of a marketing communication that *are* likely to be relied upon. Similar issues are raised by the visual images created for advertising, which naturally seek to show the product as appealingly as possible – there will be little serious concern about using mashed potato to represent easily melted ice cream in an advertising photo session. However, for some products aimed at some audiences – and children's toys are often mentioned in this context – exaggerated images may have a greater potential to delude. These questions are complex in detail: the extent to which consumers should be held responsible for critically evaluating the commercial messages is not a simple issue, since so much depends upon the circumstances of an individual case. For Attas (1999), for example, it is preferable to think about the effects of deceptive advertising

It is preferable to think about the effects of deceptive advertising in terms of the effect on society as a whole.

in terms of the effect on society as a whole (i.e. as if deception at a particular level were commonplace), rather than seeking to make firm statements about the possible effects on an individual.

The importance of context: selling complex products

The importance of context in judging ethical behaviour can be seen in the debate in the UK over the problems arising from the selling of private pensions during the 1980s. In many cases customers were persuaded by salespeople to switch out of existing pension schemes into new schemes whose subsequent performance left them worse off. In these cases the complex nature of the services, together with the unfamiliarity of many of the customers with the various types of product and how to choose between them, led them to place an unusually great reliance on the advice provided by the salesperson. Put another way, the extent to which the buyer was foreseeably *able* to 'beware' in these cases was very limited, which in turn should have placed a greater than normal ethical duty on the salesperson to ensure that the customers were properly informed of the consequences and implications of the switch. The fact that these ethical standards were clearly not met in a large number of cases has caused a great deal of loss, anxiety and inconvenience for the customers who lost out, but also a great deal of difficulty, expense and embarrassment for the pensions industry as a whole.

Writing about ethical issues in insurance selling in general, Diacon and Ennew (1996) point out that marketing transactions in financial services have greater than normal potential for ethical complications. The unavoidable complexity of many financial services products is heightened by the fact that the evaluation may depend upon individual calculations carried out for the customer by the salesperson; also, risk for the customer may be significant, in that the actual benefits received will often depend upon the performance of the economy over a long period. The authors highlight a number of other ethical issues relevant to insurance selling, including:

● the issue of 'fitness for purpose' in both the design of the products and the way in which they are matched to customer needs;

● the transparency of the price for these products, such that any commissions payable to the intermediary organisation or individual salesperson are clearly visible;

● the need for truth in promotion, not only in terms of strict factual correctness, but also in terms of what the consumer might be expected to understand from a phrase;

● the effect of the sales targeting and reward systems of the selling organisation on the behaviour of salespeople, particularly in view of the important advisory component of this type of selling.

In their survey of the industry, the authors found some awareness of these ethical issues and also evidence of initial moves to address the main cause of problems: the potentially dangerous combination of commission-based selling and imperfect information on the part of customers.

The serious problems arising from personal pension selling during the 1980s provide an example of how important it is for businesses to maintain an active awareness of the likely effects of their actions. It is difficult to escape the conclusion that a more enlightened assessment of the long-term interests of the business on the part of financial service providers would have helped to avert many of the problems, to the great benefit of all involved. This is easy to conclude with hindsight: the effective ethical businesses are those that manage to cultivate this type of *foresight*.

The relational context and expectations

The importance of the buyer/seller context in which the statement is made is also reflected in Gundlach and Murphy's (1993) paper on the ethics of relational marketing exchanges. In these exchanges the value of the arrangement for both sides depends critically upon the mutual maintenance of trust, equity, responsibility and commitment (i.e. as opposed to the more contractual regulation of shorter-term transactional relationships). Clearly, the expectations as regards the content and openness of marketing communications in the former would be different from the latter. A customer might, for example, feel upset if a car salesperson with whom he had dealt for many years failed to tell him that the model he was buying was about to be superseded, because that would seem to be inconsistent with the trust built up over the years. The same customer might not be at all upset to find the same thing happen with a personal computer bought from a discount store in London, not only because computers are known to date more quickly than models of cars, but also because there was no long-term relationship to be brought into question.

Truth-telling and PR

The practice of PR is also likely to raise many truth-telling issues. The purpose of PR is to create and manage relationships between the firm and its various publics and there must always be a temptation in so doing to place undue emphasis on the positive aspects of the firm's actions. The question of what is 'due' emphasis is no easier in this area of marketing communications than in selling or advertising: a firm must strike an ethical balance, based upon its understanding of its impact on others and its own long-term interests and reputation. Firms that make a habit of using PR techniques to mislead stakeholder groups are in effect consuming in the short term the trust upon which their long-term profitable existence may depend.

Botan (1997) distinguishes between the 'monologic' and 'dialogic' approaches to PR, suggesting that dialogue is a more ethical basis for planning PR campaigns, particularly in an information society. More pragmatically, Barton (1994) warns that, following the major business scandals of the 1980s, courts may increasingly hold PR firms liable for making false or misleading statements on behalf of their clients, placing a prudential burden of proof and research on the PR firms themselves. Onerous though such burdens may turn out to be, they appear to be little different from that which an enlightened view of long-term self-interest on the part of PR firms might indicate – PR firms above all must rely upon a basic level of public trust in their activities if they are to do any good for their clients at all.

Vulnerable groups

The question of truth-telling leads directly to the special requirements for the treatment of vulnerable groups in marketing communications campaigns. Many countries, for example, have much stricter controls on the content and timing of advertising to children than on advertising in general, based upon an enhanced concern for the potential of advertisements and other promotional material to delude and disturb this audience.

These special regulations, however, should not distract attention from the general ethical requirement to design marketing communications that show an enlightened understanding of and concern for the needs of the recipient of the communication. The often-discussed tragic problems resulting from the sale of baby milk products in some developing countries had much to do with marketing and other communications from the seller that simply did not take adequate account of the reality of life in developing countries. As De George (1999) observes:

In an attempt to increase sales, Nestlé, as well as other producers of infant formula [milk], extended the sale of their product to many countries in Africa. They followed some of the same marketing techniques that they had followed with success and without customer complaint elsewhere.

One standard technique was advertising on billboards and magazines. A second was the distribution of free samples in hospitals to new mothers as well as to doctors. In themselves, these practices were neither illegal nor unethical. Yet their use led to charges of following unethical practices and to a seven-year worldwide boycott of all Nestlé products.

(p. 264)

In retrospect, it is easy to point out that the company should have paid greater attention to the likelihood in this environment of the product being made up with water from a contaminated source or of the product being over-diluted by users who were unfamiliar with it. Again, firms that cultivate an enlightened awareness of their impact on their surroundings will have a greater chance of perceiving and anticipating these issues before they become problems.

> **Firms that cultivate an enlightened awareness of their impact on their surroundings will have a greater chance of perceiving and anticipating these issues before they become problems.**

Privacy and respect for persons

One aspect of the duty-based view of ethics referred to at the beginning of this chapter is the importance of treating others as ends in themselves, rather than merely as means: in other words, not merely using others, but treating them with the respect they deserve as fellow human beings. This ethical requirement finds a number of potential applications in the world of marketing communications, for example:

● avoiding the annoyance and harassment that can result from the inappropriate application of high-pressure sales techniques;

● respecting the wish that some may have at some times to be private, not to be approached with sales calls and – for some – not to be sent unsolicited direct mail communications;

● refraining from causing unwarranted distress or shock by ensuring that the content of any marketing communication 'remains within generally accepted boundaries of taste and decency'.

The first of these issues is perhaps easiest to deal with here: harassment is something that can be subjectively defined (i.e. by the recipient of the unwelcome attention) and no ethical business will wish to cross that line. The fact that sales harassment does take place does not undermine the principle, but rather suggests that some businesses have a flawed view of their long-term interest, or, in the most opportunistic cases, that they are making no plans to have a long-term future. As in some of the other cases discussed above, the need for regulation is primarily to support and reinforce the action that an ethical company would be likely to choose anyway.

Responding to individual preferences for privacy

The issue of privacy is a little more complex, especially if it is treated as a question of 'rights'. It is not very easy to define a separate and defensible right to privacy in respect of direct marketing approaches. Privacy is essentially a subjective concept, to do with not being perceived or disturbed at a particular time or while engaged in a particular activity. To express this as a right seems to involve a corresponding obligation on others to sense in some way that a person is in a private state and then not to perceive or disturb that person, which sounds impractical in many circumstances. In the context of a capitalist society, it is also difficult to think about general prohibitions on the making of commercial approaches.

This is not at all to argue that concerns about privacy in respect of direct marketing have no basis, but rather to suggest that they can be more productively addressed by regarding them as a reasonable request (rather than the assertion of a right) and then considering how an ethical firm ought to respond (Christy and Mitchell, 1999). Privacy-related concerns in this area seem to fall into two main categories: unwelcome sales approaches (e.g. teleselling calls in the evening) and a more general concern about the implications of large amounts of personal data being collected, stored and processed for sale to those involved in direct marketing.

Ethical firms will refrain as far as possible from making unwelcome approaches, for reasons of enlightened self-interest.

In the first case, the ethical response is the same as for sales harassment: ethical firms will refrain as far as possible from making unwelcome approaches, for reasons of enlightened self-interest. They will, for example, support and encourage the development of general schemes through which individuals can signify their general wish not to be contacted. They will also seek out and use mailing lists that are a very close match with their target segments, which will both make the mailing more effective and also reduce the chance of the mailing piece being seen as 'junk'. They will also provide a clear means for those who do not wish to be contacted to indicate their wish.

An ethical company can also respond to the second and more general concern about privacy, both by offering clear opportunities to individuals to have their details excluded from files and also by ensuring as far as possible that information about individuals used in direct marketing has been ethically collected, processed and stored (e.g. such that it is still up to date, thus minimising the risk of, say, causing distress by inadvertently mailing to deceased people). Sometimes, even these efforts may not be enough to avoid causing offence inadvertently, and an ethical firm will ensure that it has in place clear and effective systems to receive and respond to the complaint.

Taste and decency

The question of taste and decency in the content of marketing communications is also one that may have an ethical aspect. This is not only to do with the use of 'pin-up' images in corporate calendars and trade advertising; separate, but related concerns may apply to the use by a charity of particularly distressing images in order to raise funds or even the apparently innocent use of stereotypical images in advertising.

Images of women and men in advertising

The first point to be made is that public standards of what is acceptable in this area do clearly change over time. The portrayal of women in early TV advertisements, for example, now often seems so obviously inappropriate as to be hilarious: no advertiser adopting a similar tone today could expect to communicate effectively (except perhaps as a spoof). The extent to which contemporary images of women and men in advertising may also be creating stereotypes is beyond the scope of this chapter, but it should be clear that an advertisement that annoys or alienates its target audience is unlikely to be effective. Effective (and ethical) advertisers will wish to treat their prospective audiences with respect, if only because in a competitive market they cannot afford to behave otherwise. David Ogilvy's (1963) often-quoted remark that:

the consumer isn't a moron; she is your wife

(p. 96)

provided a much-needed reminder to fellow advertisers of the need to avoid insulting the intelligence of their audiences. The fact that this (no doubt entirely well-intentioned) advice would probably be expressed differently today also underlines the point that standards and expectations do change over time. Concerns are expressed not only about the portrayal of women in advertising, but also about the relative exclusion of older people (Carrigan and Szmigin, 2003) and, more broadly, the way in which advertising images may carelessly stereotype people, groups, cultures and regions for narrow commercial purposes (Borgerson and Schroeder, 2002). Ethical advertisers will seek to understand their target audiences well enough to be able to communicate effectively, without giving inadvertent offence. Building up this level of understanding is also very important in a cross-cultural context, where the risk of giving offence inadvertently is much higher. The point is obviously true for international or global marketing, but many domestic markets are also increasingly multicultural in nature.

> **Advertising images may carelessly stereotype people, groups, cultures and regions for narrow commercial purposes.**

ViewPoint 4.1   Types of public complaint

The annual report of the Advertising Standards Authority (ASA) provides a crude barometer of public attitudes towards advertising images.

For example, in its commentary on complaints received in 2003, the ASA pointed out that the number of complaints received had increased to a record level of 14,277, 2.3 per cent higher than for 2002. The ten most complained-about campaigns were responsible for about 11 per cent of these complaints. Complaints about misleading claims in adverts were the most frequent type of complaint, while complaints about matters of taste and decency rose by 18 per cent over 2002 to become the second-largest category of complaint. Reflecting developments in communications technology, a fast-growing category of complaint concerned advertising sent by email or SMS: the Internet is now the fifth most complained-about medium, ahead of regional press. On the other hand, the report gives details of a number of cases in which the ASA had decided that the complaint was 'not justified' – six of the ten most complained-about campaigns had received this verdict.

Source: ASA Web site (http://www.asa.org.uk); accessed 5 January 2005.

Images designed to shock

The question of the use of shocking images in marketing communications is one in which an organisation would do well to consider its own long-term interest as broadly as possible. In the short term, a shocking image may be effective, but used to excess the tactic will be counter-productive for a growing number of recipients of the message. The controversy resulting from Benetton's famous poster campaigns in the 1990s

ViewPoint 4.2	Finding the balance - good causes

Recent examples of shocking images illustrate the tension between the desire to make a point power-fully and the need to avoid undue offence. In April 2000 Barnardo's, the children's charity, ran a press advertisement featuring a baby sitting alone in a filthy flat and holding a syringe. The advert was headed 'John Donaldson, age 23' and the copy explained how the work of the charity sought to prevent child abuse victims from the bleak future that could await them. Protestors objected that the advertisement was shocking and offensive, but the Advertising Standards Authority did not uphold the complaints, noting that the advertiser had behaved responsibly in researching the advert among its target audience in order to ensure that the message was understood and was unlikely to cause offence.

Three years later, the ASA reported that a subsequent Barnardo's advert – showing a baby with a cockroach (rather than a silver spoon) in its mouth – had generated 475 complaints, which was more than any other national press campaign in the ASA's history. The ASA upheld these complaints, finding that the charity 'had used unduly shocking images and that the photographs used were likely to cause serious or widespread offence'. Barnardo's were saddened by this finding and commented:

While the adverts may have shocked some sensibilities, they succeeded in highlighting the very serious issue of child poverty in the UK and challenging the blinkered views of those who claim that it does not exist. Barnardo's has always fought for the nation's most disadvantaged children and its commitment to do so will continue undaunted.

The purpose of these examples is not to comment on the decisions made, but rather to illustrate the complex issues that have to be weighed in these situations in marketing communications. Barnardo's and other cause-promoting organisations are not businesses in the normal sense, but they do need to make similarly broad and balanced judgements in deciding how to communicate their ideas.

Source: ASA Web site (http://www.asa.org.uk), accessed 5 January 2005; Barnardo's Web site (http://www.barnardos.org.uk), accessed 5 January 2005.

certainly succeeded in gaining publicity for the knitwear company. As the images used in successive waves of the campaign became more and more uncomfortable, however, mounting criticism from both the public and from business partners led to the abandonment of the campaign by the company.

The same concerns may apply to a charity: those appealing for funds to help allevi-ate distressing problems around the world may be tempted to make use of shocking real-life images of the situations that they encounter. Being aware of the ever-present risk of 'compassion fatigue' on the part of donors, as well as the possibility of causing unwarranted distress to some recipients of the message, most charity fund-raising com-munications remain within limits of taste and decency for what are likely to be purely prudential reasons.

Public service organisations can also consider the use of shocking imagery to communicate important messages.

Public service organisations can also consider the use of shocking imagery to communicate important messages: adverts against drinking and driving have for many years been deliberately hard-hitting, for reasons that most would accept as justifiable. In 2004, London's Metropolitan Police published a series of very shocking photographs on posters, beer mats and nightclub flyers.[1] The images showed the physical decline over several years of real-life drug addicts, in the hope of deterring young people from choosing to go down the same road.

[1] Source: BBC News Web site (http://news.bbc.co.uk); accessed 12 November 2004.

Hospitality, incentives, inducements, and bribery and extortion

The ethical questions surrounding the payment of bribes in business feature prominently in most textbooks on business ethics. These difficult issues need to be mentioned here both because they are important and because they may well involve sales staff. Bribes are unofficial – and usually illegal – payments to individuals 'to procure services or gain influence' (*Collins Concise English Dictionary*). These payments may be to secure orders, for example, or to expedite deliveries.

Distinguishing between bribery and extortion

It is useful to draw a distinction between extortion and bribery: the former is demanded by the would-be receiver, while the latter is offered by the individual or organisation wishing to buy the influence. In a situation in which informal payments of this nature are thought to be commonplace, a company's decision to go along with extortion is ethically different from a decision to offer a bribe. But in either case, the familiar distinction between short-term and long-term benefits is important.

Difficult choices

The ethical company will need to take account of the effects on its image and wider relationships of taking part in bribery or extortion: these illegal practices have harmful effects on local economies and are likely to be regarded negatively by most stakeholders. The normal conduct of business relies heavily upon trust and the rule of law, both of which are undeniably jeopardised by corruption.

For Sternberg (2000), offering a bribe is an attempt to cheat and a violation of ordinary decency, while taking a bribe is a violation of distributive justice: decisions are made because of the bribe, rather than the relevant merits of the business offering. These are difficult questions in practice, which may involve hard choices, including the choice of whether to take part in markets in which corruption is endemic. Dunfee *et al.* (1999) examine the question of bribery in some detail from a social contract theory point of view (based upon a multilayered analysis of what affected parties and society might agree to), arguing that acceptability can only be judged by such a broad analysis.

Corporate hospitality: what are the limits?

Far less serious than actual bribery, but arguably on the same continuum, is the question of the scale of entertainment and hospitality that should be provided by the selling organisation to the buying organisation. It is entirely natural for a company to seek to build up closer relationships with its major customers, and corporate hospitality would normally be seen as an entirely legitimate part of this process. Even here, however, sales staff may be conscious of 'grey areas', in which the lavishness of the hospitality or gift-giving may seem to be out of proportion to the purpose of building a business relationship. Many companies recognise this potential hazard by providing guidelines to staff on what is to be regarded as acceptable in taking and offering corporate hospitality. Those guidelines will naturally take account of normal practice within the industry and may well differ from one industry to another and – within any given industry – from one period to another.

Again, however, the appropriate judgement about corporate entertainment is likely to be the one that maximises the company's long-term interests, within the limits of common decency and distributive justice. Hospitality expenditure, like any other business expense, needs to be assessed in terms of its intended purpose and in the context of the long-term aims of the business. At one extreme, to ban all corporate entertainment would damage a firm's commercial relationships and hence its interests in most situations; at the other end of the scale, however, a different type of damage to the firm's long-term interests would be caused by practising over-lavish hospitality.

Ethical influence of supervisory and reward systems in sales management

The previous section mentioned the beneficial role that company codes can play in promoting and facilitating ethical decision-making on the part of sales and other staff. It is also worth highlighting that the management framework itself can also exert a powerful positive or negative influence on the ethical decision-making environment. Sales recruitment, training and briefing systems, for example, can be designed to encourage ethical behaviours on the part of sales staff, but equally may (e.g. through neglect) provide an uncertain context for individual employees, in which inexperienced or opportunistic staff may start to take decisions that are against the long-term interest of the company.

Fostering ethical behaviour by the sales force

The same is true, of course, of the approach taken to sales motivation and reward: a sales targeting and reward system that has been designed without due consideration of the long-term reputation of the company may have the effect of encouraging and rewarding some highly damaging behaviours on the part of staff, especially in the run-up to year-end with everyone under pressure to meet targets. Ethical companies design sales motivation and reward systems that encourage sales behaviour which maximises the long-term company interest. In an empirical study in this area, Hunt and Vasquez-Parraga (1993) found that sales managers did consider both the behaviours of sales staff and the consequences of those behaviours: unethical behaviour was likely to be more severely disciplined, for example, if the consequences were negative for the organisation. The authors suggest that:

Ethical companies design sales motivation and reward systems that encourage sales behaviour which maximises the long-term company interest.

> A culture emphasising ethical values may be best developed and maintained by having sales people and their supervisors internalising a set of [duty-based] norms proscribing a set of behaviours that are inappropriate, 'just not done', and prescribing a set of behaviours that are appropriate, 'this is the way we do things'. In both cases, sales people and their supervisors should know that when ethical issues are involved, rewards (or punishments) flow from following (or violating) the [duty-based] norms, not from organisationally desirable or undesirable outcomes.
>
> (Hunt and Vasquez-Parraga, 1993, p. 87)

This suggestion, with its emphasis on duties for salespeople, rather than consequences, may at first sight seem to be at odds with Sternberg's (2000) general recommendation that a business should take that course of action which is consistent with maximising long-term owner value within the constraints of common decency and distributive justice. There is, however, no necessary contradiction: the recommended sales management framework may well be the best way for the firm to maximise long-term owner value, reflecting, for example, the difficulty that individual salespeople may have in judging the long-term interests of the firm reliably. It will also be very helpful to create a culture in which individual salespeople feel able to report unexpected difficulties that they encounter in applying the ethical code of practice as they understand it, either because the code seems inappropriate or because a new type of problem has arisen. In this way, a company can help to ensure that its good intentions concerning ethical behaviour are realised in practice.

Ethical decision-making models in marketing

A number of contributions to the literature have proposed models to facilitate ethical decision-making in business in general and in marketing in particular. In looking at these models, we necessarily stray beyond the specific topic of this chapter: the models offer approaches to decision-making that are certainly applicable to marketing communications, but can also be applied more widely in business affairs.

Chonko (1995) characterises the ethical decision-making process in marketing as comprising:

● the ethical situation itself (e.g. the opportunity, or scope for action, the ethical decision history and the moral intensity of the situation);

● characteristics of the decision-maker (for example, knowledge, experience, achievement, motivation, need for affiliation);

● significant influences (e.g. the organisation, the law, economics, technology);

● the decision itself;

● the outcomes of the decision (e.g. in terms of performance, rewards, satisfaction, feedback).

From a different point of view, Smith (1995) suggests that marketing ethics can be seen as depending upon the prevailing outlook, ranging along a continuum from *caveat emptor* (let the buyer beware) at one end, moving through intermediate points of industry standards, ethics codes and consumer sovereignty to the position of *caveat venditor* (let the seller beware). In his view, ethics in marketing has for some time been moving away from the simple *caveat emptor* position towards the position of consumer sovereignty. He proposes a consumer sovereignty test for companies to apply:

● *Consumer capability:* is the target market vulnerable in ways that limit consumer decision-making?

● *Information:* are consumer expectations at purchase likely to be realised? Do consumers have sufficient information to judge?

● *Choice:* can consumers go elsewhere? Would they incur substantial costs or inconvenience in transferring their loyalty?

The answers to these test questions in any situation will help the firm to realise what actions it needs to take in order to behave ethically.

Laczniak and Murphy (1991) also list some rules of thumb for marketers facing what appears to be an ethical dilemma:

- The *golden rule* – act in a way that you would expect others to act towards you.

- The *professional ethic* – take only actions that would be viewed as proper by an objective panel of your professional colleagues.

- Kant's *categorical imperative* – act in a way such that the action taken under the circumstances could be a universal law of behaviour for everyone facing those same circumstances.

- The *TV test* – a manager should always ask, would I feel comfortable explaining this action on TV to the general public?

- The *outcomes of the decision* (e.g. in terms of performance, rewards, satisfaction, feedback).

Laczniak and Murphy also propose a set of questions for marketers to help to analyse an issue in ethical terms. The questions cover issues of law, moral obligations, consequences and intent. As they point out, exploring the sometimes conflicting answers to these questions is likely to enhance the moral reasoning capabilities of managers, which – in parallel with company and other codes of ethics – is likely to result in better ethical decisions.

In these decision models, the literature provides a checklist of questions or characteristics that aim to help a firm think its way through ethical issues. As should be clear, the answers to the questions are very much up to the judgement made by the managers involved in the process.

Regulating marketing communications

As discussed above, advertising and other forms of marketing communications have the potential to offend, mislead or cause distress. An important question in this area is what – if anything – should be done to lessen this potential harm. This question has a range of possible answers, ranging from minimal or non-existent controls to extensive and detailed statutory regulation. At one end of this scale, the libertarian view of the world places ethical priority on the freedom of individuals to choose how to behave (provided that they do not unacceptably compromise the liberty of others). A libertarian argument might assert that the 'off' switch provides all of the control of TV advertising content that is needed. Individuals and groups with different views of what is acceptable or desirable must learn to tolerate each other. A libertarian would also view with caution any proposal to allow governmental control of advertising content. As has already been suggested, companies that create and publish offensive advertising are running some risk of material loss, since those who are offended may choose to buy from a less offensive competitor instead. However, a completely libertarian stance would be unsatisfactory for many: rightly or wrongly, governments are generally expected to involve themselves in a wide range of choices in everyday life – what we eat and drink, what we view and so on. In the case of marketing communications, there are a number of reasons why the self-interest of advertisers and of consumers may not be a completely reliable guarantor of harm-free content:

- Not all advertisers have competitors.

- Marketing communications may offend or harm those who are not customers of the advertiser and who therefore cannot respond by buying elsewhere.

- Whether the effect is experienced by customers or third parties, the offence caused in a particular case may be so profound and lasting as to outweigh any conceivable benefit.

- Some businesses may have little interest in the longer-term effects of their marketing communications messages, if – for example – they only plan to take part in a market for a short time and then withdraw.

- Advertisers may fail to forecast the effects of their choices properly and so cause inadvertent harm or offence.

Concerns such as these underlie the case for some form of regulation – the idea that society will be better served by regulating marketing communications than by a free-for-all. This is essentially a utilitarian ethical perspective, arguing that the greatest good of the greatest number is achieved by a system of regulation, despite the cost to some forms of individual liberty. Regulation could be statutory (based upon laws) or voluntary, based upon codes and processes run by the marketing industry. Usually, a country's regulation of marketing communications will involve elements of both types, with an emphasis on self-regulation for most of the day-to-day questions. As Harker (1998) suggests, following a review of approaches to regulation in five countries, the legal and voluntary approaches can complement each other very well: an effective combined approach seems more likely to result in acceptable advertising for the society concerned.

> **The legal and voluntary approaches can complement each other very well: an effective combined approach seems more likely to result in acceptable advertising for the society concerned.**

Self-regulation in practice

In the UK, a range of specialised codes have been developed to provide guidance on the production of acceptable marketing communications in particular circumstances. The website of the Advertising Standards Authority (ASA) (http://www.asa.org.uk) provides access to full-text versions of these codes. The ASA's main code for non-broadcast advertising (the Code of Advertising, Sales Promotion and Direct Marketing, published by the Committee of Advertising Practice) begins with a set of general principles. The first two in particular set the tone for the whole code:

- *All marketing communications should be legal, decent, honest and truthful.*

- *All marketing communications should be prepared with a sense of responsibility to consumers and to society*
  (ASA Code of Advertising, Sales Promotion and Direct Marketing (2003, p. 6.)

Notably, political advertising is exempt from this Code (section 12.1), although government communications are bound by it. The general rules of the Code discuss the requirements of legality, decency, honesty and truthfulness in more detail and also provide guidance on, for example, the protection of privacy, the use of testimonials and endorsements, on competitor comparisons and product availability.

Later sections of the main Code focus on sales promotion (sections 27 to 40) and direct marketing (sections 41 to 45), with guidance on specific issues such as free offers and free trials (section 32) and the increasingly important area of database practice (section 43). The Code also offers detailed guidance on specific marketing communications contexts, such as:

- alcoholic drinks
- children
- motoring
- health and beauty products and therapies
- weight control
- financial products
- tobacco.

This 37-page document has been developed by representatives of the advertising world over many years. Besides the advice and guidance, it defines the processes through which advertisers should comply with the Code and the sanctions that can be applied. Although very detailed, its text is characterised by clarity and a strong practical emphasis: after all, a key aim of the Code is to help those in the industry to produce 'marketing communications that are welcomed and trusted' (p. 3).

Since the broadening of its responsibilities in 2004 (see main text), the ASA also now maintains a range of Codes on broadcast advertising:

- The Radio Advertising Standards Code
- The TV Advertising Standards Code
- The Alcohol Advertising Rules
- Advertising Guidance Notes (concerning, for example, the identification of programmes likely to appeal to children and young people)
- Rules on the Scheduling of Advertising
- Code for Text Services
- Guidance on Interactive TV.

As can be seen from this list, the self-regulatory regime is having to encompass the technology-fuelled proliferation of broadcast entertainment and information services. Keeping up to date with this rapid development, as well as remaining sensitive to changes in public sensitivity or taste is a major challenge for any organisation and the ASA's library of advertising codes can be expected to continue to evolve in future.

In the United Kingdom, a major change to the regulation of marketing communications was introduced from November 2004. The main thrust of the reform was to introduce a 'one-stop shop' for consumer complaints, with the Advertising Standards Authority taking responsibility for advertising content regulation in both broadcast and non-broadcast advertising (the former by delegation from Ofcom, the general regulator for the communications industry and the latter by continuance of the ASA's former role). For this purpose the ASA, which will continue to be funded by levies from advertising, will administer a set of codes of advertising practice for the various types of advertising (see www.asa.org.uk for further details). The new system is aimed at providing clearer arrangements for consumers, as well as a better and more consistent structure for dealing with the much more diverse range of communications media that has developed in recent years. Although Ofcom retains backstop powers over the new arrangements for broadcast advertising, the system remains effectively self-regulatory[2] in approach, building on the ASA's four decades of experience as the regulator of non-broadcast advertising content.

Ethics and marketers

In closing this chapter, it is perhaps worth highlighting some of the research that has been conducted into the ethical behaviour of real-life marketing people. As Goolsby and Hunt (1992) point out, marketing as a function is often linked in the public mind with ethical abuse, mainly because of the way marketing operates at the boundary between the firm and its customers. In their study, however, the authors found that marketing people (and especially marketing women) compared favourably with those from other functions in terms of cognitive moral development (broadly, an individual's capacity for independent moral reasoning).

Singhapakdi *et al.* (1995) concluded from a survey of US marketing professionals that marketers seem to believe that ethics and social responsibility are important components of organisational effectiveness. The survey also partly indicated that ethical corporate values seem to sensitise marketers to the need to include ethics and social responsibility in marketing decisions. This view is supported by Creyer and Ross (1997), who found that many consumers do take a company's ethics into account in making purchase decisions and that they may pay a higher price to a firm whose behaviour they approve of. Clear, readily accessible and credible information about corporate behaviour is an essential element in this relationship.

These findings would seem to indicate that there may be a positive reception within the marketing profession for Thompson's (1995) suggestion:

> *For marketers, adopting a more caring orientation offers an opportunity to become ethical innovators within their organisation. In most firms, those in marketing positions are closest to consumers, in terms of direct interaction and knowledge of their lifestyles. One role for marketers would be to regard themselves as more explicit advocates of consumer interests – both immediate and long term.*

(p. 188)

This general proposal about the role of marketing in general has special relevance for the activities of marketing communications.

[2] Strictly speaking, the new system is co-, rather than self-regulatory, in that Ofcom, with its statutory powers, has delegated the responsibility for maintaining and applying codes of practice approved by the regulator (see www.ofcom.org.uk).

Summary

This chapter has provided a brief introduction to the main ideas in business ethics and looked at some of the implications of these ideas for the practice of marketing communications. Just as there are no special ethical rules for business in general, ethics in marketing communications is a matter of applying normal ethical principles to the practice of marketing communications. Some of the difficulties in business of deciding between general ethical systems based upon duties and those based upon consequences may be avoided by taking a teleological or purpose-based approach, seeking to identify actions that will have the effect of maximising the long-term interest of the firm and its owners, remaining always within the important constraints of common decency and distributive justice. Done properly, this approach obliges managers to take an intelligent and enlightened view of the likely consequences of their actions on others.

It is sometimes argued that practices such as advertising are inherently undesirable: powerful means of manipulation, with destructive consequences. This chapter, however, has taken the view that ethics in marketing communications need to be considered in the context of a market economy, meaning that advertising, selling and so on are activities which are in themselves ethically neutral, but can be carried out in ethical or unethical ways. Applying the teleological approach helps to resolve many problems in marketing communications, including those to do with truth-telling, behaviour towards vulnerable groups, privacy and respect for persons, taste and decency, inducements and approaches to sales supervision and reward.

Regulation of marketing communications content is also an important aspect of ethical decision-making: regulation may be statutory, imposed by a government, or voluntary, coordinated by the industry. Advertising regulation in most countries contains elements of both.

Marketing communications managers, with their special responsibility for the dialogue between the firm and the outside world, have every reason to take business ethics seriously (and generally, in fact, seem to do so) and may well have the opportunity to play an influential role in this respect within the firm as a whole.

Review questions

1. What are the practical problems of adopting a simple duties-based or consequences-based approach to ethics in marketing communications?

2. Explain why a practical approach to ethical business has to be based upon a clear idea of the purpose of a business.

3. What are the limitations, if any, of the principle *caveat emptor* (let the buyer beware) as a guide to ethics in personal selling?

4. What guiding principles can help a company to decide about the proposed use of a shocking image in its advertising?

5. Why is it both difficult and important for a company to take account of individual privacy in designing and implementing its marketing communications?

6. What ethical lessons for marketing communications managers in financial services companies should be learned from the private pensions scandal in the UK in the 1980s?

7. What is the difference between lying, misrepresentation and puffery in advertising? What tests should an advertiser apply to avoid misrepresentation?

8. What evidence would help to differentiate between legitimate corporate hospitality and unethical inducements, such as bribery?

9. Describe, with examples, the way in which Smith's consumer sovereignty test can help a company to design ethical marketing communications.

10. Explain the benefits of the new one-stop shop arrangements for advertising complaints handling in the UK from November 2004.

MINI-CASE
Pure and Simple Fashions

It was late in the evening and marketing director Jane Carson was reflecting on how quickly difficult situations seemed to develop in the business environment of the twenty-first century. It was only last month that she had organised a very successful launch of the new season's designs, coupled with a launch of her company's new interactive Web site, which would allow customers to order online. Recent events, however, had demonstrated that modern communications media could just as effectively carry bad news.

Pure and Simple Fashions (PSF) was a familiar retail brand on the high street, providing mid-priced fashions aimed at younger women. From its launch ten years earlier, its competitive positioning had also been pure and simple, as reflected in its advertising line: 'Fashion that doesn't cost the earth'. Pure and Simple clothes were made from natural fibres, grown organically and processed in ways that supported the environmental notion of 'sustainability': working with natural resources without reducing the future availability of those resources. This idea – coupled with some inspired and widely praised innovative designs – had connected very effectively with PSF's target segment and the organisation had built up a loyal following over the years. Indeed PSF's positioning seemed to appeal just as strongly to the new generation of young women customers as to the organisation's original clients, many of whom had stayed with PSF. The company had grown steadily, with retail outlets in most UK cities and large towns, and an enviable profit growth record, based upon its well-established positioning. This business develop-

ment had been supported by extensive and very popular press and poster advertising, based upon appealing natural images from ecosystems around the world. Two years ago, PSF had initiated an expansion into continental Europe, based upon franchised outlets in a growing number of major cities. This had now been complemented by the introduction of an interactive Web site, whose design had been nominated for a national award for ease of access and use. Customers could view the ranges in three dimensions, match colours and order clothes manufactured to exactly their own sizes. The new distribution channel was underpinned by extensive customer relationship management software, which PSF hoped would enable it to build a closer relationship with its individual customers, as well as providing the basis for increasing growth into international markets.

The current crisis for PSF had its roots in a TV documentary programme broadcast two weeks earlier. The documentary had set out to investigate what some saw as the negative effects of increasing globalisation. The agenda was a familiar one, focusing on the enormous economic power wielded by very large multinational corporations in smaller developing countries. Part of the programme had focused on working conditions in factories in developing countries, showing the manufacture of branded clothing and other products for world markets. Pure and Simple was one of many well-known brands mentioned in this part of the programme, in a sequence that also contrasted bright and appealing advertising images from Europe with distressing views of unpleasant and oppressive working environments and interviews with employees about their experiences. No specific allegations about PSF or any other brand were made in the programme, although allusions were made to earlier, well-documented allegations about the use of child labour by some manufacturers. Street interviews with shoppers in London were used to suggest a disparity between the promoted image of branded goods and the reality of life for those who made them.

In the days following the broadcast of the programme, newspapers and magazines took up the themes of the programme, resulting in a flood of letters from readers: it was clear that the programme had – at least at an emotional level – been very effective. Soon, PSF branch managers began to report increasing numbers of hostile questions from customers about the company's sourcing policy; the levels of telephone and email enquiries into PSF's headquarters confirmed this development. The problem had escalated to a new level with the threat from a previously little-known anti-capitalist lobbying group to 'jam' the communications of a number of brand-owning organisations, including PSF, by flooding their Web sites with vast amounts of communications traffic. The experiences of other organisations in the recent past had shown that threats of this nature needed to be taken seriously: the effect for PSF at the beginning of the present season could be disastrous, particularly given the strength and clear focus of its present environmentalist positioning.

Although Pure and Simple had never made any public statement about its policy concerning the manufacture of its products, Jane Carson knew that PSF had always insisted that working conditions in its suppliers were in line with – and in many cases significantly better than – local 'best practice', although of course actual wage rates were low by European standards. Objectively, PSF could argue strongly that its suppliers maintained high standards and that its participation in developing countries was of clear benefit to those economies. However, the present public debate was not being conducted objectively and Jane wondered how to regain the initiative. What seemed to be happening was that those customers who had been attracted to Pure and Simple because of its environmental commitment were those who were expressing the greatest concern about the issues raised by the TV programme. For some time it had been possible to see the growing links between previously disparate specialist lobbying organisations, together with the increasing interest on the part of affluent and well-educated customers in the values embodied in the brands they chose. Had Pure and Simple sat on its environmental laurels in recent years and been caught napping by these new developments? Or was it PSF's very strong public image and accessibility that rendered it vulnerable to these protests, whatever the reality of its case? The textbook injunction to 'balance stakeholder interests' seemed to be particularly problematic this evening, as Jane worked on her company's response.

Note: this case is wholly imaginary; no reference is intended to actual organisations or people.

Questions

1 What ethical issues for Pure and Simple Fashions arise in this case?

2 How would an evaluation of these ethical issues based on broad stakeholder theory differ from one based on Sternberg's teleological perspective?

3 Outline a possible marketing communications strategy for PSF that will allow it to respond to its current difficulties and continue its successful and profitable growth as a fashion retailer.

4 What lessons might PSF learn concerning the management of its relationship with its various stakeholders?

References

American Marketing Association (n.d.) Code of ethics. http://www.ama.org/. Accessed 1 March 2001.

Attas, D. (1999) What's wrong with deceptive advertising? *Journal of Business Ethics*, **21**, pp. 49–59.

Barton, L. (1994) A quagmire of ethics, profit and the public trust: the crisis in public relations services. *Journal of Professional Services Marketing*, **11**(1), pp. 87–99.

Borgerson, J.L. and Schroeder, J. (2002) Ethical issues of global marketing: avoiding bad faith in visual representation. *European Journal of Marketing*, **36**(5–6), pp. 570–94.

Botan, C. (1997) Ethics in strategic communication campaigns: the case for a new approach to public relations. *Journal of Business Communication*, **34**(2), pp. 188–202.

Carrigan, M. and Szmigin, I. (2003) Regulating ageism in UK advertising: an industry perspective. *Marketing Intelligence and Planning*, **21**(4), pp. 198–204.

Chonko, L.B. (1995) *Ethical Decisions in Marketing*. Thousand Oaks, CA: Sage.

Christy, R and Mitchell, S.M. (1999) Direct marketing and privacy. *Journal of Targeting, Measurement and Analysis for Marketing*, **8**(1), pp. 8–20.

Creyer, E.H. and Ross, W.T. (1997) The influence of firm behaviour on purchase intention: do consumers really care about business ethics? *Journal of Consumer Marketing*, **14**(6), pp. 421–33.

De George, R.T. (1999) *Business Ethics*. 5th edn. Englewood Cliffs, NJ: Prentice-Hall.

Diacon, S.R. and Ennew, C.T. (1996) Ethical issues in insurance marketing in the UK. *European Journal of Marketing*, **30**(5), pp. 67–80.

Dunfee, T.W., Smith, N.C. and Ross, W.T. (1999) Social contracts and marketing ethics. *Journal of Marketing*, **63**(3), pp. 14–32.

Friedman, M. (1970) The social responsibility of business is to increase its profits. *New York Times Magazine*, 13 September, pp. 32 *et seq.*

Goolsby, J.R. and Hunt, S.D. (1992) Cognitive moral development and marketing. *Journal of Marketing*, **56** (January), pp. 55–68.

Gundlach, G.T. and Murphy, P.E. (1993) Ethical and legal foundations of relational marketing exchanges. *Journal of Marketing*, **57** (October), pp. 35–46.

Harker, D. (1998) Achieving acceptable advertising. An analysis of advertising regulation in five countries. *International Marketing Review*, **15**(2), pp. 101–18.

Holbrook, M.B. (1987) Mirror, mirror, on the wall, what's unfair in the reflections on advertising? *Journal of Marketing*, **51** (July), pp. 95–103.

Hunt, S.D. and Vasquez-Parraga, A.Z. (1993) Organisational consequences, marketing ethics and salesforce supervision. *Journal of Marketing Research* (February), pp. 78–90.

Jackson, J.C. (1996) *An Introduction to Business Ethics*. Oxford: Blackwell.

Klein, N. (2000) *No Logo*. London: Flamingo.

Laczniak, G.R. and Murphy, P.E. (1991) Fostering ethical marketing decisions. *Journal of Business Ethics*, **10**, pp. 259–71.

Murphy, P.E. (1999) Character and virtue ethics in international marketing: an agenda for managers, researchers and educators. *Journal of Business Ethics*, **18**, pp. 107–24.

Ogilvy, D. (1963) *Confessions of an Advertising Man*. London: Longman.

Packard, V. (1960) *The Hidden Persuaders*. Harmondsworth: Penguin.

Pollay, R.W. (1986) The distorted mirror: reflections on the unintended consequences of advertising. *Journal of Marketing*, **50** (April), pp. 18–36.

Robin, D.P. and Reidenbach, R.E. (1993) Searching for a place to stand: toward a workable ethical philosophy for marketing. *Journal of Public Policy and Marketing*, **12**(1), pp. 97–105.

Schlegelmilch, B. (1998) *Marketing Ethics: An International Perspective*. London: International Thomson Business Press.

Singhapakdi, A., Kraff, K.L., Vitell, S.J. and Rallapalli, K.C. (1995) The perceived importance of ethics and social responsibility on organisational effectiveness: a survey of marketing. *Journal of the Academy of Marketing Science*, **23**(1), pp. 49–56.

Smith, N.C. (1995) Marketing strategies for the ethics era. *Sloan Management Review* (Summer), pp. 85–97.

Sorell, T. and Hendry, J. (1994) *Business Ethics*. Oxford: Butterworth Heinemann.

Sternberg, E. (2000) *Just Business*. 2nd edn. Oxford: Oxford University Press.

Thompson, C.J. (1995) A contextualist proposal for the conceptualization and study of marketing ethics. *Journal of Public Policy and Marketing*, **14**(2), pp. 177–91.

Tsalikis, J. and Fritzsche, D.J. (1989) Business ethics: a literature review with a focus on marketing ethics. *Journal of Business Ethics*, **8**, pp. 695–743.

Understanding how marketing communications works

Chapters 5-10

The theme of this part of the book is the contextual aspects of marketing communications.

Chapters 5 and 6 explore fundamental issues concerning information processing and buyer behaviour, important elements if marketing communication messages are to be effective. Chapter 7 develops ideas about how marketing communications might work and traces some important models and concepts that are reflected in other parts of this book.

Chapter 8 examines the potential impact of an organisation's different stakeholders and the interrelationships that organisations form with them. Chapters 9 and 10 are new to this edition and develop this theme a stage further. Chapter 9 explores the nature and characteristics of relationships and then reviews the impact marketing communications can have on relationship marketing and its development. The final chapter in this part examines new technology and the way in which digital technology in particular can assist marketing communications.

Part

2

Understanding how marketing communications works

Chapters 3–10

The theme of this part of the book is the conceptual aspects of marketing communications.

Understanding how customers process information

5

Understanding the way in which customers perceive their world, the way they learn, develop attitudes and respond to marketing communication stimuli is fundamental if effective communications are to be developed.

Aims and objectives

The aim of this chapter is to provide an introduction to the main elements of buyer information processing, in order that readers develop an appreciation of the way marketing communications can be built on an understanding of buyer behaviour.

The objectives of this chapter are to:

1. introduce cognitive theory as an important element in the development of planned communications;
2. examine personality as a main factor in the determination of successful communications;
3. explore perception in the context of marketing communications;
4. understand the main differences between conditioning and cognitive learning processes;
5. appraise the role of attitudes and the different ways in which attitudes are thought to be developed;
6. appreciate the importance of understanding an individual's intention to act in a particular way and its part in the decision process;

7. understand how marketing communications can be used to influence these elements of buyer behaviour and in particular to change attitudes;

8. provide a brief overview of the other environmental influences that affect the manner in which individuals process information.

Introduction

This chapter will explore the elements that influence the information-processing behaviour of two different types of buyer: consumers and organisational buyers. It will then establish how the identification of different behaviour patterns can influence marketing communications.

Marketing is about many things, but one of its central themes is the management of behaviour. This behaviour may be seen in the context of an exchange, in which case actions prior to, during and after a purchase will be important. In a relationship context, it is the series of behaviours manifest at the beginning, in the middle and during the decline and termination of a relationship that will be pertinent. Whichever per-

> It makes sense to underpin marketing activities with an understanding of buyer behaviour.

spective is adopted, it makes sense to underpin marketing activities with an understanding of buyer behaviour, in order that marketing strategies and communication plans in particular be more effective. It is not the intention to provide a deep or comprehensive analysis of buyer behaviour, since there are many specialist texts to which readers can refer (Solomon *et al.*, 2001; or Neal *et al.*, 2003.) However, a basic understanding of the context in which buyers process information, the way they behave, their decision-making processes and the ways in which such knowledge can be utilised in promotional plans is important and is the focus of this chapter.

There are a number of theoretical approaches that have been developed to assist our understanding of human behaviour, but the majority have their roots in one of three psychological orientations. These three (Freud's psychoanalytical theory, reinforcement theory and cognitive theory) can be seen to have influenced thinking about buyer behaviour over the last 50 years. See Table 5.1. This book will explore cognitive theory in the context of marketing communications.

Cognitive theory

> The emphasis in understanding and interpreting consumer behaviour has progressed from a reinforcement to a cognitive approach.

Mainstream psychology has moved from a behavourist to a cognitive orientation. Similarly, the emphasis in understanding and interpreting consumer behaviour has progressed from a reinforcement to a cognitive approach.

Cognitive theory is based upon an information-processing, problem-solving and reasoning approach to human behaviour. Individuals use information that has been generated by external sources (e.g. advertisements) and internal sources (e.g. memory). This information is given thought, processed, transferred into meanings or patterns and then combined to form judgements about behaviour (based on Rumelhart in Belk, 1975).

TABLE 5.1 Summary of three main psychological orientations

Theoretical approach	Explanation
Psychoanalytical theory	First developed by Freud, this approach is based on the way an individual develops over time within the context of a family and their interactions with mother and father and later with their siblings. Freud was the first to think in this way and to consider the unconscious as an important influence on behaviour. These are now referred to as psychodynamic theories and they hold that human behaviour is primarily the function of reactions to internal (thus mostly unconscious) stimuli: instincts, urges, thoughts.
Reinforcement theory	People behave in the knowledge of what will happen as a result of their behaviour. Therefore, behaviour is dependent upon the expected outcomes or consequences: Rules of Consequences. The three Rules describe the logical outcomes that typically occur after consequences: 1 Consequences that lead to Rewards increase a behaviour. 2 Consequences that lead to Punishments decrease a behaviour. 3 Consequences that lead to neither Rewards nor Punishments extinguish a behaviour.
Cognitive theory	Assumes individuals use and process information derived from external and internal sources, to solve problems and make considered decisions. See text below. Social cognitive theory considers the interaction of an individual's environment, behaviour and various personal factors such as cognitive, affective and biological events.

The cognitive orientation considers the consumer to be an adaptive problem solver, one who uses various processes in reasoning, forming concepts and acquiring knowledge. There are several determinants that are important to our understanding of the cognitive orientation because they contribute to the way in which individuals process information. These are personality, perception, learning, attitudes, certain environmental influences and issues pertinent to an individual's purchase situation (Figure 5.1). Each of these will now be considered.

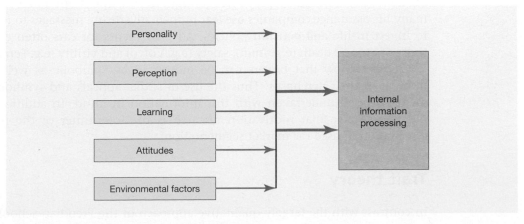

FIGURE 5.1 Elements of information processing

Personality

Personality is, essentially, concerned with the inner properties of each individual, those characteristics that differentiate each of us. Consideration is given to two main approaches: the Freudian and trait theories of personality.

Psychoanalytic theory

Freud believed that the needs which motivate human behaviour are driven by two primary instincts: life and death. The life instincts are considered to be predominantly sexual in nature, whereas the death instincts are believed to be manifested through self-destructive and/or aggressive behaviour.

The personality of the individual is assumed to have developed in an attempt to gratify these needs, and consists of the id, superego and ego; this approach is termed psychoanalytic theory. The id is the repository for all basic drives and motivations. Its function is to seek pleasure through the discharge of tension. The superego acts to restrain the id, to inhibit the impulses of the pleasure-seeking component, partly by acting within the rules of society. These two are obviously in conflict, which the ego attempts to mediate by channelling the drives of the id into behaviour acceptable to the superego.

The id is the repository for all basic drives and motivations. Its function is to seek pleasure through the discharge of tension.

The application of psychoanalytic theory to buyer behaviour suggests that many of the motives for purchase are driven by deeply rooted sexual drives and/or death instincts. These can only be determined by probing the subconscious, as in work undertaken by motivation researchers, the first of whom were Dichter and Vicary. Motivation research attempts to discover the underlying motivations for consumer behaviour. A variety of techniques have been developed, including in-depth interviews, projective techniques, association tests and focus groups.

Motivation research attempts to discover the underlying motivations for consumer behaviour.

Psychoanalytic theory has been criticised as too vague, unresponsive to the environment and too reliant on the early development of the individual. Furthermore, because the samples used are very often small and because of the emphasis on the unconscious, verification and substantiation of the results of experiments are often difficult – and some say impossible.

However, the psychoanalytic approach has been used as the basis for many advertising messages, aimed at deeply rooted feelings, hopes, aspirations and fears. For example, many life assurance companies use fear in their advertising messages to motivate people to invest in life and pension policies. Advertisements for cars often depict symbols: those of life and death (e.g. Audi), safety (e.g. Volvo) and virility (e.g. Ferrari or Porsche).

We also know that buyers can be motivated by symbolic as well as functional motives in their purchases. Thus the use of sexual appeals and symbols in advertisements is often undertaken with this information in mind. In addition, many commentators agree that motivation research is the forerunner of the psychographics research often used for market segmentation.

Trait theory

In contrast with the largely qualitative approach of the Freudian school is the empirical perspective. Under this approach, personality is measured and quantified. What is being measured are the traits or 'distinguishing, relatively enduring ways in which one individual differs from another' (Guildford, 1959). Personality tests invariably seek to measure individual differences in respect of specific traits. The end result is a label that is applied to the particular traits observed in the individuals being tested. These labels, for example, consider aspects such as the degree of assertiveness, responsiveness to change or the level of sociability an individual might exhibit.

Of specific interest to marketing communicators is the relationship between broad personality traits and general styles of behaviour. Consumer psychologists, working on behalf of advertising agencies in particular, have spent a great deal of time trying to identify specific traits and then developing consumer profiles that enable a distinct market segment to be determined. The 4Cs was one such programme, developed by Young and Rubicam in the late 1980s. Four distinct types of consumer were identified: aspirers, succeeders, mainstreamers and reformers, each of whom have particular psychographic characteristics.

Mainstreamers are motivated by a basic need for security and belonging. To satisfy that drive, they tend to buy established products and manufacturers' brands, as they perceive purchase risk to be lower. Aspirers seek status and self-esteem and this is directed through identification with materialism. Aspirers are able to express themselves through the possession of goods, which act as symbols of achievement, such as the latest hi-fi or designer clothes. Succeeders are people who are successful but who need to control the events in their lives. Typically they read the *Financial Times* or the *Daily Telegraph* and consume products that have proven quality. Reformers are the antithesis of the aspirers, in that they seek self-fulfilment rather than status. Own brands and natural products are sought by them, as it is the quality of life that is their underlying motivation (*QED*, 1989).

By combining the qualitative approach of the motivational researchers with the quantitative approach of the trait theorists, psychographic variables can be determined. Over the last 20 years this has developed into a popular segmentation technique, called psychographics.

ViewPoint 5.1   Spirito di Punto – Fiat personality

The brand advertising used to support the launch of Fiat's Punto into the UK car market was influenced partly by a previous pan-European campaign and partly by its positioning and understanding of its target market.

When a new car is launched there is usually a six-month window in which the latest technology remains unique to the car. This credibility window needs to be exploited. However, a bland, informationally based ad rarely works in this market so a couple, representative of the target market, was chosen to reflect the Fiat brand personality and values.

The campaign used two ads: the first depicted a male driver making disparaging (tongue-in-cheek) comments about how women might utilise several of the car's attributes. This ran for four or five days with the expectation of building a certain level of indignation, especially among women drivers. Then the second ad was released, which depicted a woman driver making similar derogatory comments about men, in the context of the car's attributes. The aspirational couple were chosen because they embodied the personality of Fiat and associated Italian values. He represented fun and cheekiness and she a Latin, independent feistiness.

The ads were tracked on a standard car industry-wide study that measures against awareness (recognition of the ad), branding (understanding of the brand manufacturer name) and overall likeability (did I like it?) indices. It rated so highly that the Spirito di Punto won the best car ad for 1999. See Exhibits 5.1 and 5.2.

Source: Material and photographs kindly supplied by D'arcy.

EXHIBITS 5.1 AND 5.2 Spirito di Punto
Fiat brand values and aspects of Italian personality were projected through a series of ads designed to portray aspects of the target market male and female values. Pictures reproduced with the kind permission of Fiat.

Perception

Perception is concerned with how individuals see and make sense of their environment. It is about the selection, organisation and interpretation of stimuli by individuals so that they can understand the world.

Individuals are exposed, each day, to a tremendous number of stimuli. De Chernatony (1993) suggested that each consumer is exposed to over 550 advertisements per day, while Lasn (1999) estimated that this should be 3,000 advertisements per day (cited by Dahl *et al.*, 2003). In addition there are thousands of other non-commercial stimuli that each individual encounters. To cope with this bombardment, our sensory organs select those stimuli to which attention is given. These selected stimuli are organised in order to make them comprehensible and are then given meaning; in other words, there is an interpretation of the stimuli that is influenced by attitudes, values, motives and past experiences as well as the character of the stimuli themselves. Stimuli, therefore, are selected, organised and interpreted.

Selected stimuli are organised in order to make them comprehensible and are then given meaning.

Perceptual selection

The vast number of messages mentioned earlier need to be filtered, as individuals cannot process them all. The stimuli that are selected result from the interaction of the nature of the stimulus with the expectations and the motives of the individual. Attention is an important factor in determining the outcome of this interaction: 'Attention occurs when the stimulus activates one or more sensory receptor nerves and the resulting sensations go to the brain for processing' (Hawkins *et al.*, 1989).

The nature of the stimuli, or external factors such as the intensity and size, position, contrast, novelty, repetition and movement, are factors that have been developed and refined by marketing communicators to attract attention. Animation is used to attract attention when the product class is perceived as bland and uninteresting, such as margarine or teabags. Unexpected camera angles and the use of music can be strong methods of gaining the attention of the target audience, as used successfully in the Bacardi Breezer and Renault commercials. Sexual attraction can be a powerful means of capturing the attention of audiences, and when associated with a brand's values can be a very effective method of getting attention (for example, the Diet Coke advertisement, Exhibit 5.3).

Sexual attraction can be a powerful means of capturing the attention of audiences.

The expectations, needs and motives of the individual, or internal factors, are equally important. Individuals see what they expect to see, and their expectations are normally based on past experience and preconditioning. From a communications perspective the presentation of stimuli that conflict with the individual's expectations will invariably receive more attention. The attention-getting power of erotic and sexually driven advertising messages is understood and exploited. For example, jeans manufacturers such as Levi 501s, Wranglers and Diesel often use this type of stimulus to promote their brands. However, advertising research based on recall testing often reveals that the attention-getting stimulus (e.g. the male or female) generates high recall scores, but the product or brand is very often forgotten. Looked at in terms of Schramm's model of communication (Chapter 2), the process of encoding was inaccurate, hence the inappropriate decoding.

Of particular interest is the tendency of individuals to select certain information from the environment. This process is referred to as selective attention. Through attention, individuals avoid contact with information that is felt to be disagreeable in that it opposes strongly held beliefs and attitudes.

Individuals see what they want or need to see. If they are considering the purchase of a new car, there will be heightened awareness of car advertisements and a correspondingly lower level of awareness of unrelated stimuli. Selective attention allows individuals to expose themselves to messages that are comforting and rewarding. For example, reassurance is often required for people who have bought new cars or

EXHIBIT 5.3 'Diet Coke'

Coca-Cola uses sexual overtones to gain the attention of the target market. Diet Coke is a registered trade mark of the Coca-Cola Company. This image has been reproduced with kind permission of the Coca-Cola Company.

expensive technical equipment and who have spent a great deal of time debating and considering the purchase and its associated risk. Communications congratulating the new owner on his or her wise decision often accompany post-purchase literature such as warranties and service contracts. If potentially harmful messages do get through this filter system, perceptual defence mechanisms help to screen them out after exposure.

Perceptual organisation

The four main ways in which sensory stimuli can be organised are figure–ground, grouping, closure and contour.

For perception to be effective and meaningful, the vast array of selected stimuli need to be organised. The four main ways in which sensory stimuli can be organised are figure–ground, grouping, closure and contour.

Figure-ground

Each individual's perception of an environment tends to consist of articles on a general background, against which certain objects are illuminated and stand proud. Williams (1981) gives the examples of trees standing out against the sky and words on a page. This has obvious implications for advertisers and the design and form of communications, especially advertisements, to draw attention to important parts of the message, most noticeably the price, logo or company/brand name. See Exhibit 5.4 as an example of this figure–ground approach.

EXHIBIT 5.4 Car ad which uses the foreground to highlight the object (the car) against a general background. The Figure-Ground principle in action. Picture kindly supplied by Subaru.

Grouping

Objects that are close to one another tend to be grouped together and a pattern develops. Grouping can be used to encourage associations between a product and specific attributes. For example, food products that are positioned for a health market are often displayed with pictures that represent fitness and exercise, the association being that consumption of the food will lead to a lifestyle that incorporates fitness and exercise, as these are important to the target market.

Closure

When information is incomplete individuals make sense of the data by filling in the gaps. This is often used to involve consumers in the message and so enhance selective attention. Advertisements for American Express charge cards or GM credit cards ('if invited to apply'), for example, suggest that ownership denotes membership, which represents exclusiveness and privilege.

Television advertisements that are run for 60 seconds when first launched are often cut to 30 or even 15 seconds later in the burst. The purpose is twofold: to cut costs and to remind the target audience. This process of reminding is undertaken with the assistance of the audience, who recognise the commercial and mentally close the message even though the advertiser only presents the first part.

Contour

Contours give objects shape and are normally formed when there is a marked change in colour or brightness. This is an important element in package design and, as the battle for shelf space in retail outlets becomes more intense, so package design has become an increasingly important aspect of attracting attention.

The battles between Sainsbury's and Coca-Cola in the mid-1990s regarding the introduction of an alleged 'copy-cat' (Glancey, 1994) own-label product serves to illustrate this point. This and other own-label products are often packaged in a very similar way to the branded item. This serves to diffuse the impact of the branded item on the shelves and enhances the position and credibility of the own-label item.

ViewPoint 5.2   Copycat Penguins

United Biscuits took Asda (a multiple retailer) to court when the retailer launched an own-brand chocolate biscuit (Puffin) with very similar packaging to the bar owned by United Biscuits (Penguin). Murphy (1997) reported that the court ruled that the colour, typography and use of the Puffin character were deceptively similar to those of Penguin and Asda was required to change the packaging.

These methods are used by individuals in an attempt to organise stimuli and simplify their meanings. They combine in an attempt to determine a pattern to the stimuli, so that they are perceived as part of a whole or larger unit. This is referred to as gestalt psychology.

Perceptual interpretation

Interpretation is the process by which individuals give meaning to the stimuli once they have been organised. As Cohen and Basu (1987) state, by using existing categories meanings can be given to stimuli. These categories are determined from the individual's past experiences and they shape what the individual expects to see. These expectations, when combined with the strength and clarity of the stimulus and the motives at the time perception occurs, mould the pattern of the perceived stimuli.

The degree to which each individual's ascribed meaning, resulting from the interpretation process, is realistic, is dependent upon the levels of distortion that may be present. Distortion may occur because of stereotyping: the predetermined set of images that we use to guide our expectations of events, people and situations. Another distortion factor is the halo effect that occurs when a stimulus with many attributes or dimensions is evaluated on just a single attribute or dimension. Brand extensions and family branding strategies are based on the understanding that if previous experiences with a different offering are satisfactory, then risk is reduced and an individual is more likely to buy a new offering from the same 'family'.

Distortion may occur because of stereotyping: the predetermined set of images that we use to guide our expectations of events, people and situations.

Marketing and perception

Individuals, therefore, select and interpret particular stimuli in the context of the expectations arising from the way they classify the overall situation. The way in which individuals perceive, organise and interpret stimuli is a reflection of their past experiences and the classifications used to understand the different situations each individual frames every day. Individuals seek to frame or provide a context within which their role becomes clearer. Shoppers expect to find products in particular situations, such as rows, shelves or display bins of similar goods. They also develop meanings and associations with some grocery products because of the utility and trust/emotional satisfaction certain pack types evoke. The likelihood that a sale will be made is improved if the context in which a purchase transaction is undertaken does not contradict a shopper's expectations.

Marketing communications should attempt to present products (objects) in a frame or 'mental presence' (Moran, 1990) that is recognised by a buyer, such as a consumption or purchase situation. A product has a much greater chance of entering an evoked set if the situation in which it is presented is one that is expected and relevant. However, a new pack design can provide differentiation and provoke people into reassessing their expectations of what constitutes appropriate packaging in a product category. See the Pringles case on p. 805 as an example.

ViewPoint 5.3	Changing times

The Times newspaper ran a campaign in 2004 to try to change the way the paper was perceived by people younger than the 42-year-old average reader. For infrequent readers *The Times* was a second-choice paper and in order to make it their first choice the newspaper tried to change the way it was perceived.

To do this they developed a campaign using four celebrity spokespersons: Gordon Ramsay, Jonny Wilkinson, Gabby Logan and Jodie Kidd. With the strapline 'Join the Debate' the strategy was based on the personalities debating issues about health, sport and various forms of entertainment in order to broaden the perception of the topics covered by the newspaper.

Source: Sweeney (2004).

Javalgi *et al.* (1992) point out that perception is important to product evaluation and product selection. Consumers try to evaluate a product's attributes by the physical cues of taste, smell, size and shape. Sometimes no difference can be distinguished, so the consumer has to make a judgement on factors other than the physical characteristics of the product. This is the basis of branding activity, where a personality is developed for the product that enables it to be perceived differently from its competitors. The individual may also set up a separate category or evoked set in order to make sense of new stimuli or satisfactory experiences. Consumer perception of salon- and shop-based haircare products shows important differences and indicates the different roles that marketing communication needs to play: see Figure 5.2. Within each of these sectors many brands are developed that are targeted at different segments based upon demographic, benefit and psychographic factors.

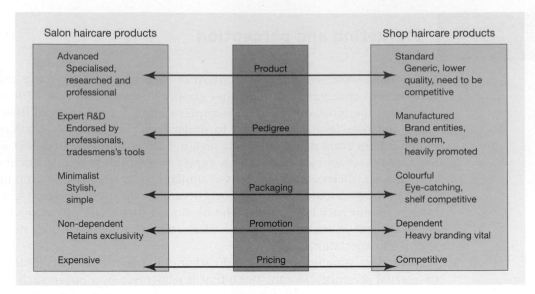

FIGURE 5.2 Comparison of salon and shop haircare products

Goodrich (1978) discusses the importance of perception, which can be seen in terms of the choices tourists make when deciding which destination to visit. The decision is influenced by levels of general familiarity, levels of specific knowledge and perception. It follows that the more favourable the perception of a particular destination, the more likely it is to be selected from its competitors.

Finally, individuals carry a set of enduring perceptions or images. These relate to themselves, to products and to organisations. The concept of positioning the product in the mind of the consumer is fundamental to marketing strategy and is a topic that will be examined in greater depth in Chapter 13. The image an individual has of an organisation is becoming recognised as increasingly important, judging by the proportion of communication budgets being given over to public relations activities and corporate advertising in particular.

Organisations develop multiple images to meet the positioning requirements of their end-user markets and stakeholders. They need to monitor and adjust their identities constantly in respect of the perceptions and expectations held by the other organisations in their various networks. For example, the level of channel coordination and control can be a function of the different perceptions of channel members. These concern the perception of the channel depth, processes of control and the roles each member is expected to fulfil. Furthermore, the perception of an organisation's product quality and its associated image (reputation) is becoming increasingly important. Both end-user buyers and channel members are attempting to ensure that the intrinsic and extrinsic cues associated with their products are appropriate signals of product quality (Moran, 1990).

Learning

There are two mainstream approaches to learning, behavioural and cognitive, as shown in Table 5.2.

Behavioural learning

There are three factors important to learning: association, reinforcement and motivation.

The behavourist approach to learning views the process as a function of an individual's acquisition of responses. There are three factors important to learning: association, reinforcement and motivation. However, it is the basic concept of the stimulus–response orientation that will be looked at in more detail.

It is accepted that for learning to occur all that is needed is a 'time–space proximity' between a stimulus and a response. Learning takes place through the establishment of a connection between a stimulus and a response. Marketing communications is thought to work by the simple process of people observing messages and being stimulated/ motivated to respond by requesting more information or purchasing the advertised product in search of a reward. Behaviour is learned through the conditioning experience of a stimulus and response. There are two forms of conditioning: classical and operant.

Classical conditioning

Classical conditioning assumes that learning is an associative process that occurs with an existing relationship between a stimulus and a response. By far the best-known example of this type of learning is the experiment undertaken by the Russian psychologist Pavlov. He noticed that dogs began to salivate at the sight of food. He stated that this was not taught, but was a reflex reaction. This relationship exists prior to any

TABLE 5.2 Types of learning

Type of learning		Explanation
Behavioural	Classical	Individuals learn to make associations or connections between a stimulus and their responses. Through repetition of the response (the behaviour) to the stimulus, learning occurs.
	Operant	Learning occurs as a result of an individual operating or interacting with the environment. The response of the individual is instrumental in getting a positive reinforcement (reward) or negative reinforcement (punishment). Behaviour that is rewarded or reinforced will be continued, whereas behaviour that is not rewarded will cease.
Cognitive		Assumes that individuals attempt to actively influence their immediate environments rather than be subject to it. They try to resolve problems by processing information from past experiences (memory) in order to make reasoned decisions based on judgements.

ViewPoint 5.4   Citroën

Citroën UK and Citroën France have both used Claudia Schiffer in their car advertising. In the UK the international model is only associated with a single product, the Xara, in two separate executions. However, research indicates that across all segments she has become the face of Citroën and an association has developed between the two.

CLAUDIA SCHIFFER ON THE SET OF THE LATEST CITROËN XSARA TV COMMERCIAL

 CITROËN
PUBLIC AFFAIRS
0870 606 9000
Neg No. 1607

EXHIBIT 5.5 Classical conditioning – Claudia Schiffer in association with Citroën
Photograph kindly supplied by Citroën UK.

In Exhibit 5.5 Claudia Schiffer is depicted next to the car. The car becomes the conditioned stimulus and the celebrity model acts as an unconditioned stimulus. See the model, think of the Xara or perhaps think of Citroën.

Source: Material and photograph kindly supplied by Citroën UK.

experimentation or learning. The food represents an unconditioned stimulus and the response (salivation) from the dogs is an unconditioned response.

Pavlov then paired the ringing of a bell with the presentation of food. Shortly the dogs began to salivate at the ringing of the bell. The bell became the conditioned stimulus and the salivation became the conditioned response (which was the same as the unconditioned response).

From an understanding of this work it can be determined that two factors are important for learning to occur:

1. To build the association between the unconditioned and conditioned stimulus, there must be a relatively short period of time.

2. The conditioning process requires that there be a relatively high frequency/repetition of the association. The more often the unconditioned and conditioned stimuli occur together, the stronger will be the association.

Classical conditioning can be observed operating in each individual's everyday life. An individual who purchases a new product because of a sales promotion may continue to buy the product even when the promotion has terminated. An association has been established between the sales promotion activity (unconditioned stimulus) and the product (conditioned stimulus). If product quality and satisfaction levels allow, long-run behaviour may develop despite the absence of the promotion. In other words, promotion need not act as a key purchase factor in the long run.

Advertisers attempt to associate their products/services with certain perceptions, images and emotions that are known to evoke positive reactions from consumers. Image advertising seeks to develop the associations that individuals have when they think of a brand or an organisation, and hence its reputation. Messages of this type show the object with an unconditioned stimulus that is known to evoke pleasant and favourable feelings. The product becomes a conditioned stimulus eliciting the same favourable response. The advertisements for Bounty Bars use images of desert islands to evoke feelings of enjoyment and pleasure and associations with coconuts.

Operant conditioning

In this form of conditioning, sometimes known as instrumental conditioning, learning occurs as a result of an individual operating or acting on some part of the environment. The response of the individual is instrumental in getting a positive reinforcement (reward) or negative reinforcement (punishment). Behaviour that is rewarded or reinforced will be continued, whereas behaviour that is not rewarded will cease.

B.F. Skinner was a pioneer researcher in the field of operant conditioning. His work, with rats that learned to press levers in order to receive food and who later only pressed the lever when a light was on (discriminative stimulus), highlights the essential feature of this form of conditioning: that reinforcement follows a specific response.

Many organisations use reinforcement in their communications by stressing the benefits or rewards that a consumer can anticipate receiving as a result of using a product or brand. For example, Sainsbury's offers 'Reward Points' and Asda offers a reward of money savings that 'make the difference'. Reinforcement theories emphasise the role of external factors and exclude the individual's ability to process information internally. Learning takes place either through direct reinforcement of a particular response or through an associative conditioning process.

Learning takes place either through direct reinforcement of a particular response or through an associative conditioning process.

However, operant conditioning is a mechanistic process that is not realistic, as it serves only to simplify an extremely complex process.

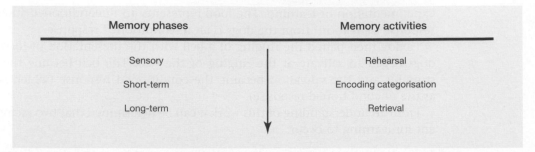

Memory phases	Memory activities
Sensory	Rehearsal
Short-term	Encoding categorisation
Long-term	Retrieval

FIGURE 5.3 Aspects of internal information processing

Cognitive learning

This approach to our understanding of learning assumes that individuals attempt to control their immediate environments. They are seen as active participants in that they try to resolve problems by processing information which is pertinent to each situation. Central to this process is memory. Just as money can be saved in short-, medium- and long-term investment accounts, so information is memorised for different periods of time. These memories are sensory, short term and long term; see Figure 5.3.

Sensory storage refers to the period in which information is sensed for a split second, and if an impression has been made the information will be transferred to short-term memory where it is rehearsed before transfer to long-term memory. *Short-term* memory lasts no longer than approximately eight seconds and a maximum of four or five items can be stored in short-term memory at any one time. Readers will probably have experienced being introduced to someone at a social event only to forget the name of the guest when they next meet them. This occurs because the name was not entered into *long-term* memory. Information can be stored for extended periods in long-term memory. This information is not lying dormant, however, it is constantly being reorganised and recategorised as new information is received.

There are four basic functions by which memory operates. These are, first, *rehearsal*, where information is repeated or related to an established category. This is necessary so that the second function, *encoding*, can take place. This involves the selection of an image to represent the perceived object. Once in long-term memory it is *categorised and stored*, the third function. *Retrieval* is the final function, a process by which information is recovered from storage.

Cognitive learning is about processing information in order that problems can be resolved.

Cognitive learning is about processing information in order that problems can be resolved. These information-handling processes can range from the simple to the complex. There are three main processes: iconic, modelling and reasoning.

Iconic rote learning involves understanding the association between two or more concepts when there is an absence of a stimulus. Learning occurs at a weak level through repetition of simple messages. Beliefs are formed about the attributes of an offering without any real understanding of the source of the information. Advertisers of certain products (low value, frequently purchased) will try to remind their target audiences repeatedly of the brand name in an attempt to help consumers learn. Through such repetition, an association with the main benefits of the product may be built, if only via the constant reminders by the spokesperson.

Learning through the *modelling* approach involves the observation and imitation of others and the associated outcomes of their behaviour. In essence, a great deal of children's early learning is developed in this way. Likewise, marketing communicators use the promise of rewards to persuade audiences to act in a particular way. By using positive images of probable rewards, buyers are encouraged to believe that they can receive the same outcome if they use the particular product. For example, clothing advertisements often depict the model receiving admiring glances from passers-by. The same admiration is the reward 'promised' to those who wear the same clothing. A similar approach is used by Kellogg's to promote their Special K breakfast cereal. The commercial depicts a (slim) mother and child playing on a beach. The message is that it is important to look after yourself and to raise your family through healthy eating, an outdoor life and exercise.

ViewPoint 5.5   Processing All-Bran

Kellogg's All-Bran, a shredded-fibre breakfast cereal, began to lose market share after achieving brand leadership. Research revealed that buyers understood the importance of fibre in their diet but had assumed that fresh fruit, vegetables and wholemeal bread were suitable and easier alternative sources of fibre. Kellogg's used a campaign that compared the fibre content with a variety of commonly assumed rich sources of fibre, such as 9 slices of brown bread (see Exhibit 5.6), 21 new potatoes and 8 bananas. The success of this campaign was largely due to both current and lapsed buyers having to rethink their view of All-Bran. They were challenged to reason why they were not using All-Bran when it is the richest source of an ingredient that they value. Buyers were encouraged to make a judgement about their current diet and an alternative that was being presented as patently superior.

Of all the approaches to understanding how we learn, cognitive learning is the most flexible interpretation. The rational, more restricted approach of behavioural learning, where the focus is external to the individual, is without doubt a major contribution to knowledge. However, it fails to accommodate the complex internal thought processes that individuals utilise when presented with various stimuli.

EXHIBIT 5.6 All-Bran advertisement – an example of the use of reasoning in an advertisement appeal
Picture supplied and used with the kind permission of Kellogg Company of Great Britain Ltd. All rights reserved.

Reasoning is perhaps the most complex form of cognitive learning.

Reasoning is perhaps the most complex form of cognitive learning. Through this process, individuals need to restructure and reorganise information held in long-term memory and combine it with fresh inputs in order to generate new outputs. Because of legislation, cigarette advertisers have had to find new ways of reaching their audiences. Benson & Hedges have used innovative complex messages to reach smokers of their Silk Cut brand. The complex messages associated with this brand require much thought and reasoning to deduce the relationship between the image (scissors and silk ribbon) and the brand.

It is useful to appreciate the way in which people are believed to learn and forget as there are several issues that are useful to media planners in particular.

Interference theory

Burke and Srull (1988) suggest that learning and brand recall can be interfered with. This may be caused either by new material affecting previously stored information or by old information being retrieved and interfered with by incoming messages. The first case, where the last message has the strongest recall, is similar to the recency effect discussed in the context of message design (Chapter 19).

In a competitive environment, where there are many messages being transmitted, each one negating previous messages, the most appropriate strategy for an advertiser would be to separate the advertisements from those of its competitors. This reasoning supports much of the positioning work undertaken by brand managers.

Decay

The rate at which individuals forget material assumes a pattern, as shown in Figure 5.4. Many researchers have found that information decays at a negatively decelerating rate. As much as 60 per cent of the initial yield of information from an advertisement has normally decayed within six weeks. This decay, or wear-out, can be likened to the half-life of radioactive material. It is always working, although it cannot be seen, and the impact of the advertising reduces through time. Like McGuire's (1978) retention stage in his hierarchy of effects model (see Chapter 7), the storage of information for future

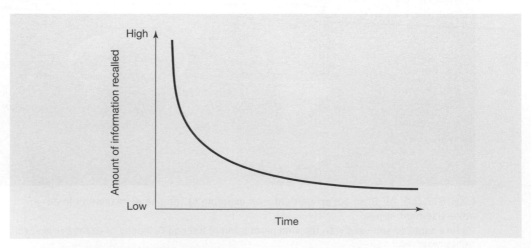

FIGURE 5.4 A standard decay curve

use is important, but with time, how powerful will the information be and what triggers are required to promote recall?

Advertising wear-out is thought to occur because of two factors. First, individuals use selective perception and mentally switch off after a critical number of exposures. Secondly, the monotony and irritation caused by continued exposure lead to counter-argument to both the message and the advertisement (Petty and Cacioppo, 1979).

Advertisements for John Smith's bitter, Gold Blend and Renault attempt to prevent wear-out by using variations on a central theme to maintain interest and yet provide consistency.

Cognitive response

Learning can be visualised as following either of the curves set out in Figure 5.5. The amount learned 'wears out' after a certain repetition level has been reached. Grass and Wallace (1969) suggest that this process of wear-out commences once a satiation point has been reached. A number of researchers (Zielske, 1959; Strong, 1977) have found that recall is improved when messages are transmitted on a regular weekly basis, rather than daily, monthly or in a concentrated or dispersed format.

An individual's ability to develop and retain awareness or knowledge of a product will, therefore, be partly dependent not only on the quality of the message but also on the number and quality of exposures to a planned message. To assist the media planner there are a number of concepts that need to be appreciated and used within the decisions about what, where and when a message should be transmitted. There are a number of other concepts that are of use to media planners: these are reach and coverage, frequency, gross rating points, effective frequency, efficiency and media source effects.

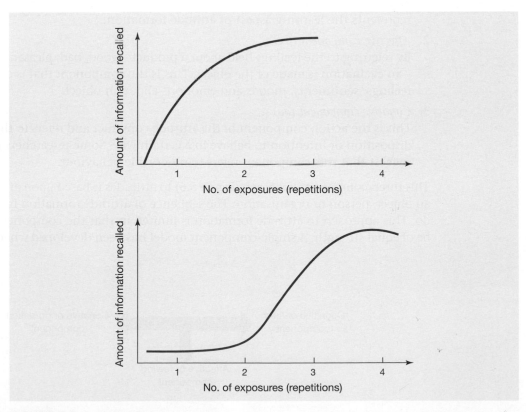

FIGURE 5.5 Learning curves

Attitudes

The perceptual and learning processes may lead to the formation of attitudes. These are predispositions, shaped through experience, to respond in an anticipated way to an object or situation. Attitudes are learned through past experiences and serve as a link between thoughts and behaviour. These experiences may relate to the product itself, to the messages transmitted by the different members of the channel network (normally mass media communications) and to the information supplied by opinion leaders, formers and followers.

Attitudes are learned through past experiences and serve as a link between thoughts and behaviour.

Attitudes tend to be consistent within each individual: they are clustered and very often interrelated. This categorisation leads to the formation of stereotypes, which is extremely useful for the design of messages as stereotyping allows for the transmission of a lot of information in a short time period (30 seconds) without impeding learning or the focal part of the message.

Attitude components

Attitudes are hypothetical constructs, and classical psychological theory considers attitudes to consist of three components.

Attitudes are hypothetical constructs, and classical psychological theory considers attitudes to consist of three components:

1. *Cognitive component (learn)*
   This component refers to the level of knowledge and beliefs held by individuals about a product and/or the beliefs about specific attributes of the offering. This represents the learning aspect of attitude formation.

2. *Affective component (feel)*
   By referring to the feelings held about a product – good, bad, pleasant or unpleasant – an evaluation is made of the object. This is the component that is concerned with feelings, sentiments, moods and emotions about an object.

3. *Conative component (do)*
   This is the action component of the attitude construct and refers to the individual's disposition or intention to behave in a certain way. Some researchers go so far as to suggest that this component refers to observable behaviour.

This three-component approach (Figure 5.6) to attitudes is based upon attitudes towards an object, person or organisation. The sequence of attitude formation is learn, feel and do. This approach to attitude formation is limited in that the components are seen to be of equal strength. A single-component model has been developed where the attitude

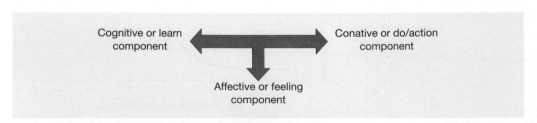

FIGURE 5.6 The three-component attitude model

only consists of the individual's overall feeling towards an object. In other words, the affective component is the only significant component.

Multi-attribute attitude models

One of the difficulties with the three- and single-component attitude models is that they fail to explain why an individual has a particular attitude. A different approach views objects as possessing many different attributes, all of which are perceived and believed by individuals with differing strengths and intensity.

Attribute analysis is an important factor in the design and consistency of marketing communication messages. For example, the UK toilet tissue market has been dominated by two main players, Andrex with 24.2 per cent market share and SCA Hygiene's Double-Velvet with 10.4 per cent share (Brabbs, 2000). In 2000 Charmin entered the market. For many years Andrex has used a puppy to symbolise the softness, strength and length of its product. Table 5.3 indicates how the softness and strength attributes valued by consumers in 1992 have changed so that by 1996 the key attributes had become slightly less significant than they were. However, strong attitudes held by Andrex's loyal customers have enabled market share to rise steadily and market leadership has been maintained. This has been achieved in the light of the increased number of high-quality products (often own label) that are now available, all of which communicate softness and strength as the key attributes; see Exhibit 5.4.

In 2000 Procter & Gamble introduced Charmin to the UK from the US where it has a 30 per cent market share. Apart from a huge £14 million ad spend and a strong outdoor, radio, press and direct marketing programme, the launch was notable for the position it took in the market. Andrex positions by features, such as strength, length and softness as symbolised by the puppy. Double-Velvet adopts a similar position but appears to focus on features such as thickness as a surrogate for quality. Charmin's approach has been to highlight a neglected attribute, namely a comfortable cleaning proposition, smooth and strong, even when wet.

Intentions

Of the many advances in this area, those made by Ajzen and Fishbein (1980) have made a significant contribution. They reasoned that the best way of predicting behaviour was to measure an individual's intention to purchase (the conative component).

TABLE 5.3 Attributes valued by consumers when purchasing toilet tissue

Attributes (%)	1992	1995	Change 1992–5
Softness	66	57	−9
Colour to match decor	47	48	1
Price	45	45	0
Brand loyalty	39	36	−3
Special offers	24	32	8
Strength	42	29	−13
Length of roll	25	24	−1
Own label	6	14	8

Source: Adapted from a Mintel Report (1996).

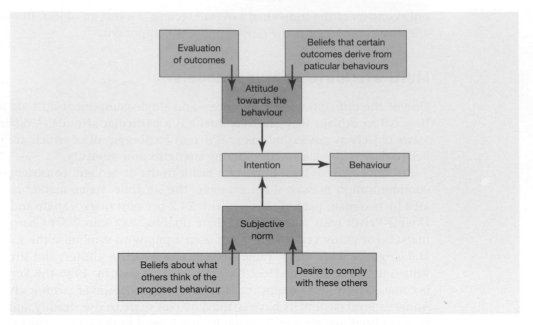

FIGURE 5.7 Theory of reasoned action model. Based on Ajzen and Fishbein (1980) and adapted from Schiffman and Kanuck (1991). Reproduced with permission of Prentice-Hall Inc., Englewood Cliffs, NJ

Underlying intentions are the individual's attitude towards the act of behaviour and the subjective norm. In other words, the context within which a proposed purchase is to occur is seen as important to the attitude that is developed towards the object.

The subjective norm is the relevant feelings others are believed to hold about the proposed purchase, or intention to purchase. Underpinning the subjective norm are the beliefs held about the people who are perceived to 'judge' the actions an individual might take. Would they approve or disapprove, or look favourably or unfavourably upon the intended action?

> Underpinning the subjective norm are the beliefs held about the people who are perceived to 'judge' the actions an individual might take.

Underpinning the attitude towards the intention to act in a particular way are the strengths of the beliefs that a particular action will lead to an outcome. Ajzen and Fishbein argue that it is the individual's attitude to the act of purchasing, not the object of the purchase, that is important. For example, a manager may have a positive attitude towards a particular type of expensive office furniture, but a negative attitude towards the act of securing agreement for him to purchase it.

The theory of reasoned action (Ajzen and Fishbein, 1980; Figure 5.7) shows that intentions are composed of interrelated components: subjective norms, which in turn are composed of beliefs and motivations about relevant others, towards a particular intention, and attitudes, which in turn are made up of beliefs about the probable outcomes that a behaviour will lead to.

This approach recognises the interrelationship of the three components of attitudes and that it is not attitude but the intention to act or behave that precedes observable behaviour which should be the focus of attention. It should be understood that attitudes do not precede behaviour and cannot be used to predict behaviour, despite the attempts of a number of researchers. Attitudes are important, but they are not the sole determinant of behaviour, and intentions may be a better indicator of behaviour.

Attitudes impact on consumer decision-making, and the objective of marketing communications is often to create a positive attitude towards a product and/or to

TABLE 5.4 Compensatory and non-compensatory models

Attribute	Weighting	Package 1 Rating	Package 1 Score	Package 2 Rating	Package 2 Score	Package 3 Rating	Package 3 Score
Price	5	5	25	6	30	5	25
Hotel cleanliness	3	3	9	2	6	4	12
Travel times	2	7	14	9	18	4	8
Attitude rating			48		54		45
Possible decisions							
Compensatory model			Not considered		Winner		Not considered
Non-compensatory model			Winner		Not considered		Considered

The objective of marketing communications is often to create a positive attitude towards a product and/or to reinforce or change existing attitudes.

reinforce or change existing attitudes. An individual may perceive and develop a belief that British Airways has a friendly and informal in-flight service and that the service provided by Lufthansa is cold and formal. However, both airlines are perceived to hold a number of different attributes, and each individual needs to evaluate these attributes in order that an attitude can be developed. It is necessary, therefore, to measure the strength of the beliefs held about the key attributes of different products. There are two main processes whereby beliefs can be processed and measured: compensatory and non-compensatory models.

Compensatory models

Through this approach, attributes that are perceived to be weak can be offset by attributes that are perceived to be strong. As a result, positive attitudes are determined in the sense that the evaluation of all the attributes is satisfactory. For example, Table 5.4 sets out a possible evaluation of three package holidays. Despite the weakness on hotel cleanliness, the strength of the other attributes in package 2 scores this the highest, so the strongest attitude is formed towards this product. Some individuals make decisions about products on the basis that their attributes must not contain any weaknesses. Therefore package 2 would not be considered, as it fails to reach a minimum level of expected satisfaction on cleanliness; thus, despite its strengths, it is relegated from the decision alternatives.

An understanding of attitude components and the way in which particular attributes can be measured not only enables organisations to determine the attitudes held towards them and their competitors but also empowers them to change the attitudes held by different stakeholders, if it is thought necessary.

Changing attitudes with marketing communications

Marketing communications is important to either maintain or change attitudes held by stakeholders. It is not the only way as product and service elements, pricing and channel decisions all play an important part in shaping the attitudes held. However, marketing communications has a pivotal role in conveying each of these aspects to the target audience. Branding (Chapter 14) is a means by which attitudes can be established and maintained in a consistent way and it is through the use of the tools of the promotional mix that brands can be sustained. The final point that needs to be made is that there is a common thread between attributes, attitudes and positioning (Chapter 13). Attributes provide a means of differentiation and positions are shaped as a consequence of the attitudes that result from the way people interpret the associated marketing communications.

Environmental influences on the attitudes people hold towards particular products and services are partly a reflection of the way they interpret the marketing communications surrounding them, partly as a result of their direct experience of using them and partly as a result of the informal messages received from family, friends and other highly credible sources of information. These all contribute to the way people position products and services and the way they understand them relative to competing products. Managing attitudes (towards a brand) is therefore very important and marketing communications can play an important part in changing or maintaining attitudes. There are a number of ways in which attitudinal change can be implemented:

1. *Change the physical product or service element*

   At a fundamental level, attitudes might be so ingrained that it is necessary to change the product or service. This may involve a radical redesign or the introduction of a significant new attribute. Only once these changes have been made should marketing communications be used to communicate the new or revised object. When VW bought Skoda it redesigned the total product offering before relaunch.

2. *Change misunderstanding*

   In some circumstances people might misunderstand the benefits of a particularly important attribute and marketing communications is required to correct the beliefs held. This can be achieved through product demonstration of functionally based communications. Packaging and even the name of the product may need to be revised.

3. *Build credibility*

   Attitudes towards a brand might be superficial and lack sufficient conviction to prompt conative behaviour. This can be corrected through the use of an informative strategy, designed to build credibility. Product demonstration and hands-on experience (e.g. through sampling) are effective strategies. Skoda supports a rally team to convey durability, speed and performance.

4. *Change performance beliefs*

   Beliefs held about the object and the performance qualities of the object can be adjusted through appropriate marketing communications. For example, by changing the perceptions held about the attributes, it is possible to change the attitudes about the object.

5. *Change attribute priorities*

   By changing the relative importance of the different attributes and ratings it is possible to change attitudes. Therefore, a strategy to emphasise a different attribute can change the attitude not only to a brand but to a product category. By stressing the importance of travel times, it might raise the importance of this attribute in the minds of potential holiday-makers and so give package 2 an advantage over its rivals, using the non-compensatory decision rule. Dyson changed attitudes to carpet cleaning equipment by stressing the efficiency of its new cyclone technology rather than the ease of use, aesthetic design or generic name (Hoover) associations used previously.

6. *Introduce a new attribute*

   Opportunities might exist to introduce a radically different and new (or previously unused) attribute. This provides a means for clear differentiation until competitors imitate and catch up. The solution for package 3 may be to introduce a fourth attribute, one in which the suppliers of package 3 know they have an advantage over the competition. This may be that they have a no-surcharge guarantee and packages 1 and 2 do not. By making prominent the new no-surcharge guarantee in the promotional messages transmitted by package 3, the introduction of a new significant attribute may lead to greater success.

7. *Change perception of competitor products*
   By changing the way competitor products are perceived it is possible to differentiate your own brand. For example, by changing the perception of packages 1 and 2 or changing the association of their packages with the others, package 3 might gain an advantage. This could be achieved by using messages that set the package apart from its rivals, suggesting, for example, that not all package holidays are the same. This is a theme that was used by Thomson Holidays, when its copy read, 'We go there, we don't stay there'.

8. *Change or introduce new brand associations*
   By using celebrities or spokespersons with whom the target audience can identify, it might be possible for package 3 to change the way the product is perceived on an emotional basis rather than relying on attributes and a more rational argument.

9. *Use corporate branding*
   By altering the significance of the parent brand relative to the product brand, it is possible to alter beliefs about brands and their overall value. In some situations there is little to differentiate competitive brands and little credible scope to develop attribute-based attitudes. By using the stature of the parent company it is possible to develop a level of credibility and brand values that other brands cannot copy, although they can imitate by using their parent brand. Procter & Gamble has introduced its name to the packs of many of its brands.

10. *Change the number of attributes used*
    Many brands still rely on a single attribute as a means of providing a point of differentiation. This was popularly referred to as a unique selling proposition at a time when attribute- and informationally-based communications reflected a *feature*-dominated understanding of branding. Today, two or even three attributes are often combined with strong emotional associations in order to provide a point of differentiation and a set of *benefit*-oriented brand values.

ViewPoint 5.6   Land-Rover seeks to change attitudes

Following a brief to sell 300 Land-Rovers, research conducted by the direct marketing agency Craik Jones found that the attitudes held by prospective Land-Rover buyers were based on serious misconceptions about the brand. Not only did they feel that Land-Rovers were essentially a rural vehicle but also that they drove like a truck rather than a luxury car.

These attitudes had been developed as a result of information and perceptions of the brand, without the prospective buyers ever having driven the car. This is typical of the order in which attitudes are formed when there is high involvement (learn–feel–do). In order to overcome this, a direct marketing strategy was developed by the agency to encourage trial in order that attitudes could be based on direct experience (learn–do–feel). Direct mail was used to stimulate a test drive and this was followed up a week later to thank the drivers and to find out their reactions to the experience of actually driving a Land-Rover. Not only were over 700 orders placed as a direct result of this campaign but the reaction and knock-on effect on the dealer network was very positive. Direct marketing had been used as part of a pull strategy to change attitudes and increase sales.

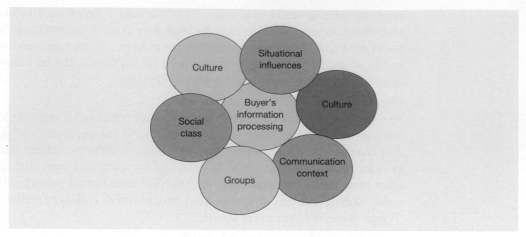

FIGURE 5.8 Environmental influences on buyer information processing

Neither organisations nor consumers exist in a vacuum. They exist in an 'open' system and therefore act upon and are affected by various environmental factors (Figure 5.8). There are a number of externally generated influences that impact upon buyer information processing and decision-making. The main factors are described below.

Culture

Culture has been referred to as the unique characteristics that identify the acceptable patterns of behaviour and social relations within a particular society. Culture embodies the norms, beliefs, artefacts and customs that are learned from society and that constitute its values. It is these values that influence consumer behaviour and are of increasing importance to the international advertiser.

> Culture embodies the norms, beliefs, artefacts and customs that are learned from society and that constitute its values.

Indeed, a more detailed consideration of the role of culture on marketing communications can be found in Chapter 30.

Culture is learned and acquired, it is not instinctive. Culture defines acceptable behaviour within a society and so sets the rules for all members who belong to the culture. For marketing communications, culture should be seen as a communication system in its own right. Through verbal and non-verbal actions a society is able to maintain stability, to bind all members with a sense of identity and to provide them with a means of continuity.

Subcultures

There are a number of subcultures within any given culture. These include age, geography, race, religion and ethnic groupings and they can all influence the way marketing communications are perceived, interpreted and understood.

Social class

Virtually all societies are stratified by class, based upon power, wealth and prestige. Society values individuals and groups on criteria such as education, occupation and level of income. This information is distilled into a social class system, such as upper, middle and lower class, which for a long time has been a main characteristic of UK society.

Marketeers have developed a socioeconomic categorisation that is used as a primary means of segmenting markets. Creative designers have always used symbols to reflect the values, lifestyles, norms and family roles associated with each perceived stratum. Among the many benefits this brings is the ability to transfer a lot of information relatively quickly and so communicate effectively. The process also allows for the continuity of the core values of society.

However, as discussed in Chapter 12, this traditional approach to segmentation is becoming increasingly difficult to utilise as consumers' purchasing habits become more complex and their lifestyles become less rigid and more open. McMurdo (1993) discusses some of the research by the advertising agency J. Walter Thompson. It is now necessary for advertisers to recognise the speed at which consumers can move between purchasing styles, even in the space of a single shopping trip. This is because the requirements of each purchase can be so different that tailor-made segmentation by product is necessary. For example, Dulux recognises that its market for paints consists of 'sloshers' and 'craftsmen'. Paint can be bought for the attic, where it will be 'sloshed', or for the lounge, where it will be applied as a 'craftsman' would do, by the same individual.

Groups

Groups are one of the primary factors influencing learning and socialisation. An individual may simultaneously be a member of several groups, each having a different degree of effect. These groups can be categorised as follows:

1. ascribed groups: one automatically belongs, e.g. family;
2. primary/secondary groups: where interaction is on a one-to-one basis, e.g. family and friends;
3. formal/informal groups: where the presence or absence of structure and hierarchy defines the group activity;
4. aspirational/membership groups: groups to which the individual wishes to belong or does belong.

All these act as reference groups for the individual and influence the individual's behaviour.

Situational influences

The design, encoding and media channels used to transmit communication messages must take into account that buyers are influenced by factors that are unique to each buying situation and are not related specifically to the product or the individual. The situational context impacts on the information-processing capabilities of the buyer. For example, the amount of light in the store or the level of store traffic can influence the amount of time given to decision-making. While this factor will normally have been accounted for in the formulation of the marketing strategy, it must be revisited if the communications are to be effective.

When considering the impact that situational influences might have on information processing, the type of situation needs to be considered. A situational determinant is a factor that is unique to each buying act. These situational influences are connected neither to the purchase object nor to the buyer, and are independent of them. Hansen (1972) identified three types of situation: usage, purchase and communications.

Usage situation

When and where is the offering to be consumed and is consumption to be largely a private act, oriented to the individual (such as chocolate bars) or part of a social activity (such as beer)? For example, some manufacturers of breakfast cereals have been repositioning (Chapter 13) their brands in an attempt to encourage use at other times of the day. Communications need to reflect this strategy and encapsulate the situation in which the desired eating behaviour occurs.

Purchase situation

The act of purchase and the associated environment can influence the behaviour of the target individual. Is shopping a monthly, biannual, weekly or last-minute activity? Mothers shopping with children are more likely to be influenced by product preferences of their children than when shopping without them. This may be due not only to the amount of time available to complete the physical act of shopping but also to the time to process the information. Engel *et al.* (1990) cite information load, format and form as important criteria. Too much information (information overload) can reduce the accuracy of an individual's decision-making, whereas the order in which information is presented both on packages and in terms of store layout can seriously retard the amount of time taken to process information, and this can also influence the motivation of the shopper.

The manner in which information is presented will affect the decision style. The manner in which information is presented will affect the decision style. For example, the ease of comparing brands, perhaps on an individual attribute basis (e.g. diabetics determining the amount of carbohydrate in competing brands), will influence both perception and purchase behaviour.

What is the environment of the shop like? Are there opportunities to influence the target with in-store promotions and advertising messages? Different individuals prefer different supermarkets and price is not the sole criterion. Store loyalty is a function of a number of issues, among them convenience, layout, product range, car-parking facilities and whether packers are available. Associated with this is the concept of corporate image. Each of the supermarket chains has a particular range of images held by its consumers. Consumer perception of store efficiency and value for money and the totality of corporate communications need to reflect, deflect or reinforce particular images. This element is pursued in greater depth in Chapter 15.

Communications situation

The settings in which marketing communications are received will affect the degree to which the message is understood and acted upon. For example, salespersons cold-calling on organisations (arriving at an organisation and requesting a sales interview without a prior appointment) are not usually received in a positive way. Furthermore, having gained an appointment through a prior arrangement does not mean that the information provided during the visit will be received as intended. The buyer may have been advised of some bad news prior to the meeting and his or her thoughts are not focused on the object of the sales meeting or presentation. Television commercials may be zipped or zapped, clutter may prevent key points of the message getting home or general noise in the form of conversation may also affect the effectiveness of the message. One of the central issues concerning the situation in which communications are received is the need to gain the attention of the receiver.

Having determined that there are particular types of situations where the consumption process occurs, Belk (1975), proposes that there are five main situation variables that should be considered. These are the physical aspects, the social surroundings, the time, the task and the antecedent states.

Physical aspects refer to the store design and layout, the location, the lighting, music, smells and sounds associated with the situation. The *social surroundings* refer to all those involved in the purchase, usage or communications. For example, a child was described in one type of situation as accompanying a mother on the shopping activity, and children have a degree of influence on such an event.

Time was considered in the context of the time available to complete the activity, but it could also be considered in the context of time of day, year or season, or time elapsed since the last purchase. The *task* itself is pertinent. Is the purchase for a third party as a present, or is it for personal consumption? Finally, *antecedent states* are the influences each individual experiences, but state is transitional. For example, states of high elation, despondency, bitterness or pleasure are experienced by all individuals, but they are not enduring characteristics.

The particular impact of various environmental influences can affect the behaviour of buyers during purchase activity, during usage and when information is being processed. Understanding the impact of the physical, time and social influences, together with the nature of the task and antecedent states, provides the marketing communications planner with fresh inputs to the exercise of positioning the product appropriately.

Summary

This chapter has reviewed some of the recent and current thinking about how individuals process information. Cognitive theory provides a valuable insight into the manner in which buyers use externally and internally generated stimuli to solve problems. Personality, perception, learning, attitudes and aspects pertinent to the wider environment and each purchase situation have been considered as major elements of the problem-solving approach adopted by both consumers and organisational buyers.

Marketing communication planners need to be aware of these elements and to understand how they operate in the target audience. Messages can be created to match the cognitive needs of the intended audience and change, for example, perception or attitudes, in such a way that communication with the target audience is likely to be more successful.

Review questions

1. Write a short description of cognitive theory. How does it differ from behaviourism?
2. What are the main elements of information processing?
3. How does trait theory differ from Freudian theories of personality?
4. Describe a purchase repertoire (or evoked set) and suggest how marketing communications might assist perceptual selection.
5. To what extent are perception and positioning interlinked?
6. Choose three printed advertisements where the user is promised a reward.
7. Attitudes are believed to comprise three elements. Name them.
8. Write a brief explanation of the theory of reasoned action.
9. How might the environment influence marketing communications?
10. Identify the different types of situational influences on the purchase process.

MINI-CASE
Changing attitudes: The Leprosy Mission

Mini-case written by Jill Brown, Senior Lecturer, University of Portsmouth Business School

Imagine pricking your finger on a pin and not feeling it! It sounds great but for millions of people this is just one of the distressing and dangerous effects of leprosy. Leprosy numbs the feeling in the fingers, toes and face and as a result those who suffer from the disease regularly injure themselves because they have no sense of pain.

Over half a million people are currently on treatment for leprosy and an estimated two to three million people today are living with the long-term devastating social, economic and physical effects of leprosy. Every day over 1,400 new cases of leprosy are reported, of whom around 10 per cent are children.

The prevailing belief about leprosy amongst people in the Western world is that it has been cured and no longer exists. In countries where the disease is most prevalent – India, Nepal, Indonesia, Bangladesh and Mozambique – beliefs about leprosy are deeply embedded in society and frequently wrong. For example it is widely believed that the disease is hereditary, and is a punishment handed down from generation to generation. In some parts of the world where animistic beliefs are influential, leprosy is believed to occur as a direct result of offending ancestors. Other widely held, incorrect beliefs about leprosy are that it is incurable, 'dirty', contagious and is a curse from God.

The treatment for leprosy is in fact very straightforward and effective. As long as the disease is diagnosed in its early stages the appropriate medicine will cure the condition completely, with no long-term effects. However many leprosy sufferers are reluctant to take a tablet to cure a hereditary disease and traditional 'medicines' and 'healers' are often preferred.

Leprosy is more than just a disease; it is enmeshed in a web of socio-religious beliefs. As a result the disease is socially unacceptable in many parts of the world and leprosy sufferers are rapidly stigmatised and cast out by their family and community. The very word 'leper' conjures up images of rejection and condemnation. For many people, leprosy means a life lived apart from society, forgotten, unable to work and condemned to a life of isolation and poverty even though they are medically cured.

The response of the medical community has been mixed. Until the late 1950s there were no orthopaedic surgeons studying the deformities caused by leprosy and although 60–70 per cent of the world's leprosy sufferers are found in India it is not unusual for doctors to deny its existence. Only priests and crackpot missionaries concern themselves with people affected by leprosy – it certainly wasn't a job for doctors!

Organisations such as The Leprosy Mission (TLM) have an uphill task when it comes to changing attitudes towards the disease. Changing beliefs and attitudes are fundamental to the fight to eradicate the disease and go hand in hand with practical programmes of patient care and rehabilitation.

Funded mainly by voluntary donations, TLM is a Christian organisation whose health and community programmes cover 255 million people worldwide. In 2003 57,886 leprosy sufferers were treated, 25,000 corrective operations were carried out and almost 6,500 children and families benefited from assistance with education or micro-enterprise development.

As part of their ongoing work TLM seeks to change attitudes in the following ways:

- of people suffering from leprosy, from one of despair to one of hope and from a sense of dependence on others to one of self-help;

- of employers in countries affected by leprosy to people disabled by leprosy, from fear and refusal to acceptance and employment;

- of governments in countries affected by leprosy, so that leprosy services are integrated with general health services and that leprosy sufferers' sense of isolation and rejection is reduced;

- of people living in the UK and other countries that are not affected by leprosy, from ignorance and apathy to enthusiastic financial support;

- of doctors in parts of the developing world, so that they acknowledge leprosy as a medical condition and its treatment as part of their job.

TLM undertakes a wide range of communication activities designed to challenge entrenched beliefs about leprosy and raise funds to support their work. Although TLM works closely with other charities such as LEPRA, World Vision and The Salvation Army 'in the field' they all compete for the same pound in the UK and there is considerable competition when it comes to fund raising.

A magazine called 'New Day' is sent to everyone on the TLM database in January and August and a smaller, cheaper newsletter is sent out in May and October.

Appeal mailings are sent to about 60,000 supporters three times per year. Carefully chosen images and stories are used to communicate the fact that leprosy is still a huge problem in many parts of the world, but that with the right treatment and adequate resources the disease can be cured and leprosy sufferers can be rehabilitated into society. These mailings generate about £1 million per year.

TLM is keen to foster appropriate attitudes in the UK, and other parts of the developed world, towards the developing world. They want to create a sense of partnership and move away from the more patronising attitudes of the past. Evidence for the change in emphasis is found in the falling number of Western missionaries who are working for TLM in developing countries. Nowadays it is far more common for local people to be recruited and trained to manage and implement the various programmes. TLM communications need to reflect this new approach and challenge existing prejudices.

Lists of potential donors for direct mailing are purchased from list brokers and inserts are targeted at publications such as the *Church Times*, the *Catholic Times*, the *Baptist Times* and the *Christian Herald*. TLM's experience is that the value of the gift generated by an insert is likely to be higher than that generated by direct mail. Around 2,000 new donors are recruited each year via a reciprocal database organisation called Occam, which many charities subscribe to.

A new 60-second radio advertisement about a 7-year-old girl who discovers she is suffering from leprosy has recently been recorded by Wendy Craig. Premier Christian Radio will be the main broadcast medium.

The more funds TLM has at its disposal the more it is able to do in terms of changing attitudes to leprosy, but the task is daunting in scale and complexity.

www.leprosymission.org.uk

Questions

1 Taking into account the organisation's limited budget, how might TLM change the attitudes of doctors, employers and governments in developing countries?

2 How can the theory of reasoned action be applied to this case?

References

Ajzen, I. and Fishbein, M. (1980) *Understanding Attitudes and Predicting Social Behavior.* Englewood Cliffs, NJ: Prentice-Hall.

Belk, R. (1975) Situational variables in consumer behaviour. *Journal of Consumer Research*, **2** (December), pp. 57–64.

Brabbs, C. (2000) Charmin characters take on the Andrex puppy. *Marketing*, 3 February, p. 15.

Burke, R. and Srull, T.K. (1988) Competitive interference and consumer memory for advertising. *Journal of Consumer Research*, **15** (June), pp. 55–68.

Cohen, J. and Basu, K. (1987) Alternative models of categorisation. *Journal of Consumer Research* (March), pp. 455–72.

Dahl D.W., Frankenberger, D. and Manchanda, R.V. (2003) Does it pay to shock? *Journal of Advertising Research*, **43**(3), September, pp. 268–80.

De Chernatony L. (1993) The seven building blocks of brands. *Management Today* (March), pp. 66–7.

Engel, F., Blackwell, R. and Minniard, P. (1990) *Consumer Behavior*, 6th edn. New York: Dryden Press.

Glancey, J. (1994) The real thing put to the test. *Independent on Sunday*, 24 April, News Analysis, p. 5.

Goodrich, J.N. (1978) The relationship between preferences for and perceptions of vacation destinations: application of a choice model. *Journal of Travel Research*, **17**(2).

Grass, R.C. and Wallace, H.W. (1969) Satiation effects of TV commercials. *Journal of Advertising Research*, **9**(3), pp. 3–9.

Guildford, J. (1959) *Personality*. New York: McGraw-Hill.

Hansen, F. (1972) *Consumer Choice Behavior: A Cognitive Theory*. New York: Free Press.

Hawkins, D., Best, R. and Coney, K. (1989) *Consumer Behavior*. Homewood, IL: Irwin.

Javalgi, R., Thomas, E. and Rao, S. (1992) US travellers' perception of selected European destinations. *European Journal of Marketing*, **26**(7), pp. 45–64.

Lasn, K. (1999) *Culture Jam. The Uncooling of America*. New York: Eagle Brook.

McGuire, W. (1978) An information processing model of advertising effectiveness. In *Behavioral and Management Science in Marketing* (eds H.J. Davis and A.J. Silk). New York: Ronald Press.

McMurdo, M.W. (1993) Chasing butterflies. *Marketing Week*, 21 May, pp. 28–31.

Mintel (1996) Household Paper Products. *Marketing Ingelligence*, January, p. 7.

Moran, W. (1990) Brand preference and the perceptual frame. *Journal of Advertising Research* (October/November), pp. 9–16.

Murphy, C. (1997) Penguin forces Asda redesign. *Marketing*, 20 March, p. 1.

Neal, C., Quester, P. and Hawkins, D. (2003) *Consumer Behaviour: Implications for Marketing Strategy*. 3rd edn. Sydney: McGraw-Hill.

Petty, R.E. and Cacioppo, J.T. (1979) Effects of message repetition and position on cognitive responses, recall and persuasion. *Journal of Personality and Social Psychology*, **37** (January), pp. 97–109.

QED (1989) It's not easy being a dolphin. BBC TV.

Schiffman, L. and Kanuck, L. (1991) *Consumer Behavior*. Englewood Cliffs, NJ: Prentice-Hall.

Solomon, M., Bamossy, G., and Askegaard, S. (2001) *Consumer Behaviour: A European Perspective*, 2nd edn. Harlow: Prentice Hall.

Strong, E.C. (1977) The spacing and timing of advertising. *Journal of Advertising Research*, **17** (December), pp. 25–31.

Sweeney, M. (2004) Times lines up stars for £4m umbrella activity. *Marketing*, 2 September, p. 3.

Williams, K.C. (1981) *Behavioural Aspects of Marketing*. London: Heinemann.

Zielske, H.A. (1959) The remembering and forgetting of advertising. *Journal of Marketing*, **23** (January), pp. 239–43.

Customer decision-making

Customers make product purchase-related decisions in different ways. Understanding the ways in which buyers make decisions and the factors that impact upon the decision process can affect the effectiveness of marketing communications. In particular, it can influence message structure, content and scheduling.

Aims and objectives

The aim of this chapter is to consider some of the different processes consumers and organisational buyers use to make purchase decisions.

The objectives of this chapter are to:

1. present a general process for purchase decision-making;
2. examine the sequence and methods used by consumers to make decisions;
3. explore the components of perceived risk;
4. introduce and explain involvement theory and relate it to planned communication activities;
5. consider the different types of individual who contribute to purchase decisions made by organisations;
6. understand the stages that organisations use to make purchase decisions;
7. appreciate the differences in approaches and content of marketing communications between consumer and organisational buying.

Introduction

An understanding of the contextual elements that impact upon individual purchase decision-making and the overall process through which individuals behave and ultimately make decisions is an important first stage in the development of any marketing

Knowledge of a buyer's decision-making processes is vital if the correct type of information is to be transmitted at the right time and in the right or appropriate manner.

communications plan. Knowledge of a buyer's decision-making processes is vital if the correct type of information is to be transmitted at the right time and in the right or appropriate manner. There are two broad types of buyer: consumers and organisational buyers. First, consideration

will be given to a general decision-making process and then an insight into the characteristics of the decision-making processes for consumers and organisational buyers will be presented. The chapter concludes with a consideration of the differences between the two main approaches.

A general buying decision-making process

Figure 6.1 shows that there are five stages in the general process whereby buyers make purchase decisions and implement them. Marketing communications can impact upon any or all of these stages with varying levels of potential effectiveness.

Problem recognition

Problem recognition occurs when there is a perceived difference between an individual's ideal state and reality. Advertisers often induce 'problem recognition' by suggesting that the current state is not desirable or by demonstrating how consumers

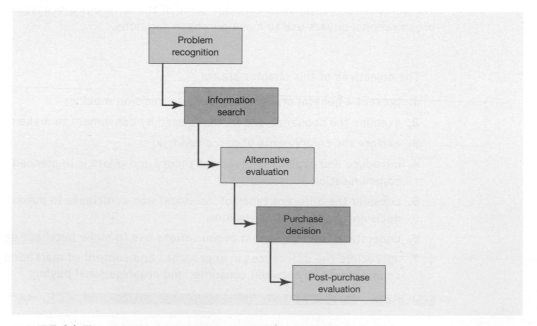

FIGURE 6.1 Five general stages of a buyer's purchase decision process

can tell whether they have a similar problem (e.g. 'Is your hair dull and lifeless?'). The difficulty in getting buyers to recognise that they have a problem invites the question, do they actually have a problem? If there is no identified need, then it is not marketing but selling that is being practised.

Information search

Having identified a problem a prospective buyer will search for information in an attempt to resolve it. There are two main areas of search activity:

1. The internal search involves a memory scan to recall experiences and knowledge, utilising the perceptual processes to see whether there is an 'off-the-shelf' solution.
2. If there is no 'off-the-shelf' solution, the prospective buyer will resort to an external search.

This will involve family and friends, reference sources and commercial guides and advertising.

Alternative evaluation

Potential solutions need to be evaluated in order that the optimum choice be made. Products considered feasible constitute the *preference set*, and it is from these seven or eight products that a smaller group of products is normally assembled. This is referred to as the *evoked set* (or repertoire) and it is from this that consumers make a choice. Attributes used to determine the sets are referred to as evaluative criteria. Very often these attributes are both objective and subjective in nature.

Attributes used to determine the sets are referred to as evaluative criteria.

Purchase decision

Having evaluated various solutions, the buyer may develop a predisposition to make a purchase. This will involve matching motives and evaluative criteria with product attributes. This necessitates the use of the processes of learning and attitude formation, discussed in the previous chapter.

Post-purchase evaluation

Direct experience of the product is an important part of the decision process. Feedback from use helps learning and attitude development and is the main contributor to long-run behaviour. Communication activity must continue to provide satisfaction and prevent the onset of cognitive dissonance. This is a state where, after the purchase decision has been made, a buyer might feel tension about a past decision either because the product fails to reach expectations or because the consumer becomes aware of a superior alternative.

Communication activity must continue to provide satisfaction and prevent the onset of cognitive dissonance.

Marketing communications, at this stage, should be aimed at reinforcing past decisions by stressing the positive features of the product or by providing more information to assist its use and application. For example, much of the advertising undertaken by car manufacturers seeks to prevent the onset of tension and purchase dissatisfaction.

Types of consumer decision-making

Buyers do not follow the general decision sequence at all times. The procedure may vary depending upon the time available, levels of perceived risk and the degree of involvement a buyer has with the type of product. Perceived risk and involvement are issues that will be covered later. At this point three types of problem-solving behaviour (extended problem solving, limited problem solving and routinised response) will be considered.

Extended problem solving (EPS)

Consumers considering the purchase of a car or house undertake a great deal of external search activity and spend a lot of time reaching a solution that satisfies, as closely as possible, the evaluative criteria previously set. This activity is usually associated with products that are unfamiliar, where direct experience and hence knowledge are weak, and where there is considerable financial risk.

Marketing communications should aim to provide a lot of information to assist the decision process. The provision of information through sales literature, such as brochures and leaflets, Web sites for determining product and purchase criteria in product categories where there is little experience, access to salespersons and demonstrations and advertisements are just some of the ways in which information can be provided.

Limited problem solving (LPS)

Having experience of a product means that greater use can be made of internal memory-based search routines, and the external search can be limited to obtaining up-to-date information or to ensuring that the finer points of the decision have been investigated.

Marketing communications should attempt to provide information about any product modification or new attributes and convey messages that highlight those key attributes known to be important to buyers. By differentiating the product, marketing communications provides the buyer with a reason to select that particular product.

Convey messages that highlight those key attributes known to be important to buyers.

ViewPoint 6.1   A magazine for Toni & Guy

Leading high street hair salon brand Toni & Guy needed to maintain their position as a fashion oriented, progressive yet slightly unconventional brand. Part of its strategy was to launch its own magazine, sent free to each of their customers four times a year.

Toni & Guy's customers are by definition familiar with the brand and have reasonable experience of what the brand offers. As with most customer magazines the intention was to remind customers of the Toni & Guy brand values and in doing so create sustainable differentiation. In addition, the marketing goals were to drive more frequent visits, increase the amount spent during each visit and encourage word of mouth communications to attract new customers. The magazine represents a classic communication device designed for audiences who experience limited brand involvement.

The content of the magazine needed to stretch beyond a focus on hair in order to appeal to their customers' overall interest in the brand. Consequently, a great deal of the content was fashion oriented, including beauty advice and tips. The magazine has a high technical specification echoing the desired positioning and customer expectations of the brand.

Source: Based on the APA Customer Magazines Awards for 2004.

Routinised response behaviour (RRB)

For a great number of products the decision process will consist only of an internal search. This is primarily because the buyer has made a number of purchases and has accumulated a great deal of experience. Therefore, only an internal search is necessary, so little time or effort will be spent on external search activities. Low-value items that are frequently purchased fall into this category, for example toothpaste, soap, tinned foods and confectionery.

Some outlets are perceived as suitable for what are regarded as distress purchases. Tesco Express and many petrol stations position themselves as convenience stores for distress purchases (for example a pint of milk at 10 o'clock at night). Many garages have positioned themselves as convenience stores suitable for meeting the needs of RRB purchases. In doing so they are moving themselves away from the perception of being only a distress purchase outlet.

Communicators should focus upon keeping the product within the evoked set or getting it into the set. Learning can be enhanced through repetition of messages, but repetition can also be used to maintain attention and awareness.

Learning can be enhanced through repetition of messages.

Perceived risk

An important factor associated with the purchase decision process is the level of risk perceived by the buyer. This risk concerns the uncertainty of the proposed purchase and the outcomes that will result from a decision to purchase a product.

Risk is perceived because the buyer has little or no experience of the performance of the product or the decision process associated with the purchase. Buyers may lack the ability to make what they see as the right decision and they may be forced to trade the decision to purchase one product in lieu of another because resources, such as time and money, are restricted. Risk is related to not only brand-based decisions but also to product categories, an especially important aspect when launching new technology products, for example. The level of risk an individual experiences varies through time, across products, and is often a reflection of an individual's propensity to manage risk. Risk is related to involvement, trust and other buyer-behaviour concepts.

The level of risk an individual experiences varies through time, across products, and is often a reflection of an individual's propensity to manage risk.

Settle and Alreck (1989) suggest that there are five main forms of risk that can be identified; the purchase of a hi-fi unit demonstrates each element. These are set out in Table 6.1 with respect to the purchase of a hi-fi system.

TABLE 6.1 Types of perceived risk

Type of perceived risk	Explanation
Performance	Will the unit reproduce my music clearly?
Financial	Can I afford that much or should I buy a less expensive version?
Physical	Will the unit damage my other systems or endanger me in any way?
Social	Will my friends and colleagues be impressed?
Ego	Will I feel as good as I want to feel when listening to or talking about my unit?

A sixth element, time, is also considered to be a risk factor (Stone and Gronhaug, 1993):

Using the hi-fi example, will purchase of the unit lead to an inefficient use of my time? Or can I afford the time to search for a good hi-fi so that I will not waste my money?

What constitutes risk is a function of the contextual characteristics of each situation, the individuals involved and the product under consideration:

1. Each situation varies according to perceptions of the shopping experience, the time the purchase is to be made in the context of the other activities that need to be completed (last chance to buy a birthday present, only 15 minutes left before meeting my partner), and the image different stores have and the risk that is associated with the products offered by the store.

2. Each individual has a propensity to higher or lower levels of risk. These levels may vary according to their experience of purchasing particular products, demographic factors such as age, level of education and religion, and various personality factors.

3. The product may, if only for price, convey a level of risk to the purchaser. For example, the purchase of a car is not only a large financial commitment for most people, but is also a highly emotive decision that has significant ego and social risks attached to it.

Perceived risk need not be constant throughout the decision process. Mitchell and Boustani (1994) suggest that the level of perceived risk may vary as depicted in Figure 6.2, although more work is required to determine the validity of their initial findings.

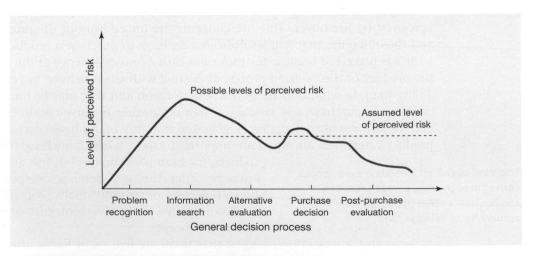

FIGURE 6.2 Varying levels of perceived risk through the purchase decision process. Adapted from Mitchell and Boustani (1994); used with kind permission

The main question is, how can buyers be helped to alleviate high levels of risk during the pre- and post-purchase stages in the decision process? The main method used by buyers is the acquisition of information. Information through the mass media, through word-of-mouth communications and through personal selling (usually sales representatives) is used to set out the likely outcomes and so reduce the levels of risk. Brand loyalty can also be instrumental in reducing risk when launching new products. The use of guarantees, third-party endorsements, money-back offers (some car manufacturers offer the opportunity to return a car within 30 days or exchange it for a different model) and trial samples (as used by many hai care products) are well-used devices to reduce risk.

Brand loyalty can also be instrumental in reducing risk.

ViewPoint 6.2   Back-page risk reducers

Many print-based direct response advertisements use a variety of ways to reduce the risk inherent in buying 'off the back page'. Holiday companies, direct wine and book clubs use a variety of sales channels but Web site-based ecommerce and direct response magazine advertisements provide a rich source of business.

Magazine advertisements, often to be found on or near the back of magazines and Sunday newspaper supplements, allow for a large amount of text as well as eye-catching visual work. The text is often used to reduce functional risk by explaining the features and extolling the benefits of the product or service. Social and ego risks are reduced by setting the right visual scene and depicting people using the product who may be seen as either aspirational or represent the target market. Financial risk is reduced through opportunities to buy now at a reduced or discounted price (credit card) and promises of warranties and money-back guarantees further reduce the uncertainty of this form of exchange. Finally, time risk is reduced through buy-now opportunities and delivery to the door, negating the need to travel, park, browse, compare, decide and carry home the purchase.

Appreciating the level and types of risk buyers perceive is important for many marketing activities. As Mitchell (1999) points out, new product development, segmentation, targeting, positioning and marketing communications can all be influenced by understanding perceived risk. Services, he points out, have been shown to carry higher levels of risk, mainly because of their characteristics of heterogeneity, perishability, inseparability and intangibility that serve to undermine buyer confidence. For example, Ashford *et al.* (2000) refer to the perceived risk associated with dental care and mentions fear and anxiety, the internal environment of the practice, dentists' social and communication skills and patient satisfaction as important elements that may interrelate and influence attitudes and behavioural intentions.

Many direct marketing advertisements in magazines seek to reduce a number of different types of risk. Companies offering wine for direct home delivery, for example, try to reduce performance risk by providing information about each wine being offered. Financial risk is reduced by comparing their 'special' prices with those in the high street, social risk is approached by developing the brand name associations trying to improve credibility and time risk is reduced through the convenience of home delivery.

Many direct marketing advertisements in magazines seek to reduce a number of different types of risk.

Involvement theory

A central framework, critical to understanding consumer decision-making behaviour and associated communications, is involvement theory. Purchase decisions made by consumers vary considerably, and one of the factors thought to be key to brand choice decisions is the level of involvement (in terms of importance and relevance) a consumer has with either the product or the purchase process.

The term 'involvement' has become an important concept in the consumer behaviour literature. The concept has its roots in social psychology, but its current form and interpretation by researchers is both interesting and revealing. There is no consensus on a definition of involvement. Kapferer and Laurent (1985) argue that involvement has five different facets. These are interest, risk importance, risk probability, sign value and hedonic value. Their approach tends to be all-consuming, whereas Ratchford (1987), quoting Zaichkowsky (1985) and others, does not perceive involvement as such a broad matter. The majority of researchers do not recognise the importance of hedonic and sign value elements in this context. To some, involvement is about the ego, perceived risk and purchase importance – a cognitive perspective. To those who favour a behavioural perspective, the search for and evaluation of product-oriented information is pertinent (Schiffman and Kanuk, 1991).

> There is no consensus on a definition of involvement.

Involvement – characteristics

The various characteristics associated with the involvement concept can be considered in three phases. These are depicted at Figure 6.3. Phase 1 considers the degree of involvement that will vary on a situational basis and will be affected by contextual elements such as the nature of the individual and their experiences, values and expectations. The situation itself concerning the purpose of the purchase (e.g. gift or own consumption) will also affect the level of involvement. The product or service will also

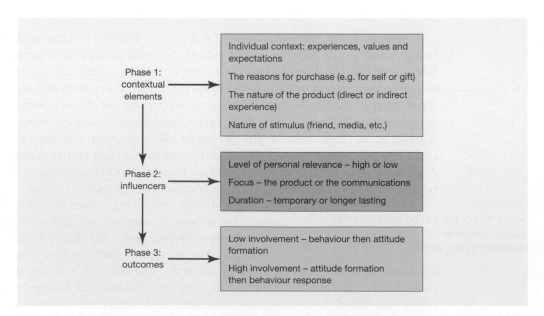

FIGURE 6.3 Three phases of individual involvement and attitude development

be a factor taking account of whether the individual has direct or indirect experience of the object. In addition, the nature of the stimulus to purchase will also be an important factor, whether this be an advertisement, friend or general need.

Phase 2 is characterised by three main factors. The intensity of involvement reflects the level or degree of personal relevance and is normally seen as either high or low involvement. The focus of the involvement refers to whether the object or the communications surrounding the product are of primary importance. The third factor concerns the duration of the involvement. Essentially this may be temporary (e.g. if motivated by an advertisement seen for the first time, or buying a gift) or it may be longer lasting or enduring, reflecting some form of loyalty, commitment or interest in the object or product category.

Phase 3 concerns the outcomes or responses individuals give as a consequence of the involvement they experience. The manner and speed at which information is processed (as a result of the level of involvement) leads primarily to either attitudes being formed prior to behaviour (high involvement) or attitudes being formed after product experience or behaviour (low involvement).

The implications for those responsible for marketing communications are many and varied. However, where high involvement is present messages should stress attributes and benefits (functional) so that they feed the more rational, considered information-processing style that accompanies this position. Where there is low involvement it is better to use more emotional (expressive) messages simply because individuals do not expend any considered or conscious effort in processing the information.

Where high involvement is present messages should stress attributes and benefits.

Where there is low involvement it is better to use more emotional (expressive) messages.

Following this analysis of the involvement process, it is interesting to consider Laaksonen's (1994) interpretation where he draws upon three perspectives of involvement from the literature. These are the cognitive, predisposition to act and response-based interpretations.

He proposes that the *cognitive view* of involvement regards the perceived personal relevance of an object to an individual as of paramount importance. This approach refers to the strength or extent of the cognitive/attitude structure towards an object. The strength of the psychological linkage between an individual and a stimulus object determines the intensity of involvement. How important is it to purchase PlayStation2? This intensity of attitude is seen to have originated from social judgement theory, where involvement is seen as a variable affected by how others might interpret a purchase; that is, their predisposition to respond to PlayStation2.

The second perspective regards involvement as an individual state or *predisposition to act*. Here, involvement focuses on the mental state of an individual, evoked by a stimulus. It is the degree of perceived importance, the interest or level of emotional attachment, arousal, drive or motivation that defines the intensity of involvement, either present in an individual or present in any given situation. Using the previous analogy, how motivated is the individual to purchase PlayStation2? Therefore, involvement refers to the motivational state of an individual in a specific situation. The goals and their importance (hierarchy) defined by individuals determine the direction (towards an object/advertisement or perhaps the act of purchasing) and the level (high, medium, low) of involvement. Again, involvement is regarded as a mediating variable in information processing and a predisposition to act.

The third perspective is the *response view*. Here involvement is regarded as a reaction to an external stimulus or stimuli such as marketing communications. These responses are typically characterised by the form of cognitive and behavioural processing (learn–feel–do) directed to accomplishing a task. So the response view of involvement is based on the reaction of an individual to a stimulus, which will affect the learn–feel–do sequence and the depth to which processing occurs. Therefore, the impact of promotional messages for PlayStation2 is likely to be most important in determining the direction and purchase intentions of potential game station purchasers. Here, involvement is considered as a cognitive response to the marketing communication messages (Batra and Ray, 1983). These views do not see involvement as a mediating variable, simply because involvement is regarded as 'an actualised response in itself' (Laaksonen, 1994).

Of these three, no one view can be determined as a correct interpretation. In a way all are wrong and all are right simultaneously. There is agreement among many researchers that involvement should be seen in the context of three main states. These are high, low and zero involvement. The last of these is self-explanatory and requires no additional comment. The other two states are portrayed as two discrete ends of a continuum. Consumers are thought to move along this continuum, from high to low, as purchase experience increases, perceived risk is reduced and levels of overall knowledge improves.

The approach taken here is that involvement is about the degree of personal relevance and risk perceived by members of the target market in a particular purchase situation (Rossiter *et al.*, 1991). This implies that the level of involvement may vary through time as each member of the target market becomes more (or less) familiar with the purchase and associated communications. At the point of decision-making involvement is either high or low, not some point on a sliding scale or a point on a continuum between two extremes. Involvement is a cognitively bound concept, the strength and depth of which varies among and between individuals.

> Involvement is about the degree of personal relevance and risk perceived by members of the target market in a particular purchase situation.

High involvement

High involvement occurs when a consumer perceives an expected purchase that is not only of high personal relevance but also represents a high level of perceived risk. Cars, washing machines, houses and insurance policies are seen as 'big ticket' items, infrequent purchases that promote a great deal of involvement. The risk described is financial but, as we saw earlier, risk can take other forms. Therefore the choice of

---

ViewPoint 6.3   Web-involved Mazdas

Loch (2003) refers to involvement branding, a concept that brings together direct response and value-added branding work. He cites work on the UK's Mazda 2 campaign where the company used a couple of Web-only video clips and distributed them through a network of targeted sites. By placing tracking codes in the clips Mazda could measure the number of occasions each clip was viewed, and on which sites.

At the end of the clips a 'hot spot' links to a landing page where visitors can request a brochure or even book a test drive. This in turn is linked to a tracking system, connected to Mazda HQ and its dealership network. Through this networked approach Mazda can not only identify how many brochures/test drives were requested directly as a result of the campaign, but also how many cars were sold on the back of it.

Source: Adapted from Loch (2003).

perfume, suit, dress or jewellery may also represent high involvement, with social risk dominating the purchase decision. The consumer, therefore, devotes a great deal of time to researching the intended purchase and collecting as much information as possible in order to reduce, as far as possible, levels of perceived risk.

Low involvement

A *low-involvement* state of mind regarding a purchase suggests little threat or risk to the consumer. Low-priced items such as washing powder, baked beans and breakfast cereals are bought frequently, and past experience of the product class and the brand cues the consumer into a purchase that requires little information or support. Items such as alcoholic and soft drinks, cigarettes and chocolate are also normally seen as low involvement, but they induce a strong sense of ego risk associated with the self-gratification that is attached to the consumption of these products.

ViewPoint 6.4   Grooming men with special words

Men's grooming products have traditionally been regarded as evoking low involvement, but the sector has started to change in recent years, especially within the younger male age groups. Encouraged by key opinion formers such as David Beckham and Brad Pitt, men are becoming more overtly involved with their appearance, health and fitness. As a result some parts of the sector are now becoming more involved with the products and the category.

In a sector where brands such as Nivea, King of Shaves, Easy4men and the recently launched Gillette Complete have grown to satisfy this new market opportunity, care over the presentation of these products is important. Care over the packaging, naming and merchandising of these products is necessary in order to communicate effectively with those men who prefer to be 'involved' with grooming products. It is necessary to use male vocabulary and to avoid effeminate or softer suggestive words. Gray (2004) reports that the focus should be on the functionality of the product and conveying masculinity through acronyms such as DDS (Dual Delivery Systems) rather than phrases such as natural herbs, essence or plant extracts. Brand names such as Perfector, Enhancer, Defender and Improver are more likely to resonate well with the modern man.

Source: Adapted from Gray (2004).

Hedonic consumption

There is a range of products and services that can evoke high levels of involvement based upon the emotional impact that consumption provides the buyer. This is referred to as hedonic consumption, and Hirschmann and Holbrook (1982) describe this approach as 'those facets of consumer behaviour that relate to the multi sensory, fantasy and emotive aspects of one's experience with products'. With its roots partly in the motivation research and partly in the cognitive processing schools, this interpretation of consumer behaviour seeks to explain how and why buyers experience emotional responses to the act of purchase and consumption of particular products. *Historical imagery* occurs when, for example, the colour of a dress, the scent of a perfume

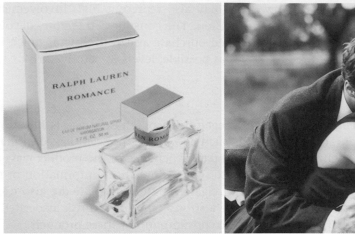 

EXHIBIT 6.1 *Romance* by Ralph Lauren
An example of romantic fantasy used for fragrance advertising. Picture reproduced with the kind permission of Ralph Lauren and Neville McCarthy Associates.

or aftershave, or the aroma of a restaurant or food can trigger an individual's memory to replay an event. In contrast, *fantasy imagery* occurs when a buyer constructs an event, drawing together various colours, sounds and shapes to compose a mental experience of an event that has not occurred previously. Consumers imagine a reality in which they derive sensory pleasure. Some smokers were encouraged to imagine themselves as 'Marlboro Men': not just masculine, but as idealised cowboys (Hirschmann and Holbrook, 1982).

> Consumers imagine a reality in which they derive sensory pleasure.

The advertising of fragrances and luxury brands is often based on images that encourage individuals to project themselves into a desirable or pleasurable environment or situation, for example those which foster romantic associations. The Ralph Lauren *Romance* ad is an excellent example of a romantic/fantasy message. To some extent this is a sophisticated example of features and benefits. The left-hand page (features) shows what the brand is, how it is presented (the packaging) and prominently displays the brand name around the neck of the bottle. The right-hand page shows the benefits of usage, namely the depiction of a romantic embrace, presumably fuelled by *Romance* and one that users perceive as desirable. See Exhibit 6.1. Readers should also observe the thematic consistency of the brand name through the visual associations that the ad seeks to make.

There are a number of problems with the hedonic approach, namely measurement factors of reliability and validity, but, nevertheless, appreciating the hedonic needs of the target audience can be an important contribution to the creation of promotional messages.

Consumer decision-making processes

From this understanding of general decision-making processes, perceived risk and involvement theory, it is possible to identify two main approaches to consumer decision-making.

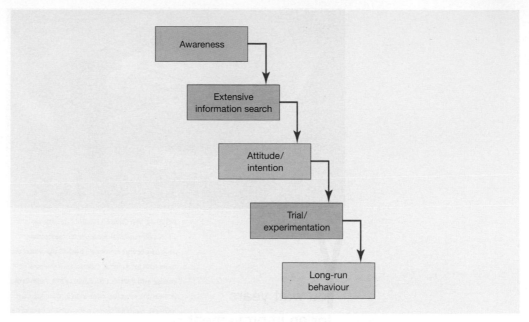

FIGURE 6.4 High-involvement decision-making process

High-involvement decision-making

If an individual is highly involved with the initial purchase of a product, EPS is the appropriate decision sequence, as information is processed in a rational, logical order.

When high-involvement decision-making is present individuals perceive a high level of risk and are concerned about the intended purchase.

Individuals who are highly involved in a purchase are thought to move through the process shown in Figure 6.4. When high-involvement decision-making is present individuals perceive a high level of risk and are concerned about the intended purchase. The essential element in this sequence is that a great deal of information is sought initially and an attitude is developed before a commitment or intention to trial is determined.

Information search is an important part of the high-involvement decision-making process. Because individuals are highly motivated, information is actively sought, processed and evaluated. Many media sources are explored, including the mass media, word-of-mouth communications and point-of-sale communications. As individuals require a lot of information, print media are more appropriate as a large volume of detailed information can be transmitted and this allows the receiver to digest the information at a speed they can control. Exhibit 6.2 depicts an advertisement for a car. Note the amount of information presented and the balance between the copy and the visual elements of the message.

Evaluation of the information and of the alternatives that have been derived from the information search needs to be undertaken. By comparing and implicitly scoring the different attributes of each alternative, a belief about the overall competitiveness of each alternative can be established. In Chapter 5 a compensatory model was examined. In this approach, individuals do not reject products because an attribute scores low; rather, a weakness is offset or compensated for by the strength and high scores accredited to other attributes. An individual's attitude to a purchase is the sum of the scores given to the range of evaluative criteria used in the decision-making process. As observed in Chapter 5, Fishbein states that an attitude towards the act of purchasing and the subjective norm (the perceived attitude of others to the act being considered)

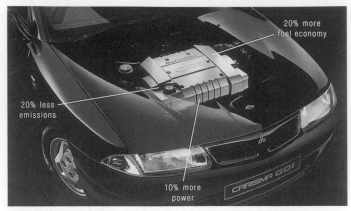

INSIDE THE NEW Carisma is Mitsubishi's revolutionary 1.8 L Gasoline Direct Injection engine. It's been specially designed to be more economical, up to 20% improvement over conventional petrol engines. It releases fewer emissions, including a reduction of carbon dioxide by 20%. Performance is increased too, with a 10% improvement in power output and torque over normal fuel injected petrol engines of the same size. Of course the Carisma GDI® still has all the other important features such as twin airbags, side impact door beams, engine immobiliser and multi-link suspension with passive rear wheel steering. And everything is covered by Mitsubishi's unbeatable 3 year unlimited mileage warranty package. We haven't just re-designed the engine, we've re-invented it.

Prices start from £14,515 on the road.

For more information, simply

Freecall **0800 123 363**.

The Colt Car Company Ltd., Watermoor, Cirencester, Glos GL7 1LF.
www.mitsubishi-cars.co.uk

GDI is a registered trademark of Mitsubishi Motors Corporation. Price includes delivery, number plate and 12 months road fund licence.

EXHIBIT 6.2 A print advertisement for a product that often evokes high involvement
Picture reproduced with the kind permission of Mitsubishi.

combine to form an *intention* to act in a particular way. This part of the process is facilitated by the use of credible sources of information. Therefore personal selling is important to bring individuals closer to the product, in order that it may be demonstrated and allow intense learning to occur.

Trial behaviour will follow if the perceived quality of the product is satisfactory and sufficient triggers, from internal searches, stimulate experimentation. Likewise, long-run behaviour, the goal of all marketing activities, will be determined if the guarantees and product quality combine to meet the expectations of the individual, generated by the information search.

Low-involvement decision-making

If an individual has little involvement with an initial purchase of a product, LPS is the appropriate decision process. Information is processed cognitively but in a passive, involuntary way. Information is processed using right-brain thinking so information is stored as it is received, in sections, and this means that information is stored as a brand association (Heath, 2000). An advertisement for Andrex toilet tissue featuring the puppy is stored as the 'Andrex Puppy' without any overt thinking or reasoning.

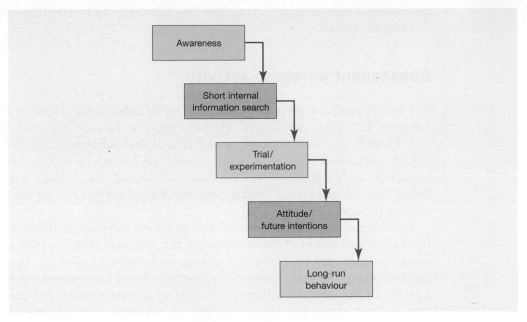

FIGURE 6.5 Low-involvement decision-making process

Because of the low personal relevance and perceived risk associated with this type of processing, message repetition is necessary to define brands and create meaningful brand associations. Individuals who have a low involvement with a purchase decision choose not to search for information and are thought to move through the process shown in Figure 6.5.

Communications can assist the development of awareness in the low-involvement decision-making process. However, as individuals assume a passive problem-solving role, messages need to be shorter than in the high-involvement process and should contain less information. Broadcast media are preferred as they complement the passive learning posture adopted by the individual. Repetition is important because the receiver has little or no motivation to retain information, and his or her perceptual selection processes filter out unimportant information. Learning develops through exposure to repeated messages, but attitudes do not develop at this part of the process (Harris, 1987).

> However, as individuals assume a passive problem-solving role, messages need to be shorter than in the high-involvement process and should contain less information.

Where low involvement is present, each individual relies upon internal, rather than external, search mechanisms, often prompted by point-of-purchase displays. Using non-compensatory decision rules (Chapter 5), where product weaknesses are not offset by strengths, individuals make decisions, often at the point of purchase, to try established or new brands.

> Where low involvement is present, each individual relies upon internal, rather than external, search mechanisms.

Price can be a very important factor by which individuals can discriminate between low-involvement purchase decisions. In high-involvement decisions there is a wide variety of attributes that individuals can use to discriminate between purchase decisions. In low-involvement purchases price, packaging and point-of-purchase displays, and promotions, work together to cue and stimulate an individual into trying a product.

As a direct result of trying a product (or experimenting) and hence product experience, an attitude develops. By judging the quality of the experience, an attitude is formed that acts as the basis for future decisions. Long-run behaviour is a function of promotional messages, product quality and the degree of loyalty that can be sustained towards the brand.

Subsequent purchase activity

The initial purchase decision process frames all subsequent decisions in the product category. If a high-involvement decision process ends satisfactorily, then levels of brand loyalty are normally high, which means that subsequent decisions can be processed much more quickly. Routinised response behaviour occurs safely, as any risk associated with a purchase can be dispelled through the security associated with a brand. Brand loyalty is the normal outcome of a successful high-involvement decision-making process.

If the high-involvement process ends in partial satisfaction then, depending upon the nature and extent of the outstanding risk, the next decision may also be EPS. For example, if the purchase of a first savings or investment product results in total dissatisfaction, any second purchase of a similar or financially related product will require a review of the critical attributes to provide up-to-date product and provider information, but not necessarily to inform about what a savings/investment policy is.

If the initial decision was motivated by a low level of involvement and the outcome was satisfactory, then subsequent decisions will be based upon a state of brand ambivalence. This means that individuals relegate these decisions to a habitual process but will consider a number of different brands, and will switch to one of them if they perceive that the circumstances in which the decision is being made are changing. For example, a typical habitual decision concerns the purchase of tinned tomatoes. Most consumers will decide upon their usual brand until they notice a price promotion, special offer or incentive to purchase a different brand. A switch may also be actuated by different merchandising and positioning within the store, different personal requirements (e.g. dietary changes) and levels of brand awareness.

Repeat purchase decisions are often unstable on the grounds that buyers are content to switch between products in their evoked set unless there is a high level of brand loyalty. Manufacturers of products that are associated with low-involvement decision-making are required to engage in promotional activities that keep the awareness of the brand at the top of each individual's mind-set. Otherwise there is a danger that a competitor may change the circumstances in which an individual makes a decision and trigger a motivation to try its offering.

Impact on communications

Involvement is a theory central to our understanding of the way in which information is processed and the way in which consumers make decisions about product purchases.

There are two main types of involvement: high and low.

It was established that there are two main types of involvement: high and low. This concept of involvement leads to two orderings of the hierarchy of effects. In decisions where there is high involvement, attitude precedes trial behaviour. In low-involvement cases this position is reversed. In the former a positive and specific position is assumed by the consumer, whereas in the latter attitudes to the product (not the product class) develop after product use.

As discussed earlier, where there is high involvement, consumers seek out information because they are concerned about the decision processes and outcomes. Because they have these concerns, consumers develop an attitude prior to behaviour. Products

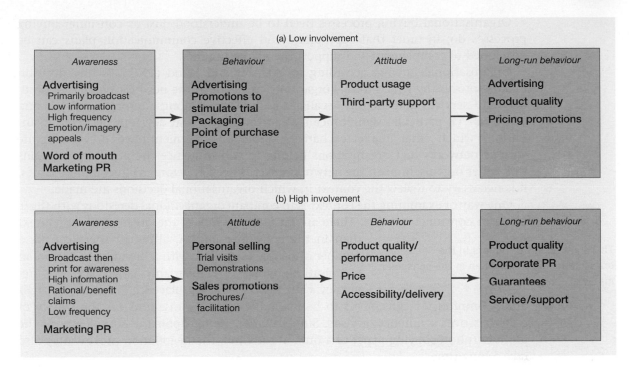

FIGURE 6.6 Promotional strategies for different levels of involvement

that evoke high-involvement decision processes tend to be high cost, to be bought relatively infrequently, to be complex, to elicit feelings of risk and to be visible to others.

Where there is low involvement, consumers are content to select any one of a number of acceptable products and often rely on those that are in the individual's evoked set. Low involvement is thought to be a comfortable state, because there are too many other decisions in life to have to make decisions about each one of them, so an opportunity not to have to seek information and make other decisions is welcome.

This suggests that high and low positions are not static or permanent. Involvement is said by some (Vaughn, 1980; Ratchford, 1987) to be a continuum where consumers can move from a high- to a low-involvement position, as their experience of a product increases and their perceived risk is reduced. Figure 6.6 indicates the advertising and promotion strategies best suited for each level within both involvement spectra.

Involvement impacts therefore on what is said, how it is said and when it is said. Readers are advised that other material relating to involvement and the strategic implications for marketing communications can be found in Chapters 12 and 18.

Organisational buying decision processes

Organisations have so far been viewed in the context of sellers, but in order to function they need to buy materials, parts, general supplies and services from a range of other organisations. Some texts refer to this as industrial marketing or, in the more current terminology, business-to-business marketing, reflecting the growth and importance of the public sector and the increasing use of the services sector within mature economies. However, the term 'organisational marketing' is used here to reflect the wide range of organisations involved in such activities.

Organisational buying processes need to be understood, just as consumer buying processes do, in order that appropriate and effective communication plans can be developed to complement and support the marketing mix.

Organisational buying, according to Webster and Wind (1972), is 'the decision making process by which formal organisations establish the need for purchased products and services and identify, evaluate and choose among alternative brands and suppliers'. Of particular significance is the relationship that develops between organisations which enter market exchange transactions. As mentioned previously, the various networks that organisations belong to will influence the purchase decisions that other organisations in the network make. However, before exploring these issues, it is necessary to review the context in which organisational decisions are made.

One way of examining the context is to compare organisational decisions with those made in consumer markets. There are far fewer buyers in the organisational context than in the consumer market, although there can be a number of people associated with a buying decision in an organisation. Orders are invariably larger and the frequency with which they are placed is much lower. It is quite common for agreements to be made between organisations for the supply of materials over a number of years. Similarly, depending upon the complexity of the product (photocopying paper or a one-off satellite), the negotiation process may also take a long time.

> There are far fewer buyers in the organisational context than in the consumer market.

ViewPoint 6.5   Hospital buying decisions

The purchase of medical supplies and equipment by hospitals is an important decision, if only because of the implications of the decisions made with regard to patient welfare. However, the wide variety of people involved in the process can lead to buying decisions becoming overly complex, sometimes over budget and delayed. For example, purchasing decisions regarding infusion pumps are influenced by various stakeholder groups: medical experts (such as doctors and consultants), administrators (such as general managers and purchasing administrators), those with financial responsibilities, purchasing agents and of course certain direct government representatives, primary care trusts and other influential stakeholders.

Many of the characteristics associated with consumer decision-making processes can be observed in the organisational context. However, organisational buyers make decisions that ultimately contribute to the achievement of corporate objectives. To make the necessary decisions a high volume of pertinent information is often required. This information needs to be relatively detailed and is normally presented in a rational and logical style. The needs of the buyers are many and complex, and some may be personal. Goals, such as promotion and career advancement within the organisation, coupled with ego and employee satisfaction, combine to make organisational buying an important task, one that requires professional training and the development of expertise if the role is to be performed optimally.

> The needs of the buyers are many and complex, and some may be personal.

TABLE 6.2 Main characteristics of the buyclasses

Buyclass	Degree of familiarity with the problem	Information requirements	Alternative solutions
New buy	The problem is fresh to the decision-makers	A great deal of information is required	Alternative solutions are unknown, all are considered new
Modified rebuy	The requirement is not new but is different from previous situations	More information is required but past experience is of use	Buying decision needs new solutions
Rebuy	The problem is identical to previous experiences	Little or no information is required	Alternative solutions not sought or required

Buyclasses

Organisational buyers make decisions that vary with each buying situation and buyclass.

Organisational buyers make decisions that vary with each buying situation and buyclass. Buyclasses, according to Robinson *et al.* (1967), comprise three types: new task, modified rebuy and straight rebuy (Table 6.2):

1. *New buy*

   As the name implies, the organisation is faced with a first-time buying situation. Risk is inevitably high at this point, and partly as a consequence there are a large number of decision participants. Each participant requires a lot of information and a relatively long period of time is required for the information to be assimilated and a decision to be made.

2. *Modified rebuy*

   Having purchased a product, the organisation may request through its buyer that certain modifications be made to future purchases, for example adjustments to the specification of the product, further negotiation on price levels or perhaps the arrangement for alternative delivery patterns. Fewer people are involved in the decision process than in the new task situation.

3. *Straight rebuy*

   In this situation, the purchasing department reorders on a routine basis, very often working from an approved list of suppliers. No other people are involved with the exercise until different suppliers attempt to change the environment in which the decision is made. For example, they may interrupt the procedure with a potentially better offer.

These phases bear a strong resemblance to the extended, limited and routinised response identified earlier with respect to the consumer market.

Reference has been made on a number of occasions to organisational buyers, as if these people are the only representatives of an organisation to be involved with the purchase decision process. This is not the case, as very often a large number of people are involved in the purchase decision. This group is referred to as either the decision-making unit (DMU) or the buying centre.

Buying centres vary in size and composition in accordance with the nature of each individual task. Webster and Wind (1972) identified a number of people who make up the buying centre.

Users are people who not only initiate the purchase process but will use the product, once it has been acquired, and evaluate its performance. *Influencers* very often help set the technical specifications for the proposed purchase and assist the evaluation of alternative offerings by potential suppliers. *Deciders* are those who make purchasing decisions. In repeat buying activities the buyer may well also be the decider. However, it is normal practice to require that expenditure decisions involving sums over a certain financial limit be authorised by other, often senior, managers. *Buyers* (purchasing managers) select suppliers and manage the process whereby the required products are procured. As identified previously, buyers may not decide which product is to be purchased but they influence the framework within which the decision is made. *Gatekeepers* have the potential to control the type and flow of information to the organisation and the members of the buying centre. These gatekeepers may be technical personnel, secretaries or telephone switchboard operators.

The size and form of the buying centre is not static. It can vary according to the complexity of the product being considered and the degree of risk each decision is

The size and form of the buying centre is not static.

perceived to carry for the organisation. Different roles are required and adopted as the nature of the buying task changes with each new purchase situation (Bonoma, 1982). It is vital for seller organisations to identify members of the buying centre and to target and refine their messages to meet the needs of each member of the centre.

The task of the marketing communications manager and the corresponding sales team is to decide which key participants have to be reached, with which type of message, with what frequency and to what depth contact should be made. Just as with individual consumers, each member of the buying centre is an active problem solver and processes information so that personal and organisational goals are achieved.

Influences on the buying centre

Three major influences on organisational buyer behaviour can be identified as stakeholders, the organisational environment and those aspects the individual brings to the situation. See Table 6.3.

Stakeholders develop relationships between the focus organisation and other stakeholders in the network. The nature of the exchange relationship and the style of communications will influence buying decisions. If the relationship between organisations is trusting, mutually supportive and based upon a longer-term per-

TABLE 6.3 Major influences on organisational buying behaviour

Stakeholder influences	Organisational influences	Individual influences
Economic conditions	Corporate strategy	Personality
Legislation	Organisational culture and values	Age
Competitor strategies	Resources and costs	Status
Industry regulations	Purchasing policies and procedures	Reward structure and systems
Technological developments	Interpersonal relationships	
Social and cultural values		
Interorganisation relationships		

Source: Based on Webster and Wind (1972).

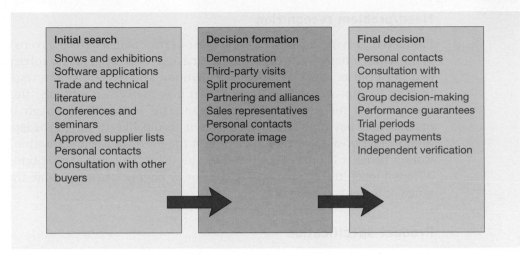

FIGURE 6.7 Risk reduction approaches for organisational purchase decisions

spective (a relational structure) then the behaviour of the buying centre may be seen to be cooperative and constructive. If the relationship is formal, regular, unsupportive and based upon short-term convenience (a market structure-based relationship) then the purchase behaviour may be observed as courteous yet distant.

Without doubt the major determinant of the organisational environment is the cost associated with switching from one supplier to another (Bowersox and Cooper, 1992). When an organisation chooses to enter into a buying relationship with another organisation, an investment is made in time, people, assets and systems. Should the relationship with the new supplier fail to work satisfactorily, then a cost is incurred in switching to another supplier. It is these switching costs that heavily influence buying decisions. The higher the potential switching costs, the greater the loss in flexibility and the greater the need to make the relationship appropriate at the outset.

Behaviour within the buying centre is also largely determined by the interpersonal relationships of the members of the centre. Participation in the buying centre has been shown to be highly influenced by individuals' perceptions of the personal consequences of their contribution to each of the stages in the process. The more that individuals think they will be blamed for a bad decision or praised for a good decision, the greater their participation, influence and visible DMU-related activity (McQuiston and Dickson, 1991). The nature and dispersal of power within the unit can influence the decisions that are made. Power is increasingly viewed from the perspective of an individual's ability to control the flow of information and the deployment of resources (Spekman and Gronhaug, 1986). This approach reflects a network approach to, in this case, intraorganisational communications.

From a communications perspective there is strong evidence that the provision/collection of information is a major contributor to risk reduction (Mitchell, 1995). Figure 6.7 sets out some of the more common approaches used by organisations to reduce risk.

There is strong evidence that the provision/ collection of information is a major contributor to risk reduction.

Buyphases

The organisational buying decision process consists of several stages or buyphases (Robinson *et al.*, 1967). The following sequence of six phases or events is particular to the new task buyclass. Many of these buyphases are ignored or compressed when either of the other two buyclasses are encountered.

Need/problem recognition

Products or services are purchased because of two main events (Cravens and Woodruff, 1986). Difficulties may be encountered first as a result of a need to solve problems, such as a stock-out or new government regulations, and, secondly, as a response to opportunities to improve performance or enter new markets. Essentially, the need/recognition phase is the identification of a gap. This is the gap between the benefits an organisation has now and the benefits it would like to have. For example, when a photocopier breaks down or fails to meet the needs of the organisation, the communication benefits it offers are missed by the users. This gap can be bridged by using a different machine on a temporary basis or by buying a new machine that provides the range of benefits required.

Product specification

As a result of identifying a problem and the size of the gap, influencers and users can determine the desired characteristics of the product needed to resolve the problem. This may take the form of a general description or may require a much more detailed analysis and the creation of a specification for a particular product. What sort of photocopier is required? What is it expected to achieve? How many documents should it copy per minute? Is a collator or tray required? This is an important part of the process, because if it is executed properly it will narrow the supplier search and save on the costs associated with evaluation prior to a final decision.

Supplier and product search

At this stage the buyer actively seeks organisations who can supply the necessary product. There are two main issues at this point. Will the product reach the required performance standards and will it match the specification? Secondly, will the potential supplier meet the other organisational requirements? In most circumstances organisations review the market and their internal sources of information and arrive at a decision that is based on rational criteria.

Organisations, as we have seen before, work wherever possible to reduce uncertainty and risk. By working with others who are known, of whom the organisation has direct experience and who can be trusted, risk and uncertainty can be reduced substantially. This highlights another reason why many organisations seek relational exchanges and operate within established networks and seek to support each other.

The quest for suppliers and products may be a short task for the buyer; however, if the established network cannot provide a solution, the buying organisation has to seek new suppliers, and hence new networks, to be able to identify and short-list appropriate supplier organisations.

Evaluation of proposals

Depending upon the complexity and value of the potential order(s), the proposal is a vital part of the communication plan and should be prepared professionally. The proposals of the short-listed organisations are reviewed in the context of two main criteria: the product specification and the evaluation of the supplying organisation. If the organisation is already a part of the network, little search and review time need be allocated. If the proposed supplier is new to the organisation a review may be necessary to establish whether it will be appropriate (in terms of price, delivery and service) and whether there is the potential for a long-term relationship or whether this is a single purchase that is unlikely to be repeated.

Once again, therefore, is the relationship going to be a market exchange or a relational exchange? The actions of both organisations, and of some of the other organisations in the network to the new entrant, are going to be critical in determining the form and nature of future relationships.

Supplier selection

The buying centre will undertake a supplier analysis and use a variety of criteria depending upon the particular type of item sought. This selection process takes place in the light of the comments made in the previous section. A further useful perspective is to view supplier organisations as a continuum, from reliance on a single source to the use of a wide variety of suppliers of the same product.

Jackson (1985) proposed that organisations might buy a product from a range of different suppliers, in other words a range of multiple sources are maintained (a practice of many government departments). She labelled this approach 'always a share', as several suppliers are given the opportunity to share the business available to the buying centre. The major disadvantage is that this approach fails to drive cost as low as possible, as the discounts derived from volume sales are not achieved. The advantage to the buying centre is that a relatively small investment is required and little risk is entailed in following such a strategy.

At the other end of the continuum are organisations that only use a single-source supplier. All purchases are made from the single source until circumstances change to such a degree that the buyer's needs are no longer being satisfied. Jackson referred to these organisations as 'lost for good', because once a relationship with a new organisation has been developed, they are lost for good to the original supplier. An increasing number of organisations are choosing to enter alliances with a limited number or even single-source suppliers.

An increasing number of organisations are choosing to enter alliances with a limited number or even single-source suppliers.

The objective is to build a long-term relationship, work together to build quality and help each other achieve their goals. Outsourcing manufacturing activities for non-core activities has increased, and this has moved the focus of communications from an internal to an external perspective.

Evaluation

The order is written against the selected supplier and immediately the supplier is monitored and performance is evaluated against such diverse criteria as responsiveness to enquiries and modifications to the specification and timing of delivery. When the product is delivered it may reach the stated specification but fail to satisfy the original need. This is a case where the specification needs to be rewritten before any future orders are placed.

Organisational buying has shifted from a one-to-one dyadic encounter, salesperson to buyer, to a position where a buying team meets a selling team. The skills associated with this process are different and are becoming much more sophisticated, and the demands on both buyers and sellers are more pronounced. The processes of buying and selling are complex and interactive.

Developments in the environment can impact on a consumer or organisation buyer and change both the way decisions are made and their nature. For example, the decision to purchase new plant and machinery requires consideration of the future cash flows generated by the capital item. Many people will be involved in the decision, and the time necessary for consultation may mean that other parts of the decision-making process are completed simultaneously.

ViewPoint 6.6   Influences on pump buying

There are a large number of influences that impact on purchasing decisions. These can be classified as macro and micro, or external and internal. However, in certain purchasing situations, and in certain sectors, there are a variety of ongoing costs that also need to be considered.

In the previous ViewPoint, infusion pumps were considered as a focus for hospital buying. In addition to the various political, social and technological influences that affect the various decision makers and members of the DMU, there are economic factors associated with running these pumps. For example, The Royal United Hospital Bath NHS Trust disclosed that they saved £35,000 on consumables by adopting a life-cycle costing approach when deciding on the supplier of their next pump order. In a sense this saving represents added value, especially in a purchasing environment that is increasingly subject to tighter controls, stricter procedures and a culture which stresses value for money. The pump supplier that lost the hospital's business would do well to consider the influences, benefits and value which they need to offer in future.

There are a number of other issues concerned with the manner in which the members of a buying centre interact and make choices. An interesting new approach to strategic management considers the subjective, cognitive thoughts of the strategist to be more important than has been considered previously. Porter (1980), Ansoff and McDonnell (1990) and others, in what is referred to as the design school of thought, assume that strategic decisions result from rational, logical analysis and interpretation of the environment.

An alternative view is that as environments are too complex and dynamic for objective analysis to be of any practical use (Simon, 1976), then strategy or choices are fashioned from individuals' interpretations of their environment. Projections of historical data in uncertain, highly unpredictable environments mean that strategists, or members of the buying centre in this case, will rely more on knowledge and experience as the main platform for decision-making.

Unifying models of buyer decision-making

The models of decision-making presented here and in the literature are important because they focus attention on key issues and bring out the priorities. They help the development of marketing communications by segregating audiences according to their situational needs. However, two points of contention concern the implied rationality of decision-making, particularly in organisational contexts and the assumption that consumer decision-making is different to organisational decision-making.

For example, there is immediate similarity between the EPS, LPS and RRB consumer-related purchase states and the new task, modified rebuy and rebuy states associated with organisational buying. Risk and involvement are relevant to both categories and, although the antecedents may vary, the marketing communications used to alleviate or reduce these conditions are essentially the same, just deployed in different ways. Wilson (2000) explores the issues related to rationality and implied differences. For example, consumers make product-related purchase decisions based on a wide array of inputs from other people and not just those in the immediate family environment. This is akin to group buying dynamics associated with the DMU. He argues that the rationality normally associated with organisational decision-making is misplaced, suggesting that in some circumstances the protracted nature of decision-making is more a reflection of organisational culture and the need to follow bureaucratic procedures and to show due diligence. In addition, issues concerning established behaviour patterns, difficulties and reluctance to break with established (purchasing) practices, intra- and interorganisational politics and relationships, and the costs associated with supplier switching, all contribute to a more interpretative understanding of organisational decision-making. Further support for this view is given by Mason and Gray (1999), who refer to the characteristics of decision-making in the air business passenger travel market and note some strong similarities between the two main groups.

What needs to be considered is that many of the characteristics of both consumer and organisational decision-making show greater similarities than normally assumed (or taught). The implication for marketing communications is that a richer, deeper understanding of these processes and characteristics may encourage the development of more effective communications.

> A richer, deeper understanding of these processes and characteristics may encourage the development of more effective communications.

Summary

The processes that buyers use to make purchase decisions differ according to a variety of factors. These vary with the nature of the purchase situation; that is, whether the purchase is oriented to consumer or organisational buying and the depth of experience held by the buyer. Other factors concerned are the levels of perceived risk, involvement, knowledge and the number of others who are contributing to the final outcome.

Some of the decision processes that have been presented in this chapter appear to be linear and based upon logic and reason. This is not the case, as decisions are often the result of experience, knowledge and an interpretative view of the environment. Therefore the decision processes used by buyers are not always sequential, nor do they reflect a rational approach to resolving problems and needs.

Marketing communications needs to be based on an understanding of the decision processes used by buyers in the targeted market. This means that the content and style of messages and the form of delivery by the tools of the promotional mix (Chapters 20–31) can be dovetailed closely to the needs of the receivers. This also demonstrates how the realm of understanding is an important issue in effective communications.

Review questions

1. Describe the general decision-making process.
2. What are EPS, LPS and RRB?
3. Select a product and a service that you have used recently and relate the six elements of perceived risk to both of them. How do the elements of risk differ?
4. Explain the three broad interpretations of involvement. How does involvement differ from perceived risk?

5. Describe the high- and low-involvement decision-making processes.
6. Highlight the differences between consumer and organisational buying.
7. What are buyclasses and buying centres?
8. How might a salesperson successfully utilise knowledge about the buying centre?
9. Explain the components of the various buyphases.
10. What are the main communication differences between consumer-oriented and business-to-business-oriented marketing communications?

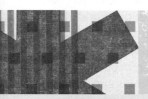

MINI-CASE
Sunny Cottage Holidays

Sunny Cottage Holidays was considering its marketing communications and trying to determine how best to communicate with its different audiences. The company operates in the holiday cottage market and until now employed traditional processes and procedures to attract business.

Of demand for rented holiday cottages 58 per cent is concentrated in the A, B and C1 social groups. Very often customers want an independent family holiday rather than to be part of a group. The notion of 'escaping to the countryside' for a short break is significant for those holidaying out of season in rented cottages. For those holidaying in the main summer months, the prime reasons for renting a cottage, apart from the geographic scenery, appear to be the informality associated with these types of holidays and the wide range of activities available to families of all ages. Some 94 per cent of bookings are for periods of four or more nights in the period June to September. The purchase decision process is inevitably one of high involvement and based upon high levels of trust.

portfolio) and to customers in order to obtain revenue and profit on the cottages they rent out.

An agent's attractiveness to property owners is related to their ability to be seen to be active in securing bookings and to the development of an image with which property owners are happy to be associated. Focused geographic markets permit advertising in the local press, in local authority guides and in Tourist Information Centres (TICs). Word of mouth and participation at local exhibitions are further important means of developing visibility. By instigating a system to check the standards of accommodation, agents demonstrate their concern and orientation to quality and tourist satisfaction.

Agents also use advertising to encourage property owners to place their accommodation with them in order that they secure bookings on their behalf. Both placements and bookings are generated partly through advertising in such publications as *Exchange and Mart*, *Dalton's Weekly*, the *Sunday Times* and the *Observer*, a variety of provincial newspapers, and travel magazines.

The agents' view

Cottage owners require bookings, and to assist them they choose either to undertake their own marketing, to use an agent, or to use a combination of the two methods. When using an agent (such as Sunny Cottage Holidays) responsibility for marketing properties and managing bookings passes to the agent, who receives a 20 per cent commission for each successful booking.

Agents such as Sunny Cottage Holidays need to market themselves to cottage owners (to develop a

The Tourist Board view

One of the roles of the Regional Tourist Board (RTB) is to encourage people to visit and take their holidays in a particular area and to encourage the provision and improvement of tourist amenities and facilities. They accomplish these aims by, in broad terms, providing financial assistance to certain tourism projects, by investing in promotional activities and by providing advisory and information services. TICs and TIPs (Tourist Information Points) are vital supporting elements of the tourism industry. TIPs are unmanned information points, whereas TICs are usually staffed and provide tourists with authoritative information and assist them with arrangements associated with their visit.

The RTB inspects tourist accommodation at the request of owners and managers. Accommodation that reaches the necessary standard is said to be 'verified' and described as such in RTB publications. Verification is justified on the grounds that it helps to protect consumer interests by giving customers a greater guarantee of appropriate standards. It also provides a potential advantage to scheme participants in that the endorsement is seen to be granted by a third party which has no pecuniary interest in the accommodation. Finally, it is claimed that the system helps to advance improvements in the quality of accommodation offerings.

The customers' view

The primary purchasing procedure is based around a colour brochure, mailed to customers by agents and/or cottage owners. These colour brochures are traditionally large and require customers to identify their preferred cottages by thumbing through pages of photographs, categorised first by geographical area and then size of accommodation. Most photographs are of the exterior of the cottages, although some of the more expensive or desirable properties have some interior views. The limited descriptive text is normally supported by a coding system in order to provide some comparative measure of quality and content. To determine the price of renting a cottage for a week, reference has to be made to particular price bands that are correlated with different weeks of the year. The next step is to telephone Sunny Cottage Holidays to find out if the identified and preferred cottage is available in the week(s) required.

Sunny Cottage Holidays' view

Sunny Cottage Holidays is considering the way it communicates with its customers as it feels there are certain problems associated with the way it currently does business; for example, the high cost of producing the colour brochures, the long lead times involved in changing and updating them, combined with the wastage involved in mailing to people who may not be actively interested in renting a holiday cottage. The call centre is perceived as an important part of the process and is effective in both clarifying information for customers and building trust through 'personal' contact. However, Sunny Cottage Holidays believes that there is a more effective and efficient way of using its marketing communications and providing customers with a more customer-friendly communication process.

Questions

1 How might the provision of a Web site assist SCH?

2 Compare the levels of risk and involvement present for both visitors and cottage owners.

3 How might an understanding of involvement assist the development of a marketing communications campaign for SCH?

4 Consider the different types of decision making (business-to-customer and business-to-business) and apply them to the SCH case.

References

Ansoff, H.I. and McDonnell, E.J. (1990) *Implanting Strategic Management.* 2nd edn. Hemel Hempstead: Prentice Hall.

Ashford, R., Cuthbert, P. and Shani, N. (2000) Perceived risk and consumer decision making related to health services: a comparative study. *International Journal of Nonprofit and Voluntary Sector Marketing,* 5(1), pp. 58–72.

Batra, R. and Ray, M.L. (1983) Operationalizing involvement as depth and quality of response. In *Advances in Consumer Research* (eds R.P. Bagozzi and A.M. Tybout), Vol. 10, pp. 309–13. Ann Arbor, MI: Association for Consumer Research.

Bonoma, T.V. (1982) Major sales: who really does the buying? *Harvard Business Review* (May/June), p. 113.

Bowersox, D. and Cooper, M. (1992) *Strategic Marketing Channel Management*. New York: McGraw-Hill.

Cravens, D. and Woodruff, R. (1986) *Marketing*. Reading, MA: Addison-Wesley.

Gray, R. (2004) The changing faces of man. *Marketing*, 27 October, pp. 28–30.

Harris, G. (1987) The implications of low involvement theory for advertising effectiveness. *International Journal of Advertising*, **6**, pp. 207–21.

Heath, R. (2000) Low-involvement processing. *Admap* (March), pp. 14–16.

Hirschmann, E.C. and Holbrook, M.B. (1982) Hedonic consumption: emerging concepts, methods and propositions. *Journal of Marketing*, **46** (Summer), pp. 92–101.

Jackson, B. (1985) Build customer relationships that last. *Harvard Business Review*, **63**(6), pp. 120–8.

Kapferer, J.N. and Laurent, G. (1985) Consumer involvement profiles: a new practical approach to consumer involvement. *Journal of Advertising Research*, **25**(6), pp. 48–56.

Laaksonen, P. (1994) *Consumer Involvement: Concepts and Research*. London: Routledge.

Loch, R. (2003) *Involvement Branding: Offering the Best of Both Worlds*. Retrieved 18 November 2004 from www.marketingvox.com/archives/2003/05/14/.

McQuiston, D.H. and Dickson, P.R. (1991) The effect of perceived personal consequences on participation and influence in organisational buying. *Journal of Business*, **23**, pp. 159–77.

Mason, K.J. and Gray, R. (1999) Stakeholders in a hybrid market: the example of air business passenger travel. *European Journal of Marketing*, **33**(9/10), pp. 844–58.

Mitchell, V.-M. (1995) Organisational risk perception and reduction: a literature review. *British Journal of Management*, **6**, pp. 115–33.

Mitchell, V.-M. (1999) Consumer perceived risk: conceptualisations and models. *European Journal of Marketing*, **33**(1/2), pp. 163–95.

Mitchell, V-W. and Boustani, P. (1994) A preliminary investigation into pre- and post-purchase risk perception and reduction. *European Journal of Marketing*, **28**(1), pp. 56–71.

Porter, M.E. (1980) *Competitive Strategy: Techniques for Analysing Industries and Competitors*. New York: Free Press.

Ratchford, B.T. (1987) New insights about the FCB grid. *Journal of Advertising Research* (August/September), pp. 24–38.

Robinson, P.J., Faris, C.W. and Wind, Y. (1967) *Industrial Buying and Creative Marketing*. Boston, MA: Allyn & Bacon.

Rossiter, J.R., Percy, L. and Donovan, R.J. (1991) A better advertising planning grid. *Journal of Advertising Research* (October/November), pp. 11–21.

Schiffman, L. and Kanuk, L. (1991) *Consumer Behavior*. Englewood Cliffs, NJ: Prentice-Hall.

Settle, R.B. and Alreck, P. (1989) Reducing buyers' sense of risk. *Marketing Communications* (January), pp. 34–40.

Simon, H.A. (1976) *Administrative Behavior: A Study of Decision Making Processes in Administrative Organizations*. New York: Free Press.

Spekman, R.E. and Gronhaug, K. (1986) Conceptual and methodological issues in buying centre research. *European Journal of Marketing*, **20**(7), pp. 50–63.

Stone, R.N. and Gronhaug, K. (1993) Perceived risk: further considerations for the marketing discipline. *European Journal of Marketing*, **27**(3), pp. 39–50.

Vaughn, R. (1980) How advertising works: a planning model. *Journal of Advertising Research* (October), pp. 27–33.

Webster, F.E. and Wind, Y. (1972) *Organizational Buying Behavior*. Englewood Cliffs, NJ: Prentice-Hall.

Wilson, D.F. (2000) Why divide consumer and organisational buyer behaviour? *European Journal of Marketing*, **34**(7), pp. 780–96.

Zaichkowsky, J. (1985) Measuring the involvement constraint. *Journal of Consumer Research*, **12**, pp. 341–52.

How marketing communications might work

7

An attempt to understand how marketing communications might work must be cautioned by an appreciation of the complexity and contradictions inherent in this complex commercial activity. Understanding how marketing communications might work, with its rich mosaic of perceptions, emotions, attitudes, information and patterns of behaviour is challenging in itself.

Aims and objectives

The aims of this chapter are to consider some of the theoretical concepts associated with ideas about how marketing communications might work and to consider the complexities associated with understanding how clients can best use marketing communications.

The objectives of this chapter are to:

1. explore some of the fundamental ideas about the role of marketing communications;

2. examine the strengths and weaknesses of the sequential models of how marketing communications works;

3. explain cognitive processing as a means of understanding how people use marketing communications messages;

4. discuss the contribution that the elaboration likelihood model can make to comprehending how motivation and attitude change can be brought together;

5. consider the concept, significant value;

6. present a composite model of how marketing communications might work.

Introduction

This chapter considers ways in which marketing communications might work and introduces a number of concepts and frameworks that have contributed to our understanding. This chapter should be read prior to Chapters 11 and 18 in which ideas about integrated marketing communications and ways in which advertising is considered to work are explored. In addition, Chapter 19 complements this chapter as it considers the content of advertising messages, or what is to be conveyed.

Ideas about how advertising works dominate the literature, whereas ideas about how marketing communications is thought to work are often regarded as of secondary consideration. Although the author recognises the importance of both these approaches it is important to change this priority, if only in recognition of the principles of integrated marketing communications. This chapter therefore deals with ideas concerning ways to explain and interpret how marketing communications might work.

Context – strategy & marketing communications

For a long time many considered marketing communications to be a purely operational issue, one which worked by delivering messages about products to audiences, who then, if the communication was effective, purchased the product. No real consideration was given to combining and synchronizing the tools, reinforcing messages, understanding the target audience or keying the communications into the overall organisational strategy.

This silo approach has changed. Propelled by the emerging focus on a wider range of stakeholders (Chapter 8), the excitement about relationship management (Chapter 9), surging developments in technology (Chapter 10) and the emerging controversy over integrated marketing communications (Chapter 11) has raised the profile and importance of a strategic orientation for marketing communications.

The corporate strategy that organisations pursue should be supported by business, operational and functional level strategies. Therefore, to be effective, marketing communications should be used to complement the marketing, business and corporate strategies. Such complementarity serves to reinforce core messages, reflect the mission and provide a means of using resources efficiently yet at the same time provide reinforcement for the whole business strategy.

ViewPoint 7.1   AA – that's the strategy

The relationship between corporate strategy and marketing communications can be observed quite clearly by looking at the UK market leader for roadside assistance, the AA.

The AA used to position itself as the 'Fourth emergency service' and in doing so conveyed very clearly its main business activity and key values for audiences. Centrica, whose core business rests with providing a range of household services, bought the organisation partly because it saw value in the 9.5 million members and the opportunities to cross sell their products. This strategy was reflected in the new strapline 'Just AAsk', introduced in 2002. See Exhibit 7.1. This drew attention not just to the breakdown facilities, but to insurance, publishing, driving lessons, retailing and other travel related services.

However, CVC Capital Partners, in partnership with Permira, bought the AA from Centrica, partly because they could see opportunities to exploit unrealised value. Their business strategy is about splitting the company into independent businesses, and selling off parts such as publishing and insurance because they are not core to roadside assistance. As a result the 'Just AAsk' strategy has been abandoned, the centralised marketing department collapsed and, according to Bold (2004), the AA will return to being the 'fourth emergency service'. See Exhibit 7.2.

It could be argued that marketing communications works when it effectively reflects the corporate level strategy and supports the marketing plan and other related activities. It does not work simply because it complements strategy but it certainly will not work unless it does reflect the marketing and business imperatives.

The emergence of marketing communications

It is important to appreciate how marketing communications has developed in order to understand how it might work. Before marketing communications there was promotion and before that separate individual promotional tools, and one overriding tool, advertising. The broad task of advertising was to deliver the unique selling proposition (USP) that all products were considered to have. These USPs were based on product

ViewPoint 7.2   USP with Ronseal

Ronseal has a range of products in the specialist paint sector. One of its major products is called *No Rust* that, unlike other paints, can be applied directly to rust and its 3 in 1 formulation means – no primer, no undercoat, no fuss.

Ronseal claims that the unique formulation contains 'anti-rust agents, anti-sag agents and advanced silicone technology to create a paint that locks out moisture to give superior, long-lasting protection'.

This USP is reflected in the company's hard-hitting advertising and universally applied message, which says: RONSEAL – Does exactly what it says on the tin®. See Exhibit 7.3.

EXHIBIT 7.3 Ronseal USP

USPs were based on product features and related to particular attributes that differentiated one product from another.

features and related to particular attributes that differentiated one product from another. If this uniqueness was of value to a consumer then the USP alone was thought sufficient to persuade consumers to purchase. However, the reign of the USP was short lived when technology enabled me-too and own-label brands to be brought to market very quickly and product life cycles became increasingly shorter. The power of the USP was eroded and with it the basis of product differentiation as it was known then. In addition the power and purpose of advertising's role to differentiate was challenged.

What emerged were emotional selling propositions or ESPs. Advertising's role became more focused on developing brand values that were based on emotion and imagery.

Became more focused on developing brand values that were based on emotion and imagery.

This approach to communication builds brand awareness, desire and aspirational involvement. However, it often fails to provide customers with a rationale or explicit reason to purchase, what is often referred to as a 'call to action'. Other tools were required to provide customers with an impetus to act and sales promotions, event marketing, roadshows and later direct marketing, evolved to fulfil this need. These tools are known collectively as below-the-line communication tools (see Chapter 1) and their common characteristic is that they are all capable of driving action or creating behavioural change. For example, sales promotions can be used to accelerate customer behaviour by bringing forward sales that might otherwise have been made at some point in the future. Methods such as price deals, premiums and bonus packs are all designed to change behaviour by calling customers into action. This may be in the form of converting or switching users of competitive products, creating trial use of newly introduced products or encouraging existing customers to increase their usage of the product.

ViewPoint 7.3   Dental ESPs

Toothpaste, the biggest part of the oral hygiene market (including dental floss, mouthwashes, dental gum and dental cleaners and fixatives) has experienced declining sales. This is due in part to the increasing use of electronic toothbrushes, which require less toothpaste, and competitive price deals and bonus packs.

Toothpaste has traditionally been presented on an attribute basis, with each brand focusing on a particular USP, such as Sensodyne for sensitive teeth and gums and Colgate for decay prevention/tartar control.

In the 1990s manufacturers started to move towards using ESPs, principally whitening agents with cosmetic benefits. The use of ESPs in this market is becoming increasingly common as products are launched for smokers, children and, for example, Crest's Revitalise, which is targeted at women and uses Ulrika Jonsson in the advertising. The focus is now about lifestyle and how teeth contribute to an individual's overall beauty, appearance and feelings about oneself. Growing interest in the cosmetic benefits of toothpaste has led Crest's owners, Procter & Gamble, to move the brand from the oral care to the beauty division.

Source: Bainbridge, 2004.

The shift in focus away from mass communications towards more personalised messages delivered through different media.

The shift in focus away from mass communications towards more personalised messages delivered through different media has been demonstrated by the increased use of direct marketing by organisations over the past 10 years. It can also be argued that the development of direct marketing is a response to some of the weaknesses, to do with cost and effectiveness, of the other tools, most notably advertising.

The promotional mix has expanded and become a more complex managerial instrument.

The promotional mix has expanded and become a more complex managerial instrument, but essentially it is now capable of delivering two main solutions. On the one hand it can be used to develop and maintain brand values, and on the other it could be used to change behaviour through the delivery of calls to action. From a strategic perspective, the former is oriented to the long term and the latter to the short term. It is also apparent that the significant rise of below-the-line tools within the mix is partly a reflection of the demise of the USP but it is also a reflection of the increasing financial pressures experienced by organisations to improve performance and improve returns on investment.

Organisations, therefore, are faced with a dilemma. On the one hand they need to create brands that are perceived to be of value but on the other they need to prompt or encourage customers into purchase behaviour. To put it another way, marketing communications should be used to encourage buyers along the purchase decision path, but how many resources should be used to create brand values and how many should be used to prompt behaviour?

The role of marketing communications

Extending these ideas about values and action leads to a consideration of the role of marketing communications. In Chapter 1 the notion of engagement was introduced to explain the different forms of marketing communication. Engagement, or 'buy-in' as it is referred to by Thomson and Hecker (2000), when considering employee-oriented communications, consists of two main components, an intellectual and an emotional element. The intellectual element is concerned with audiences engaging with a brand on the basis of processing rational, functional information. The emotional element is

Communication strategies should be based on the information processing styles of audiences and their access to preferred media.

concerned with audiences engaging and aligning themselves with a brand's values on the basis of emotional and expressive information. It follows that communication strategies should be based on the information processing styles of audiences and their access to preferred media. Communications should reflect a suitable balance between the need for rational information to meet intellectual needs and expressive types of communication to meet the emotional needs of an organisation's different audiences. The better the quality of communication, the higher the level of engagement.

Also in Chapter 1, the idea that marketing communications had a DRIP role was introduced. The idea that marketing communications can be used to differentiate, reinforce, inform or persuade audiences to think or behave in a particular way reveals not only the inherent complexity in this subject but also the wide expectation associated with the use of this aspect of marketing. See Table 7.1.

Marketing communications is used extensively to enable individuals to progress through the decision-making process. The first role is to *inform* or make potential customers aware of a product's availability, of its new attributes or its revised facilities. However, this element has other tasks that may need implementing. Indeed information may be necessary to instruct audiences about *how* to use products, or to advise *when* a product should be used or to suggest *who* might be the optimal users. In other words marketing communications is used to engage audiences intellectually.

TABLE 7.1 Aspects of DRIP

Role	Tasks	Explanation
Differentiate	Attribute Whole product	To make a product or service stand out in the category
Reinforce	Remind Reassure	To consolidate and strengthen previous messages and experiences
Inform	Make aware Educate	To make known and advise of availability and features
Persuade	Purchase Further enquiry	To encourage further positive purchase-related behaviour

In addition to informing, customers need to know how a product differs from other competitor brands. This differentiation role of marketing communications has two sub-tasks attached to it. The first is to clarify for audiences, either directly or indirectly, the degree to which certain attributes are unique or superior to other competing brands. The second task is to convey how the product (service) as a whole is superior to other brands in the category. When customers perceive and believe in the strength of both of these claims a sense of conviction and preference can develop. Marketing communications can be used to engage audiences both intellectually and emotionally.

Marketing communications can be used to engage audiences both intellectually and emotionally.

One of the more popular perceptions of marketing communications is that it can be used to *persuade* customers to purchase products or to behave in new ways. Packard (1958) wrote about the 'Hidden Persuaders' and regarded advertising as an undesirable force that relentlessly drove customers to buy products they did not want or need. This is no longer a widespread or popular view, but there can be no doubt that marketing communications has a role to *persuade* current and potential customers to act in particular, desirable ways. Readers should remember that product purchase is just

---

ViewPoint 7.4   Changing consumption times

Many seasonal products try to deseasonalise their sales by reminding markets of their products and demonstrating new ways or fresh occasions when customers can buy and consume their brands. For a long time ice cream was a summer food, but Walls and then the super premium brands such as Häagen Dazs and Ben & Jerry's used communications to extend consumption across the year.

Liqueur brands are heavily oriented to the Christmas market but summer barbecues, parties and Father's Day have been used by such brands to stimulate new reasons to buy (Solley, 2004). Baileys has made extensive use of television to show younger age groups enjoying the brand and has also sponsored the Channel 4 series *Sex in the City*, in order to reinforce the repositioning and develop new brand associations.

Camelot seeks to remind players of the benefits of playing the National Lottery, both personal and social. As if to demonstrate this neatly, one recent campaign was based on the good causes that lottery money has been used to fund, and this was replaced at the end of 2004 with an umbrella theme called 'Be lucky': from the social to the individual.

one of several tasks that marketing communications might persuade individuals to undertake. For example, new behaviour might be to visit a Web site, engage in word-of-mouth (or mouse) communications, send for a brochure, phone a number or download wallpaper or ringtones. Persuasion might be achieved intellectually or emotionally depending upon the product offering and the degree of uncertainty felt by the audience towards the purchase.

In an era when customer retention and loyalty are dominant marketing goals, the use of planned and coordinated communications to reinforce previous messages and product experiences is of vital importance. The two main sub-tasks are to *remind* people of a need they might have or to remind them of the benefits of past transactions and so convince them that they should enter into a similar exchange. A further task is to *reassure* audiences, to comfort them by reaffirming the correctness of their original thoughts or purchase decisions. Through reassurance in particular marketing communications can be used to retain current customers. This approach to business is much more cost effective than constantly striving to lure new customers. Reinforcement is essentially a function of emotional engagement.

Reinforcement is essentially a function of emotional engagement.

How does marketing communications work?

For a message to be communicated successfully, it should be meaningful to the recipient. Messages need to be targeted at the right audience, be capable of gaining attention, be understandable, relevant and acceptable. For effective communication to occur, messages should be designed that fit the cognitive capability of the target audience and follow 'the model of how marketing communications works'. Unfortunately, there is no such single model, despite years of research and speculation by a great many people. However, from all of the work undertaken in this area, mainly with regard to advertising, a number of views have been expressed, and the following sections attempt to present some of the more influential perspectives. For an interpretation of how advertising might work, this chapter should be read in conjunction with Chapter 18.

Sequential models

Various models have been developed to assist our understanding of how these promotional tasks are segregated and organised effectively. Table 7.2 shows some of the better-known models. These models were developed primarily to explain how advertising worked. However, the principle of these hierarchical models also applies to marketing communications.

AIDA

The AIDA model was designed to represent the stages that a salesperson must take a prospect through in the personal selling process.

Developed by Strong (1925), the AIDA model was designed to represent the stages that a salesperson must take a prospect through in the personal selling process. This model shows the prospect passing through successive stages of attention, interest, desire and action. This expression of the process was later adopted, very loosely, as the basic framework to explain how persuasive communication, and advertising in particular, was thought to work.

TABLE 7.2 Sequential models of advertising

Processing	AIDA sequence[a]	Hierarchy of effects sequence[b]	Information sequence[c]
Cognitive		Awareness ↓	Presentation ↓
			Attention ↓
	Attention ↓	Knowledge ↓	Comprehension ↓
	Interest	Liking ↓	Yielding
Affective	↓	Preference ↓	↓
	Desire ↓	Conviction ↓	Retention ↓
Conative	Action	Purchase	Behaviour

Source: [a] Strong (1925); [b] Lavidge and Steiner (1961); [c] McGuire (1978).

Hierarchy of effects models

An extension of the progressive staged approach advocated by Strong emerged in the early 1960s. Developed most notably by Lavidge and Steiner (1961), the hierarchy of effects models represent the process by which advertising was thought to work and assume that there is a series of steps a prospect must pass through, in succession, from unawareness to actual purchase. Advertising, it is assumed, cannot induce immediate behavioural responses; rather a series of mental effects must occur with fulfilment at each stage necessary before progress to the next stage is possible.

The information processing model

McGuire (1978) contends that the appropriate view of the receiver of persuasive advertising is as an information processor or cognitive problem solver. This cognitive perspective becomes subsumed as the stages presented reflect similarities with the other hierarchical models, except that McGuire includes a retention stage. This refers to the ability of the receiver to retain and understand information that is valid and relevant. This is important, because it recognises that marketing communication messages are designed to provide information for use by a prospective buyer when a purchase decision is to be made at some time in the future.

Difficulties with the sequential approach

For a long time the sequential approach was accepted as the model upon which advertising was to be developed. However, questions arose about what actually constitute adequate levels of awareness, comprehension and conviction and how it can be determined which stage the majority of the target audience has reached at any one point in time.

The model is based on the logical sequential movement of consumers towards a purchase via specified stages. The major criticism is that it assumes that the consumer moves through the stages in a logical, rational manner: learn, then feel and then do. This is obviously not the case, as anyone who has taken a child into a sweet shop can confirm. There has been a lot of research that attempts to give an empirical validation of some of the hierarchy propositions, the results of which are inconclusive and at times ambiguous (Barry and Howard, 1990). Among these researchers is Palda (1966), who found that the learn–feel–do sequence cannot be upheld as a reflection of general buying behaviour and who provided empirical data to reject the notion of sequential models as an interpretation of the way advertising works.

The sequential approach sees attitude towards the product as a prerequisite to purchase.

The sequential approach sees attitude towards the product as a prerequisite to purchase, but as discussed earlier (Chapter 5) there is evidence that a positive attitude is not necessarily a good predictor of purchase behaviour. What is important, or more relevant, is the relationship between attitude change and an individual's intention to act in a particular way (Ajzen and Fishbein, 1980). Therefore it seems reasonable to suggest that what is of potentially greater benefit is a specific measure of attitude *towards* purchasing or *intentions* to buy a specific product. Despite measurement difficulties, attitude change is considered a valid objective, particularly in high-involvement situations.

A great deal of time and money must be spent on research, determining what needs to be measured. As a result, only large organisations can utilise the model properly: those with the resources and the expertise to generate the data necessary to exploit this approach fully.

All of these models share the similar view that the purchase decision process is one in which individuals move through a series of sequential stages. Each of the stages from the different models can be grouped in such a way that they are a representation of the three attitude components, these being cognitive (learn), affective (feel) and conative (do) orientations. This could be seen to reflect the various stages in the buying process, especially those that induce high involvement in the decision process but do not reflect the reality of low-involvement decisions.

Cognitive processing

Reference has already been made to whether buyers actively or passively process information. In an attempt to understand how information is used, cognitive processing tries to determine 'how external information is transformed into meanings or patterns of thought and how these meanings are combined to form judgements' (Olsen and Peter, 1987).

By assessing the thoughts (cognitive processes) that occur to people as they read, view or hear a message, an understanding of their interpretation of a message can be useful in campaign development and evaluation (Greenwald, 1968; Wright, 1973). These thoughts are usually measured by asking consumers to write down or verbally report the thoughts they have in response to such a message. Thoughts are believed to be a reflection of the cognitive processes or responses that receivers experience and they help shape or reject a communication.

Researchers have identified three types of cognitive response and have determined how these relate to attitudes and intentions. Figure 7.1 shows these three types of response, but readers should appreciate that these types are not discrete; they overlap each other and blend together, often invisibly.

Product/message thoughts

These are thoughts that are directed to the product or communication itself. Much attention has been focused upon the thoughts that are related to the message content. Two particular types of response have been considered: counter-arguments and support arguments.

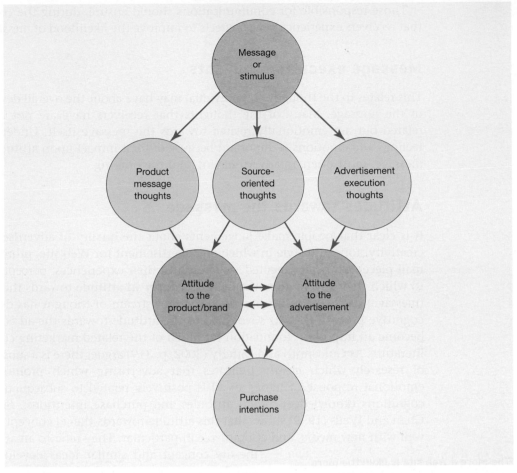

FIGURE 7.1 A cognitive processing model. Adapted from Lutz *et al.* (1983); used with kind permission

A counter-argument occurs when the receiver disagrees with the content of a message. According to Belch and Belch (1990),

> *The likelihood of counter-argument is greater when the message makes claims that oppose the beliefs or perceptions held by the receiver. Not surprisingly, the greater the degree of counter-argument, the less likely the message will be accepted. Conversely, support-arguments reflect acceptance and concurrence with a message. Support-arguments, therefore, are positively related to message acceptance.*

Use of the social value groups, discussed in Chapter 5, can provide important input to this aspect of message generation. Communications planners should ensure that advertisements and general communications encourage the generation of support arguments.

> Planners should ensure that advertisements and general communications encourage the generation of support arguments.

Source-oriented thoughts

A further set of cognitive responses is aimed at the source of the communication. This concept is closely allied to that of source credibility (Chapter 19), where, if the source of the message is seen as annoying or untrustworthy, there is a lower probability of message acceptance. Such a situation is referred to as source derogation; the converse as a source bolster.

Those responsible for communications should ensure, during the context analysis, that receivers experience bolster effects to improve the likelihood of message acceptance.

Message execution thoughts

This relates to the thoughts an individual may have about the overall design and impact of the message. Many of the thoughts that receivers have are not always product related but are emotionally related towards the message itself. Understanding these feelings and emotions is important because of their impact upon attitudes towards the message, most often an advertisement, and the offering.

Attitudes towards the message

It is clear that people make judgements about the quality of advertisements and the creativity, tone and style in which an advertisement (or Web site, promotion or direct mail piece) has been executed. As a result of their experiences, perception and degree to which they like an advertisement they form an attitude towards the advertisement (message) itself. From this base an important stream of thought has developed about cognitive processing. Lutz's work led to the attitude-towards-the-ad concept that has become an important foundation for much of the related marketing communications literature. As Goldsmith and Lafferty (2002, p. 319) argue, there is a substantial amount of research which clearly indicates that advertising which promotes a 'positive emotional response of liking an ad is positively related to subsequent brand-related cognitions (knowledge), brand attitudes and purchase intentions'. Similar work by Chen and Wells (1999) shows that this attitude-towards-the-ad concept applies equally well with new media, and eCommerce in particular. They refer to an attitude-towards-the-site concept and similar ideas developed by Bruner and Kumar (2000) conclude that the more a Web site is liked the more attitudes improved to the brand and purchase intentions.

The more a Web site is liked the more attitudes improved to the brand and purchase intentions.

It seems highly plausible, therefore, to conclude that attitudes-towards-the-message (and delivery mechanism) impact on brand attitudes, which in turn influence consumers' propensity to purchase. It is also known that an increasing proportion of advertisements attempt to appeal to feelings and emotions, simply because many researchers believe that attitudes towards both the advertisement and the product should be encouraged and are positively correlated with purchase intention. Similarly, time and effort is placed with the design of sales promotion instruments, increasing attention is given to the design of packaging in terms of a pack's communication effectiveness, and care is taken about the wording in advertorials and press releases. Perhaps above all else, more and more effort is being made to research and develop Web sites with the goal of designing them so that they are strategically compatible, user friendly and functional, or to put it another way – liked. Any model that is developed to explain how marketing communications works should therefore be based around the important concept, attitude-towards-the-message.

Elaboration likelihood model

What should be clear from the preceding sections is that neither the purely cognitive nor the purely emotional interpretation of how marketing communication works is realistic. In effect it is probable that both have an important part to play in the way the

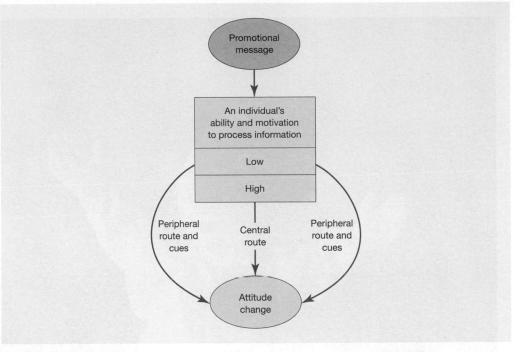

FIGURE 7.2 The elaboration likelihood model. Based on Aaker *et al.* (1992)

various tools, and advertising in particular, work. However, the degree of emphasis should swing according to the context within which the marketing communication message is expected to work.

One approach to utilise both these elements has been developed by Petty and Cacioppo (1983). The Elaboration Likelihood Model (ELM) has helped to explain how cognitive processing, persuasion and attitude change occur when different levels of involvement are present. Elaboration refers to the extent to which an individual needs to develop and refine information necessary for decision-making to occur. If an individual has a high level of motivation or ability to process information, elaboration is said to be high. If an individual's motivation or ability to process information is poor, then his or her level of elaboration is said to be low. The ELM distinguishes two main cognitive processes, as depicted in Figure 7.2.

> Elaboration refers to the extent to which an individual needs to develop and refine information necessary for decision-making to occur.

Under the central route the receiver is viewed as very active and involved. As the level of cognitive response is high, the ability of the message (advertisement) to

ViewPoint 7.5   Peripheral cues and Twinings

Consumers tend to stay with their preferred brands of food and drink and will only switch if their preferred brand fails to reach threshold levels of satisfaction or a new brand offers sufficient curiosity and engagement such that trial is induced. Many brands in the tea market, for example, use peripheral cues in order to get the brand noticed, remembered and enjoyed. Twinings used a Jack-in-the Box to symbolise the stimulating effects of their breakfast tea and as an easy means by which customers can make associations with the Twinings brand.

Spring into

life

*with a brisk,
full-bodied tea*

ENGLISH
BREAKFAST

www.twinings.com

There's more to tea with **TWININGS**

EXHIBIT 7.4 Twinings

Through the use of peripheral cues, Twinings have been able to enrich the way their brand is perceived while at the same time improve the level of awareness. Picture reproduced with the kind permission of Twinings.

persuade will depend upon the quality of the argument rather than executional factors. For example, the purchase of a consumer durable such as a car or washing machine normally requires a high level of involvement. Consequently, potential customers would be expected to be highly involved and willing to read brochures and information about the proposed car or washing machine prior to demonstration or purchase. Their decision to act would depend upon the arguments used to justify the model as suitable for the individual. For the car purchase these might include the quiet and environmentally friendly engine, the relatively excellent fuel consumption and other safety and performance indicators, together with the comfort of the interior and the effortless driving experience. Whether the car is shown as part of a business executive's essential 'kit' or the commercial is flamboyant and rich will be immaterial for those in the central route.

Under the peripheral route, the receiver is seen to lack the ability to process information and is not likely to engage cognitive processing. Rather than thinking about and evaluating the message content, the receiver tends to rely upon what have been referred to as 'peripheral cues', which may be incidental to the message content. Twinings use peripheral cues to attract attention to their brand. See Exhibit 7.4.

In low-involvement situations, a celebrity may serve to influence attitudes positively. This is based upon the creation of favourable attitudes towards the source rather than engaging the viewer in the processing of the message content. For example, Gary Lineker has been used as a celebrity spokesperson to endorse Walkers Crisps. The power of Gary Lineker would be more important as a major peripheral cue (more so than the nature of the product) in eventually persuading a consumer to try the brand or retaining current users. Think crisps, think Gary Lineker, think Walkers. Where high involvement is present, any celebrity endorsement is of minor significance to the quality of the message claims.

Communication strategy should be based upon the level of cognitive processing that the target audience is expected to engage in.

Communication strategy should be based upon the level of cognitive processing that the target audience is expected to engage in and the route taken to affect attitudinal change. If the processing level is low (low motivation and involvement), the peripheral route should dominate and emphasis needs to be placed on the way the messages are executed and on the emotions of the target audience (Heath, 2000). If the central route is expected, the content of the messages should be dominant and the executional aspects need only be adequate.

Interaction, dialogue and relationships

Marketing communications is traditionally perceived and developed as a planned managerial activity. This in itself is perfectly fine, to be encouraged, and is a central platform for the development of integrated marketing communications (see Chapter 11). However, much of marketing practice and theory has moved towards a more relational rather than transactional perspective (see Chapter 9). Marketing communications is in transition as it adapts in order to complement this new approach. Therefore, any explanation about how it works should be articulated in the light of relationship marketing principles.

Mass media-based communications generate one-way communication and is based on informing, telling and educating audiences.

As a generalisation, mass media-based communications generate one-way communication and is based on informing, telling and educating audiences with a view to persuading them to act in a particular way, ultimately to purchase a product (Ballantyne, 2004). New media and digital technologies have given organisations radically different methods to communicate with audiences. New media offer opportunities for audiences to respond to the messages they receive and give rise to opportunities for people to interact with those organisations with whom they wish to be involved and to whom they grant permission to continue sending messages. One-way communication begins to look like two-way communication.

Interaction is about actions that lead to a response and direct marketing helped make significant inroads, in the 1990s, in the transition from one-way to two-way and then interactive-based communication. New technology has further enabled this inter-action process. However, interaction alone is not a sufficient goal, simply because the content of the interaction could be about a radical disagreement of views, an exchange of opinion or a social encounter. Dialogue occurs through mutual understanding and a reasoning approach to interactions, one based on listening and adaptive behaviour. Dialogue is concerned with the development of knowledge that is specific to the relationship of the parties involved. Ballantyne refers to this as 'learning together' (Ballantyne, 2004, p. 119) and it is referred to by Gronroos (2004) as a critical aspect of marketing communication's role within relationship marketing (see Chapter 9).

Ballantyne refers to two-way communication with audiences in two ways. First, as a '*with*' experience, as manifest in face to face encounters and contact centres. He also distinguishes a higher order of two-way communication based on communication '*between*' parties. It is this latter stage that embodies true dialogue where trust, listening and adaptive behaviour are typical. These are represented diagrammatically in Table 7.3.

The adoption of dialogue as the basis for communication changes an organisation's perspective of its audiences. Being willing and able to enter into a dialogue indicates that there is a new emphasis on the relationships organisations

The adoption of dialogue as the basis for communication changes an organisation's perspective of its audiences.

TABLE 7.3 Communication matrix (Ballantyne, 2004); used with permission

Direction	Mass markets	Portfolio/mass-customised	Networks
One-way	*Communication 'to'*	*Communication 'for'*	
Planned communications designed to inform and persuade Medium to high wastage	Planned persuasive messages aimed at securing brand awareness and loyalty; e.g. *communication of USPs and ESPs*	Planned persuasive messages with augmented offerings for target markets; e.g. *communicating targeted lifecycle products, guarantees, loyalty programmes*	
Two-way		*Communication 'with'*	*Communication 'between'*
Formal and informal with a view to listening and learning Minimal wastage		Integrated mix of planned and interactively shared knowledge; e.g. *face to face, direct (database), contact centres, interactive b2b Internet portals*	Dialogue between participants based on trust, learning and adaptation with co-created outcomes; e.g. *key account liaison, expansion of communities, staff teamwork*

TABLE 7.4 The five features of a dialogical orientation (Kent and Taylor, 2002); used with permission

Role	Explanation
Mutuality	The recognition of the presence of organisational stakeholder relationships
Propinquity	The temporality and spontaneity of organisation–stakeholder interactions
Empathy	Support for stakeholder interests and their goals
Risk	Willingness to interact with others on their terms
Commitment	The extent to which an organisation actually interprets, listens to and practises dialogical communications

hold with their stakeholders. Kent and Taylor (2002) argue that there are five main features of a dialogical orientation. These are presented in Table 7.4.

It can be seen in Table 7.4 that many aspects of dialogue require interaction as a precursor. In other words, for dialogue to occur there must first be interaction and it is the development and depth of the interaction that leads to meaningful dialogue.

Ideas about how marketing communication works must be founded, in part, on the notion and significance of the level of interaction and dialogue that the organisation and their stakeholder audiences desire. One-way communication, as reflected in traditional planned mass media-based communication, still has a significant role, especially for audiences who prefer transactional exchanges. Two-way communication based on interaction with audiences who desire continuing contact, or dialogue for those who desire a deeper, more meaningful relationship will form an increasingly important aspect of marketing communications strategy in the future.

Developing significant value

Marketing communications consists of a set of disciplines and media that are used in varying ways to convey messages to audiences. Depending upon the context in which the message is created, delivered and interpreted, the brand and the individual have an opportunity to interact. Marketing communication messages normally pass individuals unobserved. Those that are remembered contain particular characteristics (Brown, 1991; Fletcher, 1994). These would appear to be that the product must be different or new, that the way the message is executed is different or interesting and that the message proclaims something that is personally significant to the individual in their current context. The term 'significance' means that the message is meaningful, relevant (e.g. the individual is actually looking to buy a new car or breakfast cereals tomorrow or is planning to gather information on a new project) and is perceived to be suitably credible. These three characteristics can be tracked from the concept of ad likeability (Chapter 17), which many researchers believe is the only meaningful indicator of the effectiveness of an advertisement.

To be successful therefore, it is necessary for marketing communication messages to:

● present an object that is new to the receiver
● be interesting and stimulating
● be personally significant.

Any one message may be *significantly valuable* to an individual.

The object referred to in the first element refers to both products and services (or an offering that is substantially different from others in the category) and to organisations as brands. The net effect of all these characteristics might be that any one message may be *significantly valuable* to an individual.

Messages announcing new brands or new attributes may convey information that is perceived to be significantly different. As a result individuals may be intrigued and interested enough to want to try the brand at the next purchase opportunity. For these people there is a high level of personal relevance derived from the message, and attitude change can be induced to convince them that it is right to make a purchase. For them the message is significantly valuable and as a result may well generate a purchase decision that, from a market perspective, will drive a discernible sales increase.

However, the vast majority of marketing communications are about products that are not new or which are unable to proclaim or offer anything substantially different. These messages are either ignored or, if interest is aroused, certain parts of the message are filed away in memory for use at a later date. The question is, if parts are filed away, which parts are filed and why and how are they retrieved?

Marketing communications can provide a rationale or explanation for why individuals (cognitive processors) have bought a brand and why they should continue buying it. Normally, advertising alone does not persuade – it simply reminds and reassures individuals. Or, to put it another way, individuals use advertising and public relations to remind themselves of preferred brands or to reassure themselves of their previous (and hence correct) purchase behaviour. Sales promotions, personal selling and direct marketing are used by consumers to take particular action.

Consumers, particularly in FMCG markets, practise repertoire-buying based on habit, security, speed of decision-making and to some extent self-expression. The brands present in any single individual repertoire normally provide interest and satisfaction. Indeed, advertising needs to ensure that the brand remains in the repertoire or is sufficiently interesting to the individual that it is included in a future repertoire. Just consider the variety of messages used by mobile phone operators, such as MM02, T-Mobile, Vodafone, 3 and Orange. These are continually updated and refreshed using particular themes, all of which are intended to be visually and cognitively engaging.

Messages, in particular advertising messages, that are interesting, immediately relevant or interpreted as possessing a deep set of personal meanings (all subsequently referred to as likeable; see Chapter 17) will be stored in long-term memory (Chapter 5). Research shows, repeatedly, that only parts of an advertisement are ever remembered – those parts which are of intrinsic value to the recipient and are sometimes referred to as 'the take-out'. The Brown (1991) example in ViewPoint 7.6 provides suitable evidence of this phenomenon. This selectivity, or message take-out, is referred to as the *creative magnifier* effect. Figure 7.3 illustrates the effect that parts of a message might have on the way a message is remembered.

Messages work best through the creation of interest and likeable moments, from which extracts are taken by individuals.

The implication of this is that messages work best through the creation of interest and likeable moments, from which extracts are taken by individuals and stored away in memory. However, it might also be reasonable to suggest that the other tools of the mix are also capable of enabling individuals to take extracts. For example, the size of a sales promotion offer, or the tone of a sales presentation, the professionalism of a direct mail piece or the immediacy of an online promotion might all give due reason for an individual to generate a take-out. Interest is generated through fresh, relevant ideas where the brand and the messages are linked together in a meaningful and relevant way. This in turn allows for future associations to be made, linking brands and marketing communication messages in a positive and experiential way.

ViewPoint 7.6 Cadbury's Flake

Brown (1991) reports about research concerning ads for Cadbury's Flake. This chocolate bar crumbles easily when bitten. An advertisement was devised that depicted the bar being eaten by three different people in three different contexts. The first was a secretary, who collected the crumbs in the wrapping paper. The second was a man on a train, who collected the crumbs on a plate, and the third was a small boy, who used a straw to suck up the crumbs. Each character was shown for 10 seconds, but in the tracking studies that followed it was the small boy who was recalled most, in disproportion to the time of the message exposure. See Figure 7.3 and Exhibit 7.3.

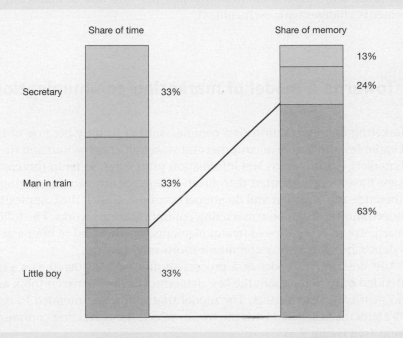

FIGURE 7.3 The creative magnifier (From Brown (1991); used with kind permission.)

EXHIBIT 7.5 Cadbury's Flake Bar

Advertising is used to trigger brand associations and experiences for people.

Advertising is used to trigger brand associations and experiences for people, not only when seated in front of a television, PC or when reading a magazine or reading text messages but also when faced with product purchase decisions. Of all low-value FMCG purchase decisions 70 per cent are said to be made at the point of purchase. All forms of marketing communication, but principally advertising, can be used to generate brand associations, which in turn are used to trigger advertising messages or, rather, 'likeable' extracts. The other tools of the mix can benefit from the prior use of advertising to create awareness so that the call to action brought about through below-the-line communications can occur naturally and unhindered by brand confusion or uncertainty.

This last point is of particular importance because advertising alone may not be sufficient to trigger complete recall of brand and communication experiences. The brand, its packaging, sales promotion, digital media, POP and outdoor media all have an important role to play in providing consistency and interest and prompting recall and recognition. Integrated marketing communications is important, not just for message take-out or likeable extracts, but also for triggering recall and recognition and stimulating relevant brand associations.

Messages that customers perceive as being of significant value to them as individuals is a key to developing effective marketing communications. In order to create these messages of significant value a complex array of disciplines, media, people, technology and intuition need to be coordinated and deployed. These principles apply equally to consumer and business markets, it is just that the mix of marketing communication elements changes with each context.

Towards a model of marketing communications

Marketing communications is a complex subject, if only because of the large number of variables, the nature of customer and stakeholder behaviour and the dynamic nature of markets, organisations and information processing. So far in this chapter a number of issues have been presented that, taken independently, are interesting but lack overall coherence and direction and do not necessarily deal with the complexity or advance our understanding about how marketing communications works. The following represents an attempt to bring these different elements together and to offer a general framework to depict how marketing communications might work.

Any descriptive model of a process should be considered as a generalisation and intended only to represent the key elements, the flow between them and the outcomes and possible consequences. The model that follows is intended to bring together the key elements associated with the way in which the marketing communications process works (see Figure 7.4).

The starting point depicting how marketing communications may work should be the audience or individual person receiving messages. The context therefore is an important aspect of marketing communications, not the message itself, the media or the tools used.

To reflect the different marketing communications needs of those individuals who are engaged with both transactional and relationship exchanges.

This model seeks to accommodate marketing communications in both consumer and b2b markets. It attempts to reflect the different marketing communications needs of those individuals who are engaged with both transactional and relationship exchanges, although it does not indicate how marketing communications might assist transition from the former to the latter.

The task of marketing communications is to present key messages in such a way that the meanings which people (the target audience) ascribe to them are relevant and capable of being memorised, acted upon and recalled at some point in the future. Advertising can be regarded as a potentially powerful means of enabling buyers to attribute meanings to messages they receive about brands. Messages conveyed through the below-the-line communications enable people to decide if and *how* they should respond to the message. Lannon (1992) argues that we should be concerned with what people do *with* advertising, how they assign meaning, and Gronstedt (1997) echoes this thought with

Messages conveyed through the below-the-line communications enable people to decide if and *how* they should respond to the message.

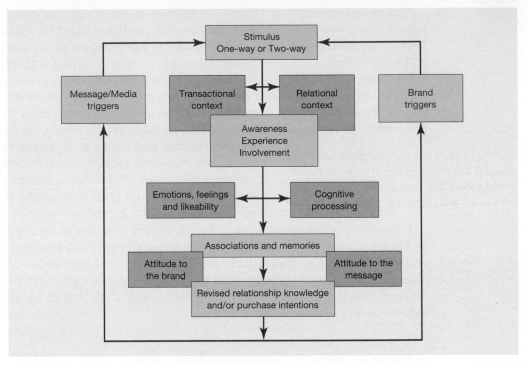

FIGURE 7.4 A model of how marketing communications might work

respect to public relations. He suggests that the focus should be on what stakeholders do with messages as opposed to what the message does to the stakeholder.

Customers are problem solvers, and their capability is partly determined by their level of elaboration. They can be regarded as active information processors (to varying degrees) in all product categories. Advertising is a convenient and often cost-effective way of conveying information about brands to people, who then have an opportunity to reappraise their understanding of the brand and its related elements. Advertising can either make people aware or promote interest in a new brand or remind buyers of the values and experiences of previous usage. More direct forms of communication may enable people to make brand associations but are more likely to pose challenges with regard to persuasion and how they should act in response to a message. These marketing communication messages are processed internally and are used to achieve two main outcomes. One is to update an individual's knowledge about a brand and/or the generic category of products as they see it ('Oh, that is a different type of ice cream'). The second is to prompt individuals into further action, either to seek more information or to purchase.

Our understanding of perception suggests that people organise filtered and selected stimuli according to the context of their current situation and past experiences. Therefore, marketing communication messages need to be consistent in order that people can organise information about a brand in the same way as they processed the information the last time they perceived the stimuli. As suggested above, the stimulus need not be just an advertisement: it could be any element of the promotional or marketing mix, or indeed the brand itself. Therefore, the presence of either the product or the communication event may act as a stimulus. It is not surprising that integrated marketing communications require that whatever the contact with a brand, the message should be the same and be expected in the context with which information was processed previously.

The model presented in Figure 7.4 attempts to bring together those elements that influence the way in which marketing communications might be considered to work. Stimuli are considered in the context of the probable exchange environment that will reflect a transactional or relational emphasis. These stimuli will act upon levels of elaboration, which in turn determine levels of cognitive processing. Likeable extracts are taken out of the messages and stored for future use. Marketing communication messages and/or brand experiences then allow for these extracts to be recalled. This impacts on the attitude to the brand and towards the message, which affects purchase intentions.

Each is capable of reinforcing the others and triggers are required to establish or recall brand values and then prompt the action processes and reinforce previous behaviour.

Therefore brands and all the tools of the marketing communication mix work together: each is capable of reinforcing the others and triggers are required to establish or recall brand values and then prompt the action processes and reinforce previous behaviour.

For marketing communications to work and for messages to be effective, they must be likeable (interesting, meaningful and relevant to the brand and the target audience) and must therefore be contextually compatible with the target audience and the brand. If these twin factors (likeability and contextual compatibility) are established then positive emotional attitudes towards the message may form that in turn lead to positive influences on purchase intentions.

Summary

Over time a variety of models have been developed, each of which has attempted to explain how advertising works. AIDA and sequential models, such as the hierarchy of effects approach, were for a long time the received wisdom in this area. Now they are regarded as quaint but out of date, for a number of hard-hitting reasons.

The developing interest in integrated marketing communications, and in particular the complementary influence of brand values with calls to action and behaviour change, has stimulated a move away from an advertising-only perspective. Developments concerning cognitive processing, feelings, likeability and elaboration enable a broader perspective on marketing communications as a whole to be achieved. At the same time many writers have become sceptical of advertising's power to persuade consumers to change their purchasing habits, USPs have given way to ESPs and industry and commerce have shifted the focus of their marketing spend away from above- to below-the-line activities, as if to emphasise the need to affect behavioural change. Therefore understanding the way marketing communications works, rather than just the way advertising works, is now more important.

We now understand that marketing communication messages tend to be more successful when they are of particular significance to each individual. When significant they are of value, hence the need to generate messages that are of significant value to the target audience. To be significantly valuable messages should present a new product or a product that is substantially different from the other products in the category, be interesting and stimulating and be personally meaningful.

Reality suggests that the majority of marketing communication messages cannot claim to be of significant value to most people. Those messages that are of value are normally dissected so that only parts of the message are extracted and stored for future use. Messages or extracts of messages can be recalled or released from long-term memory when triggered by an association, such as new incoming messages or experiences with a particular brand. Marketing communication messages and brands should be regarded as complementary elements that need to work together if marketing communications and their respective brands are to be successful.

Review questions

1. Explain the role that marketing communications plays within relationship marketing.
2. Write brief notes outlining the difference between three sequential models and evaluate the ways in which they are considered to work.
3. Which element in McGuire's model separates it from other similar models?
4. Explain the concepts of USPs and ESPs.
5. Discuss the primary roles of marketing communications.
6. Cognitive processing consists of three main elements. Name them.
7. Give examples of peripheral and central route cues to attitude change using the Elaboration Likelihood Model.
8. Describe the creative magnifier effect. Why is it important?
9. What is the likely impact of triggers and brand associations in determining how advertising works?
10. Evaluate the concept of significant value.

MINI-CASE
Of course I'm worth it . . . aren't I?

L'Oréal is one of the world's leading cosmetics and fragrances companies, operating in more than 130 countries around the world. The company is structured around four distinct customer markets: luxury goods, consumer goods, professional and pharmacies (drugstores). In each of these sectors L'Oréal has a limited range of brands, a policy that enables the organisation to generate economies of scale in production, advertising and packaging. However, while there are benefits from these shared resources, each brand retains its own individual style and consumer appeal. The international flavour of the company is demonstrated by brands that not only promote a French way of life (as with *Lancôme* and *L'Oréal Paris*), but also reflect Italian style (*Giorgio Armani* fragrances and cosmetics) and American vitality (*Maybelline New York*, *Redken 5th Avenue NYC* and *Matrix*). Such diversity might help ensure that L'Oreal appeals to a large number of different consumer segments.

Lancôme is a brand from the luxury goods division, one that seeks to maintain very high levels of quality with regard to the product, packaging, merchandising and all associated communications.

One of the brand's principles is to provide personal relationships with its customers. Selective distribution is through department stores and fine perfumeries and this helps to ensure that official beauty consultants are able to help customers maximise their relationship with the brand.

The *L'Oréal Paris* and *Garnier* brands are both part of the consumer products division, whose aim is to offer consumers innovative, high-technology beauty products at competitive prices. This is a global strategy yet it is intentionally combined with a local understanding of the needs of women and men of all ages. Synonymous with the *'Because you're worth it'* strapline, this division remains the premium mass-market offering, allowing consumers accessible luxury through high-performance products. Distribution is through mass market retail outlets such as supermarkets and leading independent and chain store chemists.

The L'Oréal professional products division is dedicated to providing the world's hairdressing industry not only with the most technologically advanced haircare and styling products but also in helping to develop hairdressers' businesses through technical

TABLE 7.5 Summary of L'Oreal's markets and distribution outlets

Division	Market	Distribution channel outlets	Promotional message
Luxury	Affluent/prestige	Department stores	Sophistication and exclusivity
Consumer	Mass market	Supermarkets and high street chemists	Image and value
Professional	Hair stylists	Hair salons	Technical supremacy
Drugstore	Pharmacists	Drugstores and pharmacies	Efficacy

education, management seminars and fashion shows. Many professional haircare products are developed for use solely in salons, while others can also be sold through salons, to clients for use at home.

The final division, Active Cosmétique, develops dermo-cosmetic healthcare brands for sale through pharmacies and drugstores. These skincare products, which are subject to extensive pharmaceutical research, are only available through pharmacists and dermatologists.

L'Oréal markets a range of brands internationally, through different distribution channels, to reach mass market customers, hair salons, department stores and drugstores. These are summarised in Table 7.5.

The traditional industry approach to consumer cosmetic advertising is based upon a formula that involves prestigious locations, glamorous models and exaggerated messages which promise life enhancement based on unique product attributes. The media used are normally rich, high-quality glossy magazines, although television is used for some leading brands.

Brand promotion at L'Oreal is partly based upon the use of various supermodels such as Andie MacDowell, Milla Joovich, and Judith Gidreche, and celebrities such as Catherine Deneuve and Jennifer Aniston, who become the face of the brand. However, marketing communications messages used to support these brands vary considerably. At one extreme some brands (e.g. *Lancôme's* anti-ageing cream targeted at the over-55s) are supported by advertising messages that are stylish, luxurious and supported with minimal packaging and substantial product-based information delivered across the counter by experts. At another extreme consumer division brands such as *L'Oréal Paris* and *Garnier* attempt to convey brand images based upon

spokespersons, beauty, price and attractive packaging. At yet another extreme messages targeted at the professional (and exclusive) hair stylists, such as Charles Worthington, are detailed and supported with a range of ancillary technical information.

Some luxury and consumer cosmetic brands have tried to overcome an increasingly cluttered market by trying to stimulate both awareness and trial through online communications. For example, *L'Oreal Paris* developed a virtual make-over site 'Easy Make-up', allowing customers to upload digital photos of themselves on to the site and then experiment on-screen with different colours and techniques.

Questions

1 Evaluate the marketing communication messages used to support brands in both the professional and consumer products divisions, using the DRIP framework.

2 Evaluate the extent to which L'Oréal uses USPs and ESPs as the core of its communication strategy.

3 Using the creative magnifier approach identify different aspects of L'Oréal's advertising that might be used by audiences as 'take-out'.

4 Apply the cognitive processing model, developed by Lutz, to the L'Oréal context.

5 Of the three elements in Lutz's model, which might have the most influence on L'Oréal's audiences and how might this impact on the company's marketing communications?

6 What might be the significant value in L'Oréal's communications?

References

Aaker, D.A., Batra, R. and Myers, J.G. (1992) *Advertising Management.* 4th edn. Englewood Cliffs, NJ: Prentice-Hall.

Ajzen, I. and Fishbein, M. (1980) *Understanding Attitudes and Predicting Social Behavior.* Englewood Cliffs, NJ: Prentice-Hall.

Bainbridge, J. (2004) Dental diversification. *Marketing,* 12 September, pp. 36–7.

Ballantyne, D. (2004) Dialogue and its role in the development of relationship specific knowledge. *Journal of Business and Industrial Marketing,* **19**(2), pp. 114–23.

Barry, T. and Howard, D.J. (1990) A review and critique of the hierarchy of effects in advertising. *International Journal of Advertising,* **9**, pp. 121–35.

Belch, G.E. and Belch, M.A. (1990) *An Introduction to Advertising and Promotion Management.* Homewood, IL: Richard D. Irwin.

Brown, G. (1991) *How Advertising Affects the Sales of Packaged Goods Brands.* Warwick: Millward Brown Publications.

Bruner, G.C. and Kumar, A. (2000) Web commercials and advertising hierarchy of effects. *Journal of Advertising Research,* January/April, pp. 35–42.

Chen, Q. and Wells, W.D. (1999) Attitude toward the site. *Journal of Advertising Research,* September/October, pp. 27–37.

Fletcher, W. (1994) The advertising high ground. *Admap* (November), pp. 31–4.

Goldsmith, R.E. and Lafferty, B.A. (2002) Consumer response to web sites and their influence on advertising effectiveness. *Internet Research: Electronic Networking Applications and Policy,* **12**(4), pp. 318–28.

Greenwald, A. (1968) Cognitive learning, cognitive response to persuasion and attitude change. In *Psychological Foundations of Attitudes* (eds A. Greenwald, T.C. Brook and T.W. Ostrom). New York: Academic Press.

Gronroos, C. (2004) The relationship marketing process: communication, interaction, dialogue, value. *Journal of Business and Industrial Marketing,* **19**(2), pp. 99–113.

Gronstedt, A. (1997) The role of research in public relations strategy and planning. In *The Handbook of Strategic Public Relations and Integrated Communications* (ed. C.L. Caywood), pp. 34–59. Boston, MA: McGraw-Hill.

Heath, R. (2000) Low involvement processing. *Admap* (April), pp. 34–6.

Kent, M.L. and Taylor, M. (2002) Toward a dialogic theory of public relations. *Public Relations Review,* **28**(1), (February), pp. 21–37.

Lannon, J. (1992) Asking the right questions: what do people do with advertising? *Admap* (March), pp. 11–16.

Lavidge, R.J. and Steiner, G.A. (1961) A model for predictive measurements of advertising effectiveness. *Journal of Marketing* (October), p. 61.

Lutz, J., Mackensie, S.B. and Belch, G.E. (1983) Attitude toward the ad as a mediator of advertising effectiveness. *Advances in Consumer Research X.* Ann Arbor, MI: Association for Consumer Research.

McGuire, W.J. (1978) An information processing model of advertising effectiveness. In *Behavioral and Management Science in Marketing* (eds H.L. Davis and A.J. Silk). New York: Ronald/Wiley.

Olsen, J.C. and Peter, J.P. (1987) *Consumer Behavior.* Homewood, IL: Irwin.

Packard, V. (1958) *The Hidden Persuaders.* Harmondsworth: Penguin.

Palda, K.S. (1966) The hypothesis of a hierarchy of effects: a partial evaluation. *Journal of Marketing Research,* **3**, pp. 13–24.

Petty, R.E. and Cacioppo, J.T. (1983) Central and peripheral routes to persuasion: application to advertising. In *Advertising and Consumer Psychology* (eds L. Percy and A. Woodside). Lexington, MA: Lexington Books.

Solley, S. (2004) Not just for Christmas. *Marketing,* 4 August, pp. 34–5.

Strong, E.K. (1925) *The Psychology of Selling.* New York: McGraw-Hill.

Thomson, K. and Hecker, L.A. (2000) The business value of buy-in. In *Internal Marketing: Directions for Management* (eds R.J. Varey and B.R. Lewis), pp. 160–72. London: Routledge.

Wright, P.L. (1973) The cognitive processes mediating the acceptance of advertising. *Journal of Marketing Research,* **10** (February), pp. 53–62.

Stakeholders: supply chains and interorganisational relationships

8

Contemporary marketing communications should recognise and reflect the growing significance of relationship marketing. Therefore understanding the whole system of relationships between organisations is important, if only because the relationship between any two is contingent upon the direct and indirect relationships of all the actors (Andersson, 1992). A network of relationships therefore provides the context within which exchange and associated marketing communication behaviour occur.

Aims and objectives

The aims of this chapter are to introduce the concepts of networks and stakeholders with a view to understanding business-to-business relationships, of which marketing channel relationships and associated supply chain networks are important elements.

The objectives of this chapter are to:

1. introduce fundamental issues concerning network analysis;
2. develop a methodology for stakeholder analysis and network mapping;
3. show how organisations combine to form partnerships with particular stakeholders, coordinating their efforts to provide buyer satisfaction;
4. establish marketing communications as a vital management process between stakeholders in a network of organisations;
5. introduce two main common distribution networks, the conventional and vertical marketing systems;
6. examine some of the behavioural issues involved with the management of channel networks, including conflict and leadership;
7. explain how planned communications, in both network and intra-organisational contexts, can be improved by focused responsibilities and integration of communications activities.

Introduction

Although distribution is a vital part of the marketing mix and accounts for a large percentage of the cost of a product, its significance is often overlooked by managers and students of marketing, and marketing communications in particular.

The distribution of products concerns two main elements. The first is the management of the tangible or physical aspects of moving a product from the producer to the end-user. This must be undertaken in such a way that the customer can freely access an offering and that the final act of the buying process is as easy as possible. The second element is the management of the intangible aspects or issues of ownership, control and flows of communication between parties responsible for making the offering accessible to the customer. The focus of this chapter will be on the second of these elements, commonly referred to as channel management or, as it is increasingly referred to, supply chain management and, by some, demand chain management.

Products flow through a variety of organisations, which coordinate their activities to make the offering readily available to the end-user. Coordination is necessary to convert raw materials into a set of benefits that can be transferred and be of value to the end-user. These benefits are normally bundled together and represented in the form of a product or service. The various organisations that elect to coordinate their activities each perform different roles in a chain of activity. Some perform the role of manufacturer, some act as agents and others may be distributors, dealers, value-added resellers, wholesalers or retailers. Whatever their role, it is normally specific and geared to refining and moving the offering closer to the end user.

> Coordination is necessary to convert raw materials into a set of benefits that can be transferred and be of value to the end-user.

ViewPoint 8.1   Snapple brand

Quaker Oats bought the Snapple drink in 1994 for $1.7 billion, when the drink's turnover had reached $674 million, having risen threefold in as many years. Quaker saw synergies with its existing drink Gatorade and the logic of the acquisition looked sound (Miles, 2000).

By 1997 Quaker had sold the drink to Triarc Companies of New York for just $300 million, a drop of $1.4 billion, or a loss of $1.3 million per day. The reasons for this disaster were thought to be a failure to understand the previous distribution channels and the lack of synergy in logistics and the associated brand values.

Source: Adapted from *Marketing Business*, the magazine for The Chartered Institute of Marketing, Issue 91. Used with kind permission.

Each organisation is a customer to the previous organisation in an industry's value chain. Some organisations work closely together, coordinating and integrating their activities, while others combine on a temporary basis. In both cases, however, these organisations can be observed to be operating as members of a partnership (of differing strength and dimensions) with the express intention of achieving their objectives with their partner's assistance and cooperation. So, in addition to the end-user, a further set of customers (partners) can be determined: all those who make up the distribution channel.

It was seen in Chapter 2 that effective communications are developed by building a positive realm of understanding with all those who impact upon the organisation and with whom communication is necessary and important: the target audiences. It is important, therefore, to identify who these other organisations (the target audiences) are, what their needs are and how important they are to the focus organisation and its products. Further questions include what the aims and objectives of these other organisations are and what the nature of the relationships between them is. Having undertaken this analysis it is then possible to develop complementary messages, to coordinate their transmission and to monitor and assess their effectiveness.

To help accomplish this, organisations must not only understand which other organisations interact with them but also determine the nature and the form of the relationships between organisations both inside and outside of the distribution channel. For example, organisations operating within the 'fast-moving consumer goods' or the 'over-the-counter' markets will invariably be able to identify two particular clusters: first, all those that contribute to the value-adding activities and directly affect the performance of the focus organisation, such as dealers, distributors, wholesalers and retailers, and secondly, all those that affect the performance in an indirect way, such as banks, market research agencies, recruitment organisations and local authorities.

The stakeholder concept

All organisations develop a series of relationships with a wide variety of other organisations, groups and indeed consumers who buy their products. These relationships and individual partnerships vary considerably in their intensity, duration and function. Nevertheless, these partnerships are entered into on the grounds that each organisation anticipates benefit from mutual cooperation.

The concept of different groups influencing an organisation and in turn being influenced is an important element in the development of integrated marketing communications. The concept enables an organisation to identify all those other organisations and individuals who can be or are influenced by the strategies and policies of the focus organisation. Understanding who the stakeholders are also helps to determine where power is held, and this will in turn influence strategy at a number of levels within the focus organisation. According to Freeman (1984), stakeholders are 'any group or individual who can affect or is affected by the achievement of an organisation's purpose'. These stakeholders may be internal to the organisation, such as employees or managerial coalitions, or external to the organisation in the form of suppliers, buyers, local authorities, shareholders, competitors, agencies or the government.

> Understanding who the stakeholders are also helps to determine where power is held.

The essential purpose of stakeholder analysis is to determine which organisations influence the focus organisation and what their aims, objectives and motivations are. This enables the development of a more effective strategy, one that considers the power and interests of those who have a stake in the focus organisation. Freeman suggested that the stake held by any organisation could be based upon one of three forms. The first is a stake based upon the equity held in the organisation, the second is a stake based upon an economic perspective, reflecting a market exchange-based relationship, and the third is a stake based upon the influence of organisations that affect the focus organisation but 'not in marketplace terms'.

The horizontal dimension reflects the type of power that stakeholders can have over the focus organisation. Again, Freeman highlights three elements. The first is the

	Formal or voting	Economic	Political
Equity	Shareholders Directors Minority interests	Employers/owners	Dissident shareholders
Economic	Preferred debt holders	Suppliers Debt holders Customers Employees Competitors	European Union Local governments Foreign governments Consumer lobbies Unions
Influencers	Outside directors Licensing bodies	Regulatory agencies	Trade associations Environmental groups

(Stake — vertical axis label; Power — horizontal axis label)

FIGURE 8.1 Participant stakeholders: the grid location denotes the primary but not necessarily sole orientation of the stakeholder (From Freeman (1984); used with kind permission.)

formal power to control the actions of the organisation. The second is economic power to influence the organisation through the markets in which they operate, and the final element is political power generated by the stakeholders' ability to influence an organisation through legislation and regulation. He constructed a matrix, Figure 8.1, which represents the dominant influence of each stakeholder. This acknowledges that stakeholders could be placed in a number of different cells, but as Stahl and Grigsby (1992) point out, by showing their dominant role the focus organisation is in a better position to gauge the influence of each stakeholder group.

Stakeholder models

Following Freeman's work various authors have attempted to interpret or develop our understanding of the stakeholder concept (e.g. Carroll, 1993; Donaldson and Preston, 1995; Mason and Gray, 1999; Johnson and Scholes, 2000). However, following the work of Rowe *et al.* (1994), there are several frameworks that underpin the way organisations cope with the diversity of interests of a variety of stakeholders. Figure 8.2 sets out the first two of these, the autocratic and coordinator frameworks. The autocratic framework clearly suggests that the power and the right to lead a marketing channel is placed in a single organisation that uses one-way communication to tell and inform stakeholders.

> The autocratic framework clearly suggests that the power and the right to lead a marketing channel is placed in a single organisation.

The second framework, the coordinator approach, suggests that the power and right to govern the channel is still vested in the focus organisation but this time power is dispersed symmetrically rather than just top down and there is a greater sense of orchestration and involvement. Communication is still one-way and is used, essentially, in order to provide information for each of the other organisations in order that they can fulfil their roles.

Figure 8.3 depicts two further stakeholder frameworks. Model C reflects a set of integrated relationships, where power is non-existent or is dispersed equally among the different stakeholders. Relationships are essentially two-way and symmetrical, as reflected in the communications that are between each of them. The organisation, as

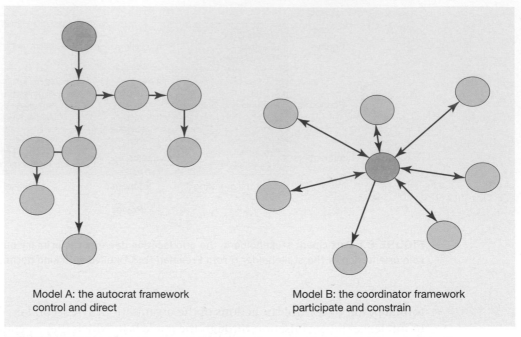

Model A: the autocrat framework
control and direct

Model B: the coordinator framework
participate and constrain

FIGURE 8.2 The autocrat and coordinator frameworks of stakeholder management

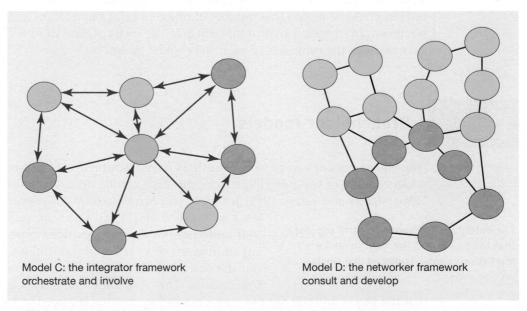

Model C: the integrator framework
orchestrate and involve

Model D: the networker framework
consult and develop

FIGURE 8.3 The integrator and networker models of stakeholder management

an integrator, attempts to balance the conflicting aims and objectives and hence 'weave' a path through the conflicting influences on the organisation. The final model depicts the organisation as a networker, where there is consultation, interaction and involvement in different networks or groups of organisations. The organisation works with a variety of stakeholders and in doing so interacts with organisations from a variety of networks. Communications are 'between' organisations and are based on dialogue where participants listen and act in accordance with the needs of all organisations in each network.

These models set out the key ways in which organisations manage their stakeholders.

These models set out the key ways in which organisations manage their stakeholders. In reality organisations and stakeholder groups consist of different types of organisations, some of whom do not fit neatly within one of these frameworks or models. However, the principles are that organisations seek to manage their stakeholders in different ways and as a result the nature of the relationships and the flows of communication differ. It also illuminates the direct and indirect interaction between the different stakeholders and the power positions relative to the focus organisation.

Stakeholder analysis

The first step in stakeholder analysis is to list all stakeholders and then position them on a map. Those organisations with a primary relationship are then linked together so that 'patterns of interdependence emerge' (Rowe *et al.*, 1994). Figure 8.4 is a stakeholder map for WorkSpace Ltd, an office furniture manufacturer. Here it can be seen not only that WorkSpace interacts with primary and secondary stakeholders but that there is also interaction between the different stakeholders. This application of systems theory is important, as it highlights the point that stakeholders who may be far removed or distant from an original change to the system may well be affected to a greater degree than a number of other stakeholders who are closer to the point of change. This aspect of change within a system is referred to as 'structural change' and can affect stakeholders regardless of their distance from the focus organisation or the point within the system where change was initiated

'Structural change' can affect stakeholders regardless of their distance from the focus organisation or the point within the system where change was initiated.

It is also important to recognise that coalitions and individuals can belong to more than one stakeholder group. For example, lorry drivers/transport owners and the UK government may be in conflict over the latter's position on fuel tax. However, the two parties may also be locked together in opposition to a European Union ruling that the maximum weight of lorries be increased to allow larger European juggernauts wider access to the UK road network, even though UK hauliers are discriminated in other ways when travelling across the Continent.

Stakeholder groups can also emerge as a result of a specific event. This is of particular relevance to organisations planning for disaster and crisis situations. Relatives of patients who have been afflicted or harmed as a result of using particular drugs or who have been involved in an accident, such as an aircraft disaster, often form action groups when lobbying for compensation. For example, the friends and relatives of the Lockerbie disaster, those who claim their children have been damaged through the MMR vaccine, those associated with the Countryside Alliance and fighting over the ban on fox hunting and victims of Gulf War Syndrome have all acted collaboratively in an attempt to get their cases heard and sanctioned.

The current position an organisation holds within the stakeholder map is partly a result of the past decisions of the organisation and its other stakeholders, and is also a reflection of the balance of forces acting on an organisation: those that drive it forward and those that try to restrain it. As Rowe *et al.* (1994) suggest:

> *the present status of the organisation is at best, a temporary balance of opposing forces. Some of these forces provide resources and support to the organisation, while some serve as barriers or constraints. The forces are generated by stakeholders in the course of pursuing their own interests, goals, and objectives.*

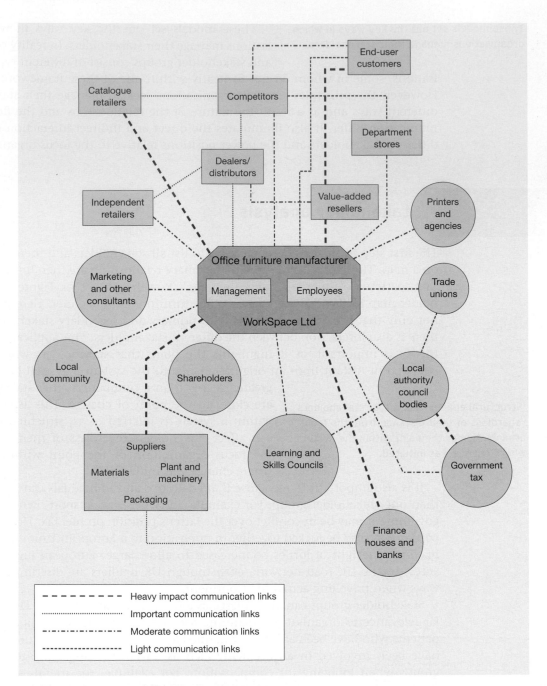

FIGURE 8.4 A stakeholder map for WorkSpace

Having mapped the different stakeholders and made judgements about the interrelationships between different stakeholders, the next task is to make assumptions about the effects a proposed strategy might have on them. For example, a marketing strategy to terminate a particular product line and substitute it with one that is targeted at a different market, one which will require different types of distribution, may well arouse opposition from particular members of the channel network. These assumptions then need to be listed as supporting or resisting the strategy and then be evaluated by the use of two simple rules. The first rule determines the importance of the assumption and the second its reliability. While the numerical analysis may be prone to subjectivity and bias, the exercise is useful because, as Greenley (1989) says, 'it helps focus attention upon those influences or forces that are likely to be extremely beneficial or detrimental'.

The outcome of this process is an evaluation of the likelihood of the success of a proposed strategy. Should the support be greater than the resistance, management has a better basis upon which to proceed with the proposed strategy.

Stakeholder networks

Stakeholders represent actors within marketing channel analysis.

Stakeholders represent actors within marketing channel analysis. Indeed, the degree of congruence between stakeholder analysis and channel analysis is strong. Stakeholder maps reflect the complex web of relationships that all organisations weave. These maps also suggest that the focus organisation operates within a dynamic system of interacting organisations. As mentioned earlier, the map indicates the primary relationships and patterns of interdependence. These patterns and webs suggest the existence of a number of networks within each stakeholder map. Owing to the relative positions of stakeholders, particular networks focus upon functional activities and so have priority over others, or are perceived as more important than certain other networks. This suggests that certain organisations and individuals within each network may have a disproportionate level of power and influence.

The marketing channel represents a vitally important network of organisations.

The marketing channel represents a vitally important network of organisations, and in order to distinguish between the traditional linear and vertical interpretation of distribution channels, which emphasises a bipolar and dyadic relationship (Andersson, 1992), a perspective of *a network of organisations, collaborating and working together in partnership, to provide end-user satisfaction*, is introduced as a more useful, realistic but conceptually more challenging approach. These networks not only constitute those organisations that make up the marketing channel but also seek to integrate all those other organisations that assist the channel members to achieve their objectives of satisfying customer needs. Therefore a stakeholder network can be identified, which in turn can be subdivided into two major sub-networks: the performance and support networks.

The performance network consists of organisations that are directly involved with the value-adding processes in the production and distribution of the product or service. Examples would be producers, manufacturers, suppliers, distributors (such as wholesalers and retailers) and also competitors. The performance network for WorkSpace is shown in Figure 8.5.

The support network consists of those organisations or groups that influence, indirectly, the value-adding processes. For some organisations these may be financial institutions, local and national government and legislature, consultancies and support agencies, training and professional bodies, and pressure groups, such as consumer interest organisations. All of these organisations may influence the value-adding processes in an indirect way and on an irregular basis, and are characterised by their irregular, infrequent and low level of interaction in comparison with members of the performance network. Membership of the different networks will vary. For example, the government is a key stakeholder in the performance network of an NHS hospital. However, the same government is a member of the support network for a retailer or provider of wholesale services in the food or clothing markets. The support network for WorkSpace is shown in Figure 8.6.

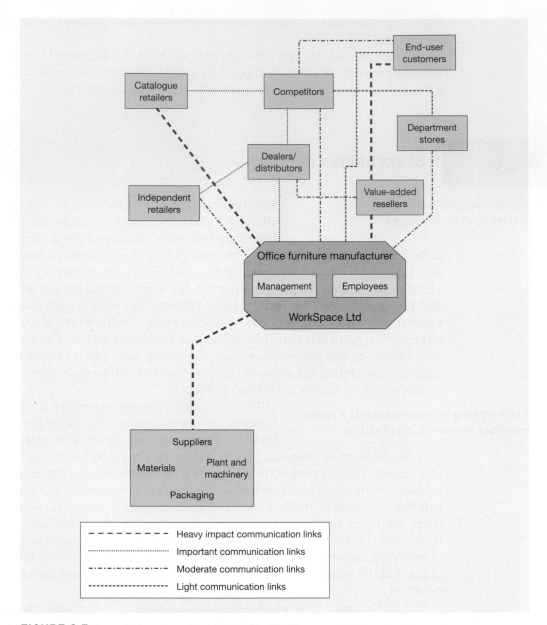

FIGURE 8.5 A performance network map for WorkSpace

It should be remembered that these two sub-networks are not mutually exclusive. Indeed, they are interdependent and interactive. However, for ease of analysis it is often appropriate to distinguish between the two. The identification of these networks is an important foundation for the development of marketing communications. As seen in Chapter 2, when examining communication theory, relational communication networks take into account the context in which the communication takes place, and in particular the roles participant organisations play in the network.

Relational communication networks take into account the context in which the communication takes place.

The context for the performance network is the interdependence between organisations in the value-adding processes, each with the common aim of satisfying buyer needs. The context for the support network is a market exchange relationship between each actor and the focus organisation, and the absence of any mutual interdependence. For

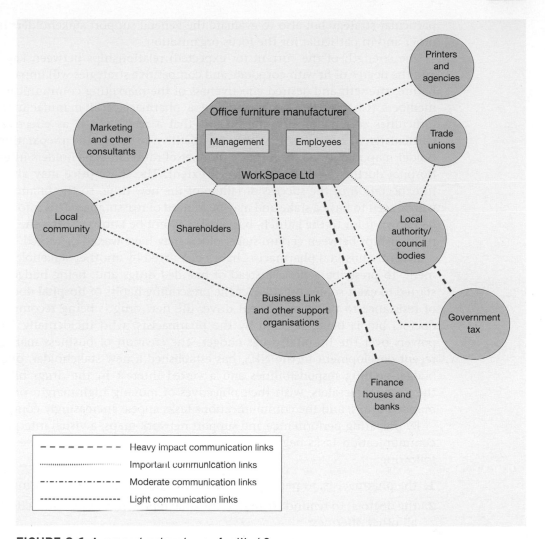

FIGURE 8.6 A support network map for WorkSpace

example, a bank may provide loan facilities to the focus organisation, but the arrangement is relatively short term. The loan is normally only 'discussed' by both parties at the initiation and at periodic reviews and, while important, is not necessarily vital to the long-term process of adding value or to the performance of the organisation or the other organisations involved in the value chain.

Stakeholder analysis is an important concept for developing knowledge and understanding about the other organisations in the environment. From the stakeholder map it is possible to distinguish or at least derive particular networks of organisations. The performance and support networks help identify groups of organisations that have different needs and relationships, which in turn will affect the marketing communications undertaken by the focus organisation, in particular those organisations in the performance network with whom tight couplings or partnerships are formed.

Stakeholder analysis is seen, increasingly, as a significant part of corporate strategy (analysis, formulation, implementation and evaluation). However, its use as a tool within marketing communications has generally been overlooked, but is of importance. Of particular interest are the mapping and assumption rating exercises. Mapping is important in its own right to identify stakeholders and their interrelationships. The assumption rating exercise is important not only to evaluate the support for a particular strategy but also to evaluate the general support stakeholders have for each other and in particular for the focus organisation.

The strength of the current (or expected) relationships between key stakeholders and the degree of fit with corporate and competitive strategies will impact on the form, nature, strength and desired effectiveness of the marketing communications between members (Chapter 9). For example, if a pharmaceutical manufacturer experiences difficulties convincing hospital doctors that a new drug is as effective as claimed, particularly in comparison with a competitive offering, the preparation of a stakeholder map may well reveal that a number of different stakeholders interact with the hospital doctors to a greater or lesser extent. The share price may also be wavering in expectation of the success or failure of the new drug, so the financial community will be seen to have a stake and may be in need of reassurance. This information should be known prior to the launch, but what may not be known is that the strength of the relationships between certain stakeholders may have waxed or waned.

Recently hospital pharmacists have been urged by another stakeholder, the government, to prescribe generic instead of branded drugs and, being budget driven, have started to exert some control over the prescribing habits of hospital doctors. As a form of resistance to the management drive, the new drug is being recommended by the doctors but is being rejected by the pharmacists, who incidentally have increased powers over the hospital drugs budget. The creation of business managers, another recent development in the NHS, has established a new stakeholder, once again with budget-holding responsibilities and a vested interest in the drugs bill. Add to this the drug wholesalers, with their objectives of moving high-margin offerings such as branded drugs, and the communications tasks appear increasingly complex.

By preparing performance and support network maps, a visual interpretation of the communication tasks begins to emerge. Communications have to be targeted at the following:

1. the pharmacists, to persuade them of the efficacy and value of using the drug;

2. the doctors, to remind them that the drug represents better value effectiveness than all other offerings;

3. the financial community, to ensure continuing confidence in the manufacturer and all the manufacturer's related activities;

ViewPoint 8.2   Networking pallets

Palletways is a growing haulage business that was originally based on the principle of carrying clients' goods on pallets stacked on lorries to destinations all over the country. Of several problems, two were crucial. The first concerned collecting sufficient orders to make the outward journey profitable and hoping that there might even be an order to contribute to the costs of the homeward journey. The second concerned the fragmented nature of the market and the territories that were owned by local 'warlords'.

Palletways introduced a new approach, whereby it coordinated networks of hauliers from across the country. By bringing the different parts of the industry together, it has reduced conflict and brought some new values to this part of the distribution system. Hauliers now bring their clients goods to a central depot in the Midlands where they offload and pick up other loads from other members, for distribution in their own geographic areas. This helps ensure economic load factors, reduces costs and environmental damage and improves the service for all clients.

Source: Adapted from Gracie (2001).

4. the business managers, to keep the drug at the top of their awareness, or in their evoked set;

5. the wholesalers, to keep them informed of developments, to involve them in the management of the network and to maintain their distribution facilities and stock levels;

6. the sales representatives of the manufacturer, to support and provide continuous relevant information in order that they maintain credibility with the pharmacists whom they are trying to influence;

7. the staff of the manufacturer, to maintain morale and motivation.

Marketing channels and networks

The structural pattern that any channel assumes is a result of the relationships between the individual organisations that compose the channel. The channel is dynamic, so the structure should be flexible in order that it can respond to the changing environment. Two main channel patterns can be identified: conventional channels and vertical marketing channels. Both are representations of the performance network described earlier.

Conventional marketing channels

Traditionally, organisations group together because independently their objectives cannot be achieved. By working together each member can concentrate upon those activities that it does best. This may be retailing or manufacturing, but, whatever it is, the objectives of each organisation are best served by allowing others to perform alternative, specialist functions for them. Through this approach, organisations form temporary, often loosely aligned, partnerships with a range of organisations and retain their independence and autonomy. Bipolar relationships typify these structures, as decisions are often self-oriented and reflect the needs of just the two members (Figure 8.7).

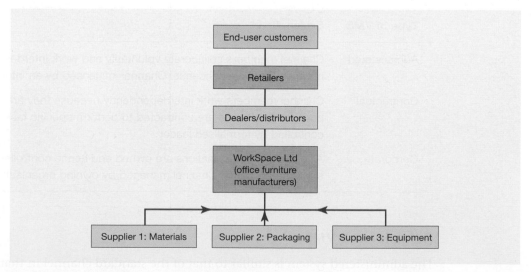

FIGURE 8.7 A conventional marketing channel

As a consequence of this self-interest, the level of control that any member has over the other members of the channel is minimal, except where access to an important raw material or product can be affected. This framework allows offerings to move through the entire system or through parts of it. There is no single controlling organisation and the framework is viewed as a set of independent organisations working in free association with one another. There is, as Oliver (1990) puts it, 'no controlled coverage of the market'. Attempts to secure coverage usually result in a loss of control in the marketing channel. Furthermore, the level of loyalty is low, which is indicative of the instability that exists in these configurations (as organisations are able to enter and exit with relative freedom) and the lack of impact on the remaining actors in the overall system.

Communication within these channels is often framed within the needs of any two partners, and a wider systems perspective is absent. As a result, communications tend to be ad hoc, reactionary, unidirectional (in the sense that messages are not reciprocated) and do not occur on a very frequent basis.

> Communication within these channels is often framed within the needs of any two partners.

Vertical marketing systems

Vertical marketing systems (VMSs) attempt to trade off coverage against the lack of control – more control means less coverage. They have developed since the mid-1970s and consist of vertically aligned and coordinated marketing partners. They function as a system, centrally driven by a controlling organisation, designed to achieve economies of scale and to maximise market impact in a collaborative partnership attempting to satisfy customer needs. The tighter cooperation and interdependence of member partners is formally recognised and a planned approach ensures that a greater degree of stability is achieved. The entry and exit of partners to the system is controlled to meet the needs of the channel and not any one member. The coupling between members is tight and the level of connectedness is similarly strong.

> The entry and exit of partners to the system is controlled to meet the needs of the channel and not any one member.

There are three types of VMS: administered, contractual and corporate. See Table 8.1.

TABLE 8.1 Types of vertical marketing systems

Type of VMS	Explanation
Administered	Channel members collaborate voluntarily and work interdependently yet maintain their independence. Channel influenced by an informal leader.
Contractual	Channel members work interdependently because they are legally bound together and are contracted to perform specific tasks. Channel controlled by formalised leader.
Corporate	All participant organisations are owned and hence controlled by a single organisation. Channel managed by owning organisation.

Administered VMSs

The administered system is similar to that of the standard channel in that the participants work together, tied by the attraction of potential rewards. 'The point at which the conventional channel stops and the administered one begins must be made on the basis of judgements about the degree of effective interorganisational management taking place in the channel' (Rosenbloom, 1983).

Organisations work together to fulfil strategies developed by a limited number of channel partners. These strategies are then administered through informal 'voluntary' collaborative agreements by all interested parties. It is important to recognise that members retain their own authority and that each member's commitment to the system is largely determined by self-interest, but a system-wide perspective and a view of the longer term helps bind members together.

Contractual VMSs

Developing out of administered VMSs are contractual partnerships that consist, essentially, of a written agreement between a dominant member and the other members of the channel. These contracts set out members' rights and obligations. There are three kinds of contractual arrangement:

1. *Wholesaler-sponsored chains*
   These consist of organisations that agree to work together to obtain discounts and other advantages in purchasing, distribution and promotion, e.g. Booker.

2. *Retailer-sponsored chains*
   These are similar to the wholesaler chains and, for the individual organisation, represent a trade-off between independence and performance potential. The sponsored chain approach allows small and medium-sized organisations to compete against the purchasing power of many retail and wholesale multiples. Spar and VG are examples of retailer cooperatives.

3. *Franchise*
   There are three forms of franchise:
   (a) manufacturer-driven retailer systems, e.g. Ford;
   (b) manufacturer-driven wholesaler systems, e.g. Coca-Cola;
   (c) service-driven retailer systems, e.g. McDonald's.

ViewPoint 8.3   TUI - a vertical marketing system

TUI Northern Europe is part of TUI AG, the largest tourism and services group in the world. It is a market leader in Europe and includes:

Specialist Holidays Group
TUI Ireland
TUI Nordic
TUI UK.

TUI UK, the largest holiday company in the UK, in turn includes Thomson Holidays (a holiday and tour operator) and Lunn Poly (a branded chain of high street travel retailers) plus smaller agencies. Therefore TUI UK owns a substantial share of holiday capacity and the travel agencies to enable customers to buy holidays. The company claims to have about a third of the UK market. It offers a wide range of holiday types and resorts, but attempts to be consistent with 'best value for money' brand messages. The Glasgow call centre deals with around 1 million holidays a year, including direct bookings for Thomson, Lunn Poly and Portland.

Source: Adapted from http://www.thomsontravelgroup.com/companyback/index.htm (accessed 04/03/03); used with kind permission.

Franchise arrangements have grown in popularity over the last 25 years. Under these arrangements the right to market a particular offering is agreed between two parties (a bipolar arrangement).

There are two main approaches to franchising. The first is a *product franchise*, where the channel's dominant organisation authorises particular organisations to distribute their offering. In other words, organisations are selected into a channel and each is permitted to use the trade name and promotional materials (which are deemed to be of value to the customer) of the dominant organisation. Various German kitchen appliance and furniture manufacturers use this form of authorisation to allow particular UK retailers (independent kitchen design and fit organisations) to distribute their offerings. The second form of franchise can be referred to as a *business franchise*. Under this format not only is the product permitted to be used by the franchisee but the whole trading approach must be utilised. McDonald's restaurants are an example of the latter, with franchisees having to adopt the entire established trading style.

The relationships between the franchisor and franchisee can determine the style, breadth and form of the communications between partners.

What is of importance to those responsible for marketing communications is that the relationships between the franchisor and franchisee can determine the style, breadth and form of the communications between partners. For example, under the product franchise arrangement, the relationship is such that, once each new franchise operation is established, contact between the two parties is limited to periodic performance review, a relationship often characterised by non-involvement and a market-structured orientation.

Under the business franchisee arrangement, a closer relationship, formed partly to protect the brand and the associated investment, means that the communications can be more relational and hence supportive, rather than market structured. As McGrath and Hardy (1986) point out, those organisations that seek to develop understanding through substantial communications programmes will improve relationships and reduce the level of channel conflict. It will be shown later (Chapter 31) that the form of the relationship is an important factor in the communications strategy adopted by organisations. Whether the franchise arrangements are product or business formats is not necessarily important in itself, but the outcomes of the arrangements are important for subsequent analysis and strategy formulation.

Corporate VMSs

A corporate vertical marketing system is a discrete grouping of organisations that are owned, and hence controlled, by one dominant member.

A corporate vertical marketing system is a discrete grouping of organisations that are owned, and hence controlled, by one dominant member. This form provides for the greatest control in comparison with the other two systems. Laura Ashley not only designs and makes products but distributes them through its own retail outlets. TUI, the tour operator, owns Thomsons, Lunn Poly travel agencies and Britannia Airways and in turn controls not only the distribution of its own offerings (and is therefore not dependent upon other travel agencies) but also the carrier with whom clients travel. Of the many benefits that this format provides, control over the information flow is an important one. Information can be dispersed to selected areas of the organisation at a time that meets management's requirements.

Corporate systems are achieved through vertical integration. Organisations can choose to integrate upstream to control their sources of supply (their inputs), or they can move downstream and seek to control the distribution of their offerings. Complete control is virtually impossible and the scale economies and cost savings that are important attractions of vertical integration can often only be achieved through large investment.

Indeed some writers feel that contractual systems can provide many of the benefits that corporate systems provide and that there must be sound reasons to enter into a corporate system (Buzzell, 1983). The inherent lack of flexibility associated with corporate systems has been a prime reason for organisations to move away from such rigidity.

Channel design

The design of a marketing channel can only be predetermined if the focus organisation is considering the development of a VMS; otherwise, the decision is normally based upon whether to enter a particular system or how to adjust a system in which they are currently operating. These decisions need to be made on the basis of the answers to the following two questions: how many sales outlets are required to provide optimal service for current and future customers and how should the outlets participate in order for customer satisfaction to be achieved? These questions are answered by the level of market coverage offered to the customer segment. There are three choices available: intensive, selective and exclusive.

1. *Intensive distribution*

   This is normally applicable to items that are low priced and frequently purchased, where customer involvement is low and perceived risk minimal. Chewing gum, newspapers and soft drinks are good examples. By offering the product through a large number of outlets, the wide availability promotes the opportunity for high-volume sales.

2. *Selective distribution*

   By placing the offering in a limited number of outlets a more favourable image can be generated and the producer can determine which intermediaries would be best suited to meet the needs of the channel. Customers are more involved with the purchase, and the level of perceived risk is correspondingly higher. As a result, buyers are prepared to seek out appropriate outlets, and those that best match the overall requirements of the customer will be successful. Televisions, hi-fi equipment and clothing are suitable examples of this form of distribution.

   As the costs of each channel are evaluated by a greater number of organisations, so it is likely that they will determine that the commonly accepted guide that 80 per cent of sales are often driven by just 20 per cent of outlets will apply. It is therefore highly probable that in the future selective distribution will be used by an increasing number of organisations.

3. *Exclusive distribution*

   Some customers may perceive a product to be of such high prestige or to be positioned so far away from the competition that just a single outlet in a particular trading area would be sufficient to meet the needs of the channel. For example, BMW cars are normally only available from a single outlet in any one area. If the offering requires complex servicing arrangements or tight control then the exclusive form of distribution may be best, as it fosters closer relationships.

Coughlan *et al.* (2001) warn against the temptation of moving to an intensive distribution strategy in the expectation that sales volume will improve. For example, if Jaeger, the manufacturer of high-quality clothing, now distributed through selective outlets, decided to use multiples, discount stores and variety stores, any short-term sales improvement would rapidly fall away for the following reasons:

1. New outlets would use Jaeger products as loss leaders to attract customers. Prices generally would fall and the smaller margins might not be attractive to the original outlets.

2. Service and customer care would vary from store to store and generally deteriorate.

3. Promotion would have to be increased and more stock held by Jaeger rather than channel members. Increased costs and smaller margins would lead eventually to an unattractive business characterised by poor profitability and conditions in which no participant can win.

The selection criteria for entry to a performance network are a function of the following factors, as identified by Cravens and Woodruff (1986):

1. anticipated revenue flows and costs

2. legal considerations

3. level of channel control required

4. channel availability.

To this list should be added the expected levels of cooperation and goodwill that will frame the relationship between members. Indeed a further question should be asked of the focus organisation itself: if accepted into an established channel will it be able to fulfil the role expected of it and what will be the form of the relationship with the other members? Will it fit in?

Coordination, conflict and power

As noted previously, if a marketing channel is to function effectively, cooperation between members is paramount. To work effectively and efficiently the interdependence, specialisation and expertise of individual organisations should be encouraged (Rosenbloom, 1983). However, interdependence is rarely distributed in a uniform and equitable way. This inequality is a major source of power for members of the channel configuration. This disproportionate distribution means that no single organisation can have absolute power (Stern and Gorman, 1969). For example, by owning and controlling resources that are valued by another organisation, channel power can be established. Relationships between members can be seen to be a reflection of the balance of power that exists between them. Emerson (1962) referred to power as a function of dependence. The more dependent X is on Y, the greater power Y has over X. As all members of the channel network are interdependent then all members have a degree of power. It is therefore imperative that the power held by constituent members is utilised to further the development of the superorganisation and the achievement of its objectives and goals. If used otherwise, power may lead to negative consequences for the member and in turn for the channel network.

Social exchange theory is used by Stern and El-Ansary (1992) to look at the issue of dependence: 'This theory rests on two major constructs: comparison level (CL) and comparison level of alternatives (CLalt)'. The former concerns the expected performance levels of channel members based on experience. The latter is based on the expected performance of the best alternative organisation to a current channel member. As this is true for all channel members, there is a certain level of dependence upon each other. This means that each channel member can affect, by its own actions, the performance of others. It is this ability to influence the performance of others that is seen by advocates of social exchange theory as a source of power.

> Interdependence is rarely distributed in a uniform and equitable way.

Sources of power

Determined five bases for power: rewards, coercion, expertise, legitimate and reference.

French and Raven (1959), in a classic study, determined five bases for power: rewards, coercion, expertise, legitimate and reference bases. *Rewards* are one of the more common, where, for example, a manufacturer might grant a wholesaler particular discounts dependent upon the volume of products bought during an agreed period. *Coercion* is the other side of the 'reward-based' coin, where negative measures may be brought in to sanction a channel member. If a wholesaler becomes dissatisfied with the payment cycle adopted by a retailer, deliveries may be slowed down or the discount structure revised. Power based upon *expertise*, perceived by other channel members, makes them dependent upon the flow of information from the source. Interestingly, the expert power exercised by leading pharmaceutical manufacturers is derived from the dependence of the pharmacies and general practitioners (GPs) on them and not so much on the dependence of the wholesalers. *Legitimate* power, whereby the authority to manage the channel is recognised rather like a manager recognises the authority of an executive director, is uncommon in conventional channels. Only in contractual and corporate vertical marketing systems (for example, franchisors) can legitimate power be exercised. Finally, *reference* power works on the basis of association and identification – 'being in the same boat' as Rosenbloom (1983) refers to it. If members of a network are able to share and empathise with the problems of their 'network partners', then a channel-wide solution to a common problem may well result in increased understanding, collaboration and trust.

By recognising and understanding the bases of power, the levels of cooperation and the form of the relationships between members, the nature of communication, its pattern, its frequency and its style can be adjusted to complement the prevailing conditions. Furthermore, such an understanding can be useful to help shape the power relationships of the future and to enhance the corporate/marketing strategy. Once the current and expected power bases are determined, marketing communications can assist the shaping process. Of the power propositions provided by French and Raven, reward and coercion seem more apt for use within channels, where market exchange-based transactions predominate.

Reward and coercion seem more apt for use within channels, where market exchange-based transactions predominate.

Legitimate and expert power might be better applied in channels with a high level of relational exchanges.

Channel conflict

Conflict within and between all channels is endemic. Indeed Hunt and Nevin (1974) found conflict to be widely prevalent in channel relationships. Conflict represents a breakdown or deterioration in the levels of cooperation between partners (Shipley and Egan, 1992). Cooperation is important because members of any channel are, to varying degrees, interdependent; hence their membership in the first place.

The reasons for conflict need to be clearly appreciated, as identification of the appropriate cause can lead to communication strategies that remedy, or at least seek to repair, any damage. Some of the more common reasons for channel conflict, suggested by Stern and Gorman (1969), are failure to enact a given or agreed role, issues arising among the participant organisations, selective perception and inadequate communications. For example, because channel members undertake particular *roles*, any failure to fulfil the expected role may be a cause of conflict. An *issue* may arise within the channel that causes conflict. For example, a wholesaler and a manufacturer may disagree about margins, training, marketing policies or, more commonly, territorial issues. McGrath and Hardy (1986) see conflict emanating from manufacturers' policies, such as sales order policies. The tighter and more constricting they are, the greater the likelihood that conflict will erupt than if the policies are flexible and can be adjusted to meet the needs of both parties.

All of these reasons can be distilled into three main factors (Stern and Heskett, 1969). These concern differences relating to:

● competing or incompatible goals
● domains
● perceptions of reality.

Underpinning all of them is inadequate communication.

Competing goals

This is a common form of conflict and typically occurs when one upstream member changes strategy so that its goals become difficult for other downstream members to support. For example, a manufacturer may decide that it wants to reach new market sectors but current dealers might resist this strategy as it is not in their interest to supply other (new) channels with the same products. Indeed, if actioned it might give rise to increased channel competition and then impact on dealer revenues and profits.

Another example of competing goals can be seen when retailers try to increase performance by lowering their stock levels. Conflict is likely as the manufacturer's goal is to increase the level of stock in the channel while intermediaries prefer to be able to pull down stock on demand, and hence avoid working capital costs.

Alternatively, a department manager in a retail organisation may not be too concerned which of its product offerings in a particular category helps the department achieve its volume and margin contributions. However, the manufacturer of an individual brand will be most concerned if their brand is not included as part of the retailer's portfolio of category brands. Different goals yet same product focus.

Domain differences

A channel domain refers to an area, field or sphere of function.

A channel domain refers to an area, field or sphere of function. According to Stern *et al.* (1996) it has four main elements: population, territory, member roles and issues concerning technology and marketing. So disputes can arise because one channel member perceives another member operating outside of the previously designated (agreed) area, perhaps geographically, or in terms of its role. For example, a wholesaler and a manufacturer may disagree about margins, training, marketing policies or, more commonly, territorial issues. McGrath and Hardy (1986) see conflict emanating from manufacturers' policies, such as sales order policies. The tighter and more constricting they are, the greater the likelihood that conflict will erupt than if the policies are flexible and can be adjusted to meet the needs of both parties.

So, a wholesaler who starts to sell direct to end user-consumers, or retailers who begin to sell to other retailers are blatantly adopting a new role and this may infringe upon another member's role and prevent or impede them from achieving their objectives.

A more common example exists when a manufacturer decides to sell through a dealer's competitors, to the extent of even breaking an exclusivity arrangement. The reverse of this intra-channel type of conflict can also cause conflict, when a manufacturer perceives an intermediary selling another (competing) manufacturer's products at the expense of its own range of products.

ViewPoint 8.4	Domain-based conflict at Miller Electric

Miller Electric, a manufacturer of welding equipment, and Linweld, a key distributor of industrial and medical gases and welding supplies, experienced domain-based conflict concerning a change in channel strategy.

Miller Electric's Web site receives 60,000 visitors every month and over half result in sales. Miller Electric wanted to move to a direct channel strategy with distributors responsible for delivering the goods. However, ownership of the sales transaction meant that Miller Electric would be able to set prices and eventually cut the channel out completely. The intermediaries rejected the strategy.

Miller Electric compromised and sales leads generated by Miller Electric's Web site were given to distributors. Once customers designate items they want to buy on Miller Electric's site, they must choose from a list of nearby distributors. The customers and their shopping lists are then whisked off to the selected distributor's Web site, where they receive pricing and availability information prior to completing the order.

However, another problem arose concerning which distributor gets the lead. Miller Electric's process for listing distributors works on the basis that when a customer inputs a zip code, the three closest distributors pop up. Moreover, only the distributor's name, address and contact information are provided. Such a simple process does not reflect Linweld's power, importance and size of investment compared to many smaller and more provincial distributors. In reaching a solution, Miller had to recognise Linweld's powerful position based on the volume and value of business placed through Miller Electric.

Source: Adapted from: Kaneshige (2001) http://www.line56.com/articles/default.asp?NewsID=2382 (accessed 3 December 2003); used with kind permission.

Another cause of domain-based conflict concerns the emergence of multiple channels. An intermediary might feel threatened by increased competition and reduced financial performance opportunities.

Disagreements about pricing, sales areas or sales order processing, for example, are sensitive issues that can also lead to channel conflict. Once agreement has been made about policy terms or operational formats, any changes should be negotiated and managed in a cooperative and considered way. Indeed, some channels often stipulate the way that changes to key domain-based issues should be managed.

Perceptions of reality

Through the process of selective perception any number of members may react to the same stimulus in completely different and conflicting ways. The objectives of each of the channel members are different, however well bonded they are to the objectives of the distribution system. It is also likely that each member perceives different ways of achieving the overall goals, all of which are recipes for conflict. As each member organisation perceives the world differently, their perception of others and their actions may lead to tensions and disagreements. So, an action taken by member X might be perceived differently by member Y to that intended. Any action that Y takes as a result of this perception may result in conflict. Perceptions about a product attribute, its applications and appropriate segments can all give rise to perceptually based conflict.

Apart from poor or incomplete communication, the main reason for this tendency to see different information or actions differently to that intended may arise because, in the absence of a strong cooperative relationship, different channel members are focused on different business elements (Coughlan *et al.* 2001). A manufacturer might be focused on products and processes and a dealer may be focused on their customers and the functions and processes necessary to meet their needs. Differences in perception may arise because member focus is culturally driven. What may be an appropriate behaviour in one culture may not be understood, known or be just different to that in another. This can obviously be a problem for internationally based organisations.

The final reason is perhaps one of the most important, and central to the issue of this particular key factor. *Communication* is a coordinating mechanism for all members

Communication **is a coordinating mechanism for all members of the system.**

of the system. Its absence or failure will inevitably lead to uncoordinated behaviour and actions that are not in the best interests of the channel system. The channel can become destabilised through poor or inadequate communication, as the processes of selective perception can distort encoded messages and lead to conflict and disunity.

Conflict can emerge in a previously stable system, as certain members see their corporate and marketing objectives capable of being achieved through new channels that require new members and new roles. When Heinz withdrew television advertising to use direct mail and coupons, the response of the supermarkets was to threaten not to redeem any Heinz coupons that had been sent to customers. This is against the food manufacturers' rules about misredemption, but the disequilibrium was easy to observe. The performance network broke down as a result of a shift in the perceptions of members of the best way to achieve their own objectives.

Management of channel communications

Communications between members of marketing channels, and VMSs in particular, are normally the responsibility of a particular member in the channel system. This member assumes this dominant role by virtue of the dependence of the other actors (members). This dependence provides for the exercise of power, as set out earlier. The organisations that are perceived to be powerful in the context of the distribution channel are said to be channel leaders or channel captains.

Channel leadership carries a responsibility to coordinate the activities of the other members. Therefore, all communications should be designed to assist the network as a whole and not just those of the leader. As Frazier and Sheth (1985) suggest, the objective of channel leadership is to contribute to the improved performance of the channel network. If the channel performance improves, then the channel leader is likely to benefit and its role as leader will be confirmed for a further period.

The communications that the channel leader masterminds consist of two main strands. The first is the operational data flow, enhancing the performance of the network at an operational level. The advances in information technology (IT) have been crucial to the distribution of data between organisations. Indeed, IT now provides an opportunity for organisations to develop competitive advantage. For example, the installation of computerised reservation systems in travel agencies by tour operators not only helps to provide for a high level of customer satisfaction through real-time processing but also signals the existence of a considerable mobility barrier. Those travel agents who wish to exit the network and those tour operators wishing to enter a more compelling relationship with certain travel agents must now account for all the costs of changing systems, including the hardware, software, training and support associated with information technology.

The second strand is marketing communications. This concerns the deployment of the range of tools in the promotional mix, established earlier. These flows of largely persuasive information are designed to influence organisations and individuals to take a particular course of action. Information is distributed in order to influence the decisions that members make about the marketing mix they each adopt.

Particular organisations can be seen to adopt the role of channel leader and to become responsible for the discharge and regulation of the information in the network or superorganisation.

Management of organisational communications

As a broad generalisation, formal communication with all other organisations and individuals, that is all stakeholders, has been the responsibility of two individual managers, each within different departments and reporting to different senior executives:

1. The first of these is the brand manager, who traditionally has been responsible for the communications and, in particular, the promotion of the brand. Recently a number of organisations have been appointing trade or channel managers, reflecting the increasing recognition of the significance and power associated with certain channel intermediaries, such as the multiple retailers. These channel managers have many responsibilities, including the establishment of suitable relationships with all organisations in the performance network.

2. The second is the public relations manager, whose department has historically been responsible for communications with other non-trade organisations and the establishment of goodwill with organisations in the wider environment.

By spreading responsibility for an organisation's communications across two separate departments, each trying to accomplish different, often conflicting, objectives, organisations can only suboptimise and fail to communicate effectively. Different and uncoordinated messages, conveyed at different times, lead to confusion and misunderstanding by stakeholders. At worst, there may be a change to a more negative perception and a fall in confidence and goodwill towards the organisation, which, unless corrected, can in the long term affect not only consumer perception and sales but also the share price and value of the organisation.

Other problems brought about by this divided approach to the management of organisational communications are changes to employees' motivation and the shared values held by the organisation. Changes in attitude and the image held of the organisation by all stakeholders, and failure to communicate corporate strategy and marketing plans to particular organisations, are illustrative of further problems, as are the missed opportunities to develop strategic alliances and to satisfy changing customer needs.

Many researchers (Mallen, 1969; Rosenbloom, 1978) have concluded that channel conflict is reduced, but never eliminated, by building cooperation among members of the channel. To help build cooperation it is essential that there is consensus about the overall objectives and sound communication. To assist the development of a cooperative network of relationships, the generation of integrated marketing communications by all members, particularly channel leaders, is fundamental. One of the first steps is to appoint a communications coordinator. This person should be responsible for the development and implementation of a communications strategy that controls all the message outputs of the organisation and assists the organisation through the complex web of channels to which all organisations belong.

Networks

The ideas expressed so far in this chapter are well founded, accepted and researched but use, as their focus, the dyadic relationship between organisations based upon the functionality whereby each organisation is able to achieve their own goals. This perspective, while still current in many respects, has been challenged, and some now consider a supply chain perspective as more valid, one where interorganisational functionality across the whole network of interacting organisations is more prevalent.

Business-to-business relationships are characterised by organisations that choose to coordinate their activities in such a way that their individual goals are achieved, but not necessarily at the expense of other organisations with whom they interact. Relational exchanges are sought with a variety of organisations and McLoughlin and Horan (2000) identify five main exchange elements:

● financial and economic exchange
● technological exchange
● knowledge exchange
● legal exchange
● information exchange.

These exchanges are both formal and informal and occur in different degrees between two or more organisations through time.

These exchanges are both formal and informal and occur in different degrees between two or more organisations through time.

In marketing channels, organisations manage a trade-off between the desire to remain independent (autonomous) and the need to be interdependent (cooperative). Much of the literature and the discussion so far depicts these channels as a vertical alignment of organisations, one that is linear and essentially bipolar. That is, the interorganisational relationships are regarded as one to one or dyadic in nature, as if to exclude the impact and influence that other organisations bring to the relationship. One of the difficulties of this approach is that organisations are regarded out of the true context in which they operate. It is necessary to consider the whole system of relationships because the relationship of any two actors (organisations) is contingent upon the direct and indirect relationships of all the actors (Andersson, 1992). A network of relationships therefore provides the context within which exchange behaviour occurs.

A systems view accepts that the actions of an organisation impact, to a greater or lesser degree, upon many other organisations.

A systems view accepts that the actions of an organisation impact, to a greater or lesser degree, upon many other organisations, not just the one to whom action is directed. Indeed, it is the interdependence and web of relationships that organisations develop with one another which characterises the nature and intensity of network behaviour.

Networks hold together partly through 'an elaborate pattern of interdependence and reciprocity' (Achrol, 1997). Indeed the development of relationship marketing appears to coincide with the emergence of network approaches to interorganisational analysis. This approach is referred to as industrial network analysis, and has evolved from its original focus on dyadic relationships (Araujo and Easton, 1996). Now the position of an organisation in a network is regarded as important. Positions are determined by the functions performed, their importance, the strength of relationships with other organisations and the identity of the organisations with which there are direct and indirect relationships (Mattsson, 1989). Some researchers (e.g. Lancioni, 2000) argue

ViewPoint 8.5   Informal distribution networks

Many organisations, especially start-up companies, have little opportunity or insufficient resources to set up formal chains of distributors and retailers. The alternative is to rely on informal networks developed through satisfied customers passing on word-of-mouth recommendation. Ecoflow, which makes watch-like devices that can boost the flow of blood, adopted a network marketing system whereby those who decide to resell products as a result of being introduced to them by other customers are rewarded with a discount on future purchases. Ecoflow has 8,000 worldwide distributors and although the credibility is high and the cost structure low, issues arise concerning branding, distribution development and coordination and direction of customer communications.

Network marketing is often confused with pyramid selling, which can be troublesome for companies such as Ecoflow, because pyramid selling is basically illegal. Pyramid selling usually requires new members to pay a joining fee and all people hierarchically associated with someone who makes a sale, earns a commission. Ecoflow uses discounts to reward and retain its distributors.

Source: Adapted from Terry (2004).

that there has been a transition from thinking of channels of distribution where the focus is upon making each constituent firm more productive and hence more efficient (an intrafunctional view) to one which looks at enhancing the level of efficiency of the entire network by focusing on the need for collaboration and mutual support (an interfunctional view). A more recent step holds that the objectives and strategies of constituent firms become one and the same, such that the network assumes a customer focus so that improvements are achieved by firms acting together (an interorganisational approach). Those supporting this supply chain management perspective maintain that management's role is to ensure that the coalition runs smoothly and that a focus on conflict resolution is paramount (Ballou *et al.*, 1999). This view is not shared (e.g. Achrol, 1997) as, although a customer focus is regarded as important, others regard the current paradigm to be built around cooperating and coordinating networks that are built upon trust and commitment and in which there is a noticeable absence of power, overt conflict and political jousting. However, there is agreement that networks of interacting organisations is a more acceptable interpretation of management practice than the more rigid distribution channels approach so widely accepted in the 1970s and 1980s.

The position an organisation has and the degree to which an organisation is connected or coupled to other organisations partly determines the extent to which

> The degree to which an organisation is connected or coupled to other organisations partly determines the extent to which organisations are able to mobilise resources and achieve corporate goals.

organisations are able to mobilise resources and achieve corporate goals. As Achrol states, the strength and duration of a relationship are partly dependent upon 'the network of relationships that collectively define and administer the norms by which dyadic relationships are conducted'. He goes on to quote Macneil (1978) who suggested that the more relational an exchange becomes the more it takes on the properties of 'a minisociety with a vast array of norms beyond those centered on the exchange and its immediate processes'. Network approaches provide a more dynamic interpretation of the relationships that organisations have with one another. Networks provide a context for understanding the actions that actors take and in particular provide a means for understanding or interpreting the communications used to maintain or enhance relationships. This text uses a network approach to understand the context within which organisations interact.

Outsourcing

A significant recent structural development within the network concept has been the use of outsourcing. Under this approach organisations devolve responsibility for the manufacturing or servicing of key or core activities to other organisations. These organisations could be within a company group or, as is normal, independent organisations. The idea pivots on the concept that activities should be undertaken by those who are expert in that area, who are more able to be innovative and whose cost structure is lower than that which could be reasonably expected by the focus organisation. As a result the outsourcer is free to concentrate on what they do best, their area of core capability.

There are of course a large number of variations concerning the degree to which outsourcing can be undertaken but two main aspects emerge. The first concerns the degree to which the outsourced organisation is tied into or coupled by the outsourcer, and the second concerns the processes by which the organisations interact.

Tightly coupled organisations are effectively making a trade-off between flexibility and customer service. The lower flexibility provides for lower costs but threatens customer service should the outsourced provider be unable to deliver products due to a manufacturing or production problem. More loosely coupled networks might experience higher costs because of the greater number of alternative providers, but at least the opportunity to maintain customer service levels exists as production can be switched as problems arise.

ViewPoint 8.6	Li & Fung: the orchestrators

Li & Fung, a Hong Kong-based trading company, outsources the production of all its goods to others. Li & Fung make no products at all. By orchestrating its global network of highly focused providers it arranges private-label manufacturing, primarily on behalf of US and European clothiers. For a specific product or client, Li & Fung puts together a set of partner organisations to manage product development, the sourcing of raw materials, production planning and management, manufacturing and shipping. Any problems are resolved by shifting activities from one network partner to another.

Brown *et al.* (2002) argue that this level of flexibility 'promotes high-output performance'. Li & Fung gains efficiencies through the specialisation of suppliers rather than by squeezing supply chain costs by tightly integrating activities. Loose coupling frees up processes and enables greater levels of specialisation. The results confirm the efficacy of this approach. The return on equity has been over 30 per cent a year for each year since 1996 and in 2001 revenues amounted to just over $1 million per employee.

Source: Adapted from Brown *et al.* (2002); used with permission.

The processes used by the lead organisations to manage their providers are often the same ones used internally, rigid. As a result the possibilities for innovation and development are limited, constricted by cost and time criteria. Brown *et al.* (2002) argue that outsourcers should behave as orchestrators which enable the network organisations to concentrate on processes as well as outcomes. Process networks lead to an increase in the number of participants that add to the network's value to customers, as the more providers the network includes, the more opportunity each has to specialise and innovate. One of the outcomes of this exploration is the emphasis and importance that is placed upon communication between the various stakeholders, if only to enable the network to continue.

Summary

This chapter has introduced network theory as a means of exploring some of the issues associated with an organisation's interorganisational relationships, in particular those actor organisations involved with what is traditionally viewed as the marketing channel.

Stakeholder theory provides a similar perspective to network analysis, and issues concerning the manner in which stakeholder maps can be drawn to assist marketing communications were presented. Following this, the distribution channels were presented as a network of interacting organisations, some of whom contribute directly to the value-added activities of the focus organisation (referred to as performance networks) and some of whom provide activities and services that support the focus organisation (referred to as support networks) but do not contribute directly to the channel of distribution.

Understanding who the key stakeholders are, and knowing their positions and roles in the various networks, represents an important key factor in the development of planned communications. Communications are regarded as an important element in the smooth working of, and reduction in the level of conflict in, any network. Understanding the quality and form of the current relationships helps to shape future marketing communications with members of the different networks.

Review questions

1. What are the four factors that are considered to determine the position of an organisation in a network?

2. Explain the central characteristics of industrial network analysis.

3. Determine the main stakeholders for an organisation with which you are familiar and rank them in order of importance.

4. Select those that directly influence the value-adding processes performed by the organisation.

5. Prepare a performance network map. Indicate on the map the main flows of marketing communications currently established and the promotional flows that should be in position.

6. Suggest ways in which new flows of promotional information can be established.

7. What are the differences between conventional channel networks and vertical marketing systems?

8. How might marketing communications be influenced by the type of franchise in place?

9. To what extent might the emergence of a powerful organisation reflect levels of interdependence in a network?

10. French and Raven identified several bases for power. What are they?

MINI-CASE
Understanding the stakeholder network for a new 'private' university

Mini-case written by Richard Scullion, Senior Lecturer, Bournemouth University

Becoming a university

It might not have the spires of Oxford or the beautiful river of Cambridge but things have been happening and causing quite a stir at the new 'private' University of Westbridge (UW) based in the south of England. Government approval was given under a year ago, after quite a battle in parliament for the management of UW to win approval. Many MPs were opposed on a matter of principle – for them universities should be public bodies for the general public good, not for profit making. Others were also opposed – many local residents in Westbridge argued that the town was too small to cope with an invasion of 10,000 undergraduate students and 500 postgraduate students. They pointed to a lack of facilities and accommodation as reasons for their concern. Many were worried about likely increased road congestion and parking problems too given that it was anticipated that over 70 per cent of the students would have their own car. Another university some 20 miles from Westbridge also voiced anxiety about the new form of competition it would face with the opening of a new, well-funded university. It fought for concessions from UW, seeking and getting assurances that the new university would not offer the same degree programmes as those currently run by their neighbour.

Despite these concerns Westbridge was successful in being granted university status, in part because it has excellent financial backing. Two large multinational companies support it with million-pound plus sponsorship deals, and several other commercial companies are minor sponsors. All buildings, lecture and seminar rooms, student bar and sports facilities are sponsored and heavily branded with the sponsor's messages. UW therefore gets very little money from taxpayers compared to all other universities. Student fees at UW are about 10 per cent higher than at most other UK universities. It also has a string of prestigious professors willing to work for it on a part-time basis setting up degree programmes and delivering some of the keynote sessions to students. Some rather sceptical observers suggest the most likely reason why the University of Westbridge was successful in its application to become a university was due to its high profile public relations agency Stir. It was able to lobby members of the government and backbench MPs. Through the PR agency's contacts in the national media it was also influential in gaining favourable coverage for the UW cause.

First year of operation

UW management was determined to ensure excellent recruitment for the first year of operation. They employed a leading London advertising agency, Levy & Co., which devised a 48-sheet poster campaign aimed at school sixth formers and their teachers. The campaign ran within a 100-mile radius of the campus and focused on the relative luxury of Westbridge. Another campaign ran in Beijing, China aimed at attracting postgraduate students, and focused on the pleasures of student life in Britain. *Marketing Week* ran a front-cover feature on these campaigns calling them groundbreaking; a university using blatantly persuasive messages in such a populist manner was considered favourably. The *Times Higher Education Supplement* however published letters from alarmed academics who argued that such an approach diminished what higher education should be all about, creating a challenging rather than a fun environment. Despite (or perhaps in part because of) the controversy surrounding the advertising campaign it was successful in filling 95 per cent of all courses for year one.

Student experiences were in many ways very similar to those at other universities. However there were some big differences. Students were fined for missing classes, any student engaged in part-time work was strictly limited to no more than 10 hours per week and assignments were linked to one of the sponsors of the university. In addition students were able to pay for extra private tutoring (subject to a maximum of three extra hours per week). They each had a dedicated laptop and space in the learning resource centre for their laptop; and they had access to the 'student leisure village', full of subsidised bars, restaurants, shops, a huge sports centre and even a nightclub.

Reviewing the situation

Senior managers reviewed the first year of operation in order to make careful assessment of their strengths and weaknesses to date. Generally they were delighted, student numbers and therefore revenue was over target. Sponsors were pleased with the benefits they were getting by being associated with a university. Student feedback was generally very positive; the only points of concern seemed to be: (a) the assignments were too similar from one module to the next and (b) they had to pay extra for lecture handouts and all other printed material. However despite retaining the PR agency the university had continued to receive some poor publicity in the educational press. Stories expressed worries about standards of student achievement and possible lack of impartiality over issues that concern the university's sponsors; for example they questioned whether the sponsors' influence was undermining freedom of speech, and wondered if the university was limiting engagement in the critical thinking of students and staff. Local residents had held a public meeting earlier in the year to raise their concerns about traffic levels, inappropriate parking by some students, noise levels late into the evening and increased litter being dropped in the vicinity. The two local councillors had addressed the meetings and assured the residents that they would raise these issues at the Town Hall. The Vice-Chancellor of UW subsequently gave a presentation to all councillors about what the new university was doing to benefit the town, ranging from employment opportunities to gaining a higher national profile. Most councillors remain supportive of having the university in the town and for its future plans for expansion.

A small number of other universities, mainly in the north of England, and a college of further education based in Jersey have approached UW with proposals for joint ventures. These institutions are interested in gaining any benefits they can from the relatively wealthy, well-connected and innovative approach to higher education that UW is seen to take. No firm agreements have been reached as yet and in recent weeks some of the academic staff at these other universities have expressed opposition to any joint venture. They are uneasy about making formal links that might impact their existing terms and conditions of employment (UW does not recognise trade unions, unlike all other UK universities). There are plans for academic staff from other universities to hold a rally in London to make their collective views more widely known.

Planning for the future

A meeting has been called for all senior managers of the university in order to finalise a detailed strategic plan for year two. Most of the managers essentially believe in a 'more of the same' approach given how well year one had gone. A few members want the university to be even more radical by increasing student fees substantially (30–40 per cent) but at the same time reducing targets for the numbers being recruited. Essentially this would be a high-quality positioning so that each student had more space, more contact with tutors, more access to resources, etc., but at a premium. With revenue from sponsors set to increase there is a healthy promotional budget to use and so retaining both a PR and advertising agency seems highly desirable too. Both Stir and Levy & Co. have submitted proposals outlining what UW need to do in year two. In brief the PR agency wants to hold a major exhibition in conjunction with UW sponsors showcasing the relevance of the students' work to the wider world of commerce. The advertising agency is keen to push for what it calls a 'brand positioning' to make UW a unique place for unique students. It based its arguments on the student experience being superior to that at other universities. The meeting of senior managers clearly has some vital decisions to make.

Questions

1a Draw a stakeholder network map for the University of Westbridge.

1b Include lines of communication between UW and each other part of the network, differentiating between the levels of importance of that communication link: vital, important, moderate, not important.

2a From UW's perspective, how might it be useful to segment the various stakeholders you have identified on the network map?

2b What are the implications of such segmentation from a marketing communication point of view?

3 You are UW's PR/advertising agency. Work out justified recommendations that would help it to develop long-term partnerships with others in its network.

4 How might an understanding of the different methods of channel management assist UW's senior managers?

References

Achrol, R.S. (1997) Changes in the theory of interorganisational relations in marketing: toward a network paradigm. *Journal of the Academy of Marketing Science*, **25**(1), pp. 56–71.

Andersson, P. (1992) Analysing distribution channel dynamics: loose and tight coupling in distribution networks. *European Journal of Marketing*, **26**(2), pp. 47–68.

Araujo, L. and Easton, G. (1996) Networks in socioeconomic systems: a critical review. In *Networks in Marketing* (ed. D. Iacobucci). Thousand Oaks, CA: Sage.

Ballou, R., Gilbert, S. and Mukherjee, A. (1999) New managerial challenges from supply chain opportunities. *Industrial Marketing Management*, **29**, pp. 7–18.

Brown, J.S., Durchslag, S. and Hagel III, J. (2002) Loosening up: how process networks unlock the power of specialization. *The McKinsey Quarterly*, Number 2, retrieved from www.mckinseyquarterly.com/article/page.aspx?ar=1202&L2=1&L3=24.

Buzzell, R.D. (1983) Is vertical integration profitable? *Harvard Business Review*, **61** (January/February), pp. 96–100.

Carroll, A.B. (1993) *Business and Society: Ethics and Stakeholder Management*. Cincinnati, OH: South-Western.

Coughlan, A.T., Anderson, E., Stern, L. and El-Ansary, A. (2001) *Marketing Channels*. 6th edn. Englewood Cliffs, NJ: Prentice-Hall.

Cravens, D.W. and Woodruff, R.B. (1986) *Marketing*. Reading, MA: Addison-Wesley.

Donaldson, T. and Preston, L.E. (1995) The stakeholder theory of the corporation: concept, evidence, implications. *Academy of Management Review*, **20**(1) (January), pp. 65–91.

Emerson, R. (1962) Power–dependence relations. *American Sociological Review*, **27** (February), pp. 32–3.

Frazier, G.L. and Sheth, J. (1985) An attitude–behavior framework for distribution channel management. *Journal of Marketing*, **43**(3), pp. 38–48.

Freeman, R.E. (1984) *Strategic Management*. Boston, MA: Pitman.

French, J.R. and Raven, B. (1959) The bases of social power. In *Studies in Social Power* (ed. D. Cartwright). Ann Arbor, MI: University of Michigan Press.

Gracie, S. (2001) Haulage network changes culture to roll into Europe. *Sunday Times*, 19 August, p. 9.

Greenley, G. (1989) *Strategic Management*. Hemel Hempstead: Prentice Hall.

Hunt, S.B. and Nevin, J.R. (1974) Power in channels of distribution: sources and consequences. *Journal of Marketing Research*, **11**, pp. 186–93.

Johnson, G. and Scholes, K. (2000) *Exploring Corporate Strategy*. 6th edn. Harlow: Prentice Hall.

Kaneshige, T. (2001) Avoiding channel conflict. *Line56 Magazine*, March. http://www.line56.com/articles/default.asp?NewsID=2382 (accessed 3 December 2003).

Lancioni, R. (2000) New developments in supply chain management. *Industrial Marketing Management*, **29**(1), pp. 1–6.

McGrath, A. and Hardy, K. (1986) A strategic paradigm for predicting manufacturer–reseller conflict. *European Journal of Marketing*, **23**(2), pp. 94–108.

McLoughlin, D. and Horan, C. (2000) Perspectives from the markets-as-networks approach. *Industrial Marketing Management*, **29**(4), pp. 285–92.

Macneil, I.R. (1978) Contracts: adjustment of long-term economic relations under classical, neoclassical and relational contract law. *Northwestern University Law Review*, **72** (January–February), pp. 854–905.

Mallen, B.E. (1969) A theory of retailer–supplier conflict. In *Distribution Channels: Behavioural Dimensions* (ed. L.W. Stern). New York: Houghton Mifflin.

Mason, K.J. and Gray, R. (1999) Stakeholders in a hybrid market: the example of air business passenger travel. *European Journal of Marketing*, **33**(9/10), pp. 844–58.

Mattsson, L.-G. (1989) Development of firms in networks: positions and investments. *Advances in International Marketing*, 3, pp. 121–39.

Miles, L. (2000) Sleeping with the enemy. *Marketing Business* (July–August), pp. 17–19.

Oliver, G. (1990) *Marketing Today*. 3rd edn. Hemel Hempstead: Prentice Hall.

Rosenbloom, B. (1978) Motivating independent distribution channel members. *Industrial Marketing Management*, 7 (November), pp. 275–81.

Rosenbloom, B. (1983) *Marketing Channels: A Management View*. Hinsdale, IL: Dryden Press.

Rowe, A.J., Mason, R.O., Dickel, K.E., Mann, R.B. and Mockler, R.J. (1994) *Strategic Management: A Methodological Approach*. 4th edn. Reading, MA: Addison-Wesley.

Shipley, D. and Egan, C. (1992) Power, conflict and co-operation in brewer–tenant distribution channels. *International Journal of Service Industry Management*, 3(4), pp. 44–62.

Stahl, M. and Grigsby, D. (1992) *Strategic Management for Decision Making*. Boston, MA: P.W.S. Kent.

Stern, L. and El-Ansary, A. (1992) *Marketing Channels*. 4th edn. Englewood Cliffs, NJ: Prentice-Hall.

Stern, L., El-Ansary, A. and Coughlan, A.T. (1996) *Marketing Channels*. 5th edn. Englewood Cliffs, NJ: Prentice-Hall.

Stern, L.W. and Gorman, R.H. (1969) Conflict in Distribution Channels: An Exploration. In *Distribution Channels: Behavioral Dimensions* (ed. L.E. Stern). Boston, MA: Houghton Mifflin.

Stern, L.W. and Heskett, J.L. (1969) Conflict management in interorganisational relations: a conceptual framework. In *Distribution Channels: Behavioral Dimensions* (ed. L.W. Stern). Boston, MA: Houghton Mifflin.

Terry, F. (2004) Building on magnetic therapy. *Sunday Times*, 18 July, p. 15.

Marketing: relationships and communications

9

The importance of relationship marketing has become a key aspect of both consumer and business marketing. There are a number of dimensions associated with organisational and consumer relationships, many of which encompass established concepts such as trust, commitment and loyalty. The role that marketing communications can play in establishing and nurturing key relationships can be pivotal, yet the ways in which marketing communications might be best deployed depends to a large extent on the context in which both the relationship and the communications are configured.

Aims and objectives

The aims of this chapter are to explore concepts and ideas concerning marketing relationships and the role marketing communications can play in developing and sustaining such relationships.

The objectives of this chapter are to:

1. explore the concept of value and its role in developing marketing relationships;
2. consider the characteristics of relationship marketing;
3. appraise the theoretical concepts underpinning relationship marketing;
4. understand the principles of the customer life cycle;
5. consider the importance of customer retention and the use of loyalty programmes to reduce customer defection;
6. examine trust and commitment as important relationship concepts;
7. explore issues concerning the development of trust in online environments;
8. explore ways in which marketing communications can help organisations develop relationships.

Introduction

Value has become an increasingly significant concept, to both marketing practitioners and academics. Indeed many believe that the only viable marketing strategy should be to deliver improved shareholder value (Doyle, 2000). However, the importance of providing value for customers is not a new idea. Concepts of differentiation, unique and emotional selling propositions (USPs and ESPs) and positioning are founded on the idea that superior perceived value is of primary significance to customers. It has been understood for a long time that customers buy benefits not features, that they buy products and services as solutions which enable them to achieve their goals. The majority of women buy lipstick because of a mixture of both tangible and intangible attributes or even features and benefits. They buy particular brands because they feel different as a result of using them. What they do buy will vary from person to person, but in terms of tangible attributes they prefer to buy colour and smudge-free lips (no 'bleed'), that the lipstick stays on the lips, prevents dryness, is long lasting and smooth (Puth *et al.*, 1999). However, among the intangible attributes are self-confidence, a coordinated fashion accessory, trust, perhaps an alter ego or, as Revlon once claimed, hope.

It has been understood for a long time that customers buy benefits not features.

The same principle applies to organisational marketing. Business customers buy solutions to business problems, not just stand-alone products. These benefits and solutions constitute added value for the customer, and represent the reason why one offering is selected in preference to another. For both consumers and business customers, value is determined by the net satisfaction derived from a transaction, not the costs incurred to obtain it.

So, if customers seek to satisfy their needs through their purchase of specific products and services then it can be said that the satisfaction of needs is a way of delivering value. Kothandaraman and Wilson (2001) argue that the creation of value is dependent upon an organisation's ability to deliver high performance on the benefits that are important to the customer and this in turn is rooted in their competency in technology and business processes, or core competences. Doyle (2000) regards the creation of customer value as being based on three principles:

The creation of value is dependent upon an organisation's ability to deliver high performance on the benefits that are important to the customer.

- Customers will choose between alternative offerings and select the one that (they perceive) will offer them the best value.

- Customers do not want product or service features, they want their needs met.

- It is more profitable to have a long-term relationship between a customer and a company rather than a one-off transaction.

Value is the customer's estimate of the extent to which a product or service can satisfy their needs.

Value is the customer's estimate of the extent to which a product or service can satisfy their needs. However, there are normally costs associated with the derivation of benefits such that a general model of value would identify the worth of the benefits received for the price paid (Anderson and Narus, 1998). Therefore, value is relative to customer expectations and experience of competitive offerings within a category and can be derived from sources other than products, such as the relationships between buyers and sellers (Simpson *et al.*, 2001).

The value concept

The value chain concept developed by Porter (1985), is based on the premise that organisations compete for business by trying to offer enhanced value, which is developed, internally, through a coordinated chain of activities. The value chain was devised as a tool to appraise an organisation's ability to create what Porter terms differential advantage. It consists of nine activities, five primary and four support, all of which incur costs but together can (and should) lead to the creation of value. The primary activities are those direct actions necessary to bring materials into an organisation, to convert them into final products or services, to ship them out to customers and to provide marketing and servicing facilities. Support activities facilitate the primary activities. Customers perceive they are getting superior value when these activities are linked together. These linkages can be achieved through systems and processes such as those offered by new technology. Doyle refers to three processes:

Customers perceive they are getting superior value when these activities are linked together.

- innovation processes to generate a constant stream of new products and hence ability to maintain margins;
- operations processes to deliver first-class performance and costs;
- customer creation and support processes to provide a consistent and positive cash flow.

ViewPoint 9.1   Added value OnAir

As part of its customer development Airbus has developed facilities for airlines to offer a range of consumer communications while in flight. The system will enable passengers to use email and text messages, send and receive voice messages and Web browse, all through the use of their own phones, laptops and PDAs.

Airbus has identified a major opportunity in the market and believes the system, branded as OnAir, represents significant added value for major premium travel airlines to offer their passengers. It is expected that Boeing will offer a similar system, with both manufacturers recognising the need for their customers to offer passengers additional value in what is a highly competitive market.

The processes used by an organisation become a critical part of the way in which they can add value. Customers, however, lie at the heart of the value chain. Only by understanding particular customer needs and by focusing value chain activities on satisfying them can superior value be generated. Value might be perceived in terms of price, low cost and accessibility. For others, price may be relatively inconsequential and the other benefits associated with a brand or organisation, such as continuity of supply, innovation and prestige, are signals that a longer-term association is of greater value to them. However, according to Ryssel *et al.* (2004) there is an increasing amount of evidence that the relationships organisations form are themselves a generator of value and hence an important aspect of contemporary marketing.

There is an increasing amount of evidence that the relationships organisations form are themselves a generator of value and hence an important aspect of contemporary marketing.

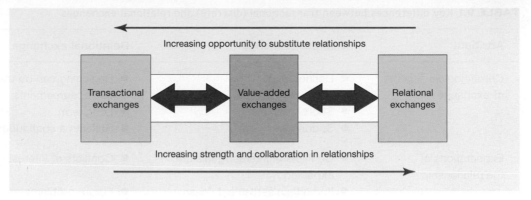

FIGURE 9.1 A continuum of value-oriented exchanges
Source: Adapted from Day (2000).

Development of relationship marketing

Interaction between customers and sellers is based around the provision and consumption of perceived value.

Interaction between customers and sellers is based around the provision and consumption of perceived value. However, the quality, duration and level of interdependence between customers and sellers can vary considerably. The reasons for this variance are many and wide-ranging but at the core are perceptions of shared values and the strength and permanence of any relationship that might exist. Relationship value can be visualised as a continuum (see Figure 9.1).

At one end of the continuum are transactional exchanges, characterised by short-term, commodity or price oriented exchanges, between buyers and sellers coming together for one-off exchanges independent of any other or subsequent exchanges. Both parties are motivated mainly by self-interest. Movement along the continuum represents increasingly valued relationships. Interactions between parties are closer and stronger. The focus moves from initial attraction to retention and mutual understanding of each other's needs.

At the other end of the continuum are relational exchanges or what Day (2000) refers to as collaborative exchanges. These are characterised by a long-term orientation, where there is complete integration of systems and processes and the relationship is motivated by partnership and mutual support. Trust and commitment underpin these relationships and these variables become increasingly important as relational exchanges become established.

Perceived value may take many forms and be rooted in a variety of attributes, combined in different ways to meet segment needs. However, the context in which an exchange occurs between a buyer and a seller provides a strong reflection of the nature of their relationship. If the exchange is focused on the product (and the price) then the exchange is considered to be essentially transactional. If the exchange is focused around the needs of both the customer and the seller then the exchange is considered

If the exchange is focused on the product (and the price) then the exchange is considered to be essentially transactional.

to be relational. The differences between transactional and relational exchanges are set out in Table 9.1 and provide an important starting point in understanding the nature of relationship marketing.

TABLE 9.1 Key differences between transactional (discrete) and relational exchanges

Attribute	Discrete exchange	Relational exchange
Chronological aspects of exchange	● Defined beginning ● Short term ● Sudden end	● Beginning can be traced back to earlier agreements ● Long term ● Reflects a continuous process
Expectations of the relationship	● Conflicts of interest/goals are expected ● Immediate settlement ('cash payment') ● No problems expected in future	● Conflicts of interest expected ● Future problems are overcome by trust and joint commitment
Communication	● Minimal personal relations ● Ritual-like communication predominates	● Both formal and informal communication used
Transferability	● Totally transferable ● It makes no difference who performs contractual obligations	● Limited transferability ● Exchanges are highly dependent on the identity of the parties
Cooperation	● No joint efforts	● Joint efforts at both planning and implementation stages ● Modifications endemic over time
Division of burden and benefit	● Sharp distinction between parties ● Each party has its own, strictly defined obligations	● Burden and benefits likely to be shared ● Division of benefits and burdens likely to vary over time

Source: Wagner and Boutellier (2002). Reprinted with permission from *Business Horizons*, 45, 6 (November–December 2002). Copyright © (2002) by The Trustees at Indiana University, Kelley School of Business.

The product marketing approach is rooted in the traditional 4Ps model of marketing and to a large extent reflects the transactional approach. For a long time consumer marketing has been regarded as something that generally take place between anonymous individuals. Relationship marketing considers the value inherent in a longer-term series of exchanges that occur between individuals who are, in general, known to each other. Relationship marketing acknowledges the changing lifetime needs of customers and emphasises the importance of both the product and customer life cycles. This in turn leads to a focus on customer retention.

Relationship marketing considers the value inherent in a longer-term series of exchanges.

Relationship marketing is also characterised by the frequency and intensity of the exchanges between customers and sellers. As these exchanges become more frequent and more intense so the strength of the relationships between buyers and sellers improves. It is this that provided the infrastructure for a new perspective of marketing, one based on relationships (Spekman, 1988; Rowe and Barnes, 1998), rather than the objects of a transaction, namely products and services.

Principles of retention

Marketing has been characterised by its potential to influence and attract customers. Indeed early ideas considered marketing to be a social anathema due to the perception that it persuaded and manipulated people into purchasing goods and services they did not want. While these fears and misgivings have generally been overcome, a further fallacy concerned the notion that all customers are good customers. As most commercial organisations will now agree, some customers are far more attractive than other customers, on the grounds that some are very profitable, others are marginally profitable but offer great potential and others offer little and/or incur losses.

> Some customers are far more attractive than other customers, on the grounds that some are very profitable, others are marginally profitable but offer great potential and others offer little and/or incur losses.

Through the use of relationship cost theory it was possible to identify the benefits associated with stable and mutually rewarding relationships. Such customers avoid costly switching costs that are associated with finding new suppliers, while suppliers experience reduced quality costs incurred when adapting to the needs of new customers. Reichheld and Sasser (1990) identified an important association between a small (e.g. 5 per cent) increase in customer retention and a large (e.g. 60 per cent) improvement in profitability. Therefore, a long-term relationship leads to lower relationship costs and higher profits. Since this early work there has been general acceptance that customers who are loyal not only improve an organisation's profits but also strengthen its competitive position (Day, 2000) because competitors have to work harder to dislodge or destabilise their loyalty. It should be noted that some authors suggest the link between loyalty and profitability is not that simple (Dowling and Uncles, 1997), while others argue that much more information and understanding is required about the association between profitability and loyalty, especially when there may be high costs associated with customer acquisition (Reinartz and Kumar, 2002).

By undertaking a customer profitability analysis it is possible to identify those segments that are worth developing, and hence build a portfolio of relationships, each of varying dimensions and potential. These relationships provide mutually rewarding benefits and offer a third dimension of the customer dynamic, namely customer development.

> By undertaking a customer profitability analysis it is possible to identify those segments that are worth developing.

> Customer relationships can be considered in terms of a series of relationship development phases: customer acquisition, development, retention and decline.

Customer relationships can be considered in terms of a series of relationship development phases: customer acquisition, development, retention and decline. The duration and intensity of each relationship phase will inevitably vary and it should be remembered that this representation is idealistic. A customer relationship cycle is represented at Figure 9.2.

Customer acquisition

The acquisition phase is characterised by three main events: search, initiation and familiarisation. See Table 9.2.

The logical sequence of acquisition activities moves from search and verification through the establishment of credentials. The length of this period of initiation will depend partly on the importance of the buying decision, the complexity of the products, and partly upon the nature of the introduction. If the parties are introduced by an established and trusted source then certain initiation rights can be shortened.

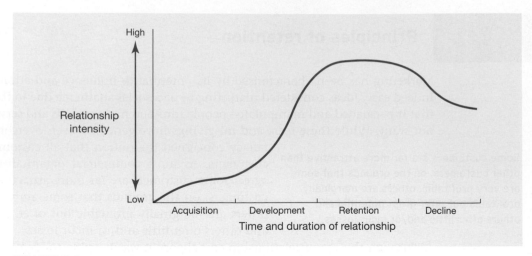

FIGURE 9.2 Customer relationship life cycle

Once a transaction occurs the buyer-seller start to become more familiar with each other and gradually begin to reveal more information about themselves.

Once a transaction occurs the buyer-seller start to become more familiar with each other and gradually begin to reveal more information about themselves. The seller receives payment, delivery and handling information about the buyer, and as a result is able to prepare customised outputs. The buyer is able to review the seller's products and experience the service quality of the seller.

TABLE 9.2 Customer acquisition events

Acquisition event	Explanation
Search	Buyers and sellers search for a suitable pairing
Initiation	Both parties seek out information about the other before any transaction occurs
Familiarisation	The successful completion of the first transaction enables both parties to start revealing more information about themselves

Customer development

The development phase is characterised by the seller attempting to reduce buyer risk and enhancing credibility.

The development phase is characterised by the seller attempting to reduce buyer risk and enhancing credibility. This is achieved by encouraging cross-selling whereby the buyer consumes other products, by improving the volume of purchases, by engaging the buyer with other added-value services and by varying delivery times and quantities. The buyer's acquiescence is dependent upon their specific needs and the degree to which the buyer wishes to become more involved with the supplier. Indeed it is during this phase that the buyer is able to determine whether or not it is worth developing deeper relationships with the seller.

Customer retention

The retention phase is the most profitable, where the greatest level of relationship value is experienced. The retention phase will generally last as long as both the buyer and seller are able to meet their individual and joint goals. If the relationship has

ViewPoint 9.2   Retaining office accounts

The office products division of the Cantrell Corporation had been an important part of the company's overall performance, with 40 per cent of its revenue derived online. However, office products' customers rely on flawless ecommerce performance of their suppliers to help reduce their administrative overheads, and as a result competition within this sector is strong.

One of the challenges facing Cantrell is that their Web site was not integrated with customer account information, so customers with questions about order status or account balances flooded the call centres. Costs were rising, customers were leaving and performance targets were being missed with increasing regularity. Cantrell resolved to reassert their prominence in the market by creating a world-class shopping experience, with CRM capabilities, automatic fulfilment and integration with its largest customers.

The company developed a new Web site and as a result customers are now able to research their questions on the Web, and the company no longer needs to fund an additional call centre.

Customers can now shop online for office supplies, order online training courses and read online newsletters that are customised for them. They can quickly and efficiently find the items they need in the online catalogue, order them and check stock. Cantrell's order fulfilment system now reads Web orders just as if they had been generated from the call centre, and fulfils them automatically. As a result, instead of customers leaving, new accounts are being registered at record levels, order fulfilment cycles have been reduced and costs lowered, all in the name of using technology to improve customer management and retention.

become more involved greater levels of trust and commitment between the partners will allow for increased cross-buying and product experimentation and, for b2b relationships, joint projects and product development. However, the very essence of relationship marketing is for organisations to identify a portfolio of customers with whom they wish to develop a range of relationships. This requires the ability to measure levels of retention and also to determine when resources are to be moved from acquisition to retention and back to acquisition.

Customer decline

Customer decline is concerned with the closure of a relationship. Termination may occur suddenly as a result of a serious problem or episode between the parties. The more likely process is that the buying organisation decides to reduce their reliance on the seller because their needs have changed, or an alternative supplier who offers superior added value has been found. The buyer either formally notifies the established supplier or begins to reduce the frequency and duration of contact and moves business to other, competitive organisations.

Theoretical concepts of relationship marketing

There have been numerous theoretical attempts to explain relationship marketing. Three are presented here: social exchange, social penetration and interaction theories.

Social exchange theory

Relationships are based upon the exchange of values between two or more parties.

The central premise associated with social exchange theory (Blau, 1964) is that relationships are based upon the exchange of values between two or more parties. Whatever constitutes the nature of an exchange between the participants, equality or satisfaction must be felt as a result. An absence of equality means that an advantage might have been gained by one party and this will automatically result in negative consequences for another. Therefore, in a b2b context, organisations seeking to maintain marketing channel relationships should not raise prices past threshold levels or allow levels of service output to fall below those of competitors. If channel partners perceive a lack of added value from these exchanges they are more likely to compare performance with other potential suppliers, and even withdraw from the relationship by establishing alternative sources of supply.

Relationships evolve from exchange behaviour that serves to provide the rules of engagement.

Exchanges can occur between two parties, three parties in sequence, or between at least three parties within a wider network and not necessarily sequentially. Relationships evolve from exchange behaviour that serves to provide the rules of engagement. They are socially constructed and have been interpreted in terms of marriage and social relationships (Tynan, 1997). Social norms drive exchange reciprocity within relationships, and serve to guide behaviour expectations.

Whether in personal or interorganisational relationships, exchanges are considered to consist of two main elements. First there are value exchanges that are based on the exchange of resources (goods for money) and secondly there are symbolic exchanges where, in an interorganisational context, goods are purchased for their utility plus the feelings and associations that are bestowed on the user.

Social exchange theory serves to explain customer retention on the basis that the rewards derived through exchanges exceed the associated costs. Should expectations about future satisfaction fall short of the levels established through past exchanges, or alternative possibilities with other organisations suggest potentially improved levels of satisfaction, then the current partner may be discarded and a new relationship encouraged.

Social penetration theory

This theory is based on the premise that as relationships develop individuals begin to reveal more about themselves.

This theory is based on the premise that as relationships develop individuals begin to reveal more about themselves. Every encounter between a buyer and seller will allow each party to discover more about the other and make judgements about assigning suitable levels of relationship confidence. Consequently the behaviour and communications exhibited between parties may well change from a very formal and awkward introduction to something more knowledgeable, relaxed and self-assured.

Altman and Taylor (1973) refer to personality depth and personality breadth as two key aspects of the social penetration approach. *Personality breadth* is concerned with the range of topics (or categories) discussed by the parties and the frequency with which organisations discuss each topic. Unsurprisingly, products and customer needs are two main categories that are discussed by organisations. The analogy of an onion is often used to describe the various layers that make up the depth of a personality. The outer layers are generally superficial, contain a number of elements (of personality) and are relatively easy to determine. However, the key personality characteristics, those that influence the structure of the outer levels, are embedded within the inner core. The

EXHIBIT 9.1 Marmite Smile
Brand personality which openly proclaims contrasting consumer preferences and brand relationships.

term *personality depth* refers to the difficulties associated with penetrating these inner layers, often because of the risks associated with such revelations.

Personality depth can be interpreted in terms of the degree to which a seller understands each of its customers. This client knowledge will vary, but may include the way they use the products, their strategies, resources, culture and ethos, difficulties, challenges, successes and other elements that characterise buying organisations. Through successive interactions each organisation develops more knowledge of the other, as more information is gradually exposed, revealed or made known. At the outset of relationships buyers tend to restrict the amount of information they reveal about themselves, but as confidence and trust in the other party develops so the level of openness increases. Likewise, as relationships develop so the degree of formality between the parties decreases, becoming more informal. This relationship intensity impacts on the quality of the relationship between two or more organisations.

> Through successive interactions each organisation develops more knowledge of the other, as more information is gradually exposed, revealed or made known.

Deconstructing a relationship reveals that it is composed of a series, or layers, of interactions. Each interaction results in judgements about whether to terminate or proceed with the relationship. The judgement is based on the accumulation of interactions, the history of the relationship and the level of customer knowledge that has been revealed.

Interactional theory

The development of relationship marketing appears to coincide with the emergence of network approaches to interorganisational analysis. This is referred to as industrial network analysis, and has evolved from the original focus on dyadic relationships

TABLE 9.3 Elements of exchange episodes

McLoughlin and Horan (2000)	IMP Group
Financial and economic exchange	Product/service exchange
Technological exchange	Information exchange
Information exchange	Financial exchange
Knowledge exchange	Social exchange
Legal exchange	

(Araujo and Easton, 1996). The International Marketing and Purchasing Group (IMP), a significantly strong and influential research group, focuses on the interaction between members of a network. The IMP Group analyses relationships rather than transactions between buyers and sellers but, unlike relationship marketing theorists, it believes that both parties are active participants. Relationships between buyers and sellers are regarded as long term, close and complex and, through episodes of exchange, the links between organisations become institutionalised. Processes and roles become established, ingrained and expected of one another. It is particularly significant in this interactional approach that other organisations are considered to influence the relationship between a buyer and a seller. This incorporates ideas concerning network interpretations of business to business and channel configuration, considered in Chapter 8.

> The IMP Group analyses relationships rather than transactions between buyers and sellers but, unlike relationship marketing theorists, it believes that both parties are active participants.

The interactional approach is based on relational exchanges with a variety of organisations within interlocking networks. An important aspect of network operation is the high degree of cooperation and reciprocity necessary between participants. This cooperation is manifest through the various exchanges that organisations undertake. McLoughlin and Horan (2000) identify five main exchange elements, while the IMP Group determine four. These are set out in Table 9.3.

These two lists are largely similar and both encompass formal and informal exchanges. These occur with varying levels of intensity between two or more organisations, over time.

Building marketing relationships

As discussed earlier, relationships are developed through interaction and dialogue. Exchanges that occur as a result of interaction are influenced by four main factors: technology, organisational determinants (size, structure and strategy), organisational experience and individuals. The result of this is an atmosphere in which a relationship exists that reflects issues of power-dependence, the degree of conflict or cooperation and the overall closeness or distance of the relationship.

Relationships consist of much more than just interaction or a series of exchanges so a deconstruction of the relationship construct can provide a deeper understanding of the nature of relationships and in doing so indicate how marketing communications might best be used. Holmlund (1997) cited by Gronroos (2004) suggests that an ongoing relationship can be considered to consist of four components. These are set out in Figure 9.3.

> A deconstruction of the relationship construct can provide a deeper understanding of the nature of relationships.

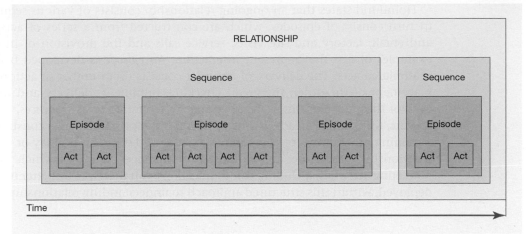

FIGURE 9.3 Interaction levels in a relationship
Source: Holmlund (1997, p. 96).

ViewPoint 9.3　Building snappy relationships

The recently forged partnership between HP and Lego demonstrates aspects of relationship development not only between the two organisations but also with their shared target customers.

The two organisations operate in very different markets, HP in high technology and Lego in building blocks and child development. Put together they offer advantages. For example, Lego's roadshows of UK town centres allows children access to, and opportunities to play with, the Lego brand. Now, through use of HP digital cameras, a physical memory of the event can be taken away, one which should reinforce positive memories and brand triggers. At the same time as the photo is handed over, parent details are recorded, opt-in permission requested and the possibilities for two-way communication established. HP then lead the initiative phase of the relationship offering online games and competitions, which lead to regular emails and newsletters, cross selling and customer satisfaction as the communications become customised around individual needs, purchasing history and declared requirements.

So, from an initial meeting in a high street, HP and parents meet each other, share an episode in the parents' lives, and then gradually begin to exchange more and more information as parents develop increased levels of trust and confidence in HP. Lego fulfilled the role of agent bringing the parties together, but then email communication becomes the primary means by which HP and parents begin to know each other in more detail. The onion is unravelled.

In terms of acts and episodes, the roadshows consist of a series of interrelated acts (playing with Lego, photographs, recording information) all of which constitute an episode. The email communications, from which deeper information is provided, enables opportunities for buying and selling to occur and these might be regarded a sequence. From this position a relationship might be said to have developed between HP and their Lego derived customers.

Source: based on May (2004).

Holmlund states that an ongoing relationship consists of various sequences, which in turn consist of episodes, which are constructed from a series of acts. Phone calls and email, factory and site visits, service calls and the provision of information are examples of *acts* that represent interaction. An *episode* is developed from a series of interrelated acts. The delivery of an order consists of a number of actions such as the placement of the order, the credit checking, fulfilment, delivery and unloading and each of these are acts. Interrelated episodes are referred to as *sequences*, which are time specific; for example an advertising or sales promotion campaign, a construction project, a training programme, or all activities experienced during a holiday or visit to a hotel. Relationships, therefore, are composed of sequences, many of which might overlap. Marketing activities, including communications, can therefore be better understood, and deployed, within this structured approach to understanding relationship development.

Related relationship concepts

Among the many concepts associated with relationship marketing three stand out. Trust, commitment and loyalty are considered in turn.

Trust

Many writers contend that one of the crucial factors associated with the development and maintenance of interorganisational relationships is trust (Morgan and Hunt, 1994; Doney and Cannon, 1997). However, Cousins and Stanwix (2001) believe that the concepts, although important, are difficult to define and suggest that many authors fail to specify clearly what they mean when using them. A review of the literature indicates that trust is an element of personal, intraorganisational and interorganisational relationships, and is both necessary for and results from their perpetuation. As Gambetta (1988) argues, trust is a means of reducing uncertainty in order that effective relationships can develop.

> Trust is a means of reducing uncertainty in order that effective relationships can develop.

Cousins and Stanwix also suggest that, although trust is a term used to explain how b2b relationships work, often it actually refers to ideas concerning risk, power and dependency, and these propositions are used interchangeably. From their research of vehicle manufacturers it emerges that b2b relationships are about the creation of mutual business advantage and the degree of confidence that one organisation has in another.

Interorganisational trust is based on two main dimensions: credibility and benevolence. Credibility concerns the extent to which one organisation believes (is confident) that another organisation will undertake and complete its agreed roles and tasks. Benevolence is concerned with goodwill, that the other organisation will not act opportunistically, even if the conditions for exploitation should arise (Pavlou, 2002). In other words, interorganisational trust involves judgements about another organisation's reliability and integrity.

> Interorganisational trust involves judgements about another organisation's reliability and integrity.

It has been suggested that interorganisational trust consists of three main elements (Zucker, 1986; Luo 2002). *Characteristic* trust, based on the similarities between parties; *process* trust, developed through familiarity and typically fostered by successive exchange transactions; and *institutional* trust, see below. This third category might be considered the most important, especially at the outset of a relationship when familiarity and similarity factors are non-existent or hard to discern respectively.

TABLE 9.4 Elements of institutional trust

Element of institutional trust	Key aspect
Perceived monitoring	Refers to the supervision of transactions by, for example, regulatory authorities or owners of b2b market exchanges. This can mitigate uncertainty through a perception that sellers or buyers who fail to conform with established rules and regulations will be penalised.
Perceived accreditation	Refers to badges or symbols that denote membership of externally recognised bodies that bestow credibility, authority, security and privacy on a selling organisation.
Perceived legal bonds	Refers to contracts between buyers, sellers and independent third parties, so that the costs of breaking a contract are perceived to be greater than the benefits of such an action. Trust in the selling organisation is therefore enhanced when bonds are present.
Perceived feedback	Refers to signals about the quality of an organisation's reputation and such feedback from other buyers about sellers, perhaps through word-of-mouth communication, can deter sellers from undertaking opportunistic behaviour.
Perceived cooperative norms	Refers to the values, standards and principles adopted by those party to a series of exchanges. Cooperative norms and values signal good faith and behavioural intent, through which trust is developed.

Source: Adapted from Pavlou (2002).

Pavlou (2002) argues that there are six means by which institutional trust can be encouraged. See Table 9.4.

Institutional trust is clearly vital in b2c markets where online perceived risk is present and known to prevent many people from purchasing online. In the b2b market, institutional trust is also important but more in terms of the overall reputation of the organisation. The development and establishment of trust is valuable because of the outcomes that can be anticipated. Three major outcomes from the development of trust have been identified by Pavlou, namely satisfaction, perceived risk and continuity. Trust can reduce conflict and the threat of opportunism and that in turn enhances the probability of buyer satisfaction, an important positive outcome of institutional trust.

Perceived risk is concerned with the expectation of loss and is therefore tied closely with organisational performance. Trust that a seller will not take advantage of the imbalance of information between buyer and seller effectively reduces risk. Continuity

> Perceived risk is concerned with the expectation of loss and is therefore tied closely with organisational performance.

is related to business volumes, necessary in online b2b marketplaces, and the development of both on and offline enduring relationships. Trust is associated with continuity and when present is therefore indicative of long-term relationships. Ryssel *et al.* (2004, p. 203) recognise that trust (and commitment) have a 'significant impact on the creation of value and conclude that value creation is a function of the atmosphere of a relationship rather than the technology employed'.

Trust within a consumer context is equally important as a means of reducing uncertainty. In particular brands are an important means of instilling trust mainly because

TABLE 9.5 Components of Trust (Morrison and Firmstone, 2000).

Trust component	Explanation
Reputation	Provides a summary statement of the likelihood that purchase and experience expectations will not disappoint.
Familiarity/closeness	Personal or human trust is a significant component witnessed by organisations recruiting people with skills and experience that potential buyers can identify with. Sales force representatives and slice of life advertising typify ways in which organisations seek to establish familiarity.
Performance	The performance of the product or service becomes regularised and habitual.
Accountability	The use of trade associations, credit agencies and professional organisations to underwrite and enforce performance standards give consumers the necessary confidence to trust and can be important in areas where consumers have limited specialised knowledge.

they are a means of condensing and conveying information so that they provide sufficient information for consumers to make calculated purchase decisions in the absence of full knowledge. In a sense consumers transfer their responsibility for brand decision-making, and hence brand performance, to the brand itself. Through extended use of a brand purchasing habits develop or what is termed routinised response behaviour. This is important not just because complex decision-making is simplified but because the amount of communication necessary to assist and provoke purchase is considerably reduced.

The establishment of trust can be based around the existence of various components (Morrison and Firmstone, 2000). These are set out in Table 9.5.

According to Young and Wilkinson (1989) the presence of trust within a relationship is influenced by four main factors. These are the duration of the relationship, the relative power of the participants, the presence of cooperation and various environmental factors that may be present at any one moment.

The presence of both commitment and trust leads to cooperative behaviour and this in turn is conducive to successful relationship marketing.

Extending these ideas into what is now regarded by many as a seminal paper in the relationship marketing literature, Morgan and Hunt (1994) argued, and supported with empirical evidence, that the presence of both commitment and trust leads to cooperative behaviour and this in turn is conducive to successful relationship marketing.

Online trust and security

These components can be substantiated through experience but in terms of information systems and technology and the Internet in particular, problems arise when attempting to apply these criteria. There is a total lack of accountability on the Internet that may explain why a substantial proportion of the population are reluctant to engage in ecommerce exchanges. Many consumers do not understand the performance characteristics of the Internet and of various aspects of the modern digital world, which suggests to Morrison and Firmstone that there is too much missing knowledge for a sufficient level of trust to be present. This factor may dissipate as successive generations become more conversant and confident in technology and its performance characteristics. However, at the moment a lack of familiarity might partly explain why sufficient numbers of consumers do not place their trust when there is so much that is unknown. In addition the cues by which trust is established offline have yet to become established in the online world. Symbols, trade marks and third party endorsements need to be available so that the trust inducing cues can be interpreted and relied on. Finally, brand reputation is a summary statement of performance and reputation conveys signals that others do and, for long-established brands, have in the past trusted the brand. Morrison and Firmstone (2000, p. 621) argue that 'existence confers an invitation to trust and a long existence gives strength to the presumption that one should trust'. This means that pure play ecommerce operations will have a more challenging task to establish reputation than bricks and clicks operations that are able to transfer part of their offline reputation into their online world.

> Symbols, trade marks and third party endorsements need to be available so that the trust inducing cues can be interpreted and relied on.

Technology is available to provide virtually secure online transactions and despite the relatively small amount of online crime there is a strong consumer perception that online transactions are not safe, even though many of these same people willingly give their credit card details over the telephone to complete strangers. Eretailers should use marketing communications to reduce levels of perceived risk associated with online shopping and to provide a strong level of consumer reassurance. Thomas (2000) suggests that there are a number of things that can be done to provide such reassurance. These are:

1. Strong off-line brands immediately provide recognition and an improved level of security although care needs to be taken to convince audiences that the operator's online work is as effective as that of the off-line brand.

2. Ensure that Web pages where sensitive data are stored are hosted on a secure server. Use the most up-to-date security facilities and then tell consumers the actions you have taken to create a feel-good association and trust with the online brand. It is also worthwhile listing any physical, tangible addresses the company might have in order that consumers feel they are dealing with a modern yet conventional business.

3. Provide full contact details, fax, telephone, postal addresses and the names of people they can refer to. Again, this enables a level of personalisation and may soften the virtual atmosphere for those hesitant to immerse themselves in online transactions.

4. Provide an opportunity for the consumer to lock into the online brand by registering and subscribing to the site. Many organisations offer an incentive such as a free email newsletter or introductory offer.

5. By satisfying criteria associated with transparency, security and customer service it is possible to earn accreditation or cues that signal compatibility and compliance. The Academy of Internet Commerce operates a best practice called the Academy Seal of Approval. The logo appears on the site and when clicked provides a full text of the charter itself, a powerful form of reducing functional and financial risk.

> By satisfying criteria associated with transparency, security and customer service it is possible to earn accreditation or cues that signal compatibility and compliance.

6. Post-purchase communications are just as important in the online as well as the off-line environment. Email acknowledgement of an order provides reassurance that the company actually exists and prompt (immediate/next day) delivery or, if on extended delivery, an interim progress report (email) will provide confidence. Online order tracking is now quite common, so that it is possible to see the exact location of an order.

ViewPoint 9.4   Online trust

A survey of 1,700 online users by Thomson (2004) found that 1 in 20 online consumers have been victims of attempts to defraud or steal financial or personal details while undertaking transactions online. The study also found that 73 per cent of UK consumers were more concerned about security than convenience, price or quality when shopping online. In the UK 20 million consumers shop online, so a security failure should represent a crisis for online retailers. The study revealed that 24 per cent of discontented buyers defect to alternative online brands after security failures and 12 per cent made (word-of-mouth) complaints to friends and family about the companies that had let them down.

The overall finding is that if consumers lose trust when shopping in an online environment they will switch brands readily. So, the need for online security systems and processes is absolutely fundamental and cannot be overstressed.

Source: Adapted from Thomson (2004).

Commitment

Morgan and Hunt regard commitment as the desire that a relationship continue (endure) in order that a valued relationship be maintained or strengthened. They postulated that commitment and trust are key mediating variables between five antecedents and five outcomes. See Figure 9.4.

According to the KMV model the greater the losses anticipated through the termination of a relationship the greater the commitment will be expressed by the exchange partners. Likewise, when these partners share the same values commitment increases. Trust is enhanced when communication is perceived to be of high quality but decreases when one organisation knowingly takes action to seek to benefit from the relationship, which will be to the detriment of the other.

> Trust is enhanced when communication is perceived to be of high quality but decreases when one organisation knowingly takes action to seek to benefit from the relationship, which will be to the detriment of the other.

Kumar *et al.* (1994) distinguish between *affective* and *calculative* commitment. The former is rooted in positive feelings towards the other party and a desire to maintain the relationship. The latter is negatively oriented and is determined by the extent to which one party perceives it is (not) possible to replace the other party, advantageously.

The centrality of the trust and commitment concepts to relationship marketing has thus been established and they are as central to marketing channel relationships as to other b2b relationships (Achrol, 1991; Goodman and Dion, 2001).

Customer loyalty and retention

Implicit within this customer relationship cycle is the notion that retained customers are loyal. However, this may be misleading as 'loyalty' may actually be a term used to convey convenience or extended utility. Loyalty, however presented, takes different forms, just as there are customers who are more valued than others. Christopher *et al.* (2002) depict the various types of relationships as stages or steps on a ladder, the Relationship Marketing Ladder of Loyalty (Figure 9.5).

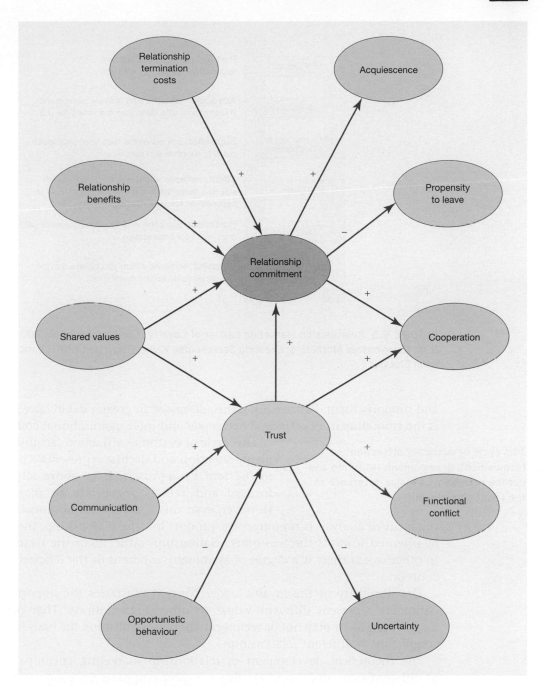

FIGURE 9.4 The KMV model of commitment and trust (Morgan and Hunt, 1994); used with kind permission of the American Marketing Association

A prospect becomes a purchaser, completed through a market or discrete exchange. Clients emerge from several completed transactions but remain ambivalent towards the seller organisation. Supporters, despite being passive about an organisation, are willing and able to enter into regular transactions. Advocates represent the next and penultimate step. They not only support an organisation and its products but actively recommend it to others by positive, word-of-mouth communications. Partners, who represent the top rung of the ladder, trust and support an organisation just as it trusts

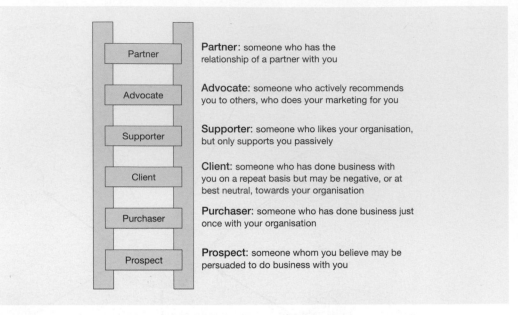

FIGURE 9.5 Relationship Marketing Ladder of Loyalty (Christopher *et al.*, 2002). 'Reprinted from *Relationship Marketing: Creating Stakeholder Value*, Copyright (2002), with permission from Elsevier'.

and supports them. Partnership status, discussed in greater detail later in this chapter, is the embodiment of relational exchanges and interorganisational collaboration.

> This cycle of customer attraction (acquisition), development, retention and decline represents a major difference to the four Ps approach.

This cycle of customer attraction (acquisition), development, retention and decline represents a major difference to the four Ps approach. It is, above all else, customer focused and more appropriate to marketing values. However, even this approach is questionable as, although the focus of analysis is no longer the product but the relationship, the focus tends to be oriented towards the 'customer relationship' rather than the relationship per se. In other words there is a degree of asymmetry inherent in the relationship marketing concept.

The simplicity of the loyalty ladder concept illustrates the important point that customers represent different values to other organisations. That perceived value (or worth) may or may not be reciprocated, thus establishing the basis for a variety and complexity of different relationships.

The theoretical development of relationship marketing encompasses a number of different concepts. These involve a greater emphasis on cooperation rather than competition and the identification of different development phases within customer relationships, namely customer acquisition, development and retention.

Types and levels of loyalty

The concept of loyalty has attracted much research attention if only because of the recent and current popularity of this approach. Table 9.6 represents some of the more general types of loyalty that can be observed.

These hierarchical schemes suggest that consumers are capable of varying degrees of loyalty. This type of categorisation has been questioned by a number of researchers.

TABLE 9.6 Types of loyalty

Emotional loyalty	This is a true form of loyalty and is driven by personal identification with real or perceived values and benefits.
Price loyalty	This type of loyalty is driven by rational economic behaviour and the main motivations are cautious management of money or financial necessity.
Incentivised loyalty	This refers to promiscuous buyers: those with no one favourite brand who demonstrate through repeat experience the value of becoming loyal.
Monopoly loyalty	This class of loyalty arises where a consumer has no purchase choice owing to a national monopoly. This, therefore, is not a true form of loyalty.

Fournier and Yao (1997) doubt the validity of such approaches and Baldinger and Rubinson (1996) support the idea that consumers work within an evoked set and switch between brands. This view is supported on the grounds that many consumers display elements of curiosity in their purchase habits, enjoy variety and are happy to switch brands as a result of marketing communication activities and product experience.

Loyalty at one level can be seen to be about increasing sales volume, that is, fostering loyal purchase behaviour. High levels of repeat purchase, however, are not necessarily an adequate measure of loyalty, as there may be a number of situational factors determining purchase behaviour, such as brand availability (Dick and Basu, 1994).

Loyalty can be regarded as an attitudinal disposition.

At another level, loyalty can be regarded as an attitudinal disposition. O'Malley (1998) suggests that customer satisfaction has become a surrogate measure of loyalty. However, she points out that there is plenty of evidence to show that many satisfied customers buy a variety of brands and that polygamous loyalty, as suggested by Dowling and Uncles (1997), may be a better reflection of reality.

Another interesting perspective on relationship marketing concerns the role of consumer satisfaction. Garbarino and Johnson (1999) researched the attitudes and motivations of people who held long-term subscriptions to a theatre. While this group might be said to hold a strong relationship with the theatre, it was possible to determine two subgroups of customers. Some had a functional orientation towards the service provider and others were determined as holding partnership characteristics. These they termed low and high relational customers respectively. Their research found that the long-term intentions of the low relational customers are driven by overall satisfaction measures. In contrast, high relational customers are driven by trust and commitment, which means that satisfaction is an irrelevance for this customer group. They will continue subscribing regardless of whether the plays and performances are entertaining and enjoyable. The implication for the design of marketing communication programmes is that transactional-based communications that focus on developing measures of satisfaction will be suitable for customers who have a functional yet long-term relationship with a brand. For those more passionately involved, communications should focus on building trust and commitment.

Transactional-based communications that focus on developing measures of satisfaction will be suitable for customers who have a functional yet long-term relationship with a brand.

At whichever level of loyalty, customer retention is paramount and neither behavioural nor attitudinal measures alone are adequate indicators of true loyalty.

O'Malley suggests that a combination of the two is of greater use and that the twin parameters of relative attitudes (to alternatives) and patronage behaviour (the recency, frequency and monetary model), as suggested by Dick and Basu, when used together offer more accurate indicators of loyalty. See Chapter 23 for a consideration of loyalty programmes.

The role of marketing communications in relationships

Having considered ideas about relationship marketing and established its centrality within contemporary marketing thought, it now remains to explore ways in which marketing communications can contribute to relationship marketing. Transaction marketing, where the focus is on product and price, uses mass communications with persuasion as a central element. Relationship marketing, with its focus on the relationship between the participants, encourages interaction and dialogue. This is compatible with the concepts of integrated marketing communications (IMC). Gronroos (2004) suggests that although IMC cannot be synonymous with relationship marketing, IMC is an important aspect of relationship marketing. He argues that within an interaction and planned communication context customer messages can be divided into five groups. These are set out in Table 9.7.

> Gronroos (2004) suggests that although IMC cannot be synonymous with relationship marketing, IMC is an important aspect of relationship marketing.

Gronroos develops the view that there are two main types of message that customers receive, process and use to determine the extent to which a relationship delivers value. The first of these messages are planned marketing communication messages, those that are predetermined and delivered through various media and tools of the promotional mix. These planned messages set out an organisation's promises. In addition, there are messages generated through the product and service aspects of the interaction that occurs between organisations and their customers. The degree to which these two

TABLE 9.7 Source of messages about an organisation. Derived from Gronroos (2000) who acknowledges the work of Duncan and Moriarty (1997) and Calonius (1989)

Message Source	Explanation
Planned marketing communications	Make promises about how solutions to customer problems should occur – for example, mass communications, brochures, sales, direct response, WWW pages
Product messages	For example: the design, technical features, utility, appearance, production process, durability and distribution
Service messages	Derived from interactions with an organisation's customer service – deliveries, invoicing, claims handling, product documentation
Unplanned messages	News stories, references, gossip, Internet chat groups, word-of-mouth communications
Absence	A lack of communication or silence following service breakdown

streams of messages support or counter each other will influence the type of unplanned communications that ensue. The greater the degree that the two sets of messages support or reinforce one another the more favourable the unplanned communication which should result in positive word-of-mouth communication (Gronroos and Lindberg-Repo, 1998). This can lead to dialogue, an increasing propensity to share information, the establishment of two-way communication and a process of reasoning. Reasoning is important because it enables a sharing of values and a deeper under-

Through shared meaning trust increases.

standing of the other parties' needs and position. Through shared meaning trust increases. Gronroos argues that relationship marketing develops, not from planned marketing communications, but through the interaction and personal experience of products and services and the degree to which these two sets of messages and meanings complement the promises and messages transmitted previously. He suggests that when these two processes come together a single, two-way communication process emerges. Put precisely he says (p. 107) 'the two processes merge into a relationship dialogue'.

Communication during the customer life cycle

Marketing communications can play an important role throughout all relationship phases and at all stages of the customer life cycle. Indeed, marketing communications should be used to engage with audiences according to the audiences' needs, whether transactional and remote or relational and close. According to Ryssel *et al.* (2004) the use of IST, which enables communication to be timely, accurate and direct has a positive impact on trust. During the *acquisition* phase marketing communications

During the *acquisition* phase marketing communications needs to be geared towards creating awareness and access to the brand.

needs to be geared towards creating awareness and access to the brand. Included within this period will be the need to help potential customers become familiar with the brand and to help them increase their understanding of the key attributes, possible benefits from use and to know how the brand is different and represents value that is superior to the competition. Indeed marketing communications has to work during this phase because it needs to fulfil a number of different roles and it needs to be targeted at precise audiences. Perhaps the main overriding task is to create a set of brand values that are relevant and which represent significant value for the target audience. In DRIP terms differentiation and information will be important and, in terms of the promotional mix, advertising and direct marking in the b2c market and personal selling and direct marketing in the b2b market.

The main goals during the development phase are for the selling organisation to reduce buyer-perceived risk and to simultaneously enhance their own credibility. In order to reduce risk a number of messages will need to be presented through marketing communications. The selection of these elements will depend upon the forms of risk that are present either in the market sector or within individual customers. Marketing communications needs to engage by communicating messages concerning warranties and guarantees, finance schemes, third-party endorsements and satisfied customers, independent testing and favourable product performance reports, awards and the attainment of quality standards, membership of trade associations, delighted customers, growth and market share, new products and alliances and partnerships, all of which seek to reduce risk and improve credibility. In DRIP terms information and persuasion will be important and in terms of the promotional mix, public relations, sales promotion and direct marking in the b2c market and personal selling, public relations and direct marketing in the b2b market.

Messages need to be relational and reinforcing

The length of the retention phase will reflect the degree to which the marketing communications is truly interactional and based on dialogue. Messages need to be relational and reinforcing. Incentive schemes are used extensively in consumer markets as a way of retaining customers and minimising customer loss or churn. They are also used to cross-sell products and services and increase a customer's commitment and involvement with the brand. Through the use of an integrated programme of communications value can be enhanced for both parties and relational exchanges are more likely to be maintained. In business markets personal contact and key account management are crucial to maintaining interaction, understanding and mutual support. Electronic communications have the potential to automate many routine transactions and allow for increased focus on one-to-one communications. In DRIP terms reinforcement and information will be important and, in terms of the promotional mix, sales promotion and direct marking in the b2c market and personal selling (and key accounts), public relations and direct marketing in the b2b market.

The final phase of decline concerns the process by which a relationship is eventually terminated. This process may be sharp and sudden or slow and protracted. Marketing communications plays a minor role in the former but is more significant in the latter. During an extended termination, marketing communications, especially direct marketing in the form of telemarketing and email, can be used to deliver orders and profits. These forms of communication are beneficial because they allow for continued personal messages but do incur the heavy costs associated with field selling (b2b) or advertising (b2c). In DRIP terms reinforcement and persuasion will be important and, in terms of the promotional mix, direct marketing in both markets and sales promotion in the b2c will be significant.

Summary

The development of customer-perceived value is now regarded not only as crucial for commercial success but there is an increasing amount of evidence which indicates that the relationships organisations form, with a range of stakeholders, not just customers, are themselves a generator of value and hence an important aspect of contemporary marketing. Relationship marketing is based upon various ideas about costs and profitability but at the heart of the concept is that it is more profitable to have a long-term relationship between a customer and a company rather than a one-off transaction. Therefore, an organisation's marketing activities should be directed towards servicing those customer groups that offer the highest (potential) lifetime value. Understanding the characteristics of relationship concepts can help organisations manage and direct their resources more profitably. Some of these concepts concern the theoretical explanations about how relationships develop (social exchange theory, social penetration theory and interaction theory), the phases of development (customer acquisition, development, retention and decline) and concepts concerning trust, commitment and customer satisfaction.

At the heart of many relationship marketing strategies are loyalty or customer retention programmes. Whether these are loyalty or perhaps convenience programmes may be debatable but organisations in the b2c market should always question whether consumers really desire a relationship with a brand and whether their actions are those bred of loyalty or inertia. Questions concerning trust and commitment have far-ranging implications for marketing communications, whether these be delivered off-line or in an online context.

Review questions

1. Discuss the view that the notion of customer value is too abstract to be of worth to organisations when loyalty is so hard to establish.

2. Identify the three principles Doyle established for the development of customer value.

3. Without looking back, draw the figure depicting the range of value-oriented exchanges.

4. Make a list of the main differences between transactional and relationship marketing.

5. Write brief notes explaining relationship marketing in terms of social exchange, penetration and interaction theories.

6. Explain the concepts of trust and commitment and outline the linkages between them.

7. Evaluate reasons why it has been difficult for organisations to establish online customer trust.

8. Identify two different commercial loyalty programmes and consider the marketing communications used to support them.

9. Prepare brief notes explaining different types of loyalty.

10. Discuss ways in which marketing communications can be used to develop relationships with customers.

MINI-CASE

The Royal International Pavilion: changing times – developing partnerships

Mini-case written by Jeremy Miles, Consultant and Lecturer, Manchester Metropolitan University

The Llangollen International Musical Eisteddfod was started over 50 years ago by a group of musical and cultural enthusiasts who wished to create a showcase of international talent in Llangollen, a small rural town in North Wales with a population of around 3,000 people. The week-long Eisteddfod (festival in English) has developed into one of the country's most prestigious festivals, attracting participants and audiences from around the globe.

During the day musicians and dancers from approximately 50 different countries compete in various competitions. In the evenings both competitors and professional artists take to the stage. Previous performers include world-famous names such as Kiri Te Kanawa, Pavarotti, Montserrat Caballe, Lesley Garratt and Dame Shirley Bassey.

The festival, which traditionally takes place during July, is staged in a giant tented canvas structure raised specially for Eisteddfod Week, and caters for over 80,000 visitors.

By the early 1980s Llangollen's success brought new challenges. Substantial increases in the numbers of competitors and visitors began to create pressure upon the Eisteddfod's primitive facilities. Other music festivals with more modern facilities and infrastructure began to be established in competition. Support for the International Eisteddfod is widespread throughout Wales, providing a unique high-profile tourism product contributing towards economic regeneration and the tourism product in this rural area.

Working with a vision

As a result the various County, District and Town Councils, the Wales Tourist Board, the Welsh Development Agency and the Eisteddfod agreed to meet the International Eisteddfod's need for improved accommodation. The aim was to enhance Llangollen's profile and positioning as a tourist

EXHIBIT 9.2 The Royal Pavilion at The Eisteddfod

destination. This required the construction of a 5,000-seat auditorium.

The project gained instant credibility in 1989 when the Wales Tourist Board developed a plan that awarded Llangollen LEAD resort status. The document supported the proposal for the International Eisteddfod to establish permanent facilities for the exclusive use of the Eisteddfod for four weeks in the year. For the other 48 weeks the complex and its facilities would be available for regional and community use. The Eisteddfod agreed to lease their site to the County Council (now Denbighshire) to develop the project.

Following a successful bid for European grant aid, a unique complex was planned. A canvas structure was designed as a permanent facility, resembling a giant tent to maintain the canvas tradition of previous festivals. The permanent 'core' 400-seat building, constructed in traditional materials, has many backstage services, including changing-rooms, showers and catering facilities. The main 1,500-seat auditorium encloses a vast stage. The facility may be extended on a temporary basis during the summer months to accommodate a further 3,000 people, again under canvas. All of this was completed in 1992 and named the Royal International Pavilion.

Developing a mutually beneficial trading partnership

The Eisteddfod is a registered charity, and has been able to develop and maximise the potential of this unique and world-renowned festival. Denbighshire County Council has adopted trading responsibilities for the facility during the remainder of the year. Branding by the two trading partners remained separate.

Under the County Council, the centre was positioned as a multi-purpose arts, events and cultural centre catering for large indoor and outdoor events. A variety of events and festivals is hosted throughout the remainder of the year at the site. For example, the Llangollen Hot Air Balloon Festival attracted in excess of 12,000 people, and a Celtic Food Festival for both the public and traders was successful in showcasing local produce to regional and national audiences. These festivals were established through partnerships to gain funding, and also because the venue was seen to have a pivotal role in stimulating economic regeneration in the rural economy by extending the tourism season.

Conferences and exhibitions were targeted as a further market opportunity. Despite fierce competition from alternative venues such as universities and

EXHIBIT 9.3 'Llangollen Nightfire' – use of sponsorship to engage with festival events

stately homes, the Llangollen site has proved to be attractive and unique. Export fairs have been utilised to make the best of international links. The Export Association, Chambers of Trade, economic regeneration departments and colleges have all contributed towards these events, aiming to achieve new business contacts and opportunities in global markets.

Concerts and events have always been popular, even in the face of alternative venues in North Wales, Chester, Manchester and Liverpool. The emotional message relating to the idyllic countryside, historic sites and the internationally recognised Eisteddfod location has proved successful. However, event organisers and promoters have some considerable choice in the range of alternative venues and commercial entertainment complexes located in and on the periphery of urban conurbations.

The partnership between the Eisteddfod and Denbighshire County Council has developed signi-

ficantly in recent years. With a jointly funded chief executive responsible for the effective liaison between the many stakeholders and the strategic development of the facilities, the future of the Llangollen site looks exciting.

Questions

1   What would you consider to be the marketing and communications objectives for a not-for-profit facility of this nature?

2   Why do you think it would be important for the organisation to draw up a network of stakeholders?

3   Recommend ways in which marketing communications might be used to help improve relationships and reduce levels of potential conflict among stakeholders.

References

Achrol, R.S. (1991) Evolution of the marketing organisation: new forms for turbulent environments. *Journal of Marketing*, **55**(4), pp. 77–93.

Altman, I. and Taylor, D.A. (1973) *Social Penetration: The Development of Interpersonal Relationships*. New York: Holt, Rinehart & Winston.

Anderson, J.C. and Narus, J.A. (1998) Business marketing: understand what customers value. *Harvard Business Review*, **76** (June), pp. 53–65.

Araujo, L. and Easton, G. (1996) Networks in socioeconomic systems: a critical review. In *Networks in Marketing* (ed. D. Iacobucci). Thousand Oaks, CA: Sage.

Baldinger, A. and Rubinson, J. (1996) Brand loyalty: the link between attitude and behaviour. *Journal of Advertising Research*, **36**(6) (November–December), pp. 22–34.

Blau, P. (1964) *Exchange and Power in Social Life*. New York: John Wiley.

Calonius, H., Avlontis, G.J., Papavasiliou, N.K. and Kouremeos, A.G. Market communication in service marketing, *Marketing Thought and Practice in the 1990s*, Proceedings from the XVIIIth Annual Conference of the European Marketing Academy, Athens.

Christopher, M., Payne, A. and Ballantyne, D. (2002) *Relationship Marketing: Creating Stakeholder Value*. Oxford: Butterworth Heinemann.

Cousins, P. and Stanwix, E. (2001) It's only a matter of confidence! A comparison of relationship management between Japanese and UK non-owned vehicle manufacturers. *International Journal of Operations and Production Management*, **21**(9) October, pp. 1160–80.

Day, G. (2000) Managing market relationships. *Journal of the Academy of Marketing Science*, **28**(1), Winter, pp. 24–30.

Dick, A.S. and Basu, K. (1994) Customer loyalty: toward an integrated framework. *Journal of the Academy of Marketing Science*, **22**(2), pp. 99–113.

Doney, P.M. and Cannon, J.P. (1997) An examination of the nature of trust in buyer–seller relationships. *Journal of Marketing*, **62**(2), pp. 1–13.

Dowling, G.R. and Uncles, M. (1997) Do customer loyalty programmes really work? *Sloan Management Review* (Summer), pp. 71–82.

Doyle, P. (2000) *Value Based Marketing*. Chichester: Wiley.

Duncan, T. and Moriarty, S. (1997) *Driving Brand Value*. New York: McGraw-Hill.

Fournier, S. and Yao, J.L. (1997) Reviving brand loyalty: a reconceptualisation within the framework of consumer–brand relationships. *International Journal of Research in Marketing*, **14**(5), pp. 451–72.

Gambetta, D. (1988) *Trust: Making and Breaking Co-operative Relations*. New York: Blackwell.

Garbarino, E. and Johnson, M.S. (1999) The different roles of satisfaction, trust and commitment in customer relationships. *Journal of Marketing*, **63** (April) pp. 70–87.

Goodman, L.E. and Dion, P.A. (2001) The determinants of commitment in the distributor–manufacturer relationship. *Industrial Marketing Management*, **30**(3) April, pp. 287–300.

Gronroos, C. (2000) Creating a relationship dialogue: communication, interaction, value. *Marketing Review*, **1**(1), pp. 5–14.

Gronroos, C. (2004) The relationship marketing process: communication, interaction, dialogue, value. *Journal of Business and Industrial Marketing*, **19**(2), pp. 99–113.

Gronroos, C. and Lindberg-Repo, K. (1998) Integrated marketing communications: the communications aspect of relationship marketing. *The IMC Research Journal*, **4**(1), pp. 3–11.

Holmlund, M. (1997) *Perceived Quality of Business Relationships*. Hanken Swedish School of Economics, Finland/CERS, Helsingfors.

Kothandaraman, P. and Wilson, D. (2001) The future of competition: value creating networks. *Industrial Marketing Management*, **30**(4) (May), pp. 379–89.

Kumar, N., Hibbard, J.D. and Stern, L.W. (1994) The nature and consequences of marketing channel intermediary commitment. Marketing Science Institute, pp. 94–115.

Luo, X. (2002) A framework based on relationship marketing and social exchange theory. *Industrial Marketing Management*, **31**(2) February, pp. 111–18.

McLoughlin, D. and Horan, C. (2000) Perspectives from the markets-as-networks approach. *Industrial Marketing Management*, **29**(4), pp. 285–92.

Morgan, R.M. and Hunt, S.D. (1994) The commitment-trust theory of relationship marketing. *Journal of Marketing*, **58** (July), pp. 20–38.

Morrison, D.E. and Firmstone, J. (2000) The social function of trust and implications of e-commerce. *International Journal of Advertising*, **19**, pp. 599–623.

O'Malley, L. (1998) Can loyalty schemes really build loyalty? *Marketing Intelligence and Planning*, **16**(1), pp. 47–55.

Pavlou, P.A. (2002) Institution-based trust in interorganisational exchange relationships: the role of online b2b marketplaces on trust formation. *The Journal of Strategic Information Systems*, **11**(3–4), (December), pp. 215–43.

Puth, G., Mostert, P. and Ewing, M. (1999) Consumer perceptions of mentioned product and brand attributes in magazine advertising. *Journal of Product Brand Management*, **8**(1), pp. 38–50.

Porter, M.E. (1985) *Competitive Advantage: Creating and Sustaining Superior Performance*. New York: Free Press.

Reichheld, F.F. and Sasser, E.W. (1990) Zero defections: quality comes to services. *Harvard Business Review* (September), pp. 105–11.

Reinartz, W.J. and Kumar, V. (2002) The mismanagement of customer loyalty. *Harvard Business Review* (July), pp. 86–94.

Rowe, W.G. and Barnes, J.G. (1998) Relationship marketing and sustained competitive advantage. *Journal of Market-Focused Management*, **2**(3), pp. 281–97.

Ryssel, R., Ritter, T. and Gemunden H.G. (2004) The impact of information technology deployment on trust, commitment and value creation in business relationships. *Journal of Business and Industrial Marketing*, **19**(3), pp. 197–207.

Simpson, P.M., Sigauw, J.A. and Baker, T.L. (2001) A model of value creation; supplier behaviors and their impact on reseller-perceived value. *Industrial Marketing Management*, **30**(2) (February), pp. 119–34.

Spekman, R. (1988) Perceptions of strategic vulnerability among industrial buyers and its effect on information search and supplier evaluation. *Journal of Business Research*, **17**, pp. 313–26.

Thomas, R. (2000) How to create trust in the net. *Marketing*, 2 March, p. 35.

Thomson, J. (2004) Businesses need help with e-security. Retrieved 5 January 2005 from www.nu-riskservices.co.uk/news/articles/.

Tynan, C. (1997) A review of the marriage analogy in relationship marketing. *Journal of Marketing Management*, **13**, pp. 695–703.

Wagner, S. and Boutellier, R. (2002) Capabilities for managing a portfolio of supplier relationships. *Business Horizons*, November–December, pp. 79–88.

Young, L.C. and Wilkinson, I.F. (1989) The role of trust and co-operation in marketing channels: a preliminary study. *European Journal of Marketing*, **23**(2), pp. 109–22.

Zucker, L. (1986) Production of trust: institutional sources of economic structure 1840–1920. *Research in Organisation Behaviour*, **8**(1), pp. 53–111.

The impact of technology on marketing communications

10

The development of digital-based technologies and Web-enabled communications has had a profound effect on marketing communications. However, the full potential of these new technologies has yet to be realised as customer behaviour adapts and learns new ways of incorporating these facilities. Interactivity and rapid two-way communications enabled by technology require the development of new communication strategies and a fresh understanding of what customers might need.

Aims and objectives

The aim of this chapter is to consider some of the ways technology has influenced the use by both customers and organisations of marketing communications. The intention is not to describe the many aspects and features of new technology but to explore some of the ways marketing communications has been influenced by these new facilities. It is recommended that this chapter be read in conjunction with Chapter 21.

The objectives of this chapter are to:

1. briefly review the nature and breadth of the available technology and new media applications;
2. examine the characteristics of the business-to-business and business-to-consumer ecommerce models and to introduce related marketing communications issues;
3. consider the nature and characteristics of CRM systems;
4. explore the impact new technology has had on marketing communications;
5. briefly appreciate strategic influence of IST on marketing communications;
6. touch upon some of the technologies that are currently being developed and to see how they might influence marketing communications.

Introduction

The phrase 'information systems and technology' (IST) is used in this book to embrace the wide variety of new technologies that have been developed to improve the quality of life for the people who use IST and for those who benefit from their deployment. Ryssel *et al.* (2004) consider IST a term that embraces 'all forms of technology utilized to create, capture, manipulate, communicate, exchange, present and use information in its various forms (business data, voice conversations, still images, motion pictures, multimedia presentations and other forms, including those not yet conceived'. They conceptualise the range of IST in terms of where the IST are used (internal or external) and across which broad functions (information, communication and decision support). See Figure 10.1.

However, it is not the intention to provide a detailed examination of each of these systems or of the various technologies as that is beyond the scope of this book. Readers interested in this aspect of technology are referred to Chaffey *et al.* (2003) or Rayport and Jaworski (2001). The intention here is twofold; first, to consider the broad scope of different aspects of IST and in particular attention is given to the Internet, database, mobile and WAP technologies with subsequent sections given over to ecommerce, customer relationship management (CRM) and software applications. The second intention is to explore ways in which new technology influences marketing communications. Consideration is given to the strategic impact of technology before the chapter concludes with a reflection on how technology might evolve and affect marketing communications in the future.

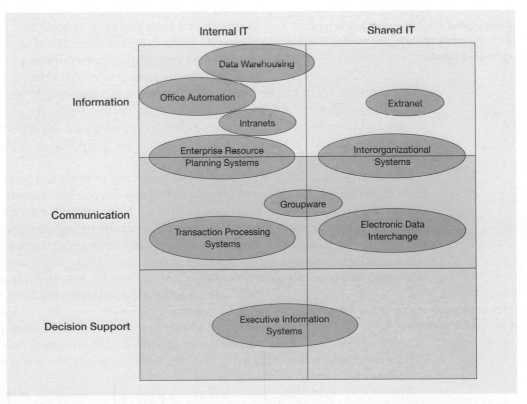

FIGURE 10.1 Types of information systems and their classification (Ryssel *et al.*, 2004); used with permission

Information systems and technology

The Internet

The Internet provides a wide variety of activities, which include electronic mail, global information access and retrieval systems, discussion groups, multiplayer games and file transfer facilities, all of which are helping to not only transform the way we think about marketing communications but are also impacting on business strategy, marketing channel structures, interorganisational relationships and the configuration of the marketing communications mix.

Are also impacting on business strategy, marketing channel structures, interorganisational relationships and the configuration of the marketing communications mix.

The Internet impacts upon marketing in two main ways: distribution and communication. The first concerns distribution and marketing channels. The Internet provides a new, more direct route to customers, which can either replace or supplement current distribution/channel arrangements. The second element concerns the Internet as a communication medium. It provides a means of reaching huge new audiences and enabling the provision of vast amounts of information. These two elements, distribution and communication, combine as ebusiness and ecommerce to provide benefits for both buyers and sellers.

The World Wide Web (WWW) can be considered as a network within which there are a number of nodes, called Web sites. These sites are created and maintained by organisations and individuals who wish to participate in Internet activities with the expectation that they can benefit (often profitably) from such participation. Web sites are intended to be visited by those who purposely want to access the site's content or by those browsing the Internet. Once visited the opportunity to interact with the site's content and form a dialogue increases rapidly. The commercial attractiveness of a Web site is based around the opportunities to display product and company information, often in the form of catalogues,

Once visited the opportunity to interact with the site's content and form a dialogue increases rapidly.

as a corporate identity cue and for internal communications, to generate leads, to provide on-screen order forms and customer support at both pre- and post-purchase points and to collect customer and prospect information for use within a database or as a feedback link for measurement and evaluative purposes. A more detailed consideration of Web sites can be found in Chapter 21.

The Internet is an important new way of providing product and service information and can enable organisations to provide new levels of customer support. With it come doubts about its ability to deliver competitive advantage and whether it could offer suitable levels of privacy, security and measures of advertising effectiveness.

The Internet is not a panacea for a manager's marketing communications problems. It is a relatively new and different means of communication, one that should be integrated into the marketing communications mix. Off-line communications are used to raise site awareness and interest among a wide audience and to provide them with the site address. Once at the Web site, in-depth product information can be exchanged for customer-specific details to refresh the database and fuel future communication activity. It is this holistic perspective of the new media that should be developed.

Should be integrated into the marketing communications mix.

Traditional marketing communications strategies employ a mix of tools and normally an emphasis is put on one type of promotional device depending on the

IBM
ibm.com/ondemand/uk

NAPSTER
IS ON

Napster is back. Over 700,000 songs strong. And IBM is helping students get the music they want without swamping university networks.

ON DEMAND BUSINESS

EXHIBIT 10.1 IBM Ad featuring Napster
IBM On Demand Business ad, referencing how IBM has helped students and universities to use Napster.

context. Broadly it has been the norm to weight advertising over the other tools, when dealing with consumer markets, and to weight personal selling when operating in the b2b sector. This reflects advertising's ability to raise awareness and develop brands and personal selling's prime skill at provoking behavioural action and closing orders. These general approaches have begun to be relaxed as audience and media fragmentation gathers speed and new ways of doing business (e.g. ecommerce) are developed. The prime benefit of the Internet, as a hybrid medium, is that it is good at all of these activities but not as good for any one task as a single promotional tool might be. Interestingly, it excels as a part of the communication and decision-making process that the established promotional tools fail to properly address, namely the search for and retrieval of information pertinent to purchase behaviour. It might be said, therefore, that the Internet provides a complementary facility to the other marketing communication tools and as such should be used with, and not instead of, the established means of marketing communication.

> The Internet provides a complementary facility to the other marketing communication tools and as such should be used with, and not instead of, the established means of marketing communication.

Database technologies

A marketing database is a collection of records that can be related to one another in multiple ways and from which information, usually customer related, can be obtained in a variety of formats. This can be analysed to determine appropriate segments and target markets and used to stimulate and record individual responses to marketing communications. It therefore plays a role as a storage, sorting and administrative device to assist direct, personalised communications.

When customer related transactional and response data is combined with additional information from external sources, such as a list broker, the database can become a potent source for marketing communication activities. Indeed, the increasing sophistication of information retrieval from databases enables much more effective targeting and communications.

Databases provide a means of monitoring changes in customer behaviour, identifying new target markets, and cross-selling products and services. The purpose of cross-selling is to reduce customer churn and increase switching costs (Kamakura *et al.*, 2003). While increasing a customer's potential switching costs may not be compatible with relationship marketing principles, the result of successful implementation may be improved levels of customer retention and satisfaction where relationships are more discrete and transactional rather than collaborative in nature.

> Databases provide a means of monitoring changes in customer behaviour.

There are many potential operational problems associated with interrogating and processing information within live databases. Ryals and Payne (2001) point out that the transaction processing performance may be slowed down when interrogating customer information and the structure of the database itself is constantly changing in response to the large volume of transactions. Many organisations have moved towards the use of data warehouses (and smaller data marts). These are integrated stores of data collected from a variety of sources (e.g. customer contact centres, the sales force and market research) and are updated at intervals, making it non-volatile and easier for interrogating customer information.

Short message services (SMS)

Although different in format, short message services (SMS), or 'texting', can be regarded as an extension of email communication. SMS is a non-intrusive but timely way of delivering information and as Doyle (2003) points out, the Global System for Mobile Communication (GSM) has become a standard protocol, so that users can send and receive information across geographic boundaries. Apart from pure text other simple applications consist of games, email notifications, and information-delivery services such as sports and stock market updates.

SMS is a non-intrusive but timely way of delivering information.

Organisations have been relatively slow at adopting SMS despite the low costs and high level of user control (target, content and time). It is these types of benefits that are attracting marketing professionals to consider SMS for more complex services. However, marketers also need to consider the potential concerns of consumers, most notably security and privacy. Just as with email, there is the potential for unwanted messages (i.e. spam) and Internet service providers (ISP) need to manage the increasing numbers of unsolicited messages through improved security systems as SMS becomes more widespread. Given that most consumers pay for SMS functionality, marketers should realise that invading personal privacy greatly reduces the potential value and effectiveness of SMS.

Marketers also need to consider the potential concerns of consumers, most notably security and privacy.

Multimedia

The term multimedia has not achieved universal agreement. Strictly speaking the term refers to any presentation of information or material that uses two or more media. However, the term multimedia has only gained prominence since the advent of digital technologies. So, multimedia is generally assumed to refer to the integration of text, audio and images in order to enhance the user interface with computer-based applications. As a result the 'streaming' of video and audio over the Internet typifies multimedia applications. As hardware and communications technology evolve so new systems and applications develop to provide the delivery of personalised email and marketing communication messages. See ViewPoint 10.1.

The 'streaming' of video and audio over the Internet typifies multimedia applications.

ViewPoint 10.1   Expert Web sites

Integrated Project Services (IPS) provides services to the pharmaceutical and biotech industries. Its original Web site was little more than brochureware and its competitors were growing partly because of their online facilities. IPS decided that it needed an uprated Web site.

The site needed to show IPS's expertise, flexibility and technological ability and also be an effective sales and marketing tool. IPS wanted a Web site that would better represent the organisation as innovative industry leaders capable of servicing large pharmaceutical giants. Additionally, IPS knew it needed a cost-effective forum to test new ideas. Since the industry is fast paced, traditional print advertising is not an efficient way to test ideas. In other words it was required to deliver both product- and corporate-related content.

Advance Design developed the new Web site using:

- content management
- interactive flash movies
- flash animation
- custom-designed banners
- database-driven content.

An interactive multimedia campaign was created to accompany the launch of the Web project. The campaign included:

- multimedia trade show and presentation
- print brochures with ecards
- IPS mascot trade show floor cutouts
- Internet marketing campaign.

The interactive Web site changed both the business strategy and the approach to marketing and sales activities. The results were impressive, as the number of new visitors to the Web site increased by 39 per cent, Internet visibility increased from 10 per cent to 23 per cent on the primary search engines, page views doubled from an average of 11,000 to 22,000 per month and IPS reached a milestone in sales, adding a record breaking 55 new clients in the first year.

IPS recently won a contract with a major pharmaceutical company for over $20 million. As IPS's visibility increased on the search engines, so did the number of leads. Managing the increased traffic became crucial to IPS's interactive marketing strategy. After thorough review of the daily list of visitors, the marketing department relays potential leads to the sales department, allowing them to capitalise on the interest of the client while IPS is fresh in their mind.

Source: http://www.advancewebdesign.com/clients/exam4.asp and http://www.ipsdb.com; used with permission.

Mobile phones and WAP technologies

Mobile phone technologies have advanced considerably and have enjoyed huge commercial success. Wireless application protocol or WAP phones possess the usual email and text information services but they also have an Internet browser facility. As a result, messages can be not only location specific but also time specific, for example a message sent when someone is in a town centre at lunch time, promoting a café, restaurant or shop. However, market growth in WAP technologies has been far less than originally expected, partly because of the text input facilities and the need for improved information displays.

Market growth in WAP technologies has been far less than originally expected.

New and faster technologies, such as General Packet Radio Service (GPRS) and third-generation (3G) services enabling sound and image transfers, are expected to herald a successful relaunch of m-commerce. Bluetooth is the name given to a short-range radio technology which enables any kind of electronic equipment to be connected. Bluetooth's founding members include Ericsson, IBM, Intel, Nokia and Toshiba and the goal is to let Bluetooth's radio communications take the place of wires for connecting peripherals, telephones and computers.

Business applications

A raft of increasingly sophisticated application programmes have evolved to meet the needs of the market. Initially electronic data interchange (EDI) via public networks, and now the Internet, managed the direct transmission between different companies' computer systems of data relating to business transactions. The applications tended to focus on systems designed by suppliers to assist customers in their purchasing procedures, processes and overall decision-making. The level of sophistication and scope of these applications now embrace a network of transactions and flow of information between a number of organisations. Radjou (2003 p. 25) refers to 'supply network processes', which encompass the following categories:

● product life cycle management
● supply chain management
● enterprise asset management
● production network management
● continuous demand management
● order fulfilment and distribution management
● aftermarket service management.

These applications serve to reduce costs, speed up processes, improve accuracy and provide added value for end-user customers. In terms of the relationships between organisations and their customers these applications can serve to improve collaboration, both internally and externally. For example, enterprise-wide solutions such as complete enterprise resource planning (ERP) systems attempt to integrate all business processes across an organisation's accounting, manufacturing, sales and human resource departments. Further downstream electronic point of sale (EPOS), which involves computerised tills linked back to a company's central computer(s), enables the data of every retail sale to be transmitted back to the organisation to facilitate sales and inventory management and, in a marketing context,

Enterprise resource planning (ERP) systems attempt to integrate all business processes across an organisation's accounting, manufacturing, sales and human resource departments.

can be used to better understand customer demand and buying behaviour. As networks, including the Internet, have extended to connect multiple businesses in the supply chain, sophisticated point-of-sale data has enabled collaborative marketing. For example, the leading supermarkets have systems that enable selected suppliers to 'find out information such as the repeat purchase rate of individual products, profiles of customers purchasing particular products and the most appropriate tools to attract customers' (Thomas, 2003).

Interorganisational use of network technologies to share business information and coordinate supply chain activities has been termed 'ecollaboration' and represents a major area of development, particularly for high-technology-based companies.

Interactive television

Another important technological development is digital broadcasting and the opportunities for interactive television. Digital television and interactive services are two related but different facilities. Digital television is now a reality, but full interactivity has yet to be delivered to the majority of the population. Potential advantages are

Digital television and interactive services are two related but different facilities.

consumer familiarity, the full-screen, high-quality sound and picture format, fast channel and picture/text 'hopping', combining entertainment and shopping. The disadvantages include the current high cost of the sets to consumers and of broadcasting for companies. Also, it cannot deal with individual customers until TV-based email is widely established. Penetration rates will rise as analogue services in the UK are phased out.

ViewPoint 10.2   Interactive chicken?

Unilever ran the first UK interactive TV ad for its Chicken Tonight brand, endorsed by the ex-footballer and emerging entertainer Ian Wright. According to Reid (2001), the ad provoked response rates 70 per cent higher than those normally associated with DRTV. The next major phase of the Unilever interactive strategy was to run two (digital) spots for its brands Colman's and Olivio spread. Each interactive ad offered click-throughs to the company's portal, Creative Kitchen, containing all of the company's food brands.

Digital services provide many benefits for consumers, one of which will be the opportunity to screen out current intrusive advertising. Interactive advertising will be driven by consumers who will decide which advertisements they want to watch, when, and how long they will stay involved. The creative possibilities are far ranging but in order to retain audiences it will become increasingly important to develop creative ideas based upon a sound understanding of the target audience and their interactive and buying patterns. Currently on UK teletext there are pages about holiday bargains that direct potential users to the Internet (www.teletext.co.uk/holidays) where they will find a searchable database, plus weather reports, resort reviews and advice. This service claims a choice of preferred operators, competitive pricing, confidence – full financial protection, up-to-date offers and human interaction at the point of sale. It states that, in the future, customers will be able to access the full functionality of the Web site via digital TV and/or mobile phone. The point is that digital television and interactive marketing communications are unlikely to thrive isolated from other methods of communication. Just as online facilities need off-line drivers, and just as bricks and clicks appear to be a more profitable format than clicks only, so an integrated perspective is required if digital television and interactive advertising are to be successful.

> Digital television and interactive marketing communications are unlikely to thrive isolated from other methods of communication.

Video conferencing

There are currently two main types of video conferencing systems: PC based and room based. PC-based, or desktop, systems are suitable for a small number of people, for short time periods. The cameras are usually fixed focus, with small field capability, and viewing screens are also small. Transmission speeds are limited by modem and telephone line capabilities. An advantage is that software applications and files can be shared and viewed jointly.

Room-based systems use large, sophisticated (pan–tilt–zoom) cameras and wide TV screens. More people can participate. Transmission via ISDN (integrated services digital network), including satellite links, facilitates better picture/sound quality. Sessions have to be pre-booked and are costlier than PC based (Source: www.videocom.co.uk, 7 July 2000).

Video conferencing can be used in marketing communications for research (audience polling), product promotion/launch, training, employee and/or channel member briefings and sales negotiations. The advantages of video conferencing include speed and convenience as travel costs are minimised, potential reduction in message ambiguity as there is joint and simultaneous viewing of materials and instant feedback.

One of the disadvantages is that all participants have to be available at the same time, which can be difficult across time zones. The connections are not always reliable and room time-slots often cannot be extended beyond the original booking. Some people are uneasy in front of cameras, which may impair effectiveness.

The use of video conferencing has increased because of major technical advances, which have improved the clarity and reliability of many commercial systems. This combined with periods of major global crisis, which have lead to a rapid decrease in the volume of air travel, appear to have spurred on the use of video conferencing.

> The use of video conferencing has increased because of major technical advances, which have improved the clarity and reliability of many commercial systems.

Kiosks

Electronic kiosks are terminals that can be accessed by the public for information and services. Very often kiosks are operated via touch-screens and video displays and incorporate card readers, coupon printers and other devices specific to their application. Increasingly electronic kiosks provide not only multimedia facilities but also enable access to the Internet (www.scala.com).

ViewPoint 10.3   REI in kiosks

The outdoor climbing, hiking and mountain biking clothes made by REI require a high degree of touch and trial as well as significant information prior to purchase. REI has exploited these characteristics by building in-store climbing walls as well as hiking boot and mountain bike test areas. Due to limited retail floor space, REI installed Web kiosks through which customers research 68,000 items as well as 45,000 Web pages of product information.

By exploiting the fundamental nature of its products and through the instalment of kiosks in its stores, REI has effectively engaged its customers in a multi-channel experience. Kiosk implementation has allowed it to dedicate floor space to test areas while simultaneously attending to its breadth of inventory. Customers can utilise the strength of each channel and have consequently increased their spending. According to Jupiter Communications, existing REI customers who shopped online for the first time increased their store spending by 22 per cent and customers shopping on more than one channel spent overall more than in the previous year.

Ecommerce

Ecommerce, the electronic buying and selling of goods and services, either in a b2b or b2c context, provides potentially huge benefits for participants. The essential attraction for sellers is that a global market becomes available and transaction costs are reduced. For buyers, search convenience combined with lower prices make ecommerce a compelling option. There are a number of ecommerce or business models that can be identified operating over the WWW. The range of business models is shown in Table 10.1.

Other dotcom models include what are known colloquially as 'clicks' (or pure play) and 'bricks and clicks' operations. 'Bricks and clicks' operations refer to organisations that retain a physical presence (high street or business park) and online facilities are added either to reach discrete segments/new markets or as a supplement to the current distribution and communication facilities. The 'clicks' model refers to dedicated Internet brands (e.g. lastminute.com) that only have a virtual presence. However, long-established businesses have added dotcom facilities to their business and promotional activities. There are several implications for marketing communications and branding activities for both of these two types of Internet operations and these will be examined later.

It is not surprising, therefore, that out of this complexity of formats and styles, markets and customer needs, a number of hybrid business formats have emerged, principally to meet the needs of the new electronic marketplace.

However, despite the complexities associated with formats and services provided, there are two main models. One concerns interorganisational communications and transaction activity, referred to as business-to-business (b2b). The other concerns activities with consumers and is referred to as business-to-consumer (b2c). In the United States the development of b2c is much further advanced than it is in Europe, where the emphasis has been on b2b. These two models will now be looked at in turn but readers are advised that references to other aspects of Internet-based communications are made throughout the book.

TABLE 10.1 Ecommerce business models

Model	Explanation
eauction	Demand- and supply-oriented bidding processes for both consumers and organisations
ecollaboration	Demand and supply orientation for mutual benefit
emalls	Demand-led collection of eretail 'shops' that seek common synergies
epurchase	Demand-led buying and selling for businesses
eprocurement	Supply-led services for the purchase of materials and equipment
eretail	Demand-led buying opportunities for the public
eservice providers	Supply-led provision of speciality business services

Business-to-business ecommerce

In b2b markets organisational buying behaviour is more complex than that observed in consumer markets. This is because of the increased number of people involved in the decision-making process and the nature of the

Marketing communications in the b2b market are traditionally characterised by the predominance of personal selling.

relationships between individuals and organisations. As a result of this and other factors, marketing communications in the b2b market are traditionally characterised by the predominance of personal selling and relatively little use of advertising (see Chapter 31). In fact, it is the complete reversal of consumer-based promotional activity (b2c) where mass media-based communications have tended to be the most important route through to the target audience (see Chapters 14 and 31).

One of the principal reasons for using the Internet as a distribution channel and communication medium between organisations is that it can drastically improve productivity. Electronic commerce saves transaction time, lowers costs and shortens the time between order and delivery. Digitally based communications can improve the accuracy of the information provided and so give a good measure of the effectiveness of marketing communication activities. However, off-line communications are still going to be important and these new communication formats should be considered as an addition to rather than a substitution for current marketing communications. For example, the collection of data for use through on- and off-line sources can be deployed to improve direct marketing activities, to target sales promotions so as to provide real and valued incentives and even benefit public relations activities by placing suitable material on the Web pages. Therefore productivity measures apply to marketing communications on- and off-line.

Communication costs can also be considerably reduced. Just as sales literature and demonstration packs take time to prepare, even longer to change/update and are quite expensive with a great deal of wastage, brochureware on the Web site is fast, easily

This can free up the sales force to visit established customers more often.

accessible and adaptable. One step further into Web site development is the collection of names and addresses, response to email questions and the provision of rich data for the sales force. If developed further, transactional Web sites enable routine orders to be processed quickly and at a lower cost. This can free up the sales force to visit established customers more often, open more new accounts and manage those accounts that are strategically important, more attentively.

There will also be some legal and information security issues that need to be addressed in order to reduce any risk to business partners. This is part of the development and maintenance of profitable relationships and marketing communications has an important role to play in the development of these relationships by reducing perceived risk and uncertainty. Marketing communications also needs to provide clarity and fast, pertinent and timely information in order that decisions can be made.

The need to reduce the frequency and intensity of conflict that is inevitable in interorganisational relationships is paramount.

Through marketing communications (and operational efficiencies and political contingencies) the development of loyalty between organisations might be observed. By targeting information and customising messages for the right people within a partner organisation, via an Extranet for example, the development of loyalty through trust and commitment might be possible. Regularised, balanced communication that is embedded within the operational interactions between organisations is much more likely to lead to higher levels of customer (intermediary) satisfaction than when it is absent. The need to reduce the frequency and intensity of conflict that is inevitable in interorganisational relationships is paramount. It will be established (Chapter 31) that the propensity to share information and to provide higher rather than lower volumes of information is perceived as an indicator of high quality (and therefore satisfying) communication. The Internet is an ideal resource for enabling these events to happen and in doing so bind partner organisations closer.

Business-to-consumer ecommerce

Using the Internet to communicate directly with consumers and encourage them to enter into financial exchanges has been an enticing goal for most businesses operating in this sector. The speed at which this sector has grown (outside of the United States) has not been as rapid or as profitable as first thought, evidenced by commentator predictions in 1999 and the failure of most dotcom brands to achieve profitability and some that have collapsed. Indeed there are a number of far-ranging b2c issues, beyond the scope of this text, concerning fraud, morality, education, family life and the nature and purpose of the current and future retail environments (e.g. the configuration and use of the high street).

There were about 22 million UK active Internet users in July 2004 (Nielsen//NetRatings, 2004) and according to a previous report by Whitely (2000) users are skewed towards higher disposable incomes (£25,000 plus) and the ABC categories. Books, music, travel and computer products make up the top purchase categories. Books and music represent low-involvement purchases and low perceived risk, so the distribution (and price) advantages of the WWW dominate. Travel and computer equipment represent high involvement and high perceived risk so the search (and price) facilities of the WWW dominate buyers' use and selection.

Whitely's report states that 31 per cent of respondents (who had bought products over the WWW) claimed that they had first heard of the site through a recommendation made by a friend or relative (active seekers), 20 per cent by surfing (passive seekers) and only 15 per cent mentioned off-line media communications and a mere 6 per cent through online advertisements. What this means is that word-of-mouth communications and the role and influence of opinion formers and especially opinion leaders (see Chapter 2) are critical to supporting interactive communications and exchanges.

> Word-of-mouth communications and the role and influence of opinion formers and especially opinion leaders are critical to supporting interactive communications and exchanges.

Fulfilment

Fulfilment of customer orders is absolutely imperative if a repeat visit to an ecommerce Web site is to be encouraged. There used to be some uncertainty as to what constitutes an acceptable delivery period but now expectations have moved from three weeks to three days. Fulfilment expectations are also raised because the online experience placing the order is characteristically convenient, quick, efficient and this is then projected by consumers on to all consequent order-processing activities. Email is often used to acknowledge orders and to advise of despatch. If this should be delayed, however, consumers may perceive this as a failure of part of the fulfilment exercise.

However, order fulfilment often requires the cooperation of outsourcing suppliers such that stock is not stored on site but in a warehouse at a distant location. According to Gray (2000), this is a key decision for organisations moving from a conventional

> Order fulfilment often requires the cooperation of outsourcing suppliers.

trading environment to a multichannel approach. Should warehousing and fulfilment be outsourced or kept in-house? Even if the decision is to undertake fulfilment in-house, slim stocking still requires suitable systems to enable suppliers to replenish stock quickly.

ViewPoint 10.4   Fulfilling food and wine

When Asda-Walmart first developed its home shopping service two independent, purpose-designed depots were built. However, this approach proved less than successful and the company soon migrated to a store-based service, the model used so successfully by Tesco. The in-store approach allows for the full range of products to be offered online so customers get a better service in terms of the range of products available.

In-store pickers use handheld systems devices to help them fulfil a number of orders simultaneously. Asda's systems are integrated with its parent company Wal-Mart, which not only assists in terms of IST and fulfilment developments in North America but also provides leading-edge technologies to integrate fulfilment with a range of corporate functions.

For Direct Wines Ltd, one of the world's largest mail order suppliers of wines, efficient fulfilment is a key to competitive factor, as even the best wines in the world need to be delivered promptly and accurately. Through the use of appropriate systems, planning and stock control Direct Wines has had to make fewer substitutions, thus improving customer service, while at the same time reducing the overall amount of stock held as working capital by around 10 per cent.

Ecommerce vendors need delivery partners and there is evidence that new providers that are able to deliver at times and locations (e.g. to work addresses) convenient to consumers will be able to gain a foothold in the marketplace. In other words, the rise of b2c ecommerce has brought about a restructuring of the delivery and fulfilment sector to meet the changing needs of customers.

Customer relationship management

Establishing what constitutes CRM is far from easy based on the various interpretations that have been placed on the term. Ang and Buttle (2003) suggest that there are three main approaches. These are *strategic*, where CRM is seen as a core business strategy; *operational*, where CRM is about automating different aspects of an organisation's selling, marketing and service functions and, finally, *analytical*, where CRM is about manipulating data to improve the efficiency and effectiveness of each phase of the customer relationship life cycle. From this it is possible to consider CRM as the delivery of customer value through the strategic integration of business functions and processes, using customer data and information systems and technology.

Early CRM applications were designed for supplier organisations to enable them to manage their end-user customers and hence they became regarded as a front-end application. Originally developed as sales force support systems (mainly sales force automation) they have subsequently evolved as a more sophisticated means of managing customers, using real-time customer information.

CRM applications typically consist of call management, lead management, customer record, sales support and payment systems.

CRM applications typically consist of call management, lead management, customer record, sales support and payment systems. These are necessary in order to respond to questions from customers (e.g. about products, deliveries, prices and order status) and questions from internal stakeholders about issues such as strategy, processes and sales forecasts.

These systems should be used at each stage of the customer life cycle, in order to develop an understanding about customer attitudes and behaviour that the organisation desires. CRM should be used to assist decisions about whom to target, which customer differences should be taken into account and what impact this will have on profitability. It is this aspect of profitability, or relative profitability of individual customers that is important and which is a core aspect of relationship marketing. As Nancarrow and Rees (2003) suggest, only by understanding the actual, potential, current and lifetime forms of individual customer profitability can different strategies be developed for different profit segments. Low-profit-generating customers may need to be treated differently from those customers that are highly profitable and those customers which incur losses for the organisation may need to be dropped.

The conceptual idea of using customer and transactional data in order to proactively shape customer relationships is appealing. IST now enables much of this to happen.

Many client organisations have voiced disappointment and even criticism.

However, many client organisations have voiced disappointment and even criticism when such systems fail to meet their expectations, while Rigby *et al.* (2002) report that very few CRM investments have proved to be successful. Table 10.2 lists some of the more prominent reasons.

Most of the reasons cited in Table 10.2 are based on the failure of a large number of organisations, both clients and vendors, to understand the central tenets of a customer-focused business philosophy. If CRM systems are to work then a central business strategy, one based on the importance of trust, commitment and customer satisfaction, has to be agreed and led by the senior managers. Only within this context can it be expected that the installation of databases, data warehouses and associated software will help influence the quality of an organisation's relationships with its customers and stakeholders. Good customer management requires attention to an organisation's culture, training, strategy and propositions and processes. Regretfully, too many organisations focus on the interface or fail to understand the broader picture.

TABLE 10.2 Reasons for CRM disappointment

Author	Reasons for CRM underachievement
Wightman, 2000	Failure to adopt CRM within a strategic orientation
Stone, 2002	CRM is regarded as a mere add-on application that is expected to resolve all customer interface difficulties
Sood, 2002	Failure of systems to accommodate the wide array of relationships that organisations seek to manage
O'Malley and Mitussis, 2002	Internal political issues concerning ownership of systems, data and budgets

Customer contact centres

Originally customer contact centres (CCC) were designed for in-house use to handle a large volume of telephone calls. They became a largely outsourced facility and manage high volumes of incoming calls through automatic call distribution (ACD) technology. ACDs distribute incoming calls to predetermined groups of agents. An ACD can hold calls in queues if necessary and play music and make announcements. Now CCCs are Internet-enabled communication solutions, designed to process and integrate a variety of media using voice messaging, interactive voice response, outbound calling and fax.

Whereas CCC were once in-house then outsourced they are often viewed as a core business activity mainly because they are a critical component when delivering customer satisfaction and driving efficiency.

ViewPoint 10.5   **Aetna's contact centre partnership**

Using phone, fax or email and the Internet-based Web chat and Web call-back features, Aetna provides its customers and insurance agents with 24-hour service. The development of the centre was characterised by Aetna's decision to select three partner organisations that each brought a unique technology to the customer contact centre.

1. CTIL, a leading Hong Kong-based customer interaction and ebusiness solution provider, brought implementation skills.

2. Interactive Intelligence provides an interaction management solution that combines the functionality of a digital PBX, ACD, IVR, voicemail system, fax server, Web gateway and computer telephony system all on a single software platform.

3. Alliance Systems provided the advanced, standards-based communication platform that enables the contact centre's multiple applications and functions to run on a single system.

As a result, Aetna has used customer contact and CRM technologies to create a multimedia based, interactive system not only to provide superior levels of customer service but in doing so have remained competitive.

Source: Adapted from www.alliancesystems.com/about/news/casestudies/aetna.asp, accessed 28 November 2003; used with kind permission.

In the near future CCCs will not be tied to a particular physical location and agents will work either from home or in various offices around the globe, each connected through a voice-over-IP network (Bocklund, 2003). CRM software will be integrated with computer-telephone integration (CTI), which means that each interaction is immediately reported (to the database) so updated information is available to agents right away.

TABLE 10.3 Benefits of digital technology

Considerably reduced transaction costs
Increased opportunities for growth and innovation
Improved competitive position
Encouragement of cooperative behaviour
Stimulates review of business and marketing strategies
Enhances communications with customers
Can improve corporate image and reputation
Information about customers improved
Enhanced measurement and evaluation of customer interaction
Customer service developed

The influence of technology on marketing communications

The various technologically driven facilities referred to above can influence an organisation's marketing communications in many different ways. The implementation and benefits derived from technology will vary across organisations. This is because the level of strategic significance afforded to these investments, the culture, managerial skills, resources and degree to which the organisation has a true customer orientation differ widely. This section considers some of the generic ways in which IST can influence marketing communications, but readers should be aware that the intensity of the influence will be variable and far from uniform. Table 10.3 sets out some of the benefits that digital technology can provide.

> The implementation and benefits derived from technology will vary across organisations.

Some of these will be revisited later in this section but readers can see that the list of benefits covers a wide range of organisational and marketing-related issues.

Interactivity

Digital technology allows for true interactively based communications, where messages can be responded to more or less instantly. Although there has been considerable media attention given to the development and potential of interactive services, the reality is that only a relatively small proportion of the public has become immersed in interactive environments, measured in terms of advertising space sold, usage and attitude research, and the number of transactions undertaken interactively. The development of interactive services may well be best served by the identification of those most likely to adopt such services and who will encourage others in their social orbits to follow their actions. This strategy would require communication with innovators and early adopters to speed the process of adoption (Rogers, 1983). This is quite crucial, as the infrastructure and associated heavy costs require an early stream of cash flows (Kangis and Rankin, 1996). The cost of equipment and time taken to learn and utilise interactive services does represent a barrier to adoption. These barriers might be substantial depending upon the background characteristics, education, personality, propensity to take risks and willingness to develop new

> Digital technology allows for true interactively based communications, where messages can be responded to more or less instantly.

skills and patterns of behaviour. This reinvention process can take individuals varying amounts of time to accomplish and hence impact on the speed of adoption.

Technological advances have made possible a range of other interactive communication opportunities. Stress so far has been placed on the Internet, but there have been many other imaginative and exciting developments and applications. One area where interactivity has been subject to experimentation is television, and some organisations have experimented with interactive messages, most notably the very first interactive advertisement for Chicken Tonight, plus Dove, Mazda and Tango. See ViewPoint 10.2.

One of the biggest factors accelerating the consumer use of digital TV will be the variety of entertainment possibilities that the Internet may struggle to provide. It is thought by many that digital TV will stimulate growth in home shopping. Digital TV will impact on home shopping, but probably not to the extent that many popular writers assume.

Home shopping represents a significant change in buyer behaviour that may affect a range of ancillary activities. Several UK supermarket operators have invested heavily in these new shopping channels and they have had to learn new fulfilment operations and new processes and procedures to meet customer expectations. Although Tesco appears to have been particularly successful there is little evidence to suggest that retailers will give up their high street presence, as predicted in the later 1990s. The physical shopping experience provides some consumers with significant entertainment and social interaction satisfactions and these are unlikely to be discarded for virtual shopping.

> Home shopping represents a significant change in buyer behaviour.

The financial services sector can be expected to undergo further change as home banking in particular becomes a secure and more convenient transaction context. Entertainment possibilities will be even more attractive, as interactive games and interactive viewing through pay per view, video on demand and time shifting (which is, as Rosen pointed out as long ago as 1997, the option to view yesterday's programmes today) become easily accessible.

The new technology and the new communication infrastructure will give increasing numbers of people the opportunity to experience interactive marketing communications and the new media. This may impact upon their expectations and bring changes to the way in which people lead their lives.

Goften (2000) reports about intuitive software that monitors a visitor's movement around a site, stores it and then adjusts the site to meet the preferred pattern each time that visitor enters the site. The implications for targeting advertising are enormous. However, despite all these developments, it appears that Cohen (1995) was quite prophetic when he commented that there was 'great uncertainty as to the level of consumer demand'. In 1995 technology and demand were uncertain but even at the beginning of the twenty-first century online profitability remains elusive to most pioneer virtual traders. The reality must be that technological advances and changes in buyer behaviour are more severely lagged than originally realised. While some consumers are ready and eager to take advantage of the new opportunities many are not, and the process of diffusion needs to move forward in order that an increasing proportion of customers have the means and motivation to participate in the interactive environments.

Multichannel marketing

Although not entirely responsible, new technology has enabled organisations to reach new markets and different segments using more than a single marketing channel. Database generated telemarketing, direct mail, email and Internet channels now

New technology has enabled organisations to reach new markets and different segments using more than a single marketing channel.

complement field sales, retail and catalogue selling and have allowed organisations to determine which customers prefer which channels and which are the most profitable. This in turn enables organisations to allocate resources far more effectively and to spread the customer base upon which profits are developed. A multichannel strategy should accommodate customers' account channel preferences, their usage patterns, needs, price sensitivities and preferred point of product and service access. So, as Stone and Shan (2002) put it, the goal is to manage each channel profitably while optimising the attributes of each channel so that they deliver value for each type of customer.

Multichannel strategies have added new marketing opportunities and enabled audiences to access products and services in ways that best meet their own lifestyle and behavioural needs. For organisations this has reduced message wastage, used media more efficiently and in doing so reduced costs and improved communication effectiveness.

ViewPoint 10.6   Multichannel banking in the UK

UK commercial banks are trying to develop new channels in a market where current distribution channels (branches, call centres and echannels) are the largest operating expense. In the UK, the majority of customers use physical branches, partly because they represent the banking experience. Even for customers who rarely use them for transactions, branches are still seen as the embodiment of the bank, and often the place at which significant changes in the relationship take place (e.g. account openings, complex financial products bought or at least investigated, serious problems resolved).

Many banks have pursued strategies based on Internet, wireless and call centre facilities while closing branches and removing the physical presence and customer experience of branch-based banking. Branch-based delivery has moved through a number of significant phases, namely the old 'bricks and personal service only', through the introduction of self-service branches, to sales branches with transactions handled in other channels. Some banks have changed strategy and are planning to increase the number of branches, often as part of a joint venture with retailers or as a franchise. However, Stone and Shan (2002) suggest that some banks may move towards the use of branch portals, which seek to combine the best of all approaches yet are still clearly centred on the branch. Such a move will re-emphasise the personal branch service facility but recognises that some customers will prefer a remote technological service based on ebanking and that abandons all personal contact with a branch.

Source: Adapted from Stone and Shan (2002).

Retailers are faced with particular problems that concern the amount of property/freehold they possess and the as yet unknown pattern of consumer shopping behaviour in the light of multichannel opportunities. The Arcadia Group (which owns Dorothy Perkins, Wallis, Top Shop, etc.) has made a significant attempt to make its own name synonymous with online shopping through the development of Zoom, an online shopping mall. Some people might think that retailers should dispose of their fixed assets and move into the Internet or perhaps reconfigure their store layouts. In most cases the optimum solution is to develop a multichannel solution whereby a range of media and experiences are offered to consumers. So, some prefer the Internet, some traditional shopping, some will use interactive TV and some will prefer catalogue shopping. This approach puts customers' needs first by determining their preferred marketing channels and also enables organisations to reconfigure their cost structures.

What may happen is that shopping activities become divided into categories that reflect particular channel options. So routine, unexciting purchases may be consigned to online and interactive channels, and the more explorative, stimulating and perhaps socially important purchases are prioritised for shopping expeditions. Stores will need to adapt themselves to provide more value than the current product focus. Related benefits and enhanced services will be important to provide differentiation and attraction. For example, the bookstore Ottakar's provides coffee bars and comfortable seating, an environment in which customers are encouraged to relax and consider their possible purchases. Larger stores and mainstream brands will need to establish themselves as 'destination' stores where the attraction for consumers is bound by excitement, entertainment and a brand experience. Jardine (1999) reports that in some destination stores it is possible to test-ride mountain bikes in an 'authentic outdoor environment', to attend cookery classes in supermarkets or perhaps shrink-fit your own Levi jeans by taking a dip in a store bathtub.

In the United States these types of store are now relatively common and experience shows that high street shopping is not about to die but take a revised shape, form and role. Mercedes has a café on the Champs-Elysées in Paris but its role is to remind, differentiate and bring the brand into people's consciousness away from the traditional frame of reference. There is no persuasion as cars cannot be bought (or sold), but the brand is reinforced. See Chapter 27 for more on multichannel strategies.

Personalisation

For the first time, digital technology has empowered organisations to personalise messages and communicate with stakeholders on a one-to-one basis, on a scale that is commercially viable. This has driven the dramatic development of direct marketing, reshaped the basis on which organisations target and segment markets, stimulated dialogue, brought about a raft of new strategies and challenged the conventional approach to mass marketing and branding techniques.

> Digital technology has empowered organisations to personalise messages and communicate with stakeholders on a one-to-one basis.

The use of email communications is now extensive and viral marketing campaigns are gaining increasing acceptance. As with all forms of communication, the successful use of email requires an understanding of the recipient's behaviour. Email communication enables a high degree of personalisation, and in order to personalise messages it is necessary to understand the attitudinal and behavioural characteristics of each email audience (Chaffey, 2003). He suggests that the following need to be considered:

● How many recipients read their emails from home and at work?

● Which times of the day and days of the week do they read their email?

● How soon after receipt is email read?

● How do recipients configure their email readers?

Understanding the email behaviour of the different audiences can influence the degree of personalisation that is given to email communications and Web site welcome messages. Many people now expect a high level of personalisation and virtual recognition. Personalisation is a sensitive area and is often twinned with privacy issues. Personalisation should be an integral aspect of relationship marketing, especially in b2b markets. The degree of personalisation will inevitably vary over the customer life cycle and become more intimate as a relationship matures. However, email communication that is based on an understanding of the audience's email behaviour should influence the message content, the time when it should be sent and, most importantly, the keys to encouraging recipients to open the email and not delete it. These keys are the 'header' of the email, which contains the subject matter, and the 'from' address, which signifies whether the sender is known and hence strongly determines whether the email is perceived positively at the outset. If it is then there is a stronger chance that the email will be opened and hence a greater opportunity for response and interactivity. A deeper consideration of email communication can be found in Chapter 21.

Mobility

Digital technologies now support a range of devices and applications that enable mobile communications. Mobile commerce (or mcommerce) refers to the use of wireless devices such as mobile phones for transactional activities and because the wireless facility enables transactions to be undertaken in real time and at any location, a feature referred to as 'ubiquity'. The impact on marketing communications could be huge. Because of the reachability, the opportunity to keep in touch, increased convenience, localisation and personalisation opportunities offered by this new technology, it will soon be possible theoretically to track people to particular locations. Then the delivery of personalised and pertinent information plus inducements and promotional offers in order to encourage specific purchase behaviour can have greater impact.

> Mcommerce refers to the use of wireless devices such as mobile phones for transactional activities and because the wireless facility enables transactions to be undertaken in real time and at any location, a feature referred to as 'ubiquity'.

SMS communications are used increasingly not just for brand awareness-based advertising but also as an effective way of delivering sales promotions, such as announcing special offers. This again reflects the increasing ubiquity of contemporary mobile communications. However, as with email, it is also important to consider the potential privacy concerns of customers, especially as the receipt of unwanted messages (i.e. spam) may well increase.

> SMS communications are used increasingly not just for brand awareness-based advertising but also as an effective way of delivering sales promotions.

Speed

IST has enabled aspects of marketing communications to be conducted at much faster, indeed electronic speeds. This impact is manifest in direct communications with end-users and in the production process itself. Draft documents, film and video clips, contracts, address lists and research and feedback reports, to name a few, can all now be transmitted electronically, saving processing time and reducing the elapsed production time necessary to create and implement marketing communication activities and events.

Efficiency

Efficiency is a broad term used to encompass a wide array of issues. New technology helps organisations to target their messages accurately to discrete groups or audiences. Indeed, one-to-one marketing is possible and when compared with mass communications and broad audiences it is clear that IST offers huge opportunities for narrow casting and reduced communication waste. Rather than shower audiences with messages that some of them do not wish to receive, direct marketing should, theoretically, enable each message to be received by all who are favourably disposed to the communication.

This principle of narrow casting applies equally well to communication costs. Moving away from mass media to direct marketing and one-to-one communications reduces the absolute costs associated with campaigns. The relative costs may be higher but these richer communications facilitate interactive opportunities with a greater percentage of the target audience than previously experienced in the mass broadcast era.

A further type of efficiency can be seen in terms of the accuracy and precision of the messages that are delivered. Marketing communications delivers product information, specifications and service details, contracts, designs, drawings and development briefs when customising to meet customer needs. The use of IST can help organisations provide customers with precise information and reduce opportunities for information deviance.

> The use of IST can help organisations provide customers with precise information and reduce opportunities for information deviance.

Relationships

As mentioned previously new technology is now used by organisations to gather and use information about customers in order to better meet their needs. Through the use of the database organisations now seek to develop longer-term relationships with customers, with programmes and strategies that are dubiously termed as customer loyalty schemes. While there may be doubt about the term loyalty, there can be no doubt that IST has helped develop new forms of sales promotion and influenced customer relationships. What should also be clear is that the existence of IST in an organisation or relationship is no guarantee that additional value will be created (Ryssel *et al.*, 2004).

Some customer service interface functions have been replaced with technology in the name of greater efficiency, cost savings and improved service. Financial services organisations are able to inform customers of their bank balances automatically without human intervention. Meyronin (2004, p. 222) refers to this as an 'infomediation' strategy and suggests that this neglect of the human interaction in the creation of joint value in service environments may be detrimental.

> Suggests that this neglect of the human interaction in the creation of joint value in service environments may be detrimental.

Relationships with intermediaries have also been affected by new technology. The development of ecommerce has given rise to channel strategies that either result in channel functions and hence members being discarded, or give rise to opportunities for new functions and members. These processes, disintermediation and reintermediation respectively, are both dynamic and potentially destabilising for organisations and their channel partners.

Client, agency and industry issues

New technology has led to changes in the balance of the tools used by many organisations. Most notably those operating in the FMCG sector that spend vast sums on above-the-line media in order to develop brand values have begun to spend more below-the-line in an effort to impact on behaviour rather than just brand development. Direct marketing has also impacted on the advertising spend, and with the development of IMC and related concepts such as media neutral planning the balance of the communications spend has moved towards either sales promotions and/or direct marketing.

The content of many marketing communication messages has therefore swung, and with it the work of advertising agencies. Agencies have had to adapt to a new environment, one in which clients expect their agencies to present strategies that involve a much broader range of tools and media and to offer new skills and resources. This has been achieved mainly through acquisition and the development of international networks of agencies, from all disciplines, pooling their talents in order to secure domestic and international business.

Tapp and Hughes (2004) refer to the impact of IST on the company–customer interface and on the internal processes and marketing resources within client companies. They report on the major impact IST has had internally and the struggle organisations have experienced coping with the disruption new technology has stimulated. In terms of marketing communications this disruption is potentially enormous. With Web sites becoming the focus of much internal communication activity, forces propelling ideas concerning the desire to integrate marketing communications and planning and strategy processes having to accommodate uncertain industry, media and audience expectations, marketing communications has been severely buffeted by IST.

> The major impact IST has had internally and the struggle organisations have experienced coping with the disruption new technology has stimulated.

However, while the changes driven by new technology might bring about an unwelcome internal production focus, these changes should be seen positively, as a primary means of moving organisations forward. New technology can help organisations communicate more effectively and more efficiently, both internally and externally. By adopting a stronger customer focus organisations can deliver improved levels of customer value and be better placed to meet their marketing goals and improve shareholder value.

Strategic implications

Organisations have had to adapt to new technologies as a means of delivering value to their stakeholders. The strategic implications are very significant although it should be noted that not all organisations have recognised or responded adequately to the strategic challenge, witnessed by the problems associated with CRM mentioned earlier. IST has not changed the value propositions or the assumptions of the value chain itself (Porter, 1985). What IST has done is change the way in which the primary and support activities work in order that value be generated. New technology has enabled organisations to reach new markets, work with different channel partners and provide value and satisfactions for a range of new audiences.

> What IST has done is change the way in which the primary and support activities work in order that value be generated.

Consideration is given here to the strategic influence of IST on the Internet and IMC-related strategies, although it is recognised that there are other areas of strategic impact which have not been considered here.

Internet strategies

The function and speed of development of Internet facilities within organisations is a function of many factors, such as the size and core skills of the organisation (it is easier for an IT organisation than a transport organisation to develop ecommerce facilities), the nature of the product offering and the market and competitor conditions. It cannot, therefore, be concluded that there is a fixed pathway for the development and incorporation of the Internet within an organisation, nor should there be one as the flexibility and adaptability to meet individual organisational requirements needs to be retained.

However, it is useful to understand the basic types of online facilities in order to appreciate the strategic thinking that needs to be undertaken. The Internet can become an integral part of the way a business operates, the way it sees its future and the way others see it, and not just be used to supplement the organisation's promotional programme. Having said that, it is this technology factor, more than any other, which has done so much to accelerate moves towards integrated marketing communications and to encourage managers to consider the totality of their activities rather than focus on an individual aspect.

Bickerton *et al.* (1998) suggest that there are three main stages to the development and implementation of the Internet within organisations: presentation, interaction and representation; and van Doren *et al.* (2000) and others present a four-stage model. What is consistent among these and the other interpretations is that the spectrum of Internet opportunities ranges from the use of the Internet as a:

● *shop window* (I would like to look at what you have to offer) through to

● *enquiry* (may I know more about that one please) to a fully

● *interactive engagement* (I would like to buy that one and have it delivered please) to one which is

● *fully integrated* or embedded within the business systems and procedures of partner organisations.

In this last phase the transactional activities between organisations are routinised and embedded in the relationship and business processes. The phases are set out in Table 10.4.

These phases of development need to be considered alongside the technological platform that the organisation wishes to operate. Essentially the Internet provides Web site access for everyone. However, an extranet platform enables an organisation to restrict access to a number of selected organisations/people. For example, end-user customers, intermediaries and suppliers might all use an extranet to provide benefits that all can share and through which the host might develop competitive advantage. An intranet platform enables the use of the same browser-based technology but access is restricted to the employees of an organisation.

IMC

The development and momentum of the IMC concept may now have reached its peak (see Chapter 11). Whether the concept of integration is accepted and indeed valid is debatable, but there can be little doubt that there are genuine benefits for organisations and their stakeholders from striving to achieve the principles of IMC.

New technology has driven the IMC concept not only through the development of direct marketing opportunities but also through ecommerce. Guens (2005) argues that IMC provides the *opportunity* for organisations to integrate their communications and that ecommerce has provided the *ability* for organisations to integrate their communications. The proposition is that these two streams converge at the organisation's Web site.

TABLE 10.4 Internet utilisation – phases of development

Phase	Explanation	Technological/organisational involvement	Departments involved
Presentation or 'shop window' – look what we have to offer	Web site projects name and identity of organisation and displays products and services	Low – externally managed Web site – Internet	Marketing, IT, external Web agency
Enquiry '. . . and contact us to find out more'	Presentation still important but site now permits registration, email enquiries and limited interrogation	Medium – externally managed Web site, staff access to email – Internet and possibly intranet	Marketing, IT, external Web agency, sales or call centre staff
Interaction – 'buy online and we will deliver'	Stronger two-way communication is established and full interaction is enabled	High – requires security and invoicing; logistics to convert online order to standard order systems – Internet and intranet	Marketing, IT, sales, accounts, dedicated process staff
Embeddedness – Web is fully integrated with business systems and procedures of partner organisations	Web integrates all business activities throughout the organisation, suppliers and customers	Fully integrated ordering, supply, marketing, sales, invoicing, delivery and customer services – Internet, intranet and extranet	All staff and external partners

The Web site has become a central point for an organisation's digital communications.

The Web site has become a central point for an organisation's digital communications. It is a point at which the complexity of messages that arise from different functional areas and departments can be integrated and managed together with the array of messages emanating from a variety of external stakeholders.

Future technologies and marketing communications

The Internet lies at the heart of current and future marketing applications of new technology but Karnell (2004) suggests that future developments will be based around three main themes: wireless networking, smart devices and intelligent communications services.

Wireless networking refers to communication between computers and related devices that does not require the use of cables and wires. It works through the use of low-powered radio frequency and infrared waves. Protocols such as Wi-FI (wireless fidelity) means that wireless-enabled computers or personal digital assistants (PDAs) can connect to the Internet if they are within 15 metres of an access point.

Radio frequency identification (RFID) tags contain chips and work on the basis that a radio signal, received by an antenna, activates the chip, which in turn transmits a

RFID tags contain chips and work on the basis that a radio signal, received by an antenna, activates the chip, which in turn transmits a unique code identifying the object that the tag is attached to.

unique code identifying the object that the tag is attached to (Blau, 2003). In addition to security applications, retail staff are able to use handheld devices to check stock and to assemble orders in the established way but these tags are also used to trigger screens within changing rooms, enabling customers to view video clips of the merchandise. Using video cameras and plasma screens, in place of mirrors, customers are able to see themselves from behind (Dean, 2003).

RFID tags do not need line-of-sight reading, as with barcodes, which means that hundreds of tags can be read in a second, saving considerable amounts of time. In addition, these radio tags are capable of providing not only the universal product codes as used in barcodes but they can also provide a unique identifying code. This means that promotions can be based on particular groups of items purchased and changed very quickly in response to changing market or competitive conditions. Consumers can use this technology to sample games and music CDs.

ViewPoint 10.7   Metro Future Store

The building used by the Metro Future Store in Germany is completely covered by a wireless network. Through this network various mobile devices such as personal shopping assistants (PSAs) and personal digital assistants (PDAs) and static devices such as electronic shelf labels (ESLs), check-out points and flat screen displays for product promotion are all interlinked.

PSAs are for the use of shoppers whose shopping trolleys have a touch screen mini-computer linked to the network and an integrated scanner. This is referred to as a PSA and allows shoppers to scan their own purchases, and the data to be transmitted to the checkout in advance of the shopper.

The PDAs are also linked to the network and are used by store employees to check stock by directly accessing Metro's merchandise management system at any time and at any point in the store. Using VoIP (Voice over Internet Protocol) technology, it is planned for the PDAs to receive 'soft phone' functionality, enabling staff to make calls in addition to sending messages or downloading information.

Source: Adapted from Fill (2005).

Barcode technology is a mature technology and will gradually be replaced by radio tags as the cost of the embedded chips reduces. RFID technology is being used to develop electronic labelling systems and smart shelves. Connected to the store network, smart shelves have readers embedded in them that will enable the main system to be informed when merchandise is removed, and will then automatically trigger a request for shelf replenishment.

Out-of-store applications of wireless technologies will grow as the Internet becomes an information utility where corporations, individuals and governments will access and interact with information anywhere, anytime and, most importantly, with any device. For marketers, this increased access means greater scope for targeted and personalised delivery of timely marketing communications messages and increased opportunities for co-branding and marketing alliances.

Increased access means greater scope for targeted and personalised delivery of timely marketing communications messages and increased opportunities for co-branding and marketing alliances.

Smart devices or information-powered devices have continuous Internet access and can be incorporated within furniture and furnishings, clocks and watches, carpets, refrigerators and freezers, and lighting and security systems. These devices can process information, signals, graphics, animation, video and audio and have the ability to exchange such information with another smart device. These devices, which will be able to receive up-to-date news, traffic, weather and sports information, have the potential to radically change the way consumers interact with brands. In addition to obvious above-the-line communications, this technology opens up opportunities for sponsorship and promotional programmes.

ViewPoint 10.8   WatchPad

IBM and Citizen have joined forces to develop the WatchPad. Among other things this device will use short-range wireless connectivity to enable users to remotely control various devices, such as laptop computers, view email messages and calendar entries, send and receive text and voice commands to other computers.

Source: Adapted from Fill (2005).

Intelligent communication services are smart devices that are integrated with the Internet. This will enable them to detect changes in their environment and in doing so prompt users to act in particular ways. Karnell suggests that this will enable marketers to track products and consumers and deliver intelligent real-time, proximity-specific and ultra-personalised information. So, as a freezer senses that the last pizza (previously tagged) has been removed it will prompt, via text, visuals or voice that a new pizza is required. This may in time be remotely linked through to a specified store, which will automatically add the item to the consumer's standing order for home delivery.

These devices could be used in store enabling retailers and brand owners to interact with consumers while they are shopping or they might be used to make purchasing and brand choice decisions in the home. Used as the ultimate form of personalised marketing communications, messages can be delivered, at the appropriate time in the consumption cycle, about products and services, lower prices or promotional offers (e.g. time-based electronic coupons); all driven by each customer's individual consumption patterns and transaction history, they have the potential to transform the shopping experience.

Biometrics

The film *Minority Report* contains a sequence in which Tom Cruise enters a futuristic store, at which point his iris/retina is scanned, checked, cross-referenced and a stream of products and services related to his preferences are then presented to him. While this futuristic view of technology-enabled, personalised marketing communications has yet to be commercially resolved and implemented, the concept and use of biometric technology applications are currently being developed. At present a range of applications are available or are at an advanced stage of development. Das (2004) refers to hand geometry, fingerprint, voice/speech, iris/retinal and face recognition facilities with earlobe, brain mapping, odour and gait recognition at an early stage of development.

The WatchPad, mentioned earlier, uses a fingerprint sensor to identify the owner of a watch, thus replacing the need for passwords, improving security and with it trust, and reducing perceived risk and reasons not to buy.

Many of these biometric technologies have been used within security-related environments to identify and authenticate individuals. Some voice recognition technologies have been used successfully in back office situations and are currently considered to be best used to gather simple information such as names, addresses and/or supporting applications such as voicemail account management through a preset menu of choices (Rockwell, 2004).

> Many of these biometric technologies have been used within security-related environments to identify and authenticate individuals.

Although these voice recognition technologies have the potential to reduce customer contact centre costs there are difficulties associated with dialects and regional accents (Rockwell). In addition, it is not yet possible to induce real-time dialogue with smart devices in order to communicate personalised product offers. Although in development it should be remembered that the advent of these facilities will also prompt a series of privacy and personal freedom-related issues.

Summary

The growth of information systems and technology has been astonishing in recent years and has had a defining impact on many aspects of marketing communications. Through the Internet and Web-enabled devices and software applications, organisations have, at varying speeds, attempted to harness and adapt new technologies in order to find a competitive advantage and drive improved added value for their stakeholders. Among the many benefits of IST interactivity has had a strong impact on the shape and nature of marketing communications. Interactivity through machines with people is now complemented with interactivity with machines. The Internet has two main elements, distribution and communication, and when these are applied together ecommerce opportunities, together with Internet marketing, provide opportunities to transform the way business is conducted, shape the relationships between organisations and provide consumers with increased search convenience, lower prices and access to a wealth of information.

New technologies are changing the way marketing communications is used by organisations, witnessed by an increased use of below-the-line tools and a renewed interest in using communications to influence customer behaviour. The establishment of the Internet has led many organisations to reconsider the pattern and format of their marketing communications strategies and some have not only taken the opportunity to reconfigure the way they communicate with their target audiences but also enabled their customers to reconfigure the way they interact with their preferred suppliers.

Perhaps above all else, advances in technology have provided a catalyst for greater degrees of personalisation and one-to-one communications. It has also challenged the balance of marketing communications mix and made IMC a more feasible strategy.

Review questions

1. Prepare brief notes explaining how the database has influenced marketing communications.

2. Discuss ways in which use of the Internet has assisted organisations to develop their marketing communications.

3. Identify different ways in which multimedia applications might be configured.

4. What are the primary differences between b2b and b2c ecmmerce models?

5. Explain CRM and identify three reasons why it appears not to have satisfied many client organisations.

6. List a range of ecommerce business models.

7. Discuss the nature of customer contact centres and consider how these might develop in the future.

8. Explain each of the four stages (phases) of Internet development in an organisation.

9. Prepare notes identifying how IST has affected the structure of the marketing communications industry.

10. Explain the meaning of biometrics and consider how biometrics and wireless technologies might affect marketing communications in the future.

MINI-CASE
'To be the best water company in the UK'

Mini-case written by Beth Rogers, Senior Lecturer, University of Portsmouth Business School

Some might think this a vision too far for a company bottom of its industry's customer service league table. However, Yorkshire Water did go from tenth out of ten to second in five years, and from being one of the most hated companies in the UK in 1996 to winning a string of customer service awards in 2003. Its turnaround involved a successful implementation of customer relationship management processes and technology.

This was at a time when many CRM projects were being dismissed as costly failures. According to an article in *Harvard Business Review* in February 2002 (Rigby *et al.*), 55 per cent of all CRM projects were not producing results and one in five users reported that CRM had actually damaged their customer relationships.

So, Yorkshire Water confronted its own history and a business trend of the day and made CRM work for the company, its customers and its shareholders. How did they manage such a massive change?

Yorkshire Water

When water management was privatised in the UK in 1989, Yorkshire Water was turned from a public body into a public limited company. It is the ninth largest water company in the world, delivering clean and waste water services to 2.2 million households and 140,000 businesses. Yorkshire Water's business customers include Ministry of Defence sites in the Portsmouth area. It handles up to 2 million calls a year from customers and completes over 1 million items of maintenance and reactive work, plus 28,000 operational visits per year.

Yorkshire Water (www.yorkshirewater.com) is part of the Kelda Group (www.kelda.com).

The background

In 1995 there was a hot, dry summer in the UK, causing a drought. Yorkshire didn't run out of water, but communication with customers was very poor and the national media lambasted the company. By 1998 Yorkshire Water was bottom of the OFWAT (UK water industry regulator) customer service league table. Pressure from the regulator and from government increased. In 2000 a 14.5 per cent price cut was imposed on the company, and deep cuts were inevitable. Great improvements in efficiency were needed to make up for this.

In the meantime, managers at Yorkshire Water had recognised the need for change. A new chairman and managing director were appointed in 1996 and following initial 'Voice of the Customer' research in 1997 work began on a programme of change to make Yorkshire Water the best water company in the UK. In March 1999 the Board approved the £28 million programme. This focused first on process change achievable within the constraints of the old system while planning a major IT overhaul. Back office systems were changed first, to avoid disruption to customers, followed by three phases of implementation from October 2001 to May 2002. By 2003 the improvement in the customers' experience was so dramatic that Yorkshire Water won two customer service awards and a poll of business customers for best utility in the UK.

Researching the customer experience

IT industry analysts Gartner praised Yorkshire Water for explicitly starting its change programme with the customer experience. The company invested considerable effort into understanding what customers wanted from them. The Voice of the Customer survey, which first identified what the company needed to do, has been regularly repeated and updated ever since. On the basis of the first survey, Yorkshire Water defined five customer service principles:

log all customer contacts – per individual
make commitments to the customer and fulfil them
offer appointments within a two-hour time-slot and keep them
own the problem to resolution – the customer should not have to chase
check that the customer feels that the job has been completed.

Strategy

As in all good plans, information and analysis resulted in robust strategy. The Board understood that enterprise-wide change and 'end-to-end'

customer processes were needed. The CRM project, which was 60 per cent of the change programme, was called ICOM (Integrated Customer and Operations Management). It was based on a strategy called 'R-cubed' – to give customers reliable service, responsiveness and fast resolution of problems – as required by the feedback from the research. The core integration was between the customer service organisation and the field service engineers. The concept of 'customer' became individuals rather than a property address. Key account management was introduced for top business customers.

Cultural change

Executive commitment to the programme was very visible. The programme manager reported to the Board every week. The change team included 100 people from different disciplines and departments, and external service partners. At least 250 briefings were held to challenge current ways of working, reduce fear, manage expectations and build commitment. There was no 'dawn of a new era', but gradual change. Call centre agents were quite adaptive. While field service engineers were more apprehensive, they were convinced by the new professionalism that the system could give them. Some 8,000 person-days of training were delivered, with 'a day in the life' format, showing people how their job should improve. Post-implementation, local area experts are in place to support colleagues and promote best practice.

Call centres/contact centres were a controversial element of CRM systems in the 1990s, causing frustration to many customers and regarded as 'white-collar sweat shops' by trade unions. Yorkshire Water's contact centre was spun off in 1999 to become a separate company within the Kelda Group, called Loop. The company has a proactive approach to employee satisfaction, and in 2003 was the only call centre in the *Sunday Times* Top 100 UK Companies To Work For. Its staff turnover is 15 per cent versus an industry average of 25–35 per cent. Each employee has a personal development plan, and attention is paid to work/life balance. The 140-seat call centre has 350 staff on varying work patterns. Yorkshire Water was also the first water company to extend its contact hours to improve customer service.

Processes

Yorkshire Water re-engineered all customer-facing and work management processes before applying technology. The single, complete view of all inter-actions with the customers was a core principle. There had to be a real-time integrated information flow between the contact centre, work management, field service engineers and contractors.

Use of technology

Yorkshire Water is an 'early adopter' of information technology – it is seen as a means to achieve stra-tegic advantage.

The ICOM system includes enterprise resource planning, CRM and work scheduling. Field service engineers have 'ruggedised' wireless laptops to access the systems. ICOM is integrated with billing, asset management, financial systems and geograph-ical information systems by a middleware product. A total of 28 systems are integrated through 213 interfaces. 'Designing, testing and implementing the integration hub was the most significant tech-nical challenge,' says Duncan Bennett, programme manager.

Since implementation, hardware and software upgrades have been applied to keep the system 'best in class'.

Measurement

In order to improve, Yorkshire Water first had to decide where it was and what it was going to meas-ure. Of course, financial measures were important, but it was also critical to climb the OFWAT customer service league table. The OFWAT table is made up of performance against a number of criteria such as time to answer a call and resolution on first call. However, some of these measures are blunt and Yorkshire Water decided that it had to do more. It has established a virtuous circle of consultative research and satisfaction feedback, enabling cus-tomers to be the qualitative judge of customer ser-vice success.

Given the functionality of the system, it has also been able to monitor operational performance on a daily basis.

Follow-up

Nothing has stood still since May 2002. Processes, technology, morale and customer service are being continually improved.

Return on Investment

According to the *Financial Times* (December 2002): 'Yorkshire Water has turned itself from one of the most ridiculed companies of the late 1990s to one of the most respected.'

£28 million is a huge investment. Any company would want a substantial return. Yorkshire Water is now seeing more than £8.5 million returns per annum from improved efficiency alone.

Revenue was not a necessary metric, given Yorkshire Water's monopoly position. However, the company has been able to win new business cus-tomers outside of Yorkshire based on its improved performance. Also, Loop, as an independent com-pany within the Kelda Group, can offer the YW multi-media contact centre model to other companies. Its external customers include the Wales Tourist Board and B&Q.

In terms of operational success, Yorkshire Water has recorded a 20 per cent decrease in call volume from 2000–3, repeat calls were down 10 per cent, written complaints were down 40 per cent, resolution on first contact reached 70+ per cent; 98 per cent of appointments are kept, 98 per cent of call backs are kept, and wasted field service visits are down 40 per cent. All these results indicate a qualitative improvement in operational effectiveness and cus-tomer service.

A milestone in customer service success was that Yorkshire Water was the first water company to open to callers in the evenings and at weekends, increas-ing contact hours from 37 to 85 without needing additional engineering staff.

In terms of improved brand value, in 2003 Yorkshire Water won the Gartner European CRM Excellence Award and the Best Use of Technology category at the UK Customer Service Awards. It was also voted top of all UK utilities for customer satisfaction in a poll of business customers.

Acknowledgement

The author of this mini-case wishes to acknow-ledge the valuable contribution of Duncan Bennett, the manager of Yorkshire Water's 'Programme for Change'. Without his willingness to be interviewed and to provide materials this case could not have been prepared. Readers might like to know that our initial enquiry via the Yorkshire Water Web site reached the right person and a response was received within 24 hours!

Sources

Material supplied by Yorkshire Water

An interview with Duncan Bennett, programme manager (current title), Yorkshire Water

Gartner research note: 'Yorkshire Water wins CRM Award with business and IT change', August 2003

AMDOC case study material

Syntegra case study material

Local Internet sites, e.g. thisisbradford.co.uk

Questions

1 What do you find particularly inspiring about this case?

2 Why do you think Yorkshire Water succeeded where others had failed? Comment on factors in the business environment and water industry, as well as internal factors.

3 Can you think of companies in highly competitive environments that have achieved 'zero to hero' customer focus transformations?

4 What can you learn from this about implementing: (a) CRM, and (b) any marketing strategy?

Further reading

'People to people: five lists for ensuring that employees drive CRM success', Ian Corner and Beth Rogers, featured on: www.wnim.com

Rogers, B. and Ryals, L. (2003) Managing 'Wicked' CRM projects: the role of marketers in best practice implementation. *Customer Management*, May/June, pp. 34–7.

If you are interested in CRM, you might like to follow these Web sites:

www.crmguru.com

www.destinationcrm.com

References

Ang, L. and Buttle, F.A. (2003) ROI on CRM: a customer journey approach. *CRM Today*. Retrieved 16 August 2004 from www.crm2day.com/library/EpFlupuEZVRmkpZCHM.php.

Bickerton, P., Bickerton, M. and Simpson-Holley, K. (1998) *Cyberstrategy*. Oxford: Butterworth-Heinemann.

Blau, J. (2003) Supermarket tunes into wireless. Available at: www.computerweekly.com/articles/. Retrieved 19 April 2004.

Bocklund, L. (2003) Building the next-generation customer contact center. *Network World*. Retrieved from www.nwfusion.com/auddev/pop/ 25 August 2004.

Chaffey, D. (2003) E-marketing insights: what's new in marketing. Retrieved 27 August 2004 from www.wnim.com/archive/issue1903/emarketing.htm.

Chaffey, D., Mayer, R., Johnston, K. and Ellis-Chadwick, F. (2003) *Internet Marketing Strategy, Implementation and Practice*. 2nd edn. Harlow: Pearson Education.

Cohen, R. (1995) Interactive demand is not as high as believed. *Precision Marketing*, 25 September, p. 8.

Das, R. (2004) The application of biometric technologies: 'The Afghan Girl-Sharbat Gula'. Available online at: http://technologyexecutivesclub.com/articles/artbiometricsapplications.htm

Dean, A. (2003) High street: the new technological battleground. Retrieved 18 April 2004 from www.raeng.org.uk/news/publications/ingenia/issue18.

van Doren, D.C., Fechner, D.L. and Green-Adelsberger, K. (2000) Promotional strategies on the World Wide Web. *Journal of Marketing Communications*, 6, pp. 21–35.

Doyle, S. (2003) The big advantage of short messaging. Retrieved 16 May from www.sas.com/news.

Fill, C. (2005) Recent developments in below-the-line communications. In *Marketing Communication: Emerging Trends and Developments* (ed. A. Kimmel). Oxford: OUP.

Goften, K. (2000) Have you got permission? *Marketing*, 22 June, pp. 28–9.

Gray, R. (2000) E-tail must deliver on Web promises. *Marketing*, 2 March, p. 37.

Guens, T.W. (2005) Current and future developments in electronic commerce. In *Marketing Communication: Emerging Trends and Developments* (ed. A. Kimmel). Oxford: OUP.

Jardine, A. (1999) Traditional retailers face their high noon. *Marketing*, 16 September, pp. 22–3.

Kamakura, W.A., Wedel, M., de Rosa, F. and Mazzon, J.A. (2003) Cross-selling through database marketing: a mixed factor analyzer for data augmentation and prediction. *International Journal of Research in Marketing*, **20**(1) (March), pp. 45–65.

Kangis, P. and Rankin, K. (1996) Interactive services: how to identify and target the new markets. *Journal of Marketing Practice: Applied Marketing Science*, **2**(3), pp. 44–67.

Karnell, I. (2004) Tech watch: the future of one-to-one marketing. Available at: www.the-dma.org. Retrieved 3 May 2004.

Meyronin, B. (2004) ICT: the creation of value and differentiation in services. *Managing Service Quality*, **14**(2/3), pp. 216–25.

Nancarrow, C. and Rees, S. (2003) Market research and CRM. Retrieved 21 August 2004 from http://www.wnim.com/issue21/pages/crm.htm.

Nielsen//NetRatings (2004) Retrieved 26 August from http://www.clickz.com/stats/big_picture/geographics/article.php/3397231.

O'Malley, L. and Mitussis, D. (2002) Relationships and technology: strategic implications. *Journal of Strategic Marketing*, **10**(3) (September), pp. 225–38.

Porter, M.E. (1985) *Competitive Advantage: Creating and Sustaining Superior Performance*. New York: Free Press.

Radjou, N. (2003) Supply chain processes replace applications: 2003 to 2008. In *Achieving Supply Chain Excellence through Technology* (ed. N. Mulani), pp. 24–8. San Francisco, CA: Montgomery Research.

Rayport, J.F. and Jaworski, B.J. (2001) *E-Commerce*. Boston, MA: McGraw-Hill/Irwin.

Reid, A. (2001) Unilever continues to defy the sceptics over digital TV spots. *Campaign*, 16 February, p. 18.

Rigby, D.K., Reichheld, F.F. and Schefter, P. (2002) Avoid the four perils of CRM. *Harvard Business Review*, February, pp. 101–9.

Rockwell, M. (2004) Can voice recognition answer the call? Available at: www.wirelessweek.com/article/. Retrieved 17 April 2004.

Rogers, E.M. (1983) *Diffusion of Innovations*. 3rd edn. New York: Free Press.

Rosen, E.M. (1997) Digital TV will soon overtake the Internet. *Revolution* (July), pp. 6–7.

Ryals, L. and Payne, A. (2001) Customer relationship management in financial services: towards information-enabled relationship marketing. *Journal of Strategic Marketing*, **9**, pp. 3–27.

Ryssel, R., Ritter, T. and Gemunden H.G. (2004) The impact of information technology deployment on trust, commitment and value creation in business relationships. *Journal of Business and Industrial Marketing*, **19**(3), pp. 197–207.

Sood, B. (2002) CRM in B2B: developing customer-centric practices for partner and supplier relationships. Available online at: http://www.intelligentcrm.com/020509/508feat2_2.shtml. Accessed 28 April 2003.

Stone, M. (2002) Managing public sector customers. *What's New in Marketing*, October. www.wnim.com/. Accessed October 2002.

Stone, M. and Shan, P. (2002) Transforming the bank branch experience for customers. *What's New in Marketing*, issue 10, September. Retrieved 23 August 2004 from http://www.wnim.com/archive/issue1003/CRM%20in%20Finance.htm.

Tapp, A. and Hughes T. (2004) New technology and the changing role of marketing. *Marketing Intelligence and Planning*, **22**(3), pp. 284–96.

Thomas, D. (2003) Sainsbury's boosts supplier collaboration. *ComputerWeekly.com*, 24 October 2003. Retrieved 10 November 2003 from http://www.computerweekly.com/articles/.

Whitely, J. (2000) Understanding the online buyer. *Admap* (July/August), pp. 14–16.

Wightman, T. (2000) E-CRM: the critical dot-com discipline. *Admap*, April, pp. 46–8.

Strategies
and planning

Chapters 11-17

The main theme of this part of the book concerns the management of marketing communications.

This part opens with a consideration of a core concept, integrated marketing communications. It explores ideas concerning the nature and validity of this concept and suggests that the concept is used in a number of ways by both academics and practitioners. This chapter adopts a strategic perspective, one that is extended into the following chapter. Here, in Chapter 12, issues about strategy and planning are discussed and readers are encouraged to consider the interaction between the two elements. The marketing communications planning framework is introduced at this point.

Chapter 13 examines the nature and role of objectives in marketing communications and then considers the importance of positioning activities. This is an important strategic aspect of this subject and one that is supported by product and corporate branding issues which are the focus of the following two chapters. The main point within these chapters is not branding itself but the role marketing communications plays in the branding process.

The final two chapters in this part review matters concerning the allocation of financial resources and how campaigns should be evaluated. Chapter 16 looks at the various techniques used by organisations to develop suitable budgets for marketing communications and debates the efficiency and effectiveness of these approaches. Chapter 17 is an important one because it looks at the evaluation of marketing communications activities from both a campaign and promotional tool perspective. It is important because evaluation is often overlooked in terms of its impact and contribution to the overall process.

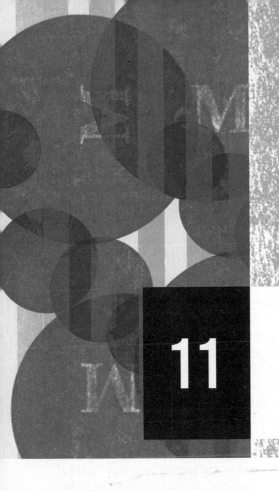

Integrated marketing communications

11

Integrated marketing communications are more likely to occur when organisations attempt to enter into a coordinated dialogue with their various internal and external audiences. The communication tools used in this dialogue and the messages conveyed should be internally consistent with the organisation's objectives and strategies. The target audiences should perceive the communications and associated cues as coordinated, likeable and timely.

Aims and objectives

The aims of this chapter are to explore the concept of integrated marketing communications with a view to appreciating the complexities associated with this relatively new strategic approach.

The objectives of this chapter are to:

1. introduce integrated marketing communications (IMC) and establish a need for this new concept;
2. understand the possible meanings that lie behind IMC;
3. illustrate the breadth and depth of IMC as applied to organisations;
4. explain the manner in which the marketing mix communicates;
5. consider how the structures and frameworks of advertising agencies might need to change so that they are better able to work with IMC;
6. appraise the reasons for the development of IMC and the main drivers propelling its growth;
7. set out some of the main reasons why IMC is resisted and how such resistance might be best overcome.

Introduction

The tools of the promotional mix have often been regarded, by practitioners and academics, as separate, individualistic methods of communication used to deliver particular messages to particular audiences. Through the use of each promotional tool, clients were able to achieve impacts or effects *on* buyers and only each specific tool was able to achieve these impacts. Consequently, clients were required to deal with a variety of functionally different and independent organisations in order to communicate with their various audiences.

As a result, clients and suppliers of the promotional tools saw specialisation as the principal means to achieve communication effectiveness. This resulted in a proliferation of advertising agencies and the development of sales promotion houses. Public relations specialists stood off from any direct association with marketing. Personal selling had already evolved as a discrete function within organisations. This specialist approach was further emphasised by the development of trade associations and professional management groups (for example, the Institute of Practitioners in Advertising (UK) and the Institute of Sales Promotion (UK)), which seek to endorse, advance, protect and legitimise the actions of their professions and members. One of the results of this individualistic perspective and functional development of the marketing communications industry has been the inevitable opposition to the desire for change driven by clients. Improvements and new approaches to create and sustain a dialogue with buyers are now central requirements. The structural inadequacies of the marketing communication industry have served to restrain the means by which client organisations can achieve their marketing and marketing communication objectives.

> This specialist approach was further emphasised by the development of trade associations and professional management groups.

It is interesting that the rapid development of direct marketing initiatives since the second half of the 1980s and the impact the Internet has made have coincided with a move towards what has become regarded as integrated marketing communications. A further significant development has been the shift in marketing philosophies, from transaction to relationship marketing, as introduced in Chapter 1. These will be considered later.

> IMC has emerged partially as a reaction to the structural inadequacies of the industry.

IMC has emerged partially as a reaction to the structural inadequacies of the industry and the realisation by clients that their communication needs can (and should) be achieved more efficiently and effectively than previously. In other words, just as power has moved from brand manufacturers to multiple retailers and now to consumers, so power is moving from agencies to clients.

There has also been a trend away from the use of traditional communication strategies, based largely on mass communications, delivering generalised messages, to one based more on personalised, customer-oriented and technology-driven approaches, referred to as integrated marketing communications. Duncan and Everett (1993) recall that this new, largely media-oriented approach, has been referred to variously as *orchestration, whole egg* and *seamless communication*. More recent notions involve the explicit incorporation of corporate communications, reflected in titles such as integrated marketing and integrated communications. See Cornelissen (2000).

What is to be integrated?

The notion that some aspects of marketing communications should be integrated begs the question – 'What is it that needs to be integrated?' While the origins of IMC might be found in the prevailing structural conditions and the needs of particular industry participants, an understanding of what elements should be integrated in order to achieve IMC needs to be established.

What is it that needs to be integrated?

The problem with answering this question is that unless there is agreement about what IMC is then identifying appropriate elements is far from easy, practical or in anyone's best interests. Figure 11.1 shows some of the elements that need integrating.

The following represents some of the fundamental elements but readers are advised to consider some of the other issues that are raised in this chapter before confirming their views about this stimulating yet young concept.

Promotional tools

One of the early and more popular views of IMC was that the messages conveyed by each of the promotional tools should be harmonised in order that audiences perceive a consistent set of meanings within the messages they receive. One interpretation of this perspective is that the key visual triggers (design, colours, form and tag line) used in advertising should be replicated across the range of promotional tools used, including point of purchase (POP) and the sales force. At another level integration is about bringing together the promotional tools. One such combination is the closer alliance of advertising with public relations. Increasing audience fragmentation means that it is more difficult to locate target audiences and communicate with them in a meaningful way. By utilising the power of public relations to get advertisements talked about, what the trade refers to as media equivalents, so a form of communications consistency, or integration to some, becomes possible.

The rapid development of direct marketing approaches has helped some organisations bring together the different tools such that they undertake more precise roles and reinforce each other. For example, the use of direct mail and telemarketing to follow

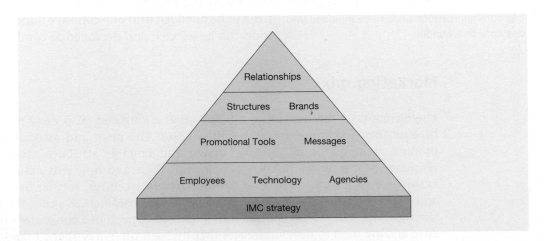

FIGURE 11.1 Elements for integration

ViewPoint 11.1   Inside-out chocolate?

UK chocolate manufacturer Cadbury's used an 'integrated' campaign, which encouraged consumers to send in special wrappers in return for free sports-related goods. The tools of the mix were coordinated – advertising, sales promotions, packaging, sponsorship and marketing public relations.

The problems with the campaign concern links between chocolate and sporting ability and between child-related obesity issues and chocolate consumption. Had the campaign been considered from an audience perspective then a different campaign strategy might have been developed.

Web-enabled communications, customer care centres and sales promotions can be linked together, through database applications, and all are designed to communicate the same core message.

through on an ad campaign is commonplace, but now Web-enabled communications, customer care centres and sales promotions can be linked together, through database applications, and all are designed to communicate the same core message.

Messages

A further interpretation, at a deeper level, is that the theme and set of core messages used in any campaign should first be determined and then deployed as an integrated whole across the promotional mix (sometimes referred to as synergy). One of the differences is the recognition that mass media advertising is not always the only way to launch consumer or business-to-business promotional activities, and that a consideration of the most appropriate mix of communication tools and media might be a better starting point when formulating campaigns.

An alternative perspective of IMC is provided by Duncan and Moriarty (1998) who state quite challengingly that stakeholders (including customers) automatically integrate brand messages. This suggests that as long as the gap between the different messages (in content and meaning) is acceptable, then management's task is to manage the process and seek to narrow those gaps that may be perceived.

The belief that above-the-line and below-the-line communications need to be moulded into one cohesive bundle.

What runs through both these approaches is the belief that above-the-line and below-the-line communications need to be moulded into one cohesive bundle, from which tools can be selected and deployed as conditions require.

Marketing mix

The elements of the marketing mix, however configured, also need to be integrated because they too communicate (Smith, 1996). The price and associated values, the product, in terms of the quality, design and tangible attributes, the manner and efficiency of the service delivery people and where and how it is made available, for example the location, Web site, customer contact centres, retailer/dealer reputation and overall service quality need to be perceived by customers as a coordinated and consistent whole. These touch points with brands are aspects of a consumer's brand experience and are used to develop images that through time may shape brand reputations. Traditionally the marketing mix was expected to deliver the brand proposition. Now it is expected that all these elements will be coordinated to maximise impact and enable customers to experience the brand through pre-, actual and post-product use.

Branding

Brands are themselves a form of integration. This means that internally organisations need to be sufficiently coordinated so that the brand is perceived externally as con-

Brands are themselves a form of integration.

sistent and uniform. However, this proposition is based on the view that a brand is prepared and delivered for a single target audience, but audience and media fragmentation make this task more challenging. Audience sizes are shrinking, which means that in many situations a single audience is no longer economically viable. Brands therefore need to appeal to a number of different audiences (White, 2000) and to do this it is necessary to develop brands that appeal to diverse consumer groups. White refers to these new brands as 'chameleon' brands, which are characterised by their ability to adapt to different situations (audiences and media) yet retain a core proposition that provides a form of continuity and recognition. For example, a top of the range music system may be seen by the owner as prestigious and technically superb, by a guest at a party as ostentatiously outrageous and overpriced and by a friend as a product of clever design and marketing. All three might have developed their attitudes through different sources (e.g. different print media, exhibitions, the Internet, retail stores, word of mouth) but all agree that the brand has a common set of values and associations that are important to each of them.

The presentation of chameleon brands requires high levels of integration, a need to develop a series of innovative messages based around a core proposition. The use of a single ad execution needs to be replaced by multiple executions delivered through a variety of media, each complementing and reinforcing the core brand proposition. This means that the audience is more likely to be surprised or reminded of the brand (and its essence) through a series of refreshingly interesting messages, so raising the

---

ViewPoint 11.2 Integrated ice cream

Media investment of £7.5 million in the market-leading Magnum ice cream was designed to provide support for an integrated promotional programme across television, press, outdoor (posters) and marketing public relations. This sum represented a 65 per cent share of voice and nearly 5,000 TVRs (television ratings) (see Chapter 22). In addition, in-store support was increased to provide for improved visibility and to cut through the own-brand imitations. Also, at a time when ideas about brand 'experiences' were becoming central, Magnum became associated with the UK's first triple-loop roller coaster 'Magnum Force'.

The public relations programme sought to build on the visibility of the brand and the coverage that the Magnum Girl gained. For example, Magnum became the first brand ever to appear on the front cover of the *Sunday Mail* magazine supplement, which has the second highest circulation of Sunday newspapers. The Magnum Girl became the central point of the campaign, featuring on posters, television, in-store and press work. Each year a competition is held to find a new Magnum Girl to front the brand, in itself a positive means of securing good public relations for the brand.

With thanks to Eileen Buckwald and Wall's Ice Cream for the original material.

EXHIBIT 11.1 Magnum
The Magnum brand has achieved market leadership through strong consistent branding and positioning.
Picture reproduced with the kind permission of Bird's Eye Walls.

probability that the likeability factor (see Chapter 19) will be strengthened, along with the brand and all relevant associations.

A further dimension of the branding factor concerns the role of corporate brands and issues of corporate communications. Should these be integrated with product brand communications, and if so what are the branding strategies that should be followed?

Strategy

IMC is regarded by some as a means of using the tools of the promotional mix in a more efficient and synergistic manner. At some level this can be true but IMC requires a deeper understanding of how and where messages are created. At a strategic level, IMC has its roots in the overall business strategy of an organisation. Using Porter's (1980) generic strategies, if a low-cost strategy (e.g. Asda-Walmart) is being pursued, it makes sense to complement the strategy by using messages that either stress any price advantage that customers might benefit from or at least do not suggest extravagance or luxury. If using a differentiation focus strategy (e.g. Waitrose), price should not figure in any of the messages and greater emphasis should be placed on particular attributes that convey the added value and enable clear positioning. There is no right way (or formula) to establish IMC but there is a need to recognise that it is a developmental exercise and that it should have a strategic orientation as well as strategic outputs.

> At a strategic level, IMC has its roots in the overall business strategy of an organisation.

Employees

The next element that should be integrated concerns the recognition that IMC cannot be sustained unless it is supported by all customer-facing employees. It is generally agreed that all employees should adopt a customer focus and 'live' the brand. While this can be achieved partially through the use of training courses and in-house documentation (including electronic forms), this usually requires a change of culture and that means a longer period of adjustment and the adoption of new techniques, procedures and ways of thinking and behaving.

> IMC cannot be sustained unless it is supported by all customer-facing employees.

Once the internal reorientation has begun (but not been completed), it is possible to take the message to external audiences. As long as they can see that employees are starting to act in different ways, do care about them as customers and do know what they are talking about in support of the products and services offered, then it is likely that customers (and other stakeholders) will be supportive. IMC should be concerned with blending internal and external messages so that there is clarity, consistency and reinforcement of the organisation's (or brand's) core proposition.

> IMC should be concerned with blending internal and external messages so that there is clarity, consistency and reinforcement of the organisation's (or brand's) core proposition.

ViewPoint 11.3   Integrated employees

The Energy4U organisation operated in a business environment that was experiencing politically and economically induced change. The government had deregulated the energy industry, increased competition, and in effect changed the rules by which business was conducted.

One of the decisions taken by Energy4U was to differentiate itself through customer service, and this meant creating a brand that was of value to its markets. To do this an external brand-awareness campaign was developed using actual employees. Prior to the launch employees received a video of the campaign and a message from the senior directors explaining the background, business argument and general rationale for the branding exercise.

A linked and integrated campaign, targeted at employees, was developed in order that staff not only understood but also actively participated in the branding process. Related to Energy4U's brand promise, the internal campaign consisted of a series of themed messages. These concerned quality service, an exciting and challenging work environment, personal and career growth opportunities, the potential rewards and the need to meet customer requirements better than the competition. By developing Energy4U as an Employer of Choice not only did the company enhance the conditions and working environment for current employees it was also able to reduce employee churn rates and attract increasingly higher quality employees.

Source: Adapted from Bergstrom and Anderson (2001).

Technology

One of the main reasons spurring the interest and debate about IMC has been the development in technology (see Chapter 10). The use of technology, and in particular database technologies, has enabled marketing managers to obtain a vastly improved view of customer behaviour, attitudes and feelings towards brands. This has enabled more precise and insightful communications and the subsequent feedback and measurement facilities have further developed the overall quality of customer communications. However, the mere presence of technology does not result in effective marketing communications. Technology needs to be integrated into not just the overall information systems strategy but the marketing strategies of organisations. Technology is an enabler and to use it effectively requires integration. The effective use of technology can touch a number of areas within the IMC orbit. For example, technology can be used to develop effective Web sites, extranets and intranets, customer contact centres, databases, advertising campaigns, fulfilment processes, CRM and sales force automation. If each of these applications are deployed independently of each other then their impact will be limited. Developed within an integrated framework the potential for marketing and customer service can be tremendous.

Associated with the use of technology are issues concerning the measurement and evaluation of IMC activities. One of the criticisms of IMC is that no evaluation system has been proposed or yet implemented so that the claims made about IMC delivering superior returns can be validated (Swain, 2004). This is of course part of the planning process and so integration of all aspects of the campaign planning process is necessary.

Technology is an enabler and to use it effectively requires integration.

Agencies

Reference was made earlier and in Chapter 3 to some of the structural issues involving agencies in the marketing communications industry and the development of IMC. Agencies play a critical role in marketing communications and if IMC is to be established it cannot be accomplished without the explicit involvement of all those working on the agency side.

Apart from questions concerning the range of promotional services offered by individual agencies and whether these are all delivered by a single agency or through a network of interacting agencies, two particular issues arise. The first concerns leadership, and the other, remuneration.

With regard to leadership, should the agency or the client lead the process of developing IMC? The consensus appears to be that this is the client's role (Swain, 2004), mainly because clients are better positioned to make integration happen across their own organisation. However, Swain then points out that there is no agreement about who in the client organisation should be responsible for implementing IMC.

The second issue, remuneration, should be regarded as interrelated to the measurement factor (Swain, 2004). This is because clients see reward as a derivative of performance. The traditional remuneration system is based on activities (Spake *et al.*, 1999, cited by Swain). Commission earned from the use of media to gain awareness or change attitudes is not measured against revenue or profit performance, and is referred to as an 'activity'. Results- or 'outcome'-based systems are considered a performance measure. A move to IMC requires a change in agency performance measures and, consequently, a change in their method of remuneration.

Remuneration should be regarded as interrelated to the measurement factor.

Closer integration of agencies within the IMC process will among other things bring changes in structure, operations, performance measures, remuneration and new responsibilities within the client relationship.

Integration summary

This list of elements that need to be integrated is not exclusive. There are other influences which are particular to individual organisations that could have been included. However, consideration of these various elements suggests strongly that what is being integrated is far more than just the communication tools. Indeed, viewed holistically integration is a strategic concept that strikes at the heart of an organisation's marketing and business orientation. The word integration has been used in various ways and it is the interpretation of the word integration that determines whether integrated marketing communications is real, achievable or even practised. In many ways, reality suggests that the claims many organisations and the communications industry make in the name of IMC are simply a reflection of improved management and coordination of the communication tools. The recent interest in media neutral planning (MNP) may be inherently a good thing for the cause of improved communications and relationship development, but MNP does not address the wider strategic issues, the importance of internal communications or the structural issues of IMC on both the client and agency side.

IMC is not a theory of marketing, but the ideas inherent in the overall approach appear to hold value. What is integration to one person may be coordination to another, and until there is a theoretical base upon which to build IMC practice the phrase will continue to be misused, misunderstood and used in a haphazard and inconsistent way.

What is integration to one person may be coordination to another.

The development of IMC

As established above, early interpretations of IMC were constructed around the idea that what was to be integrated were the promotional tools and media. Scholars such as Schultz (1993) and Duncan and Everett (1993) led much of the IMC activity and many organisations were enthusiastic about the new ideas, driven by the desire to restructure internally, reduce costs and deliver consistent messages. Kitchen *et al.* (2004) refer to this as the 'inside-out' IMC approach.

The next phase was characterised by an exploration of the nature, direction and content typified by definitions that introduced management, strategy and brand development into the IMC process. Shimp (2000) among others supported the explicit introduction of these aspects to IMC.

The current interpretation has moved the IMC concept forward, this time as an audience- or customer-driven process that incorporates the relationship marketing paradigm. Gronroos (2004) and Duncan (2002) have provided valuable insights into this dimension of IMC, one which Kitchen *at al.* refer to as the 'outside-in' IMC approach.

It should be noted that while many writers, such as Kitchen and Shultz (1997 and 1998), and Duncan (2002) have written positively and consistently promoting ideas about IMC, other authors such as Cornelissen and Lock (2000), Percy *et al.* (2001) and Spotts *et al.* (1998) to name a few, have raised criticisms and have doubted the merits inherent in the concept. This dichotomy of views reveals the inherent instability of the IMC concept. Readers interested in a fuller appraisal of IMC are referred to Kitchen *et al.* (2004).

Readers should not be surprised to learn that there is no agreement about what IMC is, what it encompasses or how it should be measured. Furthermore, apart from some anecdotal comment, there is little practical evidence of the application of a strategic, customer-oriented IMC programme. There are numerous claims of IMC practice but these are little more than coordinated promotional mix activities using themed messages (inside–out). However, the IMC concept appears to have found a stronger theoretical basis upon which to develop and the realisation that a relationship orientation requires a multidisciplinary approach to trigger dialogue will help advance the concept and provide researchers with a surer footing upon which to explore the topic.

From this review it is now possible to offer a general definition of IMC, bearing in mind that no single form of IMC can be identified:

> *IMC is a strategic approach to the planned management of an organisation's communications. IMC requires that organisations coordinate their various strategies, resources and messages in order that it engage coherently and meaningfully with target audiences. The main purpose is to develop relationships with audiences that are of mutual value.*

This definition serves to link IMC with business level strategies and the importance of coherence within the organisation of the wide use of resources and messages. Implicit is the underpinning notion that IMC is necessary for the development of effective relationships and that not all relationships need be collaborative and fully relational, as so often assumed to be in many contemporary interpretations.

Serves to link IMC with business level strategies.

Reasons for the developing interest in IMC

The explosion of interest in IMC has resulted from a variety of drivers. Generally they can be grouped into three main categories: those drivers (or opportunities) that are market based, those that arise from changing communications, and those that are driven from opportunities arising from within the organisation itself. These are set out in Table 11.1.

The opportunities offered to organisations that contemplate moving to IMC are considerable and it is somewhat surprising that so few organisations have been either willing or able to embrace the approach. One of the main organisational drivers for IMC is the need to become increasingly efficient. Driving down the cost base enables managers to improve profits and levels of productivity. By seeking synergistic advantages through its communications and associated activities and by expecting managers to be able to account for the way in which they consume marketing communication resources, so integrated marketing communications becomes increasingly attractive. At the same time, organisation structures are changing more frequently and the need to integrate across functional areas reflects the efficiency drive.

> One of the main organisational drivers for IMC is the need to become increasingly efficient.

From a market perspective, the predominant driver is the reorientation from transaction-based marketing to relationship marketing. The extension of the brand

TABLE 11.1 Drivers for IMC

Organisational drivers for IMC
- Increasing profits through improved efficiency
- Increasing need for greater levels of accountability
- Rapid move towards cross-border marketing and the need for changing structures and communications
- Coordinated brand development and competitive advantage
- Opportunities to utilise management time more productively
- Provide direction and purpose for employees

Market-based drivers for IMC
- Greater levels of audience communications literacy
- Media cost inflation
- Media and audience fragmentation
- Stakeholders' need for increasing amounts and diversity of information
- Greater amounts of message clutter
- Competitor activity and low levels of brand differentiation
- Move towards relationship marketing from transaction-based marketing
- Development of networks, collaboration and alliances

Communication-based drivers for IMC
- Technological advances (Internet, databases, segmentation techniques)
- Increased message effectiveness through consistency and reinforcement of core messages
- More effective triggers for brand and message recall
- More consistent and less confusing brand images
- Need to build brand reputations and to provide clear identity cues

personality concept into brand relationships (Hutton, 1996) requires a customer consideration in terms of asking not only 'What do our customers want?' but also 'What are their values, do they trust us and are we loyal to them?' By adopting a position designed to enhance trust and commitment an organisation's external communications need to be consistent and coordinated, if only to avoid information overload and misunderstanding.

From a communication perspective, the key driver is to provide a series of triggers by which buyers can understand the values a brand stands for and a means by which they can use certain messages to influence their activities within the relationships they wish to develop. By differentiating the marketing communications, often by providing clarity and simplicity, advantages can be attained.

ViewPoint 11.4   Coordinated Bratz

The Bratz doll brand used a mix of TV and marketing PR to get coverage in 'tween' magazines, advertorials, in-store displays and gondola positions, sponsorship (with Nickleodeon) and incorporated a competition. Bratz was also linked with an established brand targeted at four-to-seven-year-olds.

The advertising was run in three phases, each reflecting a different stage of the Nickleodeon-based competition. Typically this is referred to as an integrated campaign, and although very successful in terms of market share (up from 16 per cent to over 45 per cent and outstripping Barbie's 30 per cent share) the question remains – is this really an integrated marketing communications programme?

An integrated approach should attempt to provide a uniform or consistent set of messages. These should be relatively easy to interpret and to assign meaning to. This enables target audiences to think about and perceive brands within a relational context and so encourage behaviour as expected by the source. Those organisations that try to practise IMC understand that buyers refer to and receive messages about brands and companies from a wide range of information sources. Harnessing this knowledge is a fundamental step towards enhancing marketing communications.

> An integrated approach should attempt to provide a uniform or consistent set of messages.

It seems useful to itemise the advantages and disadvantages associated with IMC. These are set out in Table 11.2. General opinion suggests that the advantages far outweigh the disadvantages and that increasing numbers of organisations are seeking to improve their IMC resource. As stated earlier, database technology and the Internet have provided great impetus for organisations to review their communications and to implement moves to install a more integrated communication strategy.

Managing IMC

The development and establishment of IMC by organisations has not been as widespread as the amount of discussion around the subject. Recent technological advances and the benefits of the Internet and related technologies have meant that organisations have had a reason to reconsider their marketing communications and have re-evaluated their approach. Whatever route taken, the development of IMC

TABLE 11.2 Advantages and disadvantages of IMC

Advantages of IMC
Provides opportunities to cut communication costs and/or reassign budgets
Has the potential to produce synergistic and more effective communications
Can deliver competitive advantage through clearer positioning
Encourages coordinated brand development with internal and external participants
Provides for increased employee participation and motivation
Has the potential to cause management to review its communication strategy
Requires a change in culture and fosters a customer focus
Provides a benchmark for the development of communication activities
Can lead to a cut in the number of agencies supporting a brand
Disadvantages of IMC
Encourages centralisation and formal/bureaucratic procedures
Can require increased management time seeking agreement from all involved parties
Suggests uniformity and single message
Tendency to standardisation might negate or dilute creative opportunities
Global brands restricted in terms of local adaptation
Normally requires cultural change from employees and encourages resistance
Has the potential to severely damage a brand's reputation if incorrectly managed
Can lead to mediocrity as no single agency network has access to all sources of communications

> The development of IMC requires change, a change in thinking, actions and expectations.

requires change, a change in thinking, actions and expectations. The changes required to achieve IMC are large and the barriers are strong. What can be observed are formative approaches to IMC and that organisations have experimented and tried out various ideas within their resource and cultural contexts.

As with many aspects of change, there is nearly always resistance to the incorporation of IMC and, if sanctioned, only partial integration has been achieved. This is not to say that integration is not possible or has not been achieved, but the path to IMC is far from easy and the outcomes are difficult to gauge with great confidence. However, it is the expectation (what level of IMC) that really matters, as it signals the degree of change that is required.

Resistance to integration

Resistance to change is partly a reflection of the experiences and needs of individuals for stability and the understanding of their environments. However, it is also a reflection, again, of the structural conditions in organisations and industry that have helped determine the expectations of managers and employees.

Eagle and Kitchen (2000) set out four principal areas or themes concerned with barriers to IMC programmes:

● power, coordination and control issues

● client skills, centralisation/organisation and cultural issues

● agency skills/talent and overall time/resource issues

● flexibility/modification issues.

While these provide a useful general overview, the following represent some of the more common, more focused reasons for the resistance to the incorporation of IMC.

Financial structures and frameworks

Resistance through finance-led corporate goals, which have dominated industry performance and expectations, has been particularly significant. The parameters set around it and the extent to which marketing communications are often perceived as a cost rather than an investment have provided a corporate environment where the act of preparing for and establishing integrative activities is disapproved of at worst or room for manoeuvre restricted at best. Furthermore, the period in which promotion activities are expected to generate returns works against the principles of IMC and the time needed for the effects to take place.

Opposition/reluctance to change

The attitudes and opinions of staff are often predictable, in the sense that any move away from tried and proven methods to areas which are unknown and potentially threatening is usually rejected. Change has for a long time been regarded with hostility and fear, and as such is normally resisted. Our apparent need for stability and general security has been a potent form of resistance to the introduction of IMC. This is changing as change itself becomes a familiar aspect of working life. Any move towards IMC therefore represents a significantly different approach to work, as not only are the expectations of employees changed but so also are the working practices and the associated roles with internal customers and, more importantly, those providing outsourcing facilities.

> Any move towards IMC therefore represents a significantly different approach to work.

Traditional hierarchical and brand management structures

Part of the reluctance to change is linked with the structure and systems inherent in many organisations. Traditional hierarchical structures and systems are inflexible and slow to cope with developments in their fast-adapting environments. These structures stifle the use of individual initiative, slow the decision-making process and encourage inertia. The brand management system, so popular and appropriate in the 1970s and early 1980s, focuses upon functional specialism, which is reflected in the horizontally and vertically specialised areas of responsibility. Brands now need to be managed by flexible teams of specialists, who are charged with responsibilities and the resources necessary to coordinate activities across organisations in the name of integration.

Attitudes and structure of suppliers and agencies

One of the principal reasons often cited as a barrier to integration is the relationship that clients have with their agencies, and in particular their advertising agencies. Generally, advertising agencies have maintained their traditional structures and methods of operating, while their clients have begun to adapt and reform themselves. The thinking behind this is that advertising agencies have tried to maintain their dominance of mass advertising as the principal means of brand development. In doing so they seek to retain the largest proportion of agency fee income, rather than having these fees diluted as work is allocated below-the-line (to other organisations). The establishment of IMC threatens the current role of the main advertising agencies. This is not to say that all agencies think and act in this way. They do not, as witnessed by the innovative approaches to restructuring and the provision of integrated resources for their clients by agencies such as St Lukes. So, while clients have seen the benefits of integrated marketing communications, their attempts to achieve them have often been thwarted by the structures of the agencies they need to work with and by the attitudes of their main agencies.

Perceived complexity of planning and coordination

The complexity associated with integrating any combination of activities is often cited as a means for delaying or postponing action. Of greater significance are the difficulties associated with coordinating actions across departments and geographic boundaries. IMC requires the cooperation and coordination of internal and external stakeholder groups. Each group has an agenda which contains goals that may well differ from or conflict with those of other participants.

IMC requires the cooperation and coordination of internal and external stakeholder groups.

For example, an advertising agency might propose the use of mass media to address a client's needs, if only because that is where its specialist skills lie. However, direct marketing might be a more appropriate approach to solving the client's problem, but because there is no established mechanism to coordinate and discuss openly the problem/solution, the lead agency is likely to have its approach adopted in preference to others.

Implementing IMC

The restraints that prevent the development of IMC need to be overcome. Indeed, many organisations that have made significant progress in developing IMC have done so by instigating approaches and measures that aim to reduce or negate the impact of the barriers that people put up to prevent change. The main approaches to overcoming the barriers are as follows.

Adopting a customer-focused philosophy

The adoption of a customer-focused approach is quite well established within marketing departments. However, this approach needs to be adopted as an organisation-wide approach, a philosophy that spans all departments and which results in unified cues to all stakeholders. In many cases, agencies need to adopt a more customer-oriented approach and be able and willing to work with other agencies, including those below-the-line.

Training and staff development programmes

A move towards IMC cannot be made without changes in the expectations held by employees within the client and agency sectors. Some of the key processes that have been identified as important to successful change management need to be used. For example, the involvement and participation of all staff in the process is in itself a step to providing motivation and acceptance of change when it is agreed and delivered.

Appointing change agents

The use of change agents, people who can positively affect the reception and implementation of change programmes, is important. As IMC should span an entire organisation, the change agent should be a senior manager, or preferably director, in order to signal the importance and speed at which the new perspective is to be adopted. Some organisations have experimented with the appointment of a single senior manager who is responsible for all internal and external communications.

Planning to achieve sustainable competitive advantage

In order to develop competitive advantage, some organisations have restructured by removing levels of management, introducing business reprocessing procedures and even setting up outsourcing in order that they achieve cost efficiencies and effectiveness targets. Prior to the implementation of these delayering processes, many organisations were (and many still are) organised hierarchically.

Back in 1997 Brown rightly stated that the emergence and establishment of IMC will only have a real chance of success once the industry matures, becomes market oriented and leaves behind issues concerning client–agency complications and in many cases traditional brand management systems, most designed to prevent the development of synergies or shared knowledge. These issues have not yet been resolved and IMC in practice remains ill-defined, and superficial. What is required therefore is a restructuring and redesignation of who manages communications, and this requires a planned approach. It is evident that current systems, processes, procedures and structures are not suitable to support and sustain a planned approach to enable the full development and delivery of IMC.

IMC in practice remains ill-defined, and superficial.

Finally, *total* IMC (integration of all marketing and corporate communications) is achieved when all external agencies, outsourcing providers and partners work with the organisation in such a way that customers perceive consistency in the promises and actions the organisation makes, and are satisfied with the organisation's attempts to anticipate and satisfy customer needs and the results that they seek from their relationships with the brand or organisation.

Media neutral planning

The media neutral planning (MNP) approach emerged partly as a response to criticism of IMC and partly as an attempt to articulate the potential practice of IMC. For many MNP is integration under a different guise, but one of the strengths of the concept is that it openly focuses on the needs of clients and agencies. It attempts to stimulate the use of a communication mix that is driven by the needs of a target audience and not those of the communication industry. This means that rather than keep recommending that clients use mass media communications, which have traditionally rewarded agencies through a more than generous commission system, a more balanced mix of tools and media be adopted in order to be more effective and efficient. One of the main reasons for the interest in IMC is the potential to reduce costs. The rise in some media costs, most notably television through the 1990s, the specialised and independent nature of the agency side of the industry, the proliferation of media opportunities and the splintering of audiences, and the increasing clamour for measures of return on investment in communications, have led to a reappraisal of the role and nature of marketing communications and the emergence of MNP ideas. As clients have tried to reduce costs they have made greater

Attempts to stimulate the use of a communication mix that is driven by the needs of a target audience.

use of both through- and below-the-line tools. Agencies, interested in preserving margins, have attempted to maintain the prominence of advertising in their media plans but have reduced the emphasis on television advertising or have sought better deals through use of multiple TV channel mixes, improved negotiation and more alliances. Some client organisations (e.g. Kraft, Kellogg's, Unilever and Procter & Gamble) have moved, if unintentionally, towards a form of coordinated marketing communication activity. These organisations have reduced their reliance on above-the-line media and have attempted to move towards the use of below-the-line tools in order to reduce costs and deliver consistent messages in an attempt to cut through the increasing clutter. Ray (2002) refers to organisations such as Nike, Reebok and Alliance & Leicester who have practised MNP; however, he also refers to some of the problems, such as structures, areas of expertise and attitudes, faced by agencies attempting to offer a more neutral media approach for their clients.

ViewPoint 11.5   Boots uses MNP

The launch by Boots of its Intelligent Colour Foundation was an important opportunity to support the contemporary, fashionable image of the No. 7 brand. The revolutionary product blends to the colour of an individual's skin and only requires the user to decide between three shades of light, medium and dark.

As part of the planning process Boots decided to explore the use of MNP and formed a cross-disciplinary team to improve the level of interaction between departments and to optimise planning. The MNP team consisted of representatives of the brand, consumer insight, direct and relationship marketing (through the Advantage Card), PR, and communication channel planning.

It was generally accepted that PR would play a critical role, but rather than rely on TV and magazine advertising it was decided to augment the plan with direct mail using the Boots Advantage Card database. It was thought this would be more cost effective than to invest further in other media, particularly TV. In order to measure the impact of this neutral approach the planning team used two key measurement tools in order to avoid the misleading sales and awareness measures.

The first of these was a store-based model that could identify sales effect on a store-by-store basis thereby enabling the identification of stores by campaign area, e.g. with/without TV, with/without mail, with/without in-store promotions, etc. The second was a tracking study that would identify actual exposure to different media by means of a combination of viewing/reading questions together with the establishment of two matched samples to enable real comparisons of mailed versus non-mailed respondents. The tracking study measured awareness, product understanding, interest and image.

The detailed results are confidential but showed clearly that including mail in the mix added value, and Boots became more supportive of integrated communications and a media neutral approach.

For more information about this ViewPoint visit: www.brandrepublic.com/think/.

The drive behind the development of MNP appears to be concerned more with reducing the emphasis that television advertising plays in media plans, rather than the formulation of distinct media plans that deliver advertising messages in the most effective way, regardless of media selection. Many of those that support media neutral approaches are often quoted using examples that involve a mix of tools and media.

he drive behind the development of MNP
ppears to be concerned more with reducing
he emphasis that television advertising
lays in media plans.

MNP recognises that mass media advertising
is not always the most appropriate way.

MNP recognises that mass media advertising is not always the most appropriate way to launch or develop consumer or business-to-business promotional activities, and that a consideration of the most suitable mix of communication tools might be a better starting point when formulating campaigns. Advertising alone cannot carry the weight of a brand necessary to build and sustain the desired associations. Public relations, sales promotions and field marketing (merch-andising) for example, have increasingly important roles to play in establishing and sustaining a brand. However, where advertising is used, the changing media landscape and the increasing penetration of new technology means that a greater use of cross-media planning approaches is likely to enhance the effectiveness of a campaign and reduce costs, especially if previous campaigns used television as the primary media. The traditional model of media planning whereby a primary and perhaps two or three secondary media are scheduled over a five-week campaign has now to be surpassed by a more contemporary promotional mix that uses a cross-media plan combining new and old media and which is appropriate to target audience preferences and the context of the marketing communications activities.

Therefore it might be interpreted that media neutral mixes represent the response of the agency side of the marketing communications industry while IMC represents the client side approach to managing their marketing communications in a more effective and strategic manner. MNP should not be about mixing tools and media but should be regarded as an integral part of IMC. However, IMC is not the same as MNP.

The development and delivery of a marketing communications programme that repeatedly delivers significant value cannot be based solely on media-neutral planning or loose notions of IMC. What is necessary is the development of a strategic marketing communications approach that delivers a total brand experience (Tobaccowala and Kugel, 2001). This requires a coordinated approach to the selection and implementation of the right promotional tools and media that will deliver messages which are of significant value to the target audience. However, it also requires the integration of a cross-functional, multi-audience strategic approach to marketing communications, one that delivers a brand experience for the target audience.

Requires the integration of a cross-
functional, multi-audience strategic approach
to marketing communications, one that
delivers a brand experience for the target
audience.

Open Planning

In many ways media neutral planning is an approach to planning where all media have equal probability of selection and those that are chosen are deemed the best vehicles to achieve the media plan's objectives. Although there are many benefits, such as changing attitudes and perhaps reducing some costs, the neutrality perspective seeks to address industry issues about the planning process and the thinking the incumbents undertake, rather than to demonstrate concern with audience issues.

In an attempt to move thinking a step forward the Open Planning concept was developed by Jenkinson, who in 2002/3 coordinated a panel of leading marketers who shared a goal to simplify the media neutral planning concept. The main goal was to reappraise the way organisations consider their processes and thinking about marketing communication activities with a view to optimising their communication potential. The MNP group argues that this requires rethinking the way communication disciplines (tools) and media are used, to develop new methods of evaluating communication activity and to accelerate the speed at which organisations are able to integrate their communications with their business and marketing strategies.

TABLE 11.3 Action areas within the Open Planning approach (adapted from Jenkinson and Sain, 2004)

Action area	Explanation
Disciplines	Any promotional tool (i.e. discipline) can be used with any medium to achieve stated business and marketing objectives.
Media	Any medium can be used, by any tool (i.e. discipline), in almost all mixes. This means redefining media to mean anything that conveys a message to an audience. A salesperson becomes a medium.
Channels	Any mix of disciplines within a single medium becomes an open channel.
Process	All agencies (and others) should be involved with the thinking and planning process at the outset, to determine the message and goals before any resources are allocated (i.e. budgets).
Structure	The communication process should be driven by the communication preferences of a target audience (or community) rather than the silo structure-based functional specialisation present in much of the industry today.
Relationships	The relationship between client and agency should be open and functional. Agency remuneration should be based on the achievement of brand goals and not commission based on media choice.
Results	Defining more precise communication goals that enable a level playing field for all disciplines, media and agencies to maximise their contribution.
Tools	Use of media planning tools that embrace all touch points with customers.

Open Planning is concerned with eight action areas, each of which contributes to the process of MNP.

The MNP group has proposed a series of new approaches based mainly on ideas concerning Open Planning. Open Planning is concerned with eight action areas, each of which contributes to the process of MNP. These action areas are set out in Table 11.3. Readers wishing to know more should visit (www.openplanning.org.uk).

Thinking in terms of these action areas should promote marketing communications that are audience centred rather than promulgate the previous model, which was focused on the needs of the communication industry. See Figure 11.2.

Client structures and IMC

Clients have also embraced IMC and its influence on their structures. The hierarchical structures common in many organisations in the period up to the 1970s have been subject to attack. In search of survival in recession and increasing profits and dividends in times of plenty, organisations have sought to restructure and realign themselves with their environment. Hierarchies delivered a management structure that delegated authority in compartmentalised units. The brand management system that accompanied this structural approach provided a straitjacket and gave only partial authority to incumbents. At the same time, responsibility for pricing, channel management, personal selling and public relations activities was split off and allocated to a number

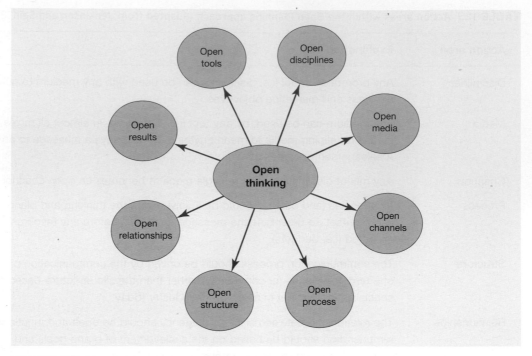

FIGURE 11.2 The eight action areas of Open Planning

The likelihood of internal integration has been hampered by the structure of the organisation and the way in which structural units were assembled.

of others. It follows from this that the likelihood of internal integration has been hampered by the structure of the organisation and the way in which structural units were assembled.

The restructuring process has resulted in organisations that are delayered and leaner. This means that the gap between senior management and those within the operating core (Mintzberg, 1996) is both smaller and now capable of sustaining viable internal communications that are truly two-way and supportive.

Increasingly organisations are operating in overseas or cross-border markets. For a deeper account of the issues concerning international marketing communications, readers are referred to Chapter 30. However, as organisations develop structurally, from international to multinational to global and transnational status, so the need to coordinate internally and to integrate internal communications becomes ever more vital to sustain integrated marketing communications (Grein and Gould, 1996). Internal marketing (Chapter 32) is becoming more popular with clients (and agencies) as it is realised that employees are important contributors to corporate identity programmes and invaluable spokespersons for the products they market. Internal communications can help not only to inform and remind/reassure but also to differentiate employees in the sense that they understand the organisation's direction and purpose, appreciate what the brand values are and so identify closely with the organisation as a whole. This is a form of integration from which marketing communications can benefit.

ViewPoint 11.6   Charities and IMC

This campaign, which sought to stop cruelty to children, had a number of integrated communication characteristics. The ambitious targets, range of activities and the huge number of people involved needed an integrated marketing communications campaign to make it succeed.

To start with there was a range of stakeholders involved: police, parents, teachers, businesses, agencies, the media and, of course, children. All needed to be part of the communications. The strategy was based around two main phases. The first was a strong pull campaign directed at the public and designed to raise awareness of child cruelty, and the second step was action oriented. In parallel there was a strategy designed to communicate with businesses in order to generate funds, goodwill and support.

The overall profile of the organisation (the NSPCC) was also to be raised and communications needed to ensure that the integrity of the organisation and those associated with it was maintained. In addition, all communications had to be consistent. The promotional mix used to create a dialogue with the public used public relations, TV, posters, field marketing, direct marketing, direct mail, telemarketing and a Web site.

In the first phase, public relations was used at the initial stages of the campaign to help create awareness. Public address systems at railway stations and airports were used as a reminder mechanism. A national TV campaign, supported by posters, broke soon after the public relations in order to raise awareness and provoke the question within each individual, 'What can I do?' The message strategy was very emotional and used strong imagery to create shock and attention.

The heavy TV campaign looked to generate 600 TVRs, 85 per cent coverage at 7.1 OTS (opportunities to see). The supporting poster campaign used 48 sheets on 3,500 sites designed to deliver 55 per cent coverage with 21 OTS. Initial enquiries in response to this wave of communications were handled by an automated telemarketing bureau.

In the second phase the aim was to provide the public with an answer to the question that the advertising had provoked, namely to sign the pledge and/or volunteer as a donor or fundraiser. An envelope picked up on the TV creative treatment, repeating as a subdued background motif the image of nursery wallpaper with a teddy bear covering its eyes with its paws: 'Don't close your eyes to cruelty to children'. This was to be delivered to 23 million postboxes, as a doordrop campaign.

It was thought that the doordrop letter addressed to 'Dear Householder' might offend established donors. To avoid this 160,000 best donors were sent an early warning letter in advance of the campaign breaking in order to get their support. Another million received personal letters just ahead of the doordrop. It was expected that the bulk of enquiries would come from the doordrop action and these were to be handled through personal telemarketing responses (inbound). The Web site was also adapted in order that it would be able to accept pledges. In addition to this, the campaign utilised a call-to-action weekend with volunteers manning 2,000 sites around the country, including most city centres, to remind and raise cash donations.

The promotional mix used to communicate with businesses involved sponsorship, direct mail/information pack and the Internet. Sponsorship deals were made available enabling businesses to align themselves more closely with the campaign. Microsoft has been closely involved with the NSPCC for a number of years and it acted as a prime mover, encouraging other businesses to pledge their support. The advertising for the campaign was sponsored by Microsoft. Other sponsorship and cause-related marketing packages were detailed in a toolkit distributed to other major organisations. Direct mail was also used to encourage businesses to make donations and electronic communications were used to promote pledges online.

At this stage it appears that the coordinated promotional plan enabled a simple yet hard-hitting message to be conveyed to a substantial part of the nation. The publicity derived from the above-the-line work and the rigorous nature of the below-the-line activities suggest that many of the objectives have been achieved. However, results declared in December 2000 showed that in its first year, of the £75 million budget, less than half was spent on child-related services, suggesting to some that the Full Stop campaign was more about brand building.

Source: Adapted from Goften (1999) and Day (2000).

Reconsidering the IMC concept

The central ideas behind the IMC concept are sound and a logical step forward for marketing communications. IMC helps provide a strategic focus and the level of debate and interest about how best to use marketing communications has advanced in recent years. The development of technology, and more importantly the relationship marketing concept, has given increased impetus to those advocates of IMC. However, concerns about pinning down the exact meaning of and interpreting IMC remain.

IMC and transactional marketing

The discussion so far has been based largely on the assumption that exchanges are (or should be) essentially relational in character and that customers are willing and eager to enter into a wide range of relationships. However, it appears that some, if not the majority of exchanges, are essentially transactional in character. Buyers do not necess-

> Buyers do not necessarily wish to enter into deep complex relationships with all suppliers.

arily wish to enter into deep complex relationships with all suppliers, neither do some consumers wish to enter into a relationship with the supplier of their favourite chocolate bar, dishwasher tablets or frozen peas. As a result these convenience-based exchanges are oriented towards a value based on the product, its price and overall availability. Depending upon the product category, after-sales and service support will be important but, by definition, customers in transactional mode do not wish to enter into a dialogue.

The target marketing process requires the development and implementation of a distinct marketing mix to meet the requirements of selected target markets. The elements are mixed together in such a way that they should meet the needs of the target segment. Each element of the marketing mix has a variable capacity to communicate (Figure 11.3).

Therefore, it may be that traditional forms of marketing communications are sufficient to reach transactional customers. Messages which focus mainly on attributes, features and benefits, emotional values, price and availability, will continue to be valid

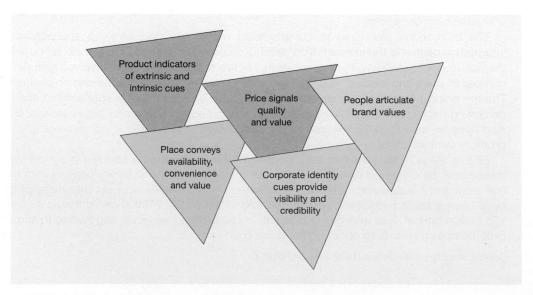

FIGURE 11.3 The marketing mix communicates

and improved if delivered through a coordinated mix of tools and media that are customer oriented. Employing communications that use a coordinated promotional mix, make greater use of a range of promotional tools and are media neutral and seek to cut waste and improve efficiency will be advantageous.

IMC and relationship marketing

There is no universally agreed definition of IMC and the development of this relatively new, embryonic concept is strewn with attempts to pin it down and label it. What can be observed, however, is that the relationship marketing paradigm has developed at the same time as IMC and that there are areas where the two concepts intertwine and reinforce each other. One of the difficulties associated with the IMC view, and with its half-sister, media neutral planning, is that successful marketing communications results from an entirely planned approach. Planning is an essential aspect of managing

Planning is an essential aspect of managing marketing communications.

marketing communications but customers interact with products and services in different ways. They experience brands through their observation of others using the products and services, through their own use, as well as through planned, unplanned and word-of-mouth communications. It is the totality of this communication experience that impacts on relationship development. IMC therefore has an important role in the development of relationship marketing because it is an important process, which seeks to generate a response from customers, to provoke interaction and, through interaction a dialogue develops that is a key characteristic of relationship marketing (Gronroos, 2004). These ideas are explored in greater depth in Chapter 9.

IMC therefore has a potentially greater role to play within relational transactions and with customers who wish to become involved in mutually rewarding relationships. To date IMC has been regarded as a concept that needs to be applied across an organisation's entire marketing communications and customer base. The suggestion is that aspects of IMC should be applied to both transactional and relationally oriented customers, but greater emphasis on interaction and dialogue should be given to communication with current and potential relationship driven customers and other stakeholders.

An incremental approach to IMC

Integrated marketing communications means different things to different people. However, if it is to be a significant development for organisations then the term should embrace the marketing mix, the promotional mix, internal communications and all those outsourced providers who contribute to the overall marketing communication process. As Figure 11.4 demonstrates, all of these elements should be linked to the overall purpose of the organisation, normally encapsulated and framed in the strategy, philosophy and mission of the organisation.

It seems logical that moves towards the establishment of IMC must be undertaken in steps: an incremental approach (Fill, 2001). What has been achieved so far can be recognised as forms of coordination. Different organisations have coordinated various aspects of their communications activities. The majority have focused upon their promotional activities and have tried to bring together their communications to provide consistency and thematic harmonisation.

Therefore, it seems that the starting point in the move towards IMC needs to reflect the context within which exchanges occur. In the majority of cases these will be transactional, where the focus is on product and price. The move from this point will be

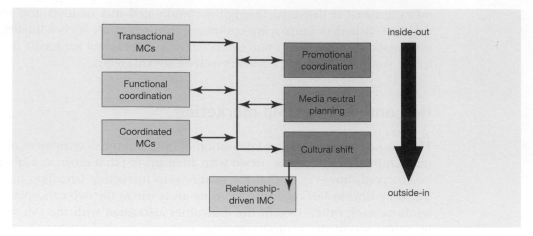

FIGURE 11.4 An incremental approach to the establishment of IMC

towards coordinating the tools and media of the promotional mix and this will take place both internally and externally with the organisation's various agencies. In order

> **Organisations need to create a technology platform necessary to provide a stream of information upon which it is possible to interact with customers.**

to make this work and to move forward, organisations need to create a technology platform necessary to provide a stream of information upon which it is possible to interact with customers. The technology will be used internally to provide an operational tie between the different departments and functional areas. This is an important part of the process as different parts of the organisation are introduced to the notion of internal marketing relationships and where internal marketing communications plays an important part of the process.

Organisations will now either adopt media neutral planning principles and/or develop fully coordinated marketing communications. This will be characterised by data-driven communications, CRM and meaningful evaluation and measurement techniques. This stage will be complemented by the organisation moving towards a strong(er) customer orientation. This requires a *cultural shift* of values and beliefs, whereby organisational, brand identity and relationship issues become paramount. This can only be implemented at this stage, as the internal systems, procedures and employee mindset need to be in place if the strategy is to be credible to customers

> **The final IMC stage is reached when planned communications and product experiences encourage interaction, and dialogue and relationships are enhanced as a result.**

and other stakeholders. The final IMC stage is reached when planned communications and product experiences encourage interaction, and dialogue and relationships are enhanced as a result. This sequential depiction sets out various incremental stages and does not require that they all be followed in strict order and neither is it intended that all organisations, should or do progress to the end (Figure 11.4). For many, perhaps small and medium-sized organisations, especially those with many transactional customers, promotional coordination or coordinated marketing communications stages may be sufficient.

In order for these incremental stages to be undertaken and completed satisfactorily, managers must be clear and agreed about what it is they wish to achieve, and communicate their intent to all who it involves, both inside and outside the organisation.

One of the key issues encouraging the establishment of IMC has been the willingness of some public relations practitioners to move closer to the marketing department. When IMC began to emerge, Miller and Rose (1994) commentated that the previously held opposition to integration by public relations practitioners had begun to dissolve as the more enlightened agencies see it as 'a reality and a necessity'. Over a decade later this movement has not moved forward with any confidence and the marketing communications industry has yet to come together and provide clients with the fully integrated services they desire.

Summary

IMC is a strategic approach to marketing communications. The development of IMC can be seen as resulting naturally from two main factors. The first concerns the way in which the tools of the promotional mix have been deployed. Their use, in the past, has been largely singular in that they have been departmentalised and managed, internally and externally, as separate and independent items. By combining tools and enabling the communication strengths of one tool to reinforce those of another, target audiences are more likely to benefit, along with the organisation.

Secondly, and following on from this first point, there has been a drive for business efficiency and increased effectiveness. IMC offers opportunities to improve effectiveness and delivery of messages in a more productive manner. Now that a genuine mixture of tools can be assembled, many managers might see IMC as a way of putting right a number of problems across the organisation, many of them structural, technological or communication oriented.

Media neutral planning is an element of IMC but IMC is not the same as MNP. With increasing levels of fragmentation and rising media (TV) costs so the need for media neutrality has increased. The main thrust of MNP is to reduce the emphasis on television and make increased use of other tools and media that are more audience focused than traditional marketing communications practice has been to date.

While the concept of IMC is attractive, the development of the approach in practical terms has to date not been very encouraging. There has been a great deal of debate about the meaning and value of an integrated approach and some attempt to coordinate the content and delivery of marketing communication messages. Most organisations have yet to achieve totally integrated marketing communications; only partially coordinated levels of activity have so far been achieved.

Review questions

1. Discuss the main reasons for the development of IMC.
2. Prepare brief notes explaining four different elements that should be part of the integration process.
3. Explain how various definitions of IMC have evolved.
4. What are the reasons for interest in IMC and is it a valid concept?
5. Appraise the main reasons offered for the failure of organisations to develop IMC.
6. What is the incremental approach to establishing IMC?
7. Explain the ideas concerning media neutral planning.
8. What is Open Planning?
9. Discuss the view that IMC is essentially the same as relationship marketing.
10. Prepare the outline for an essay arguing whether IMC is a strategic approach or just a means to correct internal operational difficulties and to reduce media costs.

MINI-CASE
IMC - still a long way to go in financial services marketing

Mini-case written by Kate Watts, Head of Knowledge, Chime Communications

The case for reviewing and renewing the way we plan and execute marketing communications could not be stronger than it is for the financial services sector. The old, mass advertising and direct model of communication is showing cracks, with diminishing returns on marketing investment reported by a number of our clients. Consumer trust in financial service brands is low and falling, and consumers are increasingly suspicious of traditional sales methods.

Financial services marketing agency, Teamspirit, has been tracking levels of trust towards financial services companies for the past few years. The problem is particularly acute for insurance and investment brands, where very few consumers have any residual levels of trust towards the sector at all. A number of high-profile cases of financial misselling and other irregularities, combined with economic uncertainty, fears over pensions shortfalls, mortgage jitters and the mounting credit burden, all mean that, if anything, mistrust of the sector is likely to continue.

In this low-trust, highly uncertain environment, financial services marketing departments should be looking for new ways to connect and re-establish trust with their customers. However, we see very little sign of this happening.

Trust me, I'm a financial service provider . . .

Re-establishing trust is not easy. It is an old cliché, but nonetheless sound – trust has to be earned. Nor can trust be simply claimed, it needs to be conferred. One of the best routes to do this is to encourage third-party endorsement, through people and/or institutions that have earned people's trust. This is the classic role for public relations. It is a more subtle, less 'in-your-face' way to generate consumer trust. Yet, in our experience, marketing campaign schedules in the retail financial services sector are, by and large, light on public relations and heavy on traditional above-the-line selling messages.

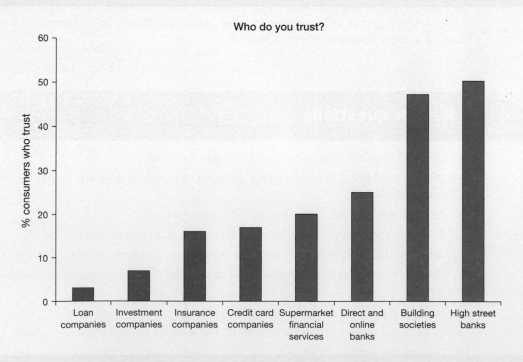

Trust in the financial services sector
Source: YouGov, Oct. 2004. N = 1981

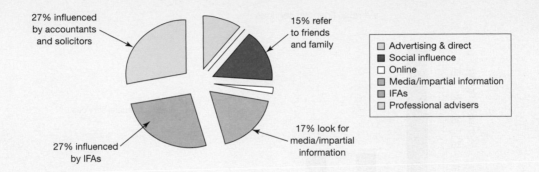

27% influenced by accountants and solicitors

15% refer to friends and family

□ Advertising & direct
■ Social influence
□ Online
▨ Media/impartial information
▧ IFAs
□ Professional advisers

27% influenced by IFAs

17% look for media/impartial information

Equity release: a high-reference product, where the influence of professional advisers is huge

An intermediated world

In a low-trust marketing environment, it makes sense for a financial services brand to build relationships of trust with a wide range of intermediaries. For many financial products, particularly the higher-value products such as mortgages, pensions and investments, consumers are influenced by a range of intermediaries, including the obvious independent financial advisers and financial journalists, but also the less obvious – knowledgeable friends, solicitors, accountants, estate agents and employers. However, subtle 'trade marketing' where relationships are actively sought and built with a wide range of intermediaries tends to be seen as a rather less important activity than the big above-the-line mass campaigns. In fact, it is probably no exaggeration to say that this kind of marketing is the Cinderella of the piece! This is perhaps because the activity is relatively unglamorous (low cost), but also highly work intensive – involving as it does the creation of a more targeted, one-on-one plan of campaign.

Who or what influences your choices?

For some time we have been using what we call the Influence Model as a planning basis for campaigns across the Chime Communications group. The Influence Model is a consumer-centric way of planning integrated communications campaigns based around identifying the web of influences on consumer attitude and behaviour. We have found such a web of influences to be present in every market we have looked at – from cars to bottled beers, from mobile telephones to a bar of chocolate. Identifying this web of influences helps us to plan more effective integrated campaigns.

When we ask consumers of financial services products who or what influences their choice these days, the message we get back is clear – planning communications in a low-trust environment means identifying and marketing to a range of more trusted intermediaries – which includes the media and other intermediary sources of professional advice. When we look at a consumer-generated map of influences, for example for an equity release (where, typically, older homeowners 'draw down' equity in their homes), we got back the web of intermediary influences shown in the next figure, including solicitors, accountants, traditional financial services advisers, friends and family, and the media.

And yet, rather than focusing on trust-generating communications methods, such as public relations and niche marketing, financial services marketing remains one of the most traditional in terms of communication spend patterns. The annual London Business School/Havas Marketing Expenditure survey shows that retail financial services clients are spending 65 per cent of their marketing budgets on advertising and direct, around 20 per cent each on sales promotion and 'brand/PR/sponsorship' and 10 per cent on interactive.

Our consumer-generated profile, based on asking who or what influences choice, suggests that this balance of spend is unlikely to yield positive results, particularly if applied to the higher risk end of the financial services market. Rather than applying the traditional filter when it comes to integrated communications planning, it would make eminent sense for clients to take a step back and ask some fundamental questions about what really influences consumer choice these days.

IMC as a concept only makes sense, in our view, if it is linked to a business imperative, and begins with the consumer perspective – it should not pursued just for its own sake. Making marketing budgets work smarter by understanding how to influence consumer behaviour in a low-trust environment is not IMC for

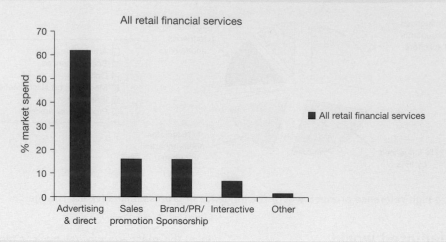

Total retail financial services spend
Source: London Business School 2004 MET report

the sake of IMC – but rather, a way of introducing integrative, influence based thinking to a sector which needs to make some fundamental changes.

Questions

1 Discuss the extent to which integrated marketing communications should be linked to business goals.

2 Find two or three organisations operating in financial services products, select a product category (e.g. savings accounts) and compare the marketing communications used to support the different brands. What is common and what is different?

3 To what extent is the success of an IMC campaign likely to be dependent upon levels of perceived trust?

References

Bergstrom, K. and Anderson, M. (2001) Delivering on promises to the market-place: using employment branding to build employee satisfaction. *Journal of Integrated Marketing Communications*. Retrieved 17 November 2004 from www.medill.nwu.edu/imc.

Brown, J. (1997) Impossible dream or inevitable revolution: an exploration of integrated marketing communications. *Journal of Communication Management*, **12**(1), pp. 70–81.

Cornelissen, J. (2000) Integration in communication management: conceptual and methodological considerations. *Journal of Marketing Management*, **16**, pp. 597–606.

Cornelissen, J.P. and Lock, A.R. (2000) Theoretical concept or management fashion? Examining the significance of IMC. *Journal of Advertising Research*, **50**(5), pp. 7–15.

Day, J. (2000) A time for gifts. *Marketing Week*, 14 December, pp. 22–5.

Duncan (2002) *IMC: Using Advertising and Promotion to Build Brand*, international edn. New York: McGraw-Hill.

Duncan, T. and Everett, S. (1993) Client perceptions of integrated marketing communications. *Journal of Advertising Research*, **3**(3), pp. 30–9.

Duncan, T. and Moriarty, S. (1998) A communication-based marketing model for managing relationships. *Journal of Marketing*, **62** (April), pp. 1–13.

Eagle, L. and Kitchen, P. (2000) IMC, brand communications, and corporate cultures. *European Journal of Marketing*, **34**(5/6), pp. 667–86.

Fill, C. (2001) Essentially a matter of consistency. *The Marketing Review*, **1**(4) (Summer) pp. 409–25.

Goften, K. (1999) NSPCC aims to convert abuse anger into cash. *Marketing*, 25 March, pp. 37–8.

Grein, A.F. and Gould, S.J. (1996) Globally integrated communications. *Journal of Marketing Communications*, **2**, pp. 141–58.

Gronroos, C. (2004) The relationship marketing process: communication, interaction, dialogue, value. *Journal of Business and Industrial Marketing*, **19**(2), pp. 99–113.

Hutton, J.G. (1996) Integrated relationship-marketing communications: a key opportunity for IMC. *Journal of Marketing Communications*, **2**, pp. 191–9.

Jenkinson, A. (2004) Open Planning: media neutral planning made simple. Retrieved 14 November 2004, from www.openplanning.org/cases/openplanning/whitepaper.pdf.

Kitchen, P., Brignell, J., Li, T. and Spickett Jones, G. (2004) The emergence of IMC: a theoretical perspective. *Journal of Advertising Research*, **44** (March) pp. 19–30.

Kitchen, P.J. and Shultz, D.E. (1997) Integrated marketing communications in US advertising agencies: an exploratory study. *Journal of Advertising Research*, **37**(5), pp. 7–18.

Kitchen, P.J. and Shultz, D.E. (1998) IMC: a UK ads agency perspective. *Journal of Marketing Management*, **14**(2), pp. 465–85.

Miller, D.A. and Rose, P.B. (1994) Integrated communications: a look at reality instead of theory. *Public Relations Quarterly* (Spring), pp. 13–16.

Mintzberg, H. (1996) *The Strategy Process*, European edn. Englewood Cliffs, NJ: Prentice-Hall.

Percy, L., Rossiter, J.R. and Elliot, R. (2001) *Strategic Advertising Management*. New York: Oxford University Press.

Porter, M.E. (1980) *Competitive Strategy: Techniques for Analyzing Industries and Competitors*. New York: Free Press.

Ray, A. (2002) How to adopt a neutral stance. *Marketing*, 27 June, p. 27.

Schultz, D. (1993) *Integrated Marketing Communications: Putting It Together and Making It Work*. Lincolnwood, IL: NTC Business Books.

Shimp, T.A. (2000) *Advertising Promotion: Supplemental Aspects of Integrated Marketing Communications*. 5th edn. Fort Worth, TX: The Dryden Press, Harcourt College Publishers.

Smith, P. (1996) Benefits and barriers to integrated communications. *Admap* (February), pp. 19–22.

Spake, D.F., D'Souza, G., Crutchfield, T.N. and Morgan, R.M. (1999) Advertising agency compensation: an agency theory explanation. *Journal of Advertising*, **28**(3), pp. 53–72.

Spotts, H.E., Lambert, D.R. and Joyce, M.L. (1998) Marketing déjà vu: the discovery of integrated marketing communications. *Journal of Marketing Education*, **20**(3), pp. 210–18.

Swain, W.N. (2004) Perceptions of IMC after a decade of development: who's at the wheel, and how can we measure success? *Journal of Advertising Research* (March), pp. 46–65.

Tobaccowala, R. and Kugel, C. (2001) Planning and evaluating cross-media programs. *Admap*, **36**(2), February, pp. 33–6.

White, R. (2000) Chameleon brands: tailoring brand messages to consumers. *Admap* (July/August), pp. 38–40.

Marketing communications: strategies and planning

12

A marketing communication strategy refers to an organisation's preferred orientation and emphasis of its communications with its customers and stakeholders, in the light of its business and marketing strategies. A marketing communications plan is concerned with the development and managerial processes involved in the articulation of an organisation's marketing communication strategy.

Aims and objectives

The aims of this chapter are to explore the nature of strategy and marketing communications strategies in particular. The goal is to familiarise readers with the elements and concepts associated with marketing communication strategy and planning, and to introduce the marketing communications planning framework.

The objectives of this chapter are to:

1. introduce the notion of marketing communication strategy as a separate concept to marketing communications plans;

2. consider three main marketing communication strategies: pull, push and profile;

3. examine involvement as a basis for developing promotional strategies;

4. consider the different elements involved in marketing communication plans;

5. highlight the linkages and interaction between the different elements of the plan;

6. present a framework for the development of marketing communication plans.

Introduction

This chapter follows on from an exploration of integrated marketing communications, which is in essence a strategic approach to marketing communications. Various issues implicit in the previous discussion are relevant in this chapter and although not developed should be considered by readers.

It is assumed by many that marketing communication strategy is simply the combination of activities in the communications mix. In other words, strategy is about the degree of direct marketing, personal selling, advertising, sales promotion and public relations that is incorporated within a planned sequence of communication activities. This is important, but it is not the essence of marketing communications strategy. From a strategic perspective, key decisions concern the overall direction of the programme and target audiences, the fit with marketing and corporate strategy, the desired position the brand is to occupy in the market, the resources to be made available, the key message and overall goals.

The chapter begins with a consideration of some fundamental ideas concerning the nature of strategy. From this a contextual and customer perspective is developed on which to build marketing communications strategy. This is used in preference to a production orientation, which is founded on the resource base. This customer orientation requires revisiting ideas concerning market segmentation and the characteristics and buying behaviour of the different target audiences. From here various dimensions of communications strategy are developed.

Understanding strategy

In order to appreciate the role and nature of communication strategy it is useful to appreciate the dimensions of the strategy concept. The management literature on strategy is extensive yet there seems to be little agreement or consensus about what it is, what it means or how it should be developed. A full discussion of this topic is beyond the scope of this book but what follows is a brief overview of some of the more general views about management strategy.

Hambrick (1983) suggested that the disparity of views about the strategy concept is due to the multidimensional nature of the strategy concept, that strategy is situational and that it varies according to industry and the environment in which it operates. In other words contextual issues determine the nature of strategy. This may be true but it does not help us understand what strategy is.

Contextual issues determine the nature of strategy.

The one main area where most authors find agreement concerns the hierarchical nature of strategy within organisations (Kay, 1993; Pearce and Robinson, 1997). This refers to the notion that there are three main levels of organisational strategy: corporate, competitive and functional. Corporate strategy is considered to be directional and sets out the broad, overarching parameters and means through which the organisation operates in order to realise its objectives. Strategies at the functional level, for example marketing, finance, production, should be integrated in such a way that they contribute to the satisfaction of the higher-level competitive strategies, which in turn should satisfy the overall corporate goals. Competitive-level strategies are important because not only do they set out the way in which the organisation will compete and use resources, but they should also provide clear messages about the way in which the organisation seeks to manage its environment.

Chaffee (1985) identifies several themes associated with the various strategic inter-pretations. The first is that strategy is used by organisa-tions as a means of adjusting to changing environmental conditions and the second is that strategy is often referred to in terms of decision-making, actions and implementa-tion. Apart from the hierarchical element mentioned pre-viously one of her other significant observations concerned the point that strategy could take various forms, most notably deliberate, emergent and realised formats.

> Chaffee (1985) identifies several themes associated with the various strategic interpretations.

Two main strategy schools of thought can be identified, namely the planning and the incrementalist approaches. The planning school is the pre-eminent paradigm and is based on strategy development and implementation, which is explicit, rational and planned as a sequence of logical steps. Andrews (1987) comments that strategy is con-cerned with a company's objectives, purpose and policies and its plans to satisfy the goals using particular resources with respect to a range of internal and external stakeholders. The organisation interacts with and attempts to shape its environment in pursuit of its goals. This perspective of strategy was first formulated in the 1950s and 1960s when the operating environments of many organisations were simple, stable and hence predictable. However, these con-ditions rarely exist in the twenty-first century and the validity of the rational model of strategy is now questionable.

> Two main strategy schools of thought can be identified, namely the planning and the incrementalist approaches.

The incrementalist school of thought considers strategy to develop step-by-step as organisations learn, sometimes through simple actions of trial and error. The core belief is that strategy is comprised of a stream of organisational activities that are continu-ously being formulated, implemented, tested, evaluated and updated. Chaffee suggested that strategy could be considered in terms of a linear, adaptive or interpretative approach, each reflecting a progressively sophisticated perspective. While the linear approach reflects the more traditional and deliberate approach to strategy (Ansoff, 1965; Andrews, 1987), the adaptive strategy is important because it reflects the view that organisations flex and adjust to changing environments while the interpretative or higher-order point of view considers strategy to be a reflection of the social order influence of strategic decision-making.

> The incrementalist school of thought considers strategy to develop step-by-step as organisations learn, sometimes through simple actions of trial and error.

> Adaptive strategy is important because it reflects the view that organisations flex and adjust to changing environments.

Two other strategic authors to be mentioned are Mintzberg (1994) and Whittington (1993). Mintzberg argues that strategy can be regarded as one or more of 5Ps of strat-egy. These are strategy as a Plan, Position, Perspective, Ploy and Pattern. Whittington (1993) offers four generic strategies: Classical, Evolutionary, Processual and Systemic. See Table 12.1.

There are a number of common points shared within these various views and per-spectives of strategy. Chaffee, Mintzberg and Whittington all agree that strategy can be considered to be deliberate in nature as reflected in their respective linear, planned and classical approaches. They also agree that strategy can be emergent and can evolve from the actions of the organisation. This can be seen in their adaptive, pattern and processual approaches. They also develop views on the extent to which an organisa-tion interacts with its environment or seeks to directly influence it. Chaffee refers to interpretative strategies, Mintzberg to strategy as a perspective and Whittington to systemic interpretations.

TABLE 12.1 Views of strategy – Mintzberg and Whittington

Author	Type of Strategy	Explanation
Mintzberg	Plan	A predetermined, deliberate course of action, implementation and evaluation.
	Position	An attempt to locate an organisation within a market.
	Perspective	A collective view of the world, one that is ingrained within the organisation and its position within it.
	Ploy	A scheme or manoeuvre to sidestep or outwit competitors.
	Pattern	A stream of actions in which there are consistent patterns of behaviour.
Whittington	Classical	Planned, rational and deliberate.
	Evolutionary	Darwinian in outlook, this strategy perceives a manager's task as trying to survive by fitting as closely as possible to the prevailing environmental conditions.
	Processual	An essentially incremental perspective whereby strategy is concerned with learning from past actions and experience. Little emphasis is given to long-term planning and horizons.
	Systemic	Strategy is a reflection of the social systems in which strategists participate.

Views on strategy have evolved as our understanding has developed. Strategy is not just about a deliberate, planned approach to business development, although it can be at the functional and competitive levels. Strategy should be considered to be about the means, speed and methods by which organisations adapt to and influence their environments in order that they achieve their goals. What is also clear is that the demarcation between an organisation and its environment is less clear than it used to be. An imaginary line was once used to refer to a border between an organisation and its environment. This line is no longer deemed valid as organisations are now viewed as boundary free. The implications of this borderless concept for marketing communications are potentially enormous. Not only do contemporary views of strategy amplify the significance of the interaction between strategy and an organisation's environment but it also stresses the importance for strategy, at whatever level, to be contextually oriented and determined.

Strategy is not just about a deliberate, planned approach to business development.

Market segmentation

The planned and deliberate perspective of strategy has had a long-term impact on marketing management. The process of market analysis and evaluation leading to planned strategies designed to meet prescribed and measurable goals is well established. It is argued that this approach enables finite resources to be used more efficiently as they can be directed towards markets which hold, potentially, greater value than other markets. Market segmentation is part of this approach and is both a functional and competitive level strategy. More importantly, the process of market segmentation is the means by which organisations define the broad context within which their strategic business units (SBUs) and products are offered.

ViewPoint 12.1   Segments galore

United Airlines segments its global markets using psychographic data about its customers. Among its categories are:

- Schedule optimisers: must reach their destination by a certain time and select their flights accordingly.
- Mile accumulators: go out of their way to take flights that will build up their air miles entitlement.
- Quality vacationers: treat the travel as part of the holiday experience and so fly with carriers that provide superior services.
- Frugal flyers: seek out the lowest-cost carriers, but still expect their flight experience to be a good one.

Source: http://www.thetimes100.co.uk/case_study.

According to T-Mobile's Web site it targets four key market segments:

- personal
- small businesses
- medium businesses
- corporate.

The segments identified for a women's portal include the following groups:

- Pillars: characterised by their family orientation, high income and broad range of interests.
- Explorers: notable for being single, thirty-something, outgoing and more social than career oriented.
- Free spirits: the youngest segment, typically unmarried, Internet savvy, and not yet committed to careers or raising a family.

Source: www.debmcdonald.com/.

Market segmentation is the division of a mass market into identifiable and distinct groups or segments, each of which have common characteristics and needs and display similar responses to marketing actions. Through this process specific target segments can be selected and marketing plans developed to satisfy the individual needs of the potential buyers in these chosen segments. The development, or rather identification, of segments can be perceived as opportunities and, as Beane and Ennis (1987) suggest, 'A company with limited resources needs to pick only the best opportunities to pursue'. The most common bases upon which markets can be segmented are set out in Table 12.2.

TABLE 12.2 Bases for segmenting markets

Segmentation base	Explanation
Demographic	Key variables concern age, sex, occupation, level of education, religion, social class and income characteristics, many of which determine, to a large extent, a potential buyer's ability to enter into an exchange relationship or transaction.
Geographic	In many situations the needs of potential customers in one geographic area are different from those in another area. For example, it is often said that Scottish beer drinkers prefer heavy bitters, Northerners in England prefer mild, drinkers in the West prefer cider, and in the South lager is the preferred drink.
Geodemographic	This type of segmentation is based on the assumption that there is a relationship between the type of housing people live in and their purchasing behaviours. At the root of this approach is the ability to use postcodes to send similar messages to similar groups of households, on the basis that where we live determines how we live. The most well-known commercial applications are Acorn (a classification of residential neighbourhoods), Mosaic and Pinpoint.
Psychographic	Through an analysis of consumers' activities, interests and opinions (AIO) it is possible to determine lifestyles or patterns of behaviour. These are a synthesis of the motivations, personality and core values held by individuals. These AIO patterns are reflected in the buying behaviour and decision-making processes of individuals. By identifying and clustering common lifestyles, a correlation with a consumer's product and/or media usage patterns becomes possible.
Behaviouristic	Usage and lifestage segments are derived from analysing markets on the basis of customer behaviour. Usage of soft drinks can be considered in terms of purchase patterns (two bottles per week), usage situations (parties, picnics or as an alcohol substitute) or purchase location (supermarket, convenience store or wine merchant). Lifestage analysis is based on the principle that people have varying amounts of disposable income and different needs at different stages in their lives. Their priorities for spending change at different trigger points and these points or lifestages do not occur at the same time.

Segmentation is necessary because a single product is unlikely to meet the needs of all customers in a mass market.

This process of segmentation is necessary because a single product is unlikely to meet the needs of all customers in a mass market. If it did, then a single type of toothpaste, chocolate bar or car would meet all of our needs. This is not so, and there are a host of products and brands seeking to satisfy particular buyer needs. For example, ask yourself the question, 'Why do I use toothpaste?' The answer, most probably, is one of the following:

1. You want dental hygiene.
2. You like fresh breath and you don't want to offend others.
3. You want white, shining teeth.
4. You like the fresh oral sensation.
5. Other products (e.g. water, soap) do not taste very good.

TABLE 12.3 Benefit segments for the toothpaste market

Segment name	The sensory segment	The sociables	The worriers	The independents
Principal benefit sought	Flavour, product appearance	Brightness of teeth	Decay prevention	Price
Demographic strengths	Children	Teens, young people	Large families	Men
Special behavioural characteristics	Users of spearmint-flavoured toothpaste	Smokers	Heavy users	Heavy users
Brands disproportionately favoured	Colgate, Stripe	Macleans, Plus White, Ultra Brite	Crest, Sensodyne	Brands on sale
Personality characteristics	High self-involvement	High sociability	High hypochondriasis	High autonomy
Lifestyle characteristics	Hedonistic	Active	Conservative	Value oriented

Source: Haley (1968); used with kind permission.

Whatever the reason, it is unlikely that given a choice everyone would choose the same product. In what is now regarded as a classic study, Russell Haley (1968) undertook some pioneering research in this field and from it established four distinct types of customer. Even after over 35 years have elapsed this typology remains a potent practical example of market segmentation: those who bought toothpaste for white teeth (sociables), those who wished to prevent decay (worriers), those who liked the taste and refreshment properties (sensors) and finally those who bought on a price basis (independents). Each of these groups has particular demographic, behaviouristic and psychographic characteristics that can be seen in Table 12.3.

It is not surprising that a range of toothpaste products has been developed that attempts to satisfy the needs of different buyers, for example Macleans for fresh breath, Crest for dental hygiene, Sensodyne for those sensitive to hot and cold drinks and numerous others promoted on special offers for those independent buyers looking for a low price. There are others who are not very interested in the product and have continued using a brand that others in their current or past households are comfortable with. Therefore, target segments constitute the environment and the context for the marketing communications strategy and activities. It is the characteristics of the target segment therefore that are the focus of an audience-centred marketing communication strategy.

The 3Ps of marketing communications strategy

The accepted approach to marketing communications (advertising) strategy has traditionally been founded upon the configuration of the promotional mix. Strategy was an interpretation of the mix and hence the resources an organisation deployed. This represents a production rather than market orientation to marketing communications and is intrinsically misplaced. This inside-out form of strategy is essentially resource driven. However, a market orientation strategy requires a consideration of the needs of the audience first and then a determination of the various messages, media and disciplines to accomplish the strategy, an outside-in approach.

A market orientation strategy requires a consideration of the needs of the audience first.

Consumer purchase decisions are characterised (very generally and see Chapter 6) by a single-person buying centre, whereas organisational buying decisions can involve a large number of different people, fulfilling different roles and all requiring different marketing communication messages. It follows from this that the approach to communicating with these two very different target sectors should be radically different, especially in terms of what, where, when and how a message is communicated. Once promotional objectives have been established, it is necessary to formulate appropriate strategies. Promotional objectives that are focused upon consumer markets require a different strategy from those formulated to satisfy the objectives that are focused on organisational customers. In addition, there are circumstances and reasons to focus communications upon the development of the organisation with a corporate brand and range of other stakeholders. Often, these corporate brands need to work closely with the development of product brands. As a result, it is possible to identify three main marketing communication strategies:

- pull strategies – to influence end-user customers (consumers and b2b);
- push strategies – to influence marketing (trade) channel buyers;
- profile strategies – to influence a range of stakeholders.

These can be referred to as the 3Ps of marketing communications strategy. Push and pull relate to the direction of the communication to the marketing channel: pushing communications down through the marketing channel or pulling consumers/buyers into the channel via retailers, as a result of receiving the communications. They do not relate to the intensity of communication and only refer to the overall approach. Profile refers to the presentation of the organisation as a whole and therefore the identity is said to be 'profiled' to various other target stakeholder audiences, which may well include consumers, trade buyers, business-to-business customers and a range of other influential stakeholders. Normally, profile strategies do not contain or make reference to specific products or services that the organisation offers. See Table 12.4.

These can be referred to as the 3Ps of marketing communications strategy.

This may be blurred where the name of a company is the name of its primary (only) product, as is often the case with many retail brands. For example, messages about B&Q are very often designed to convey meaning about the quality and prices of its consumer products and services, however, they often reflect on the organisation itself, especially when its advertising shows members of staff in workwear, doing their work. See Exhibit 12.1.

Within each of these overall strategies, individual approaches should be formulated to reflect the needs of each particular case. So, for example, the launch of a new

TABLE 12.4 Marketing communications strategy options

Strategy	Target audience	Message focus	Communication goal
Pull	Consumers	Product/service	Purchase
	End-user b2b customers	Product/service	Purchase
Push	Channel intermediaries	Product/service	Developing relationships and distribution network
Profile	All relevant stakeholders	The organisation	Building reputation

EXHIBIT 12.1 B&Q
The use of staff in television commercials provides authenticity and a sense of shared ownership with regard to the B&Q brand promise. Picture reproduced with the kind permission of B&Q.

shampoo product will involve a push strategy to get the product on the shelves of the appropriate retailers. The strategy would be to gain retailer acceptance of the new brand and to position it as a profitable new brand to gain consumer interest. Personal selling supported by trade sales promotions will be the main marketing communications tools. A pull strategy to develop awareness about the brand will need to be created, accompanied by appropriate public relations work. The next step will be to create particular brand associations and thereby position the brand in the minds of the target audience. Messages may be functional or expressive but they will endeavour to convey a brand promise. This may be accompanied or followed by the use of incentives to encourage consumers to trial the product. To support the brand, care lines and a Web site will need to be put in place to provide credibility as well as a buyer reference point. In order that these strategies be implemented, it is normal procedure to

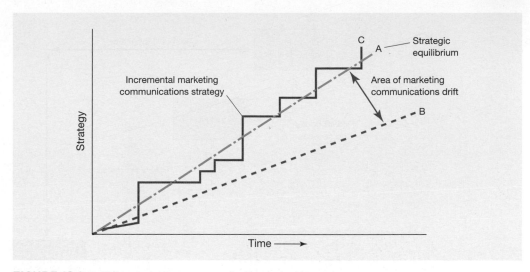

FIGURE 12.1 Drift in marketing communications strategy

develop a marketing communications plan. The degree to which these plans are developed varies across organisations and some rely on their agencies to undertake this work for them. However, there can be major benefits as a result of developing these plans in-house, for example by involving and discussing issues internally and developing a sense of ownership.

As noted earlier, planning is not necessarily the same as strategy, although the two are often used interchangeably. Strategy is about the direction, approach and implementation of an organisation's desired marketing communications (in this case) in order that it create or maintain a dialogue with particular target audiences. Planning on the other hand is usually about the formalisation of the strategy and ideas, into a manageable sequence of activities that are linked, coherent and capable of being implemented in the light of the resources that are available. Strategy is about the way an organisation prefers to communicate with its customers and stakeholders. It must do this in the light of its business and marketing strategies and the prevailing contextual conditions, in order to encourage a degree of dialogue with selected stakeholders.

> A marketing communications plan is concerned with the development and managerial processes involved in the articulation of an organisation's marketing communication strategy.

A marketing communications plan is concerned with the development and managerial processes involved in the articulation of an organisation's marketing communication strategy. This will be considered later in the chapter.

There is little doubt that planning and strategy are interlinked but it is useful to consider strategy as something that needs to be attended to on a regular basis. With so many variables and an external environment that is subject to tremendous change, marketing communications strategy can be seen to drift, to move away from its central message. The only way to correct drift is to change the marketing communications strategy by an amount according to the degree to which messages have drifted. This might be best observed in Figure 12.1.

Line B suggests that if current marketing communications remain as they are, then the size of the gap with the central theme of marketing communications will widen and any attempt to get it back will be large and expensive.

Line C depicts a brand that has adapted its marketing communications on a more frequent basis (than B) and as a result follows an incremental strategy, one that results in a more consistent message. This concept might be interpreted in terms of

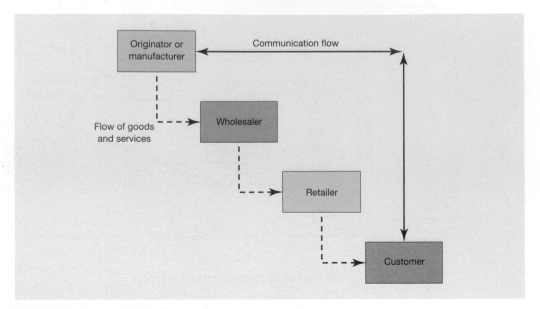

FIGURE 12.2 The direction of communication in a pull strategy

positioning and repositioning brands and the changing of agencies in order to revitalise and change the direction of the communications strategy currently being pursued.

A pull strategy

If messages are to be directed at targeted end-user customers, then the intention is invariably to generate increased levels of awareness, change and/or reinforce attitudes, reduce risk, encourage involvement and ultimately provoke a motivation within the target group. This motivation is to stimulate action so that the target audience expect the offering to be available to them when they decide to enquire, experiment or make a repeat purchase. This approach is known as a *pull* strategy and is aimed at encouraging customers to 'pull' products through the channel network. See Figure 12.2. This usually means that consumers go into retail outlets (shops) to enquire about a particular product and/or buy it, or to enter a similar transaction direct with the manufacturer or intermediary through direct mail or the Internet. B2b customers are encouraged to buy from dealers and distributors while both groups of consumers and b2b customers have opportunities to buy through direct marketing channels where there is no intermediary.

To accomplish and deliver a pull strategy, the traditional approach has been to deliver mass media advertising supported by below-the-line communications, most notably sales promotions. There has been greater use of direct marketing in non-FMCG sectors and use of the Internet presents opportunities to reach audiences in new ways and so reduce any reliance on the old formulaic approach to pull-based strategies. The decision to use a pull strategy has to be supported by a core message proposition. This will vary according to the outcomes of the context analysis and the needs of the target audience. However, it is probable that the core message will seek to differentiate (position), remind or reassure, inform or persuade the audience to think, feel or behave in a particular way. Agencies and clients have their own approach to this labelling activity. One way might be to term a communication strategy pull/remind or pull/position as this describes the audience and what the strategy seeks to achieve.

ViewPoint 12.2   Pull stratgeies

The mobile company *3* changed its business strategy to one based on driving sales of 3G by offering the lowest call tariffs on standard voice products. A pull strategy based on comparative advertising was used to demonstrate the low-cost/high-spec phones offering.

Asda-Walmart has developed a strong market share in the UK based mainly on price competition or on what is referred to as everyday low pricing (EDLP) (pull/price). Tesco runs everyday low pricing but uses sales promotions as a form of complementary positioning (pull/price/promotions). In their wake, Sainsbury's and Safeway have used differing pull strategies to try and regain lost share, increase profitability and stave off takeover threats. Sainsbury's have yet to recover and Safeway has been bought by Morrisons.

Although Sainsbury's uses EDLP on 1,000 selected lines, it has adopted a classic branding campaign, based around the celebrity chef Jamie Oliver. Making heavy use of television, the brand is positioned around a quality proposition emphasised by the personality and the associated redesign of major stores (pull/quality/repositioning).

The level and degree of involvement, explored in some depth in Chapter 6, has some implications for pull strategies. Marketing communication messages can be considered to be a stimulus that in some situations will have a strong impact on the level of involvement enjoyed by the target audience. A strategic response to this would be to adapt marketing communication messages so that they are effective at different levels of involvement, a form of differentiation.

Another approach would be to turn low-involvement decisions into high involvement that, through communications, encourage members of the target audience to reconsider their perception of a brand or of the competition. Again, this represents a form of differentiation. A third approach is to segment the market in terms of the level of involvement experienced by each group and according to situational or personality factors, and then shape the marketing communication messages to suit each group.

Refers to messages targeted at particular customer audiences and to the overall task that a campaign might seek to achieve.

A pull strategy, therefore, refers to messages targeted at particular customer audiences and to the overall task that a campaign might seek to achieve. This might be to differentiate or position a brand (e.g. by reference to specific attributes), remind/reassure, inform (by raising awareness) or persuade (stimulate action). To accomplish this, a functional or expressive branding policy needs to be agreed and understood by all relevant parties (see Chapters 14 and 15).

A push strategy

A second group or type of target audience can be identified, based first on their contribution to the marketing channel and secondly because these organisations do not consume the products and services they buy, but add value before selling the product on to others in the demand chain. The previous strategy was targeted at customers who make purchase decisions related largely to their personal (or organisational) consumption of products and services. This second group buys products and services, performs some added-value activity and moves the product through the marketing channel

ViewPoint 12.3   Crown Paints

Research undertaken by Crown Paints found that their brand was perceived to be very male, very traditional and a bit dull and staid. A pull strategy based around advertising, packaging and point-of-purchase materials was used to reposition the brand with a more contemporary identity. See Exhibit 12.2.

EXHIBIT 12.2 Crown Paints
Advertising was required to bring more emotional values to the brand and generate new levels of brand awareness. Picture reproduced with the kind permission of Akzo Nobel.

network. This group is a part of the b2b sector, and the characteristics and issues associated with trade channel marketing communications are explored in greater detail in Chapter 31.

Trade channel organisations and indeed all b2b organisations are actively involved in the development and maintenance of interorganisational relationships. The degree of cooperation between organisations will vary and part of the role of marketing communications is to develop and support the relationships that exist.

The 'trade' channel has received increased attention in recent years as the strategic value of intermediaries has become both more visible and questioned in light of the Internet. As the channel networks have developed, so has their complexity, which impacts upon the marketing communications strategies and tools used to help reach marketing goals. The expectations of buyers in these networks have risen in parallel with the significance attached to them by manufacturers. The power of multiple retailers, such as Tesco, Sainsbury's, Safeway and Asda-Walmart, is such that they are able to dictate terms (including the marketing communications) to many manufacturers of branded goods.

A *push* communication strategy involves the presentation of information in order to influence other trade channel organisations and, as a result, encourage them to take stock, to allocate resources (e.g. shelf space) and to help them to become fully aware of the key attributes and benefits associated with each product with a view to adding value prior to further channel transactions. This strategy is designed to encourage resale to other members of the network and contribute to the achievement of their own objectives. This approach is known as a *push* strategy, as it is aimed at pushing the product down through the channel towards the end-users for consumption. See Figure 12.3.

> A *push* communication strategy involves the presentation of information in order to influence other trade channel organisations.

The channel network (Chapter 8) consists of those organisations with whom others must cooperate directly to achieve their own objectives. By accepting that there is interdependence, usually dispersed unequally throughout the network, it is possible to identify organisations that have a stronger/weaker position within a network. Communication must travel not only between the different levels of dependence and role ('up and down' in a channel context) and so represent bidirectional flows, but also across similar levels of dependence and role, that is, horizontal flows; these may be from retailer to retailer or wholesaler to wholesaler.

Marketing communications targeted at people involved in organisational buying decisions are characterised by an emphasis on personal selling. Trade advertising, trade sales promotions and public relations all have an important yet secondary role to play. Direct marketing has become increasingly important and the development of the

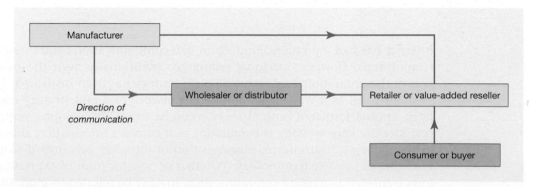

FIGURE 12.3 The direction of communication in a push strategy

ViewPoint 12.4   Makita use below-the-line branding

Black & Decker discovered that it was losing sales in the trade sector because its products were perceived to be more suitable for consumers and the do-it-yourself market. Its response was to develop a separate brand for this particular trade sector. It used a new name 'Makita', identified the product range through the colour yellow and made it available through different trade channels. The promotional materials and support documentation needed a different 'tone of voice' to reflect a more rugged and stronger position. The messages were integrated in order to reinforce the desired positioning.

EXHIBIT 12.3 Makita Products

Internet has had a profound impact on b2b communications and interorganisational relationships. However, personal selling has traditionally been the most significant part of the promotional mix where a push strategy has been instigated.

Finally, just as it was suggested that the essence of a pull strategy could be articulated in brief format, a push strategy could be treated in a similar way. The need to consider the core message is paramount as it conveys information about the essence of the strategy. Push/inform, push/position or push/key accounts/discount might be examples of possible terminology. Whether or not this form of expression is used it is important that marketing communication strategy be referred to more than just push; what is to be achieved also needs to be understood.

A profile strategy

The strategies considered so far concern the need for dialogue with customers (pull) and trade channel intermediaries (push). However, there is a whole range of other stakeholders, many of whom need to know about and understand the organisation rather than actually purchase its products and services. See Figure 12.4. This group of stakeholders may include financial analysts, trade unions, government bodies, employees or the local community. It should be easy to understand that these different stakeholder groups can influence the organisation in different ways and, in doing so, need to receive (and respond to) different types of messages. So, the financial analysts need to know about financial and trading performance and expectations, and the local community may be interested in employment and the impact of the organisation on the local environment, whereas the government may be interested in the way the organisation applies health and safety regulations and pays corporation, VAT and other taxes. It should also be remembered that consumers and business-to-business customers may also be more interested in the organisation itself and so help initiate an umbrella branding strategy, which is considered in Chapters 14 and 15.

Traditionally these organisationally oriented activities have been referred to as corporate communications, as they deal more or less exclusively with the corporate entity or organisation. Products, services and other offerings are not normally the focus of these communications. It is the organisation and its role in the context of the particular stakeholders' activities that is important. However, it should be noted that as more corporate brands appear, the distinction between corporate and marketing communications begins to become much less clear. Indeed, when considered in the light of the development and interest in internal marketing (and communications), it may be of greater advantage to consider corporate communications as part of an organisation's overall marketing communications activities.

> The distinction between corporate and marketing communications begins to become much less clear.

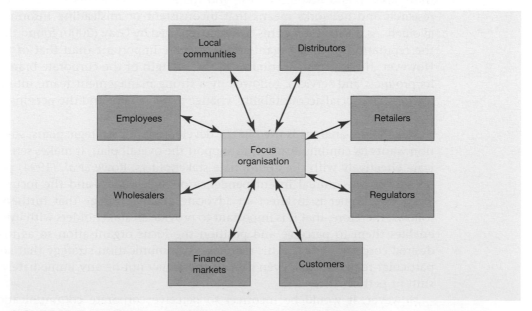

FIGURE 12.4 The direction of communication in a profile strategy

Communications used to satisfy this array of stakeholder needs and the organisation's corporate promotional goals are developed through what is referred to as a profile strategy, a major element of which is corporate branding, the subject of Chapter 15.

The awareness, perception and attitudes held by stakeholders towards an organisation need to be understood, shaped and acted upon. This can be accomplished

> The awareness, perception and attitudes held by stakeholders towards an organisation need to be understood, shaped and acted upon.

through continual dialogue, which will normally lead to the development of trust and commitment and enable relationships to grow. This is necessary in order that stakeholders act favourably towards an organisation and enable strategies to flourish and objectives to be achieved.

ViewPoint 12.5   H. Samuel raising its profile

In 2003 the UK jewellery market became increasingly competitive as stores such as Argos and Asda-Walmart began to exert control over much of the bottom end of the market while De Beers launched a chain of shops in a joint venture with the fashion company LVMH. In response to this squeeze, H. Samuel, the high street jewellery chain owned by Signet, attempted to differentiate itself by trying to create a destination lifestyle brand for its stores.

Part of this strategy required a rejuvenation of its corporate image. The goal was to enhance H. Samuel's profile and at the same time try to position it as more of a luxury brand than it has been perceived in the past.

Source: Adapted from Sweney (2003).

To build corporate brands, organisations must develop modern integrated communication programmes with all of their key stakeholder groups. Audiences demand transparency and accountability, and instant online access to news, developments, research and networks means that inconsistent or misleading information must be avoided. As if to reinforce this, a survey reported by Gray (2000) found that CEOs rated the reputation of their organisations as more important than that of their products. However, the leading contributor to the strength of the corporate brand is seen to be its products and services, followed by a strong management team, internal communications, PR, social accountability, change management and the personal reputation of the CEO.

Stakeholder analysis is used in the development of strategic plans, so if an organisation wants its communications to support the overall plan, it makes sense to communicate effectively with the appropriate stakeholders. Rowe *et al.* (1994) point out that, because of the mutual interdependence of stakeholders and the focus organisation, 'each stakeholder is in effect an advocate of any strategy that furthers its goals'. It follows, therefore, that it is important to provide all stakeholders with information that enables them to perceive and position the focus organisation so as to generate the desired corporate image. This requires a communication strategy that addresses these particular requirements, even though there may not be any immediately recognisable shift in performance.

However, it would be incorrect to perceive corporate communications as just a means of shaping or influencing the attitudes and behaviour of other stakeholders.

Organisations exist within a variety of networks, which provide a context for the roles and actions of member organisations (Chapter 8). Bidirectional communication flows exist and organisations adapt themselves to the actions and behaviour of others in the network. Therefore, corporate communications provides a mechanism by which it can learn about the context(s) in which it exists and is itself shaped and influenced by the other stakeholders with whom it shares communications. Reference is made to the work of Grunig and Hunt (1984), considered in Chapter 31.

A *profile* strategy is one that focuses an organisation's communications upon the development of corporate image and reputation, whether that be just internally, just externally or both. To accomplish and deliver a profile strategy public relations, including sponsorship and corporate advertising, become the pivotal tools of the marketing communications mix. Personal selling may remain a vital element delivering both product/service and corporate messages.

> A *profile* strategy is one that focuses an organisation's communications upon the development of corporate image and reputation.

Strategic balance

While the pull, push and profile strategies are important, it should be remembered that they are not mutually exclusive. Indeed, in most organisations it is possible to identify an element of each strategy at any one time. In reality, most organisations are structured in such a way that those responsible for communications with each of these three main audiences do so without reference to or coordination with each other. This is an example of how integrated marketing communications, which was examined in Chapter 11, needs to have one senior person responsible for all organisational communications. Only through a single point of reference is it realistically possible to develop and communicate a set of brand values that are consistent and credible.

Recognising these limitations that organisations often place on themselves, the 3Ps should be considered as part of a total communication approach. Figure 12.5 depicts how the emphasis of a total communication strategy can shift according to changing contextual elements – for example, the needs of the various target audiences, resources and wider elements such as the environment and the competition. The marketing communications eclipse provides

> The marketing communications eclipse provides a visual interpretation of the balance between the three strategic dimensions.

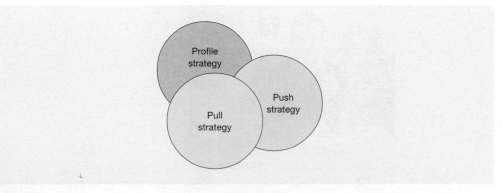

FIGURE 12.5 Marketing communication strategic eclipse

a visual interpretation of the balance between the three strategic dimensions. The more that is revealed of any one single strategy, the greater its role in any single campaign. Conversely, the less that is revealed, the smaller the contribution. In any one campaign, one or two of the three strategies might be used in preference to another and will often reflect branding approaches. For example, a brand manager's use of a profile strategy at Procter & Gamble or Mars will be virtually zero and will almost certainly be entirely pull in order to support the marketing channel or trade customers.

The role of each element of the marketing communications mix is important in promotional strategy. Each tool has different strengths and should be used accordingly. For example, direct marketing and sales promotion are more likely to be effective in persuading consumer audiences, while personal selling is likely to be more effective in b2b situations. A profile strategy designed to change perception and understanding of the organisation is more likely to utilise public relations and corporate advertising.

ViewPoint 12.6   Combining strategies

Research undertaken by the Meat and Livestock Commission identified that sales of beef and lamb for mid-week meals had been falling because consumers did not know how to prepare meat in a sufficiently quick or easy way. Consumers lacked cooking ideas and inspiration and, although meat was perceived as a traditional source of protein by consumers, other, more convenient foods were being used. Issues concerning customer and business context matters were therefore prevalent.

Convenience is a function of speed, ease and versatility. To increase consumption of meat, therefore, it was necessary to enable consumers to learn how to prepare beef and lamb in a convenient way. This was accomplished by generating a number of meal ideas and then communicating them in an informative yet credible way: a pull strategy.

It was decided that television was necessary to reach the target audience and the Harry Enfield character 'Tim Nice but Dim' would be a suitable opinion former. The reaction 'Well, if he can cook these dishes then so can I' was seen as an integral part of the way the message needed to be understood (decoded) by the target audience. See Exhibit 12.4.

The TV campaign ran for five weeks and was supported by a number of integrated promotional activities. All multiple retailers received on-pack stickers featuring a picture of 'Tim', recipe details and a reminder of the necessary ingredients. Other in-store support included shelf barkers and hanging posters.

EXHIBIT 12.4 Tim Nice but Dim

Free point-of-purchase material was received by 9,200 independent butchers and the campaign included six sheet posters placed outside Tesco and Sainsbury's stores: a push strategy. Public relations activities included the briefing of consumer journalists prior to the campaign burst, press releases to the regional press and radio interviews with celebrity chef James Martin to give a 'foodie' feel to the campaign.

A sales promotion programme using sound bites from the television commercial was used by some radio stations as part of a 'Listen and Win with Tim' campaign. Listeners had to answer a relevant question for a chance of winning some high-quality cookware. To complete the programme, the www.meatmatters.com site was refreshed and included a Tim microsite focusing solely on the campaign.

The 'Beef & Lamb, Nice & Simple' campaign had its origins in an understanding of the way consumers perceived the preparation of meat-based meals. The solutions sought to reposition beef and lamb as appropriate ingredients for modern weekday meals. This was achieved by educating consumers and helping them to learn how to use the product. They were invited to reason with the new knowledge inputs provided by the stimulus 'Tim' and then make a judgement about whether they could do the same.

By using marketing communications to inform and remind, consumers learned to reconsider their views of meat-based mid-week meals. By providing easy means to access relevant information, sales of beef and lamb increased, and qualitative research through Millward Brown found a positive shift in the way consumers perceived beef and lamb as a suitable mid-week meal. Members of the trade channel were kept informed and integrated into the campaign. Both pull and push strategies were used and they eclipsed those of a profile campaign for the Meat and Livestock Commission.

Source: Material kindly supplied by Phil Toms, Meat and Livestock Commission.

Marketing communication strategy, regardless of the overall focus, is normally composed of a number of different elements. When considering strategy there are a number of key issues that need to be considered. These are shown in Table 12.5.

Strategy needs to be understood in terms of the answers given in response to several critical questions. First, how are the communication goals that have been set going to be achieved? Secondly, how they are going to be accomplished in terms of

TABLE 12.5 Issues to be considered when developing marketing communications

Element	Issue
Target audiences	Which type of audience do we need to reach and why?
Channel strategies	How do we make our products/services available – direct or indirect?
Objectives	What do we need to achieve – what are our goals?
Positioning	How do we want to be perceived and understood?
Branding	How strong is our brand and what values and associations do stakeholders make with it?
Integration	How consistent are our communications, internally and externally?
Competitors	How do our communications compare with those of our key competitors?
Resources	What resources do we have and which do we need to secure?

complementing the business and marketing strategies? Thirdly, can current resources and opportunities support the strategy and do they encourage target audiences to respond to the communications?

Answers to these questions are not always easy to find and very often there will be conflicting proposals from different coalitions of internal stakeholders. In other words, there is a political element that needs to be considered and there may also be a strong overriding culture that directs the communication strategy and which may hinder innovation or the development of alternative methods of communication. Everyone who is involved with the development of marketing communications campaigns (internally and externally) should agree and prioritise necessary activities. The development of a marketing communications plan facilitates this process and enables the strategy to be articulated in such a way that the goals are achieved in a timely, efficient and effective manner.

> There is a political element that needs to be considered and there may also be a strong overriding culture that directs the communication strategy.

Internet strategies

The development of Internet-based facilities, once novel, is now quite commonplace for organisations and consumers. The function and speed of development of Internet facilities within organisations is a function of many factors, such as the size and core skills of the organisation (it is easier for an IT organisation than a transport organisation to develop ecommerce facilities), the nature of the product offering and the market and competitor conditions. It cannot, therefore, be concluded that there is a fixed pathway for the development and incorporation of the Internet within an organisation, nor should there be one as the flexibility and adaptability to meet individual organisational requirements needs to be retained.

However, it is useful to understand the basic types of online facilities in order to appreciate the strategic thinking that needs to be undertaken. The Internet can become an integral part of the way organisations operate, the way it sees its future and the way others see it, and not just be used to supplement the organisation's promotional programme. Having said that, it is this technology factor, more than any other, that has done so much to accelerate moves towards integrated marketing communications and to encourage managers to consider the totality of their activities rather than focus on an individual aspect.

The different Internet-related phases through which an organisation usually passes need to be considered alongside the technological platform that the organisation wishes to operate. Essentially the Internet provides Web site access for everyone. As discussed earlier, an extranet platform enables an organisation to restrict access to a number of selected organisations/people. For example, end-user customers, intermediaries and suppliers all might use an extranet to provide benefits that all can share and through which the host might develop competitive advantage. An intranet platform enables the use of the same browser-based technology but access is restricted to the employees of an organisation.

> The strategic choice of platform requires consideration of the different stakeholders with which the organisation wishes to interact.

The strategic choice of platform requires consideration of the different stakeholders with which the organisation wishes to interact. The management of these groups is then necessary in order to ensure optimum usage and the development of suitable relationships. Management needs to encourage stakeholder communities to grow and to interact with one another and this requires that users be empowered, encouraged to innovate and reviewed on a regular basis.

While the ability to reach customers directly, avoiding channel intermediaries and reducing transaction costs, is attractive strategies must be decided upon for attracting customers to a Web site (or TV-based 'shop'). Reliance on online communications alone is too limiting and unlikely to be successful so a combination of off-line and online communications is necessary to attract sufficient traffic.

The variety of off-line communications used by organisations varies according to their budgets and their overall strategy. Many online brands used television and outdoor advertising to promote not only the Web site but, more importantly for them, the brand name, to drive shareholder interest as these new entities sought stock market listings. As a result of this activity, outdoor advertising spend grew substantially. Sponsorship is also used to promote Web site addresses as well as a host of corporate literature such as company reports, brochures, calling cards and letterheads. Online communications vary from banner ads and pop-ups to viral marketing and public relations. However, research indicates that the most important factor that drives first-time visits is word of mouth and recommendations by significant others. In other words, people are more disposed to having their Web site behaviour directed by those they trust rather than risk time and effort seeking information based on communications that lack inherent credibility.

The balance between off-line- and online-generated traffic will also vary depending upon the nature of the brand itself. If a brand is being developed by a bricks and mortar company as an additional distribution and communications channel, but there is to be no visible tie to the parent company (Egg and Prudential), then the off-line branding development will need to be considerable. However, if the brand is to be tied in closely to the current channels (e.g. Argos), the initial branding can be constrained to converting current customers to the new product and to stimulating word-of-mouth recommendations, a much lower communications investment.

However, whatever the reason or branding strategy used to generate traffic, thought should be given to capitalising on the facilities to personalise the experience through the use of underlying data capture, storage, retrieval and processing abilities of integrated technologies. The ability to start with some knowledge of a customer's preferences, previous purchases, his or her already secure financial details and delivery address, for example, should be a major source of advantage. In addition, the interactive communications strategy needs to be thought through all points of customer interaction. Many companies have addressed the need to capture customers and even extract critical personal information but have failed to think through the total process and consider how the behaviour of the company communicates attitudes and degree of care. The use of email to confirm receipt and despatch details of a customer's order goes a long way to developing trust and positive customer attitudes, but unless the whole fulfilment exercise is compatible (and fulfilling), all of the investment in the front end of the exercise will be wasted.

Developing a marketing communications plan

The marketing communications planning framework (MCPF) aims to bring together the various elements of marketing communications into a logical sequence of activities. The rationale for promotional decisions is built upon information generated at previous levels in the framework. It also provides a checklist of activities that need to be considered.

The MCPF represents a way of understanding the different promotional components, of appreciating the way in which they relate to one another, and is a means of writing coherent marketing communications plans for work or for examinations, such as those offered by the Chartered Institute of Marketing in the Marketing Communications paper.

The second part of this book explored various contexts that influence or shape marketing communications. All marketing managers (and others) need to understand these contextual elements and appreciate how they contribute and influence the development of marketing communication programmes. In addition, there are a number of other elements and activities that need to be built into a programme in order that it can be implemented. These elements concern the goals, the resources, the promotional tools to be used and measures of control and evaluation. Just like the cogs in a clock, these elements need to be linked together if the plan is to work.

To help students and managers comprehend the linkages between the elements and to understand how these different components complement each other, the rest of this chapter deals with the development of marketing communication plans. To that extent it will be of direct benefit to managers seeking to build plans for the first time or for those familiar with the activity to reconsider current practices. Secondly, the material should also be of direct benefit to students who are required to understand and perhaps prepare such plans as part-fulfilment of an assessment or examination in this subject area.

The marketing communications planning framework

It has been established (Chapter 1) that the principal tasks facing marketing communications managers are to decide:

1. who should receive the messages

2. what the messages should say

3. what image of the organisation/brand receivers are expected to retain

4. how much is to be spent establishing this new established image

5. how the messages are to be delivered

6. what actions the receivers should take

7. how to control the whole process once implemented

8. what was achieved.

Note that more than one message is transmitted and that there is more than one target audience. This is important, as recognition of the need to communicate with multiple audiences and their different information requirements, often simultaneously, lies at the heart of marketing communications. The aim is to generate and transmit messages that present the organisation and its offerings to its various target audiences, encouraging them to enter into a dialogue. These messages must be presented consistently and they must address the points stated above. It is the skill and responsibility of the marketing communications planner to blend the communication tools and to create a mix that satisfies these elements.

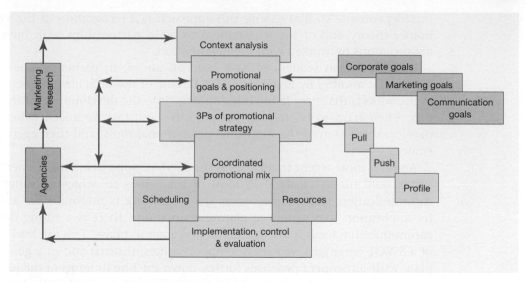

FIGURE 12.6 The marketing communications planning framework

A framework for integrated marketing communications plans

To enable managers and students to bring together the various promotional elements into a cohesive plan, which can be communicated to others, an overall framework is required.

The MCPF (Figure 12.6) seeks to achieve this by bringing together the various elements into a logical sequence of activities where the rationale for marketing communications decisions is built upon information generated at a previous level in the framework. Another advantage of using the MCPF is that it provides a suitable checklist of activities that need to be considered.

The MCPF represents a sequence of decisions that marketing managers undertake when preparing, implementing and evaluating communication strategies and plans. It

> The MCPF represents a sequence of decisions that marketing managers undertake when preparing, implementing and evaluating communication strategies and plans.

does not mean that this sequence reflects reality; indeed many marketing decisions are made outside any recognisable framework. However, as a means of understanding the different components, appreciating the way in which they relate to one another and bringing together various aspects for work or for answering examination questions such as those offered by the Chartered Institute of Marketing, this approach has many advantages and has been used by a number of local, national and international organisations.

Marketing communications requires the satisfaction of promotional objectives through the explicit and deliberate development of communication strategy. The MCPF will be used to show first the key elements, secondly some of the linkages and thirdly the integrated approach that is required.

> This framework reflects the deliberate or planned approach to strategy marketing communications.

This framework reflects the deliberate or planned approach to strategy marketing communications. The process of marketing communications, however, is not linear, as depicted in this framework, but integrative and interdependent. To that extent, this approach is a recognition of the value of stakeholder theory and of the requirement to build partnerships with buyers and other organisations networked with the organisation.

Other 'decision sequences' have been advanced, in particular one by Rothschild (1987) and another by Engel *et al.* (1994). One of the difficulties associated with their frameworks is that they fail to bring strategy into the development of the promotional mix. Their frameworks rely on the objective and task approach, whereby plans are developed for each of the individual promotional tools, and then aggregated to form strategy.

Another more recent framework is the SOSTAC approach. This is essentially a sound system and moves closer than most of the others to achieving suitable marketing communication plans. However, as the framework is multipurpose and is intended for application to a variety of planning situations, there is a strong danger that the communication focus is lost at the situation analysis phase. This can lead to a reiteration of a SWOT (strengths, weaknesses, opportunities, threats) and/or a general marketing plan, with subsequent problems further down the line in terms of the justification and understanding of the communications strategy and promotional mixes that need to be deployed. In addition, the SOSTAC model does not give sufficient emphasis to the need to identify and understand the characteristics of the target audience, which is so important for the development of a coherent marketing communications plan.

The MCPF approach presented here is not intended to solve all the problems associated with the formulation of such plans, but it is robust enough to meet the needs of employers and examiners, and is recommended.

Elements of the plan

Marketing communications plans consist of the following elements, which will be considered in turn:

- context analysis
- promotional objectives
- marketing communications strategy
- coordinated promotional mix (methods, tools and media)
- scheduling and implementation
- resources (human and financial)
- evaluation and control
- feedback.

Context analysis

Analysing the context in which marketing communication episodes occur is a necessary, indeed vital first step in the planning process. The purpose is to understand the key market and communication drivers that are likely to influence (or already are influencing) a brand (or organisation) and either help or hinder its progress towards meeting its long-term objectives. This is different from a situation analysis, because the situation analysis considers a range of wider organisational factors, most of which are normally considered in the development of marketing plans (while the communication focus is lost). Duplication is to be avoided, as it is both inefficient and confusing.

Analysing the context in which marketing communication episodes occur is a necessary, indeed vital first step in the planning process.

TABLE 12.6 The main elements of the context analysis

Context element	Dimensions
The customer context	Segment characteristics Levels of awareness, perception and attitudes towards the brand/organisation Level of involvement Types of perceived risk DMU characteristics and issues
The business context	Corporate and marketing strategy and plans Brand/organisation analysis Competitor analysis
The internal context	Financial constraints Organisation identity Culture, values and beliefs Marketing expertise Agency availability and suitability
The external context	Who are the key stakeholders and why are they important? What are their communication needs? Social, political, economic and technological restraints and opportunities.

The compilation of a context analysis (CA) is very important, as it presents information and clues about what the promotional plan needs to achieve. Information and market research data about target audiences (their needs, perception, motivation, attitudes and decision-making characteristics), the media and the people they use for information about offerings, the marketing objectives and timescales, the overall level of financial and other resources that are available, the quality and suitability of agency and other outsourced activities, and the environment in terms of societal, technological, political and economic conditions, both now and at some point in the future, all need to be considered.

At the root of the CA is the marketing plan. This will already have been prepared and contains important information about the target segment, the business and marketing goals, competitors and the timescales on which the goals are to be achieved.

The rest of the CA seeks to elaborate and build upon this information so as to provide the detail in order that the plan can be developed and justified.

The CA provides the rationale for the plan. It is from the CA that the marketing objectives (from the marketing plan) and the marketing communications objectives are derived. The type, form and style of the message are rooted in the characteristics of the target audience, and the media selected to convey messages will be based upon the nature of the tasks, the media habits of the audience and the resources available. The main components of the context analysis are set out in Table 12.6.

Promotional objectives

The role of promotional objectives in the planning process is important for a number of reasons. The first is that they provide a balance to the plan and take away the sole emphasis on sales that inevitably arises. Secondly, they indicate positioning issues, thirdly they highlight the required balance of the promotional mix, fourthly they provide time parameters for campaigns and finally they provide a crucial means by which particular marketing communication activities are evaluated.

Ideally, promotional objectives should consist of three main elements:

Corporate objectives

These are derived from the business or marketing plan. They refer to the mission and the business area that the organisation believes it should be in.

Marketing objectives

These are derived from the marketing plan and are output oriented. Normally these can be considered as sales-related objectives, such as market share, sales revenues, volumes, ROI (return on investment) and profitability indicators.

Marketing communication objectives

These are derived from an understanding of the current context in which a brand exists and the future context in the form of where the brand is expected to be at some point in the future. These will be presented as awareness levels, perception, comprehension/knowledge, attitudes towards and overall degree of preference for the brand. The choice of communication goal depends upon the tasks that need to be accomplished. In addition, most brands need either to maintain their current brand position or reposition themselves in the light of changing contextual conditions.

These three elements constitute the promotional objectives and they all need to be set out in SMART terminology (see Chapter 13). What also emerges is a refinement to the positioning that managers see as important for success. Obviously, not all plans require express attention to positioning (e.g. government information campaigns) but most commercial and brand-oriented communication programmes need to communicate a clear position in their market. So, at this point the positioning intentions are developed and these will be related to the market, the customers or some other dimension. The justification for this will arise from the CA.

Marketing communication strategy

The communication strategy should be customer not method/media oriented. Therefore the strategy depends upon whether the target audience is a consumer segment, a distributor or dealer network or whether all stakeholders need to be reached. In addition, it is imperative that the strategy be geared to the communication needs of the target audience that is revealed during the customer and business context analyses. This will show what the task is that marketing communications needs to achieve. Having established who the audience is, push-, pull- or profile-dominated strategies can be identified. The next step is to determine the task that needs to be accomplished. This will have been articulated previously in the marketing communications objectives but the approach at this stage is less quantitative and softer. The DRIP roles of marketing communications can be used to suggest the strategy being pursued. For example, if a new brand is being launched, the first task will be to inform and differentiate the brand for members of the trade before using a pull strategy to inform and differentiate the brand for the target end-user customers. An organisation wishing to signal a change of strategy and/or a change of name following a merger or acquisition may choose to use a profile strategy and the primary task will be to inform of the name change. An organisation experiencing declining sales may choose to remind customers of a need or it may choose to improve sales through persuasion.

> The strategy depends upon whether the target audience is a consumer segment, a distributor or dealer network or whether all stakeholders need to be reached.

Promotional methods

Having formulated, stated and justified the required position, the next step is to present the basic form and style of the key message that is to be conveyed. Is there to be a lot of copy or just a little? Is there to be a rational or emotional approach or some weighting between the two? What should be the tone of the visual messages? Is there to be a media blitz (e.g. a Microsoft-type day, as used for the launch of Windows 95, or Cable & Wireless yellow saturation)? It is at this point that those responsible for the development of these plans can be imaginative and try some new ideas. Trying to tie in the message to the strategic orientation is the important part, as the advertising agency will refine and redefine the message and the positioning.

> Trying to tie in the message to the strategic orientation is the important part, as the advertising agency will refine and redefine the message and the positioning.

From this the promotional mixes need to be considered *for each* of the strategies proposed, that is, a mix for the consumer strategy, a mix for the trade strategy and a distinct mix for the communications to reach the wider array of stakeholders.

The choice of promotional methods should clearly state the methods and the media to be used. A short paragraph justifying the selection is very important, as the use of media in particular is to a large extent dependent upon the nature of the goals, the target audience and the resources. The key is to provide message consistency and a measure of integration.

The schedule

The next step is to schedule the deployment of the methods and the media. This is best achieved by the production of a Gantt chart.

Events should be scheduled according to the goals and the strategic thrust. So, if it is necessary to communicate with the trade prior to a public launch, those activities tied into the push strategy should be scheduled prior to those calculated to support the pull strategy.

Similarly, if awareness is a goal then, if funds permit, it may be best to use television and posters first before sales promotions (unless sampling is used), direct marketing, point of purchase and personal selling.

Resources

This is a vitally important part of the plan, one that is often avoided or forgotten about. The resources necessary to support the plan need to be determined, and these refer not only to the financial issues but to the quality of available marketing expertise and the time that is available to achieve the required outcomes.

> The resources necessary to support the plan need to be determined.

Gantt charts and other project planning aids are best used to support this part of the plan. The cost of the media and methods can either be allocated in a right-hand column of the chart, or a new chart can be prepared. Preferably, actual costs should be assigned, although percentages can be allocated if examination time is at a premium. What is of importance is the relative weighting of the costs and that there is a recognition and understanding of the general costs associated with the proposed individual activities.

It must be understood that a television campaign cannot be run for less than £1.5 million and that the overall cost of the strategy should be in proportion to the size of the client organisation, its (probable) level of profitability and the size and dynamics of the market in which it operates.

Control and evaluation

Unless there is some form of evaluation, there will be no dialogue and no true marketing communications. There are numerous methods to evaluate the individual performance of the tools and the media used, and for examination purposes these should be stated. In addition, and perhaps more meaningfully, the most important measures are the promotional objectives set in the first place. The success of a promotional strategy and the associated plan is the degree to which the objectives set are achieved.

Feedback

The planning process is completed when feedback is provided. Not only should information regarding the overall outcome of a campaign be considered but so should individual aspects of the activity. For example, the performance of the individual tools used within the campaign, whether sufficient resources were invested, the appropriateness of the strategy in the first place, any problems encountered during implementation and the relative ease with which the objectives were accomplished are aspects that need to be fed back to all internal and external parties associated with the planning process.

This feedback is vitally important because it provides information for the context analysis that anchors the next campaign. Information fed back in a formal and

> This feedback is vitally important because it provides information for the context analysis that anchors the next campaign.

systematic manner constitutes an opportunity for organisations to learn from their previous campaign activities, a point often overlooked and neglected.

Links and essential points

It was mentioned earlier that there are a number of linkages associated with different parts of the marketing communications plan. It is important to understand the nature of these links as they represent the interconnections between different parts of the plan and the rationale for undertaking the contextual analysis in particular. The contextual analysis feeds the items shown in Table 12.7. The promotional objectives derived from the CA feed decisions concerning strategy, tools and media, scheduling and evaluation.

The marketing communications strategy is derived from an overall appreciation of the needs of the target audience (and stakeholders) regarding the brand and its competitive position in the market. The promotional mix is influenced by the previous elements and the budget that follows. However, the nature of the tools and the capacity and characteristics of the media influence scheduling, implementation and evaluation activities.

To help explain the MCPF and the linkage, a mini-case study follows the Summary and Review Questions. You are required to prepare a marketing communications plan. It is suggested that you prepare one using the material in this chapter as a guide. An answer is available on the Web site www.booknets/fillc/ that you can use to compare with your own response. The prepared answer is not the only possible answer: there are other plans that could be of equal significance and use.

TABLE 12.7 Linkages within the MCPF

Objectives	From the marketing plan, from the customer, stakeholder network and competitor analysis and from an internal marketing review
Strategic balance between push, pull and profile	From an understanding of the brand, the needs of the target audiences, including employees and all other stakeholders, and the marketing goals
Brand positioning	From users' and non-users' perceptions, motivations, attitudes and understanding about the brand and its direct and indirect competitors
Message content and style	From an understanding about the level of involvement, perceived risk, DMU analysis, information-processing styles and the positioning intentions
Promotional tools and media	From the target audience analysis of media habits, involvement and preferences, from knowledge about product suitability and media compatibility, from a competitor analysis and from the resource analysis

Summary

The development of a marketing communications strategy is important if an organisation is to communicate effectively with its various target audiences. Unlike planning, which is an articulation of strategy, marketing communications needs to be rooted in its target audiences and the task that needs to be completed.

Push, pull and profile strategies can be combined in different ways to meet the needs of different communication tasks. In addition to the broad target, it is important to express strategy in terms of the differentiation (positioning), reminding/reassuring, informing and persuading of audiences.

The marketing communications planning framework offers a sequential format for the development of marketing communication plans. In real life such plans are developed in parallel and involve different individuals and stakeholders in varying degrees. The framework presented here is practical and robust, yet the linear approach should not be accepted without question.

Communication strategy is about the direction and coordination of messages to specific audiences. It is about the delivery of timely, accurate messages that are of significant value for their recipients.

Review questions

1. Write brief notes explaining some of the key approaches to understanding strategy.

2. Explain the role strategy plays in marketing communications.

3. Compare strategy with planning. In what ways might planning be the same as strategy?

4. What are the 3Ps of marketing communications strategy? Explain the differences between each of them and use the marketing communications eclipse to support your answer.

5. Explain the key characteristics associated with a pull strategy.

6. Draw two diagrams depicting the direction of communications in both the push and the pull strategies.

7. Describe what the 'core message' is and provide four examples.

8. Sketch the marketing communications planning framework – from memory.

9. Following on from the previous question, check your version of the MCPF with the original and then prepare some bullet-point notes, highlighting the critical linkages between the main parts of the framework.

10. Discuss the extent to which Internet strategies should be considered a part of marketing communication strategies as a whole.

MINI-CASE
North West Valley Sailing Club

Mini-case written by Angela Hall, Senior Lecturer, Manchester Metropolitan University Business School

Introduction

The North West Valley Sailing Club is based at a reservoir 25 miles north of Manchester. The reservoir is located in an attractive area of moorland. The Manchester bus passes the reservoir every 15 minutes from Monday to Saturday, and hourly on Sunday. The geographical location of the 90-acre reservoir is 300 metres above sea level and lends itself to fresh, clean winds. It is noted as the north-west high wind centre. It is generally recognised to be the best inland location for dinghy and board sailing in north-east Lancashire, if not the whole region. The water itself is very clean, coming straight off the moors, and the bottom of the reservoir has no pollution.

The water is relatively shallow by reservoir/lake standards, and therefore warms up earlier and stays warmer longer than inland counterparts.

In 1998 the club managed to secure lottery funds to build a new clubhouse. This was completed in 2001. The total cost of this development was over £400,000. It provides changing facilities, showers and toilets, a bar/food/lounge area, a separate large function room, an indoor viewing area and an outdoor covered patio viewing area. An on-site business, which is independent of the club, is also attached. This business sells sailing equipment and courses for windsurfing and sailing. Outside the clubhouse there is a dinghy park where members may berth their craft. Two concrete jetties provide ease of access to the water's edge. There is a designated grass rigging-up area for windsurfers and a large car park area.

Target audience

The broad aims and objectives of the club, enshrined in its constitution, are to:

- promote and facilitate sailing and other allied non-powered watersports;
- encourage interested people of all abilities to develop the skills of sailing through the provision of training and coaching;
- provide such social and other facilities to members as may be from time to time determined by the club;
- encourage and develop the use of the water, surrounding land and clubhouse by users other than members of the sailing club.

It is recognised that a higher percentage of social grade A, B, C1 are attracted to sailing; these are therefore the groups targeted. Analysis of membership in 2002 indicated the following occupations for members:

Occupation	Percentage
School/students	17
Retired/unemployed	1
Local government	5
Fire/Police	5
Teaching	10
Medical	6
Art/Design	4
Food industry	4
Printing industry	3
Computing	9
Banking/Accounting/Surveying	8
Engineering	18
Manufacturing/Retail	9
Other	1

Analysis of the age range of the members registered in 2002 shows the following:

Age	Percentage
Over 50 years	17
30–49 years	44
21–29 years	15
Under 21 years	19

When the business plan was written for the lottery fund bid a number of key target audiences were highlighted as being important:

- young people
- women
- people with disabilities.

Young people

Watersports and in particular sailing have always held an attraction for young people; however, often the lack of facilities and the initial cost of the equipment put the sport out of the reach of many of them. By providing the necessary facilities, equipment, encouragement and training the club aims to provide opportunities for young people to progress in the sport in an enjoyable and safe environment. The club provides facilities to sail windsurfers and dinghies. It sports a thriving junior section that meets regularly and excels on the junior racing circuit.

Windsurfing is a dynamic sport similar to other youth culture sports such as surfing, snowboarding and skateboarding. It therefore has the potential 'street cred' for today's youth. Young people new to the sport have natural physical advantages. Their light weight, general fitness and athleticism give them the ability to learn quickly and to progress to more advanced equipment and techniques. Young people benefit from a lack of fear. They are naturally daredevil and have a 'go for it' attitude to sports.

School children have a lot of time available during the long school holidays. Sailing as a sport (after the initial outlay on the necessary equipment) is not expensive on a day-to-day basis. The theory of the sport will teach young people knowledge of weather patterns, the dynamics of sailing and windsurfing, and the theory of aerodynamics and resolution of forces. These can be used to build on in school education.

Women

Many of the points made about young people are also relevant for women. The advantages of light weight together with modern lightweight equipment gives women an excellent opportunity to learn and excel at the sport. The apparent restriction of a lack of basic strength can be overcome by development of good technique. Sailing is an ideal family activity. Every member of the family can enjoy the sport whatever their standard or abilities. The club wishes to change the perception by women that sailing, and windsurfing in particular, are sports for men only.

People with disabilities

The potential for people with different disabilities has been researched as shown in the following table.

Category	Windsurfing	Dinghy sailing	Canoeing	Mountain biking	Horse riding	Fishing	Walking
The deaf	A	A	A	A	A	A	A
The visually impaired	B	B	B	C	B	B	B
The blind	D	B	B	E	B	B	B
The amputee	D	B/S	B/S	C/S	B/S	B	B
The paraplegic	E/S	B/S	B/S	E	B/S	B	B
The quadriplegic	F	B/S	E	F	C	E	D/S
Those with learning difficulties	B	B	B	B	B	B	B

Key

A   No physical problems – communication is more difficult
B   Possible with assistance
C   Difficult
D   Very difficult
E   Extremely difficult
F   Almost impossible
/S   With special equipment

The club plans to provide, either directly or through other agencies, access to both the water and surrounding countryside and to welcome use of the club's facilities by all groups of people with disabilities. Club facilities will be made available as necessary. The clubhouse interior has been designed with disabled people in mind, and has had direct input into this design from disabled groups in the area.

Membership details

The club has a membership of over 100. A key objective is to increase membership by at least 12 per cent each year.

Membership details from 1995 to 2003 are shown below.

	1995	1996	1997	1998	1999	2000	2001	2002	2003
New members	30	33	35	35	40	40	35	37	35
Windsurfers					100	110	114	117	114
Dinghy sailors					35	39	41	44	41
Adult	50	55	55	60	62	64	66	66	66
Family	39	29	30	30	31	35	36	38	36
Junior	15	15	15	18	20	22	23	23	23
Temporary sailing	200	103	120	130	150	180	190	197	190
Temporary fishing	30	32	30	31	32	30	35	39	35

Notes

New members are for all categories of membership.
Windsurfers and dinghy sailors – since 1999 information has been held on each member and which type of sailing they are interested in.
Adult membership is for those over 16 years of age.
Family membership is for two people or more, living at the same address. It includes up to four children.
Junior membership is for those under the age of 16.
Temporary sailing is available for non-members on a daily basis (includes windsurfing and dinghy sailing).
Temporary fishing is available for non-members on a daily basis.

Note that figures for family/junior/adult membership do not equal number of windsurfers or sailors due to family members. One family membership could, for example, contain a family of four, or might just consist of two.

Prices for courses and membership

Membership costs

Adult membership, 1 year, per person	£95
Junior membership, 1 year, per person	£45
Family membership, 1 year, per family	£160
Unemployed/retired/student membership, 1 year, per person	£55

Occasional user costs

Day sailors	Adult, per day	£8.00
	Under-16, per day	£6.00
Hiring equipment	1st hour	£8.00
	After 1st hour, per hour	£5.50
Day fishing permit	Per day	£6.00

Courses for non-members (10 per cent reduction for members)

Learn to sail/windsurf	Adult two-day course	£75
	Junior 3 hrs × four days	£40
Improver course	Adult 3 hours individual	£40
	Junior 2 hours individual	£30
Saturday morning juniors sailing		£7.50
School parties (min. ten people) 3-hour session		£8.50
(free to staff accompanying children)		

Above prices include use of equipment and wetsuit, and prices are per person.

Competition

There are a number of competitors within the North West, details are as follows:

Club 1 – located on a reservoir around 10 miles away, also in Lancashire. The only users of the water are windsurfers. The sailing area is of a smaller size, and wind conditions are not quite as good due to its location. Membership costs are lower, but facilities are old, and there are no organised social events. There is no shop, nor bar or catering facilities.

Club 2 – located around 35 miles away in North Yorkshire. The club is located on an extremely large area of water. Wind conditions are very good. Membership costs are lower, but facilities are old and very basic. Many day sailors visit due to the large sailing area. There are mainly windsurfers, but some dinghy sailing takes place.

Club 3 – located in South Manchester, around 35 miles away. The club is situated on a large area of water and is more popular for water-skiing and jet-skiing. Membership costs are considerably higher. Good modern facilities.

There are other clubs located around the region, but the above are the only inland sailing clubs.

Marketing communications

The club communicates to existing members through a quarterly newsletter, which is sent to the home address of all members.

During the building of the new clubhouse a number of press releases were sent to local newspapers. However, since 2001 this has ceased.

Research among the existing membership in 1999 indicated that there was a definite potential to make use of word-of-mouth recommendation providing an appropriate incentive was available. This has not yet been implemented.

No marketing communications have yet been devised that promote the other facilities available for use to existing members.

A small number of leaflets have been distributed to some schools and local housing estates over the last few years. No information has been collated on whether this has been successful. These leaflets have not been updated since the new clubhouse was built.

Each year the club has an open day where anyone can come and have a look around, meet existing members, and have a free sailing lesson. This tends to be advertised by putting signs on the main road close to the entrance of the club. A number of new members have been recruited this way, but there is a feeling that these tend to be friends/family of existing members. More publicity of these open days is required. Currently these open days take place at the weekend, but could quite easily either be extended or moved to evenings (those evenings when it is light).

The club is in the process of developing a Web site. Car stickers are provided each year with each membership renewal.

The club would like to raise its profile. Its ambition is to become the premier inland windsurfing and dinghy sailing club in the region. It also wants to increase its membership by at least 12 per cent each year. Membership increases are especially sought from those thought to be underrepresented at the club (e.g. women, youngsters, the disabled, and those in lower socio-economic groups).

New developments

When writing the business plan to secure lottery funds, one of the key areas was generating increased use of the water and surrounding area. This could include canoeing, mountain biking, horse riding and walking. Some preliminary research among members found that a significant number of sailors are also involved/interested in mountain bikes. Specific groups of people underrepresented were thought to be young people, women and people with disabilities.

The reservoir and land are leased from North West Water, which does not permit the use of powerboats.

Additional information

During 2000 the club marketing secretary resigned owing to other commitments. Since this time there has been little or no marketing activity. There is no marketing communication plan in place. The club is concerned that at a time when it has some excellent and new facilities membership has not significantly increased.

The club tends to be most busy at weekends, with less use during the week. Courses are available seven days per week and it is open for sailing seven days per week. Some sailing takes place during weekdays, but this tends to be from those who work shifts, are retired, etc. Occasional courses for schools take place in the late afternoon. Wednesday evening is the Junior Club evening, which tends to be quite popular. The majority of people sail from early spring through to late autumn, although a small minority sail throughout the winter months.

The function room is currently used for committee meetings once per month, and for occasional social club events for members. Increased usage of this room is sought from existing members, local associations/clubs, etc, and by the general public. A small fee is charged for hiring the function room.

EXHIBIT 12.5 The North West Valley Sailing Club

There are no paid club members – all work undertaken is on a voluntary basis. A number of members have said that they will offer some of their free time to assist in supporting marketing activities, such as contacting various organisations, distributing literature, assisting at open days, etc.

The budget available for marketing communications is exceptionally small however; money has been found for this year only up to a maximum of £10,000.

Brief

You are a marketing communications consultant assigned to the North West Valley Sailing Club. Your task is to develop a marketing communications plan that is to be implemented in the next 12 months.

For answer visit: www.booksnet/fillc.

References

Andrews, K. (1987) *The Concept of Corporate Strategy*. Homewood, IL: Irwin.

Ansoff, H.I. (1965) *Corporate Strategy*. New York: McGraw-Hill.

Beane, T.P. and Ennis, D.M. (1987) Market segmentation: a review. *European Journal of Marketing*, **21**(5), pp. 20–42.

Chaffee, E. (1985) Three models of strategy. *Academy of Management Review*, **10**(1), pp. 89–98.

Engel, J.F., Warshaw, M.R. and Kinnear, T.C. (1994) *Promotional Strategy*. 8th edn. Homewood, IL: Irwin.

Gray, R. (2000) The chief encounter. *PR Week*, 8 September, pp. 13–16.

Grunig, J. and Hunt, T. (1984) *Managing Public Relations*. New York: Holt, Rineholt & Winston.

Haley, R.I. (1968) Benefit segmentation: a decision-oriented research tool. *Journal of Marketing*, **32** (July), pp. 30–5.

Hambrick, D.C. (1983) High profit strategies in mature capital goods industries: a contingency approach. *Academy of Management Journal*, **26**, pp. 687–707.

Kay, J. (1993) The structure of strategy. *Business Strategy Review*, **4**(2) (Summer) pp. 17–37.

Mintzberg, H. (1994) *The Rise and Fall of Strategic Planning*, Englewood-Cliffs, NJ: Prentice-Hall.

Pearce, J.A. and Robinson, R.B. Jr. (1997) *Formulation, Implementation, and Control of Competitive Strategy*. 10th edn. Chicago, IL: Irwin.

Rothschild, M. (1987) *Marketing Communications*. Lexington, MA: D.C. Heath.

Rowe, A.J., Mason, R.O., Dickel, K.E., Mann, R.B. and Mockler, R.J. (1994) *Strategic Management: A Methodological Approach*. 4th edn. Reading, MA: Addison-Wesley.

Sweney, M. (2003) Samuel aims to raise profile with BMP hiring. *Campaign*, 14 February, p. 5.

Whittington, R. (1993) *What Is Strategy and Does It Matter?* London: Routledge.

Marketing communications: objectives and positioning

13

The formal setting of promotional objectives is important because they provide guidance concerning what is to be achieved
and when. These objectives form a pivotal role between the
business/marketing plans and the marketing communications
strategy. The way in which a product or service is perceived by
buyers is the only positioning that really matters.

Aims and objectives

The aims of this chapter are to establish the nature and importance of the role that
objectives play in the formulation of promotional strategies and to explore the concept
of positioning.

The objectives of this chapter are to:

1. examine the need for organisational objectives;
2. set out the different types of organisational goals;
3. specify the relationship between corporate strategy and promotional
   objectives;
4. determine the components of promotional objectives;
5. examine the differences between sales- and communication-based objectives;
6. evaluate the concept of positioning;
7. explore the technique of perceptual mapping;
8. understand and determine various positioning strategies.

Introduction

There are many different opinions about what it is that marketing communications seeks to achieve. The conflicting views have led some practitioners and academics to polarise their thoughts about what constitutes an appropriate set of objectives. First, much effort and time has been spent trying to determine what promotion and marketing communication activities are supposed to achieve in the first place. Secondly, how should the success of a campaign be evaluated? Finally, how is it best to determine the degree of investment that should be made in each of the areas of the promotional mix? The process of resolving these different demands that are placed upon organisations has made the setting of promotional objectives very complex and difficult. It has been termed 'a job of creating order out of chaos' (Kriegel, 1986). This perceived complexity has led a large number of managers to fail to set promotional objectives. Many of those that do set them do so in such a way that they are inappropriate, inadequate or merely restate the marketing objectives. The most common promotional objectives set by managers are sales related. These include increases in market share, return on investment, sales volume increases and improvements in the value of sales made after accounting for the rate of inflation.

> This perceived complexity has led a large number of managers to fail to set promotional objectives.

Such a general perspective ignores the influence of the other elements of the marketing mix and implicitly places the entire responsibility for sales performance with the promotional mix. This is not an accurate reflection of the way in which businesses and organisations work. In addition, because sales tests are too general, they would be an insufficiently rigorous test of promotional activity and there would be no real evaluation of promotional activities. Sales volumes vary for a wide variety of reasons:

1. Competitors change their prices.
2. Buyers' needs change.
3. Changes in legislation may favour the strategies of particular organisations.
4. Favourable third-party communications become known to significant buyers.
5. General economic conditions change.
6. Technological advances facilitate improved production processes, economies of scale, experience effects and, for some organisations, the opportunity to reduce costs.
7. The entry and exit of different competitors.

These are a few of the many reasons why sales might increase and conversely why sales might decrease. Therefore, the notion that marketing communications is entirely responsible for the sales of an offering is clearly unacceptable, unrealistic and incorrect.

The role of objectives in corporate strategy

Objectives play an important role in the activities of individuals, social groups and organisations because of the following:

1. They provide direction and an action focus for all those participating in the activity.
2. They provide a means by which the variety of decisions relating to an activity can be made in a consistent way.

3. They determine the time period in which the activity is to be completed.

4. They communicate the values and scope of the activity to all participants.

5. They provide a means by which the success of the activity can be evaluated.

It is generally accepted that the process of developing corporate strategy demands that a series of objectives be set at different levels within an organisation (Johnson and Scholes, 2002; Quinn *et al.*, 2003). This hierarchy or objective consists of mission, strategic business unit or business objectives and functional objectives, such as production, finance or marketing goals.

The first level in the hierarchy (mission) requires that an overall direction be set for the organisation. If strategic decisions are made to achieve corporate objectives,

A clearly developed, articulated and communicated mission statement enables an organisation to define whose needs are to be satisfied, what needs require satisfying and which products and technologies will be used to provide the desired levels of satisfaction.

both objectives and strategy are themselves constrained by an organisation's mission. Mission statements are 'management's vision of what the organisation is trying to do and to become over the long term' (Thompson and Strickland, 1990). A mission statement outlines who the organisation is, what it does and where it is headed. A clearly developed, articulated and communicated mission statement enables an organisation to define whose needs are to be satisfied, what needs require satisfying and which products and technologies will be used to provide the desired levels of satisfaction.

Conventionally, setting the mission answers the question 'What business are we in?' (Levitt, 1960). Obvious answers such as 'engineering', 'food processing', 'import and export' or 'retailing' miss the point. These are merely activ-

Setting the mission answers the question 'What business are we in?'

ities. Missions must be linked, explicitly, first and foremost to the needs met, rather than to markets or industries (Rosen, 1995). According to IBM, its original success was tied to its founder's principle of 'offering the best customer service in the world', not to technological innovation. The mission then, should clearly identify the following:

1. the customers/buyers to be served

2. the needs to be satisfied

3. the products and/or technologies by which these will be achieved.

In some organisations these points are explicitly documented in a mission statement. These statements often include references to the organisation's philosophy, culture, commitment to the community and employees, growth, profitability and so on, but these should not blur or distract attention from the organisation's basic mission. The words mission and vision are often used interchangeably, but they have separate meanings. Vision refers to the expected or desired outcome of carrying out the mission over the agreed period of time.

The mission provides a framework for the organisation's objectives, and the objectives that follow should promote and be consistent with the mission. While the word 'mission' implies a singularity of purpose, organisations have multiple objectives because

The mission provides a framework for the organisation's objectives.

of the many aspects of the organisation's performance and behaviour that contribute to the mission, and should, therefore, be explicitly identified. However, as Rosen points out, many of these objectives will conflict with each other. In

retailing, for example, if an organisation chooses to open larger stores, then total annual profit should rise, but average profit per square metre will probably fall. Short-term profitability can be improved by reducing investment, but this could adversely affect long-term profitability. Organisations therefore have long-term and short-term objectives.

At the SBU level, objectives represent the translation of the mission into a form that can be understood by relevant stakeholders.

At the SBU level, objectives represent the translation of the mission into a form that can be understood by relevant stakeholders. These objectives are the performance requirements for the organisation or unit and these in turn are broken down into objectives or targets that each functional area must achieve, as their contribution to the unit objectives. Marketing strategies are functional strategies, as are the strategies for the finance, human resource management and production departments. Combine or aggregate them and the SBU's overall target will, in reductionist theory, be achieved.

The various organisational objectives are of little use if they are not communicated to those who need to know what they are. Traditionally, such communication has focused upon employees, but there is increasing recognition that the other members of the stakeholder network need to understand an organisation's purpose and objectives. The marketing objectives developed for the marketing strategy provide important information for the communications strategy. Is the objective to increase market share or to defend or maintain the current situation? Is the product new or established? Is it being modified or slowly withdrawn? The corporate image is shaped partly by the organisation's objectives and the manner in which they are communicated. All these impact upon the objectives of the communications plan.

Promotional objectives consist of three main components. The first component concerns issues relating to the buyers of the product or service offered by the organisation.

Promotional objectives consist of three main components.

The second concerns issues relating to sales volume, market share, profitability and revenue. The third stream relates to the image, reputation and preferences that other stakeholders have towards the organisation. Each of these three streams is developed later in this chapter.

The role of promotional objectives and plans

Many organisations, including some advertising agencies, fail to set realistic (if any) promotional objectives. There are several explanations for this behaviour, but one of the common factors is that managers are unable to differentiate between the value of promotion as an expenditure and as an investment. This issue is addressed later (Chapter 16), but for now the value of promotional objectives can be seen in terms of the role they play in communications planning, evaluation and brand development.

The setting of promotional objectives is important for three main reasons. The first is that they provide a means of communication and coordination between groups (e.g. client and agency) working upon different parts of a campaign. Performance is improved if there is common understanding about the tasks the promotional tools have to accomplish. Secondly, objectives constrain the number of options available to an organisation. Promotional objectives act as a guide for decision-making and provide a focus for decisions that follow in the process of developing promotional plans. The third reason is that objectives provide a benchmark so that the relative success or failure of a programme can be evaluated.

There is no doubt that organisations need to be flexible to be able to anticipate and adjust to changes in their environments. This principle applies to the setting of promotional objectives. To set one all-encompassing objective and expect it to last the year (or whatever period is allocated) is both hopeful and naive; multiple objectives are necessary.

The content of promotional objectives has also been the subject of considerable debate. Two distinct schools of thought emerge: those that advocate sales-related measures as the main factors and those that advocate communication-related measures as the main orientation.

The sales school

As stated earlier, many managers see sales as the only meaningful objective for promotional plans. Their view is that the only reason an organisation spends money on promotion is to sell its product or service. Therefore, the only meaningful measure of the effectiveness of the promotional spend is in the sales results.

These results can be measured in a number of different ways. Sales turnover is the first and most obvious factor, particularly in business-to-business markets. In consumer markets and the fast-moving consumer goods sector, market share movement is measured regularly and is used as a more sensitive barometer of performance. Over the longer term, return on investment measures are used to calculate success and failure. In some sectors the number of products (or cases) sold, or volume of product shifted, relative to other periods of activity, is a common measure.

Over the longer term, return on investment measures are used to calculate success and failure.

There are a number of difficulties with this view. One of these has been looked at above, that sales result from a variety of influences, such as the other marketing mix elements, competitor actions and wider environmental effects, for example the strength of the currency, changing social preferences or the level of interest rates.

A second difficulty rests with the concept of adstock or carryover. The impact of promotional expenditure may not be immediately apparent, as the receiver may not enter the market until some later date, but the effects of the promotional programme may influence the eventual purchase decision. This means that, when measuring the effectiveness of a campaign, sales results will not always reflect its full impact.

Sales objectives do little to assist the media planner, copywriters and creative team associated with the development of the communications programme, despite their inclusion in campaign documents such as media briefs.

Where direct action is required by the receiver in response to exposure to a message, measurement of sales is justifiable.

Sales-oriented objectives are, however, applicable in particular situations. For example, where direct action is required by the receiver in response to exposure to a message, measurement of sales is justifiable. Such an action, a behavioural response, can be solicited in direct-response advertising. This occurs where the sole communication is through a particular medium, such as television or print.

The retail sector can also use sales measures, and it has been suggested that packaged goods organisations, operating in markets that are mature with established pricing and distribution structures, can build a databank from which it is possible to isolate the advertising effect through sales. For example, Sainsbury's is able to monitor the stock movements of particular ingredients used in its 'celebrity recipe' commercials. This enables it to evaluate the success of particular campaigns and particular celebrities. Its use of celebrity chef Jamie Oliver is so successful that it can stock ingredients in anticipation of particular advertisements being screened. However, despite this cause-and-effect relationship, it can be argued that this may ignore the impact of changes in competitor actions and changes in the overall environment. Furthermore, the effects of the organisation's own corporate advertising, adstock effects and other family brand promotions need to be accounted for if a meaningful sales effect is to be generated.

The sales school advocates the measure on the grounds of simplicity.

The sales school advocates the measure on the grounds of simplicity. Any manager can utilise the tool, and senior management does not wish to be concerned with information that is complex or unfamiliar, especially when working to short lead times and accounting periods. It is a self-consistent theory, but one that may misrepresent consumer behaviour and the purchase process (perhaps unintentionally), and to that extent may result in less than optimal expenditure on marketing communications.

The communications school

There are many situations, however, where the aim of a communications campaign is to enhance the image or reputation of an organisation or product. Sales are not regarded as the only goal. Consequently, promotional efforts are seen as communication tasks, such as the creation of awareness or positive attitudes towards the organisation or product.

Promotional efforts are seen as communication tasks, such as the creation of awareness or positive attitudes towards the organisation or product.

To facilitate this process, receivers have to be given relevant information before the appropriate decision processes can develop and purchase activities established as a long-run behaviour.

Various models have been developed to assist our understanding about how these promotional tasks are segregated and organised effectively. AIDA and other hierarchy of effects models were considered in Chapter 7 at some length and need not be repeated here. However, one particular model was developed deliberately to introduce clear objectives into the advertising development process: Dagmar.

Dagmar

Russell Colley (1961) developed a model for setting advertising objectives and measuring the results. This model was entitled 'defining advertising goals for measured advertising results – Dagmar'. Colley's rationale for what is effectively a means of setting communications-oriented objectives was that advertising's job, purely and simply, is to communicate to a defined audience information and a frame of mind that stimulates action. Advertising succeeds or fails depending on how well it communicates the desired information and attitudes to the right people at the right time and at the right cost.

Colley proposed that the communications task be based on a hierarchical model of the communications process: awareness – comprehension – conviction – action (see Table 13.1).

Awareness

Awareness of the existence of a product or an organisation is necessary before purchase behaviour can be expected. Once awareness has been created in the target audience, it should not be neglected. If there is neglect, the audience may become distracted by competing messages and the level of awareness of the focus product or organisation may decline. Awareness, therefore, needs to be created, developed, refined or sustained, according to the characteristics of the market and the particular situation facing an organisation at any one point in time. See Figure 13.1.

Once awareness has been created in the target audience, it should not be neglected.

In situations where the buyer experiences high involvement and is fully aware of a product's existence, attention and awareness levels need only be sustained, and efforts

TABLE 13.1 Hierarchy of communications (after Colley)

Stage	Explanation
Awareness	Awareness of the existence of a product or brand is necessary before any purchase will be made.
Comprehension	Audiences need information and knowledge about the product and its specific attributes. Often the audience needs to be educated and shown either how to use the product or how changes (in attributes) might affect their use of the product.
Conviction	By developing beliefs that a product is superior to others in a category or can confer particular rewards through use, audiences can be convinced to trial the product at the next purchase opportunity.
Action	Potential buyers need help and encouragement to transfer thoughts into behaviour. Providing call-free numbers, Web site addresses, reply cards, coupons and sales people helps people act upon their convictions.

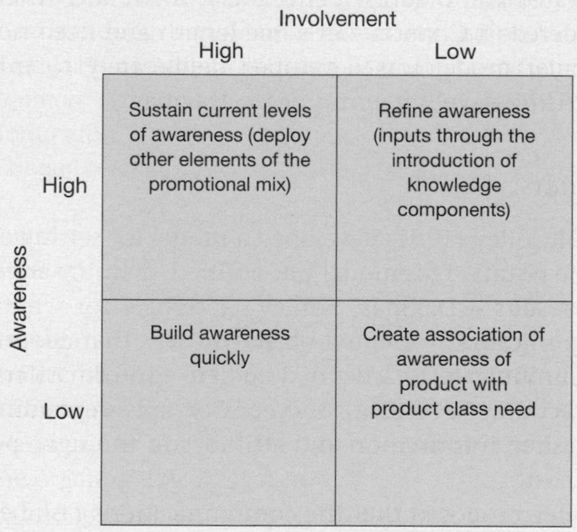

		Involvement	
		High	Low
	High	Sustain current levels of awareness (deploy other elements of the promotional mix)	Refine awareness (inputs through the introduction of knowledge components)
Awareness	Low	Build awareness quickly	Create association of awareness of product with product class need

FIGURE 13.1 An awareness grid

need to be applied to other communication tasks, which may be best left to the other elements of the communications mix. For example, sales promotion and personal selling are more effective at informing, persuading and provoking purchase of a new car once advertising has created the necessary levels of awareness.

Where low levels of awareness are found, getting attention needs to be a prime objective so that awareness can be developed in the target audience.

Where low involvement exists, the decision-making process is relatively straightforward. With levels of risk minimised, buyers with sufficient levels of awareness may be prompted into purchase with little assistance of the other elements of the mix. Recognition and recall of brand names and corporate images are felt by some (Rossiter and Percy, 1987) to be sufficient triggers to stimulate a behavioural response. The requirement in this situation would be to refine and strengthen the level of awareness in order that it provokes interest and stimulates a higher level of involvement during recall or recognition.

Where low levels of awareness are matched by low involvement, the prime objective has to be to create awareness of the focus product in association with the product class.

It is not surprising that organisations use awareness campaigns and invest a large amount of their resources in establishing their brand or corporate name. Many brands seek to establish 'top of mind awareness' as one of their primary objectives for their advertising spend.

> Many brands seek to establish 'top of mind awareness' as one of their primary objectives for their advertising spend.

ViewPoint 13.1   Changing names

One of the principal motivations for the online DVD retailer Blackstar to change its name was to secure a .com to replace its limiting .co.uk address. In order to compete more effectively with its main rivals, Amazon and Play, the new name, Sendit.com, would enable the company to reach a far greater audience.

However, one of the first tasks was to create name awareness and then to create the right brand associations and credibility to attract new customers.

Source: Adapted from Smith (2004).

Comprehension

Awareness on its own is, invariably, not enough to stimulate purchase activity. Knowledge about the product (or what the organisation does) is necessary, and this can be achieved by providing specific information about key brand attributes. These attributes and their associated benefits may be key to the buyers in the target audience or may be key because the product has been adapted or modified in some way. This means that the audience needs to be educated about the change and shown how their use of the product may be affected. For example, in attempting to persuade people to try a different brand of mineral water, it may be necessary to compare the product with other mineral water products and provide an additional usage benefit, such as environmental claims.

Conviction

Having established that a product has particular attributes that lead to benefits perceived by the target audience as important, it is then necessary to establish a sense of conviction. By creating interest and preference, buyers are moved to a position where they are convinced that one particular product in the class should be tried at the next opportunity. To do this, the audience's beliefs about the product need to be moulded, and this can be accomplished by using messages that demonstrate a product's superiority over its main rival or by emphasising the rewards conferred as a result of using the product, for example the reward of social acceptance associated with many fragrance, fashion clothing and accessory advertisements, and the reward of self-gratification associated with many confectionery messages (Cadbury's Flake).

High-involvement decisions are best supported with personal selling and sales promotion activities, in an attempt to gain conviction. Low-involvement decisions rely on the strength of advertising messages, packaging and sales promotion to secure conviction.

Action

A communications programme is used to encourage buyers to engage in purchase activity. Advertising can be directive and guide buyers into certain behavioural outcomes, for example to the use of free phone numbers (0800 in the UK), direct mail activities and reply cards and coupons. However, for high-involvement decisions the most effective tool in the communications mix at this stage in the hierarchy is personal selling. Through the use of interpersonal skills, buyers are more likely to want to buy a product than if the personal prompting is absent. The use of direct marketing activities by Avon Cosmetics, Tupperware, Betterware and suppliers of life assurance and double-glazing services has been instrumental in the sales growth experienced by organisations in these markets. Colley's dissatisfaction with the way in which advertising agencies operated led him to specify the components of a good advertising objective: 'A specific communications task to be accomplished among a defined audience to a given degree in a given period of time'. An analysis of this statement shows that it is made up of four distinct elements:

- a need to specify the communications task
- a need to define the audience
- a need to state the required degree of change
- a need to establish the time period in which the activity is to occur.

Dagmar revolutionised the approach taken by advertisers to the setting of objectives. Colley's statement is very clear – it is measurable and of assistance to copywriters. Indeed, Dagmar revolutionised the approach taken by advertisers to the setting of objectives. It helped to move attention from the sales effect to the communication effect school and has led to improved planning processes, as a result partly of a better understanding of advertising and promotional goals.

Many of the difficulties associated with sequential models (Chapter 7) are also applicable to Dagmar. In addition to problems of hierarchical progression, measurement and costs are issues concerning the sales orientation, restrictions upon creativity and short-term accountability.

Sales orientation

This criticism is levelled by those who see sales as the only valid measure of effectiveness. The sole purpose of communication activities, and advertising in particular, is to generate sales. So, as the completion of communications tasks may not result in purchases, the only measure that need be undertaken is that of sales. This point has been discussed earlier and need not be reproduced here.

Restrictions upon creativity

Dagmar is criticised on the grounds that creative flair can be lost as attention passes from looking for the big idea to concentration upon the numbers game, of focusing on measures of recall, attitude change and awareness. It is agreed that the creative personnel are held to be more accountable under Dagmar and this may well inhibit some of their work. Perhaps the benefits of providing direction and purpose offset the negative aspects of a slight loss in creativity.

Short-term accountability

To the above should be added the time period during which management and associated agencies are required to account for their performance. With accounting periods being reduced to as little as 12 weeks, the communications approach is impractical for two reasons. The first is that the period is not long enough for all of the communication tasks to be progressed or completed. Sales measures present a much more readily digestible benchmark of performance.

The second concerns the unit of performance itself. With the drive to be efficient and to be able to account for every communication pound spent, managers themselves need to use measures that they can understand and which they can interpret from published data. Sales data and communications spend data are consistent measures and make no further demands on managers. Managers do not have enough time to spend analysing levels of comprehension or preference and to convert them into formats that are going to be of direct benefit to them and their organisations. Having said that, those organisations that are prepared to invest in a more advanced management information system will enable a more sophisticated view to be taken.

> Those organisations that are prepared to invest in a more advanced management information system will enable a more sophisticated view to be taken.

The communication school approach is not accepted by some, who argue that it is too difficult and impractical to translate a sales objective into a series of specific communications objectives. Furthermore, what actually constitute adequate levels of awareness and comprehension and how can it be determined which stage the majority of the target audience has reached at any one point in time? Details of measurement, therefore, throw a veil over the simplicity and precision of the approach taken by the communication orientation school.

From a practical perspective, it should be appreciated that most successful marketing organisations do not see the sales and communications schools as mutually exclusive. They incorporate both views and weight them according to the needs of the current task, their overall experience, the culture and style of the organisation and the agencies with whom they operate.

> Most successful marketing organisations do not see the sales and communications schools as mutually exclusive.

Derivation of promotional objectives

It has been established that specific promotional objectives need to be set up if a suitable foundation is to be laid for the many communication decisions that follow. Promotional objectives are derived from understanding the overall context in which the communications will operate. Comprehending the contexts of the buyer and the organisation allows the objectives of the planned communications to be identified: the *what* that is to be achieved. For example, objectives concerning the perception that different target customers have of a brand, the perception that members of a performance network have of the organisation's offerings, the reactions of key stakeholders to previous communications and the requirements of the current marketing plan all impact upon the objectives of the communication plan. Therefore, promotional

FIGURE 13.2 The three elements of promotional goal setting

objectives evolve principally from a systematic audit and analysis of the key communication contexts, and specifically from the marketing plan and stakeholder analysis.

There are three main streams of objectives.

It was established earlier that there are three main streams of objectives. These are set out in Figure 13.2. The first concerns issues relating to the buyers of the product or service offered by the organisation. The second concerns issues relating to market share/sales volume, profitability and revenue. The third stream relates to the image, reputation and preferences that other stakeholders have towards the organisation.

All these objectives are derived from an analysis of the current situation. The marketing communication brief that flows from this analysis should specify the sales-related objectives to be achieved, as these can be determined from the marketing plan. Sales-related objectives might concern issues such as market share and sales volume.

Customer-related objectives concern issues such as awareness, perception, attitude, feelings and intentions towards a brand or product. The exact issue to be addressed in the plan is calculated by analysing the contextual information driven by the audit.

Issues related to the perception of the organisation are often left unattended or, worse, ignored. Research may indicate that the perception of particular stakeholders, in either the performance or the support network, does not complement the current level of corporate performance or may be misplaced or confused. Objectives will need to be established to correct or reinforce the perception held of the organisation. The degree of urgency may be directly related to the level of confusion or misunderstanding or be related to competitive or strategic actions initiated by competitors and other members of the network. Corporate strategy may have changed and, as identified earlier, any new strategy will need to be communicated to all stakeholders.

The need for realism when setting promotional objectives

Hierarchy of effects models that specify stages of development were first proposed as far back as 1898 by E. St Elmo Lewis (Barry and Howard, 1990) and similar views were expressed by Colley (Dagmar) in 1961. Yet despite the passage of time since their publication, a large number of organisations still either fail to set any promotional objectives or confuse objectives with strategy. Organisations seeking to coordinate their communications need to recognise the necessity of setting multiple objectives at different times in the campaign period and of being prepared to adjust them in the light of environmental changes. These changes may be due to ever-decreasing product life cycles or technological developments that may give a competitor comparative advantage, and perhaps legislative developments (or the timing of management's interpretation and implementation of certain legislation) may bring about a need to reconfigure the promotional mix.

Management's failure to set objectives is often the result of a lack of awareness of the current position, or a lack of understanding of how and why appropriate objectives need to be established. With increasingly competitive and turbulent environments, a greater number of organisations are turning their attention to ways in which they can communicate more effectively with their stakeholders. Furthermore, as more executives undertake management education programmes, so a higher level of skill is being transferred to organisations, and this in turn will bring a higher incidence of better practice.

The overall objective of any promotional programme is to increase the level of sales. While it seems unreasonable to expect the promotional mix to bear total responsibility for this, it is also unreasonable and impractical to expect the communications approach to bear total responsibility. It is imperative that organisations are willing and prepared to set promotional objectives which utilise basic communications tasks, such as awareness and intentions, and that they utilise sales benchmarks as means of determining what has been achieved and how. Promotional objectives are a derivative of both marketing and corporate strategies. Just as revenue and income targets are part of marketing strategy, so they should form part of the promotional objectives. They cannot be separated and they cannot be neglected.

Promotional objectives are a derivative of both marketing and corporate strategies.

Figure 13.2 shows the different types of objectives that can be set for a promotional strategy. The choice depends on the situation facing each manager and, in particular, whether the product or organisation is new. Establishing and maintaining levels of awareness is, however, paramount to any communications programme, and must be considered one of the primary communication objectives.

Promotional objectives need to be set which reflect the communication and sales tasks that the product or organisation needs to accomplish.

Promotional objectives need to be set which reflect the communication and sales tasks that the product or

ViewPoint 13.2   Norwich Union Flood Maps

Early in 2004 Norwich Union launched its Flood Maps, a digital method of gauging the flood danger to individual properties. This new system sought to replace the previous post code approach to risk evaluation, which failed to discriminate potential flood risk properties from high-rise flats.

The launch of the new product aimed to achieve two different objectives. The first was communication related and geared to raising awareness of the maps to property owners, especially in high-risk parts of the country. The second was sales related, as Norwich Union wanted to sell more property insurance policies.

Source: Various.

organisation needs to accomplish. It should be appreciated that promotional objectives are vitally important, as they provide the basis for a string of decisions that are to be taken at subsequent stages in the development of the communication plan.

Management's next task is to make decisions regarding which of these different promotional objectives will receive attention first. In order that decisions can be made regarding promotional strategy, the communications mix and the level of resources allocated to each promotional tool, it is necessary to rank and weight the objectives at this stage in the management process. The criteria used to weight the different objectives will inevitably be subjective. This is because they reflect each manager's perception, experience and interpretation of his or her environment. However, it is also his or her skill and judgement that are the important elements, and as long as the criteria are used and applied in a consistent manner the outcome of the communication plan is more likely to be successful.

SMART objectives

To assist managers in their need to develop suitable objectives, a set of guidelines has been developed, commonly referred to as SMART objectives. This acronym stands for specific, measurable, achievable, relevant, targeted and timed.

The process of making objectives SMART requires management to consider exactly what is to be achieved, when, where, and with which audience. This clarifies thinking, sorts out the logic of the proposed activities and provides a clear measure for evaluation at the end of the campaign:

Requires management to consider exactly what is to be achieved, when, where, and with which audience.

- *Specific*
  What is the actual variable that is to be influenced in the campaign? Is it awareness, perception, attitudes, or some other element that is to be influenced? Whatever the variable, it must be clearly defined and must enable precise outcomes to be determined.

- *Measurable*
  Set a measure of activity against which performance can be assessed; this may be a percentage level of desired prompted awareness in the target audience.

- *Achievable*
  Objectives need to be attainable, otherwise those responsible for their achievement will lack motivation and a desire to succeed.

- *Realistic*
  The actions must be founded in reality and be relevant to the brand and the context in which they are set.

- *Targeted and timed*
  Which target audience is the campaign targeted at, how precisely is the audience defined and over what period are the results to be generated?

Having determined what levels of awareness, comprehension or preference are necessary or how attitudes need to be developed, the establishment or positioning of these objectives as a task for the organisation to accomplish should be seen as a primary communication objective. The attitude held or what individuals in the target market perceive, comprehend or prefer is a focus for campaign activity and subsequent evaluation.

Sony might have set the following marketing communication objective when launching its new up-market brand of electronic consumer goods called Qualia across the European market. This goal is realistic, bearing in mind the marketing pedigree and resources available to Sony.

The marketing communications objective for the period June to September 2004 (timed) is to create 85 per cent (measurable and achievable) prompted awareness (specific) of current male customers, in the 24 to 45-year-old age group and earning £35,000 plus (targeted).

Positioning: an introduction

The final act in the target marketing process of segmentation and targeting is positioning. Following on from the identification of potential markets, determining the size and potential of market segments and selecting specific target markets, positioning is the process whereby information about the organisation or product is communicated in such a way that the object is perceived by the consumer/stakeholder to be differentiated from the competition, to occupy a particular space in the market. According to Kotler (1997), 'Positioning is the act of designing the company's offering and image so that they occupy a meaningful and distinct competitive position in the target customers' minds'.

This is an important aspect of the positioning concept. Positioning is not about the product but what the buyer thinks about the product or organisation. It is not the physical nature of the product that is important for positioning, but how the product is perceived that matters. This is why part of the context analysis (Chapter 12), requires a consideration of perception and attitudes and the way stakeholders see and regard brands and organisations. Of course, this may not be the same as the way brand managers intend their brands to be seen or how they believe the brand is perceived.

A white wine crush called Slinky, launched by Blue Nun, was positioned as a stepping stone from ready-to-drinks (RTDs) to wine. Analysis showed that there were two wine-based RTDs on the market (Bliss and Comira Coast) but they had not been marketed as a natural progression from RTDs to wine. The launch strategy was based first on a push strategy, using the trade press, which was designed to get distribution into bars. This was followed by a pull strategy, using press and broadcast media, aimed at 20 to 24-year-old women. The campaign spend was over £1 million and focused on advertising and PR, media promotions and product sampling.

Following a television-based campaign to position the Pernod brand for the 18 to 24-year-old market, attitude research revealed that the brand would be better suited to an older demographic group. McCawley (2001) reports that a campaign in 2001 was designed to reposition the brand so that it appealed to professionals in their late 20s to mid-30s and complemented their attitude set.

In the consumer market, established brands from washing powders (Ariel, Daz, Persil) and hair shampoos (such as Wash & Go, Timotei), to cars (for example, Peugeot, Saab, Nissan) and grocery multiples (Sainsbury's, Tesco) each carry communications that enable receivers to position them in their respective markets.

The positioning concept is not the sole preserve of branded or consumer-oriented offerings or indeed those of the business-to-business market. Organisations are also positioned relative to one another, mainly as a consequence of their corporate identities, whether they are deliberately managed or not. The position an organisation takes in the mind of consumers may be the only means of differentiating one product from another. King (1991) argues that, given the advancement in technology and the high level of physical and functional similarity of products in the same class, consumers' choices will be more focused on their assessment of the company they are dealing with. Therefore it is important to position organisations as brands in the minds of actual and potential customers.

> The position an organisation takes in the mind of consumers may be the only means of differentiating one product from another.

One of the crucial differences between the product and the corporate brand is that the corporate brand needs to be communicated to a large array of stakeholders, whereas the product-based brand requires a focus on a smaller range of stakeholders, in particular the consumers and buyers in the performance network.

Whatever the position chosen, either deliberately or accidentally, it is the means by which customers understand the brand's market position, and it often provides signals to determine a brand's main competitors, or (as is often the case) customers fail to understand the brand or are confused about what the brand stands for.

The development of the positioning concept

This perspective was originally proposed by Ries and Trout (1972). They claimed that it is not what you do to a product that matters; it is what you do to the mind of the prospect that is important. They set out three stages of development: the product era, the image era and the positioning era.

The product era occurred in the late 1950s and early 1960s and existed when each product was promoted in an environment where there was little competition. Each product was accepted as an innovation and was readily accepted and adopted as a natural development. In the pharmaceuticals market, drugs such as Navidex, Valium and Lasix became established partly because of the lack of competition and partly because of the ability of the product to fulfil its claims. This was a period when the features and benefits of products were used in communications; the unique selling proposition was of paramount importance.

The image era that followed was spawned by companies with established images, which introduced new me-too products against the original brands. It was the strength of the perceived company image that underpinned the communications surrounding these new brands that was so important to their success. Products such as Amoxil, Tagamet and Tenormin were launched on an image platform.

The positioning era has developed mainly because of increasingly competitive market conditions, where there is now little compositional, material or even structural difference between products within each class. Consequently, most products are now perceived relative to each other. In most markets the level and intensity of 'noise' drives

> Most products are now perceived relative to each other.

organisations to establish themselves and their offerings in particular parts of the over-all market. It is now the ability of an offering to command the attention of buyers and to communicate information about how an offering is differentiated from the other competitive offerings that helps to signal the relative position the offering occupies in the market.

The positioning concept

All products and all organisations have a position. The position held by each stake-holder can be managed or it can be allowed to drift. An increasing number of organ-isations are trying to manage the positions occupied by their brands and are using positioning strategies to move to new positions in buyers' minds and so generate an advantage over their competitors. This is particularly important in markets that are very competitive and where mobility barriers (ease of entry and exit to a market, e.g. plant and production costs) are relatively low.

> All products and all organisations have a position.

Positioning is about visibility and recognition of what a product/service represents for a buyer. In markets where the intensity of rivalry and competition are increasing and buyers have greater choice, identification and understanding of a product's intrin-sic values become critical. Network members have limited capacities, whether this be the level or range of stock they can carry or the amount of available shelf space that can be allocated. An offering with a clear identity and orientation to a particular target segment's needs will not only be stocked and purchased but can warrant a larger margin through increased added value.

> Positioning, therefore, is the natural conclusion to the sequence of activities that constitute a core part of the marketing strategy.

Positioning, therefore, is the natural conclusion to the sequence of activities that constitute a core part of the marketing strategy. Market segmentation and target mar-keting are prerequisites to successful positioning. From the research data and the marketing strategy, it is necessary to formulate a positioning statement that is in tune with the promotional objectives.

One of the roles of marketing communications is to convey information so that the target audience can understand what a brand stands for and differentiate it from other competitor brands. Clear, consistent positioning is an important aspect of integrated marketing communication. So the way in which a brand is presented to its audience determines the way it is going to be perceived. Therefore, accepting that there are extraneous reasons why a brand's perception might not be the same as that intended, it seems important that managers approach the task of positioning in an attentive and considered manner.

> There are two main ways in which a brand can be positioned: functional and expressive.

Generally there are two main ways in which a brand can be positioned: functional and expressive (or symbolic). Functionally positioned brands stress the features and benefits, and expressive brands emphasise the ego, social and hedonic satisfactions that a brand can bring. Both approaches make a promise, a promise to deliver a whiter, cleaner and brighter soap powder (functional) or clothes that we are confident to hang on the washing line (for all to see), dress our children in and send to school and not feel guilty, or dress ourselves and complete a major busi-ness deal (symbolic).

ViewPoint 13.5   Functional positioning

Marketing communications in the consumer and trade adhesives market places heavy reliance on demonstrating the performance of the individual brands. Solvite, for example, presents a man glued to a board and suspended in dangerous situations (above sharks, towed into the sky and at a theme park on a 'vertical drop ride'). Another brand, 'No More Nails', uses a similar functional approach. One execution shows a man sitting on a chair that has been glued half-way up a wall inside a house. See Exhibit 19.7.

Adhesives provoke low-involvement decision-making and there is generally little consumer interest in the properties of each brand. The essential information that consumers require is that the brand has strong performance characteristics. This sets up umbrella brand credibility so that sub-brands for different types of glue are perceived to have the same properties as the umbrella brand and will do the 'job'.

Advertising needs to have dramatic qualities in order to attract attention and to build up a store of images that enable people to recall a brand of adhesives which do actually stick. See Exhibit 13.1.

EXHIBIT 13.1 Solvite press ad. Used to demonstrate the functional attributes of the product

ViewPoint 13.6   Expressive positioning

In 2004 British Airways developed the tagline 'The way to fly' in an attempt to build on the successful 'The world's favourite airline' tag that was dropped in 1999. The aim of BA's first corporate branding campaign since 2000 was that it become an overarching brand-positioning vehicle. It enables BA to communicate a diverse range of related offerings, such as food and service, use of primary airports, promotions, loyalty programmes and the Club World 'sleeper service', among many others.

For a while BA used rational messages based on product-led ads in the long-haul market. Campaigns that focused on flat beds in Club World, price discounts in the short haul ('Look how small our prices are') have in part been a reaction to the crisis of 11 September 2001 and the aggression of low-cost competitors.

'The way to fly' represents an emotional message and gives flyers a reason to choose the BA brand simply because it encapsulates the brand promise of reassurance and reliability.

Developing and managing a position

To develop a position, managers should be guided by the following process:

1. Which positions are held by which competitors? This will almost certainly require consumer research to determine attitudes and perceptions and possibly the key attributes that consumers perceive as important. Use perceptual mapping.

2. From the above, will it be possible to determine which position, if any, is already held by the focus brand?

3. From the information gathered so far, will it be possible to determine a positioning strategy, that is, what is the desired position for the brand?

4. Is the strategy feasible in view of the competitors and any budgetary constraints? A long-term perspective is required, as the selected position has to be sustained.

5. Implement a programme to establish the desired position.

6. Monitor the perception held by consumers of the brand, and of their changing tastes and requirements, on a regular basis.

Perceptual mapping

In order to determine how the various offerings are perceived in a market, the key attributes that stakeholders use to perceive products in the market need to be established. A great deal of this work will have been completed as part of the research and review process prior to developing a communications plan. The next task is to determine perceptions and preferences in respect of the key attributes as perceived by buyers.

The objective of the exercise is to produce a perceptual map (brand and multidimensional maps) where the dimensions used on the two axes are the key attributes, as seen by buyers. This map represents a geometric comparison of how competing products are perceived (Sinclair and Stalling, 1990). Figure 13.3 shows that the key dimensions for consumers in the shampoo market could be price and enrichment.

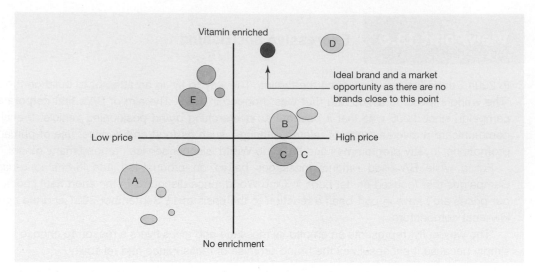

FIGURE 13.3 A perceptual map for a shampoo market

Each product is positioned on the map according to the perception that buyers have of the strength of each attribute of each product. By plotting the perceived positions of each brand on the map, an overall perspective of the market can be developed.

The closer products are clustered together, the greater the competition. The further apart the positions, the greater the opportunity to enter the market, as competition is less intense. From the map, it can be seen that brand A dominates the bottom left-hand sector where a low price and little enrichment have attracted a number of buyers and competitive brands. Brands B and C are in direct competition, positioned closely together on a fairly high price yet medium level of enrichment. Brand D is isolated and may need to be repositioned as it may start losing share to a competitor, especially if the ideal position is occupied by B or any of the brands clustered around brand E.

> The closer products are clustered together, the greater the competition.

Substitute products are often uncovered by their closeness to each other (Day *et al.*, 1979). It is also possible to ask buyers and other stakeholders what an ideal brand would consist of. This perfect brand can then be positioned on the map, and the closer an offering is to the ideal point, the greater its market share should be, as it is preferred more than its rivals. These maps are known as preference maps.

By superimposing the position of an ideal brand on the map, it is possible to extend the usefulness of the tool. Perceptions of what constitutes the right amount of each key attribute can assist management in the positioning exercise. Marketing communications can, therefore, be designed to convey the required information about each attribute and so adjust buyers' perceptions so that they are closer to the ideal position, or to the position on the map that management wants the brand to occupy. For example, brand C may wish to reposition by changing the perception that users have of the quality of the shampoo. Following any necessary adjustments to the product, marketing communications would emphasise the enrichment atribute and hope to move it away from any association with brand B.

> Marketing communications can, therefore, be designed to convey the required information about each attribute and so adjust buyers' perceptions so that they are closer to the ideal position.

Neal (1980) offered the following reasons why perceptual mapping is such a powerful tool for examining the position of products:

1. It develops understanding of how the relative strengths and weaknesses of different products are perceived by buyers.

2. It builds knowledge about the similarities and dissimilarities between competing products.

3. It assists the process of repositioning existing products and the positioning of new products.

4. The technique helps to track the perception that buyers have of a particular product, and assists the measurement of the effectiveness of communication programmes and marketing actions, intended to change buyers' perceptions.

Perceptual mapping is an important tool in the development and tracking of promotional strategy. It enables brand managers to identify gaps and opportunities in the market and allows organisations to monitor the effects of past marketing communications. For example, in the early 1980s, none of the available brands in the newly emerging lager market was seen as refreshing. All brands were perceived as virtually the same. Heineken saw the opportunity and seized the position for refreshment, and has been able to occupy and sustain the position since then.

Positioning strategies

The development of positions that buyers can relate to and understand is an important and vital part of the marketing communications plan. In essence, the position adopted is a statement about what the brand is, what it stands for and the values and beliefs that customers (hopefully) will come to associate with the particular brand. The visual images or the position statement represented in the strapline may be a significant trigger that buyers use to recall images and associations of the brand.

There are a number of overall approaches to developing a position. These can be based on factors such as the market, the customer or redefining the appeal of the brand itself; see Table 13.2.

To implement these three broad approaches various strategies have been developed. The list that follows is not intended to be comprehensive or to convey the opinion that these strategies are discrete. They are presented here as means of conveying the strategic style, but in reality a number of hybrid strategies are often used.

Product features

This is one of the easier concepts and one that is more commonly adopted. The brand is set apart from the competition on the basis of the attributes, features or benefits that the brand has relative to the competition. For example, Volvos are safe; Weetabix contains all the vitamins needed each day; and the Royal Bank of Scotland promotes its credit card by extolling the benefits of its interest rate compared with those of its competitors.

Price/quality

This strategy is more effectively managed than others because price itself can be a strong communicator of quality. A high price denotes high quality, just as a low price

TABLE 13.2 Positioning approaches

Approach	Type of application
Market related	*First into a market* 　Heineken was first to take the refreshment position *Redefine the market* 　Carlsberg claims to be 'Probably the best beer in the world' 　British Airways as 'The way to fly' 　Miller Lite said the *lite* meant not heavy; not low alcohol *Importance/leadership claim* 　H. Samuel claims to be 'The nation's favourite jeweller'
Customer related	*A unique buying reason* 　Ronseal, because 'It does exactly what it says on the can' *Particular type of buyer* 　Glenfiddich: 'Independently minded. Independently made'
Appeal related	*Distinct personality* 　Pepperami became a crazy/mad 'bit of an animal' *Decision criteria* 　Virgin Upper Class was presented as a sensible, rational business decision, 　not a whim or a risk *Imaginative or interesting* 　Castrol made oil into liquid engineering 　Dyson, because it uses cyclone technology

can deceive buyers into thinking a product to be of low quality and poor value. Retail outlets such as Harrods and Aspreys use high prices to signal high quality and exclusivity. At the other end of the retail spectrum, Matalan, BHS and Woolworths position themselves to attract those with less disposable income and to whom convenience is of greater importance. The price/quality appeal used to be best observed in Sainsbury's, 'where good food costs less', before it was changed, and with the alcoholic lager Stella Artois, which is positioned as 'refreshingly expensive'. See Exhibit 13.2.

Exhibit 13.2 shows various stills taken from a television ad for Stella Artois, called *Pilot*. The story depicts the attempt by a barman to hide a pilot who has been shot down in the Second World War. Under pressure of death to reveal where the airman is hiding the barman decides to surrender the pilot and be able to continue drinking Stella Artois. The use of subtle yet dark humour reinforces the required premium positioning of the brand.

Use

By informing markets of when or how a product can be used, a position can be created in the minds of the buyers. For example, Kellogg's, the breakfast cereal manufacturer, has repositioned itself as a snack food provider. Its marketing strategy of moving into new markets was founded on its overdependence on breakfast consumption. By becoming associated with snacks, not only is usage increased, but the opportunity to develop new products becomes feasible. The launch of Pop Tarts is a testimony to this

EXHIBIT 13.2 Stella Artois – Pilot

EXHIBIT 13.2 (continued)

strategy. Milky Way, 'The sweet you can eat between meals', informs just when it is permissible to eat chocolate; and After Eight chocolate mints clearly indicate when they should be eaten. The hair shampoo Wash & Go positions the brand as a quick and easy to use (convenience) product, for those whose lifestyles are full and demanding.

ViewPoint 13.7   Crisp sensation

Walkers is the UK's leading brand of crisp, based on supermarket sales (Simms, 2004). In 2002 they introduced a new range of crisps called Sensations and sales grew 55 per cent over the 12 months to June 2004.

These 'high-class' crisps are positioned in the snack food sector in order to reflect consumers' growing desire for premium products. They are presented as high-quality crisps aimed at adults, for consumption on special rather than everyday occasions.

EXHIBIT 13.3 Walkers Sensations

Product class dissociation

Some markets are essentially uninteresting, and most other positions have been adopted by competitors. A strategy used by margarine manufacturers is to disassociate themselves from other margarines and associate themselves with what was commonly regarded as a superior product, butter. The Alliance and Leicester Building Society used to proclaim that 'Not all building societies are the same'. The suggestion was that

A strategy used by margarine manufacturers is to disassociate themselves from other margarines and associate themselves with what was commonly regarded as a superior product, butter.

they were different from the rest and hence offered better services and customer care. The moisturising bar Dove is positioned as 'Not a soap'.

User

A sensible extension of the target marketing process is to position openly so that the target user can be clearly identified. Flora margarine was for men, and then it became 'for all the family'. American Express uses several leading business celebrities, including Sir Terence Conran and Anita Roddick, to suggest that users can have a lifestyle profile that complements those who use and endorse the Amex card. Some hotels position themselves as places for weekend breaks, as leisure centres or as conference centres. Le Creuset has recently repositioned itself to appeal to a younger customer segment (see Exhibit 13.4).

EXHIBIT 13.4 Le Creuset repositioned for a younger market
Picture reproduced with the kind permission of Le Creuset.

Competitor

For a long time, positioning oneself against a main competitor was regarded as dangerous and to be avoided. Avis, however, performed very successfully 'trying even harder' against Hertz, the industry number one. Saab contested the 'safest car' position with Volvo and Qualcast took on its new rival, the hover mower, by informing everyone that 'It's a lot less bovver than a hover', because its product collected the grass cuttings and produced the manicured lawn finish that roller-less mowers cannot reproduce.

Benefit

Positions can also be established by proclaiming the benefits that usage confers on those who consume. Sensodyne toothpaste appeals to all those who suffer from sensitive teeth, and a vast number of pain relief formulations claim to smooth away headaches or relieve aching limbs, sore throats or some offending part of the anatomy. Daewoo entered the UK offering car buyers convenience by removing dealerships and the inherent difficulties associated with buying and maintaining cars.

Heritage or cultural symbol

An appeal to cultural heritage and tradition, symbolised by age, particular heraldic devices or visual cues, has been used by many organisations to convey quality, experience and knowledge. Kronenbourg 1664, 'Established since 1803', and the use of coats of arms by many universities to represent depth of experience and a sense of permanence are just some of the historical themes used to position organisations.

Whatever the position adopted by a brand or organisation, both the marketing and promotional mixes must endorse and support the position so that there is consistency throughout all communications. For example, if a high-quality position is taken, such as that of the Ritz Carlton Hotel Group, then the product quality must be relatively high compared with competitors, the price must be correspondingly excessive and distribution synonymous with quality and exclusivity. Sales promotion activity will be minimal so as not to convey a touch of inexpensiveness, and advertising messages should be visually affluent and rich in tone and copy, with public relations and personal selling approaches transmitting high-quality, complementary cues.

> Both the marketing and promotional mixes must endorse and support the position so that there is consistency throughout all communications.

The dimensions used to position brands must be relevant and important to the target audience and the image cues used must be believable and consistently credible. Positioning strategies should be developed over the long term if they are to prove effective, although minor adaptations to the position can be carried out in order to reflect changing environmental conditions.

> Positioning strategies should be developed over the long term if they are to prove effective.

Repositioning

Technology is developing quickly, consumer tastes evolve and new offerings and substitute products enter the market. This dynamic perspective of markets means that the relative positions occupied by offerings in the minds of consumers will be challenged and shifted on a frequent basis. If the position adopted by an offering is strong, if it was the first to claim the position and the position is being continually reinforced with clear, simple messages, then there may be little need to alter the position originally adopted.

However, there are occasions when offerings need to be repositioned in the minds of consumers/stakeholders. This may be due to market opportunities and development, mergers and acquisitions or changing buyer preferences, which may be manifested in declining sales. Research may reveal that the current position is either inappropriate or superseded by a competitor, or that attitudes have changed or preferences been

> There are occasions when offerings need to be repositioned.

ViewPoint 13.8   Repositioning Green & Black's

Green & Black's, the UK's fastest growing confectionery brand, launched a £1.2 million national advertising campaign – *'Green & Black's . . . it deserves a little respect'* – as part of its programme to consolidate its repositioning from an organic to a luxury chocolate brand. Green & Black's has almost trebled its value since repositioning two years ago.

This campaign, timed to run during the key chocolate months of October and November, aims to give consumers a clear understanding of the Green & Black's taste and how it fits into their chocolate repertoire. Last year a £500,000 sampling and sponsorship programme enabled over 300,000 people to taste Green & Black's chocolate and ice cream at various high-profile English Heritage summer picnic concerts.

The new *'it deserves a little respect'* campaign highlighted the special nature of the Green & Black's brand and cues a number of usage occasions.

The advertising campaign ran nationally in food titles and Sunday supplements and was supported by London Underground posters and a commuter press schedule. An in-store sampling programme in key grocery accounts was also implemented.

Source: Green & Black's. Used with permission.

EXHIBIT 13.5 Green & Black's

surpassed; whatever the reason, repositioning is required if past success is to be maintained. However, repositioning is difficult to accomplish, often because of the entrenched perceptions and attitudes held by buyers towards brands and the vast (media) resources required to make the changes.

In an attempt to thwart the competitive threats of both rail (Channel Tunnel) and low cost airlines (e.g. easyJet), the ferry operator P&O repositioned itself as the way to 'cruise across the Channel'. By presenting the cross-Channel experience as an integral part of the holiday/travel experience, it enabled P&O to provide added value that could not be copied, and a reason to be used.

The Defence Establishment and Research Agency (DERA) was required to change its name when it ceased being a government-owned organisation and was privatised. The name QinetiQ represented a radical change of name, but the agency needed to reflect its new position in a new commercial market.

The need to reposition a brand may be stimulated because of the actions of a major competitor. The United Kingdom's car recovery and driver support service market is dominated by two mainstream organisations, the AA and the RAC. In the early 1990s the AA tried to reposition itself away from the RAC as the market became increasingly cluttered, more competitive and depressed as consumer spending became constricted with the recession. The RAC then positioned itself as the 'knights of the road', with all the heroic rescue overtones that a knight confers, while the AA, having tried to be seen as a 'a very, very nice man', portrayed itself as highly professional and demanding high standards, since a vehicle breakdown was regarded as an emergency similar in scale to that requiring the assistance of the fire, police or ambulance services. AA's new position, 'To our members we are the fourth emergency service', is an attempt to be pre-eminent and gain 'top of mind' awareness by conveying a rational benefit approach against the more emotive imagery suggested by the 'knight'. Then, in an attempt to challenge drivers with regard to the range of services provided by the AA, it changed its strapline to 'Just AAsk'. See Exhibit 13.6.

Summary

The use of objectives in the management process is clearly vital if the organisation's desired outcomes are to be achieved. Each of the objectives, at corporate, unit and functional levels, contributes to the formulation of the promotional objectives. They are all interlinked, interdependent, multiple, and often conflicting.

The major task for the promotional objectives is twofold: first, to contribute to the overall direction of the organisation by fulfilling the communication requirements of the marketing mix; secondly, to communicate the corporate thrust to various stakeholders so that they understand the focus organisation and can respond to its intentions.

Promotional objectives are derived from an initial review of the current situation and the marketing plan requirements. They are not a replication of the marketing objectives but a distillation of the research activities that have been undertaken subsequently. Such objectives consist of two main elements: sales oriented and communication oriented. A balance between the two will be determined by the situation facing the organisation, but may be a mixture of product and corporate tasks. These objectives, once quantified, need to be ranked and weighted in order that other components of the plan can be developed.

Part of the information generated at the research stage informs how buyers and stakeholders position the offering relative to the other players in the target market and how the product itself is perceived. This aspect of the management process is very important, as the

EXHIBIT 13.6 AA Poster 'Learn to Drive' demonstrates the Just AAsk strapline and its invitation to solve the problems of a particular target audience

communications undertaken by the organisation help to shape the context that individuals have of the offering (or the organisation). The way in which an organisation decides to position itself and/or its offerings determines the form, intensity and nature of the messages transmitted through the promotional mix.

Review questions

1. Why do organisations use objectives as part of their planning processes?
2. What should a mission statement clearly identify?
3. Suggest three reasons why the setting of promotional objectives is important.
4. Write a brief report arguing the case both for and against the use of an increase in sales as the major objective of all promotional activities.
5. Repeat the exercise as for the previous question but this time focus upon communication-based objectives.
6. How and from where are promotional objectives derived?
7. Why is positioning an important part of marketing communications?
8. What is perceptual mapping?
9. Select four print advertisements for the same product category and comment on the positions they have adopted.
10. What are the main positioning strategies?

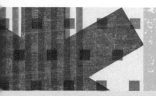

MINI-CASE
C&B positioning - hair care

Market research has shown that pharmaceutically developed shampoos were at an immature stage of market development. This was characterised by consumers' apparent ignorance about the role and use of these products. They considered that they should only be consumed if and when the need arose; in other words, the market was cause driven. Prescription brands, of which Style-Care held a substantial market share, accounted for 90 per cent of the total market. In contrast manufacturers had not developed the OTC (over the counter) market, where Factor Z held 37 per cent market share and total adspend was just €900,000.

C&B Hair Protection was launched at the end of 2000 and was targeted at AB and C1 men and women aged 25–54. Its positioning was: 'The food your hair needs' and 'A successful product now available for you'. Distribution was regulated by legislation, which required that all relevant products be channelled through pharmacies.

In 2000 the goal of all promotional activities was to educate the public regarding the benefits of pharmaceutically developed shampoos containing vitamins, encouraging them to reconsider whether their way of living influenced the quality and quantity of their hair. The C&B marketing communication strategy was tailored for each of the three different target groups: end-users, pharmacists and doctors.

During 2001 communication with the selected consumer segment included PR activities in order to achieve maximum publicity, TV commercials and inserts in magazines. Additionally, as far as doctors were concerned, a relevant newsletter was created and mailed, sales representatives were hired and a sampling programme was developed to create awareness, encourage trial and through experience develop trust for the new product. Pharmacists were approached, informed and gradually convinced through a launch presentation, constant briefing by the sales force and an attractive sales policy.

In 2001 the total cost of media expenditure in the category reached €4 million, an increase of 222 per cent from the previous year. C&B's SOV (share of voice) was 20 per cent and by the end of 2001

Style-Care market share fell by 11 per cent. The OTC market in the nutrient shampoo category increased its volume of sales by 143 per cent, with C&B becoming number two with 22 per cent market share. Among the consumers, 23 per cent had come to believe that C&B was a good, benefit-giving product, and 11 per cent had either switched from another brand or were convinced to try C&B.

In 2002 the brand continued to reach all three target groups:

- *end-users* by a TV campaign, inserts in health and lifestyle magazines, outdoor posters and sponsorships of various events;
- *pharmacists* were offered innovative POP material, educational leaflets for customers, window stickers and incentives to recommend the product;
- *doctors* were further informed through C&B's participation at medical conferences and the periodical edition of a newsletter on hair health issues.

TV advertising continued to have a strong educational message, informing of the benefits of hair products containing vitamins. They also started to build concern about people's hair health. C&B's message was differentiated from competitive brands, which only really focused on shine and beauty.

During 2001 the market changed dramatically, with Style-Care losing 47 per cent of its sales and C&B doubling its sales. The OTC hair category showed a significant increase, reaching 51 per cent of the total market, while sales in the prescription category fell by 50 per cent.

Attitudes were gradually changing towards better hair protection and care. More OTC companies were attracted to the growing market. Five new products were launched and by the end of 2001 it was obvious that competition was increasing and that different OTC brands were starting to defend their market share by increasing marketing expenditure. Total market media expenditure rose by 185 per cent, with C&B's SOV being 24 per cent, mainly allocated to TV.

Research into pharmacists' attitudes at the end of 2001 showed that 55 per cent of them were already well aware of the brand and had a good perception of it. Of these 15 per cent were persuaded to recommend it to their customers. The brand commanded 10 per cent brand loyalty.

In 2003 there were 20 OTC brands already in the market. Media expenditure remained high. C&B continued to have a high SOV. The TV ad became more aggressive, stressing the number one position of the brand in many countries and the benefits the product gives to the health of hair.

The overall market increased by 14 per cent and at the same time the only prescription brand Style-Care fell by another 22 per cent. The OTC category reached 65 per cent of the total market sales. In 2003 the C&B brand was completed with the introduction of 'C&B Men', which was developed for the special needs of young men aged 18–30.

In the same year marketing communication activities were aimed mostly at end-users, to increase spontaneous brand awareness and brand loyalty. Apart from the TV campaign, many tailored activities were addressed to different target groups. Inserts were placed in trendy magazines, outdoor work, pharmacy posters and indoor ads in sports centres. In pharmacies and doctors' surgeries educational leaflets were distributed and innovative stands were used. C&B's leader image was further imprinted through a visual presence at pharmaceutical and medical conferences.

By 2004 the market had been radically transformed. People appreciated and used pharmaceutically developed shampoos containing vitamins as a pre-emptive measure to keep hair healthy. The number of users had dramatically increased and C&B became market leader with 27 per cent volume share.

Questions

1 In your opinion to what extent has C&B demonstrated a preference for either sales- or communication-based objectives?

2 C&B targets different audiences. How might this impact on the way in which sales and communication goals are developed?

3 To what degree should the emphasis of C&B's positioning be functional or expressive?

4 How might the C&B brand be positioned other than it is? Use several (at least four) techniques.

References

Barry, T. and Howard, D.J. (1990) A review and critique of the hierarchy of effects in advertising. *International Journal of Advertising*, **9**, pp. 121–35.

Colley, R. (1961) *Defining Advertising Goals for Measured Advertising Results*. New York: Association of National Advertisers.

Day, G., Shocker, A.D. and Srivastava, R.K. (1979) Customer orientated approaches to identifying product markets. *Journal of Marketing*, **43**(4), pp. 8–19.

Hodder, R., Gordon, W. and Swan, N. (1996) From four weddings and a funeral to blue velvet? *Admap* (March), pp. 38–44.

Johnson, G. and Scholes, K. (2002) *Exploring Corporate Strategy: Text and Cases*. 6th edn. Harlow: Prentice Hall.

King, S. (1991) Brand building in the 1990s. *Journal of Marketing Management*, **7**, pp. 3–13.

Kotler, P. (1997) *Marketing Management: Analysis, Planning, Implementation and Control*. Englewood Cliffs, NJ: Prentice-Hall.

Kriegel, R.A. (1986) How to choose the right communications objectives. *Business Marketing* (April), pp. 94–106.

Levitt, T. (1960) Marketing myopia. *Harvard Business Review* (July/August), pp. 45–56.

McCawley, I. (2001) Pernod to rebrand in pursuit of older people. *Marketing Week*, 25 January, p. 8.

Neal, W.D. (1980) Strategic product positioning: a step by step guide. *Business* (USA) (May/June), pp. 34–40.

Quinn, J.B., Mintzberg, H., James, R.M., Lampel, J.B. and Ghosal, S. (2003) *The Strategy Process*. 4th edn. New York: Prentice-Hall.

Ries, A. and Trout, J. (1972) The positioning era cometh. *Advertising Age*, 24 April, pp. 35–8.

Rosen, R. (1995) *Strategic Management: An Introduction*. London: Pitman.

Rossiter, J.R. and Percy, L. (1987) *Advertising and Promotion Management*. Lexington, MA: McGraw-Hill.

Simms, J. (2004) Biggest brands. *Marketing*, 25 August, p. 30.

Sinclair, S.A. and Stalling, E.C. (1990) Perceptual mapping: a tool for industrial marketing: a case study. *Journal of Business and Industrial Marketing*, **5**(1), pp. 55–65.

Smith, P. (2004) Dotcom video star rises. *Sunday Times*, 11 July, p. 15.

Thompson, A. and Strickland, A.J. III (1990) *Strategic Management*. Homewood, IL: Irwin.

Branding and the role of marketing communications

14

The images and associations that customers make with brands and the brand identities which managers seek to create need to be closely related if long-run brand purchasing behaviour is to be achieved. Marketing communications can play an important and integral part in the development of positive brand associations that have meaning and purpose for buyers.

Aims and objectives

The aims of this chapter are to explore the nature and characteristics of branding and to identify the way in which marketing communications can be used to develop and maintain brands that are of significance to their respective target audiences.

The objectives of this chapter are to:

1. introduce and explore the nature of branding;
2. examine the common characteristics of brands;
3. determine the benefits to both buyers and owners of brands;
4. identify the different types of brands and the relationships they can have with the parent organisation;
5. appreciate the strategic importance of brands;
6. understand the contribution and the way in which marketing communications can be used to build and support brands;
7. appraise the nature and significance of brand equity.

Introduction

Successful brands create strong, positive and lasting impressions, all of which are perceived by audiences to be of value to them personally. Individuals perceive brands without having to purchase or have direct experience of them. The elements that make up this impression are numerous, and research by Chernatony and Dall'Omo Riley (1998a) suggests that there is little close agreement on the definition of a brand. They identified 12 types of definition: among them is the visual approach adopted by Assael (1990), that a brand is the name, symbol, packaging and service reputation. The dif-

Brands are a product of the work of managers who attempt to augment their products with values and associations that are recognised by and are meaningful to their customers.

ferentiation approach is typified by Kotler (2000), who argues that a brand is a name, term, sign, symbol or design or a combination of these intended to identify the goods or services of one seller or group of sellers, and to differentiate them from those of competitors. What these researchers identified was that brands are a product of the work of managers who attempt to augment their products with values and associations that are recognised by and are meaningful to their customers. In other words, brands are constructs of, first, an identity that managers wish to portray and secondly, images construed by audiences of the identities they perceive. In addition to this, it is important to recognise that both managers and customers are involved in branding as a method by which all parties are able to differentiate among similar offerings and associate certain attributes or feelings and emotions with a particular brand.

Quality and satisfaction through time can lead buyers to learn to trust a brand, which may lead to a priority position in the evoked set and repeat purchasing activity. The acceptance of buyers as active problem solvers means that branding can be seen as a way that buyers can reduce the amount of decision-making time and associated perceived risk. This is because brand names provide information about content, taste, durability, quality, price and performance, without requiring the buyer to undertake time-consuming comparison tests with similar offerings or other risk-reduction approaches to purchase decisions. In some categories brands can be developed through the use of messages that are entirely emotional or image based. Many of the 'products' in FMCG sectors base their communications on imagery, assuming low involvement and the use of peripheral cues. Other sectors, such as cars or pharmaceuticals, require rational information-based messages supported by image-based messages (Boehringer, 1996). In other words, a blend of messages may well be required to achieve the objectives and goals of the campaign.

Branding is a task that requires a significant contribution from marketing communications and is a long-term exercise.

Branding is a task that requires a significant contribution from marketing communications and is a long-term exercise. Organisations that cut their brand advertising in times of recession reduce the significance and power of their brands. The Association of Media Independents claims, not surprisingly, that the weaker brands are those that reduce or cut their advertising when trading conditions deteriorate.

In line with moves towards integrated marketing communications and media neutral planning (see Chapter 11), many organisations are moving the balance of their promotional mixes away from an emphasis on advertising towards sales promotion, public relations and direct marketing. For example, mobile phone companies have used advertising to develop brand awareness and positioning and have then used sales promotion and direct marketing activities to provide a greater focus on loyalty and reward programmes. These companies operate in a market where customer retention is a problem. Customer loss (or churn rate) used to exceed 30 per cent and there was a strong need to develop marketing and communications strategies that reduce this figure and provide for higher customer satisfaction levels and, from that, improved profitability.

Brand characteristics

Brassington and Pettitt (2004) refer to a brand's function as the creation and communication of a multidimensional character for a product, one which 'is not easily copied or damaged by competitors' efforts'. In order to develop this character it is important to understand how brands are constructed. Brands consist of two main types of attributes: intrinsic and extrinsic. Intrinsic attributes refer to the functional characteristics of the product such as its shape, performance and physical capacity. If any of these intrinsic attributes were changed, it would directly alter the product. Extrinsic attributes refer to those elements that are not intrinsic and if changed do not alter the material functioning and performance of the product itself: devices such as the brand name, marketing communications, packaging, price and mechanisms which enable consumers to form associations which give meaning to the brand. Buyers often use the extrinsic attributes to help them distinguish one brand from another because in certain categories it is difficult for them to make decisions based on the intrinsic attributes alone.

> Brands consist of two main types of attributes: intrinsic and extrinsic.

Biel (1997) refers to brands being composed of a number of elements. The first refers to the functional abilities a brand claims and can deliver. The particular attributes that distinguish a brand are referred to as brand skills. He refers to cold remedies and their skill to relieve cold symptoms, for 6 hours, 12 hours or all day.

The second element is the personality of a brand and its fundamental traits concerning lifestyle and perceived values, such as being bland, adventurous, exciting, boring or caring. The idea of brand personification is not new, but it is an important part of understanding how a brand might be imagined as a person and how the brand is different from other brands (people). Linda Barker endorses the DFS brand and, in

ViewPoint 14.1 Luxury brands

Luxury brands such as Dior, Rolex, Cartier and Donna Karan have been developed mainly by advertising that is focused not on the intrinsic but on the extrinsic attributes. The strategy has been to develop brand-narne associations that appeal to the aspirational needs and social and psychological motivations of the target audiences.

Curtis (2000) says that, in order to grow, these brands face a common problem as they need to reach new target markets. The problem they all face is that lowering the price in order to attract these audiences threatens to impact the perception of the main brand by undermining its values and reputation, the one point of differentiation that has made these brands successful. The route forward is to introduce sub-brands that cannot be seen to be part of the main brand. So, Klein Cosmetics splits its business into two, classic brands and the CK franchise line that includes CkOne and CkB fragrances. Tudor is a sub-brand of Rolex and Donna Karan uses Signature and DKNY as associate labels. See Exhibit 14.1

EXHIBIT 14.1a Luxury brand - Gucci

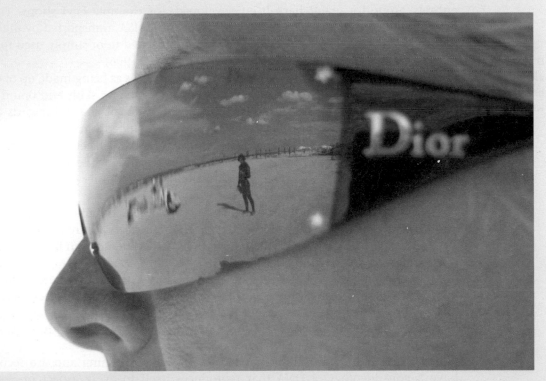

EXHIBIT 14.1b Luxury brand - Dior

doing so, makes a strong measure of association between the DFS brand (and its values) and the effervescent personality of the designer and TV presenter.

The third branding element is about building a relationship with individual buyers. People are said to interact with brands. A two-way relationship can be realistically developed when it is recognised that the brand must interact with the consumer just as much as the consumer must interact with the brand. Blackston (1993) argues that successful branding depends on consumers' perceptions of the attitudes held by the brand towards them as individuals. He illustrates the point with research into the credit card market, where different cards share the same demographic profile of users and the same conventional brand images. Some cards provide recognition or visibility of status, which by association are bestowed upon the owner in the form of power and authority. In this sense the card enhances the user. This contrasts with other cards, where the user may feel intimidated and excluded from the card because as a person the attitudes of the card are perceived to be remote, aloof, condescending and hard to approach.

For example, respondents felt the cards were saying, 'If you don't like the conditions, go and get a different card' and 'I'm so well known and established that I can do as I want'. The implications for brand development and associated message strategies become clearer.

In line with this thinking, Biel cites Fournier (1995), who considers brand/consumer relationships in terms of levels of intimacy, partner quality, attachment, interdependence, commitment and love.

> A more recent approach to brand development work involves creating a brand experience.

A more recent approach to brand development work involves creating a brand experience. The Tango roadshows, which enable Tango drinkers to bungee jump, trampoline and do other out-of-the-norm activities, are really seeking to provide extra brand-related experiences. Retail environments based entirely around a brand have been developed, for example Levi shops. The Virgin brand can be drunk as a cola or vodka, invested as an ISA, transported by flight or rail, viewed at a cinema, listened to or simply used to get married (adapted from Croft, 1996).

> Biel sees brands as being made up of three elements: brand personality, brand skills and brand relationships. These combine to form what he regards as 'brand magic'.

Therefore Biel sees brands as being made up of three elements: brand personality, brand skills and brand relationships. These combine to form what he regards as 'brand magic', which underpins added value.

Kapferer (2004) refers to a brand identity prism and its six facets. See Figure 14.1. The facets to the left represent a brands-outward expression while Kapferer argues that those to the right are incorporated within the brand, an inner expression or spirit as he refers to it.

These facets represent the key dimensions associated with building and maintaining brand identities and are set out in Table 14.1. These facets are interrelated and define a brand's identity. They represent the means by which brands can be managed, developed and even extended.

All brands consist of a mixture of intrinsic and extrinsic attributes and management's task is to decide on the balance between them. Indeed, this decision lies at the heart of branding in the sense that it is the strategy and positioning that lead to strong brands. Twivy (2000) suggests that there are two main types of brands: passionate and pseudo.

Passionate brands are those that have a strong positioning and are recognisable, have a core ideology, a DNA that reproduces itself in every aspect of the brand's behaviour and a set of values that engages an entire community of stakeholders. He cites Orange, Sony, Nike, Virgin, Channel 4 and the then new brand, the low-cost

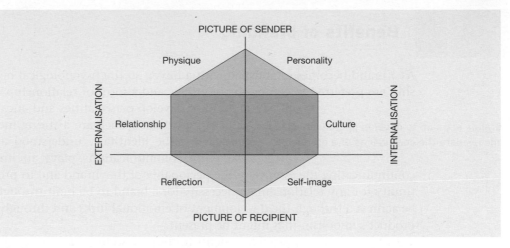

FIGURE 14.1 Brand identity prism (Kapferer, 2004); used with permission

TABLE 14.1 Brand facets (adapted from Kapferer, 2004)

Brand facet	Explanation
Physique	Refers to the main physical strength of the brand and its core added value. What does the brand do and what does it look like? E.g. the Coca-Cola bottle.
Personality	Those human characteristics that best represent the identity, best understood by the use of celebrity spokespersons who provide an instant personality.
Culture	A set of values that are central to a brand's aspirational power and essential for communication and differentiation.
Relationship	A brand's relationship defines the way it behaves and acts towards others. Apple exudes friendliness, IBM orderliness and Nike provocation. Important in the service sector.
Customer reflection	Refers to the way customers see the brand . . . for old people, for sporty people, clever people, people who want to look younger. This is an outward reflection.
Self-image	Refers to how an individual feels about themselves, relative to the brand. This is an inner reflection.

airline Go, which has subsequently been bought by and incorporated into easyJet. The corporate design for Go, undertaken by identity and design consultants Wolff Olins, was developed through association with the 'smart' Stansted airport and the use on board of Costa Coffee, which, it is argued, are all aspects that reflect attention to passionate brand detail.

Pseudo brands on the other hand lack core values and have experienced positioning drift. They might once have had such values but these have since been lost, forgotten or just abused or copied by competitors. Pseudo brands rely on USPs, redesigned logos and advertising and PR campaigns plus line extensions intended to disguise an essential lack of brand depth.

Benefits of branding

As a brand becomes established with a buyer, so the psychological benefits of ownership are preferred to competing offerings, and a form of relationship emerges. Brands are said to develop personalities and encapsulate the core values of a product. They are a strong means by which a product can be identified, understood and appreciated.

Brands are said to develop personalities and encapsulate the core values of a product.

Marketing communications plays an important role in communicating the essence of the personality of the brand and in providing the continuity for any relationship, a necessity for a brand to be built through time. This can be achieved through the development of emotional links and through support for any product symbolism that might be present.

Just as brands can provide benefits for buyers, so important direct benefits for manufacturers or resellers also exist. Brands provide a means by which a manufacturer can augment its product in such a way that buyers can differentiate the product, recognise it quickly and make purchase decisions that exclude competitive products in the consideration set. Premium pricing is permissible, as perceived risk is reduced and high quality is conveyed through trust and experience formed through an association with the brand. This in turn allows for loyalty to be developed, which in turn allows for cross-product promotions and brand extensions. Integrated marketing communications becomes more feasible as buyers perceive thematic ideas and messages, which in turn can reinforce positioning and values associated with the brand. For a summary of the benefits of branding, see Table 14.2.

TABLE 14.2 Benefits of branding

Customer benefits	Supplier benefits
Assists the identification of preferred products	Permits premium pricing
Can reduce levels of perceived risk and so improve the quality of the shopping experience	Helps differentiate the product from competitors
Easier to gauge the level of product quality	Enhances cross-product promotion and brand
Can reduce the time spent making product-based decisions and in turn reduce the time spent shopping	Encourages customer loyalty/retention and repeat-purchase buyer behaviour
Can provide psychological reassurance or reward	Assists the development and use of integrated marketing communications
Provides cues about the nature of the source of the product and any associated values	Contributes to corporate identity programmes
	Provides for some legal protection
	Provides for greater thematic consistency and uniform messages and communications

Brand portfolios: architecture and forms

The development of brand portfolios is a means of gaining and protecting brand advantage.

The way in which an organisation structures and manages its brands not only influences its overall success but also influences the marketing communications used to support them. The development of brand portfolios is a means of gaining and protecting brand advantage. The fundamental structure of a brand portfolio consists of three main levels: the architecture, the form and the individual brand. See Figure 14.2.

Brand architecture

An organisation's brand architecture represents the overall marketing interface with the community of stakeholders. Petromilli *et al.* (2002) identify the two most common types of brand architecture as branded house and the house of brands. These were formerly known as family brands and multi-brand structures.

Branded house architecture uses a single (master) brand to cover a series of offerings that may operate within descriptive sub-brand names. This corporate brand approach is used by Boeing, IBM, Virgin and Disney. Each seeks to dominate entire markets and categories through their single, highly relevant and highly leveraged master corporate brand, typical of the branded house structure.

The house of brands architecture is characterised by a group or collection of brands that have no outward connections and which operate independently of each other. These are brands that stand alone. General Motors and Procter & Gamble use this brand architecture.

These two approaches represent the two extremes of a spectrum. Many organisations operate a mix of these two architectures, and their brand architecture lies somewhere between the two, indicating that neither strategy is inherently superior.

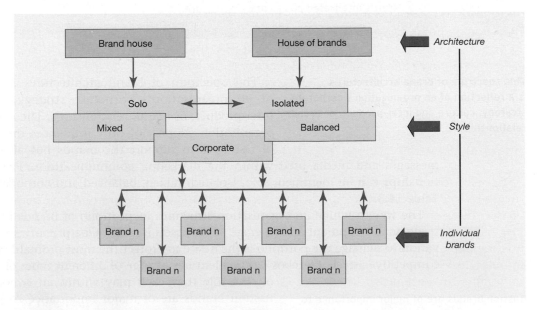

FIGURE 14.2 Basic structure of brand portfolio

Pierce and Moukanas (2002) claim that most large companies organise their portfolio of brands as a disparate collection of individual brands. This strategy becomes more effective when these brands are integrated.

ViewPoint 14.2   Pizza architectures

Kraft foods created a structure of various priced pizzas to attract different consumers. Kraft had original success in this market with the brand name Tombstone pizzas, which catered for the teenage group of consumers. Kraft saw openings at the high end of the market that would replicate the image and quality of what was seen at the upscale restaurants. Also, Kraft could see that the opportunities were no less at the lower end of the market. The structure Kraft clearly developed and benefited from was the pyramid structure. See Figure 14.3.

Source: Adapted from Pierce and Moukanas (2002).

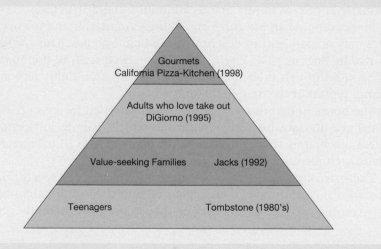

FIGURE 14.3 Kraft's integrated pizzas brand structure

This spectrum of brand architectures is a reflection of an organisation's corporate strategy, culture and inter-product, or brand, relationships.

This spectrum of brand architectures is a reflection of an organisation's corporate strategy, culture and inter-product, or brand, relationships. The approach each organisation adopts not only influences the deployment of resources to support the brands but also shapes the messages and media used within the marketing communications. Five main relationships can be identified: solo, isolated, mixed, balanced and corporate styles. See Table 14.3.

The way in which an organisation structures its portfolio of brands influences the strategic development and leverage of the assets it owns. One primary source of motivation to manage the portfolio is the desire to protect the most profitable brands from competitive attack. Riezebos (2003) identifies a range of different types of brand based on the role they each play within an overall portfolio.

Bastion brands are of major importance to an organisation.

Bastion brands are of major importance to an organisation, usually because they are the most valuable in terms

TABLE 14.3 Organisation/product brand relationships (after Gray and Smeltzer, 1985)

Relationship	Explanation
Solo style	Organisations whose brand offer is a single product type. Images of the organisation and the product tend to be the same; for example: Kwik-Fit, Pirelli, Coca-Cola.
Isolated style	Essentially a multi-product branding approach that requires promotional expenditure to support each individual brand. Should a particular brand be damaged, the other brands in the portfolio and the corporate name are protected.
Balanced style	The identity of each individual product is related to the parent organisation; for example Ford UK, where each car brand is prefixed by Ford. The Ford Fiesta 1.3L, Ford Focus and Ford Transit all convey the balance between the corporate name and the individual brands.
Mixed style	There is no pattern of relationship between the products and the parent organisation. For example, the German organisation Bosch GmbH identifies its spark plugs and power tools range under the Bosch name, but uses the name Blaupunkt for its radios.
Corporate style	Although an organisation may operate in a number of different strategic business areas, this approach requires all communications to be targeted at reinforcing the corporate image. IBM, Mars, Hewlett-Packard and Black & Decker are examples of this form.

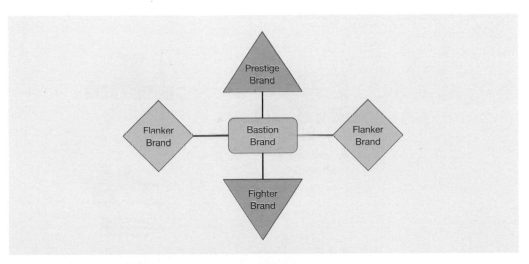

FIGURE 14.4 Portfolio of Brands (Riezebos, 2003)

of profit, revenue and market share, consequently they are prone to attack. One major form of strategic response is to develop other brands in order to protect the premier brand. See Figure 14.4.

The role of flanker brands is to protect the bastion brand by warding off competitors. By charging a slightly lower price and by offering a different set of attributes these brands make it more difficult for competitor brands to enter the market. Rather than lose sales to competitors, it is better to lose sales to an internal brand, even if the retained profits are not as high as those generated by the bastion brand.

Fighter brands are used to fend off competitors.

Fighter brands are used to fend off competitors who compete on discounted prices. Prices of fighter brands are set between the bastion brand and the competitor's low-cost offering, while the quality is adjusted to be perceived as lower than that of the bastion brand. Marketing communications should focus on name awareness, not price.

ViewPoint 14.3   Brand protectors

Riezebos (2003) refers to Procter & Gamble's shampoo Pantene as a bastion brand that is protected by Head and Shoulders and Wash & Go as flanker brands. He argues that use of these brands makes it very difficult for competitors to launch new brands to attack Pantene.

Similarly, the Volkswagen bastion brand is protected by Seat and Skoda as fighter brands. Lexus is a prestige brand for Toyota, Acura for Honda and Infinity for Nissan. These vehicle manufacturers are perceived to be strongly associated with the middle-range vehicle market. These new brands were necessary in order to enter the market and compete with Mercedes and BMW.

Source: Riezebos (2003, pp. 198–200). Used with permission.

EXHIBIT 14.2a Pantene – a classic bastion brand

EXHIBIT 14.2b Head and Shoulders and Wash & Go – both flanker brands to protect Pantene

Prestige brands can also be aimed at niche markets but this time the focus is on high quality and luxury. Prices are set high but marketing communications needs to focus on the high quality and status associated with ownership.

Brand forms

There are many forms of branding but primarily there are manufacturer, distributor, price and generic brands.

Manufacturers' brands help to identify the producer of a brand at the point of purchase. For example, Cadbury's chocolate, Ford cars and Coca-Cola are all strong manufacturers' brands. This type of brand usually requires the assistance of channel intermediaries for wide distribution, and the promotional drive stems from the manufacturer in an attempt to persuade end-users to adopt the brand, which in turn stimulates channel members to stock and distribute the brand.

Distributor (or own-label) brands do not associate the manufacturer with the offering in any way. The distributor brand is owned by a channel member, typically a wholesaler, such as Nurdin & Peacock, or a retailer, such as Tesco, Boots and Woolworths. This brand strategy offers many advantages to both the manufacturer, who can use excess capacity, and retailers, who can earn a higher margin than they can with manufacturers' branded goods and at the same time develop organisational (e.g. store) images. Channel members have the additional cost of promotional initiatives, necessary in the absence of a manufacturer's support. Some manufacturers refuse to make distributor products, and in the mid-1990s there was increased attention paid to this area, as some of the multiple grocers launched products that were alleged to be too similar to main manufacturer brands. Using a similar name and packaging the product in the same style has led to conflict in the channel network.

There has been considerable debate about the shift in volumes between manufacturers' and distributor brands. A study by Nielsen reported by Sargent (1995) attempted to isolate the key factors that contribute to longer-term brand development. The study, which focused on 45 major UK-based FMCG markets, found a decline in the volume of manufacturer brands sales and an increase in the volume of distributor sales over the three-year period of the study. TV advertising was isolated as one of the key elements in the development of the brands that had grown (at the expense of price-based sales promotions). The study also confirmed the general view that new product development and being first into a market were of major significance when seeking brand growth over the longer term.

The growth of distributor brands at the expense of manufacturer brands need not be expected to continue unchecked. Consumers value or expect a certain level of brand choice in stores, and as some store traffic and spend per visit rates have declined, some grocery multiples have taken steps to stem the volume of their distributor brand provision and increased the volume of manufacturer brands on their shelves.

Price brands are produced by manufacturers in an attempt to compete with private brands. Tesco has used this approach to respond to the arrival of a number of low-cost retailers such as Kwik Save and Aldi. The product is low priced and is further characterised by an absence of any promotional support. The effect on the other brands in the manufacturer's portfolio may be to stimulate promotional support to prevent the less loyal buyers from trading over to the low-priced offering.

The final type is the *generic brand*. This is sold devoid of any promotional materials and the packaging displays only information required by law. Manufacturers are even less inclined to produce these 'white carton' products than price brands. They are often sold at prices 40 per cent below the price of normal brands. They consume very few promotional resources, for obvious reasons, but their popularity, after a burst in the 1970s, has waned considerably, particularly in the supermarket sector where they gained their greatest success. However, generics are significant in some markets. In the early 1990s the pharmaceuticals industry experienced growth in the use of generic products, spurred by the NHS reforms of the government (Blackett, 1992) but outside of the pharmaceuticals industry generic brands have had minimal influence.

The strategic role of branding

From a strategic perspective, brands play an important role. They can be used as a means of defending market share or group brands, protecting established positions; they can be used to attack competitor brands and provide a means of deterring market entry by others, in other words, act as a market entry barrier or aid customer retention, as mentioned earlier. However, there are three broad aspects of branding that enable these strategic roles to be accomplished, namely integration, which can lead to differentiation, and finally added value. See Figure 14.5.

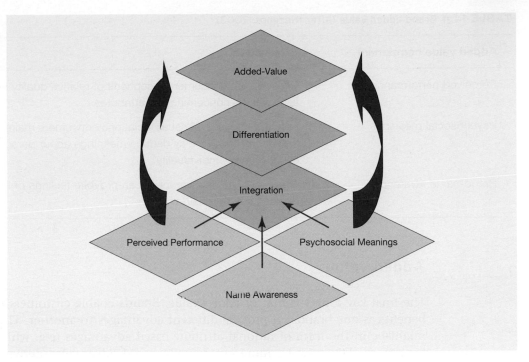

FIGURE 14.5 The strategic dimensions of branding

Integration

For a brand to be maintained and to work, it is important that the communications used to develop and maintain the brand are consistent and meaningful. Part of the essence of integrated marketing communications is that all the tools used to support a brand and the messages that are used to convey brand values must be consistent, uniform and reinforcing. Therefore, successful branding is partly the result of effective integrated marketing communications.

When Levi Strauss attempted to prevent Asda from selling its clothing it was attempting to protect the way it wanted to be perceived, that is, its positioning. If Asda continued to sell Levi Strauss products, market forces would ultimately determine whether the positioning determined by Levi Strauss was valued by customers.

Differentiation

Brands that are both enabled and which enable integration provide the means by which a product can be seen to be different, relative to a competitor's product. Branding is a method of separation and positioning so that customers can recognise and understand what a brand stands for, relative to other **Not all brands choose to be different.** brands. However, not all brands choose to be different as there is some strategic advantage for smaller new-entry brands to associate themselves closely with the market leader. This is witnessed by the disagreements between distributors and manufacturers over the packaging, names and type faces used for some products (e.g. Coca-Cola and Sainsbury's Cola, Penguin and Asda's Puffin bars).

TABLE 14.4 Brand added value (after Riezebos, 2003)

Added value component	Explanation
Perceived performance	Derived from consumer perceptions of relative quality and perceived associations concerning key attributes
Psychosocial meanings	Refers to the immaterial associations consumers make about brands from which they deduce meanings about personality and expressions of individuality
Brand-name awareness	The level of name awareness can provoke feelings of familiarity and reduced risk or uncertainty

Added value

The final key aspect is that of added value. Brands enable customers to derive extra benefits as one brand can provide different advantages to another. These advantages might be in the form of rational attribute-based advantages (e.g. whiter, stronger or longer) or they may be more emotionally based advantages derived through the augmented aspects of the products (e.g. the way you feel about a brand). This issue is evidenced by the vigour with which Levi Strauss resisted the distribution of its jeans through price-oriented distributors such as Asda. One of the arguments proposed by the company was that the inherent brand value was effectively removed through this form of distribution.

Value is added to brands through three main components: perceived performance, psychosocial meaning and the extent of brand-name awareness (Riezebos, 2003). See Table 14.4. Added value is developed using different combinations of these three components.

> Value is added to brands through three main components: perceived performance, psychosocial meaning and the extent of brand-name awareness.

Marketing communications is required to build these components so that consumers deduce particular meanings, perceive and value certain performance characteristics and of course build awareness and name familiarity.

Individual brand - fingerprinting

All branding activities need to extend across all key consumer contact points, a policy that needs to be pursued when developing integrated marketing communications (Chapter 11). One of the main tasks is to remind the market continually of the brand's presence, position and quality. When developing a marketing communications plan it is vitally important to consider the information arising from a brand audit and then develop a brand fingerprint, as Vyse (1999) refers to it. The management and development of a brand require resources and processes to ensure that the brand associations which buyers make are as intended and that the gap between managers' and buyers' expectations is tolerable. With the completion of a brand audit comes an understanding of consumers, but understanding consumers is worthless unless the information is in a form that can be read and understood by everyone involved in the brand development process.

Brands suffer mid-life crises, they lose friends and need to be vigorously rejuvenated, often through exceptional creativity (Tango, Sainsbury's, British Airways). Vyse comments that brands need to be up to date and speak the current language. Gap has a look and feel that travels across its store design, its through-the-line communications, and on packaging which expresses the visual, tactile, emotional and functional values of the clothes. Brand fingerprinting is about developing a single document that can be used by everyone involved with the brand development process. The benefits are as follows:

- It allows for continuity when brand managers move on in their careers.
- When the retail environment changes in a radical manner (e.g. ecommerce).
- It focuses on the consumer and so helps maintain the relationship.
- It fosters good team practice.

A brand fingerprint consists primarily of a document that summarises the essential character of the brand. According to Vyse, this comprises the following elements:

Target: a description of the person for whom the brand is always the first choice by defining their attitudes and values.

Insight: a description defining the elements about the consumer and his or her needs upon which the brand is founded.

Competition: a picture of the market and alternative choices as seen by the consumer and the relative values the brand offers in the market.

Benefits: the various functional and emotive benefits that motivate purchase.

Proposition: the single most compelling and competitive statement the target consumer would make for buying the brand.

Values: what the brand stands for and believes in.

Reasons to believe: the proof we offer to substantiate positioning.

Essence: the distillation of the brand's generic code into one clear thought.

Properties: the tangible things of which the merest glimpse, sound, taste, smell or touch would evoke the brand.

For a brand to grow and be sustained, the functional aspects of the product must be capable of meeting the expectations of the buyer. If the quality of the physical and functional aspects of the product is below acceptable standards, marketing communications activities alone cannot create and sustain a brand. When Jaguar cars were first exported to the United States, the car was soon rejected by the market because the first buyers of Jaguars (innovators in the process of adoption) experienced a variety of problems. These included overheating, because thermostats failed to work, and gearboxes and clutches that needed replacing too quickly. This led to a poor image of Jaguar, which meant that market penetration would be slow, at least until the product defects were corrected. A quality initiative at the production plant resulted in a car that performed at exceptionally high levels on all functions. Promotional work then built upon the new credibility, so that Jaguar became one of the most sought-after prestige cars in the United States.

The role of marketing communications in branding

Marketing communications plays a vital role in the development of brands.

Marketing communications plays a vital role in the development of brands and is the means by which products become brands, that is, how customers can see how a product is different and understand what a brand stands for and what its values are.

The way in which marketing communications is used to build brands is determined strategically by the role that the brand is expected to play in achieving an organisation's goals. Chernatony and Dall'Olmo Riley (1998b) argue that there are several roles that marketing communications can play in relation to brand development. For example, they suggest the role during brand extensions is to show buyers how the benefits from the established brand have been transferred or extended to the new brand. It may be that some of the problems currently experienced by Lego are due to a brand extension strategy that has not been suitably supported by marketing communications, or the poor financial situation may be due to a move away from core brand values (Lee, 2004). Another role might be to clarify each individual's role within the organisation. Developing Ehrenberg's (1974) ideas, it might be argued that the role of brand-based marketing communications is to remind buyers and reinforce their perceptions in order to defend market share.

Whatever the role, one major determinant that applies to all organisations is the size of the financial resources that are made available. Should the budget be high, advertising will be the main way in which brand name associations are shaped. The brand name itself will not need to be related to the function or use experience of the brand as the advertising will be used to create and maintain brand associations.

When few financial resources are available, a below-the-line approach is necessary. In particular, the brand name will need to be closely related to the function and use experience of the product, while packaging will also play a significant role in building brand associations.

Brand building through advertising

When advertising is used to enable consumers to make brand associations, two main approaches can be used, the rational and the emotional.

When a rational approach is used the functional aspects of a brand are emphasised and the benefit to the consumer is stressed. Very often product performance is the focus of the message and a key attribute is identified and used to position the brand. Typically, unique selling propositions were often used to draw attention to a single superior functional advantage that consumers find attractive. Many brands now try to present two or even three brand features as the USP has lost ground. For example, when Britvic launched Juice Up into the chilled fruit juice sector to compete with Sunny Delight, it used the higher fruit juice and lower sugar attributes as the main focus of the communication strategy. The rational approach is sometimes referred to as an informative approach (and complements functional positioning; see Chapter 13). In terms of added value (see above) this approach complements the perceived performance criteria identified by Riezebos (2003).

> When a rational approach is used the functional aspects of a brand are emphasised.

When an emotional approach is used, advertising should provide emotional selling points (ESPs). These can enable consumers to make positive brand associations based on both psychological and socially acceptable meanings, a psychosocial interpretation. Product performance characteristics are dormant while consumers are encouraged to develop positive feelings and associations with the brand.

> When an emotional approach is used, advertising should provide emotional selling points.

A further goal can be to create positive attitudes towards the advertising itself, which in turn can be used to make associations with the brand. In other words, the role of likeability, discussed later in Chapter 17, becomes paramount when using an emotional basis for advertising. Therefore these types of

ViewPoint 14.4   Diamond Trading Company

Through previous communications De Beers, now known as the Diamond Trading Company, established the idea that diamonds are forever. Diamonds have become a symbol of love and eternity as expressed through engagement rings. The problem facing the company was that they wanted new occasions in which expressions of love were made and the gift of a diamond would be appropriate.

Research showed that women need reaffirmation of love, and they perceive two aspects of the emotion. They acknowledge that love changes, yet at the same time it remains absolute. Using diamonds as a language rather than a luxury item JWT helped develop a new brand, 'The three stone diamond ring – for your past, your present and your future', which has subsequently helped drive sales of diamonds.

Source: http://www.jwt.com/case studies/. Used with permission.

advertisements should be relevant and meaningful, credible, and be of significant value to the consumer. In essence, therefore, emotional (or transformational) advertising is about people enjoying the advertisement (and complements expressive positioning; see Chapter 13).

Brand building through other techniques

When the marketing communications budget is limited or where the target audience cannot be reached reasonably or effectively through advertising, then it is necessary to use various other communication tools to develop brands. Although sales promotion is traditionally perceived as a tool that erodes rather than helps build a brand, as it has a price rather than a value orientation, it can be used strategically. In recent years new technology has enabled innovative sales promotion techniques to be used as a competitive weapon and to help build brand presence.

Direct marketing and public relations are important methods used to build brand values, especially when consumers experience high involvement. However, experience suggests that the sole use of direct marketing in FMCG markets has been less than satisfactory from those that have experimented (e.g. Heinz in the mid-1990s). The Internet offers opportunities to build new .com brands and the financial services sector has tried to harness this method as part of a multichannel distribution policy. What appear to be overridingly important for the development of brands operating with limited resources are the brand name and the merchandising activities, of which packaging, labelling and POP are crucial. In addition, as differentiation between brands becomes more difficult in terms of content and distinct symbolism, the nature of the service encounter is now recognised to have considerable impact on brand association. The development of loyalty schemes and carelines for FMCG, durable and service-based brands is a testimony to the importance of developing and maintaining positive brand associations.

> Direct marketing and public relations are important methods used to build brand values.

> Consumers develop associations about the content and positioning of the brand through advertising messages.

When advertising is the main source of brand development consumers develop associations about the content and positioning of the brand through advertising messages. As a substitute for advertising, it is the merchandising,

ViewPoint 14.5   Doritos

Doritos is regarded as an irreverent and independent brand in comparison with its sister brand, Walkers Crisps, which is positioned much more as a homely brand. Clarke (2000) reports a sales promotion undertaken for Doritos that involved over 15 million gamecards inserted into 50 million promotional packs of Doritos. The gamecards invited consumers to kiss the lips (on the card), which through a heat-seal mechanism revealed whether they had won a prize. The top prize was £10,000 and the chance to kiss a top British film star. The film theme builds on the brand's deliberate association with films and movie events and in that sense provides a form of integration and has strategic consistency.

EXHIBIT 14.3 A Doritos pack

packaging and the brand name itself that need to convey the required symbolism in such a way that the content and positioning are understood by the target audience. Indeed, the brand name needs to be closely aligned with the brand's primary function, more so than when advertising is able to convey the product's purpose and role. See Exhibit 14.4.

The below-the-line route needs to achieve a transfer of image. Apart from the clarity of the brand name (which needs to describe the product functions) and the shape, nature and information provided through the packaging and associated labelling, there are additional mechanisms through which brand associations can be developed.

ViewPoint 14.6   Bioform® goes below-the-line

When Charnos designed a revolutionary new bra it was decided not to use conventional advertising to position the brand but to use the below-the-line route. The name had to reflect some of the key product attributes and therefore needed to sound technical, suggest 'better' shape, and be perceived as 'natural'. The name 'bioform'® was generated following research into 'bio', which was found to have natural connotations, and 'form', which was perceived as meaning well formed or of good shape.

A revolutionary new pack form and structure to reflect the brand's product credentials was developed. Because it was important for consumers to handle the bra in order to check the material and structure, it was an important design objective to make the pack easy to open. Another priority was to make it easy for consumers to check the colour of the bra. This was made possible by keeping the sides of the box transparent, while fully coating the front and back panels.

Innovative new pack graphics which defied market convention were also developed so that the bioform® component became the hero of the pack and appeared centre stage, in computer-generated graphic form, on the front face. Charnos also used in-store posters, shelf-cards and leaflets announcing the arrival of bioform®. It also supplied retailers, on demand, with freestanding display units, which combined box shelving and hanging space, to present the total concept in the most effective way.

EXHIBIT 14.4 Bioform® – A new brand launch
using a below-the-line strategy
Picture reproduced with the kind permission of
Charnos and Lewis Moberly.

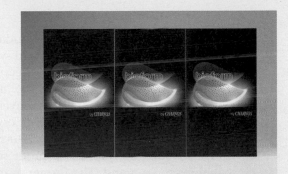

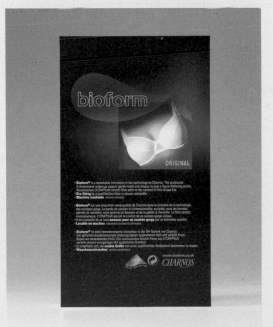

TABLE 14.5 Devices used to develop brand associations

Mechanism	Explanation
Co-branding	Refers to two or more brands that consumers can clearly identify, such as Microsoft and the NSPCC
Geographical identifiers	Attempt to provide source credibility – country of origin labels, brand names (e.g. British Airways), pictures of country origins (e.g. Cobra beer from India has a map of India on the label) and use of national symbols (e.g. flags)
Ingredient brands	Brands that are only available within other brands – Lycra, Intel and Dolby
Support services	Attempt to provide relationship strength and continuity of contact – loyalty cards (e.g. Tesco's Clubcard, Air Miles), brand-based carelines, technical help and assistance facilities (AOL)
Award symbols	Additional qualifying marks granted by independent organisations – ISO, etc.

Source: Adapted from Riezebos (2003).

There are five such devices: co-branding, geographical identifiers, the use of ingredient brands, support services and award symbols. See Table 14.5.

There are many occasions where advertising funds are not available to develop brand associations and where the brand name and merchandising needs to be the predominant force in enabling buyers to develop managed and positive brand associations. An increasing number of organisations in the b2b sector are using branding approaches and recognise the benefits of co-branding in particular. Charities and organisations in the not-for-profit sector are increasingly using commercial organisations to co-brand. The former receive commercial expertise and funding while the latter gain in terms of association with good deeds, giving (rather than taking) and being seen to care.

Marketing communications is the means by which products become brands. Buyers make associations immediately they become aware of a brand name. It is the brand manager's task to ensure that the associations made are appropriate and provide a means of differentiation. By communicating the key strengths and differences of a brand, by explaining how a brand brings value to a customer and by reinforcing and providing consistency in the messages transmitted, a level of integration can be brought to a brand, or rather the way it is perceived by the target market.

Marketing communications is the means by which products become brands.

Finally in this section, the importance of branding as a part of integrated marketing communications should not be forgotten, and to do this internal brand education is crucial. The way a brand relates internally to departments and individuals and the way the brand is articulated by senior management is an important part of brand education. Brands are not just external elements; they should be a part of the way in which an organisation operates, part of its cultural configuration.

Business-to-business branding

The branding concept has been used by a number of manufacturers (Intel, Teflon, Nutrasweet) to achieve two particular goals. Rich (1996) reports that the first goal is to develop an identity which final end-users perceive as valuable. For example, Intel has developed its microprocessors such that PCs with the Intel brand are seen to be of high quality and credibility. This provides the PC manufacturer with an added competitive advantage.

The second goal is to establish a stronger relationship with the manufacturer. Nutrasweet works with food manufacturers advising on recipes simply because the final product is the context within which Nutrasweet will be evaluated by end-users.

A b2b brand is often tied closely to the company itself, as opposed to b2c brands, which often distance themselves from the manufacturer or company name. For example, a Rolls-Royce power turbine is branded Rolls-Royce because of the perception of tradition, high quality, performance and global reach that are associated with the Rolls-Royce name.

The marketing communications should be developed so that they incorporate and perpetuate the personality of the brand. So, all the Rolls-Royce advertising materials should be in corporate colours and contain the logo. All copy should be in the house style and reinforce brand perceptions.

The use of event sponsorship, whereby an organisation provides financial support for a conference or exhibition, has become increasingly popular (Miller, 1997). Mainly because of the costs involved, event organisers have sought sponsorship aid. For sponsors, events provide a means of promoting visibility within a narrowly focused target market. In addition, they provide a means of highlighting their own particular contribution within the conference or their exhibition stand.

The use of joint promotional activities between manufacturers and resellers will continue to be an important form of communication behaviour. The desire to build networks that provide cooperative strength and protection for participants will continue. Manufacturers will use joint promotional activities as a means of forging close relationships with retailers and as a means of strengthening exit barriers (routes away from relationships).

ViewPoint 14.7   JCB

JCB is Europe's leading manufacturer of construction equipment and has developed a unique promotional style based upon demonstrating the features and versatility of its products in an entertaining way. The JCB *Dancing Diggers* consists of a series of trick routines that the company's demonstration team performs. The *Dancing Diggers* perform at exhibitions and draw huge crowds as the giant earthmoving equipment shows off its capabilities. This activity feeds advertising, sales literature and, of course, public relations work, providing a strong means of arresting attention and building tremendous levels of credibility. See Exhibit 14.5.

One little touch of personal selling and publicity skill can be observed in the development and launch of a machine called the 3D. The owner, Joe Bamford, designed the cab so that the operator could make a cup of tea. He promised to personally deliver the first 100 orders with a free kettle, which he did for each purchaser.

EXHIBIT 14.5 JCB
The Dancing Diggers are an important part of the company's publicity strategy. Picture reproduced with the kind permission of JCB.

Online branding

The major difference between online and off-line branding is the context in which the brand associations are developed and sustained. Both forms of branding are about developing and sustaining valuable relationships with consumers, but online branding occurs in a virtual context. This context deprives consumers of many of the normal cues used to sense and interpret brands. Opportunities to touch and feel, to try on and physically feel and compare products are largely removed and a new set of criteria has to be used to convey and interpret brand associations. One of the strengths of the Internet is its ability to provide copious amounts of regularly updated information, available '24/7'. As a result online brands tend towards the use of rational messages, using product attributes, quality and performance measures, third-party endorsements and price as a means of brand differentiation and advantage. However it should be remembered that online branding strategies are influenced by the nature of the brand itself. If the brand has a strong off-line presence then the amount of online branding work will be smaller than if it is a pure-play brand. Branding should be a part of an overall communications strategy, where online and off-line work are coordinated. Breen (1999) argues that online brands are stronger if the following holds true:

> The major difference between online and off-line branding is the context in which the brand associations are developed and sustained.

1. There is an overall communications strategy.

2. It is not expected to establish consumer relationships through a single Web site visit. The development of a personalised pathway for continued dialogue, such as that used by Amazon.com (which sends regular emails to customers about the status of their purchases and details of potentially interesting offers), is important.

3. A record is kept of the changing needs and interests of their consumers.

4. They attempt to be seen as a trustmark, not a trademark.

5. They try to integrate relationship-building activities with the real world. For example, financial services broker Charles Schwab opens 70 per cent of its accounts in branches where there is a face-to-face-based relationship from which account details are put online. The feeling that there is a personal element to the online relationship appears to add comfort and security.

Each Web site provides a focus for the brand identity and it is the experience consumers have with a site that determines whether a site will be revisited. The Web site acts as a prime means of differentiating online brands and those that fail to develop differential advantage will probably learn that visitors are only one click away from leaving a site (Oxley and Miller, 2000). These commentators refer to a site's 'stickiness' and ability to retain visitors, which in turn can increase advertising rate card costs.

Satisfying experiential motivations makes people stay and in doing so boosts the potency of an online brand.

However, as they point out, a long visit does not necessarily mean that the experience was beneficial as the site may try to facilitate customer transactions quickly, or enable them to find the information they need without difficulty; in other words, reduced levels of stickiness may be appropriate in some circumstances. All online branding activities need to extend across all key consumer contact points, in both off-line and online environments. Internet users generally exhibit goal-directed behaviour and experiential motivations. Goal-directed behaviour that is satisfied is more likely to make people want to return to a site. Therefore it can be concluded (broadly) that satisfying experiential motivations makes people stay and in doing so boosts the potency of an online brand.

Brand equity

The concept of brand equity has arisen from the increasing recognition that brands represent a value to both organisations and shareholders. According to Ehrenberg (1993), market share is the only appropriate measure of a brand's equity or value and, as a result, all other measures taken individually are of less significance, and collectively they come together as market share. However, this view excludes the composition of brands, the values that consumers place in them and the financial opportunities that arise with brand development and strength.

Lasser *et al.* (1995) identify two main perspectives of brand equity, namely a financial and a marketing perspective. The financial view is based on a consideration of a brand's value as a definable asset, based upon the net present values of discounted future cash flows (Farquahar, 1989). The marketing perspective is grounded in the beliefs, images and core associations consumers have about particular brands. Richards (1997) argues that there are both behavioural and attitudinal elements associated with brands and recognises that these vary between groups and represent fresh segmentation and targeting opportunities. A further component of the marketing view is the

TABLE 14.6 Five approaches to measuring brand equity

Source	Factors measured
David Aaker	Awareness, brand associations, perceived quality and market leadership, loyalty, market performance measures
Brand dynamics (Millward Brown)	Presence, relevance to consumer needs, product performance, competitive advantage, bonding
Equitrend (Total Research)	Salience, perceived quality, user satisfaction
3-D3 (TBWA Simmons Palmer)	Brand quality, quantity and future measured against a variety of stakeholders
Brand asset valuator (Young & Rubicam)	Strength (differentiation and relevance), stature (esteem and knowledge)

Source: Adapted from Cooper and Simmons (1997) and Haigh (1997).

degree of loyalty or retention a brand is able to sustain. Measures of market penetration, involvement, attitudes and purchase intervals (frequency) are typical. Feldwick (1996) used a three-part definition to bring these two approaches together. He suggests brand equity is a composite of:

- *brand value*, based on a financial and accounting base;
- *brand strength*, measuring the strength of a consumer's attachment to a brand;
- *brand description*, represented by the specific attitudes customers have towards a brand.

In addition to these, Cooper and Simmons (1997) offer *brand future* as a further dimension. This is a reflection of a brand's ability to grow and remain unhindered by environmental challenges such as changing retail patterns, alterations in consumer buying methods and developments in technological and regulative fields.

Attempts to measure brand equity have to date been varied and without a high level of consensus, although the spirit and ideals behind the concept are virtually the same. Table 14.6 sets out some of the approaches adopted.

As a means of synthesising these approaches the following are considered the principal dimensions through which brand equity should be measured:

- *brand dominance*: a measure of its market strength and financial performance;
- *brand associations*: a measure of the beliefs held by buyers about what the brand represents and stands for;
- *brand prospects*: a measure of its capacity to grow and extend into new areas.

Brand equity is considered important because of the increasing interest in trying to measure the return on promotional investments and so value brands for balance sheet purposes. A brand with a strong equity is more likely to be able to preserve its customer franchise and so fend off competitor attacks. Kish *et al.* (2001) refer to PepsiCo's attempt to build its model of brand equity, called Equitrak. See ViewPoint 14.8.

ViewPoint 14.8   Determining the value at PepsiCo

PepsiCo determined that it needed to define brand equity so that it could track the development of its various brands, benchmark them against 'icon stature' brands and enable comparisons to be made within the PepsiCo portfolio (Krish *et al.*, 2001).

The Equitrak model PepsiCo developed in the 1990s and ran into the twenty-first century, consists of two main elements: brand recognition and brand regard. See Figure 14.6. Brand recognition refers to the depth and breadth of awareness levels. Brand regard is about how people feel about a brand and measures a number of dimensions. The dimensions are weighted and then multiplied by the recognition score to provide an overall brand equity score.

By plotting the scores on a map it is possible to see how a brand is performing in particular regions, competitive analysis can be undertaken and strategic brand decisions made. See Figure 14.7.

Brand equity is a strategic related issue and whether a financial, marketing or twin approach is adopted the measurement activity can help focus management activity on brand development. However, there is little agreement about what is measured and how and when it is measured. Ambler and Vakratsas (1998) argue that organisations should not seek a single set of measures simply because of the varying circumstances and contextual factors that impinge on brand performance. In reality the measures used by most forms share many common elements.

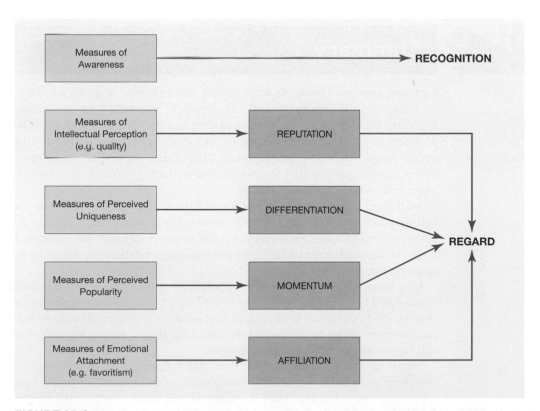

FIGURE 14.6 The structure of PepsiCo's brand equity model Equitrak (Krish *et al.*, 2001). Used with permission.

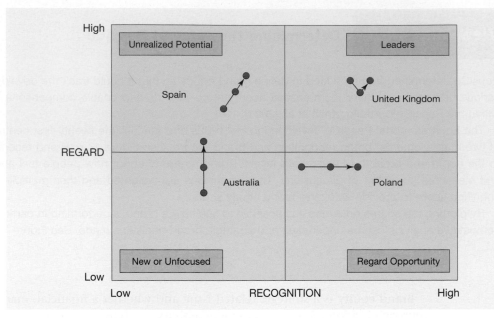

FIGURE 14.7 Brand equity development trend for a snack brand over time by country (Krish *et al.*, 2001). Used with permission.

Summary

Branding provides customers with a quick and easy way of understanding what a product is, what value it represents and can represent a measure of psychosocial reassurance. Branding provides manufacturers and distributors with a means of differentiating their products in order to gain competitive advantage in such a way that customers perceive added value. This allows for premium pricing and the improved margin can be used to invest in new opportunities for commercial initiatives through, for example, innovation or improved levels of customer service.

Marketing communications has an important role to play in brand development and maintenance. In many circumstances advertising is used to develop strong brands. To help customers make associations with brands either a rational, information-based approach might be adopted or alternatively a more emotional relationship might be forged, one based more on imagery and feelings.

In a large number of cases the opportunity to use advertising is restricted and many smaller and b2b organisations need to rely on a below-the-line approach. In these circumstances, the brand name is important as it needs to symbolise or convey meaning about the functionality of the brand. In addition, merchandising, packaging and other POP elements will be prominent in brand development.

There are many other factors that can influence the development of brands. Co-branding, geographic signals and award symbols can impact on brand associations so that ultimately risk is reduced, trust is enhanced and there is sufficient confidence to purchase the brand on a regular basis.

Branding is a key strategic communication issue and not only affects FMCG products but is increasingly used by b2b organisations as a means of differentiation and added value.

Review questions

1. Write brief notes explaining what branding is.

2. How do brands assist customers and brand owners?

3. Summarise Biel's concept of 'brand magic'.

4. Select five consumer brands and evaluate their characteristics.

5. Explain the concept of a brand portfolio and set out what you understand by the terms architecture, bastion and fighter brands.

6. Discuss the relative importance of the three elements that determine the strategic aspect of branding.

7. Explain advertising's role in the development of brands.

8. Find three non-FMCG brands and evaluate how their brand strength has been developed without the aid of advertising. How might you improve the strength of these brands?

9. Explain how business-to-business markets might benefit from adopting a branding approach.

10. Discuss two approaches to brand equity.

MINI-CASE
Car branding – from safety to sharks

Mini-case written by Graham Hughes, Principal Lecturer, Leeds Business School

The competitive nature of the car market, on a global scale, presents manufacturers with a huge challenge in branding terms. This challenge requires significant investment in marketing communications, much of which has been traditionally advertising based. In some parts of the market, particularly the mass volume sectors, many car models from different manufacturers exhibit very similar design characteristics. This puts increased pressure on branding and brand communications to provide differentiation.

Strong, effective branding is developed as a result of long-term consistency in terms of positioning platforms and the way in which brand messages are transmitted to the target audience. For many car brands this has resulted in presenting cars in ways that reflect the design of the vehicle and the enjoyment of driving. The 'classic' car advertisement is the car being driven by good-looking individuals, often male, around wide country roads in Tuscan hills or Californian freeways against a background of clear

blue skies and well-known music soundtracks. The objectives of such campaigns are awareness creation and image development. Such campaigns, however, do little in the way of supporting brand differentiation.

In branding terms, there is often a requirement to promote both the manufacturer and individual product brands. For volume car producers such as Ford, Toyota or Nissan, this usually involves a combination of both levels. For premium brands, such as BMW, Volvo and Mercedes, the emphasis is normally on the corporate brand. Models in the volume sectors are commonly identified by brand names (the Ford Mondeo or Toyota Corolla), whereas in the premium markets brands receive numbers or letters (the BMW 5 Series or the Volvo S40). The use of either names or numbers is usually to provide differentiation on the basis of car size or engine capacities and associated price ranges. It might be argued that using names provides more opportunity for creative communications development. Might using numbers or letters be considered more distinctive? The decision to use names, numbers or letters is an interesting one as it provides different opportunities to use these 'symbols' to promote brand values. Selecting a name allows the manufacturer to say something about the brand that reflects brand values and attributes. Brand names may stand alone from the manufacturer brand. Numbers and/or letters in themselves say very little, but combined with the name of the manufacturer, the BMW 5 or 7 series, they evoke a very powerful brand identity among their target audience.

The Swedish manufacturer Volvo has traditionally positioned its brands on a safety platform. The Volvo brand has long stood as a metaphor for safety, at the expense of design or style. This has meant that Volvo was never likely to be the market leader, but that it has created a loyal customer base for whom safety is a key factor in their purchase decision-making and they are happy to trade off the fact that the car they are driving is not the height of stylish or modern design. Volvo TV advertisements were unlikely to show cars in exotic locations. Instead they would show cars in test centres with dummies in the seats crashing into barriers. This clearly demonstrated the safety brand values – that, if involved in an accident, the car would be damaged but the passengers would emerge relatively unscathed. One of the features of any Volvo car is that the sidelights would always be on when the car is in operation; this is one of Volvo's essential safety characteristics. This became such a well-known symbol that urban myth suggests that, even after an old Volvo has been through a car 'crusher', each corner of the metal cube which emerges is brightly lit!

More recently Volvo has developed new models that are more attractive in design terms. Making product changes may however have a damaging effect on brand values and associations. Volvo needed to ensure that the sleeker design features would not be interpreted by the loyal customer as the car being any less safe. At the same time it was hoped that improved design would attract new customers who had previously thought of the brand as old-fashioned and ugly. The advertising and other marketing communications had to be carefully planned in order not to alienate existing customers but still provide sufficient incentive for drivers of competitive products to consider a switch in brands.

In creative terms, this has included less of an emphasis on cars being deliberately crashed to one that highlights the importance of design from a wider perspective than simply making the car look good. The brand values being claimed today by Volvo go significantly beyond safety. The company's Web site describes its brand values in terms of safety, the environment, quality and heritage (www.volvocars.co.uk). Safety per se is less at the forefront of Volvo marketing communications but nevertheless implicit in most aspects of how the business is being portrayed through a range of on- and offline communications. The Volvo director of brand strategy has recently been quoted in an attempt to explain the shift away from overt claims on safety

If you step into a BMW, it's all about driving pleasure. Of course they also have air bags and crumple zones just as we do. But why people buy a BMW is not because it's a safe car. So we have to learn from that and evolve: although I will be the first to admit that it's difficult to reinterpret what you are all about. It is our challenge to interpret functionality in an interesting way.

Josephs (2004)

In addition to advertising through TV, print and direct mail on a theme of 'Volvo. For Life', on the Volvo Web site are a series of short films that show cars being driven by different individuals in a variety of locations with the soundtrack of the conversation between the driver and their passenger. These conversations are not directly connected to the car itself but describe events in the individuals' lives that have influenced them. One of the passengers is a young girl who had her arm bitten off in a shark attack. These are a far cry from a Volvo 240 being seen crashed head-on with no damage to the dummies inside, but do say a lot about how the new brand values are being communicated.

Reference

Josephs, J. (2004) Volvo: Safe? www.brandchannel.com. Accessed 22 November 2004.

Questions

1 For a market sector of your choice, identify the leading brands and analyse their brand values.

2 Identify examples of the ways in which these values are promoted via marketing communications in both on- and offline situations.

3 Make recommendations for further developing areas of marketing communications for brand development.

References

Ambler, T. and Vakratsas, D. (1998) Why not let the agency decide the advertising. *Market Leader*, 1 (Spring), pp. 32–7.

Assael, H. (1990) *Marketing: Principles and Strategy*. Orlando, FL: Dryden Press.

Biel, A. (1997) Discovering brand magic: the hardness of the softer side of branding. *International Journal of Advertising*, 16, pp. 199–210.

Blackett, T. (1992) Branding and the rise of the generic drug. *Marketing Intelligence and Planning*, 10(9), pp. 21–4.

Blackston, M. (1993) A brand with an attitude: a suitable case for treatment. *Journal of Market Research Society*, 34(3), pp. 231–41.

Boehringer, C. (1996) How can you build a better brand? *Pharmaceutical Marketing* (July), pp. 35–6.

Brassington, F. and Pettitt, S. (2004) *Principles of Marketing*. 3rd edn. Harlow: Pearson.

Breen, B. (1999) Building stronger internet identities. *Marketing*, 16 September, pp. 25–6.

Chernatony de, L. and Dall'omo Riley, F. (1998a) Defining a brand: beyond the literature with experts' interpretations. *Journal of Marketing Management*, 14, pp. 417–43.

Chernatony de, L. and Dall'omo Riley, F. (1998b) Expert practitioners' views on roles of brands: implications for marketing communications. *Journal of Marketing Communications*, 4, pp. 87–100.

Clarke, A. (2000) Doritos' SWALK attack. *Promotions and Incentives* (June), pp. 24–6.

Cooper, A. and Simmons, P. (1997) Brand equity lifestage: an entrepreneurial revolution. TBWA Simmons Palmer, unpublished working paper.

Croft, M. (1996) Stretched marks. *Marketing Week*, 8 March, pp. 47–8.

Curtis, J. (2000) Not taking luxury for granted. *Marketing*, 24 August, pp. 26–7.

Ehrenberg, A.S.C. (1974) Repetitive advertising and the consumer. *Journal of Advertising Research*, 14 (April), pp. 25–34.

Ehrenberg, A.S.C. (1993) If you are so strong why aren't you bigger? *Admap* (October), pp. 13–14.

Farquahar, P. (1989) Managing brand equity. *Marketing Research*, 1(9) (September), pp. 24–33.

Feldwick, P. (1996) What is brand equity anyway, and how do you measure it? *Journal of Market Research*, 38(2), pp. 85–104.

Fournier, S. (1995) A consumer–brand relationship perspective on brand equity. Presentation to Marketing Science Conference on Brand Equity and the Marketing Mix, Tucson, Arizona, 2–3 March.

Gray, E.R. and Smeltzer, L.R. (1985) SMR Forum: corporate image – an integral part of strategy. *Sloan Management Review* (Summer), pp. 73–8.

Haigh, D. (1997) Brand valuation: the best thing to ever happen to market research. *Admap* (June), pp. 32–5.

Kapferer, J.-N. (2004) *The New Strategic Brand Management*. London: Kogan Page.

Kotler, P. (2000) *Marketing Management: The Millennium Edition*. Upper Saddle River, NJ: Prentice-Hall.

Krish, P., Riskey, D.R. and Kerin, R. (2001) Measurement and tracking of brand equity in the global marketplace: the PepsiCo experience. *International Marketing Review*, 18(1), pp. 91–6.

Lasser, W., Mittal, B. and Sharma, A. (1995) Measuring customer based brand equity. *Journal of Consumer Marketing*, 12(4), pp. 11–19.

Lee, J. (2004) Lego calls review of £35m European media. *Campaign*, Retrieved 23 December 2004 from www.brandrepublic.com/news/.

Miller, R. (1997) Make an event of it. *Marketing*, 5 June, p. 28.

Oxley, M. and Miller, J. (2000) Capturing the consumer: ensuring website stickiness. *Admap* (July/August), pp. 21–4.

Petromilli, M., Morrison, D. and Million, M. (2002) Brand architecture: building brand portfolio value. *Strategy and Leadership*, **30**(5), pp. 22–8.

Pierce, A. and Moukanas, H. (2002) Portfolio power: harnessing a group of brands to drive profitable growth. *Strategy and Leadership*, **30**(5), pp. 15–21.

Rich, M. (1996) Stamp of approval. *Financial Times*, 29 February, p. 9.

Richards, T. (1997) Measuring the true value of brands. *Admap* (March), pp. 32–6.

Riezebos, R. (2003) *Brand Management: A Theoretical and Practical Approach*. Harlow: Pearson.

Sargent, J. (1995) Building brands in the UK. *Admap* (January), pp. 45–7.

Twivy, P. (2000) Passionate brands will win the race. *Marketing*, 9 March, p. 19.

Vyse, K. (1999) Fingerprint clues identify the brand. *Marketing*, 30 September, p. 38.

Witt, J. (2000) Preparing Virgin Cola for the fight of its life. *Marketing*, 2 November, p. 23.

Corporate identity, reputation and branding

15

The awareness, perception and attitudes held by an organisation's various stakeholders will vary in intensity and need to be understood and acted upon. This can be accomplished through a strategy that develops the profile of an organisation, one that seeks continual dialogue and which leads to the development of trust-based relationships. This is necessary in order that stakeholders think and act favourably towards an organisation and enable the organisation to develop strategies which are compatible with the environment and its own objectives.

Aims and objectives

The aim of this chapter is to consider those communications that are designed to encourage a dialogue with stakeholders, with a view to influencing the image and reputation of the organisation.

The objectives of this chapter are to:

1. introduce the notion of corporate communications and profile strategies;
2. appraise the term 'corporate image' and the associated concepts corporate personality, identity and reputation;
3. consider the characteristics of corporate identity and corporate branding;
4. explore methods of evaluating corporate image;
5. examine the relationship between corporate identity and strategic management;
6. introduce a framework incorporating corporate identity with the process of strategic management.

Introduction

This chapter is concerned with the way in which organisations are presented, perceived and how they interact with their various stakeholder audiences. It is also concerned with the images that people form as a result of interpreting the various identity signals that organisations transmit and any interaction that may ensue. Melewar (2003) derived the following definition from a consideration of the literature. Corporate identity is concerned with 'the set of meanings by which an organisation allows itself to be known and through which it enables people to describe, remember and relate to it'.

All organisations use corporate communications to deliver their corporate identity. It is through the identity that stakeholders form images of the organisation and, through time, corporate reputations are built. People form an image of the organisation based on the cues or signals that organisations transmit. These cues may be sent deliberately or they may be accidental or unintended. Whatever the source these cues can be critical because the way they are interpreted shapes the way organisations are seen, regarded, and even whether transactions occur.

> It is through the identity that stakeholders form images of the organisation.

Hatch and Schultz (2000) refer to two schools of thought about strategic identity management. The 'Visual' school, which is concerned with operational aspects, and a 'Strategic' school, which is concerned with an organisation's aims and how it positions and distinguishes itself. This demarcation is useful because not only does it help identify the scope of the topic but it also shows how identity management, indeed reputation management, has evolved. These two aspects of identity management are referred to later in this chapter.

Organisations are said to have a personality, a persona that reflects the inner spirit and heart of the organisation. From this cultural core identities are developed and presented to the outside world. The management of the corporate identity is vital if the image held of the organisation, by all stakeholders, is to be consistent and accurately represent the personality of the organisation (Dowling, 1993).

> Organisations are said to have a personality.

Gorb (1992) refers to a continuum of differentiation where at one end there is a total loss of personality and at the other end a schizoid position is achieved. The trick is to change with the environment and maintain a differentiated position by providing continuity to the way the identity is represented and, of course, perceived. He quotes Shell, whose logo, established over a century ago, appears to have been preserved unchanged. In reality it has undergone many changes and what we see today is nothing like the original. This has occurred through careful continuity of the idea of the seashell and adaptation of it to the various contexts through time.

Corporate identity or corporate branding?

The phrase 'corporate identity' is gradually being replaced by corporate branding. Balmer (1998) suggested that corporate identity was the accepted terminology in the 1980s, and that this gave way to corporate branding in the 1990s. However, it can be argued that there are some intrinsic differences in this terminology. Balmer and Gray (2003) claim that there are strong and fundamental differences between these two concepts. All organisations have a need to address identity-related issues, such as those

TABLE 15.1 Corporate brand criteria (adapted from Balmer and Gray, 2003)

Corporate brand criteria	Explanation
Rarity	Corporate brand values (functional and emotional) developed over time that cannot be easily imitated
Durability	The value of the brand depreciates slowly, relative to product brands
Inappropriability	Only the owning organisation can derive performance-related outcomes
Imperfect imitability	It is very difficult for a competitor to copy or replicate the brand
Imperfect substitutability	Strong corporate brands maintain their position through continuous improvement and protect themselves from competitors and from being overtaken

> **The three key questions that organisations need to find answers to are, 'Who are we?' 'What business are we in?' and 'What do we want to be?'**

posed by Albert and Whetten (1985) who said the three key questions that organisations need to find answers to are, 'Who are we?' 'What business are we in?' and 'What do we want to be?' However, if corporate identity is a necessity for all organisations, corporate branding is not. Corporate brands are developed from their identity and, unlike traditional approaches to corporate messages, are primarily concerned with the delivery of specific corporate promises. These promises are often conveyed through a short strapline or 'mantra' (Keller, 1999). Balmer and Grey (2003) use Disney and Nike as examples: 'fun, family entertainment' and 'authentic athletic performance' respectively. These brands are seen to consist of certain criteria. These are set out in Table 15.1.

ViewPoint 15.1   Halifax develops split personality

In the summer of 1997 the Halifax converted from being the world's largest building society into a bank. The transition received a high level of media interest, mainly because of the volume and value of shares that were distributed to eligible members of the former building society.

The change in designation and status was enormous for the organisation to manage. From being a dominant player, indeed market leader, it became a smaller player in a different market, of which it knew less and in which it was far less influential. Some months after conversion, a customer inquired whether the Halifax offered a safe deposit service, as available in the majority of other banks. The customer was informed that the Halifax did not offer such a service. 'Why not?' was the retort, reports Wright (1997). The member of staff then investigated the matter internally with the customer relations department and relayed the answer to the customer. 'Having referred your query to head office, I have been advised that Halifax Plc is not a bank.' The question therefore is, if the Halifax Plc is not a building society and is not a bank . . . what is it? The identity crisis experienced by the few staff involved in this example may be atypical or may be replicated across the organisation. What is clear is that the personality of the organisation and the identity it wished to project are not complementary, and further self-analysis and clearer internal communication are required in order that its external communications do not lead to confusion and misunderstanding.

Source: Adapted from Wright (1997).

The organisation's ability to continually leverage its resources to deliver superior value.

Balmer and Gray developed these criteria based on the 'resource-based view of the firm', which is grounded in the brand, having considerable resources and capabilities that can be used as a major source of sustainable value. The basis therefore of a strong corporate brand and its ability to deliver its promise is the organisation's ability to continually leverage its resources to deliver superior value.

Corporate brands are a complex form of identity but not all organisations need a corporate brand, if for example they are a public utility, monopoly or work in commodities. Even though this area is of increasing interest to academics and organisations, issues concerning the development and criticality of corporate reputation appear to be of greater importance to organisations.

Corporate communications

Corporate communications are simply a part of the process that translates corporate identity into corporate image (Ind, 1992). As mentioned above, increasingly organisations are taking an active interest in corporate branding (Cowlett, 2000), mainly because of the benefits that can be achieved across the organisation. By attempting to control the messages that it transmits, an organisation can inform and motivate stakeholders of what it is, what it does and how it does it in a credible and consistent way. Traditionally the bulk of this communication work has been the responsibility of public relations.

Corporate identity programmes require good management of change. Employees are probably the most important stakeholders in the sense that they are not only an audience but also an important group of communicators to external stakeholder groups. Most programmes requiring change should attempt to adapt employee perceptions first and then their attitudes and behaviour.

The gap between organisational image and identity uncovered during research determines the nature of the communications task. A communications strategy is required to address all matters of structure and internal communications and the conflicting needs of different stakeholders so as to produce a set of consistent messages, all within the context of a coherent corporate identity programme. The British Broadcasting Corporation (BBC) changed its identity partly as a means of enabling it to compete more effectively in an environment that was changing quickly. With the advent of digital television, the emerging international competitive arena and the impending launch a range of new services it was important that the BBC logo became distinctive and reflected the BBC core values of quality, fairness, accuracy and artistic integrity. The previous identity was expensive (four colour), not suitable for the increasing volumes and range of applications, had become fragmented and reproduced in an inconsistent manner. In addition, it did not work on digital formats and was technically difficult to integrate with other graphics. The new identity signalled changes about the BBC and the culture, attitudes and behaviour of the people who work there.

Analysis of the perceptions and attitudes of stakeholders towards an organisation will reveal the size of the gap between actual and desired perception.

Analysis of the perceptions and attitudes of stakeholders towards an organisation will reveal the size of the gap between actual and desired perception. The extent of this gap will have been determined and objectives set to close the gap. This corporate perception gap may be large or small, depending upon who the stakeholder is. Organisations have multiple

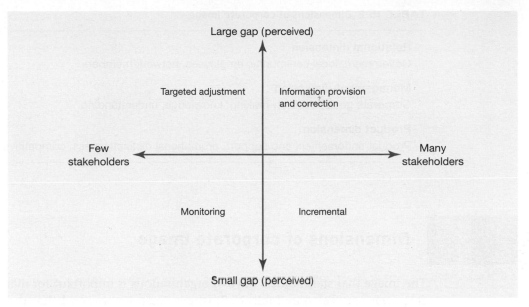

FIGURE 15.1 Corporate perception gap

images and must develop strategies that attempt to stabilise, and if possible equalise, the images held.

Using a four-cell matrix (see Figure 15.1), where the vertical axis scales the size of the perceived gap and the horizontal axis the number of stakeholders who share the same perception, a series of strategies can be identified. Should a large number of stakeholders be perceived to hold an image of an organisation that is a long way from reality, then a correction strategy is required to communicate the desired position and performance of the focus organisation. Most common of these is the gap between perceived corporate performance and the real performance of the organisation when put in the context of the actual trading conditions.

If a small number of stakeholders perceive a large gap, then a targeted adjustment strategy would be required, aimed at particular stakeholder groups and taking care to protect the correct image held by the majority of stakeholders. For example, some students perceive some financial institutions (e.g. banks) as not particularly attractive for career progression or compatible with their own desired lifestyles. A targeted adjustment strategy would be necessary by the banks to alter this perception in order that they attract the necessary number of high-calibre graduates.

Should research uncover a small number of stakeholders holding a relatively small disparity between reality and image, a monitoring strategy would be appropriate and resources would be better deployed elsewhere. The best position would be if the majority of stakeholders perceived a small difference, in which case a maintenance strategy would be advisable and the good corporate communications continued. The natural extension of this approach is to use it as a base tool in the determination of the communication budget. Funds could be allocated according to the size of the perceived perception gap.

The reasons for the gap do not necessarily rest solely with stakeholders. If the image they hold is incorrect and the organisation's performance is good, then it is poor communications that are to blame, which are the fault of the organisation. If the image is correct and accurately reflects performance, then management must take the credit or the criticism for their performance as managers (Bernstein, 1984).

TABLE 15.2 Dimensions of corporate image

Relational dimension
Government, local community, employees, network members

Management dimension
Corporate goals, decision-making, knowledge, understanding

Product dimension
Product endorsement and support, promotional distinctiveness, competitive advantages

Dimensions of corporate image

The image that stakeholders have of organisations is important for many reasons. The main ones are listed in Table 15.2, where it can be observed that the dimensions of corporate image are quite diverse.

The relational dimension refers to the exchange of attitudes and perceptions with stakeholders of the organisation itself. As will be seen later, organisations consider who they are and what they would like to be and then project identity cues to those stakeholders who it is believed need to be informed. A more advanced understanding then allows for the adaptation of the organisation based upon the feedback or the dialogue thus created.

Management also benefits from corporate identity programmes as they encourage senior staff to reflect upon the organisation's sense of purpose and then provide a decision framework for the decisions that management and others, perhaps functional managers, follow.

The final dimension refers to the advantages that a strong positive identity can give products and services. It is possible to develop more effective and efficient promotional programmes by focusing on the organisation's distinctiveness and then allow for the ripple to wash over the variety of offerings. Banks have traditionally used this approach, and car manufacturers have also partially attempted this strategy. Although the car marque is a very important decision determinant (e.g. BMW, Rover, Honda, VW, Nissan), it is common for particular models within the marque (brand) to be featured heavily.

Apart from a positive relationship between reputation and corporate performance, the principal reasons for managing the corporate identity are to make clear to all stakeholders what the values and beliefs of the organisation are and how it is striving to achieve its objectives. In addition, a strong reputation provides better opportunities to develop lasting relationships with key stakeholder groups and improved access to resources. There are a number of secondary benefits, but these distil down to creating a supportive environment for the offerings, employees and external stakeholders associated with the focus organisation. Finally, a strong reputation can provide some protection should an organisation encounter environmental turbulence or crisis.

> The principal reasons for managing the corporate identity are to make clear to all stakeholders what the values and beliefs of the organisation are.

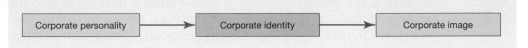

FIGURE 15.2 Elements of corporate identity (From Abratt and Shee (1989); used with kind permission.)

Elements of corporate identity

Abratt and Shee (1989) attempt to disentangle the confusion surrounding identity and image. They identify three main elements that are central to the development of corporate image. See Figure 15.2. These are corporate personality, identity and image. Individuals and organisations project their personalities through their identity. The audience's perception of the identity is the image they have of the object, in this case, the corporate body.

Corporate personality

The first of these elements requires the recognition and acceptance that organisations have personalities, or at least significant characteristics. As Bernstein (1984) states, just as individuals have personalities, so do organisations. Corporate personalities are derived partly from the cultural characteristics of the organisation: the core values and beliefs that in turn are part of a corporate philosophy. Essential to corporate personality is the strategy process adopted by the organisation. The degree to which the strategic process is either formalised and planned or informal and emergent, and whether strategy is well communicated, plays a major role in shaping the personality of the organisation.

For example, management now recognises the powerful influence that an organisation's corporate objectives have in informing and guiding the operations of each of the functional departments. The formulation of the mission statement requires management and employees to understand what the organisation seeks to achieve. To understand what the organisation wants to achieve means understanding what the organisation values and believes in, and this in turn involves and reflects the involvement of all members of the organisation, either deliberately or involuntarily. Indeed, the stated philosophy and values that are articulated through the mission statement (and other devices) are important in establishing the preferred relationship it has with its various constituencies (Leuthesser and Kohli, 1997).

The corporate personality can be considered to be composed of two main facets: the culture and overall strategic purpose (Markwick and Fill, 1997). Organisational culture is a composite of the various sectional interests and drives held by various key members. The blend of product offering, facilities, values and beliefs, staff, structure, skills and systems leads to the formation of particular characteristics or traits. Traits are rarely uniform in their dispersal throughout an organisation, so the way in which these interests are bound together impacts upon the form of the primary culture.

> The corporate personality can be considered to be composed of two main facets: the culture and overall strategic purpose.

The strategic processes adopted by organisations are relatively constant because the roots of a process are embedded within the spectrum of organisational activities.

Changing the strategic process is very different from changing the content of a strategy. Stuart (1999a) refers specifically to the contribution the organisational structure can make to an organisation's corporate identity. Interestingly she considers Mintzberg's typology of organisational structures, but what can be gathered is that structure impacts on strategy, which informs the identity process.

There was a great deal of merger activity in the late 1990s but management appears to be guilty of not paying enough attention to a vision of what the new culture will be like and how it will be expressed through the identity. The merger between Mannesmann, which was over 100 years old, and Vodafone, a mere 18 years old, was made on the basis of share value and global expansion, not cultural fit. The evidence suggests that it is the financial business model that dominates and not the brand model. Mergers do not result in amalgamated cultures, as experience shows that one will be pre-eminent, usually as a result of one or two key individuals reaching top positions. People also leave because they do not like the new way of doing things.

ViewPoint 15.2   Cultural mismerger at DaimlerChrysler

These two car companies merged in 1998 in a deal worth £28 million, a bringing together of equals designed to combine the best of German depth and American creativity and exploiting the managerial talent. The name emphasises the equality and the advertising campaign used employees from both organisations to stress the friendly nature of the merger.

Mazur (2000) reported that unfortunately a number of former Chrysler executives started to leave, disgruntled as Daimler executives began to dominate matters within the new organisation.

All members of an organisation, management and employees, are intertwined with the corporate personality; they are one and the same. The spirit and vigour with which all members of an organisation embody and articulate the mission are, according to Topalian (1984), a means by which the identity is shaped. The personality is embodied in the way the organisation carries out its business, the logic of its activities, the degree of persistence and aggression it displays in the markets in which it operates and the standards that are expected of all stakeholders.

Corporate personality is the totality of the characteristics that identify an organisation.

Corporate personality is the totality of the characteristics that identify an organisation. Consider the values held by organisations such as easyJet, HSBC, the NHS, Tesco and Oxfam. Not only are the images different but so are the values and the personalities.

The BBC and Channel 5 are interesting organisations to consider from a personality perspective. The BBC is a mature organisation where stability, security and reliability have long been regarded as important characteristics. However, these are now regarded by some as impediments to progress and innovation, not helped by the events surrounding the Hutton inquiry. Channel 5 is young and vibrant, where programme quality is measured differently to the BBC and where innovation is seen as an important part of challenging the rules of standard broadcasting.

Corporate personality is what an organisation actually is.

Corporate personality is what an organisation actually is.

Corporate identity

The second element in the image process is corporate identity. This is the formation of the cues by which stakeholders can recognise and identify the organisation. Many organisations in recent years have chosen to pay more attention to their identity and have tried to manage these cues more deliberately.

ViewPoint 15.3	Online identity

Many financial services organisations have begun to offer online banking. The chance to reduce costs and reach new customer groups has been a major force behind this development. What is interesting, however, is that many have chosen to rebrand their online offering and create a separate identity.

The Halifax uses 'If', the Cooperative Bank 'Smile' and Prudential 'Egg'. Abbey National chose to use the name 'Cahoot' in order to reach a more affluent customer, one who research shows would not normally bank with Abbey National. The disguise of the online brand identity therefore enables organisations to use communications to be directed to particular customer segments without having to overcome the negative values associated with the parent brand.

Identity is a means by which the organisation can differentiate itself from other organisations.

Identity is a means by which the organisation can differentiate itself from other organisations. Bernstein (1984) makes an important point when he observes that all organisations have an identity, whether they like it or not. Some organisations choose to deliberately manage their identities, just as individuals choose not to frequent particular shops or restaurants, drive certain cars or wear specific fabrics or colours. Other organisations take less care over their identities and the way in which they transmit their identity cues, and as a result confuse and mislead members of their networks and underperform in the markets in which they operate.

According to Olins (1989), management of the identity process can communicate three key ideas to its audiences. These are what the organisation is, what it does and how it does it. Corporate identity is manifested in four ways. These, he says, can be interpreted as the products and services that the organisation offers, where the offering is made or distributed, how the organisation communicates with stakeholders and, finally, how the organisation behaves.

The marked development of the corporate brand has been noticeable in recent years. Organisations have used it as a means of differentiating their products from competitors' products and have recognised the power of the characteristics that delineate one organisation from another. These characteristics are embodied by the organisation's personality, values and culture. The corporate brand is a means of presenting these characteristics to various audiences, such as financial markets, suppliers, employees, channel network partners, trade unions, competitors and customers.

There are three broad types of identity cues used by organisations, especially in the development of corporate brands; these are symbolism, behaviour and communication (Birkigt and Stadler, 1986).

ViewPoint 15.4   Pensionable images

Just as organisations can develop brands, so can an industry. For example, it was announced in 1999 that a consortium of pensions providers had been formed under the banner of the Association of British Insurers, to launch a £15 million advertising campaign in an attempt to rebuild the image of the industry following the prolonged public visibility of the pension misselling scandal that had cost the industry over £13 billion.

Bawden (1999) comments that the rectification process involved a six-month period consulting various stakeholder groups such as the government regulators, consumer groups and life/pension providers in order to explore issues concerning the quality and transparency of various product offerings. This is an important part of the process as the industry was anticipating a period of substantial change, caused by industry consolidation (the Prudential is industry leader and only has an 8 per cent share), the launch of stakeholder pensions and an increasing need for pension providers to become more efficient. The advertising campaign needed to build on a credible base otherwise, instead of clarifying, it would further confuse consumers and restrict growth in the sector.

Symbolism

Symbolism refers to the visual aspect of identity and was once regarded as the sole aspect of corporate identity management. Indeed, there are many today who regard visual identity as the only real element of corporate identity, mentioned earlier as the Visual school of corporate identity. Schein (1985), in his hierarchy of corporate culture, determines 'visible artefacts' as the first level. These are the more immediately observable aspects of the culture, such as the letterheads, logos, signage, emblems, colour schemes, architecture and the overall appearance of all the design aspects associated with the company. Dowling (1994) refers to visual identity and its composition consisting of four keys elements: corporate names, logos and symbols, typefaces and colour. It is thought that through the use of symbolism a level of harmonisation can be achieved by bringing all of these identity cues together.

Visual identity is also an important element in an organisation's international strategy and the way in which it wishes to be perceived in different countries and regions. In particular multinational organisations need to find new ways of identifying themselves as a result of merger, acquisition, technological developments, restructuring and other changes in their various marketplaces (Melewar, 2001).

Bosch *et al.* (2004) found in their research that a large number of organisations use templates and corporate identity manuals to help manage their visual identities and that to a large extent these were accepted by both employees and managers as appropriate tools to manage what was agreed as an important subject. However, there is little evidence to show whether this energy is well directed and importantly it appears that many managers are not consistent in their approach to managing visual identity and that they do not always 'do as they say'.

Corporate branding and names

The constituent parts of a corporate brand are many and varied. One interpretation suggests that a brand consists of the following variables: reputation, product and service performance, product brand and customer portfolio and networks in the sense of

The name of an organisation is a strong corporate cue.

Another interpretation is that each brand is perceived with varying degrees of intensity depending upon the level of involvement customers have with the brand itself.

positioning (Knox and Maklan, 1998). Another interpretation is that each brand is perceived with varying degrees of intensity depending upon the level of involvement customers have with the brand itself. According to Kunde (2000), brands can range from a product base where there is little value other than the name, through to a corporate concept brand where there is a strong and consistent relationship between the consumers, the company and the brand. At the highest level is brand religion, where the brand is paramount for consumers, a belief or a religion that enables a range of other products to be introduced within the same religious environment. He quotes Body Shop, Harley-Davidson and Coca-Cola. What is noticeable about this approach is the importance attached to the internal culture and the need to balance the internal and external positioning, a view echoed throughout contemporary corporate branding literature and one thoroughly endorsed and supported in this text.

The name of an organisation is a strong corporate cue as it is often people's first contact with the organisation.

ViewPoint 15.5   New names for new organisations

When the Defence Establishment and Research Agency (DERA) changed from public to private ownership a new name was required to represent and convey the new identity of the organisation. Research undertaken at the time revealed that the name DERA was found to have certain negative qualities. Apart from the 'civil service culture', the defence connotation in DERA's name was considered to be too limiting. As the market for defence technology and specifically its governmental applications had been declining in real terms, the name was not particularly attractive to potential investors. The new name and positioning of the brand had to reflect the core skills of scientific and technological expertise rather than their defence application. The move towards a more commercial orientation also represented a major shift in values for staff who had not previously been engaged in a fast moving, flexible, proactive commercial environment.

When British Aerospace and Marconi Electronic Systems merged in May 1999 the name and the visual identity of the new company, which was to be the third largest aerospace and defence company in the world, were important decisions.

The brand identifiers had to build on the strength of the two companies yet at the same time there was a need to signal change to both the employees and other relevant external stakeholders. The word British was extremely powerful and, although the name Marconi was not available, the new name, BAE Systems, represented an evolutionary rather than a revolutionary change. According to Mazur (2000) this represents a more practical approach, bearing in mind the strength of equity and position that both companies had in the marketplace. A revolutionary approach to the visual identity was possible to represent the increased global presence of the new company.

Abbey National changed its name to *abbey* in 2003 and at the same time removed a series of subbrands such as Scottish Provident, Scottish Mutual and Inscape. The change also offered the opportunity to remove its strapline, 'because life's complicated enough'. The change in name accompanies a change in business strategy as the organisation attempts to re-establish itself.

Names used in the telecommunications sector were for a long time dominated by purely descriptive, functionally oriented names. In 1994 this started to change when Wolff Olins created the Orange brand for Hutchinson Telecom. Orange offered instant differentiation that also reflected the 'different' service being offered for the first time.

Owning a 'colour' offered a sense of exclusivity and allowed for a number of creative advertising opportunities. Goldfish, the name given to the British Gas discount card, also allowed for immediate differentiation and an identity that challenged the norms for the sector (Murphy, 1999).

Behaviour

The behavioural aspect is largely concerned with the way in which employees and managers interact with one another and, more importantly, with external members of the organisation. The tone of voice used and the actions and consideration of customer needs by employees are often represented within a customer service policy, which is as an important part of an organisation's interface with various stakeholder groups.

Communication is used to inform stakeholders quickly of episodes concerning products and the organisation. This is normally achieved through the use of visual and verbal messages. However, a broad use can be seen in communicating not only values but also the direction the organisation is heading and notable traits that the organisation wishes to inform its audiences of. For example, in the UK Volvos were seen as very safe but very dull cars driven by people who were similarly uninteresting. Communication was used to convey interest and excitement without the loss of the stable and important 'safe' attribute.

When considering the development of a corporate brand, the stewardship dimension also needs to be considered. This refers to the degree of importance that a company places on the development and maintenance of a corporate brand. The steward of the corporate brand is responsible for the consistency of the brand, in terms of the

The stewardship dimension refers to the degree of importance that a company places on the development and maintenance of a corporate brand.

way it is presented, and for the way in which external members develop their images of the organisation. The former chairman of British Airways, Bob Ayling, might be accused of not stewarding the British Airways brand appropriately, as manifest in the inconsistency of the management of the visual identity and falling corporate performance. Vision and responsibility for this function often reside with 'the chairman but many companies who successfully take care of their corporate image also have one communications professional charged with the task' (Ferguson, 1996), operating at a very senior level within the organisation.

Much of this is an external perspective of identity, whereas much of the organisational behaviour literature sees identity as embedded within the organisation, with

ViewPoint 15.6   Questionable stewardship

The CEO of Barclays Bank decided in the summer of 2000 to announce closures to the branch network (retail outlets). One of the problems with this was that the closures affected many rural communities and attracted a great deal of hostile publicity and negative media comment. This should have been anticipated and measures put in place to ameliorate the damage. Unfortunately the bank authorised an advertising campaign to run at exactly the same time. The problem was that the corporate branding campaign was national and it focused on functional positioning issues, namely the size of the bank.

The timing was unfortunate as the credibility of the messages was lost in the welter of negative comment about the branch closures. Questionable timing may have resulted in a negative impact on the bank's reputation.

employees. Employees are members who sense identity and who are responsible for projecting their group identity to non-members, those outside the organisation. Identity develops through feelings about what is central, distinctive and enduring (Albert and Whetten, 1985) about the character of the organisation, drawn from the personality (see Chapter 32 for greater detail).

Corporate identity is the way the organisation presents itself to its stakeholders.

Corporate image

The third and final element is corporate image. This is the perception that different audiences have of an organisation and results from the audience's interpretation of the cues presented by an organisation. As Bernstein (1984) says, 'the image does not exist in the organisation but in those that perceive the organisation'. This means that an organisation cannot change its image in a directly managed way, but it can change its identity. It is through the management of its identity that an organisation can influence the image held of it.

The image held of an organisation is the result of a particular combination of a number of different elements, but is essentially a distillation of the values, beliefs and attitudes that an individual or organisation has of the focus organisation. The images held by members of the distribution network, for example, may vary according to their individual experiences, and will almost certainly be different from those that management thinks exists. This means that an organisation does not have a single image, but may have multiple images.

The identity cues upon which the image is fashioned must be based on reality and reflect the values and beliefs of the organisation.

For an image to be sustainable, the identity cues upon which the image is fashioned must be based on reality and reflect the values and beliefs of the organisation.

Images can be consistent, but are often based upon a limited amount of information. Images are prone to the halo effect, whereby stakeholders shape images based upon a small amount of information. The strategic credibility of Microsoft may be based largely on the image of Bill Gates rather than the current financial performance of Microsoft and the actual strategies being pursued by the organisation. Stakeholders extrapolate that Bill Gates has a high reputation for business success, therefore, anything to do with Bill Gates is positive and likely to be successful.

Corporate images are shaped by stakeholder interpretations of the identity cues they perceive at an individual level. These cues are the identity signals transmitted by organisations, either deliberately planned and timed or accidental, often unknown to the organisation and very often unwelcome. Planned corporate communications reflected through symbolism, communication and behaviour are accompanied by unplanned communications such as those generated by competitors, through word of mouth and the personal experiences and memories of the individual (Cornelissen, 2000).

Corporate image is what stakeholders perceive the organisation to be.

Corporate reputation

An individual's reflection of the historical and accumulated impacts of previous identity cues.

A deeper set of images constitute what is termed corporate reputation. This concept refers to an individual's reflection of the historical and accumulated impacts of previous identity cues, fashioned in some cases by near or actual transactional experiences. It is much harder and takes a lot longer to change reputation, whereas images may be influenced quite quickly. The latter is more transient and the former more embedded.

This view of reputation, that image is different to reputation, is regarded as part of the 'differentiated' school of thought but is a view not held by all writers. Gotsi and Wilson (2001) argue that although in the minority, authors such as Kennedy (1977) see the two terms as having the same meaning while authors such as Alvesson (1998), Dichter (1985) and Dutton *et al.* (1994) regard the terms as interchangeable. The view held here is that they are not interchangeable but interrelated, if only because reputations are developed through time, whereas images can be instantaneous and reality superficial.

A strong reputation is considered strategically important.

A strong reputation is considered strategically important for three main reasons: as a primary means of differentiation when there is little difference at product level, as a support facility during times of turbulence and as a measure of corporate value (Greyser, 1999). An even more tangible impact of a strong reputation is the effect on a company's share price, perhaps as much as 15 per cent (Cooper, 1999).

In a survey reported by Gray (2000) the importance of a company's reputation was regarded by 1,005 CEOs consulted to be either important or very important. Fombrun (1996) claims that in order to build a favourable reputation four attributes need to be developed. These are credibility, trustworthiness, reliability and responsibility. Using these criteria it may be possible to speculate about the reputation developed by a company such as Nokia, the mobile phone manufacturer. Credibility is established through its range of products, which are perceived to be of high quality and branded. Trustworthiness has been developed through attention to customer service and support. Reliability and consistency have been achieved by setting and adhering to particular standards of quality, and responsibility is verified through a strong orientation to service and values manifested through the company's strong product development and innovation policy.

Reputation itself is developed through a number of variables. Greyser (1999) suggests that the key drivers are competitive effectiveness, market leadership, customer focus, familiarity/favourability, corporate culture and communications. It is the combination

ViewPoint 15.7   Damaged reputations

McDonald's, British Airways, Microsoft, Nike, Coca-Cola and Perrier are just some of the leading global brands that have been subject to media or judicial investigation. As a result of being in the public spotlight, their corporate reputation might be questioned, spoof Web sites created and doubt expressed about their integrity and well-being.

Many of these brands represent a benchmark for marketing performance. Using highly recognisable visual identity cues (e.g. 'golden arches', 'national flags', packaging or unique logos) consistently throughout the world, these brands are normally associated with high standards of service, good value for money and being widely available. To help maintain their identity, huge sums are spent each year on advertising, public relations and relevant in-house training and support.

Despite their overall and continued marketing success, it would appear that the reputation of corporate brands can be tarnished. However, it is the strength of the brand, management's flexibility and willingness to be open and transparent with inquisitive publics that can protect reputation in the long run.

of these elements that drives corporate reputation. However, he states that the most important dimension which impacts on reputation is the relationship between expectation and action. Whether this be at corporate level or at product/brand level, the brand promise must be delivered if reputation is to be enhanced, otherwise damage to the corporate reputation is most likely.

Strategy and corporate identity/image

It is taken for granted that measurements of the perceptions which consumers have of brands and offerings are taken periodically. This practice varies with each organisation and industry, but the overall tendency is to take such measurements on an ad hoc basis. As well as measuring the strength of perception of the organisation's offerings, measurements should also be taken of the perceptions that stakeholders have of the organisation. It may be that the marketing communications have to realign perceptions of the organisation before new offerings can be launched successfully.

In Figure 15.3 the perceptions that customers have of four recruitment companies are presented. The axes used show the levels of awareness and attitude towards the service provided by each of the companies, and for the sake of discussion each company is depicted in one of the four quadrants. Company A is in the strongest position and its communications should be aimed at maintaining its current position. Company B is liked just as much as A, but known only to a limited audience. Work needs to be undertaken to improve levels of awareness by reaching a larger number of stakeholders. Company C, to those that are aware of it, is seen as a poor organisation, but fortunately only a few know about it. Management's task is to bring about improvements to its offering and delay informing stakeholders until the level of service is satisfactory. Company D is seen to suffer from poor service delivery and everyone knows about it. Management's task is to lower the level of awareness, or not actively increase it, and put right the service offering before seeking stakeholder attention.

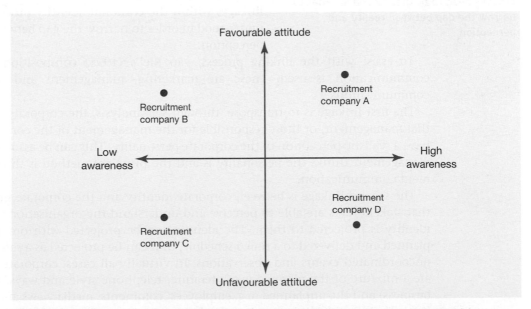

FIGURE 15.3 Images held by stakeholders of four recruitment companies (Adapted from Barich and Kotler (1991) by permission of the publisher. Copyright 1991 by the Sloan Management Review Association. All rights reserved.)

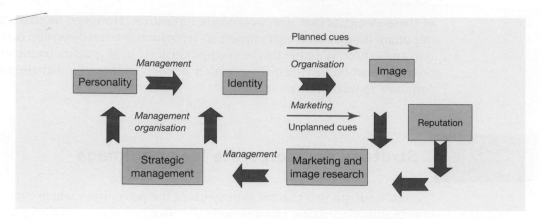

FIGURE 15.4 The corporate identity management process (adapted from Markwick and Fill, 1997)

This depiction is obviously a simplification, as corporate image is multidimensional (Dowling, 1986) and there is no single indicator that can adequately reflect the corporate personality. As different stakeholders will inevitably have different images, the measurement of corporate image is made difficult.

Various models have been developed to provide a visual interpretation of the elements involved in corporate identity (Kennedy, 1977; Dowling, 1986; Abratt and Shee, 1989; Stuart, 1999b). These models reflect the development of the subject and the growing integrative nature of corporate identity within an organisation's overall strategy. One such framework, presented by Markwick and Fill (1997), is entitled the corporate identity management process (CIMP). See Figure 15.4, which depicts the three main elements of the process as identified by Abratt and Shee (1989): corporate personality, corporate identity and corporate image. In order for management to be able to use such a model there must be understanding of the linkages between the components. Just as the linkages in the value chain determine the extent of competitive advantage that may exist, so the linkages within the corporate identity process need to be understood in order to narrow the gap between reality and perception.

> The linkages within the corporate identity process need to be understood in order to narrow the gap between reality and perception.

To assist with the linking process, van Riel's (1995) composition of corporate communication is used. These are marketing, management and organisational communications.

The first linkage is to transpose, through self-analysis, the corporate personality so that management, or those responsible for the management of the corporate identity, have a realistic perception of the corporate personality. This can be assumed to be what management thinks the personality is and the principal method is through management communication.

The second linkage is between corporate identity and the corporate image. In order that stakeholders are able to perceive and understand the organisation, the corporate identity is projected to them. The identity can be projected with orchestrated cues, planned and delivered to a timed schedule, or it can be projected as a series of random, uncoordinated events and observations. In virtually all cases, corporate identity cues are a mixture of the planned (e.g. literature, telephone style and ways of conducting business) and the unplanned (e.g. employees' comments, media views and product failures). The principal linkages are through organisation and marketing communications.

All organisations communicate all the time; everything they make, do, say or do not say is a form of communication. The totality of the way the organisation presents itself, and is visible, can be called its identity (Olins, 1989). Corporate image is how stakeholders actually perceive the identity. It is, of course, unlikely that all stakeholders will hold the same image at any one point in time. Owing to the level of noise and the different experiences stakeholders have of an organisation, multiple images of an organisation are inevitable (Dowling, 1986). It is important that organisations monitor these images to ensure that the (corporate) position is maintained.

The third linkage is between the image that stakeholders have of an organisation and the corporate strategy formulation and implementation processes that an organisation adopts. This research-based linkage provides feedback and enables the organisation to adjust its personality and its identity, thus consequently affecting the cues presented to stakeholders. Image research is an important method of linking back into the strategy process.

The cues used to project the corporate identity are many and varied; some are controllable and others beyond the reach of management. These cues include the logo and letterheads, the way employees speak of the organisation, the buildings and architecture, the perception of the ability of the organisation to fulfil its obligations, its technical skills, prices, dress code, competitor communications, word of mouth and the way the telephone is answered. Of all these and the many others, however, research needs to determine those attributes that key stakeholders perceive as important.

> **Cues used to project the corporate identity are many and varied.**

Having determined the important attributes, stakeholders should be asked to evaluate how well the organisation rates on each of them and how well it performs on each

ViewPoint 15.8   Simply never stirred

When BMW (GB) was first established in 1979 it replaced a distributor that had sold a range of performance cars. The business goal was to treble sales volumes to 40,000 cars a year and to maintain the high margins.

The advertising strategy was to build on the core brand values and move the perception of BMW cars from one of *performance* to one of *reward*. The line 'ultimate driving machine' was first used in 1979 and has been used to underline the BMW brand ever since. A consistent tone of voice was adopted whereby the advertising messages are always factually correct and removed from other types of glamour car advertising. Because of the need to focus on the technological strengths and benefits of BMW, a policy not to include any people in the advertisements was developed. The reasoning is that people are fallible, whereas BMW technology is not.

Robin Wight at WCRS, the advertising agency responsible for the continued success of BMW in the UK, leads what is referred to as a 'product interrogation' team each year. The team visits the factory and tries to uncover from the engineers new information and developments about BMW technology.

He recalls a time when he spent half a day trying to understand why six-cylinder engines were smoother than those with four cylinders. The exasperated engineer was finally asked how he would convince his next-door neighbour not to buy a Mercedes (arch rival) but a BMW. He thought for a while and then said that he would place a glass of water on both engines. When revving the Mercedes the glass would not move but the imperfections in the balance of the engine would destabilise the water in the glass. No matter how much he revved the BMW, the water would not move.

Wight arrived back in London and tested the claim. It worked. Within 15 minutes the 'Shaken, not stirred' advertisement was created (see Exhibit 15.1).

Source: Adapted from publicity materials kindly provided by BMW (1994 publicity documents) and Broadbent (1994).

EXHIBIT 15.1 BMW
Shaken not stirred. This BMW is a classic advertisement which portrays comparative product attributes, originality and message consistency. Picture reproduced with the kind permission of BMW and WCRS.

attribute in comparison with competitors. Figure 15.5 sets out the possible results of such research along two dimensions, the importance of the attribute to the stakeholder and the perceived performance of the organisation against the attribute. It can be seen that the ideal position lies to the right of the curve, and communication strategy should be aimed at achieving such a position. By introducing a third dimension, an evaluation of relative competitors against the same attributes, it is possible to determine a number of strategies that could lead to sustainable competitive advantage.

Stakeholder images can also be determined on three dimensions: the importance of attributes, organisational performance against the attributes and performance with respect to competitors on the same attributes. A three-dimensional perception matrix (Figure 15.6) draws out the significant points. The ideal position occurs when high customer and competitor ratings are recorded for important attributes. When the attribute has a low level of importance it may be that the organisation's effort is misdirected, and management should reduce the effort spent on developing this image or seek alternative markets where this attribute has higher levels of importance. The worst position occurs when the organisation underperforms with respect to the customers' requirements and the competition on an attribute that is important. A change of strategy is required.

Effort should be concentrated on developing either corporate identity or personality in areas where the customer rating is poor and competitor rating is high on a factor that is important.

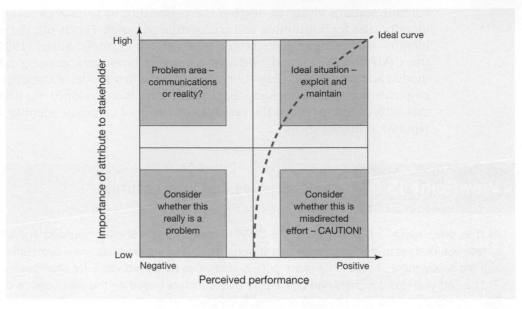

FIGURE 15.5 A two-dimensional attribute perception matrix (From Markwick (1993); used with kind permission.)

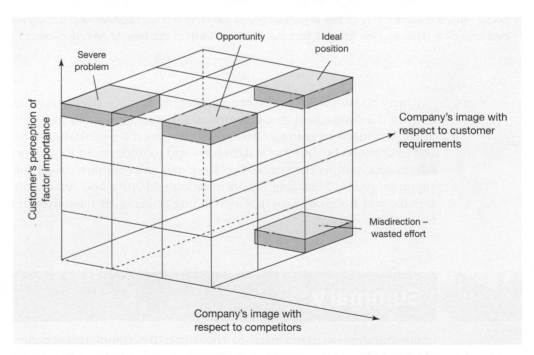

FIGURE 15.6 A three-dimensional attribute perception matrix (From Markwick (1993); used with kind permission.)

This model reveals that, by understanding the strength of images held by key stakeholders across attributes that are important to them, corrective action may be required to the personality and cues presented to stakeholders as part of the identity process. Strategic development therefore can result from an understanding of the images held about an organisation by its stakeholders.

Therefore, for the CIMP framework to be complete, management is required to analyse and interpret the research data and then use management and marketing communications either to develop the personality or to provide adjusted corporate identity cues for positioning and goal-setting purposes. This is not the only corporate identity framework to have been developed. For example, Stuart (1999b) developed the CIMP framework and offered a composite framework drawing on a variety of models and Balmer and Gray (1999) formulated a new model of the corporate identity-corporate communications process. Each of these has developed our understanding of this subject and extended the breadth and depth of corporate identity, branding and reputation management.

ViewPoint 15.9   Shell reserves and restructures

As if to demonstrate the principles of the CIMP framework cycle Shell announced in 2004 that it was to restructure itself in the light of the catastrophe relating to the organisation's overstated oil reserves and the subsequent impact of its share price and obvious perceived value for shareholders.

The 100-year-old company had operated a dual structure based on the joint venture between Shell Transport and Trading (the UK arm) and the Royal Dutch of the Netherlands. The announcement saw an end to this structure and a single organisation established, making it leaner, tighter and much more capable of making faster decisions. However, the cycle of poor performance, damaged reputation, structural and strategy change will impact on the culture and values of the organisation and alter, in some way, the personality of the organisation. In turn this will be seen to feed through to the identity and branding cues and the images that stakeholders form of the new Shell organisation.

It may be concluded that corporate identity is not a peripheral tool to be used ad hoc but is a component that is central to the strategic management process. It should be used regularly by managers to understand how the organisation is being interpreted and understood by different stakeholders and to understand the essence of the organisation and whether the symbolic, behavioural and communication cues are contextually appropriate. Managing an organisation's identity and reputation is a complex, variable and necessary aspect of developing stakeholder relationships in the twenty-first century.

Summary

Communication strategies need to encompass the communication needs of all those other stakeholders, those other constituencies that might influence the organisation or be influenced by it. These approaches are referred to as the profile strategy and so complete the 3Ps for communication: push, pull and profile.

Profile strategies are essentially concerned with communication about the organisation itself rather than its products and/or services. The focus rests with the corporate body; who it is, what it is, what it is seeking to do and how it is important to other stakeholders.

At the root of this strategic approach is the notion of corporate identity. Organisations project themselves (as they want to be seen/understood) through a series of cues. These are then interpreted by stakeholders and used to create an image of the organisation. This corporate image may or may not be a correct interpretation of the organisation but this perception is an important one and must be treated seriously. Reputations over time are developed from the image and can be seen to feed back to the corporate personality and impact upon the way members of an organisation think about themselves and determine what is central, distinctive and enduring.

Profile strategies are an important part of communication strategy and should be regarded as an integral part of any total or integrated marketing communications approach (Chapter 11) that might be developed.

Review questions

1. Define corporate communications. What is a profile strategy?

2. Explain what a corporate brand is. How does it differ from a product brand?

3. Discuss the differences between corporate branding and corporate identity. Are the differences of any value?

4. What are the main facets of corporate personality?

5. Describe the personality or defining characteristics of five organisations. What are their distinctive differences?

6. Prepare brief notes explaining what corporate identity is. Set out the differences between personality and identity.

7. Suggest ways in which planned and unplanned corporate identity cues are presented to stakeholders. Use an organisation with which you are familiar to illustrate your answer.

8. What is corporate image and how does it differ from corporate identity?

9. Draw the CIMP model, paying particular attention to the linkages between the components.

10. Discuss the view that there is nothing intrinsically different between corporate image and reputation.

MINI-CASE
Corporate branding in the business-to-business sector – Bruntwood

Mini-case written by Stuart Roper, Senior Lecturer, Manchester Business School

Everybody can name the great consumer brands. Is there a place for branding in the business-to-business sector, however? Bruntwood Estates is one of the largest privately owned property companies in Manchester and has built its business rapidly in its home city, as well as in Liverpool and Leeds, on the back of its corporate brand.

Commercial landlords do not normally have a close, proactive relationship with their customers. Many office blocks in the UK's cities are owned by pension companies that are quite happy to adopt a *white label* approach to branding, preferring to keep a low profile, offering only standard long-term leases and an impersonal service. Although Bruntwood only has approximately 750 customers it has invested in its corporate brand, which it sees as the key to its long-term success. Rather than take the white label approach Bruntwood visibly displays its corporate image on buildings that it owns. Bruntwood's red corporate logo is displayed on the exterior of its buildings and is illuminated at night. With only a limited budget for marketing communications it is logical to make use of free advertising space that city-centre buildings provide. As all business customers are also consumers it makes sense to reinforce the brand name in this way. The visible presence of the brand is leading to an increasing amount of unsolicited business for the company.

However, building a corporate brand involves more than thoughtful placing of the corporate image. A service brand such as a commercial landlord is intangible, inseparable from the people who deliver the service and can be homogeneous. The internal culture of the organisation is therefore crucial to its success. Bruntwood staffs are encouraged to deliver a quality product to customers by being innovative and flexible and concentrating on customer care and satisfaction at all times. With only a small number of customers, the loss of even one would have an impact on the business. The company has grown from 60 employees seven years ago to 260 employees today. It is easy for corporate culture to change as a business expands and particular attention is therefore paid to the personality of new staff during the recruitment process. Decisions to employ new people are made on a 60:40 basis, 60 per cent on cultural fit and 40 per cent on the skills that they bring to the organisation. Employees are required to have a positive personality and they take part in annual training that is aimed at developing and maintaining a positive mental attitude. It is unusual for a business-to-business organisation to spend money on such non-core training but it is part of the differentiation necessary in the building and maintenance of a successful corporate brand. Twelve core values that underpin and reflect the Bruntwood brand have been identified and these values are reinforced via internal marketing and projected externally by employees in their dealings with customers.

With only a modest communications budget, Bruntwood cannot afford ill-designed and wasteful promotions. It guards its brand image carefully and all communications, both internal and external, must conform to specific corporate guidelines. As with a consumer brand its trademark is protected and the laws of intellectual property applied. The organisation has had to work hard to move from being a price-led commodity to a service-led corporate brand and all aspects of the brand must therefore be safeguarded. The company does not believe that slick marketing

communications are the preserve of consumer goods brands; its customers may be business people but they are not property experts. They appreciate the security that the Bruntwood brand provides.

Bruntwood is proud of its place in the community and its marketing communication spend reinforces this. The company was a major sponsor of the 2002 Commonwealth Games held in Manchester and it used this opportunity not just to reward customers with hospitality at the Games but to considerably increase awareness of itself among the wider population. The company sponsors a new play annually at Manchester's Royal Exchange Theatre and invites customers, suppliers and employees. Likes and dislikes of individual customers and suppliers are recorded and this intimate knowledge allows true customer relationship management to take place.

Brands and relationships can only be built over the long term and Bruntwood has developed lasting relationships with its suppliers as well as its customers. There is no competitive retendering process for Bruntwood's suppliers as this would not be in line with the company's value system and the importance it places on lasting affiliation. It is important that a corporate brand projects its values to all stakeholders, not just customers.

Bruntwood is demonstrating that there is a place for corporate branding within the business-to-business sector and that it need not cost a fortune in marketing communications spends. The company believes that branding has not only helped it build its current strength in the commercial property market but that the values displayed by the corporate brand will allow it to diversify more easily into other areas of business in the future. This attitude demonstrates an important point about corporate brands – that they are defined by their underpinning and clearly demonstrated values and not by the business they happen to be in at the present moment.

Questions

1. Who are the stakeholders that the Bruntwood brand must communicate with?

2. Suggest some cost-effective marketing communications activities that would enhance the Bruntwood brand.

3. What are the advantages and disadvantages of adopting a corporate branding strategy?

References

Abratt, R. and Shee, P.S.B. (1989) A new approach to the corporate image management process. *Journal of Marketing Management*, **5**(1), pp. 63–76.

Albert, S. and Whetten, D.A. (1985) Organisational identity. In *Research in Organizational Behavior* (eds L.L. Cummings and B.M. Straw). Greenwich, CT: JT Press.

Alvesson, M. (1998) The business concept as a symbol. *International Studies of Management and Organisation*, **28**(3), pp. 86–108.

Balmer, J.M.T. (1998) Corporate identity and the advent of corporate marketing. *Journal of Marketing Management*, **14**(8), pp. 963–96.

Balmer, J.M.T. and Gray, E.R. (1999) Corporate identity and corporate communications: creating a competitive advantage. *Corporate Communications, an International Journal*, **4**(4), pp. 171–6.

Balmer, J.M.T. and Gray, E.R. (2003) Corporate brands: what are they? What of them? *European Journal of Marketing*, **37**(7/8), pp. 972–97.

Barich, H. and Kotler, P. (1991) A framework for marketing image management. *Sloan Management Review*, **94** (Winter), pp. 94–104.

Bawden, T. (1999) Can advertising fix pensions industry? *Marketing Week*, 8 July, pp. 18–19.

Bernstein, D. (1984) *Company Image and Reality: A Critique of Corporate Communications*. London: Holt, Rinehart & Winston.

Birkigt, K. and Stadler, M.M. (1986) Corporate identity. In *Principles of Corporate Communication* (ed. C.B.M. van Riel). Hemel Hempstead: Prentice Hall.

van den Bosch, A.L.M., de Jong, M.D.T. and Elving, W.J.L. (2004) Managing corporate visual identity: use and effects of organisational measures to support a consistent self-presentation. *Public Relations Review*, **30**(2) (June), pp. 225–34.

Broadbent, T. (1994) How 15 years of consistent advertising helped BMW treble sales without losing prestige. IPA Advertising Effectiveness Awards. London: WCRS.

Cooper, A. (1999) What's in a name? *Admap*, **34**(6), pp. 30–2.

Cornelissen, J. (2000) Corporate image: an audience centred model. *Corporate Communications: an International Journal*, **5**(2), pp. 119–25.

Cowlett, M. (2000) Buying into brands. *PR Week*, 24 November, p. 13.

Dichter, E. (1985) What's in an image? *Journal of Consumer Marketing*, **2**, pp. 75–81.

Dowling, G.R. (1986) Measuring your corporate images. *Industrial Marketing Management*, **15**, pp. 109–15.

Dowling, G.R. (1993) Developing your company image into a corporate asset. *Long Range Planning*, **26**(2), pp. 101–9.

Dowling, G.R. (1994) *Corporate Reputations: Strategies for Developing the Corporate Brand*. London: Kogan Page.

Dutton, J.E., Dukerich, J.M. and Harquail, C.V. (1994) Organisational images and member identification. *Administrative Science Quarterly*, **39**, pp. 239–63.

Ferguson, J. (1996) The image. *Communicators in Business*, **9** (Summer), pp. 11–14.

Fombrun, C. (1996) *Reputation: Realising Value from the Corporate Image*. Cambridge, MA: Harvard Business School Press.

Gorb, P. (1992) The psychology of corporate identity. *European Management Journal*, **10**(3) (September), pp. 310–13.

Gotsi, M. and Wilson, A.M. (2001) Corporate reputation: seeking a definition. *Corporate Communications: an International Journal*, **6**(1), pp. 24–30.

Gray, R. (2000) The chief encounter. *PR Week*, 8 September, pp. 13–16.

Greyser, S.A. (1999) Advancing and enhancing corporate reputation. *Corporate Communications: an International Journal*, **4**(4), pp. 177–81.

Hatch, M.J. and Schultz, M. (2000) Scaling the Tower of Babel: relational differences between identity, image and culture in organisations. In *The Expressive Organisation:*

Linking Identity, Reputation and the Corporate Brand (eds M. Schultz, M.J. Hatch and M.H. Larsen). Oxford: Oxford University Press.

Ind, N. (1992) *The Corporate Image: Strategies for Effective Identity Programmes*. London: Kogan Page.

Keller, K.L. (1999) Brand mantra: rationale, criteria and examples. *Journal of Marketing Management*, 15(1–3) Jan–April, pp. 43–51.

Kennedy, S. (1977) Nurturing corporate images. *European Journal of Marketing*, 11(3), pp. 120–64.

Knox, S. and Maklan, S. (1998) *Competing on Value: Bridging the Gap Between Brand and Customer Value*. London: Financial Times.

Kunde, J. (2000) *Corporate Religion*. London: Financial Times.

Leuthesser, L. and Kohli, C. (1997) Corporate identity: the role of mission statements. *Business Horizons*, 40(3) (May–June), pp. 59–67.

Markwick, N. (1993) Corporate image as an aid to strategic development. Unpublished MBA project, University of Portsmouth.

Markwick, N. and Fill, C. (1997) Towards a framework for managing corporate identity. *European Journal of Marketing*, 31 (5/6), pp. 396–409.

Mazur, L. (2000) Anatomy of a new identity. *Marketing*, 16 March, p. 22.

Melewar, T.C. (2001) Measuring visual identity: a multi-construct study. *Corporate Communications: an International Journal*, 6(1), pp. 36–42.

Melewar, T.C. (2003) Determinants of the corporate identity construct: a review of the literature. *Journal of Marketing Communications*, 9, pp. 195–220.

Mintzberg, H. and Quinn, J. (1988) *The Strategy Process: Concepts, Contexts and Cases*. 3rd edn. Englewood Cliffs, NJ: Prentice-Hall.

Murphy, C. (1999) The real meaning behind the name. *Marketing*, 14 October, p. 31.

Olins, W. (1990) *Corporate Identity: Making Business Strategy Visible Through Design*. London: Thames & Hudson.

van Riel, C.B.M. (1995) *Principles of Corporate Communication*. Hemel Hempstead: Prentice Hall.

Schein, E.H. (1985) *Organizational Culture and Leadership*. San Francisco, CA: Jossey-Bass.

Stuart, H. (1999a) The effect of organisational structure on corporate identity management. *Corporate Reputation Review*, 2(2), pp. 151–64.

Stuart, H. (1999b) Towards a definitive model of the corporate identity management process. *Corporate Communications: an International Journal*, 4(4), pp. 200–7.

Topalian, A. (1984) Corporate identity: beyond the visual overstatements. *International Journal of Advertising*, 3, pp. 55–62.

Wright, D. (1997) Comment: Halifax facts. *Sunday Times*, Money, 10 August, p. 2.

Financial resources for marketing communications

16

Organisations need to ensure that they achieve the greatest possible efficiency with each unit of resource (pounds sterling, dollars, rubles, Swedish kronor) they allocate to promotional activities. They cannot afford to be profligate with scarce resources and managers are accountable to the owners of the organisation for the decisions they make, including those associated with the costs of their marketing communications.

Aims and objectives

The aim of this chapter is to examine the financial context within which organisations undertake promotional campaigns.

The objectives of this chapter are to:

1. determine current trends in advertising and promotional expenditure;
2. discuss the role of the promotional budget;
3. clarify the benefits of using promotional budgets;
4. examine various budgeting techniques, both practical and theoretical;
5. provide an appreciation of the advertising-to-sales (A/S) ratio;
6. set out the principles where share of voice (SOV) can be used as a strategically competitive tool.

Introduction

The rate at which advertising and associated media costs have outstripped the retail price index has been both alarming and troublesome. This disproportionate increase in the costs of advertising has served to make it increasingly less attractive to clients and has spurred the development of other forms of promotion, most notably direct marketing.

Some advertising agencies have argued that this disproportionately high increase is necessary because of the increasing number of new products and the length of time it takes to build a brand. Levels of advertising spend have continued to grow. Between 2000 and 2002 cinema admissions grew 23 per cent before falling back slightly in 2003. Outdoor grew by over 10 per cent in 2003 as clients continued to see this as a cost-effective approach to brand development. Procter & Gamble spent £189 million in the UK across their product portfolio, while 3 spent £49.4 million and McDonald's spent £40.7 million on their brands respectively. See Table 16.1.

Large investment and commitment are required over a period of years if long-term, high-yield performance is to be achieved. Many accountants, however, view advertising from a different perspective. Their attitude has been, for a long time, to consider

Large investment and commitment are required over a period of years.

advertising as an expense, to be set against the profits of the organisation. Many of them see planned marketing communications as a variable, one that can be discarded in times of recession.

These two broad views of advertising and of all promotional activities, one as an investment to be shown on the balance sheet and the other as a cost to be revealed in the profit and loss account, run consistently through discussions of how much should be allocated to the promotional spend. For management, the four elements of the promotional mix are often divided into two groups. The first contains advertising, sales promotion and public relations, while the second group contains the financial aspects that relate to personal selling.

This division reflects not only a functional approach to marketing but also the way in which, historically, the selling and marketing departments have developed. This is often observed in older, more established, organisations that find innovation and change more difficult to come to terms with. Accountability and responsibility for promotional expenditure in the first group often fall to the brand or product manager. The second group is managed by a sales manager, often at national level, reporting to a sales director.

TABLE 16.1 Top five UK advertisers January–December 2003

Organisation	£ million total (2003)
Procter & Gamble	188.9
Central Office of Information	139.5
BT	96.4
L'Oréal	90.4
Ford Motor Company	79.0
Total	**3,189.3**

Source: ACNeilsen MMS. Used with kind permission.

The promotional costs that need to be budgeted include the following. First, there is the airtime on broadcast media or space in print media that has to be bought to carry the message to the target audience. Then there are the

There are the production costs associated with generating the message.

production costs associated with generating the message and the staff costs of all those who contribute to the design and administration of the campaign. There are agency and professional fees, marketing research and contributions to general overheads and to expenses such as cars, entertainment costs and telephones that can be directly related to particular profit centres. In addition to all these are any direct marketing costs, for which some organisations have still to find a suitable method of cost allocation. In some cases a particular department has been created to manage all direct marketing activities, and in these cases the costs can be easily apportioned.

The budget for the sales force is not one that can be switched on and off like an electric light. Advertising budgets can be massaged and campaigns pulled at the last minute, but communication through personal selling

The budget for the sales force is not one that can be switched on and off.

requires the establishment of a relatively high level of fixed costs. In addition to these expenses are the opportunity costs associated with the long time taken to recruit, train and release suitably trained sales personnel into the competitive environment. This process can take over 15 months in some industries, especially in the fast-changing, demanding and complex information technology markets.

Strategic investment to achieve the right sales force, in terms of its size, training and maintenance, is paramount. It should be remembered, however, that managing a sales force can be rather like turning an ocean liner: any move or change in direction has to be anticipated and actioned long before the desired outcome can be accomplished. Funds need to be allocated strategically, but for most organisations a fast return on an investment should not be expected.

This chapter will concentrate on the techniques associated with determining the correct allocation of funds to the first group of promotional tools and, in particular, emphasis will be placed upon advertising. Attention will then be given to the other measures used to determine the correct level of investment in sales promotion, public relations and the field sales force. Finally, in an era in which shareholder value is becoming increasingly prominent and a means of distinguishing between alternative strategic options, the question about how a brand's value might influence the budget setting is considered.

Trends in promotional expenditure

It was stated earlier that advertising expenditure in the United Kingdom has risen faster than consumer expenditure. While this is true, the rapid increases in advertising spend in the 1980s slowed at the beginning of the 1990s, then speeded up again as the economy recovered only to waver again in 2001 after a buoyant previous year fuelled by the dotcom excitement. After a few years during which the advertising spend levels stabilised, only online advertising grew substantially, in percentage terms. However, there were signs early in 2005 that real growth was emerging once again, although only time will tell if this encouraging development is to be consolidated.

This noticeable cutback in off-line advertising expenditure when trading conditions tighten reflects the short-term orientation that some organisations have towards brand development or advertising. What is also of interest is the way in which the promotional mix has been changing over the past 10–15 years. For a long time the spend on media advertising dominated the promotional budget of consumer products and services. Sales promotion became a strong influence but spend on this tool has stagnated over the past few years. Now sponsorship, direct marketing and online activities show greatest investment. The reasons for this shift, first reported by Abraham and Lodish (1990), are indicative of the increasing attention and accountability that management is attaching to the promotional spend. Increasingly, marketing managers are being asked to justify the amounts they spend on their entire budgets, including advertising and sales promotion. Senior managers want to know the return they are getting for their promotional investments, in order that they meet their objectives and that scarce resources can be used more effectively in the future.

> Indicative of the increasing attention and accountability that management is attaching to the promotional spend.

In recent years some organisations have deliberately reallocated their budgets in order to make more funds available for price cutting and discounting. Procter & Gamble, Safeway, Citröen and Heinz are just some of the organisations that have made these decisions. The Royal Mail slashed its advertising budget in May 2004. See Viewpoint 16.1.

ViewPoint 16.1 Slashed Mail

The Royal Mail announced in May 2004 that it was cutting back on its advertising by at least 40 per cent, approximately £8 million. It also announced that it was postponing further marketing activities, including £5 million assigned to promoting its Parcelforce brand.

These cuts were made in the light of strikes the previous autumn, a series of reported financial losses and the reduction in headcount of about 350 staff.

The news of the reduction in communications spend coincided with a report from the industry watchdog Postwatch that over 14 million items of post are lost each year.

While the cuts affect a number of roster agencies and the brand was receiving poor publicity, the Royal Mail was under huge pressure to turn the operation around. Interestingly, at the time of writing this in November 2004, the Royal Mail reported that its six-monthly results had shown a turnaround from a previous loss to a profit of £217 million. So, were the £8 million cuts in advertising really necessary? Perhaps it was the need to avoid publicity when so many items were not being delivered?

It is not uncommon to find companies that are experiencing trading difficulties deciding to slash their adspend, if only on a temporary basis. Marks & Spencer and Sainsbury's are also experiencing difficulties but have either increased or maintained their above-the-line spend. According to Hall (1999), Procter & Gamble set 'strict guidelines about how much can be spent below-the-line if a brand's equity is to be maintained'.

> Companies which maintain or even increase their adspend during a recession are likely to grow three times faster.

Research by Profit Impact on Market Strategy (PIMS) (Tylee, 1999; Tomkins, 1999) found that companies which maintain or even increase their adspend during a recession are likely to grow three times faster than those companies that cut the adspend when the economy turns round. The Renault Clio and the Nescafé Gold Blend brands were cited as examples of advertisers that had increased their adspends during the last downturn and succeeded in increasing their profitability and market performance.

A report undertaken for the Advertising Association, however, found that the majority of brand leaders which use advertising as a substantial proportion of the promotional mix continue to dominate their markets, just as they did 30 years ago. In doing so, the report concludes, they have thwarted the challenge of own brands. In other words, advertising can protect brands, as long as the adspend is substantial.

The role of the promotional budget

The role of the promotional budget is the same whether the organisation is a multi-national, trading from numerous international locations, or a small manufacturing unit on an industrial estate outside a semi-rural community. Both organisations want to ensure that they achieve the greatest efficiency with each pound they allocate to promotional activities. Neither can afford to be profligate with scarce resources, and each is accountable to the owners of the organisation for the decisions it makes.

There are two broad decisions that need to be addressed. The first concerns how much of the organisation's available financial resources (or relevant part) should be allocated to promotion over the next period. The second concerns how much of the total amount should be allocated to each of the individual tools of the promotional mix.

Benefits of budgeting

The benefits of engaging in budgeting activities are many and varied.

The benefits of engaging in budgeting activities are many and varied, but in the context of marketing communication planning they can be considered as follows:

1. The process serves to focus people's attention on the costs and benefits of undertaking the planned communication activities.

2. The act of quantifying the means by which the marketing plan will be communicated to target audiences instils a management discipline necessary to ensure that the objectives of the plan are capable of being achieved. Achievement must be at a level that is acceptable and will not overstretch or embarrass the organisation.

3. The process facilitates cross-function coordination and forces managers to ensure that the planned communications are integrated and mutually supportive.

4. The process provides a means by which campaigns can be monitored and management control asserted. This is particularly important in environments that are subject to sudden change or competitive hostility.

5. At the end of the campaign, a financial review enables management to learn from the experiences of the promotional activity in order that future communications can be made more efficient and the return on the investment improved.

The process of planning the communications budget is an important one. Certain elements of the process will have been determined during the setting of the promotion objectives. Managers will check the financial feasibility of a project prior to committing larger resources. Managers will also discuss the financial implications of the communication strategy (that is, the push/pull dimension) and those managers responsible for each of the individual promotional tools will have estimated the costs that their contribution to the strategy will involve. Senior management will have some general ideas about the level of the overall appropriation, which will inevitably be based partly upon precedent, market and competitive conditions and partly as a response to the pressures of different stakeholders, among them key members of the performance network. Decisions now have to be made about the viability of the total plan, whether the appropriation is too large or too small and how the funds are to be allocated across the promotional tools.

Communication budgets are not formulated at a particular moment in a sequence of management activities. The financial resources of an organisation should be constantly referred to, if only to monitor current campaigns. Therefore, budgeting and the availability of financial resources are matters that managers should be constantly aware of and be able to tap into at all stages in the development and implementation of planned communications.

Difficulties associated with budgeting for communications spend

There are a number of problems associated with the establishment of a marketing communications budget.

There are a number of problems associated with the establishment of a marketing communications budget. Of them all, the following appear to be the most problematic. First, it is difficult to quantify the precise amount that is necessary to complete all the required tasks. Secondly, communication budgets do not fit neatly with standard accounting practices. The concept of brand value is accepted increasingly as a balance sheet item, but the concept of investment in communication to create value has only recently begun to be accepted, for example by Jaguar and Nestlé. Third, the diversity of the promotional tools and the means by which their success can be measured renders like-for-like comparisons null and void. Finally, the budget-setting process is not as clear-cut as it might at first appear.

ViewPoint 16.2   What is the right level of spend?

Back in 1987 Nike's marketing president was pitching to the board for a revised advertising budget. The previous year Nike had spent $8 million, and the marketing chief wanted to raise this to $34 million, an astronomical increase, particularly for a company that was just getting going. The CEO, Philip Knight, turned to the marketing man and asked the question: 'How do I know if you are asking for enough?'

Source: Holmes (2004).

There are four main stakeholder groups that contribute to the budget decision. These are the focus organisation, any communication agencies, the media whose resources will be used to carry the designated messages and the target audience. It is the ability of these four main stakeholders to interact, to communicate effectively with each other and to collaborate in a way that will impact most upon the communications budget.

The allocation of scarce resources across a promotional budget presents financial and political difficulties.

However, determining the 'appropriate appropriation' is a frustrating exercise for the marketing communications manager. The allocation of scarce resources across a promotional budget presents financial and political difficulties, especially where the returns are not easily identifiable. The development and significance of technology within marketing can lead to disputes concerning ownership and control of resources. For example, in many companies management and responsibility for the Web site rests with the IT department, which understandably takes a technological view of issues. Those in marketing, however, see the use of the Web site from a marketing perspective and need a budget to manage it. Tension between the two can result in different types of Web site design and effectiveness and this leads to different levels of customer support.

Smallbone (1972) suggested a long time ago that the allocation of funds for promotion is one of the primary problems facing marketers, if not one of the major strategic problems. Audience and media fragmentation, changed management expectations and a more global orientation have helped ensure that budgeting remains problematic.

Models of appropriation

At a broad level there are a number of models proposed by different authors concerning the appropriation of the promotional mix. In particular, Abratt and van der Westhuizen (1985) who refer, among others, to Smallbone's (1972) and Gaedeke and Tootelian's (1983) models of promotional appropriation. Abratt and van der Westhuizen have determined, among other things, that personal selling dominated the promotion mix of all their respondents in a particular study of business-to-business markets and that the models themselves were too simplistic to be of any direct benefit.

These broad approaches to budget allocation are not therefore appropriate, and it is necessary to investigate the value of using particular techniques. It is useful to set out the theoretical approach associated with the determination of communication and, in particular, advertising budgets.

Techniques and approaches

Theoretical approaches: marginal analysis and response curves

This method is normally depicted as a tool for understanding advertising expenditures but, as Burnett (1993) points out, it has been used for all elements of the promotional mix, including personal selling, so it is included here for understanding the overall promotional allocation.

Marginal analysis (or response curve analysis) enables managers to determine how many extra sales are produced from an extra unit of promotional spend. A point will be reached when an extra pound spent on promotion will generate an equal amount (a single pound's worth) of revenue. At this point marginal revenue is equal to marginal costs, the point of maximum promotional expenditure has been reached and maximum profit is generated.

> Marginal analysis enables managers to determine how many extra sales are produced from an extra unit of promotional spend.

Another way of looking at this approach is to track the path of sales and promotional expenditure. Even with zero promotional effort some sales will still be generated.

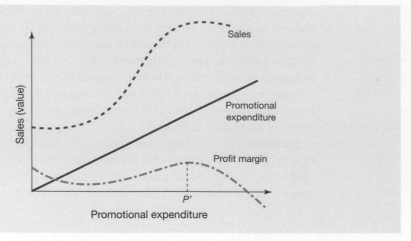

FIGURE 16.1 Marginal analysis for promotional expenditures. P′ is the point of maximum profit, the optimal level of promotional expenditure

In other words, sales are not totally dependent upon formal promotional activity, a point we shall return to later. When there is a small amount of promotion effort, the impact is minimal, as the majority of potential customers are either unaware of the messages or they do not think the messages are sufficiently credible for them to change their current behaviour. After a certain point, however, successive increments in promotional expenditure will produce more than proportionate increments in sales. The sales curve in Figure 16.1 can now be seen to rise steeply and the organisation moves into a position where it can begin to take advantage of the economies of scale in promotion. Eventually the sales curve starts to flatten out as diminishing returns to promotion begin to set in. This is because the majority of the potential target market have become aware of the offering and have decided whether or not to become customers.

This model suffers from a number of disadvantages (Table 16.2). First, it assumes that communications can be varied smoothly and continuously. This is not the case.

This model suffers from a number of disadvantages.

Secondly, it assumes that communications are the only influence upon sales. As discussed previously, sales are influenced by a variety of factors, of which planned communications is but one. Controllable and uncontrollable elements in the environment influence sales. Next, no account is taken of the other costs associated indirectly with the presentation of the offering, such as those allied to distribution. Each promotional thrust will often be matched, or even bettered, by the competition. Furthermore, the actions of rivals may even affect the sales performance of all products in the same category.

TABLE 16.2 Difficulties with the marginal analysis as a way of setting promotional budgets

Assumes promotional activities can be varied in a smooth and uniform manner.
Requires perfect data that in reality are very difficult to obtain.
Assumes only promotional activities impact upon sales.
Does not consider all the costs associated with promotional activities.
No account is made of the actions of direct and indirect competitors.
Adstock effects are ignored.
All messages are regarded as having equal impact. No consideration is given to the quality of messages.

It is fair to say, therefore, that the marginal approach fails to account for competitor reactions. The model assumes that sales are the result of current promotional campaigns. No attempt is made to account for the effects of previous campaigns and that adstock (or carryover) may well be a prime reason for a sale occurring. The time parameters used to compute the marginal analysis could be totally inaccurate.

One of the most important shortcomings of the theory is its failure to account for the qualitative effects of the messages that are transmitted. It is assumed that all messages are of a particular standard and that relative quality is unimportant. Clearly this cannot be the case.

The marginal approach is suspect in that it operates outside the real world, and it requires data and skill in its implementation that are difficult and expensive to acquire. Theoretically, this approach is sound but the practical problems of obtaining the necessary information and the absence of qualitative inputs render the technique difficult for most organisations to implement.

However, before moving to some of the more pragmatic approaches, it should be noted that marginal analysis is not entirely without practical foundation. For example, Weaver and Merrick (2004) consider ways in which response-curve approaches can be combined with econometrics and management judgement and through the merged processes a more accurate and meaningful budget can be determined.

Practical approaches

If the marginal approach is not practical then a consideration of the alternative approaches is necessary. Practitioners have developed a range of other methods that tend to reflect simplicity of deduction and operation but raise doubts over their overall contribution and effectiveness.

The following represent some of the more common approaches. It should be noted, at this point, that none of the techniques should be seen in isolation. Organisations should use a variety of approaches and so reduce any dependence, and hence risk, on any one method. The main methods are arbitrary, inertia, media multiplier, percentage of sales, affordable, quantitative, and objective and task.

Arbitrary

Sometimes referred to as 'chairperson's rules', this is the simplest and least appropriate of all the techniques available. Under chairperson's rules, what the boss says or guesses at is what is implemented. The fact that the boss may not have a clue what the optimal figure should be is totally irrelevant. Very often the budget is decided on the hoof, and as each demand for communication resources arrives so decisions are made in isolation from any overall strategy.

> This is the simplest and least appropriate of all the techniques available.

Apart from the merit of flexibility, this method has numerous deficiencies. It fails to consider customer needs, the demands of the environment or marketing strategy, and there is an absence of any critical analysis. Regretfully this approach is often used by many small organisations.

Inertia

An alternative to guesswork is the 'Let's keep it the same' approach. Here all elements of the environment and the costs associated with the tasks facing the organisation are ignored. Not an impressive approach.

Media multiplier

One step more advanced is the method that recognises that media rate card costs may have increased. So, in order to maintain the same impact, the media multiplier rule requires last year's spend to be increased by the rate at which media costs have increased.

Percentage of sales

One of the more common and thoughtful approaches is to set the budget at a level equal to some predetermined percentage of past or expected sales. Invariably, organisations select a percentage that is traditional to the organisation, such as 'We always aim to spend 5.0 per cent of our sales on advertising'. The rationale put forward is that it is the norm for the sector to spend about 4.5–5.5 per cent or that 5.0 per cent is acceptable to the needs of the most powerful stakeholders or is set in recognition of overall corporate responsibilities. For example, a local authority will be mindful of the needs of its council taxpayers, whose finances contribute to the funding and maintenance of local tourism activities, for example a museum or park facilities.

Invariably, organisations select a percentage that is traditional to the organisation.

There are a number of flaws with this technique. It is focused upon the sales base on which the budget rests. Planned communications, and advertising in particular, are intended to create demand, not to be the result of past sales. If the demand generators of the promotional mix are to be based on last period's performance, then it is likely that the next period's results will be similar, all things being equal. This must be the logical implication when the percentage is based on past performance.

Another way of looking at this method is to base the spend on a percentage of the next period's sales. This overcomes some of the problems, but still constrains the scope and the realistic expectations of a budget. No consideration is given to the sales potential that may exist, so this technique may actually limit performance.

Affordable

This approach is still regarded by many organisations as sophisticated and relatively free of risk. It requires each unit of output to be allocated a proportion of all the input costs and all the costs associated with the value-adding activities in production and manufacturing, together with all the other costs in distributing the output. After making an allowance for profit, what is left is to be spent on advertising and communication. In other words, what is left is what we can afford to spend.

The affordable technique is not in the least analytical, nor does it have any market or task orientation. It is a technique which is used by organisations of differing sizes (Hooley and Lynch, 1985), that are product rather than customer oriented. Their view of advertising is that it is a cost and that the quality of their product will ensure that it will sell itself. Organisations using this technique will be prone to missing opportunities that require advertising investment. This is because a ceiling on advertising expenditure is set and borrowings are avoided. As sales fluctuate in variable markets, the vagueness of this approach is unlikely to lead to an optimal budget.

The affordable technique is not in the least analytical.

Quantitative approaches

Various quantitative approaches have been offered in an attempt to determine a precise, all-encompassing model to derive a budget. Weaver and Merrick (2004) refer to Dyson

(1999), who published a mathematical model to help apportion a budget within a brand portfolio. They also mention Harper and Bridges (2003), whose scoring system approach was offered as a contrast to the algorithms of Dyson. Neither is entirely satisfactory, if only for their lack of flexibility and interpretation of the competitive environment.

Objective and task

The methods presented so far seek to determine an overall budget and leave the actual allocation to products and regions to some arbitrary method. This is unlikely to be a realistic, fair or optimal use of a critical resource.

The objective and task approach is different from the others in that it attempts to determine the resources required to achieve each promotion objective. It then aggregates these separate costs into an overall budget.

The objective and task approach is different from the others in that it attempts to determine the resources required to achieve each promotion objective.

For example, the costs associated with achieving a certain level of awareness can be determined from various media owners who are seeking to sell time and space in their media vehicles. The costs of sales promotions and sales literature can be determined and the production costs of these activities and those of direct marketing (e.g. telemarketing) and PR events and sponsorships can be brought together. The total of all these costs represents the level of investment necessary to accomplish the promotion objectives that had been established earlier in the marketing communications plan.

The attractions of this technique are that it focuses management attention upon the goals which are to be accomplished and that the monitoring and feedback systems which have to be put in place allow for the development of knowledge and expertise. On the downside, the objective and task approach does not generate realistic budgets, in the sense that the required level of resources may not be available and the opportunity costs of the resources are not usually determined. More importantly, it is difficult to determine the best way to accomplish a task and to know exactly what costs will be necessary to complete a particular activity. Very often the actual costs are not known until the task has been completed, which rather reduces the impact of the budget-setting process. What is also missing is a strategic focus. The objective and task method deals very well with individual campaigns, but is not capable of providing the overall strategic focus of the organisation's annual (period) spend. The case of Procter & Gamble illustrates this point.

The use of this approach leads to the determination of a sum of money. This sum is to be invested, in this case in promoting the offerings of the organisation, but it could equally be a new machine or a building. To help discover whether such a sum should be invested and whether it is in the best interests of the organisation, a 'payout plan' can be undertaken:

1. *Payout plans*
   These are used to determine the investment value of the advertising plan. This process involves determining the future revenues and costs to be incurred over a two- or three-year period. The essential question answered by such an exercise is 'How long will it take to recover the expenditure?'

2. *Sensitivity analysis*
   Many organisations use this adjusting approach to peg back the advertising expenditure because the payout plan revealed costs as too large or sales developing too slowly. Adjustments are made to the objectives or to the strategies, with the aim of reducing the payback period.

Competitive parity

In certain markets, such as the relatively stable FMCG market, many organisations use promotional appropriation as a competitive tool. The underlying assumption is that advertising is the only direct variable that influences sales. The argument is based on the point that while there are many factors that impact on sales, these factors are all self-cancelling. Each factor impacts upon all the players in the market. The only effective factor is the amount that is spent on planned communications. As a result, some organisations deliberately spend the same amount on advertising as their competitors spend: competitive parity.

Many organisations use promotional appropriation as a competitive tool.

Competitive parity has a major benefit for the participants. As each organisation knows what the others are spending and while there is no attempt to destabilise the market through excessive or minimal promotional spend, the market avoids self-generated turbulence and hostile competitive activity.

There are, however, a number of disadvantages with this simple technique. The first is that, while information is available, there is a problem of comparing like with like. For example, a carpet manufacturer selling a greater proportion of output into the trade will require different levels and styles of advertising and promotion from another manufacturer selling predominantly to the retail market. Furthermore, the first organisation may be diversified, perhaps importing floor tiles. The second may be operating in a totally unrelated market. Such activities make comparisons difficult to establish, and financial decisions based on such analyses are highly dubious.

The competitive parity approach fails to consider the qualitative aspects of the advertising undertaken by the different players. Each attempts to differentiate itself, and very often the promotional messages are one of the more important means of successfully positioning an organisation. It would not be surprising, therefore, to note that there is probably a great range in the quality of the planned communications. Associated with this is the notion that, when attempting to adopt different positions, the tasks and costs will be different and so seeking relative competitive parity may be an inefficient use of resources.

The competitive parity approach fails to consider the qualitative aspects of the advertising undertaken by the different players.

The final point concerns the data used in such a strategy. The data are historical and based on strategies relevant at the time. Competitors may well have embarked upon a new strategy since the data were released. This means that parity would not only be inappropriate for all the reasons previously listed, but also because the strategies are incompatible.

Advertising-to-sales ratio

Approach attempts to account for the market shares held by the different players and to adjust promotional spend accordingly.

An interesting extension of the competitive parity principle is the notion of advertising-to-sales (A/S) ratios. Instead of simply seeking to spend a relatively similar amount on promotion as one's main competitors, this approach attempts to account for the market shares held by the different players and to adjust promotional spend accordingly.

If it is accepted that there is a direct relationship between the volume of advertising (referred to as weight) and sales, then it is not unreasonable to conclude that if an organisation spends more on advertising then it will see a proportionate improvement in sales. The underlying principle of the A/S ratio is that, in each industry, it is possible to determine the average advertising spend of all the players and compare it with the value of the market. Therefore, it is possible for each organisation to determine its own A/S ratio and compare it with the industry average. Those organisations with an A/S ratio below the average may conclude either that they have advertising economies of scale working in their favour or that their advertising is working much harder, pound for pound, than some of their competitors. Organisations can also use A/S ratios as a means of controlling expenditure across multiple product areas. Budgets can be set based upon the industry benchmark, and variances quickly spotted and further information requested to determine shifts in competitor spend levels or reasons leading to any atypical performance.

Each business sector has its own characteristics, which in turn influence the size of the advertising expenditure. In 2002 the A/S ratio for female fragrances was 6.9 per cent, chewing gum 5.81 per cent, analgesics 4.87 per cent, digital cameras 13.19 per cent, toilet tissue 1.57 per cent, cereals 6.38 per cent and shampoo 11.5 per cent (Advertising Association). It can be seen that the size of the A/S ratio can vary widely. It appears to be higher (that is, a greater proportion of revenue is used to invest in advertising) when the following are present:

1. The offering is standardised, not customised.
2. There are many end-users.
3. The financial risk for the end-user customer is small.
4. The marketing channels are short.
5. A premium price is charged.
6. There is a high gross margin.
7. The industry is characterised by surplus capacity.
8. Competition is characterised by a high number of new product launches.

A/S ratios provide a useful benchmark for organisations.

A/S ratios provide a useful benchmark for organisations when they are trying to determine the adspend level. These ratios do not set out what the promotional budget should be, but they do provide a valuable indicator around which broad commercial decisions can be developed.

Share of voice

Brand strategy in the FMCG market has traditionally been based upon an approach that uses mass media advertising to drive brand awareness, which in turn allows premium pricing to fund the advertising investment (cost). The alternative approach has been to use price-based promotions to drive market share. The latter approach has often been regarded as a short-term approach that is incapable of sustaining a brand over the longer term.

The concept underlying the A/S ratio can be seen in the context of rival supporters chanting at a football match. If they chant at the same time, at the same decibel rating, then it is difficult to distinguish the two sets of supporters, particularly if they are chanting the same song. Should one set of supporters shout at a lower decibel rating, then the collective voice of the other supporters would be the one that the rest of the crowd, and perhaps any television audience, actually hears and distinguishes.

This principle applies to the concept of share of voice (SOV). Within any market the total of all advertising expenditure (adspend), that is, all the advertising by all of the players, can be analysed in the context of the proportions each player has made to the total. Should one advertiser spend more than any other then it will be its messages that are received and stand a better chance of being heard and acted upon. In other words, its SOV is the greater. This implies, of course, that the quality of the message transmitted is not important and that it is the sheer relative weight of adspend that is the critical factor.

When a brand's market share is equal to its share of advertising spend, equilibrium is said to have been reached.

This concept can be taken further and combined with another, share of market (SOM). When a brand's market share is equal to its share of advertising spend, equilibrium is said to have been reached (SOV = SOM).

Strategic implications of the SOV concept

These concepts of SOV and SOM frame an interesting perspective of competitive strategy based upon the relative weight of advertising expenditure. Schroer (1990) reports that, following extensive research on the US packaged goods market (FMCG), it is noticeable that organisations can use advertising spend to maintain equilibrium and to create disequilibrium in a market. The former is established by major brand players maintaining their market shares with little annual change to their advertising budgets. Unless a competitor is prepared to inject a considerable increase in advertising spend and so create disequilibrium, the relatively stable high spend deters new entrants and preserves the status quo. Schroer claims that if the two market leaders maintain SOV within 10 per cent of each other then competitive equilibrium will exist. This situation is depicted in Figure 16.2. If a market challenger launches an aggressive assault upon the leader by raising advertising spend to a point where SOV is 20–30 per cent higher than the current leader, market share will shift in favour of the challenger.

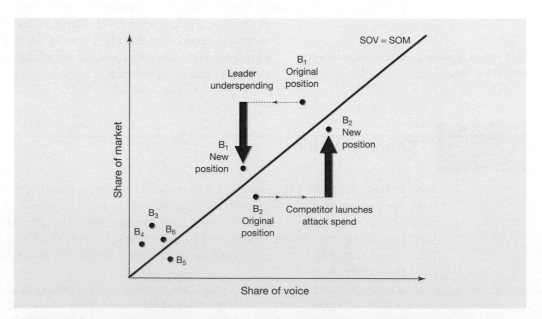

FIGURE 16.2 Strategy to gain market share by an increase in adspend. Reprinted by permission of Harvard Business School Press, from Ad spending: growing market share, *Harvard Business Review* (January/February), by J. Schroer, Boston, MA 1990, pp. 44-8, copyright © 1990 by Harvard Business School Publishing Corporation, all rights reserved

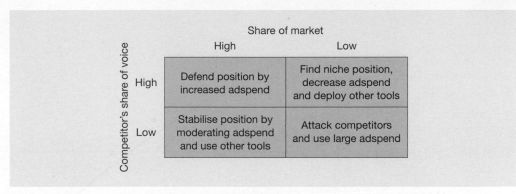

FIGURE 16.3 Strategies for advertising spend. Reprinted by permission of Harvard Business School Press, from Ad spending: growing market share, *Harvard Business Review* (January/February), by J. Schroer, Boston, MA 1990, pp. 44-8, copyright © 1990 by Harvard Business School Publishing Corporation, all rights reserved

In Figure 16.2, brands 1, 3, 4 and 6 have an SOM that is greater than their SOV. This suggests that their advertising is working well for them and that the larger organisations have some economies of scale in their advertising. Brands 2 and 5, however, have an SOM that is less than their SOV. This is because brand 2 is challenging for the larger market (with brand 1) and is likely to be less profitable than brand 1 because of the increased costs. Brand 5 is competing in a niche market and, as a new brand, may be spending heavily (relative to its market share) to gain acceptance in the new market environment.

This perspective brings implications for advertising spend at a strategic level. This is shown in the matrix, Figure 16.3, which shows that advertising spend should be varied according to the spend of the company's competitors in different markets. The implications are that advertising budget decisions should be geared to the level of adspend undertaken by competitors in particular markets at particular times. Decisions to attack or to defend are also set out. For example, promotional investments should be placed in markets where competitors are underspending. Furthermore, if information is available about competitors' costs, then decisions to launch and sustain an advertising spend attack can be made in the knowledge that a prolonged period of premium spending can be carried through with or without a counter-attack.

> Advertising budget decisions should be geared to the level of adspend undertaken by competitors in particular markets at particular times.

This traditional perspective of static markets being led by the top two brands using heavy above-the-line strategies and the rest basing their competitive thrusts on price-based promotions was challenged by Buck (1995) through reference to a study of Superpanel data by Hamilton. It was found that the brand leaders in many FMCG markets spent nearly 50 per cent more than the industry average on advertising, while the number two brand spent about 8 per cent less than the industry average. In addition, the gap with the other actors was not as significant as Schroer reported. This is, of course, a comparison of European and US markets, and there is no reason why they should be identical or at least very similar. However, the data are interesting in that the challenge of brand 2, postulated by Schroer, is virtually impossible in many of the UK, if not also in continental European, markets.

The concepts of SOV and SOM have also been used by Jones (1990) to develop a new method of budget setting. He suggests that those brands that have an SOV greater than their SOM are 'investment brands', and those that have a SOV less than or equal to their SOM are 'profit-taking brands'.

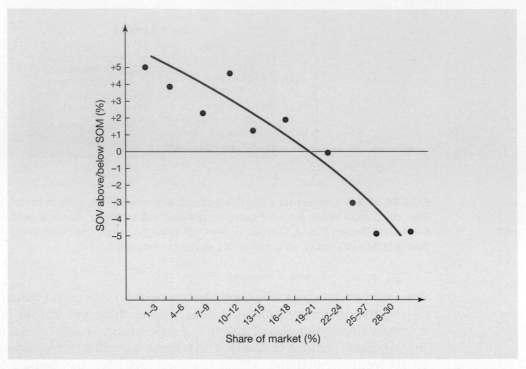

FIGURE 16.4 Curve comparing SOV with SOM. Reprinted by permission of Harvard Business School Press, from Ad spending: maintaining market share, *Harvard Business Review* (January/February), by J.P. Jones, Boston, MA 1990, pp. 38–42, copyright © 1990 by Harvard Business School Publishing Corporation, all rights reserved. One-time permission to reproduce granted by Harvard Business School Publishing 2001

There are three points to notice. First, the high advertising spend of new brands is an established strategy and represents a trade-off between the need for profit and the need to become established through advertising spend. The result, invariably, is that smaller brands have lower profitability because they have to invest a disproportionate amount in advertising. Secondly, large brands are often 'milked' to produce increased earnings, especially in environments that emphasise short-termism. The third point is that advertising economies of scale allow large brands to develop with an SOV consistently below SOM.

Using data collected from an extensive survey of 1,096 brands across 23 different countries, Jones 'calculated the difference between share of voice and share of market and averaged these differences within each family of brands'. By representing the data diagrammatically (Figure 16.4), Jones shows how it becomes a relatively simple task to work out the spend required to achieve a particular share of market. The first task is to plot the expected (desired) market share from the horizontal axis; then move vertically to the intersect with the curve and read off the SOV figure from the vertical axis.

Appropriation brand types

From this approach it is possible to determine three main types of brands, based upon the amount of advertising expenditure. In each market there are brands that are promoted without the support of any advertising. These small niche players can be regarded as zero-based brands.

Where brands are supported by token advertising, which represents a small SOV, the brand is probably being milked and the resources are being channelled into developing other brands. New launches are typified by the heavy advertising investment necessary to get them off the ground. Here the SOV will be larger than the SOM and these can be referred to as investment brands.

In situations where the SOM is very large and the SOV much smaller, these profit-taking brands are running a risk of losing market share if a competitor spots the opportunity to invest a large sum in a prolonged attack. Finally, there is a group of brands that maintain stability by respecting each other's positions and by not initiating warfare. These brands can be referred to as equilibrium brands.

1. Investment brands – SOV > SOM; heavy advertising to drive growth.

2. Milking brands – SOV < SOM; low-level advertising to take profits out of the brand.

3. Equilibrium brands – SOM = SOV; steady-level advertising to maintain position and avoid confrontation.

Assessing brands in the context of the advertising resources they attract is a slightly different way of reflecting their power and importance to their owners. If the SOV approach is limited by its applicability to stable, mature market conditions then at least it enables the promotional spend to be seen and used as a competitive weapon.

The value of brand communications

The ideas and principles associated with the SOV concept provide a foundation upon which to consider the value of marketing communications as an aid to brand development. The importance of brands cannot be understated. Indeed, many organisations have attempted (and succeeded) in valuing the worth of their brands and have had them listed as an asset on their balance sheets. While this has stimulated the accountancy profession into some debate, the concept of a brand's worth to an organisation cannot be refuted. Among other things, when companies buy other companies or brands, they are purchasing the potential income streams that these target brands offer, not just the physical assets of plant, capital and machinery. However, as discussed in Chapter 14, communications are a vital element used to develop these assets and so it is organisationally important to understand the relationship between the required level of investment in communications and the asset value that results from this activity.

> Important to understand the relationship between the required level of investment in communications and the asset value that results from this activity.

Butterfield (1999) argued that marketers will be required to account for their activities in terms of the contribution they make to the financial performance of an organisation. This will mean that markets and customers will be viewed as assets, which in turn will become subject to development, cultivation and leverage. Marketers will also be required to use different measures of performance. Market share, margin and revenues will give way to terms such as return on investment, net present value of future cash flows or just shareholder value. He said that it will not be just a question of how much your adspend is, but how much you spend relative to your main competitors' market share. Although some of his views have yet to become reality there are

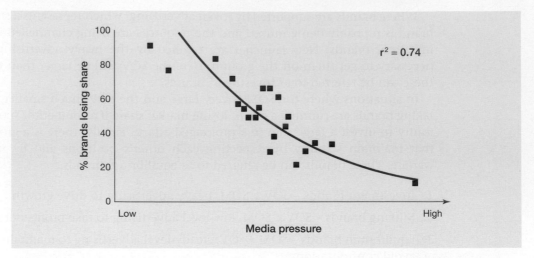

FIGURE 16.5 Communications investment to reduce risk (Farr, 2004); used with permission

signs that this longer-term, strategic value oriented approach is beginning to become part of the overall marketing communications vocabulary, if not yet part of everyday practice. Ideas concerning shareholder value as a means of developing marketing strategy have become quite common and articulated by an increasing number of authors (Doyle, 2000) since Butterfield first speculated about future techniques.

Although there are exceptional cases, it is generally accepted that stronger brands are more likely to maintain market share in the following year than weaker brands. This means that the revenue streams from stronger brands are more secure and attract lower risk than weaker brands. Farr (2004) refers to the use of brand-related communications as media pressure. He defines media pressure 'as the brand's share of communications spending minus its prior-year market share' (p. 30). A brand's strength is in (major) part due to the accumulated investments and activities in the past. It follows therefore that these investments in communications should be continued rather than truncated. Figure 16.5 shows the relationship between risk (of share loss) and media pressure.

Farr uses data from 350 brands, across a range of categories that have been divided into 20 groups based on media pressure. As media pressure grows so the risk (per cent) of losing share declines. This approach can be used to determine media budgets. Using discounted cash flows (DCFs) Farr shows that it is possible to estimate changes in the net present value (NPV) of the cash flows arising from different levels of media pressure. In the example depicted in Figure 16.6, investments up to around £40 million provide a positive impact on NPV but further investments fail to increase the value of future earnings, and should therefore not be utilised. He acknowledges that the assumption that investments in stronger brands will be more profitable may be misleading and other approaches to budget setting may need to be used when weaker (smaller) brands launch new variants or extensions.

At the end of the promotional process one of the benefits that management hopes will emerge is an overall increase in the valuation of the brand. This net value arises as a result of the investment (for example, promotional expenditures) generating a return to reward those who risked the capital invested in the brand. Some believe that this value arises from these activities and that the brand itself is worth £x; this should therefore be regarded as an asset and be placed on the balance sheet.

> At the end of the promotional process one of the benefits that management hopes will emerge is an overall increase in the valuation of the brand.

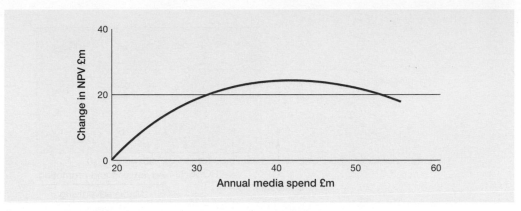

FIGURE 16.6 Media payback versus brand strength (Farr, 2004); used with permission

Profit Impact on Market Strategy (PIMS)

One of the problems with the SOV and media pressure approaches is that they fail to take into account how much of a finite budget should be allocated to the other elements of the promotional mix. Considering the relative amounts that are spent on advertising and sales promotions, let alone direct marketing, it is important to try to understand and determine how much of the budget should be spent on the other tools. In many markets a more useful strategic approach is to determine the relative spend of above- to below-the-line promotional activities. As noted earlier, Procter & Gamble actually sets limits on what proportion of a brand can be spent below-the-line.

An alternative approach is the impact of marketing communications on profitability. One of the more notable commercial research organisations is PIMS. PIMS is a major database of the performance of 3,500 business units and includes profiles of over 200 variables measured over a rolling four-year period. The database records data of business performance, enabling managers to understand and develop strategies based upon empirical results of businesses in particular sectors. One of the major findings is that total advertising spend is not correlated with profitability. What has emerged is that profitability is related to an optimum promotional mix that is dependent upon a number of key factors: again, an argument for integrated marketing communications.

The questions that brand managers need to answer are 'Should promotional investment be used to build brand image or should the goal be to drive sales off the shelf?' and 'Where is the balance?'

According to PIMS, brand leaders spend 70 per cent plus above-the-line and make 43 per cent return on capital employed (ROCE). As if to make the point, Mistry (2001) reports that market leader snack food manufacturer Walkers spends approximately 33 per cent of its overall marketing budget below-the-line. Brands ranked 2 or 3 should invest a smaller amount above-the-line but above 50 per cent, whereas brands ranked 4 or lower should only really use below-the-line investments if they are to be less than moderately successful. See Figure 16.7.

The evidence from the database reveals many statistical relationships, too many to present here. Some of the other pointers are that brands should use advertising in declining markets and use sales promotions in expanding or rapid growth markets. One other outcome appears to be that above-the-line advertising should be used when there are many distributors and where there is little innovation or sister brands.

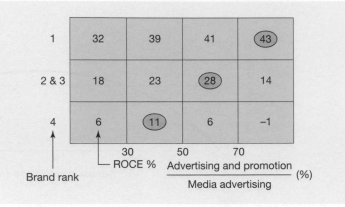

FIGURE 16.7 Brand leaders to concentrate on media advertising. From PIMS (2000)

There is some debate about the applicability and real usefulness of the PIMS data and PIMS itself points out the limitations of its work. However, the database serves to counter the arguments of the SOV school of thought that media advertising alone is the only significant variable that determines performance. One measures market share, and the other uses market share to determine ROCE.

Which methods are most used?

From this review and commentary it is necessary to draw out the degree to which these particular tools are used in practice. Mitchell's (1993) study to determine the methods and criteria used by companies to determine their advertising budgets found that 40 per cent of respondents claimed to use the objective and task approach, 27 per cent used percentage of future sales (8 per cent used past sales) and 19 per cent used a variety of company-specific methods that do not fit neatly within any one item from the list presented above.

ViewPoint 16.3   Lateral crisps at Golden Wonder

In an attempt to compete with market leader, Walkers Crisps, Golden Wonder used expensive film-style TV campaigns. It realised that this approach was not working and was failing to get the return expected. The main reason for this was that the production costs were disproportionately high to the media time Golden Wonder could purchase given its budget. The solution was to use 20-second animated TV ads, and in doing so Golden Wonder reduced its overall TV spend by 60 per cent, improved awareness and sold more product.

Although the figures resulting from the study can only be used to indicate trends of overall preferences, another set of important factors also emerged from this study. These are the range of organisational influences that impact on individual organisations. Over half the respon-

Different methods were used for new and established products.

dents reported that the method used to set these budgets

actually varied, internally, across product categories. Different methods were used for new and established products.

The criteria used by organisations to set their communication budgets are many and varied. Mitchell (1993) suggested that the criteria used could be grouped as *controllables* (41 per cent), such as financial, product, production and goals; *uncontrollables* (41 per cent), such as sales, competition, market, media and distribution and *signals* (18 per cent), such as national activities, experience, effectiveness of expenditures and awareness. He reported that the processes used to determine the budgets were found as either essentially centralised or top down (52 per cent), decentralised or bottom up (13.5 per cent) or bargaining (top down and bottom up) (21 per cent). Gullen (2003) suggests ways in which all of the techniques can be grouped but concludes that management judgement based on weighting key criteria is required to determine the optimal budget.

The main factors associated with the determination of marketing communications (advertising) budgets are:

1. organisational strategy and direction, values and cultural perspective;
2. the relative amount of financial resources that are available;
3. competitive activities and market conditions;
4. the overall level of economic confidence felt by buyers and sellers;
5. the level of product/brand development and the marketing objectives.

Over time a number of models and methods have been developed to manage these criteria to enable an appropriation to be determined.

Budgeting for the other elements of the promotional mix

The methods presented so far have concentrated on the FMCG sector. The assumption has been that only one product has been considered. In reality, a range of products will need promotional finances and the allocation decision needs to reflect the requirements of an organisation's portfolio of brands. Broadbent (1989) suggests that this situation and others (e.g. direct marketing, corporate advertising) require particular combinations of the approaches presented so far. The recommendation again is that no single method will help organisations to determine the optimal investment sum.

Sales promotion activities can be more easily costed than advertising in advance of a campaign. Judgements can be made about the expected outcomes, based upon experience, competitive conditions and the use of predictive software tools. The important variable with sales promotion concerns the redemption rate. How many of the extra pack, price deals and samples will customers demand? How much extra of a brand needs to be sold if all the costs associated with a campaign are to be covered? The production and fulfilment costs can also be determined, so in general terms a return can be calculated in advance of a sales promotion event. However, there are a large number of sales promotion activities and these will often overlap. From a management perspective the brand management system is better, since a single person is responsible for the budget, one who is able to take a wider view of the range of activities. While the objective and task approach appears to be more easily applied to this element of the mix other methods, such as competitive parity and fixed ratios, are often used.

The costs of *public relations* activities can also be predicted with a reasonable degree of accuracy. The staffing and/or agency costs are relatively fixed and, as there are no media costs involved, the only other major factor is the associated production costs. These are the costs of the materials used to provide third parties with the opportunity to 'speak' on the organisation's behalf. As with sales promotion, if a number of public relations events have been calculated as a necessary part of the overall promotional activities of the organisation, then the costs of the different tasks need to be anticipated and aggregated and a judgement made about the impact the events will make. The relative costs of achieving a similar level of impact through advertising or other elements of the mix can often be made, and a decision taken based upon relative values.

It has already been stated that the costs associated with the *sales force* are the highest of all the elements of the mix. This would indicate that the greatest degree of care needs to be taken when formulating the size and deployment of the sales force. The different approaches to the determination of the sales force are covered in Chapter 28. The costs associated with each activity of personal selling and the support facilities (e.g. car, expenses, training) can be calculated easily, but what is more difficult to predict is the return on the investment.

> Greatest degree of care needs to be taken when formulating the size and deployment of the sales force.

These approaches to calculating the amount that should be invested in promotional activities vary in their degree of sophistication and usefulness. Of all these methods, none is the ideal answer to the question of how much should be allocated to marketing communications or, more specifically, the advertising spend. Some of the methods are too simplistic, while others are too specific to particular market conditions. For example, formulating strategy to gain market share through increasing SOV seems to ignore the dynamic nature of the markets and the fact that organisations need to satisfy a range of stakeholders and not concentrate solely on winning the greatest market share.

The reader may well have reached the conclusion that the most appropriate way forward for management is to consider several approaches in order to gather a ball-park figure. Such a composite approach negates some of the main drawbacks associated with particular methods. It also helps to build a picture of what is really necessary if the organisation is to communicate effectively and efficiently.

Of all the methods and different approaches, the one constant factor that applies to them all concerns the objectives that have been set for the campaign. Each element of the promotional mix has particular tasks to accomplish and it is these objectives that drive the costs of the promotional investment. If the ultimate estimate of the promotional spend is too high, then the objectives, not the methods used, need to be revised.

Summary

The task of assigning financial resources to an organisation's marketing communications is difficult and imprecise, and as yet there is no method that can be used on a prescriptive basis. Theoretically, the task can be understood and resources allocated easily. Unfortunately, the quality and availability of information required to use marginal analysis are poor and practitioners have to rely on other methods. These other methods range from the simplistic ('This is what I think we should spend') to the more complex analysis associated with the spend incurred by competitors and the relationship of share of voice with market share that some believe is operable in certain market conditions, or purchase database information such as PIMS.

The decision to invest in marketing communications is a difficult one. This is because the direct outcomes are intangible and often distant, as the advertising effects are digested by potential buyers until such time as they are prepared and ready to purchase.

The methods presented in this chapter represent some of the more commonly used techniques. No one method is sufficient, and two or three approaches to the investment decision are required if management is to decide with any accuracy or confidence. Some commentators (Jones, 1990; Buzzell *et al.*, 1990) suggest that the actual amounts invested by some organisations are larger than is necessary. The consequence is that there is wastage and inefficiency, which contributes to a dilution of the profits that brands generate. Management has to make a trade off between investing and growing the brand to secure a position compared with relaxing the promotional investment and harvesting some profit, perhaps as a reward for the previous investment activity.

Review questions

1. How might organisations benefit from adopting an appropriation-setting process?
2. What problems might be encountered when setting them?
3. Write a brief paper outlining the essence of marginal analysis. What are the main drawbacks associated with this approach?
4. Why is the objective and task method gaining popularity?
5. What is a payout plan?
6. Discuss the view that if the A/S ratio only measures average levels of spend across an industry then its relevance may be lost as individual organisations have to adjust levels of promotional spend to match particular niche market conditions.
7. How might the notion of SOV assist the appropriation-setting process?
8. What are 'profit-taking' and 'investment' brands?
9. Determining the level of spend for sales promotion is potentially difficult. Why?
10. How might understanding brand value assist in developing a communications budget?

References

Abraham, M. and Lodish, L.M. (1990) Getting the most out of advertising and sales promotion. *Harvard Business Review* (May/June), pp. 50–60.

Abratt, R. and van der Westhuizen, B. (1985) A new promotion mix appropriation model. *International Journal of Advertising*, **4**, pp. 209–21.

Advertising Association (2004) *Advertising Statistics Year Book*. Henley: World Advertising Research Centre.

Broadbent, S. (1989) *The Advertising Budget*. Henley: NTC Publications.

Buck, S. (1995) The decline and fall of the premium brand. *Admap* (March), pp. 14–17.

Burnett, J. (1993) *Promotion Management*. New York: Houghton Mifflin.

Butterfield, L. (1999) *Excellence in Advertising: The IPA Guide to Best Practice*. Oxford: Butterworth Heinemann.

Buzzell, R.D., Quelch, J.A. and Salmon, W.J. (1990) The costly bargain of sales promotion. *Harvard Business Review* (March/April), pp. 141–9.

Doyle, P. (2000) *Value-based Marketing: Marketing Strategies for Corporate Growth and Shareholder Value*. Chichester: Wiley.

Dyson, P. (1999) How to manage the budget across a brand portfolio. *Admap*, **37**(10) (December), pp. 39–42.

Farr, A. (2004) Managing advertising as an investment. *Admap*, **39**(7) (July/August), pp. 29–31.

Gaedeke, R.M. and Tootelian, D.H. (1983) *Marketing: Principles and Application*. St Paul, MN: West.

Gullen, P. (2003) 5 steps to effective budget setting. *Admap* (July/August), pp. 22–4.

Hall, E. (1999) When advertising becomes an expensive luxury. *Campaign*, 10 December, p. 18.

Harper, G. and Bridges, D. (2003) Budgeting for healthier ROI. *Admap*, **38**(7) (July/August), pp. 25–7.

Holmes, S. (2004) What happened to 'just do it'? *The Independent on Sunday*, 12 September, pp. 8–9.

Hooley, G.J. and Lynch, J.E. (1985) How UK advertisers set budgets. *International Journal of Advertising*, **3**, pp. 223–31.

Jones, J.P. (1990) Ad spending: maintaining market share. *Harvard Business Review* (January/February), pp. 38–42.

Mistry, B. (2001) Walkers revives Tazo route. *Promotions and Incentives* (March), pp. 26–8.

Mitchell, L.A. (1993) An examination of methods of setting advertising budgets: practice and literature. *European Journal of Advertising*, **27**(5), pp. 5–21.

PIMS (2000) www.PIMS-Europe.com.

Schroer, J. (1990) Ad spending: growing market share. *Harvard Business Review* (January/February), pp. 44–8.

Smallbone, D.W. (1972) *The Practice of Marketing*. London: Staple Press.

Tomkins, R. (1999) If the return is right, keep spending. *Financial Times*, 19 March, p. 8.

Tylee, J. (1999) Survey warns against adspend cuts. *Campaign*, 12 March, p. 10.

Weaver, K. and Merrick, D. (2004) Budget allocation revisited. *Admap*, **39**(7) (July/August), pp. 26–8.

Evaluating marketing communications

17

As part of the marketing communication process it is necessary to evaluate the overall impact and effect that a campaign has on a target audience. It needs to be reviewed in order that management can learn and better understand the impact of its communications and its audiences.

Aims and objectives

The aim of this chapter is to review the ways in which marketing communications activities can be evaluated.

The objectives of this chapter are to:

1. discuss the role of evaluation as part of marketing communications;
2. explore the value and methods of pre-testing and post-testing advertisements;
3. provide an insight into the value of qualitative and quantitative testing techniques;
4. appreciate the role technology plays in the assessment and evaluation of advertising;
5. examine ways in which sales promotions can be evaluated;
6. present the methods used to evaluate direct marketing;
7. discuss the techniques and approaches used to measure and evaluate public relations;
8. explore the ways in which personal selling activities can be measured;
9. consider some of the issues associated with evaluating the effectiveness of online communications.

Introduction

All organisations review and evaluate the performance of their various activities. Many undertake formal mechanisms, while others review in an informal, ad hoc manner, but the process of evaluation or reflection is a well-established management process. The objective is to monitor the often diverse activities of the organisation so that management can exercise control. It is through the process of review and evaluation that an organisation has the opportunity to learn and develop. In turn, this enables management to refine its competitive position and to provide for higher levels of customer satisfaction.

> It is through the process of review and evaluation that an organisation has the opportunity to learn and develop.

The use of marketing communications is a management activity, one that requires the use of rigorous research and testing procedures in addition to continual evaluation. This is necessary because planned communications involve a wide variety of stakeholders and have the potential to consume a vast amount of resources.

The evaluation of planned marketing communications consists of two distinct elements. The first element is concerned with the development and testing of individual messages. For example, a particular sales promotion (such as a sample pack) has individual characteristics that may or may not meet the objectives of a sales promotion event.

An advertising message has to achieve, among other things, a balance of emotion and information in order that the communication objectives and message strategy be achieved. To accomplish this, testing is required to ensure that the intended messages are encoded correctly and are capable of being decoded accurately by the target audience and the intended meaning is ascribed to the message. The second element concerns the overall impact and effect that a campaign has on a target audience once a communications plan has been released. This post-test factor is critical, as it will either confirm or reject management's judgement about the viability of its communications strategy. The way in which the individual components of the communications mix work together needs to be understood so that strengths can be capitalised on and developed and weaknesses negated.

> Testing is required to ensure that the intended messages are encoded correctly and are capable of being decoded accurately by the target audience.

This chapter examines the testing and evaluation methods that are appropriate to all the tools of the communications mix and introduces ideas relevant to the measurement of online communications.

The role of evaluation in planned communications

The evaluation process is a key part of marketing communications. The findings and results of the evaluative process feed back into the next campaign and provide indicators and benchmarks for further management decisions. The primary role of evaluating the performance of a communications strategy is to ensure that the communications objectives have been met and that the strategy has been effective. The secondary role is to ensure that the strategy has been executed efficiently, that the full potential of the individual promotional tools has been extracted and that resources have been used economically.

Research activity is undertaken for two main reasons. The first is guidance and development and the second is prediction and evaluation (Staverley, 1993). Guidance takes the form of shaping future strategies as a result of past experiences. Development is important in the context of determining whether the communications worked as they were intended to.

Prediction and evaluation require information about options and alternatives. For example, did sales presentation approach A prove to be more effective than B and, if so, what would happen if A was used nationally? Predictably, the use of quantitative techniques is more prevalent with this set of reasons. This concluding chapter of Part 3 addresses the evaluation techniques appropriate for each of the promotional tools, in turn, before presenting a general summary of evaluation in marketing communications.

Advertising

An IPA report in 1998 stated that 23 per cent of finance directors said that if business costs were under pressure they would cut marketing and advertising before anything else (Farrow, 1999). Among the reasons offered for this view was the feeling that advertising was extremely difficult to measure and thus problematic in terms of its overall contribution to the organisation. If in doubt, cut it. On a more optimistic note Fendwick (1996) suggests that there have been four main stages to the measurement of advertising effectiveness.

1. *Direct response* – coupon response.
2. *Executions* – measurement of consumer psychological responses to the way individual ads are executed. The recognition and recall techniques were developed and refined to reflect this approach.
3. *Campaign evaluation* (current age) – the evaluation of campaigns working over a period of time. The use of econometrics and modelling techniques to examine the influence of key variables typifies this approach.
4. *Research nirvana* (future age) – through the use of computers and vast data sets it will become possible to evaluate specific individual and panel data regarding various emotional and rational impacts of a variety of marketing communication messages. The effect will be to enable managers to adjust their communications messages and media quickly, efficiently and much more effectively.

The techniques used to evaluate advertising are by far the most documented and, in view of the relative sizes of the promotional tools, it is not surprising that slightly more time is devoted to this tool. This is not to disregard or be disrespectful to the contribution each of the promotional tools can make to an integrated campaign. Indeed, it is the collective measure of success against the goals set at the outset that is the overriding imperative for measurement, as will be seen later.

Pre-testing

Advertisements can be researched prior to their release (pre-test) or after they have been released (post-test).

Advertisements can be researched prior to their release (pre-test) or after they have been released (post-test). Pre-tests, sometimes referred to as copy tests, have traditionally attracted more attention, stimulated a greater variety of methods and generated much controversy, in comparison with post-tests.

Pre-testing, that is the practice of showing unfinished commercials to selected groups of the target audience with a view to refining the commercial to improve effectiveness, is still subject to debate about its effectiveness. Reid (2000) argues that pre-testing can be used positively to support campaign development, predictively to gauge likely audience response and generally to improve advertising performance.

The methods used to pre-test advertisements are based upon either qualitative or quantitative criteria. The most common methods used to pre-test advertisements are concept testing, focus groups, consumer juries, dummy vehicles, readability, theatre and physiological tests. Focus groups are the main qualitative method used and theatre or hall tests the main quantitative test. Each of these methods will be discussed later.

The primary purpose of testing advertisements during the developmental process is to ensure that the final creative will meet the advertising objectives. It is better to help shape the way an advertising message is formed, rather like potters continuously review their progress as they craft their vases, than to make a pot and then decide that it is not big enough or that the handle is the wrong shape. The practical objective of pre-testing unfinished and finished creative work is that it is more effective for an advertiser to terminate an advertisement before costs become so large and commitment too final. Changes to an advertisement that are made too late may be resisted partly because of the sunk costs and partly because of the political consequences that 'pulling' an advertisement might have.

> The primary purpose of testing advertisements during the developmental process is to ensure that the final creative will meet the advertising objectives.

Once a series of advertisements has been roughed or developed so that its messages can be clearly understood, advertisers seek reassurance and guidance regarding which of the alternatives should be developed further. Concept tests, in-depth interviews, focus groups and consumer juries can be used to determine which of the proposed advertisements are the better ones by using ranking and prioritisation procedures. Of those selected, further testing can be used to reveal the extent to which the intended message is accurately decoded. These comprehension and reaction tests are designed to prevent inappropriate advertisements reaching the finished stage.

Pre-testing unfinished advertisements

Concept testing

The concept test is an integral part of the developmental stage of advertising strategy. The purpose is to reduce the number of alternative advertising ideas, to identify and build upon the good ideas and to reject those that the target audience feel are not suitable.

Concept testing can occur very early on in the development process, but is usually undertaken when the target audience can be presented with a *rough* outline or *storyboard* that represents the intended artwork and the messages to be used. There are varying degrees of sophistication associated with concept testing, from the use of simple *cards* with no illustrations to *photomatics*, which are films of individual photographs shot in sequence, and *livematics*, which are films very close to the intended finished message. Their use will reflect the size of the advertiser's budget, the completion date of the campaign and the needs of the creative team.

> There are varying degrees of sophistication associated with concept testing.

Concept testing, by definition, has to be undertaken in artificial surroundings, but the main way of eliciting the target's views is essentially qualitatively oriented, based

ViewPoint 17.1	Roughing it

Once a client has approved the agency's plans, ad production can begin. Very often the creative team or an independent artist will produce roughs or drawings for the agency and advertiser to see before the final artwork is finished. This is seen as necessary as the costs of producing finished work and going live without any pre-testing can be critical, and expensive.

Storyboards are a way in which it is possible to inexpensively simulate a 'rough' version of the advertisement. Pen and ink line drawings, animatics or cartoons and photoboards are some of the more common approaches. Some storyboards will consist of as many as 20 sketches, depicting key scenes, camera and product shots, close ups, and of course background scenery and essential props.

upon a group discussion. This group discussion is referred to as a focus group and is a technique used by most agencies.

Focus groups

When a small number (8–10) of target consumers are brought together and invited to discuss a particular topic a focus group is formed. By using in-depth interviewing skills a professional moderator can probe the thoughts and feelings held by the members of the group towards a product, media vehicles or advertising messages. One-way viewing rooms allow clients to observe the interaction without the focus group's behaviour being modified by external influences.

The advantage of focus groups is that they are relatively inexpensive to set up and run and they use members of the target audience. In this sense they are representative and allow true feelings and emotions to be uncovered in a way that other methods deny. They do not attempt to be quantitative and, in that sense, they lack objectivity. It is also suggested that the group dynamics may affect the responses in the 'artificial' environment. This means that there may be in-built bias to the responses and the inter-action of the group members. Focus groups are very popular, but they should not be used on their own.

> The advantage of focus groups is that they are relatively inexpensive to set up and run and they use members of the target audience.

Consumer juries

A 'jury' of consumers, representative of the target market, is asked to judge which of a series of paste-ups and rough ideas would be their choice of a final advertisement. They are asked to rank in order of merit and provide reasons for their selections.

There are difficulties associated with ranking and prioritisation tests. First, the consumers, realising the reason for their participation, may appoint themselves as 'experts', so they lose the objectivity that this process is intended to bring. Secondly, the halo effect can occur, whereby an advertisement is rated excellent overall simply because one or two elements are good and the respondent overlooks the weaknesses. Finally, emotional advertisements tend to receive higher scores than informational messages, even though the latter might do better in the marketplace.

Pre-testing finished advertisements

When an advertisement is finished it can be subjected to a number of other tests before being released.

Dummy vehicles

Many of the pre-testing methods occur in an artificial environment such as a theatre, laboratory or meeting room. One way of testing so that the reader's natural environment is used is to produce a dummy or pretend magazine that can be consumed at home, work or wherever participants normally read magazines. Dummy magazines contain regular editorial matter with test advertisements inserted next to control advertisements. These 'pretend' magazines are distributed to a random sample of households, which are asked to consume the magazine in their normal way. Readers are encouraged to observe the editorial and at a later date they are asked questions about both the editorial and the advertisements.

The main advantage of using dummy vehicles is that the setting is natural but, as with the focus group, the main disadvantage is that respondents are aware that they are part of a test and may respond unnaturally. Research also suggests that recall may not be the best measure for low-involvement decisions or where motivation occurs through the peripheral route of the ELM. If awareness is required at the point of sale, then recognition may be a more reliable indicator of effectiveness than recall.

> The main advantage of using dummy vehicles is that the setting is natural.

ViewPoint 17.2 **Dummy vehicle - Flora**

A test Flora advertisement comprising a central figure of a gingerbread man with copy above and below was inserted in *Woman* magazine and distributed on a complimentary basis to 150 housewives. Readers were asked to read the magazine in their normal manner over the course of a week, and were not told what the purpose of the exercise was.

Three objectives were determined for the exercise:

1. the impact and branding of the advertisement;
2. the level of comprehension;
3. the generation of empathy toward the brand.

Results indicated that the gingerbread man provided a strong visual focus, which in turn generated empathy towards the brand. The copy line was also liked and read by an above average number of people.

However, by utilising the results, the size of the visual was increased and toned while the typestyle for the copyline was softened. The amount of copy was reduced and the Flora logo was repositioned for greater exit impact (Colinese, 1997).

Readability tests

Rudolph Flesch (1974) developed a formula to assess the ease with which print copy could be read. The test involves, among other things, determining the average number of syllables per 100 words of copy, the average length of sentence and the percentage of personal words and sentences. By accounting for the educational level of the target audience and by comparing results with established norms, the tests suggest that comprehension is best when sentences are short, words are concrete and familiar, and personal references are used frequently.

Theatre tests

As a way of testing finished broadcast advertisements, target consumers are invited to a theatre (laboratory or hall) to preview television programmes. Before the programme commences, details regarding the respondents' demographic and attitudinal details are recorded and they are asked to nominate their product preferences from a list. At the end of the viewing their evaluation of the programme is sought and they are also requested to complete their product preferences a second time.

There are a number of variations on this theme: one is to telephone the respondents a few days after the viewing to measure recall and another is to provide joysticks, push buttons and pressure pads to measure reactions throughout the viewing. The main outcome of this process is a measure of the degree to which product preferences change as a result of exposure to the controlled viewing. This change is referred to as the *persuasion shift*. This approach provides for a quantitative dimension to be added to the testing process, as the scores recorded by respondents can be used to measure the effectiveness of advertisements and provide benchmarks for future testing.

A measure of the degree to which product preferences change as a result of exposure to the controlled viewing.

It is argued that this form of testing is too artificial and that the measure of persuasion shift is too simple and unrealistic. Furthermore, some believe that many respondents know what is happening and make changes because it is expected of them in the role of respondent. Those in favour of theatre testing state that the control is sound, that the value of established norms negates any 'role play' by respondents and that the actual sales data support the findings of the brand persuasion changes in the theatre.

A major evaluation of 400 individual advertising tests in the United States found, among many other things, that there is no clear relationship between measures of persuasion shift and eventual sales performance. This questions the use of an organisation's scarce resources and the viability of using these techniques (Lodish and Lubetkin, 1992).

This technique is used a great deal in the United States but has had limited use in the UK, until recently. However, Mazur (1993) reports that theatre testing is increasing in the UK. Agencies are concerned that the simplistic nature of recording scores as a means of testing advertisements ignores the complex imagery and emotional aspects of many messages. If likeability is an important aspect of eventual brand success then it is unlikely that the quantitative approach to pre-testing will contribute any worthwhile information.

The increasing use of, or at least interest in, theatre tests and the movement towards greater utilisation of quantitative techniques in pre-testing procedures runs concurrently with the increasing requirements of accountability, short-termism and periods of economic downturn. As no one method will ever be sufficient, a mix of qualitative and quantitative pre-test measures will, inevitably, always be required.

Physiological measures

A bank of physiological tests has been developed, partly as a response to advertisers' increasing interest in the emotional impact of advertising messages and partly because many other tests rely on the respondents' ability to interpret their reactions. Physiological tests have been designed to measure the involuntary responses to stimuli and so avoid the bias inherent in the other tests. There are substantial costs involved with the use of these techniques, and the validity of the results is questionable. Consequently they are not used a great deal in practice, but, of them all, eye tracking is the most used and most reliable. See Table 17.1.

Physiological tests have been designed to measure the involuntary responses to stimuli.

TABLE 17.1 Physiological tests

Pupil dilation

Pupil dilation is associated with action and interest and is used to measure a respondent's reaction to a stimulus. If the pupil is constricted then interest levels are low and energy is conserved. The level of arousal is used to determine the degree of interest and preference in a particular advertisement or package design.

Eye tracking

This technique requires the use of eye movement cameras that fire an infrared beam to track the movement of the eye as it scans an advertisement. The sequence in which the advertisement is read can be determined and particular areas that do or do not attract attention can be located.

Galvanic skin response

This measures the resistance the skin offers to a small amount of current passed between two electrodes. Response to a stimulus will activate the sweat glands, which in turn will increase the resistance. Therefore the greater the level of tension induced by an advertisement the more effective it is as a form of communication.

Tachistoscopes

These measure the ability of an advertisement to attract attention. The speed at which an advertisement is flashed in front of a respondent is gradually slowed down until a point (about 1/100 second) is reached at which the respondent is able to identify components of the message. This can be used to identify those elements that respondents see first as a picture is exposed, and so facilitates the creation of impact-based messages.

Electroencephalographs

This involves the use of a scanner that monitors the electrical frequencies of the brain. *Hemispheric lateralisation* concerns the ability of the left-hand side of the brain to process rational, logical information and the right-hand side handles visual stimuli and responds more to emotional inputs.

Brain activation measures the level of alpha wave activity, which indicates the degree to which the respondent is aroused by and interested in a stimulus. Therefore, the lower the level of alpha activity the greater the level of attention and cognitive processing. It would follow that, by measuring the alpha waves while a respondent is exposed to different advertisements, different levels of attention can be determined.

On the surface, pupil dilation has a number of attractions, but it is not used very much as research has shown little evidence of success. The costs are high and the low number of respondents that can be processed limits the overall effectiveness. Eye tracking can be a useful means of reviewing and amending the layout of an advertisement. Galvanic skin response is flawed because the range of reactions and emotions, the degree of learning and recall, and aspects of preference and motivation are all ignored. When these deficiencies are combined with the high costs and low numbers of respondents that can be processed, it is not surprising that this method of pre-testing has little value. The hemispheric lateralisation theory has been rejected by many researchers. Although the right side of the brain is best for recognition, and the left better for recall, only Vaughn (1980) has developed this approach in terms of advertising theory (Chapter 18). Although now superseded, his grid was regarded as an important breakthrough in our understanding of how advertising works. However, while the grid has been used extensively, there is little evidence of any commercial application of electroencephalographs. Advertisements should be designed to appeal to each hemisphere, but recent research now appears to reject this once-popular notion.

Post-testing

Testing advertisements that have been released is generally more time consuming and involves greater expense than pre-testing. However, the big advantage with post-testing is that advertisements are evaluated in their proper environment, or at least the environment in which they are intended to be successful.

There are a number of methods used to evaluate the effectiveness of such advertisements, and of these inquiry, recall, recognition and sales-based tests predominate.

Inquiry tests

These tests are designed to measure the number of inquiries or direct responses stimulated by advertisements. Inquiries can take the form of returned coupons and response cards, requests for further literature or actual orders. They were originally used to test print messages, but some television advertisements now carry 0800 (free) telephone numbers. An increase in the use of direct response media will lead to an increase in the sales and leads generated by inquiry-stimulating messages, so this type of testing will become more prevalent.

Are designed to measure the number of inquiries or direct responses stimulated by advertisements.

Inquiry tests can be used to test single advertisements or a campaign in which responses are accumulated. Using a split run, an advertiser can use two different advertisements and run them in the same print vehicle. This allows measurement of the attention-getting properties of alternative messages. If identical messages are run in different media then the effect of the media vehicles can be tested.

Care needs to be given to the interpretation of inquiry-based tests, as they may be misleading. An advertisement may not be effective simply because of the responses received. For example, people may respond because they have a strong need for the offering rather than the response being a reflection of the qualities of the advertisement. Likewise, other people may not respond despite the strong qualities of the advertisement, simply because they lack time, resources or need at that particular moment.

Recall tests

Recall tests are designed to assess the impression that particular advertisements have made on the memory of the target audience. Interviewers, therefore, do not use a copy of the advertisement as a stimulus, as the tests are intended to measure impressions and perception, not behaviour, opinions, attitudes or the advertising effect.

Normally, recall tests require the cooperation of several hundred respondents, all of whom were exposed to the advertisement. They are interviewed the day after an advertisement is screened, hence the reference to day-after-recall (DAR) tests. Once qualified by the interviewer, respondents are first asked if they remember a commercial for, say, air travel. If the respondent replies 'Yes, Virgin', then this is recorded as *unaided recall* and is regarded as a strong measure of memory. If the respondent says 'No', the interviewer might ask the question 'Did you see an advertisement for British Airways?' A positive answer to this prompt is recorded as *aided recall*.

These answers are then followed by questions such as 'What did the advertisement say about British Airways?', 'What did the commercial look like?' and 'What did it remind you of?' All the answers provided to this third group of questions are written down word for word and recorded as *verbatim* responses.

The reliability of recall scores is generally high. This means that each time the advertisement is tested, the same score is generated. Validity refers to the relationship or correlation between recall and the sales that ultimately result from an audience exposed to a particular advertisement. The validity of recall tests is generally regarded by researchers as low (Gordon, 1992).

The reliability of recall scores is generally high.

Recall tests have a number of other difficulties associated with them. First, they can be expensive, as a lot of resources can be consumed by looking for and qualifying respondents. Secondly, not only is interviewing time expensive, but the score may be rejected if, on examination of the verbatim responses, it appears that the respondent was guessing.

It has been suggested by Zielske (1982) that thinking/rational messages appear to be easier to recall than emotional/feeling ones. Therefore, it seems reasonable to assume that recall scores for emotional/feeling advertisements may be lower. It is possible that programme content may influence the memory and lead to different recall scores for the same offering. The use of a preselected group of respondents may reduce the costs associated with finding a qualified group, but they may increase their attention towards the commercials in the knowledge that they will be tested the following day. This will inevitably lead to higher levels of recall than actually exist.

On-the-air tests are a derivative of recall and theatre tests. By using advertisements that are run live in a test area, it is possible to measure the impact of these test advertisements with DAR. As recall tests reflect the degree of attention and interest in the advertisement, this is a way of controlling and predicting the outcome of a campaign when it is rolled out nationally.

Recall tests are used a great deal, even though their validity is low and their costs are high. Wells *et al.* (1992) argue that this is because recall scores provide an acceptable means by which decisions to invest heavily in advertising programmes can be made. Agencies accumulate vast amounts of recall data which can be used as benchmarks to judge whether an advertisement generated a score that was better or less than the average for the product class or brand. Having said that, and despite their popularity, they are adjudged to be poor predictors of sales (Lodish and Lubetkin, 1992).

Recall tests are used a great deal, even though their validity is low and their costs are high.

ViewPoint 17.3   Swedish Printpanel

Printpanel is a Swedish-based research project supported by 126 Swedish newspapers, and conducted by TNS-Gallup set up to measure print audiences. Using a panel of 2,300 respondents, the goal is to differentiate between the performance of the media and the performance of the ad itself. Media performance refers to the delivery of a message to an 'eyes open' audience in front of the page, as opposed to how readers react to specific print messages.

Panel members report their daily reading via mobile phones with SMS advertisement recognition questions asked via the Internet. Each panel member reports daily for 30 days, then is replaced. Since Internet and mobile phone/SMS penetration is around 80 per cent in Sweden the panel is considered reasonably representative of the adult population.

Agencies and advertisers can therefore monitor day by day how their campaigns are performing, in terms of net coverage, gross coverage and frequency. Adjustments to the campaign can be made if necessary, while the campaign is still running.

Printpanel represents a major change in syndicated print media research, simply because it eliminates two main flaws in other systems. First it reports media exposure within a few hours, and secondly it separates media exposure from how well the ad itself performs.

Source: Adapted from Randrup (2004).
See also: www.fipp.com/sadmin/1421.

Recognition tests

Recall tests are based upon the memory and the ability of respondents to reprocess information about an advertisement. A different way of determining advertising effectiveness is to ask respondents if they recognise an advertisement. This is the most common of the post-testing procedures for print advertisements. One of the main methods used to measure the readership of magazines is based on the frequency-of-reading and generally there are three main approaches:

recency: reading any issue during the last publishing interval (e.g. within the last seven days, for a weekly magazine);

specific issue: reading of a specific issue of a publication;

frequency-of-reading: how many issues a reader has read in a stated period (such as a month, in respect of a weekly magazine).

Worldwide, the recency approach is the most widely used method in national readership surveys (www.roymorgan.com). Of the many services available, perhaps the Starch Readership Report is the best known. These recognition tests are normally conducted in the homes of approximately 200 respondents. Having agreed that the respondent has previously seen a copy of the magazine, it is opened at a predetermined page and the respondent is asked, for each advertisement, 'Did you see or read any part of the advertisement?' If the answer is yes the respondent is asked to indicate exactly which parts of the copy or layout were seen or read.

> The recency approach is the most widely used method in national readership surveys.

Four principal readership scores are reported: noted, seen-associated, read most and signature. See Table 17.2.

TABLE 17.2 Principal readership scores

Readership scores	Explanation
Noted	The percentage of readers who remember seeing the advertisement
Seen-associated	The percentage of readers who recall seeing or reading any part of the advertisement identifying the offering
Read most	The percentage of readers who report reading at least 50 per cent of the advertisement
Signature	The percentage of readers who remember seeing the brand name or logo

The reliability of recognition tests is very high, higher than recall scores. Costs are lower, mainly because the questioning procedure is simpler and quicker. It is also possible to deconstruct an advertisement into its component parts and assess their individual effects on the reader. As with all interviewer-based research, bias is inevitable. Bias can also be introduced by the respondent or the research organisation through the instructions given or through fatigue of the interviewer.

The validity of recognition test scores is said to be high, especially after a number of insertions. However, there can be a problem of false claiming, where readers claim to have seen an advertisement but in fact have not. This, it is suggested, is because when readers confirm they have seen an advertisement the underlying message is that they approve of and like that sort of advertisement. If they say that they have not seen an advertisement, the underlying message is that they do not usually look at that sort of advertisement. Krugman (1988), as reported by Wells *et al.* (1992), makes the important point that these readers are passing a 'consumer vote on whether the advertisement is worth more than a passing glance'. It might be that readers' memories are a reliable indicator of what the reader finds attractive in an advertisement and this could be a surrogate indicator for a level of likeability. This proposition has yet to be fully investigated, but it may be that the popularity of the recognition test is based on the validity rating and the approval that high scores give to advertisers.

Sales tests

Counting the number of direct response returns and the number of enquiries received are the only sales-based tests that have any validity.

If the effectiveness of advertisements could be measured by the level of sales that occurs during and after a campaign, then the usefulness of measuring sales as a testing procedure would not be in doubt. However, the practical difficulties associated with market tests are so large that these tests have little purpose. Counting the number of direct response returns and the number of enquiries received are the only sales-based tests that have any validity.

Practitioners have been reluctant to use market-based tests because they are not only expensive to conduct but they are also historical by definition. Sales occur partly as a consequence of past actions, including past communication strategies, and the costs (production, agency and media) have already been sunk. There may be occasions where it makes little political and career sense to investigate an event unless it has been a success, or at the very least reached minimal acceptable expectations.

For these reasons and others, advertisers have used test markets to gauge the impact their campaigns have on representative samples of the national market.

Simulated market tests

By using control groups of matched consumers in particular geographic areas, the use of simulated test markets permits the effect of advertising on sales to be observed under controlled market conditions. These conditions are more realistic than those conducted within a theatre setting and are more representative of the national market than the limited in-house tests. This market representation is thought by some to provide an adequate measure of advertising effect. Other commentators, as discussed before, believe that unless advertising is the dominant element in the marketing mix, there are usually too many other factors which can affect sales. It is therefore unfair and unrealistic to place the sole responsibility for sales with advertising.

Single-source data

With the development and advances in technology it is now possible to correlate consumer purchases with the advertisements they have been exposed to. This is known as single-source data and involves the controlled transmission of advertisements to particular households whose every purchase is monitored through a scanner at supermarket checkouts. In other words, all the research data are derived from the same households.

The advent of cable television has facilitated this process. Consumers along one side of a street receive one set of control advertisements, while the others on the other side receive test advertisements. Single-source data provide exceptionally dependable results, but the technique is expensive, is inappropriate for testing single advertisements and tends to focus on the short-term effect, failing, for example, to cope with the concept of adstock.

Single-source data provide exceptionally dependable results.

In the UK facilities such as Adlab, then ScatScan and Homescan have helped advertisers assess their advertising effectiveness in terms of copy testing, weight testing and even the use of mixed media. The use of split regions can be very important, allowing comparisons to made of different strategies.

Other tests

There is a range of other measures that have been developed in an attempt to understand the effect of advertisements. Among these are tracking studies and financial analyses.

Tracking studies

A tracking study involves interviewing a large number of people on a regular basis, weekly or monthly, with the purpose of collecting data about buyers' perceptions of marketing communication messages, not just advertisements and how these messages might be affecting buyers' perceptions of the brand. By measuring and evaluating the impact of a campaign when it is running, adjustments can be made quickly. The most common elements that are monitored, or tracked, are the awareness levels of an advertisement and the brand, image ratings of the brand and the focus organisation, and attributes and preferences.

Tracking studies can be undertaken on a periodic or continuous basis. The latter is more expensive, but the information generated is more complete and absorbs the effect of competitor's actions, even if the effects are difficult to disaggregate. Sherwood *et al.* (1989) report that, in a general sense, continuous tracking appears more appropriate for new products and periodic tracking more appropriate for established products.

Tracking studies can be undertaken on a periodic or continuous basis.

A further form of tracking study involves monitoring the stock held by retailers. Counts are usually undertaken each month, on a pre- and post-exposure basis. This method of measuring sales is used frequently. Audited sales data, market share figures and return on investment provide other measures of advertising effectiveness.

Tracking studies are also used to measure the impact and effectiveness of online activities. These may be applied to banner ads, email campaigns and paid-for search engine placements and have for a long time been geared to measuring site visitors, clicks through or pages visited. Increasingly these studies are attending to the volume and value of traffic with regard to the behaviour undertaken by site visitors. Behaviour, or the more common term, call-to-action, can be considered in terms of the engagement through exchanges or transactions, the number of site or subscription registrations, the volume of downloads requested or the number of offline triggers such as 'call me buttons' that are activated.

Financial analysis

The vast amount of resources that are directed at planned communications, and in particular advertising, requires that the organisation reviews, on a periodic basis, the amount and the manner in which its financial resources have been used. For some organisations the media spend alone constitutes one of the major items of expenditure. For example, many grocery products incur ingredient, packaging and distribution plus media as the primary costing elements to be managed.

Variance analysis enables a continuous picture of the spend to be developed and acts as an early warning system should unexpected levels of expenditure be incurred. In addition to this and other standard financial controls, the size of the discount obtained from media buying is becoming an important and vital part of the evaluation process.

Increasing levels of accountability and rapidly rising media costs have contributed to the development of centralised media buying. Under this arrangement, the promotion of an organisation's entire portfolio of brands, across all divisions, is contracted to a single media-buying organisation. Part of the reasoning is that the larger the account the greater the buying power an agency has, and this in turn should lead to greater discounts and value of advertising spend. For example, the high street retailer Boots has six major divisions, and each had traditionally been responsible for its own media spend (Izatt, 1993). In 1993 it was decided to centralise the buying under one media-buying centre. The deal, won by BMP DDB Needham, was reported to be worth £45 million a year and is intended to bring advertising economies of scale.

Increasing levels of accountability and rapidly rising media costs have contributed to the development of centralised media buying.

The point is that advertising economies of scale can be obtained by those organisations that spend a large amount of their resources on the media. To accommodate this, centralised buying has developed, which in turn creates higher entry and exit barriers, not only to and from the market but also from individual agencies.

Likeability

A major study by the American Research Foundation investigated a range of different pre-testing methods with the objective of determining which were best at predicting sales success. The unexpected outcome was that, of all the measures and tests, the most powerful predictor was likeability: 'how much I liked the advertisement'.

From a research perspective, much work has been undertaken to clarify the term 'likeability', but it certainly cannot be measured in terms of a simple Likert scale of 'I liked the advertisement a lot', 'I liked the advertisement a little', etc. The term has a much deeper meaning and is concerned with the following issues (Gordon, 1992):

1. personally meaningful, relevant, informative, true to life, believable, convincing;

2. relevant, credible, clear product advantages, product usefulness, importance to 'me';

3. stimulates interest or curiosity about the brand; creates warm feelings through enjoyment of the advertisement.

The implication of these results is that post-testing should include a strong measure of how well an advertisement was liked at its deepest level of meaning.

Cognitive response analysis is an attempt to understand the internal dynamics of how an individual selects and processes messages, of how counter-arguing and message bolstering, for example, might be used to retain or reject an advertisement (see Chapter 19). Biel (1993) reports that there is a growing body of research evidence that links behaviour, attitude change and cognitive processing. He goes on to say that this approach, unlike many of the others, is not restricted to FMCG markets and can be deployed across service markets, durables and retailers.

> Cognitive response analysis is an attempt to understand the internal dynamics of how an individual selects and processes messages.

One of the important points to be made from this understanding of likeability is the linkage with the concept of 'significant value' considered in Chapter 7. The degree to which advertising works is a measure of the impact a message makes with a buyer. This impact is mediated by the context in which messages are sent, received and personally managed. The main factors are that the product in question should be new or substantially different, interesting and stimulating, and personally significant. For advertising to be successful, it must be effective, and to be effective it should be of personally significant value to members of the target audience (those in the market to buy a product from the category in the near future).

The future use of technology will help the measurement and evaluation of advertising. The technology is now in place to meter what people are watching, by appending meters not to sets, but to people. Strapped-on mobile people meters can pick up signals indicating which poster site, TV or radio programme is being walked past, seen or heard respectively.

> The future use of technology will help the measurement and evaluation of advertising.

Sales promotion

The measurement and evaluation of sales promotions are similar in principle to those conducted for advertising. The notion that some piloting should occur prior to launch in order that any wrinkles can be ironed out still holds strong, as does the need to balance qualitative with quantitative data. However, advertising seeks to influence awareness and image over the long term, whereas sales promotions seek to influence behaviour over the short term. As discussed earlier in this chapter, the evaluation of advertising can be imprecise and is subject to great debate. In the same way, the evaluation of sales promotions is subject to debate, but the means by which they are measured is not as ambiguous or as difficult as advertising (Shultz, 1987).

The use of quantitative methods as a testing tool leads to directly measurable and comparable outcomes, in comparison with the more subjective qualitative evaluations. Notionally, the balance in testing advertising is to use a greater proportion of qualitative than quantitative methods. The balance with sales promotions is shifted the other way. This is because the object being measured lends itself more to these kinds of measurement. If the purpose of sales promotion is to influence purchasing behaviour, then a measure of sales performance is necessary in addition to the evaluation of individual promotions.

The different types of sales promotion are discussed in Chapter 24, and there it is identified that there are a number of different target audiences for sales promotions activities; these are resellers, consumers and the sales force.

Manufacturer to reseller

The main objectives are to stimulate the resellers to try new products and to encourage them to allocate increased shelf space for established products. If campaigns are devised to meet these objectives, then a pre- and post-test analysis of the amount of allocated shelf space and the number of new products taken into the reseller's portfolio needs to be completed. These processes are called retail audits (such as those undertaken by Nielsen Marketing Research), and although the information about changes in distribution and stock levels is not usually available until after the promotion has finished, it does provide accurate information concerning the effects that the event had on these variables.

Resellers to consumers

By generating higher levels of store traffic and moving stock from the store shelves to the consumers, sales promotions in this context require two main forms of evaluation. The first requires measures of the image held of the retailer, and this needs the use of tracking studies. The second requires measures of stock turnover per product category or brand against a predetermined planned level of turnover.

Manufacturers to consumers

The objectives are to encourage new users to try a product or to increase the amount that current users consume. Targets can be set for the number of coupons to be redeemed, sales generated during and after a price deal, the volume of bonus packs sold, the speed and volume of premiums disposed of and other direct measures of activity. Consumer audits reveal changes in the penetration and usage patterns of consumers. Redemption levels give some indication of participation levels, but should not be considered as the sole method of evaluation, as there are many people who might be encouraged to purchase by the promotion but who then fail to participate for a variety of reasons.

Targets can be set for the number of coupons to be redeemed.

Manufacturers to sales forces

The objectives of these activities are to build performance, morale and allegiance to the manufacturers and their products. Apart from measuring sales performance, the effectiveness of these activities can be expensive and difficult to measure. Attitude studies of the sales force can indicate the degree to which a contest has been influential, but it is hard to isolate the effects from those of other variables acting on them.

Through systematic tracking of sales and market share, products in mature markets can be evaluated in terms of their responsiveness to sales promotions. This type of information must be treated carefully, as the impact of other environmental factors has not been determined. Redemption rates allow for quantitative analysis, that, through time, leads to the establishment of a database from which benchmarks for promotional measurement and achievement can be obtained.

> Through systematic tracking of sales and market share, products in mature markets can be evaluated in terms of their responsiveness to sales promotions.

Using technology to evaluate sales promotions

It was noted in a previous section on advertising that advances in IT have radically altered the way in which advertising and product purchases can be evaluated. The same applies to sales promotions. It is now possible to predict with a high level of accuracy the impact on sales of different combinations of in-store promotions and price deals (Nielsen, 1993). This permits greater understanding of the way in which different sales promotions work and when they are most effective. This has two main benefits: the first is to focus promotions on activities that are effective; the second is to help to target the communication spend on periods of the year, month and week that consumers are most responsive.

Homescan is an electronic household panel offered by ACNielsen that tracks day-to-day shopping patterns. It measures the household penetration and the retail distribution of a product. ACNielsen uses the system to analyse trial and repeat use and it provides data on consumer buying behaviour across most types of channel. These range from warehouse clubs and convenience stores to supermarkets, mass merchandisers, mail order and the Internet. It can measure the number of households that use the product once and it can then determine how many of these trialists adopt a product through repeat purchase activity. It follows that test promotions can be used in particular stores or geographic areas, and control promotions can be used to test impact and effectiveness. What might work in one area might be unsuccessful elsewhere.

Coupons need not only be distributed via products and media. Technology has been developed that allows coupons of competitive brands to be automatically dispensed at the checkout once a product has been scanned. This information, together with the demographics and psychographic details compiled for panel members, enables detailed profiles to be built up about the types, timing and value of sales promotions to which different consumers respond.

Sales promotions are a competitive tool that allows for swift reaction and placement. In that sense, they are not being used as part of an overall campaign, more as an ad hoc sales boost. This implies that the manageability of sales promotions is very high relative to the other elements of the promotions mix and that the opportunity to pretest might not be as large in practice as is theoretically possible (Peattie and Peattie, 1993).

The evaluation of sales promotion is potentially fast, direct, precise and easily comprehended (Doyle and Saunders, 1985). However, evaluation is not necessarily that clear cut. The synergistic qualities of the promotion mix inevitably lead to cross-over effects where the impact of other communications influences responses to particular sales promotion events. Promotions may also bring about increased awareness in addition to the trial, use and switching activities. Peattie and Peattie suggest that not only might brand and product substitution result from promotions, but store loyalty patterns might also be affected.

> The evaluation of sales promotion is potentially fast, direct, precise and easily comprehended.

Of all the tools in the promotions mix, sales promotions lend themselves more easily to evaluation rather than to testing. Testing is not realistically possible in the time frames in which some organisations operate, particularly those in the FMCG sector. Activities should be planned and research built into campaigns, but it is the availability of improved IT that will continue to improve and accelerate the quality of information that management has about its sales.

Public relations

Each of the two main forms, corporate and marketing public relations, seeks to achieve different objectives and does so by employing different approaches and techniques. However, they are not mutually exclusive and the activities of one form of public relations impact upon the others; they are self-reinforcing.

ViewPoint 17.4   Free Cone Day

For a long time Ben & Jerry's has used public relations to position itself as a socially conscious and environmentally friendly brand. Of the many aspects of its communication work the organisation often tries to gauge its corporate reputation, in addition to message penetration of its commitment to social causes.

One of the brand's important events is its annual Free Cone Day, and when planning the 2003 event a competitive aspect was noticed through mentions in the media. Some of Ben & Jerry's competitors had started similar Free Cone Days and this was picked up through shared mentions in the media.

As a response, Ben & Jerry's teamed up with 'Rock the Vote and Apple for a campaign titled, *ETOV – Turn it Around* ("ETOV" being "vote" spelt backwards)'. The one-day event featured a grand prize from Apple, retained the tradition of giving away free ice cream cones and drew 10,000 voters. As a result Ben & Jerry's secured the vast majority of the media coverage and overcame the shared mentions issue.

Source: Adapted from Iacono (2004).

Corporate public relations (CPR)

The objectives that are established at the beginning of a promotional campaign must form the basis of any evaluation and testing activity. However, much of the work of CPR is continuous, and therefore measurement should not be campaign oriented or time restricted but undertaken on a regular, ongoing basis. CPR is mainly responsible for the identity cues that are presented to the organisation's various stakeholders as part of a planned programme of communications. These cues signal the visibility and profile of the organisation and are used by stakeholders to shape the image that each has of the focus organisation.

CPR is, therefore, focused upon communication activities, such as awareness, but there are others such as preference, interest and conviction. Evaluation should, in the first instance, measure levels of awareness of the organisation. Attention should then focus upon the levels of interest, goodwill and attitudes held towards the organisation as a result of all the planned and unplanned cues used by the organisation.

> Evaluation should, in the first instance, measure levels of awareness of the organisation.

Traditionally these levels were assumed to have been generated by public relations activities. The main method of measuring their contribution to the communication programme was to collect press cuttings and to record the number of mentions the organisation received in the electronic media. These were then collated in a cuttings book that would be presented to the client. This would be similar to an explorer presenting an electric toaster to a tribe of warriors hitherto undisturbed by other civilisations. It looks nice, but what do you do with it and is it of any real use? Despite this slightly cynical interpretation, the cuttings book does provide a rough and ready way of appreciating the level of opportunities to see created by public relations activities.

The content of the cuttings book and the recorded media mentions can be converted into a different currency. The exchange rate used is the cost of the media that would have been incurred had this volume of communication or awareness been generated by advertising activity. For example, a 30-second news item about an organisation's contribution to a charity event may be exchanged for a 30-second advertisement at rate card cost. The temptation is clear, but the validity of the equation is not acceptable. By translating public relations into advertising currency, the client is expected not only to understand but also to approve of the enhanced credibility that advertising possesses. It is not surprising that the widely held notion that public relations is free advertising has grown so substantially when practitioners use this approach.

A further refinement of the cuttings book is to analyse the material covered. The coverage may be positive or negative, approving or disapproving, so the quality of the cuttings needs to be reviewed in order that the client organisation can make an informed judgement about its next set of decisions. This survey of the material in the cuttings book is referred to as a content analysis. Traditionally, content analyses have had to be undertaken qualitatively and were therefore subject to poor interpretation and reviewer bias, however well they approached their task. Today, increasingly sophisticated software is being used to produce a wealth of quantitative data reflecting the key variables that clients want evaluated.

> Traditionally, content analyses have had to be undertaken qualitatively.

Hauss (1993) suggests that key variables could include the type of publication, the favourability of the article, the name of the journalist, the audiences being reached and the type of coverage. All these and others can be built into programmes. The results can then be cross-tabulated so that it is possible to see in which part of the country the most favourable comments are being generated or observe which opinion formers are positively or negatively disposed.

Corporate image

The approaches discussed so far are intended to evaluate specific media activity and comment about the focus organisation. Press releases are fed into the media and there is a response that is measured in terms of positive or negative, for or against. This quality of information, while useful, does not assist the management of the corporate identity. To do this requires an evaluation of the position that an organisation has in the eyes of key members of the performance network. In addition, the information is not specific enough to influence the strategic direction that an organisation has or the speed at which the organisation is changing. Indeed, most organisations now experience perpetual change; stability and continuity are terms related to an environment that is unlikely to be repeated.

The evaluation of the corporate image should be a regular exercise, supported by management. There are three main aspects. First, key stakeholders (including employees, as they are an important source of communications for external stakeholders), together with members of the performance network and customers, should be questioned regarding their perceptions of the important attributes of the focus organisation and the business they are in (Chapter 12). Secondly, how does the organisation perform against each of the attributes? Thirdly, how does the organisation perform relative to its main competitors across these attributes?

The results of these perceptions can be evaluated so that corrective action can be directed at particular parts of the organisation and adjustments made to the strategies pursued at business and functional levels. For example, in the computer retailing business, prompt home delivery is a very important attribute. If company A had a rating of 90 per cent on this attribute, but company B was believed to be so good that it was rated at 95 per cent, regardless of actual performance levels, then although A was doing a superb job it would have to improve its delivery service and inform its stakeholders that it was particularly good at this part of the business.

Recruitment

Recruitment for some organisations can be a problem. In some sectors, where skills are in short supply, the best staff gravitate towards those organisations that are perceived to be better employers and provide better rewards and opportunities. Part of the task of CPR is to provide the necessary communications so that a target pool of employees is aware of the benefits of working with the focus organisation and develops a desire to work there.

Measurement of this aspect of CPR can be seductive. It is tempting just to measure the attitudes of the pool of talent prior to a campaign and then to measure it again at the end. This fails to account for the uncontrollable elements in CPR, for example the actions of others in the market, but, even if this approach is simplistic and slightly erroneous, it does focus attention on an issue. ICI found that it was failing to attract the necessary number of talented undergraduates in the early and mid-1980s, partly because the organisation was perceived as unexciting, bureaucratic and lacking career opportunities. A coordinated marketing communications campaign was targeted at university students, partly at repositioning the organisation in such a way that they would want to work for ICI when they finished their degrees. The results indicated that students' approval of ICI as a future employer rose substantially in the period following the campaign.

Crisis management

During periods of high environmental turbulence and instability, organisations tend to centralise their decision-making processes and their communications (Quinn and Mintzberg, 1992). When a crisis occurs, communications with stakeholders should increase to keep them informed and aware of developments. In Chapter 25, it will be observed that crises normally follow a number of phases, during which different types of information must be communicated. When the crisis is over, the organisation enters a period of feedback and development for the organisation. 'What did we do?', 'How did it happen?', 'Why did we do that?' and 'What do we need to do in the future?' are typical questions that socially aware and mature organisations, which are concerned with quality and the needs of their stakeholders, should always ask themselves.

Pearson and Mitroff (1993) report that many organisations do not expose themselves to this learning process for fear of 'opening up old wounds'. Those organisations that do take action should communicate their actions to reassure all stakeholders that the organisation has done all it can to prevent a recurrence, or at least to minimise the impact should the origin of the crisis be outside the control of management. A further question that needs to be addressed concerns the way the organisation was perceived during the different crisis phases. Was the image consistent? Did it change, and if so why? Management may believe that it did an excellent job in crisis containment, but what really matters is what stakeholders think; it is their attitudes and opinions that matter above all else.

The objective of crisis management is to limit the effect that a crisis might have on an organisation and its stakeholders, assuming the crisis cannot be prevented. The social system in which an organisation operates means that the image held of the organisation may well change as a result of the crisis event. The image does not necessarily become negative. On the contrary, it may be that the strategic credibility of the organisation could be considerably enhanced if the crisis is managed in an open and positive way. However, it is necessary for the image that stakeholders have of an organisation to be tracked on a regular basis. This means that the image and impact of the crisis can be monitored through each of the crisis phases. Sturges *et al.* (1991) argue that the objective of crisis management is to influence public opinion to the point that 'post-crisis opinions of any stakeholder group are at least positive, or more positive, or not more negative than before the crisis event'. This ties in with the need to monitor corporate image on a regular basis. The management process of scanning the environment for signals of change and change in the attitudes and the perception held by stakeholders towards the organisation make up a joint process that public relations activities have a major role in executing.

> The objective of crisis management is to limit the effect that a crisis might have on an organisation and its stakeholders.

Marketing public relations (MPR)

It was identified earlier that there is evidence of the increasing use of MPR. There are many reasons for this growth, but some of the more important ones quoted by organisations are rising media costs, audience fragmentation, changing consumer attitudes and increasing educational needs (Kitchen, 1993). By using public relations to support the marketing effort in a direct way, organisations are acknowledging that the third-party endorsement provided by MPR delivers a high level of credibility and cost effectiveness which the other elements of the promotions mix fail to provide.

As Kitchen rightly argues, MPR cannot exist in a vacuum; it must be integrated with the other elements of the mix and provide complementarity. It is through the use of MPR as a form of product support and as part of a planned communications mix that makes this a source of high-quality leads. However, evaluating the contribution of MPR is problematic.

Some practitioners believe that this can be overcome by coding press releases as a campaign, and with the use of particular software leads can be tracked and costed.

The number of leads that come back can be measured against sales on the database.

With the right software, the actual cost of a press release can be input and the number of leads that come back can be measured against sales on the database.

The software can not only estimate sales but also work out the number of leads required to make quota. The formula used is based on the rule that 45 per cent of leads turn into sales for someone in the market within the year. The organisation's own conversion rate can be used to adjust the 45 per cent and the quality of its lead conversion process can also be input. One of the benefits of this approach is that quantitative outcomes provide a measure of effectiveness, but not necessarily the effectiveness of the MPR campaign.

Pre- and post-test measures of awareness, preference, comprehension and intentions are a better measure of the quality and impact.

Pre- and post-test measures of awareness, comprehension and intentions are a better measure of the quality and impact that an MPR campaign might have on a target audience. Measuring the conversion ratio of leads to sales is not the only measure, as it fails to isolate the other forces that impact on market performance.

MPR in business-to-business markets is directly targeted at members of the performance network. The objectives are many and include building awareness, reducing costs, satisfying educational needs and enhancing image through improving credibility. The overriding need, however, is to improve the relationship between members of the network and to provide them with a reason to continue transactions with the focus organisation. The reasons are similar to those in the personal selling/buying formula (Chapter 28), namely to associate product adequacy when the appropriate problem is surfaced and to create pleasant feelings when the name of the product or the organisation is mentioned in the same context. MPR in this situation is being used as a competitive tool to defend established positions. Measurement of the effectiveness of MPR, therefore, should be undertaken by evaluating the degree to which members support, like, endorse or prefer the focus organisation and the products it offers. This can be achieved through the use of tracking studies that plot attitudes and opinions, against which the timings of campaigns and MPR activities can be traced and evaluated.

Other measuring techniques – PR

Of all the tools available to practitioners, Goften (1999) reports the following as the most common approaches to measuring public relations:

Set objectives and agree the criteria in advance of a campaign.

Press cuttings, radio and TV tapes, but this is a measure of volume and not quality of impact. A media equivalent value is then applied.

Media evaluation through commercial systems such as CAMMA, Impact, Precis. Under this approach, panels of readers judge whether a mention is positive or negative and whether the client's key message has been communicated. Computer programs then cut through the data.

Tracking studies are expensive but are important when changing a perception of a brand, etc.

Both CPR and MPR are difficult and elusive elements of the promotional mix to test, measure and evaluate.

Both CPR and MPR are difficult and elusive elements of the promotional mix to test, measure and evaluate. Practitioners use a variety of methods, but few provide the objectivity and validity that is necessary. For example, Comic Relief monitored the impact of media coverage on the organisation in the run-up to Red Nose Day. It was able to track which initiatives were failing to attract attention and which issues were attracting negative coverage. It evaluated coverage over six key areas: TV initiatives, education, grants (Africa and the UK), special projects, public fundraising and corporate fundraising.

The variety of measurement devices is increasing, especially as technology advances.

ViewPoint 17.5   Monitoring TeleTrax

TeleTrax is an electronic tagging system that can monitor broadcast use of its footage. Using an indelible code embedded within video tapes and through the use of approximately 100 listening posts across Europe, the company is alerted as soon as the tape is broadcast. Unfortunately it does not track the tone of the content. Monitoring the Internet for PR coverage is more taxing.

Net.Cut was set up originally to provide early warning of unfavourable corporate comment on the Internet. It can monitor comment in Internet publications, UK newsgroups and the WWW by searching the WWW at night and saving company mentions. The cuttings are then reviewed the following morning for key messages prior to warning the client as necessary. It costs about £50 a month and each alert costs an extra £1.

If, at the end of the process, evaluation and testing lack objectivity, then the method should not be used. As a greater number of organisations are beginning to recognise the impact that public relations can provide and establish a more credible balance to the promotional mix, so there is a greater requirement for planning and evaluation to be built into the process from the beginning (Watson, 1992).

Sponsorship

The measurement of sponsorship activities is problematic although the importance of doing so is accepted (Armstrong, 1998). The problem concerns the ability to separate the impact of the various elements of the promotional mix, which can be expensive and beyond the reach of smaller brands.

Many organisations attempt to measure the size of the media audience and then treat this as an indicator of effectiveness. This is misleading, as advertising and sponsorship are considered to work in different ways and cannot be measured in a similar way. Audiences consider events (a sports match, exhibition or TV programme) as their primary focus, not which organisation is sponsoring the activity, unlike advertising, where the message either dominates the screen or a page of a magazine and viewers attend according to their perceptual filters. The focus of attention is different, and so should be the means of evaluation.

Advertising and sponsorship are considered to work in different ways and cannot be measured in a similar way.

Marshall and Cook (1992) found that sports sponsors preferred to use consumer surveys to examine customer (not audience) profiles, brand-related images, attitudes and purchasing activities. This was accomplished through the use of personal interviews and telephone and postal surveys. Because the level of funding in many of the smaller sponsorships is relatively low, few if any resources are allocated to evaluative practices.

Taylor Nelson *So*fres provides a single-source data panel through which the viewing habits and purchase behaviour of a representative panel of consumers are monitored through a system called TVSpan 3000. Unlike similar competitive offerings, TVSpan 3000 uses data from 3,000 homes where TV set meters are installed that monitor each household's live television viewing, minute by minute. These homes are also equipped with AGB Superpanel scanning equipment for recording details of purchases of FMCG products. One of its prime tasks is to enable clients to monitor purchase behaviour and test advertisements at either pre- or post-test stage. Further uses are to test new creative ideas, to test the effects of advertising with or without below-the-line support and, interestingly, to test the interaction between advertising and sponsorship (Thorncroft, 1996).

The main way in which sponsorship activities should be measured is through the objectives set at the outset.

The main way in which sponsorship activities should be measured is through the objectives set at the outset. By measuring performance rigorously against clearly defined sales and communication-based measures it is more likely that a reasonable process and outcome to the sponsorship activity will be established.

Personal selling

In contrast to the other elements of the promotional mix, personal selling requires different methods of evaluation. Pre- and post-testing the performance of each salesperson is impractical and inappropriate. What is more pertinent for evaluation are the inputs and the effectiveness (measured as outcomes) of the personal selling process. Oliver (1990) suggests that performance can be seen as a factor of the effort and costs (inputs) that an organisation contributes. Outputs can be regarded as sales and profits resulting from exchanges with customers, while productivity can be deemed to be the ratio of inputs to outputs (see Figure 17.1).

Productivity can be deemed to be the ratio of inputs to outputs.

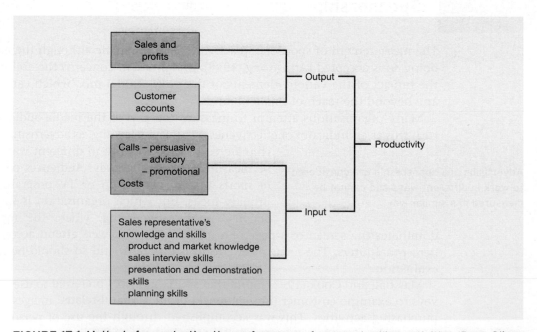

FIGURE 17.1 Methods for evaluating the performance of personal selling activities (From Oliver (1990); used with kind permission.)

This is a useful approach because it focuses attention on aspects of the promotional process that can be measured with the use of quantitative tools. This contrasts with the other tools, where qualitative measures generally predominate. In addition to this framework, it is necessary to measure the effectiveness of the sales force as a unit and the degree to which interdepartmental cooperation is achieved in synchronising the activities of the mix.

Evaluating the performance of a salesperson

The performance of a salesperson requires the use of both qualitative and quantitative methods. There are two main types of inputs to the sales process. The first of these consists of the activities undertaken and the costs incurred as a result. The second type of input concerns the knowledge and skills necessary to achieve the required outputs. These will be examined in turn.

Measuring and then evaluating the activities of each salesperson, the inputs, is an important and frequently used measuring stick. The number of planned and unplanned sales calls, the number of presentations, the frequency with which the showroom has been used and the mix of accounts visited, plus the expenses, cost of samples used and time associated with these activities, can be measured and evaluated against organisational standards and expectations. These simple quantitative measures provide for objectivity and measurement; what they do not do is provide an insight into why the input and the ultimate performance rating did or did not achieve the required standard.

Measuring and evaluating the knowledge component of the input dimension require greater subjectivity and reliance on qualitative measures. How well a salesperson uses his or her selling skills and presents him- or herself to customers is vitally important. In addition, the depth of knowledge that the subject has of the products, customers, territory and market will probably have a greater bearing on the performance outcome than the number of visits made. In other words, it is the quality of the sales call that is important, not the number of sales calls made. As Churchill *et al.* (1990) claim, the measurement of these qualitative aspects 'must invariably rely on the personal judgement of the individual or individuals charged with evaluation'.

Outputs are more easily measured than inputs. The most common technique used is that of the ratings attached to the volume or value of sales generated in a particular period in a designated area. Using a quota to measure achievement can be important for consistent tracking of performance and for motivational purposes. Volume analysis allows management to measure the effectiveness of the sales process, as comparisons can be drawn with last year's performance, with other salespersons (with similar territory potential) and with the potential in the territory.

Outputs are more easily measured than inputs.

Ratios provide a further insight into the overall performance and productivity of a salesperson. Expense ratios are a useful tool for understanding the way in which a salesperson is managing the territory. The cost/call ratio, for example, reveals the extent to which the subject is making calls and the costs of supporting the individual in the territory. Further detailed analyses are possible, for example travel expenses/call:

$$\text{sales expense ratio} = \frac{\text{expenses}}{\text{sales}}$$

$$\text{cost per call ratio} = \frac{\text{total costs}}{\text{number of calls}}$$

Servicing ratios reveal the extent to which a territory's business potential has been acquired, for example what percentage of a territory's accounts has been won, how many prospects become customers, how many customers are lost and what level of sales are achieved on average per customer or per call:

$$\text{account penetration ratio} = \frac{\text{accounts sold into}}{\text{total number of available accounts}}$$

$$\text{average order size ratio} = \frac{\text{total sales value}}{\text{total number of orders}}$$

$$\text{new account ratio} = \frac{\text{number of new accounts}}{\text{total number of accounts}}$$

The final group, activity ratios, determines the effort that is put into a territory. Calls/day, calls/account type and orders/call reveal the amount of planning and thought that is being put into an area:

$$\text{calls/accounts ratio} = \frac{\text{number of calls made}}{\text{total number of accounts}}$$

$$\text{orders/calls ratio} = \frac{\text{number of orders}}{\text{total number of calls}}$$

$$\text{calls/week ratio} = \frac{\text{number of calls}}{\text{number of weeks worked}}$$

In isolation these ratios provide some objectivity when attempting to measure the performance of a salesperson. Used in combination they become a more powerful tool, but only to the extent that they are an aid to decision-making. One major advantage of ratio analysis is the benchmarking effect. Comparisons become possible not only across the sales force but also across the industry, as norms become established through time.

While the traditional measure has been volume, increased emphasis is being placed upon measures of profitability, an efficiency measure (Burnett, 1993). The level of gross margin achieved by each salesperson and the contribution each makes to the overall profitability of the organisation are regarded by many organisations as more important than measures of volume. The approach requires the involvement of each salesperson not only in achieving the outcomes but also in the process of setting the appropriate performance targets in the first place. This requires different types of training and skills development, which in turn will affect the expectations held by each member of the sales force.

Evaluating the performance of a sales force

The methods looked at so far have been used to evaluate the performance of individual salespersons. An overall measure of the effectiveness of the larger unit, the sales force, is also necessary. The following constitute the main areas of evaluation: the objectives set in the promotion mix, the level of interaction with the other elements of the promotion mix, activity measures and achievement against quota, the effectiveness of the sales channels used and the quality of the relationships established with customers.

The sales force, as a part of the promotion mix, has a responsibility to achieve the sales objectives set out in the promotion objectives. To do this the sales force needs the support of the other elements of the mix. Measuring this interdisciplinary factor is extremely difficult, but there is no doubt that each of the elements works more efficiently if they are coordinated with one another and the messages conveyed dovetail and reinforce each other.

Many of the measures used to evaluate the performance of individual salespersons can also be aggregated and used to evaluate the performance of the sales force as a whole. The sales force will have an overall sales budget, usually by volume and value, against which actual performance can be measured. The sales force will also be expected to open an agreed number of accounts each period and the value of business as a proportion of the potential will be watched closely.

There is no doubt that the role of the sales force is changing. If the expectations of the sales force are being adapted to new environmental conditions, it is probable that alternative measures will be required to determine the progress that a sales force is making. For example, in business-to-business markets, the traditional approach of the sales force is to manage products and their allocation to selected customers. The sales force of the future is going to be responsible, to a much greater degree, for the management of customer relationships (Wilson, 1993) and the maintenance of relational transactions that will provide organisations with strategic advantage. The use of simple quantitative techniques to measure the performance of the sales force will decline, the use of qualitative techniques will become more prevalent and the techniques themselves will become sophisticated. Measures will be required to evaluate the quality of the relationships developed by the sales force rather than the quantity of outputs achieved in a particular period. The traditional emphasis upon short-term quota achievement may well change to a focus upon long-term customer alliances and an evaluation of the strength of the relationship held between partners.

One further area of evaluation that is necessary is that of the sales channels themselves. The increased use of multiple sales channels and the contribution that direct marketing will make to the sales force cannot be ignored. Measures are required of the effectiveness of the field sales force, the key account selling team and the array of direct marketing techniques. Constant monitoring of the market is required to judge whether the classification of an account should be changed, and whether different combinations of selling approaches should be introduced.

Customers need to be involved in the sales channel decision process and in the evaluation of the field sales force.

Finally, customers need to be involved in the sales channel decision process and in the evaluation of the field sales force. If customers are happy with a sales channel, then they are more likely to continue using it. It is vital that the views of customers are monitored regularly and that they contribute to the evaluation process.

The evaluation of the sales force and its individual members has for a long time been oriented to quantitative measures of input and output productivity. These are useful, as they provide for comparison within the organisation and with the industry norms. However, in future, evaluation will move from revenue to a profit perspective and much greater emphasis will be placed upon the quality of the relationships that the sales force develops with their customers. The current imbalance between the use of quantitative and qualitative measures will shift to a position where qualitative measures become more important in evaluating the performance of the sales force.

Online communications

Online research has grown as the Internet population has soared and the measures used have developed through trial and experience.

Banner ads

Not surprisingly there is disagreement about whether it is possible to measure effectively online advertising. Dreze and Zurfryden (1998) rightly point out that as a viable advertising media, Internet advertising must be subject to suitable measurement standards to gauge the effectiveness of the medium. Web servers can indicate how many pages have been requested, the time spent on each page and even the type of computers that were used to request the page. However, this type of information is largely superficial and fails to provide insight into the user, their motivation to visit the site or the behavioural or attitudinal outcomes as a result of the interaction. Traditional measurement techniques of reach, frequency and target audience impressions are not capable of being readily transferred to the Internet.

Others argue that it is possible to measure online tools. For example, Briggs and Hollis (1997) point out that one of the more common measures used is the click-through rate. They indicate, however, that this normally only measures behaviour, whereas what is needed is an indicator of the user's attitudes. They claim to have developed a technique to measure attitudes (online) and show that banner advertising can be one of the most effective forms of advertising and brand development.

Web site effectiveness

Johnston cited by Gray (2000) reports that ACNielsen offers a 9,000 strong panel in the UK. The panel consists of Internet users who have special software loaded on their PCs that records every Web page they visit. The strengths and weaknesses of online qualitative and quantitative research are shown in Tables 17.3 and 17.4.

Good marketing management practice suggests that evaluation of any management activity should always include a consideration of the degree to which the objectives have been satisfied. However, the reasons organisations have for setting up a Web site are many and varied: these might be to establish a Web presence, to move to new methods of commercial activity, to enter new markets, to adhere to parent company

TABLE 17.3 Online quantitative research

Strengths	Weaknesses
Relatively inexpensive	Respondent universe
Fast turnaround	Sampling issues: narrow target audience and difficult to identify
Automated data collection	Often self-completion, hence subject to self-selection
Can show graphics and video	Technical problems
No interviewer bias	
Quality of data	
Seamless international coordination	

TABLE 17.4 Online qualitative research

Strengths	Weaknesses
Slightly faster and cheaper than traditional focus group	Loss of non-verbal communications
Avoids the dominance of loud personalities	Less useful for emotional issues
More client control	Online moderation requires new skills pattern
Can show concepts and/or Web sites	Slow keyboard skills can hamper some respondents
Allows for international coordination and permits mixed nationalities	Technical problems Sampling issues: difficult to identify a narrow target audience

TABLE 17.5 Criteria to assess Web site effectiveness

Visitor type	Cognitive state	Management action
All surfers	Level of awareness that a site exists: aware or not aware	Provide off-line and online information and directions
Those aware	Level of interest in the site: interested or not interested	Create interest and curiosity
Those interested	Known route to the site: determined or accidental	Enable greater opportunities for site hit
Determined visitors	Was the visit completed successfully? Transaction or no transaction	Encourage bookmarking and post-purchase communication to permit legitimate dialogue
Those who transacted	Will these visitors return to the site? Retained or not retained	Maintain and enhance top-of-mind site recall

Source: Adapted from Berthon *et al.* (1996); used with kind permission.

demands or to supplement current distribution channels. Consequently, it is not practicable to set up a definitive checklist to use as a measure of Web site effectiveness, although certain principles need to be followed.

One of the basic approaches is to develop profiles of Web site visitors built up by presenting every tenth visitor with a questionnaire. The next stage will be to provide media planners with these data to optimise banner ad placement. Based upon the work of Berthon *et al.* (1996), Table 17.5 suggests the criteria that might be used to test a site's effectiveness, but different criteria will have a different impact depending upon each organisation's situation.

Dreze and Zurfryden (1998) were apprehensive of the difficulties associated with measuring the number of unique site visitors, mainly because of various technology-related factors and the difficulties of isolating who is a unique visitor.

As mentioned earlier in this chapter, tracking studies are used to measure online brand values (site visits) and various forms of calls-to-action.

Summary

The evaluation of a marketing communications plan, once implemented, is an essential part of the total system. The evaluation provides a potentially rich source of material for the next campaign and the ongoing communications that all organisations operate, either intentionally or not.

The degree to which the promotional objectives set for a campaign (Chapter 13) have been achieved has to be the focus of the evaluation process. The next important factor is the measurement of the contribution each part of the marketing communications mix may have made. Again, this can be determined from a holistic perspective or it can be usefully explored by employing some of the particular techniques and methodologies outlined in this chapter.

It would appear that, should resources be made available and should management appreciate the importance of measuring the effectiveness of their investment in marketing communications, then testing before and after exposure to each campaign activity is advisable, in order that a degree of change can be determined. While pre- and post-testing is normally an advertising-related approach the principle can be applied across all the tools of the mix, to some extent.

There are many issues involved with the assessment of each of the tools of the promotional mix, some associated with their individual characteristics. There is no perfect or ideal technique, but research must be undertaken if the communication performance of an offering is to be built or maintained. An important question is why so many managers choose not to measure effectiveness. The immediate answer is that all managers do measure the effectiveness as demonstrated through their observation of the sales results at the end of each period. However, proper testing and analysis is a practice rejected for many reasons. Some of the more prevalent ones are that research uses resources which some managers would prefer to sink into the product, to build sales or to build market awareness.

There can be disagreement about what is to be researched on the grounds that the many different people associated with a campaign have different needs, and as the budget is restricted the net result is that there is no research. Others argue that as it is very difficult, if not impossible, to isolate the effects of one particular tool, why waste resources on testing?

All these points can and should be refuted. Only by attempting to measure effectiveness will our understanding improve and lead to a more effective utilisation and more efficient use of marketing communications. Sales measurement is used most commonly because it is relatively cheap to administer and quick to implement, and to many managers sales and profits are derived from communications (and advertising in particular), so this constitutes the only meaningful measure.

Review questions

1. If the process is difficult and the outcomes imprecise, why should organisations evaluate and monitor their marketing communications?

2. What is pre- and post-testing?

3. Write a brief report comparing recall and recognition tests.

4. What are the principal dimensions of likeability as a measure of advertising effectiveness?

5. Identify four ways in which sales promotions can be evaluated.

6. Write brief notes explaining why the use of media comparison techniques are insufficient when measuring the impact of public relations.

7. Why should the measurement of sales results be considered an inadequate measure of personal selling performance?

8. What are the techniques used to measure Web site effectiveness? Are they any good?

9. Many organisations fail to undertake suitable research to measure the success of their campaigns. Why is this and what can be done to change this situation?

10. Comment on the view that, if a method of evaluation and testing lacks objectivity and testing, then the method should not be used.

MINI-CASE
Not as simple as black and white

Developing an anti-racism campaign for Scotland
TNS (formerly NFO WorldGroup Edinburgh) and the Scottish Executive

Mini-case written by Chris Eynon, Managing Director – TNS System Three; Julie Tinson, Lecturer, University of Stirling

Background

On the surface, racism was not a significant issue in Scotland, yet police records suggested otherwise. From 2,242 racist incidents reported to the police in 1998–9, the latest figures showed that these had risen in number to over 3,000 in 2000–1. At the time of the research this was likely to represent an increase of approximately 50 per cent in reported racist incidents over a period of two years.

To the Scottish Executive, it was clear that racism was indeed a growing problem in Scotland and one that needed to be addressed before the situation worsened. A mass media campaign was identified as having a key role to play, not only in raising public awareness of racism as a very real concern for Scotland but also in influencing attitudes and behaviour in support of a more racially cohesive society.

Objectives

The objectives of the research programme were relatively straightforward:

● To explore current beliefs, attitudes and behaviour among the population of Scotland on race-related issues, first to establish beyond doubt the need for an anti-racism campaign, and secondly to facilitate creative development for this campaign.

● To evaluate alternative strategies and routes for the campaign in terms of potential impact,

EXHIBIT 17.1 The Scottish flag used to symbolise unity and the people of Scotland all pulling together to eradicate racism

communication and effectiveness in meeting campaign objectives. This encompassed both overall theme/branding and specific executional approaches.

● To set up a mechanism for monitoring the effectiveness of the campaign in meeting its objectives over time. It was strongly believed that, to change behaviour, attitudes must first be changed.

Key findings

The research programme was evolutionary, involving both quantitative and qualitative approaches in sequential stages conducted by TNS.

The research confirmed that Scots are to a large extent in denial and that racism is an important issue for Scotland. There is a reluctance to accept that Scots are anything other than warm and friendly towards people from other backgrounds who live in Scotland. Similarly, the vast majority are not inclined to recognise racist tendencies in their own attitudes or behaviour.

However, the extent to which one acknowledges the existence of racism depends largely on how this is defined. The research identified the tendency to associate racism primarily with behaviour rather than attitudes, and with intent to offend. In many cases,

then, what might be construed as racist behaviour may occur through ignorance or lack of understanding, such as use of colloquial language.

Shaping the campaign

It was evident from the research that a 'traditional' hard-hitting, aggressive campaign along the lines of 'Don't be racist', as requested by many from minority ethnic community pressure groups, would achieve little. Indeed it was likely to be counter-productive and serve only to exacerbate the situation as most Scots do not accept there is a problem and it could be seen as anti-white.

In contrast, there was general support from both indigenous white Scots and members of minority ethnic communities for a more positive and inclusive approach, encapsulated in the campaign theme and strapline of 'One Scotland. Many cultures'. This sought to motivate rather than accuse or put on the defensive by appealing to national pride and aspiration for Scotland as a diverse country where all live and work together for the benefit of all. It is significant that, across all media and creative executions, the word 'racism' is featured on only one poster. At the same time, the campaign recognised the need to challenge the comfortable perception of

Scotland as non-racist, and to educate on what does in fact constitute racist attitudes and behaviour, for all the lack of intent. This was achieved through a combination of executions.

The Scottish Executive and Barkers Advertising created a bold and imaginative campaign to tackle racism in Scotland, and the TNS research programme played a major role in informing its development.

Supporting material

Campaign launch

The campaign used a range of media, including television, cinema, radio and outdoor.

The contribution of the research to the campaign development was recognised at its launch to the news media on 24 September 2002. In her launch address the Minister for Social Justice referred to 'a campaign based on solid research'.

Campaign impact and effectiveness

Although the initial burst of the campaign lasted only five weeks, a further omnibus wave was conducted immediately following this, primarily to establish campaign cut-through (claimed spontaneous recall of the ad), reach, recognition and communication. Attitudinal measures were also repeated, to detect any immediate effect on public opinion. Among the key findings were the following:

● verified cut-through level of 44 per cent for the television ads, demonstrating high impact;

● overall reach of 66 per cent;

● 70 per cent recognition of the strapline 'One Scotland. Many cultures';

● higher recognition of different types of behaviour as racist among those aware of the campaign, directly reflecting incidents featured in the ads;

● perceptions of racism as at least a serious problem in Scotland increasing to 61 per cent from 56 per cent at the previous wave, and significantly higher among those aware of the campaign (65 per cent) than those unaware (53 per cent).

Questions

1 What are the factors other than the advertising campaign that might influence the target audience and how can these issues be addressed?

2 Why was the research so significant and effective in facilitating the communications approach and to what extent does this illustrate an integrated campaign?

3 What are the problems of measuring and monitoring the success of a campaign such as this?

References

Armstrong, C. (1998) Sport sponsorship: a case study approach to measuring its effectiveness. *European Research*, **16**(2), pp. 97–103.

Berthon, P., Pitt, L. and Watson, R. (1996) The world wide web as an advertising medium: toward an understanding of conversion efficiency. *Journal of Advertising Research*, **6**(1) (January/February), pp. 43–53.

Biel, A.L. (1993) Ad research in the US. *Admap* (May), pp. 27–9.

Briggs, R. and Hollis, N. (1997) Advertising on the Web: is there response before click-through? *Journal of Advertising Research*, **37**(2), pp. 33–46.

Burnett, J. (1993) *Promotion Management*. New York: Houghton Mifflin.

Churchill, G.A., Ford, N.M. and Walker, C. (1990) *Sales Force Management*. Homewood, IL: Irwin.

Colinese, R. (1997) Pretesting in the press. *Admap* (June), pp. 53–5.

Doyle, P. and Saunders, J. (1985) The lead effect of marketing decisions. *Journal of Marketing Research*, **22**(1), pp. 54–65.

Dreze, X. and Zurfryden, F. (1998) Is Internet advertising ready for prime time? *Journal of Advertising Research* (May/June), pp. 7–18.

Farrow, C. (1999) If it doesn't sell it isn't creative . . . true or false? *Marketing News* (October/ November), pp. 4–5.

Fendwick, P. (1996) The four ages of ad evaluation. *Admap* (April), pp. 25–7.

Flesch, R. (1974) *The Art of Readable Writing*. New York: Harper & Row.

Goften, K. (1999) The measure of PR. *Campaign Report*, 2 April, p. 13.

Gordon, W. (1992) Ad pre-testing's hidden maps. *Admap* (June), pp. 23–7.

Gray, R. (2000) The relentless rise of online research. *Marketing*, 18 May, p. 41.

Hauss, D. (1993) Measuring the impact of public relations. *Public Relations Journal* (February), pp. 14–21.

Iacono, E. (2004) Making measurement count. *PR Week USA*, 15 November. Retrieved 4 January 2005 from www.brandrepublic.com/news/newsArticle.

Izatt, J. (1993) Swayed Boots. *Media Week*, 1 October, pp. 20–1.

Kitchen, P.J. (1993) Public relations: a rationale for its development and usage within UK fast-moving consumer goods firms. *European Journal of Marketing*, **27**(7), pp. 53–75.

Krugman, H.E. (1988) Point of view: limits of attention to advertising. *Journal of Advertising Research*, **38**, pp. 47–50.

Lodish, L.M. and Lubetkin, B. (1992) General truths? *Admap* (February), pp. 9–15.

Marshall, D.W. and Cook, G. (1992) The corporate (sports) sponsor. *International Journal of Advertising*, **11**, pp. 307–24.

Mazur, L. (1993) Qualified for success? *Marketing*, 23 January, pp. 20–2.

Nielsen, A.C. (1993) Sales promotion and the information revolution. *Admap* (January), pp. 80–5.

Oliver, G. (1990) *Marketing Today*. 3rd edn. Hemel Hempstead: Prentice Hall.

Pearson, C.M. and Mitroff, I. (1993) From crisis prone to crisis prepared: a framework for crisis management. *Academy of Management Executive*, **7**(1), pp. 48–59.

Peattie, K. and Peattie, S. (1993) Sales promotion: playing to win. *Journal of Marketing Management*, **9**, pp. 255–69.

Quinn, J.B. and Mintzberg, H. (1992) *The Strategy Process*. 2nd edn. Englewood Cliffs, NJ: Prentice-Hall.

Randrup R. (2004) Why newspaper ads are effective. *Admap*, **39**(6) June, pp. 47–9.

Reid, A. (2000) Testing Times. *Campaign*, 22 September, p. 40.

Sherwood, P.K., Stevens, R.E. and Warren, W.E. (1989) Periodic or continuous tracking studies: matching methodology with objectives. *Market Intelligence and Planning*, **7**, pp. 11–13.

Shultz, D.E. (1987) Above or below the line? Growth of sales promotion in the United States. *International Journal of Advertising*, **6**, pp. 17–27.

Staverley, N.T. (1993) Is it right . . . will it work? *Admap* (May), pp. 23–6.

Sturges, D.L., Carrell, B.J., Newsom, D.A. and Barrera, M. (1991) Crisis communication management: the public opinion node and its relationship to environmental nimbus. *SAM Advanced Management Journal* (Summer), pp. 22–7.

Thorncroft, A. (1996) Business arts sponsorship: arts face a harsh set of realities. *Financial Times*, 4 July, p. 1.

Vaughn, R. (1980) How advertising works: a planning model. *Journal of Advertising Research* (October), pp. 27–33.

Watson, T. (1992) Evaluating PR effects. *Admap* (June), pp. 28–30.

Wells, W., Burnett, J. and Moriarty, S. (1992) *Advertising: Principles and Practice*. 2nd edn. Englewood Cliffs, NJ: Prentice-Hall.

Wilson, K. (1993) Managing the industrial sales force of the 1990s. *Journal of Marketing Management*, 9, pp. 123–9.

Zielske, H.A. (1982) Does day-after recall penalise 'feeling' ads? *Journal of Advertising Research*, **22**(1), pp. 19–22.

The marketing communications mix: disciplines and applications

Part
4

Chapters 18-29

This part of the book explores both the nature and characteristics of the various tools or disciplines of the marketing communication mix as well as the various media necessary to carry marketing communication messages to target audiences.

Chapter 18 builds on previous work in Chapter 7 and considers the various models and concepts that have been developed to explain advertising strategy. The following chapter complements this by examining the issues associated with the way in which messages are constructed in order that the intended meaning is conveyed and understood by the target audience.

Chapters 20 and 21 consider the various media, both traditional (off-line) and new (on-line), that are used to deliver messages. Chapter 22 builds on this and examines some of the key issues that arise when planning media usage.

Chapters 23 and 24 look at sales promotion, Chapters 25 and 26 consider public relations and sponsorship respectively, while Chapters 27 and 28 look at direct marketing and personal selling.

The final chapter in this part of the book looks at some of the remaining disciplines, albeit those that do not necessarily command the major share of most communication budgets. Nevertheless, they are important sub-disciplines and many clients are beginning to put an increasing amount of resources into exhibition work, product placement, field marketing and packaging.

Advertising and strategy

18

An attempt to understand how advertising might work must be cautioned by an appreciation of the complexity and contradictions inherent in this commercial activity. Understanding how advertising might work, with its rich mosaic of perceptions, emotions, attitudes, information and patterns of behaviour, has been a challenge for many eminent researchers, authors and marketing professionals.

Aims and objectives

The aims of this chapter are to explore the different views about advertising strategy and to consider the complexities associated with understanding how clients can best use advertising.

The objectives of this chapter are to:

1. consider the role advertising plays in both consumer and business-to-business markets;
2. introduce the principal frameworks by which advertising is thought to influence individuals;
3. appraise the strong and weak theories of advertising;
4. present the alphabetical model of advertising;
5. evaluate the FCB grid as a tool for strategy development;
6. use the Rossiter–Percy grid as a means of creating strategic direction.

Introduction

The purpose of an advertising plan is to provide the means by which appropriate messages are devised and delivered to target audiences who then act in appropriate ways. This may be to buy a product, to enquire about a product or simply memorise a single aspect for future action. Guidelines for the content and delivery of messages are derived from an understanding of the variety of contexts in which the messages are to be used. For example, research might reveal a poor brand image relative to the market leader, or the different or changing media habits of target consumers. The nature of the messages and the problems to be addressed will be specified in the promotional objectives and strategy.

An advertising plan is composed, essentially, of three main elements:

1. the message, or what is to be said;
2. the media, or how the message will be conveyed;
3. the timing, or manner in which the message will be carried.

This chapter is the first of several about advertising. This one explores two main advertising issues, the first is about the way advertising might work, and consideration is given to some of the principal models and frameworks that have been devised to best describe the process by which advertising works. The second issue focuses on the strategic use of advertising, and the chapter is used to introduce a number of concepts and frameworks that have contributed to our understanding. The chapter builds on the ideas about how marketing communications might work (Chapter 7) and shares some common thoughts. Chapter 19 considers the content of the advertising message, or what is to be said. Chapter 20 looks at the characteristics of a variety of traditional media that are available to carry client messages. Chapter 21 explores the characteristics of online and interactive media; while the final chapter in this advertising section focuses upon media planning. In particular attention is given to the timing and scheduling of the selected media plus a consideration of issues concerning the way in which people use and switch between media.

The role of advertising

The role of advertising in the promotional plan is an important one. Advertising, whether it be on an international, national, local or direct basis, is important, as it can influence audiences by informing or reminding them of the existence of a brand, or alternatively by persuading or helping them differentiate a product or organisation from others in the market.

Advertising can reach huge audiences with simple messages.

Advertising can reach huge audiences with simple messages that present opportunities to allow receivers to understand what a product is, what its primary function is and how it relates to all the other similar products. This is the main function of advertising: to communicate with specific audiences. These audiences may be consumer or organisation based, but wherever they are located the prime objective is to build or maintain awareness of a product or an organisation.

Advertising cannot be said to have a single role as it can be used to achieve a number of outcomes. In DRIP terminology it can be used to differentiate and position brands, it can be used to reinforce brand messages, and it can easily inform and even persuade audiences to think and behave about and around products, services, brands and organisations. However, apart from its ability to reach large audiences, the key strengths of advertising have been to develop brand awareness, values and associations.

Management's control over advertising messages is strong; indeed, of all the elements in the promotional mix, advertising has the greatest level of control. The message, once generated and signed off by the client, can be transmitted in an agreed manner and style and at times that match management's requirements. This means that, should the environment change unexpectedly, advertising messages can be 'pulled' immediately. For example, if a campaign to encourage rail travel had been

Management's control over advertising messages is strong.

planned for December 2004, it would have to have been 'pulled' (stopped) in November following the fatalities and injuries caused as a result of the Berkshire rail crash. Difficulties associated with clearing the line and restoring rail services, plus the wider debate concerning the nature of the accident, the appropriateness of unmanned crossings and the potential of further 'accidents', would have prevented promotional messages from being received and processed in an unbiased and objective manner. It is more likely that there would have been a negative effect had the planned advertising been allowed to proceed.

ViewPoint 18.1   easyAdvertising

Rather than concentrate on differentiation or the development of brand awareness, the role of advertising at easyJet appears to be essentially about reinforcement. The airline undertakes substantial levels of in-house public relations. This is used to drive awareness levels, and is accomplished by the successful television docu-soap called 'Airline'. This fly-on the-wall-type programme, which draws audiences of over 8 million, is about the everyday working life of easyJet's staff and customers at Luton airport.

All tickets are booked online so advertising's role is partly to drive site traffic. This is typified by the use of sales promotions, which are all linked to the Internet. This means customers must go online if they wish to take advantage of promotional fares.

The advertising strategy therefore, is intended to reinforce the easyJet brand values that are based around the idea of 'consumer champion' and to drive customers to its Web site. The advertising also serves to position the easyJet brand based slightly on anarchy as well price and value for money. Interestingly the media used are essentially press, outdoor and radio plus use of its own aircraft as flying billboards. Television is not used partly because of the exposure generated by the docu-soap, partly because of the targeting and costs, and partly because of the effectiveness of the media used.

Advertising costs can be regarded in one of two ways. On the one hand, there are the absolute costs, which are the costs of buying the space in magazines or newspapers or the time on television, cinema or radio. These costs can be enormous, and they impact directly on cash flow. For example, the rate card cost of a full-page (mono) advertisement in the *Daily Mail* was £32,508 (November 2004) and a single 30-second spot, each day for one week, in the Odeon Cinema, Leicester Square in London cost £1,160 (November 2004).

On the other hand, there are the relative costs, which are those costs incurred to reach a member of the target audience with the key message. So, if an audience is measured in hundreds of thousands, or even millions on television, the cost of the advertisement spread across each member of the target audience reduces the cost per contact significantly. This aspect is developed further in Chapter 22.

The main roles of advertising are to build awareness, induce an engagement (if only on a cognitive basis) and to (re)position brands, by changing either perception or attitudes. The regular use of advertising, in cooperation with the other elements of the communication mix, can be important to the creation and maintenance of a brand personality. Indeed, advertising has a significant role to play in the development of competitive advantage. In some consumer markets advertising is a dominant form of promotion. Advertising can become a mobility barrier, deterring exit and, more importantly, deterring entry to a market by organisations attracted by the profits of the industry. Many people feel that some brands sustain their large market share by sheer weight of advertising; for example, the washing powder brands of Procter & Gamble and Unilever.

> The main roles of advertising are to build awareness, induce an engagement and to (re)position brands.

Advertising can create competitive advantage by providing the communication necessary for target audiences to frame a product. By providing a frame or the perceptual space with which to pigeonhole a product, target audiences are able to position an offering relative to their other significant products much more easily. Therefore, advertising can provide the means for differentiation and sustainable competitive advantage. It should also be appreciated, however, that differentiation may be determined by the quality of execution of the advertisements, rather than through the content of the messages.

Advertising can also be regarded as an anchor for many integrated campaigns. Normally, it is necessary to use advertising to build awareness and to develop brands. Indeed, the explosion in the number of dotcom businesses and the flurry of stock market flotations that many sought in 1999 were largely driven by the use of some television and print advertising but also by a huge amount of outdoor 48- and 96-sheet poster work, trying to raise awareness of the dotcom brands and drive traffic to their Web sites. In addition, public relations and sales promotions are more effective when advertising is used to raise initial awareness and shape attitudes respectively.

> Advertising can also be regarded as an anchor for many integrated campaigns.

Advertising in the business-to-business market is geared, primarily, to providing relevant factual information upon which 'rational' decisions can be made. Regardless of the target audience, all advertising requires a message and a carrier to deliver the message to the receiver. This text will concentrate on these two main issues, while acknowledging the wider role that advertising plays in society.

Emotion in advertising

The preceding material, if taken at face value, suggests that advertising only works by people responding to advertising in a logical, rational and cognitive manner. It also suggests that people only take out the utilitarian aspect of advertising messages (cleans better, smells fresher). This is obviously not true and there is certainly a strong case for the use of emotion in advertising in order to influence and change attitudes through the affective component of the attitudinal dimensions (Chapter 5).

> There is certainly a strong case for the use of emotion in advertising in order to influence and change attitudes.

ViewPoint 18.2   Emotion-led Tesco

Emotion in advertising can be expressed in many different ways. From 1995 to 2004 Tesco used the actresses Prunella Scales and Jane Horrocks as a slightly zany and demanding mother (called Dotty) and forbearing daughter respectively. The emotion is displayed through the various scenes where the 'mother of all shoppers' is depicted demanding more and more from Tesco employees. The message was invariably about communicating low prices, a wide range of goods, and excellent customer service despite the provocation.

In one of the many ads, Dotty was shown hauling her pregnant daughter out of ante-natal classes just to register for a Tesco Clubcard. In another she buys large carrots simply to plant in her own garden to impress a visitor. The ads had a sit-com feel to them that involved and entertained viewers while developing trust and goodwill.

It should also be remembered that advertised brands are not normally new to consumers as they have some experience of the brand, whether that be through use or just through communications. This experience affects their interpretation of advertising as memories have already been formed.

The role of feelings in the way advertisements work suggests a consumerist interpretation of how advertising works rather than the rational, which is much more a researchers' interpretation (Ambler, 1998). Consumers view advertising in the context of their experience of the category and memories of the brand. Aligned with this approach is the concept of likeability, where the feelings evoked by advertising trigger and shape attitudes to the brand and attitudes to the advertisement (Vakratsas and Ambler, 1999). Feelings and emotions play an important role in advertising especially when advertising is used to build awareness levels and brand strength.

> Consumers view advertising in the context of their experience of the category and memories of the brand.

Shock strategy

Advertising strategy may also be considered in terms of the overall response a target audience might give on receipt of particular messages. Some organisations choose a consistent theme for their campaigns, a theme that is often unrelated to their products or services. One such strategy is the use of shock advertising. Shock advertising according to Venkat and Abi-Hanna (1995) 'is generally regarded as one that deliberately, rather than inadvertently, startles and offends its audience'.

ViewPoint 18.3   Specsavers

Specsavers Opticians broke the mould of price-led competition in the UK opticians market by adopting a more expressive approach to their advertising. Using well-known endorsers, people who either use vision creatively (an artist) or think deeply and develop inner vision about high-level physics and associated activities, they helped change the way the brand was perceived and differentiate themselves from their competitors. See the mini-case at the end of this chapter and Exhibits 18.1 and 18.2.

EXHIBITS 18.1 AND 18.2 Specsavers Opticians
Using people known for the way they use their sight, Specsavers Opticians delivered
differentiation and added value to the market. Exhibit 18.1 (above) shows the artist David
Shepherd; Exhibit 18.2 (below) shows the physicist Stephen Hawking. Pictures and material
reproduced with the kind permission of Specsavers Opticians.

Dahl *et al.* (2002) suggest that shock advertising by definition is unexpected and audiences are surprised by the messages because they do not conform to social norms or their expectations. They argue that audiences are offended because there is 'norm violation, encompassing transgressions of law or custom (e.g., indecent sexual references, obscenity), breaches of a moral or social code (e.g., profanity, vulgarity), or things that outrage the moral or physical senses', for example gratuitous violence and disgusting images (p. 268). The clothing company French Connection's use of the F.C.U.K. slogan and the various Benetton campaigns depicting a variety of incongruous situations (for example a priest and a nun kissing and of a man dying of AIDS) are contemporary examples of norm violation. Shock advertising is not only used by commercial organisations such as Diesel, Egg and Sony Entertainment but is also used by not-profit organisations such as the government (anti-smoking), charities (child abuse) and human rights campaigners (Amnesty International). See ViewPoint 18.4.

> Shock advertising by definition is unexpected and audiences are surprised by the messages because they do not conform to social norms or their expectations.

The main reason for using a shock advertising strategy is that it is a good way to secure an audience's attention and achieve a longer-lasting impact than through traditional messages and attention-getting devices. The surprise element of these advertisements secures attention, which is followed by an attempt to work out why an individual has been surprised. This usually takes the form of cognitive engagement and message elaboration in order that the message be understood. Through this process a shocking message can be retained and behaviour influenced. This process is depicted in Figure 18.1.

> It is a good way to secure an audience's attention.

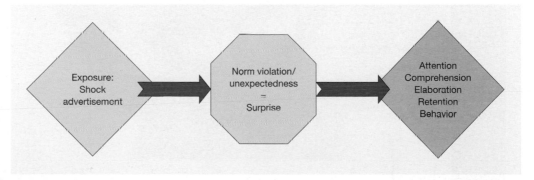

FIGURE 18.1 A preliminary model of consumer reactions to shock appeals (Dahl *et al.*, 2003)

ViewPoint 18.4   Problem? What problem?

In a campaign designed to raise awareness and to shock the public into being less complacent about domestic violence, Amnesty International used posters in the style of cosmetics advertising, featuring models using make-up to hide the damage and injuries caused by violence.

The posters, used in over 100 tube stations, depict 'Cachez', a fictional cosmetics brand, and use the slogan 'Gentle skincare for bruising relationships'.

The powerful messages show a smiling model with different injuries – a black eye, a cut cheek, a scar below her breast and three red marks on her shoulder. The aim is to address the complacency that exists about the issue and to make people think about the horror of domestic violence. Through the use of cosmetics to symbolically cover up the issue, Amnesty tried to shock people into not accepting this (or any) form of violence. See Exhibit 18.3.

THE BEST CONCEALER
KNOWN TO WOMAN

Concealer that instantly creates a flawless cover to all bruising

Cachez

Gentle skincare for bruising relationships

Problem? What problem?
www.problemwhatproblem.com

STOP
VIOLENCE
AGAINST
WOMEN
amnesty international

EXHIBIT 18.3 Amnesty International – Problem? What problem?

Shocking ads also benefit from word-of-mouth communication as these messages provoke advertisement-related conversations (Dichter, 1966). The credibility of word-of-mouth communication impacts on others who, if they have not been exposed to the original message, often seek out the message through curiousity. Associated with this pass-along impact is the generation of controversy, which can lead to additional publicity for the organisation and its advertisements. This 'free' publicity, although invariably negative, is considered to be desirable as it leads to increased brand awareness without further exposure and associated costs. This in turn can give the organisation further opportunities to provide more information about the advertising campaign and generate additional media comment (Brierley, 1996).

Advertising models and concepts

In Chapter 7 a series of sequential models was presented. These models, essentially hierarchy of effects frameworks, were the first attempts to describe how advertising works (AIDA). The sequential nature of these early interpretations was attractive because they were easy to comprehend, neatly mirrored the purchase decision process and provided a base upon which campaign goals were later assigned (Dagmar). However, as our knowledge of buyer behaviour increased and as the significance of the USP declined so these hierarchy of effects models also declined in terms of our understanding about advertising. Now they are insignificant and are no longer used as appropriate interpretations of how advertising works.

In their place a number of new frameworks and explanations have arisen, all of which claim to reflect practice. In other words these new theories about how advertising works are a reflection of practice, of the way advertising is considered to work, or at least used by advertising agencies and interpreted by marketing research agencies. The first to be considered here were developed by Hall (1992) and O'Malley (1991) and they suggest that there are four main advertising frameworks (Figure 18.2).

1. *The sales framework*

   This framework, oriented mainly to direct response work, is based on the premise that the level of sales is the only factor that is worth considering when measuring the effectiveness of an advertising campaign. This view holds that all advertising activities are aimed ultimately at shifting product – generating sales. Advertising is

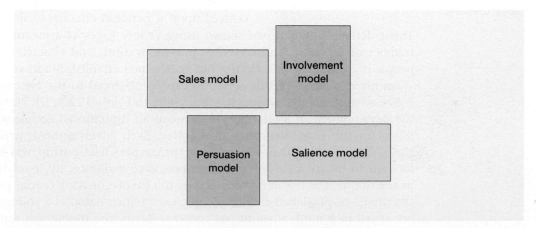

FIGURE 18.2 Four advertising frameworks (after Hall, 1991 and O'Malley, 1991)

Advertising is considered to have a short-term direct impact on sales.

considered to have a short-term direct impact on sales. This effect is measurable and, while other outcomes might also result from advertising, the only important factor is sales. On sales alone will the true effect of any advertising be felt.

2. *The persuasion framework*

The second framework assumes advertising to work rationally, because messages are capable of being persuasive. Persuasion is effected by gradually moving buyers through a number of sequential steps. These hierarchy of effects models assume that buyer decision-making is rational and can be accurately predicted. As discussed earlier, these models have a number of drawbacks and are no longer used as the basis for designing advertisements, despite great popularity in the 1960s and 1970s.

ViewPoint 18.5   Persuasive eggs

The use of advertising to persuade audiences can be key when launching new brands or when the audience experiences high involvement. When Prudential's online bank (Egg) was launched in 1998 it was the UK's first Internet bank so consumer uncertainty was high.

The advertising to back the launch used Zoe Ball and Linford Christie as spokespersons to convey the brand's quirky and essentially irreverent brand values. They were used not only to establish the brand personality and attitudes but to create name awareness. The celebrities were shown strapped to lie detectors, and the message conveyed the right modern tone of voice, trust and transparency. The message also supported the introductory interest rate of 8 per cent which, in just six months, enabled the brand to better both of its five-year targets: 500,000 customers and £5 billion funds under management.

Advertising has been used consistently and awareness levels have reached a staggering 90 per cent. However, advertising's role has had to change from persuasion to differentiation as Mint, Cahoot and IF entered the new market.

Source: Adapted from Superbrands *Brand Republic* 18 November 2004.

3. *The involvement framework*

Involvement-based advertisements work by drawing members of the target audience into the advertisement and eliciting a largely emotional response. Involvement with the product develops as a consequence of involvement with the advertisement. Yellow Pages developed a highly successful series of television commercials that centred upon a fictional character called J.R. Hartley.

Involvement with the product develops as a consequence of involvement with the advertisement.

This elderly gentleman was shown using Yellow Pages as a means of resolving a number of problems and served to provide warmth and character that involved people not only with J.R. Hartley but also helped establish brand values.

Another example of this approach can be observed in the Nescafé Gold Blend coffee advertisements. During the late 1980s and early 1990s, UK viewers witnessed the development of a relationship between an aspirational couple with a mutual liking for the Gold Blend brand of coffee. Each advertisement, which presented particular events in the development of the couple's relationship, was eagerly looked forward to by an involved and often obsessive audience. By involving the target in the drama, the brand became part of the involvement, a crucial part of each of the ritualistic playlets. Later, the couple were reincarnated as a younger couple and presented in a more adventurous context. Again, the theme was romance, which was allowed to unfold over a series of different advertisements.

4. *The salience framework*

This interpretation is based upon the premise that advertising works by standing out, by being different from all other advertisements in the product class. See Exhibit 18.4. The launch of Radion, a soap powder that used the twin propositions of cleaning and removing odours, was remarkable because of its ability to 'shout' at the audience through the use of lurid colours and striking presentations. Tango (a canned drink) was repositioned using strikingly different, zany (and interactive) messages. Pot Noodle drew attention through presentation techniques based upon a seemingly unprofessional and off-the-wall domestic camcorder production. Alternative examples of salience advertising are the Tosh campaign by Toshiba (O'Malley, 1991) and the Benson and Hedges Silk Cut campaigns (Hall, 1992).

Acceptance of the persuasion and salience frameworks is based on the assumption that the audience are active, rational problem solvers and are perfectly capable of discrimination among brands and advertisements. Furthermore, the models bring to attention two important points about people and advertising. Advertisements are capable of generating two very clear types of response: a response to the featured product and a response to the advertisement itself. As discussed earlier in Chapter 7, the cognitive responses that people make when exposed to marketing communication messages, in this case advertisements, and the Elaboration Likelihood Model (ELM) are important means of understanding how different motivations affect decision-making.

The strong and the weak theories of advertising

The explanations offered to date are all based on the premise that advertising is a potent marketing force, one that is persuasive and which is done *to* people. More recent views of advertising theory question this fundamental perspective. Prominent among the theorists are Jones, McDonald and Ehrenberg, some of whose views will now be presented. Jones (1991) presented the new views as the strong theory of advertising and the weak theory of advertising.

The strong theory of advertising

All the models presented so far are assumed to work on the basis that they are capable of affecting a degree of change in the knowledge, attitudes, beliefs or behaviour of target audiences. Jones refers to this as the strong theory of advertising, and it appears to have been universally adopted as a foundation for commercial activity.

According to Jones, exponents of this theory hold that advertising can persuade someone to buy a product that they have never previously purchased. Furthermore, continual long-run purchase behaviour can also be generated. Under the strong theory, advertising is believed to be capable of increasing sales at the brand and class levels. These upward shifts are achieved through the use of manipulative and psychological techniques, which are deployed against consumers who are passive, possibly because of apathy, and are generally incapable of processing information intelligently. The most appropriate theory would appear to be the hierarchy of effects model, where sequential steps move buyers forward to a purchase, stimulated by timely and suitable promotional messages.

That advertising can persuade someone to buy a product that they have never previously purchased.

EXHIBIT 18.4 No More Nails – a Salience ad
This ad for No More Nails literally stands out because the visual is unusual and attracts attention.

The weak theory of advertising

A consumer's pattern of brand purchases is driven more by habit than by exposure to promotional messages.

Increasing numbers of European writers argue that the strong theory does not reflect practice. Most notable of these writers is Ehrenberg (1988, 1997), who believes that a consumer's pattern of brand purchases is driven more by habit than by exposure to promotional messages.

The framework proposed by Ehrenberg is the awareness–trial–reinforcement (ATR) framework. Awareness is required before any purchase can be made, although the elapsed time between awareness and action may be very short or very long. For the few people intrigued enough to want to try a product, a trial purchase constitutes the next phase. This may be stimulated by retail availability as much as by advertising, word-of-mouth or personal selling stimuli. Reinforcement follows to maintain awareness and provide reassurance to help the customer to repeat the pattern of thinking and behaviour and to cement the brand in the repertoire for occasional purchase activity. Advertising's role is to breed brand familiarity and identification (Ehrenberg, 1997).

Following on from the original ATR model (Ehrenberg, 1974), various enhancements have been suggested. However, Ehrenberg added a further stage in 1997, referred to as the nudge. He argues that some consumers can 'be nudged into buying the brand more frequently (still as part of their split-loyalty repertoires) or to favour it more than the other brands in their consideration sets'. Advertising need not be any different from before; it just provides more reinforcement that stimulates particular habitual buyers into more frequent selections of the brand from their repertoire.

ViewPoint 18.6   Nudging chocolate

Our choice of preferred chocolate brands is fairly clear cut and considering that the amount we eat each year is so large it is difficult to see how the volume of purchases or the frequency of consumption could be improved. The role of advertising in this market is not to inform or improve awareness, as these are high enough already. The real task in this market is to assist those who are lapsed brand users to try the brand again, in other words to nudge them back to the brand.

So, rather than build brand values the focus is on consolidating or changing behaviour. Consumer buying of chocolate has also changed as impulse buying has declined and been replaced by mass purchasing at supermarkets. Consumers get cost savings and control consumption through a single weekly purchase. This pressurises advertising into helping to secure the trade listings necessary to get product on to the supermarket shelves.

According to the weak theory, advertising is capable of improving people's knowledge, and so is in agreement with the strong theory. In contrast, however, consumers are regarded as selective in determining which advertisements they observe and only perceive those which promote products that they either use or have some prior knowledge of. This means that they already have some awareness of the characteristics of the advertised product. It follows that the amount of information actually communicated is limited. Advertising, Jones continues, is not potent enough to convert people who hold reasonably strong beliefs that are counter to those portrayed in an advertisement. The time available (30 seconds in television advertising) is not enough to bring about conversion and, when combined

Consumers are regarded as selective in determining which advertisements they observe.

with people's ability to switch off their cognitive involvement, there may be no effective communication. Advertising is employed as a defence, to retain customers and to increase product or brand usage. Advertising is used to reinforce existing attitudes, not necessarily to drastically change them.

Unlike the strong theory, this perspective accepts that when people say that they are not influenced by advertising they are in the main correct. It also assumes that people are not apathetic or even stupid, but capable of high levels of cognitive processing.

In summary, the strong theory suggests that advertising can be persuasive, can generate long-run purchasing behaviour, can increase sales and regards consumers as passive. The weak theory suggests that purchase behaviour is based on habit and that advertising can improve knowledge and reinforce existing attitudes. It views consumers as active problem solvers.

These two perspectives serve to illustrate the dichotomy of views that has emerged about this subject. They are important because they are both right and they are both wrong. The answer to the question 'How does advertising work?' lies somewhere

Illustrate the dichotomy of views that has emerged about this subject.

between the two views and is dependent upon the particular situation facing each advertiser. Where elaboration is likely to be high if advertising is to work, then it is most likely to work under the strong theory. For example, consumer durables and financial products require that advertising urges prospective customers into some form of trial behaviour. This may be a call for more information from a sales representative or perhaps a visit to a showroom. The vast majority of product purchases, however, involve low levels of elaboration, where involvement is low and where people select, often unconsciously, brands from an evoked set.

New products require people to convert or change their purchasing patterns. It is evident that the strong theory must prevail in these circumstances. Where products become established their markets generally mature, so that real growth is non-existent. Under these circumstances, advertising works by protecting the consumer franchise and by allowing users to have their product choices confirmed and reinforced. The other objective of this form of advertising is to increase the rate at which customers reselect and consume products. If the strong theory were the only acceptable approach, then theoretically advertising would be capable of continually increasing the size of each market, until everyone had been converted. There would be no 'stationary' markets.

Considering the vast sums that are allocated to advertising budgets, not only to launch new products but also to pursue market share targets aggressively, the popularity and continued implicit acceptance of the power of advertising suggest that a large proportion of resources are wasted in the pursuit of advertising-driven brand performance. Indeed, it is noticeable that organisations have been switching resources out of advertising into sales promotion activities. There are many reasons for this (Chapter 22), but one of them concerns the failure of advertising to produce the expected levels of performance: to produce market share. The strong theory fails to deliver the expected results, and the weak theory does not apply to all circumstances. Reality is probably a mixture of the two.

The alphabetical model

Prue (1998) presents a framework entitled the alphabetical model, based upon the premise that advertising should be interpreted from a customer orientation. His model is an attempt to return to the simplicity inherent in the AIDA and other sequential models. See Figure 18.3. This is not so much a theory as a rather wide depository for all known interpretations of how advertising might work.

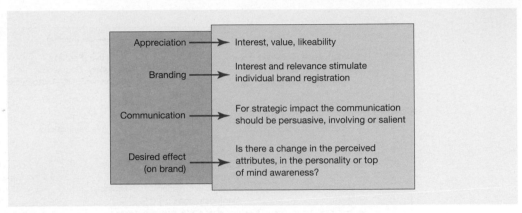

FIGURE 18.3 The alphabetical model of advertising (Adapted from Prue (1998); used with kind permission.)

Using advertising strategically

There are many varied and conflicting ideas about the strategic use of advertising. For a long time the management of the tools of the promotional mix was considered strategic. Indeed, many practitioners still believe in this approach. However, ideas concerning corporate identity and integrated marketing communications (Chapters 15 and 11) have helped provide a fresh perspective on what constitutes advertising strategy, and issues concerning differentiation, brand values and the development of brand equity have helped establish both strategic and a tactical or operational aspect associated with advertising.

One of the first significant attempts to formalise advertising's strategic role was developed by Vaughn when working for an advertising agency, Foote, Cone and Belding. These ideas (see below) were subsequently debated and an alternative model emerged from Rossiter and Percy. Both frameworks have been used extensively by advertising agencies, and although their influence has now subsided the underlying variables and approach remain central to strategic advertising thought.

The FCB matrix

Vaughn (1980) developed a matrix utilising involvement and brain specialisation theories. Brain specialisation theory suggests that the left-hand side of the brain is best handling rational, linear and cognitive thinking, whereas the right-hand side is better able to manage spatial, visual and emotional issues (the affective or feeling functions).

Vaughn proposed that by combining involvement with elements of thinking and feeling, four primary advertising planning strategies can be distinguished. These are informative, affective, habitual and self-satisfaction (see Figure 18.4). According to Vaughn, the matrix is intended to be a thought provoker rather than a formula or model from which prescriptive solutions are to be identified. The FCB matrix is a useful guide to help analyse and appreciate consumer/product relationships and to develop appropriate communication strategies. The four quadrants of the grid identify particular types of decision-making and each

> By combining involvement with elements of thinking and feeling, four primary advertising planning strategies can be distinguished.

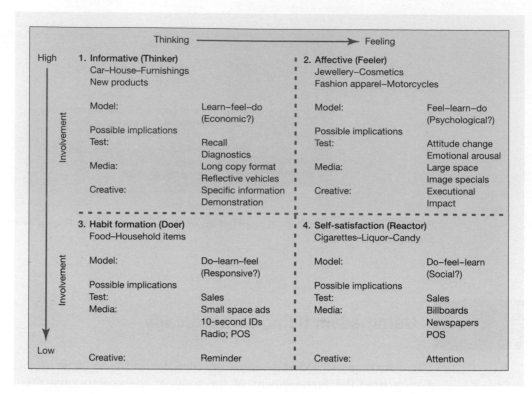

FIGURE 18.4 FCB grid (From Vaughn (1980); used with kind permission.)

requires different advertising approaches. Vaughn suggests that different orderings from the learn–feel–do sequence can be observed. By perceiving the different ways in which the process can be ordered, he proposed that the learn–feel–do sequence should be visualised as a continuum, a circular concept. Communication strategy would, therefore, be based on the point of entry that consumers make to the cycle.

Some offerings, generally regarded as 'habitual', may be moved to another quadrant, such as 'responsive', to develop differentiation and establish a new position for the product in the minds of consumers relative to the competition. This could be achieved by the selection of suitable media vehicles and visual images in the composition of the messages associated with an advertisement. There is little doubt that this model, or interpretation of the advertising process, has made a significant contribution to our understanding of the advertising process and has been used by a large number of advertising agencies (Joyce, 1991).

The Rossiter–Percy grid

Rossiter *et al.* (1991), however, disagree with some of the underpinnings of the FCB grid and offer a new one in response (revised 1997) (Figure 18.5). They suggest that involvement is not a continuum because it is virtually impossible to decide when a person graduates from high to low involvement. They claim that the FCB grid fails

> They claim that the FCB grid fails to account for situations where a person moves from high to low involvement and then back to high.

to account for situations where a person moves from high to low involvement and then back to high, perhaps on a temporary basis, when a new variant is introduced to the market. Rossiter *et al.* regard involvement as the level of perceived risk present at the time of purchase. Consequently,

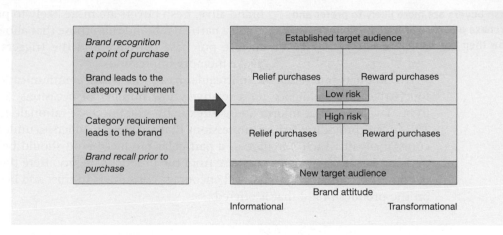

FIGURE 18.5 The Rossiter–Percy grid (Adapted from Rossiter and Percy (1997); used with kind permission.)

it is the degree of familiarity buyers have at the time of purchase that is an important component.

A further criticism is that the FCB grid is an attitude-only model. Rossiter *et al.* quite rightly identify the need for brand awareness to be built into such grids as a prerequisite for attitude development. However, they cite the need to differentiate different purchase situations. Some brands require awareness recall because the purchase decision is made prior to the act of purchasing. Other brands require awareness recognition at the point of purchase, where the buyer needs to be prompted into brand choice decisions. Each of these situations requires different message strategies, and these are explored in Chapter 19.

The other major difference between the two grids concerns the 'think–feel' dimension. Rossiter *et al.* believe that a wider spectrum of motives must be incorporated, as the FCB 'think–feel' interpretation fails to accommodate differences between product category and brand purchase motivations. For example, the decision to use a product category may be based upon a strictly functional and utilitarian need. The need to travel to another country designates the necessity of air transport. The choice of carrier, however, particularly over the North Atlantic, is a brand choice decision, motivated by a variety of sensory and ego-related inputs and anticipated outputs. Rossiter *et al.* disaggregate motives into what they refer to as informational and transformational motives. By detailing motives into these classifications, a more precise approach to advertising tactics can be developed (Chapter 19). Furthermore, the confusion inherent in the FCB grid, between the think and involvement elements, is overcome.

It should be understood that these 'grids' are purely hypothetical, and there is no proof or evidence to suggest that they are accurate reflections of advertising. It is true that both models have been used as the basis for advertising strategy in many agencies, but that does not mean that they are totally reliable or, more importantly, that they have been tested empirically so that they can be used in total confidence. They are interpretations of commercial and psychological activity and have been instrumental in advancing our level of knowledge. It is in this spirit of development that these models are presented in this text.

There are parts in both of these frameworks that have a number of strong elements of truth attached to them. However, for products that are purchased on a regular basis, pull strategies should be geared to defending the rationale that current buyers use to select the brand. Heavy buyers select a particular brand more often than light users do from their repertoire. By providing a variety of consistent stimuli, and by keeping the

Fresh buyers are more likely to prefer and purchase a particular brand than those that allow their brands to lose purchase currency.

brand alive, fresh buyers are more likely to prefer and purchase a particular brand than those that allow their brands to lose purchase currency and the triggers necessary to evoke memory impressions.

For products purchased on an irregular basis, marketing communications need only touch the target audience on a relatively low number of occasions. Strategies need to be developed that inform and contextualise the purchase rationale for consumers. This means providing lasting impressions that enable consumers to understand the circumstances in which purchase of a particular product/brand should be made once a decision has been made to purchase from the product category. Here the priorities are to communicate messages that will encourage consumers to trust and bestow expertise on the product/brand that is offered.

Advertising to engage

Advertising has traditionally been used to develop brand identities by stimulating awareness and perception. Marketing communications have evolved such that identity and values are insufficient. The growth of direct marking and one-to-one, preferably interactive, communications have become paramount and marketing budgets have swung more towards establishing a call-to-action, a behaviour rather than attitudinal response. The issue that remains is what is the role for advertising and what strategies should be used? One approach would be to maintain current advertising strategies on the grounds that awareness and perception are always going to be key factors. The other extreme approach would be to call for advertising to be used solely for direct response work. Neither of these two options seems appropriate or viable in the twenty-first century.

In an age where values and response are both necessary ingredients for effective overall communication, advertising strategy in the future will need to be based on engagement. Customers will want to engage with the values offered by a brand that are significant to them individually. However, there will also be a need to engage with them at a behavioural level and to encourage them to want to respond to the advertising. Advertising strategy should therefore reflect a brand's context and be adjusted according to the required level of engagement regarding identity development and the required level of behavioural response. Advertising will no longer be able to rightly assume the lead role in a campaign and will be used according to the engagement needs of, first, the audience, secondly the brand and thirdly the communication industry, in that order.

Advertising strategy in the future will need to be based on engagement.

Cohen (2003) refers to the gap between advertising used to develop brand identity and the need to encourage audience responses. He develops an OPC model where O refers to the offer, P to the product and C to the call-to-action. Advertising therefore should attempt to bring these elements together in a single, significant presentation. Key to his model is the brand/response (B/R) ratio, which relates to the relative levels of emphasis on the brand and response elements. The ratio refers to a line or spectrum of effects between these two elements. Traditional brand-based advertising equates with a B/R of 100/0 and direct response has a B/R of 0/100 where the sole intention is to maximise the

The gap between advertising used to develop brand identity and the need to encourage audience responses.

ViewPoint 18.7   OxiCleaned advertising

OxiClean was a newly launched brand in the US grocery sector, one noted for traditionally large advertising budgets used to develop brand identities and brand values. OxiClean's approach was based around a multichannel strategy, a small advertising budget. The advertising was founded on a memorable spokesperson, a daring product claim and a convincing demonstration of the product. This was used to build the database and build an identity for the brand. At first the brand/response ratio was 30/70 but, as the brand was introduced to standard retail outlets, a 40/60 B/R ratio was used and growth continued.

likelihood of a response. The strategic claim behind this approach may be in need of elaboration to be operationally robust, but the principle of moving the focus of advertising strategy to one that recognises the need to incorporate brand experiences is essentially sound.

Summary

A variety of models has been developed in an attempt to explain how advertising works. In addition some of these models have attempted to develop a strategic perspective for this mass communications tool. AIDA and the various sequential models, such as the hierarchy of effects approach, have now given way to new views of how advertising works.

Advertising, once considered the prime form of mass persuasion, is now subject to many different views. Those who are sceptical of advertising's power to persuade consumers to change their purchasing habits now explore ideas concerning advertising's strategic role in reinforcing brand messages and repositioning brands. The strong theory of advertising reflects the persuasion concept, and has high credibility when used with new brands. However, the contrasting view is that advertising should be regarded as a means of defending customers' purchase decisions and for protecting markets, not building them. Reality suggests that the majority of advertising cannot claim to be of significant value to most people and that the strong and the weak theories are equally applicable but not at the same time and not in the same context.

The FCB and Rossiter–Percy grids represent formalised attempts to interpret the strategic use of advertising. Intended to provide agencies with a method that might ensure consistency, meaning and value with respect to their client's brands, these are no longer considered by agencies to be sufficiently flexible, rigorous or representative of how contemporary advertising performs.

A more current perspective of advertising strategy suggests that advertising should become more engaged with the customer's experience of the brand and not be rooted just in the development of brand values.

Review questions

1. Find two advertisements and write notes explaining how they depict the roles of advertising.

2. Write brief notes outlining the difference between absolute and relative costs.

3. Name the three elements in advertising, identified by Dahl *et al.* (2002), which cause audiences to be offended. Find an example of each.

4. What are the essential differences between the involvement and salience frameworks of advertising? Find four advertisements (other than those described in the text) that are examples of these two approaches.

5. Write a short presentation explaining the differences between the strong and weak theories of advertising.

6. Select an organisation of your choice and find three ads it has used recently. Are the ads predominantly trying to persuade audiences or are they designed to reinforce brand values?

7. Evaluate the contribution of Prue's alphabetical model of advertising.

8. Draw the FCB grid and place on it the following product categories: shampoo, life assurance, sports cars, kitchen towels, box of chocolates.

9. Prepare a report explaining the differences between the Rossiter–Percy and FCB grids.

10. Write brief notes outlining the strategic role advertising plays within an organisation's overall promotional activities.

MINI-CASE
Specsavers look into it

Mini-case written by Selina Bichard, Group Communications Manager, Specsavers Optical Group

Specsavers Opticians is the UK market leader in retail optics, with 25 per cent share of the market by volume and 20 per cent by value. Its main competitors are national chains such as Dolland & Aitchison, Vision Express, Leighton's and Boots, while there are also a large number of independent, family-owned businesses. Specsavers Opticians has attained its strong position through its 'value for money' proposition and its strong commitment to marketing.

Sector advertising has tended to focus on price-led discounts and two-for-one sales promotions. Dolland & Aitchison uses celebrity actor Burt Reynolds and a two-for-one offer; Boots offers two-for-one and a Joanna Lumley voice-over; while Vision Express uses

its CEO and similar discounts. Specsavers Opticians wanted to distance themselves from this approach and find a more meaningful professional market position.

The campaign was commissioned specifically to support the Specsavers Opticians brand value of professionalism and to raise awareness of the importance of eyecare. With a long purchasing cycle (two years plus) and a low-value product, it is essential to stimulate demand for services and products; in retail optics product purchase is usually the result of a new prescription obtained during an eye examination. So although opticians make their money in the retail side of their operation, the opportunity to do this is not released until the professional side of the business has been addressed. While price-led advertising will attract customers already actively seeking to purchase in the eyecare market at the time, this campaign serves to encourage consumers to consider the importance of eyecare – i.e. to bring them back into the market.

The bulk of their marketing promotions are price led, as may be expected of their position in the market, but there is another significant factor. Opticians provide a professional service as well as a retail product and the two are more likely to be perceived as contradictory rather than as a natural partnership.

With a healthcare message, the campaign could not be overtly commercial, but had to attract and hold viewers' attention in the brash and busy medium of the TV commercial break. By using well-known and respected figures working in fields where their vision is crucial, Specsavers Opticians was able to convey the eyecare message in a thought-provoking way without resorting to the didacticism inherent in most 'good health' TV advertising, and in a visually interesting way that would stand out in the clutter of TV commercial messages.

The first commercial, featuring the famous wildlife artist David Shepherd, was highly visual and made the obvious connection between sight and the visual arts. The second, featuring Professor Stephen Hawking, reflected the two different meanings of the word vision – eyesight and the inner 'vision' that is an essential tool of the theoretical physicist. In both commercials, the focus is on the benefits of good eyesight. See Exhibits 18.1 and 18.2.

Neither commercial was strongly branded; the logo and strapline appear only on the final frames. They were not heavily supported in stores, but linked to other promotional activity through ubiquitous use of the strapline. Interviews with David Shepherd and Professor Hawking appeared in *VIEW*, Specsavers Opticians' customer magazine.

The TV campaigns ran in two bursts per year, in early spring and autumn, during the 'shoulder months' between offer-led promotions of the winter, when people have more time to shop, and product-led promotions of the summer, when protection from the sun is a key consumer interest.

The campaign has succeeded in raising awareness of the importance of eyecare and has reinforced and enhanced Specsavers Opticians' reputation as caring, professional opticians.

Questions

1 To what extent does the advertising strategy used by Specsavers better reflect the strong or weak theories of advertising?

2 How is emotion used in Specsavers Opticians' advertising?

3 Position fashion spectacles and work-wear spectacles on the FCB (Foote, Cone and Belding) framework.

4 To what extent does this campaign help or hinder cognitive processing? Does it matter?

References

Ambler, T. (1998) Myths about the mind: time to end some popular beliefs about how advertising works. *International Journal of Advertising*, **17**, pp. 501–9.

Brierley, S. (1996) The Advertising Handbook. London: Routledge.

Cohen, A. (2003) Closing the brand/response gap. *Admap*, September, pp. 20–2.

Dahl, D.W., Frankenberger, K.D. and Manchanda, R.V. (2003) Does it pay to shock? Reactions to shocking and nonshocking advertising content among university students. *Journal of Advertising Research*, **43**(3) (September), pp. 268–81.

Dichter, E. (1966) How word-of-mouth advertising works. *Harvard Business Review*, **44** (November/December), pp. 147–66.

Ehrenberg, A.S.C. (1974) Repetitive advertising and the consumer. *Journal of Advertising Research*, **14** (April), pp. 25–34.

Ehrenberg, A.S.C. (1988) *Repeat Buying*. 2nd edn. London: Charles Griffin.

Ehrenberg, A.S.C. (1997) How do consumers come to buy a new brand? *Admap* (March), pp. 20–4.

Hall, M. (1992) Using advertising frameworks. *Admap* (March), pp. 17–21.

Jones, J.P. (1991) Over-promise and under-delivery. *Marketing and Research Today* (November), pp. 195–203.

Joyce, T. (1991) Models of the advertising process. *Marketing and Research Today* (November), pp. 205–12.

O'Malley, D. (1991) Sales without salience? *Admap* (September), pp. 36–9.

Prue, T. (1998) An all-embracing theory of how advertising works? *Admap* (February), pp. 18–23.

Rossiter, J.R. and Percy, L. (1997) *Advertising, Communications and Promotion Management.* 2nd edn. New York: McGraw-Hill.

Rossiter, J.R., Percy, L. and Donovan, R.J. (1991) A better advertising planning grid. *Journal of Advertising Research* (October/November), pp. 11–21.

Vakratsas, D. and Ambler, T. (1999) How advertising works: what do we really know? *Journal of Marketing*, **63** (January), pp. 26–43.

Vaughn, R. (1980) How advertising works: a planning model. *Journal of Advertising Research* (October), pp. 27–33.

Venkat, R. and Abi-Hinni, N. (1995) *Effectiveness of visually shocking advertisements: is it context dependent?* Administrative Science Association of Canada Proceedings.

Advertising messages and creative approaches

19

The context in which people receive and interpret advertising messages must be considered thoroughly if the effectiveness of a communication is to be maximised. Ensuring that the right balance of information and emotions is achieved and that the presentation of the message is appropriate for the target audience represents a critical part of the creative process for the advertising agency and the client.

Aims and objectives

The aim of this chapter is to consider some of the ways in which advertising messages can be created by focusing on some of the principal aspects of message construction and presentation.

The objectives of this chapter are to:

1. show how messages can be constructed to account for the context in which they are to be received;
2. examine the importance and characteristics of using source credibility;
3. examine the use of emotions and feelings in advertising messages;
4. explore the advantages and disadvantages of using spokespersons in message presentation;
5. consider how advertising messages might be best presented;
6. suggest how informational and transformational motives can be used as tactical tools in an advertising plan.

Introduction

Whether advertising converts people into becoming brand-loyal customers or acts as a defensive shield to reassure current buyers, and whether central or peripheral cues are required, there still remains the decision about the nature and form of the message to be conveyed: the creative strategy.

In practice, the generation of suitable messages is derived from the creative brief. For the sake of discussion and analysis, four elements will be considered. First considerable attention is given to the source of a message and issues relating to source credibility. This is followed by a consideration of the *balance, structure,* and *presentation of the message* itself to the target audience.

Message source

Messages are perceived in many different ways and are influenced by a variety of factors. However, a critical determinant concerns the credibility that is attributed to the source of the message itself. Kelman (1961) believed that the source of a message has three particular characteristics. These are the level of perceived credibility as seen in terms of perceived objectivity and expertise, the degree to which the source is regarded as attractive and message recipients are motivated to develop a similar association or position and the degree of power that the source is believed to possess. This is manifest in the ability of the source to reward or punish message receivers. The two former characteristics are evident in various forms of marketing communications but the latter is directly observable in personal selling situations, and perhaps in the use of sales promotions.

> Believed that the source of a message has three particular characteristics.

Following this work on source characteristics three key components of source credibility can be distinguished:

1. What is the level of perceived expertise (how much knowledge the source is thought to hold)?

2. What are the personal motives the source is believed to possess?

3. What degree of trust can be placed in the source concerning the motives for communicating the message in the first place?

No matter what the level of expertise, if the level of trust is questionable, credibility will be adversely affected.

Establishing credibility

> Credibility can be established in a number of ways.

Credibility can be established in a number of ways. One simple approach is to list or display the key attributes of the organisation or the product and then signal trustworthiness through the use of third-party endorsements and the comments of satisfied users.

A more complex approach is to use referrals, suggestions and association. Trustworthiness and expertise, the two principal aspects of credibility, can be developed by using a spokesperson or organisation to provide testimonials on behalf of the sponsor of the advertisement. Credibility, therefore, can be established by the initiator of the advertisement or by a messenger or spokesperson used by the initiator to convey the message.

Effectively, viewers trade off the validity of claims made by brands against the perceived trustworthiness (and expertise) of the individuals or organisations who deliver the message. The result is that a claim may have reduced impact if either of these two components is doubtful or not capable of verification but, if repeated enough times, will enable audiences to accept that the products are very effective and of sufficiently high performance for them to try.

Credibility established by the initiator

The credibility of the organisation initiating the communication process is important. An organisation should seek to enhance its reputation with its various stakeholders at every opportunity. However, organisational credibility is derived from the image, which in turn is a composite of many perceptions. Past decisions, current strategy and performance indicators, level of service and the type of performance network members (e.g. high-quality retail outlets) all influence the perception of an organisation and the level of credibility that follows.

One very important factor that influences credibility is branding. Private and family brands in particular allow initiators to develop and launch new products more easily than those who do not have such brand strength. Brand extensions (such as Mars ice cream) have been launched with the credibility of the product firmly grounded in the strength of the parent brand name (Mars). Consumers recognise the name and make associations that enable them to lower the perceived risk and in doing so provide the platform to try the new product.

> One very important factor that influences credibility is branding.

The need to establish high levels of credibility also allows organisations to divert advertising spend away from a focus upon brands to one that focuses upon the organisation. Corporate advertising seeks to adjust organisation image and to build reputation.

ViewPoint 19.1   *Max Factor*'s source credibility

Max Factor claims that its products are so good that they are used by the experts in their industry: 'The Make-up of Make-up Artists'. Many of its recent campaigns feature expert make-up artists who work on blockbuster Hollywood movies, although most of these experts themselves are not known to the general public. The development of 'trustworthiness' therefore relies on the film credential.

As with all use of spokespersons, *Max Factor* needs to ensure that its use of experts is perceived by the target audiences as genuinely believable. In this case Max Factor uses these experts because they are perceived to be objective and independent simply because their job gives them freedom of choice with regard to the products they use.

Potential new customers seeing these advertisements are challenged on the grounds that if the brand is good enough for these experts then it should be good enough for them. If a viewer is already a *Max Factor* customer, then product experience will contribute to a support argument and these advertising messages are used to reinforce previous brand choice decisions. Either way these *Max Factor* advertisements are extremely powerful.

EXHIBIT 19.1 *Max Factor*: used with the kind permission of Leo Burnett, London, Eugenia Silva and the photographer Darren Feist

Credibility established by a spokesperson

People who deliver the message are often regarded as the source, when in reality they are only the messenger. These people carry the message and represent the true source or initiator of the message (e.g. manufacturer or retailer). Consequently, the testimonial they transmit must be credible. There are four main types of spokesperson: the expert, the celebrity, the chief executive officer and the consumer.

The expert has been used many times and was particularly popular when television advertising first established itself in the 1950s and 1960s. Experts are quickly recognisable because they either wear white coats and round glasses or dress and act like 'mad professors'. Through the use of symbolism, stereotypes and identification, these characters (and indeed others) can be established very quickly in the minds of receivers and a frame of reference generated that does not question the authenticity of the message being transmitted by such a person. Experts can also be users of products, for example professional photographers endorsing cameras, secretaries endorsing word processors and professional golfers endorsing golf equipment (Exhibit 19.2).

> Through the use of symbolism, stereotypes and identification, these characters can be established very quickly in the minds of receivers.

Entertainment and sporting celebrities were used increasingly in the 1990s, not only to provide credibility for a range of high-involvement (e.g. David Beckham for Vodafone and Linda Barker for DFS) and low-involvement decisions (e.g. Jamie Oliver for Sainsbury's) but also to grab the attention of people in markets where motivation to decide between competitive products may be low. The celebrity enables the message to stand out among the clutter and noise that typify many

> The celebrity enables the message to stand out among the clutter and noise that typify many markets.

"As Virgin Atlantic we like to feel we've always put people first.' So we've created Hot Air, a magazine that people actually want to read. Perhaps that's why Hot Air has so often been voted the best inflight magazine in the world"

Richard Branson
Chairman, Virgin Atlantic Airways

CUSTOMER MAGAZINES WORK
To find out what they could do for you,
call Sarah Farmer on 0171 404 4166
http://www.apa.co.uk e-mail: sarah@apa.co.uk

EXHIBIT 19.2 Sir Richard Branson being used to endorse APA
Picture kindly supplied by APA. Photograph by Steve Pike.

markets. It is also hoped that the celebrity and/or the voice-over will become a peripheral cue in the decision-making process: Joanna Lumley for Privilege car insurance, Gary Lineker for Walkers Crisps and Nicole Kidman for Chanel No. 5.

ViewPoint 19.2   Lineker keeps scoring for Walkers

Walkers Crisps has embarked upon a series of campaigns that have incorporated a consistent communications mix. The objective was to revive and reposition the brand, and this has been achieved using television and Gary Lineker as the central spokesperson to appeal to both adults and teenagers. Lineker has been a consistent element throughout all the campaigns and is presented and perceived as a cheeky but fun endorser of the brand. Advertisements with a number of related spokespersons, such as Paul Gascoigne and the Spice Girls, have been mixed with messages with unrelated spokespersons, such as everyday people and even a nun. These campaigns have been used to promote sales promotions such as competitions, from which a tremendous amount of PR media coverage has been generated. The market has grown by 11 per cent, but Walkers has achieved growth of 19 per cent. It has revived its brand, achieved market leadership and profitability and repositioned itself as the number one snack food brand in the UK.

There are some potential problems that advertisers need to be aware of when considering the use of celebrities. First, does the celebrity fit the image of the brand and will the celebrity be acceptable to the target audience? Consideration also needs to be given to the longer-term relationship between the celebrity and the brand. Should the lifestyle of the celebrity change, what impact will the change have on the target audience and their attitude towards the brand?

ViewPoint 19.3   Running endorsement

According to the *Sunday Times* the athlete Paula Radcliffe who failed to complete the Marathon and 10,000 metres at the Athens Olympic Games in 2004, was dropped by Quaker Oats as the endorser of their Oatso Simple brand. The line 'Quaker Oats – helps you go the distance' might not have been in the best taste but the decision to cancel the ads was made because the Broadcast Advertising Clearance Centre would not pass the scripts.

This matching process can be used to change brand attitudes as well as reinforce them. BT wanted to change the attitude that men had to telephone calls. Rather than being just the bill payer and the gatekeeper of calls to other members of the family, the role Bob Hoskins had was to demonstrate male behaviour and to present a solution that was acceptable to all members of the family. Attitudes held by men towards the telephone and its use changed significantly as a result of the campaign, partly because Hoskins was perceived as a credible spokesperson, someone with whom men could identify and feel comfortable.

EXHIBIT 19.3 Gary Lineker – Walkers spokesperson

There is a danger that the receiver remembers the celebrity but not the message or the brand.

The second problem concerns the impact that the celebrity makes relative to the brand. There is a danger that the receiver remembers the celebrity but not the message or the brand that is the focus of the advertising spend. The *celebrity* becomes the hero, rather than the product being advertised. Summers (1993) suggests that the Cinzano advertisements featuring Joan Collins and Leonard Rossiter are a classic example of the problem: 'The characters so dwarfed the product that consumers may have had trouble recalling the brand'.

Issues such as brand development can also be impeded when identification by an audience with the celebrity is strong. Sony had to fade audiences away from its association with John Cleese by using a Robot/Cleese lookalike for a period.

Richard Branson is used to promote Virgin Financial products and Victor Kiam 'so liked the razor that he bought the company' (Remington). Here, the CEO openly promotes his company. This form of testimonial is popular when the image of the CEO is positive and the photogenic and on-screen characteristics provide for enhanced credibility. Bernard Mathews has established authenticity and trustworthiness with his personal promotion of Norfolk Roasts. See also Chapter 32 and the concept of strategic credibility.

The final form of spokesperson is the consumer. By using consumers to endorse products, the audience is being asked to identify with a 'typical consumer'. The identification of similar lifestyles, interests and opinions allows for better reception and understanding of the message. Consumers are often depicted testing similar products, such as margarine and butter. The Pepsi Challenge required consumers to select Pepsi from Coca-Cola through blind taste tests. By showing someone using the product, someone who is similar to the receiver, the source is perceived as credible and the potential for successful persuasion is considerably enhanced.

Sleeper effects

The assumption so far has been that high credibility enhances the probability of persuasion and successful communication. This is true when the receiver's initial position is opposite to that contained in the message. When the receiver's position is favourable to the message, a moderate level of credibility may be more appropriate.

Whether source credibility is high, medium or low is of little consequence, according to some researchers (Hannah and Sternthal, 1984). The impact of the source is believed to dissipate after approximately six weeks and only the content of the message is thought to dominate the receiver's attention. This sleeper effect (Hovland *et al.*, 1949) has not been proved empirically, but the implication is that the persuasiveness of a message can increase through time.

The impact of the source is believed to dissipate after approximately six weeks.

Furthermore, advertisers using highly credible sources need to repeat the message on a regular basis, in order that the required level of effectiveness and persuasion be maintained (Schiffman and Kanuk, 1991).

Message balance

It is evident from previous discussions that the effectiveness of any single message is dependent upon a variety of issues. From a receiver's perspective, two elements appear to be significant: first, the amount and quality of the information that is communicated and, secondly, the overall judgement that each individual makes about the way a message is communicated.

This suggests that the style of a message should reflect a balance between the need for information and the need for pleasure or enjoyment in consuming the message. Figure 19.1 describes the two main forms of appeal. Messages can be product oriented and rational or customer oriented and based upon feelings and emotions.

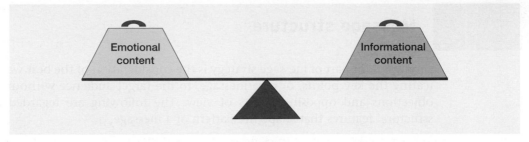

FIGURE 19.1 The balance of emotions and information provision

It is clear that when dealing with high-involvement decisions, where persuasion occurs through a central processing route, the emphasis of the message should be on the information content, in particular the key attributes and the associated benefits. This style is often factual and product oriented. If the product evokes low-involvement decision-making, then the message should concentrate upon the images that are created within the mind of the message recipient. This style seeks to elicit an emotional response from receivers. There are, of course, many situations where both rational and emotional messages are needed by buyers in order to make purchasing decisions.

ViewPoint 19.4   Salon brand messages

Salon brands of haircare products, such as Toni & Guy, Paul Mitchell, Fudge and Tigi, are distributed through hair salons and use the credibility that consumers bestow upon their 'regular' hairdressers as an important means to judge salon brands. Consumers delegate decision responsibilities to their professional

Decisions about salon brands are made as a result of interpreting both rational and emotional messages. Rational messages are driven by the superior quality of the product, the strength of the relationship held with their hairdresser and the diagnosis that hairdressers provide. Emotional messages are derived from the packaging, the quality of the relationship with the hairdresser and the imagery associated with the relative exclusivity that salon brands afford. Younger buyers perceive increased 'shower cred' and older customers perceive indulgence and a treat factor.

EXHIBIT 19.4 Toni and Guy - a salon brand

Message structure

An important part of message strategy is the consideration of the best way of communicating the key points, or core message, to the target audience without encountering objections and opposing points of view. The following are regarded as important structural features that shape the pattern of a message.

Conclusion drawing

Should the message draw a firm conclusion for the audience or should people be allowed to draw their own conclusions from the content? Explicit conclusions are, of course, more easily understood and stand a better chance of being effective (Kardes, 1988). However, it is the nature of the issue, the particular situation and the composition of the target audience that influence the effectiveness of conclusion drawing (Hovland and Mandell, 1952). Whether or not a conclusion should be drawn for the receiver depends upon the following:

1. *The complexity of the issue*

   Healthcare products, central heating systems and personal finance services, for example, can be complex, and for some members of the target audience their cognitive ability, experience and motivation may not be sufficient for them to draw their own conclusions. The complexity of the product requires that messages must draw conclusions for them. It should also be remembered that even highly informed and motivated audiences may require assistance if the product or issue is relatively new.

   > Even highly informed and motivated audiences may require assistance if the product or issue is relatively new.

ViewPoint 19.5   Sure conclusion

The deodorant brand Sure used screen icons Steve McQueen, Elvis and James Dean to promote its Crystal for Men range. The message was that this simple antiperspirant product minimises the white marks on clothes and to convey this it used doctored pictures of the celebrities showing white stains on their clothes.

The message drew a conclusion for the audience whose low involvement required a clear one-sided message: white stains are bad, so use this product and you will avoid such problems.

---

2. *The level of education possessed by the receiver*

   Better-educated audiences prefer to draw their own conclusions, whereas less educated audiences may need the conclusion drawn for them because they may not be able to make the inference from the message.

3. *Whether immediate action is required*

   If urgent action is required by the receiver, then a conclusion should be drawn very clearly. Political parties can be observed to use this strategy immediately before an election.

4. *The level of involvement*

   High involvement usually means that receivers prefer to make up their own minds and may reject or resent any attempt to have the conclusion drawn for them (Arora, 1985).

One- and two-sided messages

This concerns whether the cases for and against an issue or just that in favour are presented to an audience. Messages that present just one argument, in favour of the product or issue, are referred to as one-sided. Research indicates that one-sided messages are more effective when receivers favour the opinion offered in the message and when the receivers are less educated.

Two-sided messages, where the good and bad points of an issue are presented, are more effective when the receiver's initial opinion is opposite to that presented in the

Two-sided messages tend to produce more positive perceptions of a source than one-sided messages.

message and when they are highly educated. Credibility is improved and two-sided messages tend to produce more positive perceptions of a source than one-sided messages (Faison, 1961).

Order of presentation

Further questions regarding the development of message strategy concern the order in which important points are presented. Messages that present the strongest points at the beginning use what is referred to as the *primacy* effect. The decision to place the main points at the beginning depends on whether the audience has a low or high level of involvement. A low level may require an attention-getting message component at the beginning. Similarly, if the target has an opinion opposite to that contained in the message, a weak point may lead to a high level of counter-argument.

A decision to place the strongest points at the end of the message assumes that the *recency* effect will bring about greater levels of persuasion. This is appropriate when the receiver agrees with the position adopted by the source or has a high positive level of involvement.

The order of argument presentation is more relevant in personal selling than in television advertisements. However, as learning through television is largely passive,

The order of argument presentation is more relevant in personal selling than in television advertisements.

because involvement is low and interest minimal, the presentation of key selling points at the beginning and at the end of the message will enhance message reception and recall.

 ## Message presentation

The presentation of the promotional message requires that an appeal be made to the target audience. The appeal is important, because unless the execution of the message appeal (the creative) is appropriate to the target audience's perception and expectations, the chances of successful communication are reduced.

There are two main factors associated with the presentation. Is the message to be dominated by the need to transmit product-oriented information or is there a need to transmit a message that appeals predominantly to the emotional senses of the receiver? The main choice of presentation style, therefore, concerns the degree of factual information transmitted in a message against the level of imagery thought necessary to make sufficient impact for the message to command attention and then be processed. There are numerous presentational or executional techniques, but the following are some of the more commonly used appeals.

Appeals based upon the provision of information

Factual

Sometimes referred to as the 'hard sell', the dominant objective of these appeals is to provide information. This type of appeal is commonly associated with high-involvement decisions where receivers are sufficiently motivated and able to process information. Persuasion, according to the ELM, is undertaken through the central processing route. This means that advertisements should be rational and contain logically reasoned arguments and information in order that receivers are able to complete their decision-making processes.

Slice of life

As noted earlier, the establishment of credibility is vital if any message is to be accepted. One of the ways in which this can be achieved is to present the message in such a way that the receiver can identify immediately with the scenario being presented. This process of creating similarity is used a great deal in advertising and is referred to as slice-of-life advertising. For example, many washing powder advertisers use a routine that depicts two ordinary women (assumed to be similar to the target receiver), invariably in a kitchen or garden, discussing the poor results achieved by one of their washing powders. Following the advice of one of the women, the stubborn stains are seen to be overcome by the focus brand.

The overall effect of this appeal is for the receiver to conclude the following: that person is like me; I have had the same problem as that person; he or she is satisfied using brand X, therefore I, too, will use brand X. This technique is simple, well tried, well liked and successful, despite its sexist overtones. It is also interesting to note that a number of surveys have found that a majority of women feel that advertisers use inappropriate stereotyping to portray female roles, these being predominantly housewife and mother roles.

Demonstration

A similar technique is to present the problem to the audience as a demonstration. The focus brand is depicted as instrumental in the resolution of a problem. Headache remedies, floor cleaners and tyre commercials have traditionally demonstrated the pain, the dirt and the danger respectively, and then shown how the focus brand relieves the pain (Panadol), removes the stubborn dirt (Flash) or stops in the wet on a coin (or the edge of a rooftop – Continental tyres). Whether the execution is believable is a function of the credibility and the degree of lifelike dialogue or copy that is used.

> The focus brand is depicted as instrumental in the resolution of a problem.

Comparative advertising

Comparative advertising is a popular means of positioning brands. Messages are based upon the comparison of the focus brand with either a main competitor brand or all competing brands, with the aim of establishing and maintaining superiority. See Exhibit 19.4. The comparison may centre upon one or two key attributes and can be a good way of entering new markets. Entrants keen to establish a presence in a market have little to lose by comparing themselves with market leaders. However, market leaders have a great deal to lose and little to gain by comparing themselves with minor competitors. See ViewPoint 19.6.

ViewPoint 19.6   Duracell uses comparative bunnies

Duracell has established itself as the leading battery manufacturer in many markets, including the UK. Its advertising messages are information based and use the strength and longevity of its batteries as the key attribute upon which it wants to be evaluated. Independent tests verify the Duracell attribute claims and prevent any counter claim by competitors. Its positioning, with regard to ordinary zinc carbon batteries, is emphasised through the use of the strapline 'Duracell . . . lasts longer, much longer'.

One of the interesting aspects of Duracell's approach is its use of pink bunnies to symbolise the attribute. From a consumer perspective, batteries evoke little enthusiasm or engagement, yet the use of the bunnies as peripheral cues (see Chapter 7) enables consumers to connect with the Duracell brand, provides standout in the category and enables consumers to remember the key brand messages.

EXHIBIT 19.5 Duracell using comparative messages. Used with permission.
© Duracell 2004 . . . 'Lasts longer, much longer*.'
*versus ordinary zinc carbon batteries.

Appeals based upon emotions and feelings

Appeals based on logic and reason are necessary in particular situations. However, as products become similar and as consumers become more aware of the range of available products, so the need to differentiate becomes more important. Increasing numbers of advertisers are using messages that seek to appeal to the target's emotions and feelings, a 'soft sell'. Cars, toothpaste, toilet tissue and mineral water often use emotion-based messages to differentiate their products.

There are a number of appeals that can be
used to solicit an emotional response.

There are a number of appeals that can be used to solicit an emotional response from the receiver. Of the many techniques available, the main ones that can be observed to be used most are fear, humour, animation, sex, music, and fantasy and surrealism.

Fear

Fear is used in one of two ways. The first type demonstrates the negative aspects or physical dangers associated with a particular behaviour or improper product usage. Drink driving, life assurance and toothpaste advertising typify this form of appeal. The second approach is the threat of social rejection or disapproval if the focus product is not used. This type of fear is used frequently in advertisements for such products as anti-dandruff shampoos and deodorants and is used to support consumers' needs for social acceptance and approval.

Fear appeals need to be constrained, if only to avoid being categorised as outrageous and socially unacceptable. There is a great deal of evidence that fear can facilitate attention and interest in a message and even motivate an individual to take a particular course of action: for example to stop smoking. Fear appeals are persuasive, according to Schiffman and Kanuk (1991), when low to moderate levels of fear are induced. Ray and Wilkie (1970), however, show that should the level of fear rise too much, inhibiting effects may prevent the desired action occurring. This inhibition is caused by the individual choosing to screen out, through perceptive selection, messages that conflict with current behaviour. The outcome may be that individuals deny the existence of a problem, claim there is no proof or say that it will not happen to them.

ViewPoint 19.7   The Scottish 'Widow'

Since the mid-1980s Scottish Widows has used the 'Widow' as a symbol of its brand. The 'Widow' has become synonymous with the brand – even taking on iconic status – especially as research shows that four out of five people can link the image with the company.

Recently, in a campaign designed to allay people's anxiety about long-term finances, the Widow has been shown interacting with other people, displaying confidence and providing reassurance and support to others.

Humour

The use of humour as an emotional appeal is attractive because it can draw attention and stimulate interest. A further reason to use humour is that it can put the receiver in a positive mood. Mood can also be important, as receivers in a positive mood are likely to process advertising messages with little cognitive elaboration (Batra and Stayman, 1990). This can occur because there is less effort involved with peripheral rather than central cognitive processing, and this helps to mood protect. In other words, the positive mood state is more likely to be maintained if cognitive effort is avoided. Yellow Pages has used humour quietly to help convey the essence of its brand and to help differentiate it from the competition.

It is also argued that humour is effective because argument quality is likely to be high. That is, the level of counter-argument can be substantially reduced. Arguments against the use of humour concern distraction from the focus brand, so that while

Humour does not travel well.

attention is drawn, the message itself is lost. With the move to global branding and standardisation of advertising messages, humour does not travel well. While the level and type of humour are difficult to gauge in the context of the processing abilities of a domestic target audience, cultural differences seriously impede the transfer of jokes around the world. Visual humour (lavatorial, Benny Hill-type approaches) is more universally acceptable (Archer, 1994) than word-based humour, as the latter can get lost in translation without local references to provide clues to decipher the joke. Humour, therefore, is a potentially powerful yet dangerous form of appeal. Haas (1997) reports that UK advertising executives have significantly higher confidence in the use of humour than their US counterparts, but concludes that 'humour is a vague concept and that its perception is influenced by many factors'. These factors shape the context in which messages are perceived and the humour conveyed.

Animation

Animation techniques have advanced considerably in recent years, with children as the prime target audience. However, animation has been successfully used in many adult-targeted advertisements, such as those by Schweppes, Compaq, Tetley Tea, Direct Line Insurance and the Electricity Board. The main reason for using animation is that potentially boring and low-interest/involvement products can be made visually interesting and provide a means of gaining attention. A further reason for the use of animation is that it is easier to convey complex products in a way that does not patronise the viewer.

The main reason for using animation is that potentially boring and low-interest/involvement products can be made visually interesting.

Sex

Sexual innuendo and the use of sex as a means of promoting products and services are both common and controversial. Using sex as an appeal in messages is excellent for gaining the attention of buyers. Research shows, however, that it often achieves little else, particularly when the product is unrelated. Therefore, sex appeals normally work well for products such as perfume, clothing and jewellery but provide for poor effectiveness when the product is unrelated, such as cars, photocopiers and furniture. Häagen Dazs premium ice cream entered the UK market using pleasure as central to the message appeal. This approach was novel to the product class and the direct, natural relationship between the product and the theme contributed to the campaign's success.

The use of sex in advertising messages is mainly restricted to getting the attention of the audience.

The use of sex in advertising messages is mainly restricted to getting the attention of the audience and, in some circumstances, sustaining interest. It can be used openly, as in various lingerie, fragrance and perfume advertisements, such as WonderBra and Escape; sensually, as in the Häagen Dazs and Cointreau campaigns; and humorously in the Locketts brand.

Music

Music can provide continuity between a series of advertisements and can also be a good peripheral cue. A jingle, melody or tune, if repeated sufficiently, can become associated with the advertisement. Processing and attitudes towards the advertisement may be directly influenced by the music. Music has the potential to gain attention and assist product differentiation. Braithwaite and Ware (1997) found that music in advertising

Music in advertising messages is used primarily either to create a mood or to send a branded message.

messages is used primarily either to create a mood or to send a branded message. In addition, music can also be used to signal a lifestyle and so communicate a brand identity through the style of music used.

Many advertisements for cars use music, partly because it is difficult to find a point of differentiation (*Independent*, 18 October 1996), and music is able to draw attention, generate mood and express brand personality (e.g. BMW, Nissan Micra, Peugeot, Renault).

Some luxury and executive cars are advertised using commanding background music to create an aura of power, prestige and affluence, which is combined with strong visual images in order that an association be made between the car and the environment in which it is positioned. There is a contextual juxtaposition between the car and the environment presented. Readers may notice a semblance of classical conditioning, where the music acts as an unconditioned stimulus. Foxall and Goldsmith (1994) suggest that the stimulus elicits the unconditioned emotional responses that may lead to the purchase of the advertised product.

Fantasy and surrealism

The use of fantasy and surrealism in advertising has grown partly as a result of the increased clutter and legal constraints imposed on some product classes. By using fantasy appeals, associations with certain images and symbols allow the advertiser to focus attention on the product. The receiver can engage in the distraction offered and become involved with the execution of the advertisement. If this is a rewarding experience it may be possible to affect the receiver's attitudes peripherally. Readers may notice that this links to the earlier discussion on 'liking the advertisement'.

Can engage in the distraction offered and become involved with the execution of the advertisement.

Finally, an interesting contribution to the discussion of message appeal has been made by Lannon (1992). She reports that consumers' expectations of advertisements can be interpreted on the one hand as either literal or stylish and on the other as serious or entertaining, according to the tone of voice. This approach vindicates the view that consumers are active problem solvers and willing and able to decode increasingly complex messages. They can become involved with the execution of the advertisement and the product attributes. The degree of involvement (she argues implicitly) is a function of the motivation each individual has at any one moment when exposed to a particular message.

Advertisers can challenge individuals by presenting questions and visual stimuli that demand attention and cognitive response. Guinness challenged consumers to decode a series of advertisements that were unlike all previous Guinness advertisements and, indeed, all messages in the product class. The celebrity chosen was dressed completely in black, which contrasted with his blond hair, and he was shown in various time periods, past and future, and environments that receivers did not expect. He was intended to represent the personification of the drink and symbolised the individual nature of the product. Audiences were puzzled by the presentation and many rejected the challenge of interpretation. 'Surfer' and 'Bet on Black' are more recent Guinness campaigns that seek to convey the importance and necessity to wait (for the drink to be poured properly). To accomplish this, it portrays a variety of situations in which patience results in achievement.

When individuals respond positively to a challenge, the advertiser can either provide closure (an answer) or, through surreal appeals, leave the receivers to answer the questions themselves in the context in which they perceive the message. One way of achieving this challenging position is to use an appeal that cognitively disorients the receiver

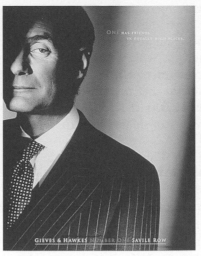

EXHIBIT 19.6 A series of print advertisements designed to challenge readers by encouraging the question 'what is going on here?'
Picture reproduced with kind permission of Gieves and Hawkes.

(Parker and Churchill, 1986). If receivers are led to ask the question 'What is going on here?' their involvement in the message is likely to be very high. See Exhibit 19.6 for an excellent example of a print advertisement for Gieves and Hawkes that deliberately seeks to stimulate the reader to ask the question 'What is this?' Benetton consistently raises questions through its advertising. By presenting a series of messages that are socially disorienting, and for many disconcerting, Benetton continually presents a challenge that moves away from involving individuals into an approach where salience and 'standing out' predominates. This high-risk strategy, with a risk of rejection, has prevailed for a number of years.

The surrealist approach does not provide or allow for closure. The conformist approach, by contrast, does require closure in order to avoid any possible counter-arguing and message rejection. Parker and Churchill argue that, by leaving questions unanswered, receivers can become involved in both the product and the execution of the advertisement. Indeed, most advertisements contain a measure of rational and emotional elements. A blend of the two elements is necessary and the right mixture is dependent upon the perceived risk and motivation that the target audience has at any one particular moment.

> The surrealist approach does not provide or allow for closure.

The message appeal should be a balance of the informative and emotional dimensions. Furthermore, message quality is of paramount importance. Buzzell (1964) reported that 'Advertising message quality is more important than the level of advertising expenditure'. Adams and Henderson Blair (1992) confirm that the weight of advertising is relatively unimportant, and that the quality of the appeal is the dominant factor. However, the correct blend of informative and emotional elements in any appeal is paramount for persuasive effectiveness.

Advertising tactics

The main creative elements of a message need to be brought together in order for an advertising plan to have substance. The processes used to develop message appeals need to be open but systematic.

The level of involvement and combination of the think/emotional dimensions that receivers bring to their decision-making processes are the core concepts to be considered when creating an advertising message. Rossiter and Percy (1997) have devised a deductive framework which involves the disaggregation of the emotional (feel) dimension to a greater degree than that proposed by Vaughn (1980) (see Chapter 18 for details). They claim that there are two broad types of motive that drive attitudes towards purchase behaviour. These are informational and transformational motives and these will now be considered in turn.

Informational motives

Individuals have a need for information to counter negative concerns about a purchase decision. These informational motives (see Table 19.1) are said to be negatively charged feelings. They can become positively charged, or the level of concern can be reduced considerably, by the acquisition of relevant information.

Transformational motives

Promises to enhance or to improve the user of a brand are referred to as transformational motives. These are related to the user's feelings and are capable of transforming a user's emotional state, hence they are positively charged. Three main transformational motives have been distinguished by Rossiter *et al.* (1991) (see Table 19.2). Various emotional states can be associated with each of these motives, and they should be used to portray an emotion that is appropriate to the needs of the target audience.

> Promises to enhance or to improve the user of a brand are referred to as transformational motives.

One of the key promotion objectives, identified earlier, is the need to create or improve levels of awareness regarding the product or organisation. This is achieved by determining whether awareness is required at the point of purchase or prior to purchase. Brand recognition (at the point of purchase) requires an emphasis upon visual stimuli,

TABLE 19.1 Informational motives

Motive	Possible emotional state
Problem removal	Anger – relief
Problem avoidance	Fear – relaxation
Incomplete satisfaction	Disappointment – optimism
Mixed approach–avoidance	Guilt – peace of mind
Normal depletion	Mild annoyance – convenience

TABLE 19.2 Transformational motives

Motive	Possible emotional state
Sensory gratification	Dull – elated
Intellectual stimulation	Bored – excited
Social approval	Apprehensive – flattered

the package and the brand name, whereas brand recall (prior to purchase) requires an emphasis on a limited number of peripheral cues. These may be particular copy lines, the use of music or colours for continuity and attention-getting frequent use of the brand name in the context of the category need, or perhaps the use of strange or unexpected presentation formats.

ViewPoint 19.8   Cancer UK messages

Cancer Research UK changed the approach it used to communicate with donors. For a while its campaigns used to convey messages about family loss and in that sense adopted a negative approach. The charity's 'All Clear' campaign conveyed messages about people diagnosed with cancer and their improved chances of recovery due to the benefits of the research.

For many people this will be a low-involvement with transformational motives situation, in which case the use of an emotional-based claim in the message is important. The happy ending based on people surviving achieves this while the endline uses a voice-over that requests a donation so that the words 'all clear' can be heard by more people in the future.

Advertising tactics can be determined by the particular combination of involvement and motives that exist at a particular time within the target audience. If a high-involvement decision process is determined, with people using a central processing route, then the types of tactics shown in Figures 19.2 and 19.3 are recommended by Rossiter and Percy (1997). If a low-involvement decision process is determined, with the target audience using a peripheral processing route, then the types of tactics shown in Figures 19.4 and 19.5 are recommended.

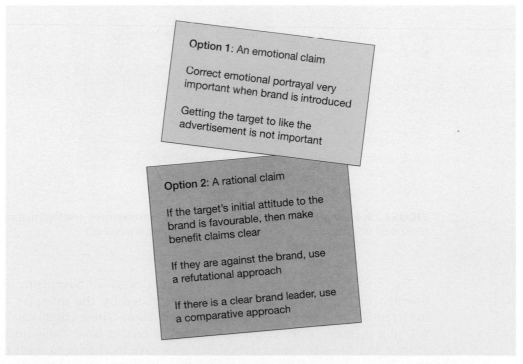

Option 1: An emotional claim

Correct emotional portrayal very important when brand is introduced

Getting the target to like the advertisement is not important

Option 2: A rational claim

If the target's initial attitude to the brand is favourable, then make benefit claims clear

If they are against the brand, use a refutational approach

If there is a clear brand leader, use a comparative approach

FIGURE 19.2 Message tactics where there are high involvement and informational motives (Based on Rossiter and Percy (1997); used with kind permission.)

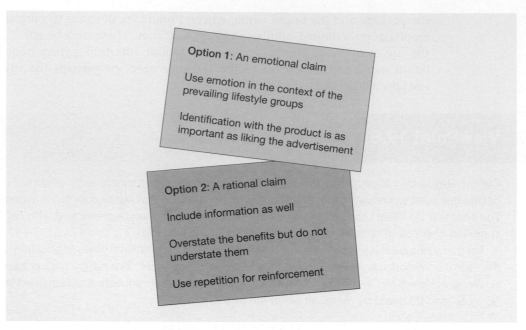

FIGURE 19.3 Message tactics where there are high involvement and transformational motives (Based on Rossiter and Percy (1997); used with kind permission.)

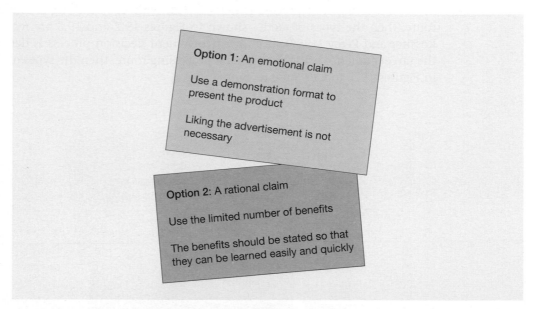

FIGURE 19.4 Message tactics where there are low involvement and informational motives (Based on Rossiter and Percy (1997); used with kind permission.)

The Rossiter–Percy approach provides for a range of advertising tactics that are oriented to the conditions which are determined by the interplay of the level of involvement and the type of dominant motivation. These conditions may only exist within a member of the target audience for a certain time. Consequently, they may change and the advertising tactics may also have to change to meet the new conditions. There are two main points that emerge from the work of Rossiter and Percy. The first is that all messages should be designed to carry both rational, logical information

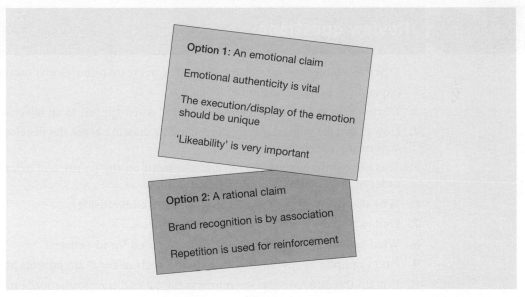

FIGURE 19.5 Message tactics where there are low involvement and transformational motives (Based on Rossiter and Percy (1997); used with kind permission.)

Persuasion through the central processing route is characterised by an evaluation of the alternatives within any one product category. and emotional stimuli, but in varying degrees and forms. Secondly, low-involvement conditions require the use of just one or two benefits in a message, whereas high-involvement conditions can sustain a number of different benefit claims. This is because persuasion through the central processing route is characterised by an evaluation of the alternatives within any one product category.

Summary

Advertising has an important role to play in most promotional plans. It is used primarily to build awareness and to usher in the other tools of the mix. The tasks that advertising is expected to achieve will have been set out in the promotional objectives and they will require communication with target consumers and organisational buyers.

Advertising is normally regarded as a tool that can persuade and change the behaviour of individuals, but there are a growing number of researchers who believe that its prime use is to defend loyal customers from the attacks of competitor products, by reinforcing attitudes.

The design and assembly of advertising messages is crucially important. Through establishment of a good realm of understanding, messages can be created in such a way that they stand a far greater opportunity of building a dialogue between members of the target audience and the brand. By appreciating the underlying emotions of the target buyer and the motivations that drive attitudes and purchase intentions, the balance and the pattern they assume can be shaped in such a way that they lead to effective advertising.

Review questions

1. Describe each of the four elements needed to create promotional messages.
2. Explain the concept of source credibility.
3. Discuss what is meant by the term 'balance' when applied to an advertising message.
4. How might an understanding of conclusion drawing assist the development of an advertising message?
5. Select five print advertisements and comment on the nature and extent to which the order of presentation features in each of them.
6. Why do advertisers use spokespersons in their advertising?
7. Find examples of each type of spokesperson.
8. What are the main types of appeal that are used by advertisers?
9. Find examples of advertising messages for each of the main appeals identified.
10. Explain the difference between informational and transformational motivations.

MINI-CASE
No More Nails

An alternative to drilling, nailing, screwing and bolting items together is to stick them. Indeed, many professional builders on the Continent have long preferred to use this method as it is quicker, faster and ultimately cheaper. These products are referred to as instant grab, gap-filling adhesives and in the UK brands such as Gripfill are well established, in the trade. However, apart from a single, rather little-known brand, the UK consumer market was wide open to instant grab products.

Henkel, with sales in excess of £50 million, is the UK market leader in DIY adhesives. The organisation has developed two main products: Solvite and Pritt Stick. The other products that drive revenue have been acquired, with brands such as UniBond, Nitromors and Loctite.

The Henkel new product development programme identified the market opportunity for an instant grab product targeted at the consumer market. Various business and marketing plans were developed, including the following:

- 200,000 unit sales per annum
- a minimum annual turnover of £400,000
- clear brand leadership of the DIY category
- improved key customer perceptions.

To introduce the product to the market an advertising agency, BDH TBWA, was given the brief to introduce the concept to the DIY market and recruit *new* users. This would both help sales for Henkel and also enable DIY retailers to develop add-on sales opportunities among these new users. The agency developed the name No More Nails, which gave a clear, crisp, direct view of the product and its capabilities. User group research clearly advocated a no-nonsense direct tone of voice, similar to the Ronseal message '*It does exactly what it says on the can*'. Research also found that it would be important to stress the convenience as well as the performance attributes.

Marketing communications – phase 1

The first phase of the marketing communications strategy was focused on the Henkel sales force, which was required to sell the product to DIY retailers with the backing of a visually striking campaign based on in-store posters and point-of-sale materials.

One of the first key roles for the in-store advertising was to inform current consumers about this new product and to educate them in terms of its various applications. In addition, it was important to give them a reason to buy. The initial in-store advertising communicated the product's fundamental proposition (it sticks anything to virtually anything) in original and eye-catching ways at the point of purchase. See Exhibit 18.4.

At first this strategy proved successful but sales began to level off within 12 months. The marketing strategy had to change if the original sales targets were to be reached.

Marketing communications – phase 2

The next significant phase therefore was to use mass media advertising in order to attract new users. How-ever, there were problems in determining the market size and potential in what was an unknown market – just how much should be spent? It was decided to use a small amount of advertising (£100,000) to create the impression of a much larger campaign, one of at least a £500,000 national equivalent figure. As a result, a television campaign was developed, targeted at both reluctant and irregular DIY consumers as well as enthusiasts. The campaign followed the simplicity of the original in-store posters. Using the power of television to demonstrate the powerful properties of No More Nails Henkel was able to differentiate its brand from all others and deliver a strong call-to-action. See Exhibit 19.7.

The campaign was shown in three test market areas. Store managers and retail buyers were sent

EXHIBIT 19.7 TV ad for No More Nails

video mailings of the television advertisements and they were also invited to trade roadshows at local TV studios. The power of TV was used to add credibility to the sales pitch.

This campaign drove sales vigorously and soon it was rolled out in other ITV areas. EPoS data shows an immediate sales response to adspend. Comparisons with non-advertised regions show a marked rate of sale benefits where media investment takes place. Not only did the advertising impact heavily on sales, but in areas where TV advertising was used more people were aware of No More Nails than all of its major competitors put together. Results also show that the campaign's visual impact and recall is high.

Each campaign was tracked with quantitative as well as qualitative research. The analysis shows a strong correlation between advertising and sales increases and it can be shown that, via control comparisons, the media investment is significantly raising the profile of No More Nails as well as that of its UniBond parent brand.

The use of advertising by UniBond is interesting, not just because of the impact on sales but because of the way in which product advertising was used to support the sales force and Henkel's wider product range. In a market where sales promotions and trade deals are very common, Henkel concentrated on brand development, maintained a price premium (on average 22.3 per cent *above* the number two brand, Vallance's Liquid Nails) and has been able to launch a series of brand extensions, such as No More Cracks, No More Sealant Guns and No More Big Gaps, each a premium convenience DIY consumer product group in its own right.

In addition, the advertising has provided credibility for Henkel and helped to enhance its reputation. The largely *regional* media investment had *national* impact on the stocking policies of national multiple retailers. It is this TV-related distribution and display effect that has largely driven the non-ad region increases.

Advertising was used to deliver a new brand into a relatively new market. Advertising was used to first inform and educate consumers and trade buyers. It was then used to differentiate the No More Nails brand from the large number of copycat brands that entered the market on the back of Henkel's generic market development work.

No More Nails now accounts for some 10 per cent of Henkel's DIY sales in the UK. Yet despite the increased competition, No More Nails continues to outstrip its rivals. The DIY instant grab adhesives category is currently worth £128 million a year and is still growing. In fact, it has driven the growth of the overall value of DIY adhesives sales. Yet, prior to the TV investment, the sector pottered along with a DIY value of just £1.5 million.

By being first into the market Henkel has been able to build a dominant level of category awareness or, as it is often phrased, developed top of mind awareness. This was built on with strong rational and emotional claims so that users, it appears, prefer to stay with the Henkel product, and in doing so secure Henkel's competitive advantage.

The author would like to acknowledge the kind help and materials supplied by Henkel.

Questions

1   To what extent is the message strategy based on an emotional or informational approach?

2   Discuss the reasons why Henkel decided not to launch immediately with a television campaign.

3   Why was the functionality of the product sufficient to establish credibility? If you had to use a spokesperson to endorse the brand who would you select and why?

4   Consider each of the emotional and information-based appeals and apply them to No More Nails. Which of them works and which do not work? Justify your reasoning.

References

Adams, A.J. and Henderson Blair, M. (1992) Persuasive advertising and sales accountability. *Journal of Advertising Research*, **32**(2) (March/April), pp. 20–5.

Archer, B. (1994) Does humour cross borders? *Campaign*, 17 June, pp. 32–3.

Arora, R. (1985) Consumer involvement: what it offers to advertising strategy. *International Journal of Advertising*, **4**, pp. 119–30.

Batra, R. and Stayman, D.M. (1990) The role of mood in advertising effectiveness. *Journal of Consumer Research*, **17** (September), pp. 203–14.

Braithwaite, A. and Ware, R. (1997) The role of music in advertising. *Admap* (July/August), pp. 44–7.

Buzzell, R. (1964) Predicting short-term changes in market share as a function of advertising strategy. *Journal of Marketing Research*, **1**(3), pp. 27–31.

Faison, E.W. (1961) Effectiveness of one-sided and two-sided mass communications in advertising. *Public Opinion Quarterly*, **25** (Fall), pp. 468–9.

Foxall, G.R. and Goldsmith, R.E. (1994) *Consumer Psychology for Marketing*. London: Routledge.

Haas, O. (1997) Humour in advertising. *Admap* (July/August), pp. 14–15.

Hannah, D.B. and Sternthal, B. (1984) Detecting and explaining the sleeper effect. *Journal of Consumer Research*, 11 September, pp. 632–42.

Hovland, C.I., Lumsdaine, A. and Sheffield, F.D. (1949) *Experiments on Mass Communication*. New York: Wiley.

Hovland, C.I. and Mandell, W. (1952) An experimental comparison of conclusion drawing by the communicator and by the audience. *Journal of Abnormal and Social Psychology*, **47** (July), pp. 581 8.

Kardes, F.R. (1988) Spontaneous inference processes in advertising: the effects of conclusion omission and involvement on persuasion. *Journal of Consumer Research*, **15** (September), pp. 225–33.

Kelman, H. (1961) Processes of opinion change. *Public Opinion Quarterly*, **25** (Spring), pp. 57–78.

Lannon, J. (1992) Asking the right questions – what do people do with advertising? *Admap* (March), pp. 11–16.

Parker, R. and Churchill, L. (1986) Positioning by opening the consumer's mind. *International Journal of Advertising*, **5**, pp. 1–13.

Ray, M.L. and Wilkie, W.L. (1970) Fear: the potential of an appeal neglected by marketing. *Journal of Marketing*, **34** (January), pp. 54–62.

Rossiter, J.R., Percy, L. and Donovan, R.J. (1991) A better advertising planning grid. *Journal of Advertising Research* (October/November), pp. 11–21.

Rossiter, J.R. and Percy, L. (1997) *Advertising and Promotion Management*. 2nd edn. New York: McGraw-Hill.

Schiffman, L.G. and Kanuk, L. (1991) *Consumer Behavior*. 4th edn. Englewood Cliffs, NJ: Prentice-Hall.

Summers, D. (1993) Dangerous liaisons. *Financial Times*, 18 November, p. 12.

Vaughn, R. (1980) How advertising works: a planning model. *Journal of Advertising Research*, **20**(5), pp. 27–33.

Traditional media

In order that messages can be delivered to specified audiences they need to utilise (and pay for) the services of particular media. The array of media is continually growing, all of which have strengths and weaknesses that impact on the quality, effectiveness and meaning attributed to the message by the audience.

This chapter focuses upon the characteristics of traditional off-line media and the following chapter considers new media, mainly in the form of Web sites and interactive media.

Aims and objectives

The aim of this chapter is to establish the principal characteristics of each type of off-line media. This will assist understanding of the management processes by which media are selected and scheduled to deliver advertiser's messages. These planning and scheduling processes are looked at in Chapter 22.

The objectives of this chapter are to:

1. determine the variety and types of media available to advertisers;
2. establish the primary characteristics of each type of medium;
3. examine the strengths and weaknesses of each type of medium;
4. provide a brief summary of the main trends in advertising expenditure on each type of medium in the United Kingdom;
5. compare the media used by direct marketers with those of general marketers.

Introduction

This chapter is the first of three that considers the media. This chapter explains some of the main characteristics associated with each of the primary off-line and traditional media while the next, Chapter 21, focuses on new and online media. Chapter 22 considers issues relating to media switching and planning. Information concerning in-store media, product placement and packaging are considered in Chapter 29.

Organisations use the services of a variety of media in order that they can deliver their planned messages to target audiences. Of the many available media, six main classes can be identified. These are broadcast, print, outdoor, new, in-store and other media classes. Within each of these classes there are particular media types. For example, within the broadcast class there are television and radio, and within the print class there are newspapers and magazines.

Of the many available media, six main classes can be identified.

Within each type of medium there are a huge number of different media vehicles that can be selected to carry an advertiser's message. For example, within UK television there are the terrestrial networks (Independent Television Network, Channel 4 and Channel 5) and the satellite (BSkyB) and cable (e.g. NTL) networks. In print, there are consumer and business-oriented magazines and the number of specialist magazines is expanding rapidly. These specialist magazines are targeted at particular activity and interest groups, such as *Amateur Photographer*, *Golf World* and the infamous *Sponge Divers Gazette*! This provides opportunities for advertisers to send messages to well-defined homogeneous groups, which improves effectiveness and reduces wastage in communication spend. There are, therefore, three forms of media: classes, types and vehicles. See Table 20.1.

TABLE 20.1 Summary chart of the main forms of media

Class	Type	Vehicles
Broadcast	Television	*Coronation Street*, *Big Brother*
	Radio	Virgin 1215, Classic FM
Print	Newspapers	The *Sunday Times*, The *Mirror*, The *Daily Telegraph*
	Magazines: Consumer	*Cosmopolitan*, *FHM*, *Woman*
	Business	*The Grocer*, *Plumbing News*
Outdoor	Billboards	96 and 48 sheet
	Street furniture	Adshel
	Transit	London Underground, taxis, hot-air balloons
New media	Internet	Web sites, email, intranet
	Digital television	Teletext, SkyText, Ceefax
	CD-ROM	Various: music, educational, entertainment
In-store	Point of purchase	Bins, signs and displays
	Packaging	The Coca-Cola contour bottle
Other	Cinema	Pearl & Dean
	Exhibitions	Ideal Home, The Motor Show
	Product placement	Films, TV, books
	Ambient	Litter bins, golf tees, petrol pumps
	Guerrilla	Flyposting

Evaluative criteria

One of the key marketing tasks is to decide which combination of vehicles should be selected to carry the message to the target audience. The means by which this decision is reached is the subject of Chapter 22. First, however, it is necessary to consider the main characteristics of each media type in order that media planning decisions can be based upon some logic and rationale. The fundamental characteristics concern the costs, delivery and audience profile associated with a communication event.

Costs

One of the important characteristics that needs to be considered is the costs that are incurred using each type of medium. There are two types of cost: absolute and relative.

There are two types of cost: absolute and relative.

Absolute costs are the costs of the time or space bought in a particular media vehicle. These costs have to be paid for and directly impact upon an organisation's cash flow. Relative costs are the costs of contacting each member of the target audience. Television, as will be seen later, has a high absolute cost but, because messages are delivered to a mass audience, when the absolute cost is divided by the total number of people receiving the message the relative cost is very low.

Communication (of the message)

The way in which an advertiser's message is delivered to the target audience varies across media types. Certain media, such as television, are able to use many communication dimensions, and through the use of sight, sound and movement can generate great impact with a message. Other types of media have only one dimension, such as the audio capacity of radio. The number of communication dimensions that a media type has will influence the choice of media mix. This is because certain products, at particular points in their development, require the use of different media in order that the right message be conveyed and understood. A new product, for example, may require demonstration in order that the audience understands the product concept. The use of television may be a good way of achieving this. Once understood, the audience does not need to be educated in this way again and future messages need to convey different types of information that may not require demonstration, so radio or magazine advertising may suffice.

The number of communication dimensions that a media type has will influence the choice of media mix.

Audience profile

The profile of the target audience (male, female, young or old) and the number of people within each audience that a media type can reach are also significant factors in media decisions. For example, 30 per cent of adults in the socio-economic grade A read the *Sunday Times*. Only 4 per cent of the C2 group also read this paper. Messages appropriate to the A group would be best placed in the *Sunday Times* and those for the C2 group transmitted through the *News of the World*, which 34 per cent of the C2 group read. It is important that advertisers use media vehicles that convey their messages to their target markets with as little waste as possible. Newspapers enable geographically based target audiences to be reached. The tone of their content can be controlled, but the cost per target reached is high. Each issue has a short lifespan, so for positive learning to occur in the target audience a number of insertions may be required.

A large number of magazines contain specialised material that appeals to particular target groups. These special-interest magazines (SIMs) enable certain sponsors to reach interested targets with reduced wastage. General-interest magazines (GIMs) appeal to a much wider cross-section of society, to larger generalised target groups. The life of these media vehicles is generally long and their 'pass along' readership high. It should not be forgotten, however, that noise levels can also be high owing to the intermittent manner in which magazines are often read and the number of competing messages from rival organisations.

ViewPoint 20.1   *Glamour*

When *Glamour* was launched in March 2001 the new publication from Condé Nast received huge marketing communications support. This included a £4.5 million campaign featuring television, print, outdoor and cinema. In addition, public relations generated a huge amount of publicity about the A5 'handbag-sized' format.

Part of the rationale for the radically different size was not only the success experienced in the United States and Italy, where the format has been successful for over seven years, but also the trend towards miniaturisation (Walkmans, mobile phones) and the fashion appeal that the smaller size might represent. In addition, however, is the high impact the smaller size has in standing out on the shelves of newsagents among the clutter of the established, larger, heavyweight competitors.

Television reaches the greatest number of people, but although advertisers can reach general groups, such as men aged 16–24 or housewives, it is not capable of reaching specific groups and incurs high levels of wastage. This blanket coverage offers opportunities for cable and satellite entrepreneurs to offer more precise targeting, but for now television is a tool for those who wish to talk to mass audiences. Television is expensive from a cash flow perspective but not in terms of the costs per target reached.

Radio offers a more reasonable costing structure than television and can be utilised to reach particular geographic audiences. For a long time, however, this was seen as its only real strength, particularly when its poor attention span and non-visual dimensions are considered. Research in the 1990s, however, indicates that it is not destined to remain the poor relation to television, as radio has been shown to be capable of generating a much closer personal relationship with listeners, witnessed partly by the success of Classic FM and Virgin 1215, than is possible through posters, television or print.

The interesting point about outdoor and transit advertising is that exposure is only made by the interception of passing traffic. Govoni *et al.* (1986) make the point that

Interception represents opportunistic coverage.

such interception represents opportunistic coverage. Consequently the costs are low, at both investment and per contact levels.

The use of direct marketing has grown in recent years, as technology has developed and awareness has increased. The precise targeting potential of direct mail and its ability to communicate personally with target audiences is impressive. In addition, the control over the total process, including the costs, remains firmly with the sponsor.

The size of the industry should not be underestimated as UK advertising expenditure reached £17.2 billion in 2003. See Table 3.1 in Chapter 3.

Print media

Print media are very effective at delivering a message to the target audience.

Of the total amount spent on advertising, across all media, most is spent on the printed word. Newspapers and magazines are the two main types of media in this class. They attract advertisers for a variety of reasons, but the most important is that print media are very effective at delivering a message to the target audience.

Most people have access to either a newspaper or a magazine. They read in order to keep up to date with news and events or to provide themselves with a source of entertainment. People tend to have consistent reading habits and buy or borrow the same media vehicles regularly. For example, most people read the same type of newspaper(s) each day and their regular choice of magazine reflects either their business or leisure interests, which are normally quite stable. This means that advertisers, through marketing research, are able to build a database of the main characteristics of their readers. This in turn allows advertisers to buy space in those media vehicles that will be read by the sort of people they think will benefit from their product or service.

The printed word provides advertisers with the opportunity to explain their message in a way that most other media cannot. Such explanations can be in the form of either a picture or a photograph, perhaps demonstrating how a product is to be used. Alternatively, the written word can be used to argue why a product should be used and detail the advantages and benefits that consumption will provide the user. In reality, advertisers use a combination of these two forms of communication.

The print media are most suitable for messages designed when high involvement is present in the target market. These readers not only control the pace at which they read a magazine or newspaper but also expend effort to read advertisements because they care about particular issues. Where elaboration is high and the central processing route is preferred, messages that provide a large amount of information are best presented in the printed form.

Magazines are able to reach quite specialised audiences and tend to be selective in terms of the messages they carry. In contrast, newspapers reach a high percentage of the population and can be referred to as a mass medium.

Magazines are able to reach quite specialised audiences.

The messages that newspapers carry are usually for products and services that have a general appeal.

Newspapers

Expenditure on newspaper advertising increased steadily in the 1980s, fell back sharply with the recession in the early 1990s and has since slowly redeveloped its position. Since 1986 newspaper readership has fallen, but the biggest shift has been away from the popular press with some movement towards the quality press. In 2003 expenditure on national newspaper advertising reached £2.4 billion or 14 per cent of the total UK advertising spend (Advertising Association, 2004).

Strengths

Newspaper advertisements are seen positively by readers because they are in control of the speed and depth of reading the newspaper. This means that they choose which advertisements to read. This facilitates what is referred to as comparison shopping. Newspapers provide wide exposure for advertisements, and market coverage in local, regional or national papers can be extensive. These media vehicles are extremely flexible as they present opportunities for the use of colour and allow advertisements of variable sizes, insertions and coupons.

Weaknesses

The combination of a high number of advertisements and the small amount of reading time that readers give to newspapers means that most newspaper advertisements receive little exposure. Statistics show that newspaper circulation has fallen behind population growth; furthermore, teenagers and young adults generally do not read newspapers.

Newspaper circulation has fallen behind population growth.

Advertising costs have risen very quickly and the competition to provide news, not just from other newspapers but other sources such as cable, satellite and terrestrial television, means that newspapers are no longer one of the main providers of news. One of the consequences of this has been the development of price wars between many of the broadsheets, with *The Times* and The *Sunday Times* leading the battle by discounting the Sunday and Monday papers at various times.

Printing technologies advanced considerably during the 1980s and 1990s, but the relatively poor quality of reproduction means that the impact of advertisements can often be lost.

Magazines

In a market that is extremely competitive, the overall trend is that the number of monthly consumer magazines has grown, mainly at the expense of weekly magazines. Advertising revenue was fairly static in 2002–3 at around £785 million (Advertising Association, 2004), whereas advertising in business magazines fell by 3.8 per cent. Business magazines attract nearly a third as much advertising revenue as the consumer sector, despite being highly fragmented and complex. The fastest growing part of the consumer magazine market has been the men's lifestyle sector, where titles such as *Loaded*, *FHM* and *Men's Health* established themselves quickly. However, circulation and advertising revenues have started to fall.

Strengths

The visual quality of magazines is normally very high.

The visual quality of magazines is normally very high, a result of using top-class materials and technologies. This provides advertisers with greater flexibility in the way in which the visual dimension is used to present their messages, which can be used to create impact and demand the attention of the reader.

The large number and wide range of specialised titles means that narrow, specific target audiences can be reached much more successfully than with other media vehicles. For example, messages concerning ski equipment, clothing and resorts will be best presented in specialist ski magazines on the basis that they will be read by those who have an interest in skiing, and not knitting, snooker or fishing. Magazines can provide a prestigious and high-quality environment, with the editorial providing authority, reassurance and credibility to the advertising that they contain.

Magazines are often passed along to others to read once the original user has finished reading it. This longevity issue highlights the difference between circulation (the number of people who buy or subscribe to a magazine) and readership (the number of people who actually read the vehicle, perhaps as a friend or partner at home, in a doctor's waiting room or at the instigation of a department head or workplace superior).

Weaknesses

Magazine audience growth rates have fallen behind the growth in advertising rates. Therefore the value of advertising in magazines has declined relative to some other types of media. The long period of time necessary to book space in advance of publication dates and to provide suitable artwork means that management has little flexibility once it has agreed to use magazines as part of the media schedule. Apart from specialist magazines, a single magazine rarely reaches the majority of a market segment. Several magazines must be used to reach potential users.

The absolute and relative costs associated with magazines are fairly high.

Having reached the target, impact often builds slowly, as some readers do not read their magazine until some days after they have received it. The absolute and relative costs associated with magazines are fairly high, particularly costs for general-interest magazines. Special-interest magazines, however, allow advertisers to reach their target audiences with little waste and hence high levels of efficiency. Customer magazines differ from consumer magazines because they are sent to customers direct, often without charge, and contain highly targeted and significant brand-related material. These have made a big impact in recent years and, partly because of high production values, have become a significant aspect of many direct marketing activities.

ViewPoint 20.2   Parenting-based customer titles

The number of customer magazines has grown in recent years across a variety of sectors. *M&S Magazine*, Waitrose's *Food Illustrated*, Honda's *Dream* and Boots' *Health and Beauty* are just some of the more prevalent titles. In Spring 2005 the NSPCC, in a co-branding alliance with Woolworths, launched *Your Family*. This is a quarterly magazine and is part of the charity's positive parenting campaign. Distributed free through Woolworths' stores, the magazine will be funded through advertising and compete against paid-for consumer magazine titles, *Practical Parenting* and *BBC Parenting*.

One final form of print media yet to be discussed concerns directories. Advertising expenditure on directories has continued to increase. One of the largest consumer directories is Yellow Pages, or Yell as they are now called as they have diversified across new media (e.g. Yell.com).

Broadcast media

Broadcast media are quite young in comparison with the printed word. Fundamentally, there are two main forms of broadcast – television and radio – to which attention will be given here. Advertisers use these classes of media because they can reach mass audiences with their messages at a relatively low cost per target reached.

Approximately 99 per cent of the population in the United Kingdom has access to a television set and a similar number have a radio. The majority of viewers use television passively, as a form of entertainment; however, new technological applications, such as digitalisation, indicate that television will be used proactively for a range of services, such as banking and shopping. Radio demands active participation, but can reach people who are out of the home environment.

Broadcast media allow advertisers to add visual and/or sound dimensions to their messages. The opportunity to demonstrate or to show the benefits or results that a particular product can bring gives life and energy to an advertiser's message. Television uses sight, sound and movement, whereas radio can only use its audio capacity to convey meaning. Both media have the potential to tell stories and to appeal to people's emotions when transmitting a message. These are dimensions that the printed media find difficulty in achieving effectively within the time allocations that advertisers can afford.

Advertising messages transmitted through the broadcast media use a small period of time, normally 60, 30 or 20 seconds, that the owners of the media are prepared to sell. The cost of the different time slots varies throughout a single transmission day and with the popularity of individual programmes. The more listeners or viewers that a programme attracts, the greater the price charged for a slice of time to transmit an advertising message. This impacts upon the costs associated with such advertising.

> The cost of the different time slots varies throughout a single transmission day.

The time-based costs for television can be extremely large. For example, as at 17 November 2004, the rate card cost of a nationwide 30-second spot in the middle of *Coronation Street* was £82,932 (www.itvsales.com). However, this large cost needs to be put in perspective. The actual cost of reaching individual members of the target audience is quite low, simply because all of the costs associated with the production of the message and the purchase of time to transmit the message can be spread across a mass of individuals, as discussed earlier.

The costs associated with radio transmissions are relatively low when compared with television. This reflects the lack of prestige that radio has and the pervasiveness of television. People are normally unable, and usually unwilling, to become actively involved with broadcast advertising messages. They cannot control the pace at which they consume such advertising and as time is expensive and short, so advertisers do not have the opportunity to present detailed information. The result is that this medium is most suitable for low-involvement messages.

> The costs associated with radio transmissions are relatively low when compared with television.

Where the need for elaboration is low and the peripheral processing route is preferred, messages transmitted through electronic media should seek to draw attention, create awareness and improve levels of interest.

As the television and radio industries become increasingly fragmented, so the ability to reach particular market segments improves. This means that the potential effectiveness of advertising through these media increases. These media are used a great deal by consumer markets, mainly because of their ability to reach mass audiences. Messages targeted at other organisations need to be delivered by other media that are more selective and controlled more effectively.

Television

For a number of years there was above inflation growth in television advertising expenditure but annual growth in 2003 was just 1 per cent. When the dotcom bubble burst revenue growth stopped abruptly and station average prices have been falling by anything up to 30 per cent, causing major difficulties for the various television owners.

The number of households connected to cable networks represented 13.7 per cent of all homes by December 2003. More importantly, the percentage of homes connected as a percentage of the number of homes who could be connected has risen from 21 per cent in 1996 to 26.6 per cent in 2003. This slow but increasing acceptance of cable television is expected to encourage advertisers, who will be able to target their audiences much more easily and communicate with them with less wastage.

Strengths

From a creative point of view, this medium is very flexible and the impact generated by the combination of sight and sound should not be underestimated. Consumer involvement and likeability of an advertisement is dependent upon the skill of the creative team. The prestige and status associated with television advertising is higher than that of other media: in some cases, the credibility and status of a product or organisation can be enhanced significantly just by being seen to be advertising on television.

The prestige and status associated with television advertising is higher than that of other media.

The costs of reaching members of large target segments are relatively low, so the medium is capable of a high level of cost efficiency.

Weaknesses

Because the length of any single exposure is short, messages have to be repeated on television in order to enhance learning and memory. This increases the absolute costs of producing and transmitting television commercials, which can be large, making this medium the most expensive form of advertising.

Television audiences are increasingly fragmented as the number of entertainment and leisure opportunities expands. For example, terrestrial television networks are suffering from the competition from cable and satellite broadcasters plus video recorders and other sources of entertainment. This proliferation of suppliers has led to television clutter. In order to keep viewers, programmes are now promoted vigorously by television companies and a variety of techniques are being used to prevent viewers from channel grazing (switching).

The trend towards shorter messages has led to increased clutter.

The trend towards shorter messages has led to increased clutter. Management flexibility over the message is frustrated, as last-minute changes to schedules are expensive and difficult to implement. The only choices open to decision makers are either to proceed with an advertisement or to 'pull' it, should circumstances change in such a way that it would be inappropriate to proceed.

Technological developments, most notably the development of interactive television (iTV), have been slow to be adopted. However this is changing as iTV is increasingly recognised as the way forward (see Chapter 10 for more on iTV). However, as technology advances to create better, more commercially viable interactive opportunities so it also develops disruptive potential to benefit viewers who dislikeadvert interruptions. First there was TiVo, a device to blank out ads when recording programmes, which was slow to catch on but is now gathering momentum. Now there are personal video recorders that enable viewers to pause live programmes, 'time-shift' programming to suit their on lifestyles and convenience and to fast forward through commercial breaks in six seconds (Sherwin, 2004). He reports that advertisers are developing 'intelligent' ads which impart information, so that they are recognised when the fast forward button is activated.

Radio

There has been a rapid increase in the number of commercial radio services offered in the United Kingdom since 1973. Advertising expenditure on radio reached £582 million in 2003, a growth of 6.8 per cent on the previous year. This renewed interest in radio is possibly due to a trend away from television and a recognition of the versatility of what is often regarded as a secondary medium.

Strengths

Radio permits specialised programming, which in turn attracts selective audiences. Radio is a mobile medium (that is, one that can travel with audiences), so that messages can be relayed to them, for example, even when shoppers are parking their cars near to a shopping precinct. The production costs are low and radio has great flexibility, which management can use to meet changing environmental and customer needs. If it is raining in the morning, an advertiser can implement a promotional campaign for umbrellas in the afternoon.

From a creative point of view the medium needs the active imagination of the listener. Radio has a high level of passive acceptance and the messages that are received are more likely to be retained than if they were delivered via a different medium. This combination of features makes radio an excellent support medium.

Radio has a high level of passive acceptance.

Weaknesses

Because there is an absence of visual stimuli, the medium lacks impact and the ability to hold and enthuse an audience. Levels of inattentiveness can be high, which means that a high number of messages are invariably ignored or missed. When this is combined with low average audiences, high levels of frequency are required to achieve acceptable levels of reach.

Outdoor media

The range of outdoor media encompasses a large number of different media, each characterised by two elements. First, they are observed by their target audiences at locations away from home. Secondly, they are normally used to support messages that are transmitted through the primary media: broadcast and print. Outdoor media can, therefore, be seen to be a secondary but important support media for a complementary and effective communications mix.

Media spend on outdoor advertising declined in the earlier 1990s after steady growth in the 1980s. Growth returned once again to the sector as the UK economy moved out of recession and has since grown consistently. In 2003 strong growth in 6-sheet posters helped advertising revenues to £901 million (Advertising Association, 2004).

Outdoor media consist of three main formats: street furniture (such as bus shelters); billboards (which consist primarily of 96-, 48- and 6-sheet poster sites); and Transit (which covers the Underground, buses and taxis). Outdoor media accounted for approximately 5.3 per cent of total advertising expenditure in 2003, and have been taking an increasing percentage of organisations' media spend.

Outdoor media consist of three main formats: street furniture, billboards and Transit.

ViewPoint 20.3   London and the 2012 Olympic bid

In 2004 Transport for London (Tfl) provided £8.4 million of media space to support the London bid for the 2012 Olympics. Using more than 50,000 outdoor sites on the London Underground and bus networks, plus 40 double-decker buses carrying the livery of the bid programme, the aim was to provide full backing for the bid, raise support and promote interest ahead of the visit of the Olympic Committee early in 2005.

Tfl wanted a successful bid as that would bring the financial resources necessary to redevelop the transport system, funds that otherwise would not be secured.

EXHIBIT 20.1 Promotional boards used in The Mall at The London Marathon

Other reasons for the growth in outdoor expenditure are that it can reinforce messages transmitted through primary media, act as a substitute media when primary media are unavailable (e.g. tobacco organisations deprived of access to television and radio) and provide novelty and interest (electronic, inflatable and three-dimensional billboards), which can help avoid the clutter caused by the volume of advertising activity.

Billboards and street furniture

These are static displays and, as with outdoor media generally, are unable to convey a great deal of information in the short period of time available that people can attend to the messages. However, advances in technology permit precise targeting of poster campaigns on a national, regional or individual audience basis, or by their proximity to specific outlets, such as banks, CTNs (confectioner, tobacconist and newsagent) and off-licences. Evaluation through the POSTAR system allows for measurement of not only the size and type of audience but also the traffic flows, travel patterns and even how people read posters.

ViewPoint 20.4   Golfing media

Sports events represent prime promotional opportunities, if only because of the television coverage. The picture at Exhibit 20.2 depicts a golf tournament at the Forest of Arden. Here on the final hole British golfer David Howell is shown teeing off, surrounded by promotional media. The flowers on the bank remind audiences of the location, the perimeter boards reinforce messages from the main sponsors of the event, the clock and timing of the event is sponsored by Omega, the caddies' bibs carry advertising messages and even the bins receive financial support.

EXHIBIT 20.2 A variety of promotional messages communicated at an important golfing event

Strengths

One of the main advantages of this medium springs from its ability to reach a large audience. This means that most members of a target audience are likely to have an opportunity to see the message, so the cost per contact is very low. It has become recognised that outdoor media can provide tremendous support to other tools in the media mix, particularly at product launch, as back-up and when attempting to build brand name recognition.

The medium is characterised by its strong placement flexibility.

The medium is characterised by its strong placement flexibility. Messages can be placed geographically, demographically or by activity, such as on the main routes to work or shopping. The potential impact is high, as good sites can draw the eye and make an impression. Gross rating points (GRPs; see Chapter 22) can be developed quickly by reaching a large percentage of the target audience many times in a short period.

Weaknesses

Messages transmitted by this medium do not allow for the provision of detailed information. Posters are passed very quickly and the potential attention span is therefore brief. This means that the message must be short, have a high visual impact and be capable of selling an idea or concept very quickly. Printing and production lead times are long; therefore while control over message content is high, the flexibility in delivery once showings are agreed can be a limiting factor. The final disadvantage of outdoor media to be discussed is that the effectiveness of message delivery is very difficult to measure, and in an age when accountability is becoming an increasingly important factor, this drawback does not help to promote the usage of this medium.

Transit

Transit or transport advertising is best represented by the names and signs that are painted on the sides of lorries. These moving posters, which travel around the country, serve to communicate names of organisations and products to all those who are in the vicinity of the vehicle. Indeed, transport advertising includes all those vehicles that are used for commercial purposes. In addition to lorries, transport media include buses, the Underground (trains, escalators and walkways), taxis, aeroplanes, blimps and balloons, ferries and trains, plus the terminals and buildings associated with the means of transport, such as airports and railway stations. For example, at Milan airport, the walls of terminal 1 are dominated by huge advertisements for the Giorgio Armani brand. The difference between outdoor and transport media is arbitrary, although the former are media static and the latter are media mobile.

Messages can be presented as inside cards, where the messages are exposed to those using the vehicle. An example of this would be the small advertising messages displayed on the curvature of the roof of London Underground trains. Outside cards are those that are displayed on the exterior of taxis, buses and other commercial vehicles.

> Outside cards are those that are displayed on the exterior of taxis, buses and other commercial vehicles.

Strengths

The exposure time given to messages delivered via transport media can be high, but is dependent upon the journey time of the reader. The high readership scores that are recorded are due, possibly, to the boredom levels of travellers. The cost is relatively low, mainly because no extra equipment is necessary to transmit the message. Local advertisers tend to benefit most from transport advertising, as it can remind buyers of particular restaurants, theatres and shops.

Weaknesses

The medium fails to cover all market segments, as only particular groups use transportation systems. In comparison with other media it lacks status, is difficult to read (particularly in the rush hour) and suffers from the high level of clutter associated with inside cards.

Cinema

There has been a revival in the level of expenditure on cinema advertising, reflecting the trends in audience sizes. In 2003 cinema advertising was worth £180 million, or approximately 1 per cent of total advertising spend. With decreasing audiences until 1985, advertisers were reluctant to utilise this high-impact medium. However, since the boom years of the mid-1980s and the recessionary early 1990s, the number of people visiting cinemas in the United Kingdom has grown considerably, and attendances reached 167 million in 2003 (CAA/EDI). This growth is linked to the increase in multiplex cinemas (multiple screens at each site). With customer satisfaction levels improving, advertisers have consistently increased the adspend in this medium.

The number of people visiting cinemas in the United Kingdom has grown considerably.

Advertising messages transmitted in a cinema have all the advantages of television-based messages. Audio and visual dimensions combine to provide high impact. However, the audience is more attentive because the main film has yet to be shown and there are fewer distractions or noise in the communication system. This means that cinema advertising has greater power than television advertisements. This power can be used to heighten levels of attention and, as the screen images are larger than life and because they appear in a darkened room that is largely unfamiliar to the audience, the potential to communicate effectively with the target audience is strong.

Strengths

The mood of the audience is generally positive, particularly at the start of a show. This mood can be carried over into the commercials. Furthermore, the production quality of cinema messages is usually very high and transmission is often assisted by high-quality audio (digital surround-sound systems) that is being installed in the new multiplex arenas.

The production and transmission costs are quite low, which makes this an attractive media vehicle. The attention-getting ability and the power of this medium contribute to the high recall scores that this medium constantly records, often four times higher than the average recall scores for television commercials.

ViewPoint 20.5   Kidman turns heads in cinemas

Cinema advertising was boosted by the debut of Chanel No. 5's new ad in the premiere of *Bridget Jones: The Edge of Reason*. The production costs of the ad, at £18 million, were reputed to be the most expensive ad made to date and the decision to show the ad in the cinema before breaking it on television was greeted as a positive endorsement for the medium.

The celebrity star was Nicole Kidman, who at the time was reputedly considering the role as Coco Chanel in a film to be made about the fashion designer's life. The only reference to the brand appears at the end of the ad when Kidman is shown wearing a pendant saying No. 5.

Weaknesses

The costs associated with reaching local audiences are low; however, if an advertiser wishes to reach a national audience, the costs can be much higher than those for television.

The audience profile for UK cinema admissions indicates that approximately 80 per cent of visitors are aged 15 to 34. With an increasing proportion of the population aged over 55 (the grey market), cinema advertising is limited by the audience profile and the type of products and services that can be realistically promoted.

The third and final weakness is to some the most important. The irritation factor associated with viewing advertising messages when customers have paid to see a film has been found to be very high. Some respondents, to a number of studies, have expressed such an intensity of feeling that they actively considered boycotting the featured products. So despite the acclaim and positive reasons for using cinema advertising, advertisers are advised to be careful about the films they select to run their commercials against (audience profile will also be affected) and whether they should use this medium.

In-store media

Advertisers have become aware of the need to provide suitable in-store communications.

As an increasing number of brand choice decisions are made during the shopping experience, advertisers have become aware of the need to provide suitable in-store communications. The primary objective of using in-store media is to direct the attention of shoppers and to stimulate them to make purchases. The content of messages can be easily controlled by either the retailer or the manufacturer. In addition, the timing and the exact placement of in-store messages can be equally well controlled.

As mentioned previously, both retailers and manufacturers make use of in-store media although, of the two main forms (point-of-purchase displays and packaging), retailers control the point-of-purchase displays and manufacturers the packaging. Increasingly there is recognition of the huge potential of retail stores becoming an integrated media centre, with retailers selling and managing media space and time. Attention is given here to in-store media and the retail media format, while a consideration of packaging issues can be found in Chapter 29.

Point of purchase

The most used are window displays, floor and wall racks to display merchandise, posters and information cards, plus counter and check-out displays.

There are a number of POP techniques, but the most used are window displays, floor and wall racks to display merchandise, posters and information cards, plus counter and check-out displays. The most obvious display a manufacturer has at the point of purchase is the packaging used to wrap and protect the product until it is ready for consumption. This particular element is discussed in detail later.

Supermarket trolleys with a video screen attached have been trialled by a number of stores. As soon as the trolley passes a particular infrared beam a short video is activated, promoting brands available in the immediate vicinity of the shopper. Other advances include electronic overhead signs, in-store videos at selected sites around the store and coupons for certain competitive products dispensed at the check-out once the purchased items have been scanned. Indirect messages can also play a role in in-store communications: for example, fresh bread smells can be circulated from the super-market bakery at the furthest side of the store to the entrance area, enticing customers further into the supermarket. Some aroma systems allow for the smell to be restricted to just 45 cm (18 inches) of the display.

End-of-row bins and cards displaying special offers are POP media that aim to stimu-late impulse buying. With over 75 per cent of supermarket buying decisions made in store, a greater percentage of communication budgets will be allocated to POP items.

ViewPoint 20.6   Out of the home and into the community

The use of new technology to reach targeted audiences outside the home is a reflection of the break-down in the use of traditional media. With audiences fragmenting, clients are searching for new ways and techniques of reaching customers. One of these approaches involves using outdoor media where communities or naturally forming groups of people gather outside the home.

One such group forms in stores and supermarkets and the rapid development of in-store media (see below) is a sign of the media industry's search for pull- rather than push-based media. Another approach has been to use media in order to engage audiences. For example, Yahoo used the 22-storey-high Reuters giant screen in New York to display a public virtual car-racing game, in order to promote its motoring pages at the time of the New York motor show (Silverman, 2004).

Strengths

Point-of-purchase media are good at attracting attention and providing information. Their ability to persuade is potentially strong, as these displays can highlight particular product attributes at a time when shoppers have devoted their attention to the pur-chase decision process. Any prior awareness a shopper might have can be reinforced.

From management's point of view, the absolute and relative costs of POP advertise-ments are low. Furthermore, management can easily fine tune a POP advertisement to

The absolute and relative costs of POP advertisements are low.

reflect changing conditions. For example, should stock levels be high and a promotion necessary to move stock out, POP displays can be introduced quickly.

Weaknesses

These messages are usually directed at customers who are already committed, at least partly, to purchasing the product or one from their evoked set. POP messages certainly fail to reach those not actively engaged in the shopping activity.

There can be difficulties maintaining message continuity across a large number of outlets. Signs and displays can also be damaged by customers, which can impact upon the status of a product. Shoppers can therefore be negatively influenced by the temporary inconvenience of damaged and confusing displays. Unless rigorously con-trolled by store management, the large amount of POP materials can lead to clutter and a deterioration in the perception shoppers have of a retail outlet.

Retail media centres

Supermarkets have begun to recognise the media potential that lies within their stores. Traditionally retailers allow their stores to be used in a variety of ways by a variety of organisations to communicate messages to their audiences. These audiences are jointly owned, not necessarily in equal proportion, by the branded food manufacturers that use stores for distribution purposes, and the retailers which try to build footfall or store traffic through retail branding approaches. As a result the management of the media opportunities and the messages that are communicated are uncoordinated, inconsistent and the media potential, to a large extent, ignored. In the past retailers will have argued that their core business rests with retailing not selling and managing media. However, the media world has developed considerably in recent years, often in tandem with developments in technology. Retailers have for a long time built databases using customer information and developed sales promotion-based loyalty programmes as a result. Street furniture has been used in the immediate vicinity of supermarkets and shopping centres and malls to drive local traffic. In-store radio has been used, first as background and now, in many cases, as a radio station based on entertainment. In-store posters, promotions, merchandising and various ambient media opportunities have been used haphazardly or, at best, in an uncoordinated way. All of these have been managed by a variety of specialists, typical of the way in which the marketing communications industry has developed (see Chapter 3). However, as Reid (2004) points out, this may be about to change. For a start Tesco and Asda-Walmart have installed various in-store plasma television screens and are selling television time according to product category, some of which equates directly with particular aisles and store space. In addition, Asda-Walmart has created its own media (or sales) centre through which media activities are to be coordinated. Based on its own publishing facilities this change may impact on media planning and change the way established media houses account for the new retail media environment. Tesco understands the media potential of each of its stores and the opportunities that advertisers value by reaching the 27 per cent of all UK shoppers who visit Tesco each week. Indeed, some of the time sold on the Tesco TV channels has been sold to advertisers that are not stocked in store (e.g. finance, travel and cars). It appears that the retail channel can be expected to grow considerably in volume, value and media presence, besides influencing the nature and structure of the media industry.

> Tesco and Asda-Walmart have installed various in-store plasma television screens and are selling television time according to product category.

Ambient media

Ambient media are a fairly recent innovation and represent a non-traditional alternative to outdoor media. Ambient media are regarded as out-of-home media that fail to fit any of the established outdoor categories. Ambient-driven advertising revenue, although relatively small, has grown from £101 million in 2001 to £113 million in 2002. Ambient media can be classified according to a variety of factors. See Table 20.2. Of these standard posters account for the vast majority of ambient activity (59 per cent) with distribution accounting for 24 per cent and the four remaining categories just 17 per cent.

TABLE 20.2 Ambient media categories

Ambient category	Explanation
Standard posters	Washrooms, shopping trolleys, phone boxes
Distribution	Tickets, receipts, carrier bags
Digital	Video screens, projections, LED screens
Sponsorships	Playgrounds, golf holes, petrol pump nozzles
Mobile posters	Lorries, barges, sandwich boards
Aerials	Balloons, blimps, towed banners

Source: Advertising Association (2003).

EXHIBIT 20.3 Petrol pumps deliver ambient messages

Guerrilla tactics

Guerrilla media tactics are an attempt to gain short-term visibility and impact in markets where the conventional media are cluttered and the life of the offering is very short. Traditionally, flyposting was the main method, practised most often by the music business. Now the term refers to a range of activities that derive their power and visibility from being outside the jurisdiction of the paid-for media. Sabotage is a stronger interpretation, as the tactics require the hijacking of conventional media events. Lanigan (1996) reports on the use of spray paint to sabotage other advertisers' posters, while the launch of the *Blah Blah Blah* music magazine involved sticking speech bubbles over posters carrying messages for other advertisers.

> Guerrilla media tactics are an attempt to gain short-term visibility and impact in markets where the conventional media are cluttered.

Direct response media

Finally, this chapter on the media would not be complete without reference to direct response media. The principal use of the media is to convey one of two types of message: one is oriented towards the development of brands and attitudes; the other is aimed at provoking a physical (and mental) response. It follows that attitude and response-based communications require different media.

Conventional media (television, print or radio) once used just to develop brands and attitudes are now used as a mechanism or device to provoke a response, through which consumers/buyers can follow up a message, enter into an immediate dialogue and either request further information or purchase goods. The main difference with new media is the time delay or response pause between receiving a message and acting upon it. Through direct response mechanisms the response may be delayed for as long as it takes to make a telephone call, press a button or fill out a reply coupon. However, the response pause and the use of a separate form of communication highlight the essential differences.

> **The main difference with new media is the time delay or response pause between receiving a message and acting upon it.**

Estimates vary, but somewhere between 30 per cent and 40 per cent of all television advertisements now carry a telephone number or Web address. Direct Response Television (DRTV) is attractive to those promoting service-based offerings and increasingly FMCG brands such as Tango, Pond's face creams and Pepperami are using it. Also reports how DRTV can be likened to a video game. Level one is viewing the commercial, while Level two requires the respondent to phone in and receive more information and derive greater entertainment value. Only at Level three will there be an attempt to sell directly to the respondent. The main purpose for all advertisers using this route is to extract personal information for the database and subsequent sales promotion and mailing purposes.

One aspect that is crucial to the success of a direct response campaign is not the number of responses but the conversion of leads into sales. This means that the infrastructure to support these promotional activities must be thought through and put in place, otherwise the work and resources put into the visible level will be wasted if customers are unable to get the information they require.

The provision of the infrastructure itself is not sufficient. The totality of the campaign should support the brand. Indeed, this is an opportunity to extend brand opportunities and provide increased brand experiences. For example, Martini used direct response to involve the consumer in the brand and to encourage greater identification with the brand and its values. By thinking through the voice and the content that respondents would hear on phoning in, it was possible to provide entertainment, add value and extend the television advertisement by providing a direct audio extension (Croft, 1996).

Summary

Each of the main classes and types of media that are available to advertisers has its own strengths and weaknesses. In addition, each medium type and vehicle has properties that are important to each situation faced by individual advertisers. Their selection and deployment should be based upon a contingency approach.

The general media are facing increased competition from technology-driven media, such as cable and satellite. This has resulted in fragmentation of the market and increased choice for advertisers in an attempt to customise messages for particular, precise and well-defined target audiences. Direct marketing is a relatively new approach that, through the use of direct response media and database support, permits the generation and feedback of messages for and from individual customers. The overarching objectives are to build and sustain a mutually rewarding relationship with each customer, reduce media costs and improve effectiveness and measurement.

The use of direct response media will continue to grow, while for some organisations their whole marketing approach can be built around the concept (e.g. insurance and financial services) as changes in distribution drive whole strategic shifts. Increasingly, direct response is becoming attractive to FMCG brands in an effort to provide additional brand experiences for customers.

Review questions

1. Explain the differences between media classes, types and vehicles. Give two examples of each to support your answer.

2. Describe the main characteristics of the print media. Find examples to illustrate your points.

3. Compare and contrast newspapers and magazines as advertising media.

4. What do you think will be the impact on broadcast television of the growth in penetration by cable television? How will this affect advertisers?

5. If radio is unobtrusive, why should advertisers use it?

6. What are the strengths and weaknesses of outdoor advertising media? Why is it sometimes referred to as the last true broadcast medium?

7. Why are the relative costs of each medium different?

8. Under what conditions might cinema be used as the primary media?

9. List the main types of ambient media.

10. Explain the role of primary and secondary media. Is this a valid demarcation in a period of media neutral planning?

MINI-CASE
Galaxy 105-106

Mini-case written by Yvonne Dixon, Senior Lecturer, Marketing, University of Sunderland; Andy Saxton, Marketing Manager, Galaxy Radio

Steve and Karen Breakfast Show Campaign April–May 2003

Background

Galaxy 105–106, based in Newcastle upon Tyne, commissioned research into radio listening in the North East of England marketplace.

This research revealed that there was no clear breakfast show market leader. Competitor radio stations had been promoting their own breakfast shows using more conventional media; however, it seemed their activity was not having any impact. Galaxy 105–106 recognised the opportunity and began work on a promotional campaign to cut through other radio stations' activity. Budgets were limited (approximately £20,000) and thus any campaign had to create and sustain awareness and interest.

The aims of the campaign

The brief was simple: first to make existing listeners aware of who Steve and Karen actually were (breakfast show presenters), that is, putting faces to names. Secondly, to convert those who listen to the station from time to time into core Galaxy 105–106 listeners.

The solution

The answer to the first part of the brief was simple: use and design media that was suitable to carry Steve and Karen's photographs, giving maximum geographical coverage in the North East.

The answer to the second part of the brief was to be creative, to target in a way that was novel and adhered to Galaxy 105–106's brand values of being edgy, engaging, non-conformist and rewarding.

The media choices

A range of media was used. A bus-side campaign was booked for an initial one-month period at a cost of just over £15,000, including media space, artwork and materials. This did not leave much of the budget and so the Galaxy team became creative, utilising internal resources. The bus sides were backed up by the Galaxy ground crew distributing branded cereal packets at busy breakfast-time commuter locations, such as outside Tyne and Wear Metro (underground) stations, bus depots, railway stations and school drop-off points. The ground crew also distributed Galaxy branded beer mats, and acted as ticket inspectors, placing spoof parking tickets on car windscreens all over the region. Additionally a competition was run on air, which provided that essential initial interest.

Bus-side advertising

As a more conventional media platform, bus-side advertising allowed Galaxy 105–106 to reach a large number of people and to present the Steve and Karen Breakfast Show as being a breakfast show that was real and one to which listeners could relate.

The message was that, whoever you were, the Steve and Karen Breakfast Show would have something for you – something you could relate to – and give you situations you could find yourself in. See Exhibits 20.4 and 20.5.

Beer mats

Galaxy 105–106 targets the 15–34-year-old listener, and as such it wanted to make existing and potential listeners aware of the Steve and Karen Breakfast Show in a way they would appreciate.

Bars, pubs and clubs in the North East region were identified as a key way of reaching the target market. Galaxy 105–106 wanted a way to get into these venues without having to pay a fee to an agency, or the venues themselves, as budgets were relatively tight – providing beer mats was the ideal answer! Additionally there was the element of surprise – not many people would expect a radio station to advertise itself, or a show, on the reverse of a beer mat.

CRUMPET OR CROISSANT?   IT'S JUST BREAKFAST STEVE & KAREN   Galaxy 105-106

BUTTY OR BAGEL?   IT'S JUST BREAKFAST STEVE & KAREN   Galaxy 105-106

PORRIDGE OR PANCAKES?   IT'S JUST BREAKFAST STEVE & KAREN   Galaxy 105-106

EXHIBIT 20.4 Bus advertising

EXHIBIT 20.5 Use of buses (transport media) to communicate Galaxy radio

Using the 'What's That Noise?' competition as a hook, listeners were enticed into the Breakfast Show with the chance of winning thousands of pounds.

Branded cereal packets

Galaxy 105–106 decided to market the Steve and Karen Breakfast Show to an audience that would take notice of the message given to it – free food gifts provided the ideal medium.

After clearing the shelves of the North East's biggest Cash 'n' Carry's, and then adding a Galaxy-branded sticker to the front of each packet, the Galaxy ground crew distributed Kellogg's Variety packs at busy breakfast-time commuter locations all around the North East.

The message was simple: 'Gain a few pounds over breakfast'.

Spoof parking tickets

Galaxy 105–106 wanted to create a very quick awareness rate. All over the North East region, free car parking spaces were becoming something of a novelty. With more and more Councils starting parking meter schemes, parking tickets on car windscreens were becoming more of a nuisance for motorists.

With this in mind a spoof parking ticket was created. The parking tickets were then placed in a clear plastic envelope, and deposited on to car windscreens in residential areas, in supermarket car parks, in out-of-town shopping centre car parks, and in any other areas where there was a high density of parked cars.

Once opened, the reverse of the parking ticket led with the line 'GOTCHA!' – Play What's That Noise and win £1000s!

Effectiveness

The effectiveness of this campaign can be measured in a number of ways.

First and foremost, the audience figures: during RAJAR survey weeks 38 2002–12 2003, the breakfast show had 281,000 listeners per week. This rose during RAJAR survey weeks 2–25 2003 to 313,000 listeners per week. This equates to a rise of 5,000 listeners in average daily audience.

Secondly, it is evident from the number of calls to the radio station from listeners wanting to take part in the 'What's That Noise?' competition that all the off-air marketing activity carried out had worked, and allowed Galaxy 105–106 to increase the amount of cash available in the prize fund.

Thirdly, feedback from core Galaxy listeners on the ground, from focus groups recently carried out, and from existing advertising clients confirmed that the spoof car parking tickets were a particular hit. Listeners, and clients, had seen them across the region and had thought they were particularly

EXHIBIT 20.6 Beer mat for Galaxy Radio campaign

EXHIBIT 20.7 Cereal packet used to promote the *Its Just Breakfast* show on Galaxy Radio

EXHIBIT 20.8 Spoof parking tickets used to attract attention to the breakfast show

amusing. Some listeners had also contacted the radio station to ask if it was possible to supply them with a batch of car parking tickets, as they wanted to 'wind up' their friends, parents, etc.

And finally, it is evident from the latest set of RAJAR audience figures that, even though there has been a downturn in radio listening as a whole, Galaxy 105–106 has managed to overcome all competition from other radio stations (with bigger marketing budgets!) in terms of sheer audience size. Only Galaxy 105–106 can say it has more listeners than any other radio station in the North East – commercial or BBC!

Questions

1 How does Galaxy 105–106 use marketing communications to enhance not only awareness of the breakfast show but also brand values?

2 When considering likeability, do you believe that the spoof parking tickets could have alienated target customers?

3 How could new media have been used to encourage interaction?

4 Thinking about the 4C's framework, which media choices do you think are the most suitable?

5 If you were marketing manager for Galaxy 105–106 what other media might you have selected?

References

Advertising Association (2004) *Advertising Statistics Year Book*. Henley: NTC and at www.adassoc.org.uk/inform/.

Croft, M. (1996) Right to reply. *Marketing Week*, 12 April, pp. 37–42.

Govoni, N., Eng, R. and Galper, M. (1986) *Promotional Management*. Englewood Cliffs, NJ: Prentice-Hall.

Lanigan, D. (1996) Guerrilla Media. *Campaign*, 5 April, pp. 26–7.

Reid, A. (2004) Asda leads charge as retail media comes of age. *Campaign*, 2 July, p. 15.

Sherwin, A. (2004) Instant adverts to counter digital TV viewers. *The Times*, 24 July, p. 15.

Silverman, G. (2004) Back to the future: advertisers get out of the living room and onto the street. *Financial Times*, 25 October, p. 15.

Online and interactive media

21

The use of the Internet as a means of communicating with specific audiences is becoming an increasingly important aspect of contemporary marketing communications. The role of the Web site and the deployment of the promotional tools, online, has now to be considered an integral part of an organisation's overall communication activity.

Aims and objectives

The aim of this chapter is to explore some of the essential characteristics concerning Web site development and design and its ability to be a medium for marketing communications.

The objectives of this chapter are to:

1. explore issues concerning the management of Web sites;
2. examine Web site characteristics and understand their strengths and weaknesses;
3. compare the content and potential of traditional media with Web sites;
4. understand Web site visitor behaviour and consider its impact on Web site design;
5. examine the primary techniques and issues relating to advertising online;
6. consider some of the issues relating to the way in which each of the tools of the promotional mix can be deployed online;
7. explore the characteristics of online communities and consider how they might best be used in a relationship-building programme.

Introduction

Issues relating to technology and marketing communications were considered earlier in Chapter 10. This chapter follows on from that point and explores issues related to both online and interactive marketing communications.

After first considering the intrinsic qualities of digital media and exploring their key characteristics, considerable time is given in the first part of the chapter to examining the nature and characteristics of Web sites. This is followed by an exploration of the degree to which each of the promotional tools can or should be deployed online before looking at some of the other new media. The chapter concludes by considering the impact of digital media on audiences in the form of Internet communities.

Digital media

In comparison with traditional media, the Internet and new media facilities provide an interesting contrast. See Table 21.1. Space (or time) within traditional media is limited and costs rise as demand for the limited space/time increases. On the Internet, space is unlimited so absolute costs remain very low and static, while relative costs plummet as more visitors are recorded as having been to a site. Another aspect concerns the focus of the advertising message. Traditionally advertisers tend to emphasise the emotional rather than information aspect, particularly within low-involvement categories. Digital media allows focus on the provision of information and so the emotional aspect of advertising messages tends to have a lower significance. As branding becomes a more important aspect of Internet activity, it is probable that there will be a greater use of emotions, especially when the goal is to keep people at a Web site, rather than driving them to it.

> It is probable that there will be a greater use of emotions, especially when the goal is to keep people at a Web site.

Apart from the obvious factor that digital media and the Internet in particular provide interactive opportunities that traditional media cannot provide, it is important to remember that opportunities-to-see are generally driven by customers rather than by the advertiser that interrupts viewing or reading activities. People drive the interaction at a speed that is convenient to them; they are not driven by others.

TABLE 21.1 Comparison of new and traditional media

Traditional media	New media
One-to-many	One-to-one and many-to-many
Greater monologue	Greater dialogue
Active provision	Passive provision
Mass marketing	Individualised marketing
General need	Personalised
Branding	Information
Segmentation	Communities

TABLE 21.2 Comparison of information content

Web sites/Internet	Traditional media
Good at providing rational, product-based information	Better at conveying emotional brand values
More efficient as costs do not increase in proportion to the size of the target audience	Costs are related to usage
Better at prompting customer action	Less effective for calling to action except point-of-purchase and telemarketing
Effective for short-term, product-oriented brand action goals and long-term corporate identity objectives	Normally associated with building long-term values
Poor at generating awareness and attention	Strong builders of awareness
Poor at managing attitudes	Capable of changing and monitoring attitudes
Measures of effectiveness weak and/or in the process of development	Established methodologies, if misleading or superficial (mass media); direct marketing techniques are superior
Dominant orientation – cognition	Dominant orientation – emotion

Management control over Internet-based marketing communications is relatively high.

Management control over Internet-based marketing communications is relatively high as not only are there greater opportunities to control the position and placement of advertisements, promotions and press releases but it is possible to change the content of these activities much more quickly than is possible with traditional media. The goals outlined above indicate the framework within which advertising needs to be managed.

In addition to considering the attributes of the two different forms of media it is also worth considering the content of the information that each is capable of delivering. These are set out in Table 21.2.

As mentioned earlier, digital media is superior at providing rational, product-based information whereas traditional media are much better at conveying emotional brand values. The former has a dominant cognition orientation and the latter an emotional one. There are other differences but the predominant message is that these types of media are, to a large extent, complementary, suggesting that they should be used together, not one independently of the other.

Web site characteristics

Web sites are the cornerstone of Internet activity.

Web sites are the cornerstone of Internet activity for organisations, regardless of whether they are operating in the b2b, b2c or not-for-profit sectors and whether the purpose is merely to offer information or provide fully developed embedded ecommerce (transactional) facilities. The characteristics of a Web site can be crucial in determining the length of stay, activities undertaken and the propensity for a visitor to return to the site at a later time. When the experience is satisfactory, then both the visitor and the Web site owner might begin to take on some of the characteristics associated with relationship marketing.

To understand the characteristics associated with Web site interaction, consideration will first be given to their strengths and weaknesses, then the issues associated with the development of a Web site will be identified and finally the processes involved in attracting and managing Web site activity will be examined.

Web sites can be used for a variety of purposes but essentially they are either product-oriented or corporate-oriented. Product-oriented Web sites aim to provide product-based information such as brochureware, sales-based enquiries, demonstrations and endorsements through to online transactions and ongoing technical support as the main activities.

> Corporate-oriented Web sites aim to provide information about the performance, size, prospects, financial data and job opportunities relating to the organisation.

Corporate-oriented Web sites aim to provide information about the performance, size, prospects, financial data and job opportunities relating to the organisation. They also need to relate to issues concerning the ethical expectations and degree of social responsibility accepted by the company, if only to meet the needs of prospective investors and employees. The demarcation is not necessarily as clear cut as this might suggest but the essence of a site's orientation is to a large extent derived from the organisation's approach to branding.

The strengths and weaknesses of Web site facilities are set out in Table 21.3; however, it should be remembered that these are generalised comments and that some organisations have attended to these issues and have been able to develop the strengths and negate some of the weaknesses such that their Web sites are particularly attractive, user friendly and encourage repeat visits.

TABLE 21.3 Strengths and weaknesses of Web site-based communications

Strengths	Weaknesses
Quick to set up and easy to maintain	Slow access and page downloading speeds
Flexibility	Huge variability in Web site design and user friendliness
Variety of information	
High level of user involvement	Unsolicited email
Potentially high level of user convenience (and satisfaction)	Security and transaction privacy issues
	Relatively poor Internet penetration across UK households
Range of service facilities	
Global reach and equal access opportunities	Inconsistent fulfilment standards (information to online transactions only)
Open all hours – reduced employment costs	Variability and speed of technology provision
Very low relative costs (per person reached)	Lack of regulation concerning content and distribution
Can provide cost efficiencies in terms of marketing research	Online search time costs prohibitive for many users

ViewPoint 21.1 Online tea requirements

Marketing tea online is not the easiest of challenges but in the autumn of 2004 Tetley launched a range of specialist teas with the various options/flavours communicated through mood options such as 'relaxing', 'invigorating', with lifestyle tips and health information about tea in general.

The target market of 45 to 64 year olds are aware of health issues, are independently minded and positively involved with the Internet. Therefore allowing them to access information that they prefer is a crucial Web site design feature.

Strengths

Any WWW user can create a Web site, consisting of a home page and a number of linked pages. Business pages can carry advertising, product catalogues, descriptions, pricing, special offers, press releases – all forms of promotional material. They can link to online order pages, so that potential customers can order directly, or to email facilities for requesting further information or providing feedback. Consumer interest and activity can be monitored easily, allowing for timely market research, rapid feedback and strategy adaptation.

Barriers to entry are low, it is relatively inexpensive to create/maintain a site and share of voice is theoretically equal for all participants, although in practice this is clearly not the case. Large organisations can buy banner ads and have a better chance of appearing in the first few results presented by search engines. Good design can add to brand appeal and recognition. Potential customers actively seek products and services, which is both time and cost effective from a company's point of view, and indicative of positive attitudes, perception and involvement. Channel communications can also be swift and supportive. Coverage is global, without the need for huge investment or expensive staff to be employed around the clock. Savings can be made in advertising budgets, travel, postage and telephone costs. Different time zones no longer matter in the virtual environment and language barriers are less of an issue. However, it has been suggested that cultural and language issues have been partly responsible for the relatively slow take-up of the Internet through PCs, which is in essence a geographic and cultural variance in the process of diffusion (Curtis, 2000).

> It is relatively inexpensive to create/maintain a site and share of voice is theoretically equal for all participants.

Weaknesses

Some of the disadvantages are that the speed of access, page location and loading are still too slow for many users, especially from home PCs. Potential customers are easily put off by slow or unreliable connections and this frustration can result in negative images of the company or product. Poorly designed Web sites, which confuse rather than clarify, also leave a lasting poor impression, one that deters a return visit.

> Poorly designed Web sites, which confuse rather than clarify, also leave a lasting poor impression.

Unsolicited email is extremely annoying to many users and may be counter-productive. The worries over the security of financial details and transactions online, while not discouraging people from seeking information, may still be a barrier to full ecommerce. Fulfilment issues, principally delivery problems (such as long delays), wrong items, incorrect billing, plus the associated inconvenience of returning products or otherwise seeking resolution, may deter repeat purchase.

It is interesting to note that the UK supermarket chain Somerfield announced in June 2000 that it was closing its Web site and three associated distribution centres. A spokesman said on the radio that this operation had been 'a distraction'. While this is potentially true, consideration must be given to the marketing strategy and the overall context, internal resources, audience requirements, available computing and tele-communications facilities, prior to the design and build of any marketing Web site. In 2004, Somerfield does have a Web site but does not provide online shopping facilities.

Some regard ecommerce as transactional Web sites or extended enterprises but it is more to do with information/communication management and the impact on relationships. Ecommerce should be aimed at building new relationships with established customers and providing potential customers with a reason to change. The idea that ecommerce provides process efficiencies is correct but these features need to be transformed into benefits for customers. A fuller consideration of ecommerce-related matters can be found in Chapter 10.

Web site design

The design and functionality of a Web site is now recognised as an important integral aspect of an organisation's communication strategy. Indeed many organisations now update their sites on a regular basis. What constitutes a suitable Web site has also been the subject of much debate and speculation, marked by a lack of substantial empirical work to determine a common framework. Of the many ideas available two are featured here, if only because of their currency at the time of writing and the background of the researchers involved.

> The design and functionality of a Web site is now recognised as an important integral aspect of an organisation's communication strategy.

Karayanni and Baltas (2003) suggest that Web sites have four main characteristics. These are set out in Table 21.4 and were presented in the context of b2b markets.

This breakdown is useful becomes it indicates the main facilities that a successful site should provide. However, what it does not provide is a depth of insight and balance that would help organisations design their sites more appropriately. Rayport and Jaworski (2004) offer a 7Cs framework that they subsequently develop into a map which can be used to analyse sites and to design sites more effectively.

The 7Cs of the Customer Interface design are intended to cover the range of elements necessary for good Web site design. These are set out in Table 21.5.

Context

> The Context of a site is concerned with the balance between the functional and aesthetic look and feel.

The Context of a site is concerned with the balance between the functional and aesthetic look and feel. Some sites will be designed such that their functionality dominates the aesthetic and will try to provide text-based information rather than emphasising the visual elements of the site. Conversely other sites attempt to provide warm feelings for visitors and use multimedia facilities to create an emotional engagement with the site, often at the expense of long loading times. The balance between the functional and emotional can be termed balanced (although Rayport and Jaworski call it integrated). In this approach visitors experience a site that

TABLE 21.4 Four aspects of Web site design (Karayanni and Baltas, 2003)

Web site characteristic	Explanation
Interactivity	The provision of solutions in response to the provision of personal information and the ability of users to customise preferences. This can be delivered through memory storage/organisation and response to individual needs.
Navigability	The structure and organisation of the site combined with the ease with which information can be retrieved.
Multimedia design	The Internet offers all the facilities that each of the other media provide individually. This provides opportunities for stimulation as well as flexibility and visitor involvement with a site.
Content	
Company content	Information relating to the organisation, its markets, culture and values are important to establish credibility and reduce risk.
Customer content	This concerns both the provision of information, for example a *frequently asked questions* facility, and the collection of information about customers and the market.

TABLE 21.5 The 7Cs of the Customer Interface (Rayport and Jaworski, 2004); used with permission

Type of Community	Explanation
Context	Layout and design of web site
Content	Text, sound, pictures and video material
Community	Site enabled user-to-user communication
Customization	Site facilities to tailor itself to user needs
Communication	The ways in which 2 way communication is enabled
Commerce	Ability to enable commercial transactions
Connection	The number of other linked sites

provides a suitable level of information, is easy to navigate and yet is interesting and stimulating in terms of the emotional satisfaction derived from using the site. This need not be the optimal site design for all organisations as the context should reflect the values and purpose of the organisation itself. At one extreme, high fashion and luxury brands will focus on aesthetic styled sites while the Driving Vehicle Licensing Agency would be expected to be predominately functional.

Content

This refers to what is presented on the site in terms of audio, text, graphics, images and video.

This refers to what is presented on the site in terms of audio, text, graphics, images and video. The content can be considered in terms of the following:

- *Offering mix* – the balance between information, products and services.
- *Appeal mix* – the balance between functional (attribute and benefits) and the emotional (feelings and brand engagement) appeals.
- *Multimedia mix* – the selected combination of audio, text, graphics, images and video.
- *Timeliness mix* – the time sensitivity of the information determines how often a site needs to be updated. For example, www.BBC.co.uk/news has to be updated on a frequent and regular basis whereas a site dealing with largely historical or archive data (e.g. family trees) needs less regular attention.

Community

The increasing role and significance of online communities indicates that site design should reflect the needs and significance of these communities to organisations. Online communities are about the interaction between the users of a site, not between the site and users. These interactions may be one to one (email) or among many (chat rooms) but are significant to organisations as they can be a source of information about customer feelings and attitudes that may be strong or weak. A deeper consideration of these communities can be found at the end of this chapter.

Site design should reflect the needs and significance of these communities to organisations.

Customisation

The extent to which a site is capable of being adapted to the individual needs of visitors.

This is concerned with the extent to which a site is capable of being adapted to the individual needs of visitors. When customisation is initiated by customers it is referred to as personalisation but when driven and managed by the organisation it is called tailoring. Of course different sites will provide varying levels of customisation, from low through medium to high levels, and this will be reflected in the users' site experience.

Communication

The type of communication provided by a site is to some extent a reflection of the type of relationship offered by the organisation. The communication may be broadcast (content update reminders or mass mailings) in which case one-way communication prevents user response and with it opportunities for dialogue. Alternatively, interactive communication (user ratings or feedback) enables user response that can lead to dialogue.

Interactive communication (user ratings or feedback) enables user response that can lead to dialogue.

Connection

With the degree to which a site is linked or connected to other sites.

Connection is concerned with the degree to which a site is linked or connected to other sites. These links may be located on other Web pages and, when clicked, take the user to another site. If a transaction then occurs a commission is payable to the affiliate

ViewPoint 21.2   MondeMail

Of the many dynamic aspects of online marketing, rich media email, personalisation and ecustomer relationship management are key. The MondeMail system brings these together and generates a professional and personalised multimedia experience for the receiver. They can see their name and other personalised content animated and integrated within the email addressed to them. The recipient of the email can then personalise and forward the multimedia email to others simply by typing text into a form. Not only does MondeMail track all email that is forwarded but its reporting functions enable post-campaign analysis.

One of the features of the system is that it uses Macromedia Flash to create personalised multimedia files automatically from the database. The benefit is that it saves a huge amount of time and enables tailored rich media emails that otherwise could not be produced.

Monde On-line was developed for the Jaguar Web site – www.jaguar.com.au – as part of the campaign to develop Jaguar sales in Australia. Using fast to load Flash into the email itself (rather than clunky email attachments that take time to download) the system is not only fast to download but also avoids having to use executable files as multimedia attachments. These are often stripped by many corporate firewalls because of the fear of virus infection. Flash streaming media technology allows the multimedia to play immediately on being opened.

Source: www.monde.com.au/control.cfm?page=Case_Study_1. Retrieved 23 August 2004.

site. Outside links make it difficult for the user to return to the original page and are therefore not used a great deal. Framed links attempt to overcome this problem. Pop-up windows present a new site within the original site but can be annoying to users.

Commerce

The ability of a site to support financial transactions is an important feature of product-dominated Web sites. Apart from the need to provide a secure and risk-free trading environment, the key activities associated with these sites are: registration, shopping carts, credit card approval, one-click shopping, orders through affiliate sites, configuration facilities (different combinations of products and services), order tracking and delivery options. All of these 7Cs can be mapped and a site analysed against this criteria. See Table 21.6. Use of this mapping approach, that is the identification of which element applies to a Web site, can enable Web site designers to better understand how their site appears to visitors and enables sites to be developed according to the planned needs of organisations.

> The ability of a site to support financial transactions is an important feature.

To conclude this section it should be noted that there is little empirical research which shows how different Web site design features impact on visitor responsiveness. Indeed Kent *et al.* (2003) make the point that there is a gulf between what many organisations expect of a Web site capability to foster relationships and the actual Web sites that are designed to facilitate these relationships. They argue that there is an inconsistency in what is thought to be possible through a Web site and practice, that it is generally recognised that Web sites are poorly used dialogic tools, and that the actual design of a Web site can have a strong impact on the way in which visitors perceive the organisation and hence influence its relationship-building potential.

TABLE 21.6 7Cs Framework Map (Rayport and Jaworski, 2004); used with permission

Context	Aesthetically dominant	Functionally dominant		Integrated
Content	Product-dominant	Information-dominant		Service-dominant
Community	Nonexistent	Limited		Strong
Customization	Generic	Moderately customized		Highly customized
Communication	One-to-many, nonresponding user	One-to-many, responding user	One-to-one, nonresponding user	One-to-one, responding user
Connection	Destination	Hub		Portal
Commerce	Low	Medium		High

Web sites – visitor behaviour

It is possible to deconstruct users' Web site behaviour into a number of discrete activities, but the resultant list would be far too complex to be of any practical assistance. However, several authors have tried to discriminate among Internet users and segment the market accordingly. Lewis and Lewis (1997) have segmented the Internet on the basis of people who use the Internet and Forsyth *et al.* (2002) on the basis of those who are active online consumers, a behavioural approach to segmentation. These are shown at Table 21.7.

Several authors have tried to discriminate among Internet users and segment the market accordingly.

The design of Web sites should account for the needs of these different types of users and also the different stages each has reached in terms of their experience in using the Internet, their stage in the adoption process (see Chapter 2) and different stages users have reached in the buying process. For the purposes of the rest of this text, reference is made to two broad categories, active (goal directed) and passive (experiential) information seekers. Figure 21.1 depicts a process framework which describes the path that visitors follow when visiting a Web site.

The initial goal is to generate awareness of the Web site.

The initial goal is to generate awareness of the Web site and this needs to be understood in the knowledge that there are many Web users who have no interest in a particular (your) Web site and those who do are said to have a potential interest. The task is therefore to drive awareness levels among those who might find the site useful.

The second phase is to encourage the potential segment to actually visit the site. The problem is that there are two types of information seeker, passive and active. Passive seekers have no intention of hitting any particular site, whereas active seekers do have the express intention of visiting a particular site. Part of the communication strategy must therefore be geared to facilitating active seekers and attracting passive information seekers.

TABLE 21.7 Online segments

	Group of Internet users	Explanation
Lewis and Lewis (1997)	Directed information seekers	Experienced users who know what information they require and where to find it.
	Undirected information seekers	Inexperienced users (generally) who surf looking for information or who browse for leisure and pleasure.
	Directed buyers	Experienced users who are online with the express intention of purchasing specific goods/services.
	Bargain hunters	Users in search of free offers and sizeable discounts.
	Entertainment seekers	Users whose intentions are primarily to exploit sales promotions and competition opportunities and use chat rooms.
Forsyth *et al.* (2000)	Simplifiers	Simplifiers like readily available product information, reliable customer service and easy returns, and they respond positively to any evidence conveyed through advertising or on-site messages.
	Surfers	Surfers move quickly among sites, continually seeking new online experiences. Sites must offer a strong online brand, cutting-edge design and features, constant updates, and a rich variety of products and services.
	Bargainers	Bargainers care mainly about getting a good deal and enjoy the search for a good price, control over transactions, and the sense of community that sites such as eBay offer.
	Connectors	Connectors tend to be novices who use the Internet mainly to relate to other people through chat services.
	Routiners	Routiners use the Internet for news and financial information and spend more than 80 per cent of their online time surfing through their ten favourite sites.
	Sportsters	Sportsters behave like Routiners but gravitate to sports and entertainment sites. They view content as entertainment, so sites must be fresh, colourful and interactive to attract them.

The next phase is to ensure that active seekers, once on the Web site, are able to find the information they need quickly and efficiently so that they are inclined to revisit. This entails good site access and, once found, good site design so that navigation is easy, simple and fast. This normally means that the design of the site is simple and is user, rather than technologically, oriented. Passive information seekers on the other hand need to be made curious and stimulated to want to know more about the site and the products and services available. Here the objective is to convert hitters into visitors. A site registration book, supported perhaps with sales promotion devices, or a site design that is sufficiently intriguing may allow these goals to be met. Research suggests that there are three main elements that strongly influence the perceived quality of a Web site visit (Oxley and Miller, 2000):

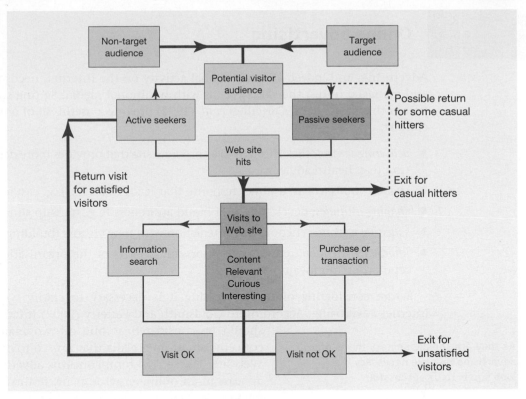

FIGURE 21.1 A framework depicting Web site visitor behaviour

- all are content oriented and refer to whether the site material is relevant to the needs of the visitor;
- the degree to which the content (and design) encourages curiosity to explore the site;
- whether the content is presented in an interesting way.

These three points correlate strongly with the idea of 'likeability', that advertising effectiveness improves when an individual assigns significant value (represented by relevance, curiosity and interest) to any particular form of marketing communication discipline but advertising in particular in this case (Chapters 7 and 18). Therefore, the main factors that might influence the way an individual perceives a Web site may be similar to the way they process and evaluate other marketing communications and, in particular, advertising messages. Goldsmith and Lafferty (2002) have made similar observations and consider theories concerning attitudes towards the ad as developed by Lutz *et al.* (1983) and Bruner and Kumar (2000). Attitudes developed towards advertisements can also impact on attitudes towards the brand and hence are better indicators of purchase intentions (see Chapter 5). Goldsmith and Lafferty also refer to advertisement brand recall and the fact that those consumers who have strong emotional feelings towards a brand (a positive attitude) are more likely to be able to recall it. Therefore, investment in marketing communications that seeks to establish top-of-mind awareness of a brand and also creates positive attitudes are more likely to be successful. The next section considers the role of each of the main tools of the promotional mix, when used in an online context.

Attitudes developed towards advertisements can also impact on attitudes towards the brand.

Online advertising

Advertising, and indeed all promotional activity on the Internet, needs to be planned and managed in just the same way as with traditional media. Setting suitable goals is part of this process and Cartellieri *et al.* (1997) provide a useful set of objectives in this context:

● *delivering content*: click through to a corporate site that provides more detailed information (e.g. health advice);

● *enabling transactions*: a direct response that leads to a sale (e.g. easyJet);

● *shaping attitudes*: development of brand awareness (e.g. start-up situations);

● *soliciting response*: encouraging interaction with new visitors (building market share);

● *improving retention*: reminding visitors and seekers of the organisation (developing reputation and loyalty).

Before considering online advertising it is necessary to clarify what constitutes Internet advertising. According to Goldsmith and Lafferty (2002) Internet advertising should be considered as one of two main forms. One concerns all off-line media that is used to drive traffic to a Web site. The second form concerns advertising that only appears in an online environment. Both need to be used together in a coordinated way as they are complementary forms of advertising that are necessary if a Web site is to be successful.

> As they are complementary forms of advertising that are necessary if a Web site is to be successful.

Online advertising is not confined to an organisation's Web site. Traffic needs to be directed from other sites so advertisements need to be placed on other Web sites where it is thought the target audience is most likely (or known) to visit. Therefore, advertisements are bought and placed on other Web sites and through careful analysis it is possible to place the ads on sites where it is thought that members of the target market will pass and not only see the advertisements but also be prompted to click the banner and be taken to the advertiser's own corporate site.

The most common form of ads are referred to as banner ads (see below), but as technology and marketing knowledge improves so more sophisticated versions of the banner ad have evolved. Some of these are outlined below.

Banner ads

These are the dominant form of paid-for communication on the Web. Fifty-five per cent of all Web ads are banner ads, which are responsible for 96 per cent of all Internet ad awareness. Banner ads use a link through to an advertiser's chosen destination and therefore can act as a gateway to other Web sites but are also effective in their own right. Banner ads are linked to key words submitted by a seeker into a search engine. The ad should therefore be strategically positioned to catch the optimum, or even greatest, traffic flow. Certain product groups such as computer-related products represent 56 per cent of all banner ads, whereas financial products account for only 7 per cent. An extension of the banner concept is e*banners. These allow for media-rich content that enables a depth of material and even ecommerce transactions. Therefore banners are said to signpost and e*banners provide action.

> These allow for media-rich content that enables a depth of material and even ecommerce transactions.

EXHIBIT 21.1 AA banner ad

TABLE 21.8 Determinants for click through

Source of predisposition	Factor
Audience related	Innate tendency to click through
Audience related	Immediate relevance of product
Audience related	Pre-existing source appeal (product or organisation)
Advertising related	Immediate relevance of the message
Advertising related	Level of curiosity generated by the banner

Source: Briggs and Hollis (1997); used with kind permission.

The aim of the banner ad is to attract attention and stimulate interest but the problem is that click-through rates are low, some reports suggest just 4 per cent, which leads to the question about whether banner ads are worthwhile. Briggs and Hollis (1997) found that click-through rates are determined by five main factors; see Table 21.8.

An interesting outcome from the Briggs and Hollis work was that banner ads are an important and effective form of communication. Making allowances for the scope of their research, click through was seen as unnecessary for the development of brand awareness and even the development of brand attitudes.

Pop-ups

Instead of transferring users to an orthodox Web site, banner ads can also be used to transfer users to an interactive site based upon games or a competition. These games provide entertainment and seek to develop user involvement and an incentive to return to the site at a later date. In addition, data can be captured about the user in order to refine future marketing offers. These ads can be saved for later use and are therefore more adaptable and convenient than interstitial ads that appear as users move between Web sites and cannot be controlled by the user.

Banner ads can also be used to transfer users to an interactive site.

Superstitials or interstitials

Also known as transitional online ads, these appear during the time when pages are being downloaded. They are intended to appear as a relief to the boredom that might set in when downloading can take a long time. In that sense they are not regarded as intrusive but supportive. One of the first of these was run by British Airways with a three-second media rich advertisement that was triggered when users clicked on either the travel or the business link on *The Times* home page. In turn there was a link to the British Airways Web site.

Micro sites

This type of site is normally product or promotion specific and is often run as a joint promotion with other advertisers. Creating a separate site avoids the difficulty of directing traffic to either of the joint partners' sites. Micro sites are much less expensive to set up than the traditional site and are particularly adept at building awareness as click throughs to micro sites are higher than through just banners.

> Micro sites are much less expensive to set up than the traditional site.

Email

Email can be used with high levels of frequency, which is important when building awareness. It is extremely cost effective in that each message costs less than a penny (Goften, 2000). Email communications are easily customised, enabling tailored messages for different segments. Brands such as www.FT.com send out customised messages to 14 different sectors and Goften reports that this is likely to increase. Email is also a part of direct marketing (see below).

ViewPoint 21.3   Houses by email

One of the problems encountered by estate agents (and house buyers and sellers) is the inordinate amount of time it takes to complete the cycle of transactions necessary to sell and buy a house. Paul Smith, an established estate agent, developed email systems in order to shorten the cycle.

As soon as a property came to the market his agency would email the particulars to preselected target buyers. Customers appreciated the promptness, detail and personal attention (sales rose 11 per cent), while Smith slashed his mailing and copying costs (by £729,000).

Now he uses SMS and texts his customers at 8 in the morning and queues often form outside some of his 250 nationwide branches.

Source: Armistead (2002); used with permission.

The use of email to attract and retain customers has become a main feature of many organisations' marketing communications programmes. Using appropriate email lists is a fast, efficient and effective way to communicate regularly with a market. Email-based marketing enables organisations to send a variety of messages concerning public relations-based announcements, newsletters and sales promotions, to distribute online catalogues and to start and manage permission-based contact lists. Many organisations build their own lists using data collected from their CRM system. By acquiring email responses and other contact mechanisms, addresses and contact details can be captured for the database and then accessed by all customer support staff.

> The use of email to attract and retain customers has become a main feature of many organisations' marketing communications programmes.

The use of viral marketing, that is email messages conveyed to a small part of the target audience where the content is sufficiently humorous, interesting or persuasive that the receiver is compelled to send it on to a friend, is limited in the b2b market. However, apart from just preparing lists and messages, organisations must be equally prepared to manage responses. The majority of responses are likely to be received within a day of transmission and organisations must be prepared to act upon the requests of those responding by at least acknowledging their message. The next step may require the activation of some form of internal processing and fulfilment, very often off-line and outsourced.

Another approach is to identify affinity groups such as those used within the financial services industry. Given the increasingly goal-directed nature of much Web activity, communicating to people through an affinity site can be more cost effective than trying to bring people to a site.

The use of the Internet should not be restricted to a series of independent, isolated communication activities. Through coordination with other tools and media the influence of the Internet can be considerably enhanced. The Web site lies at the heart of an organisation's Internet activities but it is necessary to use other tools and media to drive traffic to the site. Direct mail to generate leads and permission-based email lists plus print advertising for product and company awareness are effective at directing potential visitors and customers to a Web site. Once at the Web site the quality and relevance of the content will be paramount at retaining and developing interest.

> But it is necessary to use other tools and media to drive traffic to the site.

Email strategies require a central creative proposition around which all communications are linked. This might be related to particular attributes such as product features, for example colour, size or speed of service. The benefits of the attributes might also be used, for example no production downtime or improved staff efficiency might be valid claims. In contrast, an emotional feeling might be generated through the use of a tag line, gimmick, slogan, music or perhaps a mood. In other words, some form of branding needs to be used to differentiate the Web site and create longer-lasting memories that can be easily recalled through the mention of the brand name or perhaps an attribute or central theme.

Rich media banner ads

The essential difference between regular and rich media banner ads is that the latter allow for significantly more detailed and enhanced messages to be communicated to the target audience. Video, and other more visitor-engaging material, provide depth and interest. Millward Brown argues that the media-rich banner ads are highly effective mainly because the medium enhances the message.

> Media-rich banner ads are highly effective mainly because the medium enhances the message.

Offline media

In the late 1990s it was a common strategy to use TV advertising to build awareness and provide information about the Web site address. This TV approach cost £11 million in 1999 but in 2000 this figure fell 25 per cent (McCawley, 2000). This was partly due to a fall in the number of dotcom flotations and some bad publicity following the failure of some high-profile organisations such as boo.com. However, experience and research suggest that newspaper ads, magazines, word of mouth and online ads are far more effective in driving Web site traffic.

Online sales promotions

In principle these have been used either to attract and retain customers or as a way of providing interest and involvement with the brand by encouraging return visits. In reality price deals and competitions have been the main tools used. Bol.com used a viral campaign to announce a three-hour window in which it offered spectacular discounts. The information spread quickly, thousands of new customers registered and Bol had a huge number of new names and addresses on its database.

Virtual sales promotions are generally cheaper than hard copy versions but to date it appears that WWW sales promotions have not been used to develop brand differentiation or added value. The issue is, of course, that sales promotions are normally used to bring forward future sales, to provide a reason to buy now. On the Internet this motivation does not exist in the same way and for many people the only reason to use the Internet is to find information and to compare prices. However, digital media is being used increasingly to deliver sales promotion activity. Indeed there has been a decline in the use of traditional on-pack promotions (Barrand, 2004) and a significant growth in the use of SMS, email and the Internet as means of delivering sales promotion activity. While traditional forms of sales promotion are in need of innovation, the use of the Internet to deliver promotions and the use of text-to-win strategies are signs of the industry adapting and reinventing itself.

Digital media is being used increasingly to deliver sales promotion activity.

McLuhan (2000) refers to Amazon, which emails occasional users offering them a £3 voucher that is instantly redeemable and of immediate value. Beenz is a cyber currency that can be collected at a number of sites and then 'cashed' in for goods at other sites. Honda used Beenz to encourage test drives but the real value of Beenz collection is questioned by McLuhan as all that is involved is site registration. iPoints works in much the same way but the major difference is that these points can only be accessed at one appointed trader in each sector. This offers competitive advantage and the benefit of horizontal cooperation between iPoints traders (e.g. database knowledge). However, these currency collection devices (similar to old-fashioned Green Shield Stamps) serves only to foster 'site grazing' for Web points and are hardly a suitable way to develop brand value. They are also in danger of being abused through the development of automated software designed to scan and collect points by cheating.

Online direct marketing

The most obvious form of direct marketing on the Internet is email. However, direct marketing has an important part to play off-line to drive site traffic. Interestingly, advertising was the primary off-line tool used to drive traffic but following the reassessment and consolidation of dotcom growth at the beginning of 2000 direct marketing (and direct mail in particular) appears to have taken on the mantle as primary traffic generator. It does this in one of two main ways. The first way is to launch a teaser campaign appealing to people's innate curiosity or, secondly, the direct mail piece is part of a sales promotion campaign where the promise of a reward lures people to the Web site.

The most obvious form of direct marketing on the Internet is email.

EXHIBIT 21.2 NSPCC catalogue
Online Christmas catalogue designed to promote additional revenue.

In order to utilise this potency, by far the most influential aspect of email is what is referred to as viral marketing. This works on the principle that brand-based email messages are conveyed to a small part of the target audience and the content is sufficiently humorous, interesting or persuasive that the receiver is compelled to send it on to a friend. Felix pet food used this approach so that recipients ended up with cartoon cats walking around their screens. This is effectively word-of-mouth (word-of-mouse) communication and as such has very high credibility and penetration.

ViewPoint 21.4   Viral Crystal

The use of a viral campaign backed up by an off-line direct mail activity can only be really successful if there is a large database. Crystal Holidays, which offers action-based holidays and is a part of the TUI Group, holds both email and postal address details of their customers so this combined approach was perfectly feasible.

In addition to a personalised message about Crystal, the email contained a Mpeg movie about a hang glider that appears to fly out of the film and knock over items on the recipient's desktop. This was followed up by an oversized postcard with images of the various holiday options.

Another approach is to identify affinity groups. Given the increasingly goal-directed nature of much Web use, communicating to people through an affinity site can be more cost effective than trying to bring people to your site. Many online retailers sell via other sites, using the visitors of that site and the relationship that those visitors have with the site content. While the potential through email advertising and communications is high and often quite legitimate when a user has registered his/her email address at a particular site, the risk of being accused of sending spam or junk mail is equally high as it is perceived as unethical and intrusive. The development of permission marketing has brought about a change in perspective as contemporary approaches are now based upon communication with people who have already agreed to receive such marketing communications, very often agreed when registering at a site.

> Communicating to people through an affinity site can be more cost effective than trying to bring people to your site.

Online public relations

The use of public relations on the Internet, and extranets in particular, is claimed by many as a viable and active part of the promotional mix. The claim is that Web site hosts become media owners in the sense that they are free to publish materials and information without recourse to the origin. The problem is that the information they present or convey (on behalf of themselves) has not been influenced by an independent third party, such as an opinion former, and may be no more than brochureware. However, the role is more complex because the Web site assumes the role of the fax machine, with press releases posted so that those interested can view (at their discretion and initiative) and then enter into a dialogue in order to expand on the information provided.

Online and new media developments have been instrumental in assisting public relations move from a predominantly one-way model of communication to a two-way model. Hurme (2001) suggests that public relations practitioners can be divided into two main groups: those that use traditional media and those which adopt online communications. Since that paper was written an increasing number of practitioners will have moved over to online communications, but the realisation of the potential to develop true dialogue with stakeholders remains unfilled in most cases. Therefore opportunities for interactivity and dialogue have increased even if Web sites are not being designed to fulfil this requirement completely.

Other forms of public relations are more easily observable. Sponsorship activity is an important part of online marketing communications, whether it be a partnership deal or direct sponsorship of a site. Web sites can also play an important role in terms of crisis management. In the event of an organisational crisis or disaster, up-to-date information can be posted quickly either providing pertinent information or directing visitors to off-line facilities should it be appropriate.

> Web sites can also play an important role in terms of crisis management.

Online personal selling

Face-to-face personal communications over the Internet for the purposes of buying and selling remain the one part of the promotional mix that the Internet cannot address. Increasingly video conferencing (see later) does provide this facility but costs and logistics limit the practical application of this tool to conferencing and non-sales meetings. The

Internet is an impersonal medium and as such does not allow for direct personal communication. The recognition of this limitation should direct management attention to the use of the Internet as a complementary role within the promotional mix. However, it has been determined that the Internet can impact upon sales performance indirectly through sales management activities (Avlonitis and Karayanni, 2000). They describe how managing and analysing data can refine segmentation and customer classification schemes, allowing sales people to spend more time on core activities.

ViewPoint 21.5   Web site to build sales

Zyrotech Project Management (ZPM) provides design/build services, engineering, validation and compliance solutions that are customised for companies in the biotech and pharmaceutical industries.

Its original Web site was little more than brochureware and limited the perception visitors had of the company. There were several goals attached to the new site design. First it should display ZPM's expertise, flexibility and technological ability; secondly it needed to convey credibility such that large pharmaceutical organisations would be comfortable dealing with the company; and finally it also had to have a strong sales presence and be capable of delivering good quality sales leads.

The result was a site designed using content management, interactive flash movies, flash animation, custom-designed banners and database driven content. To launch the site a multimedia campaign was used. This was an interactive programme that incorporated print brochures with ecards, a multimedia trade show and presentation plus an Internet marketing campaign.

The results suggest that the new design was extremely successful. In essence the new site changed the way the company approached its business. Site visitors rose 52 per cent, the number of new clients increased by a record 43, including a deal with a major pharmaceuticals company, and page views doubled to 32,000 per month.

Sales leads are now handled very quickly on the basis that it is far better to contact potential clients as soon as possible after they visit the site. So, the marketing department relays potential leads to the sales department at the close of each day. Closely monitoring the behaviour of the Web visitors has sparked ZPM to create an entirely new marketing strategy for 2004.

The Web site remains at the core of Internet marketing and ecommerce activities and therefore it is important to attempt to evaluate a site's overall effectiveness if progress and goals are to be achieved. Many researchers have formulated methodologies and techniques to achieve this (e.g. Dreze and Zurfryden, 1997; Evans and King, 1999) and this topic is explored in greater detail in Chapter 17. However, a Web site does appear to have particular general parameters that need to be in position if the site is to be successful. These parameters concern access to the page (and ease of initial location), the technical specification of the page (e.g. page loading times) and the design and content in order that seekers can complete their visit goals as quickly and efficiently as possible, yet be stimulated in order to want to return another time.

> The Web site remains at the core of Internet marketing.

Online communities

Armstrong and Hagel (1996) were two of the first to propose the benefits of virtual communities and the development of these communities is one of the key elements that differentiates interactive from traditional media. Through communities people

TABLE 21.9 Four types of virtual community

Type of community	Explanation
Purpose	Those attempting to achieve the same goal or who are experiencing a similar process.
Position	Those experiencing particular circumstances. These might be to do with lifestage issues (the old or the young), health issues or perhaps career development opportunities.
Interest	Those sharing a hobby, pastime or who are passionately involved with, for example, sport, music, dance, family trees, jigsaws, gardening, film, etc.
Profession	Those involved with the provision of b2b services. Often created by publishers these portals provide information about jobs, company news, industry issues and trading facilities (e.g. auctions).

who share a common interest(s) interact, share information, develop understanding, build relationships and add value through their contribution to others involved with the Web site. In a sense user groups and special interest groups are similar facilities but the key with all these variations is the opportunity to share information electronically, often in real time.

There are four main types of community defined by their purpose, position, interest and profession.

Chaffey *et al.* (2003) refer to Durlacher (1999), who argues that there are four main types of community defined by their purpose, position, interest and profession. See Table 21.9.

Communities are characterised by several determining elements. Muniz and O'Guinn (2001) identify three core components:

● consciousness of kind: an intrinsic connection that members feel towards one another;

● the presence of shared rituals and traditions that perpetuate the community's history, culture and consciousness;

● a sense of moral responsibility, duty or obligation to the community as a whole and its individual members.

Within virtual communities five particular characteristics can be identified. The first concerns the model of communication, which is essentially visitor to visitor and in some cases customer to customer. Secondly, communities create an identity that arises from each individual's involvement and sense of membership and belonging. The more frequent and intense the interaction the stronger the identity. Thirdly, relationships, even friendships develop among members, which facilitates mutual help and support. The fourth characteristic concerns the language that the community adopts. Very often specialised languages or codes of (electronic) behaviour emerge that have particular meaning to members. The fifth and final characteristic refers to the methods used to regulate and control the behavior and operations of the community. Self-regulation is important in order to establish acceptable modes of conduct and inter-action among the membership.

The role that members assume within these communities and the degree to which they participate also varies. There are members who attend but contribute little to those who create topics, lead discussion, those who summarise and those who perform brokerage or intermediary roles among other members.

ViewPoint 21.6   Sharwoods in the community

Sharwoods, the Asian food brand, relaunched its Web site in 2004 as a fully interactive site for customers. The expectation was to build a community and to use this to add value and to help respond to increased competitive pressures.

The site is to be core to Sharwoods' communication strategy and to help achieve this the URL, www.sharwoods.com, appears on all forms of communication, including packaging and advertisements.

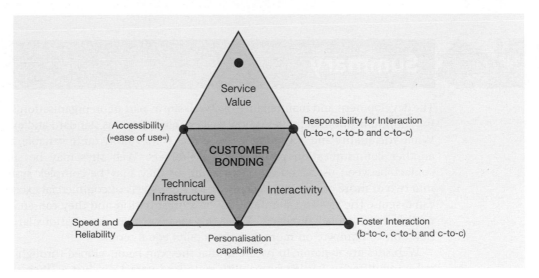

FIGURE 21.2 The Customer Bonding Triangle framework (Szmigin and Reppel, 2004); used with permission

The provision and form of online communities will inevitably develop and frameworks will emerge in order that understanding about the way they operate (effectively) is disseminated. Szmigin and Reppel (2004) have offered their Customer Bonding Triangle framework, which is built on interactivity, technical infrastructure and service value elements. See Figure 21.2.

The fit between the elements which determine the level of bonding between community members.

It is argued by the authors of this framework that it is the fit between the elements which determine the level of bonding between community members. Further work is required in this area but this framework provides an interesting conceptualisation of the elements that characterise this relatively new relationship developing approach.

Affiliate marketing

Associated with the concepts of communities and networks, affiliate marketing has become an essential aspect of online marketing communications and ecommerce.

Affiliate schemes are based on a network of Web sites on which advertisements or text links are placed.

Affiliate schemes are based on a network of Web sites on which advertisements or text links are placed. Those who click on them are taken directly to the host site. If this results in a sale, only then will the affiliate receive a commission (payment for the ad). Cookies are used to track, monitor and record transactions and pay commission plus any agreed charges. As with many online marketing schemes management can be undertaken in-house or outsourced. If the latter approach is adopted then many of the relationship issues discussed earlier need to be considered and managed.

Affiliate schemes are popular because they are low-cost operations, paid on a results-only basis and generating very favourable returns on investment. Rigby (2004) reports that the low-cost airline Flybe has an affiliate network of over 1,450 Web sites, which generates 10 per cent of sales, an ROI twice as big as that earned through direct response press activity and all at zero risk.

Summary

The development and maintenance of a Web site as part of an organisation's overall marketing communications activities is now well established and is standard and expected practice. While the quality and 'stickiness' of Web sites is inevitably quite variable, they do provide another communication point with stakeholders. Web sites may be simple points of contact between users and an organisation or they may be complex systems embedded into two or more organisations allowing for high levels of commercial exchange. Web sites can disguise the size and stature of the host organisation and they can enable all organisations to reach global audiences. What this means is that organisations large and small are now able to compete on more (but not totally) equal terms.

Web sites are dynamic in nature in that they can be developed through different phases reflecting different levels of capability and user interaction. Just as Web sites vary in user friendliness and capabilities, so the behaviour of site visitors is variable and every attempt should be made to accommodate their varying needs.

All the tools of the promotion mix can be deployed, to a greater or lesser extent, online. Advertising, through a variety of techniques, is a prime method of online communication but all the tools are able to fulfil particular online roles. Off-line communications are also important, particularly for driving visitors to Web sites.

Other forms of interactive communications, and in particular digital television services, are beginning to provide new forms of entertainment, shopping and banking facilities as well as marketing communications opportunities. In the longer term fully interactive services will bring increased leisure and entertainment facilities to a greater number of people and new opportunities for advertisers through interactive advertisements.

Review questions

1. List five strengths and five weaknesses attributed to Web sites.
2. Identify the different categories of Internet user. What are the principal characteristics of each type of user?
3. Prepare brief notes explaining the different phases of Web site visitor behaviour.
4. Explain how the communication capability of a Web site compares with traditional media.

5. Discuss the validity of the five goals suggested by Cartellieri *et al.* as a necessary part of Web site design.

6. What is the role of the Web site in terms of marketing communications? Explain four types of online advertising.

7. Find three examples of online sales promotion and evaluate their effectiveness.

8. To what extent is online public relations just online advertising?

9. Write a report examining the use of email online as a form of marketing communications. Find examples to support the points you make.

10. The development of Web sites has been a feature of recent organisational communications for reaching members and non-members. Prepare short notes outlining the problems in developing such sites and argue the case for developing a Web site for a manufacturer of household electrical goods, a Premier League football club and a department store.

MINI-CASE
Flowersbypost.com

Mini-case written by Mike Molesworth, Senior Lecturer, Bournemouth University

Flowersbypost (FBP) is an Internet-based florist and gift retailer operating from a warehouse in Hampshire, UK. It has been trading for 18 months. The company is run by partners Daisy Campbell and Harvey McCraken. Daisy has over 15 years' experience as a florist and Harvey gave up his highly paid job in the computer industry to start FBP. Neither have any real marketing experience.

FBP specialises in next-day delivery of bouquets of flowers, but also offer other gifts: chocolates, muffins, cuddly toys and up-market food hampers through a 'sister' website, Giftsbypost (GBP). Flowers account for 89 per cent of sales by value. FBP uses the Royal Mail for deliveries and each day goods are collected from its warehouse, where orders are also made up. Delivery is 'guaranteed' next day, or the Royal Mail will refund the full cost. In the event of a failed delivery, FBP will refund the full cost of the order. Currently failed deliveries happen in less than 1 in 200 orders.

Competition is fierce in this market and currently FBP is one of over 200 firms offering online flower purchase in the UK. Many of its competitors are also small specialists, but it also competes against large florist chains, Interflora and the major supermarkets. The large players always get the top slots on the major search engines and the rest of the competitors, including FBP, fight for the next spaces through search engine optimisation. Daisy and Harvey feel that they are doing pretty much all they can with search engine optimisation and have also made regular use of expensive paid-for links. Like many of their competitors, FBP also makes extensive use of affiliate sites and directories, but this too is very expensive. The advantage of affiliate programmes is that they are paid on a commission basis and therefore only have to be paid if they produce a sale. However most affiliates promote several online florists and gift retailers and it seems clear that when a customer uses an affiliate loyalty to the retailer is likely to be much lower. Overall, Harvey and Daisy feel that it is something of a 'lottery' as to whether a potential customer clicks on to a particular retailer's site. They are therefore putting most of their effort into ensuring that the experience of a visitor once they arrive at FBP is as good as possible. This means that they have invested heavily in the site. They pay for studio photography of the flowers and gifts, for example, and employ an external Web design company to help build the site. They also use a third-party-secure payment service. Harvey feels that, together, all these things give the impression that the company is a lot bigger than it really is. Sales since the start of trading are given in Table 1.

Although sales in the second year of trading are showing healthy increases and the company is in profit, both Daisy and Harvey are aware that with so much competition they need to grow the company as fast as possible. As a result they have employed an external marketing consultant, Lily Chalk, who quickly identified several key aspects of the operation that may inform further strategies for growth.

TABLE 1 FBP/GBP sales data by source

	Flower sales (£)				Gift sales (£)				
Quarter	Total flowers	Direct (new)	Affiliate	Repeat	Total gifts	Direct (new)	Affiliate	Repeat	Total (3)
2005 1st	69,100	31,871	29,876	7,353	9,100	4,337	2,798	1,965	78,200
2004 4th	339,100	297,899	10,178	31,023	47,900	23,433	14,867	9,600	387,000
2004 3rd	86,800	44,190	36,634	5,976	13,500	7,867	3,780	1,853	100,300
2004 2nd	128,000	68,815	52,642	6,543	9,000	5,034	2,254	1,712	137,000
2004 1st	40,300	20,842	17,982	1,476	6,400	4,457	1,476	467	46,700
2003 4th	176,300	105,263	70,675	362	21,800	17,117	4,531	152	198,100

First Lily notes that FBP and almost all its competitors offer a very similar product – simple gifts and bouquets, although GBP is more innovative than many others in the way it packages and combines gifts. Daisy explains that the similarity in offerings is because none of them use trained florists, but rather rely on casual labour. This is necessary because business is highly seasonal and because the cost of recruiting and retaining qualified staff would be too high. Experienced florists would almost certainly prefer to work in a shop where they get to talk with customers. Bouquets are therefore simple tied bunches designed by Daisy. Daisy is confident however that her years of experience mean that FBP uses the very best quality flowers and comparisons suggest that its gifts are at least as good as their main competitors and in many ways better. Harvey also points out that over 95 per cent of orders are delivered to an address different from the billing address. As gifts are received by a third party, they are less likely to question value for money. Again, this suggests that as long as quality is acceptable, the focus should be on promoting the company and on developing the site itself. But Lily notes that despite its professional appearance and the recognition of the importance of the user experience by Daisy and Harvey, the site lacks innovative interactive functions. It is simply presented as an online catalogue. She further observes that the same is true of almost all the competitors. Currently few, if any, offer competitive advantage through the use of interactive functions such as personal choice helpers, personalised pages, chat with a florist, or special event reminders.

Secondly, Lily also observes that a large proportion of sales seem to be coming from expensive affiliate sites, and that there is relatively little repeat business. The customer database currently holds 30,630 unique entries (total customers over the 18 months of trading). Fewer than 5,000 of these have ordered more than once. Lily further notes that a high proportion of repeat business is from business addresses and a significant number of the direct sales come from overseas addresses. Currently the site has a very English feel and focuses on private buyers. Daisy and Harvey confess that they have done little to encourage repeat business, or overseas business, although they do get customers to click a box allowing future communication from FBP and GBP in line with the Data Protection Act. They also confirm that a problem with affiliate business is that net profits from sales are reduced by about a half where business comes through an affiliate.

Finally, Lily reviewed existing marketing communication. Other than the expensive affiliate links and paid-for search results, FBP and GBP have done almost no promotion. They were lucky enough to get good PR coverage in a major Sunday newspaper in the run-up to Christmas 2004, but this was not planned. However budgets for marketing communications are very low. It is unlikely that the company could afford more than about £20,000 in total on marketing in the next year and this would include any major additions to the existing Web site.

Lily feels that there are several key issues that need to be addressed. First the company needs to consider ways in which it can differentiate itself from other retailers. In particular, this might be through the way gifts are presented on the site and the overall experience of using the site. Daisy and Harvey might also consider a focus on specific markets. Secondly, the company needs to consider ways of gaining more repeat business. Finally, the company needs to consider ways of gaining new customers who do not rely on expensive affiliate programmes that produce little loyalty. Lily considers it important that the brands FBP and GBP are built so that consumers seek out the specific stores rather than stumble on them via searches or affiliates. Lily now sits down with Harvey and Daisy to discuss options for the future.

Questions

1 Do you agree with Lily's analysis? Are there any other issues that you think might be important?

2 Consider the issue of site development and differentiation. Should the company focus on just some sections of the gift market, and if so which? How might this be reflected in site development? Which specific interactive functions should be included and why?

3 What can be done to encourage more repeat business?

4 Given the very limited budget, what approaches might be taken to drive new customers to the site?

5 How might the various online developments be integrated with off-line marketing communications approaches?

References

Armistead, L. (2002) Forms sold short by bad sales technique. *Sunday Times*, 20 October, p. 17.

Armstrong, A. and Hagel III, J. (1996) The real value of on-line communities. *Harvard Business Review*, **74**(3) (May/June), pp. 134–41.

Avlonitis, G.J. and Karayanni, D. (2000) The impact of Internet use on business-to-business marketing. *Industrial Marketing Management*, **29**, pp. 441–59.

Barrand, D. (2004) Promoting change. *Marketing*, 6 October, pp. 43–5.

Briggs, R. and Hollis, N. (1997) Advertising on the web: is there response before click-through? *Journal of Advertising Research* (March/April), pp. 33–45.

Bruner, G.C. and Kumar, A. (2000) Web commercials and advertising hierarchy of effects. *Journal of Advertising Research*, January/April, pp. 35–42.

Cartellieri, C., Parsons, A., Rao, V. and Zeisser, M. (1997) The real impact of Internet advertising. *McKinsey Quarterly*, **3**, pp. 44–63.

Chaffey, D., Meyer, R., Johnston, K. and Ellis-Chadwick, F. (2003) *Internet Marketing*. 2nd edn. Harlow: Pearson.

Curtis, J. (2000) Can Japan wipe out? *Revolution*, 13 December, pp. 41–4.

Dreze, X. and Zurfryden, F. (1997) Testing web site design and promotional content. *Journal of Advertising Research* (March/April), pp. 77–91.

Durlacher (1999) UK on-line community. *Durlacher Quarterly Internet Report*, Q3, 7–11, London.

Evans, J.R. and King, V.E. (1999) Business-to-business marketing and the world wide web: planning, managing and assessing web sites. *Industrial Marketing Management*, **28**, pp. 343–58.

Forsyth, J.E., Lavoie, J. and McGuire, T. (2002) Segmenting the e-market. *The McKinsey Quarterly*, **4**. Retrieved 10 November 2004 from www.mckinseyquarterly.com/article.

Goften, K. (2000) Have you got permission? *Marketing*, 22 June, pp. 28–9.

Goldsmith, R.E. and Lafferty, B.A. (2002) Consumer response to web sites and their influence on advertising effectiveness. *Internet Research: Electronic Networking Applications and Policy*, **12**(4), pp. 318–28.

Hurme, P. (2001) On-line PR: emerging organisational practice. *Corporate Communications: an International Journal*, **6**(2), pp. 71–5.

Karayanni, D.A. and Baltas, G.A. (2003) Web site characteristics and business performance: some evidence from international business-to-business organisations. *Marketing Intelligence and Planning*, **21**(2), pp. 105–14.

Kent, M.L., Taylor, M. and White, W.J. (2003) The relationship between web site design and organisational responsiveness to stakeholders. *Public Relations Review*, **29**(1) (March) pp. 63–77.

Lewis, H. and Lewis, R. (1997) Give your customers what they want. Cited in Chaffey *et al.* (2003).

Lutz, J., Mackensie, S.B. and Belch, G.E. (1983) Attitude toward the ad as a mediator of advertising effectiveness. *Advances in Consumer Research X*. Ann Arbor, MI: Association for Consumer Research.

McCawley, I. (2000) Are TV ads a waste of dot-com money? *Marketing Week*, 31 August, p. 12.

McLuhan, R. (2000) A lesson in on-line brand promotion. *Marketing*, 23 March, pp. 31–2.

Muniz, A.M. Jr and O'Guinn, T.C. (2001) Brand community. *Journal of Consumer Research*, **27**(4), pp. 412–32.

Oxley, M. and Miller, J. (2000) Capturing the consumer: ensuring website stickiness. *Admap* (July/August), pp. 21–4.

Rayport, J.F. and Jaworski, B.J. (2004) *Introduction to E-commerce*. 2nd edn. New York: McGraw-Hill.

Rigby, E. (2004) E-tail affiliate marketing. *Revolution* (October), pp. 66–9.

Szmigin, I. and Reppel, A.E. (2004) Internet community bonding: the case of macnews.de. *European Journal of Marketing*, **38**(5/6), pp. 626–40.

Media behaviour and planning: delivering the message

22

Media planning is essentially a selection and scheduling exercise. The selection refers to the choice of media vehicles to carry the message on behalf of the advertiser. With media fragmentation audiences are switching between media with greater regularity, which impacts on media scheduling. Decisions regarding the number of occasions, timing and duration that a message is exposed, in the selected vehicles, to the target audience have become increasingly critical.

Aims and objectives

The aims of this chapter are to introduce the fundamental elements of media planning and to set out some of the issues facing media planners.

The objectives of this chapter are to:

1. consider various theories concerning the content of different media and related media switching behaviours;

2. explain the role of the media planner and highlight the impact of media and audience fragmentation;

3. examine the key concepts used in media selection: reach and cover, frequency, duplication, rating points and CPT;

4. appreciate the concept of repetition and the debate concerning effective frequency and recency planning;

5. understand the concepts of effectiveness and efficiency when applied to media selection decisions;

6. introduce media source effects as an important factor in the selection and timing of advertising in magazines and television programmes;

7. explore the different ways in which advertisements can be scheduled.

Introduction

Once a message has been created and agreed, a media plan should be determined. The aim of the media plan is to devise an optimum route for the delivery of the

The aim of the media plan is to devise an optimum route for the delivery of the promotional message to the target audience.

promotional message to the target audience. This function is normally undertaken by specialists, either as part of a full service advertising agency or as a media independent whose sole function is to buy air time or space from media owners (e.g. television contractors or magazine publishers) on behalf of their clients, the advertisers. This traditional role has changed since the mid-1990s, and many media independents now provide consultancy services, particularly at the strategic level, plus planning and media research and auditing services.

Media departments are responsible for two main functions. These are to 'plan' and to 'buy' time and space in appropriate media vehicles. There is a third task – to monitor a media schedule once it has been bought – but this is essentially a subfunction of buying. The planner chooses the target audience and the type of medium, while the buyer chooses programmes, frequency, spots and distribution, and assembles a multichannel schedule (Armstrong, 1993). In the past the media planner has been pre-eminent, but the role of the buyer is changing. Some feel the role of the buyer is in the ascendancy, but there are others who feel that the role is capable of increased automation and that many software packages now fulfil many functions of the media buyer. Such a move has implications for the type of person recruited. In the United States, for example, many semi-skilled people have been recruited on a part-time basis to do many parts of the traditional media planner's job.

Media planning is essentially a selection and scheduling exercise. The selection refers to the choice of media vehicles to carry the message on behalf of the advertiser. Scheduling refers to the number of occasions, timing and duration that a message is exposed, in the selected vehicles, to the target audience. However, there are several

Media planning is essentially a selection and scheduling exercise.

factors that complicate these seemingly straightforward tasks. First, the variety of available media is huge and rapidly increasing. This is referred to as media fragmentation. Secondly, the characteristics of the target audience are changing equally quickly. This is referred to as audience fragmentation. Both these fragmentation issues will be discussed later. The job of the media planner is complicated by one further element: money. Advertisers have restricted financial resources and require the media planner to create a plan that delivers their messages not only effectively but also efficiently.

Three sets of decisions need to be made about the choice of media, vehicles and schedules.

The task of the media planner, therefore, is to deliver advertising messages through a selection of media that match the viewing and/or reading habits of the target audience at the lowest possible cost. In order for these tasks to be accomplished, three sets of decisions need to be made about the choice of media, vehicles and schedules.

Decisions about the choice of media are complex. While choosing a single one is reasonably straightforward, choosing media in combination and attempting to generate synergistic effects is far from easy. Advances in IT have made media planning a much faster, more accurate process, one that is now more flexible and capable of adjusting to fast-changing market conditions.

One of the key tasks of the media planner is to decide which combination of vehicles should be selected to carry the message to the target audience. In addition,

McLuhan (1966) said that the medium is the message. He went on to say that the medium is the massage, as each medium massages the recipient in different ways and so contributes to learning in different ways. For example, Krugman (1965) hypothesised that television advertising washes over individuals. He said that viewers, rather than participate actively with television advertisements, allow learning to occur passively. In contrast, magazine advertising requires active participation if learning is to occur.

The characteristics of the target audience, should be considered when deciding on the optimal media mix.

The various media depicted at Table 22.1 have wide-ranging characteristics. These, and the characteristics of the target audience, should be considered when deciding on the optimal media mix. It should be clear that deciding on which media to use is alone fraught with difficulties, let alone deciding on the optimal combination, how much of each media should be used before even considering the cost implications.

Media switching behaviour

The range of media has grown dramatically in the past 30 years and is continuing to grow as technology, in particular, advances. However, even before digital media started to change the media landscape, researchers had recognised that different media have different capabilities and that media were not completely interchangeable. In other words, different tasks can be accomplished more effectively using particular media. This implies that there is a spectrum of media depending upon the content they carry.

Daft and Lengel (1984) were the first to propose that this content issue concerned the richness of the information conveyed through each medium. As a result the tasks facing managers should be considered according to the degree of fit with the most appropriate media based on the richness of the information.

Communication media help resolve ambiguity and facilitate understanding in different ways and to different degrees.

Communication media help resolve ambiguity and facilitate understanding in different ways and to different degrees. They established that there were four main criteria which determined what level of richness a medium possessed:

1. the availability of instant feedback
2. the capacity to transmit multiple cues
3. the use of natural language
4. the degree of personal focus.

Media Richness Theory (MRT) holds that there is a hierarchy or spectrum of media ranging from personal or face-to-face encounters as the richest media through to single sheets of text-based information as lean media at the other end. Rich media facilitates feedback, dialogue iteration and an expression of personal cues such as tone of voice, body language and eye contact that in turn helps establish a personal connection. In descending order of richness the other media are telephone, email, letter, note, memo, special report, and fliers and bulletins. At this end of the richness scale numeric and formal written communication is slow, often visually limited and impersonal.

MRT suggests that rich media reduce ambiguity more effectively than others.

MRT suggests that rich media reduce ambiguity more effectively than others but are more resource intensive than lean media. If rich media allow for more complex and

TABLE 22.1 A summary of media characteristics

Type of media	Strengths	Weaknesses
Print		
Newspapers	Wide reach	Short lifespan
	High coverage	Advertisements get little exposure
	Low costs	Relatively poor reproduction, gives
	Very flexible	poor impact
	Short lead times	Low attention-getting properties
	Speed of consumption controlled by reader	
Magazines	High-quality reproduction that allows high	Long lead times
	impact	Visual dimension only
	Specific and specialised target audiences	Slow build-up of impact
	High readership levels	Moderate costs
	Longevity	
	High levels of information can be delivered	
Television	Flexible format, uses sight, movement	High level of repetition necessary
	and sound	Short message life
	High prestige	High absolute costs
	High reach	Clutter
	Mass coverage	Increasing level of fragmentation
	Low relative cost so very efficient	(potentially)
Radio	Selective audience, e.g. local	Lacks impact
	Low costs (absolute, relative and	Audio dimension only
	production)	Difficult to get audience attention
	Flexible	Low prestige
	Can involve listeners	
Outdoor	High reach	Poor image (but improving)
	High frequency	Long production time
	Low relative costs	Difficult to measure
	Good coverage as a support medium	
	Location oriented	
New media	High level of interaction	Segment specific
	Immediate response possible	Slow development of
	Tight targeting	infrastructure
	Low absolute and relative costs	High user set-up costs
	Flexible and easy to update	Transaction security issues
	Measurable	
Transport	High length of exposure	Poor coverage
	Low costs	Segment specific (travellers)
	Local orientation	Clutter
In-store POP	High attention-getting properties	Segment specific (shoppers)
	Persuasive	Prone to damage and confusion
	Low costs	Clutter
	Flexible	

TABLE 22.2 Media richness grid (Adapted from McGrath and Hollingshead, 1993.)

	Computer text systems	Audio systems	Video systems	Face-to-face communication
Generating ideas and plans	**Good fit**	Marginal fit: medium too resource intense	Poor fit: medium too resource intense	Poor fit: medium too resource intense
Choosing correct answer: intellective tasks	Marginal fit: medium too constrained	**Good fit**	**Good fit**	Poor fit: medium too resource intense
Choosing preferred answer: judgement tasks	Poor fit: medium too constrained	**Good fit**	**Good fit**	Marginal fit: medium too resource intense
Negotiating conflicts of interest	Poor fit: medium too constrained	Poor fit: medium too constrained	Marginal fit: medium too constrained	**Good fit**

difficult communications then lean media are more cost effective for simple or routine communications. McGrath and Hollingshead (1993) developed a matrix showing the levels of richness required to perform certain tasks successfully and efficiently. Their media richness grid identifies the level of fit between the information richness requirements of the tasks and the information richness capacity of the media. See Table 22.2.

Social influence theory (SIT) was developed by Fulk *et al.* (1990). This is intended to complement MRT as it also assumes that the relatively objective features of media do influence how individuals perceive and use media. However, these researchers argue that SIT has a strong social orientation because different media properties (such as ability to transmit richness) are subjective and are influenced by attitudes, statements and the behaviour of others. This approach recognises that members of groups influence other people in terms of their perceptions of different media. The main difference between MRT and SIT is that MRT identifies rich media as inefficient for simple or routine communication whereas SIT suggests rich media can be just as appropriate for simple messages as it is for ambiguous communication.

SIT has a strong social orientation.

A third approach, the technology acceptance model (TAM) relates to the utility and convenience a medium offers. The perceived usefulness and perceived ease of use are regarded as the main issues that are considered when selecting media (King and Xia, 1997). Perceived usefulness refers to the user's subjective assessment that using a specific computer application will increase his or her job performance. Perceived ease of use addresses the degree to which a user expects the identified application to be free of effort.

(TAM) relates to the utility and convenience a medium offers.

Influential factors for media selection

In addition to these richness, social and utility issues of media selection, other factors are also of importance. Duarte and Snyder (2001) propose a list of factors influencing technology selection. See Table 22.3.

TABLE 22.3 Factors influencing the choice of technology

Factor	Explanation
Experience and familiarity	With virtual operations the amount of experience using a particular interactive medium
Permanence	The degree to which users need an historical record of team interactions or decisions
Symbolic meaning	The subjective meanings attached to the use of a particular medium
Time constraints	The amount of time available to the user to use a medium in order to execute their tasks
Access to technology and/or support	The number of and access to available media influences media choice

Switching behaviour

It is clear therefore that different media have different properties and that people will switch between media according to their tasks, social environment and familiarity and access to different media. What is important therefore is to understand switching behaviour and the decision-making process that people use. Decisions are made through *rational* and *systematic* processes or alternatively there are unaccountable factors that 'bound' decision-making. The classic eight stage rational–linear decision-making model (situation analysis, objectives setting, through to choosing and evaluating alternatives, making the decisions, evaluation and consequences) is well known and its criticisms well documented. Simon (1972, 1987) showed that people make decisions within 'bounded rationality', performing limited searches and accepting the first acceptable alternative, what is regarded as 'satisficing behaviour'.

> People will switch between media according to their tasks, social environment and familiarity and access to different media.

Srinavasan (1996) developed a satisfaction-loyalty curve whereby an individual's level of satisfaction is the biggest determinant of their switching behaviour. As their satisfaction increases, so does loyalty and of course the reverse is equally true. For each person there is a point at which decreasing satisfaction intersects with the decreasing loyalty levels. This is the point at which switching occurs and the current brand is abandoned in favour of another.

> There is a point at which decreasing satisfaction intersects with the decreasing loyalty levels. This is the point at which switching occurs.

Keaveney (1995) distinguishes between involuntary, simple and complex switching behaviours. Involuntary switching may be due to factors beyond an individual consumer's control (e.g. business liquidated) whereas simple switching is characterised by individual events where consumers can identify a single incident or factor causing the switch, for example a price change. Complex switching behaviour occurs when a customer's loyalty has decreased due to a variety of factors, which might include core product failure, price changes and poor service. It should be noted that switching is very often a routine behaviour influenced by the expectations of the context in which the media decision is made. For example, when sending text-based documents to team members, most people would select email and use file attachments.

> Complex switching behaviour occurs when a customer's loyalty has decreased.

TABLE 22.4 Reasons for moving to richer or leaner media

Movement	Reasons
Towards a richer medium	Message complexity
	Increased comfort
	Time pressure
	Timely discussion required
	Need to rest from computer-based medium
Towards a leaner medium	Desire for written record
	Reducing cost
	Convenience (of being asynchronous or distant)
	Share individual written work (attachment)
	External pressure or requirement

As a final comment on media switching behaviour it is useful to return to MRT and to consider the reasons why individuals move towards richer or lean media. These are set out in Table 22.4.

Therefore, movement between media is based on a range of criteria and will vary according to the context and individual skills and preferences.

Vehicle selection

The discussion so far has explored unpaid media, and increasingly the Internet and the use of email communications fits this range. However, organisations need to use media that is owned by others in order to convey their messages. These paid-for media have particular characteristics and ability to deliver rich or lean content. The discussion now moves on to consider different paid-for media and the ways in which organisations develop a media mix to meet their communications needs.

Increasingly, organisations are required to prove how advertising adds value to the bottom line. While this is not a new question, it is one that is being asked more often and in such a way that answers are required. As advertisers attempt to demonstrate effectiveness, contribution and return on investment, questions concerning the choice of media, how much should be spent on message delivery and how financial resources are to be allocated in a multichannel environment increasingly haunt senior managers.

Media decisions have become significantly more important and certainly more visible areas, attracting management attention in the late 1990s and the early years of the new millennium. For example, Brech (1999) reports that companies such as Scottish Courage need to make choices about the split between the Internet, mass media, digital TV and consumer press. Companies such as BT, IKEA and ScottishPower need to use media strategically in order that they reach the right audience, in the right context, at the right time and at an acceptable cost. To help organisations achieve these goals a variety of approaches has been adopted. For example, New PHD is an agency retained by BT to advise about strategic (media) planning and budget allocation. However, ZenithOptimedia implements

Reach the right audience, in the right context, at the right time and at an acceptable cost.

decisions for press and radio and the Allmond Partnership manages TV and cinema while Outdoor Connections handles poster buying. This division provides objectivity, reduces partisan approaches and can deliver more effective media plans. Cost per response is certainly one way of measuring effectiveness but the communication impact, or share of mind, is also important. There has also been a move away from volume of media to one where media decisions are made by looking at media in the context of the brand's total communications.

> Cost per response is certainly one way of measuring effectiveness.

A further problem facing clients and media concerns the integrated media experience. For a long time, some organisations have used above-the-line media to reach audiences of 20 million people. With fragmented media it is difficult to generate consistent levels and types of impact. Increasingly media management is being outsourced so there are fewer in-house areas of expertise. All this means that, to forge appropriate solutions, advertisers and media agencies need to work closely together so that the relationship becomes so close that it acts more as an extension to the marketing department.

Decisions regarding which vehicles are to carry an advertiser's message depend upon an understanding of a number of concepts: reach and coverage, frequency, gross rating points, effective frequency, efficiency and media source effects.

Media planning concepts

Reach and coverage

> Reach refers to the percentage of the target audience exposed to the message at least once during the relevant time period.

Reach refers to the percentage of the target audience exposed to the message at least once during the relevant time period. Where 80 per cent of the target audience has been exposed to a message, the figure is expressed as an '80 reach'.

Coverage, a term often used for reach, should not be confused or used in place of reach. Coverage refers to the size of a potential audience that might be exposed to a particular media vehicle. For media planners, therefore, coverage (the size of the target audience), is very important. Reach will always be lower than coverage, as it is impossible to reach 100 per cent of a target population (the universe).

Building reach within a target audience is relatively easy as the planner needs to select a range of different media vehicles. This will enable different people in the target audience to have an opportunity to see the media vehicle. However, a point will be reached when it becomes more difficult to reach people who have not been exposed. As more vehicles are added, so repetition levels (the number of people who have seen the advertisement more than once) also increase.

Frequency

Frequency refers to the number of times a member of the target audience is exposed to a media vehicle (not the advertisement) during the relevant time period. It has been stated that targets must be exposed to the media vehicle, but to say that a target has seen an advertisement simply because they have been exposed to the vehicle is incorrect. For example, certain

> Frequency refers to the number of times a member of the target audience is exposed to a media vehicle during the relevant time period.

viewers hop around the channels as a commercial break starts. This has been referred to as 'channel grazing' by Lloyd and Clancy (1991). Individuals have different capacities to learn and to forget, and how much of a magazine does a reader have to consume to be counted as having read an advertisement? These questions are still largely unanswered, so media planners have adopted an easier and more consistent measure: opportunities to see (OTS).

This is an important point. The stated frequency level in any media plan will always be greater than the advertisement exposure rate. The term OTS is used to express the reach of a media vehicle rather than the actual exposure of an advertisement. However, a high OTS could be generated by either a large number of the target audience being exposed once (high reach) or a small number being exposed several times (high frequency).

This then raises the first major issue. As all campaigns are restricted by time and budget limitations, advertisers have to trade off reach against frequency. It is impossible to maximise both elements within a fixed budget and set period of time.

ViewPoint 22.1   Haier than the weather

Haier, the major Chinese global manufacturer of consumer durables, uses television in China to reach its main audiences. In a country where it is estimated that over 250 million Chinese families watch CCTV programmes, Haier sponsors the weather forecast, which is the highest-rated programme in China. Guaranteeing large audiences on a repeat basis ensures Haier achieves high OTS based on a large frequency.

Source: Adapted from unpublished student coursework and www.zaobao.com/.

To launch a new product, it has been established that a wide number of people within the target audience need to become aware of the product's existence and its salient attributes or benefits. This means that reach is important but, as more and more people become aware, so more of them become exposed a second, third or fourth time, perhaps to different vehicles. At the outset, frequency is low and reach high, but as a campaign progresses so reach slows and frequency develops. Reach and frequency are inversely related within any period of time, and media planners must know what the objective of any campaign might be: to build reach or frequency.

Gross rating point

GRPs are a measure of the total number of exposures (OTS) generated within a particular period of time.

To decide whether reach or frequency is the focus of the campaign objective, a more precise understanding of the levels of reach and frequency is required. The term gross rating point is used to express the relationship between these two concepts. GRPs are a measure of the total number of exposures (OTS) generated within a particular period of time. The calculation itself is simply reach × frequency:

$$\text{reach} \times \text{frequency} = \text{gross rating point}$$

Media plans are often determined on the number of GRPs generated during a certain time period. For example, the objective for a media plan could be to achieve 450 GRPs in a burst (usually four or five weeks). However, as suggested earlier, caution is required when interpreting a GRP, because 450 GRPs may be the result of 18 message exposures to just 25 per cent of the target market. It could also be an average of nine exposures to 50 per cent of the target market.

Rating points are used by all media as a measurement tool, although they were originally devised for use with broadcast audiences. GRPs are based on the total target audience (e.g. all women aged 18–34, or all adults) that might be reached, but a media planner needs to know, quite rightly, how many GRPs are required to achieve a particular level of effective reach and what levels of frequency are really required to develop effective learning or awareness in the target audience. In other words, how can the effectiveness of a media plan be improved?

Effective frequency

There are a number of reasons why considering the effectiveness of a media plan has become more important. First, there is the combination of media and audience fragmentation and rising media costs. Secondly, there is short-termism, increased managerial accountability and intensifying competition. This last point about competition refers to the media planning industry itself and the restructuring and concentration of media buying points (centralisation) in response to clients' globalisation strategies and their need for more cost-effective ways of buying media.

Frequency refers to the number of times members of the target audience are exposed to the vehicle. It says nothing about the quality of the exposures and whether any impact was made. Effective frequency refers to the number of times an individual needs to be exposed to an advertisement before the communication is effective. Being exposed once or possibly twice is unlikely to affect the disposition of the receiver. But

Effective frequency refers to the number of times an individual needs to be exposed to an advertisement before the communication is effective.

the big question facing media planners is, how many times should a message be repeated for effective learning to occur? The level of effective frequency is generally unknown, but there has been some general agreement following work by Krugman (1972) that, for an advertisement to be effective (to make an impact), a target should have at least three OTS, the three-hit theory. The first exposure provokes a 'What is this?' reaction, the second reaction is 'What does this mean to me?' The reaction to the third is 'Oh I remember' (du Plessis, 1998). More than ten will be ineffective and a waste of resources. The level of three was determined by messages that first provide understanding, secondly provide recognition and thirdly actually stimulate action.

Determining the average frequency partially solves the problem. This is the number of times a target reached by the schedule is exposed to the vehicle over a particular period of time. For example, a schedule may generate the following:

10 per cent of the audience is reached ten times ($10 \times 10 = 100$)

25 per cent of the audience is reached seven times ($25 \times 7 = 175$)

65 per cent of the audience is reached once ($65 \times 1 = 65$)

Total = 340 exposures

Average frequency = 340/100 = 3.4

This figure of average frequency is misleading because different groups of people have been reached with varying levels of frequency. In the example above, an average

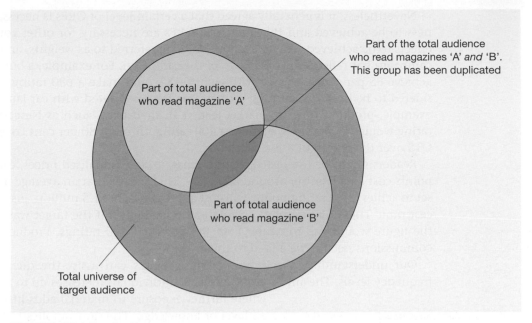

Part of the total audience who read magazines 'A' *and* 'B'. This group has been duplicated

Part of total audience who read magazine 'A'

Part of total audience who read magazine 'B'

Total universe of target audience

FIGURE 22.1 Duplication

frequency of 3.4 is achieved but 65 per cent of the audience is reached only once. This means that the average frequency, in this example, may lead to an audience being underexposed.

Members of the target audience do not buy and read just one magazine or watch a single television programme. Consumer media habits are complex, although distinct patterns can be observed, but it is likely that a certain percentage of the target audience will be exposed to an advertisement if it is placed in two or more media vehicles. Those who are exposed once constitute unduplicated reach. Those who are exposed to two or more are said to have been duplicated. Such overlapping of exposure, shown in Figure 22.1, is referred to as duplicated reach.

Duplication provides an indication of the levels of frequency likely in a particular schedule, so media plans need to specify levels of duplicated and unduplicated reach. Duplication also increases costs, so if the objective of the plan is unduplicated reach, duplication brings waste and inefficiency.

ViewPoint 22.2   Optimising media schedules

Multi-media Optimisers (MMO) are software programs that plan and schedule the placing of advertising campaigns across more than one medium. MMOs use single-source or fused database information rather than survey based information, which is prone to inaccuracies.

MMOs take into account duplication rates when deciding which combination of media vehicles to use (not types such as TV and magazines). They also facilitate media neutral planning (see Chapter 11).

However, MMOs work on responses and this can pose problems in terms of agreeing what form of response is valid, while audiences have to be converted to ad exposures/impacts in order to base evaluation on equivalent measures. Accounting for decay rates and adstock features ('ad impact retention') by medium, through time is also problematic.

Source: Adapted from Jarvis and McElroy (2004) and www.fipp.com/sadmin/1418.

Nevertheless, it is generally agreed that a certain level of GRPs is necessary for awareness to be achieved and that increased GRPs are necessary for other communication effects to be achieved. These levels of GRPs are referred to as weights, and the weight a campaign has reflects the objectives of the campaign. For example, a burst designed to achieve 85 per cent coverage with eight OTS would make a 680 rating, which is considered to be heavy. Such high ratings are often associated with car launches and, for example, products that are market leaders in their class, such as Nescafé. An average rating would be one set to achieve a 400 rating, through 80 per cent coverage and five OTS over the length of a five-week period.

Readers might be interested to know that, at deseasonalised prices, each 100 rating points cost an advertiser around £300,000. That means that an average five-week burst set to achieve 400 rating points will cost approximately £1.5 million, just for the broadcast time. These figures relate to an all-adult audience. If the target was all men, then the figure would rise to nearer £500,000 for each 100 ratings. Production costs and commissions need to be added to this figure.

Our understanding about how learning works can assist the quest for effective frequency levels. The amount of learning in individuals increases up to a certain point, where further exposure to material adds little to our overall level of knowledge. The same applies to the frequency level and the weightings applied to exposures. Table 22.5 shows the spread of weights for a burst bought by a major advertiser. The ratings are spread in such a way that greater weight is 'laid down' at the beginning of the campaign, to get attention, and in some areas (WCTV) the weight in week 4 is only 33 per cent of the first week's activity.

> Understanding about how learning works can assist the quest for effective frequency levels.

The figures that coverage and reach provide only show the numbers of people who are exposed to the vehicle. Effective reach measures those that are aware of the message. This ties in with the previous discussion on effective frequency levels. Essentially, media planners recognise that effective advertising requires that, in addition to the other aspects of advertising planning, a single transmission (reach) of an advertisement will be unproductive (Krugman, 1975; Naples, 1979). A minimum of two exposures and a reach threshold of 45 per cent of the target audience are required for reach to be regarded as effective (Murray and Jenkins, 1992).

TABLE 22.5 A television laydown for a national burst

	3–9 January	10–16 January	17–23 January	24–30 January	Total (including satellite)
London	125	100	100	86	411
Central	125	100	100	77	402
Granada	125	112	111	111	459
North	125	100	100	68	393
STV	125	125	115	115	480
HTV	125	100	100	53	378
Meridian	125	100	100	47	372
Anglia	125	100	100	48	373
WCTV	125	100	100	41	366
Border	125	100	100	72	397
Grampian	125	118	100	100	443

Recency planning

A new perspective to counter the effective frequency model has emerged from the United States. This is known as recency planning, and has developed at a time when the weak theory of advertising has started to gain greater acknowledgement as the most acceptable general interpretation of how advertising works. It is also more generally accepted that advertising is not the powerful marketing tool it was once thought to be (Jones, 1990) and that the timing and presentation of advertising messages need to be reconsidered in the light of the way advertising is currently thought to work.

If it is accepted that consumer decision-making is more heavily influenced by running out of particular products (opening empty fridges and store cupboards) rather than exposure to advertising messages that are repeated remorselessly, then it follows that advertising needs to be directed at those people who are actually in the market and prepared to buy (Ephron, 1997).

As many fast-moving consumer goods products are purchased each week, Jones (1995) argues that a single exposure to an advertising message in the week before a purchase is to be made is more important than adding further messages and so increasing frequency. Recency planning considers reach to be more important than frequency.

The goal of this new approach is to reach those few consumers who are ready to buy (in the market). To do this the strategy requires reaching as many consumers as possible in as many weeks as possible (as far as the budget will extend).

This requires a lower weekly weight and an extended number of weeks to a campaign. Advertising budgets are not cut; the fund is simply spread over a greater period of time. According to Ephron, this approach is quite different from effective frequency models and quite revolutionary; see Table 22.6.

This approach has been greeted with a number of objections. It has not been accepted universally and has not been widely implemented in the UK market at the time of writing.

Rejects the notion of recency planning because effectiveness will vary by brand, category and campaign.

Gallucci (1997), among others, rejects the notion of recency planning because effectiveness will vary by brand, category and campaign. He claims that reaching 35 per cent of a cola market (Indonesia) once a week will not bring about the same result as reaching 65 per cent four times a week.

The development of banner advertising on the Internet raises interesting questions concerning effective frequency in new media. Is the frequency rate different and if so how many times is exposure required in order to be effective? Research into this area is in its infancy and no single accepted body of knowledge exists. Broussard (2000)

TABLE 22.6 The differences between effective frequency and recency planning

Recency planning model	Effective frequency model
Reach goal	Frequency goal
Continuity	Burst
One-week planning cycle	Four-week planning cycle
Lowest cost per reach point	Lowest cost per thousand
Low ratings	High ratings

Source: Adapted from Ephron (1997).

reports that, in a limited study concerning the comparison of a direct response and a branding-based campaign on the Internet, the lowest cost per lead in the direct response campaign was achieved with low frequency levels. Results from the branding campaign suggest that up to seven exposures were necessary to improve brand awareness and knowledge of product attributes.

The debate concerning the development of recency planning and effective frequency will continue. What might be instrumental to the outcome of the debate will be a better understanding of how advertising works and the way buyers use advertising messages that are relevant to them.

Media usage and attitudes

Research from a variety of sources (e.g. CIA MediaLab reported by Beale, 1997) consistently reveals that a large proportion of the population (50 per cent plus) has a negative attitude towards advertising. Advertising is seen by this large body of people as both intrusive and pervasive. Beale's work led to the development of a four-part typology of personality types based upon respondents' overall attitudes towards advertising (see Table 22.7). Through an understanding of the different characteristics, it is possible to make better (more informed) decisions about the most appropriate media channels to reach target audiences.

It is common for advertisers and media planners to discuss target markets in the context of heavy, medium, light and non-users of a product. It is only now that consideration is being given to the usage levels of viewers and readers. Zenith Optimedia has determined that TV audiences can be categorised as heavy, medium and light users based upon the amount of time they spend watching television. Table 22.8 presents a breakdown of the general categories, where the amount of time spent viewing can be seen to vary considerably between the summer and winter periods.

> TV audiences can be categorised as heavy, medium and light users based upon the amount of time they spend watching television.

One of the implications of this approach is that if light users consume so little television, then perhaps it is not worthwhile trying to communicate with them and

TABLE 22.7 Advertising attitudes for media determination

Cynics (22%)	**Enthusiasts (35%)**
This group perceives advertising as a crude sales tool. They are resentful and hostile to advertisements, although they are more likely to respond to advertisements placed in relevant media.	Enthusiasts like to get involved with advertising and creativity is perceived as an important part of the process. Apart from newspapers, which are regarded as boring, most types of media are acceptable.
Ambivalents (22%)	**Acquiescents (21%)**
While creativity is seen as superfluous and irrelevant, Ambivalents are more disposed to information-based messages or those that promise cost savings. The best advertisements are those that use media which reinforce the message.	As the name suggests, this group of people has a reluctant approach to advertising. This means that they see advertising as unavoidable and an inevitable part of their world. Therefore they are open to influence through a variety of media.

Source: Adapted from Beale (1997); used with kind permission.

TABLE 22.8 Usage patterns of television consumption (Zenith Optimedia)

Season/Consumption	Minutes spent watching TV[a] per day
Winter	
Heavy	195–500+
Medium	106–200
Light	Less than 100
Summer	
Heavy	150–500+
Medium	60–150
Light	Less than 60

[a] ITV + CH4.

resources should be directed to the medium and heavy user groups. The other side of the argument is that light users are very specific in the programmes that they watch, therefore it should be possible to target messages at them and so use a heavy number of GRPs. Questions still remain about the number of ratings necessary for effective reach in each of these categories.

The question concerning how many rating points should be purchased was addressed by Ostrow (1981). He said that, rather than use average frequency, a decision should be made about the minimum level of frequency necessary to achieve the objectives and then maximise reach at that level. Ostrow (1984) suggested that consideration of the issues set out in Table 22.9 would also assist.

The traditional approach of using television to reach target audiences to build awareness is still strong. For example, Procter & Gamble, Lever Brothers, Nestlé, Kellogg's and British Telecom all spend in excess of 70 per cent of their budgets on television

TABLE 22.9 Issues to be considered when setting frequency levels

Issues	Low frequency	High frequency
Marketing issues		
Newness of the brand	Established	New
Market share	High	Low
Brand loyalty	Higher	Lower
Purchase and usage cycle times	Long	Short
Message issues		
Complexity	Simple	Complex
Uniqueness	More	Less
Image versus product sell	Product sell	Image
Message variation	Single message	Multiple messages
Media plan issues		
Clutter	Less	More
Editorial atmosphere	Appropriate	Not appropriate
Attentiveness of the media in the plan	Holds	Fails to hold
Number of media in the plan	Less	More

Source: Adapted from Ostrow (1981); used with kind permission.

Some major advertisers are moving slowly from a dominant above-the-line approach to a more integrated and through-the-line approach.

advertising. However, there are signs that some major advertisers are moving slowly from a dominant above-the-line approach to a more integrated and through-the-line approach as a more effective way of delivering messages to target audiences. Nescafé now uses 48-sheet posters and Unilever, traditionally a heavy user of television, has begun to use radio and posters as support for its television work.

Efficiency

All promotional campaigns are constrained by a budget. Therefore a trade-off is required between the need to reach as many members of the target audience as possible (create awareness) and the need to repeat the message to achieve effective learning in the target audience. The decision about whether to emphasise reach or frequency is assisted by a consideration of the costs involved in each proposed schedule or media plan.

This is the cost of the space or time required for the message to be transmitted.

There are two main types of cost. The first of these is the *absolute cost*. This is the cost of the space or time required for the message to be transmitted. For example, the cost of a full-page, single-insertion black-and-white advertisement, booked for a firm date in *The Sunday Times*, is £56,150 (November 2004). Cash flow is affected by absolute costs.

Relative costs are the costs incurred in making contact with each member of the target audience.

In order that an effective comparison be made between media plans the *relative costs* of the schedules need to be understood. Relative costs are the costs incurred in making contact with each member of the target audience.

Traditionally, the magazine industry has based its calculations on the cost per thousand people reached (CPT). The original term derived from the print industry is CPM, where the 'M' refers to the Roman symbol for thousand. This term still has limited use but the more common term is CPT:

$$CPT = \text{space costs (absolute)} \times 1,000/\text{circulation}$$

The newspaper industry has used the milline rate, which is the cost per line of space per million circulation.

Broadcast audiences are measured by programme ratings (United States), and television audiences in the UK are measured by television ratings or TVRs. They are essentially the same in that they represent the percentage of television households that are tuned to a specific programme. The TVR is determined as follows:

$$TVR = \text{number of target TV households tuned into a programme} \times 100/\text{total number of target TV households}$$

A single TVR, therefore, represents 1 per cent of all the television households in a particular area that are tuned into a specific programme.

A single TVR, therefore, represents 1 per cent of all the television households in a particular area that are tuned into a specific programme.

A further approach to measuring broadcast audiences uses the share of televisions that are tuned into a specific programme. This is compared with the total number of televisions that are actually switched on at that moment. This is expressed as a percentage and should be greater than the TVR. Share, therefore, reveals how well a programme is perceived by the available audience, not the potential audience.

The question of how to measure relative costs in the broadcast industry has been answered by the use of the rating point or TVR. Cost per TVR is determined as follows:

$$\text{Cost per TVR} = \text{time costs (absolute costs)/TVR}$$

Intra-industry comparison of relative costs is made possible by using these formulae. Media plans that only involve broadcast or only use magazine vehicles can be evaluated to determine levels of efficiency. However, members of the target audience do not have discrete viewing habits; they have, as we saw earlier, complex media habits that involve exposure to a mix of media classes and vehicles. Advertisers respond to this mixture by placing advertisements in a variety of media, but have no way of comparing the relative costs on an inter-industry basis. In other words, the efficiency of using a *News at Ten* television slot cannot be compared with an insertion in *The Economist*. Attempts are being made to provide cross-industry media comparisons, but as yet no one formula has yet been provided that satisfies all demands. The television and newspaper industries, by using CPT in combination with costs per unit of time and space respectively, have attempted to forge a bridge that may be of use to their customers.

Finally, some comment on the concept of CPT is necessary, as there has been speculation about its validity as a comparative tool. There are a number of shortcomings associated with the use of CPT. For example, because each media class possesses particular characteristics, direct comparisons based on CPT alone are dangerous. The levels of wastage incurred in a plan, such as reaching people who are not targets or by measuring OTS for the vehicle and not the advertisement, may lead to an overestimate of the efficiency that a plan offers.

Similarly, the circulation of a magazine is not a true representation of the number of people who read or have an opportunity to see. Therefore, CPT may underestimate the efficiency unless the calculation can be adjusted to account for the extra or pass-along readership that occurs in reality. Having made these points, media buyers in the UK continue to use CPT and cost per rating point (CPRP) as a means of planning and buying time and space. Target audiences and television programmes are priced according to the ratings they individually generate. The ratings affect the cost of buying a spot. The higher the rating, the higher the price to place advertisements in the magazine or television programme.

> The circulation of a magazine is not a true representation of the number of people who read or have an opportunity to see.

Media source effects

CPT is a quantitative measure, and one of its major shortcomings is that it fails to account for the qualitative aspects associated with media vehicles. Before vehicles are selected, their qualitative aspects need to be considered on the basis that a vehicle's environment may affect the way in which a message is perceived and decoded.

An advertisement placed in one vehicle, such as *Cosmopolitan*, may have a different impact upon an identical audience to that obtained if the same advertisement is placed in *Options*. This differential level of 'power of impact' is caused by a number of source factors, of which the following are regarded as the most influential:

1. *vehicle atmosphere* – editorial tone, vehicle expertise, vehicle prestige;
2. *technical and reproduction characteristics* – technical factors, exposure opportunities, perception opportunities;
3. *audience and product characteristics* – audience/vehicle fit, nature of the product.

Vehicle atmosphere

Editorial tone

This refers to the editorial views presented by the vehicle and the overall tone of the material contained. Understandably, some clients do not want to be associated with particular television shows or certain specialist magazines that are characterised by sex or violence.

Vehicle expertise

Magazines and journals can reflect a level of expertise and represent source credibility. Readers who regard particular magazines, especially some of the consumer SIMs (e.g. *Golf Monthly*), business-to-business magazines (e.g. *Fire & Rescue*) and academic journals (e.g. *Harvard Business Review*), as important sources of credible information are more relaxed and open to persuasion.

Vehicle prestige

The message strategy adopted for each advertisement should be appreciated, as this can have a strong effect upon the scheduling. The prestige of a vehicle is important to some products, especially when targeted at audiences where vehicle status is important, for example *Country Life*. Transformational advertisements have been shown to be more effective in prestige-based vehicles than in expertise-based vehicles (and vice versa for information-based advertisements).

Technical and reproduction characteristics of a vehicle

Technical factors

The technical characteristics of the vehicle, such as its visual capability, may influence the impact of the message. The use of colour, movement and sound may be necessary for the full effectiveness of a message to be realised. Other messages may need only a more limited range of characteristics, such as sound. For example, the promotion of inclusive tour holidays benefits from the communication of an impression (photograph/drawing) of the destination resort. This is important, as each destination needs to be differentiated, in the minds of the target audience, from competing destinations.

Exposure opportunities

The possibility that an advertisement will be successfully exposed to the target increases as more consideration is given to the likelihood of successful communication. Each vehicle has a number of time slots or spaces that provide opportunities for increased exposure. The back pages of magazines or facing matter often command premium advertising rates, just as prime time spots or film premieres on television always generate extra revenue for the television contractors.

Perception opportunities

Being exposed to the message does not mean that the message is perceived. A reader may not perceive an advertisement when searching for the next page of an article. Similarly, a car driver may not 'hear' a radio message because his or her attention may be on a passing car or a strange engine noise. The solution is to use strong attention-gaining materials, such as loud or distinctive music or controversial headlines. In addition new, imaginative ways of attracting attention are being developed. Car dealers have used incentives to attract audiences to test drive a car and receive vouchers for a free video film or have free subscriptions to particular magazines.

Audience/product characteristics

Audience/vehicle fit

The media plan should provide the best match between the target market and the audience reached by the vehicles in the media schedule. The more complex the target market description or consumer profile, the greater the difficulty of matching it with appropriate vehicles. Weilbacher (1984) argues that media evaluation based on product usage may be better than using demographics and psychographics. These may be inappropriate and inefficient when matching markets with audiences. As advertising is directed at influencing consumer behaviour, product usage is a more logical measure of media evaluation. This view is supported by media planners targeting heavy, medium and light users.

> The more complex the target market description or consumer profile, the greater the difficulty of matching it with appropriate vehicles.

ViewPoint 22.3   Monday is Horlicks night

Horlicks is a rich milky drink made with malt that contains high levels of calcium and various other vitamins. Traditionally it is associated with older people and helps relaxation and inducing sleep. MediaCom was given the task of finding a new target audience and to reposition the brand. Planning and research identified women aged 35+ who were trying to manage both their careers and their family as a very stressed group and MediaCom was also able to identify Mondays as the night when they were most likely to have a poor night's sleep.

This information enabled MediaCom to target the Monday night schedule, and the end of evening section, or the 'wind-down ritual' in particular. With a 13-week concentration Horlicks was able to target its customers at a time when they would be most receptive and as a result a new market was won. It was reported that sales climbed 28 per cent in the first four weeks of the campaign.

Source: Adapted from Grimshaw (2004).

This perspective contrasts with the view of Rothschild (1987). He sees demographic and psychographic factors as being relatively stable and enduring factors, and thus as suitable influences upon the media selection decision. By contrast, the dynamic factors (those that vary within an individual with respect to brand choice, purchase behaviour and time of adoption between products) are seen as being more suitable for influencing media strategy.

Nature of the product

In addition to this, consideration needs to be given to the nature of the product itself. Audiences have particular viewing patterns, therefore it does not make sense to advertise when it is known that the target audience is not watching (for example, promoting children's sweets late at night or photocopiers in consumer-interest magazines).

Prime television spots such as *Coronation Street* or major sporting occasions such as the Olympic Games will attract many major competitive brands. It may be wise to avoid competing for time and look for other suitable programmes.

Vehicle mood effects

The mood that a vehicle creates can also be an important factor. Aaker *et al.* (1992) report on the work of a number of studies in this area. These suggest that food advertisements using transformational appeals are more effective when placed in situation comedies than in thrillers and mystery programmes. Adverts for analgesics work better in both adult westerns and situation comedies (Crane, 1964).

Vehicle-related source effects need to be considered as support for the quantitative work.

These qualitative, vehicle-related source effects need to be considered as support for the quantitative work undertaken initially. They should not be used as the sole reason for the selection of particular media vehicles, if only because they are largely subjective.

Scheduling

This seeks to establish when the messages are transmitted in order that the media objectives be achieved at the lowest possible cost. The first considerations are the objectives themselves. If the advertising objectives are basically short term, then the placements should be concentrated over a short period of time. Conversely, if awareness is to be built over a longer term, perhaps building a new brand, then the frequency of the placements need not be so intensive and can be spread over a period so that learning can occur incrementally.

The second consideration is the purchasing cycle. We have seen before that the optimum number of exposures is thought to be between three and ten, and this should occur within each purchasing cycle. This, of course, is only really applicable to packaged goods, and is not as applicable to the business-to-business sector. However, the longer the cycle, the less frequency is required.

People who are highly involved actively seek information and need little assistance to digest relevant information.

The third consideration is the level of involvement. If the objective of the plan is to create awareness, then when there is high involvement few repetitions will be required compared with low-involvement decisions. This is because people who are highly involved actively seek information and need little assistance to digest relevant information. Likewise, where there is low involvement, attitudes develop from use of the product, so frequency is important to maintain awareness and to prompt trial.

Finally, the placement of an advertisement is influenced by the characteristics of the target audience and their preferred programmes. By selecting compatible 'spots' message delivery is likely to improve considerably.

Timing of advertisement placements

The timing of placements is dependent upon a number of factors. One of the overriding constraints is the size of the media budget and the impact that certain placement patterns can bring to an organisation's cash flow. Putting cost to one side, many researchers have identified and labelled different scheduling patterns. Govoni *et al.* (1986), Sissors and Bumba (1989), Burnett (1993) and Kotler (1997) all suggest different approaches to scheduling. Figure 22.2 and the following are presented as a synthesis of the more common scheduling options.

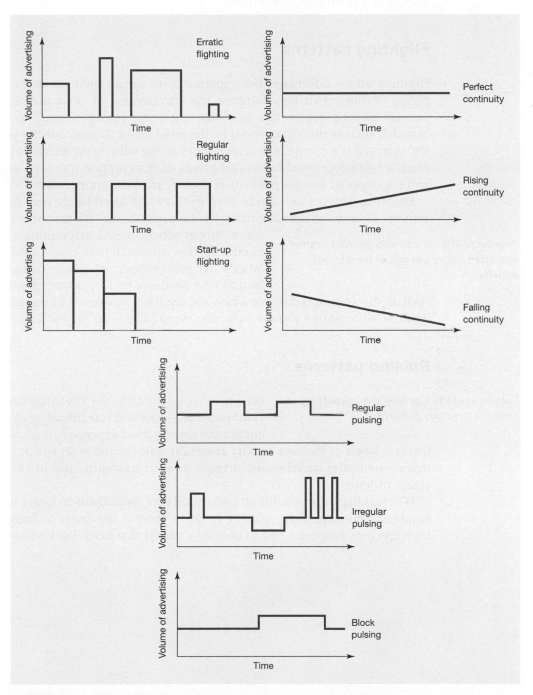

FIGURE 22.2 Media scheduling patterns

Continuity patterns

Continuous patterns involve regular and uniform presentation of the message to the target audience. Over the long term, a continuous pattern is more appropriate for products and services where demand is crisis led, e.g. plumbing, or where there is a long purchase cycle. These continuous patterns are often used for mature products, where reminder advertising is appropriate. A rising pattern is used when activity centres around a particular event, such as the FA Cup Final, the Olympic Games or a general election. A fading pattern may follow an initial burst to launch a new product or to inform of a product modification.

Flighting patterns

Flighting allows advertisers the opportunity to spread their resources across a longer period of time. This may improve the effectiveness of their messages. A flighting pattern may be appropriate in situations where messages need to reflect varying demand, such as that experienced by the retail sector throughout the year. Flighting is also adopted as a competitive response to varying advertising weights applied by rivals. These schedules are used for specific events, such as support for major sales promotions and responses to adverse publicity or one-off market opportunities.

Flighting patterns can also be used in short and often heavy periods of investment activity. Because of the seasonality of the product (e.g. for inclusive tour operators),

Flighting patterns can also be used in short and often heavy periods of investment activity.

advertising at other times is inappropriate and a waste of resources. This approach can also be used to respond quickly to a competitor's potentially damaging actions, to launch new products or to provide unique information, such as the announcement of a new organisation as a result of merger activity, or to promote information about a particular event such as an impending share offer.

Pulsing patterns

Pulsing seeks to combine the advantages of both the previous patterns.

Pulsing seeks to combine the advantages of both the previous patterns. As a result it is the safest of all the options, but potentially the most expensive. It allows advertisers to increase levels of message activity at certain times of the year, which is important for times when sales traditionally increase, as with fragrance sales in December and ice cream in June.

Whereas flighting presents an opportunity for individuals to forget messages during periods of no advertising, pulsing helps to prevent the onset of forgetting, to build high levels of awareness and to provide a barrier that holds back competitor attack.

Summary

The task of buying the time or space in media vehicles in order that an advertising message be carried to a target audience appears seductively straightforward. It is not. It is complicated by a number of factors, ranging from the size and dispersion of the target audience to the increasing number and variety of available media. These factors are referred to as audience and media fragmentation, which bring both benefits to and difficulties for media planners and advertisers. For example, it is easier to target more specialised and compact target audiences using new and specialised media. However, audience profiles are changing rapidly and there is little control information about these audiences that allows advertising funds to be allocated 'properly' (Mueller-Heumann, 1992).

Another major difficulty, increasing in its importance, is the question of how many times a message must be repeated before an impression, awareness or learning occurs. The search for effective frequency continues, particularly by product class. However, it is generally accepted that three exposures are necessary as a minimum and ten as a maximum.

Decisions regarding the media cannot be made in isolation from the qualitative factors associated with each vehicle. Known as vehicle source effects, these are concerned with the quality of the vehicle in terms of its atmosphere, technical aspects and audience/product fit.

The final task concerns the timing or scheduling of advertisements. As with most things in life, timing is of the essence. Scheduling calls for subjectivity and, while there are numerous quantitative measures to assist decision-making, media planning is essentially about management making judgements about where best to place its client's messages to maximise their effectiveness and the efficiency of the spend.

Review questions

1. Compare media richness theory, social influence theory and the technology adoption model.

2. What are the main tasks facing media planners?

3. If the rate at which information decays within individuals is known, then the task of the media planner is simply to place messages at suitable intervals in the path of decay. Discuss.

4. Why is it important that a media planner knows whether reach or frequency is the main objective of a media plan?

5. Why are frequency levels so important? Explain the concept of effective frequency.

6. How does recency planning differ from effective frequency?

7. What is a TVR and how does it relate to GRPs?

8. How is CPT flawed as a measure of media efficiency?

9. Write a brief report outlining the principal characteristics of media source effects.

10. What are the main ways in which media plans can be scheduled?

MINI-CASE
Targeting *movers* and *shakers*

Mini-case written by Clive Nancarrow, Bristol Business School; Julie Tinson, University of Stirling; Lucy Bristowe, Channel 4

Sophisticated targeting

Channel 4 TV offers its advertising clients a more sophisticated way of targeting consumers who are the key to the successful launch and relaunch of products. Media choice to date has been based in part on the size of audience as well as the profiles of various media in terms of demographics, product and brand use or purchase. In the case of TV the demographics of specific TV programmes is a further consideration. However, a Channel 4 and Bristol Business School study examined a new angle on media choice, namely the TV viewing preferences of consumers who are more influential than others (early adopters and opinion shapers). Consumers who are first to try new products (early adopters) are of considerable interest when launching a new product. More generally, it also makes sense to try and target consumers who potentially influence the consumption of others – opinion shapers (see Figure 1).

Opinion shaping

The research team broadened the definition and measure of opinion leadership to include copycat behaviour (see Figure 2). They note sometimes consumers are unconsciously on the look-out for ideas in certain areas and on other occasions see something in an area of no previous interest that captures their imagination. This has been described as 'in your face' experience. Some previous measures relied solely on opinion leadership through word of mouth (verbal recommendation). Observation of what others do is also potentially very influential – what others wear, use or consume publicly.

The term opinion leader was dropped on this account because it can suggest passive acceptance of what others say or do rather than an accommodation of new opinions with one's own. Instead the term 'opinion shaper' is used as opinions could evolve from either observing others' consumption or verbal recommendation and, at the same time, it seems to better describe the merging of one's own thoughts and behaviour with that of others.

Connectors

Notably, the team recognised that some opinion shapers are potentially more influential than others either because they had a bigger social network or their influence spread across several communities or groups (family, work/study groups, various interest groups or friends and so on). In the latter case this might help spread the word or desired consumption into new sectors of the population.

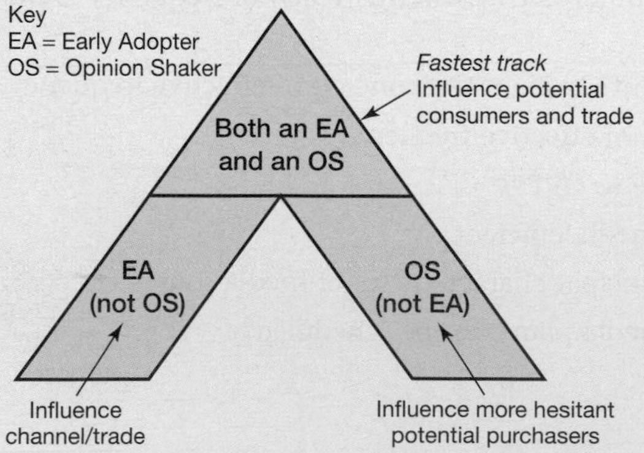

Key
EA = Early Adopter
OS = Opinion Shaker

Fastest track
Influence potential consumers and trade

Both an EA and an OS

EA (not OS)

OS (not EA)

Influence channel/trade

Influence more hesitant potential purchasers

FIGURE 1 Marketing relevance
Source: Nancarrow *et al.* (2004).

	VERBAL	VISUAL
Initiated by SELF	Ask for a view about product X	On the look out for ideas about X
Initiated by OTHERS	Told about X	X *in your face (unexpected)*

FIGURE 2 Word of mouth and copycat
Source: Nancarrow and Tinson (2004).

TV programme preferences

Finally, the TV programme preferences of opinion shapers and early adopters, particularly those with good social networks, were examined. Such data clearly improves the efficiency in media targeting either in terms of advertising or sponsorship of TV programmes.

The importance of word of mouth and copycat behaviour

As media continues to fragment and groups of individuals become less well defined, so word of mouth is a powerful marketing tool. It is the opinion shapers and early adopters whose word of mouth is seen as crucial in the adoption process. These are the agents of change. This underlines the importance of studying such consumers and their media habits.

The other two groups are influential in different ways. Early adopters will quickly influence trade support and opinion shapers may reassure hesitant purchasers who are not early adopters but are likely to come into the market later. Early adopters are particularly relevant where the trade may have some doubts about the product. The opinion shapers are likely to be particularly relevant where there is perceived to be a high risk associated with purchase, consumption, use or display (if there is an opportunity for conspicuous consumption – use or display).

The study examines the TV programme preferences (types of programmes and specific programmes such as *Friends*, *Coronation Street*, etc.) of over 3,000 people representative of adults aged 16–60 randomly selected from the Taylor Nelson Sofres online panel early in 2004.

Key findings

It was no surprise to note that those consumers who scored highest* in terms of opinion shaping in a specific field were typically twice as likely to watch a relevant TV programme. Thus fashion opinion shapers were more likely than others to watch fashion programmes; opinion shapers on cars were the more likely to watch motoring programmes; opinion shapers for financial services were the more likely to watch money programmes. Also there were higher levels of claimed product recommendation by opinion shapers (within their product field).

The incidence of opinion shapers and early adopters among people who watch non-terrestrial channels is much higher than average. In the fashion category, for example, people who viewed MTV in the last week are almost 60 per cent more likely than average to be early adopters of products in general and E4 viewers are 50 per cent more likely to be opinion shapers in the category of fashion.

The study profiled 33 specific TV programmes in terms of the incidence of early adopters and well-connected opinion shapers. So the research facilitates those interested in targeting these key groups in various product fields and categories by providing accurate profiles of specific TV programmes. This ultimately assists advertisers to fast-track new developments in the marketplace either through advertising in specific programmes or sponsoring programmes.

Questions

1 This information on early adopters and opinion shapers will assist with media planning. What marketing communication vehicles, other than TV, might be used to facilitate early adoption?

2 What is the difference between sought and unsought recommendation and how might this influence behaviour associated with word-of-mouth advice?

3 In what way could Channel 4 and their advertising clients measure the success of identifying opinion shapers and early adopters?

* In the top 16 per cent of scores (based on the principle underlying the Diffusion of Innovation distribution).

References

Aaker, D., Batra, R. and Myers, J.G. (1992) *Advertising Management*. 4th edn. Englewood Cliffs, NJ: Prentice-Hall.

Armstrong, S. (1993) The business of buying: time, lads, please. *Media Week*, 3 September, pp. 26–7.

Beale, C. (1997) Study reveals negativity towards ads. *Campaign*, 28 November, p. 8.

Brech, P. (1999) When the media buck stops with you. *Media Week*, 19 November, pp. 22–3.

Bristowe, L., Nancarrow, C. and Tinson, J. (2004) Targeting consumer movers and shakers. Media Research Group, Madrid, 3–6 November.

Broussard, G. (2000) How advertising frequency can work to build online effectiveness. *International Journal of Market Research*, **42**(4), pp. 439–57.

Burnett, J. (1993) *Promotion Management*. New York: Houghton Mifflin.

Crane, L.E. (1964) How product, appeal, and program affect attitudes towards commercials. *Journal of Advertising Research*, **4** (March), p. 15.

Daft, R.L. and Lengel, R.H. (1984) Information richness: a new approach to managerial behavior and organizational design. In *Research in Organizational Behavior 6* (eds L.L. Cummings and B.M. Straw). Homewood, IL: JAI Press.

Daft, R.L. and Lengel, R.H. (1986) Organizational information requirements, media richness and structural design. *Managerial Science*, No. 32.

Duarte, D.L. and Snyder, N.T. (2001) *Mastering Virtual Team*. 2nd edn. San Francisco, CA: Jossey-Bass.

Ephron, E. (1997) Recency planning. *Admap* (February), pp. 32–4.

Fulk, J., Schmitz, J.A. and Steinfield, C.W. (1990) A social influence model of technology use. In *Organizations and Communication Technology* (eds J. Fulk and C. Steinfield). Newbury Park, CA: Sage.

Gallucci, P. (1997) There are no absolutes in media planning. *Admap* (July/August), pp. 39–43.

Govoni, N., Eng, R. and Galper, M. (1986) *Promotional Management*. Englewood Cliffs, NJ: Prentice-Hall.

Grimshaw, C. (2004) MediaCom – media agency of the year. *Marketing Agency*, December, p. 7.

Jarvis, T. and McElroy, B. (2004) Can optimisers provide a lifeline for media? *Admap* **39**(2) (February), pp. 32–5.

Jones, P. (1990) Advertising: strong or weak force? Two views an ocean apart. *International Journal of Advertising*, **9**(3), pp. 233–46.

Jones, P. (1995) *When Ads Work: New Proof that Advertising Triggers Sales*. New York: Simon & Schuster, The Free Press/Lexington Books.

Keaveney, S.M. (1995) Consumer switching behavior in service industries: an exploratory study. *Journal of Marketing*, **59**(2), pp. 71–82.

King, R.C. and Xia, W. (1997) Media appropriateness: effects of experience on communication media choice. *Decision Sciences*, **28**(4), pp. 877–909.

Kotler, P. (1997) *Marketing Management: Analysis, Planning, Implementation and Control*. 9th edn. Englewood Cliffs, NJ: Prentice-Hall.

Krugman, H.E. (1965) The impact of television advertising: learning without involvement. *Public Opinion Quarterly*, **29** (Fall), pp. 349–56.

Krugman, H.E. (1972) How potent is TV advertising? Cited in du Plessis (1998).

Krugman, H.E. (1975) What makes advertising effective? *Harvard Business Review* (March/April), pp. 96–103.

Lloyd, D.W. and Clancy, K.J. (1991) CPMs versus CPMis: implications for media planning. *Journal of Advertising Research*, **31**(4) (August/September), pp. 34–44.

McGrath, J.E. and Hollingshead, A.B. (1993) Putting the 'Group' back into group support systems: some theoretical issues about dynamic processes in groups with technological enhancements. In *Group Support Systems: New Perspectives* (eds L.M. Jessup and J.S. Valacich). New York: Macmillan.

McLuhan, M. (1966) *Understanding Media: The Extensions of Man*. New York: McGraw-Hill.

Mueller-Heumann, G. (1992) Market and technology shifts in the 1990s: market fragmentation and mass customisation. *Journal of Marketing Management*, **8**, pp. 303–14.

Murray, G.B. and Jenkins, J.R.G. (1992) The concept of effective reach in advertising. *Journal of Advertising Research*, **32**(3) (May/June), pp. 34–42.

Nancarrow, C. and Tinson, J. (2004) Presentation on opinion shaping to Channel 4, London, October.

Naples, M.J. (1979) *Effective Frequency: The Relationship Between Frequency and Advertising Effectiveness*. New York: Association of National Advertisers.

Ostrow, J.W. (1981) What level of frequency? *Advertising Age* (November), pp. 13–18.

Ostrow, J.W. (1984) Setting frequency levels: an art or a science? *Marketing and Media Decisions*, **24**(4), pp. 9–11.

Plessis, E. du (1998) Memory and likeability: keys to understanding ad effects. *Admap* (July/August), pp. 42–6.

Rothschild, M.L. (1987) *Marketing Communications*. Lexington, MA: D.C. Heath.

Simon, H. (1972) Theories of bounded rationality. In *Decision and Organisation* (eds C.B. McGuire and R. Radner). London: North-Holland.

Simon, H. (1987) Bounded rationality. In *The New Palgrave* (eds J. Eatwell, M. Milgate and P. Newman). London: Macmillan.

Sissors, J.Z. and Bumba, L. (1989) *Advertising Media Planning*. 3rd edn. Lincolnwood, IL: NTC Business Books.

Srinivasan, M. (1996) New insights into switching behaviour: marketers can now put a numerical value on loyalty. *Marketing Research*, **8**(3), pp. 26–34.

Weilbacher, W. (1984) *Advertising*. New York: Macmillan.

Sales promotion: principles and approaches

23

Sales promotion seeks to offer buyers additional value as an inducement to generate an immediate sale. These inducements can be targeted at consumers, distributors, agents and members of the sales force. Sales promotions can form an important part of the communication mix and are often of strategic importance to number three and four brands in fast-moving consumer goods markets.

Aims and objectives

The aim of this chapter is to consider the nature and role of sales promotion and to appraise its position within the marketing communications mix.

The objectives of this chapter are to:

1. explain the role of sales promotion in the promotional mix;
2. discuss the reasons for the increased use of sales promotions;
3. examine the way in which sales promotions are considered to work;
4. appraise the value of this promotional tool;
5. discuss the nature of loyalty programmes and issues associated with customer retention;
6. appreciate how sales promotions can be used strategically.

Introduction

One of the main tasks of advertising is to develop awareness in the target audience. The main task of sales promotion is to encourage the target audience to behave in a particular way, usually to buy a product. These two tools set out to accomplish tasks at each end of the attitudinal spectrum: the cognitive and the conative elements. Just as advertising seeks to work over the long term, sales promotion can achieve short-term upward shifts in sales.

Sales promotion offers buyers additional value.

Sales promotion offers buyers additional value, as an inducement to generate an immediate sale. These inducements can be targeted at consumers, distributors, agents and members of the sales force. A whole range of network members can benefit from the use of sales promotion.

This promotional tool is traditionally referred to as a form of below-the-line communication because, unlike advertising, there are no commission payments from media owners with this form of communication. The promotional costs are borne directly by the organisation initiating the activity, which in most cases is a manufacturer, producer or service provider.

Understanding the value of sales promotions

There are many sales promotion techniques, but they all offer a direct inducement or an incentive to encourage receivers of these promotional messages to buy a product/service sooner rather than later. The inducement (for example, price deals, coupons, premiums) is presented as an added value to the basic product and is intended to encourage buyers to act 'now' rather than later. Sales promotion is used, therefore, principally as a means to accelerate sales. The acceleration represents the shortened period of time in which the transaction is completed relative to the time that would have elapsed had there not been a promotion. This action does not mean that an extra sale has been achieved, just that a potential future exchange is confirmed and transacted upon now.

The inducement (for example, price deals, coupons, premiums) is presented as an added value to the basic product. Sales promotion is used, therefore, principally as a means to accelerate sales.

Sales promotions consist of a wide range of tools and methods. These instruments are considered in more detail in the following chapter but consideration of what constitutes sales promotion methods is important. In many cases price is the determinant variable and can be used to distinguish between instruments. Sales promotions are often perceived purely as a price discounting mechanism through price deals and the use of coupons. This, however, is not the whole picture, as there are many other ways in which incentives can be offered to buyers.

Reference has already been made to the idea that sales promotions are a way of providing value and it is this value orientation that should be used when considering the nature and essential characteristics of sales promotions. Peattie and Peattie (1994) established a useful way of discriminating between price and non-price sales promotion instruments. They refer to sales promotions that are value increasing and sales promotions that are value adding. See Table 23.1.

Sales promotions that are value increasing and sales promotions that are value adding.

TABLE 23.1 A value orientation of sales promotions (Peattie and Peattie, 1994)

Value element	Explanation
Value increasing	Value is increased by offering changes to the product quantity/quality or by lowering the price. Generally used and perceived as effective over the short term.
Value adding	Value is added by offering something to augment the fundamental product/price offering. Premiums (gifts), information or opportunities can be offered as extras and the benefits realised over different periods of time: delayed (postal premiums), accumulated (loyalty programmes) or instant (scratch and win competitions). These have the potential to add value over the longer term.

This demarcation is important because a large amount of research into sales promotion has been based on value-increasing approaches, most notably price deals and coupons (Gupta, 1988; Blattberg and Neslin, 1990; Krishna and Zhang, 1999). This tends to distort the way sales promotions are perceived and has led to some generalisations about the overall impact of this promotional discipline. There is a large range of other sales promotion instruments that add value and enhance the offering and which provide opportunities to drive longer-term benefits. See Table 23.2. However, research into these is limited (Gilbert and Jackaria, 2002).

As a result of this diversity of sales promotion instruments it should be no surprise to learn that they are used for a wide range of reasons. Sales promotions can be targeted, with considerable precision, at particular audiences and there are three broad audiences to whom sales promotions can be targeted: consumers, members of the distribution or channel network, and the sales forces of both manufacturers and resellers. It should be remembered that the accuracy of these promotional tools means that many subgroups within these broad groups can be reached quickly and accurately. These are presented in Table 23.3.

> The accuracy of these promotional tools means that many subgroups within these broad groups can be reached quickly and accurately.

TABLE 23.2 A sales promotion typology as used in the commercial sector

Value increasing (alters price/quantity or price/quality equation)	Value adding (offers 'something extra' while leaving core product and price unchanged)
Discount pricing	Samples
Money-off coupons	Special features (limited editions)
Payment terms (e.g. interest-free credit)	Valued packaging
Refunds	Product trial
Guarantees	In-pack gifts
Multipack or multi-buys	In-mail gifts
Quantity increases	Piggy back gifts
Buybacks	Gift coupons
	Information (e.g. brochure, catalogue)
	Clubs or loyalty programmes
	Competitions/prize draws

TABLE 23.3 Reasons for the use of sales promotions

Reach new customers	They are useful in securing trials for new products and in defending shelf space against anticipated and existing competition.
Reduce distributor risk	The funds that manufacturers dedicate to them lower the distributor's risk in stocking new brands.
Reward behaviour	They can provide rewards for previous purchase behaviour.
Retention	They can provide interest and attract potential customers and in doing so encourage them to provide personal details for further communications activity.
Add value	Can encourage sampling and repeat purchase behaviour by providing extra value (superior to competitors' brands) and a reason to purchase.
Induce action	They can instil a sense of urgency among consumers to buy while a deal is available. They add excitement and interest at the point of purchase to the merchandising of mature and mundane products.
Preserve cash flow	Since sales promotion costs are incurred on a pay-as-you-go basis, they can spell survival for smaller, regional brands that cannot afford big advertising programmes.
Improve efficiency	Sales promotions allow manufacturers to use idle capacity and to adjust to demand and supply imbalances or softness in raw material prices and other input costs, while maintaining the same list prices.
Integration	Provide a means of linking together other tools of the promotional mix.
Assist segmentation	They allow manufacturers to price discriminate among consumer segments that vary in price sensitivity. Most manufacturers believe that a high-list, high-deal policy is more profitable than offering a single price to all consumers. A portion of sales promotion expenditures, therefore, consists of reductions in list prices that are set for the least price-sensitive segment of the market.

Lee (2002) suggests that the main reasons for the use of sales promotions can be reduced to four:

1. as a reaction to competitor activities
2. as a form of inertia – this is what we have always done
3. as a way of meeting short-term sales objectives
4. as a way of meeting long-term objectives.

ViewPoint 23.1   Competitive sales promotions

As if to demonstrate the competitive use of sales promotions the UK supermarkets, Tesco and Sainsbury's, engaged in a coupon-based mini-battle in 2002.

Tesco announced that it would accept vouchers issued by Sainsbury's for its home delivery service. Sainsbury's responded by issuing a flood of vouchers and sending them to customers where it did not have a store presence, just so that they would be redeemed at Tesco.

It appears that the first three are used widely and Lee comments that many brand owners use sales promotion as a panic measure when competitors threaten to lure customers away. Cutting prices is undoubtedly a way of prompting a short-term sales response but it can also undermine a longer-term brand strategy.

Not too many years ago sales promotions were regarded as a key way of developing sales. However, the use of sales promotions has stagnated and in particular the use of on-pack promotions, bonus packs, competitions and price deals have failed to maintain the growth of previous years. Reasons for the decline include changing consumer behaviour, the rise of new media and a distinct lack of innovation in the industry.

Supermarkets have become media owners.

Another important factor has been the expectations and drive of resellers, and the main supermarket chains in particular. They desire sales promotion programmes that are exclusive to them as this is seen as a major way of developing their retail brands. Supermarkets have become media owners and realise the value of their store space as a means of exposing others' brands. Therefore, any form of sales promotion activity within their environments should be exclusive and tied into their brand. On-pack promotions for individual stores is too expensive and uneconomic so this form of promotion has suffered a great deal.

New solutions have had to be found and as Barrand (2004) suggests the use of digital media and the integration of sales promotion within other campaigns has been

The use of digital media and the integration of sales promotion within other campaigns has been successful.

successful. The use of SMS, email, viral campaigns and the Internet are being used increasingly to drive sales by providing the veritable call-to-action, for a long time the province of sales promotion activities.

The role of sales promotion

The role of sales promotion has changed significantly over recent years. At one time, the largest proportion of communications budgets was normally allocated to advertising. In many cases advertising no longer dominates the communications budget and sales promotion has assumed the focus of the communications spend, for reasons that are described below. This is particularly evident in consumer markets that are mature, have reached a level of stagnation, and where price and promotion work are the few ways of inducing brand switching behaviour.

Short termism

The short-term financial focus of many industrialised economies has developed a managerial climate geared to short-term performance and evaluation, over periods as short as 12 weeks. To accomplish this, communications tools are required that work quickly and directly impact upon sales. Many see this as leading to an erosion of the brand franchise.

Managerial accountability

Following on from the previous reason is the increased pressure upon marketing managers to be accountable for their communications expenditure. The results of sales promotion activities are more easily justified and understood than those associated with advertising. The number of coupons returned for redemption and the number of bonus packs purchased can be calculated quickly and easily, with little room for error or mis-judgement. Advertising, however, cannot be so easily measured in either the short or the long term. The impact of this is that managers can relate the promotional expenditure to the bottom line much more comfortably with sales promotion than with advertising.

Brand performance

Technological advances have enabled retailers to track brand performance more effectively. This in turn means that manufacturers can be drawn into agreements that promulgate in-store promotional activity at the expense of other more traditional forms of mass media promotion. Barcode scanners, hand-held electronic shelf-checking equipment and computerised stock systems facilitate the tracking of merchandise. This means that brand managers can be held responsible much more quickly for below-par performance.

Brand expansion

As brand quality continues to improve and as brands proliferate on the shelves of increasingly larger supermarkets, so the number of decisions that a consumer has to make also increases. Faced with multiple-brand decisions and a reduced amount of time to complete the shopping expedition, the tension associated with the shopping experience has increased considerably over the last decade.

ViewPoint 23.2	Sales promotions in Boots

In August 2003 Boots, the high street chemist and retailer, announced that it had reviewed its use of sales promotions, which until then had been a central part of its marketing offer. In particular, its three-for-two product offers had been a prominent part of its communications.

Using the incentive of extra product in order to create store traffic was considered not to be a viable or compatible strategy with the desire to make Boots a must-visit high street destination.

Associated with this development was the evolution of its loyalty card scheme (Advantage card). Through improved data-mining it hoped to better understand its customers and then create improved cross-selling opportunities. Boots wants to be perceived as more exclusive and to achieve that it needs to give consumers more powerful reasons for shopping there than those provided through traditional product promotions.

Source: Adapted from Kleinman (2003).

Promotions make decision-making easier for consumers: they simplify a potentially difficult process. So, as brand choice increases, the level of shopping convenience falls. The conflict this causes can be resolved by the astute use of sales promotions. Some feel that the cognitive shopper selects brands that offer increased value, which makes decision-making easier and improves the level of convenience associated with the shopping experience. However, should there be promo-

Promotions make decision-making easier for consumers.

tions on two offerings from an individual's repertoire then the decision-making is not necessarily made easier.

Competition for shelf space

Sales promotions help manufacturers win valuable shelf space.

The continuing growth in the number of brands launched in the 1980s and 1990s and the fragmentation of consumer markets mean that retailers have to be encouraged to make shelf space available. Sales promotions help manufacturers win valuable shelf space and assist retailers to attract increased levels of store traffic and higher utilisation of limited resources.

The credibility of this promotional tool is low, as it is obvious to the receiver what the intention is of using sales promotion messages. However, because of the prominent and pervasive nature of the tool, consumers and members of the trade understand and largely accept the direct sales approach. Sales promotion is not a tool that hides its intentions, nor does it attempt to be devious (which is not allowed, by regulation).

The absolute costs of sales promotion are low, but the real costs need to be evaluated once a campaign has finished and all redemptions received and satisfied. The relative costs can be high, as not only do the costs of the premium or price discount need to be determined, but also the associated costs of additional transportation, lost profit, storage and additional time spent organising and administering a sales promotion campaign need to be accounted for.

ViewPoint 23.3   Sales promotions to drive car sales

Sales promotions are used in the UK car market to drive customers into dealerships. However, the retail landscape for car buyers has changed enormously following allegations that car prices in the UK were 10–15 per cent higher than in continental Europe.

In addition to the pressure to reduce prices, the opportunities and marketing channels (Internet driven) for purchasing new cars has expanded considerably. Therefore the primary role for sales promotions now appears to be one of presenting the car to the customer in the channel environments that customers are more likely to inhabit (Miller, 2000). It would appear that sales promotions started to be used as a strategic and integrated tool in order to develop brands.

In its favour, sales promotion allows for a high degree of control. Management is able to decide just when and where a sales promotion will occur and also estimate the sales effect. Sales promotions can be turned on and off quickly and adjusted to changed market conditions. The intended message is invariably the one that is received, as there is relatively little scope for it to be corrupted or damaged in transmission.

Sales promotion plans: the objectives

The objectives of using this tool are sales oriented and are geared to stimulating buyers either to use a product for the first time or to encourage use on a routine basis.

One objective of sales promotion activity is to prompt buyers into action, to initiate a series of behaviours that result in long-run purchase activity. These actions can be seen to occur in the conative stage of the attitudinal set. They reflect high or low involvement, and indicate whether cognitive processing and persuasion occur via the central or peripheral routes of the ELM (Chapter 7). If the marketing objectives include the introduction of a new product or intention to enter a new market, then the key objective associated with low-involvement decisions and peripheral route processing is

	Involvement	
	High	**Low**
New product or market	Withhold sales promotion	Use sales promotion to stimulate trial
Established product or market	Non-loyals – use for switching Loyals – use carefully	Non-loyals – use sales promotions to attract for trial Loyals – use sales promotion to reward for increased usage

FIGURE 23.1 A sales promotion objectives grid

to stimulate trial use as soon as possible. When high-involvement decisions and central route processing are present, then sales promotions need to be withheld until a suitable level of attitudinal development has been undertaken by public relations and advertising activities.

If a product is established in a market, then a key objective should be to use sales promotions to stimulate an increase in the number of purchases made by current customers and to attract users from competing products. See Figure 23.1. The objectives, therefore, are either to increase consumption for established products or to stimulate trial by encouraging new buyers to use a product. Once this has been agreed then the desired trial and usage levels need to be determined for each of the target audiences. Before discussing these aspects, it is necessary first to review the manner in which sales promotions are thought to influence the behaviour of individuals.

> If a product is established in a market, then a key objective should be to use sales promotions to stimulate an increase in the number of purchases made by current customers.

An overview of how sales promotions work

If the overriding objectives of sales promotions are to accelerate or bring forward future sales, the implication is that a behavioural change is required by the receiver for the sales promotion to be effective. The establishment of new behaviour patterns is the preferred outcome. If sales promotions are to work over the longer term, that is to bring about repeat purchase behaviour, then the new behaviour patterns need to be learned and adopted on a permanent basis.

This is a complex task, and is referred to by behaviourists as shaping. The behaviourist's view is advocated, for example, by Rothschild and Gaidis (1981). They suggest that by breaking the overall task into its constituent parts a series of smaller sequential tasks can be learned. When the successive actions are aggregated the new desired pattern of behaviour emerges. This view emphasises the impact of external stimuli in changing the behaviour of people.

> When the successive actions are aggregated the new desired pattern of behaviour emerges.

The cognitive view of the way sales promotions operate is based on the belief that consumers internally process relevant information about a sales promotion, including those of past experiences, and make a reasoned decision in the light of the goals and objectives that individuals set for themselves.

The ELM suggests that individuals using the peripheral route will only consider simplistic cues, such as display boards and price reduction signs. Individuals using the central route of the ELM have a higher need for information and will develop the promotional signal to evaluate the relative price and the salient attributes of the promoted product before making a decision (Inman *et al.*, 1990).

The main difference between the views of the behaviourists and those of the cognitive school of thought is that the former stress the impact of externally generated stimuli, whereas the latter recognise the complexity of internal information processing as the most significant element.

ViewPoint 23.4　Sharwood's use of sales promotions

As part of a strategy to develop and maintain the position of the Sharwood's brand of Asian foods (www.sharwoods.com), the organisation used a £5 million above-the-line television campaign as part of its strategy to build a more engaging brand. This has included its first investment in interactive digital television. Via banner advertising on the NTL digital platform consumers were directed to a microsite to participate in an interactive competition to win two Virgin flights and one of 10,000 money-off coupons for Sharwood's products. The promotion not only developed an extensive database for use in future emarketing but added value through entertainment and built the brand in a lighthearted, involving context. See Exhibit 23.1.

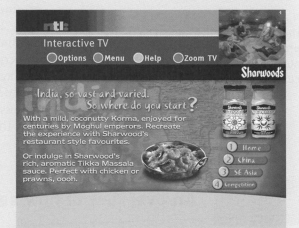

EXHIBIT 23.1 Sharwood's brand development using an interactively based sales promotion campaign
Picture reproduced with the kind permission of Centura Foods Ltd.
Material Kindly provided by Caroline Clarke, Senior Brand Manager, Sharwood's.

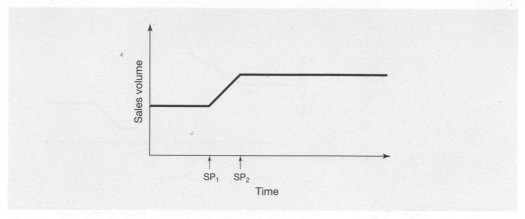

FIGURE 23.2 Expected response to a sales promotion event: SP₁ is the start of the event; SP₂ is the end

The increasing proportion of budgets being allocated to sales promotions, and temporary price reductions (TPRs) in particular, has prompted concern about the costs and overall impact of these activities. It might be reasonable to expect that the sales curve following a price-based promotion would look like that depicted in Figure 23.2.

There is plenty of evidence that sales volumes can be increased following use of a TPR.

There is plenty of evidence that sales volumes can be increased following use of a TPR (Ehrenberg, 2000). However, a long-term upward shift in demand is unrealistic, particularly in mature markets. Extra stock is being transferred to consumers, and therefore they have more than they require for a normal purchase cycle. Ehrenberg suggests that most people who use TPRs are actually infrequent purchasers of a given category. Research suggests that these types of promotion do not attract new buyers.

The graph shown in Figure 23.3 is more likely to occur, with sales volume falling in the period when buyers are loaded with stock and temporarily removed from the market. However, Dawes (2004) found that there were as many buyers in a market in the period following a promotion as there were when the TPR was running.

Promotional activity does not take place in a vacuum with new products.

Promotional activity does not take place in a vacuum with new products: competitors will be attracted and some customers lost to competitive offerings; in mature markets, non-loyals will take advantage of a sales promotion and then revert to competitors' sales promotions when they re-enter the market. So, the third scenario is shown in Figure 23.4. The result is that overall demand for a brand *may* be reduced owing to the combined effects of competitive promotional activity. However, Dawes found that

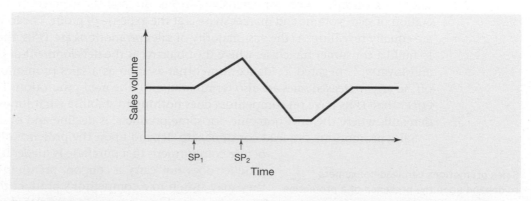

FIGURE 23.3 Realistic response to a sales promotion event: SP₁ is the start of the event; SP₂ is the end

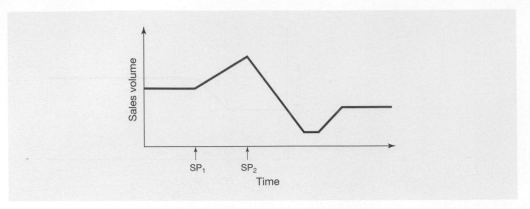

FIGURE 23.4 The destructive effect of competitive sales promotions

price promotions have a neutral impact on a brand, with the benefits of volume increases being countered by the consequent fall in profitability. It may be therefore that the second scenario is the more accurate interpretation.

Sales promotions incur a large number of hidden costs. It was stated earlier that the cost of a sales promotion is thought to be relatively low but, as Buzzell *et al.* (1990) and others have demonstrated, there are a host of other indirect costs that must be considered. Manufacturers, for example, use promotional deals to induce resellers to buy stock at a promotional price, in addition to their normal buying requirements. The additional stock is then held for resale at a later date, at regular retail prices. The effect of this forward buying on the costs of the reseller can be enormous. Buzzell *et al.* point out that the promotional stock attracts higher interest charges, storage costs, expenses associated with the transfer of stock to different geographical areas of the organisation and the costs associated with keeping normal and promotional stock separate. When these are added to the manufacturer's forward buying costs it is probable, they conclude, that the costs outweigh the benefits of the sales promotion exercise.

These activities suggest that the relationship between the members of the network is market oriented rather than relational. However, many of these extra costs are unknown, and the resellers are unaware of the costs they are absorbing as a result of the deal. In the future, resellers and manufacturers should work together on such promotions and attempt to uncover all the costs involved to ensure that the exercise is successful for both parties.

> **Resellers and manufacturers should work together on such promotions and attempt to uncover all the costs.**

Not only the short-term costs associated with a sales promotion but also the long-term costs must be evaluated. Jones (1990) refers to this as the double jeopardy of sales promotions. He argues that manufacturers that participate extensively in short-term sales promotions, mainly for defensive reasons, do so at the expense of profit. The generation of sales volume and market share is at the expense of profit. The long-term effects are equally revealing. As the vast majority of sales promotions are TPRs, the opportunity to build a consumer franchise, where the objective is the development of brand identity and loyalty, is negated. Evidence shows that as soon as a sales promotion is switched off, so any increased sales are also terminated until the next promotion. The retaliatory effect that TPRs have on competitors does nothing to stabilise what Jones calls volatile demand, where the only outcome, for some products, is decline and obscurity.

Sales promotions can lead consumers to depend upon the presence of a promotion before commitment to a purchase is made. If the preferred product does not carry a coupon, premium or TPR, then they may switch to a competitor's product that does offer some element of increased value. A related issue concerns

> **Sales promotions can lead consumers to depend upon the presence of a promotion before commitment to a purchase is made.**

the speed at which sales promotions are reduced following the introduction of a new product. If the incentives are removed too quickly, it is probable that consumers will have been unable to build a relationship with the product. If the incentives are sustained for too long, then it is possible that consumers have only identified a product by the value of the incentive, not the value of the product itself. The process by which a sales promotion is removed from a product is referred to as fading, and its rate can be crucial to the successful outcome of a product launch and a sales promotion activity.

Loyalty and retention programmes

Despite questions about the use of sales promotions to build loyalty the growth of loyalty programmes has been a significant promotional development in recent years. One of the more visible schemes has been the ClubCard offered by Tesco, which has been partly responsible for Tesco dominating the UK retail market. The response of its nearest rival Sainsbury's, at the time, was to publicly reject loyalty cards, but some 18 months later it launched its Reward Card and then subsequently joined the group scheme, Nectar.

Loyalty schemes have been encouraged through the use of swipe cards.

Loyalty schemes have been encouraged through the use of swipe cards. Users are rewarded with points each time a purchase is made. This is referred to as a 'points accrual programme', whereby loyal users are able to build up the necessary points, which are stored (often) on a card, and 'cashed in' at a later date for gifts or merchandise. The benefit for the company supporting the scheme is that the promised rewards motivate customers to accrue more points and in doing so increase their switching costs, effectively locking them into the loyalty programme and preventing them from moving to a competitor brand.

Recent technological developments mean that smart cards (a card that has a small microprocessor attached) can record enormous amounts of information, which is updated each time a purchase is made.

ViewPoint 23.5   Loyalty to Qantas

The reasons behind the development of the Frequent Flyer Programme (FFP), run by the airline Qantas, are very similar to other loyalty programmes. Essentially they are used to nurture brand loyalty and repeat business, to deter smaller airlines from entering the market and to collect information about their customers in order to provide them with more personalised communications and product offers.

Points are awarded according to the distance flown and class of travel or fare paid. There are four different levels of membership: bronze at entry level, silver, gold and platinum, and each level confers different privileges.

To some extent all airlines need such a programme but each incurs heavy administrative and IT costs and a potential liability in terms of the accumulation of unredeemed points. Apart from a small number of very loyal customers, these types of loyalty schemes do not appear to reflect true relationship development. In view of the financial problems facing the airline industry the long-term value of FFPs has to be questioned.

Source: Adapted from Whyte (2004).

Not only have loyalty schemes for frequent flyers (e.g. BA Executive Club and Virgin Freeway) been very successful, but the cards are also used to track individual travellers. Airlines are able to offer cardholders particular services, such as special airport lounges and magazines; the card through its links to a database also enables a traveller's favourite seat and dietary requirements to be offered. In addition, the regular accumulation of air miles fosters continuity and hence loyalty, through which business travellers reward themselves with leisure travel. However, the airlines' desire to develop relationships with their customers might not be fully reciprocated as customers seek only convenience.

The potential number of applications for smart cards is tremendous. However, just like swipe cards the targeting of specific groups of buyers can be expected to become more precise and efficient and it is also easier to track and target individuals for future promotional activities.

Perhaps the attention given to loyalty and retention issues is misplaced because marketing is about the identification, anticipation and satisfaction of customer needs (profitably). If these needs are being met properly it might be reasonable to expect that customers would return anyway, reducing the need for overt 'loyalty' programmes. The demise of Safeway's ABC loyalty card suggested that their investment did not provide a competitive advantage and did not differentiate the supermarket sufficiently to drive profits and provide shareholder value. The demise of Safeway itself (taken over by Morrisons in 2003) is indicative of the poor value that it offered customers and the potential value that Morrisons believes it can leverage.

Because the programme allows for the collection of up-to-date customer information.

There is an argument that these schemes are important not because of the loyalty aspect but because the programme allows for the collection of up-to-date customer information and then the use of the data to make savings in the supply chain. It was estimated that Tesco had saved over £500 million through the use of its customer data (Jardine, 2000). That information has not been updated, but one of the main logistical problems concerning the management and analysis of the huge volumes of data collected has largely been overcome. Some organisations use less than half the data they collect and then it was argued that the data actually used can be bought in at a much lower cost than these loyalty schemes cost to run. This may be partly true but vastly improved data-mining and warehousing techniques have led to more effective use of customer data.

Reflecting the increased emphasis upon keeping customers rather than constantly finding new ones.

There has been a proliferation of loyalty cards, reflecting the increased emphasis upon keeping customers rather than constantly finding new ones and there is evidence that sales lift by about 2 or 3 per cent when a loyalty scheme is launched. However, there is little evidence to support the notion that sales promotions, and in particular the use of premiums, are capable of encouraging loyalty, whether that be defined as behavioural and/or attitude. 'The notion of hard core loyals is fast becoming extinct' (Yim and Kannan, 1999) as the proliferation of brands has led customers to prefer to actively select from a repertoire of favourite brands, each of which serves to satisfy slightly different needs. Schemes do enable organisations to monitor and manage stock, use direct marketing to cross and up-sell customers, and manage their portfolio in order to consolidate (increase?) customer's spending in a store. Whether loyalty is being developed by encouraging buyers to make repeat purchases or whether the schemes are merely sales promotion techniques that encourage extended and consistent purchasing patterns is debatable. Customer retention is a major issue and a lot of emphasis has been given to loyalty schemes as a means of achieving retention targets.

There are views that loyalty schemes are not only misguided but have cost industry a huge amount of money. Hastings and Price (2004) for example have expressed strong views about the notion and viability of so-called loyalty and points-based schemes.

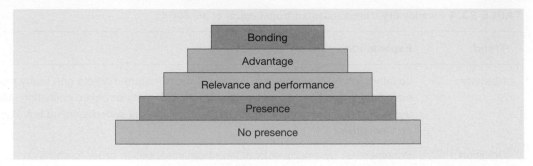

FIGURE 23.5 The brand emotional loyalty pyramid (Hallberg, 2004); used with permission

They claim that loyalty schemes are misunderstood for two main reasons. The first is the assumption that loyalty can be bought when, like love, true loyalty can only be given. Secondly, there is an assumption that points-based schemes can be profit centres.

Hallberg (2004) reports a major study involving in excess of 600,000 in-depth consumer interviews. The study identifies different levels of loyalty and concludes that significant financial returns are gained only when the highest level of loyalty is achieved. These levels of loyalty are set out in Figure 23.5.

> **And concludes that significant financial returns are gained only when the highest level of loyalty is achieved.**

Hallberg refers to the impact of emotional loyalty, a non-purchase measurement of attachment to a brand:

- At the 'No Presence' level consumers are unaware of a brand and so there is no emotional loyalty.
- At the 'Presence' level there is awareness but emotional loyalty is minimal.
- At the 'Relevance and Performance' level the consumer begins to feel that the brand is acceptable in terms of meeting their needs.
- At the 'Advantage' level consumers should feel that the brand is superior with regard to a particular attribute.
- At the 'Bonding' level emotional loyalty is at its highest because consumers feel the brand has several unique properties. They love the brand.

Loyalty schemes are exponentially effective when the consumers reach the bonding stage. Although sales generally increase the further up the pyramid consumers move it is only at the Bonding stage that sales start to reflect the emotional attachment people feel towards the brand. Hallberg refers to the success and market leadership that Tesco has achieved but the principles established through this study should apply to loyalty programmes regardless of category or sector.

There are a proliferation of loyalty programmes to the extent that Capizzi *et al.* (2004) suggest that the market is mature. They also argue that five clear trends within the loyalty market can be identified. These are set out in Table 23.4.

These trends suggest that successful sales promotions schemes will be those that enable members to perceive significant value associated with their continued association with a scheme. That value will be driven by schemes run by groups of complementary brands, which use technology to understand customer dynamics and communications that complement their preferred values. The medium-term goal might be that these schemes should reflect customers' different relationship needs and recognise the different loyalty levels desired by different people.

> **Value will be driven by schemes run by groups of complementary brands, which use technology to understand customer dynamics and communications that complement their preferred values.**

TABLE 23.4 Five loyalty trends (adapted from Capizzi *et al.*, 2004)

Trend	Explanation
Ubiquity	Loyalty programmes have proliferated in most mature markets and many members have little interest in them other than the functionality of points collection. Managers are trying to reduce communication costs by moving the scheme online but also need to be innovative.
Coalition	Schemes run by a number of different organisations in order to share costs, information and branding (e.g. Nectar) appear to be the dominant structure industry model.
Imagination	Opportunities to exploit technologies and niche markets will depend on creativity and imagination in order to get customer data to feed into the loyalty system. Employ IST imaginatively.
Wow	To overcome consumer lethargy and boredom with loyalty schemes, many rewards in future will be experiential, emotional, unique in an attempt to appeal to life stage and aspirational lifestyle goals – wow them. Differentiate to stand out.
Analysis	To be competitive the use of customer data analytics and business intelligence is becoming critical, if only to feed CRM programmes. Collect and analyse customer information effectively.

The strategic use of sales promotions

For a long time sales promotions have been regarded as a short-term tactical tool whose prime purpose is to encourage customers to try a brand or to switch brands (within their repertoire), attracted by the added value of the sales promotion. Indeed Papatia and Krishnamurthi (1996) claim that coupons can actively promote switching behaviour and so reduce levels of loyalty. As discussed earlier what happens after a sales promotion activity finishes is debatable. Some claim that once a promotion is withdrawn satisfied customers will return to the brand unsupported by a sales promotion, but supported by other elements of the marketing communications mix: in particular advertising, to maintain awareness of the brand and its values; direct marketing, to provide personal attention and the opportunity to take immediate action; and public relations to sustain credibility and relevance.

By way of contrast it can be argued that sales promotion serves to discount a brand, either directly through price-based reductions or indirectly through coupons and premiums. Customer alignment is to the deal rather than to the brand itself. This serves to lower expectations of what a brand stands for and what it is capable of delivering. So, once a sales promotion is removed, the normal price is perceived as representing inferior value and so repeat purchase behaviour is deterred.

However, despite these less than positive views, some writers (Davis, 1992; O'Malley, 1998) argue that sales promotions have a strategic role to play in the promotional mix. Traditionally they have been viewed as short-term tactical tools that can be used offensively to induce the trial of new products, or defensively for established products to retain shelf space and consumers. Sales promotions that do not work as intended may have been used to support inappropriate products or may have been devised without adequate planning. An example of the latter issue may be the Hoover free flights

> Sales promotions oriented to consumer deals and TPRs, in particular, do little to contribute to the overall strategy adopted for an organisation or even a product.

misjudgement and the associated over-subscription which followed the launch of that particular sales promotion activity. There can be no doubt that sales promotions oriented to consumer deals and TPRs, in particular, do little to contribute to the overall strategy adopted for an organisation or even a product.

One of the consequences of competitive sales promotions, especially in consumer markets, is the spiral effect that retaliatory actions can have on each organisation. A sales promotion 'trap' develops when competitors start to imitate each other's activities, often based upon price reductions. This leads eventually to participants losing profitability and consumers losing value and possibly choice as some products are forced to drop out of the market.

With the development of relationship marketing and the move towards integrated marketing communications has been the realisation that employees are an important target audience. There is a strong need to motivate the workforce and sales promotion activities have an important role to play. However, employee incentives need to be made accessible to everyone and not just a few (such as the sales force). This means that rewards need to be more broadly spread and there needs to be choice. Vouchers, for example, enable the prizewinner to make a choice based on their circumstances and they are easier to administer than many of the other types of reward. Incentive schemes should be designed in such a way that they do not fall into the trap of creating winners and losers which can be the case when, for example, the top 20 in a scheme win a prize, which effectively creates 80 losers out of every 100 employees.

Many schemes are based around product prizes, typically electrical goods. However, for many people these are no longer attractive (or sufficiently motivating) as rewards. Virgin vouchers provide activity-based rewards where there is an experience that gives the recipient a memory. Activities such as hot-air ballooning, sky diving, visits to the theatre or to health farms appeal to a wide cross-section of people.

> The true strategic effect of sales promotion activities can only be achieved if they are coordinated with the other activities of the promotional mix.

The true strategic effect of sales promotion activities can only be achieved if they are coordinated with the other activities of the promotional mix, and this requires planning. In particular, the complementary nature of sales promotion and advertising should be exploited through

---

ViewPoint 23.6   Integrated promotions at Kellogg's

Kellogg's entered into an on-pack promotion to donate a minimum of £500,000 to the charity Childline. Under the Kellogg's strapline 'Helping Kids Grow', consumers sent six tokens from Kellogg's cereal packs in return for a three-track CD. Consumers could select three tracks from a list of ten. For every CD requested, Kellogg's donated 30p to Childline and, for a submission of tokens and no CD, Kellogg's donated £1. The record company BMG was enlisted as it had recording rights to a wide range of artists.

The cereal packs together with leaflets, a dedicated Web site and direct mail to 30,000 teachers all helped to raise awareness of the ways in which children at risk could help themselves. A TV campaign was used to support the promotion and the music artists, ad agency and fulfilment houses all gave their time and services free of charge. The important aspect of this promotion is that Kellogg's was able to associate itself with a cause and at the same time underline its own proposition of healthy eating and care for others.

Source: Clarke, 2000.

the use of common themes and messages, timing, targeting and allocation of resources (in particular budgets). Sales promotions that are planned as a sequence of predetermined activities, reflecting the promotional requirements of a product over the longer term, are more likely to be successful than those sales promotions that are simply reactions to competitors' moves and market developments.

The strategic impact of sales promotions is best observed when they are designed or built into a three- to four-year plan of promotional activities, coordinated with other promotional tools and integrated with the business strategy.

The manner in which many of the loyalty programmes are managed signals a move from pure sales promotion to direct marketing. The integration of these two approaches has become necessary in order that the advantages of both are realised. This does raise an interesting conflict, in that sales promotion is essentially a short-term tool, and direct marketing needs to work over the long term. The former is product oriented (albeit giving added value to consumers) and often oriented to mass audiences, whereas the latter is based upon developing a personal dialogue (Curtis, 1996).

A further strategic issue concerns the use of joint promotions with other leading brands. With the intention of promoting the health aspects of its oil for frying purposes, Goldenfields rapeseed oil joined up with Morphy Richards to offer a two-tier campaign. The first involved 20 stainless steel fat fryer prizes in return for coupons from the oil bottle label and the second was a health farm prize and a further 20 fat fryers (Clarke, 2001). By twinning brand names increased promotional impact can assist both partners. However, there is a danger that such a pairing will be short lived, and hence the strategic perspective may be limited.

Finally, the huge sums of money involved in some of the mainstream loyalty or reward-based programmes suggest that these should be seen as longer-term promotional investments. As the return will spread over many years, a medium-term perspective may be more appropriate rather than a short-term view based on a sales 'blip'.

Summary

Sales promotions now command the lion's share of the promotional budget. This is because it has been proved that they are very effective as a communication tool with consumers, members of the performance network and the sales force. The range of techniques and methods used to add value to offerings is enormous, but there are growing doubts about the effectiveness and profitability associated with some sales promotions.

In comparison with advertising and public relations, many of the sales promotion techniques are easier to evaluate, if only because the number of variables is smaller and they are easier to isolate. Having said this, there is a lack of effective sales promotion measurement and control. This often leads to a short-term focus. Retailers are the same, except for the evaluation on a pre- and post-test basis of their own-brand promotions. Store traffic, sales volume and consumer attitude studies prevail.

Sales promotions have a strategic role to play, particularly when they are used to complement the other activities in the promotional mix. By attempting to develop a consistent theme to a promotional plan, sales promotions can follow advertising's awareness-building activities with a series of messages that continue the theme already established. Success is much more likely when consumers are invited to take advantage of a promotion for a product that they are not only aware of but are conscious of through recent promotional messages.

Review questions

1. Why is sales promotion referred to as a below-the-line communication tool?

2. What are the purposes of using sales promotion and why has it assumed such a large share of promotional expenditure?

3. Write a brief note explaining how shaping works.

4. Identify the major differences between the behavioural and the cognitive explanations of how sales promotions work.

5. Does sales promotion have a strategic or a tactical role to play in the promotional mix?

6. Write brief notes outlining some of the issues associated with loyalty programmes and customer retention initiatives.

7. How would you advise a newly appointed assistant brand manager on the expected outcomes of a sales promotion programme? (Choose any sector/industry of your choice.)

8. Find three examples of sales promotion activity and determine the extent to which they are strategic or tactical.

9. What is the value of joint sales promotion activities?

10. How might use of technology assist the development of loyalty and retention programmes?

MINI-CASE
Using sales promotion in the IT industry

Mini-case written by Angela Hall, Senior Lecturer in Marketing, Manchester Metropolitan University (formerly a Product Marketing Manager within the Fujitsu group)

The first computer was developed in the 1940s by Howard Aiken (Encyclopedia of Global Industries, 1999). By the early 1950s there were still only around 100 computers worldwide; this increased to hundreds of millions by the end of the century.

Worldwide PC shipments of 45.3 million units were achieved in the first quarter of 2004 (Gartner, 2004), with a figure of 13.6 per cent market growth rate from the same quarter in the previous year. The PC market in 2004 was largely driven by replacement PCs, and is likely to surpass PC sales in the run up to 2000 in 1998 and 1999. The top five PC vendors for unit shipments in the first Quarter of 2004 are (in order): Dell; Hewlett-Packard; IBM; Fujitsu/ Fujitsu Siemens and Acer. Competition has continued to increase, with reduced selling prices and more efficient ways of manufacturing. Product life cycles have become much shorter in recent years, with a typical product life cycle being as little as one year (Panorama of EU Industry, 1997).

Distribution of PCs has also changed through the use of direct selling, computer superstores and the general selling of PCs alongside other household electrical goods (Mintzberg and Quinn, 1996; Panorama of EU Industry, 1997). As business buyers became more knowledgeable about purchasing PCs they became more confident in where they bought them from, often using computer superstores that offered reduced prices. Another type of reseller emerged known as the VAR (value-added reseller), who would buy in large quantities, and therefore be able to offer low prices, bundle with software and offer to configure to a network (Mintzberg and Quinn, 1996). Also some computer manufacturers decided to sell direct (for example Dell), and were able to offer their products at a much reduced price.

The IT industry has always seen a wide variety of sales promotions, often with substantial budgets available. These may be in the form of bundles offered to b2b or b2c customers (e.g. a PC with extra software and/or printer for a lower price than the component price), or those from the PC manufacturer aimed at the sales force of the intermediary. During the 1980s IBM put substantial money into air miles incentives for those selling IBM PCs over the competitors. Toshiba offered free luxurious ski holidays to top-selling intermediary salespeople for many years, and many other incentives were offered, usually with substantial budgets attached.

Intermediaries usually received a marketing fund from the manufacturer, sometimes as much as 5 per cent of sales. Although it was usual for the manufacturer to approve the incentive, the intermediary usually decided how the money was to be spent. One such incentive ran with a large intermediary, with the objective of increasing the sales of Toshiba mobile PCs, and for the intermediary to be the top-selling UK intermediary for this manufacturer. The incentive ran for nine months. There was a lavish launch event at a top hotel, where all salespeople were invited. Each salesperson was given a monthly Toshiba sales target. This was based upon their sales history at Toshiba, with a percentage increase to challenge each individual. Therefore, the incentive was attractive to both senior and junior salespeople alike, as both had equal chance of achieving their own personal target. Every salesperson to achieve their target each month received vouchers (of their choice). This increased as they went over their target. No upper limit was given. Amounts paid out to individuals *per month* ranged from around £30–40 at the lower end, up to as much as £1,000+ for some top-selling salespeople. In addition to vouchers, the top ten salespeople who were the highest over target (in percentage terms) were invited to a monthly event. These events were extremely attractive to the typically young salespeople and included:

● learn how to fly day (two-seater plane, and helicopter), and treasure hunt by air
● water activity day – water-skiing, etc.
● rally driving day

● all expenses paid weekend in Edinburgh
● learn how to drive a tank day.

Those salespeople who were the highest over target throughout the nine months spent a long weekend in Monte Carlo, including transfer to the hotel via helicopter and a variety of entertainment, including a visit to a casino.

The incentive was very attractive to all salespeople. The monthly events stimulated discussion among the large sales force of over 120, and enthused them to promote Toshiba. The objectives were fully met, but the cost of this incentive was substantial. Moreover, sales of other mobile PCs dropped considerably throughout the Toshiba promotion.

References

European Communities (1997) Panorama of EU Industry. **3**, Brussels: European Communities/Union.

Gale Research (1999) Encyclopedia of Global Industries. 2nd edn. Detroit, MI: Gale Research.

Gartner (2004) Gartner says business segment drives worldwide PC shipments to 13 per cent growth in first quarter of 2004. Retrieved 15 April 2004 from http:/www4.gartner.com/5_about/press_releases/asset_66788_11.jsp.

Mintzberg, H. and Quinn, J.B. (1996) *The Strategy Process: Concepts, Contexts, Cases*. NJ: Englewood Cliffs.

Questions

1 Discuss why this Toshiba nine-month sales promotion was so attractive and considered successful by those who devised it.

2 Discuss whether the Toshiba nine-month sales promotion was really a success for the intermediary overall.

3 Discuss what ethical considerations may need to be considered by the intermediary for the Toshiba nine-month sales promotion, and for sales promotions generally.

References

Barrand, D. (2004) Promoting change. *Marketing*, 6 October, pp. 43–5.

Blattberg, R.C. and Neslin, S.A. (1990) *Sales Promotion: Concepts, Methods and Strategies.* Englewood Cliffs, NJ: Prentice-Hall.

Buzzell, R.D., Quelch, J.A. and Salmon, W.J. (1990) The costly bargain of trade promotion. *Harvard Business Review* (March/April), pp. 141–9.

Capizzi, M., Ferguson, R. and Cuthbertson, R. (2004) Loyalty trends for the 21st century. *Journal of Targeting Measurement and Analysis for Marketing*, **12**(3), pp. 199–212.

Clarke, A. (2000) Kellogg's in CD push for Childline. *Promotions and Incentives* (October), pp. 28–30.

Clarke, A. (2001) Finger on the pulse. *Promotions and Incentives* (February), pp. 41–4.

Curtis, J. (1996) Opposites attract. *Marketing*, 25 April, pp. 28–9.

Davis, M. (1992) Sales promotions as a competitive strategy. *Management Decision*, **30**(7), pp. 5–10.

Dawes, J. (2004) Assessing the impact of a very successful price promotion on brand, category and competitor sales. *Journal of Product and Brand Management*, **13**(5), pp. 303–14.

Ehrenberg, A.S.C. (2000) Repeat buying: facts, theory and applications. *Journal of Empirical Generalizations in Marketing Science*, **5**, pp. 392–770.

Gilbert, D.C. and Jackaria, N. (2002) The efficacy of sales promotions in UK supermarkets: a consumer view. *International Journal of Retail & Distribution Management*, **30**(6), pp. 325–32.

Gupta, S. (1998) Impact of sales promotions on when, what and how much we buy. *Journal of Marketing Research*, **25**(4), pp. 342–55.

Hallberg, G. (2004) Is your loyalty programme really building loyalty? Why increasing emotional attachment, not just repeat buying, is key to maximizing programme success. *Journal of Targeting Measurement and Analysis for Marketing*, **12**(3), pp. 231–41.

Hastings, S. and Price, M. (2004) Money can't buy me loyalty. *Admap*, **39**(2) (February), pp. 29–31.

Inman, J., McAlister, L. and Hoyer, D.W. (1990) Promotion signal: proxy for a price cut? *Journal of Consumer Research*, **17**(June), pp. 74–81.

Jardine, A. (2000) Why loyalty's not as simple as ABC. *Marketing*, 18 May, p. 19.

Jones, P.J. (1990) The double jeopardy of sales promotions. *Harvard Business Review*, (September/October), pp. 145–52.

Kleinman, M. (2003) Boots to overhaul loyalty strategy. *Marketing*, 28 August, p. 1.

Krishna, A. and Zhang, Z.J. (1999) Short or long duration coupons: the effect of the expiration date on the probability of coupon promotions. *Management Science*, **45**(8), pp. 1041–57.

Lee, C.H. (2002) Sales promotions as strategic communication: the case of Singapore. *The Journal of Product and Brand Management*, **11**(2), pp. 103–14.

Miller, R. (2000) Car pricing battles boost promotions. *Marketing*, 13 July, p. 29.

O'Malley, L. (1998) Can loyalty schemes really build loyalty? *Marketing Intelligence and Planning*, **16**(1), pp. 47–55.

Papatia, P. and Krishnamurthi, L. (1996) Measuring the dynamic effects of promotions on brand choice. *Journal of Marketing Research*, **33**(1) (February), pp. 20–35.

Peattie, S. (2003) Applying sales promotion competitions to nonprofit contexts. *International Journal of Nonprofit and Voluntary Sector Marketing*, **8**(4), pp. 349–62.

Peattie, S. and Peattie, K.J. (1994) Sales promotion. In *The Marketing Book* (ed. M.J. Baker). 3rd edn. London: Butterworth-Heinemann.

Rothschild, M.L. and Gaidis, W.C. (1981) Behavioural learning theory: its relevance to marketing and promotions. *Journal of Marketing Research*, **45**(2), pp. 70–8.

Whyte, R. (2004) Frequent flyer programmes: is it a relationship, or do the schemes create spurious loyalty? *Journal of Targeting Measurement and Analysis for Marketing*, **12**(3), pp. 269–80.

Yim, C.K. and Kannan, P.K. (1999) Consumer behavioural loyalty: a segmentation model and analysis. *Journal of Business Research*, **44**(2), pp. 75–92.

Sales promotion: methods and techniques

24

The range and sophistication of the main sales promotion techniques reflect the variety of audiences, their needs and the tasks that need to be accomplished. By adding value to the offer and hoping to bring forward future sales, these techniques are a source of competitive advantage, one that is invariably short rather than long run.

Aims and objectives

The aim of this chapter is to consider the nature and characteristics of the main sales promotion tools and techniques.

The objectives of this chapter are to:

1. examine the sales promotional techniques used by manufacturers to influence resellers;
2. examine the sales promotional techniques used by manufacturers to influence consumers;
3. examine the sales promotional techniques used by resellers to influence consumers;
4. examine the sales promotional techniques used by manufacturers to influence the sales force;
5. clarify the particular objectives sales promotions seek to satisfy.

Introduction

As established in the previous chapter, sales promotions seek to offer buyers additional value, as an inducement to generate an immediate sale. These inducements can be targeted at consumers, distributors, agents and members of the sales force. A whole range of network members can benefit from the use of sales promotion. The purpose of this chapter is to consider each of the principal sales promotion techniques.

The techniques considered in this chapter attempt to reflect the range and variety of techniques that are used to add value and induce a sale sooner rather than later. The nature and characteristics of the target audiences mean that different techniques work in different ways to achieve varying objectives. Therefore, consideration is given to the range of tasks that need to be accomplished among the following audiences: resellers, consumers and the sales force.

Sales promotions: manufacturers to resellers

Manufacturers and retailers see sales promotions as important devices to encourage trials among non-users and stimulate repeat purchase among users.

Manufacturers and retailers see sales promotions as important devices to encourage trial among non-users and stimulate repeat purchase among users. Retailers prefer instore promotions (push) instead of promotions aimed at consumers (pull) strategies. This has implications for the promotional mixes deployed by manufacturers.

Objectives for new products: trial

For manufacturers launching new products, the main marketing objective is to establish distribution. This is because the use of awareness advertising at the launch of a new product is pointless unless the product is available for consumers to purchase at retail outlets. Therefore, a distribution network needs to be set up in anticipation of consumer demand. The task of marketing communications is to encourage resellers to distribute a new product and to establish trial behaviour.

Objectives for established products: usage

Sales of established products need to be maintained and encouraged. The active support and participation of resellers is crucial. One of the main objectives of manufacturers is to develop greater exposure for their products; this means motivating distributors to allocate increased shelf space to a product thereby (possibly) reducing the amount of shelf space allocated to competitors. The task of marketing communications, therefore, is to encourage resellers to buy and display increased amounts of the manufacturer's products and establish greater usage.

Means motivating distributors to allocate increased shelf space to a product thereby (possibly) reducing the amount of shelf space allocated to competitors.

It is an interesting point that the trial objective for retailers is to increase the number of new customers visiting a store. The usage objective aims to increase levels of store loyalty and the overall number of visits made by current customers. In the same way that manufacturers seek to establish brand loyalty, so retailers seek to build store loyalty.

Resellers (in particular, retailers) and manufacturers have conflicting objectives. Manufacturers want to increase the amount of shelf space and attention paid to their products, whereas resellers want to increase the number of people using the store; they want to develop store traffic.

Methods

The main type of sales promotion used to motivate trade customers is an allowance.

The main type of sales promotion used to motivate trade customers is an *allowance*. Allowances can take many forms, some of the more common ones being buying, count and recount, buy-back allowances, merchandising and advertising allowances. Trade allowances are a means of achieving a short-term increase in sales. They can be used defensively to protect valuable shelf space from aggressive competitors. By offering to work with resellers and providing them with extra incentives, manufacturers can guard territory gained to date.

Buying allowances

The most common form of discount is the buying allowance.

The most common form of discount is the buying allowance. In return for specific orders between certain dates, a reseller will be entitled to a refund or allowance of *x* per cent off the regular case or carton price. The only factor that the reseller must consider is the timing of the order. Manufacturers often use these sales promotions so that they coincide with a main buying period, reducing risk to the distributor.

For the manufacturer, these types of allowances can lead to an increase in the average size of orders, which in turn can utilise idle capacity and also prevent competitors securing business at their expense. This technique can also be used to encourage new stores to try the manufacturer's products or to stimulate repeat usage (restocking).

Count and recount allowances

Manufacturers may require resellers to clear old stock before a new or modified product is introduced. One way this can be achieved is to encourage resellers to move stock out of storage and into the store. The count and recount method provides an allowance for each case shifted into the store during a specified period of time.

ViewPoint 24.1   Trade promotions on Mars

One of the problems faced by Mars Confectionery has been its rival's (Wall's) dominance of ice cream freezer cabinets in the independent sector. Most shops have only enough space for one cabinet and that, historically, has been Wall's. A promotion was targeted at familiarising customers with the location of Mars freezers and its product range. The 'Find a Freezer' game required consumers to locate Mars freezers in 6,000 outlets. Freezers were given a name sticker and the Capital FM radio station invited listeners to find them in return for cash and Mars merchandise rewards.

The arithmetic for this transaction is as follows:

opening stock + purchases – closing stock
= stock entitled to receive the agreed allowance

This technique can also be used to prevent a store becoming out of stock, and as such is essentially a usage-only technique. If a promotional campaign is to be launched, count and recount can prevent stock-out, loss of custom and wastage of promotional resources.

Buy-back allowances

Buy-backs can be used to follow up count and recount promotions. Under this scheme, the purchases made after the count and recount scheme (up to a maximum of the count and recount) are entitled to an allowance to encourage stores to replenish their stocks (with the manufacturer's product and not that of a competitor). By definition this is a usage-only technique.

Merchandise allowances

The previous three methods require the exchange of money, in the form of either a credit or a cash refund. Merchandising allowances benefit resellers by providing extra goods for which no payment is required. These free goods are only delivered if a reseller's order reaches a specific size. The benefit to the manufacturer is that the administrative and transportation costs for the allowance are very low and are tied to those associated with the costs of the regular order.

Merchandising allowances benefit resellers by providing extra goods for which no payment is required.

For resellers, the incentive is that they can earn above-average profits with the free units. Manufacturers use this type of allowance to generate trials and to open up new distributors. However, this sales promotions technique needs the support of other activities, such as advertising, to provide security and confidence before potential resellers commit themselves to a new product.

Advertising allowances

Advertising allowances can be made if resellers can show that they have undertaken a promotional campaign featuring a manufacturer's product. A percentage allowance is given against a reseller's purchases during a specified period of time. This is a useful technique in stimulating trial by new stores. By weighting the allowances, resellers can be encouraged to take stock and create shelf space for new products.

Dealer listings are advertisements and notices that identify resellers and the range of products that each carries. Issued by manufacturers to help consumers locate their nearest store, they are effective in generating store traffic and for providing source credibility.

A further refinement of the advertising allowance is a scheme which involves the collaboration of a reseller so that an advertising campaign can be jointly funded. Instead of providing an allowance against product purchases, an allowance is provided against the cost of an advertisement or campaign. Govoni *et al.* (1986) suggest that there are two forms of cooperative advertising, vertical and horizontal:

1. *Vertical advertising allowances*
   In vertical advertising, a manufacturer agrees to contribute to the reseller's campaign. A common approach is for a retailer to take out a full-page newspaper advertisement in which a number of different products are highlighted. Each manufacturer then

Each manufacturer then contributes a share of the total cost, proportionate to its space/share of the advertisement.

contributes a share of the total cost, proportionate to its space/share of the advertisement. This omnibus approach is popular, as costs are shared and store traffic (usage) can be considerably improved. In addition to these benefits, manufacturers will invariably provide materials, such as artwork and schedules, to assist the promotion and coordinate the activities with their national campaigns.

Direct mail is used increasingly, as lower unit costs and low wastage (relative to the mass appeal of advertising) encourage resellers to devote more time and resources to this form of promotion.

2. *Horizontal advertising allowances*

In horizontal advertising, competitors join together to promote the product class and so stimulate primary demand. This form of promotion is often organised and controlled by a trade association. For example, the Milk Marketing Board's award-winning promotion of the home delivery service served to inform and remind people that the doorstep delivery service provided a range of benefits on behalf of relatively small delivery services that individually could not have undertaken the campaign and reached their target audiences so effectively.

Retailers have participated in horizontal programmes, but are normally reluctant to do so for competitive reasons. Retailers stocking products that have a territorial franchise associated with them are more willing to participate; the Southern Ford Dealers programme is a good example of retailer collaboration.

There are, of course, advantages and disadvantages with advertising allowance schemes. The manufacturer is able to buy more space, or time, for each pound spent on advertising, because the spend is often made at local, not national rates. A further factor in their favour is that the scheme encourages those who do not use advertising to participate. Finally, advertising allowances can also induce new resellers to become distributors when the objective is trial.

One of the main drawbacks concerns the cooperative aspect of the allowance arrangements. Resellers are able to assume control over the process and this can lead to circumstances where inappropriate messages and media are used. Furthermore, fraudulent claims have been submitted for advertising that either did not take place or duplicated a previous claim. This lack of control can lead to conflict, and the

This lack of control can lead to conflict.

very scheme that was designed to foster collaborative behaviour can degenerate into a conflict of opinion and a deterioration in reseller/manufacturer relationships. It is interesting to observe that the organisations in the network that have the responsibility for distributing the manufacturer's products are the same ones which may (theoretically) be penalised by their supplier (Grey, as cited in Govoni *et al.*, 1986), following abuse of sales promotions.

Hostaging

Hostaging is a process whereby a retailer/reseller is able to exert power over a manufacturer in order to pressurise or force it into providing trade promotions on a more

Hostaging is a process whereby a retailer/reseller is able to exert power over a manufacturer in order to pressurise or force it into providing trade promotions on a more or less continual basis.

or less continual basis. A less dependent firm may use influence strategies, such as requests and information exchange (Anderson and Narus, 1990). In contrast, the more dependent firm should seek to add value (or reduce costs) to the exchange for the partner firm, at a relatively small cost to itself.

The more dependent firm in a working relationship needs to protect its transactions-specific assets by taking various actions, such as close bonding with end-user firms. Strategies to avoid 'hostaging' would include reducing the frequency of trade deals, converting trade spending into advertising and consumer promotions, and focusing on differentiating the brand with less reliance on price (Blattberg and Neslin, 1990).

Other forms of sales promotions aimed at resellers

There are a number of other techniques that can be used to achieve sales promotion objectives. These include dealer contests, which should be geared to stimulating increased usage. By encouraging resellers to improve their performance, growth can be fostered and the reseller's attention focused on the manufacturer's products, not those of the competition. Motivation and the provision of information are necessary at the launch of new products and at the beginning of a new selling season. To assist these objectives, dealer conventions and meetings are used extensively, often in conjunction with a dealer contest. The informal interaction between the focus organisation and its resellers that these events facilitate can be an invaluable aid to the development and continuance of good relations between the two parties and, of course, at a horizontal level between resellers.

Many manufacturers provide extensive training and support for their resellers. This is an important communications function, especially when products are complex or subject to rapid change, as in the IT markets. Such coordination means that a stronger relationship can be built and manufacturers have greater control over the messages that the reseller's representatives transmit. It also means that the switching costs of the reseller are increased, since the training and support costs will be incurred again if a different supplier is adopted. Coordination through training and support can be seen as a form of marketing communications.

> A stronger relationship can be built and manufacturers have greater control over the messages that the reseller's representatives transmit.

Personal selling is an important tool used to persuade buyers, the objective being to ensure that the reseller follows the guide of the manufacturer. As products become more similar and as channel power becomes concentrated in the retail sector, so resellers are able to select products from a variety of suppliers and determine the most appropriate sales promotions necessary for the markets in which they operate. This means that manufacturers can no longer assume control over members of the performance network, and they must find different ways of accessing the sales force of their distributors.

Marketing communications between manufacturers and resellers is vitally important. Sales promotions play an increasingly important role in the coordination between the two parties. Resellers look for sales promotions to support their own marketing initiatives. Supplier selection decisions depend in part upon the volume and value of the communications support. In other words, will supplier X or Y provide the necessary level of promotional support, either within the channel or direct to the consumer?

> Sales promotions play an increasingly important role in the coordination between the two parties.

Sales promotions: resellers to consumers

Objectives

There are two overall objectives that retailers wish to achieve. The first is to promote the store as a brand. Growth at the retail level can be achieved by generating store traffic and increasing the number of people who become store (brand) loyal. This, as stated previously, is the equivalent to the *generation of trial*. To do this they need to communicate with those who are store switchers and non-store users. Therefore store image advertising is undertaken by retailers and is executed away from the store. The aim is to convert switchers and non-loyals into store-loyal customers.

The second main objective, according to a study undertaken by Blattberg *et al.* (1981), is to transfer stock and its associated costs from the retailer's shelves to the cupboards and refrigerators of consumers. In an attempt to increase usage, marketing communications, and sales promotion activity in particular, are oriented to shifting particular stock at particular times. This means that turnover is increased (and targets are reached) and shelves are cleared to receive new products.

Methods

Sales promotion by retailers is normally tied to the activities of manufacturers, but some price-off techniques are retailer driven. Joint advertising and sales promotion in the local press combine to attract customers to the store. However, as discussed earlier, many of these advertising campaigns are cooperative exercises and so cannot be classed as retailer sales promotions. The attention-getting devices of in-store displays are normally regarded as merchandising, in that they are geared to gaining attention, not moving product.

Promotions that do occur in store, regardless of origin, appear to affect non-store loyals to a greater extent than store loyals. Rossiter and Percy (1987) report the work of a Nielsen study in which sales promotions in supermarkets were tracked and sales correlated with the degree of store loyalty. The main finding was that non-store loyals recorded a 20-fold increase in sales following the promotion, whereas store loyals increased their sales by a factor of only 10.

Sales promotions: manufacturers to consumers

Objectives

Manufacturers use sales promotions to communicate with consumers because they can be a cost-effective means of achieving short-term increases in sales. The objectives are to stimulate trial use by new users or to increase product usage among those customers who buy the product on an occasional or regular basis.

The success of any new offering is partly dependent on the number of consumers encouraged to try the product in

The success of any new offering is partly dependent on the number of consumers encouraged to try the product in the first place.

the first place and partly upon the number who repurchase the product at a later point in the purchase cycle. The importance of stimulating trial use cannot be underestimated. Through the use of coupons, sampling and other techniques (see below), sales promotions have become an important element in the new product launch and introduction processes.

ViewPoint 24.2   Sampling and SMS at Brylcreem

Brylcreem used sampling and SMS to launch its Next Generation Ultra Gel product. Samples of the brand were handed out to young males at welcome meetings at Club 18–30 holiday destinations. Each sample pack carried a code, encouraging recipients to text in for a chance to win prizes such as holidays and PlayStation games and consoles. They are also asked to text in their opinions on Brylcreem.

The simplicity of the campaign was intended to reflect Brylcreem's brand values and was designed to complement the fact that increasingly people are taking their phones on holiday and using SMS.

In addition to trial, organisations need to encourage consumers to repurchase products. In markets that are mature, sales growth can only be realistically achieved by encouraging users of competitive products to switch their allegiance. This can be achieved by offering them superior benefits and added value. Attracting non-users is an alternative route, but this requires convincing them, first, that they have a need for the product class and, secondly, that they should try the promoted product. A more productive approach is to find new uses for the product. For example, breakfast cereals have been promoted as nourishing snacks, suitable for consumption at different times of the day. Dairies have distributed recipe books where many of the meals use milk as a prime ingredient.

Just as sales promotions are used to attract customers of competing products, so competitors use sales promotions to counter-attack and defend their markets. Sales promotions, sometimes in combination with advertising, must be used to defend a customer base from competitive attacks. By using bonus packs (extra product), price-offs, competitions and coupons to encourage increased usage, customers can be loaded with stock, effectively removing them from the market for a period longer than the normal purchase cycle.

> Sales promotions, sometimes in combination with advertising, must be used to defend a customer base from competitive attacks.

There are two prime reasons for using sales promotions with consumers. The first is to collaborate with resellers in an attempt to defend the shelf space or franchise. This helps build a close and supportive relationship and also creates a mobility barrier that has to be overcome by competitive organisations. The second reason is the need to transfer the cost of stock from the reseller to the consumer, boosting revenue and clearing the way for new products with better margins.

Methods for encouraging new users to try a product

There are three main approaches to encouraging new customers to try a product for the first time: sampling, coupons and a range of consumer deals.

Sampling

When a product is introduced, whether it be a new product category or an improved or modified product, sampling is one of the most effective sales promotion techniques available. For decisions that evoke low involvement, where there is little thought or elaboration undertaken by the consumer, attitudes are confirmed as a result of product experience. It makes sense, therefore, to provide a risk-free opportunity for consumers to test a product.

> It makes sense, therefore, to provide a risk-free opportunity for consumers to test a product.

Samples are very often free miniature versions of the actual product and can be used to win new customers and to protect a customer base. Samples can take the form of demonstrations, trial size packs that have to be purchased or free use for a certain period of time. The recent offers by car manufacturers to allow purchasers to return their cars after a four-week period if not satisfied provide a good example of a high-involvement decision where attitudes are formed prior to trial and are used to confirm a purchase decision. The use of scented page folds in women's magazines to demonstrate new scents and perfumes is an innovative and interesting example of making trial easier. Previously, the only method of testing perfume was through the use of samplers, available on the counters in cosmetic departments of retail outlets. Marketing communications and sales promotions in particular were aimed at enticing people to the store. Using scent folds means that it is easier for consumers to try a perfume. A far greater number of people can try a new scent, while the reader's attention can be focused on the accompanying advertisement. Readership and recall scores increase remarkably.

> Samples can take the form of demonstrations, trial size packs that have to be purchased or free use for a certain period of time.

EXHIBIT 24.1 Distributing samples

EXHIBIT 24.2 A sampling point

Sampling is expensive.   Sampling is expensive. Of all the available sales promotion techniques, the costs associated with sampling are the
largest. To offset the high cost, the potential rewards can be equally dramatic, especially if the audience is familiar with or predisposed to the product class, and if the
sample has some superior benefits. Sampling is best undertaken when the following
apply:

ViewPoint 24.3   Philips Softone samples

In order to introduce the new range of Softone light bulbs to a newer, younger audience, Philips Lighting used a two-stage sampling approach. Utilising a door-to-door approach, the first phase consisted of the delivery of a questionnaire to collect database material and to ask which colour of bulb the house-holder would like to receive. The following day, phase 2 kicked in with the collection of the question-naire and the delivery of the appropriate colour bulb (so avoiding the problem of delivering a glass product through a letterbox too small to accept it).

Awareness rose to 82 per cent, 10 per cent of targeted households requested a sample and from the 1,100,000 questionnaires that were completed, Philips was able to pinpoint innovators, early adopters and early majority individuals and use these data to roll the campaign out nationwide, and in doing so substantially reduce its costs and improve its efficiency and effectiveness.

1. Advertising alone is unable to communicate the key benefits.
2. The product has benefits that are superior to its competitors and which are clearly demonstrable.
3. Competitive attacks require loyal customers to be reminded of a product's advantages. A further use occasion of sampling is to introduce the product to customers of competitive products, in an effort to encourage them to switch.

Apart from the size, mass and degree of perishability associated with the physical characteristics, the main constraints concern the number of people who are required to receive the samples and when they are to receive them: the timing of the trial. Samples are often distributed to consumers free of charge, with the twin goals of introducing the product to new users and hopefully encouraging them to switch brands. In addition to this, sampling provides an ideal opportunity to gather valuable market research data from the field.

However, some retailers prefer miniature products that customers are expected to purchase. This approach encourages consumers to use the sample, and because they paid for it they will be likely to use it. For the retailer, this approach provides a margin in part compensation for the risk associated with any stock purchased in advance and for the floor or shelf space allocated for the trial.

Rossiter and Percy (1987) have compiled a table that sets out the main sampling media. See Table 24.1.

Coupons

Coupons are a proven method by which manufacturers can communicate with consumers and they are a strong brand-switching device. They may be distributed via resellers or directly to consumers. Coupons are vouchers or certificates that entitle consumers to a price reduction on a particular product. The value of the reduction or discount is set and the coupon must be presented when purchasing the product. The objective, therefore, is to offer a price deal, a discount off the full price of the product. Retailers and wholesalers act as agents for manufacturers by allowing consumers to redeem the value of coupons from them at the point of purchase. They in turn recover the cost of the deal, the value of the coupon, from the manufacturer.

> Coupons are a proven method by which manufacturers can communicate with consumers and they are a strong brand-switching device.

TABLE 24.1 Eight methods of distributing samples

Methods	Uses	Limitations
Door to door	● Virtually any product can be delivered in this way	● Most expensive means of sampling ● Problem with leaving perishables if occupant absent ● Illegal in some areas
Direct mail	● Best for small, light products that are non-perishable	● Rising postal costs
Central location	● Best for perishables such as food, or when personal demonstration is required	● If in-store, same offer must be made to all retailers (Robinson–Patman Act) ● Usually involves cost of sales training ● If in public place, may be illegal in some areas
Sample pack in stores	● Best method for attracting retail support, because retailers sell the packs at a premium unit price	● Requires retail acceptance like any other new product ● May necessitate special production for trial sizes
Cross-product sampling in or on pack	● Good for low-cost sampling of a manufacturer's other products	● Trial limited to users of 'carrier' product ● Restricted to large products
Co-op package distribution	● Good for narrow audiences such as college students, military personnel, brides	● Little appeal to trade
Newspaper or magazine distribution	● Relatively low-cost method of sample distribution for flat or pouchable products	● Seem to be regarded by media vehicle recipients as 'cheap' and are often disregarded, resulting in less trial than with other sampling methods ● Obviously limited to certain product types
Any of above with coupon	● Increases post-sample trial rate by using purchase incentive	● Additional cost of coupon handling

Source: Rossiter and Percy (1987); used with permission.

Coupons provide precision targeting of price-sensitive customers, without harming those regular customers who are prepared to pay full price. In reality, however, some coupons are redeemed by regular product users, and their use reduces margins unnecessarily. The level of perceived risk experienced by new users can be reduced through the use of coupons. Users of competitive products can also be encouraged to try the product, so coupons can be effective for product introductions and established products in stable markets.

'Smart shoppers' are those consumers who feel some exclusivity and control as a result of using coupons to try new brands. They receive a psychological and economic benefit. While retailers like coupons because they merely switch the brand bought and so do not lose a sale, manufacturers are less keen, as they consider they may lose out. The evidence suggests that consumers tend to revert to their pre-coupon preferred brand after redemption of the coupon (Kahn and Louie, 1990).

This form of sales promotion allows management to set a specific period of time in which a promotion is to run. This in turn allows the other elements of the promotional mix to be integrated. For example, advertising can be used to create awareness, and print media can then be used to display a coupon for the reader to cut out for redemption at the next purchase opportunity. When attempting to generate trial, advertising must be used to create awareness, since a coupon for an unknown product will be totally ineffective and usually discarded by consumers. Personal selling can be timed to inform resellers of a forthcoming coupon offer and give time for shelves to be fully stocked when the campaign breaks. Unfortunately, it is difficult to estimate when and how many coupons will be redeemed. There are certain guides developed through experience and a redemption rate of between 3 per cent and 5 per cent can be considered good. The variance, however, can be marked, and the promotional cost of a stock-out can be considerable.

Couponing is an expensive activity. Not only has the face value of the coupons to be considered, but the production and distribution costs must also be accounted for.

Couponing is an expensive activity.

General Mills, the US food group, decided to reduce the number of coupons it issues on the grounds that it sees them as a waste of money (Tomkins, 1994). At 2 per cent redemption, the cost in terms of time, print and distribution, plus the face value of the coupon itself, mean that the exercise was costing General Mills money. It has moved back to an 11 per cent price reduction on its products instead. Many organisations such as General Mills consider that a saving of 30 per cent in the promotional budget and a cut in the price on the shelf is a better and more profitable way to do business. This approach is sometimes referred to as everyday low pricing.

There are three primary ways in which coupons can be distributed:

1. Consumer direct distribution allows management to focus the coupons upon particular target audiences. Coupons can be sent through the post, delivered on a door-to-door basis or, with new media, delivered via a Web site. This last approach works through the use of a smart card inserted into a PC that can then receive the downloaded coupon, which the user can then present to a retailer (either bricks or clicks) for redemption.

   An average redemption rate of 6 per cent makes this one of the more effective methods of distributing coupons, although a major disadvantage is that its costs are increasing. Consequently, some manufacturers are collaborating with other manufacturers (non-competitively) to distribute coupons on a joint basis.

2. Media direct distribution allows management to gain a broad level of exposure for a product. Free-standing inserts are a popular way of distributing coupons. These are separate sheets containing a number of different coupons.

   Free-standing inserts are a popular way of distributing coupons.

   This contrasts with the normal method of printing the coupon in a newspaper or magazine. However, the redemption rates of this second approach are low because of the short life of such media vehicles, particularly newspapers, and the extra effort required by readers to cut out and store the coupon until the next purchase opportunity arises.

   Various alternative methods have been developed in response to the need to find novel ways of attracting readers' attention. On-page coupons can be found in magazines coupled with an advertisement. Pop-ups are coupons printed on card and bound into a magazine. Finally, tip-ins are coupons glued to the cover of a magazine.

3. Package direct distribution generates the highest redemption rates of all the methods available. By inserting (in) or imprinting (on) coupons on the packaging of a product (in/ons), distribution costs can be minimised. However, coupons distributed in this way only reach users; they fail, therefore, to reach non-users.

Instant coupons are an effective point-of-purchase incentive.

Instant coupons are an effective point-of-purchase incentive, which allow purchasers literally to rip the coupon off the package for redemption at the check-out. This can generate very high levels of redemption and is administratively easier to manage than price deals, as the latter require the active participation of the reseller.

Coupons that are redeemable off the next purchase of the same item are referred to as bounce-back coupons. Coupons that are redeemable against different products are referred to as cross-ruff coupons. These are particularly effective in encouraging consumers to try other products in a manufacturer's product range. Soap, frozen foods and breakfast cereals are product ranges where this couponing approach has been successful.

Over 5 billion coupons were issued in the UK in 2002 (Advertising Association, 2004) and this represents a great deal of business activity. Of these coupons, 75 per cent were distributed by direct mail and 452 million were redeemed. Fulfilment houses undertake the work for brand managers, acting as brokers for the issuers and retailers who accept them. Manufacturers outsource coupon work, if only because it is so labour intensive. New software systems threaten to replace some of this work, especially the tracking of vouchers, which can be undertaken in-house.

Over 5 billion coupons were issued in the UK in 2002.

Many technological advances, and in particular the use of barcode scanners, present opportunities for manufacturers and retailers to use couponing more effectively. Fraudulent use of coupons can be cut considerably and checkout speeds increased. More importantly, however, this technology has the potential to monitor an individual customer's purchases, establish buying patterns and dispense coupons to users of competitive products at the checkout. This will lead inevitably to the identification of those customers who use coupons more frequently and the development of coupon user profiles. Manufacturers will also gain by the reduced distribution costs and the reduction in time spent handling coupons.

One such system, the Catalina Marketing System, claims a redemption rate of 6–8 per cent. Asda-Walmart became one of the first UK users that, after an initial proving period, installed the system in all of its UK stores. Somerfield also used the system extensively. Catalina claims a number of advantages for both manufacturers and retailers. For manufacturers it provides for exclusivity, as only one manufacturer per product category can be installed. For retailers the overall incentive is that the system encourages return visits and increases store traffic, and volume grows.

Catalina and other similar systems provide money-off coupons plus the opportunity to deliver a variety of messages to specific shoppers. In addition, it is possible to provide incentives to the right target customers to encourage participation in research exercises. Sampling opportunities increase as well. Asda-Walmart uses the system to target those customers most likely to use free telephone numbers in order to receive a free sample of a new/other product or hear a pre-recorded message. This is referred to as *confined target advertising*, or in other words a blend of sales promotion, direct marketing and advertising.

By providing coupons at the point a purchase decision is made, at the shelf and not after the decision, at the till, a greater uplift in sales is to be expected.

A more recent initiative concerns machines that dispense coupons but at the POP not POS. In other words, by providing coupons at the point a purchase decision is made, at the shelf and not after the decision, at the till, a greater uplift in sales is to be expected. One such facility, the Instant Coupon Machine, allows consumers to withdraw a paper coupon, for either a single or group of brands, and redeem it at the till or use at a later date. Sales increases of up to 60 per cent were reported by companies taking part in some of the trials (Mathews, 1999).

Consumer deals

These forms of sales promotion are only effective in the short term. They are not used to build consumer franchises or brand personalities. Their function is to bring about a short-term increase in sales by moving the product from the shelves of the reseller to the homes of consumers. They can encourage trial behaviour by new users and also stimulate repurchase by existing users. The techniques are as follows.

Price-offs

By far the simplest technique is to offer a direct reduction in the purchase price with the offer clearly labelled on the package or point of purchase display. These are simply referred to as 'price-offs'. A minimum reduction of 15 per cent appears to

---

ViewPoint 24.4   Train offers

Following the Hatfield rail crash in the UK and the consequent rail inspections and track relaying programme by Railtrack, which was responsible for the track systems and infrastructure, a huge number of rail travellers reverted to other forms of transport. In an effort to encourage these lapsed customers back to the rail network the various rail operating companies (which provide the trains and services) entered into a massive sales promotion campaign to incentivise people to use the train network.

Some operators gave away boxes of chocolates, some gave heavily discounted weekends in London, and Virgin offered £10 million in the form of price reductions over a one-month period. Virgin referred to it as 'The world's biggest train offer', and Benady and Barrett (2001) draw similarities to the British Airways 'World's biggest offer' in the early 1990s, in the attempt to revive air travel after the Gulf War and a growing fear of terrorism.

---

be required for optimal effect (Della Bitta and Monroe, 1980). Others suggest that this figure varies according to the store and the type of brand under consideration. Research indicates that consumers are sceptical of price deals, in particular those concerning price-offs. This may result in individuals discounting the discounts (Gupta and Cooper, 1992).

The mere presence of a price-off for those with a low need for elaboration, regardless of the value of the sales promotion, appears to be sufficient to bring about a change in an individual's disposition towards the promoted product (Inman *et al.*, 1990). They suggest that it is theoretically possible to bring about an increase in sales from those

TABLE 24.2 Five types of customer and their attitudes towards sales promotion

Branded EDLP seekers (19 per cent)

This group has a restricted income but is brand loyal. These customers, therefore, look around for the best deal they can get for their preferred brand. In their search for everyday low prices they ignore coupons and money-off promotions.

Low-price fixture ferrets (23.3 per cent)

Again, income is restricted in this group, which is mainly populated by young families. They are very budget conscious and are store rather than product loyal. They like promotions and are quick to switch brands.

Promotion junkies (18.4 per cent)

These people are referred to as professional shoppers because of their desire to seek out bargains. They have zero loyalty and are keen to tell their contacts of their shopping successes. They are a hazard to both manufacturers and retailers.

Stockpilers (21 per cent)

These shoppers are loyal to both manufacturers and retailers. They have no income difficulties and are happy to buy up large quantities of their preferred brands, regardless of the cost. Of the five types of shopper, these are the second most promotionally active, as they search for bargains but they do not switch brands for promotional reasons.

Promotionally oblivious (18.3 per cent)

This group is totally unaware of any promotions. Described as rather old-fashioned, this group is not interested in pursuing low prices. Therefore these customers will buy a preferred brand regardless of the existence of a promotion and so represent a reliable group of buyers.

Source: Miller (1997); used with kind permission.

with a low need for information simply by placing a promotional display without actually reducing the price.

In a study by ACNielsen (reported by Miller, 1997) of consumer attitudes towards price-offs and sales promotions, five different types of people were identified. These are set out in Table 24.2.

> Retailers see price deals as a necessary activity to stimulate short-term sales.

Whatever the decision regarding the value of the price-off, the entire price reduction should be carried by the manufacturer, as the retailer must be continually motivated and a reduction in margin will be adversely received. Retailers see price deals as a necessary activity to stimulate short-term sales. Manufacturers regard price deals as effective when tied into media advertising.

Bonus packs

Bonus packs offer more product for the regular pack price. They provide direct impact at the point of purchase, and this, combined with the lure of lower unit costs and extra value, means that this is a popular technique with consumers and manufacturers. The poster at Exhibit 24.3 depicts a price deal where the AA are offering 3 lessons for the price of 2.

However, resellers do not gain from bonus packs: there is no additional margin and extra shelf space is required.

EXHIBIT 24.3 AA Bonus Pack – 3 for the price of 2

Refunds and rebates

Refunds and rebates are used to invite consumers to send in a proof of purchase and in return receive a cash refund. These are very effective in encouraging the trial of new products and have proved exceptionally popular with consumer durables (rebate) as

The process of redeeming refunds may evoke negative feelings.

well as fast-moving consumer goods (refunds). The process of redeeming refunds may evoke negative feelings, as consumers do not like the trouble and inconvenience associated with claiming refunds and, when combined with the negative perception that consumers have of manufacturers which offer such rebates, the conclusion has to be that any redemption procedure should be clear, simple and easy to implement.

Methods for encouraging increased consumption – usage

There are two main ways in which sales promotions can be used to encourage increased usage: premiums, and contests and sweepstakes.

Premiums

Premiums are items of merchandise that are offered free or at a low cost in return for purchase of one or many products or services. Premiums are used as a direct incentive to motivate people to purchase a specific product. The premium merchandise is used to add value to the product and represent an advantage over competitor products. Finding suitable low-cost premiums for the adult market, however, is difficult, as a poor premium may deter people from buying the product. Consumers are required to show proof that a purchase has been made. However, Internet facilities now allow consumers to collect digital currencies that can be redeemed for gifts or discounts. MyPoints and Mutualpoints are online retention systems each supported by a variety of mainstream retailers such as Boots, the Kingfisher Group, Virgin and Argos. Witthaus (2000) reports, however, that instead of points being awarded in return for purchases made, points can be collected as a result of accepting advertising, either by visiting an advertiser's site or by accepting emails. An added point of differentiation is that MyPoints can be redeemed either online or by visiting the bricks and mortar store. This system appears to recognise that a large number of people prefer (understand) high street shopping and it provides a gradual transfer rather than imposing a totally dedicated online shopping experience and reward.

MyPoints can be redeemed either online or by visiting the bricks and mortar store.

Premiums are used to increase sales by attracting repeat buyers, stimulating impulse purchase and brand-switching behaviour, and to offset competitor moves. There are two main forms of premium: direct and self-liquidating.

Direct premiums are provided for the consumer at the point of purchase. They are free of charge and require the consumer to do nothing other than buy the package. The premium merchandise may be attached to the product as an on-pack premium. This can result in improving the shelf display, which is attractive to resellers as it presents an instant stimulus–response opportunity to potential buyers. Unfortunately, on-packs take up extra space, and this can mean increased labour in shelf replenishment. The extra costs involved with packaging also need to be taken into account when designing on-pack premiums.

Gillette UK attempted to switch users of competitive shaving products by offering free gel with its disposable razors. Blister packaging makes for an attractive, attention-getting display and provides an incentive for consumers to receive a free product.

Premium merchandise that is packaged inside the product is referred to as an in-pack premium. This obviously saves space and reduces costs for the manufacturer, as there is virtually no requirement to change the packaging. Breakfast cereals have traditionally used this approach.

Self-liquidating premiums require consumers to contribute to the cost of the incentive.

In contrast to direct premiums, *self-liquidating* premiums require consumers to contribute to the cost of the incentive. Manufacturers seek only to cover their costs and, by buying the premium merchandise in volume, can offer the merchandise at prices considerably below the regular retail price. In many ways these can be referred to as delayed premiums, as proof of purchase needs to be sent through the mail (d'Astous and Jacob, 2002).

ViewPoint 24.5   Premium Pepsi and Robbie

Robbie Williams wrote a track that was used in a television advertisement. Consumers had to collect 25 ring pulls for a CD-ROM of the exclusive track, plus backstage footage, an interview with RW and a screensaver. The ring pulls are redeemable at HMV stores and by mail order. Fulfilment rates are equivalent to number 8 in the charts.

Dunmore (2000) reports that the Pepsi Web site features audio and video clips of the ad, with a chance to win RW concert tickets in exchange for an email address and personal details.

The effectiveness of self-liquidating premiums is not as strong as that of direct premiums because they do not provide the same immediate impact, as the time delay between awareness of the offer and the reward can often be a number of weeks. Consequently, the redemption rate for these types of sales promotion is very low (0.1 per cent). They can be used to stimulate resellers and create attention in the market, and they can deflect attention from competitor brands. Proposed new regulations from the European Union threaten the abolition of self-liquidating premiums.

In an attempt to understand consumer reactions to premium-based sales promotions d'Astous and Landerville (2003) isolated four key variables. See Table 24.3. Their research proved inconclusive other than it became clear that the interaction of these four elements shaped consumer reactions toward premium-based offers.

Manufacturers can also offer mail-in premiums to customers if they send several proofs of purchase. The premium is technically free to the customer and the multiple purchases that are stimulated generate revenue, take stock off the shelves and take customers out of the market for a period of time because they are loaded with stock.

TABLE 24.3 Four key variables affecting premiums (Adapted from d'Astous and Landerville, 2003; used with permission.)

Premium variable	Explanation
Attractiveness	Does the premium add positive or negative associations with the brand?
Immediacy	Is the premium available immediately on purchase (direct) or is the premium delayed (self-liquidating)?
Mention of the premium's value	Does mention of a premium increase or decrease the perceived value of a promotional offer?
Fit between premium and category	Is the premium integrated with the brand's intended positioning or is there a lack of fit?

Contests and sweepstakes

A contest is a sales promotion whereby customers compete for prizes or money on the basis of skills or ability. Entry requires a proof of purchase and winners are judged against a set of predetermined criteria. Completing the line 'I like XXX because . . .', writing one-line slogans, suggesting names, and drawing posters and pictures are some of the more common contests used to involve consumers with products.

A sweepstake is a sales promotion technique where the winners are determined by chance and proof of purchase is not required. There is no judging and winners are drawn at random. A variant of the sweepstake is a game that also has odds of winning associated with it. Scratchcards have become very popular games, mainly because consumers like to participate and winners can be instantly identified.

> A sweepstake is a sales promotion technique where the winners are determined by chance.

Sweepstakes are more popular than contests because they are easier to enter and, because there is no judging, administration is less arduous and less expensive. Both contests and sweepstakes bring excitement and attention to campaigns, and if the contest or sweepstake is relevant, both approaches can bring about increased consumer involvement with the product.

Great care and preparation must be put into contests and sweepstakes. Because of the legal implications and requirements of these sales promotions, many organisations contract the event to organisations that specialise in such activities.

Sales promotions: the sales force

Just as consumers and resellers benefit from the motivation provided by sales promotions, so too can members of the sales force. To stimulate performance, sales promotions can be directed at the sales force of either the manufacturer or the reseller. Incentives such as contests and sales meetings are two of the most used motivators.

Contests

Contests have been used a great deal, and if organised and planned properly can be very effective in raising the performance outcomes of sales teams. By appealing to their competitive nature, contests can bring about effective new product introductions, revive falling sales, offset a rival's competitive moves and build a strong customer base. To do this, contests must be fair, so that participants have a roughly equal chance of being successful, and the winners should not be those who have high-density and high-potential territories. A further consideration is the duration of the contest: too short and the full effects may not be realised; make it too long and interest and support for the incentive may wane.

Sales meetings

Sales meetings provide an opportunity for management to provide fresh information to the sales force about performance, stock positions, competitor activities, price deals, consumer or reseller promotions and new products. Sales training exercises can be introduced and short product training sessions can often be included. These formal agenda items are supplemented by the informal ones of peer reassurance and competitive stimulus, as well as information exchange and market analysis. Meetings can be held annually, quarterly, monthly or at local level on a weekly basis. The time that representatives are off territory needs to be considered, but generally such meetings are of benefit to people who spend the greater part of their working week away from the office, at the boundary of the organisation.

The time that representatives are off territory needs to be considered.

Other sales promotion aids

Brochures are a sales promotion that can be used to assist consumers, resellers and sales forces. Apart from the ability of the brochure to impart factual information about a product or service, brochures and sales literature stimulate purchase and serve to guide decisions. For service-based organisations, the brochure represents a temporary tangible element of the product. Inclusive tour operators, for example, might entice someone to book a holiday, but consumption may take place several months in the future. The brochure acts as a temporary product substitute and can be used to refresh expectations during the gestation period and remind significant other people of the forthcoming event (Middleton, 1989). Just as holiday photographs provide opportunities to relive and share past experiences, so holiday brochures serve people to share and enjoy pre-holiday experiences and expectations. Consumption of inclusive tours, therefore, can be said to occur at the booking point, and the brochure extends or adds value to the holiday experience.

The brochure acts as a temporary product substitute and can be used to refresh expectations during the gestation period.

Sales literature can trigger awareness of potential needs. As well as this, it can be useful in explaining technical and complex products. For example, leaflets distributed personally at DIY stores can draw attention to a double-glazing manufacturer's products. Some prospective customers may create an initial impression about the manufacturer, based on past experiences triggered by the literature, the quality of the leaflet and the way it was presented. The leaflet acts as a cue for the receiver to review whether there is a current need and, if there is, then the leaflet may be kept longer, especially where high involvement is present; value is thus added to the purchase experience.

Financial services companies use sales literature at various stages in the sales process. Mailers are used to contact prospective customers, corporate brochures are used to provide source credibility, booklets about the overall marketplace are left with clients after an initial discussion and product guides and brochures are given to customers after a transaction has been agreed. To help prevent the onset of cognitive dissonance, a company magazine is sent soon after the sale and at intermediate points throughout the year to cement the relationship between client and company.

Corporate brochures are used to provide source credibility.

An increasingly important and expensive approach is to license a TV cartoon character from *The Simpsons*, *Rugrats* or *South Park* or a cyber person such as Lara Croft who was used by Lucozade. These characters are used to attract the attention of children and provide the parental agreement necessary for a purchase to be made. There are, of course, issues concerning consistency of brand values and the need to prevent competitors using the same or similar characters to support their brands. It is also argued that apart from a short-term sales increase there is a residual sales increase following promotions utilising these prime characters, especially if the promotion is based upon a free gift or the chance to win an instant gift.

Character licensing is used strategically to build brands. Murphy (1999) reports how Disney has long-term contracts with McDonald's and Nestlé that grant them first refusal on tie-ins to new films. Warner Bros and Cadbury's have established a similar arrangement.

Summary

The range of techniques and methods used to add value to offerings is enormous but there are growing doubts about the effectiveness and profitability associated with some sales promotions.

Sales promotions used by manufacturers to communicate with resellers are aimed at encouraging resellers to either try new products or purchase more of the ones they currently stock. To do this, trade allowances, in various guises, are the principal means.

Sales promotions used by resellers (largely retailers) to influence consumers are normally driven by manufacturers, although some price deals and other techniques are used to generate store traffic. The majority of sales promotions are those used by manufacturers to influence consumers. Again, the main tasks are to encourage trial or increase product purchase. A range of techniques, from sampling and coupons to premiums, contests and sweepstakes, are all used with varying levels of success, but there has been a distinct shift away from traditional promotional instruments to the use of digital media in order to reflect consumers' preferences and media behaviour.

Review questions

1. Explain the objectives that manufacturers might have when encouraging resellers to take more product.

2. List the main sales promotion methods used by manufacturers and targeted at consumers.

3. Evaluate the allowance concept.

4. Consider whether hostaging is conducive to relationship marketing.

5. Collect four examples of sampling and determine whether you feel they were effective in achieving their objectives.

6. Name five different methods of distributing samples.

7. How can coupons be used to reduce levels of perceived risk?

8. Which of the two forms of premiums is generally regarded as the less successful and why do you think this is?

9. What role does the sales brochure play in marketing communications?

10. Consider the view that the sales force does not require incentivising through sales promotion as it is motivated sufficiently through other means.

MINI-CASE
Denby Toiletries

Richard Littlejohn was delighted when he was invited to join Denby Toiletries as marketing and sales director. He was already one of three national line sales managers for a leading FMCG food organisation and he was ambitious to take full responsibility for the sales and marketing of a single company.

Denby Toiletries

Denby Toiletries offers two main brands: 'Caress', a soap in toilet- and bath-size packages, and 'Splash', a shower gel. Both brands are distributed throughout the UK. The recommended retail price for a Caress toilet bar is 88p. This places the brand in the upper third by price, among the quality brands, although some soaps are considerably more expensive. The Splash brand has been positioned in a similar way in the top third of the national market. Littlejohn calculated that in real terms Denby's sales appeared to have been decreasing around 5 per cent per annum over the past four years. Nevertheless, the Caress brand is widely recognised and the firm made a profit before tax of 4 per cent on sales last year. The Caress brand had been sold for over 50 years and has a good, sound quality image, appealing to AB women in the grey market (50+-year-olds) with above-average disposable incomes. Distribution is through the independent sector, not supermarkets. The Splash shower gel was launched in 1994 but has failed to establish a strong position in the market. It is seen by supermarket buyers as a third-rate product and, so far, they have failed to list it, let alone devote shelf space to it.

Group net turnover was about £9.2 million last year, giving Denby Toiletries less than 2 per cent of the market. Both the Caress and the Splash brands are targeted at the independent sector (high street chemists, retail chains) and most are serviced through wholesalers. Very large chains are able to buy direct from Denby. During the Second World War, Denby had been forced to use general manufacturers' representatives working on commission to cover its accounts. Thereafter, Denby never fully returned to an employee sales force. The firm now operates through a field marketing organisation in six regions, although its own sales director covers a

seventh – London West – operating from the head office at Ealing. Representatives work on 2 per cent commission for all orders from their regions, including national, wholesale and retail chains that purchase for delivery to other regions.

Research

When he arrived at Denby, Littlejohn was confident he could change the situation by repositioning both brands. He is on first-name terms with many of the buyers for national supermarket and retail chains, comes into frequent contact with them to arrange special deals and promotions, and has entertained and been 'out on the town' with a number of them.

One of Littlejohn's first actions on joining his new company was to meet the current advertising agency, Parsons, Smith and Brown (PSB). The agency commissioned a series of research activities including a study of the representation of the Denby brands in different outlets and its share of the market through those outlets. The results confirmed that Caress (and to a lesser extent Splash) had a strong presence in the independent chemist sector, had a moderate share of the retail grocery chains and virtually no representation through the supermarkets.

Even more revealing were PSB's findings about people's attitudes towards the Caress and Splash brands. Research indicated that while a substantial market existed for the Caress brand (for those who wished to reward themselves with a luxury soap), a new segment was emerging for technology-based products. The target market appears to be characterised by ABC1 women, aged 18–35, who have busy careers and who pursue modern lifestyles. This group wants a soap product that has a highly technical formulation, provides reassurance and protection for sensitive skin, and hints at some expression of the user's awareness of environmental issues.

Several competitors had an SOV double that of Caress but Littlejohn has said that he is not impressed with the advertising strategies being used to increase market share. He referred to the heavy advertisers as 'adland's puppets'. These strategies were based on highly emotional messages where differentiation was based upon self-indulgence and reward. Littlejohn believed that to achieve market share customers wanted added value, a tangible reason to buy.

Virtually all housewives buy toilet soap and some 9 per cent – disproportionately grouped in the 35–44 age bracket – were classified as heavy users. To get at these heavy users PSB argued that there was no substitute for brand advertising. Littlejohn recognised the argument but favoured trying to reach occasional users of both Caress and competitor brands. He believed an emphasis was needed on below-the-line work and in particular sales promotion, merchandising and packaging.

The Nurella brand

Littlejohn's idea is to withdraw Splash from the market, continue with Caress and launch a soap brand as Nurella. A new shower gel should then follow, to be called 'Nurella Protein Plus', thus extending the Nurella brand. Littlejohn saw Nurella positioned as a scientifically, hi-tech, modern and credible brand.

Access to supermarket shelves should be possible with Nurella, as long as Denby was prepared to invest in a promotional campaign to support the multiple grocers. Meanwhile, the Caress brand would be unaffected and so the risk to Denby, he reasons, is limited to the possible loss of the current volume of Splash sales through the independent sector.

Questions

1 Do you believe Littlejohn can build the Caress and Nurella brands without using advertising?

2 If Littlejohn is to use sales promotion, which techniques do you advise he uses? Why?

3 Who might be the target audiences for the sales promotions?

4 If asked whether premiums or sampling would be appropriate to support the Caress brand, what would be your answer and why?

5 What role might advertising play if sales promotions are to dominate the promotional strategy?

References

Advertising Association (2004) *Marketing Statistics*. Henley: WARC.

Anderson, J.C. and Narus, J.A. (1990) A model of distributor firm and manufacturer firm working partnerships. *Journal of Marketing*, **54** (January), pp. 42–58.

Benady, D. and Barrett, L. (2001) Virgin terrain. *Marketing Week*, 18 January, pp. 28–9.

Blattberg, R.C., Eppen, G.D. and Lieberman, J. (1981) A theoretical and empirical evaluation of price deals for consumer nondurables. *Journal of Marketing*, **5**(1), pp. 116–29.

Blattberg, R.C. and Neslin, S.A. (1990) *Sales Promotion: Concepts, Methods and Strategies*. Englewood Cliffs, NJ: Prentice-Hall.

d'Astous, A. and Jacob, I. (2002) Understanding consumer reactions to premium-based promotional offers. *European Journal of Marketing*, **36**(11), pp. 1270–86.

d'Astous, A. and Landerville, V. (2003) An experimental investigation of factors affecting consumers' perceptions of sales promotion. *European Journal of Marketing*, **37**(11/12), pp. 1746–61.

Della Bitta, A.J. and Monroe, K.B. (1980) A multivariate analysis of the perception of value from retail price advertisements. In *Advances in Consumer Research*, Vol. 8 (ed. K.B. Monroe). Ann Arbor, MI: Association for Consumer Research.

Dunmore, T. (2000) Can net music help sell your products? *Marketing*, 14 September, p. 39.

Govoni, N., Eng, R. and Gaper, M. (1986) *Promotional Management*. Englewood Cliffs, NJ: Prentice-Hall.

Gupta, S. and Cooper, L.G. (1992) The discounting of discounts and promotion brands. *Journal of Consumer Research*, **19** (December), pp. 401–11.

Inman, J., McAlister, L. and Hoyer, D.W. (1990) Promotion signal: proxy for a price cut? *Journal of Consumer Research*, **17** (June), pp. 74–81.

Kahn, B.E. and Louie, T.A. (1990) Effects on retraction of price on brand choice behaviour for variety seeking and last purchase-loyal-consumers. *Journal of Marketing Research*, **18** (August), pp. 279–89.

Mathews, V. (1999) Return of the 'instant redemption'. *Financial Times*, 30 April, p. 14.

Middleton, V.T.C. (1989) *Marketing in Travel and Tourism*. Oxford: Heinemann.

Miller, R. (1997) Does everyone have a price? *Marketing*, 24 April, pp. 30–3.

Murphy, C. (1999) Using cartoons to build brands. *Marketing*, 24 June, pp. 25–6.

Rossiter, J.R. and Percy, L. (1987) *Advertising and Promotion Management*. New York: McGraw-Hill.

Tomkins, R. (1994) Time to cut it out. *Financial Times*, 21 April, p. 25.

Witthaus, M. (2000) Baiting the buy. *Marketing Week*, 16 November, pp. 71–3.

Public relations

25

Public relations is a management activity that attempts to shape the attitudes and opinions held by an organisation's stakeholders. Through dialogue with these stakeholders the organisation may adjust its own position and/or strategy. Therefore there is an attempt to identify with, and adjust an organisation's policies to, the interests of its stakeholders. To do this it formulates and executes a programme of action to develop mutual goodwill and understanding. Profile communication strategies make substantial use of public relations when developing understanding about who they are and what their intentions are.

Aims and objectives

The aim of this chapter is to explore public relations in the context of promoting organisations and their products.

The objectives of this chapter are to:

1. discuss the role of public relations in the communications mix;
2. clarify the differences between corporate public relations and marketing public relations;
3. highlight the main audiences to which public relations activities are directed;
4. provide an overview of some of the main tools used by public relations;
5. appreciate the development and significance of corporate advertising;
6. examine the nature and context of crisis management;
7. determine the manner in which public relations complements the other tools of the promotional mix.

Introduction

The shift in the degree of importance given by organisations to public relations over recent years is a testimony to its power and effectiveness. An increasing number of organisations are now recognising that the role that public relations can play in the external and internal communications of organisations is a tool for use by all organisations, regardless of the sector in which they operate. Therefore all organisations in the public, hybrid, not-for-profit and private sectors can use this tool to raise visibility, interest and goodwill.

Is a testimony to its power and effectiveness.

Traditionally public relations has been a tool that dealt with the manner and style with which an organisation interacted with its major 'publics'. It sought to influence other organisations and individuals by public relations, projecting an identity that would affect the image that different publics held of the organisation. By spreading information and improving the levels of knowledge that people held about particular issues, the organisation sought ways to advance itself in the eyes of those it saw as influential. This approach is reflected in the definition of public relations provided by the Institute of Public Relations: 'Public Relations practice is the planned and sustained effort to establish and maintain goodwill and mutual understanding between an organisation and its publics'. Another definition has been provided by delegates attending a world convention of public relations associations in 1978, entitled the Mexican Statement: 'Public Relations is the art and social science of analysing trends, predicting their consequences, counselling organisations' leadership and implementing planned programmes of action which will serve both the organisation's and the public interest' (Public Relations Educational Trust, 1991). A more recent definition from Bruning and Ledingham (2000) is that public relations is the management of relationships between organisations and their stakeholders (publics). This last definition indicates the direction in which both public relations and marketing theory is moving.

Public relations is the management of relationships between organisations and their stakeholders.

For a long time public relations has been concerned with the development and communication of corporate and competitive strategies. Public relations provides visibility for an organisation, and this in turn, it is hoped, allows it to be properly identified, positioned and understood by all of its stakeholders. What some definitions do not emphasise or make apparent is that public relations should also be used by management as a means of understanding issues from a stakeholder perspective. Good relationships are developed by appreciating the views held by others and by 'putting oneself in their shoes'.

Public relations should also be used by management as a means of understanding issues from a stakeholder perspective.

Through this sympathetic and patient approach to planned communication, a dialogue can be developed that is not frustrated by punctuated interruptions (anger, disbelief, ignorance and objections). Public relations is a management activity that attempts to shape the attitudes and opinions held by an organisation's stakeholders. It attempts to identify its policies with the interests of its stakeholders and formulates and executes a programme of action to develop mutual goodwill and understanding and through this relationships that are in the long-run interests of all parties.

Characteristics of public relations

Public relations should, therefore, be a planned activity, one that encompasses a wide range of events. However, there are a number of characteristics that single out this particular tool from the others in the promotional mix. Public relations does not require the purchase of airtime or space in media vehicles, such as television or magazines. The decision on whether an organisation's public relations messages are transmitted or not rests with those charged with managing the media resource, not the message sponsor. Those that are selected are perceived to be endorsements or the views of parties other than management. The outcome is that these messages usually carry greater perceived credibility than those messages transmitted through paid media, such as advertising.

The degree of trust and confidence generated by public relations singles out this tool from others in the promotional mix as an important means of reducing buyers' perceived risk. However, while credibility may be high, the amount of control that management is able to bring to the transmission of the public relations message is very low. For example, a press release may have been carefully prepared in-house, but as soon as it is passed to the editor of a magazine or newspaper, a possible opinion former, all control is lost. The release may be destroyed (highly probable), printed as it stands (highly unlikely) or changed to fit the available space in the media vehicle (almost certain, if it is decided to use the material). This means that any changes will not have been agreed by management, so the context and style of the original message may be lost or corrupted.

An important means of reducing buyers' perceived risk.

The costs associated with public relations also make this an important tool in the promotional mix. The absolute costs are minimal, except for those organisations that retain an agency, but even then their costs are low compared with those of advertising. The relative costs (the costs associated with reaching members of the target audiences) are also very low. The main costs associated with public relations are the time and opportunity costs associated with the preparation of press releases and associated literature. If these types of activity are organised properly, many small organisations could develop and shape their visibility in a relatively inexpensive way.

A further characteristic of this tool is that it can be used to reach specific audiences, in a way that paid media cannot. With increasing media fragmentation and finer segmentation (customisation) of markets, public relations represents a cost-effective way of reaching such markets and audiences.

New technology has played a key role in the development and practice of public relations. Gregory (2004) refers to the Internet and electronic communication 'transforming public relations'. With regard to the use of the Internet by public relations practitioners she identifies two main schools. One refers to those who use the Internet as an extension to traditional or pre-Internet forms of communication. The second see opportunities through the Internet to develop two-way, enhanced communication. There can be little doubt that new technology has assisted communication management in terms of improving the transparency, speed and reach of public relations messages and at the same time enabling interactive communication between an organisation and its specific audiences.

New technology has played a key role in the development and practice of public relations.

The main characteristics of public relations are that it represents a very cost-effective means of carrying messages with a high degree of credibility. However, the degree of control that management is able to exert over the transmission of messages can be limited.

Publics or stakeholders?

The first definition of public relations quoted earlier used, as indeed does most of the public relations industry, the word *publics*. This word is used traditionally to refer to the various organisations and groups with which a focus organisation interacts. So far, this text has referred to these types of organisation as *stakeholders*. 'Stakeholders' is a term used increasingly in the field of strategic management, and as public relations is essentially concerned with strategic issues the word 'stakeholders' is used in this text to provide consistency and to reflect the strategic orientation and importance of this promotional tool.

The stakeholder concept has been discussed earlier, at great length, in Chapter 8. Various networks of stakeholders were identified, with each network consisting of members who are oriented towards supporting the focus organisation either in an indirect way or directly through the added-value processes.

For the purposes of this chapter it is useful to set out who the main stakeholders are likely to be. Stakeholder groups, it should be remembered, are not static and new groups can emerge in response to changes in the environment. The main core groups, however, tend to be the following.

Employees (internal public relations)

The employees of an organisation are major stakeholders and represent a major opportunity to use word-of-mouth communications. It has long been established that employees need to be motivated, involved and stimulated to perform their tasks at a high level. Their work as external communicators is less well established, but their critical role in providing external cues as part of the corporate identity programme was discussed earlier in Chapter 15.

Financial groups (financial or investor relations)

Shareholders require regular information to maintain their continued confidence in the organisation.

Shareholders require regular information to maintain their continued confidence in the organisation and to prevent them changing their portfolios and reducing the value of the organisation.

In addition to the shareholders, there are those individuals who are either potential shareholders or who advise shareholders and investors. These represent the wider financial community but nevertheless have a very strong influence on the stature, strength and value that an organisation has. Financial analysts need to be supplied with information in order that they be up to date with the activities and performance outcomes of organisations, but also need to be advised of developments within the various markets that the organisation operates.

Organisations attempt to supply analysts with current information and materials about the organisation and the markets in which they are operating, to ensure that the potential and value of publicly quoted organisations is reflected in the share price. The success of any further attempts to increase investment and to secure any necessary capital will be determined by the confidence that the financial community has in the organisation. Public relations, or investor relations, is an important form of communication in that it can create and shape these relationships. By developing confidence in this way the perception of risk held by investors can be lowered, funds are released and new products are developed and launched.

Customers (media relations)

The relationships that organisations develop with the media are extremely important in order that their messages reach their current and potential customers. Customers represent a major stakeholder audience and are often the target of public relations activities, because although members of the public may

The relationships that organisations develop with the media are extremely important.

not be current customers the potential they represent is important. The attitudes and preferences towards the organisation and its products may be unfavourable, in which case it is unlikely that they will wish to purchase the product or speak positively about the organisation. By creating awareness and trust it is possible to create goodwill and interest, which may translate into purchase activity or favourable word-of-mouth communications. This is achieved through media relations.

ViewPoint 25.1   MRP for Jersey potatoes

As part of the preparations for the launch of the new season's crop of Jersey potatoes to its main market, the UK, Hammond Communications research uncovered a case of potato rustling on the island. The company discovered that not only was poaching a current problem for farmers but they were unaware of the extent of the problem.

By referring to the potatoes as 'brown gold' and using the television detective Bergerac (John Nettles) to organise a 'Spud Watch' with local farmers an event was staged. The resultant photocall and subsequent interviews were covered by BBCTV News 24, Channel 5 News, GMTV, 7 national and 31 regional daily newspapers and three national radio stations.

Source: Adapted from PR Awards 2000.

Of all the media, the press is the most crucial, as it is always interested in newsworthy items and depends to a large extent on information being fed to it by a variety of corporate press officers. Consequently, publicity can be generated for a range of organisational events, activities and developments.

Organisations and communities (corporate public relations)

There are a variety of public, private, commercial and not-for-profit organisations and communities with whom organisations need to communicate and interact on a regular basis.

Corporate public relations (sometimes referred to as corporate communications) are used to reach this wide spectrum of audiences and cover a range of activities. Each audience and set of issues have particular characteristics that lead to individual forms of public relations practice:

- *public affairs* – government and local authorities
- *community relations* – members of local communities
- *industry relations* – suppliers, associations and other trade stakeholders
- *issues management* – various audiences concerning sensitive industries (e.g. tobacco or pharmaceuticals).

Public relations should be aimed at informing audiences of their strategic intentions.

Organisations should seek to work with, rather than against, these stakeholder groups. As a result, public relations should be aimed at informing audiences of their strategic intentions and seeking ways in which the objectives of both parties can be satisfied.

A framework of public relations

Communications with such a wide variety of stakeholders need to vary to reflect different environmental conditions, organisational objectives and form of relationship. Grunig and Hunt (1984) have attempted to capture the diversity of public relations activities through a framework. They set out four models to reflect the different ways in which public relations is, in their opinion, considered to work. These models, based on their experiences as public relations practitioners, constitute a useful approach to understanding the complexity of this form of communication. The four models are set out in Figure 25.1.

	Model			
Characteristic	Press agentry/publicity	Public information	Two-way asymmetric	Two-way symmetric
Purpose	Propaganda	Dissemination of information	Scientific persuasion	Mutual understanding
Nature of communication	One way; complete truth not essential	One way; truth important	Two way; imbalanced effects	Two way; balanced effects
Communication model	Source→Rec.*	Source→Rec.*	Source ⇌ Rec.* Feedback	Group ⇌ Group
Nature of research	Little; 'counting house'	Little; readability, readership	Formative; evaluative of attitudes	Formative; evaluative of understanding
Leading historical figures	P.T. Barnum	Ivy Lee	Edward L. Bernays	Bernays, educators, professional leaders
Where practised today	Sports, theatre, product promotion	Government, not-for-profit associations, business	Competitive business, agencies	Regulated business, agencies
Estimated percentage of organisations practising today	15%	50%	20%	15%

* Receiver.

FIGURE 25.1 Models of public relations (From Grunig and Hunt (1984); used with kind permission.)

The press agentry/publicity model

The essence of this approach is that communication is used as a form of propaganda. That is, the communication flow is essentially one way, and the content is not bound to be strictly truthful as the objective is to convince the receiver of a new idea or offering. This can be observed in the growing proliferation of media events and press releases.

The public information model

There is little focus on persuasion, more on the provision of information.

Unlike the first model, this approach seeks to disseminate truthful information. While the flow is again one way, there is little focus on persuasion, more on the provision of information. This can best be seen through public health campaigns and government advice communications in respect of crime, education and health.

The two-way asymmetric model

Two-way communication is a major element of this model. Feedback from receivers is important, but as power is not equally distributed between the various stakeholders and the organisation, the relationship has to be regarded as asymmetric. The purpose remains to influence attitude and behaviour through persuasion.

The two-way symmetric model

This represents the most acceptable and mutually rewarding form of communication. Power is seen to be dispersed equally between the organisation and its stakeholders and the intent of the communication flow is considered to be reciprocal. The organisation and its respective publics are prepared to adjust their positions (attitudes and behaviours) in the light of the information flow. A true dialogue emerges through this interpretation, unlike any of the other three models, which see an unbalanced flow of information and expectations.

A true dialogue emerges through this interpretation.

The model has attracted a great deal of attention and has been reviewed and appraised by a number of commentators (Miller, 1989). As a result of this and a search for excellence in public relations, Grunig (1992) revised the model to reflect the dominance of the 'craft' and the 'professional' approaches to public relations practices. That is, those practitioners who utilise public relations merely as a tool to achieve media visibility can be regarded as 'craft' oriented. Those organisations whose managers seek to utilise public relations as a means of mediating their relationships with their various stakeholders are seen as 'professional' practitioners. They are considered to be using public relations as a longer-term and proactive form of planned communication. The former see public relations as an instrument, the latter as a means of conducting a dialogue.

These models are not intended to suggest that communication planners should choose among them. Their use and interpretation depend upon the circumstances that prevail at any one time. Organisations use a number of these different approaches to manage the communication issues that exist between them and the variety of different stakeholder audiences with whom they interact. However,

Their use and interpretation depend upon the circumstances that prevail at any one time.

there is plenty of evidence to suggest that the press/agentry model is the one most used by practitioners and that the two-way symmetrical model is harder to observe in practice.

Public relations and relationship management

In addition, it is important to remember that the shift to a relationship management perspective effectively alters the way public relations is perceived and practised by organisations. Ehling (1992) suggests that instead of trying to manipulate audience opinion so that the organisation is of primary importance, the challenge is to use sym-

> It is the ability of organisations to encourage and practise dialogue that really enables truly symmetrical relationships to develop.

bolic visual communication messages with behaviour such that the organisation–audience relationship improves for all parties. Kent and Taylor (2002) and Bruning and Ledingham (2000) develop this theme by suggesting that it is the ability of organisations to encourage and practise dialogue that really enables truly symmetrical relationships to develop. What follows from this is a change in evaluation, from measuring the decimation of messages to one that measures audience influence and behavioural and attitudinal change and, of course, relationship dynamics. Bruning and Ledingham phrase this as a change from measuring outputs to outcomes.

In addition to this discernible shift in emphasis has been a change in the way public relations is used by organisations. Traditionally, public relations has been used as a means of managing communication between parties, whereas now communication is regarded as a means of managing relationships (Kent and Taylor, 2002). In order to use communication to develop the full potential within relationships many argue that dialogic interaction should be encouraged. In Chapter 7 five tenets of dialogue were presented: mutuality, empathy, propinquity, risk and commitment. These have been offered by Kent and Taylor as the elements that may form a framework through which dialogue may be considered and developed. On a practical level they argue that organisations should place email, Web addresses, 0800 telephone numbers and organisational addresses prominently in all forms of external communication, most notably advertisements and Web sites, to enable dialogue.

Corporate public relations and marketing public relations

Many writers and organisations are now challenging the traditional view of public relations. The marketing dimension of public relations has been developed considerably in recent years. This is a response to media rates increasing ahead of inflation, media and markets becoming increasingly fragmented and marketing managers seeking more effective communication mixes. As a result, public relations is being used actively to support and reinforce other elements of the communications mix (Kitchen, 1991).

The development of integrated marketing communications has helped bring marketing and public relations closer together. The advantage of utilising a number of tools together is that through coordination message impact is improved. One of the best examples of this is the Wonderbra campaign by Playtex. It is estimated that the poster campaign was enhanced by £50 million worth of 'extra' media coverage based on the stories and publicity generated by the programme (Barrett, 1997).

It was established earlier (Chapter 8) that a performance network consists of those organisations (stakeholders) who directly influence or are influenced by the value-added processes of the focus organisation. They can engage in relational exchanges and often seek to develop long-term collaborative relationships. The support network consists of those organisations that influence and are influenced by the value-adding processes in an indirect way. They tend to engage in market exchanges that encourage a short-term perspective.

They tend to engage in market exchanges that encourage a short-term perspective.

Both these networks require public relations, but in different ways. The support network needs public relations to help build and sustain goodwill between members and to create relationships that acknowledge the direction and intent of the strategy being pursued by each of them. This requires the work of a more traditional approach to public relations. The performance network needs public relations to sustain an environment where there is not only goodwill but also collaboration and trust, one where the satisfaction of particular target segments is the goal of all members. This requires a marketing orientation where there is a greater emphasis on the need to achieve certain levels of profitability as a result of meeting and satisfying customer needs.

Bearing these points in mind and recalling the professional and craft designations set out previously, it is not surprising that two types of public relations have begun to emerge: corporate public relations and marketing public relations. Corporate public relations, according to Cutlip *et al.* (1985), is 'a function of management seeking to identify, establish and maintain mutually beneficial relationships between an organisation and the various publics on whom its success and failure depend'. They define marketing public relations as 'not only concerned with organisational success and failure but also with specific publics: customers, consumers and clients with whom exchange transactions take place'.

This dichotomy is not intended to suggest that these are mutually exclusive forms of public relations, since they are not, and, as Kitchen and Proctor (1991) rightly point out, they are mutually interactive. The use of corporate communications has an effect similar to that of ink being injected into a bottle of water: the diffusion produced can assist all parts of an organisation and its stakeholders, whether they be in the performance or support networks. Similarly, public relations at the product level can have an immediate effect upon the goodwill and perspective with which stakeholders perceive the whole organisation.

They are mutually interactive.

For example, an airline opening a new route and using marketing PR activities focused on customers in the hinterland of each destination will impact on both the product and the airline as a whole. Further examples of MPR can be observed by companies installing 'carelines' that can be used by customers to contact them (to seek advice and complain) about aspects of the company's products and services. The telephone number, which can be made visible on posters, receipts, catalogues, advertisements and shopping bags, serves to feed negative and positive aspects and through the use of data analysis can assist the development of new products and services. Indeed, Burger King has used this to develop new menus and merchandising items.

The net impact of either approach has to be reflected in the performance of the organisation, and for many that is the profitability of the unit. The identification of these two forms of public relations does not mean that this approach is a widely used practice. Indeed, at this stage only a minority of organisations recognise the benefits that this approach can bring. However, as an increasing number of organisations, in a variety of sectors, are expanding their use of PR, so more sophisticated approaches are likely to emerge, aimed at improving product, corporate and overall performance and satisfaction levels.

Objectives of a public relations plan

It can be seen that the main broad objectives of public relations activities are to provide visibility for the corporate body and support for the marketing agenda at the product level. The promotional objectives, established earlier in the plan, will have

> The task of the public relations plan is to provide a series of coordinated programmes that complement the overall marketing communications strategy.

identified issues concerning the attitudes and relationships stakeholders have with an organisation and its products. Decisions will have been made to build awareness and to change perception, preferences or attitudes. The task of the public relations plan is to provide a series of coordinated programmes that complement the overall marketing communications strategy and which develop and enhance some of the identity cues used by stakeholders. The overall goal should be to develop the relationship between the organisation and its different audiences.

Public relations can be used to address issues identified within the support and performance networks (Chapter 8). These will be concerned with communications that aim to develop positive attitudes and dispositions towards the organisation and generally concern strategic issues. Public relations can also contribute to the marketing needs of the organisation and will therefore be focused at the product level in the performance network and on consumers, seeking to change attitudes, preferences and awareness levels with respect to products and services offered. Therefore a series of programmes is necessary: one to fulfil the corporate requirements and another to support the marketing of products and services.

ViewPoint 25.2   Heinz Salad Cream

Cowlett (2000) reports that established food brands need to be refreshed and repositioned on a regular basis in order to be of value to successive generations. Heinz Salad Cream, for example, is a brand that has been around for over 85 years and was generally perceived as a salad dressing preferred mainly by the older generation. Many adults have not even tried it as they have been brought up using mayonnaise.

Rather than discontinue the brand, Heinz decided to reposition the product by introducing it to a new generation of young adults and surrounding it with a new set of associations and brand values. This was accomplished using public relations, advertising, radio and in-store promotions in concert with the Web site. A launch event using Denise van Outen and Graham Norton was used to generate media attention and, through sponsorship of a comedy tour, tasting opportunities were increased among the target audience.

Cause-related marketing

One major reason for the development of public relations and the associated corporate reputation activities has been the rise of cause-related mar-

> Many brand owners have become aware of the need to be perceived as credible, responsible and ethically sound.

keting, which over the last six years in particular has been a significant influence as many brand owners have become aware of the need to be perceived as credible, responsible and ethically sound. Developing a strong and socially oriented corporate reputation has become a major form of differentiation in many markets where price, quality and tangible attributes are relatively similar. Being able to present their corporate brands as contributors to the wider social framework, a role beyond that of simple profit generators, has enabled stronger positive positions to be achieved.

By which profit-oriented and not-for-profit organisations form partnerships to exploit, for mutual benefit, their association in the name of a particular cause.

One of the methods used by brands is cause-related marketing. This is a commercial activity by which profit-oriented and not-for-profit organisations form partnerships to exploit, for mutual benefit, their association in the name of a particular cause.

The benefits from a properly planned and constructed campaign accrue to all participants. Cause-related marketing helps improve corporate reputation, enables product differentiation and appears to contribute to improved customer retention through enhanced sales. In essence, cause-related marketing is a means by which relationships with stakeholders can be developed effectively. As organisations outsource an increasingly larger part of their business activities and as the stakeholder networks become more complex, so the need to be perceived as (and to be) socially responsible becomes a critically important dimension of an organisation's image.

ViewPoint 25.3   NSPCC uses cause-related marketing

The NSPCC has entered into a number of different cause-related marketing programmes.

Among the organisations it has worked with are the House of Fraser, which it helped to promote its range of collectable soft toys, Fraser Bear and Fraser Bunny. A £2 donation is given to the 'Full Stop' campaign for each toy sold at Christmas. Programmes with Masterfoods, based on consumers collecting 10 tokens from Funsize and Snickers packs, have resulted in over £100,000 being raised for the charity. The Yorkshire Building Society set up and ran a Happy Kids Saver Account for eight years based on a donation of £1 for every account opened; while the Skipton Building Society raised £400,000 based on the value of the opening balances of new accounts.

Finally, the Dixons Group (PC World, Dixons, Currys and The Link) raised £200,000 during 2000–1 based on encouraging customers to return/recycle computer ink jet cartridges, with each cartridge contributing £1 to the NSPCC.

Source: Adapted from www.nspcc.org.uk.

A public relations programme consists of a number of planned events and activities that seek to satisfy communication objectives. The following represent some of the broad tools and techniques associated with public relations, but it should be noted that the list is not intended to be comprehensive.

Public relations methods and techniques

An organisation's corporate identity consists of those activities that reflect, to a large extent, the personality of an organisation (see Chapter 15). Public relations provides some of the deliberate cues that enable stakeholders to develop images and perceptions by which they recognise, understand and converse with organisations.

The range of public relations cues or methods available to organisations is immense. Different organisations use different permutations in order that they can communicate effectively with their various stakeholder audiences. For the purposes of this text a general outline is provided of the more commonly used methods.

Public relations cues are largely visual, whereas those provided by sales promotion, for example, may appeal to a broad range of senses, such as taste, touch and sight. Kitchen and Moss (1995) report how a number of fast-moving consumer goods companies in the UK have categorised the tools used in both these types of public relations. For these organisations, media and sports sponsorships, publicity and sales promotion tie-ups constitute the core activities of marketing public

What also emerges is a profound recognition of the need to integrate the various communication activities.

relations. Corporate public relations activities revolve around corporate publicity, issues management, public affairs, lobbying, financial/investor relations and corporate advertising. This demarcation should not be regarded as typical or indeed desirable, but it serves as a useful means of understanding the focus of these two types of public relations. What also emerges is a profound recognition of the need to integrate the various communication activities, which itself requires objective and coordinated management attention.

ViewPoint 25.4   Launching Harry Potter

The launch date of the eagerly awaited fourth book in the Harry Potter series was announced in February 2000, a full five months before actual publication. During this period J.K. Rowling, the author, suggested that there not be any reviews of the book, in an attempt to keep secret the plot of the new story.

When the launch was made the author undertook an eight-day book-signing tour, conducting her tour of the UK by a steam engine that was painted and branded the Hogwart's Express, as per one of the character's journeys in previous books (Bold, 2000).

In May, prior to the launch, *The Times*, following an invited pitch of all national newspapers, had an exclusive interview with the author. In a novel sales promotion event each bookshop was sent 'golden tickets' that it could distribute in any way (e.g. competitions), enabling children to have their copy of the book signed on the train itself.

The launch achieved massive publicity, not only in the UK but also in Australia, the United States and Canada. Advance book orders reached £5 million and a huge number of bookshops ran out of stock.

No further attempt is made in this book to segregate the cues used by organisations for either marketing or corporate public relations. The main reason for this is that there is no useful benefit from such a subdivision. Cues are interchangeable and can be used to build credibility or to provide visibility for an organisation. It is the skill of the public relations practitioner that determines the right blend of techniques. The various types of cue are set out in Table 25.1.

While there is general agreement on a definition, there is a lower level of consensus over what constitutes public relations. This is partly because the range of activities is diverse and categorisation problematic. The approach adopted here is that public relations consists of a range of communication activities, of which media relations, publicity and event management appear to be the main ones used by practitioners.

TABLE 25.1 Cues used by PR to project corporate identity

Cues to build credibility	Cues to signal visibility
Product quality	Sales literature and company publications
Customer relations	Publicity and media relations
Community involvement	Speeches and presentations
Strategic performance	Event management
Employee relations	Promotional messages
Crisis management skills	Media mix
Third-party endorsement	Design (signage, logo, letterhead)
Perceived ethics and environmental awareness	Dress codes
Architecture and furnishing	Exhibitions/seminars
	Sponsorships

Media relations

Media relations consists of a range of activities designed to provide media journalists and editors with information. The intention is that they relay the information, through their media, for consumption by their audiences. Of course the original message may be changed and subject to information deviance as it is processed but audiences perceive much of this information as highly credible simply because opinion formers (Chapter 2) have bestowed their judgement on the item. Of the various forms of media relations, press releases, interviews, press kits and press conferences are most used.

Press releases

The press release is a common form of media relations activity. A written report concerning a change in the organisation is sent to various media houses for inclusion in the media vehicle as an item of news. The media house may cover a national area, but very often a local house will suffice. These written statements concern developments in the organisation, such as promotions, new products, awards, prizes, new contracts and customers. The statement is deliberately short and written in such a style that it attracts the attention of the editor. Further information can be obtained if it is to be included within the next publication or news broadcast.

The press release is a common form of media relations activity.

Press conferences

Press conferences are used when a major event has occurred and where a press release cannot convey the appropriate tone or detail required by the organisation. Press conferences are mainly used by politicians, but organisations in crisis (e.g. accidents and mergers) and individuals appealing for help (e.g. police requesting assistance from the public with respect to a particular incident) can use this form of communication. Press kits containing a full reproduction of any statements, photographs and relevant background information should always be available.

Interviews

Interviews with representatives of an organisation enable news and the organisation's view of an issue or event to be conveyed. Other forms of media relations concern bylined articles (articles written by a member of an organisation about an issue related

EXHIBIT 25.1 An example of a press release issued by Alton Towers

to the company and offered for publication), speeches, letters to the editor, and photographs and captions.

Media relations can be planned and controlled to the extent of what is sent to the media and when it is released. While there is no control over what is actually used,

ViewPoint 25.5	Press for Dyson

When James Dyson launched his revolutionary, upright vacuum cleaner he did not have the resources to fund an advertising campaign to support the launch. Although the design enabled the product to stand out in showrooms there was little to inform customers of the advantages of the product and to justify the starting price, which was double that of the competition.

One solution was to hang a brochure and a point-of-sales tag on the handle of each machine. The brochure folded out, provided basic information about each component and avoided any superlatives or attempts at persuasion. The sales tag however was used to tell the story about the experiences Dyson encountered trying to design and bring the new product to the market. People would be seen bending over avidly reading the Dyson story.

The second solution was to use press journalists to recall the same story because they could reach the target market and their messages would be highly credible in the eyes of the target audience. Rather than write press releases Dyson gave interviews to selected reporters, many of whom were from the quality press. The articles tended to be extremely positive about the product but concentrated more on the life experiences of James Dyson himself and reinforced the messages conveyed through the sales tags. The personalised account of the development process and the frequency with which these articles appeared provided readers with a way of identifying and becoming emotionally engaged with the whole Dyson experience. The language used and the repetition of the messages only served to increase the overall intensity of these marketing communication messages.

Source: Adapted from Boyle (2004); used with permission.

media relations allow organisations to try to convey information concerning strategic issues and to reach particular stakeholders.

The quality of the relationship between an organisation and the media will dramatically affect the impact and dissemination of news and stories released by an organisation. The relationships referred to are those between an organisation's public relations manager and the editor and journalists associated with both the press and the broadcast media.

Publicity and events

Control over public relations events is not as strong as that for media relations. Indeed, negative publicity can be generated by other parties, which can impact badly on an organisation by raising doubts about its financial status or perhaps the quality of its products.

Three main event activity areas can be distinguished: product, corporate and community events.

1. *Product events*

   Product-oriented events are normally focused upon increasing sales. Cookery demonstrations, celebrities autographing their books and the opening of a new store by the CEO or local MP are events aimed at generating attention, interest and sales of a particular product. Alternatively events are designed to attract the attention of the media and, through stories and articles presented in the news, are able to reach a wide audience. See Exhibit 25.2 regarding an event concerning the launch of the Gatwick Express.

EXHIBIT 25.2 Event designed to attraction media attention for the Gatwick Express

2. *Corporate events*

   Events designed to develop the corporate body are often held by an organisation with a view to providing some entertainment. These can generate a lot of local media coverage, which in turn facilitates awareness, goodwill and interest. For example, events such as open days, factory visits and donations of products to local events can be very beneficial.

3. *Community events*

   These are activities that contribute to the life of the local community. Sponsoring local fun runs and children's play areas, making contributions to local community centres and the disabled are typical activities. The organisation attempts to become more involved with the local community as a good employer and good member of the community. This helps to develop goodwill and awareness in the community.

The choice of events an organisation becomes involved with is critical.

The choice of events an organisation becomes involved with is critical. The events should have a theme and be chosen to satisfy objectives established earlier in the communications plan. See Chapter 26 for an example of sponsorship of local community events.

In addition to these key activities the following are important forms of public relations:

- lobbying (out of personal selling and publicity)
- sponsorship (out of event management and advertising); see Chapter 26
- corporate advertising (out of corporate public relations and advertising)
- crisis management (which has developed out of issues management, a part of corporate public relations).

Lobbying

They also ensure that the views of the organisation are heard in order that legislation can be shaped appropriately.

The representation of certain organisations or industries within government is an important form of public relations work. While legislation is being prepared, lobbyists provide a flow of information to their organisations to keep them informed about events (as a means of scanning the environment), but they also ensure that the views of the organisation are heard in order that legislation can be shaped appropriately, limiting any potential damage that new legislation might bring.

Moloney (1997) suggests that lobbying is inside public relations as it focuses on the members of an organisation who seek to persuade and negotiate with its stakeholders in government on matters of opportunity and or threat. He refers to in-house lobbyists (those members of the organisation that try to influence non-members) and hired lobbyists contracted to complete specific tasks.

His view of lobbying is that it is one of 'monitoring public policy-making for a group interest; building a case in favour of that interest; and putting it privately with varying degrees of pressure to public decision makers for their acceptance and support through favourable political intervention'.

Where local authorities interpret legislation and frame the activities of their citizens and constituent organisations, the government determines legislation and controls the activities of people and organisations across markets. This control may be direct or indirect, but the power and influence of government are such that large organisations and trade associations seek to influence the direction and strength of legislation, because any adverse laws or regulations may affect the profitability and the value of the organisation. Recent initiatives by the UK government to reduce the length of time that new drugs are protected by patent were severely contested by representatives from drug manufacturers and their trade association, the Association of British Pharmaceutical Industries. Despite a great deal of lobbying the action was lost, and now manufacturers have only eight years to recover their investment before other manufacturers can replicate the drug. The pharmaceutical industry has also been actively lobbying the EU with respect to legislation on new patent regulations and the information that must be carried in any promotional message. The tobacco industry is well known for its lobbying activities, as are ICI and many other organisations.

Corporate advertising

In an attempt to harness the advantages of both advertising and public relations, corporate advertising has been seen by some as a means of communicating more effectively with a range of stakeholders. The credibility of messages transmitted through public relations is high, but the control that management has over the message is limited. Advertising, however, allows management virtually total control over message dispersion, but the credibility of these messages is usually low. Corporate advertising is the combination of the best of advertising and the best of public relations.

The credibility of messages transmitted through public relations is high.

Corporate advertising, that is advertising on behalf of an organisation rather than its products or services, has long been associated with public relations rather than the advertising department. This can be understood in terms of the origins and former

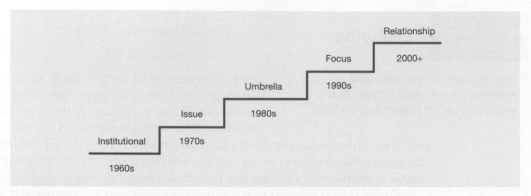

FIGURE 25.2 The development of corporate advertising

use that organisations made of corporate advertising (Figure 25.2). The first major period was the 1960s, when institutional advertising became prominent. According to Stanton (1964), the primary task of institutional advertising was to create goodwill. The next period was the 1970s, when corporate image advertising became popular. During this decade, organisations used issue and advocacy advertising as a means of promoting political and social ideas in an attempt to generate public support for the position adopted by an organisation.

During the 1980s, which witnessed a large number of mergers and takeovers, there was an increase in the use of umbrella advertising. Organisations used the name of the organisation as a broad banner, under which a range of products and services was promoted. As discussed previously, there has been a movement towards the incorporation of products and services in the use of public relations. This is reflected in the use of corporate advertising in the 1990s. Although the generation of goodwill continues to be a dominant theme, there is also a need to focus upon organisations as discrete units. As many organisations delayer and return to core business activities, so there is a need to focus communications on what they do best. Such focusing also enables them to reduce advertising expenditure on products because of increased media costs.

Corporate advertising provides some opportunity for organisations to achieve these objectives. However, the main purpose of corporate advertising appears to be the provision of cues by which stakeholders can identify and understand an organisation.

Cues by which stakeholders can identify and understand an organisation.

This is achieved by presenting the personality of the organisation to a wide range of stakeholders, rather than presenting particular functions or products that the organisation markets. Schumann *et al.* (1991) conclude that a number of US studies indicate that the first goal of corporate advertising is to enhance the company's reputation and the second is to provide support for the promotion of products and services. Table 25.2 sets out the most important goals that executives see corporate advertising as responsible for satisfying.

Reasons for the use of corporate advertising

The need to improve and maintain goodwill and to establish a positive reputation among an organisation's stakeholders has already been mentioned. These are tasks that need to be undertaken consistently and continuously, with the aim of building a reputational reservoir. In addition, however, there are particular occasions when organisations need to use corporate advertising:

TABLE 25.2 Goals of corporate advertising

Enhance corporate reputation
Improve credibility
Provide a point of differentiation
Support for products and services
Attract higher-quality employees
Underpin shareholder value
Easier access to new markets and suppliers
Advocacy of a position
Public communication of the company's social and environmental actions

- during change and transition
- when the organisation has a poor image
- for product support
- recruitment
- repositioning
- advocacy or issues.

Change

When an organisation experiences a period of major change, perhaps the transition before, during and after a takeover or merger, corporate advertising can be used in a variety of ways. The first is defensively, to convince stakeholders, particularly shareholders, of the value of the organisation and of the need not to accept hostile offers; secondly to inform and to advise of current positions; finally to position any 'new' organisation that may result from the merger activity. The defence of Marks & Spencer led by Stuart Rose, when Philip Green attempted a takeover in 2004, was based around messages communicated to current shareholders of the superior future value of the business under the current ownership and managers. This was intended to raise credibility and hence prevent a takeover based on differing projected values.

Poor image

Corporate advertising can also be used to correct any misunderstanding that stakeholders might have of corporate reality (Reisman, 1989). For example, financial analysts may believe that an organisation is underperforming, but reality indicates that performance is good. As we have seen before, this can be a result of poor communication, and through corporate advertising the organisation can correct such misunderstandings and help establish strategic credibility with the financial community and other stakeholders.

Product support

Corporate advertising can also assist the launch of new products. The costs normally associated with a launch can be lowered, and it is feasible to assume, although difficult to measure, that the effectiveness of a product launch can be improved when corporate advertising has been used to establish good reputational equity.

ViewPoint 25.6   Recruiting police

In order to recruit sufficient numbers for the police force, M & C Saatchi used a self-selection process. The purpose of the exercise was not to generate a volume of enquiries but to attract the right type of person and in effect reduce the ratio of enquiries to recruits. In the past too many people failed to follow through with their enquiries when they found out not only what the job entailed but what the rewards and conditions of employment were like. Until this campaign, police recruitment was managed on a local force basis. This approach broke with the local approach and went national.

The approach adopted asks potential recruits the question 'Could you?' Using a series of characters believed to be perceived by the public as highly credible and of high esteem (Patsy Palmer from *EastEnders*; a Falklands war hero, Simon Weston; and the ex-footballer John Barnes, representing females, bravery and ethnic minorities) they enlarge on what is required in the job, namely to break the news of a death, protect a drug dealer's girlfriend or face a gang of thugs . . . and they all say that they could not do it.

Source: Newland (2000).

Recruitment

Corporate advertising is used to recruit employees by creating a positive and attractive image of the organisation.

Corporate advertising is used to recruit employees by creating a positive and attractive image of the organisation. The development of source credibility, in particular trust, is fundamental, and through the process of identification individuals can become attracted to the notion of working for a particular organisation and are stimulated to seek further information.

Repositioning

Organisations periodically undergo self-review that may lead to repositioning. Hewlett-Packard launched its 'Invent' campaign as part of a process of preparing stakeholders for the future. The campaign sought to take the company back to its roots, its original ideology 'the rules of the garage' in which the founders first developed the organisation and the values that are part of the corporate philosophy. The campaign sought to encourage invention and to legitimise exploration and risk taking, remembering, of course, that the HP way determines how employees work and that the customer defines whether the job is well done. See Exhibit 25.3.

Organisations can be repositioned by the activities of competitor organisations. New products, new corporate messages, an improved trading performance or the arrival of a new CEO and the implementation of a new strategy can displace an organisation in the minds of its different stakeholders. This may require an adjustment by the focus organisation to re-establish itself. The Pepsi Challenge, referred to earlier, effectively dislodged Coca-Cola from its position as brand leader and led to a stream of product adjustments and messages from Coca-Cola aimed at repositioning itself.

Advocacy

The reasons presented so far for the use of corporate advertising are strongly related to image. A further traditional reason for the use of this tool is the opportunity for the organisation to inform its stakeholders of the position or stand that it has on a particular issue. This is referred to as advocacy advertising. Rather than promoting the

It's because they're not afraid
to get their hands filthy.
To eat the paste.
To use a hammer as a brush.
To break something just to see how it works.
And to start with the impossible,
which is where grownups usually stop.
Just a few of the things we're keeping in mind
as we invent the new hp.
Want to come along?
www.hp.com

All kids are inventors.

EXHIBIT 25.3 HP invent

As part of the process of preparing for the future, Hewlett Packard used corporate advertising to reaffirm corporate values, with staff and major stakeholders. Picture reproduced with the kind permission of Hewlett Packard Ltd.

organisation in a direct way, this form of corporate advertising associates an organisation with an issue of social concern, which public relations very often cannot achieve alone.

The organisation can be seen as a brand in much the same way as products and services are branded. Just as a product-based brand can be tracked, so can the corporate entity be tracked for levels of awareness, attitudes and preferences held by stakeholders.

The corporate entity can be tracked for levels of awareness, attitudes and preferences held by stakeholders.

Crisis management

A growing and important part of the work associated with public relations is crisis communications. At one time, when a crisis such as a threat of takeover or workplace accident struck an organisation, the first stakeholders to be summoned by the CEOs were merchant bankers. Today the public relations consultant is first through the door. The power of corporate and marketing communications is beginning to be recognised and appreciated. Indeed, the astute CEO summons the public relations consultant in anticipation of crisis, on the basis that being prepared is a major step in diffusing the energy with which some crises can affect organisations.

Organisational crises can be usefully considered in the context of chaos theory (Seeger, 2002). Chaos occurs when complex systems break down and the established order and equilibrium is broken by events that are often abrupt and discontinuous. Chaos

Chaos occurs when complex systems break down.

TABLE 25.3 Common causes of disasters

Origin of crisis	Explanation
Economic	As the Western world currently experiences growth and high levels of employment and countries in the developing world follow a fluctuating path of revitalisation and competition, this has brought some organisations and industries in the West to collapse (e.g. UK shipbuilding).
Managerial	Human error and the pursuit of financial goals by some organisations give rise to the majority of disasters. For example, cutting costs at the expense of safety and repair of systems.
Political	Issues concerning war and terrorism have encouraged kidnapping, as well as organisations having to change the locations of their business.
Climate	The climate is changing substantially in certain parts of the world, and this has brought disaster to those who lie in the wake of natural disturbances. For example, the hurricanes in 2004 that decimated the Cayman Islands and Grenada in the Caribbean; south-east Asia's December 2004 tsunami.
Technology	The rate at which technology is advancing has brought about crises such as those associated with transportation systems and aircraft disasters. Human error is also a significant factor, often associated with the rate of technological change.
New media	The age of electronic media and instant communication means that information can be disseminated throughout the world within 30 minutes of an event occurring.
Consumer groups	The rise of consumer groups (e.g. Amnesty International and Greenpeace) and their ability to investigate and publicise the operations and policies of organisations.

theory considers system breakdown as a necessary event in order that the system be refreshed. Seeger phrases this process as 'disorder necessary for order, decay a precursor to renewal, decline a step in growth and collapse a prelude to rebuilding as one of the most attractive and optimistic features of chaos theory'.

Crises can occur because of a simple or minor managerial mistake, an incorrect decision or because of a seemingly distant environmental event. All organisations face the prospect of managing a crisis or as Fink (2000) phrases it 'a crisis looms on the horizon of every organisation'. Crises are emerging with greater frequency as a result of a number of factors. Table 25.3 sets out some of the main factors that give rise to crises for organisations.

'A crisis looms on the horizon of every organisation'.

Figure 25.3 describes organisational crises in the context of two key variables. On the horizontal axis is the degree to which management has control over the origin of the crisis. Is the origin of the crisis outside management's control, such as an earthquake, or is it within its control, such as those crises associated with poor trading results? The vertical axis reflects the potential impact that a crisis might have on an organisation. All crises, by definition, have a potential to inflict damage on an organisation. However, some can be contained, perhaps on a geographic basis, whereas others have the potential to cause tremendous damage to an organisation, such as those experienced through product tampering and environmental pollution.

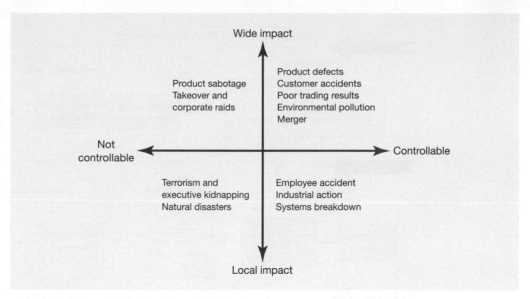

FIGURE 25.3 An organisational crisis matrix

The increasing occurrence of crises throughout the world has prompted many organisations to review the manner in which they anticipate managing such events, should they be implicated. It is generally assumed that those organisations which take the care to plan in anticipation of disaster will experience more favourable outcomes than those that fail to plan. Quarantelli (1988) reports that there is only a partial correlation between those which plan and those that experience successful outcomes. He attributes this to the fact that only some of the organisations that take care to prepare do so in a professional way.

There is only a partial correlation between those which plan and those that experience successful outcomes.

Poor planning can only deliver poor results. Fink (2000) reports that organisations that do not plan experience crises that last over twice as long as those that do plan.

The second reason concerns the expectations of those who design and implement crisis plans. It is one thing to design a plan; it is entirely another to implement it. Crisis planning is about putting into position those elements that can effect speedy outcomes to the disaster sequence. When a crisis strikes, it is the application of contingency-based tactics by all those concerned with the event that will determine the strength of the outcome. Spillan (2003) sought to determine whether the experience of a crisis encourages concern and attention to preventing further crisis events. This was based on the evidence of Barton (2001) and Mitroff and Anagnos (2001) that most organisations only prepare crisis management plans after suffering from and recovering from a disaster. The central issue appears to revolve around the need to assess an organisation's vulnerabilities at the earliest opportunity, before a crisis occurs (Caponigro, 2000, as cited by Spillan, 2003).

Crisis phases

The number of phases through which a crisis passes varies.

The number of phases through which a crisis passes varies according to author and the management model they are proposing. For example, Penrose (2000) mentions

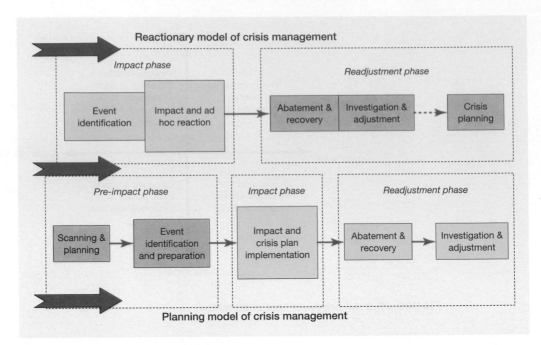

FIGURE 25.4 Twin models of crisis management

Littlejohn's six-step model, Fink's audit, Mitroff's portfolio planning approach and Burnett's crisis classification matrix. The number of phases is also influenced by the type of crisis management an organisation uses. Essentially there are two main models: organisations that plan in order to manage crisis events and in doing so attempt to contain the impact; secondly there are organisations that fail to plan and manage by reacting to crisis events. See Figure 25.4.

The differences between these two approaches are that there are fewer phases in the shorter 'reactionary' model and that the level of detail and attention given to the anticipation, management and consideration of crisis events is more deliberate in the planning model. Time is spent here considering the sequence of events within the planning model. A three-phase (and five episodes) framework is adopted: Pre-impact, Impact and Readjustment phases. It should be remembered that the duration of each phase can vary considerably, depending upon the nature of the crisis and the manner in which management deals with the events associated with the crisis.

The first period is referred to as the Pre-impact phase and consists of two main episodes, Scanning and planning and Event identification and preparation. Good strategic management demands that the environment be scanned on a regular basis to detect the first signs of significant change. Organisations that pick up signals which are repeated are in a better position to prepare for disaster than those that do not scan the environment. Penrose (2000) reports that those who perceive the impact of a crisis to be severe or very damaging and plan accordingly tend to achieve more successful outcomes. Those that fail to scan are often taken by surprise and have to react with less time and control to manage the events which hit them. Even if they do pick up a signal, many organisations not only ignore it but also attempt to block it out (Pearson and Mitroff, 1993). It is as if management is attempting to deny the presence of the signals in order that any stability and certainty they may have could continue.

The environment be scanned on a regular basis to detect the first signs of significant change.

Many of the signals detected during the Pre-impact phase wither and die. Some gather strength and develop with increasing force. The next episode is characterised by the identification of events that move from possible to probable status. There is

The objective is not to prevent the crisis but to defuse it as much as possible.

increasing activity and preparation in anticipation of the crisis, once its true nature and direction have been determined. Much of the activity should be geared to training and the preparation and deployment of crisis teams. The objective is not to prevent the crisis but to defuse it as much as possible, to inform significant stakeholders of its proximity and possible effects, and finally to manage the crisis process.

The Impact phase is the period when the 'crisis breaks out' (Sturges et al., 1991). Management is tested to the limit and if a plan has been developed it is implemented with the expectation of ameliorating the damage inflicted by the crisis. One method of reducing the impact is to contain or localise the crisis. By neutralising and constraining the event, it is prevented from contaminating other parts of the organisation or stakeholders. Pearson and Mitroff (1993) suggest that the containment of oil spills and the evacuation of buildings and aircraft are examples of containment and neutralisation. Through the necessity to talk to all stakeholders, management at this point will inevitably reveal its attitude towards the crisis event. Is its attitude one of genuine concern for the victims and stakeholders? Is the attitude consistent with the expectations that stakeholders have of the management team? Alternatively, is there a perception that management is making lame excuses and distancing itself from the event, and is this consistent with expectations? Readers should note that within the Reactionary model the Pre-impact and Impact phases are merged into one, simply because there is little or no planning, no scanning and by definition no preparation in anticipation of a crisis.

The Readjustment phase within the planning model consists of three main episodes. The period concerns the recovery and realignment of the organisation and its stakeholders to the new environment, once the deepest part of the crisis event has passed. The essential tasks are to ensure that the needs of key stakeholders can still be met and, if they cannot, to determine what must be done to ensure that they can be. For example, continuity of product supply is critically important. This may be achieved by servicing customers from other locations.

Common characteristics of this phase are the investigations, police inquiries, public demonstrations, court cases and media probing that inevitably follow major crises and

ViewPoint 25.7   Crisis at Firestone Tyres

Bridgestone-Firestone, a major manufacturer of car tyres, experienced a problem of tread separation where the binding within a tyre gives way and a 'blow out' happens. The problem was first observed in 1992 when the first complaints were received. The complaints were received from different parts of the world and Ford, a major customer, gradually replaced Firestone tyres on its vehicles in different parts of the world, in many cases before the American public was told of the problem.

A total of 271 lives were lost due to this defect and Bridgestone-Firestone took several steps to manage their image in the light of the gathering problems. They denied the problem existed, concealed information, refused to take suitable corrective action and even tried to pass blame to both Ford and to consumers, blaming them for poor maintenance. All of this did little to enhance the company's reputation.

Source: Blaney et al. (2002).

TABLE 25.4 Image restoration approaches (Benoit, 1997)

Damage retrieval	Explanation
Simple denial	Outright rejection that the act was caused by them or even occurred in the first place, or shifting the blame by asserting that another organisation (person) was responsible for the act.
Evasion (of responsibility)	Provocation . . . a reasonable response to a prior act. Defeasibility . . . the act occurred because of a lack of time or information. Accident . . . the act was not committed purposefully. Good intentions . . . the wrongful act was caused despite trying to do well.
Reducing offensiveness	This involves demonstrating that the act was of minor significance or by responding so as to reduce the impact of the accusor.
Corrective action	This may involve putting right what was damaged and taking steps to avoid a repeat occurrence.
Mortification	An apology or statement of regret for causing the act that gave offence.

disasters. The manner in which an organisation handles this fall-out and tries to appear reasonable and consistent in its approach to such events can have a big impact on the perception that other stakeholders have of the organisation.

The rate at which organisations readjust is partly dependent upon the strength of the image held by stakeholders prior to the crisis occurring. If the organisation had a strong reputation then the source credibility attributed to the organisation will be high. This means that messages transmitted by the organisation would be received favourably and trusted. However, if the reputation is poor, the effectiveness of any marketing communications is also going to be low. The level of source credibility held by the organisation will influence the speed with which stakeholders allow an organisation to readjust and recover after a crisis.

> The rate at which organisations readjust is partly dependent upon the strength of the image held by stakeholders prior to the crisis occurring.

Benoit (1997) developed a theory concerning image restoration in the light of an organisational crisis. The theory states that there are five general approaches: denial, evade responsibility, reduce offensiveness, use corrective action and lastly mortification. See Table 25.4.

Benoit has used these approaches to evaluate the responses given by a variety of organisations when faced by different disasters and crises. See ViewPoint 25.7.

Organisations that have not planned their management of crisis events and have survived a disaster may decide to instigate a more positive approach so as to mitigate the impact of future crisis events. This is not uncommon and crisis management planning may occur at the end of this cycle.

Crisis for online brands

The development of the Internet may have forced many organisations to reconsider the significance of corporate reputation as part of their communication strategies. With so much information available instantaneously about each organisation it is important that brands that have gone online be transparent

> It is important that brands that have gone online be transparent and open in the way they communicate.

TABLE 25.5 Forms of cyber attack

Method	Explanation
Cyber squatting	By registering and setting up domain names similar to established brand names, an attempt is made to mislead (gone out of business signs), misdirect (send them to other sites) or exploit (extract personal details) users.
Anti-corporate sites	Sometimes referred to as 'suck sites', these attempt to niggle large corporations (e.g. Mcspotlight) to extend their complaint or gripe.
Distributed denial of service	A DDOS attack comprises several hijacked computers simultaneously feeding information requests to a single site. This causes it to slow down or deny access.
Firewall attack	The defence shield surrounding a site becomes insecure and the host prone to data loss, misuse and corruption.
IP and Web spoofing	These sites look and feel just like the master site. However, the intention may be to use the customer data fraudulently, to spy on the host site or just present a nuisance factor.
Direct/indirect site attacks	There are number of forms of attack which vary from the indirect form by changing the style of the site text (e.g. to a biblical style) or by using Post-it style notes (e.g. 'Will never use this xxxx service again') to the more direct approach such as rewriting the Web pages in real time and changing the prices.
Email	This is a potential problem for organisations – cyber harassment, defamation and the spread of viruses by email are unfortunately quite common.
Password capture	Entering networks with fake identities is a problem for companies as data destruction, corruption and misuse can seriously undermine customer confidence.

Source: Hollingworth (2000); used with kind permission.

and open in the way they communicate. The problem is that they are prone to attack from a variety of stakeholders. There are customers who have gripes, and there are others who despise the company on trading, moral and ethical stances. There are others who enjoy the fun of the chase. Hollingworth (2000) lists the areas of attack in Table 25.5.

ViewPoint 25.8   Cahoot in crisis

Online brands are also prone to attack from inside the organisation, whether accidentally or deliberately. In November 2004 Cahoot, the Internet banking brand of Abbey, was forced to shut for ten hours once it had been revealed that account access processes could be circumnavigated avoiding key security and protection features. The problem appears to have been due to a system upgrade installed 12 days previously and was not a malicious attack.

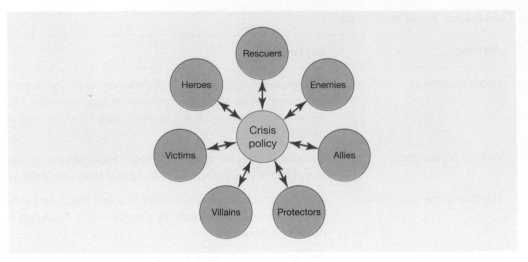

FIGURE 25.5 Crisis roles for stakeholders (From Pearson and Mitroff (1993); used with kind permission.)

Who is affected by crisis events? When a crisis hits an organisation, many different stakeholders are vulnerable to the repercussions. Pearson and Mitroff (1993) suggest that stakeholders may perceive the focus organisation adopting a particular role. This role may be as a hero, villain or even protector. Figure 25.5 depicts some of the roles that the focus organisation might be cast in; in much the same way, stakeholders themselves might be cast in a role that reflects the perception of the focus organisation. It is interesting to monitor the ascribed roles and to see whether stakeholders actually fulfil their designated role or perhaps another when crisis strikes. Perhaps a move from rescuer to enemy is not uncommon.

The importance of this perspective is that attention has to be focused on the different organisations, not just the one on which the crisis has had immediate impact. The stakeholder net is wide and the sensitivity among cohesive groups in particular can be acute. The organisation that has a crisis plan of value is one which has considered the impact upon its stakeholders.

Integration of public relations in the promotional mix

Public relations has three major roles to play within the communications programme of an organisation. These are the development and maintenance of corporate goodwill, the continuity necessary for good product support and through these the development and maintenance of suitable relationships.

The traditional role of creating goodwill and stimulating interest.

The first is the traditional role of creating goodwill and stimulating interest between the organisation and its various key stakeholders. Its task is to provide a series of cues by which the stakeholders can recognise, understand and position the organisation in such a way that the organisation builds a strong reputation. This role is closely allied to the corporate strategy and the communication of strategic intent.

The second role of public relations is to support the marketing of the organisation's products and services, and its task is to integrate with the other elements of the promotional mix. Public relations and advertising have complementary roles. For example, the launch of a new product commences not with advertising to build awareness in target customers but with the use of public relations to inform editors and news broadcasters that a new product is about to be launched. This news material can be used within the trade and consumer press before advertising occurs and the target buyers become aware (when the news is no longer news). To some extent this role is tactical rather than strategic, but if planned, and if events are timed and coordinated with the other elements of the promotional mix, then public relations can help build competitive advantage.

The third role is to provide the means by which relationships can be developed. To do this public relations has a responsibility to encourage dialogue to provide the means

The means by which relationships can be developed.

through which interaction, discourse and discussion can occur and to play a full part in the communication process and the messages that are conveyed, listened to, considered and acted upon.

Summary

Public relations, whether oriented primarily to product support or to the development of corporate goodwill, plays an important role within the communications mix. According to Haywood (1991), public relations can support marketing in a number of ways, from improving awareness and projecting credibility to the creation of direct sales leads and motivating the sales force and members of the performance network. However, public relations is now recognised as a communication discipline that can develop and maintain a portfolio of relationships with a range of key stakeholder audiences.

By providing all stakeholders with cues by which they can develop an image of an organisation, public relations enables organisations to position themselves and provide stakeholders with a means of identifying and understanding an organisation. This may be accomplished inadvertently through inaction or deliberately through a planned presentation of a variety of visual cues. These range from publicity through press releases to the manner in which customers are treated, products perform, events are managed and expectations are met.

Finally, the area referred to as crisis communications management has grown in significance during recent years. Public relations plays an important role in preparing for and constraining the impact of a crisis and re-establishing an organisation once a crisis has passed.

By creating campaigns targeted at individual stakeholders, or at least identifying the needs of the performance network as separate from those of the support network, the effects intended at the outset can be measured at the close of different campaigns.

Review questions

1. Define public relations and set out its principal characteristics.
2. Using an organisation of your choice, identify the main stakeholders and comment on why it is important to communicate with each of them.
3. Highlight the main objectives of using public relations.
4. What is the difference between corporate public relations and marketing public relations? Is this difference of importance?

5. Write a brief paper describing the main methods of publicity.

6. Why do you think an increasing number of organisations are using sponsorship as a part of their promotional mix?

7. Suggest occasions when corporate advertising might be best employed.

8. Identify the main phases associated with crisis management.

9. What roles might stakeholders adopt when a crisis occurs?

10. Discuss the view that public relations can only ever be a support tool in the promotional mix.

MINI-CASE
eBay: PR building the online person-to-person brand

Mini-case written by Dr Ruth Ashford, Principal Lecturer, Manchester Metropolitan University Business School; Peter Betts, Senior Lecturer, Manchester Metropolitan University Business School

Background

eBay has been in existence for less than a decade, yet the brand name is synonymous with the excitement of online auctions. The eBay brand is very well known and has been a new phenomenon that has changed the way people do business throughout the world.

Back in 1998, the communications agency Manning, Selvage and Lee (San Francisco and Los Angeles) was commissioned to introduce the media and consumers to the emerging auction category and position eBay as a recognisable market leader, and ultimately make eBay a household name.

The agency was faced with introducing an infant company into an emerging market. Yahoo! and Amazon already had millions of registered users and had started their own online auctions. So research was undertaken and there were several attributes that distinguished eBay from the hundreds of other online sites in the noise of the Internet. The most important one was that collectors, general consumers and other people, including the media, could find virtually anything that interested them on eBay. However, research had shown that there was concern arising over fraud on the Internet and this could have an impact on trading online.

The agency recognised that even reporters could easily become hooked to eBay, making them more inclined to cover eBay news, by emphasising their interests in published press releases.

Although in 1998 it had been trading for only three years, eBay also had a very active community offering a good supply of interesting stories and eager ambassadors for the brand. Also, the eBay site was, and still is, organised into collectors' interests, with categories such as Sports, Antiques and Toys. This meant that eBay was a very accessible place to find popular items or the latest trends, thus allowing public relations to position eBay as a barometer on pop-culture.

Campaign objectives

The following key communications objectives were set:

● to educate the media and consumers about, and encourage personal use by them of, online auctions;

● to make the eBay brand synonymous with this emerging space on the Internet;

● to introduce eBay into mainstream culture;

● to brand eBay as a secure online destination in which to experience safe trading;

● to convert eBay users to advocates for the brand.

PR tactics employed

Manning, Selvage and Lee devised a number of creative approaches for the brand, linked to awareness, testimonial campaigns, pop culture and safety:

Awareness – PR tactics were designed to appeal to reporters' personal interests in an effort to drive them to eBay and have them become users. When speaking with the media, reporters were asked what they liked to collect and about their hobbies, then introduced to the site, unveiling a range of items relating to their interests on eBay. When they had logged in, the reporters were directed to a message board where they were given up-to-the-minute happenings. A list of more than 150 'special friends' of eBay received press releases and other eBay news. This effort resulted in reporters writing personal accounts of their own experiences on eBay and keeping their audiences informed of the latest events.

Testimonial campaign – human interest angles relating to eBay user stories were offered. A database of user profile stories was developed to pitch to the media, such as the story of a businessman whose business on eBay had enabled him to generate enough income to buy a house and a car for his father in Malaysia.

Pop cultures – the eBay brand was positioned as a barometer of pop culture trends. By using current news events around entertainment and pop culture icons, PR was able to spotlight eBay in front of high-profile national print and broadcast entertainment media that were setting the tone of what was 'hot' with consumers. This was done by, for example, linking to the 'Furbies' phenomenon with stories of eBay being the world's largest collection of Furbies and where they were available online to purchase. Also, the camera that was used to film *The Blair Witch Project* was put on the eBay site, and this was used as an opportunity to place top stories with entertainment television programmes and publications.

Safety – eBay aimed to take a leadership position to endorse safe trading online by introducing Safe Harbor programmes designed to eliminate much of the risk often associated with ebusiness sites. Close interaction with users of the site on a daily basis, discovering their likes and dislikes of the site, allowed the team to take on the issues of fraud. There was an aggressive campaign positioning eBay as a responsible company dedicated to solving problems in order to maintain users' confidence. Being proactive was quite different behaviour in contrast with the competition and thus received coverage.

Evaluation

Within the first six months of the campaign 6 billion impressions had been achieved. The campaign achieved the objectives set in that, now, eBay is one of the best-known brands on the Internet, and consistently one of the top five ecommerce sites. The eBay brand has become so mainstream that it has appeared in comic strips in the national papers, and has frequent mentions on popular programmes such as *Friends*, *Who Wants to Be a Millionaire?* and many other programmes in both Europe and the United States. Indeed the online community has since grown substantially to more than 10 million registered users and continues to grow daily. This was achieved with little to no advertising support and has been a phenomenal success for the development of an online brand.

Dr Ruth Ashford and Peter Betts, have adapted this case from the Manning, Selvage and Lee submission to the IPRA Golden World Awards, with kind permission.

Questions

1 In this case study, what was the role of public relations in the communications mix?

2 Discuss the strengths and weaknesses of employing PR methods for this campaign.

3 Evaluation of the public relations effort is one of the main problems which communications managers face, discuss how further evaluation could have been undertaken for this case.

References

Barrett, P. (1997) A marriage of PR and ads. *Marketing*, 30 October, p. 15.

Barton, L. (2001) *Crisis Organisations II*. Cincinnati, OH: South Western Publishing.

Benoit, W.L. (1997) Image repair discourse and crisis communication. *Public Relations Review*, **23**, pp. 177–86.

Blaney, J.R., Benoit, W.L. and Brazeal, L.M. (2002) Blowout! Firestone's image restoration campaign. *Public Relations Review*, **28**(4) (October), pp. 379–92.

Bold, B. (2000) Bloomsbury casts spell for Potter sequel. *PR Week*, 21 July, p. 22.

Boyle, E. (2004) Press and publicity management: the Dyson case. *Corporate Communications: an International Journal*, **9**(3), pp. 209–22.

Bruning, S.D. and Ledingham, J.A. (2000) Perceptions of relationships and evaluations of satisfaction: an exploration of interaction. *Public Relations Review*, **26**(1), pp. 85–95.

Caponigro, J.R. (2000) *The Crisis Counsellor: A-Step-by-Step Guide to Managing a Business Crisis*. Chicago, IL: Contemporary Books.

Cowlett, M. (2000) Cooking up a recipe for long-term success. *PR Week*, 16 August, p. 8.

Cutlip, S., Center, A.H. and Broom, G.J. (1985) *Effective Public Relations*. Englewood Cliffs, NJ: Prentice-Hall.

Ehling, W.P. (1992) Estimating the value of public relations and communication to an organisation. In *Excellence in Public Relations and Communication Management* (eds J.E. Grunig, D.M. Dozier, P. Ehling, L.A. Grunig, F.C. Repper and J. Whits), pp. 617–38. Hillsdale, NJ: Lawrence Erlbaum.

Fink, S. (2000) *Crisis Management Planning for the Inevitable*. New York: AMACON.

Gregory, A. (2004) Scope and structure of public relations: a technology driven view. *Public Relations Review*, **30**(3) (September), pp. 245–54.

Grunig, J. (1992) Models of public relations and communication. In *Excellence in Public Relations and Communications Management* (eds J.E. Grunig, D.M. Dozier, P. Ehling, L.A. Grunig, F.C. Repper and J. Whits), pp. 285–325. Hillsdale, NJ: Lawrence Erlbaum.

Grunig, J. and Hunt, T. (1984) *Managing Public Relations*. New York: Holt, Rineholt & Winston.

Haywood, R. (1991) *All About Public Relations*. 2nd edn. Maidenhead: McGraw-Hill.

Hollingworth, C. (2000) Cyber-Attack, Communications Directors Forum, June.

Kent, M.L. and Taylor, M. (2002) Toward a dialogic theory of public relations. *Public Relations Review*, **28**(1) (February), pp. 21–37.

Kitchen, P.J. (1991) Developing use of PR in a fragmented demassified market. *Marketing Intelligence and Planning*, **9**(2), pp. 29–33.

Kitchen, P.J. and Moss, D. (1995) Marketing and public relations: the relationship revisited. *Journal of Marketing Communications*, **1**, pp. 105–19.

Kitchen, P.J. and Proctor, R.A. (1991) The increasing importance of public relations in FMCG firms. *Journal of Marketing Management*, **7**(4) (October), pp. 357–70.

Miller, G. (1989) Persuasion and public relations: two 'Ps' in a pod. In *Public Relations Theory* (eds C. Botan and V. Hazelton). Hilldale, NJ: Lawrence Erlbaum.

Mitroff, I. and Anagnos, G. (2001) *Managing Crises Before They Happen*. New York: American Management Association.

Moloney, K. (1997) Government and lobbying activities. In *Public Relations: Principles and Practice* (ed. P.J. Kitchen). London: International Thomson Press.

Newland, F. (2000) Can this campaign strengthen the thin blue line? *Campaign*, 8 September, p. 28.

Pearson, C.M. and Mitroff, I. (1993) From crisis prone to crisis prepared: a framework for crisis management. *Academy of Management Executive*, **7**(1), pp. 48–59.

Penrose, J.M. (2000) The role of perception in crisis planning. *Public Relations Review*, **26**(2), pp. 155–71.

Public Relations Educational Trust (1991) *The Place of Public Relations in Management Education*. London: Institute of Public Relations.

Quarantelli, E.L. (1988) Disaster crisis management: a summary of research findings. *Journal of Management Studies*, **25**(4), pp. 373–85.

Reisman, J. (1989) Corporate advertising in disguise. *Public Relations Journal* (September), pp. 21–7.

Schumann, D.W., Hathcote, J.M. and West, S. (1991) Corporate advertising in America: a review of published studies on use, measurement and effectiveness. *Journal of Advertising*, **20**(3), pp. 35–56.

Seeger, M.W. (2002) Chaos and crisis: propositions for a general theory of crisis communication. *Public Relations Review*, **28**(4) (October), pp. 329–37.

Spillan, J.E. (2003) An exploratory model for evaluating crisis events and managers' concerns in non-profit organisations. *Journal of Contingencies and Crisis Management*, **11**(4) (December), pp. 160–9.

Stanton, W.J. (1964) *Fundamentals of Marketing*. New York: McGraw-Hill.

Sturges, D.L., Carell, B.J., Newsom, D.A. and Barrera, M. (1991) Crisis communication management: the public opinion node and its relationship to environmental nimbus. *SAM Advanced Management Journal* (Summer), pp. 22–7.

Sponsorship

26

Sponsorship is a commercial activity, whereby one party permits another an opportunity to exploit an association with a target audience in return for funds, services or resources. Organisations are using sponsorship activities in a variety of ways to generate awareness, brand associations and to cut through the clutter of commercial messages.

Aims and objectives

The aims of this chapter are to introduce and examine sponsorship as an increasingly significant form of marketing communications.

The objectives of this chapter are to:

1. appreciate the variety and different forms of sponsorship activities;
2. understand the reasons why sponsorship has become an important part of the promotional mix;
3. provide an insight into the main characteristics of this form of communication;
4. consider where in the promotional mix sponsorship may best be placed;
5. explore ways in which sponsorship can be best evaluated.

Introduction

In Chapters 8 and 25 it was suggested that an organisation should contribute to the local community with a view to being seen as participative, caring and involved with local affairs. The degree of control that can be levied against this type of activity

As a means of reaching wider target audiences.

is limited once a commitment has been made. By adopting a more commercial perspective, some organisations have used sponsorship, particularly of sports activities, as a means of reaching wider target audiences. Sponsorship can provide the following opportunities for the sponsoring organisation:

1. Exposure to particular audiences that each event attracts in order to convey simple awareness-based brand messages.

2. To suggest to the target audiences that there is an association between the sponsored and the sponsor and that by implication this association may be of interest and/or value.

3. To allow members of the target audiences to perceive the sponsor indirectly through a third party and so diffuse any negative effects associated with traditional mass media and direct persuasion.

4. Sponsorship provides sponsors with the opportunity to blend a variety of tools in the promotional mix and use resources more efficiently and arguably more effectively.

A commercial activity, whereby one party permits another an opportunity to exploit an association with a target audience in return for funds, services or resources.

From this it is possible to define sponsorship as a commercial activity, whereby one party permits another an opportunity to exploit an association with a target audience in return for funds, services or resources.

It is necessary to clarify the distinction between sponsorship and charitable donations. The latter are intended to change attitudes and project a caring identity, with the main returns from the exercise being directed to society or the beneficiaries. The beneficiaries have almost total control over the way in which funds are used. When funds are channelled through sponsorship the recipient has to attend to the needs of the sponsor by allowing it access to the commercial associations that are to be exploited, partly because they have a legal arrangement, but also to ensure that the exchange becomes relational and longer term; in other words, there is repeat purchase (investment) activity. The other major difference is that the benefits of the exchange are intended to accrue to the participants, not society at large.

The growth and development of sponsorship

The development of sponsorship as a communication tool has been spectacular.

The development of sponsorship as a communication tool has been spectacular since the early 1990s. This is because of a variety of factors, but among the most important, according to Meenaghan (1991), are the government's policies on tobacco and alcohol, the escalating costs of advertising media, the proven ability of sponsorship, new opportunities due to increased leisure activity, greater media coverage of sponsored events and the recognition of the inefficiencies associated with the traditional media. In addition to this list of drivers can be added regulations and technology. The Independent

TABLE 26.1 Growth and development of sponsorship

Increased media coverage of events
Relaxation of government and industry regulations
Increased incidence of sponsorship event supply (and demand)
Relationship orientation and association between sponsorship participants
Positive attitude change toward sponsorship by senior management
Awareness and drive towards integrated marketing communications
Increasing rate of other media costs
Need to develop softer brand associations and to reach niche audiences

Television Commission, which is now subsumed with Ofcom, acted to restrict the nature and form of programme (or broadcast) sponsorship. However, a recent relaxation in the regulations has allowed for the development of this type of sponsorship. The reference to technology concerns systems such as TiVo that allow users to skip over advertising breaks (and eventually block them out altogether). Should these machines achieve strong consumer penetration then the sponsorship credits could become more important than advertising in achieving brand presence. See Table 26.1.

ViewPoint 26.1   Timed sponsorship

Many watch manufacturers have developed associations with particular sports personalities or sporting events. The main goals of these sponsorships have been to develop brand awareness, associations and favourable values. The following examples are just some of the associations that have been developed between particular events and watch manufacturers (Balfour, 2000):

Motor racing
The TAGHeuer brand has been associated with precision technology and Grand Prix motor racing for a long time.
Omega sponsors Michael Schumacher, the World Formula 1 Racing Champion (2004).
Chopard makes the Mille Liglia chronograph at the time of the road race and presents one to all competitors.

Water sports
Omega promotes its Seamaster in association with the America's Cup.

Polo
Cartier sponsors many prestige polo events.

Golf
Alfred Dunhill sponsors the annual Alfred Dunhill Golf Championship at St Andrews.

Football
Tissot sponsors Michael Owen, the Real Madrid and England footballer.
The Bregeut Type XX Aéronavale watch was used in association with the Football France promotion in 1998.

Aviation
Breitling has developed an association with aviation.

It has been suggested that the rapid worldwide development of sponsorship is such that it is now seen as a standardised method of communicating a brand name (Witcher *et al.*, 1991). This form of communication has certainly gained in popularity, but not to the extent of standardisation. Sponsorship remains a communication tool, part of the promotional mix, but as with other tools it needs to be used with a purpose and as part of an integrated communications approach. In other words, sponsorship provides a further tool that, to be used effectively, needs to be harnessed strategically. For example, many companies and brands originating in south-east Asia and the Pacific regions have used sponsorship as a means of overseas market entry in order to develop name or brand awareness (e.g. Panasonic, JVC and Daihatsu).

It needs to be used with a purpose and as part of an integrated communications approach.

In addition, many sponsorships have survived recessionary periods. This may be because of the two- to three-year period that each sponsorship contract covers and the difficulty and costs associated with terminating such agreements. It may also be because of the impact that sponsorship might have on the core customers who continue to buy the brand during economic downturns. Easier targeting through sponsorship can also assist the reinforcement of brand messages. Readers are reminded of the weak theory of advertising (Chapter 18), and it may be that sponsorship is a means of defending a market and of providing additional triggers to stimulate brand recall/recognition.

Sponsorship objectives

The primary reasons are to build awareness, developing customer loyalty and improving the perception (image) held of the brand or organisation.

There are both primary and secondary objectives associated with using sponsorship. The primary reasons are to build awareness, developing customer loyalty and improving the perception (image) held of the brand or organisation. Secondary reasons are more contentious, but generally they can be seen to be to attract new users, to support dealers and other intermediaries and to act as a form of staff motivation and morale building (Reed, 1994).

Sponsorship is normally regarded as a communications tool used to reach external stakeholders. However, if chosen appropriately sponsorship can also be used effectively to reach internal audiences. Care is required because different audiences transfer diverse values (Grimes and Meenaghan, 1998). According to Harverson (1998), one of the main reasons IT companies sponsor sports events is that this form of involvement provides opportunities to 'showcase' their products and technologies, in context. Through application in an appropriate working environment, the efficacy of a sponsor's products can be demonstrated. The relationship between sports organisers and IT companies becomes reciprocal as the organisers of sports events need technology in order for the events to run. Corporate hospitality opportunities are often taken in addition to the brand exposure that the media coverage provides. EDS claims that it uses sponsorship to reach two main audiences, customers (and potential customers) and potential future employees. The message it uses is that the EDS involvement in sport is sexy and exciting.

EDS claims that it uses sponsorship to reach two main audiences, customers and potential future employees.

A further interesting point arises from a view of a company sponsor through time. Meenaghan (1998) suggests that, at first, the sponsor acts as a donor, through the pure exchange of money in order to reach an audience. The next stage sees the sponsor acting as an investor, where, although large sums of money may well be involved, the sponsor is now actively involved and is looking for a return on the investment made. The third stage is reached when the sponsor assumes the role of an impresario. Now the sponsor is vigorously involved and seeks to control activities so that they reflect corporate/brand values and thus assist the positioning process.

Following on from this is the issue about whether sponsorship is being used to support a product or the organisation. Corporate sponsorships, according to Thwaites (1994), are intended to focus upon developing community involvement, public awareness, image, goodwill and staff relations. Product- or brand-based sponsorship activity is aimed at developing media coverage, sales leads, sales/market share, target market awareness and guest hospitality. What is important is that sponsorship is not a tool that can be effective in a stand-alone capacity. The full potential of this tool is only realised when it is integrated with some (or all) of the other tools of the promotional mix. As Tripodi (2001) comments, the implementation of integrated marketing communications is further encouraged and supported when sponsorship is an integral part of the mix in order to maximise the full impact of this communication tool.

Sponsorship is not a tool that can be effective in a stand-alone capacity.

How sponsorship might work

Interpretations about how sponsorship might work are varied, but assuming a cognitive orientation sponsorship works through associations that consumers make with a brand (which will be an accumulation of previous advertising and other promotional activities) and the event being supported. In addition, people make a judgement based upon the fit between the event and sponsorship such that the greater the degree of compatibility the more readily acceptable the sponsorship will be.

If a behavourist orientation is used to explain how sponsorship works, then the sponsorship will be perceived as a reinforcement of previous brand experiences. An event generates rewards by reminding individuals of pleasurable brand experiences. However, this assumes that individuals have previous brand experience and fails to explain adequately how sponsorship works when launching new products.

Sponsorship will be perceived as a reinforcement of previous brand experiences.

Generally, sponsorship plays a supporting or secondary role in the communication mix of many organisations and is not an important source of corporate information. This is largely because the communication impact of sponsorship is limited as sponsorship only reinforces previously held corporate (or product) images (positive or negative) rather than changes them (Javalgi *et al.*, 1994). It is also suggested that the only significant relationship between sponsorship and corporate image occurs where there has been direct experience of the brand. This in turn raises questions about whether sponsorship should be used to influence the image of the product category and its main brands in order to be of any worthwhile effect (Pope and Voges, 1999).

As Dolphin (2003) suggests, the range of activities, events, goals and the variety of ways in which it is used by organisations suggest that it is not entirely clear how sponsorship might best be used to help an organisation achieve its business goals. It is used to shape and assist corporate image, develop name association and awareness, drive product sales, build brands, help with recruitment, defend against hostile competitors and as a means of developing and providing opportunities for corporate hospitality. However, the primary goal for its use will generally reflect the context within which it is used. In situations where transactional exchanges are predominant within the target audience, broad-based sponsorship activities are likely to be preferred. In contexts where the target audience is relatively small or geographically discrete and where relational exchanges are preferred or sought, then relationship development sponsorship activities are more likely to be successful.

ViewPoint 26.2   Chichester supported by Tennyson

Sponsorship at music festivals is certainly not new but according to McCormack (2000) brand managers now realise the potential by being imaginative and creative and by bringing some added value to an event. For example Tennyson, a growing sales management agency, supports the Chichester Festival each year in an attempt to raise and maintain its local profile. The company's goal is to be regarded as a major local employer in an area where employment is high and it is difficult to recruit suitably qualified employees. Through its sponsorship Tennyson seeks to raise awareness and establish credibility.

Theoretical aspects of sponsorship

The notable lack of research into sponsorship, from a theoretical point of view, suggests that the role of sponsorship within the marketing communications mix has not been clearly understood. Problems associated with goals, tools and measurement methods and approaches have hindered both academics and practitioners. However, two developments have helped resolve some of these dilemmas. First, the development of relationship marketing and an acknowledgement that there are different audiences each with different relationship needs has helped understanding about which types of sponsorship should be used with which type of audience. Secondly, our understanding of the nature and role of integrated marketing communications within relationship marketing has helped focus thinking about the way in which sponsorship might contribute to the overall communication process.

> Suggests that the role of sponsorship within the marketing communications mix has not been clearly understood.

Relationship marketing is concerned with the concept of mutual value rather than the mere provision of goods and services (Gummesson, 1996) and is therefore compatible in many ways with the characteristics and range of benefits, both expected and realised, associated with sponsorship (Farrelly *et al.*, 2003). Sponsorship represents a form of collaborative communication, in the sense that two (or more) parties work together in order that one is enabled to reach the other's audience. Issues regarding the

> Sponsorship represents a form of collaborative communication.

TABLE 26.2 Basic variables underpinning interorganisational networks (Adapted from Olkkonen, 2001)

Network variable	Explanation
Actors	These are organisations and individuals who are interconnected. They control the other two variables.
Activities	Activities are created through the use of resources, and complex activity chains arise with different organisations (actors) contributing in different ways.
Resources	There are many different types of resource that can be combined in different ways to create new resources. The relationships that organisations develop create resource ties and these ties become shaped and adapted as the relationship develops.

relationship between the parties concerned will impact on the success of a sponsorship arrangement and any successive arrangements. As Farrelly *et al.* quite rightly point out, further work concerning the key drivers of sponsorship and relationship marketing is required as sponsorship matures as an increasingly potent form of marketing communications.

Olkkonen (2001) adopted a similar approach as he considered sponsorship within an interactional, relationships and ultimately network approach. The network approach considers the range of relationships that impact on organisations within markets and therefore considers non-buyers and other organisations, indeed all who are indirectly related to the exchange process. This network concept is considered in Chapters 8 and 9. In doing so this approach moves beyond the simple dyadic process adopted by the interaction interpretation. Some scholars have advanced a broad conceptual model within which to consider interorganisational networks (Hakansson and Snehota, 1995, cited by Olkkonen). These are actors, activities and resources. See Table 26.2.

> Considered sponsorship within an interactional, relationships and ultimately network approach.

A relationship consists of activity links based on organisations working together. Some of the activities will use particular resources in different configurations and differing levels of intensity. These activities will impact on other organisations and affect the way they use resources. In addition, organisations try to develop their attractiveness to other organisations in order to access other resources and networks. This is referred to as network identity and is a base for determining an organisation's value as a network partner. Sponsorship, therefore, can be seen as a function of an organisation's value to others in a network. The sponsored and the sponsor are key actors in sponsorship networks but agencies, event organisers, media networks and consultancies are also actors, each of whom will be connected (networked) with the sponsor and sponsored. See ViewPoint 26.3.

> A function of an organisation's value to others in a network.

Sponsorship has, traditionally, lacked a strong theoretical base, relying on managerial cause and effect explanations and loose marketing communications mix interpretations. The network approach may not be the main answer but it does advance our thought, knowledge and research opportunities with respect to this subject.

ViewPoint 26.3   Networked Snowboards

Nokia Mobile Phones (the sponsor) contracted to be the title sponsor for the International Ski Federation's (the sponsored) Snowboard World Cup. In addition to these key actors, various marketing communication agencies, hospitality agencies, Halva (which distributes media rights), Nokia's production team for its own television interests and local event organisers combine in various ways to construct outcomes seen to be of value to all actors in the network. The relationship between the key actors was largely legalistic but all possessed resources that were not only attractive to the others but which also helped form resource ties as a result of the activity chains that formed between them.

Source: For a detailed account and analysis of this ViewPoint and associated issues, see the source paper by Olkkonen (2001).

Types of sponsorship

It is possible to identify particular areas within which sponsorship has been used. See Table 26.3. These areas are sports, programme/broadcast, the arts, and others that encompass activities such as wildlife/conservation and education. Of all of these, sport has attracted most attention and sponsorship money.

Sport has attracted most attention and sponsorship money.

Sports sponsorship

Sports activities have been very attractive to sponsors, partly because of the high media coverage they attract. Sport is the leading type of sponsorship, mainly for the following reasons:

1. Sport has the propensity to attract large audiences, not only at each event but more importantly through the media that attach themselves to these activities.

TABLE 26.3 Long-term trends in the UK sponsorship market by sector, 1980–2003 (£ million)

	Sports	Arts	Broadcast	Other	Total
1980	30	3	–	2	35
1990	223	35	7	16	281
1995	285	83	75	35	478
2000	401	150	176	80	807
2002	429	111	193	58	791
2003	411	120	199*	63*	793

* estimated.
Source: Mintel, Ipsos.

EXHIBIT 26.1 Siemens, sponsors of Real Madrid Football Club

2. Sport provides a simplistic measure of segmentation, so that as audiences fragment generally, sport provides an opportunity to identify and reach often large numbers of people who share particular characteristics.

3. Visibility opportunities for the sponsor are high in a number of sporting events because of the duration of each event (e.g. the Olympics or the FIFA World Cup).

Barclaycard's sponsorship of the football Premier League and Coca-Cola's sponsorship of the football Championship have been motivated partly by the attraction of large and specific target audiences with whom a degree of fit is considered to exist. The constant media attention enables the sponsors' names to be disseminated to distant audiences, many of them overseas.

Marshall and Cook (1992) found that event sponsorship (e.g. the Olympics or the Ideal Home Exhibition) is the most popular form of sponsorship activity undertaken by organisations. This was followed by team, league and individual support.

Golf has attracted a great deal of sponsorship money, mainly because it has a global upmarket appeal and generates good television and press coverage. Golf clubs are also well suited for corporate entertainment and offer the chance of playing as well as watching. Volvo sponsored the European Golf Championship for the period 1996–2000 for £20 million. Johnny Walker has put £11 million into the game throughout the world (Wighton, 1995). Toyota used to support the World Matchplay Championship at Wentworth each year because the tournament fitted into a much wider promotion programme. Toyota dealers sponsored competitions at their local courses,

ViewPoint 26.4 Sailing sponsorship

Ellen MacArthur's second place in the Vendée Globe solo round-the-world yacht race that ended in February 2001 resulted in considerable media exposure for her main sponsor, the Kingfisher Group, after whom her boat was named. The Group's recent purchase of several French companies (France being a country enthusiastic about sailing) meant that the heroism and media interest in MacArthur's achievement was extremely high.

Kingfisher's investment of £2 million was easily recouped if the strong positive media coverage was correctly valued at about £50 million media equivalents. However, as Hill (2001) reports, the overall success of the sponsorship lay in the supporting promotional campaign.

with qualifiers going through to a final at Wentworth. The winner of that played in the pro-am before the World Matchplay. Toyota incorporated the tournament into a range of incentive and promotional programmes and flew in top distributors and fleet customers from around the world. In addition the environment was used to build customer relationships.

Programme sponsorship

While becoming established in North America in the 1980s, television programme sponsorship only began to receive serious attention in the UK in the late 1990s. The market was worth around £200 million (estimates vary) in 2003 and is growing, partly because of a relaxation by the Independent Television Commission in the regulations. However, the visibility that each sponsor is allowed has been strictly controlled

The visibility that each sponsor is allowed has been strictly controlled.

ViewPoint 26.5 Rugby World Cup

The Rugby World Cup finals held in Australia in 2003 attracted a number of different sponsors, termed official worldwide partners.

Heineken was the official beer and one of its goals was to add to the experience of the event for rugby fans and beer drinkers all over the world, regardless of whether they are at the game, at home or at their local bar or pub.

Visa's sponsorship was partly shaped by its desire to be associated with some of the world's most recognised brands. One brand in particular was Avis, with whom a competition was run.

British Airways and Qantas were the official airlines of the tournament and were responsible for flying teams, officials and international visitors into Australia and carrying Australian fans to matches around the country.

Peugeot was the official car of the tournament and it used the occasion to help launch its 307 Tourer model. This was used to transport players and officials between locations.

EXHIBIT 26.2 Sports sponsorship in action. England national rugby team sponsored by O2
Jonny Wilkinson, captain of the England national rugby team shown supporting the O2 sponsorship.

to certain times, and before, during the break and after each programme with the credits. Allen (2000) reports that while it is still not intended that sponsors influence the content or scheduling of a programme so as to affect the editorial independence and responsibility of the broadcaster, it is now permissible to allow the sponsor's product to be seen along with the sponsor's name in bumper credits and to allow greater flexibility in terms of the use of straplines. There is a requirement on the broadcaster to ensure that the sponsored credit is depicted in such a way that it cannot be mistaken as a spot advertisement. So, Hedburg (2000) gives the example of Nescafé sponsoring *Friends* and shows a group of people sitting on a sofa and drinking coffee and of *Coronation Street* sponsor Cadbury's, which presents a whole chocolate street and chocolate characters.

Masthead programming, where the publisher of a magazine such as *Amateur Photographer* sponsors a programme in a related area, such as *Photography for Beginners*, is generally not permitted, although the regulations surrounding this type of activity are being relaxed.

There are a number of reasons why programme sponsorship is appealing. First, it allows clients to avoid the clutter associated with spot advertising. In that sense it creates a space or mini-world in which the sponsor can create awareness and provide brand identity cues unhindered by other brands. Secondly, it represents a cost-effective medium when compared with spot advertising. It is expected that the cost of programme sponsorship will increase as the value of this type of communication is appreciated by clients (Fry, 1997). Thirdly, the use of credits around a programme offers opportunities for the target audience to make associations between the sponsor and the programme.

> The use of credits around a programme offers opportunities for the target audience to make associations between the sponsor and the programme.

Research by the Bloxam Group suggests that for a sponsorship to work there needs to be a linkage between the product and the programme. Links that are spurious, illogical or inappropriate are very often rejected by viewers. For example, Summers (1995) argues that 'Tango's sponsorship of the youth programme *The Word* was regarded as about right but the Prudential's link with *Film on Four* was not seen to link at all well'.

The same research suggests that viewers claim to own their favourite programmes. Therefore sponsors should acknowledge this relationship and act accordingly, perhaps as a respectful guest, and not intrude too heavily on the programme. They should certainly resist any active participation in the programme. 'If Pop Larkin starts asking for a cup of Tetley, then that's not right', claims Summers, and product placement issues begin to confuse matters.

Programme sponsorship is not seen as a replacement for advertising; indeed, the argument that sponsorship is not a part of advertising is demonstrated by the point that many sponsors continue with their spot advertising when running major sponsorships.

Cadbury's sponsorship of the premier UK soap opera, *Coronation Street*, which began in 1996, is reported to have cost £10 million each year, when all the additional promotional activities and requirements are considered. The linkage established between the two parties (Cadbury's and *Coronation Street*) exemplifies the view about the relationship and the linkages. 'The best sponsorships are those where there is an equivalence of stature between the two partners', according to Richard Frost, Cadbury's head of public relations. Research indicates that those aware of the sponsorship regarded the chocolate and the company more positively than those unaware of the linkage. Cadbury's was also awarded higher marks for being up to date and a supporter of the local community (Smith, 1997).

ViewPoint 26.6   Imperial Leather tops the Games

Imperial Leather undertook a leading sponsorship role within the Commonwealth Games in 2002. Rather than attempt to build a sports performance association for the luxury soap brand and to adopt the normally serious tone of an official endorser the sponsorship was used to develop a set of fun values that matched the unofficial name 'The Friendly Games'.

This was implemented by a media neutral approach aimed at trade, consumers and employees. During the Games, three different TV advertisements were run featuring diving, athletics and gymnastics. In addition to normal public relations and sales promotions (including competitions and sampling events) the main media used were outdoor and press, signage, ambient plus online microsites. During the two weeks of the games £880,000 worth of extra sales were found to be definitively related to the sponsorship. In direct comparison to many of the other leading sponsors, all of who spent far more on advertising prior to the Games than Imperial Leather, research showed that the soap brand recorded the highest spontaneous awareness of all the sponsors.

Source: Adapted from Hawtin (2004).

Arts sponsorship

Arts sponsorship was very successful in the 1980s and 1990s, as responsibility for funding the arts in the UK has shifted from the government to the private sector and business in particular. Growth has slowed down, partly because of the increasing need to justify such investments, partly because of the increasing opportunities to reach target audiences and also because it is difficult to engage in these very visible activities when profits are declining and company restructuring activities are of greater concern to those being made redundant or being displaced.

Arts sponsorship, according to Thorncroft (1996), began as a philanthropic exercise, with business giving something back to the community. It was a means of developing corporate image and was used extensively by tobacco companies as they attempted to reach their customer base. It then began to be appreciated for its corporate hospitality opportunities: a cheaper, more civilised alternative to sports sponsorship, and one that appealed more to women.

Many organisations sponsor the arts as a means of enhancing their corporate status.

Many organisations sponsor the arts as a means of enhancing their corporate status and as a means of clarifying their name. Another important reason why organisations use sponsorship is to establish and maintain favourable contact with key business people, often at board level, together with other significant public figures. Through related corporate hospitality, companies can reach substantial numbers of their targeted key people.

NTL uses the benefits of sponsorship to enhance the corporate body, to increase awareness of the company and to change part of the corporate image. Others use sponsorship to influence image and awareness factors at the brand level, such as 7-Up, Foster's and Budweiser (Meenaghan, 1998).

Most recently, sponsorship has been used to reach specific groups of consumers. Beck's, part of Scottish & Newcastle Breweries, has used sponsorship to position the brand as an upmarket beer for free-spending young professionals. To accomplish this, exhibitions by avant-garde artists such as Gilbert and George and Damien Hirst have been supported (Thorncroft, 1996).

The sponsorship of the arts has moved from being a means of supporting the community to a sophisticated means of targeting and positioning brands. Sponsorship, once part of corporate public relations, has developed skills that can assist marketing public relations.

ViewPoint 26.7   Community sponsorship - R&S

Royal & SunAlliance has many commercial offices around the UK, but one of the more substantial is located in Horsham, West Sussex. It is by far the town's largest employer, with over 2,000 staff. For some time sections of the local community were alienated against the organisation despite the provision of considerable financial support. It transpires that one of the major reasons for the negative feelings stemmed from the huge building programme when the main campus building was developed in the town centre. The scale of the work was so large that the layout of the town centre was radically altered.

Royal & SunAlliance decided that it was important to generate positive, warmer feelings towards the organisation. So, in addition to financial assistance, the company now provides practical support, targeted where the community informs the company that it is most needed:

- *Photocopying*: charity newsletters, church magazine event programmes, information leaflets, posters and publicity material for events.

- *Design*: production of artwork for small groups.

- *Hosting*: provision of meeting, lecture and function rooms that are not used by the company during the weekends or evenings. Staff act as hosts and ushers as necessary.

- *Catering*: in-house facilities to support the hosting activities above.

- *Professional advice*: business advice delivered to voluntary groups through attendance at local committees.

- *Raffle prizes*: gifts surplus to the requirements of the direct marketing division are donated to charities for raffles to raise funds.

- *Minibuses*: company minibuses are used regularly to support local events, such as sponsored walks, students' educational trips and taking disabled children to swimming galas.

- *Town centre events*: major town events, such as festivals, Christmas decorations and the biennial Arts Fanfare, are rigorously supported, as are the local churches, schools, Chamber of Commerce and local health and emergency services.

- *Staff support*: the staff themselves are actively involved in voluntary activities in and around Horsham, and again the company seeks to support its employees in these pursuits.

The change from finance provider to resource facilitator appears to have had a major impact on the attitudes held by the community towards Royal & SunAlliance in Horsham. A corporate image study will be undertaken shortly to measure the degree of change. This use of sponsorship and public relations activities has been used to the benefit of all concerned and it seems that a positive dialogue has resulted in mutual understanding and goodwill.

Source: Information kindly supplied by Ann Seabrook, Community Liaison Manager for Royal & SunAlliance in Horsham.

These three main forms of sponsorship, sports, arts and programme, are not mutually exclusive and use of one does not necessarily prevent use of either of the others. NTL sponsors four major English and Scottish football teams to achieve brand awareness, particularly in areas where it seeks to develop cable services. NTL also undertakes programme sponsorship and work with *Who Wants to Be a Millionaire?*. This helps to develop brand values and may be more cost effective than spot advertising, especially at peak times. In addition to these two major sponsorships, NTL also supports the MacMillan Cancer Relief fund, perhaps to present a more caring or balanced identity for its various audiences. However, because of targeting issues many organisations find it more efficient to use one major form of sponsorship, supported by a range of secondary sponsorship activities.

Other forms of sponsorship

It has been argued that there is little opportunity to control messages delivered through sponsorship, and far less opportunity to encourage the target audiences to enter into a dialogue with sponsors. However, the awareness and image opportunities can be used by supporting either the local community or small-scale schemes.

Volkswagen wanted to be associated with the motoring environment rather than just the motorist.

Whitbread has been involved in supporting school programmes, environmental developments and other locally oriented activities because that is where its customers are based. Volkswagen wanted to be associated with the motoring environment rather than just the motorist. To help achieve this goal it sponsored the jackets worn by road-crossing wardens (lollipop people) so that the local authority was free to use the money once spent on uniforms on other aspects of road safety (Walker, 1995).

A fresh form of sponsorship emerged in 1997 as brands sought to leverage each other and achieve greater efficiencies and impact through association with each other. For example, Cable & Wireless (C&W) supported Barnardo's in its campaign to increase awareness of current issues, generate funds and redefine the image held of the charity. C&W provided the funds for the TV campaign and in return had a credit at the end of the commercial. The integrated campaign included radio, newspapers, direct marketing and leaflets in each of the 320 Barnardo's shops. C&W had previously involved Barnardo's in its own launch through direct response advertisements and also sponsored a major report published by Barnardo's about child care. Its has stated its intention to become involved with local community projects (Campbell, 1997).

The majority of sponsorships, regardless of type, are not the sole promotional activity undertaken by the sponsors. They may be secondary and used to support above-the-line work or they may be used as the primary form of communication but supported by a range of off-screen activities, such as sales promotions and (in particular) competitions.

This section would not be complete without mention of the phenomenon called 'ambush marketing'. This occurs when an organisation deliberately seeks an association with a particular event but does so without paying sponsorship fees. Such hijacking is undertaken with the purpose of influencing the audience to the extent that they believe the ambusher is legitimate. According to Meenaghan (1998), this can be achieved by overstating the organisation's involvement in the event, perhaps through major promotion activity using theme-based advertising or by sponsoring the media coverage of the event.

The role of sponsorship in the promotional mix

Whether sponsorship is a part of advertising, sales promotion or public relations has long been a source of debate. It is perhaps more natural and comfortable to align sponsorship with advertising. Since awareness is regarded as the principal objective of using sponsorship, advertising is a more complementary and accommodating part of the mix. Sales promotion from the sponsor's position is harder to justify, although from the perspective of the sponsored the value-added characteristic is interesting. The more traditional home for sponsorship is public relations (Witcher *et al.*, 1991). The sponsored, such as a football team, a racing car manufacturer or a theatre group, may be adjudged to perform the role of opinion former. Indirectly, therefore, messages are conveyed to the target audience with the support of significant participants who endorse and support the sponsor. This is akin to public relations activities.

Hastings (1984) contests that advertising messages can be manipulated and adapted to changing circumstances much more easily than those associated with sponsorship. He suggests that the audience characteristics of both advertising and sponsorship are very different. For advertising there are viewers and non-viewers. For sponsorship there are three groups of people that can be identified. First there are those who are directly involved with the sponsor or the event, the active participants. The second is a much larger group, consisting of those who attend sponsored events, and these are referred to as personal spectators. The third group is normally the largest, and comprises all those who are involved with the event through various media channels; these are regarded as media followers.

> The audience characteristics of both advertising and sponsorship are very different.

As if to demonstrate the potential sizes of these groups, estimates suggest that in excess of 4 million people attend the Formula 1 Grand Prix championship races (active participants) and over half a billion people (media followers) watch the races on television.

Exploratory research undertaken by Hoek *et al.* (1997) suggests that sponsorship is better able to generate awareness and a wider set of product-related attributes than advertising when dealing with non-users of a product, rather than users. There appears to be no discernible difference between the impact that these two promotional tools have with users.

The authors claim that sponsorship and advertising can be considered to work in approximately the same way if the ATR model developed by Ehrenberg (1974) is adopted (Chapter 18). Through the ATR model, purchase behaviour and beliefs are considered to be reinforced by advertising rather than new behaviour patterns being established. Advertising fulfils a means by which buyers can meaningfully defend their purchase patterns. Hoek *et al.* regard this approach as reasonably analogous to sponsorship. Sponsorship can create awareness and is more likely to confirm past behaviour than prompt new purchase behaviour. The implication, they conclude, is that, while awareness levels can be improved with sponsorship, other promotional tools are required to impact upon product experimentation or purchase intentions.

> Advertising can be considered to work in approximately the same way if the ATR model developed by Ehrenberg is adopted.

It was suggested earlier in this chapter that one of the opportunities that sponsorship offers is the ability to suggest that there is an association between the sponsored and the sponsor which may be of value to the message recipient. This implies that there is an indirect form of influence through sponsorship. This is supported by

Crimmins and Horn (1996), who argue that the persuasive impact of sponsorship is determined in terms of the strength of links that are generated between the brand and the event that is sponsored.

These authors claim that sponsorship can have a persuasive impact and that the degree of impact that a sponsorship might bring is as follows:

$$\begin{array}{c} \text{persuasive} \\ \text{impact} \end{array} = \begin{array}{c} \text{strength} \\ \text{of link} \end{array} \times \begin{array}{c} \text{duration} \\ \text{of the link} \end{array} \times \left\{ \begin{array}{c} \text{gratitude felt} \\ \text{due to the link} \end{array} + \begin{array}{c} \text{perceptual change} \\ \text{due to the link} \end{array} \right\}$$

The strength of the link between the brand and the event is an outcome of the degree to which advertising is used to communicate the sponsorship itself. Sponsors that failed to invest in advertising during the Olympic Games have been shown to be far less successful in building a link with the event than those who chose to invest.

The *duration of the link* is also important. Research based on the Olympic Games shows that those sponsors who undertook integrated marketing communications long before the event itself were far more successful than those who had not. The use of mass media advertising to communicate the involvement of the sponsor, the use of event graphics and logos on packaging, and the creative use of promotional tie-ins and in-store, event-related merchandising facilitated the long-term linkage with the sponsorship and added value to the campaign.

Gratitude exists if consumers realise that there is a link between a brand and an event.

Gratitude exists if consumers realise that there is a link between a brand and an event. Sixty per cent of US adults said that they 'try to buy a company's product if they support the Olympics'. They also stated that 'I feel I am contributing to the Olympics by buying the brands of Olympic sponsors'.

Perceptual change occurs as a result of consumers being able to understand the relationship (meaning) between a brand and an event. The sponsor needs to make this clear, as passive consumers may need the links laid out before them. The link between a swimwear brand and the Olympics may be obvious, but it is not always the case. Crimmins and Horn (1996) describe how Visa's 15 per cent perceived superiority advantage over MasterCard was stretched to 30 per cent during the 1992 Olympics and then settled at 20 per cent ahead one month after the Games had finished. The perceptual change was achieved through the messages that informed audiences that Visa was the one card that was accepted for the Olympic Games; American Express and MasterCard were not accepted.

This research, while based only upon a single event, indicates that sponsorship may bring advantages if care is taken to invest in communications long before and during the event to communicate the meaning between the brand and the event, which will leverage gratitude from a grateful audience.

Summary

Sponsorship of events, activities and organisations will continue to grow in significance, if only because of its effectiveness and value as a tool of marketing communications relative to the other tools in the mix. Organisations believe that sponsorship allows them access to specific target audiences and enhances their corporate image (Marshall and Cook, 1992). Other areas will become subject to sponsorship, such as the development of television programme sponsorship (for example the weather forecasts by Portman Building Society on Meridian and Tulip Computers on Sky).

There seems little doubt that the introduction of new products and brands can be assisted by the use of appropriate sponsorships. Indeed, it appears that sponsorship, in certain contexts, can be used to prepare markets for the arrival and penetration of new brands.

The evaluation of sponsorship arrangements poses a problem in that measurement is little better than that used for advertising. However, the impact and approach that sponsorship can have suggest that the two tools should be used together, coordinated, if not integrated, to develop awareness and strong brand associations and triggers. There is a warning, and that concerns the degree to which sponsorship is capable of changing purchase behaviour through persuasion. Organisations considering the use of sponsorship as a means of directly impacting upon the bottom line are likely to be disappointed. Other tools are required to stimulate behaviour; sponsorship alone is not capable of persuading target audiences to behave differently.

Review questions

1. What are the main opportunities that sponsorship opens up for organisations?
2. Why has sponsorship become such a major promotional tool in recent years?
3. If the objective of using sponsorship is to build awareness (among other things), then there is little point in using advertising. Discuss this view.
4. Name four types of sponsorship.
5. Why is sport more heavily sponsored than the arts or television programmes?
6. Chose eight sporting events and name the main sponsors. Why do you think they have maintained their associations with the events?
7. Consider five television programmes that are sponsored and evaluate how viewers might perceive the relationship between the programme content and the sponsor.
8. How might sponsorship have a persuasive impact on its target audiences? What is the formula used to measure this impact?
9. Explain the role of sponsorship within the promotional mix.
10. How might sponsorship develop in the future?

MINI-CASE
Tiger Beer

Mini-case written by Shauna Li Roolvink, Founder and Managing Director of BrandHub; Schubert Neo, Manager of International Sponsorship at Asia Pacific Breweries based in Singapore

The origins of Tiger Beer

The first Tiger Beer brew was launched in 1932 in Singapore by Malayan Breweries, a joint venture set up by Fraser & Neave Limited (F&N) and Heineken NV.

Over the years, Tiger Beer has become synonymous with quality, having won over 30 gold medals and awards throughout the world, including the prestigious Beer Industry International Award (BIIA) in the UK in 1998. In 2004, the brand also won the World Beer Cup for European-style Pilsners beating 44 international entries in the same category.

Today, Tiger Beer is the biggest selling premium beer in Singapore and Indochina and is enjoyed by millions of drinkers in over 60 countries in Asia, Australasia, Europe, North America, and Africa.

The Tiger brand

In European and other western-style markets such as North America and New Zealand, Tiger Beer is positioned as a premium foreign beer brand targeted at trend-setting, cosmopolitan consumers.

In Asia, where Tiger Beer is long established and enjoys market leadership in the premium beer segment within a number of markets, the brand's core target audiences are modern professional men from 25 to 35 years of age. In these markets, Tiger Beer is positioned as an everyday reward and recognition for Asians on their path to success. Tiger Beer's communication personifies masculinity, drive and determination within a social environment. It aims to maintain its perception as a world class and award-winning quality lager.

The role of sponsorship

In Asian markets where Tiger Beer is well established, sponsorship is one of the key pillars of the brand. As a powerful business tool, sponsorship is used to cut through advertising clutter and build brand affinity through customer experiential engagement. This is achieved through such platforms as football, golf and music events, which are popular with the target market. The correct choice of sponsorship is important to help build appropriate associations with world class and popular/prestigious events and in doing so develop premium brand status and equity.

The association with sports in particular helps to reinforce Tiger Beer's brand personality (masculinity, drive and determination in a social setting) and it also complements with Tiger Beer's core target market of professional males aged between 25 and 35.

Tiger Beer believe that sponsorship helps to build customer loyalty and affinity, which is then translated to consumption and sales revenue. However, in today's competitive environment, the challenge is to find ways to engage consumers with the brand through the right sponsorship platform(s) and remain ahead of the pack.

Multi-level sponsorship

For Tiger Beer sponsorship is approached at three levels: international, regional and local. Sponsorship of international events helps to reinforce Tiger Beer's brand credentials as an international and world class lager which helps bring world-class events to their consumers. Examples of such brand sponsorships include the broadcast sponsorship of the English Premier League in Southeast Asia. Tiger is the official beer brand for the Arsenal team in Singapore, Vietnam and Thailand and the Tiger Skins – a golf skins competition which has featured golfers such as VJ Singh, Sergio Garcia and other top PGA players.

Regional sponsorship events help to solidify Tiger's position as one of the leading beer brands in the region. Tiger beer's regional sponsorship property is the Tiger Cup, Southeast Asia's premier football tournament.

Local sponsorship events help to strengthen Tiger Beer's bond with local consumers in each market. Tiger's local event sponsorship programmes help to complement the regional and international platforms of football and golf whilst at the same time catering for the local market requirements for music and other food and beverage relevant platforms.

Events are selected based on their appeal to the brand's target market as well as the fit with Tiger Beer's brand personality.

Tiger Beer and Football

Football has long been regarded as the most popular sport in Southeast Asia and Tiger Beer has a long tradition of supporting football at all levels – international, regional and local.

As stated earlier, at an international level, Tiger Beer is one of the four main sponsors of the English Premier League broadcast in Southeast Asia. The others are the multinational brands Nokia, Toyota and Toshiba. The EPL games are broadcast live to 210 million homes across Asia on ESPN Star Sports.

The programme sponsorship allows Tiger Beer to enjoy the regional association with EPL, broadcast through a combination of on-air and online branding plus advertising entitlements around all 'live' matches and repeats on ESPN and Star Sports. Together with the official beer sponsorship of Arsenal FC, these sponsorships also give Tiger Beer the opportunity to engage consumers through EPL viewing parties, consumer promotions and actual trips to watch the EPL matches live.

Chris Kidd, Asia Pacific Breweries Director of Group Marketing, said, 'The EPL has a huge following in Asia and for Tiger Beer, this sponsorship, as well as our tie-up with Arsenal in several Southeast Asian countries, allows our customers the chance to watch and experience the number one league in the world.'

At the regional level, Tiger Beer is the title sponsor of the Tiger Cup. Launched in 1996 by the

EXHIBIT 26.3 Tiger Beer, sponsors of the Tiger Cup

ASEAN Football Federation, the biennial competition comprises members from 10 countries in Southeast Asia. Now in its 5th tournament, the Tiger Cup has become the most prestigious football championship of ASEAN. This has been primarily due to Tiger Beer's extensive promotional and PR activities to popularise and raise the profile of the tournament.

At the local level, Tiger Beer sponsors local leagues such as the S-League in Singapore.

Maximising value of the sponsorship

Tiger Beer's marketing activities are closely aligned to these sponsorship events in order to maximise their value. The approach is to provide 360 degree consumer engagement via ATL communication, sponsorship packaging, retail promotions, trade relationship building, PR, on ground leveraging and engagement through the website.

In the case of the Tiger Cup, the entire range of activities are launched at least six weeks prior to the event, along with trade/retail promotions, point-of-sales materials, promotion packs and the Web site.

Evaluating sponsorship

Pre- and post-sponsorship evaluation is regarded as essential in order to measure the effectiveness and value of any sponsorship activity. In general, these evaluations cover total costs of sponsorship, the media value of the sponsorship, the impact on consumer attitudes, usage of the brand and the incremental sales that are generated. Such feedback is necessary when deciding on the renewal of sponsorship contracts and for fine tuning Tiger Beer's marketing and sponsorship programmes and tactics.

Key learning points

Over the years, Tiger Beer has gained much insight into the effectiveness of sponsorships. Some key learning points include:

1 Use of the correct sponsorship platform in new markets can be a very cost effective way of establishing brand recognition and recall.
2 When activated effectively and consistently, sponsorship can build brand affinity, loyalty and leadership in markets where brand presence is fairly established.
3 It is crucial to use the media and PR to communicate the sponsorship to as wide an audience as possible so as to co-opt more consumers to the sponsorship event and the brand.

Questions

1 Which methods and techniques might Tiger Beer use to measure the effectiveness of their different sponsorships?
2 Suggest other events that Tiger Beer might choose to sponsor. What might be the key criteria management might use when deciding which events to support?
3 To what extent should Tiger Beer use the other tools of the marketing communication mix to support their programme sponsorship?
4 In a country of your choice, determine the key regulations which control the use of programme sponsorship.

References

Allen, D. (2000) TV sponsorship rules are eased. *Media Week*, 14 April, p. 3.

Balfour, M. (2000) Precision technology delivered in record time. *Financial Times*, 25 March.

Campbell, L. (1997) C&W underpins Barnardos' ads. *Marketing*, 30 October, p. 4.

Crimmins, J. and Horn, M. (1996) Sponsorship: from management ego trip to marketing success. *Journal of Advertising Research* (July/August), pp. 11–21.

Dolphin, R.R. (2003) Sponsorship: perspectives on its strategic role. *Corporate Communications: an International Journal*, **8**(3), pp. 173–86.

Ehrenberg, A.S.C. (1974) Repetitive advertising and the consumer. *Journal of Advertising Research*, **14** (April), pp. 25–34.

Farrelly, F., Quester, P. and Mavondo, F. (2003) Collaborative communication in sponsor relations. *Corporate Communications: an International Journal*, **8**(2), pp. 128–38.

Fry, A. (1997) Keeping the right company. *Marketing*, 22 May, pp. 24–5.

Grimes, E. and Meenaghan, T. (1998) Focusing commercial sponsorship on the internal corporate audience. *International Journal of Advertising*, **17**(1), pp. 51–74.

Gummesson, E. (1996) Relationship marketing and imaginary organisations: a synthesis. *European Journal of Marketing*, **30**(2), pp. 31–45.

Hakansson, H. and Snehota, I. (1995) *Developing Relationships in Business Networks*. London: Routledge.

Harverson, P. (1998) Why IT companies take the risk. *Financial Times*, 2 June.

Hastings, G. (1984) Sponsorship works differently from advertising. *International Journal of Advertising*, **3**, pp. 171–6.

Hawtin, L. (2004) Imperial Leather: a winning performance. *Admap* (April), pp. 23–5.

Hedburg, A., (2000) Bumper crop. *Marketing Week*, 19 October, pp. 28–32.

Hill, A. (2001) On the crest of a sponsorship wave. *PR Week*, 23 February, p. 9.

Hoek, J., Gendall, P., Jeffcoat, M. and Orsman, D. (1997) Sponsorship and advertising: a comparison of their effects. *Journal of Marketing Communications*, **3**, pp. 21–32.

Javalgi, R.G., Traylor, M.B., Gross, A.C. and Lampman, E. (1994) Awareness of sponsorship and corporate image: an empirical investigation. *Journal of Advertising*, **24** (June), pp. 1–12.

McCormack, D. (2000) Music festivals grow up. *PR Week*, 18 August, p. 11.

Marshall, D.W. and Cook, G. (1992) The corporate (sports) sponsor. *International Journal of Advertising*, **11**, pp. 307–24.

Meenaghan, T. (1991) The role of sponsorship in the marketing communications mix. *International Journal of Advertising*, **10**, pp. 35–47.

Meenaghan, T. (1998) Current developments and future directions in sponsorship. *International Journal of Advertising*, **17**(1), pp. 3–28.

Olkkonen, R. (2001) Case study: the network approach to international sport sponsorship arrangement. *The Journal of Business and Industrial Marketing*, **16**(4), pp. 309–29.

Pope, N.K.L. and Voges, K.E. (1999) Sponsorship and image: a replication and extension. *Journal of Marketing Communications*, **5**, pp. 17–28.

Reed, D. (1994) Sponsorship. *Campaign*, 20 May, pp. 37–8.

Smith, A. (1997) UK sponsors look to US. *Financial Times*, 24 March, p. 16.

Summers, D. (1995) Sponsors' careful link with TV. *Financial Times*, 2 March, p. 14.

Thorncroft, A. (1996) Business arts sponsorship: arts face a harsh set of realities. *Financial Times*, 4 July, p. 1.

Thwaites, D. (1994) Corporate sponsorship by the financial services industry. *Journal of Marketing Management*, **10**, pp. 743–63.

Tripodi, J.A. (2001) Sponsorship: a confirmed weapon in the promotional armoury. *International Journal of Sports Marketing and Sponsorship*, **3**(1) (March/April) paper 5.

Walker, J.-A. (1995) Community service. *Marketing Week*, 20 October, pp. 85–90.

Wighton, D. (1995) The FT guide to golf: the price of playing. *Financial Times*, 20 July, p. xxvii.

Witcher, B., Craigen, G., Culligan, D. and Harvey, A. (1991) The links between objectives and functions in organisational sponsorship. *International Journal of Advertising*, **10**, pp. 13–33.

Direct marketing

27

Direct marketing is a strategy used to create a personal and intermediary-free dialogue with customers. This should be a measurable activity and it is very often media based, with a view to creating and sustaining a mutually rewarding relationship. The development and use of direct marketing principles by a variety of organisations are testimony to the power of this personal form of communication.

Aims and objectives

The aim of this chapter is to explore the characteristics of direct marketing and to develop an understanding of interactive marketing communications.

The objectives of this chapter are to:

1. introduce and define direct marketing;
2. consider the reasons behind the growth and development of this new marketing communications tool;
3. examine the relationship of direct brands and direct response media and their role within the marketing communications mix;
4. appreciate the significance of the database in direct marketing;
5. identify and consider different direct response media;
6. consider the value of integrating the activities of direct marketing with other elements of the mix.

Introduction

From previous discussions about relational and marketing exchanges (Chapters 1 and 9), it should be apparent that the long-term goal of most organisations is to build a long-term relationship with each of their customers. Most of the marketing communications disciplines use mass media to address huge audiences, in what is essentially one-way communication – not an ideal way of developing relationships. Advertising communicates with large audiences and primarily seeks to provide certain information, affect emotions and frame intentions when the next purchase opportunity arises. Advertising is not capable of talking personally to individual customers, nor is it used to generate personal responses. Furthermore, those who choose to use advertising are constrained by the page sizes, paper types, fonts and style or the available spots, the skill of the media planner and the programmes that are available.

> The long-term goal of most organisations is to build a long-term relationship with each of their customers.

Sales promotions are designed to generate an immediate sale, but the information is not stored or used in such a way that a relationship is deliberately created and sustained and the perceived value of a brand can be diluted. Public relations seeks to develop favourable interest and goodwill by piggy-backing on other media. Personal selling is certainly founded upon the need to establish long-term personal relationships. However, the range of tasks that the sales force is expected to complete means that only a small percentage of its time can be focused upon generating an immediate response. Personal selling is expensive and there is variable control over the messages that are transmitted by individual members of the sales force.

In addition to these promotional tool deficiencies, the distribution element of the marketing mix was the last to receive attention. Faced with an increasing lack of product/service differentiation and margins being eroded through price competition, the marketing channel was ripe for investigation and review. It became clear that many cost advantages could be achieved through a more direct approach to the market. This meant sidelining or avoiding expensive intermediaries (channel network members) and providing opportunities to improve quality and service provision. For these main reasons, direct marketing has developed and flourished in recent years.

The role of direct marketing

Direct marketing is a term used to refer to all media activities that generate a series of communications and responses with an existing or potential customer. Early on there was considerable debate about the term 'direct marketing' itself. It was often referred to as direct mail or as 'curriculum marketing, dialogue marketing, personal marketing and database marketing' (Bird, 1989). This proliferation of terms reflects the range of activities that are undertaken in an attempt to prompt a response from a customer.

> Direct marketing is a term used to refer to all media activities that generate a series of communications and responses with an existing or potential customer.

Terminology has settled in favour of direct marketing, and this broad approach will be adopted here. However, readers are advised that this chapter on direct marketing should not be read in isolation, as issues concerning direct communications are embedded throughout this text. Particular reference should be made to Chapters 1, 9, 10 and 21.

Primarily direct marketing is concerned with the management of customer behaviour.

Primarily direct marketing is concerned with the management of customer behaviour and is used to complement the strengths and weaknesses of the other communication disciplines. To put this is a very basic way, advertising and public relations provide information and develop brand values but sales promotion and direct marketing drive response, most notably behaviour.

For a long time direct mail was the main tool of direct marketing but the development of information technology and, in particular, the database, have enabled the introduction of a range of other media. These are used to communicate directly with individual customers and often carry a behavioural (call-to-action) message. Typically, direct marketing agencies work across a variety of media including the telephone, Internet, direct mail, email, press and posters. No single media channel dominates their work. In an era where the talk is about integration and media neutrality (Chapter 11) the direct marketing industry is in a strong position to provide a wide range of client communication services. All the elements of the promotional mix can be used with direct marketing to support and build meaningful relationships with consumers and members of the various stakeholder networks.

For a long time direct mail was the main tool of direct marketing.

ViewPoint 27.1　Bailey's call-to-action

Direct marketing's ability to provoke action is demonstrated by Baileys appointing a direct marketing agency, Craik Jones, to encourage more frequent drinking of its product.

Research indicated that Baileys was perceived as a special occasion drink, but in order to drive future growth this perception needed to be changed. By presenting the drink as one that can be consumed on different, more informal occasions, and by developing the database into a resource that can be used to support a number of campaigns across various communication channels, it was intended to reposition the drink and achieve the organisation's goals. Targeted, individual special offers, celebratory free gifts and providing advice about general promotions would also be possible as part of the move towards CRM. The budget for this was set at £500,000 but the above-the-line spend was also increased by 40 per cent to support the brand.

Source: Adapted from Kleinman (2000).

Direct marketing is a strategy used to create and sustain a personal and intermediary-free dialogue with customers, potential customers and other significant stakeholders. In most cases this is a media based activity and offers great scope for the collection and utilisation of pertinent and measurable data. There are a number of important issues associated with this definition. The first is that the activity should be measurable. That is, any response(s) must be associated with a particular individual, a particular media activity and a particular outcome, such as a sale or enquiry for further information. The second issue concerns the rewards that each party perceives through participation in the relationship. The customer receives a variety of tangible and intangible satisfactions. These include shopping convenience, time utility and the satisfaction and trust that can develop between customers and a provider of quality products and services when the customers realise and appreciate the personal attention they appear to be receiving.

This is a media based activity and offers great scope for the collection and utilisation of pertinent and measurable data.

Underpinning the direct marketing approach are the principles of trust and commitment, just as they support the validity of the other promotional tools. If a meaningful relationship is to be developed over the long term and direct marketing is an instrumental part of the dialogue, then the pledges that the parties make to develop commitment and stability are of immense importance (Ganesan, 1994).

Indeed, the concept of establishing trust is vital if relational exchanges are to be developed. Trust is a multidimensional construct (Morgan and Hunt, 1994) and the need to ensure that it is recognised and accepted by parties where direct marketing is used is highly important (Fletcher and Peters, 1997).

The direct marketer derives benefits associated with precision target marketing and minimised waste, increased profits and the opportunities to provide established customers with other related products, without the huge costs of continually having to find new customers. In addition, direct marketing represents a strategic approach to the market. It actively seeks to remove channel intermediaries, reduce costs, and improve the quality and speed of service for customers, and through this bundle of attributes presents a new offering for the market, which in itself may provide competitive advantage. First Direct, Virgin Direct and the pioneer, Direct Line, all provide these advantages, which have enabled them to secure strong positions in the market.

Types of direct brand

Direct marketing is assumed to refer to direct promotional activity, but this is only part of the marketing picture. Using direct response media in this way is an increasingly common activity used to augment the communication activities surrounding a brand and to provide a new dimension to the context in which brands are perceived.

In addition to these promotional advantages there are two main types of direct brands: *pedigree direct* brands and *hybrid direct* brands (Foster, 1996). These reflect their origins in the sense that the pedigree direct brand is developed to deliberately exploit a market-positioning opportunity. Hybrid direct brands are essentially the same except that the brand heritage is rooted in traditional distribution channels, which may well continue to be a route to market used in parallel to the direct route. Therefore, as Foster points out, the main difficulty facing the hybrid direct brand is the organisational culture: its context and heritage. With these brands there is a generally accepted approach to the market and commonality as to the way things should be done. Even the systems and processes associated with the intermediary-based approach are established and need to be altered to meet the needs of a new type of customer.

There are two main types of direct brands.

However, there is further difficulty, which lies with the image that the customer base and other stakeholders have of the hybrid direct brand. It represents a change from the frame in which stakeholders expect to see the brand. Care therefore needs to be taken with the marketing communications to ensure that the transition is carried out in such a way that the credibility of the brand is maintained.

To ensure that the transition is carried out in such a way that the credibility of the brand is maintained.

From this review it is possible to see direct marketing as part of one of the types shown in Figure 27.1. These are not hierarchical in the sense that there has to be progression from one type to another. They are reflections of the way different organisations use direct marketing and the degree to which the tool is used strategically.

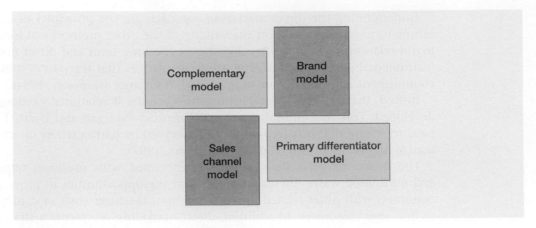

FIGURE 27.1 Types of direct marketing

Type 1: complementary tool

At this level, direct response media are used to complement the other promotional activities used to support a brand. Their main use is to generate leads and to some extent awareness, information and reinforcement. For example, financial services companies, tour operators and travel agents use DRTV to stimulate enquiries, loans and bookings, respectively.

Type 2: primary differentiator

Rather than be one of a number of promotional tools, at this level direct response media are the primary form of communication. They are used to provide a distinct point of differentiation from competitor offerings. They are the principal form of communication. In addition to the Type 1 advantages they are used to cut costs, avoid the use of intermediaries and reach finely targeted audiences (for example book, music and wine clubs).

Type 3: sales channel

A third use for direct marketing and telemarketing in particular concerns its use as a means of developing greater efficiency and as a means of augmenting current services. By utilising direct marketing as a sales tool, multiple sales channels can be used to meet the needs of different customer segments and so release resources to be deployed elsewhere and more effectively. This idea is developed further later in this chapter.

> Multiple sales channels can be used to meet the needs of different customer segments.

Type 4: brand vehicle

At this final level, brands are developed to exploit market space opportunities. These may be the pedigree or hybrid brands identified earlier (for example, Direct Line, Virgin Direct and Eagle Star Direct). The strategic element is most clearly evident at this level.

Indeed, the entire organisation and its culture are oriented to the development of customer relationships through direct marketing activities.

The growth of direct marketing

There can be little doubt that, of all the tools in the marketing communications mix, direct marketing has experienced the most growth in the last ten years. The reasons for this growth are many and varied, but two essential drivers behind the surge in direct marketing have been technological advances and changing buyer lifestyles and expectations. These two forces for change demonstrate quite dramatically how a change in the context can impact on marketing communications.

Growth driver 1: technology

As discussed previously in Chapter 10, rapid advances in technology have heralded the arrival of new sources and forms of information. Technology has enabled the collection, storage and analysis of customer data to become relatively simple, cost effective and straightforward. Furthermore, the management of this information is increasingly available to small businesses as well as the major blue chip multinational organisations. Computing costs have plummeted, while there has been a correspondingly enormous increase in the power that technology can deliver.

Technology has enabled the collection, storage and analysis of customer data.

The technological surge has in turn stimulated three major developments. The first concerns the ability to capture information, the second to process and analyse it and the third to represent part or all of the information as a form of communication to stimulate dialogue and interaction to collect further information. See Table 27.1.

Organisations have been able to make increasing use of technological developments within marketing communications. Indeed, all areas of the mix have benefited as new and more effective and efficient processes and methods of communication evolve. Advances in technology are responsible for the demise of some traditional forms of communication. For example, the impact of mass communications and advertising in particular as a single device has diminished in favour of a more personalised and integrated approach to communications, enabled by technology. This gives the ability to target potential customers much more precisely, at any location and at lower cost.

TABLE 27.1 Advances in technology

Data capture and collection
Web site registration data, scanners, smart cards, loyalty schemes, marketing research

Information processing
Database marketing, warehousing, mining

Communication and interaction
Greater precision in segmentation and targeting effectiveness, direct mail, telemarketing, SMS and mobile marketing plus a simultaneous decline in traditional media consumption/effectiveness.

TABLE 27.2 Changing market context

Lifestyles and expectations
Inner directedness, pluralism, individualism

Fragmentation
Audience, media

Management requirements
Costs, accountability, competition, speed of response

Growth driver 2: changing market context

The lifestyles of people in Western European and North American societies, in particular, have evolved and will continue to do so. Generally, the brash phase of *selfishness* in the 1980s gave way to a more caring, society-oriented *selflessness* in the 1990s. The start of the twenty-first century suggests that a *self-awareness* lifestyle might predominate and be reflected in brand purchase behaviour and a greater emphasis on long-term value and different brand values. Continued fragmentation of the media and audiences requires finely tuned segmentation and communication devices. Direct marketing offers a solution to this splintering and micro market scenario and addresses some of the changing needs of management, namely for speed of response and justification for the use and allocation of resources. See Table 27.2.

> **Fragmentation of the media and audiences requires finely tuned segmentation and communication devices.**

The twin impact of these drivers can be seen within the emergence of ideas about integrated marketing communications and an overall emphasis on relationship marketing principles. The enhanced ability of organisations to collect, store and manage customer lifestyle and transactional data, to generate personalised communications and their general enthusiasm for retention and loyalty schemes have combined to provide a huge movement towards an increased use of direct and interactive marketing initiatives.

The role of the database

At the hub of successful direct marketing and CRM activities is the database. A database is a collection of files held on a computer that contain data that can be related to one another and which can reproduce information in a variety of formats. Normally the data consist of information collected about prospects and customers that are used to determine appropriate segments and target markets and to record responses to communications conveyed by the organisation. A database therefore plays a role as a storage, sorting and administrative device to assist direct and personalised communications.

Age and lifestyle data are important signals of product usage. However, there will be attitudinal variances between people in similar groups demanding further analysis. This can, according to Reed (2000), uncover clues concerning what the direct mail piece should look like. So, older customers do not like soft colours and small type and sentences should not begin with 'and' or 'but'.

> **Age and lifestyle data are important signals of product usage.**

ViewPoint 27.2   Supermarkets direct

The lead organisations in the UK grocery market use databases to hold detailed information about their customers' purchases. The database holds information about its customers that they can mine and then target sales promotions, advertising and direct marketing communications. For example, each quarter Tesco sends out a statement to its 10 million regular Clubcard users and includes promotional vouchers and coupons mirroring each customer's purchases. As a result, there are 100,000 different promotional messages reflecting the preferences and buying habits of customers rather than the supermarket's desire to sell particular products (Marsh, 2001).

Increasingly, the information stored is gathered from transactions undertaken with customers, but on its own this information is not enough and further layering of data is required. The recency/frequency/monetary (RFM) model provides a base upon which lifestyle data, often bought in from a list agency, can be used to further refine the information held. Response analysis requires the identification of an organisation's best customers, and then another layer of data can be introduced which points to those that are particularly responsive to direct mail or mail order (Fletcher, 1997). It is the increasing sophistication of the information held in databases that is enabling more effective targeting and communications. The database now consists of several layers of information whereby traditional segmentation data, which set out customer profiles, can be fused with transactional data so that biographics (Evans, 1998) emerges as a potent new approach to developing a dialogue with individual customers.

However the merging of data generated through transactions with attitudinal and lifestyle data poses a further problem. In essence this paints a picture of what has been achieved, it describes behaviour. What it does not do is explain why the behaviour occurred. It may be possible to track back through a campaign to examine the inputs, isolate variables and make a judgement, but the problem remains that the data itself, what has been collected, does not provide insight into what underpins the behaviour. Pearson (2003) suggests that direct marketing and market

Direct marketing and market research data sets should be brought together into what has been referred to as 'consilience'.

ViewPoint 27.3   Data-rich BSkyB

It is generally assumed that members of loyalty schemes are less likely to leave, although it is recognised that they will probably be members of several other schemes, some in the same sector. First T, a joint venture of the British Market Research Bureau and Dunnhumby designed to bring together market research with database marketing, represents an attempt at achieving a level of consilience. BSkyB used First T to analyse its subscribers using Target Group Index data to find out about their aspirations, hobbies, pastimes and interests; what inspired them; what drove and what motivated them. From this information BSkyB was better placed not only to adapt the rewards offered within its loyalty scheme but also better placed to communicate with prospects and potential new members.

Source: Adapted from Pearson (2003); used with permission.

research data sets should be brought together into what has been referred to as 'consilience' (Wilson, 1998) or a unity of knowledge. This data-rich information should then be capable of providing organisations with data intelligence and an opportunity to predict behaviour and offer a new form of data value.

Databases provide the means by which a huge range of organisations, large and small, can monitor changes in customer lifestyles and attitudes or, in the business-to-business sector, the changing form of the interorganisational relationships and their impact on other members in the network as well as the market structure and level of competitive activity (Gundach and Murphy, 1993). It is through the use of the database that relationships with participants can be tracked, analysed and developed. Very importantly, database systems can be used not only to identify strategically important customers and segments but also to ascertain opportunities to cross-sell products (Kamakura *et al.*, 2003).

> It is through the use of the database that relationships with participants can be tracked, analysed and developed.

However, there are a number of tensions associated with the use of the database. For example, customers have varying tolerances regarding the level of privacy that a database can exploit. The tolerance or thresholds (Goodwin, 1991) vary according to the information itself, how it was collected and even who collected it. The information exists on a database very often because a customer entered into a transaction. The business entity that received the information as part of a transaction has a duty to acknowledge the confidential nature of the information and the context in which it was collected before selling the details to a third party or exploiting the information to the detriment of the individual who provided it in the first place. Breaking privacy codes and making unauthorised disclosures of personal details lays open the tenuous relationship an organisation thinks it has with its 'loyal' customers.

ViewPoint 27.4   Great British bollards

The simple yet successful use of a database as part of a direct marketing campaign is demonstrated by the launch of 'Ferrocast' by the Great British Bollard Company (GBBC) and reported by Gardiner and Quinton (1998). GBBC had developed a new traffic bollard that provides a high level of user benefits. UK local authorities were identified as the main customer base and direct marketing was seen as the most cost-efficient means of reaching buyers. Lists of three or four key decision-makers within each local authority were developed from the *Municipal Year Book* and the list was cleaned using telephone research. A market database of 200 architects and 400 engineers was constructed and used as the basis of a direct mail campaign. Samples were produced and used in response to enquiries and as demonstration units for the sales director when meeting potential customers.

Analysis of the database indicated that there were certain specifiers and key decision-makers who would never consider Ferrocast or the GBBC as a supplier. These individuals were labelled 'traditionalists' and were flagged on the database so that they did not receive any further communications from GBBC, even if they moved to a new local authority. This saved sending out unwanted communications, reduced costs, improved targeting and subsequent calling activity and helped develop corporate reputation by focusing on potential customers.

Source: Adapted from Gardiner and Quinton (1998); used with kind permission.

Direct response media

The choice of media for direct marketing can be very different from those selected for general advertising purposes. The main reason for using direct response media is that direct contact is made with prospects and customers in order that a direct response is solicited and a dialogue stimulated or maintained. In reality, a wide variety of media can be used, simply by attaching a telephone number, Web site address or response card. However, if broadcast media such as television and radio are the champions of the general advertiser, their adoption by direct marketers in the UK has been relatively slow. Direct mail, telemarketing and door-to-door activities are the main direct response media, as they allow more personal, direct and evaluative means of reaching precisely targeted customers.

> The main reason for using direct response media is that direct contact is made with prospects.

Direct mail

> The largest direct response media expenditure is direct mail.

The largest direct response media expenditure is direct mail, which has grown steadily year on year. However, the industry has since struggled to maintain momentum and reached £2.43 billion in 2003 (Goften, 2004). Direct mail refers to personally addressed advertising that is delivered through the postal system. It can be personalised and targeted with great accuracy, and its results are capable of precise measurement.

The generation of enquiries and leads together with the intention of building a personal relationship with customers are the most important factors contributing to the growth of direct mail. However, the intention to build loyalty is not reflected in the statistics as Ridgeway (2000) reports that mailings appear to be focused on customer acquisition, not retention. Other factors include the increased market and media fragmentation, which have combined to reduce the overall effectiveness of general advertising. Direct mail can be expensive, at anything between £250 and £500 per 1,000 items dispatched. It should, therefore, be used selectively and for purposes other than creating awareness.

Expenditure on direct mail advertising increased rapidly in the late 1980s. Despite a slight dip in 1990, adspend on direct mail has continued to increase and demands an increasing proportion of advertisers' budgets. In 1992, £945 million was spent on direct mail, equating to 11 per cent of total promotional expenditure (DMIS, 1993). By 2000, direct mail volumes had increased so that they accounted for nearly half of the overall letterbox (DMIS, 2000) and 15 per cent of total promotional expenditure (Ridgeway, 2000). However, Day (2000) reports that levels of opening and reading of direct mail items have fallen, with 75 per cent opened and 53 per cent read. So, the volumes sent out have increased but response rates have fallen, and as reported by Reed (2000) 'we mail the customer until they give in'. In other words, this persistent approach to marketing is used to overcome a failure in segmentation and targeting.

> Organisations in the financial services sectors are the main users of this medium.

Organisations in the financial services sectors are the main users of this medium and the financial health of the sector is dependent to a large extent on some of the major financial services companies maintaining their spend on direct mail. However, an increasing number of other organisations are experimenting with this approach, as they try to improve the effectiveness of their promotional expenditure and reduce television advertising costs. The growth in consumer-based direct mail activities has outstripped that of the business-to-business sector. The number of direct mail items sent to consumers has increased considerably in comparison with the b2b sector.

Telemarketing

The prime qualities of the telephone are that it provides for interaction, is flexible and permits immediate feedback and the opportunity to overcome objections, all within the same communication event. Other dimensions of telemarketing include the development and maintenance of customer goodwill, allied to which is the increasing need to provide high levels of customer service. Telemarketing also allows organisations to undertake marketing research which is both highly measurable and accountable in that the effectiveness can be verified continuously and call rates, contacts reached and the number and quality of positive and negative responses are easily recorded and monitored.

Growth in telemarketing activity in the business-to-business sector has been largely at the expense of personal selling. The objectives have been to reduce costs and to utilise the expensive sales force and their skills to build on the openings and leads created by telemarketing and other lead generation activities.

> Growth in telemarketing activity in the business-to-business sector has been largely at the expense of personal selling.

Some of the advantages of using the telephone as part of the media mix are that it allows for interaction between participants, it enables immediate feedback and sets up opportunities to overcome objections, all within the same communication event when both the sender and the receiver are geographically distant.

All of these activities can be executed by personal selling, but the speed, cost, accuracy and consistency of the information solicited through personal visits can often be improved upon by telemarketing. The complexity of the product will influence the degree to which this medium can be used successfully. However, if properly trained professional telemarketers are used, the sales results, if measured on a call basis, can outperform those produced by personal selling.

> Contact centres use a variety of IST.

Contact centres use a variety of IST with the prime goals of reducing costs, improving efficiency and improving the client's reputation through quality of customer interaction. The following are just a few of the ways in which technology is used in these environments:

ViewPoint 27.5   Alton Towers calling

The brand development of Oblivion, the world's first vertical drop roller-coaster, at Alton Towers incorporated the use of telemarketing. Gray (1999) reports that a special telephone number was set up for a promotion aimed at the young adult market. A mocking voice explained the ride to callers, goading and daring callers to try the ride:

> Pilots can experience black-out, grey-out or even red-out; Oblivion may be enough for some people to experience what is commonly known as a cop-out.
> If you decide not to, no one will consider it a weakness or a lack of nerve. Honest.

Callers were challenged to book a special time slot by transferring within the same call to live telemarketers at Alton Towers or Telecom Potential. Branding was extended to the queue for the ride with a series of TV monitors showing the face behind the sneering voice, and still goading consumers towards the ride. See Exhibit 27.1.

EXHIBIT 27.1 The experience of a ride at Alton Towers
The *Whizzer* ride at Alton Towers. Picture reproduced with the kind permission of Alton Towers.

- Automatic call distribution systems enable inbound calls to be distributed efficiently among contact centre operators. Interactive voice response (IVR) systems
allow callers to perform self-help functions without speaking with an individual.
Using simple phone keypad selections these systems have the capability to connect
calls to employees who may be working at home or in remote geographic offices.

- Call recording systems, which consist of voice recording, logging, monitoring and
call management that can be vital in a CRM environment.

- Computer telephony integration (CTI) allows telephone applications and services
to be merged with computer applications. CTI enables the simultaneous arrival of a
call and associated caller data to be displayed on an agent's desktop.

- Customer interaction management (CIM) systems are used to support the contact
centre's operations. Technologies such as predictive dialling, live chat applications
as well as email response systems are often used together with conventional communications technology.

- Predictive diallers (PDs) are used in outbound telemarketing to increase the number
of successful calls and optimise the operators time speaking to customers. PDs
enable engaged lines, no response and answering machines to be avoided (ignored),
thus allowing operators to spend an increased proportion of their time talking to
potential customers rather than wasting time dialling and listening to telephones
ringing. Estimates vary, but now operators can talk for 45 minutes in every hour,
compared with 25 minutes before the development of predictive dialling facilities
(Cook, 1997).

EXHIBIT 27.2 A typical call centre layout and design

Operator contact with customers can be also be supported by technology. Computer-assisted telephone interviewing (CATI) can provide varying degrees of technical support. The degree to which this is used depends on the task, the product and the nature of the target audience. Calls might be driven through a prepared script, often regardless of the interjections of the receiver. This rather crude approach can be quite sophisticated, as computer software prepares scripts that 'branch', as in a decision tree, to respond to a prospect's different answers (Roberts and Berger, 1989). Another approach is to use a semi-structured interview, where the caller has a number of topics that need to be covered but the order and the style in which the issues are dealt with are immaterial. A third method is based on a personal sales presentation. Undertaken by professionally trained callers, the conversation is tuned to the needs of the receiver, not those of the caller. When the call is completed, regardless of whether an order has been placed, it is intended that recipients finish the call feeling satisfied that they have used their time appropriately and in full expectation that they will receive further calls.

The costs of telemarketing are high: for example, £15 to reach a decision-maker in an organisation. When this is compared with £5 for a piece of direct mail or £150+ for a personal sales call to the same individual, it is the effectiveness of the call and the return on the investment that determines whether the costs are really high.

The costs of telemarketing are high.

Carelines

Another reason to use telemarketing concerns the role carelines can play within the consumer brand relationships. Manufacturers use contact centres to enable customers to:

● complain about a product performance and related experience

● seek product related advice

● make suggestions regarding product or packaging development

● comment about an action or development concerning the brand as a whole.

What binds these together is the potential all of these people have for repurchasing the brand, even those who complain bitterly about product performance and experience. If these people have their complaints dealt with properly then there is a reasonable probability that they will repurchase.

The previous letter-based mechanism did not encourage customer response especially when research by Sitel (McLuhan, 2000) found that 98 per cent of customers switched brands rather than complain. Telephone and email encourage greater contact and the chance to talk to customers because it is easier and quicker to implement. The majority of the careline calls are not about complaints but seek advice or help about products. Food manufacturers can provide cooking and recipe advice, cosmetic and toiletries companies can provide healthcare advice and application guidelines while white goods and service-based organisations can provide technical and operational support.

Carelines are essentially a post-purchase support mechanism that facilitates market feedback and intelligence gathering. They can warn of imminent problems (product defects), provide ideas for new products or variants and of course provide a valuable method to reassure customers and improve customer retention levels. Call operators, or agents as many of them are now being called, have to handle calls from a variety of new sources – Web, email, interactive TV and mobile devices – and it is appreciated that many are more effective if they have direct product experience. Instant messaging channels enable online shoppers to ask questions that are routed to a call centre for response. Sales conversion ratios can be up by 40–50 per cent and costs are about £1 to answer an inbound question, compared with £3.50 by phone (Murphy, 2000). Kellogg's reports that its careline makes a 13:1 return on investment (Bashford, 2004).

> **Carelines are essentially a post-purchase support mechanism.**

Expenditure on telemarketing increased rapidly in the late 1980s and early 1990s, but this rapid growth then subsided. Some organisations began undertaking their outbound calls themselves rather than using tele-agencies to do the work on their behalf but as technology improved outsourcing resumed normal growth. In recent years the telemarketing sector has experienced huge growth. There were signs of oversupply in the market and so there is huge pressure on costs and margins.

As the application of digital technologies gathered pace so telemarketing and call centres became threatened. Rather than persist in a potentially declining business activity, call centres repositioned themselves so that they could provide multimedia support services such as eCRM, Internet and even email management. The name has changed to (customer) contact centres and the accent is now on strategic partnerships to assist clients develop customer relationships. Bashford (2004) explains that L'Oréal runs a careline staffed by former hairdressers and skincare consultants. This first-hand product knowledge reflects the attention given to understanding the brand and being able to relate to customer questions. In order that staff can communicate effectively they must believe in the brand values themselves. Davenge refers to the current terminology that expresses this level of involvement as 'emotional connectivity' and 'emotional congruence'. This may be a new form of temporary hyper language but at least this idea of involvement in the brand or category should be of comfort to customers in need.

> **Call centres repositioned themselves so that they could provide multimedia support services such as eCRM, Internet and even email management.**

While the Internet has provided further growth opportunities, it will also take on a number of the tasks currently the preserve of telemarketing bureaux. Web sites enable

ViewPoint 27.6   Careline approaches

Nestlé Purina, whose petfood brands include Purina ONE, Felix, Go Cat, Bakers and Winalot, refers to its contact centre as a relationship centre. Using a strapline 'Your pet, our passion™', the careline is used not only to get feedback on campaigns and products, but is used by a variety of people internally who 'listen in' in an attempt to get close to the consumer.

The extent of the company's involvement with consumers is demonstrated by the fact that contact staff have been trained in bereavement counselling, to help people who have recently lost a pet.

Source: Bashford (2004).

EXHIBIT 27.3 Felix cat food

product information and certain support advice to be accessed without the call centre costs and focus attention on other matters of concern to the customer. Chat room discussions, collaborative browsing and real-time text conversations are options to help care for customers in the future. However, it is probably the one-to-one telephone dialogue between customer and agent that will continue to provide satisfaction and benefits for both parties.

Inserts

Inserts are media materials that are placed in magazines or direct mail letters. These not only provide factual information about the product or service but also enable the recipient to respond to the request of the direct marketer. This request might be to place an order or post back a card for more information, such as a brochure.

Inserts have become more popular, but their cost is substantially higher than a four-colour advertisement in the magazine in which the insert is carried. Their popularity is based on their effectiveness as a lead generator, and new methods of delivering inserts to the home will become important to direct mailing houses in the future. Other vehicles, such as packages rather than letter mail, will become important.

Print

There are two main forms of direct response advertising through the printed media: first, catalogues and, secondly, magazines and newspapers.

Catalogues mailed direct to consumers have been an established method of selling products for a long time.

Catalogues mailed direct to consumers have been an established method of selling products for a long time. Mail order organisations such as Freeman's, GUS and Littlewoods have successfully exploited this form of direct marketing. Organisations such as Tchibo and Kaleidoscope have successfully used mini-catalogues, but instead of providing account facilities and the appointment of specific freelance agents, their business transactions are on a cash-with-order basis.

Business-to-business marketers have begun to exploit this medium, and organisations such as Dell and IBM now use online and off-line catalogues, partly to save costs and partly to free valuable sales personnel so that they can concentrate their time selling into larger accounts. Direct response advertising through the press is similar to general press advertising except that the advertiser provides a mechanism for the reader to take further action. The mechanism may be a telephone number (call free) or a coupon or cut-out reply slip requesting further information. Dell has transformed its marketing strategy to one that is based around building customised products for both consumers and business customers. Consumer direct print ads, such as the one at Exhibit 27.4 offering an incentive, are designed explicitly to drive customers to the Dell Web site, where transactions are completed without reference to retailers, dealers or other intermediaries.

Door to door

This delivery method can be much cheaper than direct mail as there are no postage charges to be accounted for. However, if the costs are much lower, so are the response rates. Responses are lower because door-to-door drops cannot be personally addressed, as can direct mail, even though the content and quality can be controlled in the same way.

Avon Cosmetics and Betterware are traditionally recognised as professional practitioners of door-to-door direct marketing. Other organisations, such as the utility companies (gas, electricity and water), are using door to door drops to create higher levels of market penetration. For more information on this see Chapter 29.

EXHIBIT 27.4 A fine example of a direct response print ad driving offline readers and potential customers online to Dell's Web site

Radio and television

Of the two main forms discussed earlier, radio and television, the former is used as a support medium for other advertising, often by providing enquiry numbers. Television has greater potential because it can provide the important visual dimension, but its use in the UK for direct marketing purposes has been limited. One of the main reasons for this has been the television contractors' attitude to pricing. However, the industry has experienced a period of great change and has introduced greater pricing flexibility, and a small but increasing number of direct marketers have used the small screen success-fully, mainly by providing freephone numbers for customers. Direct Line, originally a motor insurance organisation, has been outstanding in its use of television not only to launch but also to help propel the phenomenal growth of a range of related products.

The Internet and new media

The explosion of activity around new media and the Internet has been quite astonish-ing in recent years and now represents a major new form of interactive marketing com-munications. The development of digital television services will herald the birth of a new form of interactivity during the first ten years of the new century as analogue services are withdrawn. Initially home shopping and banking facilities will be attractive to those whose lifestyles complement the benefits offered by the new technology. In the longer term fully interactive services will bring increased leisure and entertainment opportunities to a greater num-ber of people. A much fuller consideration of interactive communications can be found in Chapters 2, 10 and 21.

In the longer term fully interactive services will bring increased leisure and entertainment opportunities to a greater number of people.

Integration and direct marketing

This brief review of the media used in direct marketing activities has tended to present them as separate, independent resources. Increasingly, successful direct marketing programmes are using these media in combination, as a team of complementary tools. Many organisations, regardless of whether their marketing activities are oriented solely to direct marketing or not, are using direct response media to support and supplement their other promotional activities (Emerick, 1993; Gardiner and Quinton, 1998).

Other organisations are using integrated direct marketing, which Eisenhart (1990) identified as 'the orchestration of various direct marketing vehicles so that they work together in a synergistic fashion'. An example of this orchestration might be the dis-patch of a direct mailing using a well-qualified list followed by contacting addresses through a telemarketing programme within 24 hours of the mailing arriving. In some cases response rates have doubled by using telemarketing in this way.

Some doubt whether organisations can justify the cost and the administrative and managerial implications of com-plex integrated direct campaigns. Advocates of the approach claim that each contact with a prospect helps to create a wave effect, with response rates increasing at each contact.

Some doubt whether organisations can justify the cost and the administrative and managerial implications of complex integrated direct campaigns.

There are two aspects to direct marketing integration. One is the integration of direct marketing activities themselves and the other concerns the integration of direct marketing within marketing communications activities. There is plenty of evidence to support the view that the distinction between above- and below-the-line communications is blurring and that this is reflected in the structure and work of agencies working in the market (Acland, 2003). This is set to continue as media fragments further and agencies of all disciplines diversify in an attempt to grow and meet their own goals. The pattern of communications spend is continuing to move from above- to below-the-line channels. The IPA reported direct marketing budgets up by 5.7 per cent in quarter three of 2003 compared with media advertising budgets down by 3.4 per cent. There can be little doubt, therefore, that integrated direct response media will be used increasingly in the future as organisations realise its power and continue to build the direct approach. As general media rates continue to increase ahead of inflation, and as managers seek new ways of providing evidence of their astute use of marketing and, in particular, promotional resources, so direct response media will play an increasingly important role in the marketing activities of a large number of organisations. Whether

> It is probable that direct marketing will play a more influential role within the marketing communications industry.

direct marketing agencies have the necessary credentials, in particular the account planning skills necessary to attract clients completely away from brand based agencies and the media budgets that are attached to them, is highly unlikely. However, it is probable that direct marketing will play a more influential role within the marketing communications industry as it seeks to become more integrated and offer a more integrated range of services for its clients.

It should not be forgotten, however, that commitment to the direct route or to a combination of general and direct response media means that organisations must ensure that they are transmitting a consistent or complementary message through each medium used.

Supporting the sales force

In an effort to increase the productivity of the sales force and to use their expensive skills more effectively, direct marketing has provided organisations with an opportunity to improve levels of performance and customer satisfaction. In particular, the use of an inside telemarketing department is seen as a compatible sales channel to the field sales force. The telemarketing team can accomplish the following tasks: they can search for and qualify new customers, so saving the field force from cold calling; they can service existing customer accounts and prepare the field force should they be required to attend to the client personally; they can seek repeat orders from marginal or geographically remote customers, particularly if they are low-unit-value consumable items; finally, they can provide a link between network members that serves to maintain the relationship, especially through periods of difficulty and instability. Many organisations prefer to place orders through telesales teams, as it does not involve the time costs associated with personal sales calls. The routine of such orders gives greater efficiency for all concerned with the relational exchange and reduces costs.

Direct mail activities are also becoming more important in areas where personal contact is seen as unnecessary or where limited field sales resources are deployed to key accounts. As with telesales, direct mail is often used to supplement the activities of the field force. Catalogue and electronic communications such as fax can be used for accounts, which may be regarded as relatively unattractive.

In addition to this, use of the Internet and mobile-based communications have provided new opportunities to reach customers. The Web site itself symbolises the changing orientation of marketing communications. Whereas once the brochure, mass media advertising and perhaps a promotional incentive represented the central channel of communication, now the Web site and the database serve to integrate directed, sometimes interactive, one-to-one communications. These are supported in many cases by more call-to-action messages channelled through a variety of coordinated off-line and digital media.

All of these activities free the field sales force to increase their productivity and to spend more time with established customers or those with high profit potential.

Multichannel selling

A number of different sales channels have been identified so far and many organisations, in their search to reduce costs, have restructured their operations in an attempt to better meet the 'touchpoints' of their different customers.

Restructuring has often taken the form of introducing multiple sales channels.

Restructuring has often taken the form of introducing multiple sales channels with the simple objective of using less expensive channels to complete selling tasks that do not require personal, face-to-face contact. Technology-enhanced channels, mainly in the form of Web-based and email communications, have grown considerably, often at the expense of telephone and mail facilities. Payne and Frow (2004) have developed a categorisation of sales channels and these are depicted in Table 27.3.

In order to better meet the needs of customers, organisations need to evolve their mix of channels. Customers will then be able to interact with their supplying organisations using the mix of channels that they prefer to use. Therefore, marketing communications needs to be used in order to best complement the different audiences, channel facilities and characteristics. Through mixing channels and communications in a complementary way higher levels of customer service can be achieved. The proliferation of channels may, however, lead organisations to believe that the greater the number of channels the greater the chances of commercial success. In addition to the view that multichannel customers are known to spend up to 30 per cent more than single channel customers, the Internet and overseas call centres also offer substantial

ViewPoint 27.7   Oarsman uses many channels

FiveGold is a company developed by five times Olympic gold medallist Sir Steve Redgrave. The company supplies good quality clothing to catalogue retailers such as Freeman's and Grattan, independent menswear clothing shops and department stores. In addition the brand uses the Internet, which accounts for 20 per cent of sales. Online catalogues, email and viral marketing campaigns are used online. FiveGold uses advertising in Sunday newspaper supplements and attends particular sporting events to merchandise the brand. Sir Steve was even dressed in FiveGold clothing when commentating for the BBC and being seen greeting the British Olympic rowers after their latest famous victory.

The range of channels used by FiveGold is designed to meet the needs of particular target audiences. The chosen channels do not cannibalise sales from other channels and serve the mass market that the brand was designed to serve.

Source: Adapted from Crush (2004).

TABLE 27.3 Comparison of channel characteristics

Channel	Breadth	Dominant form of communication	Cost/contact
Field sales	Key account, service and personal representation	Dialogue	High
Outlets	Retail branches, stores, depots and kiosks	Interactive	Medium
Telephony	Traditional telephone, facsimile, telex and contact centres	One way and two way	Low to Medium
Direct marketing	Direct mail, radio and traditional television	One way and two way	Low
ecommerce	Email, Internet, interactive television	Interactive	Very low
mcommerce	Mobile telephony, SMS, WAP and 3G	Interactive	Very low

(short-term) cost savings (Myers *et al.*, 2004). However, there is a word of caution and that is although cost savings per transaction might be achieved the use of multiple channels can incur higher overall costs. Myers *et al.* (2004) cite retail off-line banks as an example of false economies. The introduction of ATMs helped reduce the average transaction cost by 15 per cent but the number of transactions more than doubled compared with the times when queuing in a bank represented the only operating format. As a result, they argue, the cost of serving customers has actually increased. This may or may not be true, but what is not accounted for is the value customers place on the convenience of the services provided, the closer the organisation is able to get to customers increases the opportunities to cross-sell and develop new products. The move from a cost to a customer perspective is readily made, although the banks have some way to go before they are truly customer oriented.

Categorising customers

One simple approach to managing channels is to categorise accounts (customers) according to their potential attractiveness and the current strength of the relationship between supplier and buyer. See Figure 27.2. A strong relationship, for example, is indicative of two organisations engaged in mutually satisfying relational exchanges. A weak relationship suggests that the two parties have no experience of each other or, if they have, that it is not particularly satisfying. If there have been transactions, it may be that these can be classified as market exchange experiences. Attractiveness refers to the opportunities a buying organisation represents to the vendor: how large or small the potential business is in an organisation.

> One simple approach to managing channels is to categorise accounts (customers) according to their potential attractiveness.

For reasons of clarity, these scales are presented as either high or low, strong or weak. However, they should be considered as a continuum, and with the use of some relatively simple evaluative criteria accounts can be positioned on the matrix and strategies formulated to move accounts to different positions, which in turn necessitate the use of different sales channel mixes.

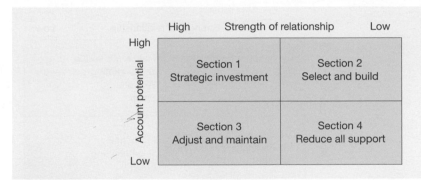

FIGURE 27.2 Account investment matrix

ViewPoint 27.8 Multichannel BUPA Wellness

BUPA Wellness offers an onsite corporate dental service. Rather than use the expensive and time-poor field sales force to generate leads and new business it decided to manage the process of customer acquisition through technology. BUPA outsourced the task to Inbox Media, whose goals were to develop a database as a foundation for the project, create awareness and impact in the market and generate leads for the sales force to convert.

Inbox Media used telemarketing to create a list of HRM managers who agreed to receive emails from it in the future. Their details were used in the database and then each were sent personalised video emails informing them about the services of BUPA Wellness and, more particularly, the number of days that their organisation lost each year through dental visits and associated oral health problems. While the results were entirely satisfactory (52 per cent of emails were opened, 21 per cent clicked through and approximately 50 leads were turned into appointments), one of the interesting elements of the campaign concerned the dynamics associated with the email part of the programme. Inbox Media was able to monitor who opened the emails, how long they spent reading them and who they forwarded them to. It thus built a picture of email opening and behaviour characteristics.

Although the opportunity was declined it was technically possible to use the sales team to call recipients as they opened their video email or even when or just after it had been played. However, this coordinated approach was considered inappropriate as it would raise strong concerns about privacy, trust, intrusion, reputation and the ethics associated with over-aggressive selling strategies.

Source: Adapted from Anon (2003).

Based on the original approach developed by Cravens *et al.* (1991) appropriate sales channels are superimposed on the grid so that optimum efficiency in selling effort and costs can be managed (Figure 27.3). Accounts in Section 1 vary in attractiveness, as some will be assigned key account status. The others will be very important and will require a high level of selling effort (investment), which has to be delivered by the field sales force. Accounts in Section 2 are essentially prospects because of their weak relationship but high attractiveness. Selling effort should be proportional to the value of the prospects: high effort for good prospects and low for the others. Care should be given to allocating a time by which accounts in this section are moved to other parts of the grid, and in doing so save resources and maximise opportunities for growth. All the main sales channels should be used, commencing with direct and email to identify prospects, telesales for qualification purposes, field sales force selling directed at the

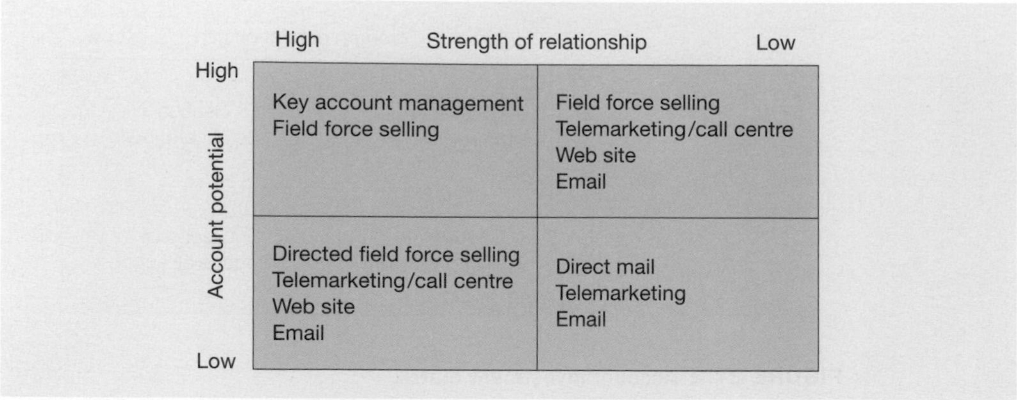

FIGURE 27.3 Multichannel mix allocation

strong prospects and telesales and Web site for the others. Web site details provide support and information for those accounts that wish to remain distant. As the relationship becomes stronger, so field selling takes over from telemarketing and the coordinating activities of the contact or call centre. If the relationship weakens, then the account may be discontinued and selling redirected to other prospects.

Accounts in Section 3 do not offer strong potential and, although the relationship is strong, there are opportunities to switch the sales channel mix by reducing, but not eliminating, the level of field force activity and to give consideration to the introduction of telemarketing for particular accounts. Significant cost reductions can be achieved with these types of accounts by simply reviewing the means and reasoning behind the personal selling effort. Accounts in Section 4 should receive no field force calls, the prime sales channels being telesales, email, the Web site and perhaps catalogue selling depending upon the nature of the Web site.

Establishing a multiple sales channel strategy based on the grid suggested above may not be appropriate to all organisations. For example, the current level of performance may be considered as exceeding expectations, in which case there is no point in introducing change. It may be that the costs and revenues associated with redeployment are unfavourable and that the implications for the rest of the organisation of implementing the new sales channel approach are such that the transition should be either postponed or rejected. Payne and Frow (2004) suggest a range of channel options or strategies can be identified that relate to the channel needs of target segments. These range from a single dominant channel such as those used by Amazon and Egg, a customer segment approach designed for use with different channel types such as intermediaries, b2b end-user customers and consumers, one based on the different activity channels that customers prefer to use, such as a mix off online and off-line resources to identify, see, demonstrate, select and pay for a computer and finally a truly integrated multichannel strategy utilising CRM systems to integrate all customer information at whichever contact point the customer chooses to

> Experience has shown that costs can be reduced through the introduction of a multiple sales channel approach.

use. These strategies reflect some of the approaches that can be used and indeed various combinations can be used to meet customers' channel needs. However, experience has shown that costs can be reduced through the introduction of a multiple sales channel approach and that levels of customer satisfaction and the strength of the relationship between members of the network can be improved considerably. In addition, it is vital to remember that customers will move into and use new channel mixes over the customer life cycle and that channel decisions should be regarded as fluid and developmental.

Summary

Direct marketing has become an established communications discipline. The various ways in which direct marketing can be used is increasing, mainly due to developments within technology. Direct marketing uses direct response media based on database support and permits the generation and feedback of messages with individual customers. The over-arching objectives are to build and sustain a mutually rewarding relationship with each customer, reduce media costs and improve effectiveness and measurement.

The use of direct marketing has grown considerably in recent years and will undoubtedly continue to grow as new efficiency and effectiveness measures are developed. For some organisations their whole marketing approach has been built around the direct concept (e.g. First Direct in financial services), whereas for others the approach has been used to complement their use of the other tools in the promotional mix. Direct marketing will not replace mass media-based communications but it is likely that an increasing proportion of marketing budgets will move towards direct communication activities.

Review questions

1. Set out a definition of direct marketing and consider the key words in the definition.
2. Explain the differences between direct response media and direct marketing.
3. Direct response media have many advantages over general mass advertising. What are they and why is this form of promotional communication increasing so quickly?
4. What are the different levels of direct marketing? What is the fundamental difference between levels?
5. Evaluate the main drivers behind the growth of direct marketing. How might these drivers change in the future?
6. Discuss the role of the database as the hub of marketing communications.
7. Telemarketing has become an integral feature of the promotional mix for reaching consumer and business-to-business markets. Why is this and what particular features of telemarketing attract clients?
8. Identify and then evaluate three different media for delivering direct response communications.
9. Find two examples of organisations using carelines. Comment on their effectiveness.
10. Explain why direct marketing activities should be integrated with other elements of the promotional mix.

MINI-CASE
Recovering cars with direct marketing

In the UK car recovery and breakdown market the Royal Automobile Club (RAC) is regarded as the challenger brand with the Automobile Association (AA) as the undisputed market leader. In addition, Direct Line Rescue (DLR) has entered the market and taken a 10 per cent market share.

Customers in this market are no longer simply users of the vehicle breakdown services but expect a broad range of products and services, which the motoring organisations aim to satisfy in different ways.

Traditionally marketing communications messages have been based on advertising and the development of brand values. Messages have been very product focused, typified by ads for speed of recovery, get you home services, helpfulness of staff and a range of ancillary products such as car finance, legal and advisory services.

The perceived benefits of motor organisation membership have changed. Factors concerning reassurance have become more important while economic factors have become less so. For example, research shows that many motorists are more concerned about getting home, with or without their car, than they are with the relative merits of membership costs and the variety of ad hoc services most motoring organisations now provide.

One of the main reasons for the change in attitude towards motor organisation membership is the change in profile of the UK motorist. The dominance of middle-aged male drivers has diminished as the percentage of young and female drivers has increased. Drivers are less willing to perform roadside repairs while, at the same time, cars are becoming more complex. Cars are becoming more reliable but it is becoming increasingly difficult for drivers to repair them by the roadside, partly as a result of sealed accessories and the need for specialised diagnostic equipment.

During the 1990s the promotional emphasis of the main motoring organisations changed from one that emphasised economic and tangible attributes to ones that gave higher prominence to driver safety and reassurance. In addition to changes in the core messages used by the RAC and AA, greater emphasis has been placed on the other promotional tools, partly in response to the entry and aggression of DLR.

One of the strategies used by both the AA and RAC has been to change the organisational culture, although some commentators feel this has been at the expense of customer service. A recently published *Which?* magazine survey revealed that the RAC fared badly against the AA. In addition, a BBC consumer affairs programme, *Rogue Traders*, revealed that some RAC patrolmen were selling car batteries to stranded drivers who did not need them.

In the face of competitive pressures, profit margins declining on recovery services and private membership rising only slightly, the RAC has moved into direct response TV to support its ancillary services. This required a move to a more emotionally based message to convey the idea that the RAC can help people afford their dream car, regardless of what it is, and secure the finance from a trusted brand to help them buy it. The ads encouraged viewers to call an 0800 number to apply for a loan and get an instant decision. Every successful loan applicant received free RAC Breakdown cover. In addition, the RAC has developed its 36-page *RAC Magazine* as a means of communicating with its different markets. Of the several million copies mailed out three times a year everyone receives the standard 20 pages of content but, in addition, there is also a 16-page insert that takes account of a person's lifestage and their length of membership.

Direct Line Rescue (DLR) is a very strong brand that lends itself to strong imagery and no-nonsense messaging. DLR wants to develop a much closer relationship with its customers and it too has strategies that are designed to offer more than just vehicle breakdown services. A recent campaign was designed to target customers of the RAC and AA and to reinforce the Rescue brand, which has nearly 1 million customers. Through its DM agency DLR developed a series of mail packs, each containing a letter, envelope and insert, targeting different messages to existing AA and RAC members. These messages instructed recipients to 'Stop paying too much' by switching to Direct Line. The company's own car insurance customers received a third pack which said that 'First we save u money, then we save u'. This was intended to highlight the breakdown cover offer from £35 and to reassure people about the high level of service while prompting them to respond through bold calls to action and guaranteed low prices.

Questions

1 Explain ways in which use of a database might assist the RAC with its direct marketing programme.

2 Discuss the extent to which the use of customer magazines could help the RAC develop relationships with customers.

3 Prepare a list of sales channels that the RAC could use to reach its different types of customers. Select the four top channels and explain their advantages in respect of the RAC.

4 Which direct response media would you recommend the RAC should consider? Justify your selections.

5 Discuss the role of the telephone in the marketing communications programme.

References

Acland, H. (2003) Direct marketing: championing the direct route. *Campaign*, 5 December. Retrieved 7 January from www.brandrepublic.co.uk/news/newsArticle.

Anon (2003) Royal Mail. Data 2003. *Marketing Direct*, Sponsored Supplement.

Bashford, S. (2004) Telemarketing: customers calling. *Marketing*, 8 September. Retrieved 16 October 2004 from www.brandrepublic.com/news/.

Bird, D. (1989) *Commonsense Direct Marketing*. 2nd edn. London: Kogan Page.

Cook, R. (1997) The future of telemarketing. *Campaign*, 20 June, pp. 27–8.

Cravens, D.W., Ingram, T.N. and LaForge, R.W. (1991) Evaluating multiple channel strategies. *Journal of Business and Industrial Marketing*, 6(3/4), pp. 37–48.

Crush, P. (2004) FiveGold, *Marketing*, 1 December, p. 21.

Day, J. (2000) Battle for mats and minds. *Marketing Week*, 14 September, pp. 42–3.

DMIS (1993) *Letterbox Fact File*. Bristol: Direct Mail Information Service.

DMIS (2000) *Letterbox Fact File*. Bristol: Direct Mail Information Service.

Eisenhart, T. (1990) Going the integrated route. *Business Marketing* (December), pp. 24–32.

Emerick, T. (1993) The multimedia mix. *Direct Marketing* (June), pp. 20–2.

Evans, M. (1998) From 1086 and 1984: direct marketing into the millennium. *Marketing Intelligence and Planning*, 16(1), pp. 56–67.

Fletcher, K. (1997) External drive. *Marketing*, 30 October, pp. 39–42.

Fletcher, K.P. and Peters, L.D. (1997) Trust and direct marketing environments: a consumer perspective. *Journal of Marketing Management*, 13, pp. 523–39.

Foster, S. (1996) Defining the direct brand. *Admap* (October), pp. 33–6.

Ganesan, S. (1994) Determinants of long-term orientation in buyer–seller relationships. *Journal of Marketing*, 58 (April), pp. 1–19.

Gardiner, P. and Quinton, S. (1998) Building brands using direct marketing: case study. *Marketing Intelligence and Planning*, 16(1), pp. 6–11.

Goften, K. (2004) Top 85 direct marketing agencies. *Marketing*, 25 March, pp. 25–31.

Goodwin, C. (1991) Privacy: recognition of a consumer right. *Journal of Public Policy & Marketing*, 10(1), pp. 149–66.

Gray, R. (1999) Using the voice at the end of the line. *Marketing*, 16 September, pp. 29–30.

Gundach, G.T. and Murphy, P.E. (1993) Ethical and legal foundations of relational marketing exchanges. *Journal of Marketing*, 57 (October), pp. 93–4.

Kamakura, W.A., Wedel, M., de Rosa, F. and Mazzon, J.A. (2003) Cross-selling through database marketing: a mixed factor analyzer for data augmentation and prediction. *International Journal of Research in Marketing*, **20**(1) (March), pp. 45–65.

Kleinman, M. (2000) Baileys database task awarded to Craik Jones. *Marketing*, 24 August, p. 16.

McLuhan, R. (2000) How a complaint can offer insights. *Marketing*, 3 August, pp. 25–6.

Marsh, H. (2001) Dig deeper into the database goldmine. *Marketing*, 11 January, pp. 29–30.

Morgan, R.M. and Hunt, S.D. (1994) The commitment–trust theory of relationship marketing. *Journal of Marketing*, **58** (July), pp. 20–38.

Murphy, D. (2000) Call centres ponder price of technology. *Marketing*, 14 September, pp. 43–4.

Myers, J.B., Pickersgill, A.D. and Metre van, E.S. (2004) Steering customers to the right channels. *The McKinsey Quarterly*, **4**, 16 November.

Payne, A. and Frow, P. (2004) The role of multichannel integration in customer relationship management. *Industrial Marketing Management*, **33**(6) (August) pp. 527–38.

Pearson, S. (2003) Data takes centre stage. Data 2003. *Marketing Direct*, Sponsored Supplement.

Reed, D. (2000) Too much, too often. *Marketing Week*, 12 October, pp. 59–62.

Ridgeway, J. (2000) DirectWatch in 2000. *Marketing*, 21 December, pp. 24–5.

Roberts, M.L. and Berger, P.D. (1989) *Direct Marketing Management*. Englewood Cliffs, NJ: Prentice-Hall.

Wilson, E.O. (1998) *Consilience: The Unity of Knowledge*. New York: Random House.

Personal selling

28

This form of marketing communication involves a face-to-face dialogue between two persons or by one person and a group. Message flexibility is an important attribute, as is the immediate feedback that often flows from use of this promotional tool.

Aims and objectives

The aims of this chapter are to examine personal selling as a promotional tool and to consider management's use of the sales force.

The objectives of this chapter are to:

1. consider the different types, roles and tasks of personal selling;
2. determine the strengths and weaknesses of personal selling as a form of communication;
3. explore the ways in which personal selling is thought to work;
4. establish the means by which management can organise a sales force;
5. compare some of the principal methods by which the optimum size of a sales force can be derived;
6. introduce the concept of multiple sales channels;
7. discuss the future role of the sales force.

Introduction

Personal selling characterises the importance of strong relationships between vendor and buyer.

In an era where relationship marketing has become increasingly understood and accepted as the contemporary approach to marketing theory and practice, so personal selling characterises the importance of strong relationships between vendor and buyer.

The traditional image of personal selling is one that embraces the hard sell, with a brash and persistent salesperson delivering a volley of unrelenting, persuasive messages at a confused and reluctant consumer. Fortunately this image is receding quickly as the professionalism and breadth of personal selling become more widely recognised and as the role of personal selling becomes even more important in the communications mix.

Personal selling activities can be observed at various stages in the buying process of both the consumer and business-to-business markets. This is because the potency of personal communications is very high, and messages can be adapted on the spot to meet the requirements of both parties. This flexibility, as we shall see later, enables objections to be overcome, information to be provided in the context of the buyer's environment and the conviction and power of demonstration to be brought to the buyer when the buyer requests it.

Personal selling is different from other forms of communication in that the transmitted messages represent, mainly, dyadic communications.

Personal selling is different from other forms of communication in that the transmitted messages represent, mainly, dyadic communications. This means that there are two persons involved in the communication process. Feedback and evaluation of transmitted messages are possible, more or less instantaneously, so that these personal selling messages can be tailored and be made much more personal than any of the other methods of communication.

Using the spectrum of activities identified by the hierarchy of effects, we can see that personal selling is close enough to the prospective buyer to induce a change in behaviour. That is, it is close enough to overcome objections, to provide information quickly and to respond to the prospects' overall needs, all in the context of the transaction, and to encourage them directly to place orders.

Types of personal selling

One way of considering the types of personal selling is to examine the types of customer served through this communication process:

1. *Intermediaries*

   This involves selling offerings onward through a particular channel network to other resellers. They in turn will sell the offering to other members who are closer to the end-user. For example, computer manufacturers have traditionally distributed their products through a combination of direct selling to key accounts and through a restricted number of dealers, or value-added resellers. These resellers then market the products (and bundle software) to their customers and potential customer organisations.

2. *Industrial*

   Here the main type of selling consists of business-to-business marketing and requires the selling of components and parts to others for assembly or incorporation within larger offerings. Goodman manufactures car radio systems and sells them to Ford, which then builds them into its cars as part of the final product offering.

3. *Professional*

   This type of selling process requires ideas and offerings to be advanced to specifiers and influencers. They will in turn incorporate the offering within the project(s) they are developing. For example, a salesperson could approach an architect to persuade him or her to include the alarm system made by the salesperson's organisation within the plans for a building that the architect has been commissioned to design.

4. *Consumer*

   This form of personal selling requires contact with the retail trade and/or the end-user consumer.

It will be apparent that a wide range of skills and resources is required for each of these types of selling. Selling to each of these types of customer requires different skills; as a result, salespersons usually focus their activities on one of these types.

Selling to each of these types of customer requires different skills.

The tasks of personal selling

The generic tasks to be undertaken by the sales force have been changing because the environment in which organisations operate is shifting dramatically. These changes, in particular those associated with the development and implementation of new technologies, have had repercussions on the activities of the sales force and are discussed later in this chapter.

The tasks of those who undertake personal selling vary from organisation to organisation and in accord with the type of selling activities on which they focus. It is normally assumed that they collect and bring into the organisation orders from customers wishing to purchase the offering. In this sense the order aspect of the personal selling tool can be seen as one of four order-related tasks:

1. *Order takers* are salespersons to whom customers are drawn at the place of supply. Reception clerks at hotels and ticket desk personnel at theatres and cinemas typify this role.

2. *Order getters* are sales personnel who operate away from the organisation and who attempt to gain orders, largely through the provision of information, the use of demonstration techniques and services and the art of persuasion.

3. *Order collectors* are those who attempt to gather orders without physically meeting their customers. This is completed electronically or over the telephone. The growth of telemarketing operations was discussed in the previous chapter, but the time saved by both the buyer and the seller using the telephone to gather repeat and low-value orders frees valuable sales personnel to seek new customers and build relationships with current customers.

4. *Order supporters* are all those people who are secondary salespersons in that they are involved with the order once it has been secured, or are involved with the act of ordering, usually by supplying information. Order processing or financial advice

TABLE 28.1 Tasks of personal selling

Prospecting	Finding new customers
Communicating	Informing various stakeholders and feeding back information about the market
Selling	The art of leading a prospect to a successful close
Information gathering	Reporting information about the market and reporting on individual activities
Servicing	Consulting, arranging, counselling, fixing and solving a multitude of customer 'problems'
Allocating	Placing scarce products and resources at times of shortage
Shaping	Building and sustaining relationships with customers and other stakeholders

services typify this role. In a truly customer-oriented organisations all customer-facing employees will be order supporters.

However, this perspective of personal selling is narrow because it fails to set out the broader range of activities that a sales force can be required to undertake. Salespersons do more than get or take orders. The tasks listed in Table 28.1 provide direction and purpose, and also help to establish the criteria by which the performance of members of the personal selling unit can be evaluated. The organisation should decide which tasks it expects its representatives to undertake.

Salespersons do more than get or take orders.

One view of personal selling is that the sales force is responsible for selling, installing and upgrading customer equipment and another is they are responsible for developing, selling and protecting accounts. The interesting point from both these examples is that responsibilities, or rather objectives, are extended either vertically upstream, into offer design, or vertically downstream, into the development and maintenance of long-term customer relationships, or both. It is the last point that is becoming increasingly important. In the business-to-business sector the sales activity mix is becoming more oriented to the need to build and sustain the relationships that organisations have with their major customers. This will be discussed later. Some of the key questions that need to be addressed when preparing a communications plan are 'What will be the specific responsibilities of the sales force?' and 'What role will personal selling have relative to the other elements of the mix?'

Personal selling is the most expensive element of the communications mix. The average cost per contact can easily exceed £150 when all markets and types of businesses are considered. It is generally agreed that personal selling is most effective at the later stages of the hierarchy of effects or buying process, rather than at the earlier stage of awareness building. Therefore, each organisation should determine the precise role the sales force is to play within the communication mix.

Personal selling is the most expensive element of the communications mix.

The role of personal selling

Personal selling is often referred to as interpersonal communication and from this perspective Reid *et al.* (2002) determined three major sales behaviours, namely getting, giving and using information:

- Getting information refers to sales behaviours aimed at information acquisition, for example gathering information about customers, markets and competitors.

- Giving information refers to the dissemination of information to customers and other stakeholders, for example sales presentations and seminar meetings designed to provide information about products and an organisation's capabilities and reputation.

- Using information refers to the sales person's use of information to help solve a customer's problem. Associated with this is the process of gaining buyer commitment through the generation of information (Thayer, 1968, cited by Reid *et al.*, 2002).

As the complexity of a purchase situation increases so the amount of giving information behaviours decline and getting information behaviours increase.

These last authors suggest that the using information dynamic appears to be constant across all types of purchase situations. However, as the complexity of a purchase situation increases so the amount of giving information behaviours decline and getting information behaviours increase. This finding supports the need for a sales person to be able to recognise particular situations in the buying process and then to adapt their behaviour to meet buyer's contextual needs.

However, sales people undertake numerous tasks in association with communication activities. Guenzi (2002) determined that some sales activities are generic simply because they are performed by most sales people across a large number of industries. These generic activities are selling, customer relationship management and communicating to customers. Other activities such as market analysis, pre-sales services and the transfer of information about competitors to the organisation are industry specific. Interestingly he found that information-gathering activities are more likely to be undertaken by organisations operating in consumer markets than in b2b, possibly a reflection of the strength of the market orientation in both arenas.

The role of personal selling is largely one of representation.

The role of personal selling is largely one of representation. In business-to-business markets sales personnel operate at the boundary of the organisation. They provide the link between the needs of their own organisation and the needs of their customers. This linkage is absolutely vital, for a number of reasons that will be discussed shortly, but without personal selling communication with other organisations would occur through electronic or print media and would foster discrete closed systems. Representation in this sense therefore refers to face-to-face encounters between people from different organisations. Wright and Fill (2001) found that the sales force was used by doctors as a means of forming images of pharmaceutical companies. In other words the sales force, whether intentionally or not, served as a corporate identity cue and gave signals.

In other words the sales force, whether intentionally or not, served as a corporate identity cue.

Many authors consider the development, organisation and completion of a sale in a market exchange-based transaction to be the key part of the role of personal selling. Sales personnel provide a source of information for buyers so that they can make the right purchase decisions. In that sense they provide a good level of credibility, but they are also perceived, understandably, as biased. The degree of expertise held by the salesperson may be high, but the degree of trustworthiness will vary, especially during the formative period of the relationship, unless other transactions with the selling organisation have been satisfactory. Once a number of transactions have been completed and product quality established, trustworthiness may improve.

As the costs associated with personal selling are high, it is vital that sales personnel are used effectively. To that end, some organisations are employing other methods to decrease the time that the sales force spends on administration, travel and office work and to maximise the time spent in front of customers, where they can use their specific selling skills.

The amount of control that can be exercised over the delivery of the messages through the sales force depends upon a number of factors. Essentially, the level of control must be regarded as low, because each salesperson has the freedom to adapt messages to meet changing circumstances as negotiations proceed. In practice, however, the professionalism and training that many members of the sales force receive and the increasing accent on measuring levels of customer satisfaction mean that the degree of control over the message can be regarded, in most circumstances, as very good, although it can never, for example, be as high as that of advertising.

ViewPoint 28.1   Message control - hay fever

It can be argued that members of the sales team must be free to adapt messages at the point of delivery because individual clients are themselves different and have different needs and requirements. Lloyd (1997) believes that, when selling to doctors, medical representatives enter into conversations that are appropriate for individual doctors.

An example concerns two products manufactured by Schering-Plough. They have two hay fever products (one nasal and the other an oral antihistamine), and sales representatives are expected to decide which to present (in detail) to doctors, based upon the representatives' knowledge and experience of each individual doctor's preferences and the needs of his or her patients.

This flexibility is framed within the context of the product strategy. Decisions that impact upon strategy are not allowed. There is freedom to adapt the manner in which products are presented, but there is no freedom for the sales representatives to decide the priority of the products to be detailed.

Strengths and weaknesses of personal selling

There are a number of strengths and weaknesses associated with personal selling. It is interesting to note that some of the strengths can in turn be seen as weaknesses, particularly when management control over the communication process is not as attentive or as rigorous as it might be.

Strengths

Dyadic communications allow for two-way interaction that, unlike the other promotional tools, provides for fast, direct feedback. In comparison with the mass media, personal selling allows for the receiver to focus attention on the salesperson, with a reduced likelihood of distraction or noise.

There is a greater level of participation in the decision process by the vendor than in the other tools. When this is combined with the power to tailor messages in response to the feedback provided by the buyer, the sales process has a huge potential to solve customer problems.

Weaknesses

One of the major disadvantages of personal selling is the cost. Costs per contact are extremely high, and this means that management must find alternative means of communicating particular messages and improve the amount of time that sales personnel spend with prospects and customers. Reach and frequency through personal selling are always going to be low, regardless of the amount of funds available.

Control over message delivery is very often low and, while the flexibility is an advantage, there is also the disadvantage of message inconsistency. This in turn can lead to confusion (a misunderstanding perhaps with regard to a product specification), the ramifications of which can be enormous in terms of cost and time spent by a variety of individuals from both parties to the contract.

> The quality of the relationship can, therefore, be jeopardised through poor and inconsistent communications.

The quality of the relationship can, therefore, be jeopardised through poor and inconsistent communications.

When personal selling should be a major part of the promotional mix

In view of the role and the advantages and disadvantages of personal selling, when should it be a major part of the communications mix? The following is not an exhaustive list, but is presented as a means of considering some of the important issues: complexity, network factors, buyer significance and communication effectiveness.

Complexity

Personal selling is very important when there is a medium to high level of relationship complexity. Such complexity may be associated either with the physical characteristics of the product, such as computer software design, or with the environment in which the negotiations are taking place. For example, decisions related to the installation of products designed to automate an assembly line may well be a sensitive issue. This may be due to management's attitude towards the operators currently undertaking the work that the automation is expected to replace. Any complexity needs to be understood by buyer and seller in order that the right product is offered in the appropriate context for the buyer. This may mean that the buyer is required to customise the offering or provide assistance in terms of testing, installing or supporting the product.

> Personal selling is very important when there is a medium to high level of relationship complexity.

When the complexity of the offering is high, advertising and public relations cannot always convey benefits in the same way as personal selling. Personal selling allows the product to be demonstrated so that buyers can see and, if necessary, touch and taste it for themselves. Personal selling also allows explanations to be made about particular points that are of concern to the buyer or about the environment in which the buyer wishes to use the product.

Buyer significance

The significance of the product to the buyers in the target market is a very important factor in the decision on whether to use personal selling. Significance can be measured as a form of risk, and risk is associated with benefits and costs.

The absolute cost to the buyer will vary from organisation to organisation and from consumer to consumer. The significance of the purchase of an extra photocopier for a major multinational organisation may be low, but for a new start-up organisation or for an established organisation experiencing a dramatic turnaround, an extra photo-copying machine may be highly significant and subject to high levels of resistance by a number of different internal stakeholders.

The timing of a product's introduction may well be crucial to the success of a wider plan or programme of activities. Only through personal selling can delivery be dove-tailed into the client's scheme of events.

Communication effectiveness

There may be a number of ways to satisfy the communication objectives of a campaign, other than by using personal selling. Each of the other communication tools has strengths and weaknesses; consequently differing mixes provide different benefits. Have they all been considered?

One of the main reasons for using personal selling occurs when advertising alone, or any other medium, provides insufficient communications. The main reason for this inadequacy surfaces when advertising media cannot provide buyers with the informa-

When advertising media cannot provide buyers with the information they require to make their decision.

tion they require to make their decision. For example, someone buying a new car may well observe and read various magazine and newspaper advertisements. The decision to buy, however, requires information and data upon which a rational decision can be made. This rationality and experience of the car, through a test drive perhaps, balances the former, more emotional, elements that contributed to the earlier decision.

The decision to buy a car normally evokes high involvement, and motivation occurs through the central route of the ELM. Therefore, car manufacturers provide a rich balance of emotional and factual information in their literature, from which the prospective buyer seeks further information, experience and reassurance from car dealers, who provide a personal point of contact. Car buyers sign orders with the presence and encouragement of sales persons. Very few cars are bought on a mail order basis, although some are bought over the Internet.

Personal selling provides a number of characteristics that make it more effective than the other elements of the mix. As discussed, in business-to-business marketing the complexity of many products requires salespeople to be able to discuss with clients their specific needs; in other words, to be able to talk in the customer's own language, to build source credibility through expertise and hopefully trustworthiness, and build a relationship that corresponds with the psychographic profile of each member of the DMU. In this case, mass communications would be inappropriate.

There are two further factors that influence the decision to use personal selling as part of the communications mix.

There are two further factors that influence the decision to use personal selling as part of the communications mix. When the customer base is small and dispersed across a wide geographic area it makes economic sense to use sales-persons, as advertising in this situation is inadequate and ineffective.

TABLE 28.2 When personal selling is a major element of the communications mix

	Advertising relatively important	Personal selling relatively important
Number of customers	Large	Small
Buyers' information needs	Low	High
Size and importance of purchase	Small	Large
Post-purchase service required	Little	A lot
Product complexity	Low	High
Distribution strategy	Pull	Push
Pricing policy	Set	Negotiate
Resources available for promotion	Many	Few

Source: Adapted from Cravens (1987).

Personal selling is the most expensive element of the communications mix. It may be that other elements of the mix may provide a more cost-effective way of delivering the message.

Channel network factors

If the communications strategy combines a larger amount of push rather than pull activities, then personal selling is required to provide the necessary communications for the other members of the channel network. Following on from this is the question regarding what information needs to be exchanged between members and what form and timing the information should be in. Handling objections, answering questions and overcoming misconceptions are also necessary information exchange skills.

When the number of members in a network is limited, the use of a sales force is advisable, as advertising is inefficient. Furthermore, the opportunity to build a close collaborative relationship with members may enable the development of a sustainable competitive advantage. Cravens (1987) has suggested that the factors in Table 28.2 are important and determine when the sales force is an important element of the communications mix.

The roles of personal selling and the sales force are altering because the environment in which organisations operate is changing dramatically.

The roles of personal selling and the sales force are altering because the environment in which organisations operate is changing dramatically. The repercussions of these changes will become evident following the discussion of the tasks that personal selling is expected to complete.

How personal selling works: sales processes

A number of conceptual schemes have been proposed to explain the various stages in the sale process. These can be distilled into nine main stages, set out in Figure 28.1. The alignment and rigidity of the sequence should not be overstated, as the actual activities undertaken within each of these stages will vary not only from organisation to organisation but also between salespeople.

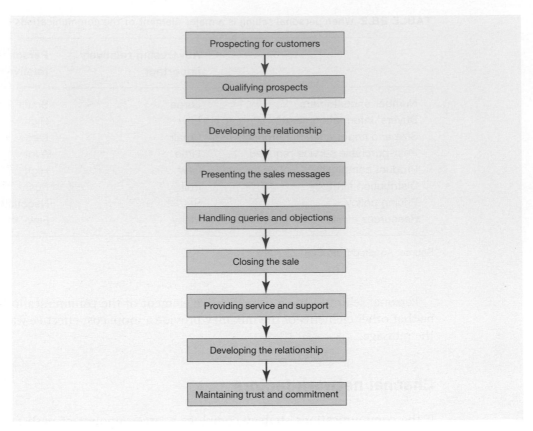

FIGURE 28.1 The main stages in the sales process

This rather simplistic approach to the sales process fails to explain how a sales-person should approach a customer or why some negotiations are successful and others are not. There have been many attempts to explain how the personal selling process works. One of the first methods proposed was discussed in Chapter 18 when exploring the hierarchy of effects models. The AIDA sequence put forward by Strong (1925) says that prospects must be drawn along a continuum of mental states, from attention to interest, desire, and finally stimulation to act in accordance with the vendor's wishes. This approach allows for a good deal of flexibility in the salesperson's approach and permits movement around a central theme.

A further model, the stimulus–response model, suggests that if the salesperson can create the right set of circumstances then it is probable that the buyer will react in a particular way. Therefore, by controlling the circum-stances of the sales process it is possible to induce the desired response. The salesperson is trained to deliver a particular stimulus (that is, what to say) and the buyer provides predictable responses, to which the salesperson has a number of expected responses. The sales presentation is therefore 'canned', ensuring that all aspects of the sale are covered in a logical order.

> By controlling the circumstances of the sales process it is possible to induce the desired response.

Jolson (1975) studied the results of such canned or prepared presentations with those that are personalised and determined more 'on the hoof'. His results indicated that buyers learned more through on-the-hoof presentations, but revealed that buyers had greater intentions to buy after the prepared presentation. This behavioural view is vendor led and discounts the cognitive processes of the buyer in its attempt to control the process and the differing needs of different buyers.

The role of the salesperson is to assist buyers to find solutions to their problems.

A third model focuses upon buyers and their needs. The role of the salesperson is to assist buyers to find solutions to their problems. According to Still *et al.* (1988), the salesperson needs to understand the cognitive processes of buyers in respect of their decision to buy or not to buy. This approach has been termed the 'buying formula' and is based upon the satisfactions that a buyer experiences when placing orders as a solution to perceived problems (from work based on Strong, 1938).

The sequence of the model, therefore, is that the buyer first recognises a problem or a need. A solution is then found, which is purchased, and the buyer experiences a level of satisfaction. This formula can be seen in Figure 28.2. The solution contains two components, the product or service and the name of the organisation or the salesperson who facilitated the solution. When a buying habit is formed, the formula adjusts to that in Figure 28.3. To complete the formula, buyers must regard the product and the source as adequate and experience pleasant feelings when thinking of the components to the solution (Figure 28.4).

Still *et al.* (1988) emphasise the need for salespersons to ensure that all the components of the buying habit are in place. For example, it is important that the buyer knows why the product is the best one for the identified problem and he or she must also have a pleasant feeling towards the source. This means that any competitor attack will be rebuffed because the current solution is deemed adequate. Reasons and pleasant feelings constitute the major elements of defence in a buying habit.

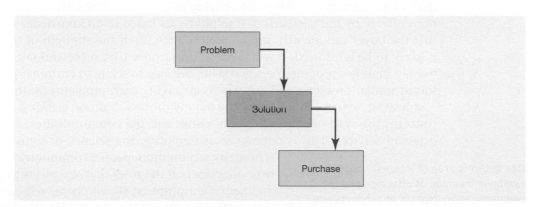

FIGURE 28.2 The mental stages involved in a purchase

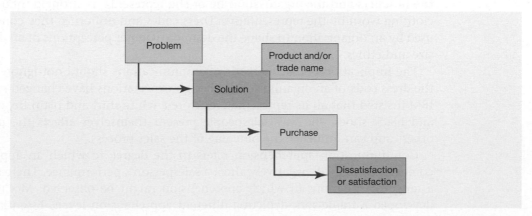

FIGURE 28.3 The buying formula (From Still *et al.* (1988); reproduced by kind permission of Prentice-Hall Inc., Englewood Cliffs, NJ.)

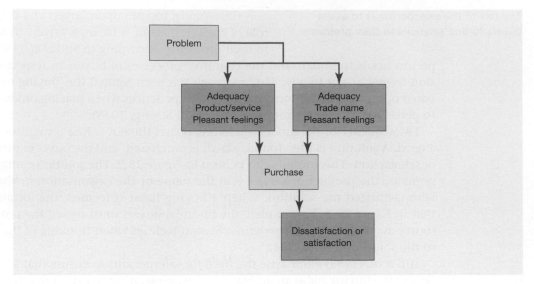

FIGURE 28.4 The complete buying formula (From Still *et al.* (1988); reproduced by kind permission of Prentice-Hall Inc., Englewood Cliffs, NJ.)

While some people might reject this approach, the essence of the buying formula is that a long-term relationship can develop as a result of the satisfaction with the solutions offered by the salesperson. If solutions are based upon knowledge and experience that the buyer can identify and empathise with, then the strength of the relationship is likely to be reinforced. It will come as no surprise that successful salespeople appear to hold high levels of interpersonal skills, are able to relate to customer problems, have solved similar problems and are experts at solving such problems (Rothschild, 1987).

A host of factors can influence the buying process, but one growing area of interest concerns the symbolic meaning of offerings and the communication aspects of products and services. This is referred to as semiotics, the science of signs and meaning.

One growing area of interest concerns the symbolic meaning of offerings and the communication aspects of products and services.

Through consumption, people communicate non-verbally who they are and the roles they are playing at a particular moment. Consumption allows people self-expression. This perspective is important to the salesperson, as the perception that buyers have of them can influence the sales process. Stuart and Fuller (1991) found that a buyer's initial perception of a salesperson, the products and the organisation he or she represents, is strongly influenced by the clothing worn by the representative. Dress codes and uniforms, they conclude, can be used by an organisation to shape the desired customer perceptions of an organisation's size and ethics.

The implication is that marketing communications should not ignore issues about the dress code of an organisation. Although expectations have changed radically since IBM insisted that all its representatives wore a white shirt and plain tie, dark blue suit and black shoes, the way salespeople present themselves affects the perception of others and can influence the outcome of the sales process.

Communication apprehension refers to the degree to which an apprehension of communication will negatively affect a salesperson's performance. There appears to be a range of situations in which apprehension might be observed. McCroskey (1984) developed a framework depicting different apprehension levels. Essentially there are two main conditions. One is a condition that affects individuals in situations which normal people would not consider threatening. The other is a state that refers to the

ViewPoint 28.2   Different selling approaches

Having repeatedly failed to get appointments with major organisations in order to sell his services about compliance with the regulations in the technology sector, Steve Kerner tried a different approach. He wrote to Dell and offered to pay for their time if they agreed to meet him. Not only did they meet but he got the job, didn't have to pay and they gave him a referral to AT&T.

Richard Knight runs an advertising agency in Hampshire, which concentrates on poster-sized advertisements. However, he sensed that prospects were bored and cynical of standard presentations so he has adopted a number of different approaches. One of these requires him to fold a poster until it is small and proclaim that this size will cost £300 (in a local paper). He unfolds it once and announces that will cost £600 and then completely unfolds it and states that he will put this at bus stops for just £40. The response is immediate and based on the visual impact of the value that was so clearly demonstrated.

Source: Armistead (2002); used with permission.

normal apprehension felt by people when speaking in meetings, group situations, dyadic communications and public speaking situations. Generally speaking, it is not uncommon to find that above-average sales performance is achieved by individuals who have the lowest level of communication apprehension. Not surprisingly, those with low levels of sales performance tend to have high levels of communication apprehension (Pitt *et al.*, 2000).

A further issue concerns the degree of ambiguity that both parties to a sales meeting might experience.

A further issue concerns the degree of ambiguity that both parties to a sales meeting might experience. Such ambiguity might refer to specific product-related information, failure to understand the problem that needs to be resolved, the time available to resolve it or the impact on other stakeholders related to the specific situation.

Sales force management and organisation

The target market and profile of the customer will have been established previously during the development of the communication plan. In particular, the communication strategy will have indicated the degree of push and pull to be used and will have illuminated detail about the nature of the channels in which the salesperson is to operate. Such information is important, as it helps to shape the sales strategy and the messages to be transmitted. Essentially, the salesperson acts as a link between a supplier and a customer, the primary role being to arrange matters so that the relationship can be continued and developed to the mutual benefit of both organisations and their participants.

The primary and traditional sales channel is the field sales force.

The primary and traditional sales channel is the field sales force. These are people who are recruited and trained to find prospective customers, to demonstrate or explain the organisation's products and services and to persuade prospects that they should buy the offering. Orders are then signed, and the salesperson reports the order to his or her organisation, which then fulfils the details of the

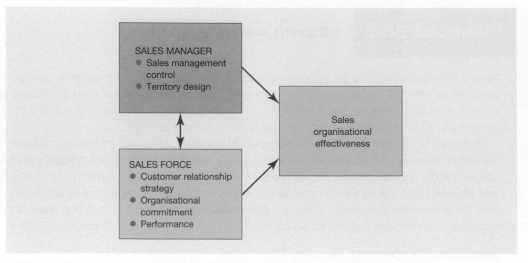

FIGURE 28.5 Antecedents of sales organisational effectiveness (From Grant and Cravens (1999); used with kind permission.)

customer's order, as agreed. However, while life is not this simple, this broad perspective is assumed to be the primary sales channel of many organisations, particularly those operating in the business-to-business sector.

Salespersons are like any other unit of resource in that they need to be deployed in a way that provides maximum benefit to the organisation. Grant and Cravens (1999) suggest that the effectiveness of the sales organisation (or unit) is determined as a result of two main antecedents: the sales manager and the sales force itself. These are shown in Figure 28.5.

An organisation is linked to its customers through three main processes that Srivastava *et al.* (1999) refer to as core business capabilities, namely product development management, supply chain management and customer relationship management. See Table 28.3. Ingram *et al.* (2002) make the point that the centrality of the customer to the organisation highlights the crucial role of sales strategy with regard to the organisation's overall customer interaction process.

> The centrality of the customer to the organisation highlights the crucial role of sales strategy with regard to the organisation's overall customer interaction process.

In order to decide on an appropriate sales strategy, the nature of the desired communication needs to be examined. Are there to be salespersons negotiating individually, or as a team with a single buyer or buying team? Is a sales team required in

TABLE 28.3 Core business capabilities (adapted from Srivastava *et al.*, 1999)

Category	Explanation
Product development management	Developing and maintaining suitable products and services to meet customer needs and provide customer value
Supply chain management	The acquisition and transformation of resources (inputs) into valued customer offerings, throughout the supply chain
Customer relationship management	Creating, sustaining and developing customer relationships for mutual benefit

order to sell to buying teams or will conference and seminar selling achieve the desired goals? What is the degree of importance of the portfolio of accounts, and how should the organisations be contacted?

The primary, and traditional, sales channel is the field sales force. These are people who are fully employed by the organisation and are referred to as the direct sales force. Salespersons, like any other unit of resource, should be deployed in a way that provides maximum benefit to the organisation. Sales organisation effectiveness results from the performance of salespeople, organisational factors and various environmental factors (Baldauf *et al.*, 2002).

The performance of sales people is a measure of both their work, or task-related, behaviours and the results of their activities and inputs. Therefore, a sales management control strategy should refer to the degree to which sales managers actively manage the inputs as a well as reward against targeted outcomes (sales, market share, etc).

From this it is possible to identify two main sales management approaches, Behaviour based- and Outcome-based control systems (Baldauf *et al.*, 2002). Essentially, control through Behaviour-based systems is founded upon managing the inputs or processes to a salesperson and rewarding them with a high fixed salary and low commission. Conversely, control through Outcome-based approaches is characterised by a focus on results, little managerial supervision and direction, and high levels of commission as an incentive to perform.

Many organisations use a hybrid approach but research by Baldauf *et al.* indicates that sales managers appear to utilise a 'coaching rather than command and control management styles'. The emphasis appears to be on the long term and the value of developing relationships. The performance of salespeople is therefore enhanced by sales management strategies that are based on generating positive behaviour. However, results from previous work undertaken by Piercy *et al.* (1998) supported many previous findings that sales people with high levels of behaviour performance also exhibit high levels of outcome performance. This implies that sales managers should spend a greater amount of their time selecting, training and developing sales people rather than just selecting, directing and measuring results.

From this brief overview of sales management responsibilities it can be concluded that they are responsible for five broad activities associated with sales people. These are:

- selection and recruitment
- training
- size and deployment
- motivation and supervision
- evaluation, control and reward.

Of these space is devoted only to the issue of size and deployment.

Sales force size and structure

One of the first questions that needs to be addressed concerns the type of sales force to be used (assuming the decision has been made that some form of personal selling is required in the communications mix). Further questions are concerned with how many salespersons are required and where and how they should operate. Decisions regarding the type, structure, size and territory of the sales force will be discussed on the basis that this is the only sales channel used by an organisation.

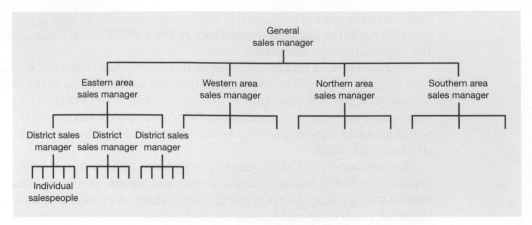

FIGURE 28.6 A geographically based sales force structure

There are a number of ways in which an organisation can structure the sales force, but there are three broad approaches (geographic, product and market/customer) that most organisations have used. The following examples are based upon Tgi PLC, which designs, manufactures and distributes loudspeaker products. These are purely examples of how it might organise its sales force and are not intended to represent the way in which Tgi approaches its markets.

Geographic-based sales force

> The most common and straightforward method of organising a sales force is to assign individuals to separate geographic territories.

The most common and straightforward method of organising a sales force is to assign individuals to separate geographic territories (Figure 28.6). In this type of sales force the salesperson is responsible for all the activities necessary to sell all products to all potential customers in the region or area in which the territory is located. This method of assignment is used by new companies, in situations where customers tend to buy a range of products, where there is little difference in the geographic spread of the products or when resources are limited.

Strengths

This approach provides for the lowest cost, concentrates the selling effort throughout the territory and allows for a quick response to regional or local needs. This structure also ensures that customers only see one person from the selling organisation and are not at risk of becoming the recipient of multiple and conflicting messages.

Weaknesses

The level of specialised knowledge is reduced, as many products have to be promoted by each salesperson. Furthermore, salespeople under this structure tend to be allowed greater freedom in the design and execution of their working day. Consequently, the number of new customers is often low and the line of least resistance is usually pursued. This may also conflict with the objectives of the organisation, as, for example, call patterns may not be compatible with the overall goals of the sales force.

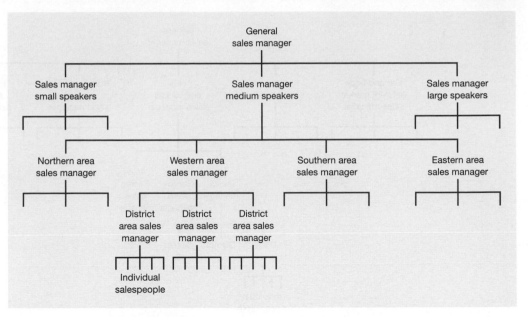

FIGURE 28.7 A product-based sales force structure

Product-based sales force

The organisation has different sales teams, each carrying a particular line of products.

Under this type of structure, the organisation has different sales teams, each carrying a particular line of products (Figure 28.7). This is often used by organisations with large and diverse product lines. Also, organisations with highly technical and complex products, which require specialist knowledge and particular selling techniques, prefer this form of sales force structure.

Strengths

The most important advantage of this approach is that it allows the development of product knowledge and technical expertise. In business-to-business markets this factor can lead to improved source credibility, since the level of expertise, and possibly trustworthiness, can be important if the messages are to be persuasive and effective. If the organisation's production facilities are organised by product (separate factories), each with a sales team operating out of the unit, then there can be increased cooperation, which in turn benefits the customer.

Sales management is better able to control the allocation of the selling effort across all products under this type of structure. If greater focus is required upon a particular product, then more salespersons can be allocated appropriately.

Weaknesses

The major disadvantage is that there is a high probability that there will be duplication of sales effort. A customer could be called on by a number of different salespeople, all from the same organisation.

Selling expenses are driven higher and management time and costs rise as the company attempts to bring coordination.

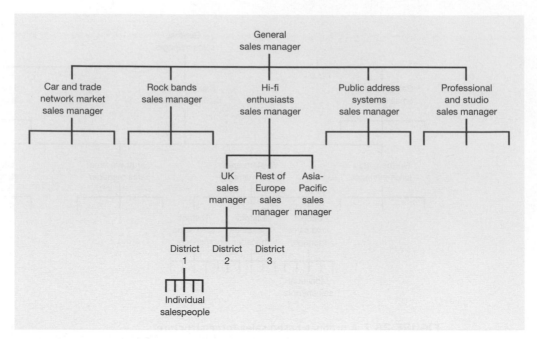

FIGURE 28.8 A market-based sales force structure

Market-based sales force

Organising a sales force by market
or customer type is an activity
complementary to the marketing
concept.

Organising a sales force by market or customer type is
an activity complementary to the marketing concept
(Figure 28.8). This form of sales force organisation has
increased in popularity, as it allows products with many
applications to be sold into many different markets and
hence to different customers.

Strengths

By calling on a single type of customer, a greater understanding of customer needs
develops. Such customer specialisation can be used to foster specialist selling approaches for different markets. The size of the specialist sales forces can be varied by sales
management in accordance with internal and external requirements. This is important
for organisations operating in highly competitive and quickly changing environments.

Weaknesses

As with the product structure, duplication is a primary difficulty. The costs, however,
of operating under this form of structure are higher than any of the others.

These three approaches to sales force design are not mutually exclusive, and most
major organisations use a combination of them to meet the needs of their various
stakeholders. As Still *et al.* (1988) state, the subdivision of the structure is usually
related to primary and secondary needs for marketing success. Most organisations use
geography as a subdivision, but whether this is a primary or secondary subdivision
depends largely upon the importance of customer or product subdivisions for the
achievement of competitive advantage. Such hybrid structures are not static and

should evolve as the organisation and the environment in which it operates develop. Tgi uses the customer approach not only for the sales force but at an SBU level as well.

Sales force size and shape

The size of the sales force needs to be determined on a regular basis because the environments in which sales forces are operating are changing rapidly. The decision regarding the size of the sales force presents a dilemma.

Because the environments in which sales forces are operating are changing rapidly.

Increasing the size of the sales force will increase the sales revenue, but it will also increase costs. A balance needs to be achieved, and according to Govoni *et al.* (1986) the decision is a blend of the following factors: the number of potential customers, the sales potential of each of these accounts, the geographic concentration of the customers and the availability of financial resources.

There are many different approaches to the determination of the appropriate sales force size. Many of the more recent ones are based upon sophisticated software, but these are derived essentially from three main approaches: the *breakdown*, *workload* and *sales potential* methods.

The intuitive method is a label for all of the methods not based on reason, logic, market information or, in some cases, sense. At one extreme are the hunch and the 'I have been in this business for *x* years' approach, while at the other extreme there is the 'If it is good enough for the competition, then it is good enough for us' approach. These are to be rejected.

The breakdown method

This is the simplest method. Each salesperson is viewed as possessing the same sales productivity potential per period. Therefore, divide the total expected sales by the sales potential and the resultant figure equates to the number of salespeople required:

$$n = \frac{sv}{sp}$$

where *n* is the number of salespeople required, *sv* is the anticipated sales volume and *sp* is the estimated sales productivity of each salesperson/unit.

This technique is flawed in that it treats sales force size as a consequence of sales, yet the reverse is probably true. A further difficulty concerns the estimate of productivity used. It fails to account for different potentials, abilities and levels of compensation. Furthermore, there is no account of profitability as it treats sales as an end in itself.

The workload method

Underlying this method is the premise that all salespeople should bear an equal amount of the work necessary to service the entire market.

Underlying this method is the premise that all salespeople should bear an equal amount of the work necessary to service the entire market. The example offered is based upon work by Govoni *et al.* (1986).

The first task is to classify customers into categories based on the level of sales to each account. The ABC rule of account classification holds that the first 15 per cent of customers account for 65 per cent of sales (A accounts), the next 20 per cent will produce 20 per cent of sales (B accounts) and the final 65 per cent will yield only 15 per cent (C accounts).

- *Task 1.* Classify customers into categories:
  Class A: large/very attractive   = 300
  Class B: medium/moderately attractive   = 400
  Class C: small/unattractive   = 1,300

- *Task 2.* Determine the frequency and desired duration of each call for each type of account:
  Class A: 15 times/pa 95 mins/call   = 23.75 hours
  Class B: 10 times/pa 63 mins/call   = 10.50 hours
  Class C: 6 times/pa 45 mins/call   = 4.50 hours

- *Task 3.* Calculate the workload in covering the market:
  Class A: 300 accounts 23.75 hours/account   = 7,125 hours
  Class B: 400 accounts 10.50 hours/account   = 4,200 hours
  Class C: 1,300 accounts 4.50 hours/account = 5,850 hours
  Total workload   = 17,175 hours

- *Task 4*: Determine the time available per salesperson:
  40 hours/week × 46 weeks/pa   = 1,840 hours

- *Task 5.* Determine selling/contact time per salesperson:
  Contact: 45%   = 828 hours
  Travelling: 31%   = 570 hours
  Non-selling: 24%   = 442 hours

- *Task 6.* Calculate the number of salespersons required:

$$\text{number of salespersons} = \frac{\text{total work load}}{\text{contact hours}} \frac{17,175}{828} = 20.74$$

A total of 20 or 21 salespeople would be required using this method. While this technique is easy to calculate, it does not allow for differences in sales response among accounts that receive the same sales effort. It fails to account for servicing and assumes that all salespersons have the same contact time. This is simply not true. One further shortcoming is that the profitability per call is neglected.

The sales potential method

Semlow (1959) was one of the earliest to report the decreasing-returns principle when applied to sales force calculations. The principle recognises that there will be diminishing returns as extra salespeople are added to the sales force. For example, one extra salesperson may generate £120,000, but two more may only generate a total of £200,000 in new sales. Therefore, while the first generates £120,000, the other two only generate £100,000 each.

Semlow found, for example, that sales in territories with 1 per cent potential generated £160,000, whereas sales in territories with 5 per cent averaged £200,000. Therefore 1 per cent potential in the second territory equates to £40,000 (200,000/5) and £160,000 (160,000/1) in the first.

The conclusion reached was that a higher proportion of sales per 1 per cent of potential could be realised if the territories were made smaller by adding salespeople. As asked above, what is the optimum number of salespersons, because costs rise as more salespeople are added?

Semlow's work provides the basis for some of the more sophisticated techniques and derivatives of the incremental or marginal approach.

Semlow's work provides the basis for some of the more sophisticated techniques and derivatives of the incremental or marginal approach. It is relatively simple in concept but exceedingly difficult to implement. The conclusion, that a salesperson in a low-potential territory is expected to achieve a greater proportion of the potential than a colleague in a high-potential territory is, as Churchill *et al.* (1990) say, 'intuitively appealing'.

Territory design

Having determined the number of salespeople that are necessary to achieve the set promotion objectives, attention must be given to the shape, potential and equality of the territories to be created. The decomposition of the total market into smaller units facilitates easier control of the sales strategy and operations. A sales territory is a grouping of customers and prospects assigned to an individual or team of salespeople. The reason for the establishment of sales territories is mainly oriented to aspects of planning and control. Sales territories enable the organisation to cover the designated market, to control costs, to assist the evaluation of salesperson performance, to contribute to sales force morale and to provide a bridge with other promotional activities, most notably advertising (Still *et al.*, 1988).

Churchill *et al.* (1990) suggest that the steps depicted in Figure 28.9 are the most appropriate. The objective is to make all territories as equal as possible with respect to, first, sales potential, as this facilitates performance evaluation, and, secondly, work effort, as this tends to improve morale and reduce levels of conflict.

The most basic unit is a small geographic area. Small units permit easier adjustments to be made and allow for the reassignment of accounts from one salesperson to another. Units can be based on counties, local authority areas, postcodes (important in Greater London and other metropolitan areas), cities and regions.

Once the market potential in each unit has been established, approximate territories can be set up. From this point account analysis helps to determine the call frequency and duration necessary for the larger accounts. A matrix approach, based upon the attractiveness of the account and the ability of the organisation to exploit the opportunities presented, can help this part of the management process, as in Figure 28.10.

Adjustments are designed to equalise potential and workload in each area.

The penultimate step is to make adjustments to the boundaries of the tentative territories established earlier. These adjustments are designed to equalise potential and workload in each area.

It should be remembered that sales potential is never static, at the market, the territory or the account level. In particular, potential will vary with call frequency. It will be apparent that there is a relationship between account attractiveness (AA) and account effort (AE). While AA determines how hard the account should be worked, the frequency and duration will affect the sales derived from each account. There is a need to balance potentials and workloads if computer programs, such as Callplan, are not being used.

There are several methods available. Empirically based methods use regression analysis to represent the relationship between sales and a number of key sales variables such as the number of calls, potential or workload. Judgement-based methods require the salesperson to estimate the sales/sales call ratio so that the optimum number of calls can be made on each account. The subjectively based method involves executives

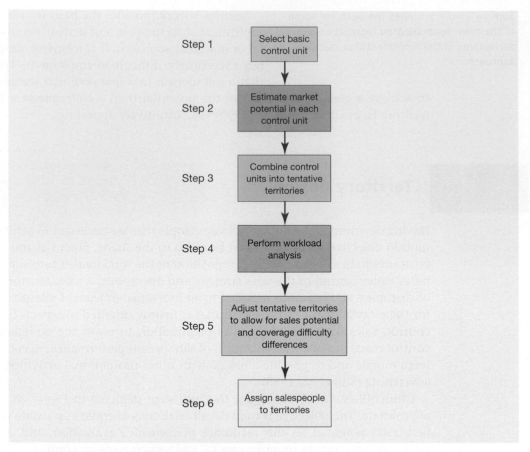

FIGURE 28.9 Key steps in territory design (From Churchill *et al.* (1990); used with kind permission.)

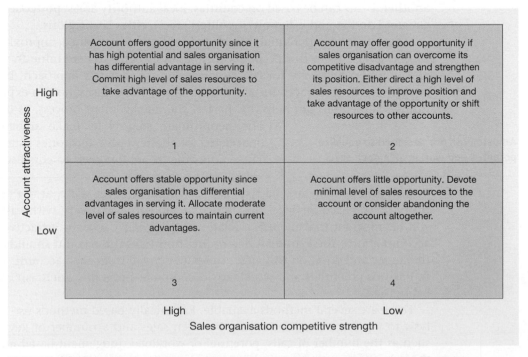

FIGURE 28.10 Account planning matrix (From Churchill *et al.* (1990); used with kind permission.)

making changes in call frequency to reflect changes in the market or to achieve a specific objective.

The final task is to assign salespeople to territories. It should be remembered that salespeople have varying levels of ability. To overcome this disparity, the most able is allocated an index of 1.00 and all others rated relative to that individual. For example, an index of 0.75 means that a salesperson could achieve 75 per cent of the business that a salesperson with an index of 1.0 could achieve in the same territory. Salespeople can then be allocated on a basis that maximises the return to the organisation.

Grant and Cravens (1999) found that the effectiveness of a sales organisation is partly determined by the design of sales territories. For sales organisations that place high value on directing, evaluating, rewarding and monitoring, territory design and sales force commitment appear to be linked to sales unit effectiveness. From their research they state that territory design plays a 'pivotal role in sales unit effectiveness'. Decisions regarding the size, shape and form of the sales force need to be made once a strategic decision has been made to employ a sales force. An alternative approach is to hire or rent a sales force, by region, product or time, to suit the needs of the task at hand. These temporary sales forces are recruited from companies in the field marketing sector. This sector has grown in significance and stature over the past few years, and more detail is provided in Chapter 29.

Changing channels

The previous discussion of the role of the field sales force was pre-empted by the statement that this is the primary sales channel for many organisations in the business-to-business sector. There are, however, a growing number of organisations that see a different role for the sales force and which are introducing other sales channels in order to improve productivity and the bottom line. These have been explored in other parts of the book, most notably Chapter 27. There are many implications for organisations arising from the development of a multichannel approach. Two of these include team selling and sales force automation, which are discussed below. Others include key and global account management, which are discussed in Chapter 31, and direct marketing, which is the subject of Chapter 27.

Team selling

Three distinct selling strategies can be identified: transactional, consultative and alliance sales.

Three distinct selling strategies can be identified: transactional, consultative and alliance sales (Rackham and DeVincetis, 1999). See Table 28.4. These strategies represent different eras of thought and approaches to selling and sales management. However, they also represent phases through which individual organisations can develop their selling practices.

In order that partnership and more collaborative selling approaches be implemented it has become increasingly necessary and common for organisations to assign a team of salespeople to meet the needs of key account customers. A variety of different skills are thought necessary to meet the diversity of personnel making up the DMUs of the larger organisations. Consequently, a salesperson may gain access to an organisation, after which a stream of engineers, analysts, technicians, programmers, training executives and financial experts follow.

TABLE 28.4 Three selling strategies (adapted from Rackham and DeVincetis, 1999)

Selling strategy	Explanation
Transactional selling	This is the traditional form of selling and the strategy is characterised by the planned development of a large volume of sales accounts, each of which has individual and unrelated buyers.
Consultative selling	Due to better understanding about relationships and the need to limit the number of buyers consultative selling evolved in the mid-1980s. Partnerships were formed with customers and a form of preferred supplier status was established. Sometimes referred to as solution selling.
Alliance sales	An alliance sales strategy was developed when various processes of the selling organisation were integrated with those of the partner. Sales moved from a quantitative perspective (transactional) to a qualitative perspective (both consultative and alliance based).

For example, when one of Goodman's (a division of Tgi discussed earlier) car-manufacturing clients plans a new model, a salesperson opens the door to provide a communication link between the two organisations. Soon, a project team evolves, consisting of engineering, manufacturing, purchasing, production and quality staff, all working to satisfy the needs of their client. Goodman even uses the same project code number as the client to provide for clarity and avoid confusion. It also helps to build the relationship and identification between the partners.

Most leading IT-based organisations used to sell the hardware and then leave the customer to work out how to use it. Team selling is now used by Digital, Hewlett-Packard, IBM and others to provide customised combinations of hardware, software and technical support as solutions to their customers' business problems. This requires teams of salespeople and technical experts working closely with the customer's DMU throughout the sales/purchasing cycle and beyond.

The sales team approach requires high levels of coordination and internal communication if it is to be successful and sell across product lines from various locations (Cespedes *et al.*, 1989). In addition, the range of activities associated with team selling requires a culture that is focused on customers' needs and the team must be supported and self-driven to deliver on these internally recognised performance barriers. Indeed, Workman *et al.* (2003) refer to the need to develop an *esprit de corps* in order that selling teams, primarily used for key accounts, be successful.

The sales team approach requires high levels of coordination and internal communication.

Team selling requires a different approach to both the customer and also the associated internal activities than those required for regular field force selling. Both the levels of commitment and costs associated with cross-functional team selling are large, and these reasons alone restrict the use of this selling approach to those accounts that are strategically important.

Sales force automation (SFA)

The use of technology to assist field force selling has grown substantially, and the advent of 3G technology is likely to accelerate usage of digital technology in the sales and selling context. There are a number of reasons for this interest, most notably the

TABLE 28.5 The use of technology in sales (adapted from Widmier *et al.*, 2002)

Sales function	Use of technology
Organising	Call schedules, route plans, contacts, sales plans
Presenting with	Portable multimedia presentations, customised proposals
Reporting on	Call reports, expense claims, monthly performance
Informing about	Prospecting, product performance and product configuration information
Communicating via	Mobile phones, pagers, the Internet, email, personal organisers, fax machines
Supporting transactions	Order status and tracking, stock control, stock availability

attraction of lower selling costs, improved communication effectiveness and enhanced market and customer information. Various forms of technology have been employed (Engle and Barnes, 2000). What constitutes sales force automation is questionable, simply because of the breadth of internal and external activities undertaken in the name of selling. One perspective is that such technology embraces sales force automation, communication technology and customer relationship management (Widmier *et al.*, 2002). These authors identify six main sales-related functions, namely organising, presenting, reporting, communicating, informing and supporting transactions. These are set out in Table 28.5.

Embraces sales force automation, communication technology and customer relationship management.

Research by these authors shows that technology is used extensively to assist all of the selling functions but is used least by salespersons when in the field for actually supporting transactions (e.g. order status and stock enquiries and qualifying customers). It also indicates that technology is more likely to be used by salespersons in the office (preparing presentations, proposals, route planning, scheduling and reporting) than the field.

The deployment of SFA varies among organisations and its effectiveness will, to a large extent, be dependent upon appropriate implementation, proper utilisation by the sales force and suitable support processes. Indeed, Morgan and Inks (2001) report SFA failure rates between 25 and 60 per cent, a large proportion of which can be accredited to poor management of change and sales force resistance to change. The factors that relate to the successful implementation of SFA will vary according to industry and organisation and perhaps even individual sales people. Research by Morgan and Inks identified four main elements associated with the successful implementation of SFA: management commitment, training, user involvement and accurate expectation setting. They also determined that implementation will be less than satisfactory when there are fears of technology, of interference in an individual's selling activities, or a loss of power (over the information they have on their customers), and where there is a general resistance to change.

It would appear logical that the adoption of SFA should lead to substantial productivity gains. However, high implementation costs, sales force resistance and under-utilisation have been cited as some of the key reasons for the failure to substantially increase productivity. This apparent conflict of views should be considered in the light of varying industry characteristics, operational circumstances and different definitions of SFA and technology. To date, there is little research evidence to show the impact of SFA on relationships.

It may be that technology is used by sales force personnel to engage with internal colleagues more than their customers.

There can be little doubt that most sales people use technology much more in their work than their counterparts of 15 years ago. However, it may be that technology is used by sales force personnel to engage with internal colleagues more than their customers. The greater adoption of SFA will only come through appropriate management leadership, training, accurate expectations and the influence and encouragement of users themselves (Morgan and Inks, 2001).

The future role of the sales force

The performance networks of many markets are in transition; this in turn affects the structure and strategy of network members and has stimulated recognition that organisations should seek cooperative relationships (Jarillo, 1993) rather than be competitive in the manner which Porter (1985) and the Design School advocate.

Transition has also been brought about because of changing customer needs, the buoyancy of the European economy in the mid-1980s and its subsequent recession, and the shifting balance of key stakeholders. The expectations of organisational buyers and consumers have shifted so that new skills are required of a salesperson. Internally, organisations have moved their focus. For example, the manner in which performance is measured and resources are deployed has moved from a sales to a profit basis, while the sharp rise in costs of personal selling has required organisations to seek new ways of reaching and communicating with customers.

It is not surprising that the roles salespeople are expected to undertake are changing.

In consideration of the multiple sales channel approach and the factors that have brought significant change to the way in which field sales forces are organised, it is not surprising that the roles salespeople are expected to undertake are changing. Some of these roles are set out in Figure 28.11.

When these factors are brought together the salesperson, who was seen earlier as working at the boundary of the organisation to generate sales, is now expected to act as a network coordinator and as a manager of customers (Wilson, 1993). In Chapters 9 and 31 it is identified that a collaborative communication strategy seeks to establish long-term relational transactions. The short-term market exchange perspective hinders the development of strategic advantage. Strong personal interaction with clients, based upon a problem–solution perspective to buyer needs, can provide a source of sustainable competitive advantage for organisations.

Integrating and coordinating the efforts of both the buying and the selling teams will become an important role for the salesperson, particularly as the effects of concentration lead to even greater levels of centralisation of the buying function.

The integration of personal selling with the other elements of the promotional mix

Personal selling cannot work effectively in isolation from the other elements in the promotional mix.

Personal selling cannot work effectively in isolation from the other elements in the promotional mix. For example, members of the sales force are literally representative of

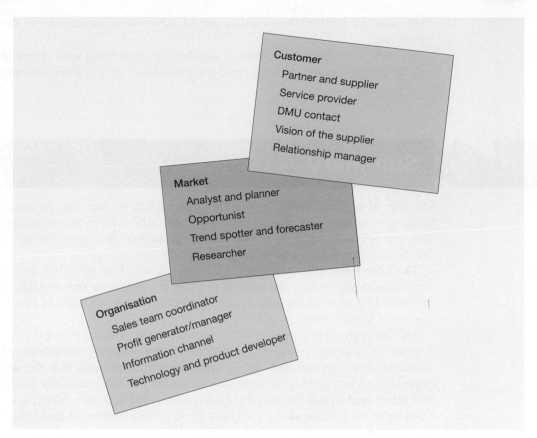

FIGURE 28.11 New roles for the sales force (Adapted from Wilson (1993) and Anderson and Rosenbloom (1982).)

the organisation for whom they work: they are mobile PR representatives. Stakeholders perceive them and partly shape their image of the selling organisation on the way in which, for example, the salesperson dresses, speaks and handles questions, the type of car driven and the level of courtesy displayed to the support staff.

The integration and compatibility of direct marketing with the sales force have been discussed and the degree of impact should not be underestimated. The sales force's role within sales promotions can be strong, especially with activities directed at members of the performance network. Members of the sales force are often used to distribute promotional merchandise to both consumers and the trade.

It is with advertising that the strongest degree of integration with personal selling can be observed. As determined earlier, it would appear that these two elements of the communications mix complement each other in many ways. Advertising is more effective at the initial stages of the response hierarchy, but the later stages of inducing trial and closing for the order are more appropriate for personal selling.

Rothschild (1987) has reported Levitt's (1967) work which indicated that organisations that invest in advertising to create awareness are more likely to create a more favourable reception for their salespeople than those organisations which do not invest in awareness-building activities. However, those that had invested were also expected to have a better-trained sales force.

Morrill (1970) found that selling costs were as much as 28 per cent lower if the customer had been made aware of the salesperson's organisation prior to the call. Swinyard and Ray (1977) determined that even if a sale was not made for reasons other than product quality then further use of advertising increased the probability of a future sale.

All these findings suggest that, by combining advertising with personal selling, costs will be reduced, reach extended and the probability of a sale considerably improved.

Summary

The role of personal selling in the promotional mix is changing. As organisations move to more relational exchanges, so the sales force will need to play a complementary role. This role will necessitate the execution of tasks such as managing customers and integrating the activities of the performance network.

The sales force will need to be deployed in a way that optimises the resources of the organisation and realises the greatest possible percentage of the available sales and profit potential that exists in the defined area of operation. This will result in a continuance of the growth of key accounts.

The use of the field sales force as the only means of personal selling is unlikely to remain. Technological advances and the need for increasing levels of promotional effectiveness and accountability, together with tighter cost constraints, indicate that the more progressive organisations will employ multiple sales channels. This may mean the use of telemarketing and direct mail to free the sales force from non-selling activities, which will allow management to focus the time of the sales force upon getting in front of customers and prospects, with a view to using their particular selling skills.

Review questions

1. What are the different types of personal selling?
2. Describe the role of personal selling and highlight its main strengths and weaknesses.
3. Which factors need to be considered when determining the significance of personal selling in the promotional mix?
4. What are the tasks that salespersons are normally expected to accomplish?
5. Describe two ways in which the personal selling process is thought to work.
6. Write a brief report highlighting the strengths and weaknesses of each of the main ways of structuring the sales force.
7. Identify the principal differences between the workload and the sales potential methods of determining sales force size.
8. Write brief notes outlining the way in which direct marketing might be used to assist personal selling activities.
9. Suggest four new roles that salespersons might be required to adopt in the future.
10. If an organisation seeks to establish relational exchanges with its partner organisations and customers, the size of the field sales force should be increased. Discuss.

MINI-CASE
Selling the Z5000

The Z5000 represented a major development for Reema Robotics. Not only is its design and quality superior to all competitors, but because it is also the only system in the market that is built to facilitate product developments and system enhancements. In effect, the Z5000 changed the nature of the market for all time.

Reema is a major manufacturer of robotic equipment that can be used in a variety of manufacturing and production processes. There are a number of vertical markets that offer opportunities for this type of technology but food and car production assembly lines offer major opportunities. This is because legislation is tightening in order to provide improved consumer protection and because the need to reduce car production costs and extend design platforms across a range of models is increasing. Reema has developed a major new product referred to as the Z5000. In 2004 it was thought that the UK market represented an opportunity to sell in 5,500 units each year, plus various associated service elements such as maintenance contracts, training and support.

Rupert Throgmorton is the Reema sales executive responsible for the Midlands region. Many of his customers are large national, international and even global organisations where the purchase decisions for equipment of this size and value are made by a range of different people. These are the production and operations managers, engineering designers, maintenance managers, commercial managers, finance directors, the CEO and the board of directors. These people all play different roles in the purchasing process, with some having greater or lesser degrees of influence depending upon what it is that is being bought.

In addition to these formal bodies there a number of informal groups that need to be considered when selling in high-value equipment such as the Z5000. One of these groups contains the secretaries and personal assistants. Their role is to support their line managers, and one of the ways they do this is to manage their manager's time and control the flow of information they receive. These different groups of people represent a number of different communication networks. The complexity of the information

flows requires effective project management by sales executives.

Throgmorton received a sales lead indicating that Manning's in Downston had made enquiries about the purchase of robotic equipment for use in its new assembly facility producing construction vehicles. Manning's was not a Reema customer so there was little direct experience of its purchase processes and the company had little knowledge of Reema, other than information picked up through its Web site and at exhibitions, including reference to its reputation and indirect comment.

On 2 July 2004 Throgmorton phoned Jim Bland, operations manager at Manning's. At a subsequent meeting it appeared that Bland knew a great deal about the Z5000, having researched the market, visited Reema's Web site and been sent a pack of general information when he had made his initial enquiry. He was upbeat and enthusiastic about the Z5000 and Reema.

After several meetings between Throgmorton and Bland it became apparent that the users would benefit from the Z5000, rather than the competing equipment solutions offered by GTD and Frebell Systems. Throgmorton was assured that Bland would be recommending the Z5000. However, Throgmorton wanted to make sure that the engineering team fully understood the capabilities of the Z5000 before any specification was publicised. He tried to approach the chief engineer on a number of occasions but for various reasons was unable to reach him. In the end, and after several weeks, his secretary provided the documentation relating to the assembly line technical specification. It showed that the Z5000 matched Manning's technical requirements very closely.

Throgmorton heard that the decision to purchase a robotic assembly system for the new production facility had now been agreed in principle and that Manning's understood the Reema system to be technically superior to the two competing products. However, the price of the Z5000 was a full 19 per cent higher than the nearest competitor.

Reema advised Throgmorton to meet the finance director in order to stress the capabilities of the Z5000. This he attempted to do, but he was advised that he should refer to Adam Crowbar, the commercial manager charged with responsibility for the purchase. This he did and was able to convey the various attributes of the Z5000. Crowbar was impressed but commented that all products claimed they were technologically advanced and he could not understand how the premium price was justified. This new information worried Throgmorton because he knew the Z5000 matched the specification better than those of the competing products. He offered Crowbar the opportunity of an all-expenses paid trip to visit a couple of European installations that had been piloting the Z5000 and which had worked with Reema on product development and design. This offer was declined.

Once the technical specifications were distributed, all three companies were invited to make a formal written bid. Reema took the opportunity to reduce its price so that it was only 9 per cent higher than that of their closest rivals' known bid. Once these fully documented bids had been circulated internally, Manning's invited the three companies to make a formal presentation. It was at this event that Throgmorton and his senior Reema colleagues met the finance director for the first time. Both he and Adam Crowbar referred to price on a number of occasions. In anticipation of this Reema focused on the low future support costs and the ease with which new technological developments could be easily

incorporated within the Z5000 without having to replace the entire system.

Two weeks later Reema learned that it had not been successful and that the order had been placed with a rival organisation.

This case contains fictitious information and does not relate to any organisation or individual. It is based on an original idea by Prof. Kamran Kashani.

Questions

1 What was the real added value offered by Reema and how might it have conveyed it more successfully?

2 What are the main influences acting upon Manning's purchase decision processes and how might Throgmorton have managed this aspect of the selling process?

3 To what extent can the three sales behaviours identified by Reid *et al.* (2002) be identified in Throgmorton's activities?

4 How might the use of team selling have improved Reema's chances of winning Manning's business?

5 Discuss reasons why Reema might not be too disappointed at failing to win this business.

References

Anderson, R.E. and Rosenbloom, B. (1982) Eclectic sales management: strategic responses to trends in the 1980s. *Journal of Personal Selling and Sales Management* (November), pp. 41–6.

Armistead, L. (2002) Forms sold short by bad sales technique. *Sunday Times*, 20 October, p. 17.

Baldauf, A., Cravens, D.W. and Grant, K. (2002) Consequences of sales management control in field sales organisations: a cross national perspective. *International Business Review*, **11**(5) (October), pp. 577–609.

Cespedes, F.V., Doyle, S.X. and Freedman, R.J. (1989) Teamwork for today's selling. *Harvard Business Review* (March/April), pp. 44–55.

Churchill, G.A., Ford, N.M. and Walker, C. (1990) *Sales Force Management*. Homewood, IL: Irwin.

Cravens, D.W. (1987) *Strategic Marketing*. Homewood, IL: Irwin.

Engle, R.L. and Barnes, M.L. (2000) Sales force automation usage, effectiveness and cost benefit in Germany, England and the United States. *Journal of Business and Industrial Marketing*, 15(4), pp. 216–42.

Govoni, N., Eng, R. and Galper, M. (1986) *Promotional Management*. Englewood Cliffs, NJ: Prentice-Hall.

Grant, K. and Cravens, D.W. (1999) Examining the antecedents of sales organisation effectiveness: an Australian study. *European Journal of Marketing*, 33(9/10), pp. 945–57.

Guenzi, P. (2002) Sales force activities and customer trust. *Journal of Marketing Management*, 18, pp. 749–78.

Ingram, T.N., LaForge, R.W. and Leigh, T.W. (2002) Selling in the new millennium. *Industrial Marketing Management*, 32(7) (October), pp. 559–67.

Jarillo, J.C. (1993) *Strategic Networks: Creating the Borderless Organisation*. Oxford: Butterworth-Heinemann.

Jolson, M.A. (1975) The underestimated potential of the canned sales presentation. *Journal of Marketing*, 39 (January), p. 75.

Levitt, T. (1967) Communications and industrial selling. *Journal of Marketing*, 31 (April), pp. 15–21.

Lloyd, J. (1997) Cut your rep free. *Pharmaceutical Marketing* (September), pp. 30–2.

McCroskey, J.C. (1984) The communication apprehension perspective. In *Avoiding Communication* (ed. J.A. Daley), pp. 13–38. Beverly Hills, CA: Sage.

Morgan, A.J. and Inks, S.A. (2001) Technology and the sales force: increasing acceptance of sales force automation. *Industrial Marketing Management*, 30(5) (July), pp. 463–72.

Morrill, J.E. (1970) Industrial advertising pays off. *Harvard Business Review* (March/April), pp. 159–69.

Piercy, N. F., Cravens, D.W. and Morgan, N.A. (1998) Salesforce performance and behaviour-based management processes in business-to-business sales organisations. *European Journal of Marketing*, 32(1/2), pp. 79–100.

Pitt, L.F., Berthon, P.R. and Robson, M.J. (2000) Communication apprehension and perceptions of salesperson performance: a multinational perspective. *Journal of Managerial Psychology*, 15(1), pp. 68–97.

Porter, M. (1985) *Competitive Advantage*. New York: Free Press.

Rackham, N. and DeVincctis, J.R. (1999) *Rethinking the Sales Force: Redefining Selling to Create and Capture Customer Value*. New York: McGraw-Hill.

Reid, A., Pullins, E.B. and Plank, R.E. (2002) The impact of purchase situation on salesperson communication behaviors in business markets. *Industrial Marketing Management*, 31(3), pp. 205–213.

Rothschild, M.L. (1987) *Marketing Communications*. Lexington, MA: D.C. Heath.

Semlow, W.E. (1959) How many salesmen do you need? *Harvard Business Review* (May/June), pp. 126–32.

Srivastava, R.K., Shervani, T.A. and Fahey, L. (1999) Marketing, business process and shareholder value: an organizationally embedded view of marketing activities and the discipline of marketing. *Journal of Marketing*, 63, pp. 168–79.

Still, R., Cundiff, E.W. and Govoni, N.A.P. (1988) *Sales Management*. 5th edn. Englewood Cliffs, NJ: Prentice-Hall.

Strong, E.K. (1925) *The Psychology of Selling*. New York: McGraw-Hill.

Strong, E.K. (1938) *Psychological Aspects of Business*. New York: McGraw-Hill.

Stuart, E.W. and Fuller, B.K. (1991) Clothing as communication in two business-to-business sales settings. *Journal of Business Research*, 23, pp. 269–90.

Swinyard, W.R. and Ray, M.L. (1977) Advertising–selling interactions: an attribution theory experiment. *Journal of Marketing Research*, 14 (November), pp. 509–16.

Thayer, L. (1968) *Communication and Communication Systems*. Homewood, IL: Irwin.

Widmier, S.M., Jackson Jr, D.W. and McCabe, D.B. (2002) Infusing technology into personal selling. *Journal of Personal Selling and Sales Management*, 22(3) (Summer), pp. 189–99.

Wilson, K. (1993) Managing the industrial sales force of the 1990s. *Journal of Marketing Management*, **9**, pp. 123–39.

Workman Jr, J.P., Homburg, C. and Jensen, O. (2003) Interorganisational determinants of key account management effectiveness. *Journal of Academy of Marketing Science*, **31**(1), pp. 3–21.

Wright, H. and Fill, C. (2001) Corporate images, attributes, and the UK pharmaceutical industry. *Corporate Reputation Review: an International Journal*, **4**(2) (Summer), pp. 99–112.

Exhibitions, product placement, field marketing and packaging

29

The five major tools of the communications mix work better if supported by other secondary or support tools and media. Exhibitions are a significant part of b2b promotional work, and packaging is vital to the fast-moving consumer goods sector as the majority of product decisions are made at the point of purchase. Product placement enables brands to be seen in the correct context and used by appropriate celebrities in order to help form brand associations for consumers. Field marketing offers a range of merchandising and brand experience opportunities often necessary to cut through the clutter of competitive and distracting messages.

Aims and objectives

The aims of this chapter are to consider a range of marketing communications activities that have no specific designation yet which can make a major contribution to a promotional campaign. These activities are applied to both the b2b and b2c markets.

The objectives of this chapter are to:

1. draw attention to the significance of exhibitions and trade shows;
2. highlight the main advantages and disadvantages of using exhibitions as part of the promotional mix;
3. consider the concept and issues associated with product placement;
4. introduce field marketing and explain its range of activities;
5. explore the role and key characteristics of packaging as a form of communication.

Introduction

In order to provide a difference and to cut through the noise of competing brands it is necessary to provide additional resources and communications.

The majority of marketing communications presented so far focus on the five primary tools. However, in order to provide a difference and to cut through the noise of competing brands it is necessary to provide additional resources and communications right up to the point that customers make decisions. Exhibitions fulfil a role for customers by enabling them to become familiar with new developments, new products and leading-edge brands.

Very often these customers will be opinion leaders and use word-of-mouth communications to convey their feelings and product experiences to others. In the b2b market exhibitions and trade shows are very often an integral and important component in the communications mix. Meeting friends, customers, suppliers, competitors and prospective customers is an important sociological and ritualistic event in the communication calendar for many companies.

In the consumer sector, and in particular the FMCG market, the need to provide a point of difference and offer continuity for those people who make the brand choice decisions at the point of purchase is important. Packaging not only fulfils the role of protecting a product but also conveys associations and brand cues. Product placement enables a brand to be observed in a more natural environment than that achieved on a shelf. This part of marketing communications is growing and provides income for film producers, authenticity for brand managers and relief from advertising for consumers.

Finally, this chapter also considers the impact of field marketing and the needs of both b2c and b2b brands to be flexible and adaptive to changing market conditions and reducing internal resources.

Trade shows and exhibitions

The idea of many suppliers joining together at a particular location in order to set out their products and services so that customers may meet, make comparisons and place orders is far from new. Indeed, not only does this form of promotional activity stretch back many centuries, it has also been used to explain the way the Internet works (Bertheron *et al.*, 1996). They refer to the Internet as a virtual flea circus, a forum where buyers and sellers can meet, browse, discuss, find out more information and buy products and services if appropriate.

At a basic level, trade fairs can be oriented for industrial users or consumers and the content or purpose might be to consider general or specialised products/markets.

Trade fairs can be oriented for industrial users or consumers.

According to Boukersi (2000), consumer-oriented general fairs tend to be larger and last longer than the more specialised industrial fairs and it is clear that this more highly segmented and focused approach is proving more successful, based upon the increasing number of these types of exhibitions.

Reasons to use exhibitions

There are many reasons to use exhibitions, but the primary reasons appear not to be 'to make sales' or 'because the competition is there' but because these events provide opportunities to meet potential and established customers and to create and sustain a series of relational exchanges. The main aim, therefore, is to develop long-term partnerships with customers, to build upon or develop the corporate identity and to gather up-to-date market intelligence (Shipley and Wong, 1993).

The main aim, therefore, is to develop long-term partnerships with customers.

This implies that exhibitions should not be used as isolated events, but that they should be integrated into a series of activities. These activities serve to develop and sustain buyer relationships.

ViewPoint 29.1   Trade shows

The International Motorcycle Show is run at the UK's largest exhibition complex, the National Exhibition Centre (NEC), just outside Birmingham. The 2003 event was supported by an integrated campaign using press, online, direct marketing and experiential activity at key events and biking venues.

One of the themes of the show was to extend its appeal to new riders, in addition to the seasoned bikers it regularly attracts. Over 200,000 people were expected to attend. Many new people have taken up biking partly in reaction to the ever-worsening road traffic conditions, poor and inconsistent rail services and in London the Congestion Charge that had been recently introduced to reduce the volume of traffic in London at peak times.

EXHIBIT 29.1 The National Exhibition Centre; picture used with permission

TABLE 29.1 Reasons exhibitors choose to attend exhibitions

To meet existing customers
To take orders/make sales
To get leads and meet prospective new customers
To meet lapsed customers
To meet prospective members of the existing or new marketing channels
To provide market research opportunities and to collect marketing data

After a tentative start to the 1990s, the exhibition industry has grown and is now experiencing real growth. With managers increasingly accountable for their promotional spend so a greater number of budgets are now channelled into exhibitions and related events. In 1995 visitors attended 773 exhibitions in the UK, in 2000 the number had risen to 868 and in 2003, 858 exhibitions were held where venues exceeded 2,000 square feet (Exhibitions Venue Association, 2004).

Costs can be reduced by using private exhibitions, where the increased flexibility allows organisations to produce mini or private exhibitions for their clients at local venues (e.g. hotels). This can mean lower costs for the exhibitor and reduced time away from their businesses for those attending. The communication 'noise' and distraction associated with the larger public events can also be avoided by these private showings.

> Costs can be reduced by using private exhibitions.

Characteristics of exhibitions and trade shows

> One where both have independently volunteered their time to attend; to place/take orders; to generate leads; and to gather market information.

The main reasons for attending exhibitions and trade fairs are that it enables organisations to meet customers (and potential customers) in an agreeable environment, one where both have independently volunteered their time to attend; to place/take orders; to generate leads; and to gather market information. The reasons for attending exhibitions are set out in Table 29.1.

From this it is possible to distinguish the following strengths and weaknesses of using exhibitions as part of the marketing communications programme.

Strengths

The costs associated with exhibitions, if controlled properly, can mean that this is an effective and efficient means of communicating with customers. The costs per enquiry need to be calculated, but care needs to be taken over who is classified as an enquirer, as the quality of the audience varies considerably. Costs per order taken are usually the prime means of evaluating the success of an exhibition. This can paint a false picture, as the true success can never really be determined in terms of orders because of the variety of other factors that impinge upon the placement and timing of orders.

Products can be launched at exhibitions, and when integrated with a good PR campaign a powerful impact can be made. This can also be used to reinforce corporate identity.

Exhibitions are an important means of gaining information about competitors, buyers and technical and political developments in the market, and they often serve to facilitate the recruitment process. Above all else, exhibitions provide an opportunity to meet customers on relatively neutral ground and, through personal interaction, develop relationships. Products can be demonstrated, prices agreed, technical problems discussed and trust and credibility enhanced.

Weaknesses

One of the main drawbacks associated with exhibition work is the vast and disproportionate amount of management time that can be tied up with the planning and implementation of exhibitions. However, good planning is essential if the full potential benefits of exhibition work are to be realised.

Taking members of the sales force 'off the road' can also incur large costs. Depending upon the nature of the business these opportunity costs can soar. Some pharmaceutical organisations estimate that it can cost approximately £5,000 per person per week to divert salespeople in this way.

The expected visitor profile must be analysed in order that the number of quality buyers visiting an exhibition can be determined. The variety of visitors attending an exhibition can be misleading, as the vast majority may not be serious buyers or indeed may not be directly related to the industry or the market in question.

> The expected visitor profile must be analysed.

Exhibitions as a form of marketing communications

> Exhibitions enable products to be promoted, they can build brands and they can be an effective means of demonstrating products.

As a form of marketing communications exhibitions enable products to be promoted, they can build brands and they can be an effective means of demonstrating products and building industry-wide credibility in a relatively short period of time. Attendance at exhibitions may also be regarded from a political dimension in that non-attendance by competitors may be taken as an opportunity by attendees to suggest weaknesses.

In the b2b sector new products and services are often introduced at exhibitions, especially if there are to be public relations activities and events that can be spun off the launch. In other words, exhibitions are not activities independent of the other parts of the promotional tools. Exhibitions, if used effectively, can be part of an integrated communications campaign. Advertising prior to, during and after a trade show can be dovetailed with public relations, sponsorship and personal selling. Sales promotions can also be incorporated through competitions among customers prior to the show to raise awareness, generate interest and to suggest customer involvement. Competitions during a show can be focused on the sales force to motivate and stimulate commercial activity and among visitors to generate interest in the stand, raise brand name attention and encourage focus upon particular products (new, revised or revolutionary) and generate sales leads and enquiries.

New media and exhibitions

In many ways the use of the Internet and Web site as brochureware represented a first attempt at an online exhibition. In these situations commercial organisations provided opportunities for people who physically could not get to see a product to gain some appreciation of its size, configuration and capability (through text). However, the development of multimedia technologies has given not only commercial but also not-for-profit organisations the opportunity to showcase their wares on a global basis. One type of organisation to explore the use of this technology has been museums and collections of art (static exhibits). Khoon *et al.* (2003) refer to the American History Documents (at www.indiana.edu/liblilly/histy/), Exploring Africa (at www.sc.edu/library/spcoll/sccoll/africa) and SCRAN (at www.scran.ac.uk) (which is a multimedia resource for Scottish history and culture) as examples of previous work and facilities in this area. The use of multimedia technologies enables audiences across the world to access these collections and with the use of audio, video clips and streaming video in addition to pictures and extensive text, these exhibitions can be brought to life, visited repeatedly, focus given to particular exhibits, materials updated quickly and unobtrusively and of course links made to other similar facilities. The key difference between this development and previous brochureware type facilities is the feeling of virtual reality, the sense that a digital visitor is actually in the exhibition, even though seated several thousand miles away. See ViewPoint 29.2.

ViewPoint 29.2   Online exhibition in Singapore

The process by which a country's culture and heritage is passed on to successive generations often incorporates museums, art galleries and other centres where artefacts of the nation are stored and made available to the public. However, these are generally static collections and only available to those with access to the centre concerned.

A project in Singapore to capture a physical exhibition in an online format is recognition of the power and facilities currently available. The exhibition, called 'Colours in the Wind', about Old Hill Street Police Station and its conversion into the Ministry of Information, sought to provide wider access and to promote the cultural heritage of the area.

Source: Khoon *et al.* (2003).

It is unlikely that online exhibitions will ever replace the off-line real world version, if only because of the need to make relationships.

The use of ecommerce and digital media in the management and presentation of exhibitions is likely to increase. It is unlikely that online exhibitions will ever replace the off-line real world version, if only because of the need to make relationships and to network with industry members, to touch and feel products and to sense the atmosphere and vitality that exhibitions generate. However, there is huge scope to develop specialised exhibitions, to develop online showcases that incorporate exhibits (products and services) from a variety of geographically dispersed locations.

Marketing management of exhibitions

Good management of exhibitions represents some key aspects of marketing communications in general. Successful events are driven by planning that takes place prior to the exhibition, with communications inviting a range of stakeholders, not just customers, in advance of the exhibition event. Stands should be designed to deliver key messages and press releases and press information packs should be prepared and distributed appropriately.

During the event itself staff should be well briefed, trained and knowledgeable about their role with the brand and in the exhibition process. After the exhibition it is vital to follow up on contacts made and discussions or negotiations that have been held. In other words, the exhibition itself is a planned marketing communications activity, one where activities need to be planned prior to, during and after the event. What is key is that these activities are coordinated, themed, and supported by brand-oriented staff.

Above all else, exhibitions are an important way of building relationships and signalling corporate identity. Trade shows are an important means of providing corporate

Trade shows are an important means of providing corporate hospitality.

hospitality and showing gratitude to all an organisation's customers, but in particular to its key account customers and others of strategic interest. Positive relationships with customers, competitors and suppliers are often reinforced through face-to-face dialogue that happens both formally in the exhibition hall and informally through the variety of social activities that surround and support these events.

Product placement

One way of overcoming the irritation factor associated with advertisements screened in cinemas prior to a film showing is to incorporate the product in the film that is

Is to incorporate the product in the film that is shown.

shown. This is referred to as product placement, which is the inclusion of products and services in films (or media) for deliberate promotional exposure, often, but not always, in return for an agreed financial sum. It is regarded by some as a form of sales promotion, but for the purposes of this text it is treated as an advertising medium because the 'advertiser' pays for the opportunity to present the product.

A wide variety of products can be placed in this way, including drinks (both soft and alcoholic), confectionery, newspapers, cars, airlines, perfume and even holiday destinations and sports equipment.

Characteristics of product placement

Strengths

By presenting the product as part of the film, not only is it possible to build awareness, but source credibility can be improved significantly and brand images reinforced. The audience is assisted to identify and associate itself with the environment depicted in the film or with the celebrity who is using the product.

Levels of impact can be very high, as cinema audiences are very attentive to large-screen presentations. Rates of exposure can be high, particularly now that cinema films are being released through video outlets, satellite and various new regional cable and television organisations.

Perhaps the major advantage is that the majority of audiences appear to approve of this form of marketing communications, if only because it is unobtrusive and integral to the film (Nebenzahl and Secunda, 1993).

Weaknesses

Having achieved a placement in a film there is still a risk that the product will run unnoticed, especially if the placements coincide with distracting or action-oriented parts of the film. Associated with this is the lack of control the advertiser has over when, where and how the product will be presented. If the product is noticed, a small minority of audiences claim that this form of communication is unethical; it is even suggested that it is subliminal advertising, which is, of course, illegal. The absolute costs of product placement in films can be extremely high, counteracting the low relative costs or cost per contact. The final major drawback concerning this form of medium concerns its inability to provide explanation, detail, or indeed any substantive information about the product. The product is seen in use and is hopefully associated with an event, person(s) or objects that provide a source of pleasure, inspiration or aspiration for the individual viewer.

ViewPoint 29.3   **Product placement**

Cars are often placed in films; for example, BMW is reported to have invested $20 million on a product placement campaign to support the launch of its Z3 roadster. Not only was the car featured in the James Bond film *GoldenEye*, it received great exposure in the television advertising and trailer used to promote the film prior to its release (Eisenstein, 1997).

Audi has placed cars in the films *Ronin*, *The Insider* and *Mission Impossible II*. It has also developed a futuristic car especially for the film *I, ROBOT*.

Products can also be placed in TV game shows (e.g. Coca-Cola in *American Idol*), in books (e.g. *The Bulgari Connection*), in video games (e.g. Pizza Hut and KFC *in Crazy Taxi*).

Product placement is not confined to cinema films. Music videos, television plays, dramas and soap operas can also use this method to present advertisers' products. Pervan and Martin (2002) found that product placement in television soaps was an effective communications activity. They also concluded that the way a product is used in the soap, that is positive and negative outcomes, may well have important implications for the attitudes held towards these brands. They also suggested that organisations should study the consumption imagery associated with placed products as this might yield significant information about the way in which these products are actually consumed.

> Music videos, television plays, dramas and soap operas can also use this method to present advertisers' products.

Placement issues

The nature of a placement and the impact it has on the audience appear to be affected by a number of variables. Important associations concern the placement and its association with the storyline, whether the actors use the product or it remains a background object, if the product fits the plot, the degree to which the product is prominently displayed and the amount of time that the product is actually exposed. Karrh *et al.* (2003) refer to the relative lack of control that marketers have over product placement activities but confirm the research that in comparison to adverting equivalents, product placement can have a far greater impact on audiences and in most cases at a fraction of the cost of a 30-second advertisement.

> The relative lack of control that marketers have over product placement activities.

Field marketing

Field marketing is a relatively new sector of the industry and seeks to provide support for the sales force and merchandising personnel along with data collection and research facilities for clients. The Field Marketing Council (FMC) states that field marketing is about the use of people to communicate a sales and marketing message. This is quite an open remit and reflects the wide range of activities that practitioners within the area have encompassed recently. At a basic level field marketing is concerned with getting free samples of a product into the hands of potential customers. At another level, field marketing is about creating an interaction between the brand and a new

ViewPoint 29.4   Field marketing for Lipovitan

In order to penetrate the UK market the energy drink Lipovitan used various media in an attempt to establish itself against high-sugar and caffeinated competitors. Normally PR would have been used to achieve this goal but journalists were reported to be sceptical of the claims being made. The brand turned to a sampling strategy on the grounds that getting the target market to try, taste and experience the brand would be the answer to the problem.

Rather than use a volume sampling strategy a highly targeted approach was used. Commuters were given cans of Lipovitan at underground stations in the mornings and where people sit outside for lunch. In addition a fleet of branded rickshaws was used around parts of London to raise the profile further.

EXHIBIT 29.2 Lipovitan rickshaws

Field marketing is about creating an interaction between the brand and a new customer.

customer and at still another level it is about creating a personal and memorable brand experience for potential customers. The key to field marketing is the flexibility of services provided to clients. Sales forces can be hired on short-term contracts and promotional teams can be contracted to launch new products, provide samples (both in store and door to door) and undertake a range of other activities that are not part of an organisation's normal promotion endeavours.

The decision about whether to own or to hire a sales force has to be based on a variety of criteria, such as the degree of control required over not only the salesperson but also the message to be transmitted. A further criterion is flexibility. Ruckert *et al.* (1985) identified that in environments subject to rapid change, which brings uncertainty (for example because of shortening product life cycles or large technological developments), the ability to adjust quickly the number of representatives in the distribution channel can be of major strategic importance. A further criterion is cost; for some the large fixed costs associated with a sales force can be avoided by using a commission-only team of representatives.

A large number of organisations choose to have their own sales force, but of these many use the services of a manufacturer's agent to supplement their activities. A number of pharmaceutical manufacturers use independent sales forces to supplement the activities of their own sales teams.

Range of FM activities

Research undertaken by the FMC found that there was a serious misunderstanding by clients and agencies of what field marketing activities encompass (McLuhan, 2000). Table 29.2 sets out the range of activities undertaken in the name of field marketing. To some extent it consists of tasks pulled from some of the five main promotional

TABLE 29.2 Essential features of field marketing activities

Core activities	Essential features
Sales	Provides sales force personnel on either a temporary or a permanent basis. This is for business to business and direct to the public.
Merchandising	Generates awareness and brand visibility through point-of-purchase placement, in-store staff training, product displays and leaflets.
Sampling	Mainly to the public at shopping centres and station concourses but also for business-to-business purposes.
Auditing	Used for checking stock availability, pricing and positioning.
Mystery shopping	Provides feedback on the level and quality of service offered by retail staff and the promotion of special offers.
Event marketing	Used to create drama and to focus attention at sports events, open-air concerts and festivals. Essentially theatrical or entertainment based.
Door to door (home calls)	A form of selling where relatively uncomplex products and services can be sold through home visits.

Source: Adapted from McLuhan (2000).

tools, repackaged and presented under a more contemporary title; for example, door-to-door and sales activities from personal selling, merchandising from both personal selling and sales promotion, sampling (which is a straight sales promotions task) and event marketing from public relations. Field marketing is a response to market needs and is a development practitioners have pioneered to fulfil a range of customer needs that presumably had not been adequately satisfied.

Field marketing can take place virtually anywhere but common locations are in shopping centres and supermarkets where footfall is greatest. Typically these events require agency staff to dress up in an eye-catching way in order to form associations between the clothing and the brand (e.g. dressed in Mexican ponchos and sombreros to give out free samples of Pot Noodle in a supermarket). It is regarded as a cost-effective way of demonstrating a product, getting a bit of stand-out and creating opportunities for customers to trial a product with minimum risk. Field marketing is also used to sell relatively complex products where a degree of explanation is required (e.g. computers, hi-fis or mobile phones).

> **Field marketing is also used to sell relatively complex products where a degree of explanation is required.**

ViewPoint 29.5   Field marketing out in the field

Lindemann's Wine built a living room with big comfy seats inside a trailer that was taken to events and stores. People were offered a sample of the wine and could chat informally to promotional staff who new all about wine and Lindemann's in particular.

Source: Bashford (2004).

Rimmel used a roadshow approach across 24 shopping centres to reach 48,000 stand visitors, of whom 2,500 had makeovers.

Source: Miller (2004).

> **The growing Interest in what is referred to as experiential marketing or brand experience.**

A key aspect of field marketing concerns the growing interest in what is referred to as experiential marketing or brand experience. Many in the industry see their role as delivering brand experience opportunities for their clients' customers. Others would argue that brand experience occurs through various interactions with a brand, namely purchasing, consumption and consideration. However, the term brand experience appears to be owned by those in the field marketing industry and has evolved through the development of both sampling and event/roadshow activities. Whether the brand experience industry lies inside or outside of field marketing is not particularly critical. However, what differentiates the experiential aspect from other FM activities is that it requires more precise targeting (not mass market) and it is more emotionally and physically engaging than sampling and many events or roadshows, which in turn Bashford (2004) claims can lead to stronger (positive) memories. She quotes Paul Ephremsen, a leading industry practitioner who says that field marketing is 'all about the numbers and not the interaction, and is driven by cost per sample' whereas brand experience is about 'creating an emotional bond between the brand and the consumer'.

> **Brand experience is about 'creating an emotional bond between the brand and the consumer'.**

One of the essential tasks of field marketing is to continue to make brand signals available to consumers so that they can make the necessary brand associations which they have developed through advertising, brand and category experience. It is a matter of keeping brand values alive at the point of purchase (Kemp, 2000). Field marketing has undoubtedly expanded its role in recent years and in doing so has begun to establish itself as a core marketing support activity. Indeed Moyies (2000) claims that field marketing should be cross-fertilised with direct marketing and sales promotion, and in doing so would not only benefit clients but would enhance the credibility of the industry.

Packaging

For a long time packaging has been considered a means of protecting and preserving products during transit and while they remain in store or on the shelf prior to purchase and consumption. In this sense, packaging can be regarded as an element of product strategy. To a certain extent this is still true; however technology has progressed considerably and, with consumer choice continually widening, packaging has become a means by which buyers, particularly in consumer markets, can make significant brand choice decisions. To that extent, because packaging can be used to convey persuasive information and be part of the decision-making process, yet still protect the contents, it is an important means of marketing communications in particular markets, such as FMCG.

Low-involvement decision-making requires peripheral cues to stimulate buyers into action. It has already been noted that decisions made at the point of purchase, especially those in the FMCG sector, often require buyers to build awareness through recognition. The design of packages

Low-involvement decision-making requires peripheral cues to stimulate buyers into action.

ViewPoint 29.6   Guinness bottle redesign

An innovative approach to bottle design was undertaken by Guinness in Asia. In a region where awareness of the Guinness brand is as high as that of Carlsberg and Heineken, beer drinkers were asked to vote for their favourite bottle design.

The campaign featured four different designs, one of which was based on the god of thunder, Thor, to provide a 'witty parody of conventional drinking attitudes'.

To help promote the redesign a campaign involving print ads in *Today*, *Shin Min*, *Lianhe Wanbao* and mainstream magazines such as *FHM*, *8 Days*, *Juice*, *Men's Health*, *IS* and *Banter* in Singapore was run. This was supported with outdoor work in Hong Kong, with the posters carrying a toll-free number inviting consumers to vote for their favourite design. Guinness used mobile billboards, with fully plastered trucks driving through Singapore.

Sales promotions using tent cards, column posters, table standees and coasters were used across the city. The winning bottle design was taken out on the street with promoters dressed in life-sized costumes, pitching themselves to the public as 'the better, more attractive bottle'.

Source: Hargrave-Silk (2003).

and wrappers is important, as continuity of design in combination with the power to attract and hold the attention of prospective buyers is a vital part of point-of-purchase activity. The degree of importance that manufacturers place upon packaging and design was seen in 1994, when Sainsbury's introduced its own cola. The reaction of the Coca-Cola company to the lookalike design of the own-label product is testimony to the value placed upon this aspect of brand personality.

Communication dimensions of packaging

There are a number of dimensions that can affect the power and utility of a package. Colour is influential, as the context of the product class can frame the purchase situation for a buyer. This means that colours should be appropriate to the product class, to the brand and to the prevailing culture if marketing overseas. For example, red is used to stimulate the appetite, white to symbolise purity and cleanliness, blue to signal freshness, and green is increasingly being used to denote an environmental orientation and natural ingredients. From a cultural aspect, colours can be a problem. Buckley (1993) suggests that in Germany bright bold colours are regarded as appropriate for baby products, whereas in the United Kingdom pastel shades are more acceptable.

ViewPoint 29.7	Pringles pack design

Crisps have traditionally been packaged and presented in sealed foil bags, so, when the cardboard tube format was introduced for the Pringles brand, it represented a radically new package concept. Verebelyi (2000) reports that the challenge to shoppers was whether they would accept the innovative design as an appropriate and suitable way of protecting and storing the savoury product. Once shoppers proved to themselves that the product was more likely to keep its shape in the tube, then the package (and the brand) was accepted. Indeed the Pringles tube has provided the brand with a powerful means of differentiation and enables it to stand out on the shelves. See Exhibit 29.3.

EXHIBIT 29.3 Pringles – a new packaging concept introduced into an established product category
Picture kindly supplied by Procter & Gamble UK.

EXHIBIT 29.4 Elizabeth Arden Packaging
In certain categories packaging should reflect the characteristics and personality of the brand.
Elizabeth Arden use packaging to attract attention and convey luxury values.

The shape of the package may reflect a physical attribute of the product.

The shape of the package may reflect a physical attribute of the product itself and can be a strong form of persuasion. Verebelyi (2000) suggests that this influence may be due to the decorative impact of some brands. See Exhibit 29.4.

Various domestic lavatory cleaners have a twist in the neck or a trigger action, facilitating directable and easier application. See Exhibits 29.5 and 29.6 for examples of two such products. Research indicated that Lever Brothers should develop a product that was directable.

The shape may also provide information about how to open and use the product, while some packages can be used after the product has been consumed for other purposes. For example, some jars can be reused as food containers, so providing a means of continual communication for the original brand in the home. Packaging can also be used as a means of brand identification, as a cue by which buyers recognise and differentiate a brand. The supreme example of this is the Coca-Cola contour bottle, with its unique shape and immediate power for brand recognition at the point of purchase. See Exhibit 29.7.

Package size is important, as different target markets may consume varying amounts of product.

Package size is important, as different target markets may consume varying amounts of product. Toothpaste is available in large-size family tubes and in smaller containers for those households that do not use so much. However, the size of a package can also be an important perceptual stimuli. Research by Raghubir and

 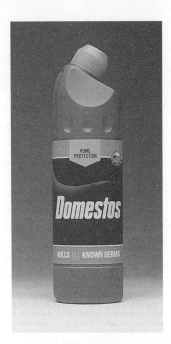

EXHIBITS 29.5 and 29.6 Dettox and Domestos cleaning fluid brands – packages designed for easier application

Pictures kindly supplied by Reckitt Benckiser and Lever Bros.

EXHIBIT 29.7 Coca-Cola contour bottle

Packaging is an important aspect of marketing communications in many sectors. Depicted here is the Coca-Cola bottle with its unique (and well-protected) shape. Coca-Cola is a registered trade mark of the Coca-Cola Company. This image has been reproduced with the kind permission of the Coca-Cola Company.

Krishna (1999) found that the height of a container was an important variable that consumers used to make judgements about the volume of the container. However, Folkes and Matta (2004) counter this by referring to Gestalt theory, which is concerned with holistic perspectives, and say that consumers use multiple dimensions to make judgements about objects (packages). Research by Folkes and Matta suggests that there is a relationship between the attractiveness of a package and the volume of the package. As a broad generalisation, the greater the attractiveness, the greater the perceived volume. The implications of this insight have been implicitly known by marketing management for years, judging by the effort that is given to create attractive packaging and shelf stand-out.

Washing and dishwasher powder manufacturers now provide plastic refill packs that are designed to provoke brand loyalty. These packs are cheaper than the original pack, partly because some of the packaging expense has been reduced as the customer has been introduced to the product at an earlier time. Purchase of the refill pack is dependent upon product quality and customer satisfaction and, as long as the brand name is prominent for identification and reminder purposes, the decision to select the refill is quicker, as most of the risk (financial, physical and social) has been removed through previous satisfactory usage.

All packages have to carry information concerning the ingredients, nutritional values and safety requirements, including sell-by and use-by dates. Non-food packages must also attempt to be sales agents and provide all the information that a prospective buyer might need and at the same time provide conviction that this product is the correct one to purchase. Labelling of products offers opportunities to manufacturers to

All packages have to carry information concerning the ingredients.

harmonise the in-store presentation of their products in such a way that buyers from different countries can still identify the brand and remain brand loyal. For example, Buckley (1993) suggests that Unilever decided not to change its different brands of washing powder in favour of a pan-European brand. It decided instead to retain the existing names (Omo, Skip, Via, Persil and All) and to package them in a similar way, using similar visual devices, typography and colours. This not only allows customers to remain loyal but also presents opportunities to save on advertising and design costs and gain access to satellite and other cross-border media.

Packages carry tangible and intangible messages. The psychological impact that packages can have should not be underestimated. They convey information about the

Packages carry tangible and intangible messages.

product but they also say something about the quality of the product (Hall, 1991) and how it differs from competitive offerings. In some cases, where there is little to differentiate products, buyers may use the packaging on its own for decision-making purposes.

Gordon and Valentine (1996) argue that 'brand packaging communicates in the context of the competition and of related products'. This is achieved by using packaging that conforms to a design code that has been established for the category. This permits consumers to identify quickly the range of brands in the product field but does not necessarily allow for the identification of individual brands. They make the important point that it is this process which allows own-label brands to become part of a category without the support of advertising to establish credibility.

Packaging has been termed passive and active (Southgate, 1994). Passive packaging relies on vast amounts of advertising to infuse the design to create interest (e.g. Heinz). Active packaging is more demonstrative and tends to work with the other marketing and communication elements. Connolly and Davison (1996) quote Tango as an example of this type of packaging. Charnos bioform® used packaging as an integral part of the overall brand. See Exhibit 14.4.

Summary

As stated earlier, the use of exhibitions as a means of communicating with a variety of stakeholders has long been established. Organisations in both the consumer and the business-to-business markets use exhibitions as part of both pull and push strategies. Point-of-purchase communications are also seen to be an integral part of a coherent marketing communications campaign. In sectors such as FMCG packaging design is necessary to continue the brand associations that have been developed through above-the-line advertising and sales promotion work. Packaging plays an important role in terms of attracting attention, consolidating brand associations and conveying product category legitimacy.

Finally, the field marketing sector has grown as a reflection of the need of companies to be able to respond quickly to changing competitive conditions and customer needs. Field marketing companies provide a range of services, from merchandising and sampling to roadshows and personal selling.

Review questions

1. Evaluate the differences between consumer- and business-oriented trade shows.
2. As sales manager for a company making plastic mouldings for use in the manufacture of consumer durables, set out the reasons for and against attendance at trade shows and exhibitions.
3. Write brief notes explaining the role exhibitions might play in a company's integrated marketing communications strategy.
4. The development of interorganisational relationships is best undertaken through personal selling rather than through exhibitions and trade shows. Discuss.
5. Explain how packaging can be an integral part of a consumer's brand experience.
6. Find three brands where the shape of a package is an integral part of the product.
7. What is the difference between active and passive packaging?
8. Name two strengths and two weaknesses of product placement.
9. Identify four examples of product placement. Evaluate their effectiveness.
10. Name five core activities associated with field marketing and explain their essential features. Do not refer to Table 29.2 until you have attempted the exercise from memory.

MINI-CASE
Hardy's – regaining a market presence

Hardy's, a long established medium-sized engineering company, distributes its range of garden equipment products through a variety of channels. Traditionally it had used ironmongers and garden centres as its main form of distribution but this had changed in the 1980s and 1990s as it had begun using discount stores, hypermarkets and DIY superstores in response to changes in the retail environment. For a long time Hardy's marketing channels and the management of its distribution was particularly successful and was regarded as a major competitive strength. This success was attributed to a high reputation, which had been established among the trade for the quality of its products, its client servicing and support, the ordering procedures and prompt delivery, which were all perceived to be trustworthy and very reliable.

The mainstay of Hardy's communications with these outlets had been its direct sales force, supported by sales literature and attendance at key garden shows and trade exhibitions. The sales force provided an important point of personal contact, mainly because they were trained engineers who could provide technical support that was valued by their retail customers. The operation was very successful, profitable, and the envy of many of Hardy's traditional competitors. However, as the business emphasis switched to DIY superstores so the support shifted as well. The focus became Web-enabled EDI, supply-chain management systems, and stock control with marketing communications oriented to an information-based Web site, the provision of leaflets and in-store merchandising. Gone was the need for high levels of personal support and advice, and attendance at the various consumer-based garden shows also ceased. A salesman's job was now oriented to maintaining relationships with the few major buyers of each of the groups who owned the DIY superstores.

Alex Bodkin, Hardy's sales and marketing manager, had recently considered a report concerning the volume and value of the business generated through the different marketing channels. The report indicated that the value of Hardy's business generated through garden centres was now worth less than 35 per cent of the whole and the trend was not looking good. The garden centre channel was no longer central to Hardy's business and many of the personal friendships and relationships with the garden centres had also withered as a result of the decline. Gone too was the technical support and the advice for garden centre sales staff and customers from the traditional gardeners' segment. Sales in this channel had declined partly because Hardy's no longer supported each garden centre in the way it used to. Sales force costs had been very high and the reduced size of the sales force meant that they had to be concentrated on the most profitable parts of Hardy's business, the DIY superstores. Although sales volumes through the superstores were strong, margins were small relative to those generated through garden centres. In addition, the level of customer service provided through these new channels had to be high in order to cope with the different types of consumer and their need for basic gardening advice, although analysis of the Web site traffic suggested that many questions were successfully answered online. Bodkin was also aware of the new systems necessary to support the high level of returns and repair work that flowed through the DIY superstores.

A separate marketing research report commissioned by Bodkin the previous summer indicated that Hardy's was perceived, by garden centre owners and managers, as distant and uncaring about their type of business. This was slightly ironic as Hardy's had tried to use advertising and direct mail to reach traditional gardeners, in a half-hearted attempt to build the Hardy's brand. However, when these potential customers arrived at garden centres to see the products and test them, they were faced with little (Hardy's) stock, sales staff with little up-to-date knowledge and large ranges of competitor equipment and products (often packed and neatly presented on racks and shelving) that were both attractive and easy to use.

Although many garden centres were independently owned and geographically isolated, others had been bought and were now part of a chain of businesses. Bodkin believed that Hardy's had made the wrong decision to reduce support for its garden centre business and that this channel represented an important part of the overall channel mix in the future, especially as more and more people were visiting them each year.

Bodkin wanted to re-establish Hardy's presence within the garden centre sector but to do this the company had to re-establish relationships with each garden centre and associated networks. Although once very costly to support, economies of scale might now be achieved by selling into the chains, rather than individual centres. To be competitive it was necessary to provide high levels of support and advice, process sales orders quickly, provide fast customer service and attend to gardeners' needs for specialist advice, not only on machinery and equipment but on other aspects of gardening as well. To achieve these goals Bodkin began to make a list of the different key issues. One of these concerned

the need for a physical presence within the garden centres, yet he knew that Hardy's could not afford a direct sales force capable of providing the necessary breadth of support to revive its business within this sector.

Questions

1　How might the need for a physical presence in the garden centre network be achieved without employing a direct sales force?

2　How might new technology assist Hardy's in the management of the garden centre business?

3　What other issues might be included on Bodkin's list? Prioritise them.

References

Bashford, S. (2004) Field marketing: The great divide? *Event*, 8 September. Retrieved 14 October from www.brandrepublic.com/news.

Bertheron, P., Pitt, L.F. and Watson, R.T. (1996) The World Wide Web as an advertising medium. *Journal of Advertising Research*, **6**(1) (January/February), pp. 43–54.

Boukersi, L. (2000) The role of trade fairs and exhibitions in international marketing communications. In *The Handbook of International Marketing Communications* (ed. S. Moyne), pp. 117–35. London: Blackwell.

Buckley, N. (1993) More than just a pretty picture. *Financial Times*, 13 October, p. 23.

Connolly, A. and Davison, L. (1996) How does design affect decisions at point of sale? *Journal of Brand Management*, **4**(2), pp. 100–7.

Eisenstein, P. (1997) Vehicles that really perform. *WorldTraveler*, January.

Exhibitions Venue Association (2004) http://www.exhibitionvenues.com/uplpdfs/EVAfactsbrochure.pdf; retrieved 16 February 2005.

Folkes, V. and Matta, S. (2004) The effect of package shape on consumers' judgments of product volume: attention as a mental contaminant. *Journal of Consumer Research*, **31**(2) September, pp. 390–402.

Gordon, W. and Valentine, V. (1996) *Buying the brand at point of choice*. MRS Conference, March.

Hall, J. (1991) Packaged good. *Campaign*, 18 October, pp. 21–3.

Hargrave-Silk, A. (2003) Guinness builds buzz with bottle's new look. *Media Asia*. Retrieved 31 October from www.brandrepublic.co.uk/news/newsArticle.

Karrh, J.A., McKee, K.B., Britain, K. and Pardun, C.J. (2003) Practitioners' evolving views of product placement effectiveness. *Journal of Advertising Research*, **43**(2) (June), pp. 138–50.

Kemp, G. (2000) Elastic brands. *Marketing Business* (October), pp. 40–1.

Khoon, L.C., Ramaiah, C. and Foo, S. (2003) The design and development of an online exhibition for heritage information awareness in Singapore. *Program: Electronic Library and Information Systems*, **37**(2), pp. 85–93.

McLuhan, R. (2000) Fighting for a new view of field work. *Marketing*, 9 March, pp. 29–30.

Miller, R. (2004) Follow the crowds. *Marketing*, 1 April, pp. 25–6.

Moyies, J. (2000) A healthier specimen. *Admap* (June), pp. 39–42.

Nebenzahl, I.D. and Secunda, E. (1993) Consumer attitudes toward product placement in movies. *International Journal of Advertising*, **12**, pp. 1–11.

Pervan, S.J. and Martin, B.A.S. (2002) Product placement in US and New Zealand television soap operas: an exploratory study. *Journal of Marketing Communications*, **8**, pp. 101–13.

Raghubir, P. and Krishna, A. (1999) Vital dimensions in volume perception: can the eye fool the stomach? *Journal of Marketing Research*, **36**, August, pp. 313–26.

Ruckert, R.W., Walker, O.C. and Roering, K.J. (1985) The organisation of marketing activities: a contingency theory of structure and performance. *Journal of Marketing* (Winter), pp. 13–25.

Shipley, D. and Wong, K.S. (1993) Exhibiting strategy and implementation. *International Journal of Advertising*, **12**(2), pp. 117–30.

Southgate, P. (1994) *Total Branding by Design*. London: Kogan Page.

Verebelyi, N. (2000) The power of the pack. *Marketing*, 27 April, p. 37.

Marketing communications for special audiences

Chapters 30-32

This last part of the book considers marketing communications in the context of special audiences.

These audiences are special in the sense that they are contextually different to mainstream audiences and can require particular strategies and configurations of the marketing communications mix. Chapter 30 for example considers some of the issues arising when dealing with marketing communications in an international or even a global environment.

Chapter 31 looks at marketing communications in the business-to-business market. Here a different emphasis on communications is required simply because the purchase decision process and the focus on relationships is very different to consumer-based marketing communications.

The final chapter in the book, 32, looks at the important issue of marketing communications when targeted at internal audiences. Although touched upon at different points in the book this chapter considers the role of employees in the branding process and the tasks marketing communications is expected to undertake.

Part
5

Marketing communications across borders

30

The management of marketing communications for audiences domiciled in two or more countries is haunted by the dilemma of whether to send the same message to all regions or adapt it to meet the needs of local markets, or do a little bit of both.

Aims and objectives

The aim of this chapter is to examine the impact that cross-border business strategies might have on marketing communications agencies and advertising strategies.

The objectives of this chapter are to:

1. consider the development and variety of organisations operating across international borders;

2. appraise different aspects of culture as a key variable affecting marketing communications;

3. examine the media as a further important variable that can influence marketing communications strategy;

4. discuss the adaptation vs. standardisation debate about marketing communications messages;

5. explore the ways in which advertising agencies have developed to meet the international communication requirements of their clients.

Introduction

For organisations the differences between operating within home or domestic markets as compared with overseas or international markets are many and varied. Most of these differences can be considered within an economic, cultural, legal, technological and competitive framework. If the core characteristics of a home market (such as prices, marketing channels, finance, knowledge about customers, legislation, media and competitors) are compared with each of the same factors in the international markets that an organisation might be operating in, then the degree of complexity and uncertainty can be illuminated easily. Management might be conversant with the way of doing business at home but, as they move outside their country/regional borders areas that represent their domain of knowledge, understanding and to some extent security, so levels of control decline and risk increases.

The objective of this chapter is not to consider these particular characteristics, as time and space restrict scope. Readers interested in these issues are recommended to consult some of the many international marketing or business texts that are available. The goal of this chapter is to consider some of the issues that impact upon marketing communications when operating across international borders. To do this it is first necessary to consider the various environments and types of organisation that operate away from their home markets.

Types of cross-border organisation

Organisations can be regarded as international, multinational, global or transnational (Keegan, 1989; Bartlett and Ghoshal, 1991) and each form is a reflection of their structure and disposition towards their chosen markets. See Table 30.1.

International organisations evolve from national organisations whose origins are to serve national customers using domestic or 'home-grown' resources. Some of these organisations, either by accident or by design, begin to undertake a limited amount of work 'overseas'. They begin to become international, first by deploying their domestically oriented marketing mix and then later by adapting it to the needs of the new local 'overseas' market. This adaption phase signals the commencement of a *multinational strategy*. What distinguishes these organisations is that they regard the world (or their parts of it) as having discrete regions. Each country/area reports to a world head office, and performance is normally geared to meet financial targets.

International organisations evolve from national organisations.

Organisations at this stage in the evolutionary process are referred to as *global*. This is characterised by centralised decision-making, where, unlike in multinational companies, the similarities as well as the differences of each country/area are sought. Customers are seen on a global rather than a country/area basis.

Characterised by centralised decision-making.

Transnational organisations are an extension of global organisations. These sophisticated organisations seek to develop advantages based on efficiencies driven by serving global customers. Using technology as a key part of the infrastructure, networks allow resources to be globally derived in response to local requirements.

Transnational organisations are an extension of global organisations.

TABLE 30.1 Organisational frameworks

International organisations	These organisations see their overseas operations as appendages or attachments to a central domestic organisation.
	The marketing policy is to serve customers domestically and then offer these same marketing mixes to other countries/areas.
Multinational organisations	These organisations see their overseas activities as a portfolio of independent businesses.
	The policy is to serve customers with individually designed country/area marketing mixes.
Global organisations	These organisations regard their overseas activities as feeders or delivery tubes for a unified global market.
	The policy is to serve a global market with a single, fundamental marketing mix.
Transnational organisations	These organisations regard their overseas activities as a complex process of coordination and cooperation. The environment is regarded as one where decision-making is shared in a participatory manner.
	The policy is to serve global business environments using flexible global resources to formulate different global marketing mixes.

Source: Based on Bartlett and Ghoshal (1001) and de Mooij (1994).

Anholt (2000), among others, suggests that in recent years a new type of transnational organisation has emerged. Primarily as a result of the Internet these organisations are conceived and born as global brands and therefore do not experience the slow development and evolution as suggested in the previous framework. These new *universal* brands, owned by either a global parent or a small independent operator, often from start-up, transcend established patterns by either minimising or negating the formal distribution channels. Dell computers, Microsoft and search engines such as Yahoo and Excite all require a global market. What characterises these new organisations is that they are generally smaller, faster and more adaptable than the established organisations. They might have a global business but some of them operate with a single office, are based in third-world nations or are simply small global businesses in their own right.

Organisations are far from static and, as domestic markets may stagnate and technology and communication opportunities in particular develop, so opportunities contract and expand. A further configuration reflects the need to be efficient and flexible in the organisation's use of materials and resources. The use of strategic alliances and outsourcing arrangements complements this goal, and network organisations, spanning the globe, emerge.

Appreciating the different types of worldwide organisation is important, not just from a structural perspective but also for the formulation and implementation of business strategy. In addition to this, other issues concerning the products, markets and the marketing communications used by these organisations also surface.

Key variables affecting international marketing communications

There are a large number of variables that can impact upon the effectiveness of marketing communications that cross international borders.

There are a large number of variables that can impact upon the effectiveness of marketing communications that cross international borders. Many of these are controllable by either local or central management. However, there are a large number that are uncontrollable, and these variables need to be carefully considered before communications are attempted. The following variables (culture and media) are reviewed here because of their immediate and direct impact on organisations and their communication activities.

Culture

The values, beliefs, ideas, customs, actions and symbols that are learned by members of particular societies are referred to as culture. The importance of culture is that it provides individuals with identity and the direction of what is deemed to be acceptable

The importance of culture is that it provides individuals with identity and the direction of what is deemed to be acceptable behaviour.

behaviour. Culture is acquired through learning. If it were innate or instinctual, then everyone would behave in the same way. Human beings across the world do not behave uniformly or predictably. Therefore different cultures exist, and from this it is possible to visualise that there must be boundaries within which certain cultures, and hence behaviours and lifestyles, are permissible or even expected. These boundaries are not fixed rigidly, as this would suggest that cultures are static. They evolve and change as members of a society adjust to new technologies, government policies, changing values and demographic changes, to mention but a few dynamic variables.

ViewPoint 30.1   Cultural Euromales

With changes to expectations about a job for life, women's increasingly independent financial and social lifestyle, and media debates concerning the role of men in society, it is not surprising that international marketing communications targeted at men are unlikely to be based on common attitudes, values and beliefs. Research by RDSi revealed, for example, the following.

Italian men are comfortable in their relationships with women, unless they are their superiors at work. The family is very important, with men aspiring to beautiful wives, beautiful children and a beautiful home. Therefore, aspirational advertisements are favoured and scenes depicting family life are approved.

Spanish men are judged to have low morale, partly as a result of the country's relatively recent move towards democracy and the high levels of unemployment when compared with the rest of Europe. The family is an important unit and with it come high levels of respect for the older generation. Cross-generation advertisements that reflect bonding and family ties are well received. There is still a strong macho theme in society, with men seeking to prove themselves.

German men see these changes as a challenge and one that needs a disciplined approach. The family is high on their list as something to be openly valued but, unlike the Italians and the French, they are uncertain about how to achieve this as it conflicts with the German work ethic.

Frenchmen are the most self-assured of all European males. They are relaxed and confident about the changing role of women in society and see opportunities to change themselves. There are some poorer sections of French society that do resent the changes and resort to displays of masculinity to reassert themselves.

British males retain a US-style work ethic and on the surface are comfortable with the changes in society. Underneath, however, the research suggests that they are in denial, and it cites the successful 'lads' magazines (e.g. *Loaded*, *FHM*) as evidence. This complexity, when combined with the most sophisticated advertising literacy and cynicism, makes it difficult to communicate with British males.

Source: Adapted from Davies (2000).

Culture is passed from generation to generation.

Culture is passed from generation to generation. This is achieved through the family, religion, education and the media. These conduits of social behaviour and beliefs serve to provide consistency, stability and direction. The extent to which the media either move society forward or merely reflect its current values is a debate that reaches beyond the scope of this book. However, there can be no doubt as to the impact that the media have on society and the important part that religion plays in different cultures around the world.

Culture has multiple facets, and those that are of direct relevance to marketing communications are the values and beliefs associated with *symbols*, such as language and aesthetics, *institutions* and *groups*, such as those embracing the family, work, education, media and religion, and finally *values*, which according to Hofstede *et al.* (1990) represent the core of culture. These will be looked at in turn.

Symbols

Language, through both the spoken and the non-spoken word, permits members of a society to enter into dialogue and to share meaning. Aesthetics, in the form of design and colour, forms an integral part of packaging, sales promotions and advertising. Those involved in personal selling must be aware of the symbolic impact of formal and informal dress codes and the impact that overall personal appearances and gestures (for example when greeting or leaving people) may have on people in different cultures. Advertisers need to take care that they do not infringe a culture's aesthetic codes when designing visuals or when translating copy into the local language.

Advertisers need to take care that they do not infringe a culture's aesthetic codes.

Institutions and groups

The various institutions that help form the fabric of societies and particular cultures provide a means by which culture is communicated and perpetuated through time. These groups provide the mechanisms by which the process of socialisation occurs. Of these groups, the family plays an important role. The form of the *family* is evolving in some Western cultures, such that the traditional family unit is declining and the number of single-parent families is increasing. In many developing economies the extended family, with several

In many developing economies the extended family, with several generations living together, continues to be a central, stable part of society.

generations living together, continues to be a central, stable part of society. Marketing communication messages need to reflect these characteristics. The impact and importance of various decision-makers need to be recognised and the central creative idea needs to be up to date and sensitive to the family unit.

ViewPoint 30.2   Colour communicates

Colours must be treated with care depending on the particular country where communications are being conducted. Griffin (1993) sets out how the colour of flowers is used to depict death and or unhappiness in different countries:

- purple flowers in Brazil
- white and yellow lilies in Taiwan
- yellow lilies in Mexico
- white lilies in Canada, Great Britain and Sweden.

Yellow flowers stand for infidelity in France and disrespect for a woman in the (ex)-Soviet Union.

Work patterns vary across regions: not all cultures expect a 9-to-5 routine. This is breaking down in the UK as delayering pressurises employees to work increased hours, while in Asia-Pacific Saturday morning work is the norm.

Literacy levels can impact heavily on the ability of target audiences to understand and to ascribe meanings to marketing communication messages. The balance between visual and non-visual components in messages and the relative complexity of messages should be considered in the light of the education levels that different countries and regions have reached. In addition to these factors, some target audiences in more developed economies have developed a high level of advertising sophistication. The meaning given to messages is in some part a reflection of the degree to which individuals understand commercial messages and what the source seeks to achieve. This high level of interaction with messages or advertising literacy suggests that advertisers need to create a dialogue with their audiences that recognises their cognitive processing abilities and does not seek to deceive or misinform.

> Advertisers need to create a dialogue with their audiences that recognises their cognitive processing abilities.

Religion has always played an important part in shaping the values and attitudes of society. Links between religion and authority have been attempted based on the highly structured nature of religion and the influence that religion can play in the family, forming the gender decision-making roles and nurturing the child-rearing process. While the results of research are not conclusive, there appears to be agreement that religion plays an important part in consumer buying behaviour and that marketing communications should take into account the level of religious beliefs held by the decision-maker (Delner, 1994).

Similarly, mass communication technologies provide audiences with improved opportunities to understand and appreciate different religious beliefs and their associated rituals and artefacts, so care needs to be taken not to offend these groups with upsetting or misinformed marketing communications.

ViewPoint 30.3   International TicTac

The 1990s advertising for the TicTac brand, owned by Ferrero, has been judged to be of the same dubious quality to that of its sister brands Ferrero Rocher and Kinder Surprise (Watts, 2000). Much of Ferrero's advertising has been based on a pan-European advertising approach, as per their infamous Ambassadors' Party ad for the Ferrero Rocher brand. For much of the 1990s TicTac's European advertising was based upon the use of German models acclaiming the virtues of just 2 calories per sweet (Watts, 2000).

The mint category in which TicTac operates has been rejuvenated by the entry of Smint and its rather unorthodox advertising. Polo, an established competitor, began to exploit the 'hole' in its adverting and with Trebor promoting its smaller mints the market has developed and become more contemporary. TicTac was beginning to be left behind and its European approach was clearly not working. Watts quotes James Lowther (chairman of M&C Saatchi) who says that 'doing a campaign that reaches all markets is not a very successful idea. In order to find something that doesn't displease, you end up reducing the things you can do to the lowest common denominator'.

Values

One of the most important international and culturally oriented research exercises was undertaken by Hofstede (1980, 1991). Using data gathered from IBM across 53 countries, Hofstede's research has had an important impact on our understanding of culture (Hickson and Pugh, 1995).

From this research, several dimensions of culture have been discerned. The first of these concerns the individualist/collectivist dimension. It is suggested that individualistic cultures emphasise individual goals and the need to empower, to progress and to be a good leader. Collectivist cultures emphasise good group membership and participation. Consequently, difficulties can arise when communications between these two types of culture have meanings ascribed to them that are derived from different contexts. To avoid the possible confusion and misunderstanding, an adapted communication strategy is advisable.

Several dimensions of culture have been discerned.

In addition to these challenges, comprehension (ascribed meaning) is further complicated by the language context. In high-context languages information is conveyed through who is speaking and their deportment and mannerisms. Content is inferred on the basis that it is implicit: it is known and does not need to be set out. This is unlike low-context languages, where information has to be detailed and 'spelled out' to avoid misunderstanding. Not surprisingly, therefore, when (marketing) communications occur across these contexts, inexperienced communicators may be either offended at the blunt approach of the other (of the low-context German or French, for example) or intrigued by the lack of overt information being offered from the other (from the high-context Japanese or Asians, for example). Referring to advertising creative strategy, Okazaki and Alonso (2003) assert that the Japanese prefer a more subtle and soft approach. In contrast North Americans prefer a more direct and hard-sell strategy with direct and explicit messages.

North Americans prefer a more direct and hard-sell strategy with direct and explicit messages.

A further cultural dimension concerns the role that authority plays in society. Two broad forms can be identified. In high-power-distance cultures, authority figures are important and guide a high proportion of decisions that are made. In low-power-distance cultures, people prefer to use cognitive processing and make reasoned decisions based on the information available. What might be deduced from this is that expert advice and clear, specific recommendations should be offered to those in high-power-distance cultures, while information provision should be the goal of marketing communications to assist those in low-power-distance cultures (Zandpour and Harich, 1996).

People in different cultures can exhibit characteristics that suggest they feel threatened or destabilised by ambiguous situations or uncertainty. Those cultures that are more reliant on formal rules are said to have high levels of uncertainty avoidance. They need expert advice, so marketing communications that reflect these characteristics and are logical, clear and provide information in a direct and unambiguous way (in order to reduce uncertainty) are likely to be more successful.

> People in different cultures can exhibit characteristics that suggest they feel threatened or destabilised by ambiguous situations or uncertainty.

From the adaptation/standardisation perspective, this information can be useful in order to determine the form of the most effective advertising messages. Zandpour and Harich used these cultural dimensions, together with an assessment of the advertising industry environment in each target country. The results of their research suggest that different countries are more receptive to messages that have high or low levels of logical, rational and information-based appeals (think). Other countries might be more receptive to psychological and dramatically based appeals (feel).

ViewPoint 30.4   Varying international regulations

Advertising of toys is not permitted in Sweden and is banned until 22.00 hours in Greece. In France all alcohol advertisements are banned, while in the Czech Republic drink can be shown but it cannot be poured, nor can advertisements show people enjoying the product. In Mexico the restrictions state that food must be visible, whereas the Costa Ricans are allowed to see a glass being filled or the drink being poured, but not both.

Tobacco advertising is about to be banned across countries in the EU while pet food advertisements are banned in Lithuania before 23.00 hours. The reason for this strict ruling is that food is scarce and this type of commercial could be considered offensive to humans.

Research concerning the effectiveness of advertising strategies in the United States and Australia (Frazer and Sheehan, 2002) found that safety appeals were more frequently used in Australia than the United States. This may well reflect varying cultural values regarding concern for safety-related issues, concern for the environment and varying regulatory requirements.

Media

The rate of technological change has had a huge impact on the form and type of media that audiences can access. However, media availability is far from uniform, and the range and types of media vary considerably across countries. These media developments have been accompanied by a number of major structural changes to the industry and the way in which

> Media availability is far from uniform.

TABLE 30.2 General trends in worldwide media

Electronic media expenditure has grown at the expense of print.

The worldwide adspend on newspapers has fallen considerably.

The number of general-interest magazines has fallen and the number of specialist-interest magazines has grown.

The growth of satellite facilities has helped generate the development of television and cable networks.

Online adspend is increasing faster than for any other medium.

Television programming and distribution have become more important.

Cinema capacity is beginning to outstrip demand.

Out-of-home media, in particular outdoor and alternative new media (e.g. ambient), have grown significantly.

the industry is regulated. Many organisations (client brands, media and agencies) have attempted to grow through diversification and the development of international networks (organic growth and alliances), and there has been an increase in the level of concentration as a few organisations/individuals have begun to own and hence control larger proportions of the media industry. For example, Rupert Murdoch, Ted Turner, Time-Warner, Bertelsmann and Silvio Berlusconi now have substantial cross-ownership holdings of international media. This concentration is partly the result of the decisions of many governments to deregulate their control over the media and to create new trading relationships. As a result, this cross-ownership of the media (television, newspapers, magazines, cable, satellite, film, publishing, advertising, cinema, retailing, recorded music) has created opportunities for client advertisers to have to go to only one media provider, which will then provide access to a raft of media across the globe. For example, the recent Time-Warner/AOL merger was intended to take the concentration and cross-industry collaboration a stage further as positions for future markets are adopted. This facility, known as one-stop shopping, has been available in North America for some time, and was attempted by Saatchi & Saatchi and WPP in the 1980s from a European base, but it is only since the 1990s that this opportunity has been offered elsewhere. The failure of the Time Warner/AOL merger is symptomatic of other cultural and business-related problems.

Deregulation has had a profound impact on media provision in nearly all parts of the world. In Korea, for example, the number of daily newspapers has grown from 60 in 1988 to 125 in 1996, while the number of television channels has grown from 3 to 4 terrestrial channels plus 26 cable services and 1 satellite broadcaster (Kilburn, 1996).

Table 30.2 sets out some of the more general worldwide trends in advertising media. The net impact of all these changes has been principally the emergence of satellite television and cable provision and the development of the international consumer press.

Cross-border communication strategy

The degree to which organisations should adapt their external messages to suit local or regional country requirements has been a source of debate since Levitt (1983) published his landmark work on global branding. The standardisation/adaptation issue is unlikely to be resolved yet is an intuitively interesting and thought-provoking subject. The cost savings associated with standardisation policies are attractive and, when these are combined with the opportunity to improve message consistency, communication effectiveness and other internally related efficiencies such as staff morale, cohesion and organisational identity, the argument in favour of standardisation seems difficult to renounce. However, in practice there are very few brands that are truly global. Some, such as McDonald's, Coca-Cola and Levi's are able to capitalise upon the identification and inherent brand value that they have been able to establish across cultures. The majority of brands lack this depth of personality, and because individual needs vary across cultures so enterprises need to retune their messages in order that their reception is as clear and distinct as possible.

Adaptation

The arguments in favour of adapting messages to meet the needs of particular local and/or regional needs are as follows:

1. Consumer needs are different and vary in intensity. Assuming there are particular advertising stimuli that can be identified as having universal appeal, it is unlikely that buyers across international borders share similar experiences, abilities and potential either to process information in a standardised way or to ascribe similar sets of meanings to the stimuli they perceive. Ideas and message concepts generated centrally may be inappropriate for local markets.

2. The infrastructure necessary to support the conveyance of standardised messages varies considerably, not only across but often within broad country areas.

3. Educational levels are far from consistent. This means that buyers' ability to give meaning to messages will vary. Similarly, there will be differing capacities to process information, so that the complexity of message content has to be kept low if universal dissemination is to be successful.

4. The means by which marketing communications are controlled in different countries is a reflection of the prevailing local economic, cultural and political conditions. The balance between voluntary controls through self-regulation and state control through legislation is partly a testimony to the degree of economic and political maturity that exists. This means that what might be regarded as acceptable marketing communications activities in one country may be unacceptable in another. For example, cold calling is not permissible in Germany but, although not popular with either sales personnel or buyers, is allowed in the Netherlands and France.

5. Local management of the implementation of standardised, centrally determined messages may be jeopardised because of a lack of ownership. Messages crafted by local 'craftsmen' to suit the needs of local markets may receive increased levels of support and motivation.

Standardisation

Just as the arguments for adaptation appear convincing at first glance, then so do those in favour of standardisation:

1. Despite geographical dispersion, buyers in many product categories have a number of similar characteristics. This can be supported by the various psychographic typologies that have been developed by advertising agencies for their clients. As brand images and propositions are capable of universal meaning, there is little reason to develop a myriad of brand messages.

2. Many locally driven campaigns are regarded as being of poor quality, if only because of the lack of local resources, experiences and expertise (Harris, 1996). It is better to control the total process and at the same time help exploit the opportunities for competitive advantage through shared competencies.

3. As media, technology and international travel opportunities impact upon increasing numbers of people, so a standardised message for certain offerings allows for a strong brand image to be developed.

4. Just as local management might favour local campaigns, so central management might prefer the ease with which they can implement and control a standardised campaign. This frees local managers to concentrate on managing the campaign and removes from them the responsibility of generating creative ideas and associated issues with local advertising agencies.

5. Following on from this point is one of the more enduring and managerially appealing ideas. The economies of scale that can be gained across packaging, media buying and advertising message creation and production can be enormous. In addition, the prospect of message consistency and horizontally integrated campaigns across borders is quite compelling. Buzzell (1968) argued that these economies of scale would also improve levels of profitability.

ViewPoint 30.5   Ford dominance

Ford unveiled its new 'roadblocks' campaign through a dominance media strategy launch. The two-minute ad was shown in 40 countries at the same time, literally. At 21.00 hours on 1 November 1999, every commercial station in the target countries showed the £9.4 million campaign. The ad featured seven of the company's brands (Ford, Volvo, Mazda, Jaguar, Lincoln, Mercury and Aston Martin) and depicted the way the brands featured in people's lives all around the world. So as to present the Ford brand as 'human', consumer oriented and not just a faceless, arrogant conglomerate, it depicted different ethnic groups greeting each other and all using Ford products in a variety of situations. Rosier (1999) also claims that the ad was a sign that global marketing initiatives can drive the creative content even at a domestic level.

Fielding (2000) and Hite and Fraser (1988) argue that the evidence indicates that, although organisations pursued standardisation strategies in the 1970s, the trend since then has been towards more local adaptation. Harris (1996) makes the point that, although the operation of a purely standardised programme is considered desirable, there is no evidence to suggest that standardisation actually works. There appears to have been little research to compare the performance of advertising that has been developed and implemented under standardisation policies with that executed under locally derived communications.

The trend since then has been towards more local adaptation.

However, while a few organisations do operate at either end of the spectrum, the majority prefer a contingency approach. This means that there is a degree of standardisation, where for example creative themes, ideas and campaign planning are driven centrally and other campaign elements such as language, scenes and models are adapted to the needs of the local environment. The cosmetic manufacturer L'Oréal distributes its Studio Line of hair care products aimed at 18–35-year-olds across 50 countries. 'These are the same

The majority prefer a contingency approach.

products with the same formulation with the same attitudinal message of personal choice' (Sennett, in Kaplan, 1994). All the advertisements have the same positioning intentions, which are developed centrally, but the executions (featuring different hairstyles) are produced locally to reflect the different needs of different markets. It is too easy to consider the internationalisation debate in terms of packaged goods companies when other sectors have approached the task in different ways. Bold (2000) refers to pharmaceutical companies that have generally made the product, as opposed to brands, the centre of their communication strategy. Drugs are launched in different countries using different names and different strategies targeted at the medical professionals. He comments that while this approach was prevalent the structure of pharmaceutical companies tended to be nation-focused even to the extent that there would be separate regionalised budgets. The merger and consolidation activity, together with the rapid rise in patient involvement in health care (e.g. AIDS), has resulted in the formation of centralised marketing departments and the development of multinational brands.

The reasons for some form of standardisation are twofold. First there is an increasing need for improved levels of internal efficiency (and accountability) in terms of the use of resources. Secondly there is an increasing awareness of the benefits that standardised advertising may have on organisational identity, employee morale and satisfaction. The pressure to make cost savings and to develop internal efficiencies, therefore, appears to override the needs of the market.

> There is an increasing awareness of the benefits that standardised advertising may have on organisational identity, employee morale and satisfaction.

However, those who argue in favour of standardisation need to be aware that the information content will often need to be correspondingly low. Mueller (1991) observes that the greater the amount of information the greater the opportunity for buyers to discriminate among alternative purchases. Conversely, the emphasis with uninformative advertising is to use imagery and indirect (peripheral) cues. Multinational organisations prepare individual marketing mixes for individual countries/areas. Products and prices will be different, so comparisons are difficult. Likewise, key attributes will vary across countries/areas, so this means that organisations need to decide whether high levels of standardisation and low levels of information are preferred to adapted campaigns with higher levels of information content.

The criterion by which organisations should decide whether to adapt or standardise their marketing (communications) activities is normally the impact that the different

ViewPoint 30.6   Adaptive Guinness

When Guinness appointed AMV and Saatchi & Saatchi as its two creative agencies (substantially reducing the number of roster agencies) the decision was made in recognition that the brand's heritage and promotional requirements were essentially twofold.

Tylee (2001) explains that in the relative sophistication of Europe and the United States the brand is perceived as a premium product supported by very emotionally led advertising reflecting years of development. In Africa and other parts of the world the brand established itself originally because it was able to be shipped long distances and still be drinkable. Now, Guinness is a mass market brand and is supported in Africa by a James Bond character, Michael Power, a black all-action hero.

Guinness recognises the need to utilise different creative approaches in respect of market perceptions.

strategies are likely to have on profit performance (Buzzell, 1968). The basis for these financial projections has to be a suitably sensitive segmentation analysis based on a layering of segment information. Country-only or arbitrary regional analysis is unlikely to be suitable. Cross-cultural and psychographic data need to be superimposed to provide the richness upon which to build effective communications.

Organisations rarely decide on a polarised strategy of total adaptation or complete standardisation. In practice, a policy of 'glocalisation' seems to be preferred. Under this approach, organisations develop standard messages centrally but expect the local country areas to adapt them to meet local cultural needs by adjusting for language and media components. There are, of course, variations on this theme. For example, head office might decide on the strategic direction and thrust of the campaign and leave the local country management to produce its own creatives.

> In practice, a policy of 'glocalisation' seems to be preferred.

The international promotional mix

International public relations

International public relations differs from domestically related activities only in the sense that it seeks to build cultural, geographical and linguistic bridges between stakeholders outside the country of origin. As if to continue the foregoing debate, the issues remain about whether to standardise communications or adapt them to meet local needs. One complication to this approach concerns the development and prevalence of trading blocs and the degree to which individuals within these blocs retain notions of national identity. This in turn will influence the relationships formed between stakeholder groups.

Public relations wherever practised needs to be based on a willingness and propensity to share information, to be prepared to adjust one's own position in the light of feedback, to be ethical in one's own behaviour.

Packaging

Product packaging fulfils two main functions. One is to protect the product so that the customer can consume the product in pristine condition at all times. The second function concerns the marketing communication needs and their potential impact on the purchase decision process. Packaging, especially in consumer markets for purchase decisions which generate low levels of involvement, need to be protective (due to possibly longer distribution chains and variations in temperature/climate) and be persuasive in such a way that it reinforces the positioning requirements and the other

> And be persuasive in such a way that it reinforces the positioning requirements and the other activities of the promotional mix.

activities of the promotional mix. Research by Berg-Weitzel and van de Laar (2000) states quite emphatically that a nation's culture has repercussions for the design of its packaging and if standardised packaging is decided upon then a neutral design should be pursued. If the decision is to adapt, then local aspects of design should be 'exploited to gain the consumer's confidence'. Colour, shape and language issues need to be carefully considered whether the decision is to standardise or localise packaging design.

> Colour, shape and language issues need to be carefully considered whether the decision is to standardise.

Trade shows and exhibitions

This is a much underestimated aspect of marketing communications and in an international dimension is of great significance. The benefits for organisations attending trade fairs are basically the same whether they be domestic or international events. What is significant, however, is that exhibitions are important, especially in the b2b market, for building and maintaining relationships with customers and members of the marketing channel (horizontally and vertically). In an international arena where the cultural backgrounds of visitors and exhibitors may be very diverse, it is essential that not only does attendance occur but that visibility is high and hospitality compatible with the local environment and those of other significant visitors.

Personal selling

As to personal local customs, culture, language and product attribute determine that a localised approach to personal selling techniques and content is vital and that a standardised approach to selling across international markets is for the vast majority of organisations a non-starter. Having said that, an international sales effort can be organised and managed with a degree of standardisation. There are four main approaches, which can be used either in sequence or simultaneously as conditions permit.

The first approach, mainly applicable for small organisations beginning to operate in international markets, enables them to use spare domestic capacity. They use a sales force that is based in the home market and which either has some international responsibilities or operates abroad exclusively. This requires the sales personnel not only to be fully conversant with the entire product range but also to understand the countries, organisations and cultures in which they seek to operate. If only from a time and expense perspective there are strong limitations to the extent to which this approach can be realistically expected to work.

A second approach requires the use of manufacturers' representatives and agents. These organisations provide local knowledge of both competitors and culture that can cut considerably the length of time necessary to enter a new market. However, there are problems associated with the commitment and bias of such agents and the level of control that management can retain. For example, agents are paid on a commission-only basis and their allegiance to a product/manufacturer is thin, such that their desire to sort out local problems of logistics, finance or product operation is questionable.

A third approach is to establish a marketing channel and appoint distributors and dealers in the target country/regions. This allows management a greater level of control but it does incur greater levels of management time and commitment to the international trade channel and the associated training if the strategy is to be successful.

The fourth and final approach is to establish a dedicated sales force in each of the countries/regions. This is expensive, and although control is considerably improved it is an approach only adopted once a market presence has been well established.

International sponsorship

Sponsorship, whether it be in a domestic (Serie A football in Italy) or an international (Olympics 2004 and 2008) context, enables support of the public relations activity either by providing a means to meet key customers or members of the marketing channel in an informal way or by improving awareness and attitudes towards the sponsor. In addition, sponsorship has an impact on the quality of relationships with a variety of

Can all be enhanced through understanding
and sympathetic alignment with the
sponsor's position regarding their social
responsibilities.

stakeholders. Relations with employees, governments and local communities can all be enhanced through understanding and sympathetic alignment with the sponsor's position regarding their social responsibilities, ethical stance and overall role as a corporate citizen (Owusu-Frimpong, 2000).

It is not surprising that the costs associated with sponsorship activities vary according to the scale (size and duration) of the activities and the size of the audience. Global brands need sponsorship on an international basis in order to reinforce their market presence and to support and reinforce the other aspects of the promotional mix. Integrated marketing communications in an international context needs to use advertising (to make aware and to reinforce brand values), public relations (to provide understanding, interest and goodwill), sponsorship (to be seen to be involved) and personal selling (to enable and drive customer action) if a brand is to be established.

Direct marketing

Most of the points concerning domestic direct marketing apply equally on the international stage. It would appear that there are four main factors that need to be considered:

1. Language is an important factor as most people prefer to receive (and give) communications in their own, first language. The focus organisation needs to consider translation costs (including time), list availability and making judgements about tone, humour and indeed what the most appropriate language might be.

2. The second factor is media availability. There may be wide variances in the range and quality of the media in the country/regions that it wishes to trade in. The quality and effectiveness of the telephone and postal services, the coverage of cable and satellite channels, the significance of magazines and the readership of the national, regional and local press all need to be carefully considered when developing an international direct marketing campaign.

The second factor is media availability.

3. The third factor to consider is the quality and breadth of the services and infrastructure necessary to support an international campaign. The quality of mailing lists, databases and supporting agencies need to be carefully reviewed before committing to an international DM campaign.

4. The quality of management control is the final international factor to be considered. Most campaigns of this nature need to be controlled centrally by the focus organisation and/or their direct marketing agency. This centralised approach is important in the light of the need for integration, control of costs and data management. There may be conditions that allow for the development of a decentralised approach whereby the planning and implementation of these direct campaigns are delegated to local management.

The centralised and decentralised positions are at two ends of a spectrum. Many organisations adopt a mid-position, with strategy and direction being determined centrally and the tactics and implementation issues determined locally.

The role of the Internet

The Internet has an important role to play for those organisations considering internationalisation or those that have already achieved transnational status. Hamill and

The Internet has an important role to play for those organisations considering internationalisation.

Gregory (1997) found that smaller organisations view the Internet as a tool to enable them to develop network communications, sales promotion and market intelligence activities.

The Internet provides global market access for all organisations and each needs a strategy to determine the role of its Web site and how it will interact with the organisation's current established distribution and communication strategies.

International advertising agencies

Just as many organisations have sought to expand internationally, so many advertising agencies have attempted to grow with their clients. This process gathered speed in the 1980s and 1990s, with varying levels of success. By trying to mirror client/brand needs and by expanding operations over increased geographic areas, organisations have experienced many financial and management challenges. These challenges have been met with varying degrees of success. The consequences of this 'natural' development are that aspects such as the structure of the industry, the configuration and work patterns of constituent agencies, the relationships between clients and advertisers and the form of advertising messages that are developed and given meaning by target audiences and agencies alike have evolved.

Agency development overseas

Operating overseas is not a recent phenomenon for advertising agencies. This strategy has been established for many decades. There are three primary routes that agencies have taken to secure international growth. These are *organic growth* through the creation of overseas subsidiaries, *acquisitive growth* through the purchase of established indigenous agencies and finally *cooperative growth*, where agencies collaborate through the formation of networks and strategic alliances.

Organic growth requires the setting up of subsidiary offices in selected regions or countries. Costs and management can be controlled, but the relatively slow speed of development has deterred many from this approach. *Acquisitive growth*, involving the merger with or purchase of advertising agencies already operating in the required market, is attractive because it is possible to use the skills and established contacts of local managers. However, these overseas operations are relatively inflexible and can incur considerable overheads as well as high initial purchase costs. *Cooperative growth* through strategic alliances and partnerships, often as part of global networks, can appear to be a more flexible and efficient approach to meeting a client's international marketing communications requirements. One of the potential problems with this approach is that the level of control over local actions can be reduced, but the reduced costs and increased speed of set-up and delivery make this an attractive option.

The level of control over local actions can be reduced.

A further variation of this method of expansion is the formation of networks of independent agencies. By contributing to a central financial fund, so giving the network a formal legal status, agencies are able to work together and provide flexibility for their clients.

International agency networks can provide clients with a number of advantages. Primarily these focus on two main areas: resource utilisation and communication effectiveness.

Resource utilisation

1. Clients and agencies help each other by avoiding costly duplication of message development work and media buying.

2. Economies of scale can reduce costs for both parties.

3. By centralising decision-making, management has increased control over the direction of campaigns and their implementation such that clients have a single main point of contact.

4. Special resources and scarce creative expertise is made available to a client globally.

Communication effectiveness

1. Creative ideas from all parts of the network can be shared and, if a largely adaptive strategy is followed, good ideas can be replicated elsewhere. Good creative ideas are rare, so by using an international agency these highly prized gems can be used to the client's benefit worldwide.

> Creative ideas from all parts of the network can be shared.

2. Internal communications are improved by a common infrastructure and management information system.

3. By using a single agency, operating across many markets, feedback and market analyses can be standardised (process, timing and format), thus facilitating common reporting and fast feedback of audience and competitor actions.

Freeman (1996) argues that, as manufacturers are re-evaluating the way in which they approach their customers, changes are also being brought about at business-to-business advertising agencies. Rapid technological advances in communications, global marketing of brands, shorter purchase decision-making cycles and heightened competition are forcing agencies to re-evaluate their internal organisation and communications strategies. This, he suggests, has already led to a number of mergers with larger organisations and internal reorganisation to better handle clients' needs.

These developments have impacted on the pitching process. When WPP agreed a deal to manage the Boots global account, the decision was made between Martin Sorrell and Steve Russell, the respective CEOs of the two organisations. The agenda, to create a unified brand and save money (White, 2000) is clear and understandable. However, the process by which the agreement was reached signalled some concern for other agencies. As a result of this 'boardroom' deal, many roster agencies (e.g. OMD) lost substantial billings and did not have an opportunity to defend their business, even though their client had, at marketing manager levels, been more than satisfied with the relationship.

Global and multinational advertising agencies work with a variety of clients generating high volumes and a broad variety of materials (e.g. storyboards, design and copy for print advertisements, media plans). Traditional methods of communication, such as telephone and mail, are often slow and inefficient. Faster alternatives, such as overnight delivery and couriers, can become expensive as projects pass through multiple review cycles. Even email has limited application. See ViewPoint 30.7.

ViewPoint 30.7   B2B Portals for Havas

Havas, a large advertising agency operating across 131 countries, developed a Web-based system to improve internal and external interaction and collaboration and to manage the huge and increasing volumes of data and information. However, it found that it did not have the most effective tools to structure and manage the increasing levels of information, and navigation became problematic.

The organisation developed a b2b portal to enable it to manage its diverse and globally distributed agencies. The goal was to enable the agencies and their clients to work more closely together with improved rapport. The portal's features include content authoring and categorisation, threaded discussions, personnel directories, calendars, templates for campaign tracking, as well as document routing and management.

Source: Adapted from http://www.kandasoft.com/success_GEM2.html; accessed 29 October 2003; used with kind permission.

The development of a b2b portal for the advertising agency Havas, cited in View-Point 30.7, required the identification of five criteria. These are set out in Table 30.3.

The success of b2b portals can be measured in terms of time savings and cost reductions. However, there are a range of other benefits associated with the ease of use and maintenance of a wide range of documents. In addition, there is improved collaboration and link management facilities, which are regarded as an important factor when attempting to improve agency performance and reduce client turnover. As part of the process of enhancing client interaction, a number of features and benefits accrue to the user and their networks. These can be seen at Table 30.4.

Havas claims its portal has increased efficiency and saved time and money. Turn-around times for client approval of creative work have been significantly reduced by as much as 50 per cent. The ability to manage global research and creative materials within the agency's network has improved dramatically, as has staff's willingness to

TABLE 30.3 Criteria for agency/client portals (Adapted from Kanda Software; used with kind permission.)

Criteria	Explanation
Simplicity of creation and operation	Client portals need to be easy for the company's account teams. A template-based system can save time, reducing duplication of effort and bringing consistency to the construction and ongoing management of such sites.
Low maintenance	The system should have built-in capabilities to keep every portal site organised and running properly with minimal intervention.
Flexible and comprehensive	The system must accommodate graphical images, audio and video files, and common office documents. In addition, multilingual capability is required.
Solid security	The system requires security features that instil confidence in the agency clients and guarantee that unauthorised personnel cannot see or access documents or collaborative areas.
Powerful and accurate searching	With the large number of documents, these systems require a powerful search capability for both document content and Meta data.

TABLE 30.4 Features and benefits of using a portal within an advertising agency (Adapted from Kanda Software; used with kind permission.)

Feature	Benefit
Content organization	Workspace views, links to other web Pages, and news updates.
Productivity tools	Secure, threaded discussions to foster and enhance collaboration; directories with phone listings; calendar functions; templates for campaign tracking.
Document routing and management	Expedites the review and approval process and improves workflow. This includes document version controls, distribution list maintenance, and automated notification agents to alert clients and account teams when new content is added or modifications are made to existing content.
Server architecture	A distributed architecture that allows several GEM servers to function as a single server. This brings increased scalability, improved load balancing and distribution, and a higher degree of reliability to the agency's portal environment.
Administrative functions	Activity audit trail reports, user profile maintenance, user definitions and access privileges, and default view definitions.

share knowledge among account teams. As a result, account teams now have more time to focus on strategic planning and delivering greater value to their clients. The agency can now communicate rapidly and more efficiently with clients, giving both the agency and its clients an improved quality of interaction and a positive working relationship. Through the use of IST this case demonstrates the opportunities to improve agency/client relationships and reduce client turnover.

Agency growth

The expansion of advertising agencies away from domestic markets is essentially an investment decision in which normal return on investment criteria need to be determined. Such decisions can be based upon the relative size of competitive advantage that an expanded operation might generate. Multinational agencies (MNAs) might be able to develop key advantages, such as size, access to capital, the loyalty given to them by multinational advertisers, their knowledge and skill, and their ability to use their foreign locations to service regional markets (West, 1996). Some of the growth has been motivated by the need to meet the expanding international requirements of clients. Kim (1995) cites Procter & Gamble's entry into Eastern Europe and the subsequent opening of offices in the same area by its adverting agency, Leo Burnett. Anholt (2000) refers to Lintas's development on the back of Unilever's growth. Offensive and defensive business strategies, to either capitalise on or counter competitor moves, can also be regarded as prime motivating factors.

A further explanation lies with the motivations of individual managers, or agency theory. This perspective suggests that managers seek growth in order to fulfil personal needs rather than those that may be in the best interests of the organisation. These advantages nevertheless have little distinguishing power if the MNA itself is unable to coordinate its activities and lever its resources to provide its clients the benefits of speed, creativity and media purchasing power.

Some implications of international growth

One of the current dilemmas facing clients and agencies is that through consolidation the number of agencies capable of and interested in international work is declining. At the same times the volume of work available is expanding as a greater number of clients seek to develop internationally. Indeed, the work is fragmenting and hence the value of individual pieces of work is getting smaller. As Anholt (2000) states quite succinctly, 'Global clients are getting more numerous, smaller and spending less, as global agencies are getting fewer, bigger and charging more'. What this means is that something has to change, probably in the way agencies think and act towards global business opportunities and the way in which they implement strategies, and involving more local creative experience to satisfy client needs.

Many advertisers have been comfortable with the way in which advertising agencies have attempted to build European and international networks to complement their own global branding initiatives. There is some evidence, however, that this one-stop shopping approach is not entirely satisfactory (*Economist*, 1996). Some client organisations want access to a range of creative teams and also want the benefits of consolidation at the same time. The response of some MNAs has been to reorganise internally. Many of the megamergers between major agency networks have resulted in further structural changes as agencies shed accounts that cause conflicts of interest. Those clients caught up in the restructuring and consequent consolidation of the industry may well regard themselves as unwitting participants.

ViewPoint 30.8   Samsung Electronics Company

Samsung Electronics is a major Korean business organisation that was founded in 1969. Because of the nature and size of the Korean market Samsung's principal activities were export focused from the beginning, so the time spent developing in domestic markets was not typical of many organisations in developed Western economies.

International stage

OEM-branded (original equipment manufacturer) exporting dominated Samsung's business activities, as this provided a convenient and less risky form of rapidly improving export volumes and cash flow. Until 1977 an export department was responsible for routine matters of shipping and courting foreign buyers. From this date an international department was created, as a more sophisticated approach was adopted, to perform market research, some product development and overseas demand forecasting. Several foreign branches were created to encourage communication with foreign buyers, and full-scale export marketing communications (with advertising, sales promotions and exhibitions) were commenced.

Corporate messages sought to establish the size and capabilities of Samsung and were targeted at importers and OEM manufacturers. Product-based messages emphasised particular brands and were targeted at distributors and dealers in the United States, Europe, Asia, the Middle East and Central and South America.

However, the product range that Samsung offered evolved during this period so that the locus moved from televisions, radios and cassette players to microwaves and VCRs. This shift meant that Samsung had to adjust the messages it conveyed in order that the company be perceived as technologically progressive. To accomplish this it adopted a corporate identity programme. This signalled the commencement of the multinational stage in Samsung's development.

Multinational stage

The message was developed centrally and the same message (standardisation) was then communicated throughout all of the markets in which Samsung was active.

Trade restraints imposed by many economies led to a change in the organisation's corporate strategy. Market penetration could now only be achieved by setting up subsidiary companies in the markets in which it wished to operate. This meant that nationals with local knowledge were required to head each of these new SBUs.

The OEM emphasis gave way to own-branded exports and, in order to support the local distribution channels and dealers, provincial marketing communications began to proliferate. Head office developed and implemented corporate communication messages and local offices (and agencies) developed product-based communications. Problems were encountered when attempting to harmonise the company awareness campaign with the vagaries of media availability in some of the markets. The 'low-cost, high-quality' message was now targeted at consumers rather than dealers, but difficulties were encountered in getting access to appropriate media. The net result of this was that uncoordinated promotional work ensued, which was relatively ineffective in achieving its goals.

Global stage

Samsung needed to change its corporate strategy, as it was unable to continue competing on a low-cost basis, mainly because of competitors' relocation of their production facilities and the increasing labour costs in Korea. By reducing the OEM activity and promoting its own high-quality brands, Samsung was better positioned to achieve one its goals of becoming one of the world's top five electronics companies.

Corporate profitability had fallen despite increased sales revenues. The company strategy highlighted the need to coordinate its activities across the group and to reduce duplication and unnecessary investments.

The group's promotional activities were also overhauled. A coordinated global corporate and brand identity programme was established with the goal of allowing its global consumers to differentiate Samsung. Korean advertising agencies were internationalising themselves either through the establishment of overseas offices or by entering into alliances with other agencies that gave them access to global networks.

Transnational stage

The company has grown considerably in the twenty-first century, and with recorded annual sales of KRW 57.63 trillion for 2004 and profits approaching US$10.8 billion it has become one of the world's leading companies. The company's rapid growth and increasing profitability is partly a direct result of its ability to utilise the Internet to source and manage a large slice of its global procurement needs and in doing so drastically reduce its cost base. Samsung appears to have moved into the transnational phase.

Source: Adapted from Cho *et al.* (1994).

The creation of the position of worldwide account director (Farrell, 1996) was an attempt to coordinate and control the global accounts of clients such as IBM and Reebok, which had centralised their international advertising activities. Another role which emerged was that of the worldwide creative director (Davies, 1996). This position, it is suggested, developed directly from clients' expectations for their agency networks to mirror their own global branding drives and management structures. But, as Martin (1996) points out, as these worldwide creative directors are invariably appointed with no department or resources and are inclined to meet resistance from local management teams, the position appears to be irrelevant and impotent.

Media planning has become increasingly difficult.

Media planning has become increasingly difficult, as not only has the provision of media services in particular regions (e.g. Asia) expanded rapidly but at the same time there have been major social changes. Kilburn (1996) reports that, in Taiwan, Ogilvy & Mather and J. Walter Thompson have formed The Media Partnership from their media buying operations, thus providing increased buying power for their clients in what is effectively a fragmented market.

Agency structures are evolving and adapting to the needs of their environments.

Agency structures are evolving and adapting to the needs of their environments. The traditional perspective of control by head office executives over the work of local network agencies, either by a disproportionate level of standardisation policies or by rather inflexible procedures that put bureaucratic needs before market requirements, is changing. Instead of control, coordination is one of the keys to competitive advantage in MNA/agency relationships. The one factor that distinguishes transnational organisations applies equally to advertising agencies. As Banerjee (1994) suggests, agency decision-making concerning the development of major multicountry brands will need to be collaborative in the future as 'agency power structures evolve to better reflect emerging revenue geographies'.

Stages of cross-border advertising development

Cho *et al.* (1994) propose a framework whereby the type of advertising deployed can be considered in the context of the stage of internationalisation that organisations have reached. Based upon studies of Korean firms, the authors propose that the advertising strategy is (or should be) a direct reflection of the marketing and business strategies employed. Therefore:

Domestic marketing   = Domestic advertising
Export marketing   = Export advertising
Multinational marketing = Multinational advertising
Global marketing   = Global advertising

From this, and utilising the information about international development, it is possible to establish the key characteristics and strategies associated with each stage of international growth. See Table 30.5.

TABLE 30.5 Strategies associated with international advertising development

	Home	International	Multinational	Global	Transnational
Advertising stage	Domestic	Export	Multinational	Global	Transnational
Key message	Product or corporate	Product and brand	Corporate and brand	Corporate and brand	Corporate and/or brand
Management	Standardisation	Standardisation	Standardisation and adaptation	Regional adaptation	Global adaptation
Management structure/support	Centralised	Centralised	Decentralised	Grouped centralisation	Network
Agency	Domestic	Domestic	Domestic and foreign local	Global	Transnational network

Summary

As organisations saturate domestic markets and seek growth opportunities overseas, so they meet new challenges and embark upon fresh strategies. Organisations operating across a number of international and/or regional borders evolve through international, multi-national, global and transnational phases and forms. The differentiating characteristics appear pronounced and convincing as growth drivers impel development.

Two of the main variables that impact upon the marketing communications deployed by organisations across these different forms are culture and the media. Culture is a composite of a number of elements, ranging from symbols such as language, groups and education, through values represented in language context and power distance.

The media are also significant drivers that have been influenced by both technological drivers and political initiatives to deregulate and open up accessibility.

The strategies used to communicate with cross-border audiences focus upon either standardisation or total adaptation to the needs of the local audience. While the debate is interesting and practice varied, the evidence suggests that a mixture of the two approaches, glocalisation, is the preferred practice of many global and transnational organisations.

Advertising agencies have had to respond to the initiatives driven by their clients. Global advertising agency development has taken a variety of forms; however there appears to be a match between the marketing strategies pursued by client organisations and the consequent advertising strategies to support them.

Review questions

1. There are four types of cross-border organisation, reflecting their structure and disposition to their markets. Name them and their key characteristics.

2. Prepare some brief notes explaining how culture impacts upon an organisation's marketing communications.

3. Select two countries of your choice. Compare the significance of cultural symbols and provide examples of how these are used.

4. Explain high- and low-context languages.

5. Discuss how deregulation of media ownership has affected marketing communications.

6. You have been asked to make a presentation to senior managers on the advantages and disadvantages of standardising the marketing messages delivered for your brand throughout the world. Prepare notes for each of the slides you will use.

7. Evaluate the different ways in which advertising agencies can grow.

8. International advertising agencies provide resource utilisation and communication effectiveness as their main advantages. Explain the detail associated with these two characteristics.

9. Determine the four stages of cross-border advertising development.

10. What are the key differences between each of these four stages?

MINI-CASE
Sexing up Asia's ads

Mini-case written by Gill Wood, The Write Marketing Consultancy

Companies in Asia are much more cautious than their counterparts in the West when it comes to making ads, partly because they are focused on building up basic product or brand knowledge in developing markets and also because they are more concerned with offending cultural mores.

Worried that marketing executives at GlaxoSmithKline in Malaysia would reject his idea for a television advertisement, Ogilvy & Mather's creative director in Kuala Lumpur dropped the storyboard approach and went straight to filming a rough version of his idea for Oxy, the spot treatment cream, paying for filming himself before showing it to the client. In the ad, a man with a stocking over his head enters a convenience store and looks furtively around. As people around him panic, the man points frantically to a tube of Oxy behind the counter – then throws some money at the assistant before running out of the shop.

When GlaxoSmithKline finally saw the film they loved it and ran the 30-second spot as part of an email campaign.

However, many multinationals in Asia often want to play it safe. The result is a stream of safe ads that do not veer from the preferred format. Hair shampoos generally feature women swishing their hair and smiling sweetly into the camera. This means it is difficult to create brands that stand out from the crowd.

One big multinational mobile phone company recently backed out of an ad that O&M Asia-Pacific's regional creative director, Tham Khai Meng, put together for the Chinese market. It featured a Beijing-based punk band called Wild Strawberries doing a rendition of Jimi Hendrix's 'Foxy Lady'. Tham had secured the rights for the song, obtained permission from Hendrix's son and had even signed up Malcolm McLaren, the former Sex Pistol's manager, to produce the song for the ad. The phone company initially liked the idea but canned it after six months' work. It wanted to tap the youth market but punk, they decided eventually, was inappropriate for China.

Many companies contend that research often shows that the nuts and bolts type of ad sells well with Asian consumers. Research conducted by the US-based advertising company Grey Worldwide shows that consumers in Asia tend to read advertising quite literally and that Asian ads work better when tested against European ads, because they tend to have a more linear, rational message.

Within multiracial Malaysia, different racial groups tend to react differently to ads. Clients put aside big budgets to test audiences and usually find that Chinese consumers want a rational message – how the product works and how much it costs – while Malay consumers fall for a more emotional appeal.

Another potential problem is that companies do not want to waste money making an ad they know will be rejected by the censors. After GlaxoSmithKline saw how successful the Oxy ad was in its email campaign, it applied to Malaysia's censorship board to run it on television. However, the board deemed the robbery scene was too graphic and permission to run the ad was denied.

Thailand, however, is recognised as producing the funniest ads in the Asia-Pacific region. Thai culture tends to be fairly laid back and Thais generally have a self-deprecating sense of humour that does not work in other Asian cultures.

One recent ad made by Leo Burnett for Thai Mobile, a network that is targeting the mass market, shows a woman on the roof of a dingy Bangkok apartment building exchanging notes, via homing pigeon, with her husband who is working on a construction site. After a dozen meaningless notes the exhausted bird vomits in her hair. On the return trip to her husband the bird collapses, convulsing on the table. The husband then laughs with colleagues: 'Look, it has a vibrating mode, just like a real cell phone.' Then the voice-over says: 'Those who don't have a cell phone, hands up', at which point the husband and his workmates all raise their hands.

Advertising, then, appears to be a social barometer, a reflection of what a society will or will not buy into. However, many Asian countries are multicultural and humour does not always cut across cultures. In addition some Confucian-influenced Asian cultures encourage conformity and discourage risk, which makes marketing directors less adventurous. Consequently many Asian advertisers tend to stick to safe ground in their advertising messages.

Questions

1 Discuss the idea that ads targeted at audiences who prefer rational product based messages should be planned, whereas ads targeted at audiences who prefer more emotional ads should be developed on a more spontaneous basis.

2 Why is it that a visually humorous ad which works in one country is very often less effective in another?

3 To what extent should advertising challenge local cultural mores and values in order to achieve commercial success?

References

Anholt, S. (2000) Updating the international advertising model. *Admap* (June), pp. 18–21.

Banerjee, A. (1994) Transnational advertising development and management: an account planning approach and a process framework. *International Journal of Advertising*, **13**, pp. 95–124.

Bartlett, C. and Ghoshal, S. (1991) *Managing Across Borders: The Transnational Solution.* Cambridge, MA: Harvard Business School Press.

Berg-Weitzel, van den, L. and Laar, van de, R. (2000) Local or global packaging. *Admap* (June), pp. 22–5.

Bold, B. (2000) Unlocking the global market. *PR Week*, 11 August, pp. 13–14.

Buzzell, R. (1968) Can you standardise multinational marketing? *Harvard Business Review*, **46** (November/December), pp. 102–13.

Cho, D.-S., Choi, J. and Yi, Y. (1994) International advertising strategies by NIC multinationals: the case of a Korean firm. *International Journal of Advertising*, **13**, pp. 77–92.

Davies, J. (1996) The rise of the super-creative. *Campaign*, 1 November, p. 18.

Davies, J. (2000) Euroman: warrior or wimp? *Campaign*, 15 October, p. 39.

Delner, N. (1994) Religious contrast in consumer decision behaviour patterns: their dimensions and marketing implications. *European Journal of Marketing*, **28**(5), pp. 36–53.

Economist (1996) A passion for variety. *Economist*, 30 November, pp. 68–71.

Farrell, G. (1996) Suits: the world is their ad oyster. *Adweek*, **37**(8), pp. 29–33.

Fielding, S. (2000) Developing global brands in Asia. *Admap* (June), pp. 26–9.

Frazer, C.F. and Sheehan, K.B. (2002) Advertising strategy and effective advertising comparing the USA and Australia. *Journal of Marketing Communications*, **8**, pp. 149–64.

Freeman, L. (1996) Client-driven change alters agency strategies. *Advertising Age – Business Marketing*, **81**(2), pp. 1–20.

Griffin, T. (1993) *International Marketing Communications*. London: Butterworth-Heinemann.

Hamill, J. and Gregory, K. (1997) Internet marketing in the internationalisation of UK SMEs. *Journal of Marketing Management*, **13**, pp. 9–28.

Harris, G. (1996) International advertising: developmental and implementational issues. *Journal of Marketing Management*, **12**, pp. 551–60.

Hickson, D.J. and Pugh, D.S. (1995) *Management Worldwide*. London: Penguin.

Hite, R.E. and Fraser, C. (1988) International advertising strategies of multinational corporations. *Journal of Advertising Research*, **28** (August/September), pp. 9–17.

Hofstede, G. (1980) *Culture's Consequences: International Differences in Work Related Values.* Thousand Oaks, CA: Sage.

Hofstede, G. (1991) *Cultures and Organisations*. London: McGraw-Hill.

Hofstede, G., Neuijen, B., Ohayv, D.D. and Sanders, G. (1990) Measuring organisational cultures: a qualitative and quantitative study across twenty cases. *Administrative Science Quarterly*, **35**(2), pp. 286–316.

Kaplan, R. (1994) Ad agencies take on the world. *International Management* (April), pp. 50–2.

Keegan, W.J. (1989) *Global Marketing Management*. Englewood Cliffs, NJ: Prentice-Hall.

Kilburn, D. (1996) Asia rising. *Adweek*, **37**(34), pp. 22–6.

Kim, K.K. (1995) Spreading the net: the consolidation process of large transnational advertising agencies in the 1980s and early 1990s. *International Journal of Advertising*, **14**, pp. 195–217.

Levitt, T. (1983) The globalization of markets. *Harvard Business Review* (May/June), pp. 92–102.

Martin, M. (1996) How essential is the role of a worldwide creative director? *Campaign*, 9 February, p. 45.

de Mooij, M. (1994) *Advertising Worldwide*. Hemel Hempstead: Prentice Hall.

Mueller, B. (1991) An analysis of information content in standardised vs. specialised multinational advertisements. *Journal of International Business Studies* (First Quarter), pp. 23–39.

Okazaki, S. and Alonso, J. (2003) Right messages for the right site: online creative strategies by Japanese multinational corporations. *Journal of Marketing Communications*, **9**, pp. 221–39.

Owusu-Frimpong, N. (2000) The theory and practice of sponsorship in international marketing communications. In *The Handbook of International Marketing Communications* (ed. S.O. Moyne). Oxford: Blackwell.

Rosier, B. (1999) Ford to 'roadblock' the world in TV campaign. *Marketing*, 28 October, p. 4.

Tylee, J. (2001) AMV and Saatchis prepare to meet over Guinness. *Campaign*, 12 January, p. 23.

Watts, J. (2000) TicTac looks to UK agencies to get a fresher image. *Campaign*, 25 August, p. 24.

West, D.C. (1996) The determinants and consequences of multinational advertising agencies. *International Journal of Advertising*, **15**(2), pp. 128–39.

White, J. (2000) Can agencies survive clients' global expansion? *Campaign*, 27 October, p. 24.

Zandpour, F. and Harich, K. (1996) Think and feel country clusters: a new approach to international advertising standardization. *International Journal of Advertising*, **15**, pp. 325–44.

Business-to-business marketing communications

31

Organisations have many reasons to enter into exchange relationships with one another, rather than with consumers. This is referred to as the business-to-business sector and marketing communications needs to reflect the characteristics of the buyer behaviour inherent in these relationships. Effective communications are important for helping to build long-term relationships, closer levels of collaboration and cooperative behaviours and help secure some advantage in the market system.

Aims and objectives

The aims of this chapter are to introduce and explore business-to-business marketing communications and to consider the factors that influence and shape relationships between organisations.

The objectives of this chapter are to:

1. establish the primary characteristics of the b2b sector;
2. develop an understanding of the particular types of risk associated with organisational decision-making;
3. introduce a model of b2b marketing communications;
4. examine trust and commitment as major components of interorganisational communications;
5. appraise the role and structural determinants of marketing communications within marketing channels;
6. explore the notions of collaborative and autonomous communication strategies;
7. consider the notion of communication quality;

8. examine issues concerning ecommerce and b2b relationships;

9. introduce key account management as an important strategic approach to communications with intermediaries.

Introduction

The characteristics of the business-to-business market are very different from those of the consumer market. The larger size of markets, the lower number of customers, the high average spend per customer, the wider geographic spread and the relatively complex nature of buyer behaviour are significant differences. Of all of these factors, it is the buyer behaviour element that is the primary distinguishing element and the one that impacts most on marketing communications. It should not be surprising therefore that the marketing communications in these two major sectors are very different.

The commercial b2b sector is made up of four main subsectors.

The commercial b2b sector is made up of four main subsectors, all of which share common buyer behaviour characteristics and communication needs, i.e. goods/services for:

1. Own consumption – vending machines, office furniture, stationery.

2. Incorporation and assembly – materials and supplies necessary for the production of your products and services. The identity of the materials can be lost within the larger product. These organisations are sometimes referred to as original equipment manufacturers.

3. Resale to another organisation – acting as a member of a marketing channel, perhaps taking ownership and possession, adding value before passing the products on to another organisation that will add value to it in some way.

4. Retail – the most common example where goods and services are sold to end-user consumers.

In all of the situations organisations are involved in the buying of products, and only in the last situation are consumers at all involved. Therefore, the nature and form of the cooperation and the interorganisational relationships that develop from the exchanges influence the nature of the marketing communication activities used.

Part of the role of marketing communications is to develop and support the relationships.

The degree of cooperation between organisations will vary and part of the role of marketing communications is to develop and support the relationships that exist between partner organisations.

In this sector organisations buy products and services and they use processes and procedures that can involve a large number of people. Fuller details about these characteristics can be found in Chapter 6. What is central, however, is the decision-making unit and the complexities associated with the variety of people and processes involved in making organisational purchase decisions and the implications for suppliers in terms of the length of time, and nature of the communications mix and messages necessary to reduce the levels of risk inherent in these situations. Mitchell (1999) refers to Haakansson and Wootz (1979), who identified need, transaction and market uncertainties, and Valla (1982) who suggested that there are five categories of risk which

TABLE 31.1 Seven types of organisational decision-making risk

Risk type	Explanation
Technical risk	Will the parts, equipment or product/service perform as expected?
Financial risk	Does this represent value for money? Could we have bought cheaper?
Delivery risk	Will delivery be on time, complete and in good order? Will our production schedule be disrupted?
Service risk	Will the equipment be supported properly and within agreed time parameters?
Personal risk	Am I comfortable dealing with this organisation? Are my own social and ego needs threatened?
Relationship risk	To what extent is the long-term relationship with this organisation likely to be jeopardised by this decision?
Professional risk	How will this decision affect my professional standing in the eyes of others and how might my career and personal development be impacted?

must be addressed by buyers and suppliers. From these it is possible to identify seven types of risk that are relevant to organisational buyers. These are shown at Table 31.1.

Personal selling is very important in b2b markets.

Personal selling is very important in b2b markets, often because of the need to help build relationships with members of buying centres and the need to demonstrate and explain technicalities associated with the products and services being marketed. In support of the personal selling effort (and exhibitions), trade promotions, trade advertising, direct marketing and public relations all play important roles. See Exhibit 31.1 for an example of b2b advertising. Increasingly, the Internet provides not only new direct routes to customers and intermediaries but also a vibrant new communications medium.

Networks and interorganisational relationships

The strategic value of marketing channels, partnerships and alliances and business networks has become increasingly more significant in recent years. As channel networks have developed so has their complexity, which impacts upon the marketing communications strategies and tools used to help reach these customers, partners and fellow intermediaries. The expectations of buyers in these networks have risen in parallel with the significance attached to them by manufacturers. The power of multiple retailers, such as Curry's, Comet, Boots and Superdrug, is such that they are able to dictate terms (including the marketing communications) to many manufacturers of branded goods. For example, many consumer-related sales promotion events are prompted by retailers in response to claims for shelf space and in-store visibility.

Many consumer-related sales promotion events are prompted by retailers.

The basic structure of any network consists of a focal organisation that is tied with a number of other functionally specialised organisations. The network uses relational exchanges to regularise and sustain cooperative activities. This is a general view and it is recognised that there is a variety of network forms, some of which were explored

It's a Chargecard.

Cut admin time and petty cash time and reduce the number of cheques issued.

It's an Information Card.

Track and control expenses with detailed monthly statements and management information.

It's a Travel Card.

Full travel booking service including free travel insurance when you use your card.

It's a Negotiation Card.

Allowing you to negotiate discounts on travel and entertainment.

It's a Security Card.

You decide each card's limit. You're also protected with free Cardholder Misuse Insurance too.

(Sorry, we forgot about the birthday card.)

For further information on our Corporate Card call 0845 721 2111 and quote 1015 or visit our website.
Company Barclaycard P.O. Box 3000 Teesdale Business Park Stockton-on-Tees TS17 6YG
www.company.barclaycard.co.uk

EXHIBIT 31.1 Company Barclaycard
An example of B2B advertising. Advertisement reproduced with the kind permission of Barclaycard

previously (Chapter 8). However, to repeat an important point, it is necessary to distinguish the type of networks an organisation belongs to from traditional perspectives, if only because it is now generally accepted that all organisations are networks in their own right and that there is a variety of internal and external networks to which all organisations belong.

Therefore, network organisations can be distinguished from traditional organisational forms because the exchanges are based upon membership, which encourages mutually determined relational transactions. This long-term perspective reflects the density, closeness and shared values that such networks seek to perpetuate.

ViewPoint 31.1	Sharwoods networks

Sharwood's network of independent retailers is vitally important in providing shelf space and visibility for its brand of sauces. However, it found that the sale of its Chinese sauces through the independent retailer network was low compared with those of Indian sauces. To help rectify the imbalance, it used a direct marketing campaign to coincide with the Chinese New Year.

Incentivised mailpacks were sent to selected independent retail outlets, inviting them to purchase cases of Oriental products and in return receive money-off coupons. The campaign also sought to educate retailers so that they provided their customers with a breadth of suitable products. After a two-week interval, telemarketing was used to identify those retailers who had either purchased or wanted to order over the phone. Darby (1997) reports that a 34 per cent take-up resulted from this approach and Sharwood's market share rose to 26 per cent over the new year period.

Many commentators have observed that organisations are forging relationships with other organisations which are based around a network in order to achieve new, fresh advantages. These advantages may be driven by competitive goals, but the behaviour exhibited is increasingly cooperative. These networks vary in the strength of their ties (degrees of interconnectedness), but success can be seen to be a function of the partnerships that are developed in these networks. A key question has to be, what determines a successful partnership and how is success characterised and replicated? An underlying principle of relational exchanges is the pivotal role of trust and commitment (Morgan and Hunt, 1994). See Figure 31.1.

Commitment to a partnership, that is the relationship with other network members, is key because of the 'enduring desire to maintain a valued relationship' (Moorman *et al.*, 1992). Of comparable importance is the degree to which partners are confident that each will act in the best interests of the relationship.

Trust, therefore, is also regarded as a key aspect of relational exchanges and is a composite of the level of reliability and integrity that exists between partners.

According to Mohr and Spekman (1994), partnership success is based upon three key parameters. These are the attributes the partnership exhibits, the communication behaviour and the techniques used to resolve conflict. See Figure 31.2. Their view is that partnership success is dependent upon a wider array of factors than just commitment and trust. These are recognised as important, but in addition they posit communication- and conflict-related issues. It could be argued that Mohr and Spekman define commitment and trust in a relatively narrow way, such that the other factors need to be made explicit. What is important, however, is that these authors state unequivocally that

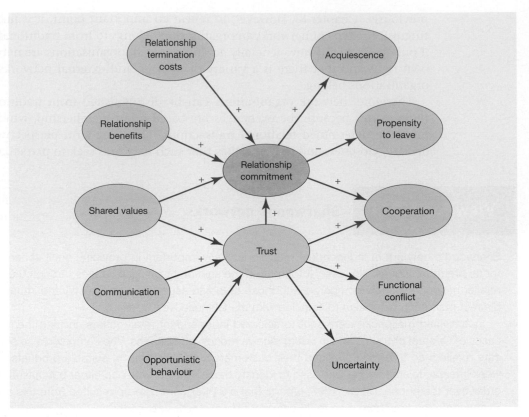

FIGURE 31.1 The role of commitment and trust in relationship marketing (From Morgan and Hunt (1994); reprinted with permission from *Journal of Marketing*, published by the American Marketing Association.)

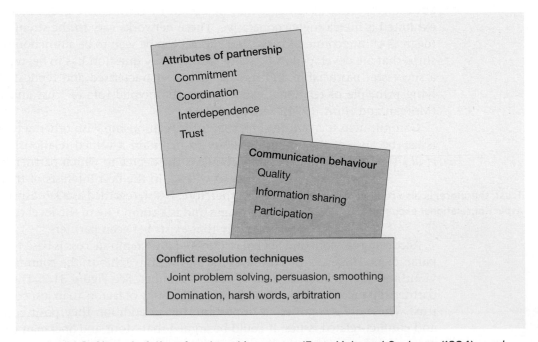

FIGURE 31.2 Characteristics of partnership success (From Mohr and Spekman (1994); used with kind permission.)

communication problems are associated with a lack of partnership success and that communication might be interpreted as an overt manifestation of more subtle phenomena, such as trust and commitment.

B2b communications

Effective communication is key to the satisfaction of buyer expectations and is the main link between an organisation and its environment. Indeed, the systems used to transfer information and meaning from people and machines, in both inter- and intra-organisational contexts, can progress or hinder the implementation of corporate and operational strategies. If the dynamics of an organisation are to be understood, for example, in order that effective and appropriate strategic change processes can be developed, then all its communication systems and networks need to be appreciated.

Effective communication is key to the satisfaction of buyer expectations.

What are their communication requirements in the light of the objectives that have been set, and more importantly what are their communication expectations? Once these have been considered, it is possible to think about the communication strategies that may be best suited to achieving these goals and then determine the means by which strategies will be implemented.

Gilliland and Johnston (1997) published a model of b2b marketing communication effects, which has been reproduced as Figure 31.3. In this model the buy task

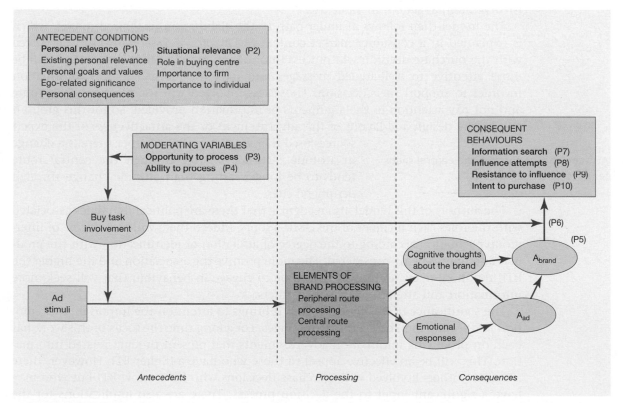

FIGURE 31.3 Model of business-to-business marketing communications (From Gilliland and Johnston (1997); used with kind permission.)

TABLE 31.2 The antecedents associated with BTI

Relevance factor	Explanation
Personal	Refers to personal goals, any ego-related significance and the perceived personal consequences of the purchase decision. The higher the personal relevance, the higher the BTI.
Situational	Refers to the importance of the decision to the individual and to the firm. The higher the situational relevance, the higher the BTI.
Opportunity to process	Refers to the level of distractions and noise that might impede exposure or prevent comprehension of a marketing message. The higher the number of opportunities to process information, the higher the BTI.
Ability to process	Refers to the knowledge an individual has about the product under consideration as the more the individual knows, the greater his/her ability to process information about it. The greater the ability to process information, the higher the BTI.

Source: Adapted from Gilliland and Johnston (1997); used with kind permission.

involvement (BTI) represents the degree to which individual members of the DMU feel personal relevance (involvement) with each purchase decision. Gilliland and Johnston identify four main elements that can impact on an individual's level of personal involvement, as set out in Table 31.2.

The model then follows a similar path to the elaboration likelihood model, which is explained in a consumer market context in Chapter 7. Essentially those involved with the purchase decision will process information via the central route, and will be more attentive to well-argued messages and look for rational logical information in order to support their decision. Those less involved will use the peripheral route and not pay attention to the arguments or information provided. So for this group it will be the design and layout of the advertisement or the attractiveness of the expert sources used that will determine whether there is a change in attitude. Attitude change through the central route tends to be longer lasting than attitude change through peripheral cues.

> Attitude change through the central route tends to be longer lasting.

The authors of this model also recognise that there are political dynamics associated with the roles each member of the DMU adopts. Indeed there will be a degree of inter-group persuasion according to the degree of affiliation or identification with the products and brands being considered. The more positive the association and the higher the BTI, the more likely an individual will be to engage in behaviour that will seek more information and attempt to influence others.

The significance of this model is that it brings to attention the importance of emotion and feeling in b2b advertising messages. For a long time the focus of this work has been on producing information advertisements that present product-related information. This will be an effective appeal to those who have a higher BTI. However, there are many others involved with purchase decisions who have a low BTI but who may have a significant input to the decision process. There are also implications for the media schedule with more reason to use television and consumer print media in particular.

Interorganisational communication

The important role that communication plays in determining the effectiveness of any group or network of organisations is widely recognised (Grabner and Rosenberg, 1969; Stern and El-Ansary, 1992). According to Mohr and Nevin (1990), communication is 'the glue that holds together a marketing channel'. It is recognised that, from a managerial perspective, communication is important because many of the causes of tension and conflict in interorganisational relationships stem from inadequate or poor communication. Communication within networks serves not only to provide persuasive information and foster participative decision-making but also to provide for coordination, the exercise of power and the encouragement of loyalty and commitment, so as to reduce the likelihood of tension and conflict.

The channel network (Chapter 8) consists of those organisations with whom others must cooperate directly to achieve their own objectives. By accepting that there is interdependence, usually dispersed unequally throughout the network, it is possible to identify organisations that have a stronger/weaker position within a network. Communication must travel not only between the different levels of dependence and role ('up and down' in a channel context) and so represent bidirectional flows, but also across similar levels of dependence and role, that is, horizontal flows – these may be from retailer to retailer or wholesaler to wholesaler.

ViewPoint 31.2 Novell

Novell, a highly influential and well-regarded network computing company, had strong relationships with IT professionals. However, in order to progress it needed to develop stronger relationships with senior business executives and those involved in strategic IT purchase decisions. Otherwise it faced losing business and clients.

J Walter Thompson decided to use a three-part strategy to reach the target market. First, rather than talk to these key influential people using technology as the main vocabulary, it was decided to converse on a business basis and to communicate messages based on the business issues and needs faced by clients. Secondly, stress Novell's ability to deliver on the promises they make and thirdly, help clients achieve their profit targets. 'We speak your language' became a meaningful tagline and became Integrated B2B campaign of the year (2003).

Source: www.jwt.com/case studies/; used with permission.

There are some specialised messages that need to be distributed across a variety of networks, for example messages proclaiming technological advances, business acquisitions and contracts won. It is also apparent that communication flows do not change radically over the short term. On the contrary, they become **Communication flows do not change radically over the short term.** established and regularised through use. This allows for the emergence of specialised communication networks (Chapter 2). Furthermore, it is common for networks to be composed of subnetworks, overlaying each other. The complexity of an organisation's networks is such that unravelling each one would be dysfunctional.

What is necessary is the establishment of those elements that contribute to the general communications in a b2b situation, and a marketing channel environment in particular. The development of a planned, channel-oriented communications strategy, a push strategy, should be based on identifiable elements that contribute to and reinforce the partnerships in the network. A number of these can be identified, namely a consideration of the movement of flows of information and in particular the timing and permanence of the flows (Stern and El-Ansary, 1992). It should also take into account the various facets of communication and the particular channel structures through which communications are intended to move (Mohr and Nevin, 1990). These will now be considered in turn.

Timing of the flows

Message flows can be either simultaneous or serial. Where *simultaneous* flows occur, messages are distributed to all members so that the information is received at approximately the same time. Business seminars and dealer meetings, together with direct mail promotional activities and the use of integrated IT systems between levels (overnight ordering procedures), are examples of this type of flow. *Serial* flows involve the transmission of messages so that they are received by a preselected number of network members who then transmit the message to others at lower levels within the network. Serial flows may lead to problems concerning the management of the network, such as those concerning stock levels and production.

Message flows can be either simultaneous or serial.

Permanence of the flows

The degree of permanence that a message has is determined by the technology used in the communication process. Essentially, the more a message can be recalled without physical distortion of the content, the more permanent the flow. This would indicate that the use of machines to record the message content would have an advantage over person-to-person messages transmitted at a sales meeting. Permanence can be improved by recording the meeting with a tape recorder or by putting the conversation on paper and using handouts and sales literature.

Mohr and Nevin (1990) suggest that the performance outcomes of a channel network are a result of the interaction of the communications strategy used within a network and the structure of the channel within which the communications flow. Figure 31.4 depicts the relationships between strategies and structure. Therefore, by examining the constituent elements and moulding the variables to meet the channel conditions, it may be possible to enhance the performance/success of the network.

Communication facets

Communication strategy results from a combination of four facets of communication.

Communication strategy results from a combination of four facets of communication. These facets are the frequency, direction, modality and content of communications:

1. *Frequency*
   The amount of contact between members of the performance network needs to be assessed. Too much information (too frequent, aggregate volume or pure repetition) can overload members and have a dysfunctional effect. Too little information can undermine the opportunities for favourable performance outcomes by failing to

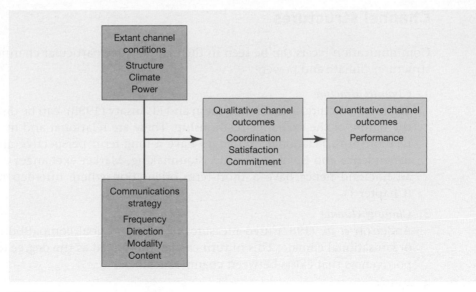

FIGURE 31.4 A model of communication for marketing channels (From Mohr and Nevin (1990); used with kind permission.)

provide necessary operational information, motivation and support. As a consequence, it is important to identify the current volume of information being provided and for management to make a judgement about the desired levels of communication.

2. *Direction*

This refers to the horizontal and vertical movement of communication within a network. Each network consists of members who are dependent upon others, but the level of dependence will vary: hence, the dispersion of power is unequal.

Communications can be unidirectional in that they flow in one direction only. This may be from a source of power to subordinate members (for example, from a major food retailer such as Sainsbury's or Tesco to small food manufacturers). Communications can also be bidirectional, that is, to and from powerful organisations. The relative power positions of manufacturer/

> Communications can be unidirectional in that they flow in one direction only.

producer and reseller need to be established and understood prior to the creation of any communication plan.

3. *Modality*

Modality refers to the method used to transmit information. Mohr and Nevin agree that there is a wide variety of interpretations of the methods used to convey information. They use modality in the sense that communications can be either formal and regulated, such as meetings and written reports, or informal and spontaneous, such as corridor conversations and word-of-mouth communications, often carried out away from an organisation's formal structures and environment.

4. *Content*

This refers to what is said. Frazier and Summers (1984) distinguish between direct and indirect influence strategies. Direct strategies are designed to change behaviour by specific request (recommendations, promises and appeals to legal obligations). Indirect strategies attempt to change a receiver's beliefs and attitudes about the desirability of the intended behaviour. This may take the form of an information exchange, where the source uses discussions about general business issues to influence the attitudes of the receiver.

Channel structures

Communication facets can be seen in the light of three particular channel conditions: structure, climate and power:

1. *Channel structure*
   Channel structure, according to Stern and El-Ansary (1988), can be distinguished by the nature of the exchange relationship. These are relational and market structure relationships. Relational exchanges have a long-term perspective and high interdependence and involve joint decision-making. Market exchanges are by contrast ad hoc and hence have a short-term orientation where interdependence is low (Chapter 1).

2. *Channel climate*
   Anderson *et al.* (1987) used measures of trust and goal compatibility in defining organisational climate. This in turn can be interpreted as the degree of mutual supportiveness that exists between channel members.

3. *Power*
   Dwyer and Walker (1981) showed that power conditions within a channel can be symmetrical (with power balanced between members) or asymmetrical (with a power imbalance).

Table 31.3 shows the relationships between communication facets and channel conditions. This is the combination of elements identified above.

Two specific forms of communication strategy can be identified. The first is a combination referred to as a 'collaborative communication strategy' and includes higher-frequency, more bidirectional flows, informal modes and indirect content. This combination is likely to occur in channel conditions of relational structures, supportive climates or symmetrical power. The second combination is referred to as an 'autonomous communication strategy' and includes lower-frequency, more unidirectional communication, formal modes and direct content. This combination is likely to occur in channel conditions of market structures, unsupportive climates and asymmetrical power.

TABLE 31.3 The relationships between channel conditions and the facets of communication

Channel conditions	Communication facets			
	Frequency	**Direction**	**Content**	**Modality**
Structure				
Relational	Higher	More bidirectional	More indirect	More informal
Market	Lower	More unidirectional	More direct	More formal
Climate				
Supportive	Higher	More bidirectional	More indirect	More informal
Unsupportive	Lower	More unidirectional	More direct	More informal
Power				
Symmetrical	Higher	More bidirectional	More indirect	More informal
Asymmetrical	Lower	More unidirectional	More indirect	More informal

Source: Mohr and Nevin (1990); used with kind permission.

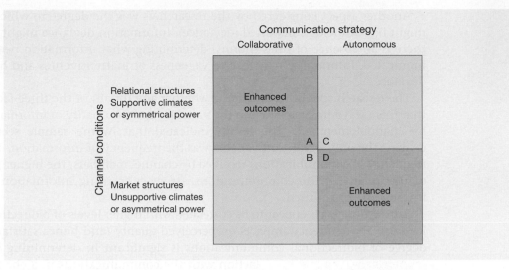

FIGURE 31.5 Proposed relationships between communication strategies and channel conditions. The pink areas represent enhanced outcome levels, or where communication strategies fit channel conditions. The blue areas represent non-enhanced outcome levels, or where communication strategies do not fit channel conditions (From Mohr and Nevin (1990); used with kind permission.)

Communication strategy should, therefore, be built upon the characteristics of the situation facing each organisation.

Communication strategy should, therefore, be built upon the characteristics of the situation facing each organisation in any particular network. Not all networks share the same conditions, nor do they all possess the same degree of closeness or relational expectations. By considering the nature of the channel conditions and then developing communication strategies that complement them, the performance of the focus organisation and other members can be considerably improved, and conflict and tension substantially reduced. Mohr and Nevin (1990) bring this together conceptually at Figure 31.5. Where channel conditions match communication strategy, the outcomes of the performance network will be enhanced. Likewise, when the communication strategy fails to match the appropriate channel conditions, the outcomes are unlikely to be enhanced.

Communication quality

Recently an interesting new perspective on marketing channel communications has emerged, namely issues concerning the quality of the communications and the success that might be attributed to the communication behaviours of the partners in any loose or tight networks.

Considered whether communication quality might be a function of the propensity to share information.

Mohr and Sohi (1995) considered whether communication quality might be a function of the propensity to share information. The inclination among members to share information could be assumed to be positive in networks where members show high levels of trust and commitment. Frequency of communication flows, the level of bidirectional communications in a network and the level of communication formality are assumed to be the main elements of the propensity to share information.

Another aspect considered by the researchers was the degree to which information might be withheld or distorted (deviance). Information deviance might be high when there is an absence of rules (norms) determining what information needs to be communicated. Informality may lead to vagueness or inattentiveness and higher levels of deviance.

The research sought to determine whether any (or all) of the three factors indicated that there was a linkage between the variables and the quality of information perceived by channel members. The results indicated that in the sample sector (computer dealers) the only significant variable was the frequency of information. The higher the frequency of communications received by channel members, the higher the perception of the quality of the communications. Issues concerning information overload and irritance are discounted.

Satisfaction levels appear to be correlated with higher levels of bidirectional communications. So, frequency impacts on perceived quality (and hence satisfaction) and the degree of bidirectional communications is significant in determining levels of satisfaction with the communications in a channel (network) environment.

Frequency impacts on perceived quality.

Ecommerce

Following on from the discussion about the propensity to share information is the rise of ecommerce and the opportunities to share information electronically. The development of extranets, in particular, enables organisations to share information for mutual benefit and to develop a form of competitive advantage through collaboration. Extranets allow organisations to work together in privacy and to deliver more efficient transactions. One of the difficulties experienced by extranet users is that all participants must use a common software system and those not hosting the system are invariably required to change the business operations

Enables organisations to share information for mutual benefit and to develop a form of competitive advantage through collaboration.

ViewPoint 31.3   Cereal collaboration

Kellogg's installed the ecollaboration software in conjunction with a number of UK supermarkets. The fuel blockades in September 1999 led shoppers to panic buying and purchase habits and patterns were soon lost. Normally, Kellogg's would adjust its production schedules according to retailers' reports of expected demand, usually with a three-day lag. However, the information would lack precision, would take considerable time to be disaggregated from the system and the amalgamation of the data from each of the supermarkets had to be completed manually.

During the panic-buying phase Hewson (2000) reports that consumer demand reverted to staple products (cornflakes rather than cinnamon muesli) but the new system allowed Kellogg's to track the emerging demand patterns quickly, to consolidate information from each of the supermarkets, and then adjust production on a daily basis. As a result of this ability to closely monitor purchasing trends, Kellogg's was able to maintain supplies, not lose sales for its business partners or itself and, of course, strengthen its relationships with the supermarkets.

Source: Hewson (2000).

behind their IT interface. New technology is changing that as ecollaboration was launched in 2000. This business model uses software that enables two different operating systems to talk to each other and to share information. All that is required is a portal through which all parties must pass.

A b2b communication strategy will often consist of a series of activities designed ultimately to influence the audience and persuade a percentage of it to take a particular action, very often to purchase the product/service itself. For example, a five-stage strategy to launch a new Web site for the purchase of office services might be to:

1. Build brand name awareness among the target audience. This would involve both off-line and online communications. The goal would be to drive site traffic and to encourage site visitors.

2. Drive site registration and generate reasons for visitors to return to the site.

3. Convert registrations into purchasers and the use of online and off-line sales promotions might be effective.

4. Ensure that a certain percentage of purchasers are retained and are encouraged to return to the site. Not necessarily loyalty but a retention facility based upon a points collection scheme could be useful.

5. Build into the communication strategy a means of personalising communications such that each buyer would receive special offers and notices of products and services that reflect their purchase patterns to date.

To support this strategy, a creative proposition will need to be developed so that there is a central theme around which all communications are linked. This might be related to particular attributes such as product features, for example a colour, size or speed of service. The benefits of the attributes might also be used, for example no production downtime or improved staff efficiency might be valid claims. In contrast, an emotional feeling might be generated through the use of a tag line, gimmick, slogan, music or perhaps a mood. In other words, some form of branding needs to be used to differentiate the Web site and create longer-lasting memories that can be easily recalled through the mention of the brand name or perhaps an attribute or central theme.

The promotional mix and b2b

As stated earlier, the use of the tools of the promotional mix is very different from that in consumer markets. The prime tool is personal selling supported by both above- and below-the-line activities. The Internet and related digital technologies have had a very significant role in changing the way business is conducted and the speed at which transactions can be undertaken and costs reduced. The WWW is of course both a new distribution channel and communication medium. As a form of communication it is impersonal and more disposed to information search and retrieval than to information that is heavily branded and has emotional overtones. The nature of communications in b2b is that they are very personal, often require face-to-face interaction and the interactive nature lends itself to tailored messages and rapid feedback.

> They are very personal, often require face-to-face interaction and the interactive nature lends itself to tailored messages.

The rest of this chapter will be spent reviewing each of the tools of the mix and the role they play within a b2b context. For a fuller exposition of these tools, readers are advised to refer to Part 4 of this text, commencing at Chapter 18.

Advertising and b2b

Apart from increasing use of online advertising, the most important form is print advertising in trade journals and newspapers. Perhaps the most important role of advertising in this context is to inform and remind, whereas differentiation and persuasion are delivered through other tools of the promotional mix, namely sales promotion and personal selling.

ViewPoint 31.4	Reebok's b2b advertising

Reebok uses advertising in trade magazines to inform its dealers and trade customers of special events, product launches and news relating to the brand. Exhibit 31.2 depicts an award-winning ad that was targeted at its dealers informing them of the launch of the new Liverpool FC kit. Using Scouse humour, Reebok drew attention to the brand and informed dealers of the kit's availability.

Source: Material kindly provided by Reebok International.

EXHIBIT 31.2 Reebok
Use of trade advertising to inform and remind dealers. Picture reproduced with the kind permission of Reebok International Ltd.

Direct marketing and b2b

Telemarketing has played an important role in recent years as a support mechanism to the sales force. It is used to facilitate customer enquiries, to establish leads, make appointments, and in certain circumstances provide a direct sales channel. One of the more common uses is as a sales order processing system to collect routine low-value orders. This frees up the sales force to concentrate on other more profitable activities.

Telemarketing has played an important role in recent years as a support mechanism to the sales force.

Direct mail has been an important part of the communications mix in b2b markets for some time. Direct mail can be used to support personal selling by building awareness, enhancing image, establishing credibility and taking orders, and it can provide levels of customer management. The significance of this part of the communications is not in doubt, even though some of it is being surpassed by the use of the Internet and ecommerce practices.

Therefore, it would appear sensible to be able to measure direct mail activities and in the b2b sector this is usually accomplished through measurement of response rates. However, this is not entirely satisfactory (Vöegle, 1992), because there are a number of stages through which a receiver of direct mail moves. These are the opening, scanning, (re)reading and response behaviours. Vriens *et al.* (1998) suggest that there are three main parts to the process. The first is the opening behaviour that is influenced by the attractiveness of the envelope and situational factors. Reading behaviour is influenced by the opening behaviour, the reader's situational characteristics and the attractiveness of the mailing and its contents. The final behaviour concerns the response generated, which is affected by the attractiveness of the offer, by the reading behaviour that preceded the response and the characteristics of the individual reader and their situation.

Wulf *et al.* (2000) used this framework to find ways in which response rates to direct mail could be increased. They found that the attractiveness of the envelope did impact on opening behaviour but so did the envelope size, material, colour and even type of postage. Surprisingly the volume of direct mail each manager received had no impact on opening behaviour. With regard to reading behaviour, it was the attitudes of the reader that were found to be significant, not the situational factors. Finally, response behaviour appeared to be determined more by the reading behaviours of the individual rather than any other factor.

> That the attractiveness of the envelope did impact on opening behaviour.

Sales promotions and b2b

The use of sales- or rather trade-based promotions is very often unnoticed by consumers. However, trade promotions and interorganisational incentives are common and generally effective. Manufacturers will use competitions and sweepstakes to incentivise the sales forces of its distributors, to motivate technical and customer support staff in retail organisations and as an inducement to encourage other businesses to place orders and business with them.

ViewPoint 31.5   Dulux targets decorators

In an effort to consolidate its position as market leader and to increase sales, Dulux used a trade-based promotion in the spring of 2004. Targeting decorators who choose paints on behalf of their largely domestic customers, rather than contractors who work on commercial accounts where the brand choice of paint is decided by the customer, a cash prize fund of £2 million was a significantly attractive promotion. The sales promotion instrument or mechanic was a scratchcard that was distributed through 1,200 trade outlets across the UK. Rather than use premium giveaways or price cuts, the scratchcard was placed inside cans of white paint so that the benefit went to the buyer (the decorator) rather than the counter staff who tend to feed their largest, by volume, customers.

Source: Adapted from Mistry (2004) and Dulux-provided materials. Used with kind permission.

Price-based promotions and delayed discounts are used to encourage organisations to place business. Another popular approach is to discount technical support and bundle up a range of support facilities. Whatever the package, the purpose remains the same, to add value in order to advance (or gain) a purchase commitment.

Public relations and b2b

The effectiveness of public relations in a b2b context should not be underestimated. The range of public relations tools and techniques enables credibility to be developed in an environment where advertising is relatively ineffective, personal selling critical to the development of relationships and sales promotion limited to short-term sales shifts. Direct marketing and particularly interactively based communications are increasingly important in this sector but public relations provides credibility and richness to an organisation's communications.

Personal selling and b2b

Personal selling is the most important tool of the marketing communications mix in b2b markets. Readers are referred to the substantial space that has been allocated to this topic in Chapter 28. In addition, exhibitions are a major part of the promotional mix used in b2b work and this was examined in Chapter 29. However, one area that has developed in recent years, owing to the use of direct marketing and interactive technology is the management of those customers who are of strategic importance to an organisation. This is explored in the sections that follow.

Strategic account management

One of the major issues concerning the development and maintenance of inter-organisational relationships is the method by which very important and/or valuable customers are managed. In many ways these methods are an extension of personal selling (Chapter 28) but as they are business-to-business matters, attention is given to these issues in this chapter. Two main forms are considered here, key account management and the emerging global account management disciplines. These are considered in turn.

Key account management

The increasing complexity of both markets and products, combined with the trends towards purchasing centralisation and industrial concentration, mean that a small number of significant accounts have become essential for the survival of many organisations. The growth in the significance of key account management (KAM) is expected to continue and one of the results will be the change in expectations of buyers and sellers, in particular the demand for higher levels of expertise, integration and professionalism of sales forces.

A small number of significant accounts have become essential for the survival of many organisations.

It has long been recognised that particular customer accounts represent an important, often large proportion of turnover. Such accounts have been referred to variously as national accounts, house accounts, major accounts and key accounts. Millman and Wilson (1995) argue that the first three are oriented towards sales, tend to the short term and are often only driven by sales management needs. However, Ojasalo (2001) sees little difference in the terminology KAM, national account marketing (NAM) and strategic account management (SAM).

Key accounts may be of different sizes in comparison to the focus organisation, but what delineates them from other types of 'account' is that they are strategically important. Key accounts are customers that, in a business-to-business market, are willing to enter into relational exchanges and which are of strategic importance to the focus organisation.

There are two primary aspects of this definition. The first is that both parties perceive relational exchanges as a necessary component and that the relationship is long term.

The key account is strategically important because it might offer opportunities for entry to new markets.

The second aspect refers to the strategic issue. The key account is strategically important because it might offer opportunities for entry to new markets, represent access to other key organisations or resources, or provide symbolic value in terms of influence, power and stature.

The importance of the long-term relationship as a prime element of key account identification raises questions about how they are developed, what resources are required to manage and sustain them, and what long-term success and effectiveness results from identifying them. Essentially this comes down to who in the organisation should be responsible for these key accounts. Generally there are three main responses: to assign sales executives, to create a key account division or to create a key account sales force. See Table 31.4.

TABLE 31.4 Three ways of managing key accounts

Category	Explanation
Assigning sales executives	Common in smaller organisations who do not have large resources. Normally undertaken by senior executives who have the flexibility and can provide the responsive service often required. They can make decisions about stock, price, distribution and levels of customisation.
	There is a tendency for key accounts to receive a disproportionate level of attention, as the executives responsible for these major customers lose sight of their own organisation's marketing strategy.
Creating a key account division	The main advantage of this approach is that it offers close integration of production, finance, marketing and sales. The main disadvantage is that resources are duplicated and the organisation can become very inefficient. It is also a high-risk strategy, as the entire division is dependent upon a few customers.
Creating a key account sales force	This is adopted by organisations who want to differentiate through service and they use their most experienced and able salespersons and provide them with a career channel.
	Administratively, this structure is inefficient as there is a level of duplication similar to that found in the customer-type structure discussed earlier. Furthermore, commission payable on these accounts is often a source of discontent, both for those within the key account sales force and those aspiring to join the select group.

The assignment of sales executives to these important accounts is common in smaller organisations. Those organisations that have the resources are able to incorporate the services of senior executives. They assume this role and with it they bring the flexibility and responsive service that are required as the account grows in stature. They can make decisions about stock, price, distribution and levels of customisation.

These accounts may be major or national accounts, as very often their strategic significance is not recognised. There is a tendency for these accounts to receive a disproportionate level of attention, as the executives responsible for these major customers lose sight of their own organisation's marketing strategy.

A further way of managing these accounts is to create a key account division. The main advantage of this approach is that it offers close integration of production, finance, marketing and sales. The main disadvantage is that resources are duplicated and the organisation can become very inefficient. It is also a high-risk strategy as the entire division is dependent upon a few customers.

Should a key account sales force be preferred then issues concerning the management of this resource arise. Key account managers require particular skills, as indeed do the executives themselves.

Key account managers

Abratt and Kelly (2002) report Napolitano's (1997) work which found that, to be successful, a KAM programme requires the selection of the right key account manager. This person should possess particularly strong interpersonal and relationship skills and be capable of managing larger, significant and often complex customers. Key account managers act as a conduit between organisations, through which high-value information flows, in both directions. They must be prepared and able to deal with organisations where buying decisions can be protracted and delayed (Sharma, 1997).

> A KAM programme requires the selection of the right key account manager.

Benedapudi and Leone (2002) agree that the key account manager is vitally important to the success of a KAM relationship but they also consider the relationship differences between the organisations as distinct to the interpersonal relationships between the customer firm's contact person and the supply side firm's key account manager, or contact employee as they refer to them. These relationships will vary in strength and there are differing consequences for the KAM relationship should the contact person leave the supply side organisation.

Among the key success factors, Abratt and Kelly report that, in addition to selecting the right key account manager, the selection of the right key account customers is also important for establishing KAM programmes. Not all large and high-volume customers are suitable for KAM programmes. Segmentation and customer prioritisation according to needs and an organisation's ability to provide consistent value should be used to highlight those for whom KAM would not be helpful.

> The selection of the right key account customers is also important.

In addition, particular sales behaviours are required at this level of operation. As the majority of key account managers are drawn internally from the sales force (Hannah, 1998, cited by Abratt and Kelly, 2002) it is necessary to ensure that they have the correct skills mix. It is also important to take a customer's perspective on what makes a successful KAM programme. Pardo (1997) is cited as claiming that the degree of impact a product has on the customer's business activity will determine the level of attention offered to the supplier's programme. Also, the level of buying decision centralisation will impact on the effectiveness of the KAM programme.

TABLE 31.5 Comparison of relational models

Ford (1980), Dwyer *et al.* (1987)	Wotruba (1991)	Millman and Wilson (1995)	McDonald (2000)
Pre-relationship awareness	Provider	Pre-KAM	Exploratory
Early stage exploration	Persuader	Early KAM	Basic
Development stage expansion	Prospector	Mid-KAM	Cooperative
Long-term stage commitment	Problem solver	Partnership KAM	Interdependent
Final stage institutionalisation	Procreator	Synergistic KAM	Integrated
		Uncoupling KAM	Disintegrated

Source: Updated from Millman and Wilson (1995); used with kind permission.

Abratt and Kelly found six factors were of particular importance when establishing a KAM programme. These are the 'suitability of the key account manager, knowledge and understanding of the key account customer's business, commitment to the KAM partnership, delivering value, the importance of trust and the proper implementation and understanding of the KAM concept'.

One final point can be made concerning key account managers. The inference is that one, multitalented individual is the sole point of contact between the supplier and customer. This is not the case as there are usually a number of levels of interaction between the two organisations. Indeed there could be 'an entire team dedicated to providing services and support to the key account' (Ojasalo, 2001). Therefore it is more appropriate to suggest that the key account manager should assume responsibility for all points of contact within the customer organisation.

Key account relationship cycles

A number of researchers have attempted to gain a greater understanding of KAM by considering the development cycles through which relationships move. Millman and Wilson offer the work of Ford (1980), Dwyer *et al.* (1987) and Wotruba (1991) as examples of such development cycles. See Table 31.5.

Millman and Wilson have attempted to build upon the work of the others (included in Table 31.5) and have formulated a model which incorporates their own research as well as that established in the literature. McDonald (2000) has since elaborated on their framework, providing further insight and explanation.

The cycle develops with the *Exploratory KAM* level where the main task is to identify those accounts that have key account potential, and those that do not, in order that resources can be allocated efficiently. Both organisations are considering each other; the buyer in terms of the supplier's offer in terms of its ability to match their own requirements and the seller in terms of the buyer providing sufficient volumes, value and financial suitability.

The next level is *Basic KAM*, where both organisations enter into a transactional period, essentially testing each other as potential long-term partners. Some relationships may stabilise at this level while others may develop as a result of the seller seeking and gaining tentative agreement with prospective accounts about whether they would become 'preferred accounts'.

At the *Cooperative KAM* level more people from both organisations are involved in communications. At the Basic KAM level both parties understand each other and the selling company has established its credentials with the buying organisation, through experience. At this next level, opportunities to add value to the relationship are considered. This could be encouraged by increasing the range of products and services transacted. As a result more people are involved in the relationship.

At the *Interdependent KAM* level of a relationship both organisations recognise the importance of the other to their operations, with the supplier either first choice or only supplier. Retraction from the relationship is now problematic as 'inertia and strategic suitability', as McDonald phrases it, holds the partners together.

Integrated KAM is achieved when the two organisations view the relationship as consisting of one entity where they create synergistic value in the marketplace. Joint problem solving and the sharing of sensitive information are strong characteristics of the relationship and withdrawal by either party can be traumatic at a personal level for the participants involved, let alone at the organisational level.

> Joint problem solving and the sharing of sensitive information are strong characteristics of the relationship.

The final level is *Disintegrating KAM*. This can occur at any time for a variety of reasons, ranging from company takeover to the introduction of new technology. The relationship may return to another, lower level and new terms of business are established. The termination, or readjustment, of the relationship need not be seen as a negative factor as both parties may decide that the relationship holds no further value.

McDonald develops Millman and Wilson's model by moving away from a purely sequential framework. He suggests that organisations may stabilise or enter the model at any level, indeed he states that organisations might readjust to a lower level. The time between phases will vary according to the nature and circumstances of the parties involved. The labels provided by McDonald reflect the relationship status of both parties rather than of the selling company (e.g. prospective) or buying company (e.g. preferred supplier). While the Millman and Wilson and McDonald interpretations of the KAM relationship cycle provide insight they are both primarily dyadic perspectives. They neglect to consider the influence of significant others, in particular those other network member organisations that provide context and interaction in particular networks and which do influence the actions of organisations and those key individuals who are strategic decision makers.

Some final aspects of KAM

In mature and competitive markets, where there is little differentiation between the products, service may be the only source of sustainable competitive advantage. Key account management allows senior sales executives to build a strong relationship with each of their customers and so provide a very high level of service and strong point of differentiation.

This approach enables an organisation to select its most experienced and able salespersons and, in doing so, provide a career channel for those executives who prefer to stay in sales rather than move into management. Administratively, this structure is inefficient as there is a level of duplication similar to that found in the customer-type structure discussed earlier. Furthermore, commission payable on these accounts is often a source of discontent, both for those within the key account sales force and those aspiring to join the select group.

The development and management of key accounts is complex and evolving. Key account relationships are rarely static and should be rooted within corporate strategy, if only because of the implications for resources, which customers seek as a result of partnering in this way (Spencer, 1999).

> The development and management of key accounts is complex and evolving.

Global account management

The development of key account management approaches highlighted the strategic importance that some customers represent to organisations. KAM represents an attempt to meet the needs of these customers in a customised and personal way. However, there are many organisations whose customers are located in many different countries, regions and even continents and the management of their needs demands different skills and resources to those adopted for KAM. The management of these customers is referred to as global account management (GAM) and in many ways is evidence of a new strategic approach to business development and marketing management in b2b organisations.

Understanding the nature of GAM is helped by Hennessey and Jeannet (2003), who provide a useful definition:

> *Global accounts are large companies that operate in multiple countries, often on two or more continents, are strategically important to the supplier and have some form of coordinated purchasing across different countries.*

(p. 1)

As if to reinforce the nature of GAM, Birkinshaw (2003) refers to Hewlett-Packard, which regards Boeing as a national (key) and not a global account as its decision-making is all US centred. One of the characteristics of global accounts is that their decision-making units are influenced through inputs from various geographical locations. Wilson *et al.* (2000) highlight the important characteristic associated with the strategic coordination associated with GAM. To them, a strategic global account is one that 'is of strategic importance to the achievement of the supplier's corporate objectives, pursues integrated and co-ordinated strategies on a worldwide basis and demands a globally integrated product/service offering from its suppliers'.

It would therefore be a mistake to think that KAM and GAM are the same. Birkinshaw (2003) is quite clear on this point when he says: 'One important point in making this assessment is to recognise that global accounts are not synonymous with key accounts'. Indeed, the roots of global account management are to be found in supply chain management, unlike KAM, which has been influenced by the sales management perspective. Hennessey and Jeannet (2003) believe that national account managers are relationship managers, whereas global account managers have a greater focus on strategic issues and coordination of personnel in different countries. Millman and Wilson (1998) refer to the importance and significance of cultural diversity and organisational issues when adopting a global account management programme.

The importance and significance of cultural diversity and organisational issues when adopting a global account management programme.

Wilson *et al.* (2000) consider how global account programmes can be delivered. They identified the need for three main global competences:

- a coordinated, globally competent supply chain;
- management of the interaction process *within* the supplying company, particularly the information and communication flows;
- the establishment of a forum, with the customer, of a collaborative design process.

This suggests that relationship management skills, in particular the use of interaction and collaboration to develop dialogue, are critical factors associated with GAM. Wilson *et al.* (2000) identify many competences that are necessary for GAM to be successful, ranging from strong communications and relationship management skills through cultural empathy and business and financial acumen. However, they make the point that global account managers need strong political skills, especially in view of the fact that they often operate without direct authority, particularly with regard to resources and processes. They refer to this role as 'political entrepreneur'.

Understanding the nature of GAM, its management and indeed associated research are at an early stage as the discipline is very young. Early work in the area suggests that there is no fixed strategic model which represents GAM if only because GAM needs to be flexible and dynamic as engagement with key global customers evolves.

Summary

The b2b market is characterised by the decision-making processes that organisational buyers use. As these can be very different from those used by consumers, it is not surprising that the marketing communications will also vary in many ways. The b2b market consists of four main types of interorganisational relationships, reflecting the role the product/service plays in the business activity of the organisation (e.g. for resale, as OEM).

Seven different types of risk were identified with organisational decision-making. Consequently, the marketing communications used to reach different organisations, predominantly personal selling, need to be adaptive to reduce different types of risk.

The model of b2b marketing communications suggests that the level of involvement experienced by the main participants in the buying process will affect the level and type of communications used. However, while the simplicity and logical reasoning associated with the model are intuitively appealing, the authors of the model accept that the political ambience in which these decisions are made does in fact 'muddy' the view and reflect the complexity of network relationships.

In order that the promotional objectives relating to members of the marketing channel network can be accomplished, it is necessary to establish and implement a communications strategy that is particular to this type of target audience. This form of marketing communications strategy is referred to as a *push* strategy. Communication strategy in the marketing channel needs to reflect the relationships that exist between members and match prevailing conditions. Commitment and trust are important variables in determining the nature of the relational exchanges that develop in networks, but in addition communications are vitally important to help build long-term relationships.

There are costs associated with communication in these networks. These costs may be direct, in the form of dealer conferences and house magazines. Costs may also be indirect in nature. For example, the views of particular retailers or manufacturers' representatives may go unheard or unreported. These views might be critical to the development of particular markets and hence be of strategic importance.

An examination of the communication networks, perhaps through a channel-wide communication audit, will reveal the need to develop communication networks appropriate to the needs of each organisation and the network as a whole.

The strategic importance of key accounts has gained increased attention in recent years. One of the prime dimensions of key accounts is the long-term relationship that can develop. McDonald (2000) has developed Millman and Wilson's (1995) interpretation of the different phases that can be associated with key account relationships. In addition global account management has recently emerged as a new strategic approach to managing customers that are represented at various locations around the world. In both these cases relationship marketing principles are important and marketing communications, principally through personal selling, is an important tool in fostering, nurturing and sustaining these strategically important accounts.

Review questions

1. Who are the principal target audiences for push-oriented communications and how do these communications differ from pull-based communication strategies?

2. Discuss the role that trust and commitment might play in marketing communications with intermediaries.

3. What are the three parameters upon which partnership success is thought to be built?

4. Prepare notes for a short article to be included in a marketing magazine about the importance of communications within marketing channels.

5. Describe the main elements of promotional informational flows in performance networks.

6. How can communication facets and channel structures be effectively combined?

7. What are the differences between collaborative and autonomous communication strategies?

8. Outline the concept of communication quality and identify the main dimension upon which quality is perceived to be based.

9. Identify the main difference between house or major accounts, key accounts and global account management.

10. Explain the concept of key account relationship cycles using the McDonald (2000) framework.

MINI-CASE
A duty to manage – changing behaviour towards asbestos

Mini-case written by Jeremy Miles, Consultant and Lecturer, Manchester Metropolitan University

Background to asbestos

Asbestos is the biggest occupational health problem ever encountered in the UK, with the level of fatalities expected to continue to rise through to the next decade. Asbestos is a naturally occurring mineral and was used extensively in building materials in the UK from the 1950s through to the mid-1970s. It has many uses, particularly for fire-proofing and insulation, but can also be deadly, with over 3,500 people currently dying each year from asbestos-related diseases (Health and Safety Executive, 2004). Claims for compensation are expected to peak in 2020 (at 10,000 deaths per year) and have an impact until 2045.

Although much asbestos has been removed over the years, it is estimated that 500,000 commercial, industrial and public buildings in the UK still contain asbestos. Changes in legislation that came into force in May 2004 place a requirement on those with responsibilities for the repair and maintenance of premises to assess and manage the risk from asbestos within their buildings. As a result, the majority of commercial businesses in the UK are affected by the change in this legislation.

To comply with the new legislation, dutyholders must find out whether their building contains asbestos and to determine its condition. They then have to assess the risk – in other words, is the asbestos likely to release fibres into the atmosphere? – and finally plan to manage that risk. This may take the form of leaving it in place and managing it through to ultimately removing it from the building totally.

Raising awareness of a new 'duty to manage'

Bill Macdonald, of the Health and Safety Executive (HSE) said:

getting the asbestos message across to those responsible for the commercial, industrial and public buildings thought to contain asbestos will be a considerable challenge – a vast and complex audience. The HSE has undertaken a five-year campaign to raise awareness of the new duty to manage and to promote effective compliance with the regulation without companies incurring excessive costs.

The HSE gave an 18-month lead-in time for businesses to work towards compliance with the new regulation. During this time, a campaign was devised to raise awareness through engaging businesses in a variety of initiatives including: a range of guidance publications; a campaign Web site; roadshows; publicity targeted at businesses nationally; presentations made at various events; publicity in company newsletters; plus the identification and utilisation of potential networks. The campaign also included working with partners who had expressed an interest in being involved as part of the push strategy. In excess of 3,000 organisations signed up to deliver conferences and workshops and to get the message across in other ways.

Changing buyer behaviour of managers in business

The threats of business interruption, potential health threats, and the risk from potential prosecution are the three main driving influences for companies. The perception for many is that asbestos removal does not 'add value', and indeed 'making good' where walls, floors or ceilings have been removed means the client may incur substantial expense – particularly for larger projects.

In general, the bigger the company, the better its understanding of the new asbestos regulations and legislation. Awareness increased by 27 per cent over the last year (2003) for companies with over 100 employees compared with an increase of only 15 per cent in companies with between 5 and 10 staff. Companies with more employees were also more likely to have plans in place to deal with the threats of asbestos. Of the companies with over 100 employees 67 per cent had plans in place compared to only 25 per cent of companies with 5–10 employees. The evidence for this is that the structure of many of the decision-making units within larger organisations has changed, with a nominated individual or department tasked with the responsibility – normally either property or the health and safety department.

Raising awareness in the smaller company continues to be a challenge. Research has revealed that 66 per cent of companies in the UK still have no plans in place to manage the risks associated with asbestos in the workplace (Zurich Risk Services, 2003). Research clearly suggests that not all companies are on track for putting asbestos management plans in place and awareness needs to increase dramatically if companies are not to be caught out by the deadlines.

Changes in demand for the asbestos industry

However, there have been some very marked changes in the industry in terms of awareness, attitude and behaviour. Demand for surveys to identify the location and condition of asbestos in buildings has soared.

The demand for removal of asbestos is starting to increase as many companies decide to adopt an 'asbestos-free' environment to reduce the risk of interruption to trading, and any threat of prosecution. However, the majority of asbestos removal works form part of refurbishment and redevelopment plans, and the total cost can often be substantial.

Danny Spicer, managing director for Silverdell, one of the leading UK contractors said, 'The profile of asbestos continues to increase, with many clients now addressing asbestos at a strategic level within their buildings management divisions. Decision-making units are being established in larger organisations that are more educated, and have formed their attitudes and approach towards managing asbestos-related issues.' He continued

Silverdell's audiences for marketing communications vary enormously. These range from the asbestos surveyor, a building contractor normally used to working with asbestos, to major clients who have a clear strategy and process for asbestos management with approved contractors that are vetted, to those clients who have a more ad hoc approach, whose first experience in dealing with asbestos is often as a result of a refurbishment/building contractor finding asbestos on site. Our promotional strategies have responded to the differing levels and changes in client understanding.

While contract work is still a substantial part of the industry, longer-term agreements are now being established by the majority of larger organisations in the public and private sector. These relationships are built around gaining efficiencies through increased understanding, clearer communication between contractors, and maintaining quality to reduce the potential threat of prosecution.

Questions

1 What would you consider to be the major influences on organisational buying behaviour that the HSE's campaign will need to take into account? These could be considered in terms of stakeholder, organisational and individual influences.

2 Explain the possible marketing communications problems the HSE could face when working with and through external agencies and partners to deliver such a campaign.

3 Explain further the elements of perceived risk that a company will need to consider, and explain how risk differs from involvement.

4 Involvement impacts on what is said, how it is said and when it is said. Identify the key components of high-involvement decision-making processes, and consider the promotional strategies an asbestos removal contractor such as Silverdell should adopt at each stage.

References

Abratt, R. and Kelly, P.M. (2002) Perceptions of a successful key account management program. *Industrial Marketing Management*, **31**(5) (August), pp. 467–76.

Anderson, E., Lodish, L. and Weitz, B. (1987) Resource allocation behaviour in conventional channels. *Journal of Marketing Research* (February), pp. 85–97.

Benedapudi, N. and Leone, R.P. (2002) Managing business-to business customer relationships following key contact employee turnover in a vendor firm. *Journal of Marketing*, **66** (April), pp. 83–101.

Birkinshaw, J.M. (2003). *The Blackwell Handbook of Global Management*. Boston, MA: Blackwell.

Darby, I. (1997) Korma chameleon. *Marketing Direct* (May), pp. 29–30.

Dwyer, F.R., Shurr, P.H. and Oh, S. (1987) Developing buyer–seller relationships. *Journal of Marketing*, **51**(2), pp. 11–28.

Dwyer, R. and Walker, O.C. (1981) Bargaining in an asymmetrical power structure. *Journal of Marketing*, **45** (Winter), pp. 104–15.

Ford, I.D. (1980) The development of buyer–seller relationships in industrial markets. *European Journal of Marketing*, **14**(5/6), pp. 339–53.

Frazier, G.L. and Summers, J.O. (1984) Interfirm influence strategies and their application within distribution channels. *Journal of Marketing*, **48** (Summer), pp. 43–55.

Gilliland, D.I. and Johnston, W.J. (1997) Towards a model of marketing communications effects. *Industrial Marketing Management*, **26**, pp. 15–29.

Grabner, J.R. and Rosenberg, L.J. (1969) Communication in distribution channel systems. In *Behavioral Dimensions in Distribution Channels: A Systems Approach* (ed. L. Stern). Boston, MA: Houghton Mifflin.

Haakansson, H. and Wootz, B. (1979) A framework of industrial buying and selling. *Industrial Marketing Management*, **8**, pp. 28–39.

Hannah, G. (1998) From transactions to relationships: challenges for the national account manager. *Journal of Marketing and Sales* (SA), **4**(1), pp. 30–3.

Health and Safety Executive (2004) http://www.willis.com/news/publications/willis_winter_Bulletin.pdf.

Hennessey, D.H. and Jeannet, J.-P. (2003) *Global Account Management: Creating Value*. Chichester: Wiley.

Hewson, D. (2000) Keeping control of panic buying. *The Sunday Times eBusiness Report*, 26 November, p. 5.

McDonald, M. (2000) Key account management: a domain review. *Marketing Review*, **1**, pp. 15–34.

Millman, T. and Wilson, K. (1995) From key account selling to key account management. *Journal of Marketing Practice: Applied Marketing Science*, **1**(1), pp. 9–21.

Millman, T. and Wilson, K. (1998) Global account management: reconciling organisational complexity and cultural diversity. The 14th Annual Industrial Marketing and Purchasing (IMP) Group Conference, Turku School of Economics and Business Administration.

Mistry, B. (2004) Dulux sets out to steal share. *Promotions and Incentives*, March, pp. 32–3.

Mitchell, V.-M. (1999) Consumer perceived risk: conceptualisations and models. *European Journal of Marketing,* **33**(1–2), pp. 163–95.

Mohr, J. and Nevin, J.R. (1990) Communication strategies in marketing channels. *Journal of Marketing* (October), pp. 36–51.

Mohr, J. and Sohi, R.S. (1995) Communication flows in distribution channels: impact on assessments of communication quality and satisfaction. *Journal of Retailing*, **71**(4), pp. 393–416.

Mohr, J. and Spekman, R. (1994) Characteristics of partnership success: partnership attributes, communication behaviour and conflict resolution techniques. *Strategic Management Journal*, **15**, pp. 135–52.

Moorman, C., Zaltman, G. and Despande, R. (1992) Relationships between providers and users of marketing research: the dynamics of trust within and between organisations. *Journal of Marketing Research*, **29** (August), pp. 314–29.

Morgan, R.M. and Hunt, S.D. (1994) The commitment–trust theory of relationship marketing. *Journal of Marketing*, **58** (July), pp. 20–38.

Napolitano, L. (1997) Customer-supplier partnering: a strategy whose time has come. *Journal of Selling and Sales Management*, **17**(4), pp. 1–8.

Ojasalo, J. (2001) Key account management at company and individual levels in business-to-business relationships. *Journal of Business and Industrial Marketing*, **16**(3), pp. 199–220.

Pardo, C. (1997) Key account management in the business-to-business field: the key accounts point-of-view. *Journal of Selling and Sales Management*, **17**(4), pp. 17–26.

Sharma, A. (1997) Who prefers key account management program? An investigation of business buying behaviour and buying firm characteristics. *Journal of Personal Selling and Sales Management*, **17**(4), pp. 27–39.

Spencer, R. (1999) Key accounts: effectively managing strategic complexity. *Journal of Business and Industrial Marketing*, **14**(4), pp. 291–310.

Stern, L. and El-Ansary, A.I. (1988) *Marketing Channels*. Englewood Cliffs, NJ: Prentice-Hall.

Stern, L. and El-Ansary, A.I. (1992) *Marketing Channels*. 4th edn. Englewood Cliffs, NJ: Prentice-Hall.

Valla, J.-P. (1982) The concept of risk in industrial buying behaviour. Workshop on Organisational Buying Behaviour, European Institute for Advanced Studies in Management, Brussels, December, pp. 9–10.

Vöegle, S. (1992) *Handbook of Direct Mail. The Dialogue Method of Direct Written Sales Communication*. Englewood Cliffs, NJ: Prentice-Hall.

Vriens, M., van der Scheer, H.R. Hoekstra, J.C. and Bult, J. (1998) Conjoint experiments for direct mail response optimisations. *European Journal of Marketing*, **32**(3/4), pp. 323–40.

Wilson, K., Croom, S., Millman, T. and Weilbaker, D.C. (2000) Global Account Management Study Report. Southampton: The Sales Research Trust.

Wotruba, T.R. (1991) The evolution of personal selling. *Journal of Personal Selling and Sales Management*, **11**(3), pp. 1–12.

Wulf, K.D., Hoekstra, J.C and Commandeur, H.R. (2000) The opening and reading behaviour of business-to-business direct mail. *Industrial Marketing Management*, **29**(2) (March), pp. 133–45.

Zurich Risk Services (2003) http://www.zurich.co.uk/professionalnews_desk/media_centre/press+release/mcasbestoscompliance.htm; retrieved 16 February 2005.

Internal marketing communications

32

The concept of 'internal marketing' recognises the importance of organisational members (principally employees) as important markets in their own right. These markets can be regarded as segments (and can be segmented), each of which has particular needs and wants which require satisfaction in order that an organisation's overall goals be accomplished. Internal (marketing) communications serve not only to convey managerial intentions and members' feelings but in many circumstances represent an integral aspect of communications with external stakeholder groups.

Aims and objectives

The aim of this chapter is to examine the context of internal marketing and how such issues might impact on an organisation's overall marketing communications.

The objectives of this chapter are to:

1. introduce the notion of internal marketing;
2. understand the significance of organisational issues when developing marketing communication strategies;
3. introduce the notion of organisational identity and the impact that employees can bring to the way that organisations are perceived by members and non-members;
4. examine the impact of corporate culture on planned communications;
5. provide an insight into the notion of strategic credibility and stakeholder perception of the focus organisation;
6. appreciate the interaction and importance of corporate strategy to planned communications;
7. examine how communication audits can assist the development of effective marketing communications;
8. introduce ideas concerning the intellectual and emotional engagement of employees.

Introduction

It was established earlier that marketing communications is concerned with the way in which various stakeholders interact with each other and with the focus organisation. Traditionally, external stakeholders (customers, intermediaries and financiers) are the prime focus of marketing communications. However, recognition of the importance of internal stakeholders as a group who should receive marketing attention has increased, and the concept of *internal marketing* emerged in the 1980s. This developed with greater impetus in the 1990s and is likely to be a major area of attention for both academics and practitioners in the first decade of the third millennium.

Recognition of the importance of internal stakeholders as a group who should receive marketing attention has increased.

Berry (1980) is widely credited as the first to recognise the term 'internal marketing', in a paper that sought to delineate between product- and service-based marketing activities. The notion that the delivery of a service-based offering is bound to the quality of the personnel delivering it has formed the foundation of a number of research activities and journal papers.

The popular view is that employees constitute an internal market in which paid labour is exchanged for designated outputs. An extension to this is that employees are a discrete group of customers with whom management interacts (Piercy and Morgan, 1991), in order that relational exchanges can be maintained (developed) with external stakeholders. Whatever view is taken, employees are, as Christensen and Askegaard (2001) state, the most central audience for organisational communication.

Both employees and managers impose their own constraints upon the range and nature of the activities the organisation pursues, including its promotional activities. Employees, for example, are important to external stakeholders not only because of the tangible aspects of service and production that they provide but also because of the intangible aspects, such as attitude and the way in which the service is provided: 'How much do they really care?' Images are often based more on the intangible than the tangible aspects of employee communications.

But also because of the intangible aspects, such as attitude and the way in which the service is provided.

Management, on the other hand, is responsible for the allocation of resources and the process and procedures used to create added value. Its actions effectively constrain the activities of the organisation and shape the nature and form of the communications the organisation adopts, either consciously or unconsciously. It is important, therefore, to understand how organisations can influence and impact upon the communication process. Therefore, as a legitimate type of 'customer' they should be subject to similar marketing practices. Each organisation is a major influence upon its own marketing communications. Indeed, the perception of others is influenced by the character and personality of the organisation.

It can be argued that the role of the employee is changing. Once they could be just part of the company but this role has been extended so that they are now recognised as and need to adopt the role of brand ambassadors (Freeman and Liedtka, 1997 and Hemsley, 1998). This is particularly important in service environments where employees represent the interface between an organisation's internal and external environments and where their actions can have a powerful effect in creating images among customers (Schneider and Bowen, 1985; Balmer and Wilkinson, 1991). It is evident that many now recognise the increasing importance of internal communications (Storey, 2001).

Member/non-member boundaries

The demarcation of internal and external stakeholders is not as clear as many writers suppose. The boundaries that exist between members and non-members of an organisation are becoming increasingly less clear as a new more flexible workforce emerges. For example, part-time workers, consultants and temporary workforces spread themselves across organisational borders (Hatch and Schultz, 1997) and in many instances assume multiple roles of employee, consumer (product) and financial stakeholder (e.g. Halifax or Northern Rock employees, who may be borrowers or savers and are now also shareholders).

According to Morgan (1997), many organisations have a problem as they do not recognise that they are themselves part of their environment. The context in which they see themselves and other organisations is too sharp. They see themselves as discrete entities faced with the problem of surviving against the vagaries of the outside world, which is often constructed as a domain of threat and opportunity. He refers to these as *egocentric* organisations. They are characterised by a fixed notion of who they are or what they can be and are determined to impose or sustain that identity at all times. This leads to an overplay of their own importance and an underplay of the significance of the wider system of relationships of which they are a part. In attempting to sustain unrealistic identities they produce identities that end up destroying important elements of the context of which they are part. The example provided by Morgan is of typewriter manufacturers that failed to see technological developments leading to electronic typewriters and then word processors.

It would appear that by redrawing or even collapsing boundaries with customers, competitors and suppliers, organisations are better able to create new identities and use internal marketing communications to better effect.

Purpose of internal marketing

Research by Foreman and Money (1995) indicates that managers see the main components of internal marketing as falling into three broad areas, namely development, reward and vision for employees. These will inevitably vary in intensity on a situational basis.

All of these three components have communication as a common linkage. Employees and management (members) need to communicate with one another and with a variety of non-members, and do so through an assortment of methods. Communication with members, wherever they are located geographically, needs to be undertaken for a number of reasons. These include the DRIP factors (Chapter 1), but these communications also serve the additional purposes of providing transaction efficiencies and affiliation needs; see Table 32.1.

> All of these three components have communication as a common linkage.

The values transmitted to customers, suppliers and distributors through external communications need to be reinforced by the values expressed by employees, especially those who interact with these external groups. Internal marketing communications are necessary in order that internal members are motivated and involved with the brand such that they are able to present a consistent and uniform message to non-members. This is an aspect of integrated marketing communications and involves

TABLE 32.1 The roles of internal marketing communications

DRIP factors	To provide information To be persuasive To reinforce – reassure/remind To differentiate employees/groups
Transactional	To coordinate actions To promote the efficient use of resources To direct developments
Affiliation	To provide identification To motivate personnel To promote and coordinate activities with non-members

product- and organisation-centred messages. If there is a set of shared values then internal communications are said to blend and balance the external communications. This process whereby employees are encouraged to communicate with non-members so that organisations ensure that what is promised is realised by customers is referred to as 'living the brand'. Hiscock (2002) claims that employees can be segmented according to the degree and type of support they give a brand. He claims that, in the UK, 30 per cent of employees are brand neutral, 22 per cent are brand saboteurs and 48 per cent are brand champions, of whom 33 per cent would talk about the brand positively if asked and 15 per cent spontaneously.

ViewPoint 32.1   'Living the brand' – British Airways

Back in the 1980s British Airways introduced a training programme that all staff attended. This was referred to as 'Putting People First' and a part of each weekly session was attended by a senior director, very often the CEO (now Lord Marshall), to reflect the importance and significance of the training and to be customer oriented. This scheme has been reintroduced as 'Putting People First – Again', partly in an effort to remind staff what the brand represents and to involve them in its development. Goften (2000) reports that the programme is about the past, the present and the future, that is pride in the past, passion for the present and faith in the future. In doing so staff are developed and encouraged to live the brand and, in a service-based business, the quality of the customer service encounter can seriously enhance or damage brand reputation. In 2003 BA started to use a similar scheme but this time called 'Passion for Service', which again is concerned about the employee contribution to the BA brand.

In a large number of both b2b and b2c organisations new products and services are often developed through the use of project teams. According to Lievens and Moenart (2000), project communication is characterised by both flows of communication among project members (intra-project communication) and flows across boundaries with external members (extra-project communication). Boundary spanners act as mediators facilitating communications flows internally (for resources) and externally to customers, suppliers, competitors and technologies. Project teams perceive differing levels of uncertainty associated with their task and these are related to external (user needs, technologies and the competition) and internal (human and financial resources) factors.

Uncertainty about the resources needs to be reduced in order to reduce uncertainty associated with external stakeholders, improve communication effectiveness and achieve project tasks. As we will see later, the integration of internal and external communications is a key factor in the development of integrated marketing communications. Project teams have an important role to play in enhancing corporate reputation, particularly in the b2b sector.

Organisational identity

Organisational identity is concerned with what individual members think and feel about the organisation to which they belong. When their perception of the organisation's characteristics accords with their own self-concept then the strength of organisational identity will be strong (Dutton *et al.*, 1994). Organisational identity also refers to the degree to which feelings and thoughts about the distinctive characteristics are shared among the members (Dutton and Dukerich, 1991). There are, therefore, both individual and collective aspects to organisational identity.

Mention was made earlier of brand ambassadors, people who identify closely with a brand and speak openly and positively about it. Albert and Whetten (1985) stated that organisations must make three main decisions: who they are, what business they are in and what they want to be. In order that these decisions be made they claim that consideration must be given to what is central, what is distinctive and what is enduring about the character of the organisation.

> Organisations must make three main decisions: who they are, what business they are in and what they want to be.

Non-members of an organisation also develop feelings and thoughts about what are the central, enduring and distinctive characteristics of an organisation. It is highly probable that there will be variances between the perceptions and beliefs of members and non-members, and this may be a cause of confusion, misunderstanding or even conflict.

This discrepancy between what Goodman and Pennings (1977) termed private and public identities can impair the 'health' of the organisation. The 'unhealthier' or greater the discrepancy, the more will be the difficulty in generating the resources required to guarantee corporate survival. In other words, the closer the member/non-member identification, the better placed the organisation will be to achieve its objectives.

Organisational identity is deemed to be important at a collective level, when an organisation is formed or when there is a major change to the continuity of the goals of the organisation or when the means of accomplishment are hindered or broken; see Table 32.2.

According to Dutton and Penner (1993), what an individual sees as important, distinctive and unique about an organisation will affect the individual's assessment of the importance of an issue facing the organisation and also the degree to which it is of personal importance.

For members, organisational identity may be conceptualised as their perception of their organisation's central and distinctive attributes, including its positional status and relevant compositional group. Consequently, external events that refute or call into question these defining characteristics may threaten the perception that organisational members have of their organisational identity (Dutton and Dukerich, 1991).

Research by Elsbach and Kramer (1996) found that members of a high-ranking organisation (MBA schools) perceived a threat because the ranking devalued their central and cherished identity dimensions and so refuted their prior claims of positional status.

TABLE 32.2 When organisational identity is important

During the formation of the organisation
At the loss of an identity-sustaining element
On the accomplishment of an organisation's *raison d'être*
Through extremely rapid growth
If there is a change in the collective status
Retrenchment

Source: Albert and Whetten (1985).

Members used selective categorisations to re-emphasise positive perceptions of their organisational identities for both themselves and their non-member audiences by highlighting identity dimensions or alternative groups with which they should be compared and that were not previously identified, the intention being to deflect attention.

Dutton and Dukerich state that there is a significant interdependence between individuals' social identities and their perceptions of their organisational identities. Thus, as they care about how their organisations are described and how they are compared with other organisations, so they experience cognitive distress (identity dissonance) when they think that their organisation's identity is being threatened by what they perceive as inaccurate descriptions or misleading (unfair) comparisons with other organisations.

In response to this distress members restore positive self-perceptions by highlighting their organisation's membership in alternative comparison groups.

It is normal to assume that identity is relatively static. However, just as organisations can experience strategic drift when the corporate strategy and performance move further away, each period, from the intended or expected pattern, so organisations can suffer from identity drift away from the expected life cycle. Kimberley (1980) argues that this can occur for three main reasons: environmental complexity, identity divestiture and organisational success.

This indicates that care must be given to understanding and managing the organisational identity to ensure that any discrepancy between members' and non-members' perceptions of what is central, enduring and distinctive is minimised and to be aware of identity dissonance should the organisation be threatened and the values upheld by its members challenged.

Organisational culture

According to Beyer (1981), organisational identity is a subset of the collective beliefs that constitute an organisation's culture. Indeed, internal marketing is shaped by the prevailing culture, as it is the culture that provides the context within which internal marketing practices are to be accomplished.

Corporate culture, defined by Schein (1985), is 'the deeper level of basic assumptions and beliefs that are shared by members of an organisation, that operate unconsciously and define in a basic taken for granted fashion an organisation's view of itself and its environment'. A more common view of organisational culture is 'the way we do things around here'. It is the result of a number of factors, ranging through the type and form of business the organisation is in, its customers and other stakeholders, its geographical position, and its size, age and facilities. These represent the more tangible aspects of corporate culture. There are a host of intangible elements

Corporate culture is 'the deeper level of basic assumptions and beliefs that are shared by members of an organisation'.

as well. These include the assumptions, values and beliefs that are held and shared by members of the organisation. These factors combine to create a unique environment, one where norms or guides to expected behaviour influence all members, whatever their role or position.

ViewPoint 32.2   B&Q shares values

B&Q is a do-it-yourself retailer employing over 22,000 people spread across 286 sites. This means that communicating a consistent message to these employees is a complex yet important task, if there is to be brand consistency.

B&Q utilises a number of different internal communications tools to undertake this task, including email, team briefs and energise sessions (early morning team work-out sessions). The company has a distinct and visible personality in that it requires employees to act as brand ambassadors. There are five main values that act as the central pillar of the organisation. These are:

- a down-to-earth approach
- respect for people
- being customer driven
- being positive
- striving to do better.

In part-fulfilment of these values B&Q staff feature in the retailer's advertising. This shows staff offering advice on tools and materials, ideas for gardening and indoor projects plus information about prices.

EXHIBIT 32.1 B&Q

As part of the process of involving staff, the daily exercise work-out seeks to bond staff as well as provide for improved health and fitness. Picture reproduced with the kind permission of B&Q.

This reflects the importance of integration because (real) staff are shown endorsing their brand and in essence challenging all customers to ask any employee about a range of matters. To make this loop work, staff need to know about the product range and how products might apply to different customers. If the message transmitted by employees (the promise) is not realised and experienced by customers, then there will be disappointment, falling expectations and a failing corporate image.

B&Q recognises that its staff are a major part of the organisation's success. It also recognises that the continuing commitment of its staff is essential, and effective internal communications are an important component in the process to gain this commitment.

Source: Material kindly provided by B&Q.

Levels of organisational culture

Corporate culture, according to Schein (1985), consists of a number of levels. The first of these, according to Thompson (1990), is the most visible level. This includes physical aspects of the organisation, such as the way in which the telephone is answered, the look and style of the reception area, and the general care afforded to visitors. Other manifestations of these visible aspects are the advertisements, logos, letterheads and other written communications that an organisation generates.

The second level consists of the values held by key personnel. For example, should particular sales teams who regularly better their targets have their targets increased or should certain members of the sales team be redeployed to less successful teams or new markets? If the decision is made to increase the target, and the outcome is successful, then the decision is more likely to be repeated when the same conditions arise again.

The second level consists of the values held by key personnel.

ViewPoint 32.3   Changing values at QinetiQ

The Defence Evaluation and Research Agency (DERA) owned by the Ministry of Defence (MoD) in the United Kingdom has recently moved from public to private ownership. Many of the staff at the organisation are scientists and engineers who under public ownership had no real need to interact with a diverse external audience and indeed knew little of the work in other divisions and parts of DERA. However, the success of the QinetiQ organisation depended on employees adopting a commercially focused value set, one that is very different to that engrained through working in a publicly owned organisation. They also needed to be committed and engaged with the new organisation.

This transformation was achieved partly through the use of CEO-led roadshows plus printed matter, cascade briefings, desk drop packs and online Web chats (with the CEO). Internal direct-looped radio, accessed through telephones and later desktop PCs, are used by the CEO to communicate key developments, to provide divisional results or just to encourage feedback. One broadcast attracted an audience of 2,000 people, of whom 300 provided immediate feedback. In addition, the use of an intranet, a variety of posters and notice boards plus face-to-face staff meetings all reflect the organisation's drive to reach employees, to actively encourage involvement and in doing so engage them within the QinetiQ brand.

Source: Hardaker and Fill (2005).

The third level in Schein's approach is achieved when the decision to increase the target becomes an automatic response to particular conditions. A belief is formed and becomes an assumption about behaviour in the organisation. This automatic approach can lead to complementary behaviour by members of the sales team. The placing of orders can become manipulated, to the extent that orders placed in month 6 may be 'delayed' or stuck in the top drawer of the sales representative's desk, until some point in month 7, when it is appropriate to release them.

The belief that the targets will be increased can lead to a behaviour that is referred to as 'the way we do things around here'. This behaviour leads to relative stability for all concerned and need not be disturbed unless a change is introduced, whose source is elsewhere in the system; that is, outside the team.

Culture and communication

Corporate culture is not a static phenomenon; the stronger the culture, the more likely it is to be transmitted from one generation of organisational members to another, and it is also probable that the culture will be more difficult to change if it is firmly embedded in the organisation. Most writers acknowledge that effective cultural change is difficult and a long-term task. Achieving a cultural fit is necessary if an organisation wishes to embrace a strategy that is incompatible with the current mind set of the organisation. Hunger and Wheelan (1993), for example, state that, to bring about cultural change, good communication, throughout the organisation, is a prerequisite for success. Mitchell (1998) considers the strong corporate culture that exists at Procter & Gamble. Depending upon one's perspective, this rigid formal hierarchical culture may be considered an advantage or a disadvantage. On the plus side it allows for strong identity, consistency and people development opportunities, as the company has a 'promote from within' policy. On the downside, the strength and penetration of the culture and need to toe the party line can restrict innovation, entrepreneurship and the use of initiative.

> The stronger the culture, the more likely it is to be transmitted from one generation of organisational members to another.

This strength of culture and the cautious approach to risk taking may be responsible for the consistent emphasis on product attributes, performance and pack shots in its advertising and communications, unlike its close rival Unilever, which makes greater use of emotions in its advertising. Procter & Gamble appears to recognise this as a limitation and has recently embarked upon a change of emphasis and has incorporated a more emotional approach in its communications. Changing the culture will be a challenge, but to be successful senior management will, among other things, need to be 'obsessive' about communicating the following to all members of the organisation (Gordon, 1985):

1. the current performance and position of the organisation in comparison with its competition and the outlook for the future;

2. the vision of what the organisation was to become and how it would achieve it;

3. the progress the organisation had made in achieving those elements identified previously as important.

The focus of this communication is internal, usually through training and development programmes. However, if the concept of the superorganisation is accepted (Chapter 8), then this level of communication activity should also occur in the channel networks, especially when the network is destabilised owing to environmental turbulence. Certain complex offerings, such as information technology-based products, require channel members to provide high levels of training and support. It is also important to communicate the objectives of the network and to share responsibility for the performance of the channel as a whole. This is partly achieved by members fulfilling their roles as successful dealers, retailers or manufacturers, but there is still a strong requirement for the channel leader to set out what is required from each member of its different networks and to report on what has been achieved to date.

Management of the communication finances, through time, will show the degree to which an organisation values such investments. Brands need time, the long term, to build and develop strength. Cutting back on investment in communications, especially advertising, in times of recession and difficulty, reveals management to view such activities as an expense, a cost against short-run needs. Furthermore, the expectation of channel members may be that a certain volume of marketing communications is necessary not only to sustain particular levels of business but also because competitors are providing established levels of communication activity. What is important is that the communications manager understands the culture of the organisation and the primary networks, values, styles, motivations and norms so that the communications work with rather than against the corporate will.

> The communications manager understands the culture of the organisation and the primary networks, values, styles, motivations and norms.

Brand engagement

The relationship between corporate strategy and communications is important. Traditionally, these communications are perceived as those that make the network between an organisation's employees and its managers. This internal perspective of communications is important, particularly when organisations are in transition. (See end of chapter case study.) This is only one part of the communication process. Employees are just one of the many stakeholders each organisation must seek to satisfy. Communications regarding strategic issues should also be targeted at members of the support and performance networks in order to gain their goodwill, involvement and understanding.

> Employees provide the main points of contact between organisations or with customers.

It is clear that long-term relationships cannot be sustained if the brand delivery is unsatisfactory and where the people behind the brand do not match the expectation generated by the promise. Apart from computer-mediated communication, employees provide the main points of contact between organisations or with customers. These interactions or 'moments of truth' as Gummesson (1999) refers to them, need to be consistent and of high quality.

Intellectual and emotional aspects

Employees are required to deliver both the functional aspects of an organisation's offering and the emotional dimensions, particularly in service environments. By attending to these twin elements it is possible that long-term relationships between sellers and buyers can develop effectively. Hardaker and Fill (2005) explore ideas concerning the notion that employees need to buy-in to organisational vision, goals and strategy (Thomson and Hecker, 2000). This buy-in, or engagement, consists of two

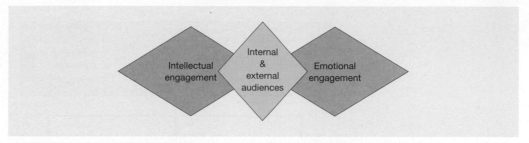

FIGURE 32.1 Brand engagement

main components, an intellectual and an emotional element. See Figure 32.1. The intellectual element is concerned with employees buying-in and aligning themselves with the organisation's strategy, issues and overall direction. The emotional element is concerned with employees taking ownership of their contribution and becoming committed to the achievement of stated goals. Communication strategies should be based on the information-processing styles of employees and access to preferred media. Communications should reflect a suitable balance between the need for rational information to meet intellectual needs and expressive types of communication to meet the emotional needs of the workforce. It follows that the better the communication, the higher the level of engagement.

Communication strategies should be based on the information-processing styles of employees and access to preferred media.

The development of internal brands based around employees can be accomplished effectively and quickly by simply considering the preferred information-processing style of an internal audience. By developing messages that reflect the natural processing style and using a diversity of media which best complements the type of message and the needs of each substantial internal target audience, the communication strategy is more likely to be successful.

Advertising and the impact on employees

Gilly and Wolfinbarger (1998) concluded that an organisation's advertising can have both a positive and a negative effect on its employees. Such advertising can serve to clarify roles, make promises which can be realistically delivered and demonstrates that the organisation values its employees. These positive outcomes can be seen in terms of improved morale and commitment.

Conversely, negative effects ensue when the advertising promises are unrealistic and cannot be delivered, messages are not true or the roles portrayed are far from flattering. For example, Boots used a campaign to inform consumers about its 'mix-and-match' offer. The ads depicted a member of staff explaining the deal to a confused colleague, who then apologises announcing that it is her first day. Staff, according to Witt (2001), complained that they were made to look stupid and incompetent. The outcome is low morale, distrust and unfavourable attitudes that can be perceived by non-members. It seems important therefore to generate advertising messages that are perceived by employees to be transparently achievable and consistent and this may involve the participation of a few staff in the development of advertising strategy.

It seems important therefore to generate advertising messages that are perceived by employees to be transparently achievable.

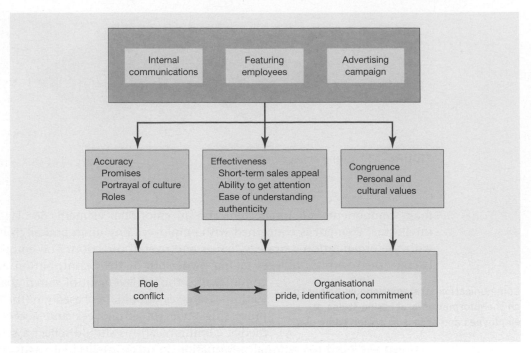

FIGURE 32.2 The impact of advertising on employees (Adapted from Gilly and Wolfinbarger (1998); used with kind permission.)

Gilly and Wolfinbarger developed a framework that presents the impact of advertising on employees. See Figure 32.2.

This model shows that employees use three main criteria when evaluating the advertising used by their employers, namely accuracy of the message, value congruence and effectiveness. In order to reduce any gap that might emerge as a result of an advertising campaign (and consequent deterioration in morale and commitment), increased vertical and horizontal communications are deemed necessary. This might require staff to be involved in both advertising development and in some cases actual participation in the advertisement, the pretesting of ideas and the dissemination of the advertising and the supporting rationale.

All stakeholders need to know what the objectives of the focus organisation are, particularly the mission and overriding vision the organisation has, as this will impact on the other organisations in the performance network. For example, if Heinz or Pedigree Petfoods were to announce that, in the future, all their products were to be presented in containers that are capable of being recycled, then current suppliers might need to reformulate their offerings and any future suppliers would be aware of the constraint this might place on them. The information is provided in order that others may work with them and continue supplying offerings to end-users with a minimum of interruption.

Barich and Kotler (1991) suggest that the concept of positioning (the process whereby offerings are perceived by consumers relative to the competition) applies at the brand and corporate level. If an organisation is pursuing a generic strategy of differentiation, then the positioning statements of the organisation need to reflect this. The image that stakeholders have of an organisation and its offerings affects their disposition towards the organisation, their intentions to undertake market transactions and the nature of the relationships between members.

Good external communications are important because, among other benefits, they can provide a source of competitive advantage. Perrier has built its share of the mineral water market on the volume and style of its planned communications. It has dominated communications in the market and has effectively set a mobility barrier which demands that any major challenger must be prepared to replicate the size of Perrier's investment in communications. The quality of the Perrier communications has also led distributors and other network members to support and want to be involved with the organisation, as evidenced by the swift recovery in market share after all world stocks had to be withdrawn because a small number of bottles had been identified as 'contaminated'. Morden (1993) refers to these positive external perceptions as intangible benefits that help to differentiate the organisation from its competitors.

All marketing strategies, such as those to harvest, build, hold and divest, require different communication strategies and messages. Similarly, market penetration, product development, market development and product penetration strategies all require varying forms of support that must be reflected in the communications undertaken by the organisation.

> All require varying forms of support that must be reflected in the communications undertaken by the organisation.

Marketing research may indicate that different stakeholders do not perceive the corporate and marketing strategies of an organisation in the same way as that intended by management. Some stakeholders may perceive the performance of an organisation inaccurately. This means that the organisation is failing to communicate in an effective and consistent way, and any such mismatch will, inevitably, lead to message confusion and relative disadvantage in the markets in which the organisation operates.

The communication of strategic intent and corporate performance must be harmonised. By understating or even misleading different stakeholders performance may be influenced, and if claims are made for an organisation that suggest a level of performance or intent beyond reality, then credibility may be severely jeopardised.

Strategic credibility

A relatively new development concerning the role of corporate strategy and corporate communications is the concept of strategic credibility. According to Higgins and Bannister (1992), strategic credibility refers to 'how favourably key stakeholders view the company's overall corporate strategy and its strategic planning processes'.

If stakeholders perceive the focus organisation as strategically capable, it is suggested that it will accrue a number of benefits. The benefits vary from industry to industry and according to each situation, but it appears from the early research that those organisations experiencing transition and that are not regulated in any way have potentially the most to gain from open corporate communication with their stakeholders. The benefits from this open attitude include improved stock market valuations and price/earnings multiples, better employee motivation and closer relationships with all members of the performance and support networks, particularly those within the financial community.

There are four main determinants of strategic credibility:

1. an organisation's strategic capability
2. past performance
3. communication of corporate strategy to key stakeholders
4. the credibility of the chief executive officer (CEO).

Strategic capability

Capability is a prerequisite for credibility. The perception that stakeholders have of the strategic processes within an organisation will influence their belief that the focus organisation can or cannot achieve its objectives. This is important in networks that are characterised by close working arrangements and high levels of interdependence. Should one organisation indicate that it lacks the necessary capability to perform strategically, then other members of the network are likely to be affected. The sharing of a strategic vision, one that may be common to all members of the stakeholder network, is a positive indicator of the existence of the acceptance that the focus organisation is strategically capable.

Capability is a prerequisite for credibility.

Past performance

The maintenance of a sustained strategic capability profile is partly dependent upon corporate performance. Poor performance does not sustain confidence, but even the existence of a strong performance is only worthwhile if it is communicated properly. The communication should inform the target audiences that the performance was planned and that there was sound reasoning and management judgement behind the performance.

Corporate communications

Organisations should inform members of the network of their strategic intentions as well as their past performance. This requires the accurate targeting and timing of the messages at a pace suitable and appropriate to the target's requirements. Higgins and Bannister refer to financial analysts, in particular, as stakeholders in need of good information. They argue that trying to evaluate the performance of a diversified organisation operating in a number of different markets, of which many of the analysts lack knowledge and expertise, is frustrating and difficult. Good information delivered through appropriate media and at particular times can be of benefit in the development of the realm of understanding between parties.

By keeping financial analysts aware of the strategic developments and the strategic thinking of the focus organisation and the industries in which it operates, the value of the organisation is more likely to reflect corporate performance. ICI experienced a major undervaluation in the 1980s because the financial markets and other key network members were not kept informed of the new strategies and thinking behind the corporate revival in the period 1982–6.

The credibility of the CEO

The fourth element proposed by Higgins and Bannister concerns the ability of the CEO to communicate effectively with a variety of audiences. By projecting strong, balanced and positive communications, it is thought that a visible CEO can improve the overall reputation of the organisation. Coupled with the improvement will be a perception of the strategic capability of the organisation. The CEO therefore can be regarded as a major determinant of the organisation's perceived strategic credibility.

The CEO therefore can be regarded as a major determinant of the organisation's perceived strategic credibility.

Haji-Ioannou, Anita Roddick, Terence Conran, Alan Sugar, James Dyson, Bernard Mathews and Richard Branson are some of the major CEOs to promote themselves on behalf of their organisations but there are many others who have tried and failed. However, research by Newell and Shemwell (1995) suggests that care should be taken when using CEOs as an endorser. They argue that the impact of source credibility may be reduced because of beliefs about product attributes, and this in turn may impact on behavioural intentions. Therefore CEOs might be best used as endorsers when informational, rather than emotional- or transformational-, based messages predominate.

ViewPoint 32.4	CEO endorsers - Vision Express

Vision Express decided to use its chairman, Daniel Abittan, to endorse the brand in its television commercials. Utilising his charisma and French accent to deliver messages about tangible product attributes (multiflex) and intangible attributes (good looks and sexiness) a high level of perceived credibility was achieved among member and non-member audiences. See Exhibit 32.2.

EXHIBIT 32.2 CEO endorser - Daniel Abittan
Picture reproduced with the kind permission of Vision Express and Webber Shandwick.

For example, Richard Branson has been used as CEO endorser of the Virgin Group. As chairman he has been a focal point in the promotion of Virgin financial products (mainly informational messages), but has not played such a central role in the persuasive communications concerning the airline Virgin Atlantic, where emotionally based messages have been used to influence brand choice decisions. In this instance celebrity spokespersons such as Helen Mirren, Marianne Faithful and Terence Stamp have all been used to endorse the airline.

Strategic credibility is an interesting concept that can be used to develop an understanding of the perception held by key support network members of an organisation's strategic management processes.

Communications audit

Research, as we have seen, is an important element in the design of communication plans. Associated with this should be an evaluation of the most recent attempts at communicating with target audiences. The accumulation of this type of short-run information is useful because it builds into a database that can be used to identify key factors over the long run. Regression analysis can eventually be used to identify key variables in the marketing communications and marketing plans.

The communications strategies of competitors should also be measured and evaluated. Organisations and offerings do not exist in isolation from each other and competitor activities; messages, styles and levels of spend should also be taken into account. If a strategy of differentiation is being pursued it would appear pointless and wasteful to position an offering in the same way as a main competitor.

> The communications strategies of competitors should also be measured and evaluated.

The process by which an organisation communicates with its target audiences is, as we have seen, extremely important. To assist the process of evaluating the effectiveness of past communication strategies, strategic credibility and the corporate image held by different members of all networks, a communications audit should be undertaken. Financial audits examine the processes by which organisations organise and systematically manage their financial affairs. Some of the underlying agenda items may be to prevent fraud and malpractice, but the positive aspects of the financial audit are to understand what is happening, to develop new ways of performing certain tasks and to promote efficiency and effectiveness. The same principle holds for the communications audit. How is the organisation communicating and are there better ways of achieving the communication objectives?

A communications audit is a process that can assist the communications planner in assessing whether or not an organisation is communicating with its consumers and other stakeholders in an effective and meaningful way. A further important goal of such an exercise is to determine whether the communications perceived and understood by the target audiences are the messages that were intended in the first place. Are the messages being decoded in the manner in which they were designed when they were encoded? This exercise helps organisations to develop their realm of understanding with their respective network members and includes all internal and external communications, whether overt or covert.

> Determine whether the communications perceived and understood by the target audiences are the messages that were intended in the first place.

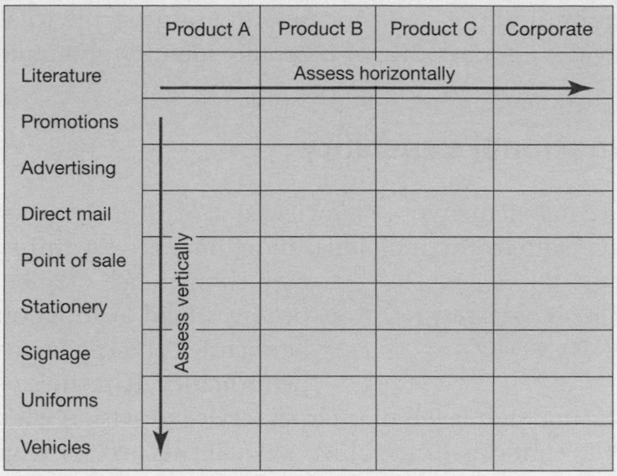

	Product A	Product B	Product C	Corporate
Literature	Assess horizontally			
Promotions				
Advertising				
Direct mail				
Point of sale				
Stationery	Assess vertically			
Signage				
Uniforms				
Vehicles				

FIGURE 32.3 A communications audit matrix (From Ind (1992); used with kind permission.)

Procedures associated with a communications audit

All forms of printed and visual communications (brochures, leaflets, annual reports, letterheads, advertisements, etc.) need to be collected and assembled in a particular location. Examples of main competitors' materials should also be brought together, as this will provide benchmarks for market evaluation. Once collated, the task is to identify consistent themes and the logic of the organisation's communications.

Ind (1992) suggests that one way of accomplishing this is to develop a communications matrix. See Figure 32.3. Information needs to be grouped by type of offering (vertically) and then by each type of medium (horizontally). The vertical grouping helps determine the variety of messages that customers receive if they are exposed to all the communications relating to a single offering. Are the messages consistent? Are the messages logically related? Is the related logic one that is intended and what is the total impact of these communications? The horizontal grouping helps determine message consistency across a number of different offerings, perhaps from different divisions. If a single dealer or end-user receives the communications relating to a product line or even a particular product mix, is the perception likely to be confusing?

Internal communications should be included in the audit. An analysis of official publications, such as in-house magazines, is obvious, but materials posted on notice boards and the way in which the telephone is answered affect the perception that stakeholders have of the organisation.

The audit needs to incorporate research into the attitudes of employees to the organisation and the perceptions held by various stakeholders. This will involve both qualitative and quantitative research. The objective is to determine whether the image of the organisation reflects reality. If corporate performance exceeds the overall image, then corporate communications are not working effectively. If the image is superior to performance, then the operations of the organisation need to be improved.

In the mid-1980s ICI's corporate performance was more advanced than its image. The organisation's communications were not working effectively. Research eventually revealed the gulf between performance and image, but had a communications audit been used on a regular basis, in conjunction with an image tracking system, then the amount of damage or loss of goodwill might have been considerably reduced.

Organisations need to understand how they are perceived by their stakeholders. A communications audit focuses attention on the totality of messages transmitted and provides a framework for corporate identity programmes.

Functional capability

The final elements to be reviewed as part of the internal marketing context are those that relate to the individual functional areas within an organisation. A firm's overall core competence may be the result of a number of competences held at functional level. Internal marketing can be regarded as a key to providing strong external marketing performance (Greene *et al.*, 1994). This is achieved by releasing high levels of internal service provision within the functional areas. As Varey (1995) confirms, 'Internal service quality is necessary for superior external service quality'.

'Internal service quality is necessary for superior external service quality'.

Financial capability

Before any communications plan can be devised in any detail, it is necessary to have a broad understanding of the financial capability of the organisation; in other words, how much money is available for communications? This is important, as it impacts upon the objectives that are to be set later and the choice of media necessary to carry the organisation's messages. For example, it is pointless asking dealers to undertake training programmes with end-users if the manufacturer does not have the sales representatives and training staff to instruct the dealers in the first place. Most medium-sized tour operators do not have the capital to fund television-based campaigns, even though some of the major national tour operators regularly use television.

Manufacturing capability

One of the main aims of the communications plan is to stimulate and maintain demand. If the production resources are limited the capacity needs to be aligned with the potential demand of a region or local area rather than nationally. Equally, the communications programme should be geared to the same area. All demand must be satisfied and likewise much of the communications programme will be ineffective in the short term if full production capacity has been reached.

Marketing capability

Discussion so far has assumed that the available corporate and marketing expertise is of sufficient calibre not only to formulate but also to implement a marketing strategy and its associated communications requirements. This raises questions about the customer orientation of the organisation, its attitude towards marketing and its general disposition towards the provision of a sustained level of customer service and satisfaction.

In a Research International study reported by Simms (2004) it was found that 47 per cent of respondents had little or no idea of what marketing does while 54 per cent believe that if marketing was abolished it would have little or no manageable impact on the company. This type of information is fairly typical of a number of studies in this area. Marketing appears to have difficulty establishing itself within many organisations although its prominence in FMCG companies is high.

Many CEOs still have a poor understanding of what marketing is: to a number of them marketing is about selling and promotion. Such a shallow perspective is unlikely to lead to an organisational culture that will support a marketing orientation, especially when so few marketing directors have a main board position. The ability of an organisation to deliver consistently effective marketing communications is dependent upon many things, but among them are the presence of a customer-oriented organisational culture and leadership with a broad mix of marketing skills.

It seems reasonable to extend these conclusions by surmising that the same values and beliefs are necessary for the successful adoption of a planned approach to marketing communications, if only because it is a subsystem of marketing planning.

Summary

Intra-organisational issues need to be appreciated when building a communications plan. One of the key factors to be considered is the corporate strategy, including the degree to which it is understood by stakeholders and the credibility that management has to manage strategic processes.

A major influence on the communication style is the prevailing culture. Culture is a reflection of the personality of the organisation, which in turn affects the corporate identity or the way in which an organisation presents itself to its stakeholders. This presentation of visual cues can be managed deliberately or left unattended. Either way, stakeholders develop a picture of the organisation that enables them to position it among others. This corporate image may well be an accurate interpretation of the real organisation. However, it may be inaccurate, in which case marketing communications needs to address the problem and narrow the gap between reality and image.

Review questions

1. Write a short definition of internal marketing and explain how marketing communications needs to assume both internal and external perspectives.

2. What is the role of internal marketing communications?

3. Write short notes explaining why organisational boundaries appear to be less clear than was once thought.

4. What is organisational identity and what do Albert and Whetten (1985) consider to be the three important aspects of identity?

5. Write a brief paper explaining why an understanding of corporate culture is important for successful marketing communications.

6. Why should marketing communications accommodate corporate strategy?

7. What are the elements of strategic credibility?

8. Select three different CEOs from a variety of organisations and evaluate their strategic credibility. What is your justification for selecting these individuals?

9. Prepare a communications matrix for an organisation (or brand/product) with which you are familiar.

10. Why might the functional capabilities of an organisation impact upon an organisation's marketing communications?

MINI-CASE
Dealer training programmes to enhance CRM

Mini-case written by Alexander Dries, CRM Consultant

The Mercedes-Benz retail UK network

Customer needs and the whole retail environment are changing. We must ensure that Mercedes-Benz offers the finest care and support the moment they begin a relationship with us.

Dermot Kelly, Managing Director,
Mercedes Car Group, DCUK

Introduction

In 1985 the automotive industry was granted an exemption, en bloc, from Article 81 of the EC Treaty – better known as the Block Exemption Regulation (BER). This regulation was installed in order to rule out anti-competitive vertical agreements between producers and distributors. In September 2002 this regulation expired and was replaced by a new BER – which has been fully effective since October 2003. This allows active sales outside of established territories and multibranded retailing in order to open up competition across the automotive value chain. Furthermore, the link between sales and after-sales services has been weakened, giving independent repairers a new role.

New challenges for automotive retailing

The new BER affected Mercedes-Benz, in line with other manufacturers, in both the distribution and servicing of cars and commercial vehicles across the EC. The changes to the regulation allowed large retail organisations, for example Tesco and Virgin, to participate in automotive retailing.

The automotive industry lagged behind in terms of CRM and customer focus in comparison to the potential new market entrants. The threat of such organisations entering the car market and changes in the consumer environment (the emergence of the 'never satisfied' customer) forced Mercedes-Benz to react. As a result, urgent changes to both structure and customer focus within the organisation and the retail network were necessary. An effective, efficient and customer-oriented retail network becomes an even more important success factor in times of such increasingly intensified competition within the industry.

The decision to meet the new set of automotive retailing challenges resulted in an unparalleled re-organisation of the distribution channels. In 2001 DaimlerChrysler UK (DCUK) introduced the market area concept, which is based on fewer dealer operations within larger territories. The newly recreated dealers, in their role as representatives of the brand within their given area of responsibility, are required to improve customer satisfaction and retention rates as well as increase profitability. The improvement of supporting processes, systems and facilities is vital for the delivery of a customer experience that is not only leading in the automotive industry but is setting a new benchmark for retailing in general.

Customer relationship management at Mercedes-Benz in the UK

CRM became a vital strategy supporting the market area concept aimed at enhancing customer relations, both internally and externally. This was necessary in order to optimise the exploitation of the Mercedes-Benz potential through consistent and appropriate customer management and retention in all areas of the operations, that is sales, marketing, after sales, parts and finance. The CRM strategy is based on four pillars, one of them being a comprehensive CRM training and mind-setting programme, which is outlined below.

CRM training at Mercedes-Benz in the UK

In 2002 DaimlerChrysler UK developed a comprehensive CRM training programme in cooperation with the Mercedes-Benz retail network and the

DaimlerChrysler headquarters in Stuttgart, Germany. The CRM training programme consists of four individual modules aimed at changing the attitude and motivation of both retail and DCUK employees and management. Furthermore, participants are provided with the skills needed in both systems, processes and their daily work as such (e.g. soft skills, communication skills). As a consequence, the individual modules address different audiences and competences.

The first two modules concern change management and provide a general foundation to understand the CRM philosophy and its benefits in order to influence and change the attitude and motivation of the participants. Modules three and four support the participants in delivering the new retail experience of Mercedes-Benz in their day-to-day work. These training modules are therefore part of the personal development of both employees and dealers.

Each module consists of several individual sections that can be used interchangeably in order to address the specific needs of the participants and to secure maximum flexibility. This helps to ensure that changes and modifications can be made within a reasonable amount of time and budget. The four modules are briefly described in the following sections.

Module 1 - CRM best practice

Target audience: Management of the retail network and DCUK

The primary aim of the first module is to encourage management buy-in in terms of the required resources (e.g. budget, management time, employees). During the event the philosophy and benefits of CRM and service excellence are communicated and transferred in various ways. In order to inspire the participants and to bring the idea of CRM to life, best-in-class companies are presented (business cases, videos and guest speakers) and visited (company visits). As a result, a mixture of both learning and motivation is achieved.

Module 2 - CRM uncovered

Target audience: Customer-facing staff

The aim of the module is to generate enthusiasm for CRM in order to bring the customer experience of Mercedes-Benz to life. The participants should understand and experience the benefits of CRM for the customer, the dealership and, at the end of the

day, for themselves. Furthermore, the course helps the participants to develop an holistic view of the organisation and its subfunction due to the exchange with members from various departments and businesses.

Module 3 - systems and processes

Target audience: Customer-facing staff

The third module aims to help the transfer of knowledge and motivation gained of CRM. This is used within the daily retail business operations in order to develop new systems and process skills. The aim of this module is to share the knowledge of systems and processes about how the various tasks are to be performed.

Module 4 - soft skills

Target audience: Customer-facing staff

CRM offers opportunities to achieve improved and superior customer interactions. However, this requires customer facing staff to have the social and communication skills to match the new processes and systems. Therefore this last module provides participants with an individual set of skills (ranging from complaint handling to time management) that are required for effective daily customer contact.

Conclusion

As a result of profound changes in the business environment, Mercedes-Benz looked for alternative ways to face the competition within the marketplace and applied changes to both the structure and the degree of customer focus for the entire organisation. CRM became a critical success factor in order to maintain the leading position within the market. In order to be successful, the CRM initiative needed cross-functional integration of the various business areas, and that emphasises the role of the company's employees as well as the supporting processes and systems. DCUK integrated its retail network and underlined its responsibility and dedication to its retail partners. Only if both parties are working together as equal partners can success in the marketplace be secured.

As a consequence of the achievements made in the UK, the programme has been rolled out to various other countries throughout continental Europe.

The author would like to acknowledge the contribution of Miles Moorhouse, CRM Manager, DaimlerChrysler UK Ltd.

Questions

1 Why might CRM initiatives fail?

2 Explain the importance of senior management support for CRM initiatives.

3 Discuss possible challenges to the adaptation of the programme in continental Europe.

4 Discuss the following statement by Herb Kelleher, former CEO of Southwest Airlines: 'People are more important than financial resources, equipment, and other material assets.'

References

Albert, S. and Whetten, D.A. (1985) Organisational identity. In *Research in Organizational Behavior* (eds L.L. Cummings and B.M. Staw). Greenwich, CT: Jai Press.

Balmer, J.M.T. and Wilkinson, A. (1991) Building societies: change, strategy and corporate identity. *Journal of General Management*, **17**(2), pp. 22–33.

Barich, H. and Kotler, P. (1991) A framework for marketing image management. *Sloan Management Review*, **94** (Winter), pp. 94–104.

Berry, L.L. (1980) Services marketing is different. *Business* (May/June), pp. 24–9.

Beyer, J.M. (1981) Ideologies, values and decision making in organisations. In *Handbook of Organisational Design* (eds P. Nystrom and W. Swarbruck). London: Oxford University Press.

Christensen, L.T. and Askegaard, S. (2001) Corporate identity and corporate image revisited. *European Journal of Marketing*, **35**(3/4), pp. 292–315.

Dutton, J.E. and Dukerich, J.M. (1991) Keeping an eye on the mirror: image and identity in organisational adaptation. *Academy of Management Review*, **34**, pp. 517–54.

Dutton, J.E., Dukerich, J.M. and Harquail, C.V. (1994) Organisational images and member identification. *Administrative Science Quarterly*, **39**, pp. 239–63.

Dutton, J.E. and Penner, W.J. (1993) The importance of organisational identity for strategic agenda building. In *Strategic Thinking: Leadership and the Management of Change* (eds J. Hendry, G. Johnson and J. Newton). Chichester: Wiley.

Elsbach, K.D. and Kramer, R.M. (1996) Members' responses to organisational identity threats: encountering and countering the *Business Week* rankings. *Administrative Science Quarterly*, **41**, pp. 442–76.

Foreman, S.K. and Money, A.H. (1995) Internal marketing: concepts, measurements and application. *Journal of Marketing Management*, **11**, pp. 755–68.

Freeman, E. and Liedtka, J. (1997) Stakeholder capitalism and the value chain. *European Management Journal*, **15**(3), pp. 286–96.

Gilly, M.C. and Wolfinbarger, M. (1998) Advertising's internal audience. *Journal of Marketing*, **62** (January), pp. 69–88.

Goften, K. (2000) Putting staff first in brand evolution. *Marketing*, 3 February, pp. 29–30.

Goodman, P.S. and Pennings, J.M. (1977) *New Perspectives on Organisational Effectiveness*. San Francisco, CA: Jossey-Bass.

Gordon, G. (1985) The relationship of corporate culture to industry sector and corporate performance. In *Gaining Control of the Corporate Culture* (eds R.H. Kilman, M.J. Saxton, R. Serpa, and associates). San Francisco, CA: Jossey-Bass.

Greene, W.E., Walls, G.D. and Schrest, L.J. (1994) Internal marketing: the key to external marketing success. *Journal of Services Marketing*, **8**(4), pp. 5–13.

Gummesson, E. (1999) *Total Relationship Marketing. Rethinking Marketing Management: From 4Ps to 30Rs*. Oxford: Butterworth-Heinemann.

Hardaker, S. and Fill, C. (2005) Corporate service brands: the intellectual and emotional engagement of employees. *Corporate Reputation Review: an International Journal*, **8**(1), pp. 365–76.

Hatch, M.J. and Schultz, M. (1997) Relations between organisational culture, identity and image. *European Journal of Marketing*, **31**(5/6), pp. 356–65.

Hemsley, S. (1998) Internal affairs. *Marketing Week*, 2 April, pp. 49–53.

Higgins, R.B. and Bannister, B.D. (1992) How corporate communication of strategy affects share price. *Long Range Planning*, **25**(3), pp. 27–35.

Hiscock, J. (2002) The brand insiders. *Marketing*, 23 May, pp. 24–5.

Hunger, J.D. and Wheelan, T. (1993) *Strategic Management*. 4th edn. Reading, MA: Addison-Wesley.

Ind, N. (1992) *The Corporate Image: Strategies for Effective Identity Programme*. rev. edn. London: Kogan Page.

Kimberley, J. (1980) Initiation, innovation and institutionalisation in the creation process. In *The Organizational Lifecycle* (eds J. Kimberley and R. Miles). San Francisco, CA: Jossey-Bass.

Lievens, A. and Moenart, R.K. (2000) Communication flows during financial service innovation. *European Journal of Marketing*, **34**(9/10), pp. 1078–110.

Mitchell, A. (1998) P&G's new horizons. *Campaign*, 20 March, pp. 34–5.

Morden, T. (1993) *Business Strategy and Planning*. London: McGraw-Hill.

Morgan, G. (1997) *Images of Organisation*. 2nd edn. New York: Sage.

Newell, S.J. and Shemwell, D.J. (1995) The CEO endorser and message source credibility: an empirical investigation of antecedents and consequences. *Journal of Marketing Communications*, **1**, pp. 13–23.

Piercy, N. and Morgan, R. (1991) Internal marketing: the missing half of the marketing programme. *Long Range Planning*, 24 (April), pp. 82–93.

Schein, E.H. (1985) *Organizational Culture and Leadership*. San Francisco, CA: Jossey-Bass.

Schneider, B. and Bowen, D. (1985) Employee and customer perceptions of service in banks: replication and extension. *Journal of Applied Psychology*, **70**, pp. 423–33.

Simms, J. (2004) You're not paranoid, they do hate you. *Marketing*, 19 May, pp. 32–4.

Storey, J. (2001) Internal marketing comes to the surface. *Marketing Week*, 19 July p. 22.

Thompson, J.L. (1990) *Strategic Management: Awareness and Change*. London: Chapman & Hall.

Thomson, K. and Hecker, L.A. (2000) The business value of buy-in. In *Internal Marketing: Directions for Management* (eds R.J. Varey and B.R. Lewis), pp. 160–72. London: Routledge.

Varey, R.J. (1995) Internal marketing: a review and some interdisciplinary research challenges. *International Journal of Service Industry Management*, **6**(1), pp. 40–63.

Witt, J. (2001) Are your staff and ads in tune? *Marketing*, 18 January, p. 21.

Author index

Subject index